Contents

Top Image Turtle Beach, Ngumuy, Northern Territory by 20000ksinacampertrailer via Instagram

KING OF THE BBQ
BMPRO
SMARTSENSE
GAS BOTTLE LEVEL MONITOR + APP
Never run out of gas unexpectedly again!
SMARTSENSE PROPANE GAS SENSOR
52%
FEATURES
Compact, tough, lightweight, water and dust resistant
Free app on Google Play and iTunes App Store
Easy DIY install with extra strong magnets
Communicates with phones via Bluetooth
Suits most small portable domestic gas bottles
Replaceable standard 3V battery CR2032
NO GAS?
NO CHANCE!
Use independently with SmartSense app or integrated with the JHub or Odyssey app*
Google play
Available on the App Store
SMARTCONNECT
JHUB
ODYSSEY
BMPRO
TEAM BMPRO .COM
*Requires ControlNode/OdysseyLink
Order online. Use code Camps10 for Camps Australia special offer.

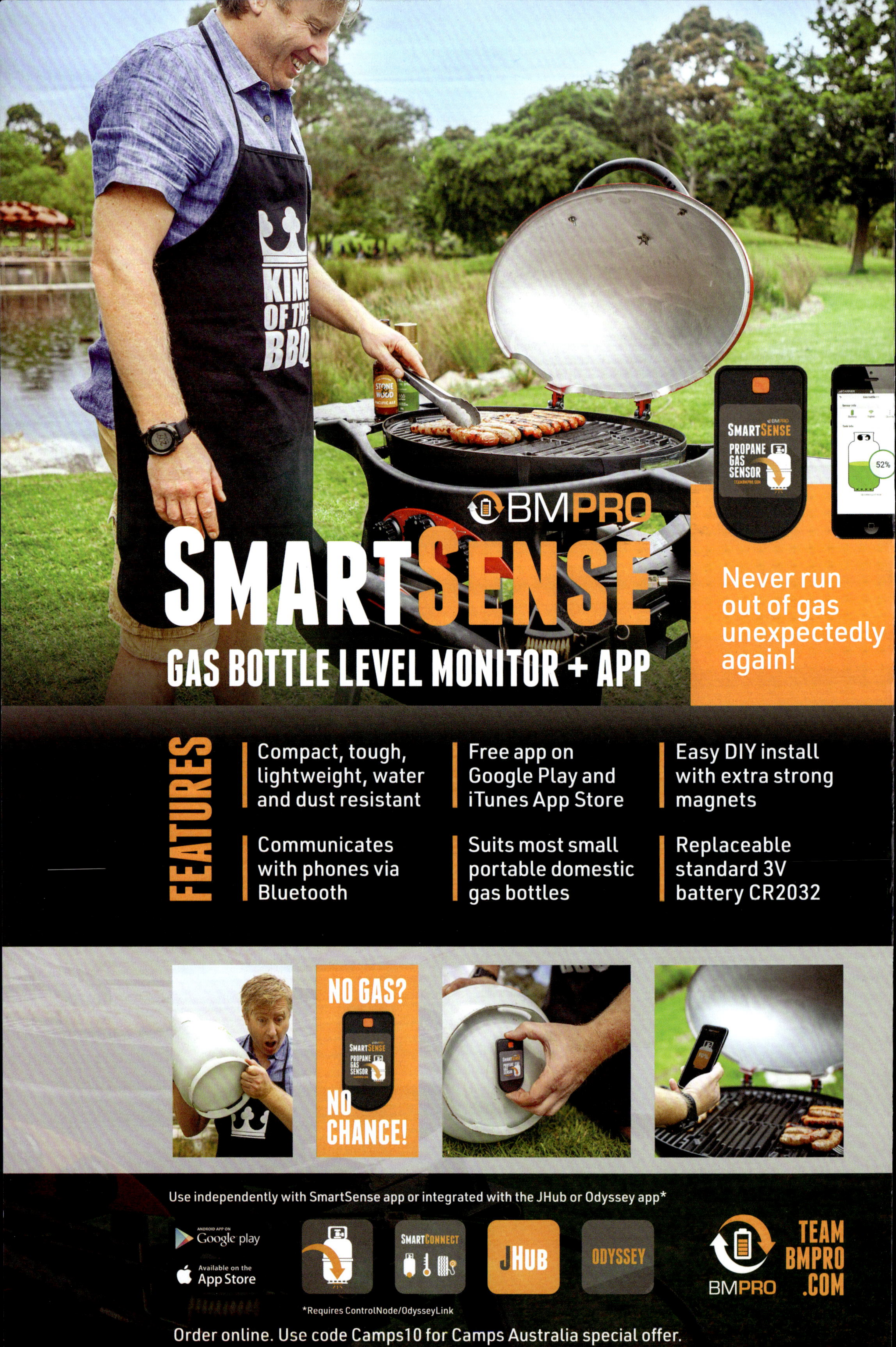

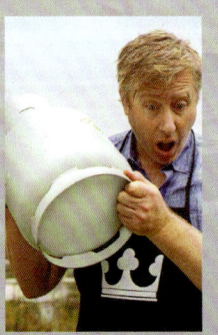

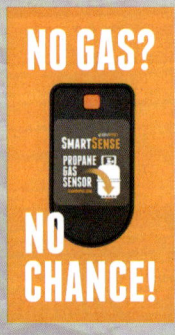

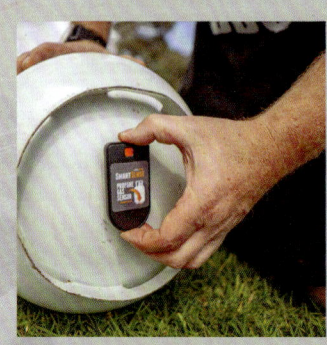

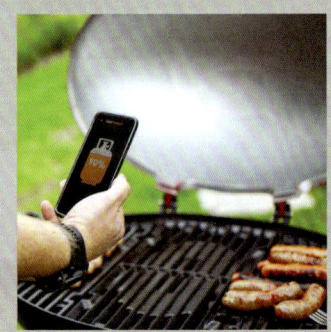

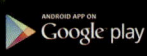

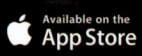

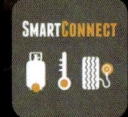

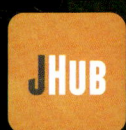

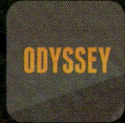

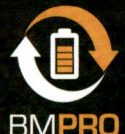

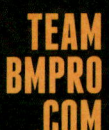

Experience adventures on the road with us

You've purchased Australia's favourite guide for freedom and low-cost camping – owned by an Aussie family and printed in Australia. We welcome you to our community of travellers across Australia. Almost 30 years of travel, research and knowledge has been transferred into our easy-to-use guides. In this edition we have some exciting new features:

New site type symbols on the maps

For the first time in the history of CAMPS, you can identify the site type at a glance on the maps. Without looking at the listing, you can see if it is pet friendly or a camp at a showground, national park, station or pub stay, state forest, RV park or other freedom or paid site.

More facilities in the listings

On top of the traditional symbols of CAMPS, we have added more symbols (some campgrounds and farm stays have playgrounds or pools, too!) and entirely new symbols like donations, pets seasonal, generators, gas bottles, glamping, laundry and games rooms.

Fishing, swimming and four wheel driving!

With more new symbols, you can easily see if you can swim (in waterholes, creeks, dams or the ocean) and fish at a site. You can also see if it is recommended as 4WD only.

Address and GPS

Not only is the GPS listed, but a street address for easy navigation is now included.

Easier to use and lighter

As well as a FREE App subscription (conditions apply), we have added hundreds of new sites to this edition, however you will find CAMPS 11 is easier to use, lighter and more manageable than previous issues. We have achieved this with our new symbols and by integrating the book and App more closely.

Free added bonuses and community

We invite you to receive added value from your book, with our newsletters. Each fortnight we share our favourite places, new listings, plus free and budget campgrounds across our beautiful country. There's even more news and tips on our Facebook and Instagram pages, and Facebook Group called "I Love Camping Australia Wide".

At CAMPS, we are passionate about giving everyone the opportunity to experience the freedom of life on the road – and we know our guides will help you and your family make priceless memories.

We look forward to many more hours on the road, chatting at happy hours, verifying camps so you can experience the best of travel in Australia. Hope to see you on the road,

Heatley & Michelle Gilmore

FREE
Scan this QR code to download your FREE Camps Australia Wide App. Conditions apply.

Link opens in Facebook Messenger
www.urlgeni.us/fb_messenger/camps-app

✉ www.campsaustraliawide.com

f www.facebook.com/CampsAustraliaWide/
www.bit.ly/iLovecamping *(FB group)*
📷 @campsaustraliawide

Top image Warrumbungles Camp Blackman, New South Wales by Bec Conroy from Look the World in the Eye via Instagram

CAMPS image by Anna Power

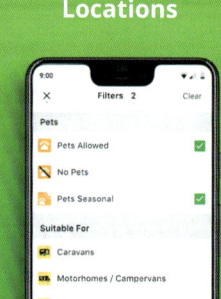

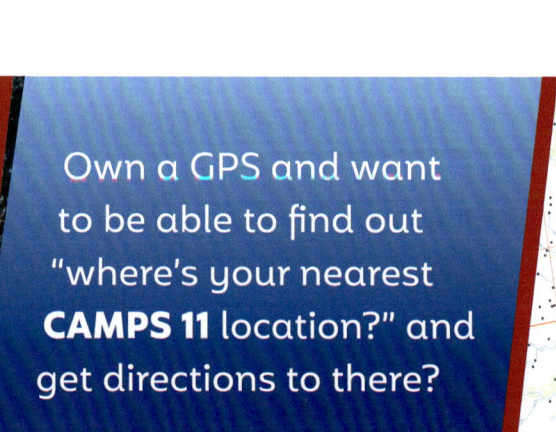

Acknowledgements

Camps Australia Wide Pty Ltd

PO Box 204 Rainbow Beach
Queensland Australia 4581
Phone: (07) 5474 2542
Email: info@campsaustraliawide.com
Website: www.campsaustraliawide.com

Eleventh edition published December 2020

ISBN: 978-0-9945327-2-5

Proprietors of Camps Australia Wide:
Compiled, Designed & Published by:
Michelle and Heatley Gilmore.

Research and Photography:
Michelle & Heatley Gilmore, Leisa Cooper, Jed & Tyla Elmer, Sheng Yee, Graham Gardiner, Rebecca Reibel, Emma Thompson.

Special Acknowledgements: Michael Brantz, & Maureen Lennon, Judy and Rebecca Gilmore.

This book is dedicated to our wonderful four, Jack, Kate, Hugh & Archie - we look forward to more adventures.

Acknowledgements: To every single traveller who has sent us a photo or site update, we appreciate each phone call, email or tip over the campfire. Please keep them coming!

Production and Prepress:
Allan and Linda Shearer, Shearer Publishing Systems
Gavin James, Mapuccino
Leanne Collett, Flowering Design
Victoria McGuin, WordforWord.com.au
Sally Joyce, SAJE Graphics
Darren Baker, Bare Graphics
Printed by C & C Offset Printing Co. Ltd.

The Publication Front Cover is a photograph of Edeowie Station, South Australia by Ross Plant.

The Publication Back Cover is a photograph on the road from Springsure to Willow Gemfields, Queensland by Michelle Gilmore.

Source of Maps
Base Maps: Hema Maps Pty Ltd.

Disclaimer
The author has attempted to ensure that the information contained in this publication is accurate at the time it was written but the author and the publisher do not warrant that it is accurate or complete.

All information provided is made available purely for general informational purposes only and is intended to be used as a guide only. It is not intended as advice and must not be relied upon as such.

Maps, directions, and other information may differ from actual conditions. Persons intending to act on any information contained herein should first check all relevant national, state and local road and parking laws, subordinate legislation and specific information provided independently by the places of interest. The author and the publisher are not liable for any loss, damage, cost or expense suffered or incurred arising directly or indirectly from the use or reliance on any information contained in this publication. It is provided in good faith without express or implied warranty.

This book includes advertisements of companies not affiliated with Camps Australia Wide. Camps Australia Wide does not guarantee these products or services.

Point Brown, South Australia by Haley Roberts
@roberts_oz.lap_no.map via Instagram

Kui Parks

Explore Australia
with Kui Parks

A network of caravan parks tailored to the travelling Nomad

- ☑ Clean
- ☑ Friendly
- ☑ Well Presented
- ☑ Reasonably Priced

Join, Save & Stay at Kui Parks

www.kuiparks.com.au

 9/10 of our parks are pet friendly.

 (03) 9730 2077
info@kuiparks.com.au

About this Guide

GPS Coordinates used

GPS coordinates used in Camps Australia Wide 11 is d°m's" (Degrees, Minutes, Seconds). Most GPS units generally have three GPS format settings. It is important that you select the correct setting in your GPS to match our format. This will ensure you are accurately guided to the site. Listed below are the three common coordinates formats:

- d.d° (-49.5000°, 123.500°) sometimes called "Degrees".
- d° m.m (49° 30.0, 123° 30.0) sometimes called "Minutes".
- d° m's" (49° 30 00S, 123° 30 00E) sometimes called "Seconds" (we use this format)

Wilpena Pound, South Australia
by Tania Dalton @bessiebusandus via Instagram

We now have GPS Point Of Interest (POI) files that have been created by our partner GPSOZ. When these files are loaded into your GPS you can view and select CAMPS 11 sites from the Custom POI section of your GPS for turn-by-turn guidance to the selected Camps listing. These files are available as a download only for Garmin, TomTom and Navman and are delivered by email. Visit our website, www.campsaustraliawide, for more information about purchasing GPS POI files.

Feedback

Our publication relies on consumer feedback to maintain accuracy and content. Your input would be most appreciated.

You can email us on talktous@campsaustraliawide.com or phone us on (07) 5474 2542. A site feedback form is available on our website under the 'Updates' tab. Any information, no matter how small, can be sent in by mail or email. It won't be ignored.

Dump Point List

Because of the ever-increasing concern for the environment, a comprehensive Public Dump Point list has been included. These dump points also have GPS coordinates to help you find their positions.

Road Conditions

Some of the sites listed are accessed by roads that may be unsuitable for some vehicles and which may also change due to weather conditions. It is recommended that you check with local authorities before travelling on roads of uncertain condition.

Maps

The maps have been customised as much as possible to make them easy to read. Due to the scale of the maps, as we add more and more sites, it is a challenge to fit the icons onto them! We do our best to ensure nothing of importance is covered over.

If you see a map page without site numbers, please check the highlighted inset maps or the Hema reference in the listing - and go to the relevant map page. The scale is much larger on these maps, and you can see site numbers more clearly.

State Regulations for Overnight Camping

There are some differences in the laws relating to overnight camping in rest areas and on private property within each state, and these laws are always changing.

Some states and local authorities are quite tolerant of overnight camping, while others will enforce the law and move you on, fine you, or both.

Conditions in Australia are constantly changing (like extreme weather events and pandemics) so sites listed in this guide, are subject to closure or change without notice.

Please obey any regulatory signs, respect people in authority and use common sense always. Do not insist that you are in the right because it says so in the book. The book is not the absolute authority. It's a guide only!

This guide prominently lists free and low-cost camping, national parks, state forests, rest areas, station stays, and show grounds. This guide is NOT a comprehensive Caravan Park Guide, only caravan parks we have categorised as budget or remote are listed. For a comprehensive list of all caravan parks across Australia, utilise our CARAVAN PARKS 5 book and Camps Australia Wide App.

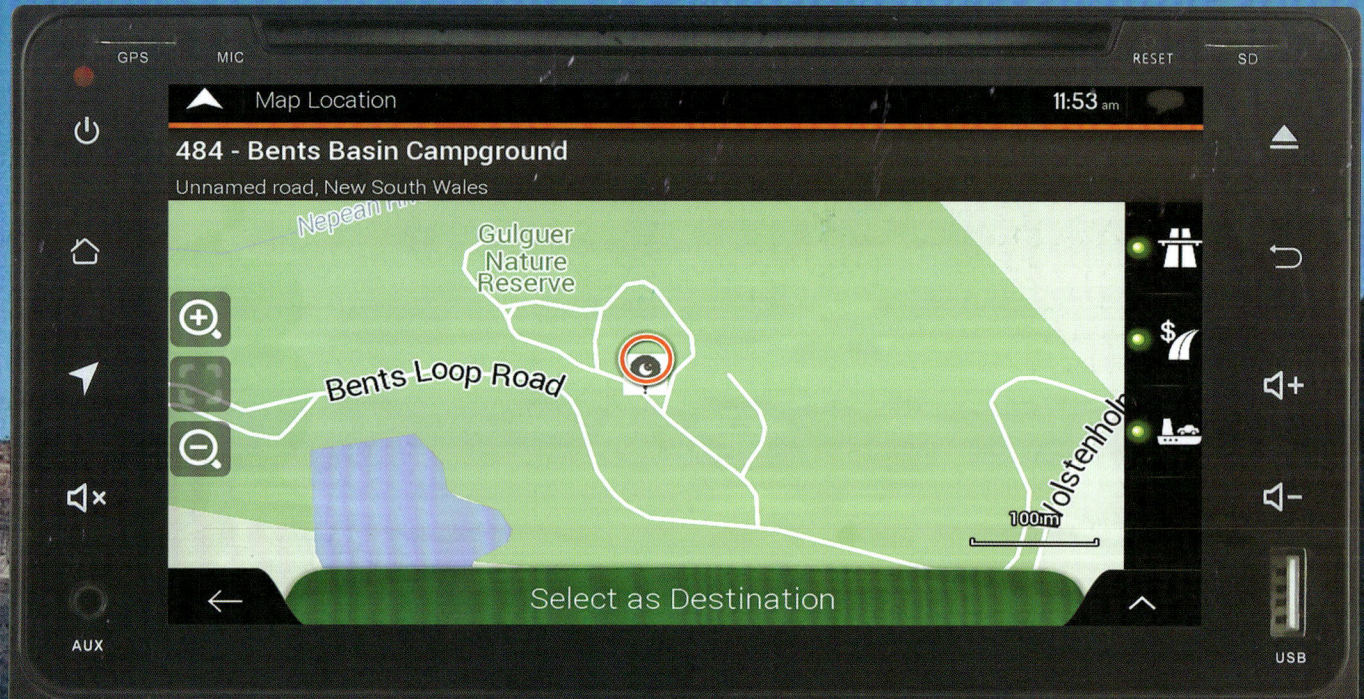

Important: Updating This Book

Changes are bound to occur, especially over time after the book's release. There are three ways you can access updates for your book.

The Camps Australia Wide App
The Camps Australia Wide App works well in conjunction with your books. You can easily compare symbols to see if a site has removed or added facilities and features.

Download your FREE version of our Camps App by scanning the QR code. Conditions apply.

Link opens in Facebook Messenger
www.urlgeni.us/fb_messenger/camps-app

Our Newsletter, Blog and Socials

Every fortnight we share new listings and site reviews in our free email newsletter. Simply send us an email or visit our website home page to sign up. All of these articles are published in our blog.

  You'll also see camp closures and new sites on our Facebook and Instagram pages, and you can join our Facebook Group called "I Love Camping Australia Wide".

Visit our website to find out more: www.campsaustraliawide.com

Free Website Update Service
Use the 'Updates' tab to find out about closed sites and major changes – it is free and user-friendly. Updates for this edition are provided for four years from the date first published.

Step 1
On the Camps Australia Wide website, select the 'Updates' tab.

Feedback
Our team always welcomes feedback on existing sites and any new site that you think worthwhile sharing with our fellow travellers.

Please email us on:
talktous@campsaustraliawide.com

Step 2
Selecting the 'Updates' tab will direct you to the 'Update Service' page which gives you an option to 'Launch Updates Program'. When that is selected, the Updates Program will display in a window floating above the web page.

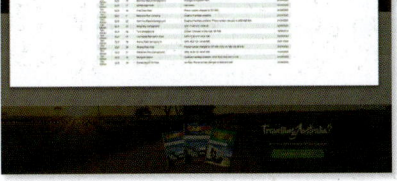

Step 3
In the Updates Program window, choices are made as to publication, edition, state, and dates. The first time you use the updates, leave the date fields blank. For subsequent updates, enter the date range using the pop-up calendar to show new updates only.

NOTE: Names of sites may change over time. As the updates are automated, we no longer use abbreviations. If the Print button is obscured, simply use the scroll bar to reveal it.

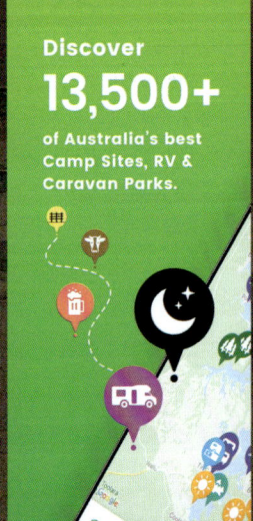

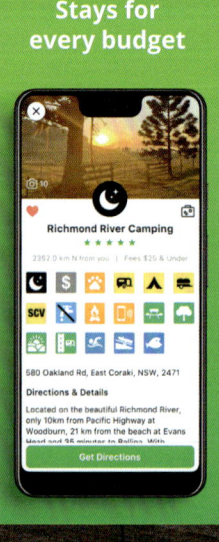
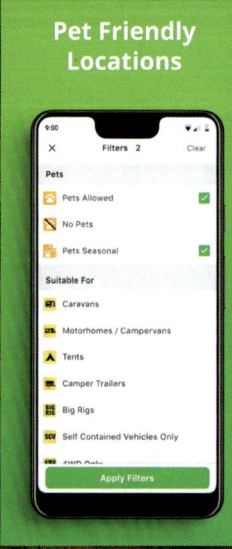
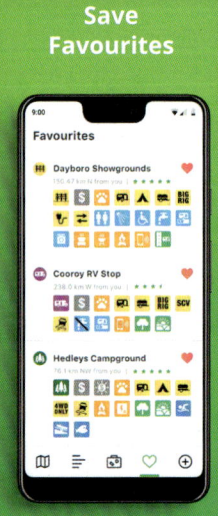

How to use this Guide

Overnight Parking and Camping Site Types

There are many new symbols for CAMPS 11. Colours now indicate site type, instead of presence of a dump point. Unlike 20 years ago when Camps was first published, dump points are now plentiful - you can see by the extensive list at the end of the book. It is also easy to see if sites are pet friendly (with ears), or not.

On Maps		In Listing	Site Type	Definition
Pets Allowed	**No Pets**			
155	155	(moon/stars icon)	**Overnight Site Free or Donation**	Any site not listed in the below categories with a money contribution or no cost. *TIP: If there is a donation box, please use it! Our cash helps the communities we travel in - keeping campsites open.*
155	155	(moon/stars icon)	**Overnight Site Paid**	Any site not listed in the below categories with a fee.
155	155	(gate icon)	**Recreation and Showgrounds Community Halls**	Often community or council run. They may be closed for events, like country shows – so best to pre-book.
155	155	(motorhome icon)	**RV Park**	For self-contained motorhomes and caravans. They do not tend to allow tents or camper trailers. Toilet facilities and power are generally not available.
155	155	(cow icon)	**Farm or Station Stays**	A camp area or bush camping on a working property. Usually in a remote location, with varied facilities. Power may be limited. GPS coordinates are at the gate or entry.
155	155	(beer mug icon)	**Pub or Club Stays**	A camping or parking area at licensed premises. If you camp at a commercial site for free, make sure you patronise the business – buy a meal or enjoy some time at the bar.
155	155	(mountains icon)	**National Park Campground***	Land protected by the Federal Government, generally pets are forbidden. Most are rich in natural beauty, trails, flora and fauna.
155	155	(trees icon)	**State Forest Nature Reserve or Conservation Area**	State protected areas of natural beauty or significance, that may or may not allow pets.
322	322	(caravan icon)	**Caravan Park (budget, remote or offer unique experiences only)**	An established area for overnight stays, providing a range of facilities and comforts. A fee is payable depending on the quality and number of facilities offered.
			Caravan Park (with fees over $25 per 2 adults per night)	For the entire list of caravan parks in Australia see our Caravan Parks book or Camps Australia Wide App.

*Some National Parks have updated their campgrounds as only suitable for camper trailer or tents, where previously it was for more vehicle types. These 4WD camper trailer and tent-only sites are listed in the Camps Australia Wide App.

The Pines - Delatite Arm, Lake Eildon, Victoria by Scott Philpotts

Cooee Point, Tasmania

Layout of the Guide

The book is divided into different coloured sections for each State or Territory for easier navigation. The listings are in a linear order along the highways and roads, following the routes on each state's contents page.

Abbreviations

Some abbreviations have been used to condense the amount of text throughout the book. They are:

Dr	Drive	**Tce**	Terrace	**Pde**	Parade
Rd	Road	**Cnr**	Corner	**Ln**	Lane
Ave	Avenue	**Jcn**	Junction	**Ct**	Court
Hwy	Highway	**Cr**	Crescent	**Is**	Island
max	Maximum	**Tr**	Track	**N**	North
PO	Post Office	**St**	Street	**S**	South
DP	Dump Point	**L**	Left	**E**	East
km	Kilometre	**R**	Right	**W**	West
m	Metre	**Rec**	Recreation		
NP	National Park	**BYO**	Bring your own		
Dev	Development/al	**SCV**	Self Contained Vehicle		

Map References

Maps are by Hema with sites and site numbers from Camps Australia Wide overlaid. All the sites are referenced to these maps. Site symbols are placed as close as possible to the exact position. Where the number of sites is quite comprehensive, more detailed maps should be used for navigation. The Hema symbol key is listed on the inside cover.

How to locate a site

If you know the name of a site, go to the Site Index, (alphabetically listed), which gives you the site number and the relevant page number.

If you want to find sites in any particular area, look at the relevant map for site numbers in that region, then look up those sites in the numerical listing. There will always be variations in odometer readings and road distance signs, so do allow for those discrepancies when locating sites.

Explanation of other terms

Rest Area An area usually located close to the highway to enable the traveller to take a break. Some rest areas provide a wide range of facilities, while others are just an area to rest for a while. Overnight camping is permitted at some sites, depending on the relevant authority's regulations. Please take notice of any regulatory signs.

Camp Area or Camp Spot An area for camping overnight or longer, that may have limited facilities, e.g. it may provide toilets and water, but not necessarily showers or power. A fee is usually charged.

Dispersed Camping Bush camping with no or limited facilities with unallocated sites, it may be across hectares e.g., in a national park or conservation reserve. GPS coordinates will usually be at entry.

Picnic Area An area that has suitable facilities for a picnic. Overnight stays may be permissible in some cases.

Parking Area An area with limited or no facilities e.g. a hotel carpark. Overnight stays may be allowed in certain cases.

Small Vehicle Only Indicates the entry into the site is tight and parking, camping or turning area is restricted, only campervans, small camper trailers or caravans are recommended.

Self Contained Vehicle (SCV) A vehicle that is fully self contained with respect to shower, toilet, washing, cooking and sleeping facilities, and which must have holding tanks for all toilet waste and sullage water sufficient for at least 48 hours' use by the occupants.

Dump Points

Only public dump points are listed on the maps - for other dump points, check individual site listings. An example of a public dump point listing, and the symbols, are shown on the introductory page of the Public Dump Point section at the end of the book.

Other Site Types

On Map	In App	Type	Definition
(caravan dump symbol)	(dump point symbol)	**Public Dump Point**	A disposal facility for RV wastewater, accessible to all. Most are free and council run, others may be privately owned with a fee.
Not Applicable	(sun symbol)	**Day Use Area**	Rest or picnic areas, where camping is not allowed, are listed in the Camps Australia Wide App.

Legend for symbols in listings

The sample below explains how each site is laid out for easy interpretation.
Most of the symbols are self-explanatory, but some have been designed to fit certain criteria.

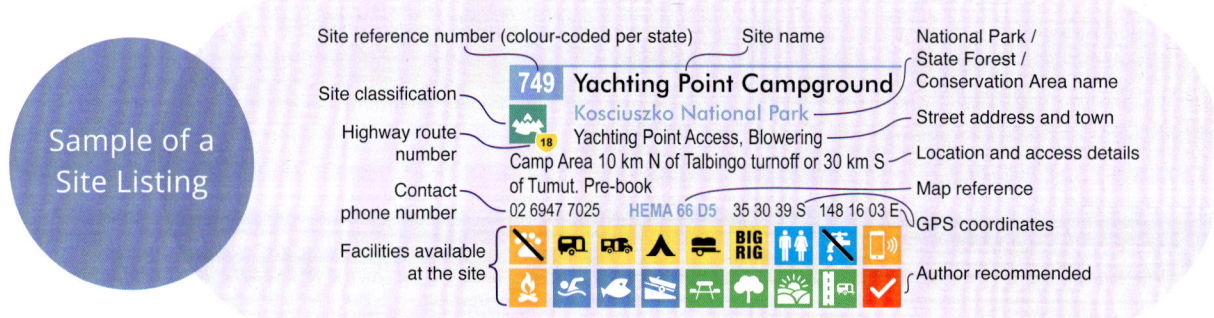

Sample of a Site Listing

- Site reference number (colour-coded per state)
- Site name
- National Park / State Forest / Conservation Area name
- Site classification
- Highway route number
- Contact phone number
- Street address and town
- Location and access details
- Map reference
- GPS coordinates
- Facilities available at the site
- Author recommended

749 Yachting Point Campground
Kosciuszko National Park
Yachting Point Access, Blowering
Camp Area 10 km N of Talbingo turnoff or 30 km S of Tumut. Pre-book
02 6947 7025   HEMA 66 D5   35 30 39 S   148 16 03 E

Explanation Of Symbols

Price Range

Prices are based on the standard off-season rate for a powered site (if available) for two adults for one night at the time of publication. Peak seasons vary across the country and fees are subject to change without notice. So it is strongly recommended that you check the fees before you arrive.

 Donation

 $25 and under

 $26 to $40

 $41 and over Sites with this symbol have been included in this edition because of their locations or because they offer something special.

 Day use fee applicable Primarily charged at state and national parks, often in addition to any camping fees.

> **TIP:** Always ask for a single or family rate, if it applies.

Pets

 Pets Not Allowed Pets are not allowed at this site.

 Pets Allowed with Conditions
Call ahead to confirm that your pet is welcome. Some operators now require a fee and/or bond as part of the conditions of entry into the area and may limit animal size. As a general rule pets must always be on a lead and must never be left unattended. As always, clean up after your pet!

 Pets Seasonal with Conditions
Pets are allowed (with conditions, see above) at this site during off-peak periods.

Maximum Stay (hours)

20 These may be Main Roads rest areas or sites provided by local authorities. Please honour the time limits as signposted, so they remain open in the future.

Suitable For

 Caravan Site is suitable for a caravan.

 Campervan or Motorhome Site is suitable for a campervan / motorhome (not a Big Rig).

 Tents
Site is suitable for setting up a tent. In a commercial camping area tent sites are usually in an open grassed area (subject to local conditions).

 Camper Trailer
Site is suitable for setting up a camper trailer.

 Big Rigs
Site is suitable for Big Rigs - rigid vehicles with an overall length of 10 metres or more. There are usually limited sites available for larger vehicles.

 Self Contained Vehicles Only
Only vehicles with shower, toilet, washing, cooking and sleeping facilities and holding tanks for all toilet waste and sullage water, sufficient for at least 48 hours' use by the occupants, are allowed here.

 4WD Only Recommended
Only vehicles with four-wheel-drive transmission can access this site. High clearance may also be required.

 Dry Weather Access Only
Roads used to access the site may become impassable during the wet season or after rain, and care is advised. Please check with local authorities for conditions. Usually recommended for 4WD only.

Accommodation and Sites

 Powered Sites
These sites may have a concrete pad and/or grassed area with a power point for your vehicle.

 Ensuite Sites
Powered sites that have individual amenities.

 Drive Through Sites
Sites that caravans or motorhomes can drive directly into and out of without having to reverse or unhitch. These sites are popular for overnight stops.

 Onsite Accommodation
Include cabins, lodges or houses with ensuites or access to communal facilities.

 Glamping
'Glamorous camping' may include yurts, pods or safari tents, and creature comforts like a real bed.

Connectivity

 Mobile Phone Service
Site has access to Telstra NextG ™ Network with a 'Blue Tick Telstra phone'.

 Wireless Internet
Wi-Fi facilities are provided. Fees may apply.

Settings and Features

 Picnic Table
Picnic tables are available and may be covered.

 Children's Playground
Play equipment may vary from a slippery dip, to a water park and jumping pillow.

 Shade
At the time of viewing this site there was shade available for your vehicle.

 Views
The site provides a pleasant outlook or vista.

 Beside Road
These sites may be noisy depending on the amount of passing traffic and time of day.

 Pool Swimming pool provided.

 Swimming Nearby
Other types of swimming, like ocean, river, waterhole, creek, lagoon are available. They may not be patrolled.

 Boat Ramp Nearby
This site has boat launch facilities nearby. The ramp may be properly built or may be adapted from local conditions. In most cases they are suitable for small 'tinnies'.

 Fishing This site has fishing nearby.

 CAMPS' Recommendation At the time they were visited, these sites were appealing, either because of the site's position or vista or because facilities were above average.

Facilities and Amenities

 Toilets
Outside of caravan parks these may be long-drops or composting types. As these are not always serviced frequently, best to BYO toilet paper.

 Showers
May be hot or cold and in some isolated areas, solar-heated only. Some are available for a fee or donation.

 Accessible Facilities
Generally, there is at least one dedicated toilet and shower for people with disabilities, in some sites this facility is unisex.

 Drinking Water
Even though it is listed as drinkable it is advisable to boil or filter before use. Please use common sense and limit your use, so that others can enjoy the availability as well.

 Non-Potable Water
Water that is not of drinking quality but may be suitable for other purposes.

 Dump Point
This park or site has a dump point to dispose of your black or grey water, either via cassettes or holding tanks.

 Laundry
An area with washing machines and clothesline, irons and dryers. They may be coin operated.

 Games or TV Room
A communal recreation area, activities may vary.

 Camp Kitchen
This covered area normally includes a BBQ, hotplate, refrigerator, dishwashing space, tables and chairs.

 BBQ
At camp sites these are usually wood-fuelled. Some parks and camps provide a free gas or electric barbeque, others may charge a small fee.

> **TIP:** Any communal cooking area needs to be cleaned ready for use by the next camper!

 Fireplace
A fireplace or fire pit is present.

Gas Bottle Refills/Exchanges
This site has facilities to top or swap your gas bottles.

Generators Allowed with Conditions
There may be a time limit or designated area if you need to operate a generator.

> **BOAT TIP:** Check local conditions for tidal flow and other hazards.

NATURE NEVER FELT SO GOOD

reflections
HOLIDAY PARKS

FERRY RESERVE
MASSY GREENE
TERRACE RESERVE
CLARKES BEACH
LENNOX HEAD
SHAWS BAY
BALLINA
EVANS HEAD
RED ROCK
CORINDI BEACH
MOONEE BEACH
COFFS HARBOUR
BOAMBEE CREEK RESERVE
MYLESTOM
URUNGA
HUNGRY HEAD
NAMBUCCA HEADS
SCOTTS HEAD
BONNY HILLS
NORTH HAVEN
TUNCURRY
FORSTER BEACH
SEAL ROCKS
HAWKS NEST
JIMMYS BEACH

COPETON WATERS
Armidale
LAKE KEEPIT
LAKE GLENBAWN
CUDGEGONG RIVER
LAKE BURRENDONG
MOOKERAWA WATERS
Orange
GRABINE LAKESIDE
WYANGALA WATERS
KILLALEA RESERVE
Hume & Hovell Track
BURRINJUCK WATERS
Canberra
BERMAGUI
PAMBULA
EDEN

Port Macquarie
Newcastle
Sydney
Wollongong

Travel Responsibly

Only camp in designated sites, obey signage and camp responsibly. At all times use common sense with fires, plants, animals and your fellow travellers, and protect the environment.

Seven Principles of Leave No Trace

1. Plan ahead and prepare
2. Travel and camp on durable surfaces
3. Dispose of waste properlyLeave what you find
4. Leave what you find
5. Minimise campfire impacts
6. Respect wildlife
7. Be considerate of your hosts and other visitors - for more information visit www.lnt.org.au

Rubbish

If there are no rubbish bins provided, please take your rubbish with you. Leave an area cleaner than you find it and consider cleaning up after someone else. A well looked after site will give the authorities a good reason to keep it open for our use.

Toilet Waste

We have provided a comprehensive Public Dump Point list at the end of the book, including caravan parks that allow use of their dump point for a fee. If you have to bury your waste in remote areas, make sure it is at least 20 centimetres deep and 200 metres away from any waterway, runoff area or camp site.

Firewood

It is advisable to carry your own supply of firewood for fires and barbeques at some of the more isolated camp spots, rather than destroy any remaining trees. Most national parks do not allow firewood collection within their boundaries. Ensure you respect all local fire bans and seasonal restrictions.

Generators

Generators can be a necessary part of travelling, but do have consideration for your neighbour and run them at respectable hours. Be aware of the noise and fumes put out by these machines and park accordingly.

> TIP: Generators are banned in some national parks.

Ballinyoo Bridge, Western Australia by Lyn Quilty

Solar Energy

Solar technology has advanced significantly in the last few years. It is a very effective way for people to travel off-grid.

Water

Although the water available at sites should be suitable for drinking, it would be wise to carry sufficient water for drinking as a backup and as an alternative if the water is drinkable but unpleasant.

Quarantine Zones

Pests, weeds and disease can travel with you. Follow the rules for restrictions as you cross quarantine and state borders to help Australia's biosecurity and farmers. On-the-spot fines apply. Check our Important Contacts page for details.

Private Property

Make sure you gain approval to travel on private land. Remember you are in someone's backyard, so behave like you would want visitors to, if they were in your home.

Be Croc-Wise, Dingo-Safe

Avoid wildlife encounters, take responsibility and follow recommendations for you and your family's safety.

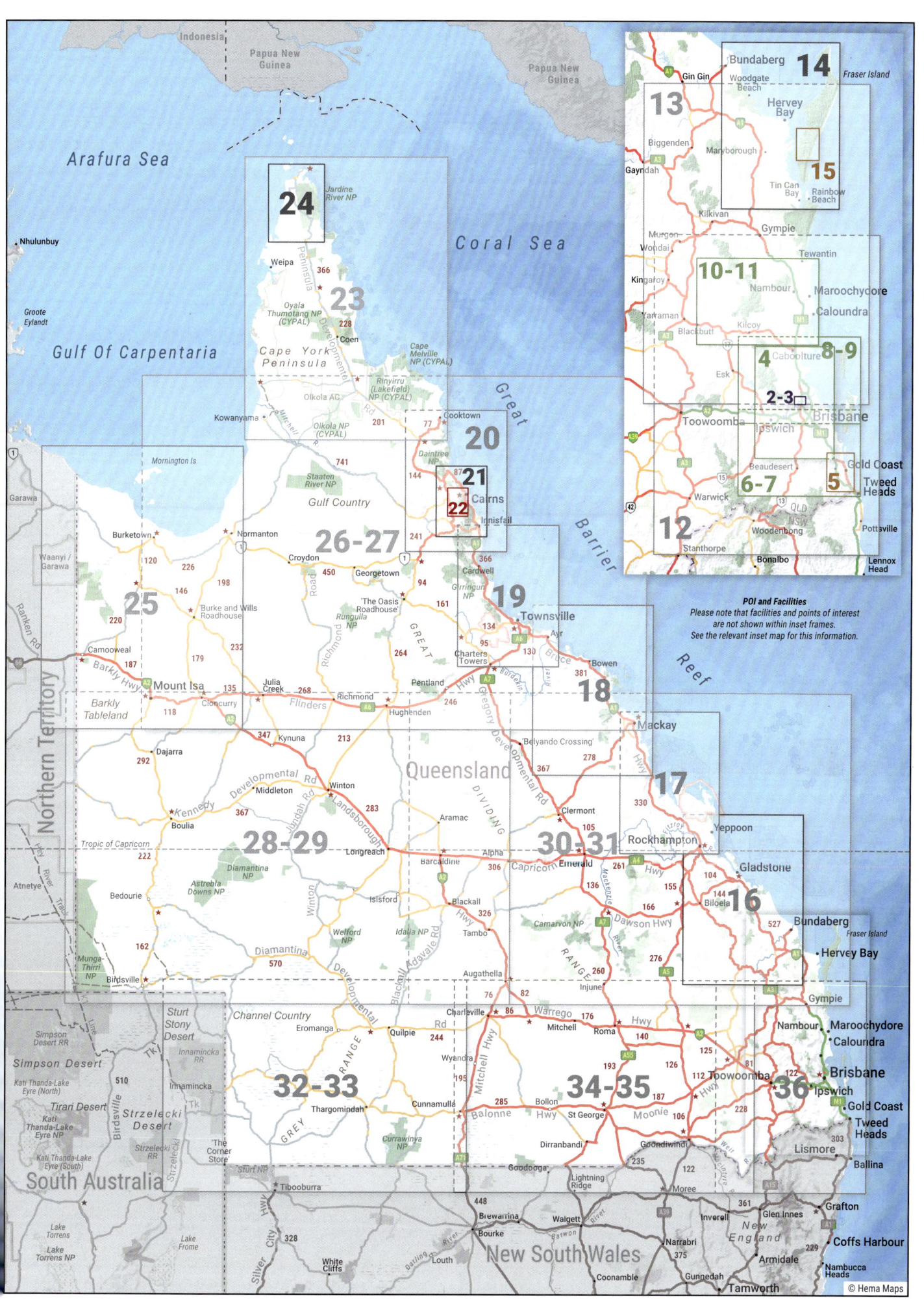

POI and Facilities
*Please note that facilities and points of interest
are not shown within inset frames.
See the relevant inset map for this information.*

© Hema Maps

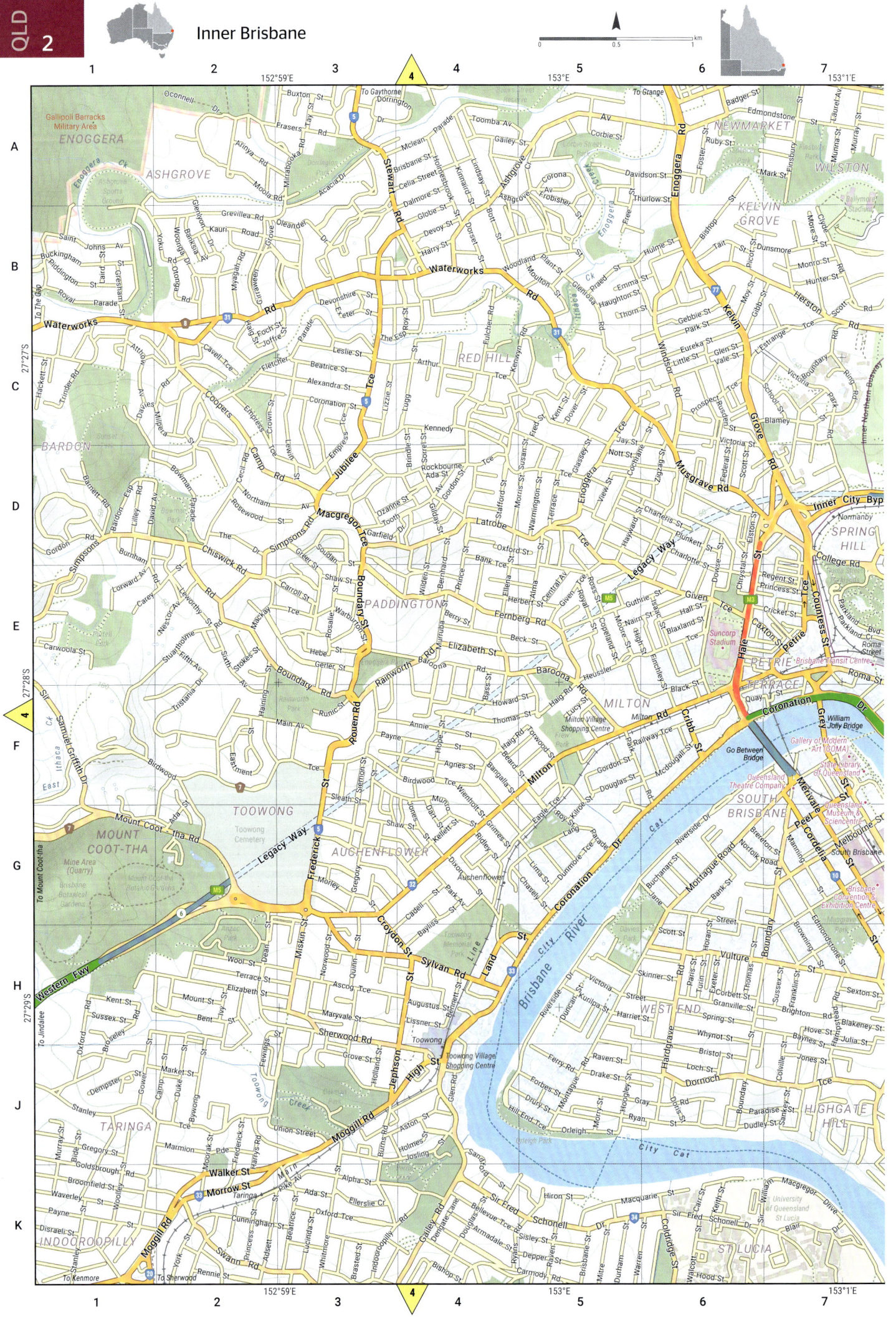

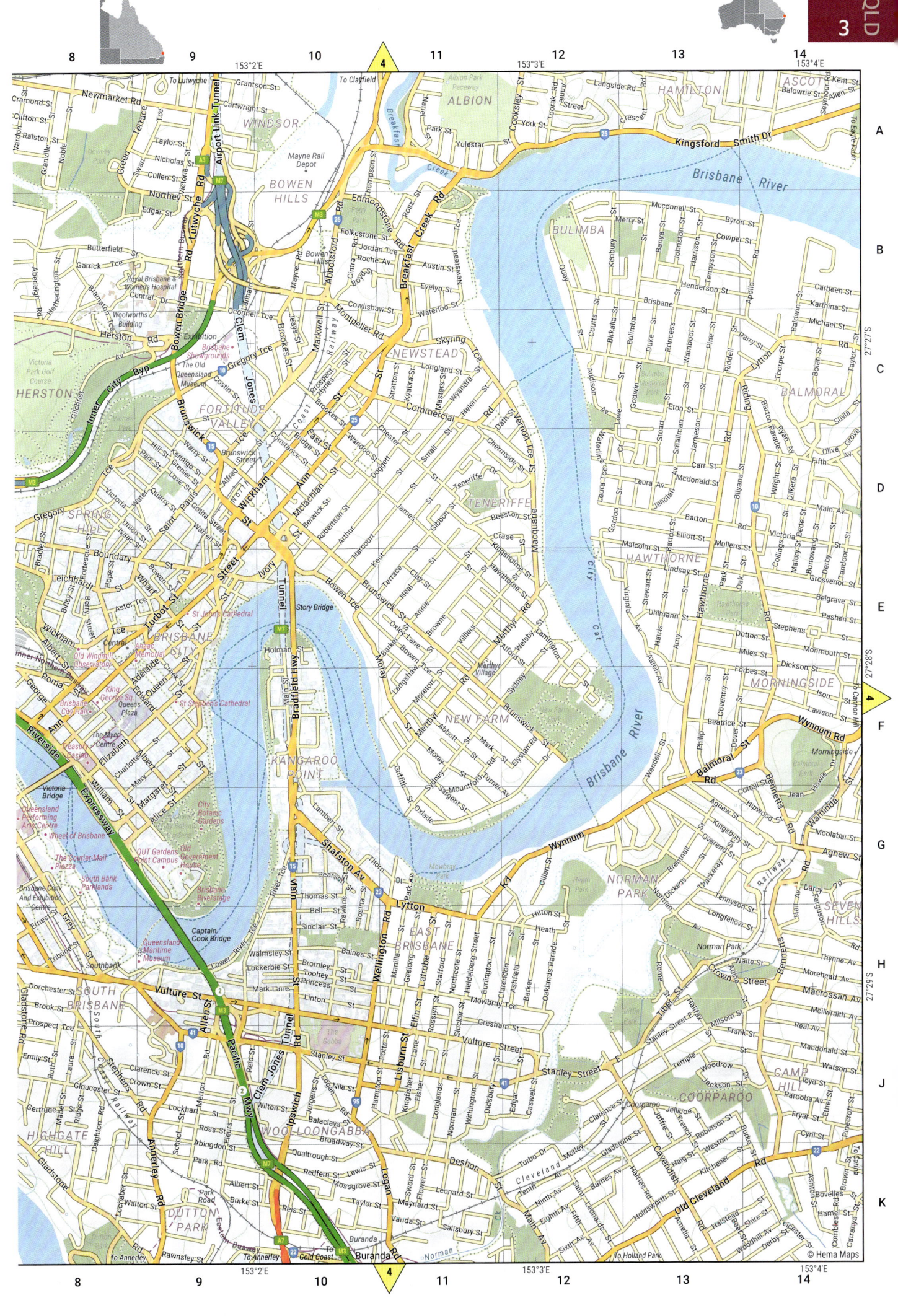

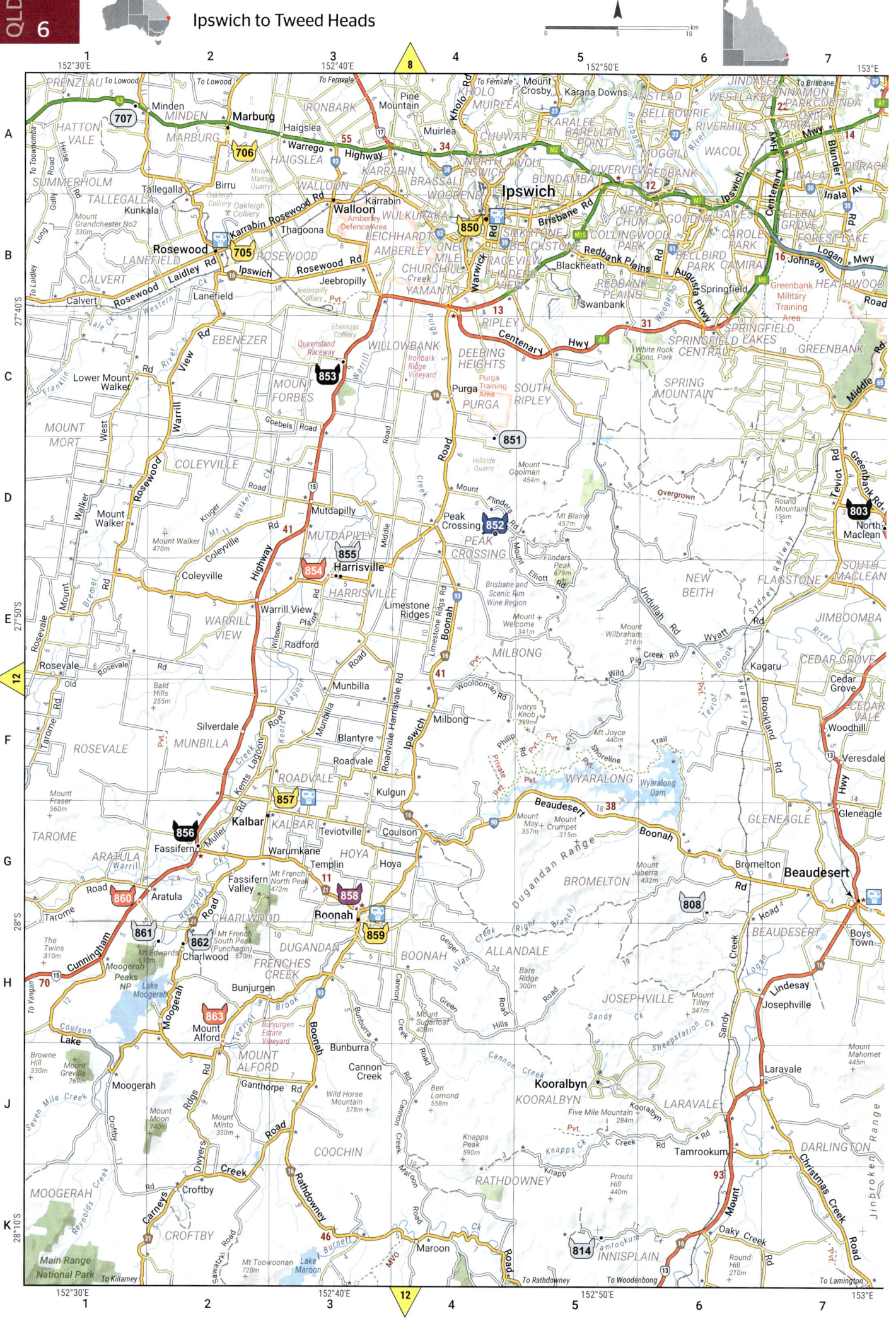

Ipswich to Tweed Heads

153°10'E
153°20'E
153°30'E
27°40'S
27°50'S
28°S
28°10'S
Moreton Bay Marine Park
Moreton Island to Broadwater
North Stradbroke Island (Minjerriba)
Moreton Bay
Moreton Bay - Offshore
Victoria Point
Redland Bay
Point Talburpin
Logan Central
Beenleigh
Jacobs Well
Russell Island
Macleay Island
Lamb Island (Ngudooroo)
Karragarra Island
Naree Budjong Djara NP
Tollways
For information on toll tags or passes for Motorways contact go via on 13 33 31 or online www.govia.com.au
Coral Sea
Jumpinpin
South Stradbroke Island
Southern Moreton Bay Islands NP
South Stradbroke Island Conservation Park
Jimboomba
Tamborine
Tamborine NP
Wickham National Park
Santa Barbara
Sanctuary Cove
Hope Island (Boykambil)
See map 5
Oxenford
Boykambil
Helensvale
Eagle Heights
North Tamborine
Mount Tamborine
Canungra
Canungra Defence Reserve
Nerang
Nerang National Park
Gold Coast
South Pacific Ocean
Advancetown
Advancetown Lake
Lower Beechmont
Burleigh Heads
Upper Mudgeeraba
Springbrook NP
Numinbah Valley
Lamington National Park
Currumbin
Tweed Heads
Coolangatta
Tweed Heads West
Piggabeen
Kerry
Hale Village
Flying Fox
Ferny Glen
Beechmont
Mt Alexander 612m
Bally Mountain 489m
Mount Dunsinane 290m
To Lamington
To Murwillumbah
To Brisbane
To Dunwich
© Hema Maps

Lake Somerset to Victoria Point

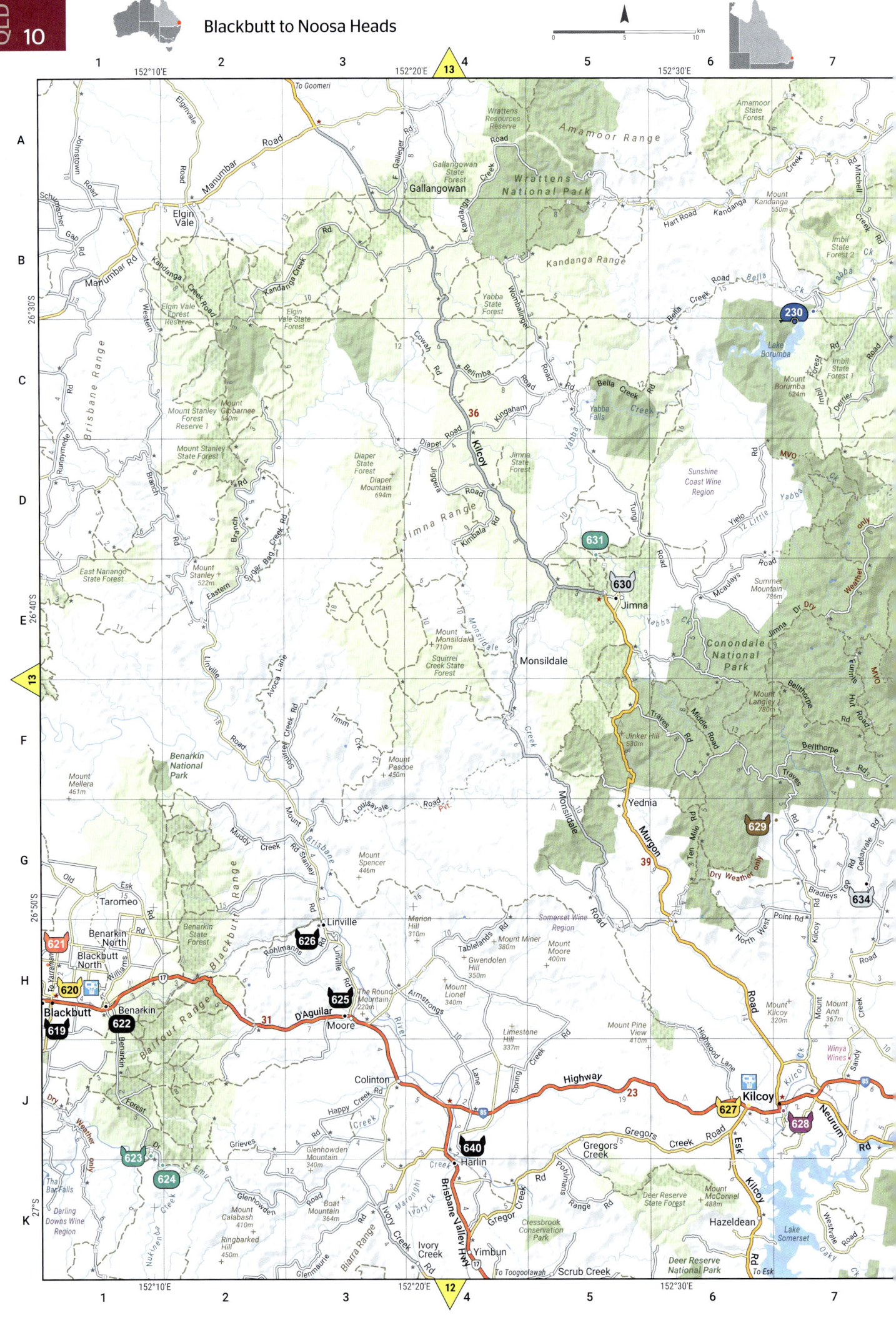

© Hema Maps

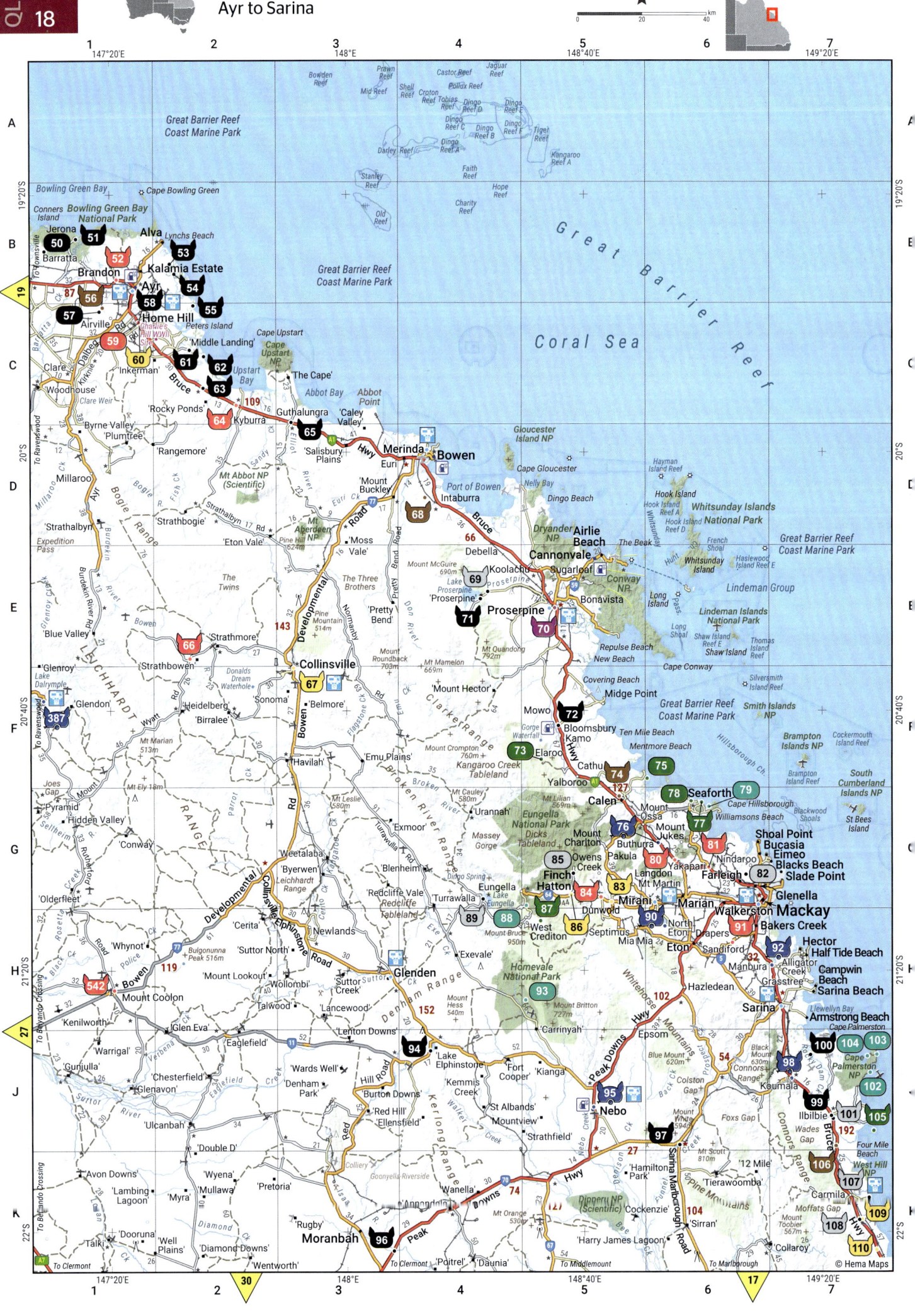

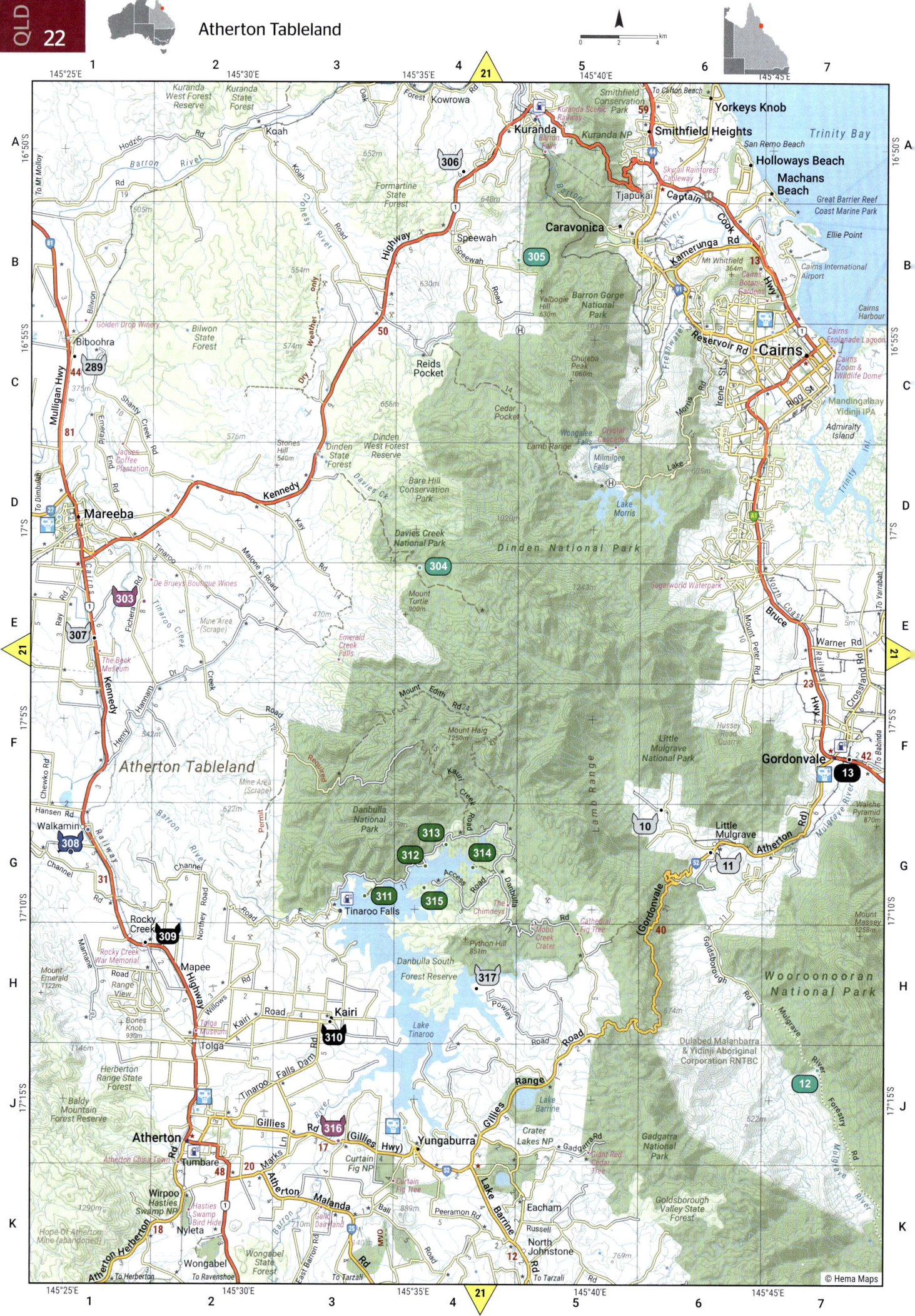

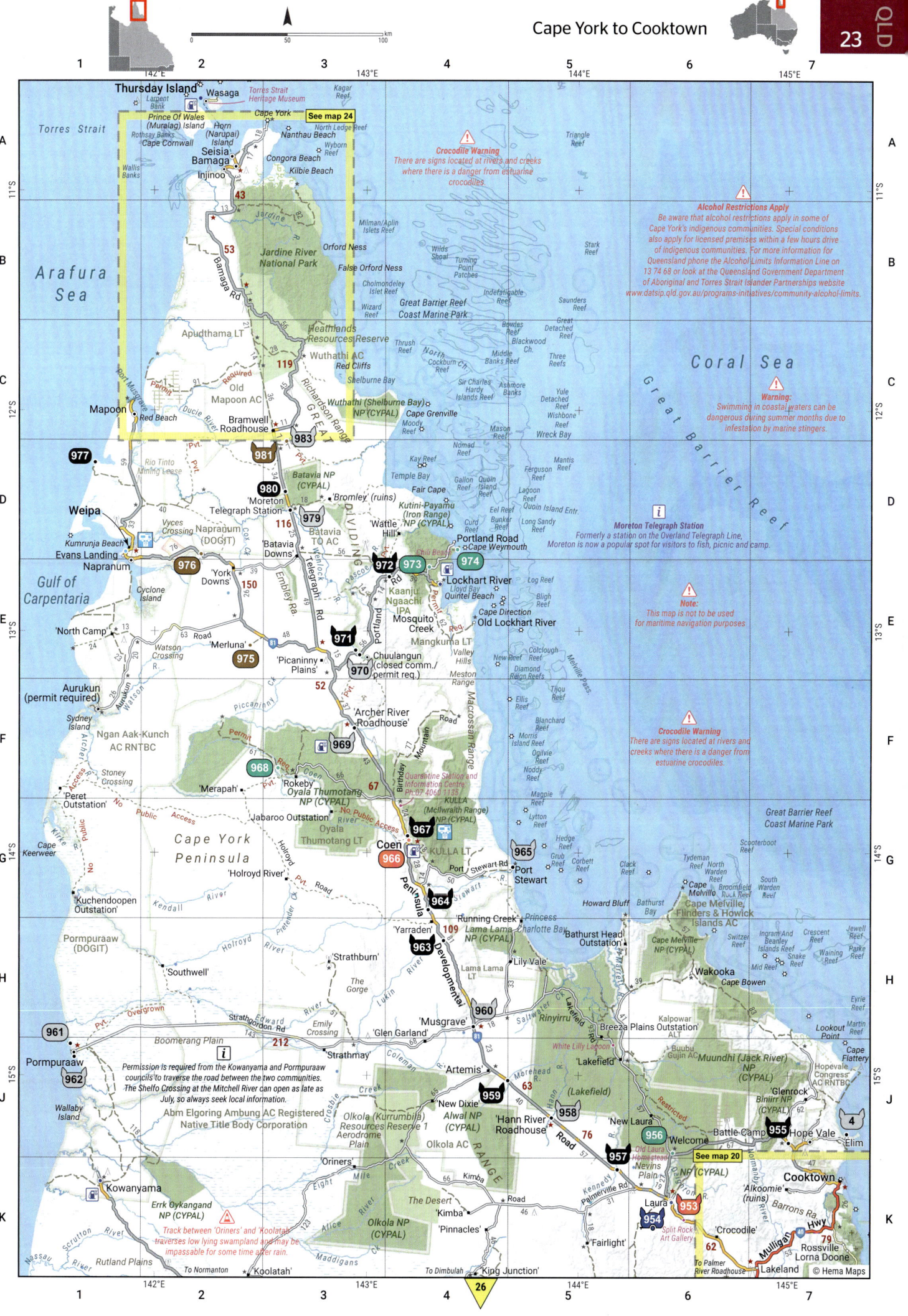

km
0   50   100

Crocodile Warning
There are signs located at rivers and creeks where there is a danger from estuarine crocodiles.

Alcohol Restrictions Apply
Be aware that alcohol restrictions apply in some of Cape York's indigenous communities. Special conditions also apply for licensed premises within a few hours drive of indigenous communities. For more information for Queensland phone the Alcohol Limits Information Line on 13 74 68 or look at the Queensland Government Department of Aboriginal and Torres Strait Islander Partnerships website www.datsip.qld.gov.au/programs-initiatives/community-alcohol-limits.

Warning:
Swimming in coastal waters can be dangerous during summer months due to infestation by marine stingers.

Moreton Telegraph Station
Formerly a station on the Overland Telegraph Line, Moreton is now a popular spot for visitors to fish, picnic and camp.

Note:
This map is not to be used for maritime navigation purposes

Crocodile Warning
There are signs located at rivers and creeks where there is a danger from estuarine crocodiles.

Quarantine Station and Information Centre
Ph.07 4060 1133.

Permission is required from the Kowanyama and Pormpuraaw councils to traverse the road between the two communities. The Shelfo Crossing at the Mitchell River can open as late as July, so always seek local information.

Track between 'Oriners' and 'Koolatah' traverses low lying swampland and may be impassable for some time after rain.

© Hema Maps

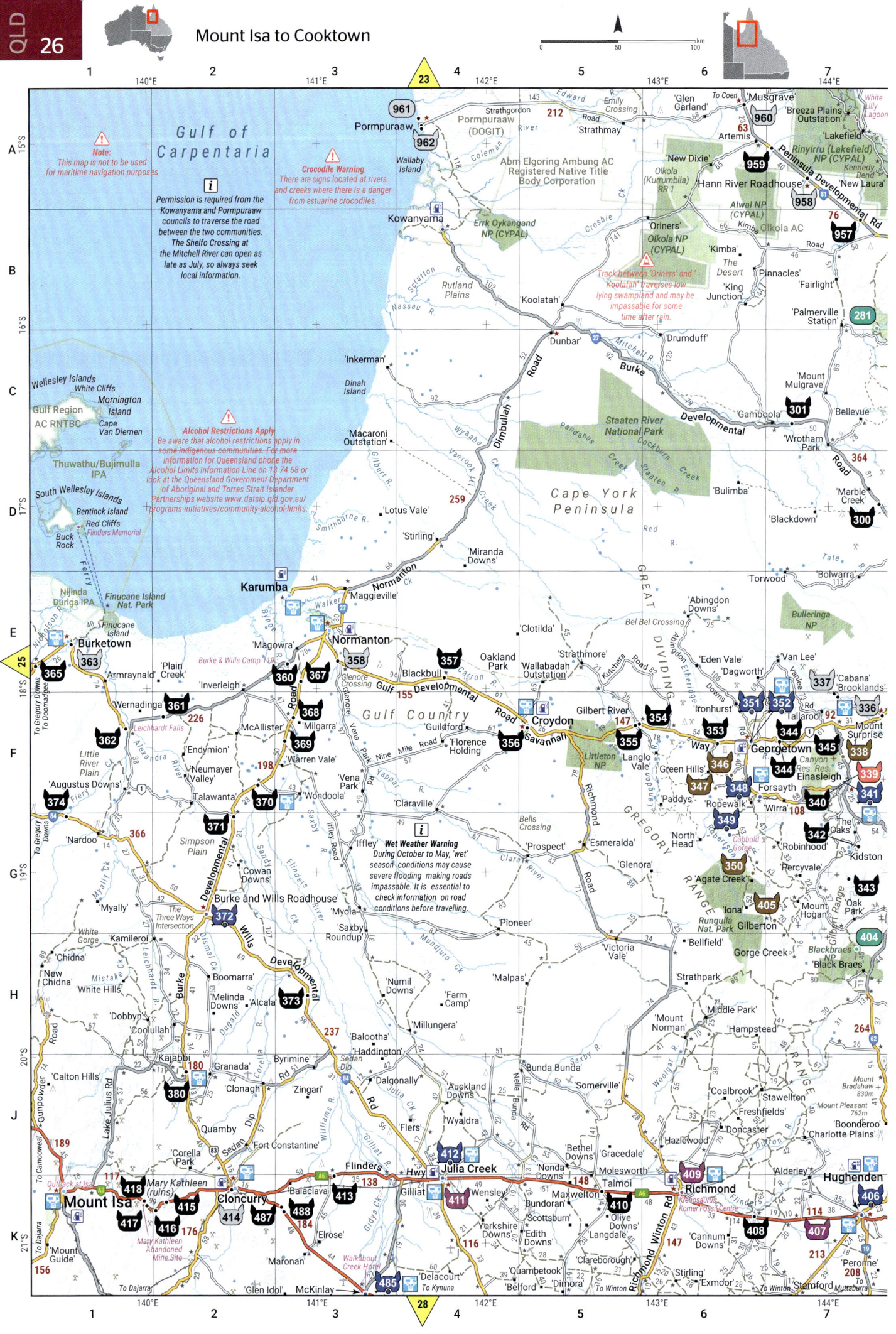

Cape Melville NP (CYPAL)
Buubu Gujin AC
Muundhi (Jack River) NP (CYPAL)
Rinyirru (Lakefield) NP CYPAL
Cape Melville, Flinders & Howick Islands AC
Helsdon Reef
Wooden Patch
Cape Flattery
Long Reef
Coconut Island
Mackay Reefs
Startle Reef

Glenrock
955
956
Welcome
Dinhara Homestead
Hope Vale
Elim
Hopevale Congress
AC RNTBC
See map 20

Laura
953
954
'Alkoomie' (ruins)
Cooktown
Osterland Reef
Split Rock Art Gallery
62
'Crocodile'
79
Rossville
Lorna Doone
Bonnie Glen
Ayton
Ngalba Bulal National Park
Agincourt Reef No.4

Lakeland
31
Wujal Wujal
The Jump Up
Bloomfield
154
Eastern Kuku
Agincourt Reefs No.3
Opal Reef

Palmer River Roadhouse
Mt Windsor NP 940m
Daintree
Daintree National Park
Yalanji IPA
Thornton Beach
41
Tongue Reef

'The Granite'
112
Mossman
Port Douglas
Craiglie
See map 21
Michaelmas Reef

'Kondaparinga'
Mount Carbine
29
72
Trinity Beach
Trinity Bay

'Mount Mulligan'
Yalkula
Kuranda
Caravonica
Cairns
Smithfield Heights
Great Barrier Reef Coast Marine Park
Thetford Reef
Elford Reef

Mungana
299
Chillagoe
Mareeba
44
63
Gordonvale
Sudbury Reef
Maori Reef

298
Royal Arch Caves
Dimbulah
81
23
42
Babinda
Flora Reef
Hadley Reef
Gibson Reef

'Crystal Brook'
Petford
Atherton
Herberton
31
17
40
18
Malanda
Howie Reef
Wardle Reef

Almaden
Emuford
Watsonville
Irvinebank
70
48
19
22
Innisfail
Peart Reef

Tate
Ravenshoe
Millaa Millaa
28
Adelaide Reef

Mount Garnet
137
62
43
Silkwood
El Arish
Potter Reef
Noreaster Reef
Yamacutta Reef

Fossilbrook
710m
Koombooloomba
Mission Beach
Wongaling Beach
Farquarson Reef
Beaver Reef
Duncan Reef

'Springfield'
332
Koombooloomba NP
Tully
Barnett Patches

56
333
'Wombinoo'
'Goshen'
Tully Heads
119
Girringun IPA
Otter Reef
Britomart Reef
Pith Reef

Undara Lava Tubes
'Yarama'
Meadowbank
330
331
Kirrama NP
Cardwell
Cape Sandwich
Hinchinbrook Island National Park
Trunk Reef
Kelso Reef

Undara Volcanic National Park
Mount McBride +911m
'Wairuna'
Girringun NP
Bramble Reef
Slashers No.2 Reef
John Brewer Reef

'Rosella Plains'
'Lake Lucy'
'Oak Hills'
Abergowrie
Trebonne
Lucinda
Macknade
Halifax
Taylors Beach
South West Cape

94
'Rhonella Park'
Ingham
Palm Island

79
334
Conjuboy
'Jervoise'
Valley Of Lagoons
'Camel Creek'
Michael Creek
Allingham (Forrest Beach)
Halifax Bay
Big Broadhurst Reef A
Shrimp Reef

The Oasis Roadhouse
Gregory
'Gadara'
Ryeburn
Barrilgie
Little Broadhurst Reef
Bowden Reef
Dingo Reef

Greenvale
335
145
'Kangaroo Hills'
Paluma
113
Balgal Beach
Bluewater
Nelly Bay
See map 18
Prawn Reef
Stanley Reef
Old Reef

Lyndhurst
'Pandanus Creek'
'New Moon'
Paluma Range NP
Deeragun
Mount Low
Townsville
Nome
Bowling Green Bay

Mount Remarkable 800m
Bluewater Springs Roadhouse
Hervey Range
158
Bohle Plains
Alligator Creek
Cungulla
Giru
Alva
Bowling Green Bay NP

Big 4 Ben 810m
Bottle Gorge
'Twelve Mile'
'Valpree'
'Dotswood'
'Granite Creek'
Lake Ross
87
Ayr
Home Hill
Cape Upstart
Great Barrier Reef Coast Marine Park

'Clarke Hills'
'Wando Vale'
'Hillgrove'
111
'Eumara Springs'
'Fanning River'
'Majors Creek'
Woodhouse
109
Upstart Bay
Abbot Bay
Abbot Point

'Pretty Plains'
King's Knob 925m
'Nulla Nulla'
'Great Basalt Wall' NP
'Myola'
'Lochwall'
'Fern Spring'
136
Kyburra
Guthalungra
Cape Edgecumbe

'Craigie'
'Cargoon'
Myrrlumbing
Charters Towers
Millaroo
Bowen
Edgecumbe Bay
Dryander NP

'Killarney'
Mount Stewart 997m
Flinders Hwy
541
Ravenswood
'Strathbogie'
66
Debella
Airlie Beach
Cannonvale
Whitsunday Islands National Park

403
'Clyde Park'
'Goldsborough'
397
Homestead
'Cameron'
Saint Pauls
'Rangeview'
'Moss Vale'
'Eton Vale'
'Pretty Bend'
Proserpine
Conway
Repulse NP

White Mtns NP
Porcupine Gorge NP
398
Pentland
246
Helenslee
'Slogan Downs'
Mount Cooper
'Blue Valley'
143
Collinsville
Heidelberg
'Havilah'
Lindeman Group

'Delbessie'
400
'Milray'
399
196
Lascelles
'New Victoria Downs'
Lake Dalrymple
Bowen R
127
Bloomsbury
Kamo
Mentmore Beach
Seaforth

Prairie
401
Torrens Creek
'Broadleigh Downs'
'Longton'
Dandenong Park
'Pyramid'
Conway
'Exmoor'
'Emu Plains'
Eungella National Park
Seaforth
Calen
Shoal Point Pt

'Redcliff'
'Curragilla'
Merlin
'Maitland'
Oxenhope Outstation
'Natal Downs'
Jumba
'Hanging Rock'
Olderfleet
119
'Redcliffe Vale'
152
'Cerita'
Newlands
Eungella NP
Walkerston
Marian
Finch Hatton
Bucasia
See map 17
Mackay

'Zara'
To Aramac
To Clermont
30
West Crediton
Turrawalla
To Nebo
Mirani

Great Barrier Reef

Coral Sea

Crocodile Warning
There are signs located at rivers and creeks where there is a danger from estuarine crocodiles.

Warning:
Swimming in coastal waters can be dangerous during summer months due to infestation by marine stingers.

© Hema Maps

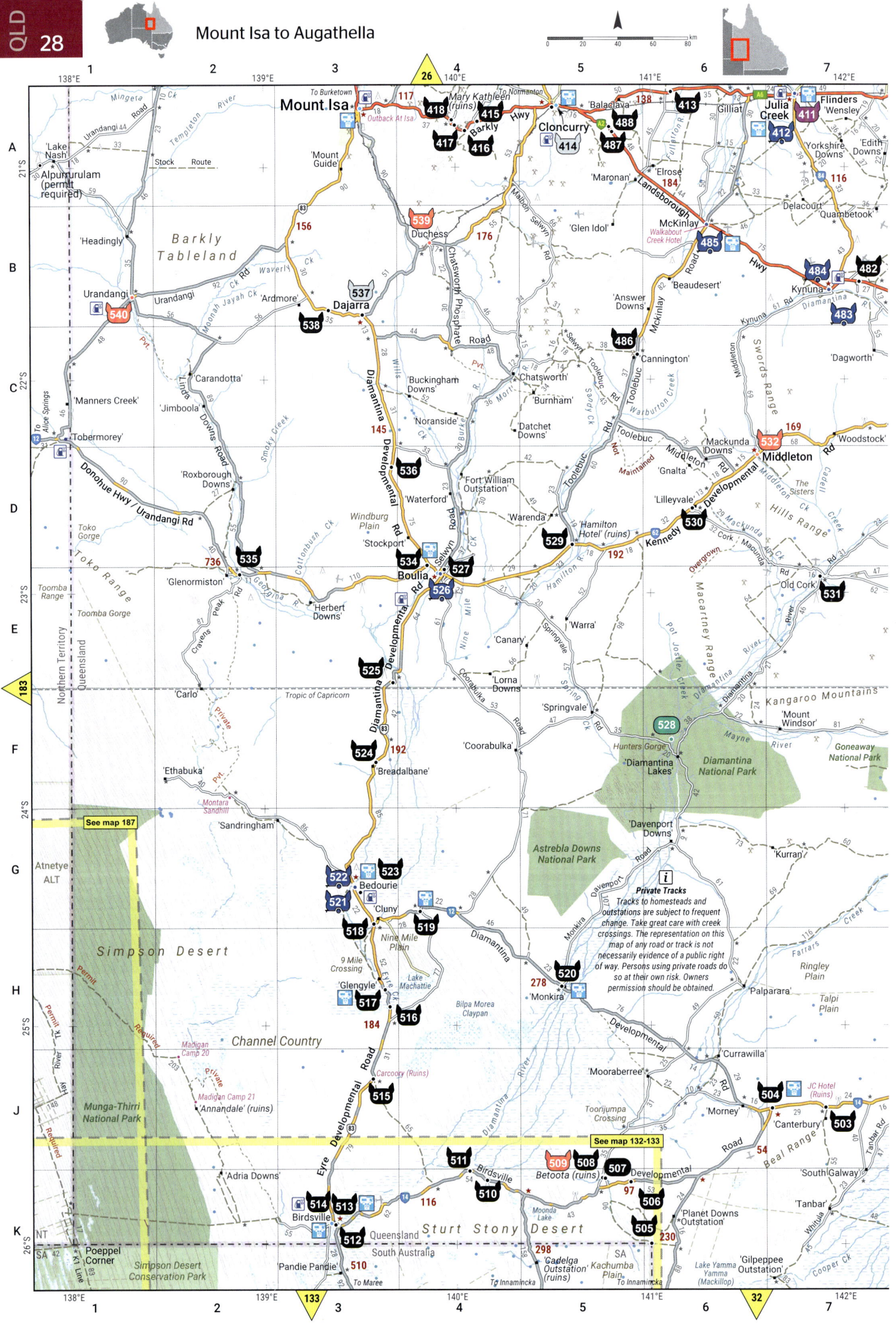

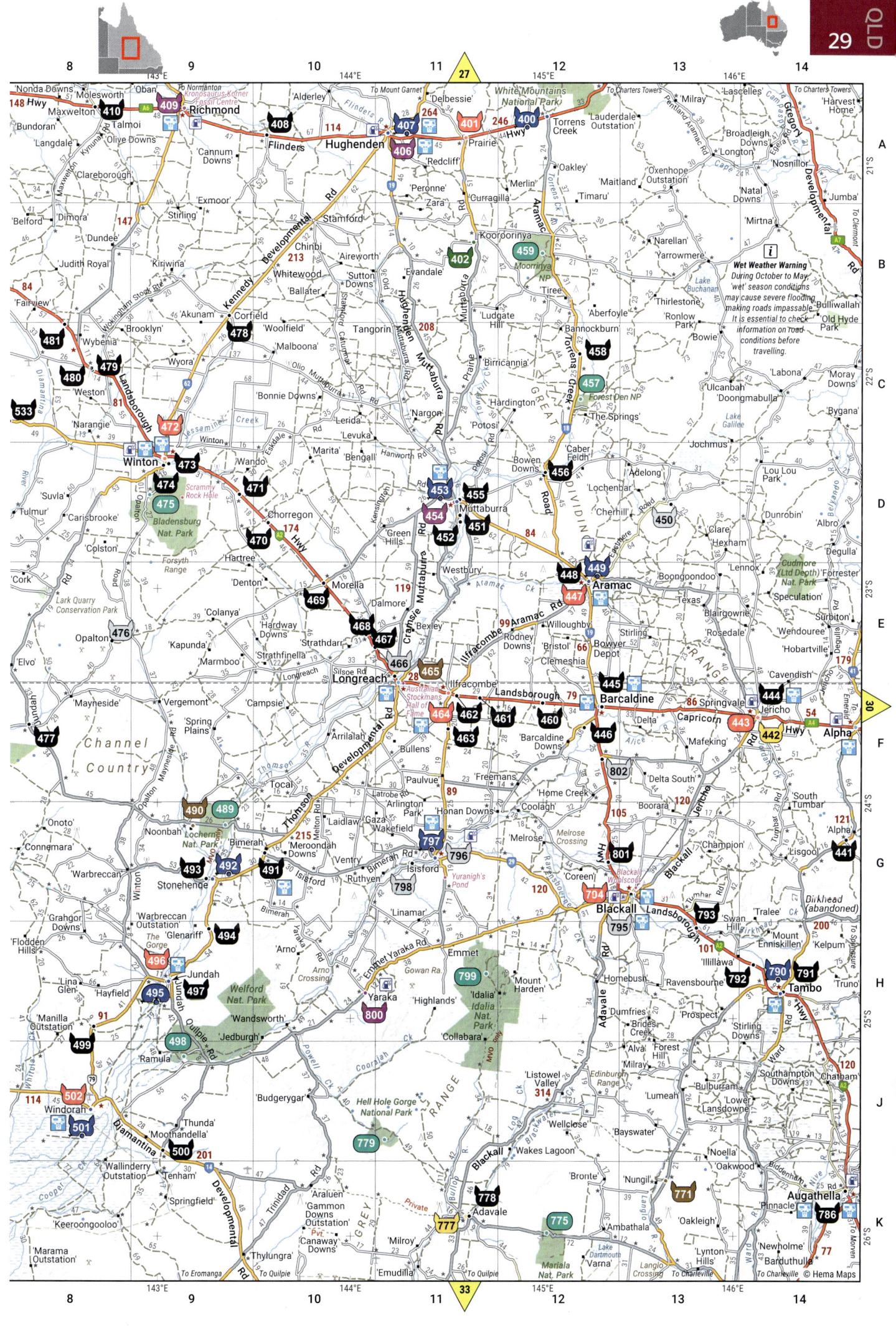

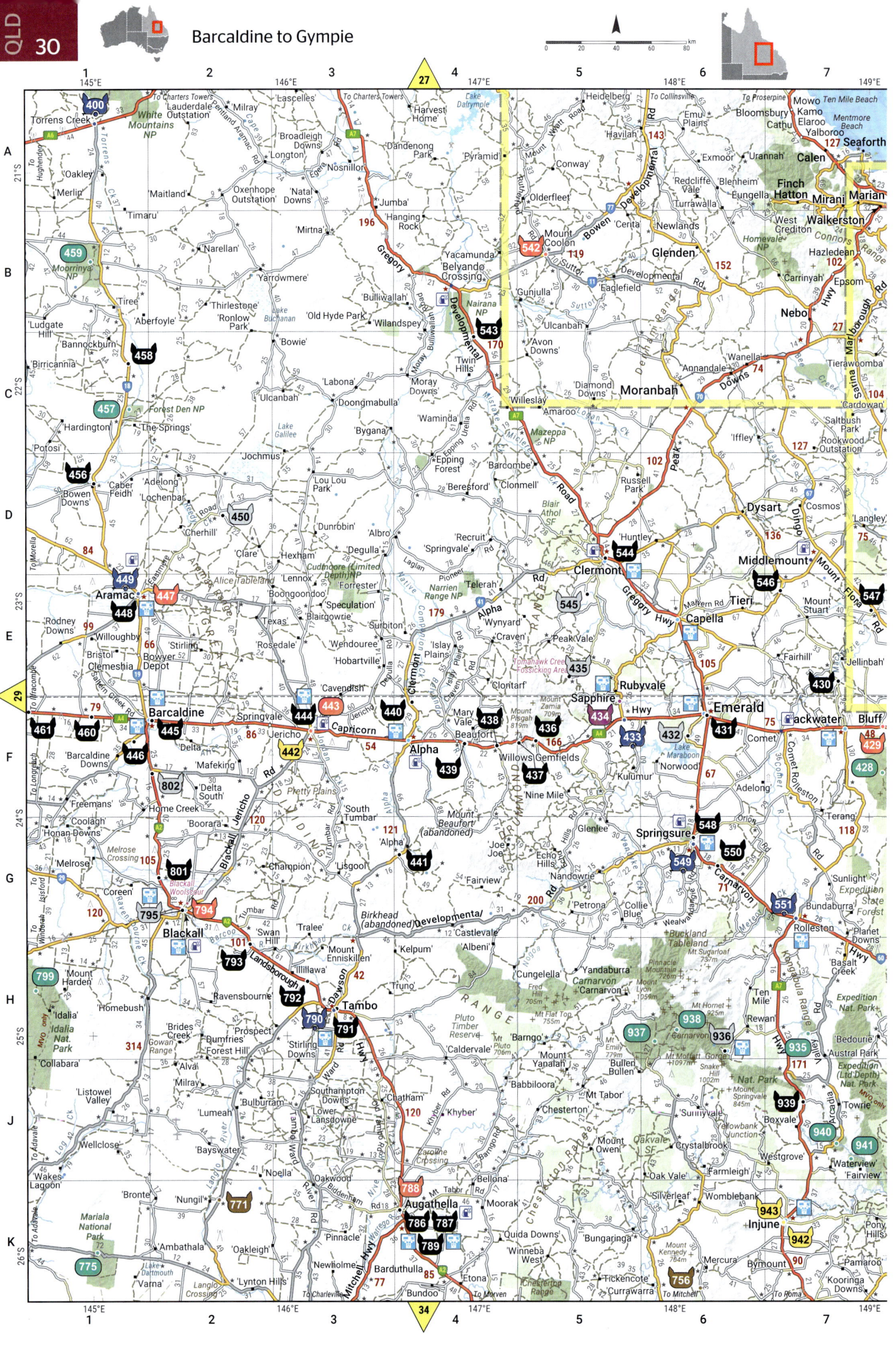

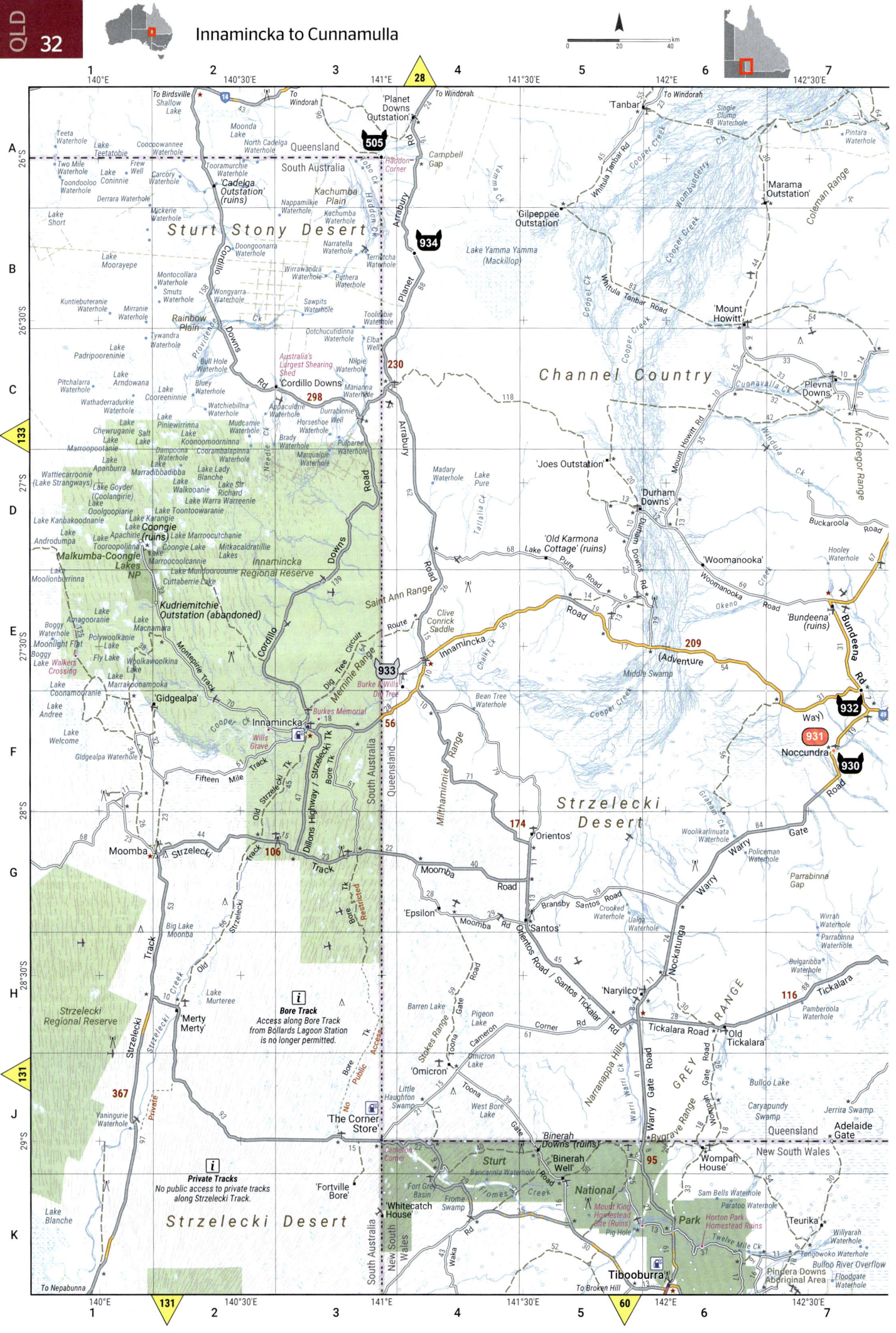

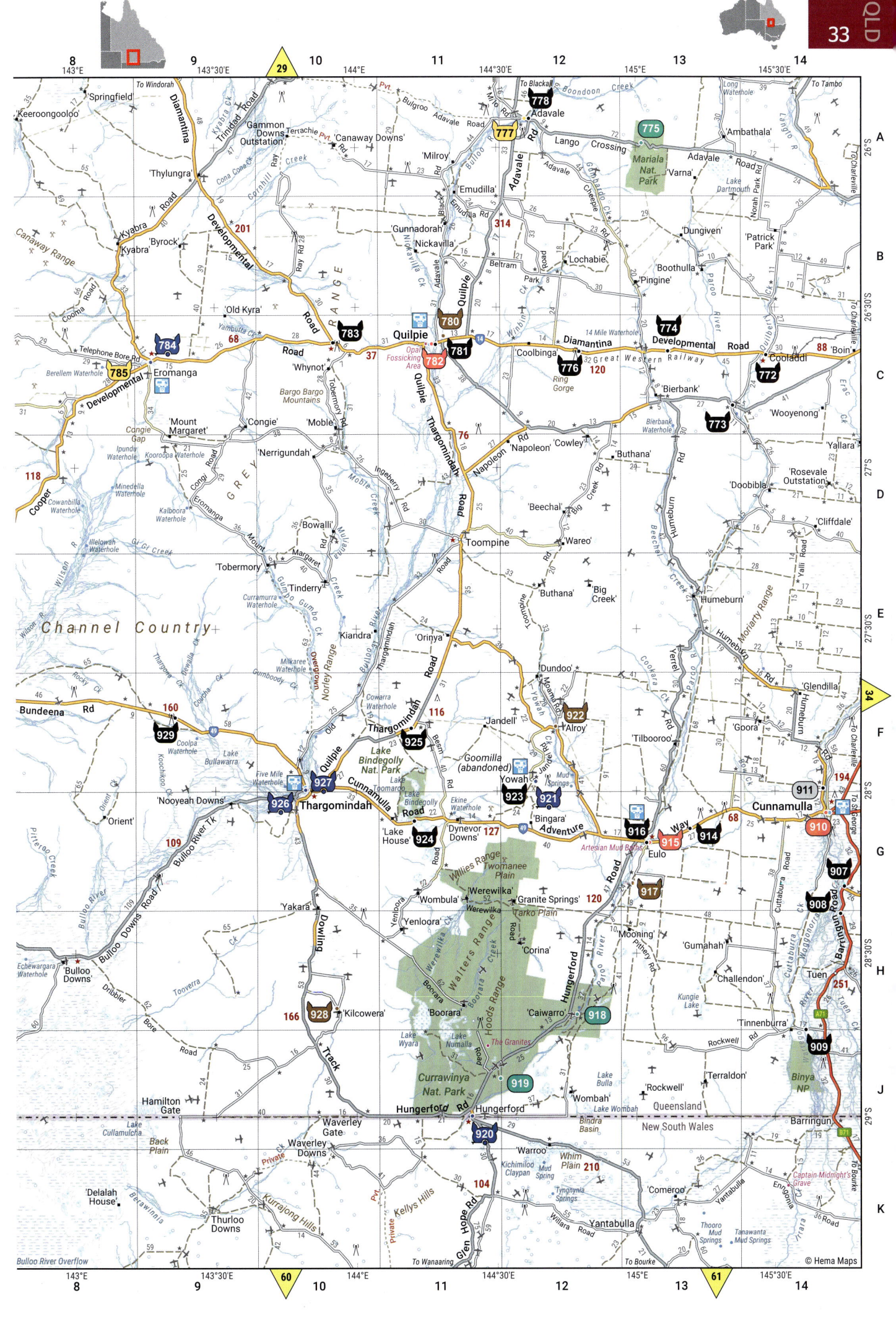

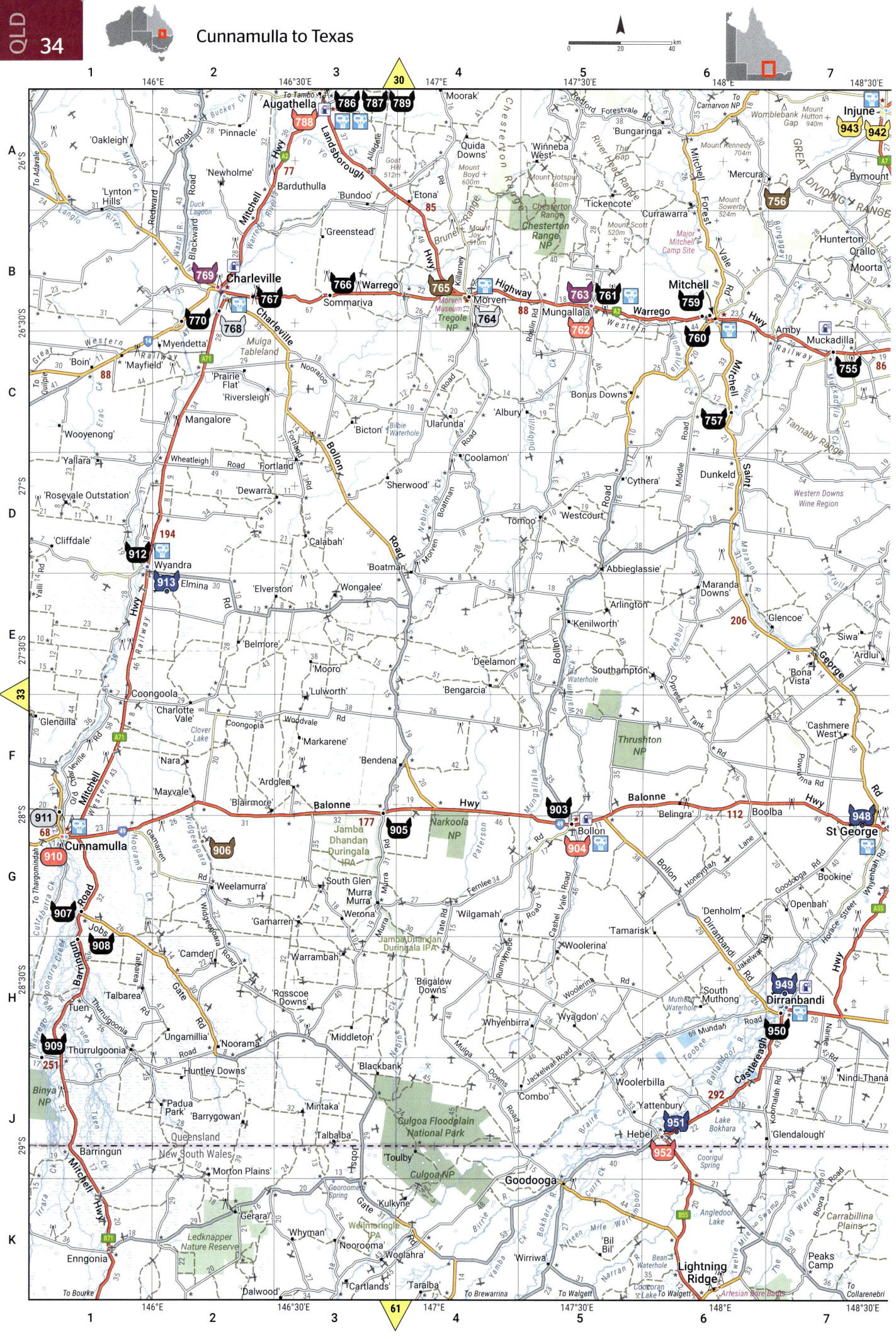

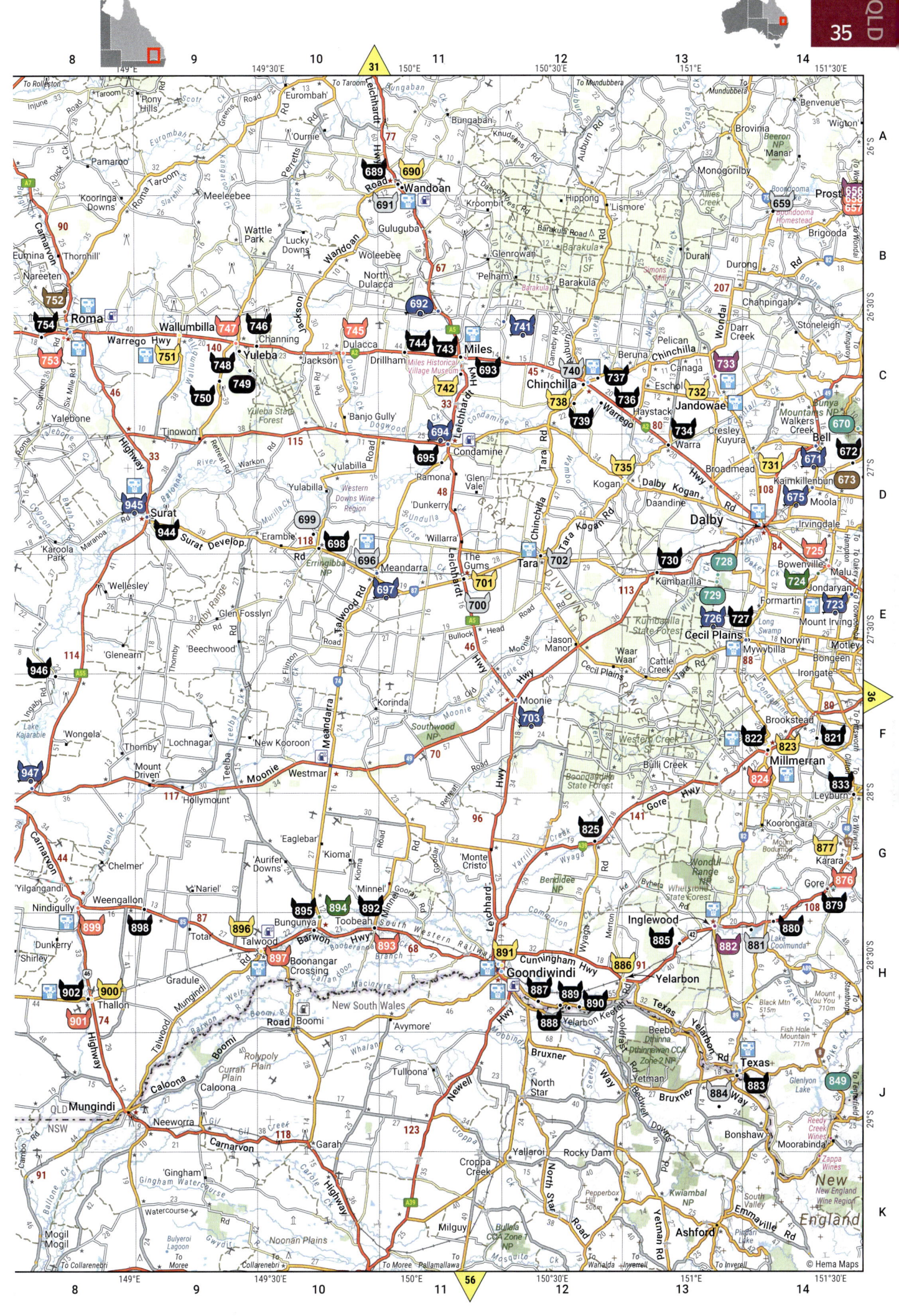

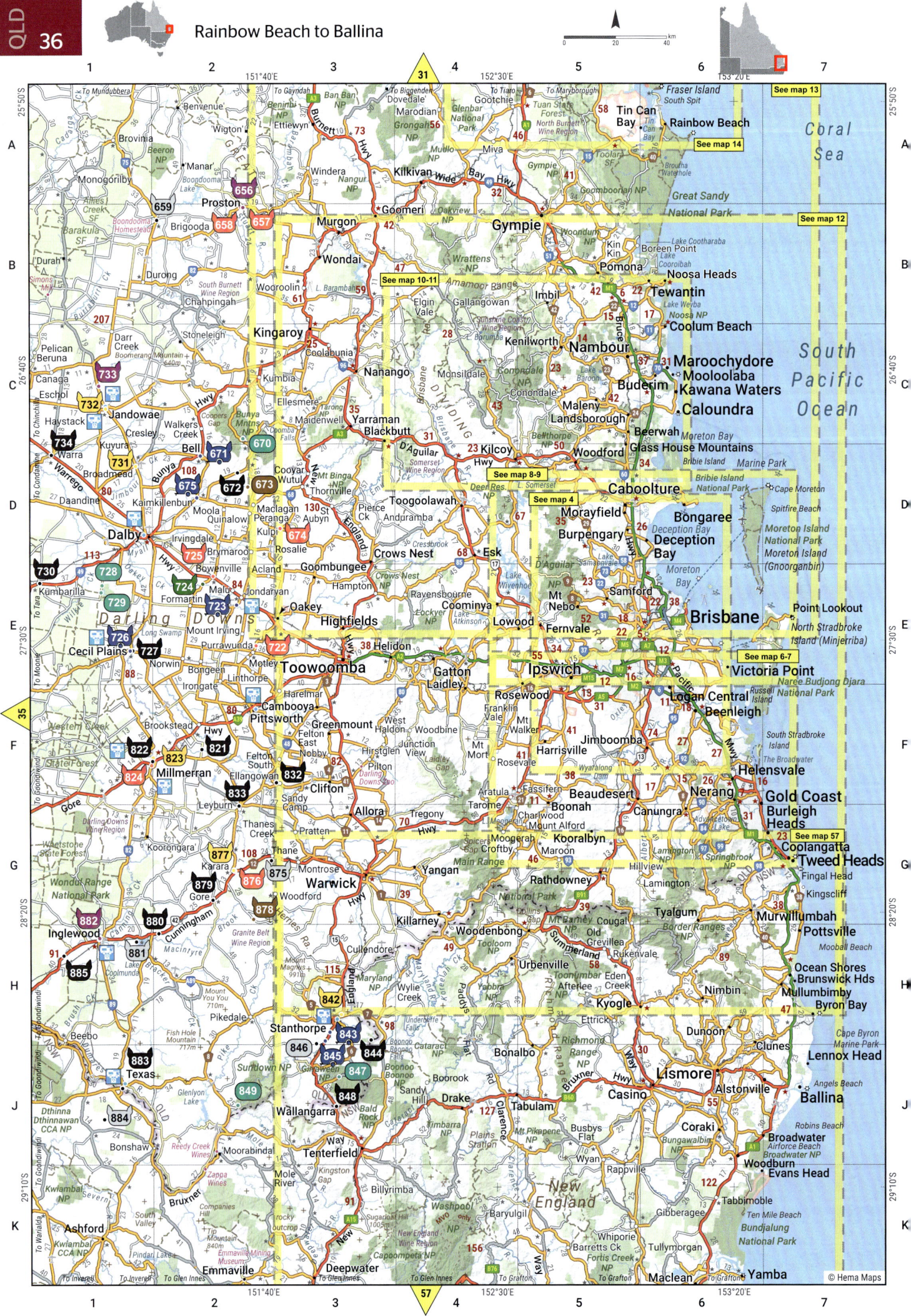

Long Waterhole, Winton, Queensland

Queensland

QUEENSLAND

Cooktown to the Gold Coast
Bruce Highway

1 Cooktown Racecourse RV Stop
Racecourse Rd, Cooktown
Parking Area off Endeavour Valley Rd
07 4082 0500   HEMA 20 A3   15 28 27 S   145 14 09 E

2 Endeavour River Escape
Barretts Creek Rd, Cooktown
Camp Area 17 km N of PO. Turn R after airport 5 km. Closed Dec - Apr
07 4069 5084   HEMA 20 A3   15 24 21 S   145 11 29 E

3 Hill Top Farm
Old Dairy Rd, Cooktown
Camp Area 23 km NW of town. Via Endeavour Valley Rd
07 4069 5058   HEMA 20 A2   15 25 05 S   145 05 16 E

4 Elim Beach - Eddies Camp
1 Beach Rd, Elim Beach
Camp Area 25 km E Hopevale. Cold showers
07 4060 9223   HEMA 23 J7   15 15 37 S   145 16 55 E

5 Archer Point Conservation Park
Archer Point Rd, Cooktown
Dispersed Camping 24 km SE Cooktown. S on Mulligan Hwy for 15 km, E for 11 km. Signposted. Dirt road, tight bends, creek crossing, narrow & steep access to lighthouse. 14 day limit. Permit applies
07 4069 6957   HEMA 20 B3   15 36 11 S   145 19 35 E

6 Lions Den Hotel
398 Shiptons Flat Rd, Bloomfield
Camp Area on the Little Annan R, at Helenvale. 4 km S of Hwy
07 4060 3911   HEMA 20 B3   15 42 21 S   145 13 23 E

7 Home Rule Rainforest Lodge
Homerule Rd, Rossville
Camp Area 34 km SE of Cooktown. At Community Hall, turn E for 2.5 km. Gravel road. Proceed to office. Pre-book July - Aug
07 4060 3925   HEMA 20 B3   15 45 14 S   145 17 24 E

8 Yindilli Camp Ground
Upper Daintree Rd, Cape Tribulation Area
Camp Area at Buru, 26 km S of Bloomfield on CREB Track, 38 km N of Daintree Village. Dry season only
07 4098 6248   HEMA 20 C3   16 03 19 S   145 18 23 E

9 Noah Beach Campground
Daintree National Park
Cape Tribulation Rd, Noah Beach
Camp Area 8 km S of Cape Tribulation. Small vehicles only. Closed wet season. Pre-book
137 468   HEMA 20 C4   16 08 06 S   145 27 05 E

10 Catch a Barra
386 Nielsen Rd, Little Mulgrave
Camp Area 14 km W of Gordonvale, via Gilles Range Rd
07 4056 1727   HEMA 22 G6   17 07 22 S   145 41 57 E

11 Little Mulgrave River Camp
880 Gillies Range Rd, Little Mulgrave
Camp Area in town near hotel, pre-book
0418 986 989   HEMA 22 G6   17 08 29 S   145 43 21 E

12 Goldsborough Valley
Wooroonooran National Park
Mulgrave River Forestry Rd, Goldsborough
Camp Area 24 km S of Gordonvale. S on Gilles Range Rd (52) for 6 km, S to Downing Rd for 600 m, S to Goldsborough Rd for 11 km, W 6 km, ebook
137 468   HEMA 22 J7   17 14 12 S   145 46 23 E

13 Greenpatch Reserve
Bruce Hwy, Gordonvale
Camp Area SE of town. N from Hwy to service road, 500 m to entry. Subject to floods
1300 692 247   HEMA 22 F7   17 06 01 S   145 47 15 E

14 The Boulders
The Boulders Rd, Babinda
Camp Area 6 km W of town. Limited sites. Cold showers
07 4067 1008   HEMA 21 H5   17 20 27 S   145 52 14 E

15 Babinda Rotary Park
Howard Kennedy Dr, Babinda
Rest Area S end of street, over railway, before bridge
07 4067 1008   HEMA 21 H6   17 20 54 S   145 55 35 E

16 Bramston Beach Camp
96 Evans Rd, Bramston Beach
Camp Area N end of road
07 4067 4121   HEMA 21 H6   17 21 08 S   146 01 25 E

17 Garradunga Hotel
191 Garradunga Rd, Garradunga
Camp Spot 9 km N of Innisfail. Free for patrons
07 4063 3708   HEMA 21 J6   17 27 41 S   145 59 43 E

18 Goondi Hill Hotel
173 Edith St, Innisfail
Camp Spot behind hotel. Register at bar
07 4223 0699   HEMA 21 J6   17 31 27 S   146 01 09 E

19 Paronella Park Camping
1671 Innisfail Japoon Rd, Mena Creek
Camp Area 19 km SW of Innisfail. Phone for site allocation. Free stay with park entry
07 4065 0000   HEMA 21 K6   17 39 07 S   145 57 24 E

20 The Paddock

5-7 Mena Creek Rd, Mena Creek
Camp Area at hotel. 19 km SW of Innisfail.
Cnr Innisfail Japoon Rd. Paronella Park overflow.
Phone for site allocation. Free stay with park entry
07 4065 0000   HEMA 21 K6   17 39 18 S   145 57 21 E

21 Kurrimine Beach Camp

Robert Johnstone Pde, Kurrimine Beach
Camp Area N side of town. 4 week limit.
Caretaker on site. No bookings
0427 639 903   HEMA 19 B2   17 46 31 S   146 06 32 E

22 Upper Liverpool Creek

Innisfail Japoon Rd, Japoonvale
Rest Area 29 km SW of Innisfail or 14 km W
of Silkwood. Creekside
132 380   HEMA 19 A2   17 43 25 S   145 56 01 E

23 Bingil Bay Campground

Alexander Dr, Bingil Bay
Camp Area 3 km N of Mission Beach. Small
vehicles only. Beachfront. 4 week limit. No bookings
07 4030 2222   HEMA 19 B2   17 49 41 S   146 06 04 E

24 Tully RV Park

1 Murray St, Tully
Camp Area in town. Book via Visitor Centre
07 4068 2288   HEMA 19 B2   17 55 55 S   145 55 39 E

25 Tully Gorge Campground

Tully Gorge National Park
Tully Gorge Rd, Cardstone
Camp Area 44 km NW of Tully. Cold showers. Pre-
book
07 4066 8601   HEMA 19 B1   17 46 22 S   145 38 59 E

26 Hull Heads Rec Area

4-18 Luff St, Hulls Heads
Camp Area 21 km SE of Tully. Limited
space, caretaker onsite
07 4068 2288   HEMA 19 B2   17 59 41 S   146 04 18 E

27 Murray Falls Campground

Murray Falls National Park
Murray Falls Rd, Tully
Camp Area 36 km SW of Tully or 41 km NW of
Cardwell. Turn W 16 km S of Tully at Murrigal or
21 km N of Cardwell at Bilyana. 3 km dirt road.
Pre-book
137 468   HEMA 19 C1   18 09 12 S   145 48 58 E

28 Bilyana Rest Area

Bruce Hwy, Bilyana
Rest Area 22 km S of Tully or 21 km N of
Cardwell
132 380   HEMA 19 C2   18 07 08 S   145 54 44 E

29 Halifax Hotel

26 Macrossan St, Halifax
Parking Area. Limited space. Free for
patrons, check in on arrival. No bookings
07 4777 7436   HEMA 19 E3   18 34 49 S   146 17 06 E

30 Mungalla Station

1236 Forrest Beach Rd, Forrest Beach
Station Stay 11 km E of Ingham. Sign at
entry
0428 710 907   HEMA 19 E3   18 42 24 S   146 15 37 E

31 Forrest Beach RV Park

20 - 24 Wattle St, Forrest Beach
Parking Area at Forrest Beach. Open Apr -
Nov. Permit from Progress Association or Venables
Real Estate. No after hours access
0428 416 608   HEMA 19 E3   18 42 38 S   146 17 49 E

32 Broadwater Campground

Abergowrie State Forest
Broadwater Park Rd, Abergowrie
Camp Area 45 km NW of Ingham, via Trebonne
along Abergowrie Rd, or turn W off Bruce Hwy 3 km
N of Ingham to Hawkins Creek Rd for 26 km. 17 km
dirt road. Pre-book
137 468   HEMA 19 D2   18 24 59 S   145 56 43 E

33 Wallaman Falls Camp

Girringun National Park
Wallaman Falls Rd, Valley of Lagoons
Camp Area 51 km W of Ingham, via Trebonne.
Steep, winding road. Cold showers. Pre-book
137 468   HEMA 19 E1   18 36 01 S   145 47 58 E

34 CMCA Ingham RV Park

Cnr Cooper & Davidson St, Ingham
Parking Area in town. Closed wet season.
Book online or at park, 5 nights in any 21 days
02 4978 8788   HEMA 19 E2   18 39 19 S   146 09 21 E

35 Ashton Hotel

9 Haberman Rd, Long Pocket
Camp Area 24 km NW of Ingham, via
Abergowrie Rd. Behind hotel. Free for patrons,
check in at bar
07 4777 4179   HEMA 19 D2   18 31 33 S   146 00 21 E

36 Tyto Wetlands RV Stop

48 Cooper St, Ingham
Parking Area at Tyto Wetlands Info Centre.
Permit from Info Centre. Open Mar - Nov
07 4776 4792   HEMA 19 E2   18 39 18 S   146 09 11 E

37 Jourama Falls

Paluma Range National Park
Jourama Falls Rd, Yuruga
Camp Area 29 km S of Ingham. W off Bruce Hwy
24 km S of Ingham or 85 km N of Townsville for
5 km. 3 km dirt road. Cold showers. Pre-book
137 468   HEMA 19 F2   18 51 22 S   146 07 35 E

38 Lake Paluma

Paluma State Forest
Paluma Dam Rd, Crystal Creek
Camp Area 11 km NW of Paluma. Not suitable for
large vehicles. Gravel road. Pre-book
134 810   HEMA 19 F2   18 57 24 S   146 08 54 E

QUEENSLAND

39 Big Crystal Creek

Paluma Range National Park
Spiegelhauer Rd, Crystal Creek
Camp Area 43 km S of Ingham. Turn W off Bruce Hwy 38 km S of Ingham to Barrett Rd, then W for 5 km. Not suitable for large vehicles after wet weather. Pre-book

137 468   **HEMA 19 F3**   18 58 49 S   146 15 23 E

40 Bushy Parker Park

Rollingstone St, Rollingstone
Rest Area 58 km S of Ingham, or 54 km N of Townsville. E off Hwy, across railway

134 810   **HEMA 19 F3**   19 02 46 S   146 23 37 E

41 Balgal Beach

3 Tooth St, Balgal Beach
Rest Area 65 km S of Ingham, or 58 km N of Townsville. 5 km E off Hwy. Limited sites, no bookings. Cold showers

134 810   **HEMA 19 F3**   19 00 37 S   146 24 18 E

42 Mystic Sands Golf Club

114 Mystic Ave, Balgal Beach
Parking Area 63 km S of Ingham, or 57 km N of Townsville. Check in at bar

07 4770 7355   **HEMA 19 F3**   19 02 31 S   146 25 16 E

43 Toomulla Beach

Herald St, Toomulla
Rest Area 69 km S of Ingham or 46 km N of Townsville. 2.5 km E off Hwy

134 810   **HEMA 19 G4**   19 05 00 S   146 28 34 E

44 Bluewater Park

Bruce Hwy, Bluewater
Rest Area 80 km S of Ingham or 29 km N of Townsville. Enter via Forestry Rd. Creekside

134 810   **HEMA 19 G4**   19 10 34 S   146 33 06 E

45 Saunders Beach

Reef St, Saunders Beach
Rest Area 87 km S of Ingham or 24 km N of Townsville. 7 km E off Hwy. Cold shower. Limited space

134 810   **HEMA 19 G4**   19 09 14 S   146 36 15 E

46 Townsville BP Overnight

Cnr Racecourse Rd & Lakeside Dr, Townsville
Parking Area at service station. Strictly no tents or fires

07 4778 3000   **HEMA 19 G5**   19 18 58 S   146 49 11 E

47 Alligator Creek Camp

Bowling Green Bay NP
Alligator Creek Rd, Mount Elliot
Camp Area 25 km SE of Townsville or 63 km NW of Ayr. Exit Hwy W for 6 km to camp. Gate locked 6.30pm, ebook. Small vehicles only. Cold shower

137 468   **HEMA 19 H5**   19 26 02 S   146 56 46 E

48 Giru Town Rest Area

Cnr Walton St & Brookes St, Giru
Camp Area via Woodstock Giru Rd

07 4783 9800   **HEMA 19 H6**   19 30 47 S   147 06 28 E

49 Cromarty Boat Ramp

Cromarty Creek Boat Ramp Rd, Giru
Parking Area 10 km N of Giru. 61 km SE of Townsville or 46 km NW of Ayr

07 4783 9800   **HEMA 19 H6**   19 28 10 S   147 05 53 E

50 Barramundi (Morris) Creek Boat Ramp

Morris Creek Rd, Giru
Parking Area 15 km N of Giru. 66 km SE of Townsville or 43 km NW of Ayr

07 4783 9800   **HEMA 18 B1**   19 28 47 S   147 09 05 E

51 Barratta Boat Ramp

Cnr SS Wakefield Ave & Esplanade, Jerona
Camp Spot 42 km NW of Ayr. Exit Hwy N to Jerona Rd. Turn E on Esplanade to boat ramp

07 4783 9800   **HEMA 18 B1**   19 26 54 S   147 14 25 E

52 Hotel Brandon

54 Drysdale St, Brandon
Caravan Park 6 km NW of Ayr

07 4782 5255   **HEMA 18 B1**   19 33 14 S   147 21 13 E

53 Ocean Creek Boat Ramp

470 Peggy Bog Rd, Airdmillan
Camp Area 13 km NE of Ayr, via Airdmillan Rd

07 4783 9800   **HEMA 18 B2**   19 31 02 S   147 30 02 E

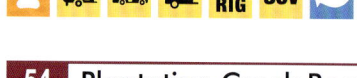

54 Plantation Creek Boat Ramp

652 Old Wharf Rd, Airdmillan
Camp Spot 12.5 km NE of Ayr via Airdmillan Rd, 5 km dirt

07 4783 9800   **HEMA 18 B2**   19 32 05 S   147 30 46 E

55 Hell Hole Boat Ramp

433 Hodder Rd, Rita Island
Camp Spot 22 km SE of Ayr via Rita Is Rd

07 4783 9800   **HEMA 18 C2**   19 37 17 S   147 33 59 E

56 Burdekin Farm Stay

171 Waterview Rd, Mount Kelly
Camp Area 16 km SW of Ayr. 8 km E of Ayr, turn S off Hwy to Five Ways Rd for 2 km, W to Aerodrome Rd for 2 km, S 3 km to sign. Pre-book, 7 days notice

0418 727 425   **HEMA 18 C1**   19 37 36 S   147 18 51 E

57 Red Lilly Rural Stopover

233 Corica Rd, Mount Kelly
Camp Spot 20 km SW of Ayr. Exit Hwy W at Katoora before river crossing. Via Sheepstation Creek Rd. Donation for wetlands. Pre-book. Closed Dec - Apr

0428 826 846   **HEMA 18 C1**   19 38 11 S   147 18 16 E

58 Home Hill Comfort Stop

Railway Ave, Home Hill
Rest Area 12 km SE of Ayr. Adjacent to old railway station. No bookings

07 4783 9800   **HEMA 18 C1**   19 39 54 S   147 24 50 E

59 Commercial Hotel Home Hill

71 Eighth Ave, Home Hill
Parking Area 12 km SE of Ayr. Behind pub
07 4782 1078   HEMA 18 C1   19 39 54 S   147 24 54 E

60 Home Hill Old Showground

Cnr Hurney Rd & Sixth Ave, Home Hill
Showgrounds 13 km SE of Ayr. Gates close
9pm - 6am
0472 636 578   HEMA 18 C1   19 40 11 S   147 24 58 E

61 Wallace Landing

217- 402 Peak Rd, Inkerman
Parking Area 21 km SE of Home Hill. Exit
Hwy E at Inkerman. Via Wallace Rd
07 4783 9800   HEMA 18 C2   19 44 10 S   147 33 20 E

62 Funny Dunny Park

246 Wunjunga Rd, Wunjunga
Camp Area 31 km SE of Home Hill. Via
Beachmount Rd. Signposted Wunjunga. 15 km dirt
road
07 4783 9800   HEMA 18 C2   19 45 09 S   147 35 45 E

63 Wilson Creek Rest Area

Bruce Hwy, Gumlu
Rest Area 28 km S of Home Hill or 11 km N
of Gumlu on NE side of Hwy
07 4783 9800   HEMA 18 C2   19 50 05 S   147 35 38 E

64 Gumlu Tavern

Lot 3 Desalis St, Gumlu
Pub Stay beside tavern. Patronage please,
fee for power
0477 847 846   HEMA 18 C2   19 52 47 S   147 41 15 E

65 Guthalungra Rest Area

Cnr Bruce Hwy & Coventry Rd,
Guthalungra
Rest Area 44 km W of Bowen. Shower at service
station for fee
132 380   HEMA 18 C3   19 55 24 S   147 50 35 E

66 Bowen River Hotel

41 Mount Wyatt Rd, Collinsville
Camp Area 32 km W of Collinsville. Via
Strathmore Rd
07 4785 3388   HEMA 18 E2   20 32 01 S   147 33 21 E

67 Collinsville Showgrounds

11 Conway St, Collinsville
Camp Area 88 km SW of Bowen. Entry on
Railway Rd
0418 556 560   HEMA 18 F3   20 33 24 S   147 50 57 E

68 Glen Erin Farmstay

222 Mookara Rd, Bowen
Camp Area 20 km S of Bowen. Turn W off
Hwy at Mookara Rd for 4 km. Signposted
0408 870 599   HEMA 18 D4   20 07 06 S   148 13 21 E

69 Camp Kanga

2396 Crystalbrook Rd, Proserpine
Camp Area 24 km W of Proserpine. Pre-book
07 4947 2600   HEMA 18 E4   20 21 37 S   148 23 53 E

70 Proserpine RV Stop

130 Main St, Proserpine
Parking Area behind St. Catherine's
Church, opposite Pioneer Park
1300 972 753   HEMA 18 E5   20 24 10 S   148 35 10 E

71 Lake Proserpine Camping

Station Rd, Lake Proserpine
Camping Area 27 km W of Proserpine
(formerly Peter Faust Dam). Past picnic area & boat
ramp
1300 972 753   HEMA 18 E4   20 22 43 S   148 22 40 E

72 Bloomsbury BP

8514 Bruce Hwy, Bloomsbury
Parking Area behind service station. 39 km
S of Proserpine
07 4947 5739   HEMA 18 F5   20 42 19 S   148 35 45 E

73 Jaxut Camping Area

Cathu State Forest

Cathu Forest Rd, Bloomsbury
Camp Area 30 km NW of Calen. Turn W off Bruce
Hwy 13 km S of Bloomsbury or 18 km N of Calen via
Cathu-O'Connell River Rd. 12 km dirt road, steep
in places
137 468   HEMA 18 F5   20 47 32 S   148 32 56 E

74 Oh Deere Farmstay

71 Zamparuttis Rd, Calen
Farm Stay 3 km NE of Calen. 500 m N of
Calen exit Bruce Hwy E to Mackenzies Rd for 1 km,
then E 1 km. Signposted. Pre-book for power
0419 873 909   HEMA 18 G5   20 53 12 S   148 45 55 E

75 St Helens Camp Reserve

Murray Rd, St Helens Beach
Camp Area 15 km NE of Calen. Via E to
Pratts Rd, N to Old Bowen Rd, E to Wewak Rd, N to
St. Helens Beach Rd, SE to Murray Rd, camping at
end. Caretaker collects fees
1300 622 529   HEMA 18 F6   20 50 28 S   148 50 38 E

76 Jolimont Caravan Park

11 Watts Rd, Kuttabul
Caravan Park 16 km S of Calen or 6 km N
of Kuttabul. Cnr Bruce Hwy
07 4954 0170   HEMA 18 G6   21 00 25 S   148 52 27 E

77 Seaforth Camp Reserve

Seaforth Reserve Rd, Seaforth
Camp Area at Seaforth. 45 km NW of
Mackay. Exit Hwy at The Leap via Yakapari Seaforth
Rd. Shower fee
0427 373 358   HEMA 18 G6   20 53 58 S   148 57 59 E

78 Ball Bay Camping Reserve
Cnr Coconut Grove & Ward Esp, Ball Bay
Camp Area 48 km NW of Mackay. Turn N,
3 km W of Seaforth to Cape Hillsborough Rd & Ball
Bay Rd. N end of Esplanade. Cold showers
07 4959 0695 **HEMA 18 G6** 20 54 11 S 148 59 44 E

79 Smalleys Beach
Cape Hillsborough NP
Smalleys Beach Rd, Cape Hillsborough
Camp Area 12 km E of Seaforth. Via Cape
Hillsborough Rd. Limited sites for larger vehicles.
1.5 km dirt road, ebook
137 468 **HEMA 18 G6** 20 54 51 S 149 01 00 E

80 Kuttabul Hotel
3024 Bruce Hwy, Kuttabul
Pub Stay 32 km NW of Mackay, or 14 km
SE of Mt Ossa. Check in with publican. Patronage
requested
07 4954 0161 **HEMA 18 G6** 21 03 05 S 148 55 16 E

81 Leap Hotel
1954 Bruce Hwy, The Leap
Pub Stay 21 km NW of Mackay. Free for
patrons
07 4954 0993 **HEMA 18 G6** 21 04 10 S 149 00 55 E

82 Rowallan Park Scout Camp
Glendaragh Rd, Farleigh
Camp Area 10 km NE of Mackay. Turn off is
7 km N of Mt Pleasant or 2 km S of Farleigh, travel
2 km, turn L at sign, over causeway and 1 km dirt
road, third grid is the entrance. 7 day limit
0408 195 834 **HEMA 18 G6** 21 05 14 S 149 07 08 E

83 Gargett Rodeo Grounds
Gargett Mia Mia Rd, Gargett
Camp Area 51 km W of Mackay, via
Mackay Eungella Rd
07 4958 5676 **HEMA 18 G5** 21 09 28 S 148 44 36 E

84 The Pinnacle Hotel
21 Child St, Pinnacle
Pub Stay 54 km W of Mackay. Via Mackay
Eungella Rd Check in with publican. Wed - Sun
5am - 8pm
07 4958 5207 **HEMA 18 G5** 21 08 46 S 148 42 51 E

85 Platypus Bushcamp
672 Gorge Rd, Finch Hatton
Camp Area 26 km NE of Eungella. Exit
Mackay Eungella Rd to Kowari Gorge Rd
07 4958 3204 **HEMA 18 G5** 21 05 03 S 148 38 10 E

86 Finch Hatton Showground
1 Peoples St, Finch Hatton
Camp Area 18 km E of Eungella. Via
Mackay Eungella Rd
07 4659 3162 **HEMA 18 G5** 21 08 22 S 148 37 51 E

87 Crediton Hall Camp
Crediton State Forest
671 Crediton Loop Rd, Crediton
Camp Area 15 km S Eungella. Via Eungella Dam
Rd, 7 km unsealed road. Steep access road
137 468 **HEMA 18 H5** 21 12 22 S 148 32 47 E

88 Broken River Bush Camp
Eungella National Park
Eungella Dam Rd, Broken River
Camping Area 5 km S from Eungella, turn E 20 m
before bridge crossing. Permit applies
137 468 **HEMA 18 G5** 21 10 03 S 148 30 20 E

89 Eungella Dam
Eungella Dam Rd, Eungella Dam
Camp Area 28 km SW of Eungella. Via
Broken River Rd. 20 km dirt road. 28 day limit. Pay
at self-registration station
131 589 **HEMA 18 G4** 21 09 01 S 148 23 03 E

90 Kinchant Waters Leisure Resort
841 Kinchant Dam Rd, Kinchant Dam
Caravan Park 15 km NW of Eton. Via North Eton Rd
07 4954 1453 **HEMA 18 H6** 21 13 14 S 148 53 34 E

91 General Gordon Hotel
777 Homebush Rd, Sandiford
Pub Stay at Homebush. 8 km W of Rosella
or 13 km E of Eton. 7 day limit
07 4959 7324 **HEMA 18 H6** 21 15 45 S 149 04 53 E

92 Moana Caravan Park
92259 Bruce Hwy, Alligator Creek
Caravan Park at Alligator Creek. 24 km S
of Mackay
07 4956 4165 **HEMA 18 H6** 21 19 15 S 149 11 30 E

93 Moonlight Dam
Homevale National Park
Homevale Rd, Hail Creek
Camp Area 40 km NW of Nebo. Travel 17 km on
Suttor Dev Rd, N into Turrawulla Rd, signed after
Homevale-Mt Britton turnoff. Pre-book
137 468 **HEMA 18 H5** 21 24 34 S 148 30 13 E

94 Lake Elphinstone
Suttor Developmental Rd, Elphinstone
Camp Area 136 km SW of Mackay. W off
Peak Downs Hwy 86 km SW of Mackay to Elphinstone.
4 km on Suttor Development Rd. Cold shower
07 4949 4100 **HEMA 18 J4** 21 32 18 S 148 14 08 E

95 Nebo Motor Inn & Van Park
58 Bowen St, Nebo
Caravan Park N side of town. Via Peak
Downs Hwy. Key deposit
07 4950 5130 **HEMA 18 J5** 21 41 00 S 148 41 34 E

96 Isaac River Rest Area

Peak Downs Hwy, Moranbah
Rest Area 7 km NE of Moranbah turnoff.
108 km NE of Clermont or 81 km SW of Nebo
1300 472 227   HEMA 18 K3   22 02 57 S   148 07 53 E

97 Funnel Creek

Marlborough Sarina Rd, Oxford
Camp Spot 92 km SW of Mackay or 32 km
E of Nebo. S side of bridge. Limited sites
HEMA 18 J6   21 46 42 S   148 55 59 E

98 Koumala Caravan Park

2 Mumby St, Koumala
Caravan Park 20 km S of Sarina
07 4950 3657   HEMA 17 C2   21 36 37 S   149 14 49 E

99 Ilbilbie Roadhouse

87249 Bruce Hwy, Ilbilbie
Parking Area 75 km S of Mackay. Back of
roadhouse. Patronage requested. Open 5am-10pm
07 4950 3944   HEMA 17 C2   21 42 17 S   149 21 26 E

100 Rocky Dam Creek

Landing Rd, Koumala
Camp Spot 10 km NE of Koumala. Exit Hwy
500 m before PO. Last 6 km dirt road
1300 622 529   HEMA 17 C2   21 32 57 S   149 18 00 E

101 Riverside RV Camping

87160 Bruce Hwy, Ilbilbie
Camp Area 77 km S of Mackay. GPS at
gates. Access 7am to 6pm
0419 824 499   HEMA 17 C2   21 42 44 S   149 21 44 E

102 Cape Palmerston Beach

Cape Palmerston National Park
Cape Palmerston Rd, Cape Palmerston
Camp Spot on E side of Cape. At Ilbilbie turn E off
Bruce Hwy to Greenhill Rd 8 km, N 6 km to entry.
5 km beach drive & low tide access, ebook. Check
tide times
137 468   HEMA 17 C3   21 35 45 S   149 28 02 E

103 Cape Creek

Cape Palmerston National Park

Via Cape Palmerston Rd, Koumala
Camp Area on NW side of Cape Palmerston. At
Ilbilbie, turn E off Hwy to Greenhill Rd 8 km, turn
6 km N to entry. 15 km track with beach section, low
tide access only, ebook. Check tide times
137 468   HEMA 17 C3   21 33 12 S   149 27 34 E

104 Windmill Bay

Cape Palmerston National Park

Via Cape Palmerston Rd, Koumala
Camp Spot on E side of Cape. At Ilbilbie turn E off
Bruce Hwy to Greenhill Rd 8 km, N 6 km to entry.
12 km track with beach section & low tide access,
ebook. Check tide times
137 468   HEMA 17 C3   21 32 57 S   149 29 09 E

105 Notch Point Campground

Yarrawonga Park Reserve

Notch Point Rd, Ilbilbie
Camp Area 14 km E of Ilbilbie. Turn E to Greenhill
Rd, SE to Notch Point Rd. 9 km to gate, 3 km
narrow rough sandy track. 7 day limit
1300 472 227   HEMA 17 D3   21 44 37 S   149 28 38 E

106 Orkabie Downs

Bruce Hwy, Carmila
Camp Area 11 km S Ilbilie or 18 km N
Carmila. Exit Bruce Hwy W, 9 km S of United
Service Station or 16 km N of Carmila. Pre-book.
GPS at entry
0413 749 614   HEMA 17 D2   21 46 57 S   149 22 15 E

107 Carmila Beach

35 Esplanade, Carmila Beach
Camp Area 6 km E of Carmila. Sealed road
to camp then sandy tracks. Pre-book. 14 day limit
1300 472 227   HEMA 17 D3   21 54 50 S   149 27 47 E

108 Flaggy Rock Cafe

83978 Bruce Hwy, Flaggy Rock
Parking Area 33 km S of Ilbilbie
0456 001 682   HEMA 17 D2   21 58 13 S   149 26 09 E

109 Flaggy Rock Community Centre

85 Flaggy Rock Rd, Flaggy Rock
Camp Area 7 km S of Carmila. Caretaker onsite.
Gates locked 6pm. Cash only
0477 545 618   HEMA 17 D2   21 58 06 S   149 26 39 E

110 Brandybottle Camping

82943 Bruce Hwy, Clairview
Camp Area at Rec Reserve. 17 km S of
Carmila or 8 km N of Clairview N turnoff. Limited
sites, pre-book. Fee includes golf. Signposted
0423 877 288   HEMA 17 E3   22 02 49 S   149 29 07 E

111 St Lawrence Rec Reserve

624 St Lawrence Connection Rd, St
Lawrence
Camp Area 1 km W of town. 6 km E of Hwy. 14 day
limit, ebook or phone
1300 472 227   HEMA 17 F3   22 21 04 S   149 31 11 E

112 St Lawrence Hotel

19 Railway Pde, St Lawrence
Parking Area behind hotel. Free for patrons,
register at bar. Fee for showers
07 4956 9165   HEMA 17 F3   22 21 05 S   149 31 27 E

113 Waverley Creek Rest Area

Bruce Hwy, St Lawrence
Rest Area 8 km S of St Lawrence turnoff or
64 km N of Marlborough
132 380   HEMA 17 F3   22 26 19 S   149 28 33 E

114 Marlborough Hotel

7 Railway St, Marlborough
Parking Area behind hotel, on Milman St.
Check in on arrival
07 4935 6103   HEMA 17 H4   22 48 48 S   149 53 22 E

115 Marlborough Roadhouse

13 Perkins Rd, Marlborough
Parking Area. Check in at counter before
camping. Shower fee, showers close 8pm
07 4935 6135   HEMA 17 H4   22 49 18 S   149 53 29 E

116 Stanage Bay
Endeavour Park
A1 Banksia Rd, Stanage Bay
Camp Area. 85 km gravel road. Donations to Plumtree Store
07 4937 3169   HEMA 17 E5   22 08 10 S   150 02 02 E

117 Yaamba Rest Area
Joan Tierney Park
1 Cnr Iris St & Yaamba Rd, Yaamba
Rest Area 37 km NW of Rockhampton
132 380   HEMA 17 J6   23 08 06 S   150 22 07 E

118 Rainforest Ranch Wilderness
Retreat
4 76 Yaxleys Rd, Byfield
Camp Area 43 km N of Yeppoon, on Adelaide Park Rd to Byfield Rd. Turn E 1.5 km N of general store. Pre-book
0447 555 186   HEMA 17 H7   22 49 31 S   150 38 35 E

119 Upper Stony Campground
Byfield State Forest
A1 Upper Stoney Creek Rd, Maryvale
Camp Area 37 km N of Yeppoon. Turn W off Byfield Rd 27 km N of Yeppoon for 11 km of dirt road. 6 tonne load limit bridge, ebook or at Byfield Store
137 468   HEMA 17 H7   22 53 31 S   150 37 05 E

120 Red Rock Campground
Byfield State Forest
A1 1708 Byfield Rd, Byfield
Camp Area 33 km N of Yeppoon. E off Byfield Rd 32 km N of Yeppoon. 1 km dirt road. 14 day limit, ebook or at Byfield Store
137 468   HEMA 17 H7   22 52 25 S   150 41 05 E

121 Water Park Creek
Byfield State Forest
A1 Sandy Creek Rd, Byfield
Camp Area 39 km N of Yeppoon. E off Byfield Rd 36 km N of Yeppoon for 3 km. 1 km dirt road. Small vehicles only, ebook or at Byfield Store. 5 more 4WD tent and camper only NP coastal camps in Camps Australia Wide App
137 468   HEMA 17 H7   22 50 10 S   150 40 18 E

122 Byfield Campstay
30 Castle Rock Rd, Byfield
A1 Camp Area 2 km N of Byfield
07 4935 1002   HEMA 17 H7   22 49 46 S   150 37 56 E

123 Ferns Hideaway Resort
67 Cahills Rd, Byfield
A1 Caravan Park 5 NE of Byfield. From Byfield Store, take Byfield Rd N 2 km, E on Yaxleys Rd 1 km, then Cahills Rd 750 m. Turn E for 800 m
0408 351 235   HEMA 17 H7   22 49 28 S   150 39 45 E

124 Fardooleys Bush Camp
40 Neslein Rd, Glendale
A1 Camp Area 19 km N of Rockhampton via Belmont Rd. Open Apr - Oct. Pre-book
0438 361 568   HEMA 16 B1   23 15 16 S   150 26 38 E

125 Kershaw Gardens
High St, Rockhampton
A1 Parking Area with entry opposite Bob Jane T-Mart
07 4932 9000   HEMA 16 B2   23 21 29 S   150 31 09 E

126 Bajool Country Hotel
86 High St, Bajool
A1 Pub Stay 27 km S of Rockhampton. Off Hwy
07 4934 6120   HEMA 16 C2   23 39 05 S   150 38 36 E

127 Alkoomi Adventure Farm
695 Old Coach Rd, Marmor
A1 Farm Stay 45 km SE of Rockhampton or 66 km NW of Gladstone. Exit Hwy S at Marmor, 2 km to camp
0423 216 412   HEMA 16 C2   23 41 43 S   150 41 39 E

128 Raglan Tavern
55739 Bruce Hwy, Raglan
A1 Pub Stay 55 km S of Rockhampton or 52 km N of Gladstone. Fee for non-patrons
07 4934 6558   HEMA 16 C2   23 42 51 S   150 48 53 E

129 Bouganvilla Caravan Park
80 399 Brendonna Rd, Burua
Caravan Park 16 km S of Gladstone or 9 km N of Calliope. Via Dawson Hwy
0420 211 121   HEMA 16 D4   23 57 03 S   151 13 08 E

130 Calliope River Rest Area
Old Bruce Hwy, River Ranch
A1 Rest Area 24 km SW of Gladstone. For S camp, exit Hwy 4 km N of Calliope turnoff, turn S to Old Bruce Hwy, 3 km to river bank. For N camp, continue on Hwy for 4 km to exit at Calliope Historical Village, no amenities
07 4970 0700   HEMA 16 D3   23 57 43 S   151 09 16 E

131 Griffiths Creek
Kroombit Tops National Park
Tableland Rd, Tablelands
Camp Area 65 km SW of Calliope via Tablelands Rd, 2 km S of The Barracks. Steep & windy road, caution when towing. Conventional vehicles in dry conditions only, ebook. More camper trailer & tent camps in the Camps Australia Wide App
137 468   HEMA 16 F3   24 22 04 S   150 58 39 E

132 Futter Creek Camp Reserve
69 Gladstone Monto Rd, Barmundu
Rest Area 21 km S of Calliope
07 4970 0700   HEMA 16 E3   24 08 17 S   151 11 45 E

133 Boynedale Bush Camp
69 Bush Camp Rd, Boynedale
Camp Area at Awoonga Lake, 31 km S of Calliope. 2 km E of Gladstone-Monto Rd, beside dam. 7 day limit. Small dogs only, on leash
07 4972 9000   HEMA 16 E4   24 13 23 S   151 15 15 E

134 Boyne Valley Discovery
Centre
69 15 McDonald St, Ubobo
Camp Area 78 km S of Gladstone or 81 NE of Monto. Via Gladstone-Monto Rd
0439 111 268   HEMA 16 F4   24 24 21 S   151 19 10 E

135 Boyne River Rest Area

48739 Bruce Hwy, Benaraby
Rest Area 1 km S of town. 49 km SE of
Mount Larcom or 49 km N of Miriam Vale. Riverside
132 380   HEMA 16 D4   24 00 39 S   151 20 26 E

136 Eurimbula & Middle Creek

Eurimbula National Park
574 Captain Cook Dr, Agnes Waters
Camp Area 24 & 28 km N of Agnes Water. Via
Eurimbula & Middle Creek Rds. Sandy track, ebook
137 468   HEMA 16 E5   24 10 25 S   151 50 55 E

137 Corsos Lowmead Hotel

3179 Lowmead Rd, Lowmead
Parking Area behind hotel. Register before
camping
07 4156 9138   HEMA 16 F5   24 31 46 S   151 45 14 E

138 Travellers Rest 1770

2143 Round Hill Rd, Agnes Water
Camp Area (The Ole Gumtree) 8 km SW
of Agnes Waters, or 59 km from Bundaberg via
Tableland Rd
0416 729 668   HEMA 16 E5   24 15 02 S   151 50 29 E

139 1770 Southern Cross

Travellers Retreat
2694 Round Hill Rd, Agnes Water
Camp Area 3 km SW of Agnes Waters. Pre-book
07 4974 7225   HEMA 16 E5   24 13 27 S   151 52 45 E

140 Horizons Kangaroo

Sanctuary
15 Fitzroy Cres, Agnes Water
Camp Area 5 km NW of Agnes Waters via Round
Hill & Rafting Ground Rds. Steep driveway
unsuitable for caravans
07 4974 7783   HEMA 16 E5   24 12 17 S   151 52 53 E

141 The Summit 1770

2741 Round Hill Rd, Agnes Water
Camp Area. Pre-book, arrive before dark.
42 day limit
0490 315 172   HEMA 16 E5   24 13 08 S   151 53 08 E

142 Middle & Wreck Rock

Deepwater National Park
Via Anderson Way, Agnes Water
Camp Area 14 & 16 km S of Agnes Water. Sandy
track. High clearance only, ebook. Detailed in
Camps Australia Wide App
137 468   HEMA 16 E6   24 17 11 S   151 57 00 E

143 Deepwater Hideaway

236 Maude Hill Rd, Deepwater
Camp Area. Via Deepwater Rd. Pre-book
0413 491 598   HEMA 16 F6   24 22 48 S   151 56 13 E

144 Rules Beach Bush Camp

299 Lindy Dr, Baffle Creek
Camp Area 9 km E of Baffle Creek. 1 km of
unsealed road. Pre-book. 18+ only
0417 968 795   HEMA 16 F6   24 29 32 S   152 00 16 E

145 Rosedale Royal Hotel

2 Wills Rd, Rosedale
Caravan Park 49 km N of Gin Gin or 59 km
NW of Bundaberg
07 4156 5322   HEMA 16 F6   24 37 44 S   151 54 59 E

146 Midskinrick Lodge

135 Newtons Rd, Rosedale
Camp Area 17 km N of Rosedale. Via
Barents Rd. Limited powered sites
0458 213 195   HEMA 16 F6   24 31 16 S   151 58 17 E

147 Rocky Point Retreat

303 Rocky Point Rd, Winfield
Camp Area 63 km N of Bundaberg. Exit
Rosdale Rd N to Winfield Rd at Watalgan. 14 day
limit. No shared amenities, portable ensuite for hire
07 4156 6111   HEMA 16 F6   24 31 02 S   152 00 42 E

148 Norval Park Campground

Norval Park Rd, Yandaran
Dispersed Camping 48 km N of Bundaberg.
Via Bundaberg - Lowmead Rd. Pre-book
1300 722 099   HEMA 16 F6   24 36 32 S   152 07 49 E

149 Avondale Homestead Tavern

4 Avondale Rd, Avondale
Parking Area 26 km NW of Bundaberg.
Check in at bar. Deposit for toilet key. SCV stay free
07 4156 1206   HEMA 16 G6   24 45 48 S   152 09 12 E

150 Colosseum Creek Motel

42651 Bruce Hwy, Colosseum
Camp Area & Roadhouse 16 km S of
Miriam Vale or 83 km N of Gin Gin
07 4974 5244   HEMA 16 F5   24 27 25 S   151 35 15 E

151 Granite Creek (Bernie

Christensen) Rest Area
Bruce Hwy, Lowmead
Rest Area 36 km S of Miriam Vale or 63 km N of Gin
Gin
132 380   HEMA 16 F5   24 36 44 S   151 40 04 E

152 Gin Gin Rest Area

34593 Bruce Hwy, Gin Gin
Rest Area 2 km N of Gin Gin
132 380   HEMA 16 H6   24 58 27 S   151 56 45 E

153 Wolca Reserve

21 Bania Rd, Mount Perry
Camp Area 6 km N of Mount Perry. W off
Gin Gin-Mount Perry Rd. Permit from council office
or call ahead
1300 696 272   HEMA 16 H5   25 07 58 S   151 37 08 E

154 Mount Perry Showgrounds

5819 Monto-Mount Perry Rd, Mount Perry
Camp Area S end of town. Pay at council
office or call ahead
1300 696 272   HEMA 16 H5   25 11 18 S   151 38 29 E

155 Tirroan Hotel
Cnr Tirroan Rd & St Kilda Rd, Tirroan
Parking Area 3.5 km W of Gin Gin. Pre-book, limited sites
07 4157 2317   HEMA 16 H6   25 00 08 S   151 55 38 E
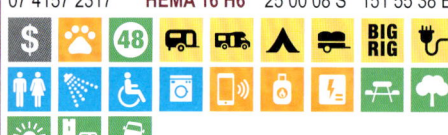

156 Bucca Hotel
5 North Bucca Rd, Bucca
Parking Area 30 km W of Bundaberg. Via Rosdale Rd
07 4157 8171   HEMA 16 G6   24 51 33 S   152 05 34 E

157 Sharon Gorge Nature Park
Lot 79 Gin Gin Rd, Sharon
Rest Area 3 km W of Sharon. 13 km W of Bundaberg
1300 722 099   HEMA 16 H7   24 53 01 S   152 14 34 E

158 Wyper Park Scout Camp
1458 Childers Rd, South Bingera
Camp Area 12 km SW of Bundaberg via Isis Hwy. GPS at entry. Cash only
07 4151 4264   HEMA 16 H7   24 56 39 S   152 15 32 E

159 Hinkler Lions Park
6 University Dr, Bundaberg
Rest Area 4 km SW of PO. Opposite airport
1300 722 099   HEMA 16 G7   24 53 49 S   152 18 51 E

160 CMCA Bundaberg RV Park
45 Burrum St, Bundaberg West
Rest Area. GPS at entry, via Pyefinch Blvd off Walker St, 5 day limit
02 4978 8788   HEMA 14 B1   24 52 45 S   152 20 46 E

161 Gin Gin Showgrounds
14 King St, Gin Gin
Camp Area at Gin Gin. N end of town off King St. Caretaker on site. 14 day limit
0409 940 925   HEMA 16 H6   24 59 16 S   151 57 07 E

162 Booyal Roadhouse
31512 Bruce Hwy, Booyal
Parking Area next to roadhouse. Grassed area
07 4126 0173   HEMA 13 A2   25 12 53 S   152 02 24 E

163 Booyal Crossing
Booyal Crossing Rd, Morganville
Camp Area 30 km N of Childers or 33 km S of Gin Gin. Turn S to Booyal Dallarnil Rd for 250 m, W to Causeway Rd for 4 km. Riverside
1300 722 099   HEMA 13 A2   25 13 45 S   152 00 34 E

164 Paradise Dam
Paradise Dam Reserve
353 Campbells Rd, Coringa
Camp Area 35 km NE of Biggenden. N off Isis Hwy to Gooroolba Biggenden Rd. Signed
07 4127 7278   HEMA 13 B2   25 21 17 S   151 55 10 E

165 Apple Tree Creek
1 Old Creek Rd, Apple Tree Creek
Rest Area 7 km N of Childers or 49 km SE of Gin Gin
1300 722 099   HEMA 13 A3   25 13 09 S   152 14 18 E

166 Wallum Reserve
Childers Rd, Childers
Rest Area 28 km SW of Bundaberg or 24 km N of Childers
1300 722 099   HEMA 13 A3   25 03 32 S   152 13 50 E

167 Childers RV
3 Crescent St, Childers
Rest Area behind PO. Facilites opposite in Millennium Park
1300 722 099   HEMA 13 A3   25 14 06 S   152 16 44 E

168 Brierley Wines
574 Rainbows Rd, South Isis
Camp Area 7 km SE of Childers. S to Taylors St, which becomes Rainbows Rd. Free for patrons. Pre-book, open Tue - Sun
07 4126 1297   HEMA 13 B3   25 17 15 S   152 17 23 E

169 Kinkuna Camping Zone
Burrum Coast National Park
Palm Beach Rd, Kinkuna
Camp Area 29 km of Bundaberg or 20 km N of Woodgate. Via Woopis Rd. Sandy track, ebook
137 468   HEMA 14 D2   25 01 49 S   152 31 07 E

170 Burrum Point Camping Area
Burrum Coast National Park
Campground Rd, Woodgate
Camp Area 7 km SE of Woodgate. Via Walkers Point Rd. Sandy track, ebook
137 468   HEMA 14 D2   25 09 17 S   152 37 48 E

171 Howard RV Stop
63 Steley St, Howard
Parking Area at Howard. 32 km SW of Hervey Bay. Via Pialba Burrum Heads Rd
1300 794 929   HEMA 14 E2   25 19 04 S   152 33 47 E

172 Buddies Road
1197 Burrum Heads Rd, Burrum Heads
Camp Area 7.2 km S of Burrum Heads or 38 km NW of Maryborough. Pre-book
0438 533 235   HEMA 14 E2   25 14 25 S   152 35 38 E

173 Lake Lenthall
Lake Lenthall Reserve
Via Wongi Waterholes Camp Area Rd, Duckinwilla
Camp Area 21 km SW of Howard. W off Bruce Hwy 12 km S of Howard, for 2 km, NW for 7 km dirt road. Cold showers. Limited sites, pre-book
07 4129 4833   HEMA 14 F2   25 24 14 S   152 32 00 E

174 Wongi Waterholes
Wongi State Forest Rec Area
Kullogum Forestry Rd, Duckinwilla
Camp Area 21 km SW of Howard. W off Bruce Hwy 12 km S of Howard or 16 km N of Maryborough, 9 km dirt road. Cold showers. Pre-book
137 468   HEMA 14 F2   25 26 15 S   152 32 37 E

175 Maryborough Showground & Equestrian Park
23349 Bruce Hwy, Maryborough West
Camp Area off Showground Rd, near Gate 5, ebook
07 4122 3584   HEMA 14 G3   25 30 22 S   152 39 46 E

176 Doon Villa RV Park
Airport Drv, Maryborough
Camp Area. Entry off Saltwater Creek Rd.
7 day limit
07 4122 1134   HEMA 14 G3   25 31 05 S   152 42 37 E

177 Cheery Nomad RV Park
113 Lawson St, St Helens
Farm Stay 6 km N of Maryborough. Off Fazio Rd
0414 754 638   HEMA 14 G3   25 29 34 S   152 42 28 E

178 Susan River Homestead
Lot 56 Noble Rd, Susan River
Camp Area at Susan River. 14 km N of Maryborough or 19 km S of Hervey Bay. First driveway. Pre-book
07 4121 6846   HEMA 14 F4   25 25 28 S   152 45 43 E

179 Hervey Bay RV Stop
227 Maryborough Hervey Bay Rd, Urraween
Parking Area at Hervey Bay Info Centre. Cnr Urraween Rd
1800 811 728   HEMA 14 E4   25 17 59 S   152 48 34 E

180 Fraser Coast RV Park
54 Bengtson Rd, River Heads
Camp Area & Caravan Park off River Heads Rd. 14 day limit
07 4125 7119   HEMA 14 F4   25 24 24 S   152 54 15 E

181 Alan & June Brown Car Park
Kent St, Maryborough
Parking Area behind police station
1300 794 929   HEMA 14 G3   25 32 12 S   152 42 01 E

182 The Wharf RV Park
71 Wharf St, Maryborough
Parking Area next to restaurant. Riverside
0427 233 081   HEMA 14 G3   25 32 24 S   152 42 27 E

183 Boonooroo Golf Course
100 Rawson Rd, Boonooroo
Parking Area & Tavern 28 km SE of Maryborough. Via Boonooroo Rd. Free for patrons. Pre-book
07 4129 8428   HEMA 14 H4   25 40 01 S   152 53 44 E

184 River Run Farm Stay
136 Burtons Rd, Antigua
Camp Area 15 km S of Maryborough
07 4129 6669   HEMA 14 H2   25 38 30 S   152 36 50 E

185 Petrie Park RV Camp
49 Van Doorn Rd, Tiaro
Rest Area 2 km NW of Tiaro. Turn W over railway line 1 km N of PO, N for 200 m, W to river bank. Limited space
1300 794 929   HEMA 14 H2   25 42 53 S   152 34 38 E

186 The Hideaway Station Hotel
Cnr Walter St & Blackmount Rd, Tiaro
Parking Area next to pub. Check in with publican
07 4129 2153   HEMA 14 H2   25 43 24 S   152 34 51 E

187 Tiaro Memorial Park
Cnr Inman & Price St, Tiaro
Rest Area at Tiaro. Behind town park. Cold showers. Toilet 100 m across park
1300 794 929   HEMA 14 J2   25 43 43 S   152 35 02 E

188 Bauple RV
14 Bauple Dr, Bauple Village
Camp Spot at 100 m N of museum
1300 794 929   HEMA 14 J3   25 48 45 S   152 37 08 E

189 Rossendale Park RV
44 Bauple Dr, Bauple
Rest Area 500 m E of Bruce Hwy
1300 794 929   HEMA 14 J2   25 50 23 S   152 35 44 E

190 Prince Alfred Hotel (The Gundy)
10 Main St, Gundiah
Camp Area. 48 km N of Gympie. Check in at bar
07 4129 3182   HEMA 14 J2   25 49 59 S   152 32 31 E

191 Boatshed Farm
Emerys Bridge Rd, Mount Urah
Farm Stay 49 km SW of Maryborough or 70 km NW of Gympie. 7 day limit. Pre-book
0400 884 657   HEMA 14 J2   25 49 36 S   152 29 14 E

192 Munna Creek Hall
Bauple Woolooga Rd, Munna Creek
Parking Area 23 km NE of Woolooga or 54 km NW of Gympie
0428 293 145   HEMA 14 K2   25 53 48 S   152 28 34 E

193 Gootchie Creek Escape
138 Gootchie Rd, Gootchie
Camp Area 45 km N of Gympie. GPS at the gate
0410 613 550   HEMA 14 K2   25 53 01 S   152 35 13 E

194 Theebine Hotel
11 Theebine Rd, Theebine
Pub Stay 36 km N of Gympie. Behind hotel. Check in with publican. Free for patrons. Power fee
07 5484 6182   HEMA 14 K2   25 56 46 S   152 32 39 E

195 Dickabram Bridge
1119 Miva Rd, Miva
Rest Area 39 km NW of Gympie. Next to bridge. Limited sites
1300 307 800   HEMA 14 K2   25 57 16 S   152 29 40 E

196 Gunna Park
433 Neerdie Rd, Gunalda
Farm Stay 5 km NE of Gunalda. Follow
Neerdie Rd 4 km, signed, ebook
0421 487 165   HEMA 14 K3   25 58 46 S   152 36 45 E

197 Gunalda Rest Area
Bruce Hwy, Gunalda
A1 Rest Area 2 km N of Gunalda turnoff. 28 km
NW of Gympie
132 380   HEMA 13 D4   25 59 10 S   152 34 14 E

198 Gunalda Bush Camping
522 Anderleigh Rd, Gunalda
A1 Camp Area 67 km S of Maryborough, or
33 km N of Gympie. 5 km E off Hwy
0418 822 803   HEMA 13 D4   26 00 24 S   152 36 43 E

199 Anderleigh Winery
131 Roberts Rd, Anderleigh
A1 Camp Area 30 km N of Gympie, or 78 km
S of Maryborough. E off Hwy to Anderleigh Rd
14 km, N 1.5 km. Open Wed - Sun. Cold shower.
Restaurant on site. Fee for power
07 5485 7999   HEMA 13 D4   25 59 24 S   152 41 08 E

200 Lake Barra Cottages
1891 Anderleigh Rd, Anderleigh
A1 Camp Area 25 km NE of Gympie
0477 477 195   HEMA 13 D4   26 00 36 S   152 43 21 E

201 Hangar O
2484 Bruce Hwy, Gunalda
A1 Camp Area 1 km S of United Service
Station. Pre-book
0412 787 829   HEMA 13 E4   26 01 07 S   152 34 05 E

202 Kookaburras On Curra
Harvey Siding Rd, Curra
A1 Camp Area 15 km N of Gympie. Pre-book.
Portable toilet required
0419 795 596   HEMA 13 E4   26 05 21 S   152 37 05 E

203 Glastonbury Creek Camp
Brooyar State Forest
49 Via Greendale Rd, Bells Bridge
Camp Area 26 km W of Gympie. 6 km W of Gympie,
turn N at Glastonbury to Diggings Rd for 10 km.
6 km dirt road. Pre-book
137 468   HEMA 13 E4   26 09 18 S   152 33 05 E

204 Chatsworth Park
Vantage Rd, Chatsworth
1 Rest Area 59 km S of Tiaro or 6 km N of
Gympie
1300 307 800   HEMA 13 E4   26 09 02 S   152 37 43 E

205 Widgee Showgrounds
22 Upper Widgee Rd, Widgee
49 Camp Area 26 km W of Gympie. Via
Gympie Woolooga Rd
0455 840 167   HEMA 13 F4   26 12 10 S   152 26 11 E

206 Marg McIntosh Park
2403 Gympie Woolooga Rd, Upper Widgee
49 Rest Area 26 km W of Gympie. 2 km N of
primary school
1300 307 800   HEMA 13 E3   26 11 30 S   152 25 55 E

207 Nomads Rest
97 Gympie Connection Rd, Gympie
15 Camp Area at Victory Heights. 7 km E of
Gympie off Tin Can Bay Rd. 21 day limit. Pre-book
0438 083 673   HEMA 13 E4   26 10 11 S   152 41 49 E

208 Chevallan Archery Park
715 Wilsons Pocket Rd, Wilsons Pocket
A1 Camp Area 18 km NE of Gympie. 7 km E of
Tin Can Bay Rd turnoff
0419 721 672   HEMA 13 E5   26 07 50 S   152 48 34 E

209 Ross Creek Store
1460 Tin Can Bay Rd, Goomboorian
A1 Rest Area 25 km NE of Gympie or 32 km
SW of Tin Can Bay
07 5486 5522   HEMA 13 E4   26 05 27 S   152 46 03 E

210 Wolvi Grove
Tagigan Rd, Wolvi
A1 Farm Stay 28 km NE of Gympie, next to
Cooloola Berries. Pre-book
0437 339 313   HEMA 13 E5   26 07 29 S   152 50 09 E

211 Silky Oak Tea Gardens
33 Priddy Road, Kia Ora
A1 Camp Area in paddock next to car park.
See publican first, patronage please
07 5486 5535   HEMA 13 E5   26 02 26 S   152 47 04 E

212 Standown Park
91 Radtke Rd, Kia Ora
A1 Caravan Park 26 km NE of Gympie. Via Tin
Cay Bay Rd. Access 8.30 - 5pm. Veteran discounts
07 5486 5144   HEMA 13 E5   26 02 08 S   152 47 32 E

213 Log Dump Campground
Tuan State Forest
A1 Via Tinnanbar Rd, Tinnanbar
Camp Area 44 km SE of Maryborough. S on
Cooloola Coast Rd for 38 km, E on Tinnanbar Rd
7 km to signed turn off. Small vehicles only, dirt
road. Pre-book
137 468   HEMA 14 J5   25 48 38 S   152 55 28 E

214 Hedleys Campground
Tuan State Forest
A1 Reserved Esplanade, Tinnanbar
Camp Area 44 km SE of Maryborough. S on
Cooloola Coast Rd for 38 km, E on Tinnanbar Rd
for 10.5 km to turn off, follow signs. Water crossings.
Pre-book
137 468   HEMA 14 J5   25 47 55 S   152 56 50 E

215 Poverty Point
Great Sandy NP - Cooloola
a1 Poverty Point Rd, Rainbow Beach
Camp Area 13 km S of Rainbow Beach via Rainbow
Beach Rd. Turnoff S of Roy Weber Plains, W to
4WD track for 6 km
137 468   HEMA 14 K5   25 57 38 S   153 01 30 E

216 Freshwater Campground
Great Sandy NP - Cooloola
A1
Campground Rd, Teewah Beach
Camp Area 8 km S of Double Island Pt or 40 km
N of 3rd cutting on Noosa North Shore. 18 km E
of Rainbow Beach via Freshwater Track. Sand &
beach tracks. Coins for shower. Permits apply
137 468　　HEMA 13 E6　26 00 13 S　153 08 55 E

217 Teewah Beach
Great Sandy NP - Cooloola
A1
Teewah Beach Access, Rainbow Beach
Dispersed Camping 16 km S of Freshwater Rd or
20 km N of 3rd cutting on Noosa North Shore. Sand
& beach tracks. Permits apply
137 468　　HEMA 13 E6　26 08 49 S　153 05 56 E

218 Inskip Point Campground
Great Sandy NP - Cooloola
A1
Inskip Point Rd, Rainbow Beach
Camp Area 12 km N of Rainbow Beach. 4WD
recommended. Permits apply
137 468　　HEMA 14 J6　25 48 35 S　153 03 16 E

219 K'gari (Fraser Island)
Great Sandy NP - Fraser Is
A1
Fraser Island Beach Rd, Fraser Island
Dispersed Camping on E and W beaches, 9
camping zones, 25 areas. Fenced areas with toilets
at Dundubara & Waddy Point. Toilets at Central
Station & Wathumba. All sites listed in Camps
Australia Wide App. High clearance only - sand &
beach tracks. Permits apply. Plan & pre-book
137 468　　HEMA 15 J5　25 34 43 S　153 06 05 E

220 Six Mile Creek Rest Area
1
Bruce Hwy, Gympie
Rest Area 6 km S of Gympie or 4 km N of
Kybong
1300 307 800　　HEMA 13 E4　26 13 54 S　152 41 49 E

221 Cedar Grove Campground
Amamoor State Forest
51
1317 Amamoor Creek Rd, Amamoor
Camp Area 12 km W of Amamoor. 5 km dirt road.
Pre-book
137 468　　HEMA 13 F4　26 21 58 S　152 35 13 E

222 Amamoor Creek Camp
Amamoor State Forest
51
1563 Amamoor Creek Rd, Amamoor Creek
Camp Area 16 km W of Amamoor. 5 km dirt road.
Pre-book
137 468　　HEMA 13 F4　26 21 26 S　152 33 24 E

223 Kandanga RV Stop
51
47 Main St, Kandanga
Parking Area opposite park with toilets &
swimming pool with showers for a fee. Donation box
07 5488 4605　　HEMA 11 A8　26 23 13 S　152 40 37 E

224 Kandanga Bowls Club
51
4 Bowling Club Rd, Kandanga
Camp Area off Kandanga Amamoor Rd
0438 843 195　　HEMA 11 A8　26 23 11 S　152 40 34 E

225 Mary Valley Koolewong Par 3 Golf Course
51
63 Barsby Rd, Imbil
Camp Spot 5 km N of Imbil. N on Kandanga Imbil
Rd for 4.5 km, turn E to Barsby Rd, 800 m to
entrance. Limited sites, pre-book
0417 762 155　　HEMA 11 A8　26 25 38 S　152 41 12 E

226 Carters Ridge RV Stop
42
8 Jubilee Rd, Carters Ridge
Parking Area 16 km E of Imbil. Cnr Poulsen
Rd, next to RFS shed. Store next door. Toilet & BBQ
opposite at Mary Fereday Park
1300 307 800　　HEMA 11 B9　26 27 04 S　152 45 52 E

227 Imbil Camping Retreat
51
5 Imbil Island Rd, Imbil
Camp Area 35 km S of Gympie
0447 135 471　　HEMA 11 B8　26 27 32 S　152 40 54 E

228 Imbil Showgrounds
51
14 Edward St, Imbil
Camp Area 35 km S of Gympie. Pre-book
0488 566 131　　HEMA 11 B8　26 27 41 S　152 40 43 E

229 Camp at Number 1
51
536 Yabba Creek Rd, Imbil
Camp Area 3 km W of Imbil. 39 km S of
Gympie. Before No. 1 Crossing
0429 845 398　　HEMA 11 B8　26 27 59 S　152 38 51 E

230 Borumba Campground
51
1484 Yabba Creek Rd, Lake Borumba
Camp Area at Borumba Dam. 12 km W of
Imbil, via Yabba Creek Rd
07 5488 6662　　HEMA 10 B7　26 30 06 S　152 35 17 E

231 Brooloo Park
51
104 Whelan Rd, Bollier
Camp Area 4.5 km SE of Imbil. 18 km N of
Kenilworth. Pre-book
0472 737 243　　HEMA 11 B8　26 28 04 S　152 42 30 E

232 Kumbak Kamping
51
3675 Mary Valley Rd, Brooloo
Camp Area 15 km N of Kenilworth or 6 km
SE of Imbil. GPS at gate. 250 m N of Brooloo Hall.
7 day limit. Pre-book
0447 945 441　　HEMA 11 B8　26 28 59 S　152 42 13 E

233 Bluff Creek Campground
51
44 Wilcox Rd, Kenilworth
Camp Area 6 km N of Kenilworth. Via
Kenilworth Brooloo Rd. 10 night limit
07 5370 2030　　HEMA 11 C9　26 33 44 S　152 44 16 E
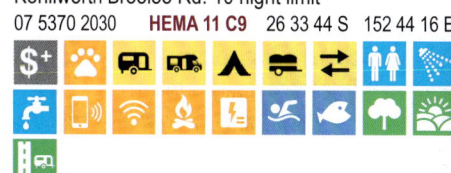

234 Puma Kybong
1
1516 Old Bruce Hwy, Kybong
Parking Area 10 km S of Gympie or 40 km
N of Cooroy. Follow Kybong offramp. Behind
roadhouse. Pay for shower at roadhouse
07 5483 5299　　HEMA 12 A4　26 18 25 S　152 43 11 E

QUEENSLAND

235 Cobb & Co Nine Mile Camp
1484 Noosa Rd, Tandur
Camp Area 10 km S of Gympie. E to Tandur Rd at Kybong Roadhouse for 6 km, S to Old Noosa Rd for 300 m. GPS at gate. 2 week limit
07 5483 5065   HEMA 12 A4   26 17 08 S   152 45 55 E

236 Warrigal Ridge Bush Camp
90 Lehman Rd, Traveston
Camp Area 17 km S of Gympie. E off Hwy to Traveston Rd 7 km, via Tandur Traveston Rd. No EFTPOS
0438 281 946   HEMA 13 F4   26 18 57 S   152 45 33 E

237 Kin Kin Oval
57 Main St, Kin Kin
Camp Area. Entry off roundabout. Call caretaker for key
07 5485 4129   HEMA 12 A5   26 15 46 S   152 52 30 E

238 Pomona Showgrounds
15 Pavilion St, Pomona
Caravan Park. Entry via Exhibition St. 6 week limit
0490 195 374   HEMA 12 A4   26 21 36 S   152 51 28 E

239 Maleny Showgrounds
13 Maleny Stanley River Rd, Maleny
Camp Area. Pay at secretary's office near Pavilion. Coin-operated showers. Donation for DP
07 5494 2008   HEMA 11 F10   26 45 47 S   152 50 44 E

240 Camp Cooroora
116 Collwood Rd, Cooroy
Camp Area 10 km NE of Cooroy. W on Noosa-Cooroy Rd for 5 km, N to Sivyers Rd, N to Gumboil Rd, follow signs. Pre-book. 7 day limit
07 5442 5285   HEMA 11 A11   26 22 51 S   152 56 14 E

241 Cooroy RV Stop
17 Mary River Rd, Cooroy
Camp Area entry between Car & Horse Clubs, ebook or caretaker collects fee
0458 650 285   HEMA 11 A11   26 24 49 S   152 54 25 E

242 Campania Hills
9 Hayward Rd, Cooroy
Camp Area 4 km E of Cooroy. Via Cooroy Noosa Rd. Pre-book
0419 305 995   HEMA 11 A11   26 24 22 S   152 56 36 E

243 Noosa Sea Scouts Camp
Badgers Wood
11 Eumundi Rd, Noosaville
Camp Area accessed via Gympie Tce roundabout. Open Fri - Tue school terms, check in 4pm - 7pm. No bookings, limited sites. Open all school holidays
07 5473 0028   HEMA 11 A13   26 23 57 S   153 03 10 E

244 Cooroys No Worries RV Stop
154 Holts Rd, Cooroy
Parking Area. Take Cooroy exit 230B off M1, follow ramp for 200 m. Turn SE to Mayall St under Hwy & SE at Holts Rd for 1.5 km. Entry signposted. 7 day limit
0411 786 247   HEMA 11 B11   26 26 31 S   152 55 08 E

245 Eumundi Mountain Retreat
116 Lone Hand Rd, Eumundi
Camp Area 6 km SE of Cooroy. Via Nandroya Rd. Pre-book
0418 743 732   HEMA 11 B11   26 26 43 S   152 57 02 E

246 Gheerulla Campground
Mapleton Forest Reserve
Sam Kelly Rd, Kenilworth
Camp Area 9 km NE of Kenilworth. NE on Eumundi Kenilworth Rd for 7km, E for 1.5 km on rough & narrow dirt road. Limited sites. Pre-book
137 468   HEMA 11 C9   26 34 12 S   152 47 29 E

247 Kenilworth Camping on the River
18 Paulger Rd, Kenilworth
Camp Area 3.5 km N of Kenilworth. Via Eumundi Kenilworth Rd
0455 176 240   HEMA 11 D9   26 34 24 S   152 44 46 E

248 Kenilworth Homestead
2760 Eumundi Kenilworth Rd, Kenilworth
Camp Area 1.5 km E of town. Pre-book
07 5440 0900   HEMA 11 D9   26 35 09 S   152 44 19 E

249 Obi Obi Creek Crossing 2
1127 Obi Obi Rd, Kenilworth
Camp Area at Kidaman Creek. 10 km SE of Kenilworth or 12.5 km W of Mapleton, via Eumundi Rd. Both sides of crossing. Facilities on W side
07 5446 0122   HEMA 11 D9   26 38 09 S   152 47 08 E

250 Kenilworth Showground
3742 Maleny Kenilworth Rd, Kenilworth
Camp Area S end of town, E of road
0438 849 947   HEMA 11 D9   26 35 57 S   152 43 35 E

251 Little Yabba Picnic Area
Imbil State Forest
3143 Maleny Kenilworth Rd, Kenilworth
Picnic Area 6 km SW of Kenilworth. E & W of bridge
07 5446 0122   HEMA 11 D8   26 37 30 S   152 41 21 E

252 Charlie Moreland Camp
Imbil State Forest
Sunday Creek Rd, Kenilworth
Camp Area 12 km SW of Kenilworth. 6 km S on Kenilworth-Maleny Rd Turn W, 7 km dirt road
137 468   HEMA 11 D8   26 36 59 S   152 39 04 E

253 Booloumba Creek No.4
Conondale National Park
Booloumba Creek Rd, Kenilworth
Camp Area 14 km SW of Kenilworth. 7 km S on Kenilworth-Maleny Rd, turn W for 7 km dirt road. Not suitable for large vehicles
137 468   HEMA 11 E8   26 38 46 S   152 38 52 E

254 Eumundi Showgrounds
1 Black Stump Rd, Eumundi
Camp Area N of town. Via Memorial Dr. Gates close 6.45pm
0490 332 627   HEMA 11 B11   26 28 13 S   152 56 34 E

255 Eumundi RV Stop Over

Cnr Napier Rd & Albert St, Eumundi
Parking Area near markets. Via Memorial
Drv. Fees collected, enter by 5pm
0412 566 671 HEMA 11 B12 26 28 34 S 152 57 13 E

256 Hidden Valley @ Gro Mad
Plantations

180 Yandina Bli Bli Rd, Yandina
Camp Area 12 km NE of Nambour. Pre-book
0432 040 751 HEMA 11 D12 26 34 34 S 152 58 31 E

257 Max & Digbys Camp

Via Wilson Rd, Ilkley
Camp Area between Eudlo & Hwy. Pre-book. Some sites 4WD only. 7 day limit
0433 677 320 HEMA 11 F12 26 44 01 S 152 59 24 E

258 Jowarra Rest Area

2859 Steve Irwin Way, Glenview
Rest Area off the Landsbrough / Caloundra roundabout exit 188A. Small parking bays
132 380 HEMA 11 G13 26 46 24 S 153 02 16 E

259 Beerwah Sportsground

32 Sportsground Dr, Beerwah
Camp Area. Entry via Simpson St off roundabout. Pre-book. Contact caretaker on arrival
07 5494 0513 HEMA 11 H12 26 51 50 S 152 57 21 E

260 Coochin Creek
Beerburrum State Forest

Roys Rd, Coochin Creek
Camp Area 30 km NE of Caboolture. Exit Bruce Hwy at Bells Creek Rd interchange, then S to Roys Rd for 5 km. Pre-book
137 468 HEMA 11 H13 26 52 52 S 153 02 46 E

261 Glass House Mountains
Caravan & Camping Park

2001 Old Gympie Rd, Glass House Mts
Camp Area 4.5 km W of Glasshouse Mountain. Via Coonowrin Rd. Enter via Mt Beerwah Rd, cash only
07 5496 9588 HEMA 11 J11 26 54 50 S 152 55 17 E

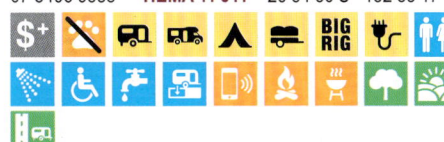

262 Gallagher Point
Bribie Island National Park

Gallagher Point Rd, White Patch
Camp Area 2 km N White Patch. Sand tracks. Pre-book, permit applies. Tent and camper trailer only listings detailed in Camps Australia Wide App
137 468 HEMA 11 K13 27 00 49 S 153 05 57 E

263 Caboolture Showgrounds

140 Beerburrum Rd, Caboolture
Camp Area 4 km N of Caboolture town centre. Gate 2. Check in with caretaker
07 5495 2030 HEMA 4 A4 27 03 54 S 152 56 54 E

264 Watson Park Convention
Centre

337 Old Gympie Rd, Dakabin
Camp Area at Seventh Day Adventist Church. Check in 9am - 4pm only. No alcohol, drugs or tobacco permitted
07 3204 6544 HEMA 4 B4 27 13 14 S 152 59 21 E

265 Dayboro Showgrounds

3512 Mount Mee Rd, Dayboro
Camp Area N side of town. 21 day limit
0403 952 198 HEMA 4 B3 27 11 25 S 152 49 24 E

266 Redcliffe Showgrounds

Scarborough Rd, Redcliffe
Camp Area N of Anzac Ave. 21 day limit
07 3284 5387 HEMA 4 C5 27 13 30 S 153 06 22 E

267 Pine Rivers Showground

757 Gympie Rd, Lawnton
Camp Area E of Gympie Rd. Check in with caretaker. 21 day limit. Deposit for key
0459 023 346 HEMA 4 C4 27 17 07 S 152 59 13 E

268 Samford Showground

40 Showgrounds Dr, Samford
Camp Area 7 km W of Samford. Pre-book, contact caretaker. 21 day limit
07 3289 7057 HEMA 4 D3 27 22 14 S 152 49 29 E

269 Baden Powell Park Scout
Camp

68 Cash Ave, Samford
Camp Area SE of town centre. Pre-book. Scout supporters fee on arrival. 14 day limit
07 3721 5700 HEMA 4 D3 27 22 33 S 152 53 26 E

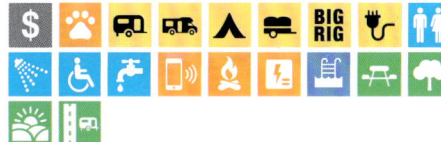

270 Karingal Scout Camp

1 Karingal Rd, Mt Cotton
Camp Area N of town. Scout membership fee
0437 486 649 HEMA 7 B10 27 36 08 S 153 13 21 E

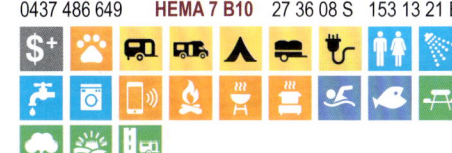

271 Tranquility Park

Springacre Rd, Thornlands
Camp Area S of Thornlands. 3 - 14 days only. Pre-book
0412 809 535 HEMA 4 G7 27 34 17 S 153 15 29 E

272 Flinders Beach
North Stradbroke Island

Beach Access Tr, Cylinder Beach
Dispersed Camping 6 km E of Amity Point or 3 km W of Cylinder Beach. Bush tracks or via beach at low tide
07 3409 9668 HEMA 9 G14 27 25 08 S 153 29 24 E

QUEENSLAND

273 Main Beach
North Stradbroke Island
Alfred Martin Way, North Stradbroke Island
Dispersed Camping 17 km S of Point Lookout. Bush
tracks or via beach at low tide
07 3409 9668   **HEMA 9 J14**   27 31 24 S   153 30 04 E

274 Hugh Muntz Park
Reisers Rd, Beenleigh
Parking Area just SE of overbridge on
Pacific Mwy. 3 night limit within 30 days
07 3412 3412   **HEMA 4 H6**   27 43 01 S   153 12 33 E

275 Beenleigh Showgrounds
1-19 Showgrounds Dr, Beenleigh
Camp Area near Mundt Pavillion. No long
term pets
07 3807 1871   **HEMA 4 H6**   27 43 14 S   153 12 00 E

276 Numinbah Valley Adventure Trails
2524 Nerang Murwillumbah Rd, Numinbah
Camp Area 21 km S of Advancetown or 37 km N of
Murwillumbah. Pre-book and check in on arrival
07 5533 4137   **HEMA 7 K10**   28 10 09 S   153 13 11 E

277 The Log Cabin Camp
3360 Nerang Murwillumbah Rd, Numinbah
Camp Area 21 km S of Advancetown or
28 km NW of Murwillumbah. 7 day limit, pre-book for
weekends
07 5533 6174   **HEMA 12 J6**   28 14 13 S   153 14 17 E

278 The Settlement Camp Area
Springbrook National Park
Carricks Rd, Springbrook
Camp Area 38 km SW of Gold Coast. Not suitable
for caravans. Pre-book
137 468   **HEMA 7 K11**   28 11 40 S   153 16 20 E

279 Mount Nimmel Lodge Camp
271 Austinville Rd, Austinville
Camp Area 10 km SW of Mudgeeraba.
SCV rates. Pre-book, 14 day limit
0448 138 086   **HEMA 5 K2**   28 08 10 S   153 19 07 E

Cairns to Cloncurry
Kennedy Highway, Gulf and Burke Developmental Roads

280 Palmer River Roadhouse
Lot 1 Mulligan Hwy, Lakeland
Camp Area 31 km S of Lakeland or 113 km
N of Mount Molloy
07 4060 2020   **HEMA 20 C1**   16 06 25 S   144 46 37 E

281 North Palmer River
Palmer Goldfield Resources Reserve
Maytown Rd, Mighell
Camp Area 97 km W of Palmer River Roadhouse. S
on Mulligan Hwy for 16 km, turn W to Whites Creek
Rd for 80 km. Pre-book epermit. Seasonal
137 468   **HEMA 26 B7**   16 01 01 S   144 17 00 E

282 Cooktown Crossing
Kondaparinga Rd, Mareeba
Camp Area 35 km NW Mount Carbine. Exit
Mulligan Hwy S to Hurricane Rd for 8 km, then E for
900 m to camp on river
HEMA 20 E2   16 33 49 S   144 53 24 E

283 Hurricane Station
Hurricane Rd, Mt Carbine
Camp Area 62 km SW Mt Carbine. 26 km N
Mt Carbine turn S to Hurricane Rd for 36 km. Open
Easter - New Year. Pre-book
07 4094 8234   **HEMA 20 E1**   16 34 33 S   144 40 35 E

284 Karma Waters Station
Karma Waters Rd, Hurricane
Station Stay 69 km SW Mt Carbine. 26 km
N of Mt Carbine turn S to Hurricane Rd for 40 km.
Continue on Karma Waters Rd, veer left towards
station. Pre-book. Closed Jan - Mar
07 4094 8337   **HEMA 20 E1**   16 37 03 S   144 36 16 E

285 Mount Carbine Caravan Park
6806 Mulligan Hwy, Mount Carbine
Caravan Park 300 m SE of roadhouse
07 4094 3160   **HEMA 20 E2**   16 31 53 S   145 08 21 E

286 Rifle Creek Rest Area
Mulligan Hwy, Mount Molloy
Rest Area 1 km N of town or 41 km N of
Mareeba. Cold showers
07 4086 4500   **HEMA 21 C2**   16 39 58 S   145 19 42 E

287 Feather & Friends
244 Clacherty Rd, Julatten
Camp Area via Mossman-Mt Molloy Rd.
Turn SE 15 km from Captain Cook Hwy Jcn, or
14 km from Mulligan Hwy Jcn for 2 km. Pre-book.
14 day limit
0412 991 175   **HEMA 21 B2**   16 34 45 S   145 21 41 E

288 Tableland Caravan Park
1045 Mossman Mount Molloy Rd, Julatten
Caravan Park 10.5 km S from Captain
Cook Hwy turnoff
07 4094 1145   **HEMA 21 B2**   16 32 44 S   145 22 59 E
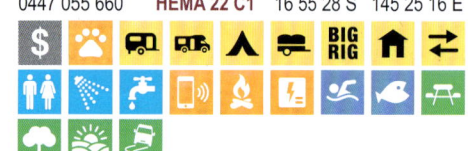

289 Birds on Barron
548 McGrath Rd, Biboohra
Camp Area 7 km N Mareeba turn E off
Mulligan Hwy, follow signs over railway track. Pre-
book. Seasonal
0447 055 660   **HEMA 22 C1**   16 55 28 S   145 25 16 E

290 Kerribee Park/Mareeba Rodeo
614 Mareeba-Dimbulah Rd, Mareeba
Camp Area 3 km W of town
07 4092 1583   **HEMA 21 E2**   16 59 34 S   145 23 43 E

291 Granite Gorge Nature Park
332 Paglietta Rd, Chewko
Camp Area 14 km SW of Mareeba. Via Rankin St & Chewko Rd. Riverside. Fee includes 3 gorge walks
07 4093 2259   HEMA 21 E2   17 02 31 S   145 21 06 E

292 Dimbulah Caravan Park
478 Burke Developmental Rd, Dimbulah
Caravan Park 750 m SW of PO. Pre-book
0472 510 833   HEMA 20 G2   17 09 05 S   145 06 20 E

293 Boonmoo Station
845 Boonmoo Rd, Dimbulah
Station Stay 14 km S of town. Pre-book, open Mar - Nov
07 4094 4129   HEMA 20 H2   17 14 56 S   145 04 26 E

294 Eureka Creek
Burke Developmental Rd, Dimbulah
Camp Spot 9 km W of Dimbulah
132 380   HEMA 20 G2   17 11 12 S   145 02 29 E

295 Emu Creek Outback Holiday Station
Burke Developmental Rd, Petford
Station Stay 30 km W of Dimbulah. Turn N 23 km W of Dimbulah, check in at house. GPS at gate. 7 km to station. Dirt road
07 4094 8313   HEMA 20 H2   17 17 14 S   144 58 34 E

296 Railway Hotel Almaden
13 Main Street, Almaden
Camp Area 33 km SE of Chillagoe. Opposite hotel
07 4094 8307   HEMA 20 H1   17 20 17 S   144 40 43 E

297 Sandy Tate River
Almaden Gingerella Rd, Almaden
Camp Area 19 km SW Almaden or 31 km N of Barwidgi
1300 308 461   HEMA 20 J1   17 28 09 S   144 37 14 E

298 Chillagoe Cockatoo Hotel
2 Tower St, Chillagoe
Parking Area and motel in town. Free for patrons. Check in at counter
07 4094 7168   HEMA 27 D8   17 09 08 S   144 31 20 E

299 Chillagoe Observatory & Eco Lodge
1 Hospital Ave, Chillagoe
Caravan Park in town. 7 night limit
07 4094 7155   HEMA 27 D8   17 08 55 S   144 31 39 E

300 Walsh River South
Burke Developmental Rd, Rookwood
Camp Area 32 km NW of Chillagoe
   HEMA 26 D7   16 59 24 S   144 17 56 E

301 Walsh River West
Burke Developmental Rd, Wrotham
Camp Area 120 km NW of Chillagoe or 183 km E of Dunbar Airport
   HEMA 26 C7   16 32 43 S   143 46 58 E

302 Mareeba Bush Stays
110 Paglietta Rd, Chewko
Camp Area 8 km SW of Mareeba. From Chewko Rd, turn W for check in at signposted house
0400 978 311   HEMA 21 F2   17 03 13 S   145 22 04 E

303 Ringers Rest RV
277 Fichera Rd, Mareeba
Camp Area 7 km SE of town. Take Kennedy Hwy E, turn S to Tinaroo Creek Rd, then S. Enter 2nd gate. Pre-book
0447 136 865   HEMA 22 E1   17 01 55 S   145 27 15 E

304 Upper Davies Creek 1 - 8
Davies Creek National Park
Davies Creek Rd, Mareeba
Camp Area 22 km E of Mareeba. E on Kennedy Hwy for 12 km, to Davies Creek Rd for 10 km. 8 sites over 5 km. GPS at first site. Pre-book
137 468   HEMA 22 D3   17 01 01 S   145 35 06 E

305 Speewah Camping Area
Speewah Conservation Park
Smiths Tr, Speewah
Camp Area 13 km S of Kuranda. Via Kennedy Hwy, Stoney Creek Rd & Smiths Tr. E-permit applies
137 468   HEMA 22 B4   16 52 54 S   145 37 51 E

306 The Billabong
186 Mount Haren Rd, Kuranda
Camp Area 4 km S of Kuranda. Via Kennedy Hwy
07 4093 7684   HEMA 22 A4   16 50 34 S   145 36 18 E

307 Mareeba Drive-In
5303 Kennedy Hwy, Mareeba
Parking Area E side of Hwy. Movie nights only, admission applies. Gates open 6.30 pm
0429 056 615   HEMA 22 E1   17 02 53 S   145 25 51 E

308 Walkamin Central Van Park
2 Wattle St, Walkamin
Caravan Park S side of town. 15 km S of Mareeba or 18 km N of Atherton
07 4093 3561   HEMA 22 G1   17 07 56 S   145 25 41 E

309 Rocky Creek Memorial Park & Camping Reserve
Kennedy Hwy, Tolga
Rest Area 23 km S of Mareeba or 12 km N of Atherton. Donation box at toilet block
1300 362 242   HEMA 22 H1   17 10 54 S   145 27 10 E

310 Kairi Lions Park
43 Irvine St, Kairi
Parking Area opposite hotel. Via Kennedy Hwy
1300 362 242   HEMA 22 H3   17 12 58 S   145 32 36 E

311 Platypus Campground
Danbulla NP & State Forest
Platypus Campground Access Rd, Tinaroo
Camp Area 6 km NE of Tinaroo off Danbulla Forest Dr. 3 km dirt road. Pre-book
137 468   HEMA 22 G3   17 09 39 S   145 33 34 E

312 Downfall Creek Camp
Danbulla NP & State Forest
Danbulla Rd, Tinaroo
Camp Area 8 km NE of Tinaroo off Danbulla Forest Dr. 5 km dirt road. Pre-book
137 468   **HEMA 22 G4**   17 08 52 S   145 35 18 E

313 Kauri Creek Campground
Danbulla NP & State Forest
Danbulla Rd, Tinaroo
Camp Area 10 km NE of Tinaroo off Danbulla Forest Dr. 7 km dirt road. Pre-book
137 468   **HEMA 22 G4**   17 08 18 S   145 35 53 E

314 School Point Campground
Danbulla NP & State Forest
School Point Access Rd, Tinaroo
Camp Area 18 km NE of Tinaroo off Danbulla Forest Dr. 13 km dirt road. Pre-book
137 468   **HEMA 22 G4**   17 08 54 S   145 36 39 E

315 Fong-On Bay Campground
Danbulla NP & State Forest
Fong-On Bay Access Rd, Tinaroo
Camp Area 22 km E of Tinaroo off Danbulla Forest Dr. 19 km dirt road. Pre-book
137 468   **HEMA 22 G4**   17 09 26 S   145 35 16 E

316 Bonadio RV & Nature Park
4756 Gillies Range Rd, East Barron
Camp Area 4 km W of Yungaburra or 9 km E of Atherton. Signposted, GPS at entry. 7 day limit
0429 682 953   **HEMA 22 J3**   17 16 06 S   145 32 51 E

317 Genazzano Campground
739 Powley Rd, Yungaburra
Camp Area 16 km NE of town. E via Gillies Hwy 9 km, N for 7 km. Open Mar - Nov. Pre-book. Small campervans only
07 4095 3232   **HEMA 22 H4**   17 12 05 S   145 36 46 E

318 Malanda Falls Caravan Park
38 Park Ave, Malanda
Caravan Park next to Malanda Falls. Firepit hire or BYO
07 4096 5314   **HEMA 21 H3**   17 21 13 S   145 35 18 E

319 Wild River Caravan Park
23 Holdcroft Dr, Moomin
Caravan Park E end of Herberton
07 4096 2121   **HEMA 21 H2**   17 22 03 S   145 23 20 E

320 Jumna Dam
Herberton Petford Rd, Irvinebank
Camp Area 7 km E Irvinebank. Turn S off Herberton-Petford Rd 21 km W Herberton. 1.5 km to dam
137 468   **HEMA 21 H1**   17 24 16 S   145 13 46 E

321 Irvinebank Town Common
2656 MacDonald St, Irvinebank
Camp Area opposite tavern. 28 km W of Herberton (12 km unsealed) or 45 km E of Petford. Coin for showers
132 380   **HEMA 21 H1**   17 25 42 S   145 12 12 E

322 Henrietta Creek
Wooroonooran National Park
Bunda St, Wooroonooran
Camp Area 22 km SE of Millaa Millaa. Via Palmerston Hwy. Pre-book
137 468   **HEMA 21 K5**   17 35 56 S   145 45 31 E

323 Ravenshoe Steam Railway
Caravan Park
63 Grigg St, Ravenshoe
Camp Area at Ravenshoe. S of town centre. 14 day limit. Limited space for big rigs
07 4097 6005   **HEMA 21 K3**   17 36 30 S   145 28 59 E

324 Ravenshoe Hotel
34 Grigg St, Ravenshoe
Parking Area central in town. Check in with publican, free with patronage
07 4097 6136   **HEMA 21 K3**   17 36 18 S   145 28 55 E

325 Koombooloomba
Conservation Park
Tully Falls Rd, Lake Koombooloomba
Camp Area 36 km S of Ravenshoe. Pre-book
137 468   **HEMA 20 K4**   17 50 15 S   145 35 46 E

326 Ravenshoe Millstream
Country Club
Lot 32 Golf Links Pde, Ravenshoe
Parking Area at Millstream. 8 km W of Ravenshoe. Check in to caretaker. 7 day limit
0487 989 568   **HEMA 21 K2**   17 38 30 S   145 25 29 E
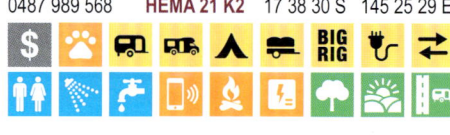

327 Archer Creek Rest Area
Kennedy Hwy, Millstream
Rest Area 16 km W of Ravenshoe or 28 km E of Mount Garnet. Large area, creekside
1300 362 242   **HEMA 21 K2**   17 38 47 S   145 20 50 E

328 Woodleigh Station
115 Woodleigh Rd, Millstream
Station Stay 24 km SW Ravenshoe. Turn S to Woodleigh Rd off Gregory Hwy. Limited powered sites. Facilities close to homestead, bush camps near river. Pre-book
07 4097 0204   **HEMA 21 K1**   17 39 57 S   145 16 39 E
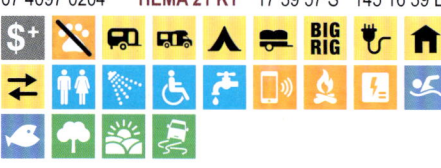

329 Mount Garnet Petrol Station
13 Silver St, Mount Garnet
Parking Area N side of Hwy. Adjoining station. Free for patrons
07 4097 9249   **HEMA 20 J2**   17 40 31 S   145 06 45 E

330 Blencoe Falls
Girringun National Park
Cashmere Rd, Kirrama
Camp Area 107 km SE of Mt Garnet. Off Kennedy Hwy, turn SE to Gunnawarra Rd for 55 km, then SE to Kirrama–Cashmere Rd for 45 km to the signposted track. 1.4 km to camp. Pre-book
137 468   **HEMA 27 F9**   18 12 30 S   145 32 20 E

331 Princess Hills

Girringun National Park
Unnamed Rd, Wairuna
Camp Area 124 km SE of Mt Garnet. Off Kennedy Hwy, turn SE to Gunnawarra Rd for 55 km, then SW to Wairuna Rd for 42 km to Princess Hills Rd turn-off. NE at intersection, 11 km to Greasy Track for 12 km. Pre-book
137 468   HEMA 27 F9   18 14 29 S 145 20 27 E

332 Pinnarendi Station Stay & Cafe

22971 Kennedy Hwy, Minnamoolka
Station Stay 55 km SW of Mount Garnet. Open April - Oct. GPS at gate. Call ahead
0401 627 315   HEMA 27 F8   18 02 24 S 144 52 08 E

333 Junction Parking Area

Cnr Kennedy Hwy & Gulf Developmental Rd, Minnamoolka
Parking Area 67 km W of Mount Garnet or 51 km E of Mount Surprise. Shared with trucks. Tracks to gravel area
132 380   HEMA 27 F8   18 08 19 S 144 48 43 E

334 Oasis Roadhouse

Kennedy Developmental Rd, Conjuboy
Camp Area at The Lynd Junction
07 4062 5291   HEMA 27 G8   18 52 47 S 144 32 37 E

335 Greenvale Caravan Park

3 Kylee Crt, Greenvale
Caravan Park E side of town. Via Gregory Hwy
0498 035 295   HEMA 27 G8   19 00 04 S 144 59 03 E

336 Planet Earth Adventures

1 Cox Ln, Mount Surprise
Camp Area S of Hwy. Via Gulf Developmental Rd
0427 406 230   HEMA 26 F7   18 08 49 S 144 19 07 E

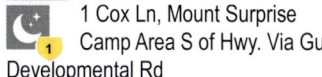

337 OBriens Creek Camp

O'Briens Creek Rd, Mount Surprise
Camp Area 36 km NW of town. 35 km dirt road, can be corrugated. No unregistered bikes/quads
07 4062 3001   HEMA 26 F7   18 02 42 S 144 03 23 E

338 Jardine Station

Gregory Developmental Road, Einasleigh
Station Stay 20 km N of Einasleigh or 25 km S of Hwy. Dirt road. GPS at road and Jardine Lagoon, 3 km to The Beach & Ellendale Hole. Pre-book for river camping. Seasonal
07 4062 5117   HEMA 26 F7   18 22 14 S 144 05 10 E

339 The Einasleigh Hotel

Daintree St, Einasleigh
Parking Area E side of town. Check in with publican. 7 day limit. Meals 7 days a week
07 4062 5222   HEMA 26 F7   18 30 45 S 144 05 40 E

340 Silks Rest on Savannah Way

Fifth St, Einasleigh
Camp Spot S side of town
07 4062 5266   HEMA 26 F7   18 31 01 S 144 05 34 E

341 Copperfield Lodge Van Park

600 Baroota St, Einasleigh
Caravan Park N side of town, W of main road. Via Burke Development Rd
07 4062 5102   HEMA 26 F7   18 30 35 S 144 05 37 E

342 Kidston Community Park

Kidston Airstrip, Einasleigh
Camp Spot 51 km S of Einasleigh. SE via Gregory Hwy for 21 km, SW on Gilberton Rd for 25 km. Next to Kidston Airstrip - signed 'River Camping'
                 HEMA 26 G7   18 51 36 S 144 10 45 E

343 Copperfield (Kidston) Dam

Dam Rd, Lyndhurst
Camp Area 72 km S Einasleigh or 98 km SW Lynd Oasis Roadhouse. Turn SW off Gregory Hwy 26 km S Einasleigh on Gilberton Rd, L to Dam Rd (46 km from Hwy). Check website for access updates
137 468   HEMA 26 G7   19 02 09 S 144 07 17 E

344 Routh Creek Campsite

Gulf Developmental Rd, Georgetown
Camp Area 72 km W of Mt Surprise or 20 km E of Georgetown. N side of road, track to waterhole. Limited space.
                 HEMA 26 F7   18 16 44 S 143 43 16 E

345 Georgetown East

Routh Creek
Gulf Developmental Rd, Georgetown
Rest Area 27 km E of Georgetown. Over the bridge, N side
137 468   HEMA 26 F7   18 17 23 S 143 42 53 E

346 Western Creek Station

Flat Creek Rd, Northhead
Camp Area 30 km SW of Georgetown. 15 km S on Forsayth Rd, turn W
07 4062 5591   HEMA 26 F6   18 28 15 S 143 26 05 E

347 Flat Creek Station

Flat Creek Rd, Northhead
Station Stay 45 km SW of Georgetown. 15 km S on Forsayth Rd, turn W to Flat Creek Rd. Open Apr - Sep. Pre-book
07 4062 5304   HEMA 26 F6   18 32 33 S 143 20 27 E

348 Forsayth Tourist Park

First St, Forsayth
Caravan Park 40 km S of Georgetown
07 4062 5324   HEMA 26 F6   18 35 16 S 143 36 06 E

349 Cobbold Gorge Village

Agate Creek Rd, Cobbold Gorge
Camp Area 45 km SW of Forsayth via Cobb
Rd. Closed Nov - Mar. Pre-book
07 4062 5470   HEMA 26 G6   18 47 45 S   143 25 23 E

350 Agate Creek Camping Ground

Agate Creek Rd, Forsayth
Camp Area 70 km S of Forsayth and 10 km from Old
Robin Hood Station. Adjacent to fossicking field, W
side of road, before Agate Ck. Signed. Gravel road,
high clearance vehicles recommended. Honesty box
07 4062 5355   HEMA 26 G6   19 00 15 S   143 33 37 E

351 Goldfields Van Park

2 St George St, Georgetown
Caravan Park N side of town. Via Gulf
Developmental Rd
07 4062 1269   HEMA 26 F6   18 17 14 S   143 32 58 E

352 Midway Caravan Park

1 North St, Georgetown
Caravan Park 500 m W of PO. Via Gulf
Developmental Rd
07 4062 1219   HEMA 26 F6   18 17 22 S   143 32 50 E

353 Cumberland Mine

Carnes Rd, Georgetown
Camp Spot at Historic Site, 20 km W of
Georgetown or 128 km E of Croydon. Via Gulf
Developmental Rd. Beside chimney & billabong
132 380   HEMA 26 F6   18 17 59 S   143 21 04 E

354 Gilbert River East

Gulf Developmental Rd, Gilbert River
Parking Area 72 km W of Georgetown or
75 km E of Croydon
132 380   HEMA 26 F5   18 11 36 S   142 53 49 E

355 Gilbert River West

Gulf Developmental Rd, Gilbert River
Rest Area 75 km W of Georgetown or
73 km E of Croydon. W side of river
132 380   HEMA 26 F5   18 12 02 S   142 52 25 E

356 Croydon Freedom Camping

2 Alldridge St, Croydon
Parking Area in town. Permits from Info
Centre when open or self register
07 4748 7100   HEMA 26 F5   18 12 49 S   142 14 31 E

357 Blackbull Siding

Gulf Devlopmental Rd, Blackbull
Rest Area 61 km W of Croydon or 94 km E
of Normanton
132 380   HEMA 26 E4   17 56 26 S   141 45 18 E

358 Leichhardt Lagoon Camping

Gulf Developmental Rd, Normanton
Camp Area 128 km W of Croydon or 24 km
SE of Normanton. Entry through white tyres at signs.
Seasonal
0487 675 173   HEMA 25 D7   17 51 02 S   141 07 43 E

359 Norman River Reserve

Burke Developmental Rd, Normanton
Parking Area 1 km NE of town. Signed.
Limited permits issued daily from Info Centre
07 4747 8422   HEMA 25 D7   17 39 48 S   141 05 19 E

360 Little Bynoe River

Burketown Normanton Rd, Normanton
Camp Spot 189 km E of Burketown or
37 km W of Normanton. Tracks on W side of river,
limited space
    HEMA 25 D7   17 52 00 S   140 49 28 E

361 Tower Layby

Burketown Normanton Rd, Carpentaria
Parking Area 100 km E of Burketown or
126 km W of Normanton
    HEMA 25 E5   18 09 11 S   140 05 48 E

362 Leichhardt River Falls

Nardoo Burketown Rd, Gregory
Camp Spot 72 km E of Burketown or
154 km W of Normanton. Camping on E & W banks
on falls
07 4745 5111   HEMA 25 E5   18 13 09 S   139 52 30 E

363 Burketown Camping

Truganini & Nardoo Burketown Rds,
Burketown
Camp Areas within 14 km of town. Permit from Info
Centre. Fee includes access, camping and fishing.
Bridge to Bottleheap (GPS listed), Deans Creek,
Meatworks & Wharf Camps. Facilities & access
varies - detailed in the Camps Australia Wide App.
7 day limit
07 4745 5111   HEMA 25 D4   17 45 24 S   139 33 09 E

364 Tirranna Springs Roadhouse

Doomadgee Rd, Gregory
Camp Area at Tirranna Springs. 103 km N
of Gregory Downs or 34 km S of Burketown
07 4748 3998   HEMA 25 D4   17 53 45 S   139 17 45 E

365 Hells Gate Roadhouse

Westmoreland Rd, Nicholson
Camp Area 202 km W of Bourketown
07 4745 8258   HEMA 25 C2   17 27 18 S   138 21 22 E

366 Beames Brook

Wills Developmental Rd, Gregory
Camp Area 93 km N of Gregory Downs or
27 km S of Burketown. 3 km S of Savannah Way
Jcn. Tracks off road, small vehicles only
137 468   HEMA 25 D4   17 52 37 S   139 20 35 E

367 QT125

Burke Developmental Rd, Normanton
Rest Area 39 km S of Normanton or 161 km
N of Burke & Wills Roadhouse
132 380   HEMA 25 D7   17 57 40 S   140 54 13 E

368 Flinders River
Burke Developmental Rd, Stokes
Camp Area 62 km S of Normanton or 138 km N of Burke & Wills Roadhouse. Sites both sides of river
07 4745 2200   HEMA 25 E7   18 09 29 S   140 51 37 E

369 QT124
Burke Developmental Rd, Normanton
Rest Area 78 km S of Normanton or 114 km N of Burke & Wills Roadhouse
132 380   HEMA 25 E7   18 17 17 S   140 48 35 E

370 Bang Bang Rest Area
Burke Developmental Rd, Stokes
Rest Area 112 km S of Normanton or 90 km N of Burke & Wills Roadhouse
132 380   HEMA 25 E6   18 31 36 S   140 39 11 E

371 Donors Hill Rest Area
Burke Developmental Rd, Stokes
Rest Area 135 km S of Normanton or 63 km N of Burke & Wills Roadhouse
132 380   HEMA 25 F6   18 41 54 S   140 30 43 E

372 Burke & Wills Roadhouse
Lot 51 Burke Developmental Rd, Four Ways
Camp Area 207 km S of Normanton or 183 km N of Cloncurry
07 4742 5909   HEMA 25 G6   19 13 37 S   140 20 51 E

373 Jack & Lil Cunningham Park
Wills Developmental Rd, Taldora
Parking Area 89 km SE of Burke & Wills Roadhouse, or 156 km NW of Julia Creek
07 4746 7690   HEMA 25 G7   19 40 07 S   140 56 33 E

374 Firey Creek
Wills Developmental Rd, Gregory Downs
Camp Spot 118 km W of Burke & Wills Roadhouse or 31 km E of Gregory Downs. Various tracks off road
07 4745 5100   HEMA 25 F4   18 41 45 S   139 31 21 E

375 Gregory Downs Hotel
Wills Developmental Rd, Gregory
Pub Stay at Gregory Downs. 148 km SW of Burketown
07 4748 5566   HEMA 25 E4   18 38 59 S   139 15 12 E
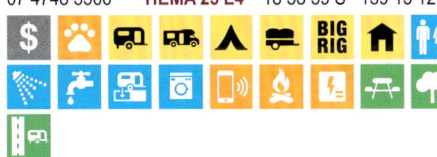

376 Gregory Downs Low Impact Camp
Gregory - Lawn Hill Rd, Gregory Downs
Camp Area at NW Cnr Wills Developmental Rd and Lawn Hill Rd. Facilities opposite hotel. Site on vacant land, no camping on river bank
07 4745 5111   HEMA 25 E4   18 38 51 S   139 15 13 E

377 Adels Grove Camping Park
Lawn Hill Rd, Lawn Hill
Camp Area 88 km W of Gregory Downs. Pre-book in high season. Dirt road
07 4748 5502   HEMA 25 F3   18 41 27 S   138 31 53 E

378 Boodjamulla (Lawn Hill)
Boodjamulla National Park
Wills Rd, Lawn Hill
Camp Area 10 km W of Adels Grove or 217 km SW of Burketown. Via Wills Developmental Rd, exit W to Gregory Lawn Hill Rd for 73 km, then S to Riversleigh Doomadgee Rd for 25 km. Pre-book in high season. Dirt road
137 468   HEMA 25 F3   18 42 05 S   138 29 16 E

379 Miyumba Bush Camp
Boodjamulla National Park
Riversleigh Rd, Lawn Hill
Camp Area 185 km N of Camooweal via Riversleigh, 48 km S of Adels Grove. 4.2 km S of Riversleigh Fossil site. Open March - Oct. Pre-book
137 468   HEMA 25 F3   19 01 06 S   138 43 21 E

380 Terry Smith Lookout
Burke Developmental Rd, Three Rivers
Rest Area 103 km S of Burke & Wills Roadhouse or 78 km N of Cloncurry
132 380   HEMA 25 H6   20 04 49 S   140 13 39 E

Townsville to Camooweal
Flinders and Barkly Highways

381 Lazy Acres Plantation
94 Major Creek Rd, Majors Creek
Farm Stay 7.4 km E Woodstock. E on Woodstock Giru Rd for 6.4 km, then N for 1 km
07 4778 8580   HEMA 19 H5   19 35 46 S   146 54 14 E

382 Reid River Rest Area
5216 Flinders Hwy, Reid River
Rest Area 58 km S of Townsville or 75 km NE of Charters Towers
132 380   HEMA 19 J5   19 45 24 S   146 50 02 E

383 Mingela Hotel
31 Hervey St, Ravenswood
Camp Area S of Flinders Hwy. W side of town. Check in with publican
07 4770 3106   HEMA 19 K4   19 52 44 S   146 37 59 E

384 Grass Hut Station
Burdekin Falls Dam Rd, Ravenswood
Station Stay 7 km SE of Mingela. Signposted. Pre-book
07 4770 3051   HEMA 19 K4   19 55 30 S   146 41 01 E

385 Railway Hotel Ravenswood
66 Macrossan St, Ravenswood
Parking Area behind hotel. Fee for power. Patrons only, register at bar
07 4770 2144   HEMA 19 K5   20 05 58 S   146 53 14 E

386 Ravenswood Showground
89 Deighton St, Ravenswood
Camp Area 39 km SE of Mingela. 3 month limit. See caretaker on arrival
07 4770 2113   HEMA 19 K5   20 05 54 S   146 53 32 E

QUEENSLAND

387 Burdekin Falls Dam Caravan Park
77 | 11950 Burdekin Falls Dam Rd, Ravenswood
Caravan Park 77 km SE of Ravenswood. 30 day limit
07 4770 3177   **HEMA 18 F1**   20 38 29 S   147 08 47 E

388 Bivouac Junction Outback Holiday Camp
A6 | 146 Bivouac Junction Rd, Dotswood
Caravan Park near Macrossan. Turn N off Flinders Hwy 111 km SW of Townsville or 22 km E of Charters Towers via Burdekin Downs Rd. 3 km dirt road
0477 873 804   **HEMA 19 K3**   19 58 58 S   146 26 04 E

389 Macrossan Park
A6 | Fanning Downs Rd, Dotswood
Rest Area 27 km SW of Mingela. 111 km SW of Townsville or 22 km E of Charters Towers. Turn S off Flinders Hwy, E of Burdekin River railway bridge. Take exit off Hwy, veer L and follow signs. 1 km dirt road. 7 day limit
07 4761 5533   **HEMA 19 K3**   20 00 12 S   146 26 22 E

390 Burdekin Duck Roadhouse
A6 | 1 School St, Sellheim
Caravan Park at Sellheim. 118 km W of Townsville or 20 km E of Charters Towers
07 4787 3587   **HEMA 19 K3**   20 00 26 S   146 24 52 E

391 Big Bend
63 | Big Bend Rd, Basalt
Dispersed Camping 32 km NW of Charters Towers or 169 km SE of Greenvale. Turn off Gregory Dev Rd to dirt road to various riverside spots
07 4761 5533   **HEMA 19 J2**   19 51 41 S   146 08 11 E

392 Fletcher Creek
63 | Gregory Hwy, Basalt
Rest Area 42 km N of Charters Towers or 157 km SE of Greenvale. Large area beside creek. Cold showers. 4 week limit
07 4761 5533   **HEMA 19 J2**   19 48 58 S   146 03 14 E

393 Burdekin River Camp Area
Dalrymple National Park
63 | Leichhardt Rd, Basalt
Camp Area 44 km NW of Charters Towers or 161 km SE of Greenvale. W on 2.6 km dirt road from Fletcher Creek Rest Area, ebook
137 468   **HEMA 19 J2**   19 48 19 S   146 05 21 E

394 Stockyard Creek
7213 | Hervey Range Development Rd, Basalt
Rest Area 80 km N of Charters Towers or 136 km W of Townsville
132 380   **HEMA 19 H1**   19 30 47 S   145 47 24 E

395 Wonderland Station
1486 Hervey Range Road, Alice River
Station Stay 32 NW of Townsville. Entry N of road, 1 km dirt road. Closed in wet season
07 4788 8222   **HEMA 19 G4**   19 18 38 S   146 35 52 E

396 Bluewater Springs Roadhouse
63 | Gregory Development Hwy, Basalt
Camp Area at Roadhouse. 112 km NW Charters Tower or 145 km SE The Lynd Jcn on Gregory Hwy
07 4788 5532   **HEMA 19 H1**   19 24 42 S   145 38 43 E

397 Campaspe River
A6 | Flinders Hwy, Pentland
Rest Area 90 km SW of Charters Towers or 16 km NE of Pentland
07 4761 5533   **HEMA 27 J9**   20 26 28 S   145 31 59 E

398 Pentland Caravan Park
A6 | Flinders Hwy, Pentland
Caravan Park E end of town. 7 am - 7pm
07 4788 1148   **HEMA 27 J9**   20 31 19 S   145 24 03 E

399 Pentland Hotel
A6 | 32 Main St, Pentland
Parking Area. Via Flinders Hwy. Check in with publican. Fee for showers
07 4788 1106   **HEMA 27 J9**   20 31 27 S   145 23 55 E

400 Exchange Hotel Torrens Creek
A6 | 34 Flinders Hwy, Torrens Creek
Caravan Park 159 km W of Charters Towers or 89 km E of Hughenden
07 4795 5990   **HEMA 27 K8**   20 46 12 S   145 01 09 E

401 Prairie Hotel
A6 | Cnr Chisholm St & Flinders Hwy, Prairie
Camp Area behind hotel. Check in with publican. Toilets available when open. Fee for shower
0427 876 750   **HEMA 27 K8**   20 52 14 S   144 36 01 E

402 Koorooorinya Falls Nature Reserve
A6 | Koorooorinya Kentle Rd, Prairie
Camp Area 60 km S of Prairie. Via Muttaburra Rd. Signposted. Permit from caretaker
07 4741 7460   **HEMA 29 B11**   21 22 04 S   144 38 25 E

403 Pyramid Campground
Porcupine Gorge National Park
Pyramids Access, Hughenden Area
Camp Area 75 km N of Hughenden. Via Kennedy Developmental Rd & Emu Plains Rd. Book online or at Info Centre Hughenden, pre-book peak season
137 468   **HEMA 27 J8**   20 20 44 S   144 27 39 E

404 Emu Swamp Campground
Blackbraes National Park
Via Oak Park Race Rd, Lyndhurst
Camp Area 170 km N of Hughenden. 2 km S of airport, W of Hwy to Bagstowe Rd for 20.5 km. High clearance. Permit applies
137 468   **HEMA 26 H7**   19 24 54 S   144 10 01 E

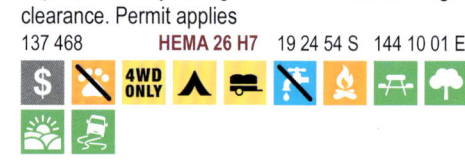

405 Gilberton Outback Retreat
Station Gravel Rd, Gilberton
Station Stay 450 km W of Townsville or 330 km N of Hughenden. From Hughenden take Kennedy Developmental Rd past Porcupine Gorge 212 km to Oak Park/Gilberton Retreat turnoff, 118 km to Station Gravel Rd. Pre-book. Baited property - strict pet policy applies
07 4062 5458   **HEMA 26 G7**   19 15 41 S   143 41 12 E

406 Hughenden Allen Terry
Caravan Park
2 Resolution St, Hughenden
Caravan Park 2 km SW of PO. Via Flinders Hwy
07 4741 1190   HEMA 26 K7   20 50 57 S   144 11 46 E

407 Hughenden RV Parking Area
2 Stansfield St, Hughenden
Camp Area E end of town next to
showgrounds. Self-registration & donation box
onsite. 7 day limit
07 4741 2900   HEMA 26 K7   20 50 40 S   144 12 22 E

408 Marathon Rest Area
Flinders Hwy, Stamford
Rest Area 65 km W of Hughenden or 47 km
E of Richmond. Share with trucks
132 380   HEMA 26 K6   20 51 31 S   143 34 07 E

409 Richmond RV Park
1 Hillier St, Richmond
Parking Area at Richmond. 300 m off Hwy,
via Harris St. Register at Kronosaurus Korner
07 4719 3390   HEMA 26 K6   20 43 44 S   143 08 36 E

410 Maxwelton Rest Area
Flinders Hwy, Maxwelton
Rest Area 49 km W of Richmond or 99 km
E of Julia Creek
07 4769 3200   HEMA 26 K5   20 43 24 S   142 40 41 E

411 Julia Creek RV Stop
Punchbowl Rd, Julia Creek
Camp Area 1 km E of town, N of Hwy, either
side of bridge. Permit from Info Centre or caretaker
07 4746 7690   HEMA 26 K4   20 39 21 S   141 45 22 E

412 Julia Creek Caravan Park
Old Normanton Rd, Julia Creek
Caravan Park 500 m N of PO
07 4746 7108   HEMA 26 K4   20 39 09 S   141 44 41 E

413 Oorindi Rest Area
Flinders Hwy, Julia Creek
Rest Area 69 km W of Julia Creek or 68 km
E of Cloncurry
132 380   HEMA 25 J7   20 38 32 S   141 06 15 E

414 Wals Camp
Lot 5 Phillips St, Cloncurry
Camp Area at Cloncurry. S at Bowls Club to
Sheaffe & Philips Sts. Follow signs. Cash only
0408 700 302   HEMA 25 J6   20 42 58 S   140 29 47 E

415 Burke & Wills Memorial
(Corella River)
Barkly Hwy, Cloncurry
Rest Area 44 km W of Cloncurry or 77 km E of Mt Isa
132 380   HEMA 25 K5   20 46 56 S   140 06 45 E

416 Clem Walton Park/Corella
Dam
Clem Walton Park Rd, Cloncurry
Camp Area 65 km E of Mt Isa or 53 km W of
Cloncurry. S off Hwy, GPS at gate, locked if the
water is high. Veer SW at first Y Jcn to camp spots
by dam. At 2nd Y Jcn veer SW to Clem Walton Park
(1.7 km). Toilets at park
07 4742 4100   HEMA 25 K5   20 49 36 S   140 02 56 E

417 Fountain Springs Rest Area
Barkly Hwy, Cloncurry
Rest Area 60 km W of Cloncurry or 61 km
E of Mt Isa
132 380   HEMA 25 K5   20 48 01 S   139 59 48 E

418 Mary Kathleen Old Mine
Township
Via Barkly Hwy, Cloncurry
Parking Area 63 km W of Cloncurry or 56 km E of Mt
Isa. Private land, no litter & no fires
HEMA 25 K5   20 46 29 S   139 58 50 E

419 World War 2 Historical Site
Barkly Hwy, Gunpowder
Rest Area 50 km NW of Mt Isa or 137 km E
of Camooweal. Near monument
07 4747 3200   HEMA 25 J4   20 22 23 S   139 15 53 E

420 David Hall Rest Area
Barkly Hwy, Gunpowder
Rest Area 90 km NW of Mt Isa or 99 km E
of Camooweal
132 380   HEMA 25 H3   20 11 23 S   138 53 52 E

421 Inca Creek Rest Area
Cnr Barkly Hwy & Thorntonia Yelvertoft Rd,
Gunpowder
Rest Area 119 km NW of Mt Isa or 70 km E of
Camooweal. Entry via side road N of Hwy
132 380   HEMA 25 H3   20 03 58 S   138 45 34 E

422 Camooweal Billabongs
Barkly Hwy, Camooweal
Camp Spot at Camooweal. W over
Georgina R Bridge, turn S immediately to dirt road.
Various camping spots next to billabongs Lake
Francis on left, 2 km to Lake Canellan
07 4749 1555   HEMA 25 H2   19 55 20 S   138 06 35 E

Rockhampton to Cloncurry
*Capricorn and Landsborough
Highways*

423 Kabra Pub
1232 Capricorn Hwy, Kabra
Parking Area 17 km SW of Rockhampton.
Free for patrons. Fee for power. Check in with
publican
07 4933 1207   HEMA 16 C1   23 27 50 S   150 24 00 E

424 Duaringa Rest Area
30 Theresa St, Duaringa
Rest Area E end of town, Mackenzie Park
1300 242 686   HEMA 31 F8   23 43 18 S   149 40 20 E

425 Duaringa Hotel
20 Edward St, Duaringa
Caravan Park 1 km off Hwy over railway line
07 4935 7202   HEMA 31 F8   23 42 46 S   149 40 11 E

426 Bridgewater Creek
Capricorn Hwy, Wallaroo
Rest Area 26 km W of Duaringa or 10 km
E of Dingo
132 380   HEMA 31 F8   23 39 51 S   149 25 41 E

427 Dingo Van & Motorhome
Park
26 Cairns St, Dingo
Caravan Park N end of town. Off Fitzroy
Developmental Rd
07 4935 9121   HEMA 31 F8   23 38 35 S   149 19 51 E

428 Munall Campground
Blackdown Tableland NP
Charlevue Rd, Blackdown
Camp Area 43 km SW of Dingo. 12 km W of Dingo
exit Capricorn Hwy SW 30 km. Steep, winding road,
suitable for small vehicles only. Pre-book
137 468   HEMA 30 F7   23 47 43 S   149 04 12 E

429 Bluff Hotel
Capricorn Highway, Bluff
Parking Area 94 km E of Emerald or 29 km
W of Dingo. Donation for amenities. Fee for power
07 4982 9158   HEMA 30 F7   23 34 56 S   149 04 14 E

430 Bedford Weir
Bedford Weir Rd, Blackwater
Camp Area 27 km N of Blackwater. Turn
N 2 km W of Blackwater to Blackwater Cooroorah
Rd. S side of weir, upper banks only, near Ski Club.
7 day limit
07 4982 4142   HEMA 30 E7   23 22 21 S   148 50 20 E

431 Emerald Botanical Gardens
100 Capricorn Hwy, Emerald
Parking Area E end of town beside Nogoa
R bridge. Facilities in gardens, but no camping
inside gardens. Limited space
07 4982 4142   HEMA 30 F6   23 31 49 S   148 09 59 E

432 Higher Ground Homestay
1467 Selma Rd, The Gemfields
Camp Area 16 km SW Emerald. Some
camping on river. 14 day limit
07 4987 4562   HEMA 30 F6   23 37 28 S   148 04 08 E

433 Anakie Gemfields Caravan
Park
7 Richardson St, Anakie
Caravan Park 45 km W of Emerald
07 4985 4142   HEMA 30 F5   23 33 07 S   147 44 41 E

434 Sapphire Reserve
Rifle Range Rd, Sapphire
Parking Area 54 km NW of Emerald.
Opposite store
1300 242 686   HEMA 30 F5   23 27 57 S   147 43 12 E

435 Tomahawk Creek Fossicking
Area
Via Clermont Rd, Argyll
Camp Spot 42 km NW of Rubyvale. Via Rubyvale
Clermont Rd for 27km, W to Recklaw Park/Mt Mica
turn off. Turn L, then L again to Recklaw Park Tr
17 km. Well signposted. Permit for fossicking &
camping
07 4987 9350   HEMA 30 E5   23 21 06 S   147 27 35 E

436 Bogantungan Rest Area
Medway St, Bogantungan
Rest Area 98 km W of Emerald or 70 km E
of Alpha. 400 m S of Hwy
07 4982 4142   HEMA 30 F5   23 38 53 S   147 17 22 E

437 Drummond Range Lookout
Capricorn Hwy, Willows
Rest Area 108 km W of Emerald or 60 km
E of Alpha. 300 m N of Hwy. Unlevel area, steep
approach, limited sites
132 380   HEMA 30 F5   23 39 30 S   147 12 09 E

438 Drummond West
Capricorn Hwy, Port Wine
Rest Area 120 km W of Emerald or 48 km
E of Alpha
132 380   HEMA 30 F4   23 40 14 S   147 05 27 E

439 Belyando River Rest Area
Capricorn Highway, Port Wine
Rest Area 138 km W of Emerald or 31 km
E of Alpha
132 380   HEMA 30 F4   23 39 40 S   146 55 51 E

440 Alpha Clermont Rd Camp
via Alpha Clermont Rd, Alpha
Camp Area 23 km N of Alpha on Alpha
Clermont Rd. High clearance vans only. Area subject
to flooding
HEMA 30 F4   23 29 04 S   146 39 20 E

441 Drummondslope Camp
Tambo Rd, Drummondslope
Camp Spot 66 km S Alpha or 100 km N of
Tambo. W to track 200 m N of Rainmore Rd. W side
of road
132 380   HEMA 30 G4   24 10 19 S   146 35 18 E

442 Jericho Showground
Showgrounds Rd, Jericho
Camp Area E end of town, turn N just E of
railway crossing
07 4651 4129   HEMA 29 F14   23 35 45 S   146 07 53 E

443 Jordan Valley Hotel
43 Darwin St, Jericho
Camp Area behind hotel. Register on
arrival. Patrons only
07 4651 4148   HEMA 29 F14   23 36 09 S   146 07 32 E

444 Redbank Park
7 Lyon St, Jericho
Camp Area S off Hwy to Bessemer St.
Riverside. Signposted. Cold showers
07 4651 5600   HEMA 29 F14   23 36 21 S   146 07 47 E

445 Barcaldine East Rest Area
Capricorn Hwy, Barcaldine
Rest Area 2 km E of Barcaldine
132 380   HEMA 29 F12   23 33 09 S   145 18 26 E

446 Lloyd Jones Weir

Lloyd Jones Wier Rd, Barcaldine
Camp Area 15 km SW of Barcaldine. Turn
W off Landsborough Hwy 5 km S of Barcaldine for
9 km. 1 km dirt road
07 4651 5600   HEMA 29 F12   23 39 00 S   145 12 57 E

447 Aramac Hotel

67 Gordon St, Aramac
Parking Area 68 km N of Barcaldine. Free
for patrons. Check in at counter
07 4651 3262   HEMA 29 E12   22 58 18 S   145 14 29 E

448 5 Emu Camp

Raven St, Aramac
Camp Spot 700 m SW Aramac. Turn W off
Barcaldine-Aramac Rd 100 m S of bridge. Camp
areas along waterway. GPS at turn off
07 4651 5600   HEMA 29 E12   22 58 31 S   145 14 13 E

449 Aramac Caravan Park

Booker St, Aramac
Caravan Park & Camping Grounds N side
of town. 69 km N or Barcaldine. Pay at council or
library after hours
07 4652 9999   HEMA 29 E12   22 58 02 S   145 14 20 E

450 Lake Dunn

Ballyneety Rd, Aramac
Camp Area 63 km NE of Aramac. Off
Eastmere Rd. Owners collect fees daily
07 4651 0565   HEMA 29 D13   22 36 16 S   145 40 24 E

451 The Broadwater

Broadwater Rd, Cornish Creek
Dispersed Camping 6 km S of Muttaburra
via Straight Rd. Riverside
07 4658 7147   HEMA 29 D11   22 39 23 S   144 34 06 E

452 Muttaburra Broadwater

Steep Gully Rd, Cornish Creek
Camp Spot 11 km S Muttaburra. S on
Straight Rd for 8 km. Veer E to Steep Gully Rd for
3 km. Various spots along the channel
07 4658 7147   HEMA 29 D11   22 41 15 S   144 34 11 E

453 Muttaburra Caravan Park

17 Bridge St, Muttaburra
Caravan Park E side of town, 84 km NW or
Aramac. Pay at library or honesty box
07 4658 7191   HEMA 29 D11   22 35 36 S   144 33 07 E

454 Muttaburra Freedom Park

Via Nev Bullen Dr, Muttaburra
Camp Area W side of town near Artesian
Bore. 84 km NW of Aramac
07 4658 7191   HEMA 29 D11   22 35 43 S   144 32 21 E

455 Pump Hole

Via Muttaburra Aramac Rd, Cornish Creek
Camp Spot 4.5 km E of Muttaburra. N off
Muttaburra-Aramac Rd, 3 km E of Muttaburra. 1 km
dirt road, limited sites
07 4658 7191   HEMA 29 D11   22 34 59 S   144 33 57 E

456 Nat Buchanan Bridge

Aramac Torrens Creek Rd, Upper Cornish
Creek
Rest Area 67 km N of Aramac or 202 km S of
Torrens Creek. N of bridge
132 380   HEMA 29 D12   22 27 16 S   145 00 36 E

457 Four Mile Waterhole

Forest Den National Park

Via Corinda Rd, Upper Cornish Creek
Camp Area 100 km N of Aramac. NW on Muttaburra
Aramac Rd for 21 km, N to Aramac Torrens Creek
Rd for 84 km, W to Corinda Rd. Signposted, 8.5 km
to camps, epermit applies
137 468   HEMA 29 C12   22 06 35 S   145 11 41 E

458 Rainsby Rest Area

Aramac Torrens Creek Rd, Upper Cornish
Creek
Rest Area 136 km N of Aramac or 134 km S of
Torrens Creek
132 380   HEMA 29 C12   21 53 43 S   145 11 24 E

459 Shirley Shearing Shed

Moorrinya National Park

Via Torrens Creek Aramac Rd, Torrens Creek
Camp Area 89 km S of Torrens Creek. S for 77 km
to entrance. 15 km W to camps, follow signs,
epermit required
137 468   HEMA 29 B12   21 25 10 S   144 59 48 E

460 Packsaddle Creek

Landsborough Hwy, Tara Station
Rest Area 30 km W of Barcaldine or 76 km
E of Longreach. Share with trucks
132 380   HEMA 29 F12   23 32 07 S   144 59 46 E

461 Dartmouth Rest Area

Landsborough Hwy, Ilfracombe
Rest Area 63 km W of Barcaldine or 43 km
E of Longreach. Share with trucks
132 380   HEMA 29 F11   23 30 45 S   144 40 14 E

462 Newstead Creek

Landsborough Hwy, Ilfracombe
Rest Area 74 km W of Barcaldine or 32 km
E of Longreach
132 380   HEMA 29 F11   23 30 08 S   144 33 06 E

463 12 Mile Hotel Site

Isisford Ilfracombe Rd, Ilfracombe
Rest Area 20 km S of Ilfracombe or 70 km
N of Isisford
137 468   HEMA 29 F11   23 39 25 S   144 30 27 E

464 Wellshot Hotel

20 Main Ave, Ilfracombe
Parking Area 27 km E of Longreach or
81 km W of Barcaldine. Check in with publican.
Limited space
07 4658 2106   HEMA 29 E11   23 29 24 S   144 30 31 E

465 Camden Park Station

Landsborough Hwy, Longreach
Station Stay 14 km NE of Longreach or
95 km W of Barcaldine. GPS at gate
0407 139 640   HEMA 29 F11   23 27 14 S   144 22 14 E

QUEENSLAND

466 Apex Riverside Park
Via Landsborough Hwy, Longreach
Camp Area 5 km NW of Longreach. 1 km E
of Hwy. Pay at Info Centre
07 4658 4150   HEMA 29 E11   23 24 37 S   144 13 47 E

467 Macsland Rest Area
Landsborough Hwy, Longreach
Rest Area 24 km NW of Longreach or
156 km SE of Winton
132 380   HEMA 29 E10   23 16 34 S   144 07 39 E

468 Darr River
55474 Landsborough Hwy, Longreach
Dispersed Camping 32 km NW of
Longreach. E side of R.L. Davison Bridge. Riverside
HEMA 29 E10   23 12 52 S   144 04 50 E

469 Morella Rest Area
Landsborough Hwy, Morella
Rest Area 68 km NW of Longreach or
112 km SE of Winton
132 380   HEMA 29 E10   22 58 31 S   143 51 36 E

470 Chorregon Rest Area
Landsborough Hwy, Chorregon
Rest Area 112 km NW of Longreach or
68 km SE of Winton
132 380   HEMA 29 D10   22 41 28 S   143 34 24 E

471 Crawford Creek
Landsborough Hwy, Corfield
Rest Area 132 km NW of Longreach or
46 km SE of Winton
137 468   HEMA 29 D9   22 33 29 S   143 25 30 E

472 North Gregory Hotel
67 Elderslie St, Winton
Parking Area behind hotel, entry off
Oondooroo St. Register at hotel
07 4657 0647   HEMA 29 D9   22 23 21 S   143 02 20 E

473 Long Waterhole
Via Winton Jundah Rd, Corfield
Camp Area 4 km S of Winton. E off the
Winton-Jundah Rd 2 km S of Winton, 2 km of dirt
road. Signposted
1300 665 115   HEMA 29 D9   22 24 46 S   143 03 33 E

474 Mistake Creek
Winton Jundah Rd, Corfield
Camp Area 3.6 km S of Winton. E side of
road, just S of Western R, tracks to various spots
1300 665 115   HEMA 29 D9   22 25 14 S   143 01 56 E

475 Bough Shed Waterhole
Bladensburg National Park
Via Bladensburg Access, Opalton
Camp Area 28 km S of Winton. Turn E off the
Winton-Jundah Rd 14 km S of Winton to Opalton Rd
for 12 km, then N along River Gums route for 2 km.
Creekside. 14 km dirt road. Pre-book
137 468   HEMA 29 D9   22 33 37 S   142 57 40 E

476 Opalton Bush Camp
Via Opalton Rd, Opalton
Camp Area 121 km S of Winton. S on
Winton Jundah Rd for 14 km, then SE on Opalton
Rd for 107 km to camp
1300 665 115   HEMA 29 E8   23 14 45 S   142 45 46 E

477 Mayne River
Via Winton Jundah Rd, Opalton
Camp Area 184 km SW Winton or 189 km
NE of Jundah. Turn E at N end causeway 500 m
HEMA 29 F8   23 38 10 S   142 19 58 E

478 Corfield Rest Area
Kennedy Developmental Rd, Corfield
Rest Area at Corfield. 86 km NE of Winton
or 128 km SW of Hughenden. Donation for RFDS.
Coin for showers at pub
07 4657 1466   HEMA 29 B9   21 42 51 S   143 22 27 E

479 Ayrshire Hills
Landsborough Hwy, Corfield
Rest Area 65 km NW of Winton or 99 km
SE of Kynuna
137 468   HEMA 29 C8   21 58 17 S   142 39 40 E

480 Dinosaur Creek - Twin Hills
Via Landsborough Hwy, Corfield
Camp Area 67 km NW of Winton or 97 km
SE of Kyuna. 1 km after rest area, head NE past
Twin Hill to camp on riverbank
1300 665 115   HEMA 29 C8   21 57 47 S   142 39 25 E

481 Wanora Downs Rest Area
Landsborough Hwy, Kynuna
Rest Area 90 km NW of Winton or 74 km
SE of Kynuna
132 380   HEMA 29 C8   21 45 20 S   142 31 07 E

482 Kynuna East Rest Area
Landsborough Hwy, Kynuna
Rest Area 18 km E of Kynuna or 146 km W
of Winton
132 380   HEMA 28 B7   21 32 25 S   142 04 37 E

483 Blue Heeler Caravan Park
Landsborough Hwy, Kynuna
 Caravan Park behind pub park area.
183 km SE of Cloncurry or 164 km NW of Winton
07 4746 8650   HEMA 28 B7   21 34 43 S   141 55 23 E

484 Kynuna Roadhouse Caravan Park
Landsborough Hwy, Kynuna
Caravan Park 183 km SE of Cloncurry or 164 km
NW of Winton. No bookings
07 4746 8683   HEMA 28 B7   21 34 44 S   141 55 13 E

485 Walkabout Creek Hotel
Cnr Middleton St & Landsborough Hwy,
McKinlay
Caravan Park 108 km SE of Cloncurry or 76 km NW
Kynuna
07 4746 8424   HEMA 26 K3   21 16 19 S   141 17 23 E

486 Toolebuc Road Bush Camp
Toolebuc Mckinlay Rd, McKinlay
Camp Spot 84 km SW McKinlay or 194 km
NE Boulia. Both sides of road
07 4746 7166   HEMA 28 C5   21 52 58 S   140 55 59 E

487 Weatherley Creek Parking
Landsborough Hwy, Kuridala
Rest Area 36 km SE Cloncurry or 71 NW McKinlay on Landsborough Hwy. NE side of Hwy
132 380   HEMA 28 A5   20 49 59 S   140 48 12 E

488 Landsborough Highway
Roadside Parking Area
Landsborough Hwy, Kuridala
Rest Area 32 km SE Cloncurry or 75 km NW McKinlay. N side of Hwy
132 380   HEMA 28 A5   20 48 30 S   140 47 17 E

Longreach - Birdsville - Mt Isa

489 Broadwater Waterhole
Lochern National Park
Via Tonkoro Rd, Stonehenge
Camp Area 100 km S Longreach or 45 km N of Stonehenge. N from Stonehenge on Thomas Developmental Rd for 50 km, W to Tonkoro Rd for 45 km to waterhole turn off. Signposted. Dirt road
137 468   HEMA 29 G9   24 06 19 S   143 21 13 E

490 Noonbah Station
12354 Tonkoro Rd, Stonehenge
Station Stay off Thomson Development Rd. 56 km dirt road. Pre-book, cash only
07 4658 5953   HEMA 29 G9   24 06 28 S   143 11 11 E

491 Isisford Road Rest Area
Jundah Longreach Rd, Stonehenge
Rest Area 121 km S of Longreach or 96 km N of Jundah
132 380   HEMA 29 G10   24 14 01 S   143 33 27 E

492 Stonehenge Caravan Park
10 Stratford St, Stonehenge
Caravan Park 155 km SW of Longreach
07 4658 5857   HEMA 29 G9   24 21 18 S   143 17 14 E

493 Thomson River North
Via Warbreccan Rd, Stonehenge
Camp Area 3 km W Stonehenge. Turn N to track after 2nd bridge
07 4658 5857   HEMA 29 G9   24 21 09 S   143 15 17 E

494 Swan Vale Rest Area
Thomson Developmental Rd, Stonehenge
Rest Area 179 km SW of Longreach or 39 km N of Jundah. Follow lookout sign, 300 m to toilets
07 4658 5857   HEMA 29 H9   24 35 09 S   143 16 08 E

495 Jundah Caravan Park
4 Dickson St, Jundah
Caravan Park 217 km SW of Longreach or 98 km NE of Windorah
0407 457 457   HEMA 29 H9   24 49 43 S   143 03 33 E

496 Jundah Hotel Caravan Park
12 Dickson St, Jundah
Caravan Park 217 km SW of Longreach or 98 km NE of Windorah. Free for patrons
07 4658 6166   HEMA 29 H9   24 49 45 S   143 03 32 E

497 Thomson River West
Thomson Developmental Rd, Jundah
Camp Area 1 km W of Jundah or 95 km N of Windorah. E side of bridge, both sides of the road
07 4658 6930   HEMA 29 H9   24 49 48 S   143 03 04 E

498 Little Boomerang Waterhole
Welford National Park
Via Hammond Downs Rd, Jundah
Camp Area 60 km SE of Jundah on the Barcoo R. Turn W off Jundah-Quilpie Rd for 10 km from turn off. Signposted. Dirt road. Pre-book
137 468   HEMA 29 J9   25 10 33 S   143 08 23 E

499 Tommy Dodd Creek
Thomson Developmental Rd, Jundah
Rest Area 46 km SW of Jundah or 46 km N Windorah. W side of road, track to large open space
HEMA 29 H8   25 02 14 S   142 40 09 E

500 Tenham Rest Area
Cnr Jundah Quilpie Rd & Quilpie Windorah Rd, Tenham
Rest Area 43 km SE Windorah
132 380   HEMA 29 J9   25 36 22 S   143 01 44 E

501 Windorah Caravan Park
1 Albert St, Windorah
Caravan Park 98 km SW of Jundah
07 4656 3063   HEMA 29 J8   25 25 13 S   142 39 09 E

502 Western Star Hotel
15 Albert St, Windorah
Camp Area behind hotel. Donation to RFDS
07 4656 3166   HEMA 29 J8   25 25 18 S   142 39 19 E

503 JC Hotel Ruins
Diamantina Development Rd, Windorah
Camp Area 75 km W of Windorah or 34 km E of Birdsville
07 4656 3063   HEMA 28 J7   25 22 38 S   141 53 55 E

504 Morney Rest Area
Diamantina Development Rd, Windorah
Rest Area 108 km W of Windorah or 95 km E of Betoota
132 380   HEMA 28 J7   25 22 50 S   141 37 24 E

505 Haddon Corner
Via Arrabury Rd, Haddon Corner
Camp Area 55 km SW of Diamantina Developmental Rd & Birdsville Developmental Rd. Sandy road, caution
07 4656 3063   HEMA 28 K6   25 59 46 S   140 59 58 E

506 Deons Lookout
Birdsville Developmental Rd, Betoota
Rest Area 200 km W of Windorah or 20 km E of Betoota. Limited space
07 4656 2000   HEMA 28 K5   25 43 00 S   140 53 39 E

507 Betoota Environmental Park
Birdsville Developmental Rd, Betoota
Camp Spot 1.5 km E of Betoota. Turn N just W of cattle grid, follow track through gate
1300 794 257   HEMA 28 K5   25 42 01 S   140 45 45 E

508 Brown Springs Creek
Birdsville Developmental Rd, Betoota
Camp Area 167 km W of Birdsville. Turn S
to track just E of hotel, follow to Betoota Waterhole
(behind hotel)
07 4746 1600   HEMA 28 K5   25 41 53 S   140 44 56 E

509 Betoota Hotel Rest Area
Birdsville Developmental Rd, Betoota
Rest Area at Betoota Hotel. 167 km W of
Birdsville. Fee for shower
0407 739 798   HEMA 28 K5   25 41 36 S   140 44 52 E

510 Durrie Rest Area
Birdsville Developmental Rd, Birdsville
Rest Area 71 km W of Betoota or 95 km E
of Birdsville
132 380   HEMA 28 K4   25 42 31 S   140 09 24 E

511 Cuppa Rest Area
Birdsville Developmental Rd, Birdsville
Rest Area 81 km W of Betoota or 85 km E
of Birdsville
132 380   HEMA 28 K4   25 40 00 S   140 04 01 E

512 Birdsville Windmill
Eyre Developmental Rd, Birdsville
Camping Area 2 km E of Birdsville. Near
windmill, riverside, both sides of road
07 5464 2000   HEMA 28 K3   25 54 22 S   139 22 24 E

513 Old Diamantina Crossing
Birdsville Developmental Rd, Birdsville
Camping Area 2 km SE of Birdsville.
Riverside, both sides of road
07 5464 2000   HEMA 28 K3   25 54 36 S   139 21 58 E

514 Birdsville Camping Area
Eyre Developmental Rd, Birdsville
Camp Area 1 km E of Birdsville. Both sides
of the road, large area with various tracks
07 5464 2000   HEMA 28 K3   25 53 58 S   139 21 41 E

515 Carcory Ruins
Eyre Developmental Rd, Birdsville
Rest Area 81 km N Birdsville or 107 km S of
Bedourie. Alternate sites on N side of creek
07 4564 2000   HEMA 28 J3   25 14 39 S   139 33 36 E

516 Cuttaburra Crossing
Eyre Developmental Rd, Bedourie
Rest Area 121 km N of Birdsville or 68 km
S of Bedourie
07 4564 2000   HEMA 28 H3   24 54 49 S   139 38 58 E

517 Eyre Creek
Eyre Developmental Rd, Bedourie
Camp Area 129 km N of Birdsville or 61 km
S of Bedourie next to creek. Tracks on E side of
road, S of bridge
07 4564 2000   HEMA 28 H3   24 50 06 S   139 37 26 E

518 King Creek
Jcn of Eyre Developmental Rd &
Diamantina Developmental Rd, Bedourie
Rest Area 25 km S of Bedourie. Various tracks along
creek
132 380   HEMA 28 G3   24 31 57 S   139 33 55 E

519 No 3 Bore Rest Area
Diamantina Developmental Rd, Bedourie
Rest Area 55 km SE of Bedourie. 24 km E
of Cluny Airport
132 380   HEMA 28 G4   24 28 31 S   139 48 33 E

520 Monkira Rest Area
Diamantina Developmental Rd, Bedourie
Rest Area 121 km E of Eyre Development
Rd Jcn or 138 km W of Birdsville Developmental
Rd Jcn
132 380   HEMA 28 H5   24 49 11 S   140 32 28 E

521 Bedourie Tourist Park
Nappa St, Bedourie
Caravan Park at Bedourie. Next to Aquatic
Spa, S end of town. Fees payable at Info Centre
07 4746 1040   HEMA 28 G3   24 21 46 S   139 28 10 E

522 Simpson Desert Oasis
1 Herbert St, Bedourie
Caravan Park at Bedourie. Opposite
roadhouse
07 4746 1291   HEMA 28 G3   24 21 23 S   139 28 16 E

523 Bedourie Racecourse
Overflow
Racecourse Rd, Bedourie
Camp Area off Diamentina Developmental Rd.
Event overflow only
1300 794 257   HEMA 28 G3   24 21 30 S   139 26 29 E

524 Breadalbane Rest Area
Boulia Bedourie Rd, Bedourie
Rest Area 120 km N of Bedourie or 121 km
S of Boulia
132 380   HEMA 28 F3   23 47 09 S   139 34 41 E

525 Eddie Jolly Miller Rest Area
Boulia Bedourie Rd, Amaroo
Rest Area 120 km N of Bedourie or 71 km
S of Boulia
132 380   HEMA 28 E3   23 24 59 S   139 40 08 E

526 Boulia Caravan Park
Diamantina Development Rd, Boulia
Caravan Park at Boulia. 191 km N of
Bedourie or 305 km S of Mt Isa
0427 021 002   HEMA 28 E4   22 54 36 S   139 55 04 E

527 Burke River
Via Selwyn Rd, Boulia
Camp Area 5 km NE of Boulia. N from Info
Centre 3 km on Selwyn Rd, E to Racecourse Rd. E
at signs to track, behind racecourse to river
07 4746 3386   HEMA 28 E4   22 53 24 S   139 56 19 E

528 Hunters Gorge
Diamantina National Park
Via Springvale Diamantina Lakes Rd,
Diamantina Lakes
Camp Area 183 km SE of Boulia via Springvale
Rd. Signposted, follow track 4 km to Mundawerra
Waterhole. 4WD tents and trailers only at Gum Hole
Camp (see Camps Australia Wide App), ebook
137 468   HEMA 28 F6   23 40 54 S   141 06 21 E

529 Hamilton Hotel Historic Site
Cnr Kennedy Developmental Rd &
Toolebuc Rd, Min Min
Rest Area 76 km E of Boulia or 286 km W of Winton
132 380   HEMA 28 D5   22 46 23 S   140 35 51 E

530 Lilley Vale
Kennedy Developmental Rd, Middleton
Rest Area 146 km E of Boulia or 216 km W
of Winton
132 380   HEMA 28 D6   22 36 14 S   141 12 54 E

531 Old Cork Homestead
Diamantina River Rd, Middleton
Camp Area 169 km SW of Winton. S
on Winton Jundah Rd for 102 km, W for 67 km,
riverside camping. Signposted
1300 665 115   HEMA 28 E7   22 55 26 S   141 52 26 E

532 Hotel Hilton
Kennedy Developmental Rd, Middleton
Parking Area opposite pub, 169 km W of
Winton or 193 km E of Boulia
07 4657 3980   HEMA 28 D6   22 21 11 S   141 32 59 E

533 Poddy Creek Rest Area
Kennedy Developmental Rd, Middleton
Rest Area 90 km W of Winton or 271 km E
of Boulia
132 380   HEMA 29 C8   22 12 48 S   142 13 49 E

534 Bengeacca Creek
Donohue Hwy, Boulia
Camp Area 9 km W of Boulia. 1 km from
turn off, both sides of creek
07 4746 3188   HEMA 28 D4   22 52 14 S   139 50 55 E

535 Georgina River Bush Camp
Donohue Hwy, Amaroo
Camp Area 122 km W of Boulia or 124 km E
of Tobermorey Station. Dirt road. Both sides of bridge
                 HEMA 28 E2   22 54 44 S   138 52 19 E

536 Peak Creek
Boulia Mount Isa Hwy, Georgina
Rest Area 64 km N of Boulia or 84 km S of
Dajarra
132 380   HEMA 28 D3   22 24 40 S   139 39 47 E

537 Dajarra Campground
Boulia Mount Isa Hwy, Dajarra
Camp Area 153 km S of Mt Isa or 149 km N
of Boulia. Limited power for fee
07 4748 4955   HEMA 28 B3   21 41 46 S   139 30 49 E

538 Dajarra Dam
Off Boulia Mount Isa Hwy, Dajarra
Camp Area 19 km W of Dajarra or 137 km
S of Mt Isa
07 4742 4100   HEMA 28 B3   21 40 30 S   139 20 21 E

QUEENSLAND

539 Duchess Hotel
1 Duke St, Duchess
Pub Stay 99 km SE of Mt Isa. Check at bar before entry
07 4748 4833   HEMA 28 B4   21 21 23 S   139 51 53 E

540 Dangi Bush Resort
Cnr Margaret & Hutton Sts, Urandangi
Pub Stay 183 km SW of Mt Isa. 7 day limit
07 4748 4988   HEMA 28 B1   21 36 33 S   138 19 00 E

Charters Towers to Banana
Gregory and Dawson Highways

541 Gregory Development Road
Gregory Hwy, Seventy Mile
Rest Area 26 km S of Charters Towers or 177 km NW Jcn of Bowen Dev Rd. Turn W off Gregory Dev Rd to Trafalgar Rd, site on R
132 380   HEMA 27 J10   20 17 18 S   146 10 44 E

542 Mount Coolon Hotel
1 Mills St, Mount Coolon
Parking Area opposite pub. Limited space, share with trucks. Free for patrons, fee for power
07 4983 5530   HEMA 30 B5   21 23 06 S   147 20 33 E

543 Belyando South
Gregory Hwy, Belyando
Parking Area 31 km S of Belyando Crossing
HEMA 30 C4   21 46 20 S   146 58 20 E

544 Clermont BP Roadhouse
Lot 133 Gregory Hwy, Clermont
Parking Area beside roadhouse. Patronise shop for free showers & parking
07 4983 1591   HEMA 30 D5   22 48 07 S   147 38 46 E

545 Theresa Creek Dam
580 Percy Albert Dr, Clermont
Camp Area 22 km SW of Clermont. Via Jellicoe St, Rubyvale & Peakvale Rds. No bookings. Pay at kiosk
07 4983 2731   HEMA 30 E5   22 58 16 S   147 33 13 E

546 Bundoora Dam
Lot 10 Connection Rd, Bundoora
Camp Area 69 km NE of Capella or 26 km SW of Middlemount. 2nd entrance from Capella or 1st entrance 3 km S of German Creek Mine. N side of Dam. Cross railway line 400 m to dam. Rough road. GPS at entry
1300 472 227   HEMA 30 E7   22 57 14 S   148 32 27 E

547 Junee Rest Area
Cnr Fitzroy Developmental & Junee Rds, MacKenzie River
Rest Area 77 km N of Dingo
132 380   HEMA 30 E7   23 02 57 S   149 02 05 E

548 Virgin Rock Rest Area
Gregory Hwy, Springsure
Rest Area 1.5 km N of Springsure or 64 km S of Emerald. W side of road. Limited space
137 468   HEMA 30 G6   24 05 37 S   148 05 48 E

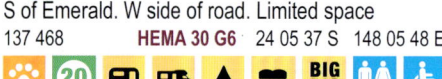

549 Springsure Roadhouse
86 William St, Springsure
Caravan Park E end of town
07 4984 1418   HEMA 30 G6   24 07 28 S   148 05 50 E

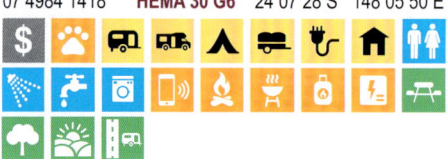

550 Staircase Range
Dawson Hwy, Orion
Picnic Area at Historical Site. 20 km SE of Springsure or 51 km NW of Rolleston. Turn N at historical marker, follow track for 600 m to picnic area, veer W at Y junction
1300 242 686   HEMA 30 G6   24 13 22 S   148 13 18 E

551 Rolleston Caravan Park
Cnr Comet St & Meteor St, Rolleston
Caravan Park in town. 72 km SE of Springsure or 76 km NW of Bauhinia
07 4984 3145   HEMA 30 G7   24 27 54 S   148 37 23 E

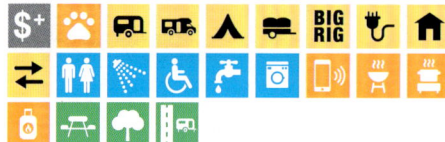

552 Bauhinia Roadhouse
25885 Dawson Hwy, Bauhinia
Camp Area 74 km W of Moura or 76 km E of Rolleston
07 4996 4146   HEMA 31 H8   24 34 13 S   149 17 31 E

553 Moura Apex River Park
Dawson Hwy, Moura
Camp Area 66 km E of Bauhinia or 7 km W of Moura. Riverside. Fee for shower. 7 day limit
07 4992 9500   HEMA 31 H9   24 35 59 S   149 54 36 E

554 Moura Rotary Park
69 Dawson Hwy, Moura
Camp Area 66 km W of Biloela. Pay fees at Mitre 10 or Culture Shack
07 4992 9500   HEMA 31 H9   24 33 56 S   149 58 38 E

Rockhampton to Toowoomba
Burnett Highway

555 Royal Hotel Bouldercombe
12 Leanne Hinchcliffe Dr, Bouldercombe
Camp Area beside closed pub. Toilets opposite in park. Cold shower
07 4934 0120   HEMA 16 C1   23 34 17 S   150 28 07 E

556 Mount Morgan Motel
Cnr Burnett Hwy & Showgrounds Rd, Mount Morgan
Caravan Park 40 km S of Rockhampton
07 4938 1952   HEMA 16 C1   23 39 41 S   150 23 15 E

557 Dululu Rest Area
Bryant St, Dululu
Rest Area 70 km SW of Rockhampton or 75 km N of Biloela. S end of town, near tennis courts
07 4992 9500   HEMA 16 D1   23 50 54 S   150 15 40 E

558 Wowan Caravan Park
Don St, Wowan
A5 Caravan Park 80 km SW of Rockhampton
or 69 km N of Banana
07 4937 1542   **HEMA 16 D1**   23 54 40 S   150 11 40 E

559 Wowan Showgrounds
223 Dee River Rd, Wowan
A5 Camp Area 2.5 km E of town
07 4992 9500   **HEMA 16 D1**   23 54 50 S   150 13 05 E

560 Lake Victoria
412 Dooneys Rd, Smoky Creek
Camp Area 25 km S of Dululu. Via Burnett
Hwy. Private property, close gates & control pets
07 4992 9500   **HEMA 16 D1**   24 02 03 S   150 17 53 E

561 Lake Pleasant
470 Lake Pleasant Rd, Goovigen
Camp Area 6 km NW of Goovigen. Via
Goovigen Rd
07 4992 9500   **HEMA 16 E1**   24 06 57 S   150 18 14 E

562 Goovigen Sportsground
5 Stone Cres, Goovigen
A3 Camp Area. Fee to hotel, 7 night limit
07 4992 9500   **HEMA 16 E1**   24 08 44 S   150 17 08 E

563 Don River
Rannes Station Access, Rannes
A5 Camp Spot N of Rannes Jcn. Sharp turn L.
Riverside
07 4992 9500   **HEMA 31 G9**   24 05 54 S   150 07 04 E

564 Myella Farm Stay
1591 Baralaba-Rannes Rd, Baralaba
A5 Farm Stay 21 km W of Rannes or 15 km E
of Baralaba. Pre-book
07 4998 1290   **HEMA 31 G9**   24 09 20 S   149 57 02 E

565 Baralaba Showgrounds
10 Wooroonah Rd, Baralaba
A5 Camp Area 49 km NW of Banana or 41 km
E of Woorabinda
0428 981 081   **HEMA 31 G9**   24 11 06 S   149 48 54 E

566 Neville Hewitt Weir
Bedford St, Baralaba
Camp Area 50 km NW of Banana or 40 km
E of Woorabinda. Turn R at end of Stopford St.
Waterside. Coin operated shower. 7 night limit
07 4992 9500   **HEMA 31 G9**   24 11 07 S   149 48 26 E

567 Jambin Hotel
Burnett Hwy, Jambin
A3 Parking Area rear of pub. Check in with the
publican. Fee for power
07 4996 5101   **HEMA 16 E1**   24 11 40 S   150 22 12 E

568 Jambin Rec Reserve
Burnett Hwy, Jambin
A3 Camp Area behind hall. Entry off Jambin
Dakenbah Rd. Donation box under hall
07 4996 5183   **HEMA 16 E1**   24 11 45 S   150 22 17 E

569 Queensland Heritage Park
11 Exhibition Ave, Biloela
A3 Camp Area E side of town. Register at
office, 9am - 4pm only
07 4992 2400   **HEMA 16 F1**   24 24 17 S   150 29 59 E

570 Lake Callide Retreat
119 Lake Callide Dr, Biloela
A3 Caravan Park 15 km NE of Biloela. S off
Dawson Hwy, 5 km NE of Biloela
07 4993 9010   **HEMA 16 F2**   24 22 22 S   150 36 40 E

571 Lawgi Dawes Hall
37715 Burnett Hwy, Lawgi Dawes
17 Rest Area 27 km SE of Biloela or 66 km
NW of Monto. Donation box by toilets
07 4992 9500   **HEMA 16 F2**   24 34 05 S   150 39 40 E

572 Coominglah Range
Coominglah State Forest
A3 Burnett Hwy, Coominglah Forest
Rest Area 75 km SE of Biloela or 22 km NW of
Monto. 100 m off Hwy
137 468   **HEMA 16 G3**   24 47 58 S   150 59 04 E

573 Monto Community Rest Stop
Lister St, Monto
69 Rest Area in Old Railway complex behind
Visitor Centre. Caretaker onsite
07 4166 9999   **HEMA 16 G3**   24 51 46 S   151 07 15 E

574 Mungungo Pub
11903 Gladstone Monto Rd, Mungungo
Parking Area 13 km NE of Monto. Free for
patrons
07 4166 5166   **HEMA 16 G3**   24 46 03 S   151 09 48 E

575 Mulgildie Hotel
12-20 Monal St, Mulgildie
17 Parking Area behind pub. 5 km S of Monto.
Contact manager. Fee for showers
07 4167 2107   **HEMA 16 H3**   24 57 50 S   151 07 56 E

576 Wuruma Dam
Wuruma Dam Rd, Eidsvold
A3 Camp Area 48 km NW of Eidsvold, via
Abercorn. Turn W 19 km N of Eidsvold. 1 km dirt
road. 2 week limit in any 4 weeks. Relocated near
dam wall
07 4165 7200   **HEMA 16 H3**   25 11 50 S   150 59 26 E

577 Ceratodus Rest Area
Burnett Hwy, Ceratodus
A3 Rest Area 65 km S of Monto or 11 km N of
Eidsvold. Beside Burnett River
132 380   **HEMA 16 J3**   25 16 53 S   151 08 20 E

578 RM Williams Australian Bush
Centre
23767 Gayndah-Monto Rd, Eidsvold
A3 Parking Area S of Burnett Hwy. Permit from Info
Centre or service station
07 4165 7272   **HEMA 16 J3**   25 22 17 S   151 07 42 E

QUEENSLAND

579 Eidsvold Showgrounds

7783 Burnett Hwy, Eidsvold
A3 Camp Area E of town. Pay at roadhouse
07 4165 1397   HEMA 16 J3   25 22 21 S   151 07 33 E

580 Tolderodden Campground
Tolderodden Conservation Park

73 Eidsvold Theodore Rd, Eidsvold
Camp Area 4.5 km W of Eidsvold or 82 km E of Cracow. Riverside. Pre-book
137 468   HEMA 16 J3   25 22 36 S   151 05 14 E

581 Lochaber Tourist Park

22172 Burnett Hwy, Malmoe
A3 Camp Area 20 km N of Mundubbera or 15 km S of Eidsvold. 700 m from Hwy
0428 654 140   HEMA 16 J4   25 28 33 S   151 12 33 E

582 Jaycees Park Black Stump

17 Burnett Hwy, Mundubbera
Rest Area 3 km N of town, 500 m E of turnoff. 35 km SE of Eidsvold or 44 km W of Gayndah
132 380   HEMA 16 K4   25 34 24 S   151 18 40 E

583 Mundubbera Showgrounds

17 Bunce St, Mundubbera
A3 Camp Area W side of town. 37 km SW of Eidsvold or 37 km W of Gayndah. 7 night limit
0402 801 163   HEMA 16 K4   25 35 09 S   151 17 50 E

584 Auburn River Campground
Auburn River National Park

75 Auburn River Rd, Mundubbera
Camp Area 42 km SW of town. W off Mundubbera-Durong Rd 15 km S of Mundubbera or 91 km N of Durong South to Hawkwood Rd 20 km, S for 7 km of dirt road. Pre-book
137 468   HEMA 16 K3   25 42 41 S   151 03 10 E

585 Binjour Range Rest Area

17 Swains Rd, Reids Creek
Rest Area 28 km E of Mundubbera or 17 km NW of Gayndah. Off Hwy
132 380   HEMA 16 J4   25 32 00 S   151 29 48 E

586 Gayndah Heritage Railway
Rail Trail

A3 9 National St, Gayndah
Camp Area N side of town, over river crossing
07 4161 1308   HEMA 16 K5   25 36 58 S   151 36 37 E

587 Zonhoven Park

17 Burnett Hwy, Gayndah
Rest Area E end of town
1300 696 272   HEMA 16 K5   25 37 44 S   151 37 33 E

588 Ban Ban Springs

17 Burnett Hwy, Ban Ban Springs
Rest Area 28 km SE of Gayndah or 74 km N of Goomeri
132 380   HEMA 13 C1   25 40 54 S   151 48 57 E

589 Biggenden RV Stop

52 Edward St, Biggenden
Parking Area at Beier Park & Old Railway Station. 46 km SW of Childers. Donation box
1300 696 272   HEMA 13 C2   25 30 44 S   152 02 40 E

590 Reeds Residence

86 Utopia Rd, Boompa
Camp Area 36 km S of Biggenden. Pre-book. 7 day limit
0413 172 822   HEMA 13 C2   25 38 48 S   152 06 27 E

591 Brooweena RV Stop

86 24 Smith Cres, Brooweena
Parking Area 48 km W of Maryborough. Facilities in park
1300 794 929   HEMA 13 C3   25 36 01 S   152 15 50 E

592 Teebar Sports Ground
86 Teebar Hall Rd, Teebar
Parking Area 53 km W of Maryborough or 32 km SE of Biggenden
1300 794 929   HEMA 13 C3   25 37 09 S   152 14 00 E

593 Springvale Eco Park

86 875 Yarrabine Rd, Gigoomgan
Farm Stay 23 km S of Teebar. Via Brooweena-Woolooga Rd. Pre-book, cash only. 7 day limit
07 5484 2109   HEMA 13 D3   25 48 50 S   152 11 40 E

594 Lawless Park (Booubyjan)

17 Cnr Ettrickdale Rd & Burnett Hwy, Booubyjan
Rest Area 40 km S of Ban Ban Springs or 34 km N of Goomeri
137 468   HEMA 13 D2   25 56 40 S   151 57 11 E

595 Kilkivan RSL Memorial Park

49 4 Bligh St, Kilkivan
Camp Area behind RSL, opposite hotel. Follow Wide Bay Hwy to town centre. Donation Box
07 5484 1415   HEMA 13 E3   26 05 06 S   152 14 11 E

596 Kilkivan Weir Oval

49 3696 Wide Bay Hwy, Kilkivan
Camp Area 100m N of Cresent St
1300 307 800   HEMA 13 E3   26 05 02 S   152 14 33 E

597 Kilkivan Bush Camping

49 577 Rossmore Rd, Kilkivan
Camp Area 8 km E of Kilkivan. E for 2 km on Wide Bay Hwy, turn S for 6 km
07 5484 1340   HEMA 13 E3   26 07 01 S   152 17 25 E

598 Fat Hen Creek

49 Wide Bay Hwy, Kilkivan
Rest Area 6 km E of Kilkivan or 32 km W of Bruce Hwy Jcn
137 468   HEMA 13 E3   26 05 24 S   152 17 18 E

599 Goomeri Roadhouse

49 61 Moore St, Goomeri
Caravan Park 26 km SW of Kilkivan
07 4168 4203   HEMA 13 E2   26 11 10 S   152 04 07 E

600 Goomeri Showgrounds

Burnett Hwy, Goomeri
Camp Area S end of town
0419 720 407   HEMA 13 E2   26 11 11 S   152 04 09 E

601 Kinbombi Falls

Kinbombi Rd, Kinbombi
Picnic Area 11 km E of Goomeri or 24 km W
of Kilkivan. S off Wide Bay Hwy 6 km E of Goomeri
or 19 km W of Kilkivan. 5 km to area
1300 307 800   HEMA 13 E2   26 13 19 S   152 09 03 E

602 Broadwater Rec Reserve

23 Broadwater Access Rd, Sandy Ridges
Camp Area 22 km N of Nanango or 40 km
S of Goomeri
07 4189 9100   HEMA 13 F2   26 29 43 S   152 01 59 E

603 Nanango RV/Caravan Park

55 Elk St, Nanango
Caravan Park 28 km SE of Kingaroy
0407 016 477   HEMA 13 G2   26 40 07 S   152 00 03 E

604 Nanango RSL Club

26 Henry St, Nanango
Parking Area at rear of club. Entry on
Drayton St via Railway Ln. Check in at bar
07 4163 1375   HEMA 13 G2   26 40 19 S   152 00 09 E

605 Nanango Showgrounds

129 Drayton St, Nanango
Camp Area. Entry off Cairns St. Pre-book
07 4163 1273   HEMA 13 G2   26 40 19 S   151 59 34 E

606 Nanango Golf Club

4 Millis Way, Nanango
Parking Area 2 km W of town. Payment via
daily greens fees or equivalent donation
07 4163 1463   HEMA 13 G2   26 39 58 S   151 58 56 E

607 Twin Gums Caravan Park

1 Scott St, Nanango
Caravan Park 1 km S of PO
07 4163 1376   HEMA 13 G2   26 40 49 S   151 59 54 E

608 Tipperary Flat Park

D'Aguilar Hwy, Nanango
Rest Area 1.5 km S of PO
07 4189 9446   HEMA 13 G2   26 40 48 S   151 59 47 E

609 Maidenwell Rest Area

Coomba Waterhole Rd, Maidenwell
Rest Area 27 km SW of Nanango or 19 km
N of Cooyar. Opposite hall. Donation for showers
132 380   HEMA 13 H1   26 50 48 S   151 48 00 E

610 Maidenwell Hotel

18 Maidenwell-Bunya Mountains Rd,
Maidenwell
Parking Area 27 km SW of Nanango or 19 km N of
Cooyar. Coin donation for showers
07 4164 6133   HEMA 13 H1   26 50 49 S   151 47 56 E

611 Maidenwell Rec Grounds

Pool St, Maidenwell
Camp Area 27 km SW of Nanango or
19 km N of Cooyar
07 4171 0100   HEMA 13 H1   26 50 53 S   151 47 54 E

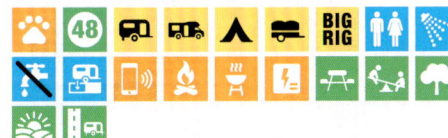

612 Swinging Bridge Park

2 Fergus St, Cooyar
Rest Area behind pub. Fee for power. Key
from pub. Toilets opposite in Memorial Park
131 872   HEMA 13 H2   26 58 52 S   151 50 02 E

613 Cooyar Showgrounds

71 Cooyar Rangemore Rd, Cooyar
Camp Area SW of town. See caretaker
07 4692 6281   HEMA 13 H2   26 59 18 S   151 49 27 E

614 Crows Nest Camp Area

Crows Nest National Park

Three Mile Rd, Crows Nest
Camp Area 7 km E of Crows Nest. Permit applies
137 468   HEMA 13 K2   27 15 15 S   152 06 25 E

615 Lake Cressbrook

Via Perseverance Dam Rd, Biarra
Camp Area 19 km E of Crows Nest. 61 km
NE of Toowoomba. Self register at entry
07 4688 6540   HEMA 13 K2   27 15 42 S   152 11 13 E

616 Chapman Park

8623 New England Hwy, Hampton
Rest Area at Visitor Information Centre
1800 009 066   HEMA 13 K2   27 21 30 S   152 04 09 E

617 Ravensbourne Rec Reserve

3217 Esk Hampton Rd, Ravensbourne
Rest Area 14 km E of Hampton or 32 km
SW of Esk
131 872   HEMA 13 K2   27 21 36 S   152 10 35 E

618 Harland Park

D'Aguilar Hwy, Yarraman
Camp Spot 8.5 km W of Blackbutt or 6 km
E of Yarraman
132 380   HEMA 13 H2   26 52 07 S   152 01 26 E

Yarraman to Ipswich
D'Aguilar and Burnett Highways

619 Blackbutt Sportscentre

11 Janice Ct, Blackbutt
Parking Area W end of town. Shower fee.
Limited hours of facilities. Pre-book
0499 812 283   HEMA 10 H1   26 53 11 S   152 05 44 E

620 Blackbutt Showgrounds

23 Bowman Rd, Blackbutt North
Camp Area 15 km W of Yarraman. Via Hart
St. 14 day limit
0437 665 199   HEMA 10 H1   26 52 52 S   152 06 08 E

621 Blackbutt Golf Course

51 Langton Rd, Blackbutt
Camp Area. Donation box on E wall of
clubhouse. Facilities available during opening hours
07 4163 0180   HEMA 10 H1   26 51 54 S   152 05 56 E

QUEENSLAND

622 First Settlers Park
11 Scott St, Benarkin
Rest Area 4 km E of Blackbutt or 42 km NW of Toogoolawah. Donations to shop opposite. Hourly fee for power
137 468　　HEMA 10 H1　26 53 18 S　152 08 10 E

623 Clancys Camping Area
Benarkin State Forest
Lot 283 Glenhowden Rd, Colinton
Camp Area 15 km SE of Blackbutt, via Benarkin Forest Dr. 4 km E of Blackbutt, turn S to dirt road 12 km. 14 day limit. Small area, ebook
137 468　　HEMA 10 K2　26 58 17 S　152 09 52 E

624 Emu Creek Camping Area
Benarkin State Forest
Lot 2 Glenhowden Rd, Anduramba
Camp Area 18 km SE of Blackbutt, via Benarkin Forest Dr. 4 km E of Blackbutt, turn S to dirt road 15 km. 14 day limit, ebook
137 468　　HEMA 10 J1　26 58 36 S　152 10 19 E

625 Stanley Gates Park
D'Aguilar Hwy, Moore
Parking Area 22 km E of Blackbutt. Opposite store
07 5424 4000　　HEMA 10 H3　26 53 38 S　152 17 21 E

626 Linville Village Railway
Ditchman Park
31 George St, Linville
Camp Area opposite hotel, through gates. Limited power
07 5424 4000　　HEMA 10 H3　26 50 36 S　152 16 33 E

627 Kilcoy Showgrounds
26 Showground Rd, Kilcoy
Camp Area 2 km W of Kilcoy off the D'Aguilar Hwy. Caretaker onsite. 7 day limit
07 5422 0440　　HEMA 10 J6　26 56 37 S　152 32 45 E

628 Kilcoy RV Stop
Seib St, Kilcoy
Parking Area S of Hope St intersection, through gates
07 5422 0440　　HEMA 10 J7　26 56 49 S　152 34 05 E

629 Yandilla Farm Stay
1785 Mount Kilcoy Rd, Mount Kilcoy
Camp Area 22 km NE of Kilcoy. Via Kilcoy Murgon Rd. Pre-book. Small dogs only
07 5498 1220　　HEMA 10 G7　26 47 07 S　152 33 50 E

630 Jimna Base Camp
21 School Rd, Jimna
Camp Area 39 km N of Kilcoy, or 79 km SW of Goomeri. Pre-book. 14 day limit
0417 756 876　　HEMA 10 E5　26 39 42 S　152 27 45 E

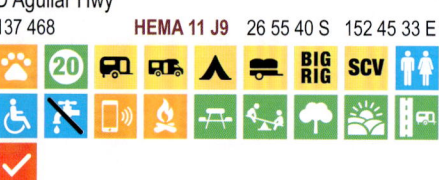

631 Peach Trees Camping Area
Jimna State Forest
Peachtrees Access, Jimna
Camp Area 4 km N of Jimna or 44 km N of Kilcoy. Permit applies. Four tonne load limit
137 468　　HEMA 10 D5　26 38 15 S　152 26 59 E

632 Cruice Park
Cruice Dr, Woodford
Rest Area 4 km NW of Woodford or 29 km W of Beerwah. At Jcn of Kilcoy-Beerwah Rd & D'Aguilar Hwy
137 468　　HEMA 11 J9　26 55 40 S　152 45 33 E

633 Running Creek Parklands
Nonmus Rd, Stanmore
Camp Area 12 km N of Woodford via Kilcoy Beerwah Rd. Caretaker 0405 930 702
07 5496 1715　　HEMA 11 H9　26 51 59 S　152 46 58 E

634 Sandy Creek Campin
229 Cedarvale Rd, Sandy Creek
Camp Area 30 km W of Woodford or 20 N of Kilcoy. Pre-book. 2 night minimum
07 5498 1032　　HEMA 10 G7　26 49 15 S　152 37 17 E

635 Bushy Browns Adventure Ski Park
2 Martin Rd, Woodford
Camp Area 7 km N of Woodford. N on D'Aguilar Hwy, N to Old Cove Rd, E to Cove Rd, E to McCabe Rd, S to the end of road. Limited sites, pre-book. 14 day limit
0419 575 032　　HEMA 11 J9　26 55 50 S　152 46 51 E

636 Woodford Showgrounds
38 Neurum Rd, Woodford
Camp Area at Woodford. Register with caretaker on arrival. Pre-book. 7 night limit
0437 390 862　　HEMA 11 J9　26 56 51 S　152 46 12 E

637 Neurum Creek Bush Retreat
268 Rasmussen Rd, Mount Archer
Camp Area 14 km W of Woodford. Pre-book, extra site fee for first night only, 2 night minimum
07 5496 3692　　HEMA 8 A3　26 59 54 S　152 41 12 E

638 Somerset Dam Campground
2210 Esk Kilcoy Rd, Somerset Dam
Camp Area at Somerset Dam. 27 km S of Kilcoy or 24 km NE of Esk
0428 180 450　　HEMA 8 C2　27 07 25 S　152 33 03 E

639 Northbrook Creek
1674 Wivenhoe Somerset Rd, Dundas
Rest Area at Dundas. Creekside, 1.5 km N of Northbrook Pkwy intersection
07 5424 4000　　HEMA 8 E2　27 17 55 S　152 36 57 E

640 Simeon Lord Park
Foggs Rd, Harlin
Rest Area 27 km W of Kilcoy. Small area
07 5424 4000　　HEMA 10 K4　26 58 33 S　152 21 34 E

641 Toogoolawah Showgrounds

30 Ivory Creek Rd, Toogoolawah
Camp Area 18 km N of Esk or 35 km SW
of Kilcoy
0417 738 590   HEMA 12 D3   27 04 41 S   152 22 31 E

642 Toogoolawah History

Museum
27 Gardiner St, Toogoolawah
Rest Area opposite Court House, toilet 50 m on
Cressbrook St. Exit Hwy to Dingyarra St
0455 177 679   HEMA 12 D3   27 05 15 S   152 22 42 E

643 Pol Crandell Park

Brisbane Valley Hwy, Toogoolawah
Rest Area S of Cressbrook Ck Crossing
07 5424 4000   HEMA 12 D3   27 05 50 S   152 22 50 E

644 Belbrooke Farms

934 Esk-Kilcoy Rd, Caboonbah
Camp Area N of Esk, 3 km via Brisbane
Valley Hwy, W for 9 km. GPS at gate. Pre-book
0427 810 026   HEMA 12 D3   27 09 30 S   152 28 06 E

645 Captain Logan Camp

Via Logan Inlet Rd, Wivenhoe Dam
Camp Area 44 km NW of Ipswich
0428 310 740   HEMA 8 F2   27 21 06 S   152 33 05 E

646 Lumley Hill Campground

Via Logan Inlet Rd, Lake Wivenhoe
Camp Area 45 km NW of Ipswich
0428 310 740   HEMA 8 F2   27 20 50 S   152 33 08 E

647 Geoff Fisher Bridge

Twin Bridges Reserve
Brisbane Valley Hwy, Fernvale
Rest Area 3.5 km N of Fernvale beside river, both
sides of Hwy
07 5424 4000   HEMA 8 G3   27 26 01 S   152 38 21 E

648 Lowood Showgrounds

14 Station St, Lowood
Caravan Park 29 km NW of Ipswich. 7 day
limit
0455 187 201   HEMA 8 H2   27 27 45 S   152 35 01 E

649 Hugos Food Forest Camp

19 -33 Schimkes Lane, Clarendon
Camp Area 11 km NW of Lowood. Pre-book
0457 602 812   HEMA 8 G1   27 26 11 S   152 30 57 E

650 Atkinson Dam Holiday Park

381 Atkinson Dam Rd, Atkinson Dam
Camp Area 18 km W of Lowood
07 5426 4211   HEMA 12 E3   27 25 12 S   152 27 11 E

Goomeri to Dalby
Bunya Highway

651 Murgon RV Stop

3 Krebs St, Murgon
Camp Area 1 km NE of PO. Deposit for
facilities key at Info Centre
07 4189 9387   HEMA 12 A1   26 14 32 S   151 56 17 E

652 Murgon Golf Club

Bunya Hwy, Murgon
Parking Area W side of town, N of Hwy.
Access water at Lions Park (100 m). Travelling
golfers and patrons welcome. Limited spaces, check
in with club
07 4168 1608   HEMA 12 A1   26 14 17 S   151 55 59 E

653 Hidden Gold Homestead

59 Waterview Dr, Moffatdale
Camp Area 23 km SW of Goomeri. Exit
Murgon Hwy S to Kilcoy Murgon Rd continue on
Murgon Barambah Rd. BYO firewood
07 4168 4784   HEMA 12 A2   26 18 46 S   152 00 25 E

654 Wondai RV Stop

Haly St, Wondai
Parking Area 15 km SW of Murgon or
29 km N of Kingaroy
07 4189 9251   HEMA 12 A1   26 19 02 S   151 52 26 E

655 Wondai Showgrounds

Cnr Baynes & Kent Sts, Wondai
Camp Area N side of town
0427 685 394   HEMA 12 A1   26 19 03 S   151 52 48 E

656 Proston Overnight Camping

Murphy St, Proston
Camp Area near bowls club
07 4189 9100   HEMA 35 B14   26 09 47 S   151 35 59 E

657 The Golden Spurs Hotel

25 Blake St, Proston
Parking Area behind hotel. Free for patrons
07 4168 9069   HEMA 35 B14   26 09 48 S   151 36 03 E

658 Proston Golf Club

81 Brigooda Rd, Proston
Camp Area W side of town. Golfers and
patrons welcome
0474 741 822   HEMA 35 B14   26 09 42 S   151 35 31 E

659 Boondooma Homestead

8262 Mundubbera-Durong Rd, Boondooma
Camp Area 81 km S of Mundubbera or
112 km NE of Chinchilla. Pay caretaker
07 4168 0159   HEMA 35 B14   26 12 10 S   151 17 35 E

660 Tingoora Rest Area

Tingoora Charlestown Rd, Tingoora
Rest Area opposite hotel. Grassed area
07 4189 9251   HEMA 12 A1   26 21 52 S   151 49 21 E

QUEENSLAND

661 Stuart River Rest Area
Chinchilla Wondai Rd, Wilkesdale
Rest Area 19 km W of Tingoora or 44 km E of Durong South
07 4189 9251 HEMA 13 F1 26 22 22 S 151 38 52 E

662 Wooroolin Rest Area
25-27 Alexander St, Wooroolin
Rest Area 16 km N of Kingaroy. Opposite PO. Coin for showers
07 4189 9251 HEMA 12 A1 26 24 38 S 151 48 58 E

663 Kingaroy Bowls Club
143 Youngman St, Kingaroy
Camp Area 800 m N of PO. 7 day limit
07 4162 1404 HEMA 12 B1 26 32 02 S 151 50 12 E

664 Kingaroy Showgrounds
31-35 Youngman St, Kingaroy
Caravan Park 1.5 km S of PO
07 4162 5037 HEMA 12 B1 26 32 49 S 151 49 56 E

665 Kingsley Grove Estate
49 Stuart Valley Dr, Goodger
Parking Area 12 km S of Kingaroy. Patrons only. Weekend lunches. Takeaway pizzas. Pre-book
0414 230 128 HEMA 12 B1 26 37 00 S 151 47 11 E

666 Coolabunia Rest Area
D'Aguilar Hwy, Coolabunia
Rest Area 7 km SE of Kingaroy or 17 km NW of Nanango. Small area
07 4189 9172 HEMA 12 B1 26 34 49 S 151 52 41 E

667 Alwyn Francis Bridge
Bunya Hwy, Taabinga
Rest Area 10 km SW of Kingaroy or 17 km NE of Kumbia. Large area, riverside
07 4189 9172 HEMA 12 B1 26 36 41 S 151 47 00 E

668 Kumbia Apex Park
26 Bell St, Kumbia
Rest Area opposite police station. Coin for power & shower, powered sites limited
07 4189 9172 HEMA 13 G1 26 41 32 S 151 39 10 E

669 Kumbia Caravan Park
Bell St, Kumbia
Caravan Park 29 km SW of Kingaroy
07 4164 4375 HEMA 13 G1 26 41 23 S 151 39 18 E

670 Dandabah Campground
Bunya Mountains National Park
Bunya Ave, Bunya Mountains
Camp Area 62 km SW of Kingaroy. Permit applies, pre-book
137 468 HEMA 35 C14 26 52 45 S 151 35 52 E

671 Bell Tourist Park
40 Cedarvale Rd, Bell
Caravan Park at Bell. 41 km NE of Dalby. Via Bunya Hwy. 200 m S of PO
07 4663 1265 HEMA 35 D14 26 55 57 S 151 26 48 E

672 Yamsion Rest Area
Old Bunya Mountain Rd, Moola
Rest Area 44 km S of Kumbia or 42 km NE of Dalby
1300 268 624 HEMA 35 D14 26 59 05 S 151 34 42 E

673 Rangemore Estate Winery
366 Malling Boundary Rd, Maclagan
Camp Area 8.5 km W of Maclagan. Via Bunya Mountains Rd 5 km, W at winery sign, follow 3.5 km. Signposted. Pre-book
0419 647 994 HEMA 35 D14 27 01 44 S 151 36 54 E

674 Pioneer Hotel
22 Oakey Cooyar Rd, Kulpi
Parking Area 61 km NW of Toowooomba. Via Kulpi Quinalow Rd, check in with publican, behind hotel. Limited sites
07 4692 8299 HEMA 36 D2 27 11 17 S 151 42 04 E

675 Glasbys Caravan Park
82 Moffatt St, Kaimkillenbun
Caravan Park 26 km NE of Dalby
07 4663 4228 HEMA 35 D14 27 03 44 S 151 26 02 E
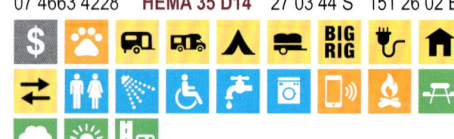

Rockhampton to Goondiwindi
Leichhardt Highway

676 Theodore Showground
127 The Blvd, Theodore
Camp Area E side of town
0487 207 373 HEMA 31 H9 24 56 22 S 150 04 34 E

677 Junction Park
The Boulevard, Theodore
Rest Area S end of road. 7 night limit
07 4992 9500 HEMA 31 H9 24 57 14 S 150 04 29 E

678 Cracow Beach
Isla Delusion Rd, Camboon
Camp Area 21 km N of Cracow. Via Eidsvold - Theodore Rd, 7 night limit
07 4992 9500 HEMA 16 H1 25 11 00 S 150 11 19 E

679 Cracow Heritage Centre
21-39 Third Ave, Cracow
Camp Area 50 km SE of Theodore. Donation box, book at hotel. 7 night limit
07 4993 7900 HEMA 16 J1 25 17 40 S 150 18 04 E

680 George Hamilton Park
Eidsvold-Theodore Rd, Cracow
Camp Area 50 km SE of Theodore. Opposite Cracow Hotel
07 4993 7118 HEMA 16 J1 25 17 43 S 150 18 11 E

681 Isla Gorge Campground
Isla Gorge National Park
Isla Gorge Rd, Isla
Camp Area 38 km S of Theodore or 58 km N of Taroom. 1 km dirt road W of Hwy
137 468 HEMA 31 J9 25 11 29 S 149 58 21 E

682 Glebe Weir

2525 Glebe Weir Rd, Spring Creek
Camp Area 93 km S of Theodore. Turn
E 66 km S of Theodore or 28 km NE of Taroom.
Honesty box. 4 week limit

07 4992 9500   HEMA 31 J9   25 27 49 S   150 02 02 E

683 Lake Murphy Conservation Park

Glenhaughton Rd, Broadmere
Camp Area 39 km NW of Taroom. 18 km N of
Taroom turn NW to Bauhinia Downs Rd 1.6 km, then
W 11 km dirt road. Pre-book

137 468   HEMA 31 J8   25 29 08 S   149 39 36 E

684 Chain Lagoons

Chain Lagoons Rd, Taroom
Parking Area 80 km S of Theodore or
16 km N of Taroom. 1 km E of Hwy. GPS at entry

07 4992 9500   HEMA 31 J9   25 31 38 S   149 46 28 E

685 Wide Water Reserve

25538 Leichhardt Hwy, Taroom
Dispersed Camping 2 km N of Taroom.
GPS at entry

07 4992 9500   HEMA 31 J9   25 38 03 S   149 46 52 E

686 Taroom Lions Park

Hutton St, Taroom
Parking Area S of main street and PO

07 4992 9500   HEMA 31 J9   25 38 35 S   149 47 42 E

687 Taroom Caravan Park

Short St, Taroom
Caravan Park 1 km NW of PO. 7 day limit

07 4627 3604   HEMA 31 J9   25 38 18 S   149 47 25 E

688 Kens Camp

Roma Taroom Rd, Taroom
Camp Area 5 km S of Taroom. Donation box

07 4992 9500   HEMA 31 K9   25 40 59 S   149 48 11 E

689 Waterloo Plains Environmental Park

West St, Wandoan
Camp Area N side of town. Toilets at football ground
next door

1300 268 624   HEMA 35 A11   26 07 02 S   149 57 31 E

690 Wandoan Showgrounds

92 Roche Creek Rd, Wandoan
Camp Area 3 km NE of PO. 7 day limit

1300 268 624   HEMA 35 A11   26 06 55 S   149 58 55 E

691 Juandah Heritage Site

92 Windeyer Rd, Wandoan
Camp Area S of town. Limited power. 7 day
limit

0475 435 737   HEMA 35 A11   26 07 40 S   149 58 23 E

692 Possum Park Camping Park

36865 Leichhardt Hwy, Miles
Caravan Park 20 km N of Miles or 46 km S
of Wandoan

07 4627 1651   HEMA 35 B11   26 30 49 S   150 06 00 E

693 Gil Weir

Gil Weir Rd, Miles
Camp Area 6 km S of Miles or 29 km N of
Condamine. W off Hwy

1300 268 624   HEMA 35 C11   26 42 33 S   150 10 46 E

694 Condamine River Caravan Park

8 Wambo St, Condamine
Caravan Park

07 4627 7179   HEMA 35 D11   26 55 36 S   150 07 59 E

695 Caliguel Lagoon

Condamine Meandarra Rd, Condamine
Picnic Area 7 km SW of Condamine

1300 268 624   HEMA 35 D11   26 59 01 S   150 06 40 E

696 Brigalow Creek

Via Condamine Meandarra Rd, Meandarra
Dispersed Camping along 1 km of creek.
Unpowered sites behind tennis courts, S end. Dump
point & BBQ at Leo Gordon Apex Park. 14 day limit.
Fees collected by ranger

0400 656 190   HEMA 35 E10   27 19 17 S   149 52 48 E

697 Meandarra Caravan Park

Gibson St, Meandarra
Caravan Park. Fees collected

0400 656 190   HEMA 35 E10   27 19 36 S   149 52 51 E

698 Glenmorgan Camping

Surat Developmental Rd, Glenmorgan
Camp Area 64 km E of Surat at Old Railway
Station

1300 268 624   HEMA 35 D10   27 14 56 S   149 40 34 E

699 Myall Park Botanic Garden

Myall Park Rd, Glenmorgan
Camp Area 5 km N of Glenmorgan.
Signposted off Riverglen Rd. Fee includes garden
entry. Follow signs to register

07 4665 6705   HEMA 35 D10   27 12 17 S   149 39 25 E

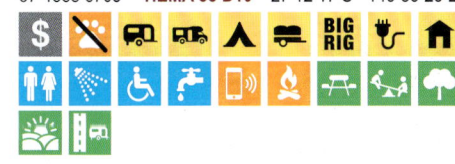

700 The Gums Roadhouse

Leichhardt Hwy, The Gums
Rest Area 49 km S of Condamine or 119 km
W of Dalby. Cnr Surat Development Rd

07 4665 9176   HEMA 35 E11   27 20 38 S   150 11 16 E

701 The Gums Sports Grounds

Surat Developmental Rd, The Gums
Camp Area 49 km S of Condamine or
119 km W of Dalby. Turn E off Hwy, 750 m

07 4665 9176   HEMA 35 E11   27 20 26 S   150 11 42 E

QUEENSLAND

702 Tara Lagoon Parklands
Showground Rd, Tara
Camp Area. Fees collected. 14 day limit
07 4679 4000   **HEMA 35 E12**   27 16 21 S   150 27 36 E

703 Moonie Crossroads Hotel
Motel Caravan Park
Cnr Moonie Hwy & Leichhardt Hwy, Moonie
Caravan Park 115 km SW of Dalby or 100 km SE of Condamine
07 4665 0200   **HEMA 35 F12**   27 43 03 S   150 22 11 E

Brisbane to Barcaldine
Warrego and Landsborough Highways

704 Tyamolum Scout Campsite
31 Bunya St, Mount Crosby
Camp Area off Mt Crosby Rd. After 6pm addtional fee. Pre-book
0404 301 603   **HEMA 8 J5**   27 31 35 S   152 50 30 E

705 Rosewood Showground
Railway St, Rosewood
Camp Area 21 km W of Ipswich. 7 night limit
0481 382 049   **HEMA 8 K2**   27 38 25 S   152 35 58 E

706 Marburg Showground
45 Queen St, Marburg
Camp Area 1 km S of Warrego Hwy. 60 day limit. Pre-book
0458 003 262   **HEMA 8 J2**   27 34 17 S   152 35 50 E

707 Minden Retreat
25 Boughens Rd, Minden
Parking Area. Sign at Hwy, self register at gate. 7 day limit
0447 681 196   **HEMA 8 J1**   27 33 15 S   152 32 20 E

708 Narda Lagoon
Pioneer St, Laidley
Parking Area S end of town. Cnr Drayton St
07 5466 3425   **HEMA 12 F3**   27 39 01 S   152 23 27 E

709 Laidley Showground
MacGregor St, Laidley
Camp Area 19 km SE of Gatton. 7 day limit. Pre-book
07 5465 1284   **HEMA 12 F3**   27 38 16 S   152 23 22 E

710 Mulgowie Hall
1 Mulgowie School Rd, Mulgowie
Camp Area 12 km S of Laidley. Via Beckman Rd. Pre-book, pay at hotel
07 5466 3426   **HEMA 12 G3**   27 43 48 S   152 21 48 E

711 Centenary Park Camp
Thornton School Rd, Thornton
Camp Area 24 km S of Laidley. Key for power via Lake Dyer Camping office. Limited powered sites. Pre-book. 7 day limit
07 5465 3698   **HEMA 12 G3**   27 47 54 S   152 22 27 E

712 Lake Dyer Camp Ground
134 Gatton Laidley Rd East, Laidley Heights
Caravan Park 1.5 km NW of Laidley. Pre-book. 7 day limit
07 5465 3698   **HEMA 12 F3**   27 37 57 S   152 22 40 E

713 William Kemp RV Stop
18 East St, Gatton
Parking Area 55 km W of Ipswich
07 5466 3426   **HEMA 12 F2**   27 33 19 S   152 16 29 E

714 Fordsdale Farmstay
171 Wagners Rd, Fordsdale
Farm Stay 30 km SW of Gatton. Pre-book
0427 584 363   **HEMA 12 G2**   27 43 36 S   152 05 41 E

715 Heifer Creek
Gatton Clifton Rd, Fordsdale
Rest Area 41 km SW of Gatton or 25 km NE of New England Hwy Thiess Memorial located here. Creekside
07 5466 3425   **HEMA 12 G2**   27 44 56 S   152 05 23 E

716 Casuarina Camping Area
Glen Rock State Forest
East Haldon Rd, East Haldon
Camp Area 42 km SW of Gatton. Via Mt Sylvia Rd & Tenthill to Junction View. Turn E. Signposted. Permit applies. 30 day limit
137 468   **HEMA 12 G2**   27 53 18 S   152 14 50 E

717 Murphys Creek Escape
356 Thomas Rd, Upper Lockyer
Camp Area 14 km N of Helidon or 17 km SE of Cabarlah. Fee for dogs. 3.7 m bridge at entry
07 4630 5353   **HEMA 12 F2**   27 28 53 S   152 05 35 E

718 Murphys Creek Tavern
3 Thursa St, Murphy's Creek
Camp Spot 20 km NE of Toowoomba. Check in at bar
07 4630 5999   **HEMA 12 E3**   27 27 42 S   152 03 18 E

719 Toowoomba Showground
Glenvale Rd, Glenvale
Camp Area for motorhomes over 30 ft & travellers with pets. Register at office. 7 day limit
07 4634 7400   **HEMA 12 F1**   27 33 36 S   151 53 04 E

720 Goombungee Haden
Showgrounds
Lau St, Goombungee
Camp Area NE side of town. 37 km N of Toowoomba. 7 day limit
0457 183 406   **HEMA 12 E1**   27 18 20 S   151 51 29 E

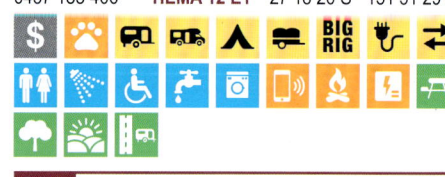

721 Gowrie Hotel
Kingsthorpe Pub
6-12 Kingsthorpe Haden Rd, Kingsthorpe
Parking Area 19 km NW of Toowoomba. Check in at reception
07 4630 0277   **HEMA 12 F1**   27 28 46 S   151 48 53 E

722 Aubigny Hotel
1277 Oakey Pittsworth Rd, Aubigny
Parking Area at rear, 13 km S of Oakey or 35 km W of Toowoomba. Pre-book. 7 day limit
07 4691 5137   **HEMA 36 E2**   27 31 03 S   151 38 37 E

723 Jondaryan Woolshed
264 Jondaryan Evanslea Rd, Jondaryan
Camp Area 3 km S of Jondaryan or 46 km NW of Toowoomba
07 4692 2229　HEMA 35 E14　27 23 32 S　151 34 30 E

724 Bowenville Reserve
Bowenville Norwin Rd, Wainui
Rest Area 5 km S of Bowenville. 59 km NW of Toowoomba. 7 day limit
131 872　HEMA 35 E14　27 19 40 S　151 27 17 E

725 Bowenville Hotel
Railway St, Bowenville
Parking Area Cnr Irvingdale St. 27 km SE of Dalby. Check in with publican, limited sites. Donation if a non patron
07 4663 7200　HEMA 35 E14　27 18 15 S　151 29 31 E

726 Cecil Plains Rural Retreat
Warfield Ave, Cecil Plains
Caravan Park 81 km W of Toowoomba. See notice board for payment & keys
0457 275 310　HEMA 35 E14　27 31 59 S　151 11 45 E

727 Cecil Plains Apex Park
Toowoomba Cecil Plains Rd, Cecil Plains
Rest Area 1 km E of PO, riverside
131 872　HEMA 35 E14　27 31 56 S　151 12 16 E

728 Wilga Bush Campground
Lake Broadwater Conservation Park
Broadwater Rd, Nandi
Camp Area 28 km SW of Dalby. Turn S off Moonie Hwy 20 km SW of Dalby or 92 km NE of Moonie along Lake Broadwater. Self-register on arrival
137 468　HEMA 35 E13　27 19 55 S　151 05 46 E

729 Lake Broadwater
Lake Broadwater Conservation Park
1040 Broadwater Rd, Ducklo
Camp Area 30 km SW of Dalby. Turn S off Moonie Hwy 20 km SW of Dalby or 92 km NE of Moonie. Register on arrival. No bookings
137 468　HEMA 35 E13　27 21 13 S　151 05 34 E

730 Kumbarilla Rest Area
4471 Moonie Hwy, Kumbarilla
Rest Area 46 km SW of Dalby or 66 km NE of Moonie
132 380　HEMA 35 E13　27 19 28 S　150 52 39 E

731 Jimbour Hall Rest Area
2413 Dalby Jandowae Rd, Jimbour East
Rest Area next to War Memorial Hall
07 4679 4000　HEMA 35 D14　26 57 50 S　151 12 59 E

732 Jandowae Showgrounds
80 Warra St, Jandowae
Camp Area 51 km NW of Dalby. Caretaker collects fees
0458 595 796　HEMA 35 C13　26 47 13 S　151 06 38 E

733 Jandowae Golf Club RV Stop
Braziers Rd, Jandowae
Camp Area between Braziers & Old Burrandowan Rds
07 4668 5349　HEMA 35 C13　26 42 58 S　151 05 10 E

734 Warra Rest Area
Talbot St, Warra
Rest Area at Richard Best Memorial Park. 46 km NW of Dalby or 35 km SE of Chinchilla
0429 457 775　HEMA 35 D13　26 55 45 S　150 55 10 E

735 Kogan Memorial Hall
9 High St, Kogan
Camp Area W side of Memorial Hall. Phone to pay & get the key
0447 490 540　HEMA 35 D13　27 02 24 S　150 45 40 E

736 Archers Crossing (South)
Archers Crossing Rd, Boonarga
Camp Area 24 km S of Chinchilla. 26 km NW of Warra or 9 km SE of Chinchilla, turn S to Hopelands Rd for 9 km to school. Turn R for 2 km, then 4 km of dirt road to river
07 4668 9564　HEMA 35 C12　26 47 57 S　150 40 46 E

737 Round Water Hole
Chinchilla Wondai Rd, Chances Plain
Rest Area 5.5 km NE of Chinchilla. Limited sites
07 4668 9564　HEMA 35 C12　26 43 18 S　150 40 03 E

738 Chinchilla Showgrounds
2 Zeller St, Chinchilla
Camp Area 84 km NW of Dalby. 7 day limit
0437 688 011　HEMA 35 C12　26 45 03 S　150 37 09 E

739 Chinchilla Weir
Chinchila Tara Rd, Crossroads
Picnic Area 9 km SW of Chinchilla. Donation to Info Centre. Limited powered sites
07 4668 9564　HEMA 35 C12　26 48 02 S　150 34 52 E

740 Clover Hill Camping
1 Braithwaite St, Chinchilla
Camp Area 1 km from PO. 7 day limit
0437 149 610　HEMA 35 C12　26 44 30 S　150 36 52 E

741 Columboola Country Vets Retreat
1381 Ryalls Rd, Hookswood
Caravan Park 29 km NE of Miles or 49 km NW of Chinchilla
07 4665 8293　HEMA 35 C12　26 32 47 S　150 19 52 E

742 Miles Showgrounds
Lot 108 Hawkins St, Miles
Camp Area. Contact caretaker on arrival
0419 028 905　HEMA 35 C11　26 39 41 S　150 10 56 E

743 Moraby Park
Warrego Hwy, Miles
Rest Area 1 km W of Miles. S side of the road. Toilets across the road
132 380　HEMA 35 C11　26 39 22 S　150 10 44 E

QUEENSLAND

744 Drillham Rest Area
Warrego Hwy, Drillham
Rest Area W side of Drillham. N side of Hwy. Cnr Forrest Rd. 21 km W of Miles.
132 380   HEMA 35 C11   26 38 27 S   149 58 50 E

745 Dulacca Hotel
Cnr Glynn Ave & Bell St, Dulacca
Camp Area 43 km W of Miles. Check in at bar, fee includes meal voucher
07 4627 6101   HEMA 35 C10   26 38 37 S   149 45 49 E

746 Yuleba East Rest Area
Warrego Hwy, Jackson South
Rest Area 17 km W of Jackson or 7.5 km E of Yuleba
132 380   HEMA 35 C10   26 37 16 S   149 27 25 E

747 Yuleba Hotel
Warrego Hwy, Yuleba
Camp Area behind hotel. 61 km E of Roma or 81 km W of Miles
07 4623 5211   HEMA 35 C9   26 36 45 S   149 23 04 E

748 Judds Lagoon
Judds Lagoon Rd, Yuleba
Camp Area 3 km SE of Yuleba, W to Forestry Rd just before Cemetery then to Moongool Rd. Signposted
0428 452 582   HEMA 35 C9   26 38 12 S   149 23 46 E

749 Old Yuleba
Mongool Rd, Yuleba South
Camp Area 13 SE of Yuleba. Via Forestry Rd for 8 km. Signposted Historic Site. 2 km dirt road
0428 452 582   HEMA 35 C9   26 41 50 S   149 25 59 E

750 The Maryanne
Yuleba Surat Rd, Yuleba
Camp Spot 16 km S of Yuleba. From the Cobb & Co Way, go past the windmill, follow track to lagoon & open area
0428 452 582   HEMA 35 C9   26 43 48 S   149 19 33 E

751 Wallumbilla Showgrounds
Warrego Hwy, Wallumbilla
Camp Area W end of town. 41 km E of Roma. Fee for shower
1300 007 662   HEMA 35 C9   26 35 14 S   149 11 01 E

752 Ups N Downs Farm Stay
78 Hartleys Ln, Roma
Farm Stay 7.5 km N of Roma. Turn W off Hwy, 5 km N of Roma. Long term stays on approval
0407 740 252   HEMA 35 B8   26 30 48 S   148 46 41 E

753 Roma Gun Club
155 Geoghegan Rd, Roma
Camp Area SW edge of town
0476 674 514   HEMA 35 C8   26 35 39 S   148 46 23 E

754 Bungeworgorai Creek
Warrego Hwy, Bungil
Camp Spot 10 km W of Roma or 31 km E of Muckadilla. Entry S of road, E of bridge
07 4622 2325   HEMA 35 C8   26 35 32 S   148 41 39 E

755 Muckadilla Community Park
Warrego Hwy, Muckadilla
Rest Area at Muckadilla. 41 km W of Roma. Donation box E side of Hall for showers & upkeep
07 4622 2325   HEMA 34 C7   26 35 07 S   148 23 17 E

756 Claravale Wilderness Experience
Warrong Rd, Kilmorey Falls
Station Stay 52 km NE of Mitchell. 500 m E of Mitchell on the Warrego Hwy turn N to Warroonga-Tooloombilla Rd. 25 km of dirt road
0428 232 721   HEMA 34 A6   26 08 43 S   148 07 51 E

757 Womalilla Creek
Mitchell Saint George Rd, Womalilla
Camp Spot 37 km S of Mitchell or 176 km NW of St George. Near bridge at Jcn of Maranoa River & Womalilla Creek
07 4624 6923   HEMA 34 C6   26 46 20 S   148 01 51 E

758 Major Mitchell Campground
Major Mitchell Rd, Mitchell
Camp Area 30 km N of Mitchell on the Forest Vale Rd, 2 km gravel road. Riverside
HEMA 34 B6   26 12 45 S   147 55 05 E

759 Neil Turner Weir
Racecourse Rd, Mitchell
Rest Area 3 km W of Mitchell. Turn N off Warrego Hwy 2 km W of Mitchell
07 4624 6923   HEMA 34 B6   26 28 28 S   147 57 21 E

760 Fishermans Rest Mitchell
Fishermans Rest Rd, Mitchell
Camp Spot 5.5 km W of Mitchell. Turn N off Warrego Hwy 5 km W of Mitchell. Donation box, cold shower
07 4624 6923   HEMA 34 B6   26 28 37 S   147 55 47 E

761 Ooline Park
Ooline Park Rd, Womalilla
Rest Area 36 km W of Mitchell or 9.6 km E of Mungallala. Turn S off Hwy, follow track for 1 km. Limited space, small vehicles only
07 4622 2325   HEMA 34 B5   26 27 53 S   147 37 49 E

762 Mungallala Hotel
12 Redford St, Mungallala
Pub Stay 44 km W of Mitchell
07 4623 6192   HEMA 34 B5   26 26 46 S   147 32 36 E

763 Mungallala RV Stop
4379 Warrego Hwy, Mungallala
Rest Area 45 km W of Mitchell or 44 km E of Morven
1300 007 662   HEMA 34 B5   26 26 44 S   147 32 29 E

764 Morven Recreation Ground
Nebine Rd, Morven
Camp Area S side of town via Victoria St.
90 km E of Charleville. Donation box. Limited power.
7 day limit
07 4656 8355   HEMA 34 B4   26 25 06 S   147 06 58 E

765 Gidgees Bush Camp
Lot 37 Old Charleville Rd, Morven
Camp Area 1.5 km W of town. Via Roma St.
Open Apr - Sept
07 4654 8380   HEMA 34 B4   26 25 14 S   147 06 06 E

766 Sommariva Rest Area
Warrego Hwy, Sommariva
Rest Area 49 km W of Morven or 39 km E
of Charleville
132 380   HEMA 34 B3   26 24 51 S   146 37 30 E

767 Charleville Rockpool
Warrego Hwy, Charleville
Camp Area 11 km E of Charleville
07 4656 8359   HEMA 34 B2   26 25 06 S   146 21 05 E

768 The Red Lizard Camp
Mitchell Hwy, Charleville
Camp Area 6 km S of Charleville
0428 928 867   HEMA 34 B2   26 27 45 S   146 14 02 E

769 CMCA Charleville Bush Camp
75 Adavale Rd, Charleville
Camp Area 1.5 km NW of Charleville. No
smoking. Pre-book. 5 night limit
02 4978 8788   HEMA 34 B2   26 23 21 S   146 13 48 E

770 Ward River
Via Diamantina Developmental Rd, Ward
Camp Area 20 km SW of Charleville. Turn
NW off Diamantina Hwy 17 km W of Charleville
to old Hwy, follow 500 m. Tracks along river.
Signposted "Ward River Fishing". 7 day limit
07 4656 8359   HEMA 34 B2   26 29 39 S   146 06 01 E

771 Nungil Station
Maruga Nungil Rd, Langlo
Station Stay 117 km NW of Charleville. Via
Charleville Adavale & Langlo Rds. Pre-book
0412 236 700   HEMA 29 K13   25 44 45 S   145 39 03 E

772 Cooladdi Foxtrap
Roadhouse
Diamantina Development Hwy, Cooladdi
Camp Area 88 km W of Charleville or 122 km E of
Quilpie. Camp near pub & river. Fee for shower
07 4654 0347   HEMA 33 C14   26 38 53 S   145 28 04 E

773 Old Quilpie Rd
Old Quilpie Rd, Cooladdi
Camp Area 25 km SW Cooladdi Roadhouse
or 114 km NW of Wyandra. Turn S off Diamantina
Dev Rd 2 km NW of roadhouse to Yarronvale Rd for
23 km, then W 500 m. Unsealed
HEMA 33 C14   26 48 20 S   145 20 53 E

774 Railway Access Rd
Diamantina Developmental Rd, Adavale
Camp Area 125 km from Charleville or
87 km E Quilpie
HEMA 33 C13   26 38 11 S   145 06 58 E

775 Mariala Roadside Camp
Mariala National Park
Adavale Rd, Adavale
Camp Area 26 km W of Adavale, next to road. No.
3 Bore & Mariala Rockholes Camps 4WD, tent and
Camper Trailer only (find in Camps Australia Wide
App). Pre-book
137 468   HEMA 33 A13   25 59 08 S   145 01 16 E

776 Winbin East Rest Area
Diamantina Developmental Rd, Adavale
Rest Area 159 km W of Charleville or 53 km
E of Quilpie
132 380   HEMA 33 C12   26 38 15 S   144 47 48 E

777 Adavale Town Camp Area
Adavale Town Hall
Blackall Adavale Rd, Adavale
Camp Area beside Hall, 99 km N of Quilpie. Visit
pub for more info. No fuel
07 4656 4656   HEMA 33 A12   25 54 29 S   144 35 59 E

778 Adavale Bush Camping
Via Charleville Adavale Rd, Adavale
Camp Area 1 km W of Adavale. 99 km N of
Quilpie. Visit pub for more info. No fuel
07 4656 4656   HEMA 33 A12   25 54 30 S   144 37 00 E

779 Hell Hole Gorge
Hell Hole Gorge National Park
Via Milo & Gooyea Rd, Adavale
Camp Area 93 km W of Adavale, ebook
137 468   HEMA 29 J11   25 33 27 S   144 10 44 E

780 The Lake (Wanco Station)
Diamantina Developmental Rd, Quilpie
Station Stay 6 km NE of Quilpie at Lake
Houdraman. E on Diamantina Developmental Rd for
4 km, turn N at orange caravan sign, cross rail line,
1 km N on dirt track to office. SCV prices
0418 947 955   HEMA 33 C11   26 35 19 S   144 18 42 E

781 Quilpie River
Diamantina Developmental Rd, Quilpie
Camp Spot at Quilpie. Turn S 1 km E of
Quilpie, just W of John Waugh Bridge (Bulloo River).
Follow track to riverside sites near old crossing
07 4656 0540   HEMA 33 C11   26 36 55 S   144 17 03 E

782 Quilpie Heritage Inn
36 Brolga St, Quilpie
Parking Area 100 m E of PO
07 4656 1427   HEMA 33 C11   26 36 49 S   144 16 11 E

783 Cooper Diamantina Corner
Cnr Cooper & Diamantina Dev Rd, Quilpie
Rest Area 38 km W of Quilpie or 209 km E
of Windorah
137 468   HEMA 33 C10   26 36 36 S   143 55 17 E

784 Eromanga Motel
Webber St, Eromanga
Caravan Park E side of town
07 4656 3276   HEMA 33 C9   26 40 10 S   143 16 20 E

QUEENSLAND

785 Eromanga Hall
Deacon St, Eromanga
14 Camp Area W side of town. Facilities in hall
07 4656 0540   **HEMA 33 C9**   26 40 12 S   143 16 00 E

786 Augathella Warrego River
Main St, Augathella
A2 Camp Area at Augathella. 85 km NE of Charleville. Opposite hotel. Donation box
07 4654 5244   **HEMA 34 A3**   25 47 43 S   146 34 53 E

787 Two Ponds Augathella
Bath St, Augathella
A2 Camp Spot S side of river. 84 km NE of Charleville
07 4654 5244   **HEMA 34 A3**   25 47 35 S   146 35 18 E

788 Ellangowan Hotel
90 Main St, Augathella
A2 Parking Area behind hotel. See publican before parking
0411 545 194   **HEMA 34 A3**   25 47 46 S   146 34 58 E

789 Fishermans Rest Augathella
Biddenham Rd, Augathella
A2 Camp Spot N side of river. 84 km NE of Charleville
07 4654 5244   **HEMA 34 A3**   25 47 32 S   146 35 15 E

790 Tambo Caravan Park
58 Arthur St, Tambo
A2 Caravan Park next to football ground
07 4654 6463   **HEMA 29 H14**   24 53 06 S   146 14 52 E

791 Stubby Bend
Racecourse Rd, Tambo
A2 Camp Spot 2 km NE of Tambo. First turn R after bridge on Alpha-Springsure Rd. Signposted
07 4654 6408   **HEMA 29 H14**   24 52 34 S   146 15 46 E

792 Tambo North Rest Area
Landsborough Hwy, Mount Enniskillen
A2 Rest Area 25 km NW of Tambo or 75 km SE of Blackall
132 380   **HEMA 29 H14**   24 45 03 S   146 06 20 E

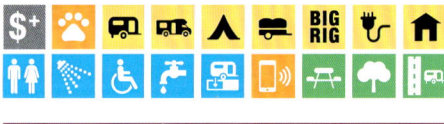

793 Barcoo River Rest Area
Landsborough Hwy, Blackall
A2 Rest Area 59 km N of Tambo or 41 km S of Blackall
132 380   **HEMA 29 H13**   24 34 53 S   145 48 34 E

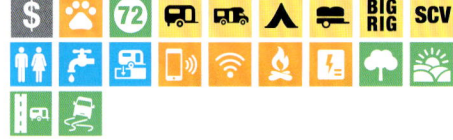

794 Barcoo Hotel Van Park
95 Shamrock St, Blackall
A2 Caravan Park enter via Spring Lane. Limited sites & space, check with publican first
07 4657 4197   **HEMA 29 G13**   24 25 24 S   145 27 53 E

795 Barcoo River Camp Blackall
Garden St, Blackall
A2 Camp Spot 500 m W of PO. Toilet opposite, shower in Short St toilets. See entry sign for payment
07 4657 4637   **HEMA 29 G13**   24 25 29 S   145 27 41 E

796 Barcoo River Weir
St Frances St, Isisford
A2 Camp Area E of town beside river. Pay at council
07 4658 8900   **HEMA 29 G11**   24 15 28 S   144 26 36 E

797 Golden West Hotel
17 Saint Mary St, Isisford
A2 Caravan Park 100 m from PO
07 4658 8380   **HEMA 29 G11**   24 15 30 S   144 26 29 E

798 Oma Waterhole
Isisford Yaraka River Rd, Isisford
A2 Camp Area 17 km SW of Isisford, next to Oma Station. Via St Helens Rd. Pay at council. Tracks in either direction
07 4658 8900   **HEMA 29 G11**   24 16 55 S   144 19 20 E

799 Monks Tank Camping Area
Idalia National Park
A2 Unnamed Rd, Blackall
Camp Area 54 km S from Blackall Emmet Rd at Benlidi Siding. Signposted. Dirt road. Pre-book
137 468   **HEMA 29 H11**   24 47 37 S   144 42 18 E

800 Yaraka Town Park & Hotel
12 Jarley St, Yaraka
79 Camp Area behind town hall. 102 km SW of Isisford. Pay at hotel
07 4657 5526   **HEMA 29 H10**   24 52 59 S   144 04 43 E

801 Douglas Ponds Creek
Landsborough Hwy, Blackall
A2 Rest Area 24 km N of Blackall or 83 km S of Barcaldine
132 380   **HEMA 29 G12**   24 16 34 S   145 20 29 E

802 Lara Wetlands
39052 Landsborough Hwy, Barcaldine
A2 Station Stay. Turn W at signpost 79 km N of Blackall or 28 km S of Barcaldine to 13 km dirt road. GPS at the gate. Apr - Oct
0457 661 243   **HEMA 29 F12**   23 47 52 S   145 18 31 E

Brisbane to Rathdowney
Mt Lindesay Highway

803 Tully Memorial Park
Beryl Pde, North MacLean
13 Rest Area 6 km N of Jimboomba. Entry via Greenbank Rd
07 3412 3412   **HEMA 4 J4**   27 47 01 S   153 00 44 E

804 Canungra Sports Ground
49 Coburg Rd, Canungra
90 Camp Area on R, past hotel on Lamington National Park Rd. Follow signs. 14 day limit
07 5543 5904   **HEMA 7 H9**   28 01 18 S   153 09 36 E

805 Spring Gully Stays
334 Sarabah Rd, Sarabah
Camp Area 15 km S of Canungra - do not drive through causeways if flooded. Bush camping sites & rates. 7 day limit, pre-book
07 5543 4490   HEMA 7 J9   28 06 29 S   153 07 01 E

806 Sharp Park River Bend
Beechmont Rd, Witheren
Camp Area 4 km SE of Canungra. Bush camping either side of Coomera R. Pre-book in peak season. 3 week limit
0409 550 745   HEMA 7 H10   28 02 59 S   153 11 18 E

807 Witheren Heights
2665 Beechmont Rd, Witheren
Camp Area E from Canungra on Beaudesert Nerang Rd, S to Beechmont Rd. Pre-book. 21 day limit
0413 879 188   HEMA 7 J10   28 04 31 S   153 11 53 E

808 Swan Gully Park
388 Swan Gully Rd, Bromelton
Camp Area 9 km W of Bromelton. 12 km W Beaudesert or 42 km E Boonah. Fee to use 4WD Park. Strictly no glass. Coins for showers
0475 630 843   HEMA 6 G6   27 59 38 S   152 54 05 E

809 Darlington Park
2505 Kerry Rd, Kerry
Camp Area 24 km S of Beaudesert. Beside Albert R. 7 day limit
07 5544 8120   HEMA 7 K8   28 11 04 S   153 02 26 E

810 Burgess Park
Christmas Creek Rd, Lamington
Camp Area 19 km SE of Laravale on Christmas Ck Rd. 3 km S of Hillview. 7 day limit
07 5544 8120   HEMA 12 J5   28 14 20 S   152 59 45 E

811 Stinson Memorial Park
2749 Christmas Creek Rd, Lamington
Camp Area 27 km SE of Laravale. 11 km S of Hillview. Pre-book. No EFTPOS. 7 day limit
07 5544 8008   HEMA 12 J5   28 17 16 S   153 02 13 E

812 Andrew Drynan Park
Running Creek Rd, Rathdowney
Camp Area 18 km SE of Rathdowney (3.8 m clearance). Turn E, 4 km N of Rathdowney. 3.5 m clearance, 5 tonne limit, steep grades & sharp curves into NSW
07 5544 1281   HEMA 12 J5   28 19 08 S   152 55 59 E

813 Running Creek Rest Area
Running Creek Rd, Running Creek
Camp Area 50 km S of Beaudesert. W of Mt Lindsay Hwy. Limited sites
132 380   HEMA 12 J5   28 19 20 S   152 56 25 E

814 Scenic Rim Adventure Park
636 Tamrookum Ck Rd, Tamrookum Ck
Camp Area 27 km SW Beaudesert off Mt Lindsay Hwy
0458 406 236   HEMA 12 H4   28 10 15 S   152 50 08 E

815 Rathdowney Caravan Park
Running Creek Rd, Rathdowney
Caravan Park just E of PO. 14 day limit
0419 522 475   HEMA 12 J5   28 12 42 S   152 51 55 E

816 Bigriggen Park
196 Bigriggan Rd, Rathdowney
Camp Area 9 km W of Rathdowney. W off Mt Lindsay Hwy 1 km S of Rathdowney to Rathdowney-Boonah Rd 7 km. S to Upper Logan Rd for 500 m, then R to dirt road
07 5463 6190   HEMA 12 J4   28 11 53 S   152 46 46 E

817 Flanagan Reserve
135 Flanagan Reserve Rd, Barney View
Camp Area 14 km W of Rathdowney. Via Rathdowney-Boonah & Upper Logan Rds (4 km). Dirt road. Coin operated showers
07 5544 3128   HEMA 12 J4   28 12 50 S   152 45 55 E

818 Lake Maroon Camp Ground
535 Burnett Creek Rd, Maroon
Camp Area 28 km W of Rathdowney or 32 km S of Boonah. Pre-book
07 5463 6256   HEMA 12 J4   28 12 05 S   152 38 43 E

819 Mount Barney Lodge
1093 Upper Logan Rd, Mount Barney
Camp Area 19 km W of Rathdowney. Dirt road. Pre-book. Move camp after 7 days
07 5544 3233   HEMA 12 J4   28 16 32 S   152 44 19 E

820 Waterfall Creek Reserve
Waterfall Creek Rd, Maroon
Camp Area 29 km W of Rathdowney. Via Boonah Rathdowney & Newman Rds. Permit applies. Steep and winding road
07 5540 5111   HEMA 12 J4   28 12 20 S   152 40 07 E

Toowoomba to Goondiwindi
Gore Highway

821 Yarramalong Weir
Yarramalong Rd, Yandilla
Camp Spot 25 km SW of Pittsworth. From Gore Hwy, turn E 11 km N of Millmerran or 33 km S of Pittsworth onto Leyburn Rd for 11 km, then N. 3 km to weir. Signposted
131 872   HEMA 35 F14   27 50 07 S   151 27 02 E

822 Walpole Park
6 Walpole St, Millmerran
Rest Area 400 m E of PO. Entry via Charles St. Cnr Charlotte St. Dump point opposite park
131 872   HEMA 35 F14   27 52 17 S   151 16 28 E

823 Millmerran Showgrounds
Millmerran Cecil Plains Rd, Millmerran
Camp Area N end of town. Entry at Gate 2
07 4695 4151   HEMA 35 F14   27 51 37 S   151 16 40 E

824 Millmerran Golf Club
8 Golf Club Rd, Millmerran
Parking Area. Play golf & stay
07 4695 1476   HEMA 35 F14   27 53 05 S   151 16 18 E

825 Wyaga Creek Rest Area
Gore Hwy, Wyaga
Rest Area 74 km SW of Millmerran or
64 km NE of Goondiwindi. At Yelarbon turnoff
132 380   HEMA 35 G12   28 09 32 S   150 39 23 E

Toowoomba to Stanthorpe
New England Highway

826 Federation Park
766 Drayton Connection Rd, Vale View
Rest Area 13 km S of Toowoomba or 71 km
N of Warwick
131 872   HEMA 12 F1   27 39 09 S   151 53 32 E

827 Shammah Park Farmstay
136 Dixon Ln, East Greenmount
Farm Stay 24 km S of Toowoomba. 14 day
limit
07 4697 1414   HEMA 12 G1   27 44 28 S   151 56 31 E

828 Nobby Town Park
12-14 Tooth St, Nobby
Rest Area opposite Rudds Pub. Fee for
power. Honesty Box
131 872   HEMA 12 G1   27 51 10 S   151 54 12 E

829 Clifton Rec Grounds
12 Morton St, Clifton
Camp Area N side of town. Pay caretaker
or shire office. 7 day limit
131 872   HEMA 12 H1   27 55 34 S   151 54 45 E

830 O'Shanleys Pub
54 Clark St, Clifton
Parking Area. Check in with publican,
shower in hotel. Free for patrons
07 4697 3288   HEMA 12 H1   27 55 54 S   151 54 24 E

831 Clifton Golf Club
1158 Clifton-Leyburn Rd, Ryeford
Camp Area 12 km W of Clifton or 57 km
SW of Toowoomba
0477 958 522   HEMA 12 H1   27 56 41 S   151 47 35 E

832 Passmore Reserve
Passmore Rd, Ellangowan
Camp Area 21 km W of Clifton or 18 km E
of Leyburn. Via Clifton Leyburn Rd, 1 km to reserve
131 872   HEMA 12 H1   27 56 11 S   151 42 55 E

833 Leyburn Rec Ground
15 Tummaville Rd, Leyburn
Camp Area across bridge near general
store. Showers behind tennis courts
1300 697 372   HEMA 35 G14   28 00 27 S   151 34 58 E

834 Spring Creek Caravan Park
616 Spring Creek Rd, Spring Creek
Caravan Park 8 km E of Clifton or 9 km N
of Allora
07 4697 3397   HEMA 12 H1   27 57 00 S   151 59 28 E

835 Allora Showgrounds
Darling St, Allora
Camp Area E side of town. 4 night limit
0427 100 210   HEMA 12 H1   28 02 19 S   151 59 24 E

836 Allora Rest Area
Dalrymple Park
Herbert St, Allora
Rest Area N side of town. Via Allora Dr. Creekside
1300 697 372   HEMA 12 H1   28 01 45 S   151 58 58 E

837 Killarney Sundown Motel
2 Pine St, Killarney
Caravan Park 35 km SE of Warwick
07 4664 1318   HEMA 12 J3   28 20 29 S   152 17 46 E

838 Berrima Camping & Farmstay
879 Cullendore Rd, Elbow Valley
Camp Area 23 km SE of Warwick. Pre-
book. GPS at gate. 5 day limit
0439 581 947   HEMA 12 J2   28 22 07 S   152 08 02 E

839 Connolly Dam
1010 Connolly Dam Rd, Silverwood
Camp Area 19 km S of Warwick. 10 km dirt
road. Self register & pay. No bookings. 7 day limit
1300 697 372   HEMA 12 J1   28 21 14 S   151 59 54 E

840 Jim Mitchell Park
Mountain Park Rd, Dalveen
Rest Area 40 km S of Warwick or 18 km N
of Stanthorpe
1300 697 372   HEMA 12 K1   28 29 21 S   151 58 14 E

841 Foxbar Falls
375 Goldfields Rd, Amiens
Camp Area 4 km NW of Amiens. 21 km NW
of Stanthorpe or 68 kms S of Warwick
0477 369 227   HEMA 12 K1   28 34 55 S   151 46 15 E

842 Stanthorpe Showground
8 High St, Stanthorpe
Camp Area NE side of town. Entry via
Showground Ln & Club Rd. Caretaker on site
07 4681 2107   HEMA 36 H3   28 38 37 S   151 56 50 E

843 Blue Topaz Campground
26806 New England Hwy, Severnlea
Caravan Park 6 km S of Stanthorpe. SCV
rates available. Diner and restaurant onsite
07 4683 5279   HEMA 36 H3   28 41 50 S   151 54 21 E

844 Hlatini

Lot 137, Ironbark Rd, Sugarloaf
Camp Spot 19 km E of Stanthorpe. Take
Sugarloaf Rd, Panoramic Dr, Central Rd, cross grid,
4 km dirt road. Private property, BYO portaloo
0447 761 129   HEMA 36 H3   28 43 13 S   152 03 05 E

845 Country Style Caravan Park

27156 New England Hwy, Glen Aplin
Caravan Park 1 km N of Glen Aplin or 9 km
S of Stanthorpe. Riverside
07 4683 4358   HEMA 36 H3   28 43 25 S   151 53 19 E

846 Mountview Wines

Mount Stirling Rd, Glen Aplin
Parking Area 3 km W of Glen Aplin. Open
Fri - Sun. Pre-book
07 4683 4316   HEMA 36 H3   28 43 55 S   151 51 21 E

847 Bald Rock & Castle Rock

Girraween National Park
Pyramids Rd, Wallangarra
Camp Area 35 km S of Stanthorpe. E off New
England Hwy 7 km S of Ballandean or 11 km N of
Wallangarra to Pyramids Rd for 9 km
137 468   HEMA 36 J3   28 49 58 S   151 56 16 E

848 Wallangarra Lions Park

80 Margetts St, Wallangarra
Picnic Area 37 km S of Stanthorpe. Behind
amenities
1300 697 372   HEMA 36 J3   28 55 18 S   151 55 41 E

849 Broadwater Campground

Sundown National Park
Permanents Rd, Mingoola
Camp Area 79 km SW of Stanthorpe or 70 km W of
Tenterfield, via Bruxner Hwy & Glenlyon Dam Rd.
5 km E of Glenlyon Dam Rd. Small vehicles only.
4 km of gravel road
137 468   HEMA 36 J2   28 55 09 S   151 34 36 E

Brisbane to Goondiwindi
Cunningham Highway

850 Ipswich Showgrounds

Cnr Warwick & Salisbury Rds, Ipswich
Camp Area. Pay at office Mon to Fri,
8.30am - 4.30pm. 7 day limit
07 3281 1577   HEMA 4 G2   27 37 38 S   152 45 33 E

851 Hardings Paddock Camp

Flinders – Goolman Conservation Estate
Carmichaels Rd, Ipswich
Camp Area 16 km S of Ipswich. Limited sites, pre-
book for gate code. 7 night limit
07 3281 0555   HEMA 6 C4   27 44 07 S   152 46 00 E

852 Ivorys Rock Campground

310 Mount Flinders Rd, Peak Crossing
Caravan Park 20 km S of Ipswich. Open
Thur - Mon. Pre-book
07 3077 9668   HEMA 6 D4   27 46 27 S   152 45 54 E

853 Albert Theaker Park

Champions Way, Willowbank
Rest Area 15 km S of Ipswich. Cnr
Cunningham Hwy (Ipswich Motorsport Precinct)
07 3810 6666   HEMA 6 C3   27 41 38 S   152 40 15 E

854 Royal Hotel Harrisville

Cnr Queen St & Dunns Ave, Harrisville
Parking Area 28 km S of Ipswich. Check in
on arrival
07 5467 1882   HEMA 6 E3   27 48 38 S   152 39 42 E

855 CHEAPaWAY Camping

38 Queen St, Harrisville
Parking Area 28 km S of Ipswich. Semi
permanent available
0438 382 666   HEMA 6 E3   27 48 39 S   152 40 00 E

---

856 Fassifern Reserve

77 Cunningham Hwy, Fassifern
Rest Area 5 km NE of Aratula or 16 km S of
Warrill View
07 5540 5111   HEMA 6 G2   27 57 30 S   152 34 46 E

857 Kalbar Showground

107 George St, Kalbar
Camp Area N end of town. 7 day limit
0499 970 119   HEMA 6 G3   27 56 15 S   152 37 32 E

858 Boonah Info Centre

20 Boonah-Fassifern Rd, Boonah
Parking Area open 4pm - 8am. Limited space
07 5463 2233   HEMA 6 G3   27 59 33 S   152 40 49 E

859 Boonah Showgrounds

8 Melbourne St, Boonah
Camp Area 40 km W of Beaudesert. Cnr
Cossart St
07 5463 4080   HEMA 6 G3   27 59 51 S   152 41 06 E

860 Aratula Hotel Motel

6841 Cunningham Hwy, Aratula
Parking Area 53 km S of Ipswich. Check in
on arrival. Free for patrons
07 5463 8100   HEMA 6 G2   27 59 20 S   152 32 32 E

861 The Gorge Campground

Gorge Rd, Charlwood
Camp Area 3 km S of Aratula. Via
Charlwood Rd, dirt road. Pre-book
07 5526 0683   HEMA 6 H2   28 00 37 S   152 33 16 E

862 Yarramalong Camping & Outdoor Recreation Centre

688 Lake Moogerah Rd, Charlwood
Camp Area 17 km E of Boonah. L off Boonah
Fassifern Rd, signposted after 4 km. Cash only.
Pre-book
0437 934 558   HEMA 6 H2   28 00 42 S   152 34 12 E

QUEENSLAND

863 Mount Alford Hotel
901 Reckumpilla St, Mount Alford
Parking Area 14 km SW of Boonah. Check in with publican, free for patrons
07 5463 0230   **HEMA 6 H2**   28 03 53 S   152 35 43 E

864 Spicers Gap
Main Range National Park
Spicers Gap Rd, Clumber
Camp Area 69 km SW of Ipswich or 74 km E of Warwick. Take Spicer's Gap turn-off from Hwy near Aratula. Signed
137 468   **HEMA 12 H3**   28 04 22 S   152 25 36 E

865 Maryvale Crown Hotel
47 Taylor St, Maryvale
Parking Area 31 km NE of Warwick. Fee for non-patrons, fee for power and water. Limited sites, overflow next door
07 4666 1148   **HEMA 12 H2**   28 04 18 S   152 14 23 E

866 Gordon Country
1698 Inverramsay Rd, Goomburra
Camp Area 20 km E of Goomburra. Vehicle fee
07 4666 6179   **HEMA 12 H3**   27 58 39 S   152 17 52 E

867 Goomburra Forest Retreat
268 Forestry Reserve Rd, Goomburra
Camp Area 25 km NW of Goomburra
07 4666 6179   **HEMA 12 H3**   27 58 44 S   152 20 16 E

868 Poplar Flat Camping Area
Main Range National Park
Forestry Reserve Rd, Goomburra
Camp Area 25 km E of Goomburra on Inverramsay Rd
137 468   **HEMA 12 H3**   27 58 44 S   152 20 32 E

869 Manna Gum Camp Site
Main Range National Park
Forest Reserve Rd, Goomburra
Camp Area 26 km E of Goomburra. E on Inverramsay Rd
137 468   **HEMA 12 H3**   27 58 51 S   152 20 49 E

870 Warrego Farm
11 Roona Rd, Junabee
Farm Stay 7 km E Warwick. Pre-book
0402 071 374   **HEMA 12 J2**   28 14 20 S   152 05 33 E

871 Washpool Camping Reserve
Washpool Rd, Leslie Dam
Camp Area 18 km W of Warwick. Turn S off Cunningham Hwy 9 km W of Warwick or 39 km E of Karara. Self registration & payment. Lakeside. 7 day limit
1300 697 372   **HEMA 12 J1**   28 14 25 S   151 54 59 E

872 Sandy Creek Pub
345 Sandy Creek Rd, Allan
Parking Area 10 km W of Warwick. 7 km W of Warwick or 41 km E of Karara turn N, travel 3 km. Patrons only, donation for charity, fee for shower
07 4661 3413   **HEMA 12 J1**   28 11 01 S   151 56 48 E

873 Bony Mountain Rec Reserve
1239 Upper Wheatvale Road, Bony Mountain
Camp Area 26 km W of Warwick or 24 km E of Karara. N of Hwy. Pay caretaker
0406 721 114   **HEMA 12 H1**   28 08 02 S   151 50 09 E

874 Victoria Hill Bush Camp
Ryeford Pratten Rd, Victoria Hill
Camp Spot 45 km NW of Warwick
HEMA 12 H1   28 00 10 S   151 45 48 E

875 Glendon Camping Grounds
222 Glendon Rd, Karara
Camp Area 38 km W of Warwick or 10 km E of Karara
0448 203 048   **HEMA 36 G2**   28 10 30 S   151 41 48 E

876 Karara Tavern
18509 Cunningham Hwy, Karara
Parking Area 49 km W of Warwick. Donation or patronage requested
07 4667 4141   **HEMA 36 G2**   28 12 24 S   151 34 01 E

877 Karara Recreation Reserve
Karara School Rd, Karara
Camp Area 49 km W of Warwick. Next to Hall. Pay at hotel. Free for SCV
07 4667 4141   **HEMA 36 G2**   28 12 15 S   151 33 49 E

878 Carbean Country Camping
Carbean Rd, Karara
Farm Stay 21 km S of Karara. Turn into Carbean Rd from Hwy 5 km S Karara. Unsealed road for 16 km. Pre-book, 2 night minimum
0428 674 142   **HEMA 36 G2**   28 21 15 S   151 38 00 E

879 Gore Rest Area
Cunningham Hwy, Gore
Rest Area 63 km W of Warwick or 47 km E of Inglewood. Next to store
07 4667 4236   **HEMA 35 G14**   28 17 42 S   151 29 19 E

880 Oman Ama Rest Area
Lot 2 Cunningham Hwy, Oman Ama
Rest Area 88 km W of Warwick or 22 km E of Inglewood. E side of closed service station
132 380   **HEMA 35 H14**   28 23 50 S   151 17 42 E

881 Lake Coolmunda
Coolmunda Access Rd, Lake Coolmunda
Camp Area 16 km E of Inglewood. Register & pay at caravan park. Deposit on key payable
07 4652 4171   **HEMA 35 H14**   28 25 20 S   151 12 54 E

882 Inglewood RV Stop
Alice St, Inglewood
Parking Area N end of town, grassed area just S of McIntyre Brook bridge. Opposite the park
0428 730 819   **HEMA 35 H13**   28 24 42 S   151 05 09 E

883 Dumaresq River
Les Jingles Myers Rest Area
Dumaresq Crossing Rd, Texas
Camp Area 1 km S Texas. N bank of Dumaresq River. 14 day limit
0428 730 819   **HEMA 35 J13**   28 52 03 S   151 09 51 E

884 Goat Rock Camping

1040 Goat Rock Rd, Texas
Camp Area 16 km S of Texas. Off Bruxner Way
0437 713 488   HEMA 35 J13   28 57 42 S   151 06 02 E

885 Cunningham Highway (The Pocket) Reserve

Cunningham Hwy, Inglewood
Rest Area at Whetstone Weir, 14.5 km SW of
Inglewood. 300 m N of McDougalls Rd, N side of
road. Riverside. 14 night limit
132 523   HEMA 35 H13   28 27 52 S   150 57 34 E

886 Yelarbon Rec Ground

27 Wyemo St, Yelarbon
Camp Area 41 km SW of Inglewood.
14 day limit
0400 018 897   HEMA 35 H13   28 34 34 S   150 45 24 E

887 Rainbow Reserve

Kildonan Rd, Goondiwindi
Camp Spot 20 km SE of Goondiwindi. Via
Border Rivers Tourist Dr (Kildonan Rd), 17 km to
reserve just before Eukabilla Rd. Riverside. 14 day limit
0428 730 819   HEMA 35 H12   28 38 27 S   150 27 04 E

888 Yellowbank Reserve

Kildonan Rd, Goondiwindi
Camp Spot 28 km SE of Goondiwindi. Via
Border Rivers Tourist Dr, 25 km to reserve. Bush
track to river. 14 day limit
0428 730 819   HEMA 35 H12   28 39 10 S   150 31 48 E

889 Lees Reserve

Kildonan Rd, Goondiwindi
Camp Area 33 km SE of Goondiwindi. E
for 29 km, then S for 1 km to riverside. Narrow bush
track. 14 day limit. 4WD only sections in wet weather
0428 730 819   HEMA 35 H12   28 39 40 S   150 33 40 E

890 Bengalla Reserve

Kildonan Rd, Yelarbon
Camp Spot 36 km SE of Goondiwindi.
33 km to gateway & reserve sign. Bush track
to river. Large area, some narrow or 4WD only
sections. GPS at track entry. 14 day limit
0428 730 819   HEMA 35 H12   28 39 29 S   150 35 56 E

891 Goondiwindi Showgrounds

Boundary Rd, Goondiwindi
Camp Area N side of town. Entry off
Leichhardt Hwy. 14 day limit
0437 809 415   HEMA 35 H12   28 31 51 S   150 19 14 E

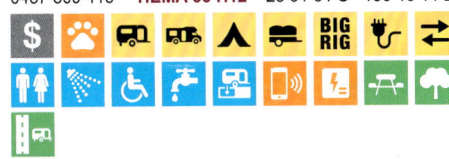

Goondiwindi to Thargomindah
Barwon and Balonne Highways

892 Toobeah Parking Area

Barwon Hwy, Toobeah
Parking Area 150 m E of the hotel
0428 730 819   HEMA 35 H10   28 25 00 S   149 52 17 E

893 Toobeah Coronation Hotel

Barwon Hwy, Toobeah
Parking Area behind hotel, check in before
parking. Fee for non-patrons
07 4677 5280   HEMA 35 H10   28 25 01 S   149 52 14 E

894 Joe Beach Bridge Reserve
Bungunya Reserve

Meandarra Talwood Rd, Bungunya
Camp Area 71 km NW Goondiwindi or 26km NE
Talwood. From Barwon Hwy turn N, 4 km to Weir R.
Sites both sides of road
0428 730 819   HEMA 35 H10   28 22 59 S   149 40 38 E

895 Bungunya Rest Area

20 Main St, Bungunya
Rest Area 69 km W of Goondiwindi or
87 km E of Nindigully
132 380   HEMA 35 H10   28 25 23 S   149 39 28 E

896 Talwood Rec Ground

Recreation St, Talwood
Camp Spot 91 km W of Goondiwindi or
65 km E of Nindigully. Donation for upkeep, to
Talwood Store. Limited power
07 4671 7400   HEMA 35 H10   28 29 12 S   149 28 08 E

897 Talwood Hotel

30 Main St, Talwood
Camp Area behind pub, check in at bar
07 4677 1109   HEMA 35 H10   28 29 05 S   149 28 08 E

898 Weengallon Rest Area

Barwon Hwy, Weengallon
Rest Area 40 km W of Talwood or 26 km E
of Nindigully. S side of Hwy
132 380   HEMA 35 G9   28 21 30 S   149 03 18 E

899 Nindigully Pub

Sternes St, Nindigully
Camp Area 1 km S of Barwon Hwy Jcn.
Camp beside Moonie River, across & along from the
hotel. Donation for upkeep
07 4625 9637   HEMA 35 G8   28 21 17 S   148 49 15 E

900 Thallon Rec Ground

William Rd, Thallon
Camp Area. Call for access key or see pub
during business hours
07 4620 8888   HEMA 35 H8   28 37 58 S   148 51 59 E

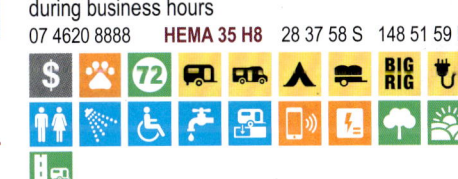

901 Francis Hotel

16 Pine St, Thallon
Camp Area next to tennis courts, behind pub.
Check in at bar before entering camp. Patrons only
07 4625 9188   HEMA 35 H8   28 38 14 S   148 52 04 E

902 Barneys Beach

Via Noondoo Thallon Rd, Thallon
Camp Area 2 km W Thallon, off Dunwinnie
Rd. NW via dirt track to river sites. NW of Hwy
07 4620 8888   HEMA 35 H8   28 37 57 S   148 51 25 E

QUEENSLAND

903 Wallam Creek

Willliam St, Bollon
Camp Area beside creek. Donation for upkeep
07 4620 8877 **HEMA 34 G5** 28 01 40 S 147 28 41 E

904 Bollon Hotel

30 Main St, Bollon
Parking Area. Check in at bar. Fee for power. Patronage required
07 4625 6188 **HEMA 34 G5** 28 01 56 S 147 28 46 E

905 Murra Murra Junction

Ballone Hwy, Nebine
Rest Area 66 km W of Bollon or 115 km E of Cunnamulla
132 380 **HEMA 34 F3** 27 59 45 S 146 48 56 E

906 Charlotte Plains Station

1993 Charlotte Plains Rd, Cunnamulla
Camp Area 135 km W of Bollon or 46 km E of Cunnamulla, 2.2 km S to artesian bore campsite, 15 km dirt road to homestead. Signposted. Pre-book
07 4655 4923 **HEMA 34 G2** 28 04 55 S 146 10 32 E

907 Jobs Gate Rest Area

Mitchell Hwy, Cunnamulla
Rest Area 34 km S of Cunnamulla or 81 km N of Barringum
132 380 **HEMA 34 G1** 28 17 37 S 145 44 57 E

908 Tuen Rest Area

Barringun Rd, Tuen
Parking Area 23 km N Tuen or 44 km S Cunnumulla
132 380 **HEMA 34 H1** 28 22 41 S 145 44 10 E

909 Warrego River Barringun

Amenda Tinnenburra Rd, Barringun
Dispersed Camping 96 km S of Cunnamulla or 39 km N of Barringum. Turn W 89 km S of Cunnamulla to Tinnenburra Rd for 6.5 km to riverside camps
HEMA 34 H1 28 44 04 S 145 36 38 E

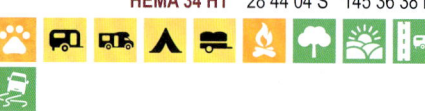

910 Hotel Cunnamulla

24 Jane St, Cunnamulla
Parking Area in main street. Check in at bar before camping. Entry off side street
07 4655 0082 **HEMA 34 G1** 28 04 06 S 145 40 58 E

911 Bowra Sanctuary

887 Humeburn Rd, Cunnamulla
Camp Area 9 km N of Cunnamulla. Turn W at signposted gate, then 6 km to house. Pre-book, limited sites & power. Closed Dec - Feb. Corrugated road. 14 day limit
07 4655 1238 **HEMA 34 F1** 27 59 32 S 145 40 22 E

912 Wyandra Camp Ground

55 Moody St, Wyandra
Camp Area N end of town, behind school
07 4655 8470 **HEMA 34 D1** 27 14 37 S 145 58 36 E

913 Wyandra General Store

35 Railway St, Wyandra
Camp Area N end of town, behind PO
07 4654 9212 **HEMA 34 D1** 27 14 46 S 145 58 48 E

914 Paddabilla Bore

Adventure Way, Eulo
Camp Area 16 km E of Eulo or 50 km W of Cunnamulla. 300 m behind bore
07 4655 8470 **HEMA 33 G13** 28 07 02 S 145 11 40 E

915 Eulo Queen Hotel

Leo St, Eulo
Caravan Park behind pub
07 4655 4867 **HEMA 33 G13** 28 09 37 S 145 02 49 E

916 Paroo River

Adventure Way, Eulo
Camp Spot 1.5 km W of Eulo or 128 km E of Thargomindah. Both sides of bridge
07 4655 8470 **HEMA 33 G13** 28 09 38 S 145 02 12 E

917 Wandilla Station

1508 Pithery Rd, Eulo
Station Stay 15 km S of Eulo. Turn at the Big Yellow Sponge Bob letterbox
07 4655 4065 **HEMA 33 G13** 28 17 04 S 144 59 09 E

918 Corni Paroo Waterhole

Pump Hole & Caiwarro Camps
Currawinya National Park
Via Warden Rd, Hungerford
Camp Areas 35 km NE of Ranger Station or 72 km S of Eulo. Small off road caravans & motorhomes. Toilets at Caiwarro Ruins. Permit applies
137 468 **HEMA 33 H12** 28 41 13 S 144 47 12 E

919 Ourimperee Waterhole

Bush Camp
Currawinya National Park
Hungerford Eulo Rd, Hungerford
Camp Area behind Currawinya Woolshed. 25 km N Hungerford entrance or 105 km S Eulo. Small off road caravans & motorhomes only. Cold showers. Permit applies
137 468 **HEMA 33 J11** 28 52 59 S 144 30 36 E

920 Southern Cross Caravan Park

Hungerford Rd, Hungerford
Caravan Park. Honesty box for outside hours. Limited powered sites
07 4655 4064 **HEMA 33 J11** 28 59 51 S 144 24 35 E

921 Artesian Waters Caravan Park

1 Blue Bonnet Blvd, Yowah Opal Field
Caravan Park 87 km NW of Eulo
07 4655 4953 **HEMA 33 F12** 27 58 18 S 144 38 15 E

922 Alroy Camping Grounds

4252 Eulo Toompine Rd, Eulo
Station Stay 61 km NW of Eulo. Turn N 18km W of Eulo, 40 km along Yowah Ck
0427 992 889 **HEMA 33 F12** 27 48 08 S 144 42 32 E

923 Yowah Rest Area
Gemwood St, Yowah
Rest Area at Yowah Opal Field. First turn after school
07 4655 8470   HEMA 33 F12   27 58 01 S   144 37 59 E

924 Lake Bindegolly Bush Camp
Bulloo Development Rd, Dynevor
Camp Spot 34 km E of Thargomindah or 90 km W of Eulo. 100 m W of NP Rest Area entrance, turn S and follow track. Signposted. Do not camp in rest area
07 4621 8095   HEMA 33 G11   28 05 37 S   144 12 18 E

925 Wild Camp
Quilpie Thargomindah Rd, Norley
Rest Area 148 km S of Quilpie or 47 km NE of Thargomindah. Sections of unsealed road
HEMA 33 F11   27 48 28 S   144 11 41 E

926 Napunyah Caravan Park
42 Powell St, Thargomindah
Caravan Park S of main street
07 4621 8000   HEMA 33 F10   27 59 49 S   143 49 31 E

927 Thargomindah Explorers
88 Dowling St, Thargomindah
Caravan Park 500 m W of PO
07 4655 3307   HEMA 33 F10   27 59 51 S   143 49 11 E

928 Kilcowera Station
Hungerford Rd, Thargomindah
Station Stay 95 km S Thargomindah or 90 km N of Hungerford. Pre-book. High clearance. Open Mar - Oct
07 4655 4960   HEMA 33 H10   28 40 07 S   143 55 45 E

929 Bulloo Development Rd
Bundeena Rd, Norley
Parking Area 75 km W of Thargomindah or 63 E of Noccundra turn off
132 380   HEMA 33 F9   27 46 26 S   143 21 22 E

930 Wilson River Camp
Via Warry Gate Rd, Nockatunga
Camp Spot at Noccundra Waterhole. Track opposite hotel. Sites beside river. Facilities at hall. BYO firewood, no collecting allowed
07 4655 4317   HEMA 32 F7   27 49 16 S   142 35 26 E

931 Noccundra Hotel
6 Wilson St, Nockatunga
Camp Area. Check in with publican. Limited powered sites, pre-book
07 4655 4317   HEMA 32 F7   27 49 04 S   142 35 20 E

932 Jackson Oil Field
Cnr of Cooper Development Rd & Adventure Way, Nockatunga
Rest Area 130 km NW of Thargamindah
132 380   HEMA 32 E7   27 37 59 S   142 41 01 E

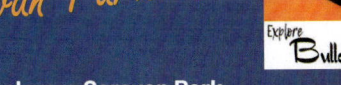

933 Burke & Wills Dig Tree
Nappa Merrie Station
Dig Tree Rd, Durham
Camp Area 46 km E of Innamincka or 225 km W of Noccundra on the Adventure Way. Signposted
07 4655 4323   HEMA 32 E4   27 37 25 S   141 04 33 E

934 Creekside near Nulla
Outstation
Arrabury Rd, Tanbar
Camp Area 76 km S of Jcn Birdsville Dev Rd Jcn, or 157 km N of Innamincka Rd Jcn. W of road near Outstation
HEMA 32 B4   26 17 35 S   141 07 07 E

Rolleston to Hebel (NSW border)
Carnarvon and Castlereagh Highways

935 Lake Nuga Nuga
Nuga Nuga National Park
Esplanade Track, Rewan
Dispersed Camping 85 km SE of Rolleston. 28 km SE of Rolleston, on Dawson Hwy via Arcadia Valley Access Rd. 58 km gravel road, W to Lake Nuga Nuga Access Rd, epermit applies
137 468   HEMA 30 H7   24 59 30 S   148 41 08 E

936 Sandstone Park
3858 Carnarvon Gorge Rd, Carnarvon Gorge
Camp Area before NP entry on a farm. Check in at reception. Sites 3 km from entry. Pre-book
07 4984 4679   HEMA 30 H6   25 04 12 S   148 15 26 E

937 Dargonelly Rock Hole
Carnarvon National Park
Via Carnarvon NP Rd, Mount Moffatt
Camp Area 153 km NW of Injune. NW on Womblebank Gap Rd 50 km, N to Mount Moffatt Rd 86 km, then N 16 km. Pre-book
137 468   HEMA 30 H6   25 01 34 S   147 53 58 E

938 West Branch
Carnarvon National Park
Unnamed Rd, Mount Moffatt
Camp Area 172 km NW of Injune. NW on Womblebank Gap Rd 50 km, N to Mount Moffatt Rd 86 km, N to Carnarvon NP Rd 34 km. Pre-book
137 468   HEMA 30 H6   24 58 26 S   148 00 43 E

939 Wallaroo Parking Area
Carnarvon Hwy, Upper Dawson
Parking Area 105 km S of Rolleston or 68 km N of Injune. Share with trucks, bitumen area
132 380   HEMA 30 J7   25 18 09 S   148 39 31 E

940 Lonesome Bush Camping
Expedition National Park
Arcadia Valley Rd, Baffle West
Camp Area 55 km NE of Injune. Travel N for 26 km on Carnarvon Hwy, E to Arcadia Valley Rd 18 km, signposted, epermit applies
137 468   HEMA 30 J7   25 29 28 S   148 49 51 E

941 Beilba Bush Camp
Expedition National Park
Via Beilba Rd, Beilba
Camp Area 55 km NE of Injune. N on Carnarvon Hwy 26 km, E to Fairview Rd 14 km, N to Beilba Rd 15 km to camp. Pre-book
137 468   HEMA 30 J7   25 33 40 S   148 54 18 E

942 Injune Rodeo Ground
Carnarvon Hwy, Injune
Parking Area 1.6 km S of town, park in fenced off area on S side of buidings
07 4626 0503   HEMA 30 K7   25 51 14 S   148 33 28 E

943 Possum Park
Racecourse Rd, Injune
Camp Area at Injune Racecourse. Off Hwy. Pay at Info Centre, caretaker will visit. Fee for shower. Stay inside fenced area
07 4626 0503   HEMA 30 K7   25 50 49 S   148 33 25 E

944 Surat Fishing & Restocking
Club Park
Carnarvon Hwy, Noorindoo
Camp Area 1 km N of Surat. Just over Balonne R
07 4626 5136   HEMA 35 D9   27 08 57 S   149 04 23 E

945 Surat Caravan Park
47 Burrowes St, Surat
Caravan Park opposite hotel. Via Marcus St. Key & pay at hotel
07 4626 5310   HEMA 35 D9   27 09 05 S   149 03 59 E

946 Warroo Bridge
Waganui Ln, Wycombe
Camp Area 60 km N of St George. Turn W to Roma Southern Rd, 66 km S of Surat or 51 km N of St George
07 4620 8877   HEMA 35 F8   27 38 34 S   148 44 28 E

947 St George Riverfront Tourist Park
12747 Carnarvon Hwy, St George
Caravan Park 187 km S of Roma (formerly Kapunda)
0408 183 134   HEMA 35 F8   27 59 17 S   148 39 24 E

948 Kamarooka Tourist Park
56 Victoria St, St George
Caravan Park. Pre-book
07 4625 3120   HEMA 34 G7   28 02 03 S   148 35 11 E

949 Dirranbandi Retreat & Caravan Park
45 Kirby St, Dirranbandi
Caravan Park 95 km SW of St George
07 4625 8707   HEMA 34 H7   28 34 53 S   148 13 44 E

950 Balonne Minor Bridge
Bollon Dirranbandi Rd, Dirranbandi
Rest Area 3 km W of Dirranbandi
07 4620 8877   HEMA 34 H7   28 35 56 S   148 12 34 E

951 Hebel Caravan Park
31 William St, Hebel
Caravan Park behind general store
07 4625 0920   **HEMA 34 J6**   28 58 18 S   147 47 44 E

952 Hebel Hotel
30 William St, Hebel
Parking area behind hotel. Check in at bar
07 4625 0923   **HEMA 34 J6**   28 58 19 S   147 47 41 E

Cairns to Cape York

This road is seasonal and more suitable to 4WD vehicles, camper trailers and off road caravans. Road conditions phone Main Roads 131 940, Cooktown Shire 07 4069 5444 or RACQ 1300 130 595

953 Peninsula (Quinkan) Hotel
Terminus St, Laura
Camp Area beside hotel & NE of the PO. Limited power. Check in with publican
07 4060 3393   **HEMA 23 K6**   15 33 29 S   144 26 45 E

954 Ang-Gnarra Aboriginal
Corporation Caravan Park
Quinkan Centre Campground
Peninsula Developmental Rd, Laura
Caravan Park at Quinkan Centre Campground. S end of town. Pay at roadhouse opposite
0474 330 109   **HEMA 23 K6**   15 33 57 S   144 26 57 E

955 Isabella Falls
Endeavour Battlecamp Rd, Cooktown
Camp Area 41 km NW of Cooktown. Off road caravan only, may be water crossing. Limited space
07 4069 5763   **HEMA 27 A1**   15 18 01 S   145 00 19 E

956 Old Laura Homestead
Rinyirru (Lakefield) NP
Endeavour Battlecamp Rd, Lakefield
Camp Area in S area of park. Near Jcn of Lakefield & Battle Camp Rds. 2 sites, either side of the road. Many camps suitable for off road camper trailer or tents only throughout NP, some with amenities or boat ramps - listed in Camps Australia Wide App. Permit applies, pre-book
137 468   **HEMA 23 J6**   15 20 42 S   144 27 20 E

957 Kennedy River Rest Area
Peninsula Developmental Rd, Laura
Rest Area 33 km N of Laura or 43 km S of Hann River Roadhouse
07 4082 0500   **HEMA 23 K5**   15 25 13 S   144 11 12 E

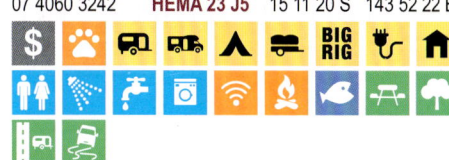

958 Hann River Roadhouse
Peninsula Developmental Rd, Laura
Camp Area at Hann River. 74 km NW of Laura or 62 km S of Musgrave
07 4060 3242   **HEMA 23 J5**   15 11 20 S   143 52 22 E

959 Morehead River Rest Area
Peninsula Developmental Rd, Laura
Rest Area 27 km N of Hann River Roadhouse or 63 km S of Musgrave Roadhouse
07 4082 0500   **HEMA 23 J4**   15 01 22 S   143 39 50 E

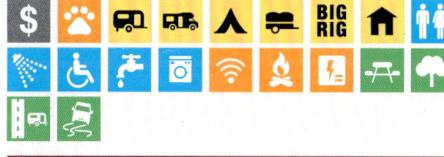

960 Musgrave Roadhouse
Peninsula Developmental Rd, Yarraden
Camp Area at Musgrave. 62 km N of Hann River Roadhouse or 107 km S of Coen. Closed Jan - Apr
07 4060 3229   **HEMA 23 H4**   14 46 51 S   143 30 14 E

961 Mungkan River Camping
Via Strathgordon Rd, Pormpuraaw
Camp Area 210 km W of Musgrave. 7.5 km N of township. May - Sept only, ebook 14 days prior. Alcohol restrictions
07 4060 4155   **HEMA 23 J1**   14 51 31 S   141 36 13 E

962 Chapman River
Via Rirranth St, Pormpuraaw
Camp Area 210 km W of Musgrave. 2.5 km S of township. May - Sept only, ebook 14 days prior. Alcohol restrictions
07 4060 4155   **HEMA 23 J1**   14 55 00 S   141 37 18 E

963 Lukin River Rest Area
Kirbys Camp
Peninsula Developmental Rd, Yarraden
Rest Area 55 km S of Coen or 53 km N of Musgrave Roadhouse. E side on N riverbank, small area
07 4082 0500   **HEMA 23 H4**   14 23 43 S   143 21 42 E

964 Kendle River
Peninsula Developmental Rd, Coen
Camp Area 41 km S Coen or 47 km N Musgrave Rd Roadhouse. Track on S side of river
07 4082 0500   **HEMA 23 G4**   14 15 23 S   143 17 23 E

965 Port Stewart Campground
Esplanade, Coen
Camp Spot at Port Stewart 73 km E of Peninsula Dev Rd. Traditional land - check in with Lama Lama Ranger Station 6.5 km W of village
07 4060 3369   **HEMA 23 G5**   14 03 54 S   143 41 13 E

966 Exchange Hotel Coen
41 Regent St, Coen
Camp Area behind hotel. Register at bar
07 4060 1133   **HEMA 23 G4**   13 56 37 S   143 11 57 E

967 The Bend
Peninsula Developmental Rd, Coen
Camp Area 3 km N of Coen. Bush camping
07 4082 0500   **HEMA 23 G4**   13 55 27 S   143 11 38 E

968 Oyala Thumotang NP
Via Rokeby Rd, Coen
Camp Areas 25 km NE of Coen. Turn W off Peninsula Dev Road, N of the airport. Formerly Mungkan Kandju NP, 14 remote sites in the Coen R (GPS at entry) Langi and Archer Bend sections (detailed in the Camps Australia Wide App). 21 day limit, ebook
HEMA 23 F4   13 37 05 S   142 34 57 E

969 Archer River Roadhouse
Peninsula Developmental Rd, Archer River Crossing
Camp Area 64 km N of Coen or 123 km S of Moreton Telegraph Station
07 4060 3266   **HEMA 23 F3**   13 26 16 S   142 56 27 E

Sites 970 — 987

QUEENSLAND

970 Chuulangun Aboriginal Corporation Campgrounds

81
Portland Rd, Archer River
Camp Area 16 km E of the Peninsula Dev Rd, 4 km from GPS. Permit applies. Alcohol prohibited. Seasonal
07 4060 3240 HEMA 23 E3 13 06 28 S 142 57 53 E

971 Batavia Goldfield Ruins

81
Via Portland Rd, Archer River
Dispersed Camping at ruins. Take L (N side) track just E of Wenlock River crossing, veer R at fork, follow narrow track 1 km
07 4082 0500 HEMA 23 E3 13 05 15 S 142 56 48 E

972 Brown Creek Crossing

81
Portland Rd, Lockhart
Camp Spot 72 km NE of Jcn with Peninsula Dev Rd, or 12 km W of entry to Kutini-Payamu NP. S side of road
07 4082 0500 HEMA 23 E4 12 45 19 S 143 06 19 E

973 Kutini-Payamu Iron Range NP

Portland Rd, Lockhart
Camp Areas 130 km NE of Archer River Roadhouse: Cooks Hut, no amenities at Rainforest & Gordon Creek South Campgrounds. N on Peninsula Developmental Rd 36 km, E to Portland Connection Rd 101 km. 4 km N of Portland & Lockhart River Rd Jcn. Permit applies
HEMA 23 E4 12 42 37 S 143 17 33 E

974 Chilli Beach Campground

Kutini-Payamu (Iron Range) NP
81
Via Portland Connection Rd, Lockhart
Camp Area 161 km NE of Archer River Rd Roadhouse. N on Penninsula Developmental Rd for 36 km, E to Portland Connection Rd for 126 km. Permit applies
137 468 HEMA 23 D4 12 37 53 S 143 25 36 E

975 Merluna Station Stay

Peninsula Development Rd, Archer River
81
Caravan Park 150 km NW of Coen or 150 km SE of Weipa. Signposted
07 4060 3209 HEMA 23 E2 13 03 54 S 142 27 01 E

976 York Downs Station

Peninsula Developmental Rd, Mission River
81
Station Stay S side of Pensinsula Dev Rd 20 km W of entry to York Downs Homestead, or 46 km E Weipa. Within fenced area only, beside dam - not at homestead. Signed. Honesty box
HEMA 23 D2 12 39 04 S 142 13 10 E

977 Pennefather River

Via Andoom Rd, Napranum
81
Camp Area 84 km N of Weipa. Turn W off Andoom Rd 50 km N Weipa to Pennefather Rd for 27 km. Access tracks N either via beach (7 km) or marginally inland track (8 km) with sand driving closer to camp at river mouth. Alcohol restrictions
07 4090 5600 HEMA 23 D1 12 14 07 S 141 43 06 E

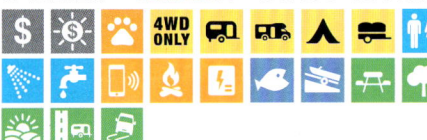

978 Cullen Point

Via Andoom Rd, Mapoon
81
Camp Area 97 km N of Weipa (partly unsealed) and 8.5 km N of Mapoon (sealed) at Andoom Rd. Permit from Jean Jimmy Land & Sea Centre (weekdays & Fri am) or Rugapayn Store, Mapoon (weekdays & Sat am). Seasonal
07 4082 5208 HEMA 24 J1 11 57 23 S 141 54 26 E

979 Moreton Telegraph Station

Telegraph Rd, Wenlock
81
Camp Area 123 km N of Archer River Roadhouse. Limited power. No ATV/Quads
07 4060 3360 HEMA 23 D3 12 27 13 S 142 38 19 E

980 Schramm Creek

Via Telegraph Rd, Wenlock
81
Camp Area between Bramwell Roadhouse & Moreton Telegraph Station. Turn E off Peninsula Dev Rd 32 km S of the roadhouse, or 10 km N of Telegraph Station. Tracks to entry 700 m from S or 300 m from NE side of Hwy
07 4082 0500 HEMA 23 D3 12 22 11 S 142 36 57 E

SCV

981 Bramwell Station

Via Telegraph Rd, Shelburne
81
Caravan Park 42 km NE of Moreton Telegraph Station or 8 km SE of Bramwell Jcn. Open May - Oct
07 4060 3300 HEMA 23 D3 12 08 26 S 142 37 19 E

982 Captain Billy Landing

Heathlands Regional Park
81
Via Bamaga Rd, Shelburne
Camp Area on Eastern Coast. 25 km narrow winding access track. High clearance, small offroad campervans, camper trailers, limited turning or passing. Large open exposed area. Pre-book, permit applies
137 468 HEMA 24 G7 11 37 54 S 142 51 21 E

983 Bramwell Junction Roadhouse

Telegraph Rd, Shelburne
81
Camp Area 46 km N of Moreton Telegraph Station. Free caravan/trailer storage
07 4060 3230 HEMA 24 K5 12 05 33 S 142 33 34 E

984 Old Telegraph Track South

Telegraph Rd, Shelburne
81
Camp Spot along 75 km of Old Telegraph track between Bramwell Jcn to S, and the Northern Bypass Rd Jcn to N. Camping at Palm, Ducie, North Alice, Dalhunty, Bertie, Gunshot, Cockatoo & Sailor Creek crossings. GPS at S end
07 4082 0500 HEMA 24 K5 12 05 33 S 142 33 29 E

985 Old Telegraph Track North

Old Telegraph Track, Jardine River
81
Camp Spots along 48 km of Old Telegraph track between the Jcn of the track & Northern Bypass Rd to S & Jardine Ferry Crossing to N. Camping at Canal, Sam, Mistake, Cannibal, Cypress & Bridge (Nolan's Brook) creek crossings. Track fringes NP (no pets in park). GPS at S end
07 4082 0500 HEMA 24 F4 11 27 15 S 142 25 04 E

986 Eliot Falls

Heathlands Regional Park
81
Via Old Telegraph Track, Shelburne
Camp Area at Eliot Falls. High clearance only, steep creek crossing. Limited sites for offroad campervans, camper trailers only. Pre-book, permit applies
137 468 HEMA 24 E4 11 23 07 S 142 24 48 E

987 North Jardine River

Jardine River National Park
81
Old Telegraph Track, Jardine River
Camp Area 14 km N Jardine Ferry Crossing, or 40 km S Bamaga via Old Telegraph Track. S to OT Track 160m N of Jcn of Northern Bypass and Peninsula Development Rds. Turn E to tracks for sites along river. Pre-book. 21 day limit
137 468 HEMA 24 D4 11 08 44 S 142 21 35 E

988 South Jardine River

Jardine River National Park

Via Old Telegraph Track, Jardine River Camp Area, E of Northern Bypass Rd via Old Telegraph Track & S of Ferry crossing. Take Nolans Brook bypass track off Northern Bypass for 18 km, or from Eliot Falls travel N on OT track for 32 km. Sites along river. Pre-book. 21 day limit

137 468   **HEMA 24 D4**   11 08 32 S   142 21 40 E

989 Jardine River Ferry

Campground & Service Station

Northern Bypass Rd, Jardine River Camp Area on W side of Jardine River at Ferry Crossing

07 4069 1369   **HEMA 24 D3**   11 06 14 S   142 16 59 E

990 Jackey Jackey Creek

Peninsula Development Rd, Injinoo Camp Area area 26 km S Bamaga or 21 km N Jardine Ferry Crossing. Turn E on Peninsula Development Rd 24 km S Bamaga or 18 km N of the Ferry for 3 km

07 4082 0500   **HEMA 24 C4**   11 01 23 S   142 23 16 E

991 Mutee Head

Mutee Heads Rd, Injinoo Camp Spot 45 km NE Jardine Ferry Crossing or 34 km SW Bamaga. Turn E off Peninsula Development Rd to Pipeline Track (becomes Mutee Head Rd) for 19 km. Well formed tracks to 2 camp areas either side of headland. GPS is entry to N camp

07 4048 6800   **HEMA 24 B3**   10 54 46 S   142 15 06 E

992 Alau Beach Campground

Namok Rd, Umagico Camp Area N coast of Cape York. 21 day limit

07 4069 3029   **HEMA 24 B4**   10 53 09 S   142 20 48 E

993 Seisia Holiday Park

6 Koraba Rd, Seisia Caravan Park 50 km NE of Jardine River Ferry Crossing or 6 km N of Bamaga. Seasonal

07 4203 0992   **HEMA 24 B4**   10 50 51 S   142 22 05 E

994 Loyalty Beach Campground

& Fishing Lodge

1 Loyalty Beach Rd, New Mapoon Camp Area at Loyalty Beach. 4 km NE of Seisia via Pajinka Back Rd. Seasonal

07 4069 3372   **HEMA 24 B4**   10 50 05 S   142 23 01 E

995 Roonga Point

Esplanade, Punsand Camp Spot along beach, W side of Northern Peninsula Area. Turn W off Punsand Rd 9 km N of The Croc Tent. Follow track for 2 km

07 4048 6600   **HEMA 24 A4**   10 43 25 S   142 25 46 E

996 Cape York Camping

Punsand Bay

Lot 11 Punsand Bay, Punsand Bay Camp Area 33 km NE of Seisa. 2 week limit

07 4069 1722   **HEMA 24 A5**   10 43 19 S   142 27 47 E

997 Somerset Beach Camping

Somerset Rd, Somerset Camp Area NE side of Northern Peninsula Area. From The Croc Tent turn E 7 km Pajinka Road, NE 11 km Somerset Rd. Signposted. Self register onsite

07 4048 6900   **HEMA 24 A5**   10 44 30 S   142 35 33 E

998 Nanthau Beach

Narau Beach Rd, Somerset Camp Spot on NE side of Northern Peninsula Area. From The Croc Tent, 7 km E on Pajinka Road, 7 km NE Somerset Rd, 3 km SE Narau Beach Rd. Sand tracks

07 4048 6900   **HEMA 24 A5**   10 46 59 S   142 35 04 E

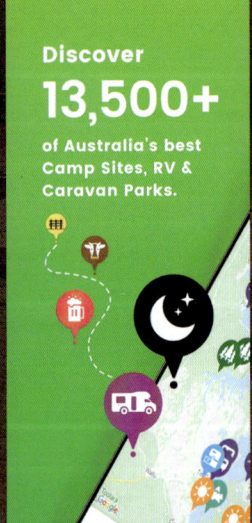

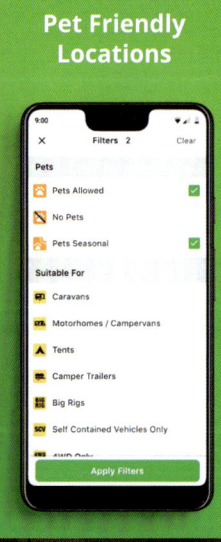

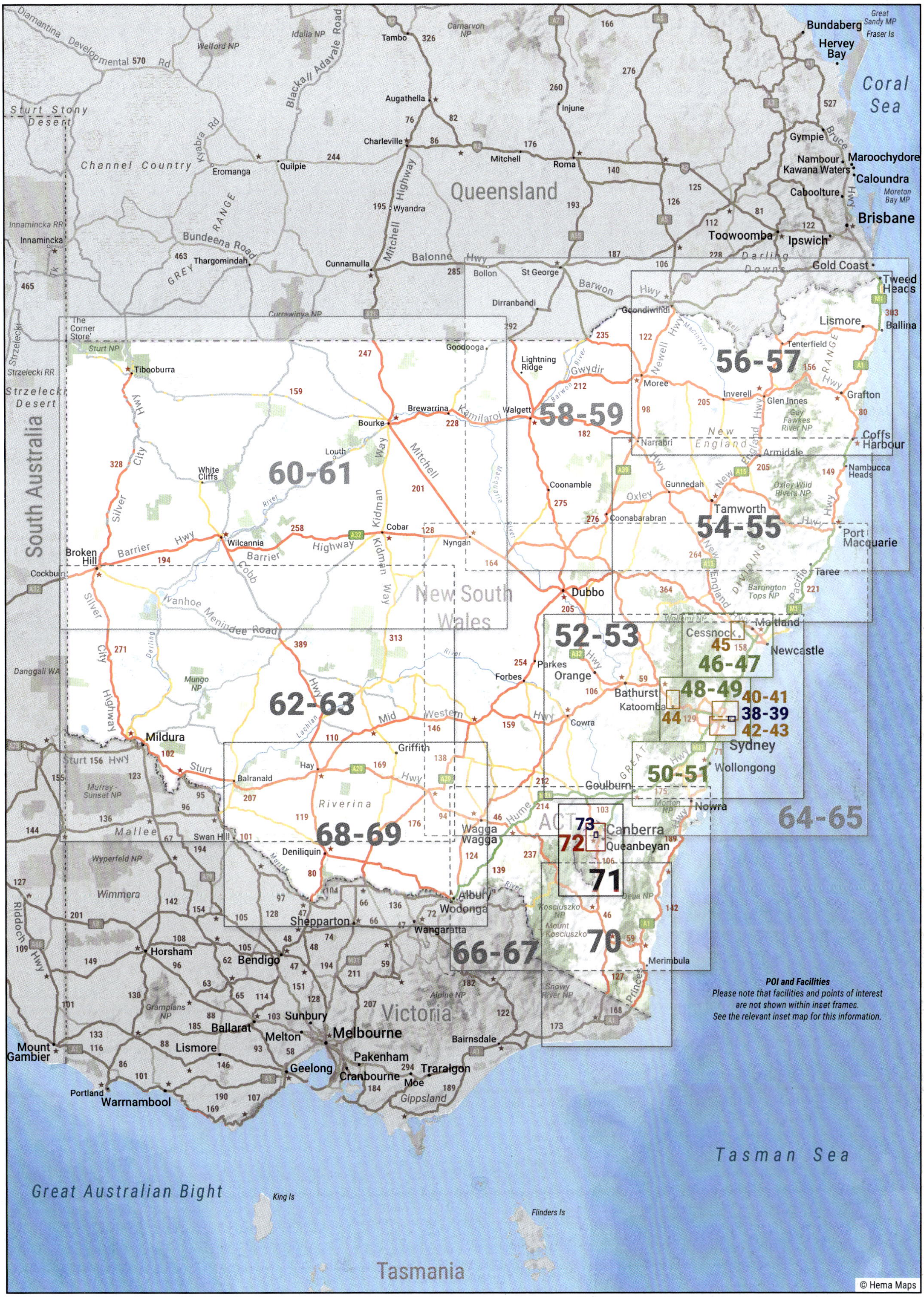

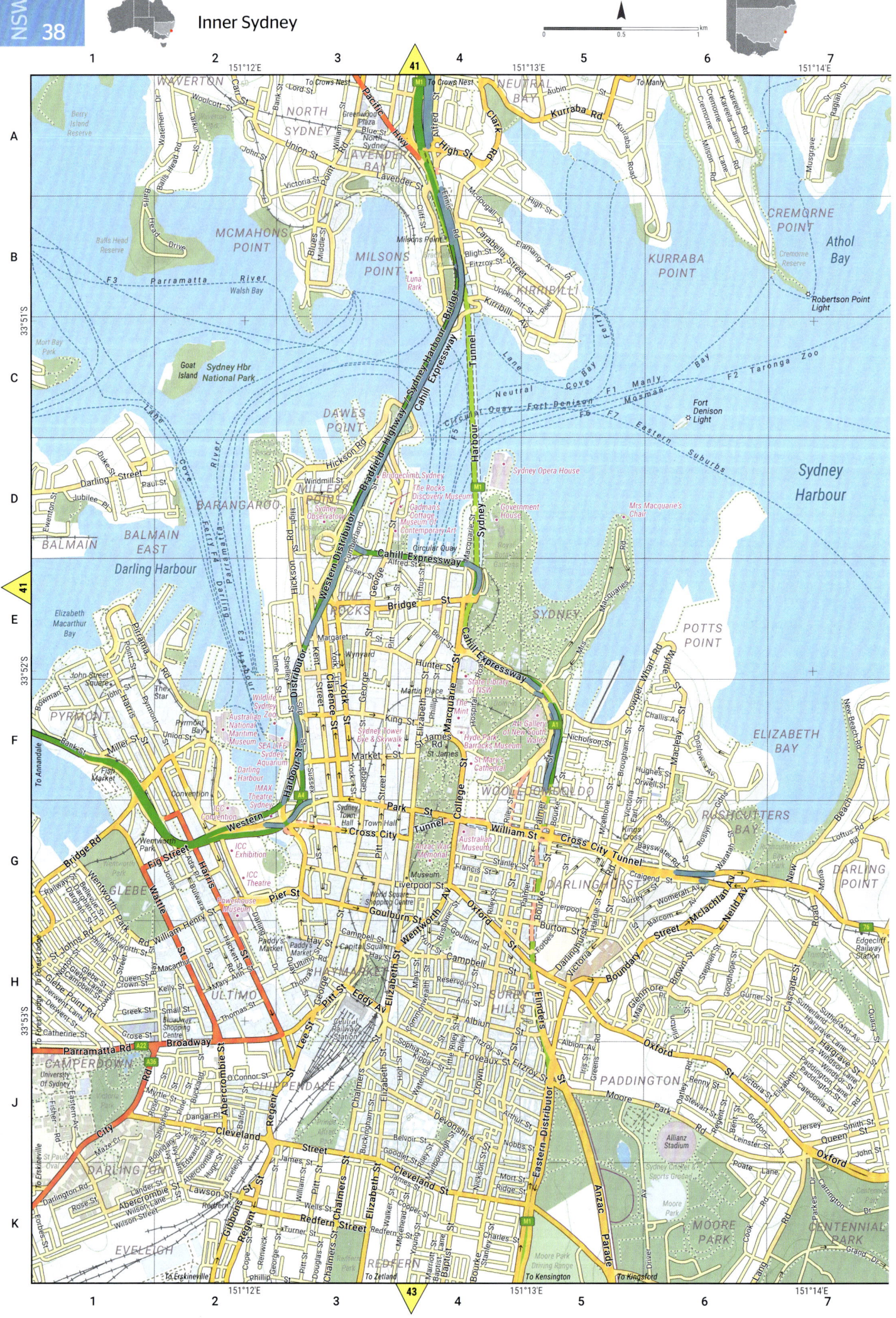

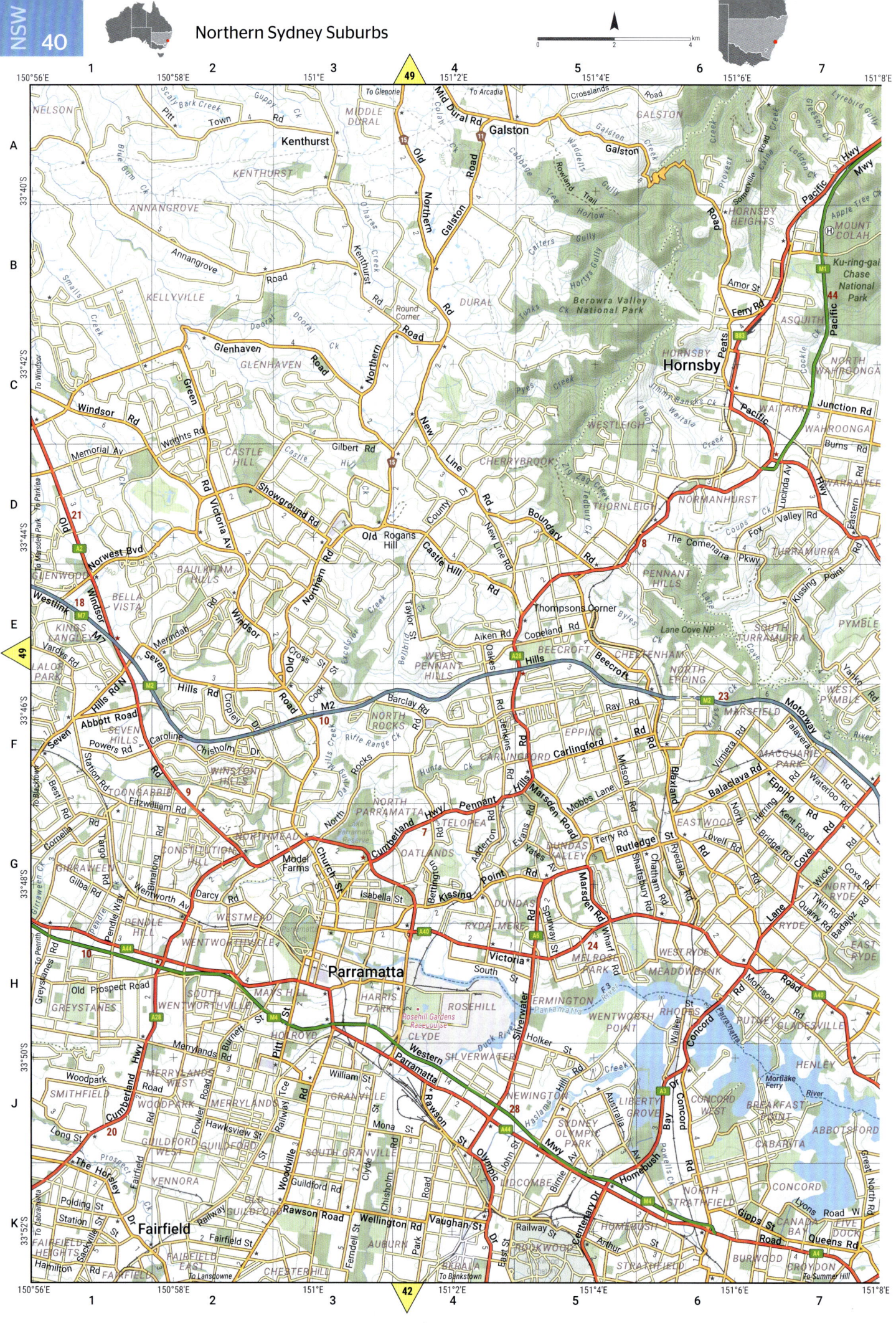

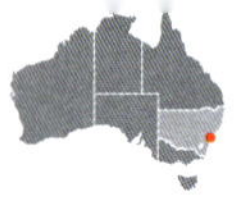

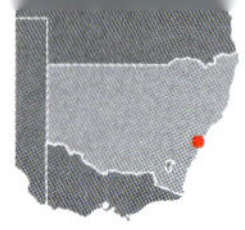

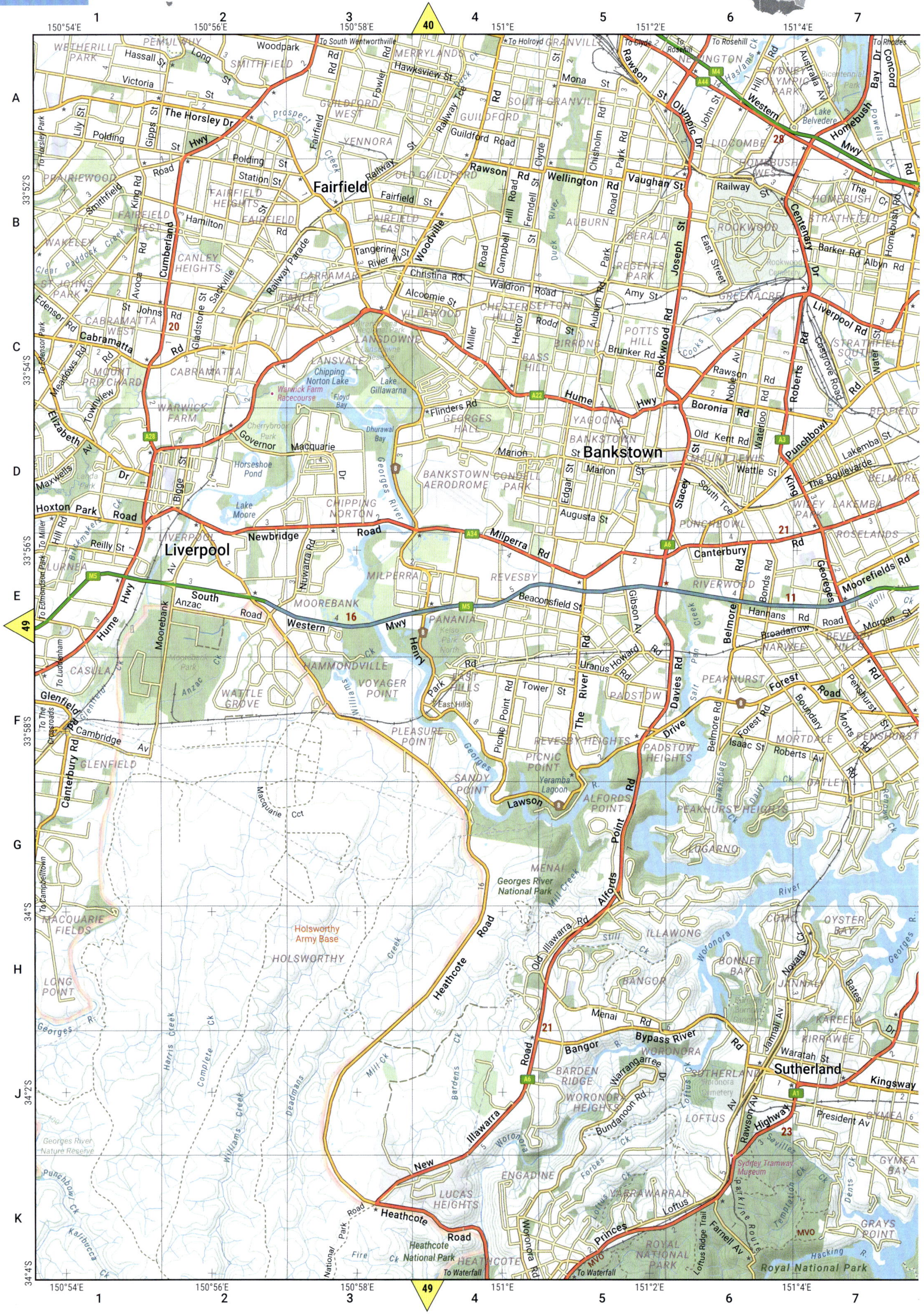

40
49
49
150°54'E
150°56'E
150°58'E
151°E
151°2'E
151°4'E
33°52'S
33°54'S
33°56'S
33°58'S
34°S
34°2'S
34°4'S
Fairfield
Bankstown
Liverpool
Sutherland
SMITHFIELD
MERRYLANDS
GRANVILLE
SOUTH GRANVILLE
GUILDFORD
GUILDFORD WEST
YENNORA
OLD GUILDFORD
FAIRFIELD HEIGHTS
FAIRFIELD WEST
FAIRFIELD EAST
CANLEY HEIGHTS
CANLEY VALE
CARRAMAR
VILLAWOOD
CHESTER HILL
SEFTON
BIRRONG
POTTS HILL
REGENTS PARK
AUBURN
BERALA
LIDCOMBE
ROCKWOOD
GREENACRE
HOMEBUSH
HOMEBUSH WEST
STRATHFIELD
STRATHFIELD SOUTH
SYDNEY OLYMPIC PARK
NEWINGTON
WETHERILL PARK
PRAIRIEWOOD
WAKELEY
ST JOHNS PARK
CABRAMATTA
CABRAMATTA WEST
MOUNT PRITCHARD
WARWICK FARM
LANSDOWNE
LANSVALE
GEORGES HALL
BASS HILL
YAGOONA
CONDELL PARK
BANKSTOWN AERODROME
CHIPPING NORTON
MILPERRA
REVESBY
PANANIA
EAST HILLS
PADSTOW
PADSTOW HEIGHTS
REVESBY HEIGHTS
PICNIC POINT
PUNCHBOWL
MOUNT LEWIS
WILEY PARK
LAKEMBA
BELMORE
BELFIELD
ROSELANDS
RIVERWOOD
NARWEE
BEVERLY HILLS
PEAKHURST
PEAKHURST HEIGHTS
MORTDALE
PENSHURST
OATLEY
LUGARNO
MOOREBANK
HAMMONDVILLE
VOYAGER POINT
PLEASURE POINT
SANDY POINT
ALFORDS POINT
WATTLE GROVE
CASULA
LURNEA
GLENFIELD
MACQUARIE FIELDS
LONG POINT
HOLSWORTHY
Holsworthy Army Base
MENAI
Georges River National Park
ILLAWONG
BANGOR
BONNET BAY
COMO
OYSTER BAY
JANNALI
KAREELA
KIRRAWEE
BARDEN RIDGE
WORONORA
WORONORA HEIGHTS
LOFTUS
ENGADINE
YARRAWARRAH
LUCAS HEIGHTS
HEATHCOTE
GYMEA
GYMEA BAY
GRAYS POINT
ROYAL NATIONAL PARK
Royal National Park
Sydney Tramway Museum
Georges River Nature Reserve
Warwick Farm Racecourse
Chipping Norton Lake
Lake Gillawarna
Lake Moore
Horseshoe Pond
Georges River
Hume Hwy
Western Mwy
Heathcote Road
Illawarra Road
New Illawarra Rd
Princes Hwy
Alfords Point Rd
Henry Lawson Dr
Milperra Rd
Canterbury Rd
Forest Road
King Georges Rd
Homebush Bay Dr
To Waterfall
To Holroyd
To Rosehill
To Rhodes

© Hema Maps

Bells Line Of Road to Wentworth Falls

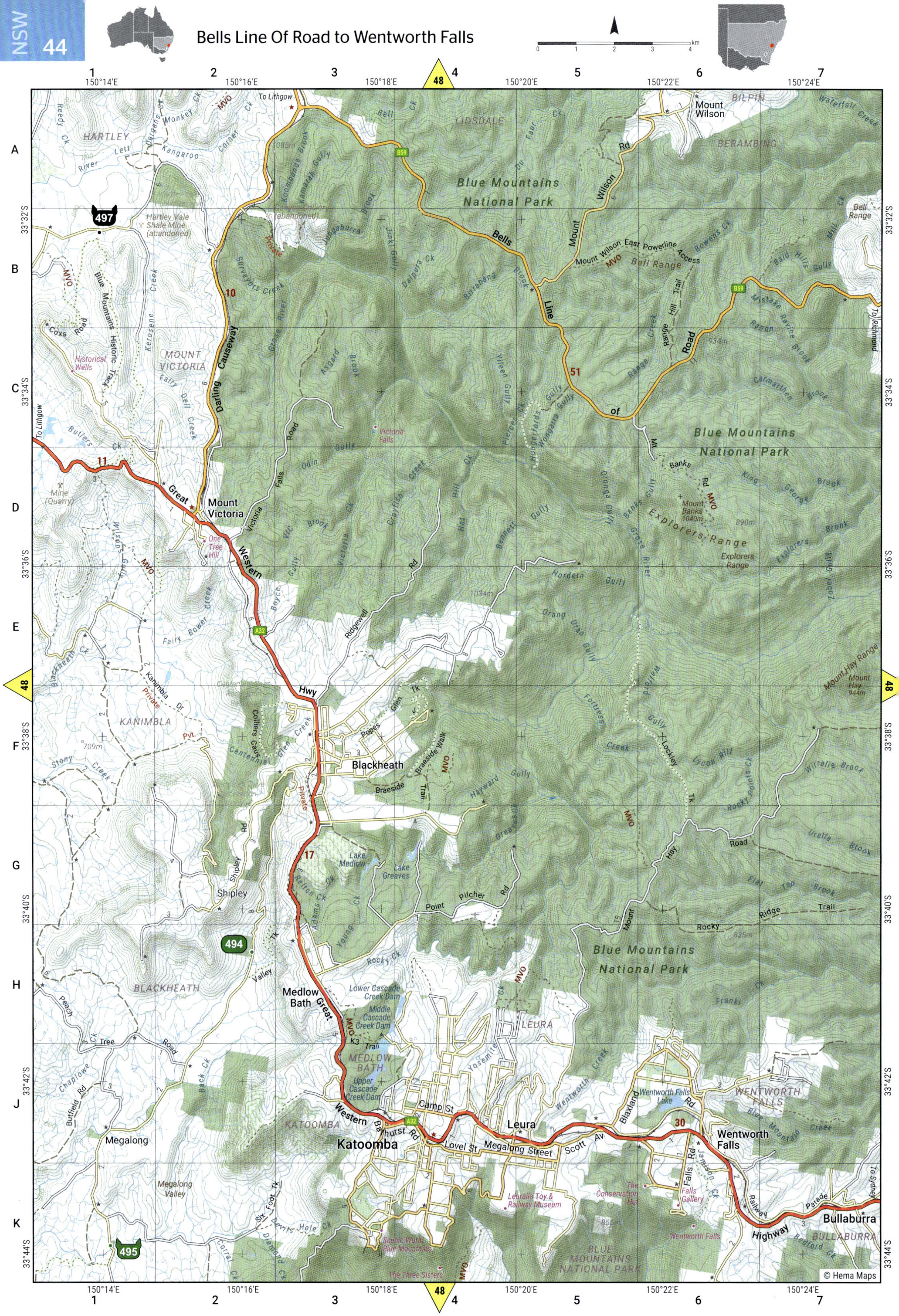

Putty Road to Newcastle

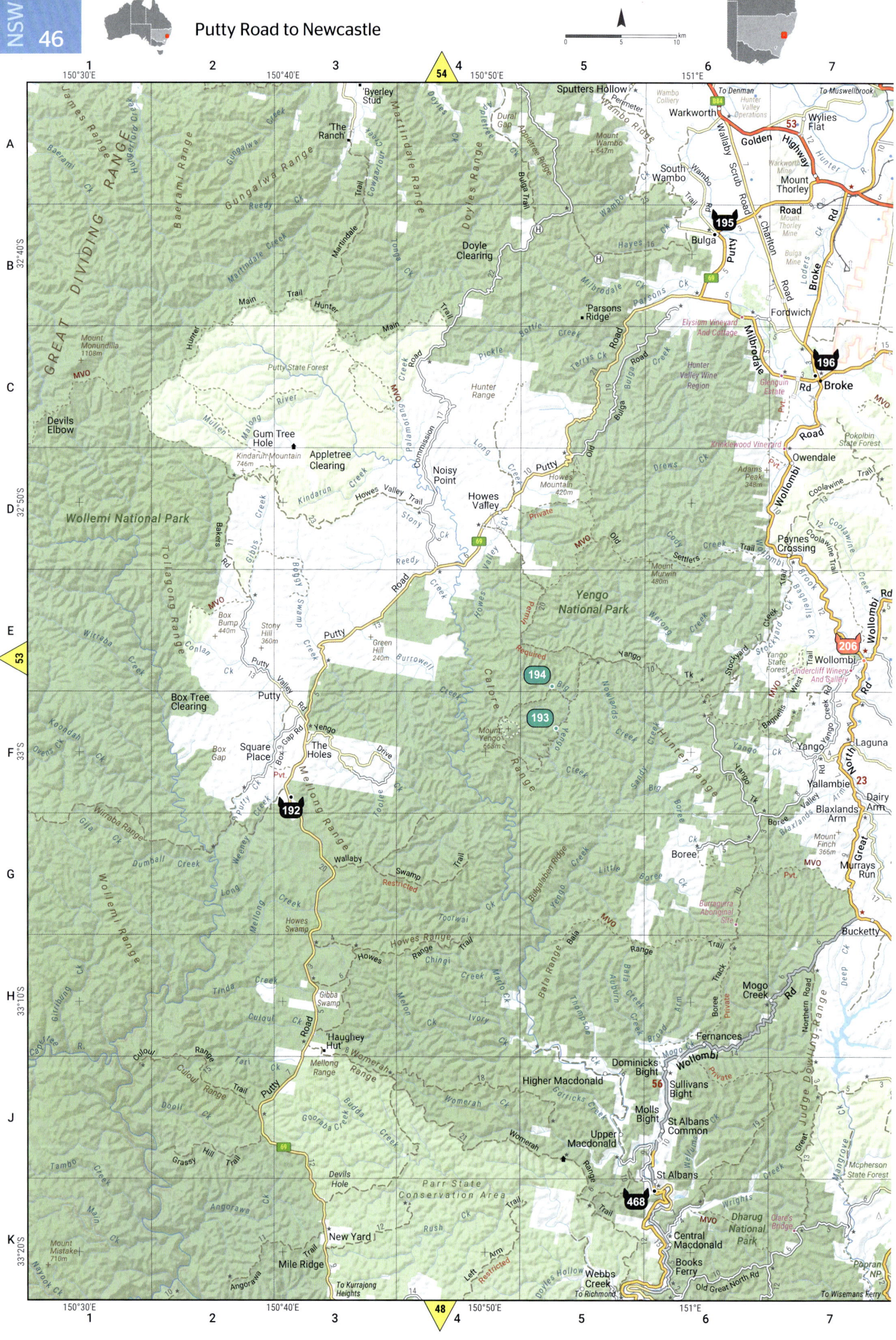

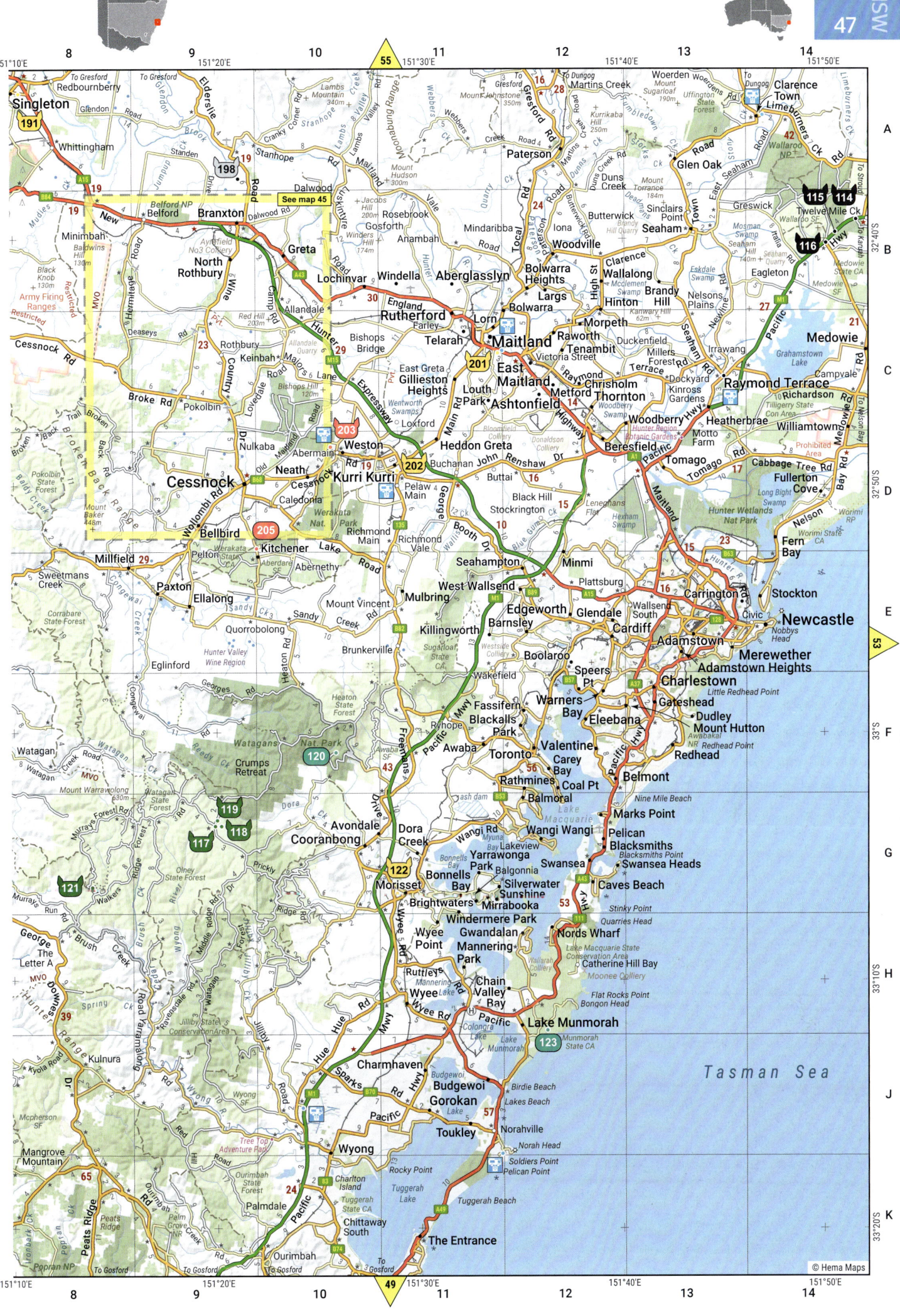

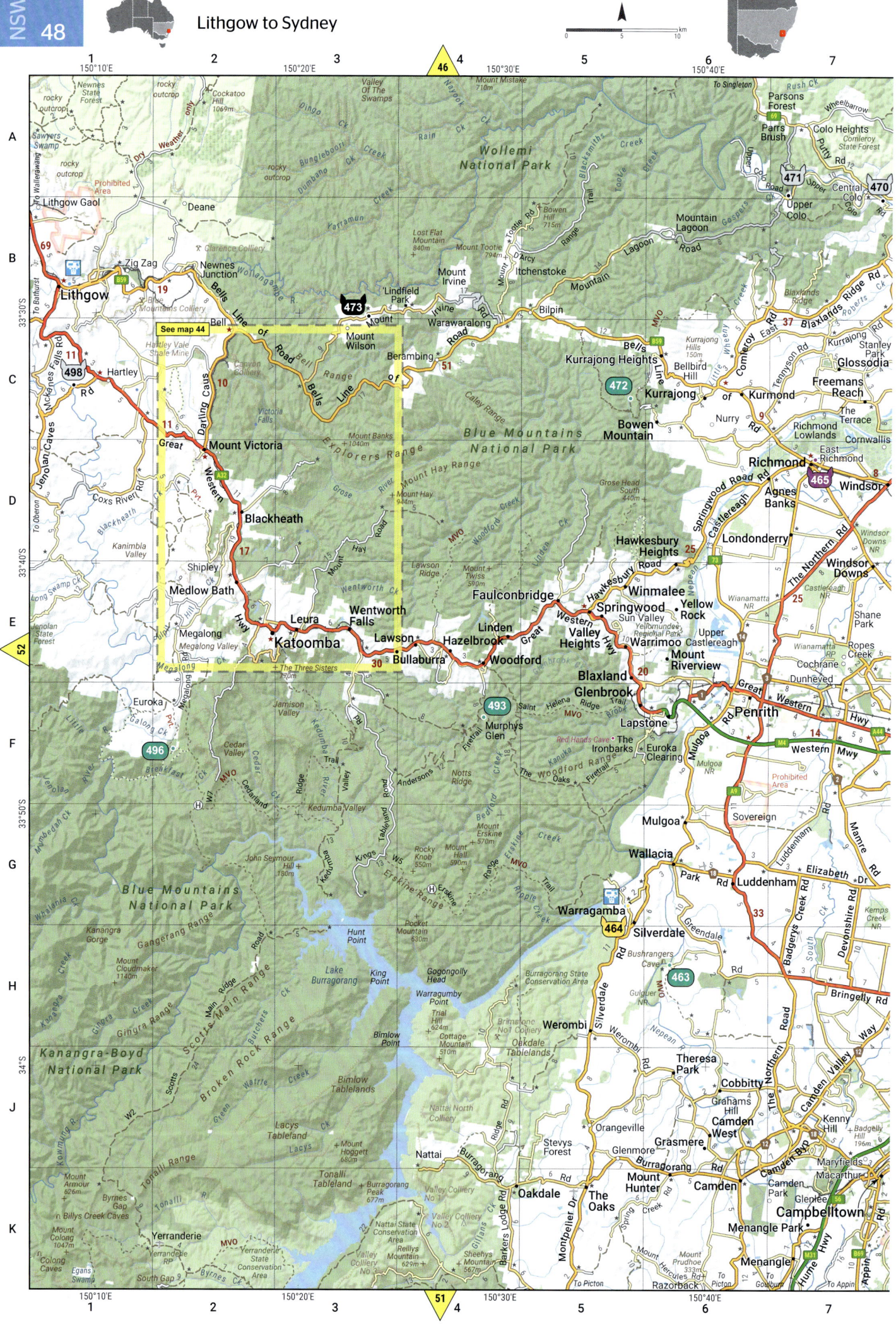

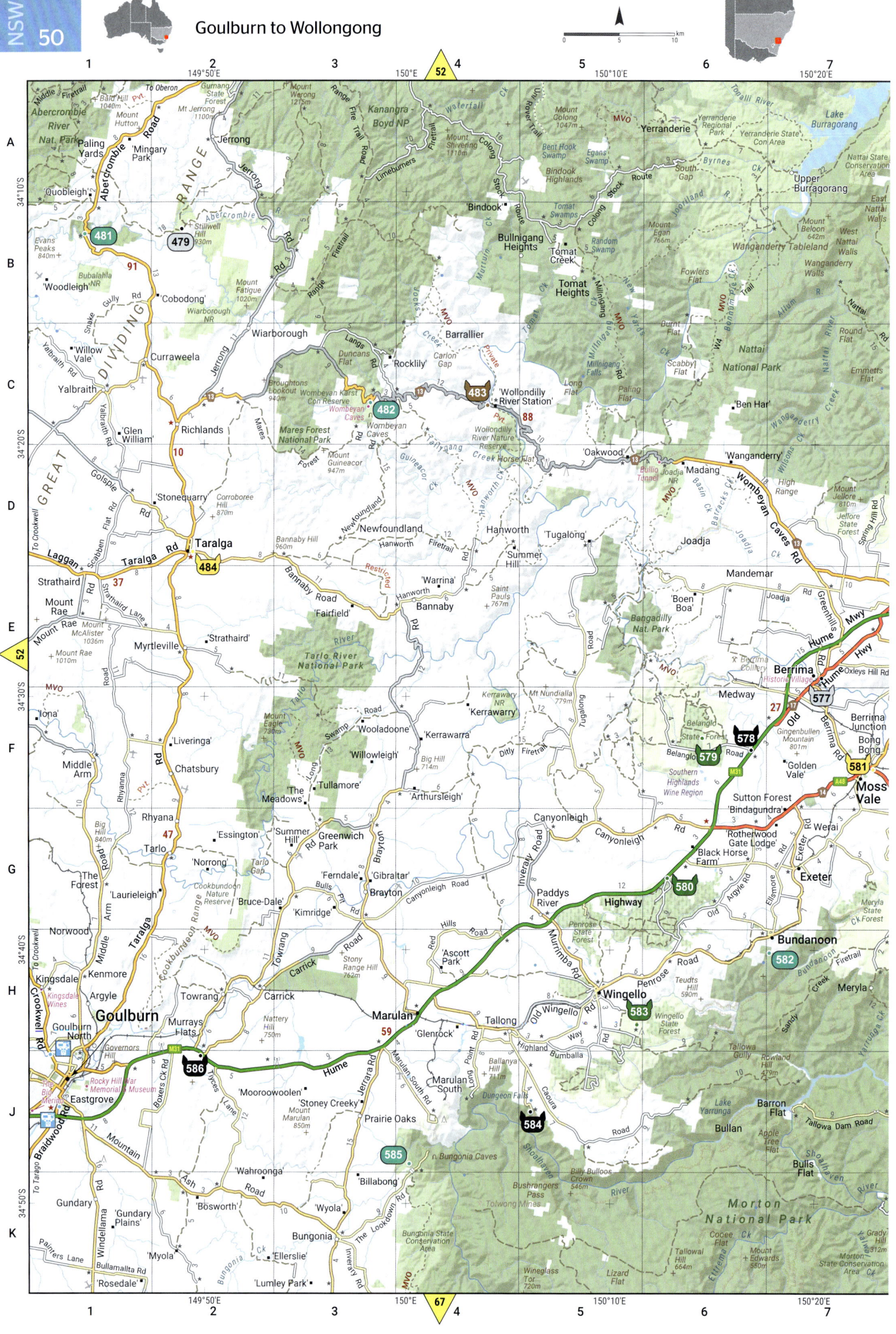

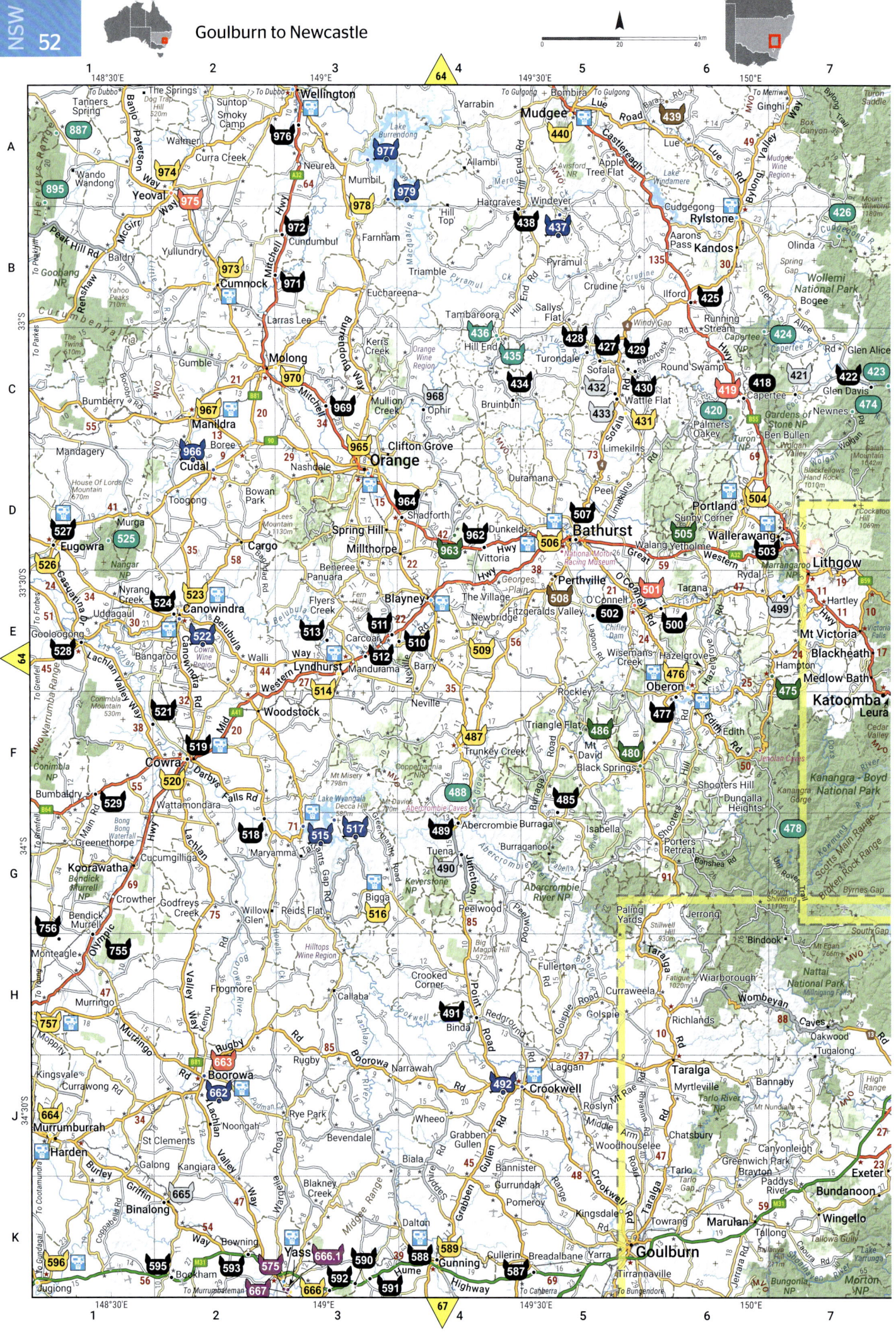

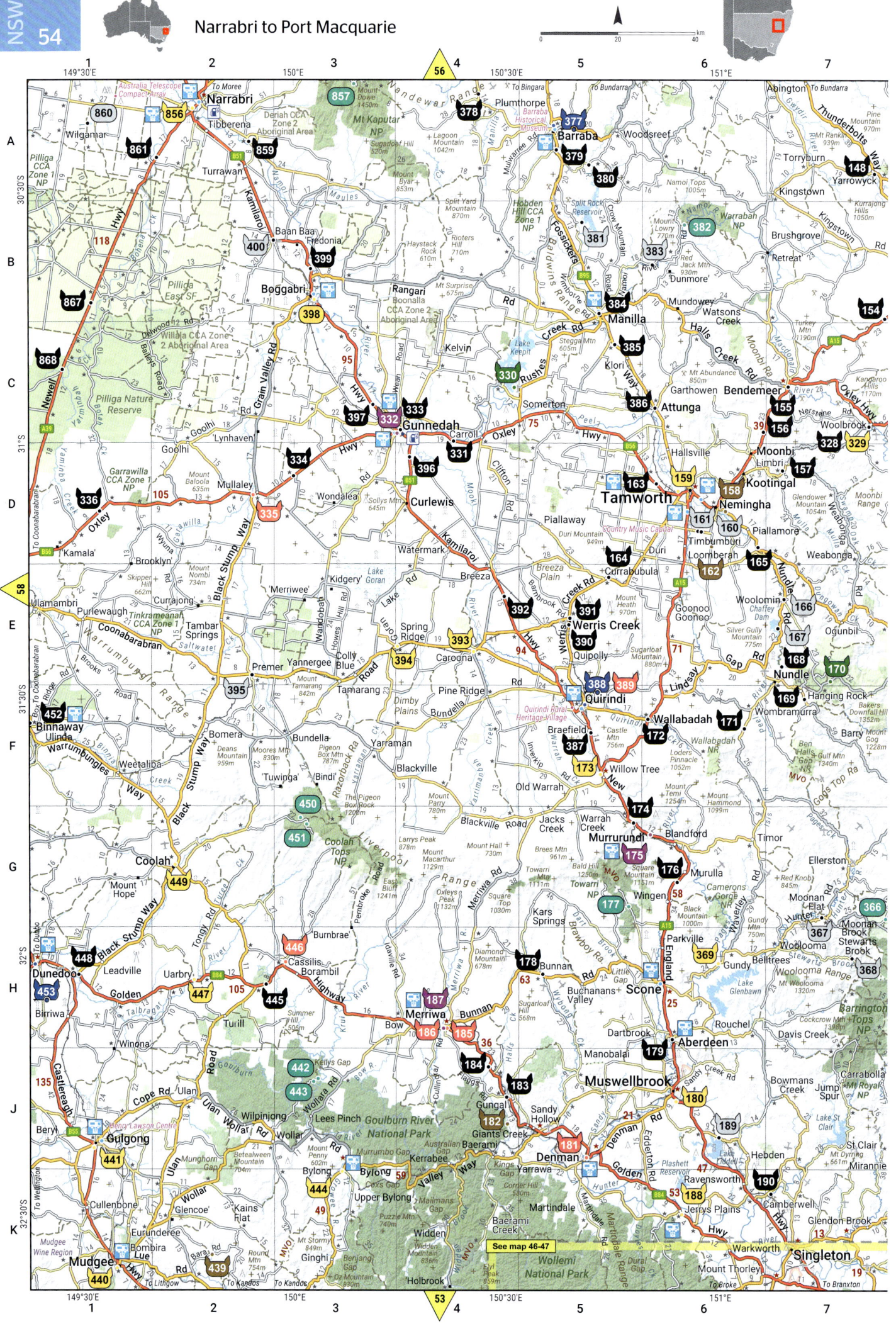

© Hema Maps

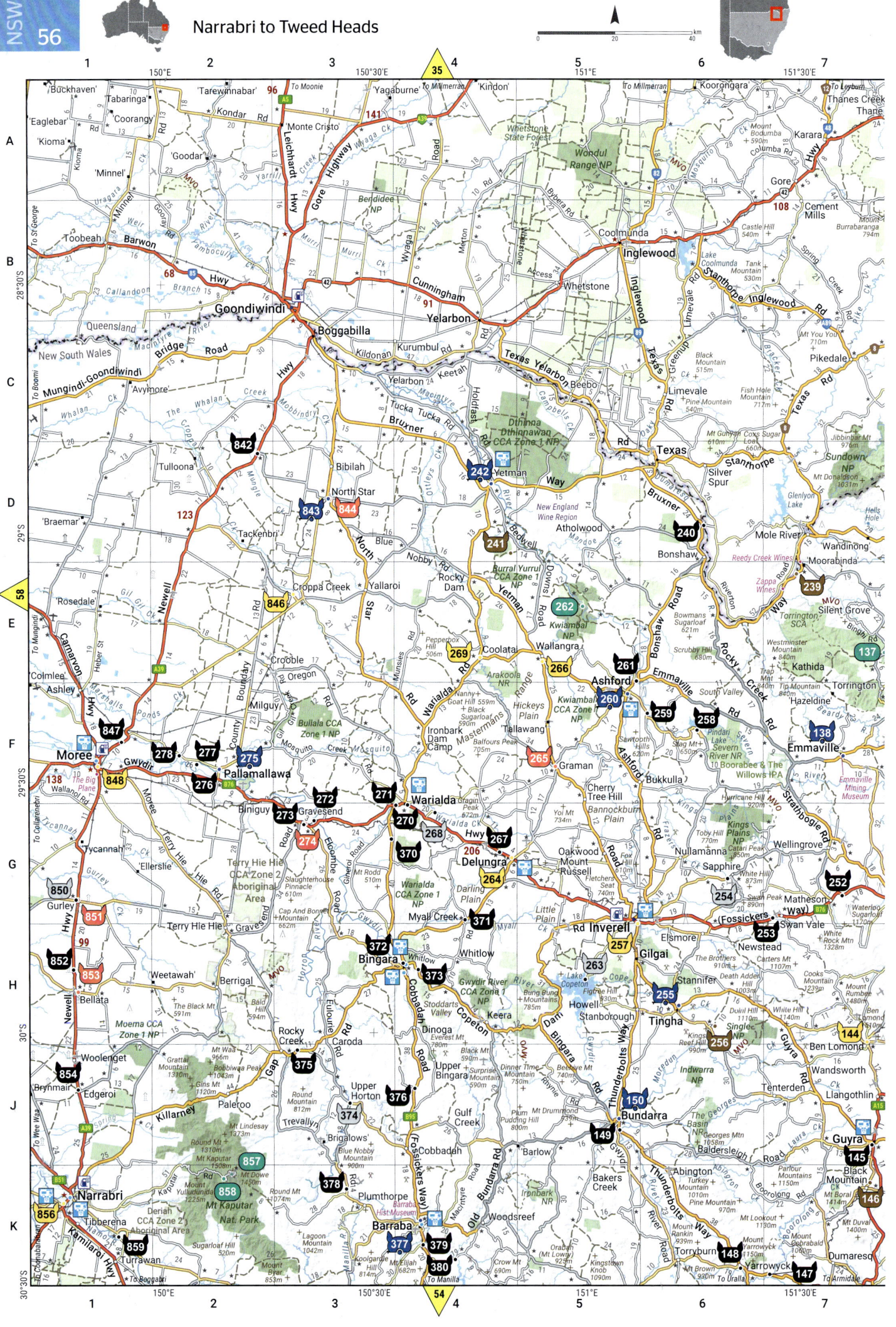

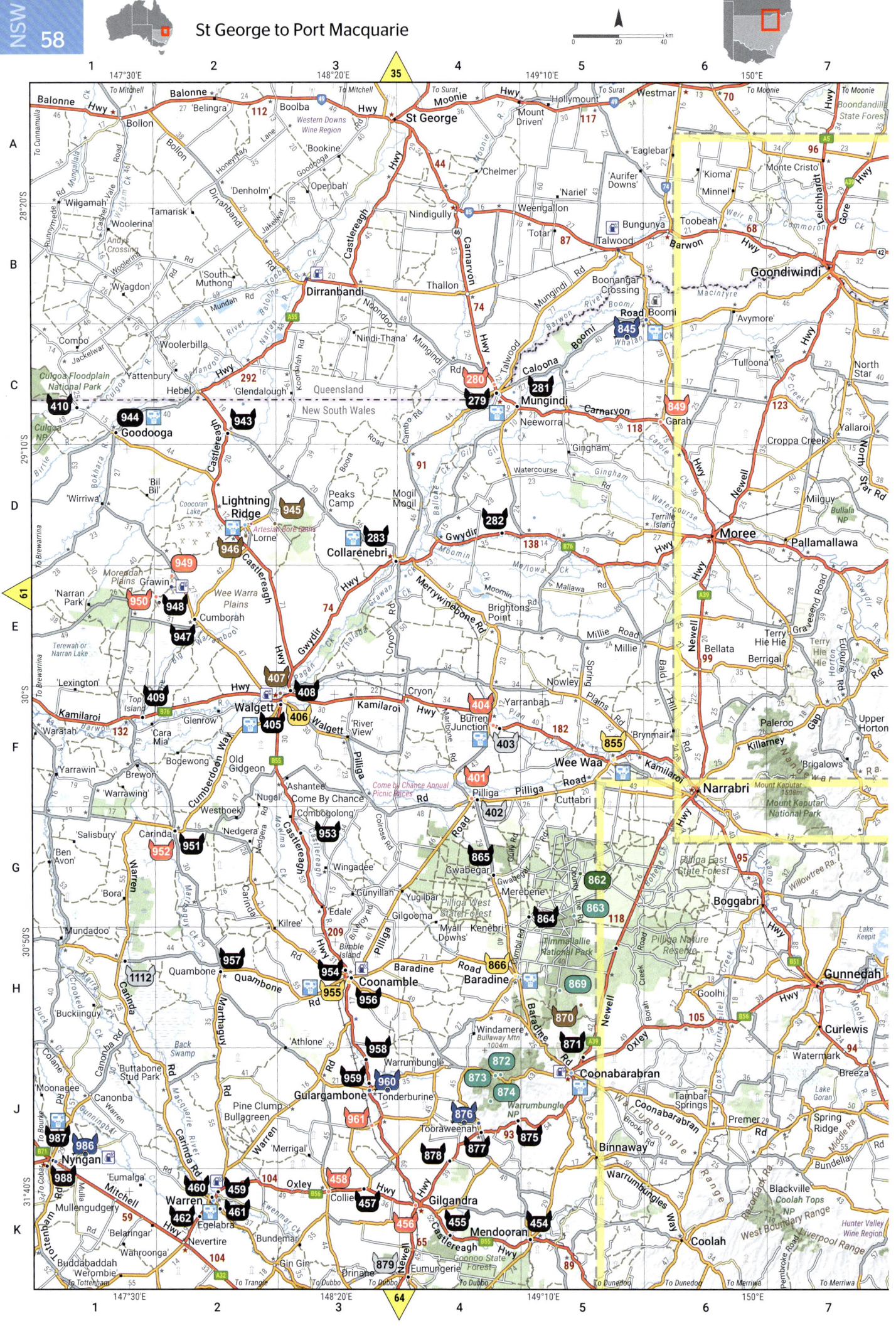

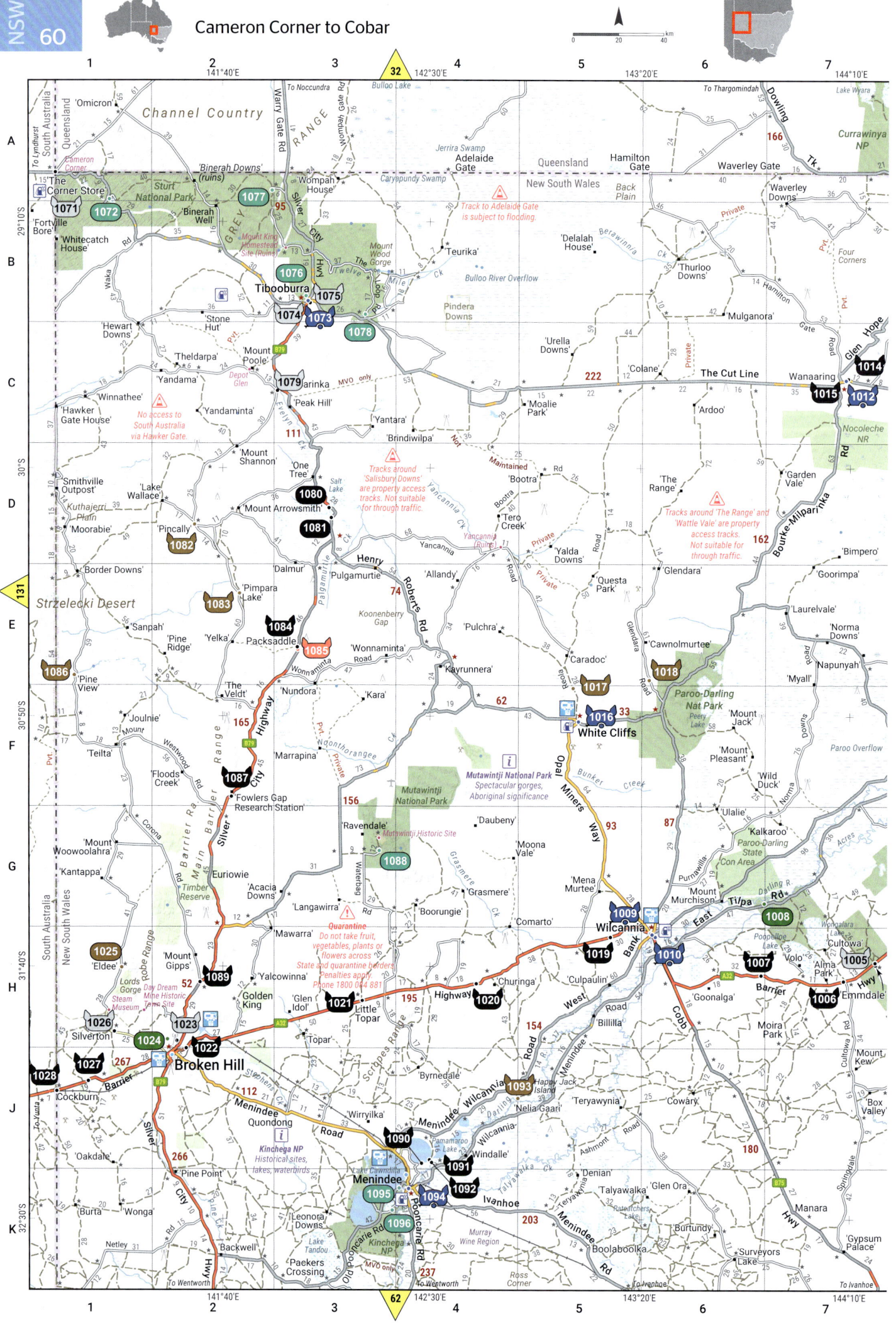

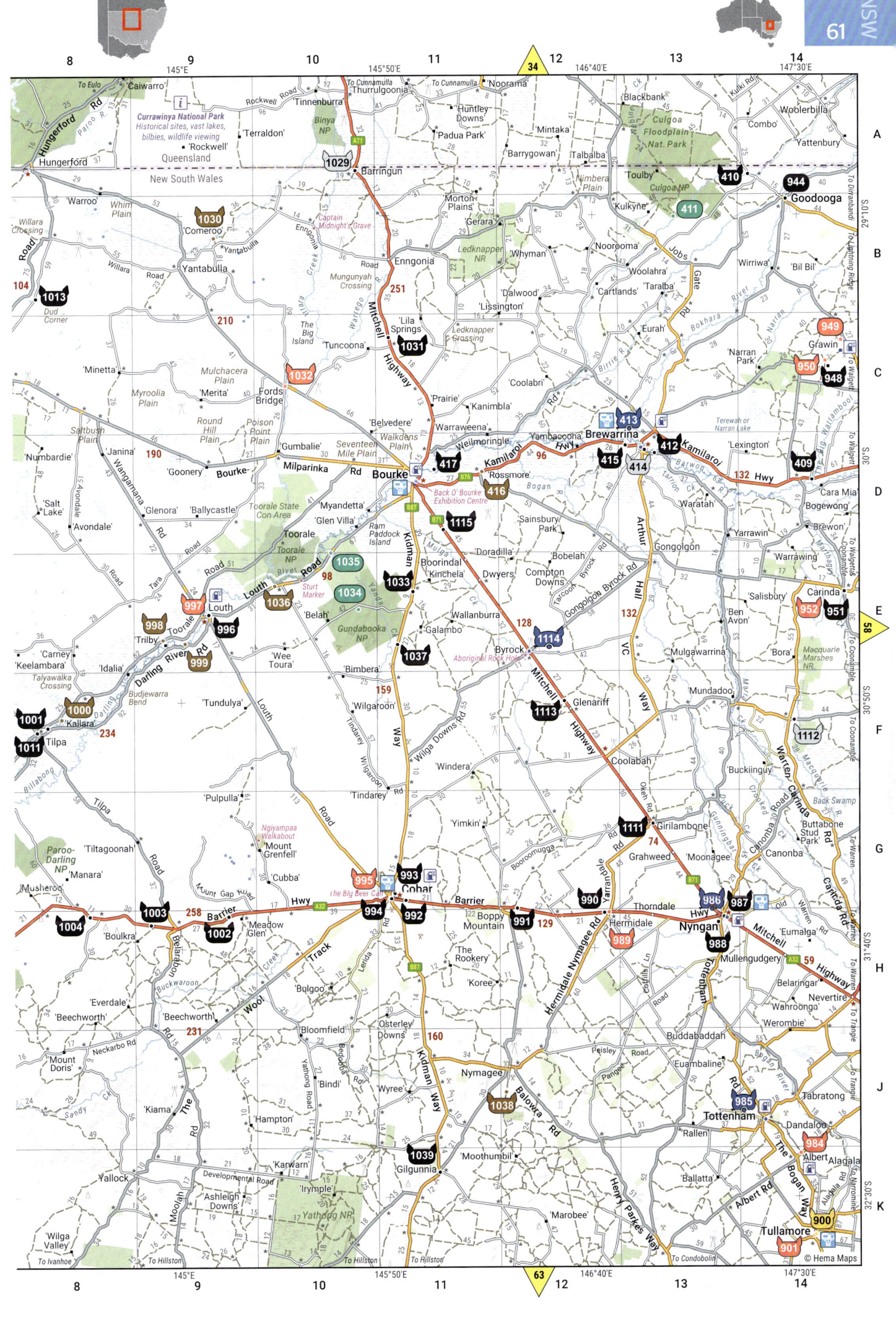

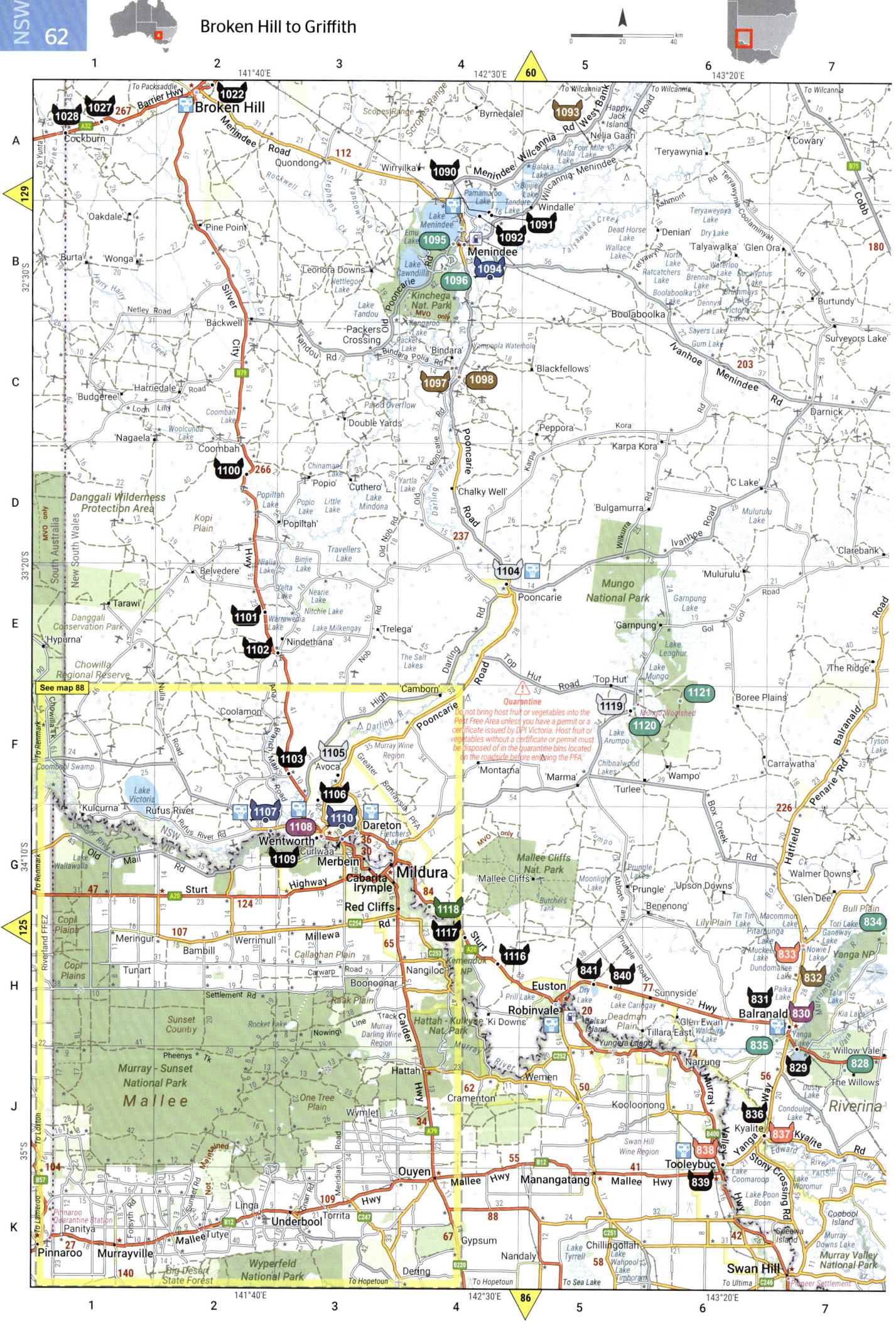

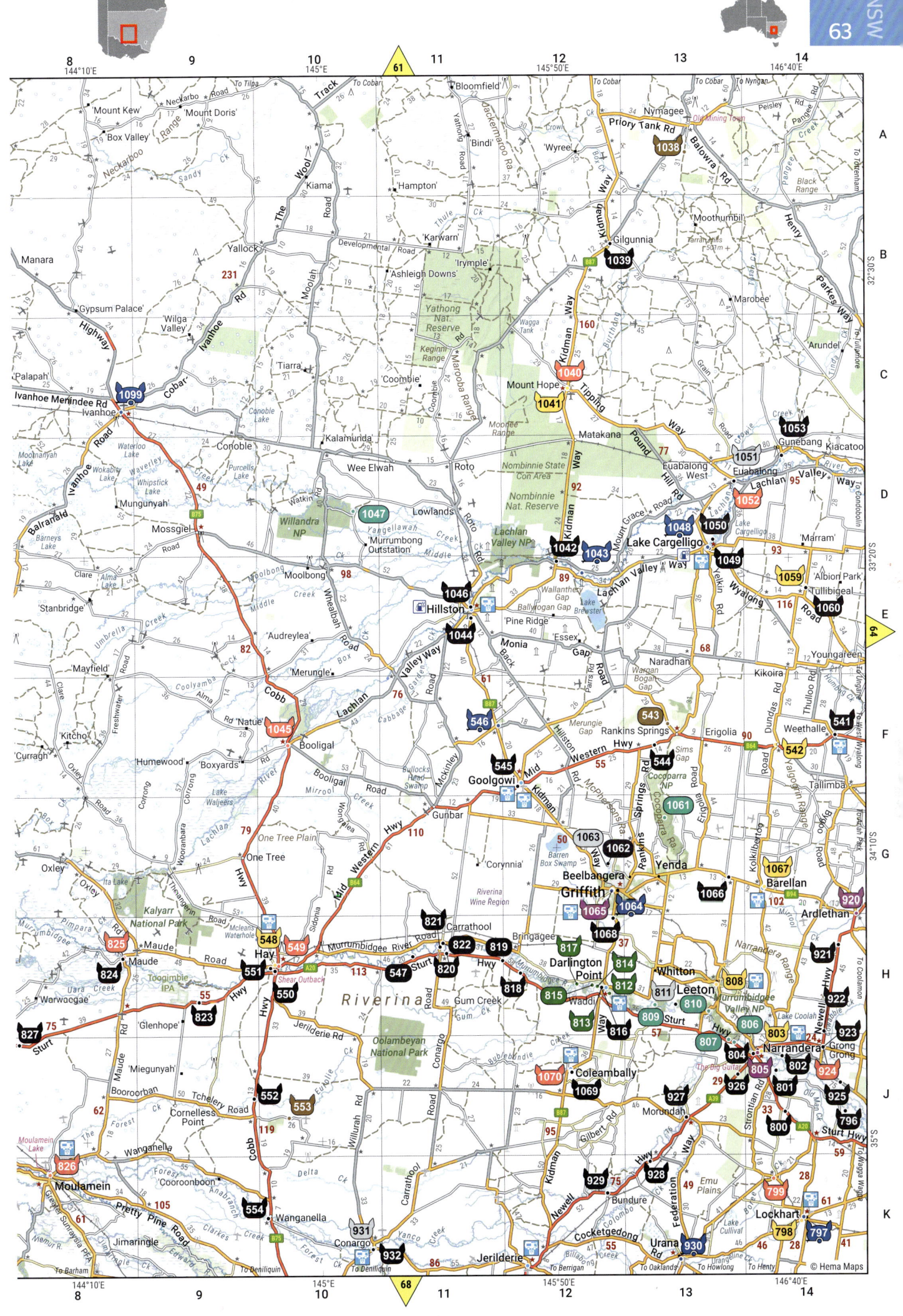

© Hema Maps

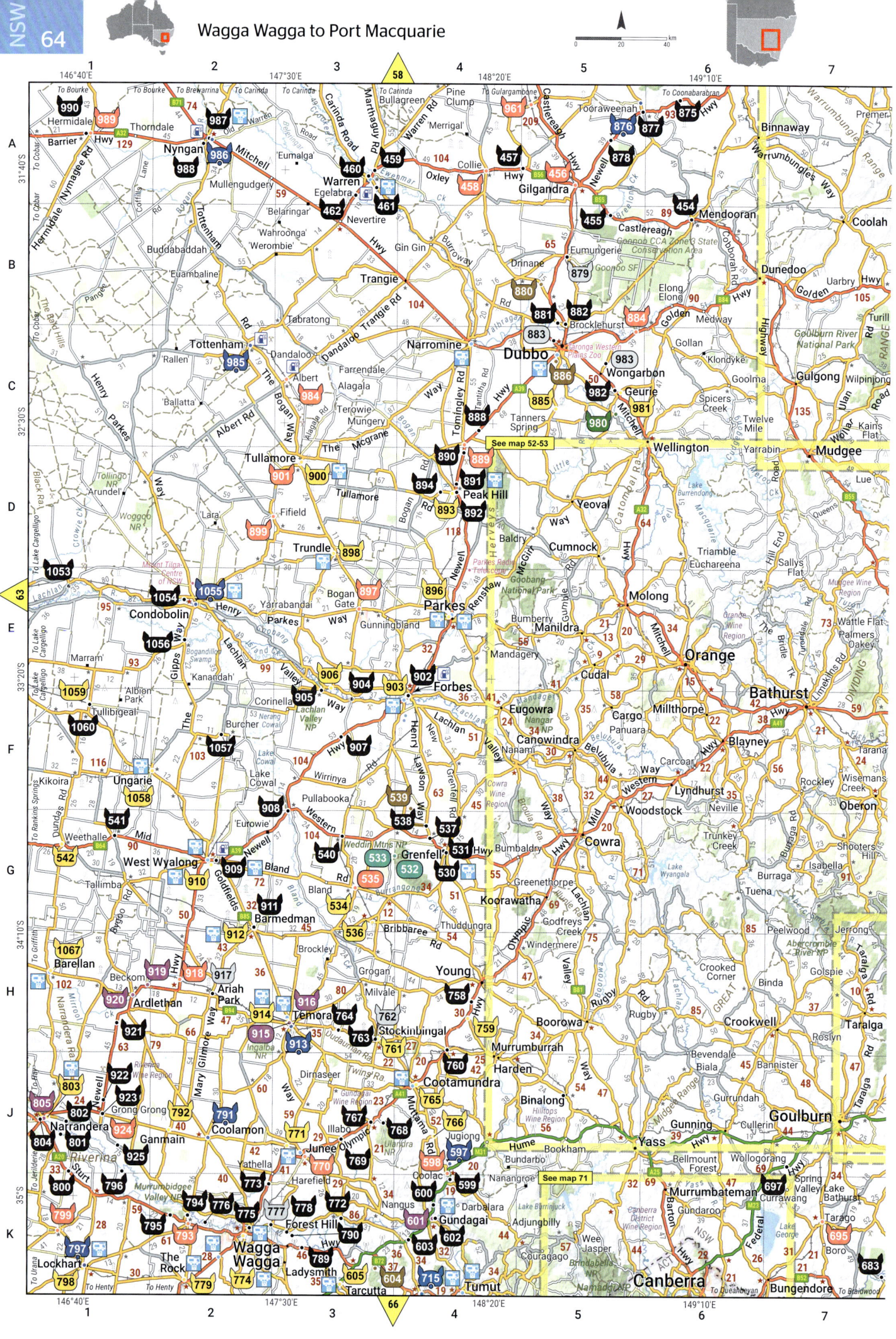

© Hema Maps

Wagga Wagga to Merimbula

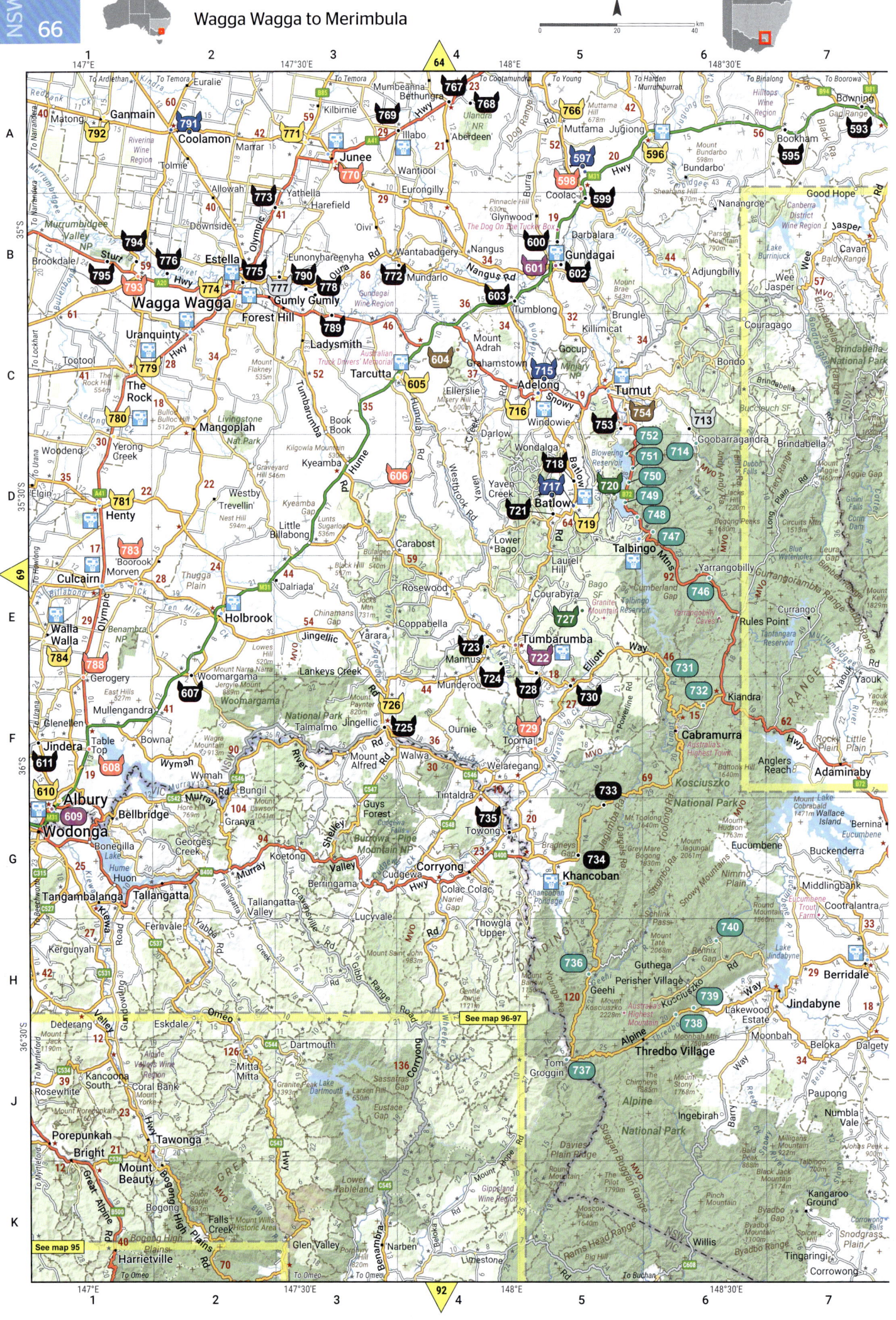

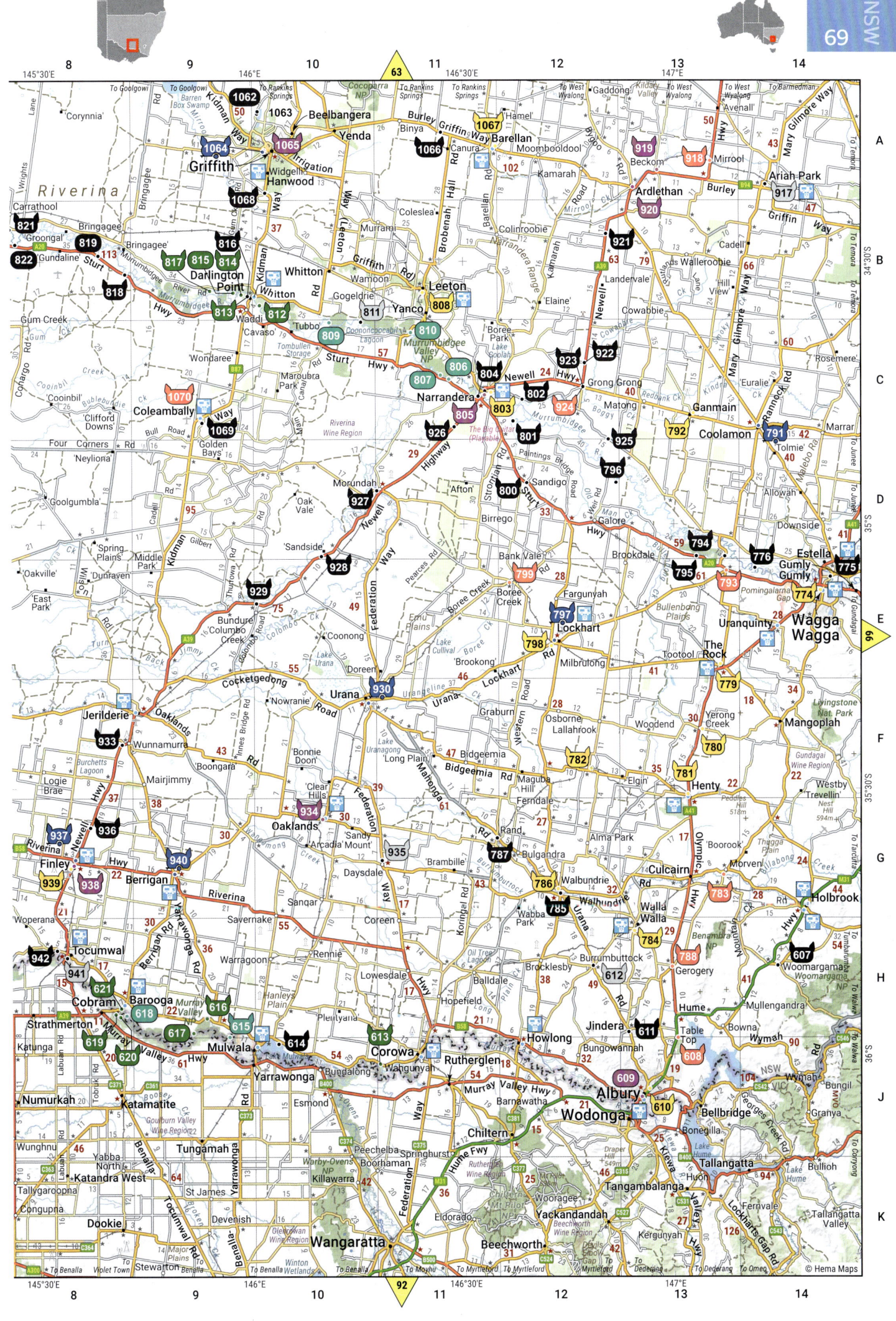

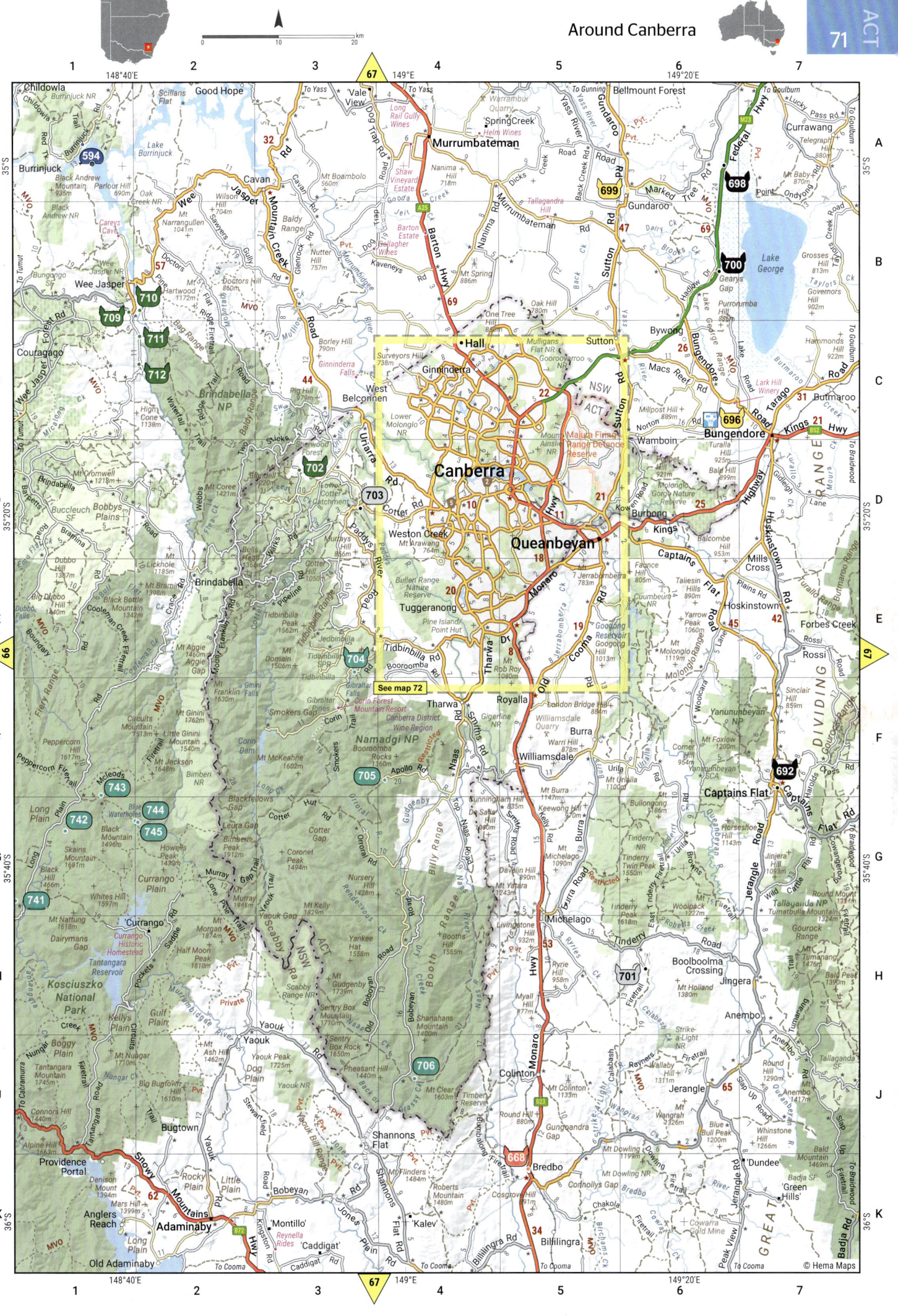

Canberra Throughroads

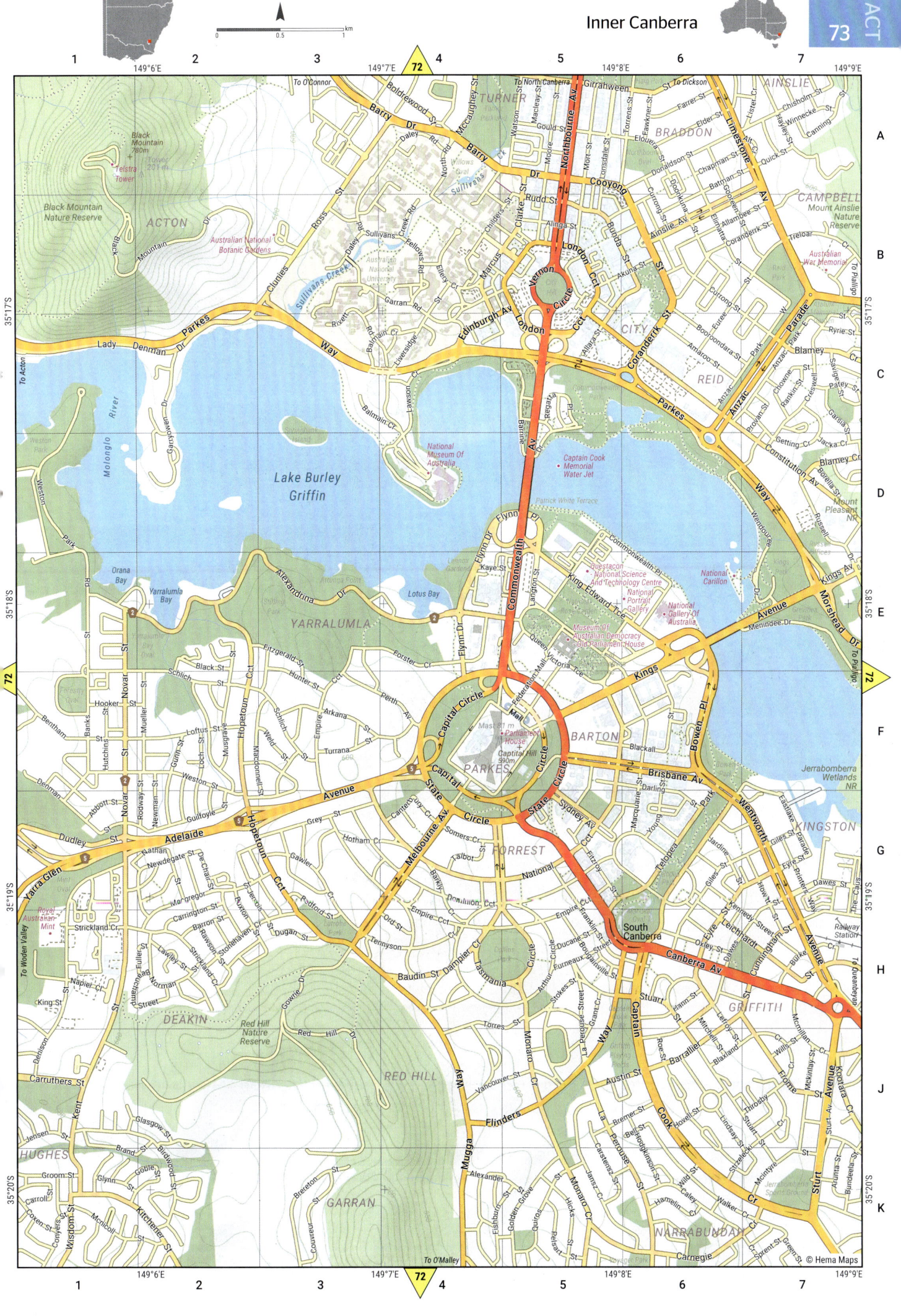

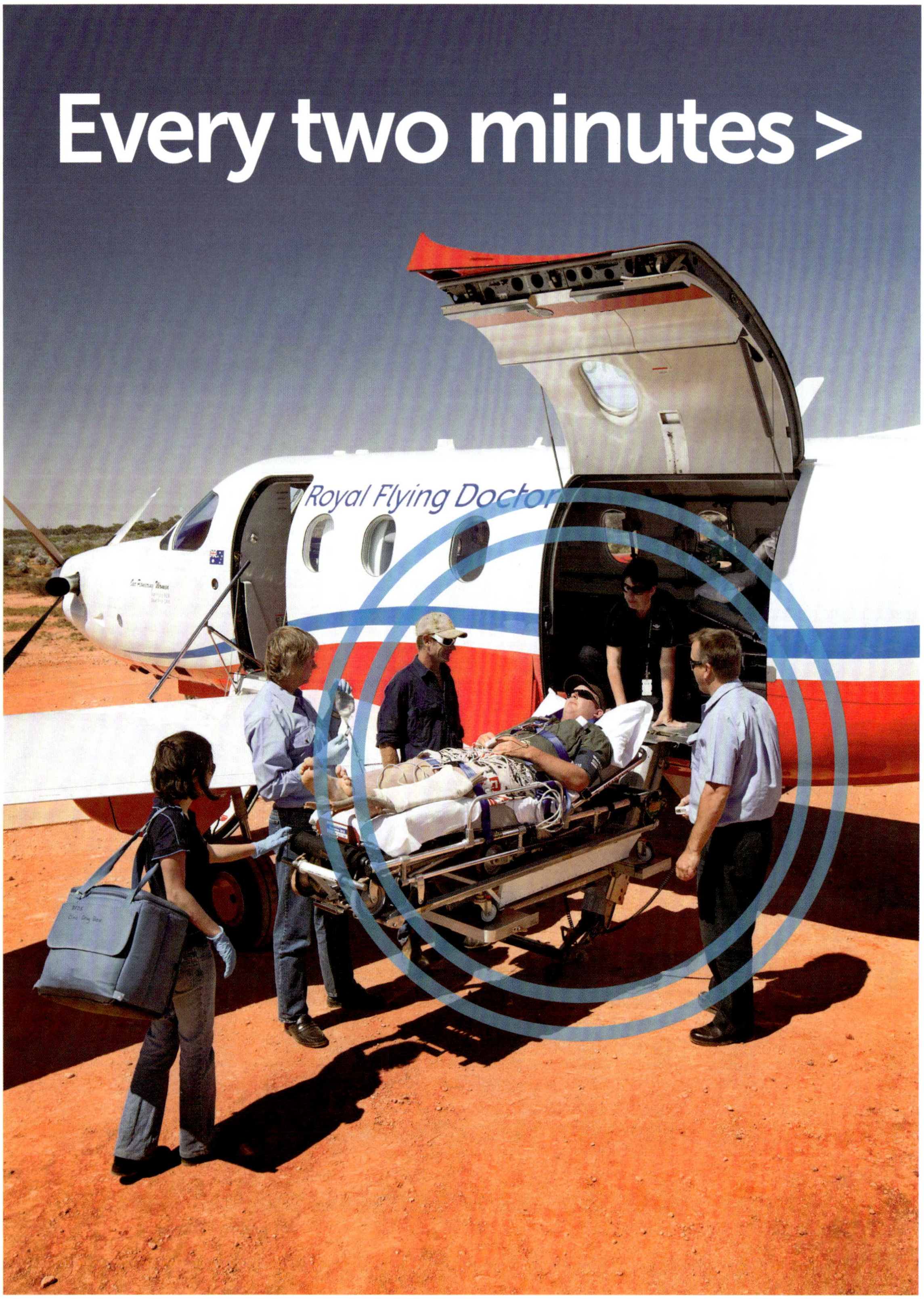

Every two minutes >

The Royal Flying Doctor Service (RFDS) delivers 24-hour emergency aeromedical and primary health care services to more than 290,000 Australians every year – that's one person every two minutes.

The RFDS relies on donations from the community to purchase and medically-equip its aircraft – at a cost of more than $6 million each – and to finance other major health initiatives.

Make a donation today and help keep the Flying Doctor flying.

1300 669 569

www.flyingdoctor.org.au

Ganmain Showgrounds, New South Wales

New South Wales

Gold Coast to Sydney
Pacific Highway

1 Tyalgum Diggers Camp

Carraboi Tce, Tyalgum
Camp Area 100 m N of town. Caretaker
collects fees. 7 day limit. Firewood for sale
0490 780 181　HEMA 57 B13　28 21 11 S　153 12 20 E

2 Murwillumbah Showground
Mooball St, Murwillumbah
Camp Area N side of town, entry via
Queensland Rd. 7 day limit. Limited sites. Pre-book
0423 327 234　HEMA 57 A13　28 19 24 S　153 23 36 E

3 Hosanna Farmstay
4 Tunnel Rd, Stokers Siding
Farm Stay 11 km S of Murwillumbah on the
Tweed Valley Way
02 6677 9023　HEMA 57 B13　28 24 02 S　153 24 33 E

4 Misty Ridge
3 Hazelbrook Rd, Smiths Creek
Farm Stay 4 km E of Uki. Via Smiths Creek
Rd, opposite mill. Fees for shower, power and
laundry, available at the house. Pre-book
0400 338 031　HEMA 57 B13　28 25 11 S　153 22 08 E

5 Cutters Camp Campground
Mebbin National Park
Mebbin Forest Rd, Mebbin
Camp Area 13 km S of Tyalgum, via Byrrill Creek
Rd. 11 km dirt road. Alternative access from Kyogle
& Cadell Rds. Small vehicles only
1300 072 757　HEMA 57 B13　28 26 40 S　153 11 41 E

6 Sleepy Hollow Southbound
Pacific Hwy, Sleepy Hollow
Rest Area 22 km S of Chinderah or 63 km
N of Ballina. Check signs
132 213　HEMA 57 B14　28 24 50 S　153 31 31 E

7 Sleepy Hollow Northbound
Pacific Hwy, Sleepy Hollow
Rest Area 24 km S of Chinderah or 61 km
N of Ballina. Check signs
132 213　HEMA 57 B14　28 25 25 S　153 31 14 E

8 Billinudgel Hotel
1 Wilfred St, Billinudgel
Parking Area behind pub. Limited space,
check in with publican before 5pm. Fee for shower
02 6680 1148　HEMA 57 B14　28 30 14 S　153 31 35 E

9 Macas Camping Ground
1156 Main Arm Rd, Upper Main Arm
Camp Area 3 km W of Main Arm. Limited
power available for fee. Pre-book
02 6684 5211　HEMA 57 B13　28 29 49 S　153 24 39 E

10 Mullumbimby Leagues Club
25 Manns Rd, Mullumbimby
Camp Area next to Leagues Club. 2 km NE
of PO. Riverside. Pre-book
0405 198 866　HEMA 57 B14　28 33 01 S　153 30 54 E

11 Mullumbimby Showground
Main Arm Rd, Mullumbimby
Camp Area 2 km W of PO. 28 day limit
0474 100 189　HEMA 57 B14　28 32 48 S　153 29 20 E

12 Tyagarah Rest Area
Pacific Mwy, Tyagarah
Rest Area 8 km S of Brunswick Heads or
40 km N of Ballina. Check signs
132 213　HEMA 57 C14　28 35 54 S　153 32 41 E

13 Alstonville Showground
South St, Alstonville
Camp Area on Cnr Commercial Rd. Contact
caretaker. 7 day limit
0427 771 512　HEMA 57 D14　28 50 23 S　153 26 26 E

14 Wardell Rest Area
Pacific Hwy, Wardell
Rest Area 14 km S of Ballina or 3 km N of
Wardell, S & N bound. Check signs
132 213　HEMA 57 D14　28 56 07 S　153 28 19 E

15 Richmond River Camping
Oakland Rd, East Coraki
Camp Area 10 km NW of Pacific Hwy at
Woodburn. 5 night limit. Pre-book
0407 815 170　HEMA 57 D13　29 02 28 S　153 17 16 E

16 Black Rocks Campground
Bundjalung National Park
Black Rocks Trail, Esk
Camp Area 24 km SE of Woodburn. Turn E off
Pacific Hwy 3.6 km from Woodburn to Gap Rd.
16 km dirt road
1300 072 757　HEMA 57 E13　29 15 02 S　153 21 59 E

17 New Italy Rest Area
8275 Pacific Hwy, New Italy
Rest Area 12 km S of Woodburn or 38 km
N of Maclean. Near museum. Cafe open 8am-5pm
02 6682 2622　HEMA 57 E13　29 09 13 S　153 17 55 E

18 Bundjalung Rest Area
Jacky Bulbin Flat, Jacky Bulbin Flat
Rest Area 13 km S of New Italy or 27 km
N of McLean. N bound only. Check signs
132 213　HEMA 57 E13　29 15 39 S　153 13 53 E

19 Beekeepers Rest Area
Pacific Hwy, Jacky Bulbin Flat
Rest Area 17 km S of New Italy or 23 km N
of Maclean. Check signs
132 213　HEMA 57 E13　29 16 56 S　153 12 56 E

20 Woody Head Campground
Bundjalung National Park
Woody Head Rd, Woody Head
Camp Area 4 km N of Iluka. Turn E off Pacific Hwy
to Iluka Rd, follow 13 km over Esk River, then
signposted
1300 072 757　HEMA 57 F13　29 21 59 S　153 22 16 E

21 Maclean Showground

12 Cameron St, Maclean
A1 Camp Area 46 km NE of Grafton. Fees collected. Limited sites, no bookings. Fire with permission
0487 101 151 HEMA 57 F13 29 27 50 S 153 11 58 E

22 Red Cliff Campground

Yuraygir National Park
A1 Red Cliff Rd, Yuraygir
Camp Area 5 km N of Brooms Head or 19 km SE of Maclean. Turn E off Pacific Hwy to Brooms Head Rd. Continue 18 km. Signposted. N & S camp areas
02 6641 1500 HEMA 57 G13 29 34 35 S 153 20 06 E

23 Lake Arragan

Yuraygir National Park
A1 Lake Arragan Rd, Brooms Head
Camp Area 5 km N of Brooms Head or 19 km SE of Maclean. Turn E off Pacific Hwy to Brooms Head Rd. Continue 18 km. Signposted. 2 km dirt road
02 6641 1500 HEMA 57 G13 29 34 00 S 153 20 10 E

24 Sandon River Campground

Yuraygir National Park
A1 Sandon River Rd, Brooms Head
Camp Area 10 km S of Brooms Head. Turn W to Brooms Head Rd 21 km SE of Maclean then to Sandon River Rd. 9 km dirt road. Not suitable for large vehicles
02 6641 1500 HEMA 57 G13 29 40 27 S 153 19 37 E

25 The Lawrence Tavern

19 Bridge St, Lawrence
A1 Parking Area behind tavern, check in with publican. Limited power
02 6647 7213 HEMA 57 F12 29 30 09 S 153 05 59 E

26 Grafton Greyhound Racing
Club Campground

B91 70 Cranworth St, Grafton
Camp Area W side of town
02 6642 3713 HEMA 57 G12 29 40 27 S 152 55 32 E

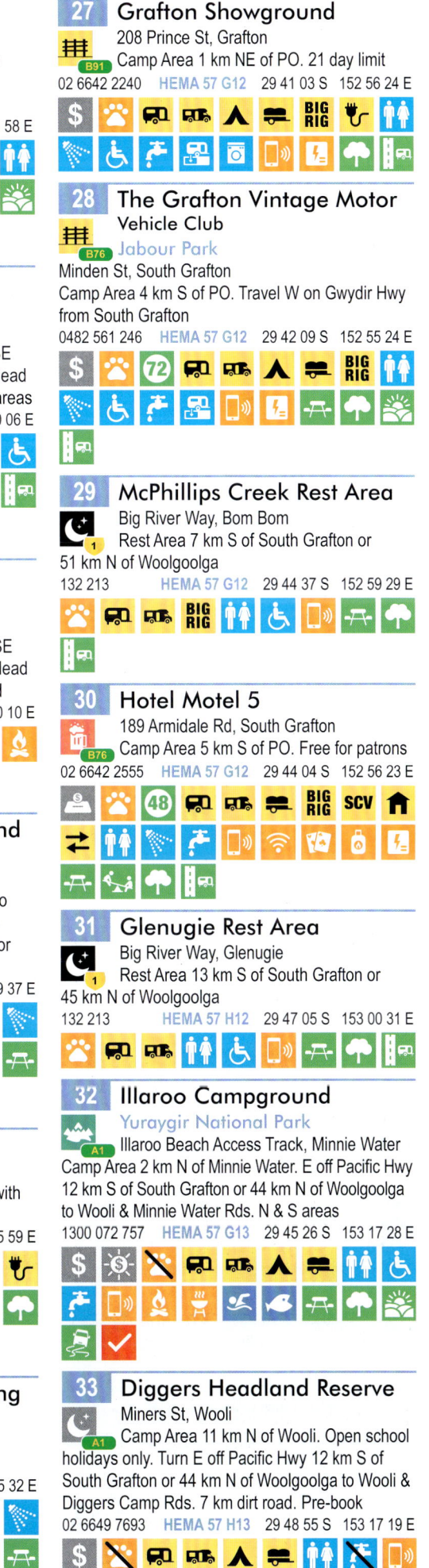

27 Grafton Showground

208 Prince St, Grafton
B91 Camp Area 1 km NE of PO. 21 day limit
02 6642 2240 HEMA 57 G12 29 41 03 S 152 56 24 E

28 The Grafton Vintage Motor
Vehicle Club

B76 Jabour Park
Minden St, South Grafton
Camp Area 4 km S of PO. Travel W on Gwydir Hwy from South Grafton
0482 561 246 HEMA 57 G12 29 42 09 S 152 55 24 E

29 McPhillips Creek Rest Area

Big River Way, Bom Bom
1 Rest Area 7 km S of South Grafton or 51 km N of Woolgoolga
132 213 HEMA 57 G12 29 44 37 S 152 59 29 E

30 Hotel Motel 5

189 Armidale Rd, South Grafton
B76 Camp Area 5 km S of PO. Free for patrons
02 6642 2555 HEMA 57 G12 29 44 04 S 152 56 23 E

31 Glenugie Rest Area

Big River Way, Glenugie
1 Rest Area 13 km S of South Grafton or 45 km N of Woolgoolga
132 213 HEMA 57 H12 29 47 05 S 153 00 31 E

32 Illaroo Campground

Yuraygir National Park
A1 Illaroo Beach Access Track, Minnie Water
Camp Area 2 km N of Minnie Water. E off Pacific Hwy 12 km S of South Grafton or 44 km N of Woolgoolga to Wooli & Minnie Water Rds. N & S areas
1300 072 757 HEMA 57 G13 29 45 26 S 153 17 28 E

33 Diggers Headland Reserve

Miners St, Wooli
A1 Camp Area 11 km N of Wooli. Open school holidays only. Turn E off Pacific Hwy 12 km S of South Grafton or 44 km N of Woolgoolga to Wooli & Diggers Camp Rds. 7 km dirt road. Pre-book
02 6649 7693 HEMA 57 H13 29 48 55 S 153 17 19 E

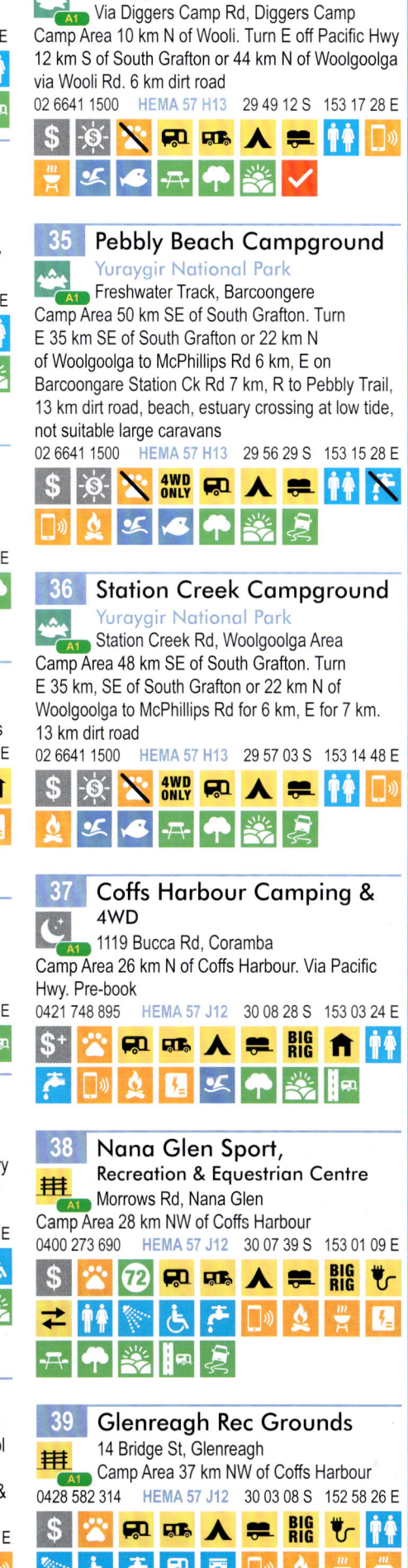

34 Boorkoom Campground

Yuraygir National Park
A1 Via Diggers Camp Rd, Diggers Camp
Camp Area 10 km N of Wooli. Turn E off Pacific Hwy 12 km S of South Grafton or 44 km N of Woolgoolga via Wooli Rd. 6 km dirt road
02 6641 1500 HEMA 57 H13 29 49 12 S 153 17 28 E

35 Pebbly Beach Campground

Yuraygir National Park
A1 Freshwater Track, Barcoongere
Camp Area 50 km SE of South Grafton. Turn E 35 km SE of South Grafton or 22 km N of Woolgoolga to McPhillips Rd 6 km, E on Barcoongare Station Ck Rd 7 km, R to Pebbly Trail, 13 km dirt road, beach, estuary crossing at low tide, not suitable large caravans
02 6641 1500 HEMA 57 H13 29 56 29 S 153 15 28 E

36 Station Creek Campground

Yuraygir National Park
A1 Station Creek Rd, Woolgoolga Area
Camp Area 48 km SE of South Grafton. Turn E 35 km, SE of South Grafton or 22 km N of Woolgoolga to McPhillips Rd for 6 km, E for 7 km. 13 km dirt road
02 6641 1500 HEMA 57 H13 29 57 03 S 153 14 48 E

37 Coffs Harbour Camping &
4WD

A1 1119 Bucca Rd, Coramba
Camp Area 26 km N of Coffs Harbour. Via Pacific Hwy. Pre-book
0421 748 895 HEMA 57 J12 30 08 28 S 153 03 24 E

38 Nana Glen Sport,
Recreation & Equestrian Centre

A1 Morrows Rd, Nana Glen
Camp Area 28 km NW of Coffs Harbour
0400 273 690 HEMA 57 J12 30 07 39 S 153 01 09 E

39 Glenreagh Rec Grounds

14 Bridge St, Glenreagh
A1 Camp Area 37 km NW of Coffs Harbour
0428 582 314 HEMA 57 J12 30 03 08 S 152 58 26 E

NEW SOUTH WALES

40 Valley Stay Campground
4 Mastons Rd, Karangi
Camp Area. Via Coramba Rd. Gravel road up driveway
0419 655 437   HEMA 57 J12   30 15 27 S   153 03 13 E

41 Coffs Harbour Leagues Club
65 Stadium Dr, Coffs Harbour
Camp Area 7 km S of Coffs Harbour. Via Pacific Hwy. Pre-book. 7 day limit
0412 722 942   HEMA 57 K12   30 19 37 S   153 05 49 E

42 Bellingen Showgrounds
Black St, Bellingen
Camp Area 35 km SW of Coffs Harbour. Entrance opposite Dowle St. 2 week limit. Contact caretaker
0490 537 047   HEMA 55 A13   30 26 55 S   152 53 53 E

43 Roses Park
2656 Waterfall Way, Thora
Rest Area 14 km W of Bellingen
132 213   HEMA 55 A12   30 25 33 S   152 46 43 E

44 Taylors Arm Reserve
Taylors Arm Rd, Taylors Arm
Parking Area at "Pub with No Beer", 27 km W of Macksville. Showers at hotel for fee. Gold coin donation
02 6564 2100   HEMA 55 C12   30 46 04 S   152 42 58 E

45 Macksville Lions Park
Ferry St, Macksville
Parking Area 12 km SW of Nambucca Heads. N side of bridge. Limited sites
02 6568 2555   HEMA 55 B13   30 42 13 S   152 55 12 E

46 River St RV Stop
River St, Macksville
Parking Area at W end of street. 4 vehicle spaces for 6 m or less
02 6568 2555   HEMA 55 B13   30 42 22 S   152 55 12 E

47 Macksville Aquatic Centre
23 Cooper St, Macksville
Parking Area S of the bridge, off Cooper St towards Kempsey. 5 vehicle spaces for RVs only
02 6568 2555   HEMA 55 B13   30 42 32 S   152 55 14 E

48 Princess Street RV Stop
Princess St, Macksville
Parking Area S of the bridge at Dawkins Park. Heading S turn R to Winifred St and L to Princess St. 5 vehicle spaces
02 6568 2555   HEMA 55 B13   30 42 40 S   152 55 08 E

49 Gumma Crossing Reserve
Boultons Crossing Rd, Macksville Area
Camp Area 7.5 km E of Macksville. E from Hwy 200 m S of bridge at Macksville to Partridge St then Gumma Rd for 5 km. L at Boltons Crossing Rd. 2 km dirt road. Fairly large area beside Warrell Creek, narrow access. Cold showers
02 6568 2555   HEMA 55 B13   30 42 24 S   152 59 00 E

50 Paddys Rest
Pacific Hwy, Eungai Creek
Rest Area 5 km S of Warrell Creek or 17 km N of Clybucca. Check signs
132 213   HEMA 55 C13   30 48 47 S   152 52 15 E

51 Yarralen Retreat
95 Mighell Rd, Yarrahapinni
Camp Area 8 km SW of Stuarts Point. Turn E off Pacific Hwy to Stuarts Point Rd for 4 km, then W. Pre-book
0448 663 009   HEMA 55 C13   30 50 15 S   152 55 46 E

52 Stuarts Point Convention Centre
250 Grassy Head Rd, Stuarts Point
Camp Area 32 km SE of Macksville
02 6569 0576   HEMA 55 C13   30 47 57 S   152 59 15 E

53 Clybucca Rest Area South
Pacific Hwy, Clybucca
Rest Area 7 km S of Stuarts Point Rd intersection or 17 km N of Frederickton intersection. Check signs
132 213   HEMA 55 C13   30 54 34 S   152 55 06 E

54 Clybucca Rest Area North
Pacific Hwy, Clybucca
Rest Area 7 km S of Stuarts Point Rd intersection or 17 km N of Frederickton Jcn. Check signs
132 213   HEMA 55 C13   30 54 31 S   152 55 03 E

55 Kempsey Showground
19 Sea St, West Kempsey
Camp Area 49 km NW of Port Macquarie. 21 day limit. Gates open 7.30am-6.30pm
0438 625 235   HEMA 55 D12   31 04 24 S   152 49 45 E

56 Trial Bay Gaol Campground
Arakoon National Park
63 Trial Bay Gaol Access Rd, Arakoon
Camp Area 4 km E of South West Rocks. 7 day bookings only and higher fees in school holidays
1300 072 757   HEMA 55 C13   30 52 41 S   153 04 16 E

57 Smoky Cape Campground
Hat Head National Park
Lighthouse Rd, Arakoon
Camp Area 9 km SE of South West Rocks. Via Arakoon Rd. Bush camping in confined area. Near beach. Small caravans only, low branches and narrow access
02 6566 6168   HEMA 55 C13   30 55 45 S   153 04 37 E

58 Hungry Gate Campground
Hat Head National Park
Hungry Campground Rd, Hat Head
Camp Area 3.5 km S of Hat Head via Gap Rd, turn R. 3 km dirt road. Not suitable for caravans
02 6561 6700   HEMA 55 D13   31 04 47 S   153 02 31 E

59 Racecourse Headland Campground
Goolawah National Park
Point Plomer Rd, Crescent Head
Camp Area 8 km S of Crescent Head via Point Plomer Rd. 7 km dirt road. Beside beach. Outside cold showers. Small vehicles only
02 6561 6700   HEMA 55 E13   31 14 57 S   152 57 37 E

60 Delicate Campground
Goolawah Regional Park
Point Plomer Rd, Crescent Head
Camp Area 10 km S of Crescent Head. 9 km dirt road. Beside beach. Outside cold showers
02 6561 6700   HEMA 55 E13   31 15 37 S   152 58 06 E

61 Waves Campground
954 Point Plomer Rd, Crescent Head
Camp Area 11 km S of Cresent Head.
21 day limit. Pre-book. Cafe on site
02 6566 0144   HEMA 55 E13   31 15 43 S   152 58 02 E

62 Melaleuca Campground
Limeburners Creek National Park
1100 Point Plomer Rd, Crescent Head
Camp Area 12 km S of Crescent Head. 14 km dirt road. Beside creek. Outside school holidays contact campground manager - 0402 779 379
02 6561 6700   HEMA 55 E13   31 16 49 S   152 57 45 E

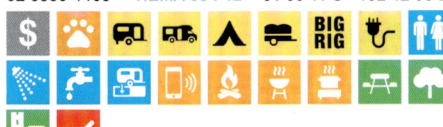

63 Point Plomer Campground
Limeburners Creek National Park
Point Plomer Rd, Limeburners Creek
Camp Area 17 km S of Crescent Head. 16 km dirt road. Beside beach. Cold showers
02 6561 6700   HEMA 55 E13   31 18 48 S   152 58 12 E

64 Kendall Showground
23 Batar Creek Rd, Kendall
Camp Area 35 km SW of Port Macquarie.
Cash only, honesty box onsite
02 6559 4463   HEMA 55 F12   31 38 11 S   152 42 06 E

65 Kew Information & Community Centre
133 Nancy Bird Walton Dr, Kew
Parking Area 32 km SW of Port Macquarie. Off Pacific Hwy. Donation box at toilet block
02 6559 4400   HEMA 55 F12   31 38 06 S   152 43 19 E

66 Diamond Head
Crowdy Bay National Park
Diamond Head Rd, Diamond Head
Camp Area 9 km S of Laurieton. 5 km dirt road. Cold showers. Beside beach
1300 072 757   HEMA 55 G12   31 43 05 S   152 47 39 E

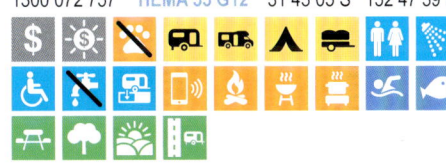

67 Indian Head Campground
Crowdy Bay National Park
Indian Head Rd, Diamond Head
Camp Area 11 km S of Laurieton. 7 km dirt road.
Cold showers
02 6588 5555   HEMA 55 G12   31 43 49 S   152 47 39 E

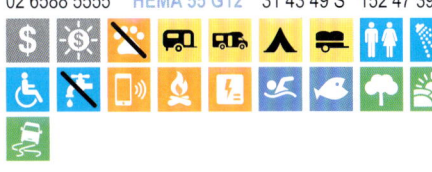

68 Kylies Beach Campground
Crowdy Bay National Park
Kylies Rd, Diamond Head
Camp Area 13 km S of Laurieton. 9 km dirt road.
Cold showers. Near beach
02 6588 5555   HEMA 55 G12   31 44 06 S   152 47 29 E

69 Crowdy Gap Campground
Crowdy Bay National Park
Crowdy Gap Rd, Crowdy Head
Camp Area 4 km N of Crowdy Head. Narrow access, small vehicles only. Dirt road. Cold showers
1300 072 757   HEMA 55 G12   31 49 59 S   152 43 48 E

70 Falls Forest Retreat
318 Isaacs Lane, Johns River
Camp Area 16 km S of Kew or 40 km N of Taree. Water crossings. Pre-book
02 6556 5000   HEMA 55 F12   31 42 52 S   152 39 50 E

71 Johns River Tavern & Cafe
28 Johns River Rd, Johns River
Camp Spot at Johns River. 400 m E of Hwy.
Toilets only open during trading hours, public toilets 350 m N
02 6556 5001   HEMA 55 G12   31 43 54 S   152 41 40 E

72 Tom Cat Creek Rest Area
Pacific Hwy, Moorland
Rest Area 20 km S of Kew or 2 km N of Moorland. Check signs
132 213   HEMA 55 G12   31 45 53 S   152 40 15 E

73 Coopernook Hotel
240 George Gibson Dr, Coopernook
Parking Area behind hotel, S end of town.
27 km NE of Taree. Check in with publican
02 6556 3150   HEMA 55 G12   31 49 57 S   152 36 23 E

74 Coopernook Forest Park
Coopernook State Forest
400 Forest Rd, Lansdowne Forest
Camp Area 4 km NW of Coopernook. Turn N to West St, N to Lansdowne Rd, then N. 4 km dirt road
1300 655 687   HEMA 55 G12   31 47 19 S   152 36 32 E

75 Taree Showgrounds
24 Muldoon St, Taree
Camp Area in centre of town
02 6552 4056   HEMA 55 G11   31 54 04 S   152 27 36 E

76 Tallowood Ridge Farm
79 Mooral Creek Rd, Cedar Party
Farm Stay 7.5 km N of Wingham via Comboyne Rd. 7 night limit
0413 825 552   HEMA 55 G11   31 48 54 S   152 22 24 E

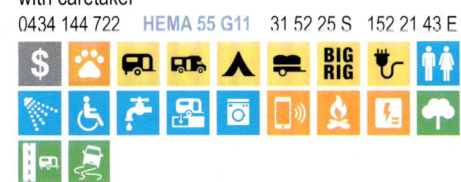

77 Wingham Showground
1274 Gloucester Rd, Wingham
Camp Area 10 km W of Taree. Check in with caretaker
0434 144 722   HEMA 55 G11   31 52 25 S   152 21 43 E

78 Wingham Riverside Reserve
Farquhar St, Wingham
Camp Area 9 km W of Taree. E of Central Park. Donation box onsite
0436 211 234   HEMA 55 G11   31 52 17 S   152 22 51 E

NEW SOUTH WALES

79 Bluebell Hill Farm

25 Bo Bo Creek Rd, Burrell Creek
Farm Stay 23 km SW of Taree via Bucketts Way. Pets on request
0421 042 165   HEMA 55 H11   31 56 55 S   152 18 49 E

80 Four Mile Hill Rest Area
Pacific Hwy, Kiwarrak
Rest Area 6 km S of Taree or 21 km N of Nabiac. Combined truck bay. Northbound only
132 213   HEMA 55 H11   31 57 49 S   152 27 53 E

81 Manning Park Rest
15510 Pacific Hwy, Rainbow Flat
Camp Area 10 km S of Taree or 10 km N of Nabiac
0411 037 949   HEMA 55 H11   32 01 45 S   152 28 11 E

82 Talawahl Creek Rest Area
15165 Pacific Hwy, Possum Brush
Rest Area 18 km S of Taree or 9 km N of Nabiac. Southbound only
132 213   HEMA 55 H11   32 02 57 S   152 26 49 E

83 The National Motorcycle Museum
33 Clarkson St, Nabiac
Camp Area 29 km S of Taree. For power, arrive prior to 3.30pm
0474 788 132   HEMA 55 H11   32 05 42 S   152 23 00 E

84 Krambach RV Park
The Bucketts Way, Krambach
Rest Area next to hotel, behind council pool
02 6559 1201   HEMA 55 H11   32 03 08 S   152 15 38 E

85 Wang Wauk Rest Area
84 Wang Wauk Rd, Wang Wauk
Rest Area 8 km S of Nabiac or 8 km N of Coolongolook. Check signs
132 213   HEMA 55 H11   32 09 16 S   152 19 19 E

86 RV Retreat Coolongolook
40 Lombard St, Coolongolook
Camp Area 29 km NE of Bulahdelah
0466 641 144   HEMA 55 J11   32 13 10 S   152 19 12 E

87 Kennedys Gap Rest Area
Pacific Hwy, Coolongolook
Rest Area 3 km S of Coolongolook or 26 km NE of Bulahdelah. S bound only. Check signs
132 213   HEMA 55 J11   32 15 04 S   152 19 24 E

88 Wootton Rest Area
Wootton Way, Wootton
Rest Area at Wootton. Check signs
132 213   HEMA 55 J11   32 17 38 S   152 18 14 E

89 Chapmans Rest Area
Pacific Hwy, Topi Topi
Rest Area 16 km S of Coolongolook or 13 km NE of Bulahdelah. Share with trucks. Both sides of the road. Check signs
132 213   HEMA 55 J11   32 21 09 S   152 18 51 E

90 Bulahdelah Showgrounds
17 Prince St, Bulahdelah
Camp Area Cnr Stuart St. Pay at Info Centre or honesty box onsite. Mon - Fri only
02 4997 4981   HEMA 55 J10   32 24 18 S   152 12 16 E

91 Bulahdelah Lions Park
Bulahdelah Way, Bulahdelah
Camp Area 1 km S of PO, entry 600 m before bridge on Old Pacific Hwy Rd. Entry only from N bound lane. Donation box
02 4997 4981   HEMA 55 K10   32 24 50 S   152 12 21 E

92 Bulahdelah Golf Club
Golf Dr, Bulahdelah
Parking Area N of town. Check in at bar. Amenities during opening hours. Closed Mon-Tue
02 4997 4327   HEMA 55 J10   32 23 34 S   152 13 16 E

93 Bulahdelah Bowling Club
50 Jackson St, Bulahdelah
Parking Area 900 m NW of PO. Check in at the bar
02 4997 4365   HEMA 55 J10   32 24 25 S   152 12 14 E

94 Violet Hill Campground
Myall Lakes National Park
Violet Hill Road, Violet Hill
Camp Area 20 km E of Bulahdelah. Turn S off The Lakes Way to Violet Hill Rd, 10 km E of Bulahdelah near Boolambayte. 10 km dirt road. Lakeside
02 6591 0300   HEMA 55 K11   32 28 16 S   152 19 37 E

95 Neranie Campground
Myall Lakes National Park
Neranie Rd, Bungwahl
Camp Area 5 km S of Bungwahl. Turn W off Seal Rocks Rd after 4 km at Fishermans Co-Op. 1 km dirt road. Lakeside
02 6591 0300   HEMA 55 J11   32 24 33 S   152 27 08 E

96 Yagon Campground
Myall Lakes National Park
Yagon Rd, Yagon
Camp Area 4 km SW of Seal Rocks. Via Thomas Rd
02 6591 0300   HEMA 55 K11   32 27 11 S   152 29 41 E

97 The Ruins Campground
Booti Booti National Park
4374 The Lakes Way, Booti Booti
Camp Area 16 km S of Forster or 5 km N of Pacific Palms
1300 072 757   HEMA 55 J11   32 18 36 S   152 31 10 E

98 Camp Elim
4859 The Lakes Way, Tiona
Camp Area 11.5 km S of Forster or 9.5 km N of Pacific Palms. Pre-book, sites limited
02 6554 0277   HEMA 55 J11   32 16 08 S   152 31 42 E

99 Tuncurry Sporties RV Park
65 Beach St, Tuncurry
Parking Area N of shops. Pay at reception
02 6554 9270   HEMA 55 H11   32 09 59 S   152 30 04 E

100 Myall River Camp
341 Mungo Brush Rd, Hawks Nest
Camp Area 4 km N of Hawks Nest
0409 836 828   HEMA 55 K10   32 38 23 S   152 10 44 E

101 Stewart and Lloyds Camp
Myall Lakes National Park
Mungo Brush Rd, Hawks Nest
Camp Area 10 km N of Hawks Nest. Signposted
02 6591 0300   HEMA 55 K10   32 36 27 S   152 13 55 E

102 Banksia Green Campground
Myall Lakes National Park
Mungo Brush Rd, Mungo Brush
Camp Area 19.5 km NE of Hawks Nest. Access also via Bombah Pt ferry from Bulahdelah (Crawford St, Ann St, Lakes Rd). Small vehicles only
02 6591 0300   HEMA 55 K11   32 32 58 S   152 18 26 E

103 Mungo Brush Campground
Myall Lakes National Park
Mungo Brush Access Rd, Mungo Brush
Camp Area 19 km NE of Hawks Nest. Access also via Bombah Pt ferry from Bulahdelah (Crawford St, Ann St, Lakes Rd)
1300 072 757   HEMA 55 K11   32 32 37 S   152 18 37 E

104 Dees Corner Campground
Myall Lakes National Park
Mungo Brush Rd, Mungo Brush
Camp Area 20 km NE of Hawks Nest. Access also via Bombah Pt ferry from Bulahdelah (Crawford St, Ann St, Lakes Rd)
02 6591 0300   HEMA 55 K11   32 32 19 S   152 18 59 E

105 White Tree Bay Camp
Myall Lakes National Park
Mungo Brush Rd, Mungo Brush
Camp Area 22 km NE of Hawks Nest. Access also via Bombah Pt ferry from Bulahdelah (Crawford St, Ann St, Lakes Rd)
02 6591 0300   HEMA 55 K11   32 31 41 S   152 19 21 E

106 Bungarie Bay Campground
Myall Lakes National Park
Violet Hill Rd, Violet Hill
Camp Area 18 km E of Bulahdelah. Turn S off The Lakes Way, 10 km E of Bulahdelah near Boolambayte. 8 km dirt road. Small area, lakeside
02 6591 0300   HEMA 55 K11   32 27 34 S   152 19 09 E

106-1 The Wells Campground
Myall Lakes National Park
Mungo Brush Rd, Mungo Brush
Camp Area 23 km NE of Hawks Nest. Access also via Bombah Pt ferry from Bulahdelah (Crawford St, Ann St, Lakes Rd)
02 6591 0300   HEMA 55 K11   32 31 31 S   152 19 22 E

107 Korsmans Landing Camp
Myall Lakes National Park
Korsmans Trail, Bombah Point
Camp Area 14 km SE of Buladelah. From Hwy turn S to Ann St at Bulahdelah, which becomes Bombah Point Rd follow for 12 km then L
02 6591 0300   HEMA 55 K11   32 28 36 S   152 17 08 E

108 Browns Flat North Rest Area
Pacific Hwy, Nerong
Rest Area 19 km S of Bulahdelah or 10 km N of Tea Gardens turnoff. N bound only. Check signs
132 213   HEMA 53 A14   32 32 54 S   152 09 13 E

109 Browns Flat South Rest Area
Pacific Hwy
Rest Area 20 km S of Bulahdelah or 9 km N of Tea Gardens turnoff. S bound only. Check signs
132 213   HEMA 53 A14   32 33 15 S   152 09 01 E

110 Tea Gardens Country Club
Yalinbah St, Tea Gardens
Parking Area. Membership fee, check in at reception. Limited sites
02 4997 0250   HEMA 53 A14   32 39 50 S   152 09 09 E

111 Station Creek Rest Area
6700 Pacific Hwy, Tea Gardens
Rest Area 30 km S of Bulahdelah or 500 m N of Tea Gardens turnoff. N bound only. Check signs
132 213   HEMA 53 A14   32 36 33 S   152 05 43 E

112 Tahlee Campground
31 Church St, Tahlee
Camp Area. Off Hwy to Carrington Rd, via Tahlee Rd
02 8328 1110   HEMA 53 A13   32 40 06 S   152 00 19 E

113 Tattersalls Campground
Karuah National Park
Tattersals Rd, Limeburners Creek
Camp Area 58 km NW of Newcastle. Turn to Bucketts Way from Pacific Hwy, 9 km then R to Hobarts Rd, past Limeburners Ck, 4 km then R to Tattersalls Rd, 2 km to campground
02 4984 8200   HEMA 53 A13   32 35 07 S   151 58 05 E

114 12 Mile Creek Southbound
Pacific Hwy, Twelve Mile Creek
Rest Area 500 m S of Bucketts Way (Stroud) intersection. S bound only. Check signs
132 213   HEMA 47 B14   32 39 13 S   151 51 35 E

115 12 Mile Hill Northbound
Pacific Hwy, Ferodale
Rest Area 17 km N of Raymond Tce. N bound only. Check signs
132 213   HEMA 47 B14   32 39 44 S   151 50 33 E

116 Medowie Rd Rest Area
Medowie Rd, Ferodale
Rest Area 12 km SW of Karuah. 1 km S of The Bucketts Way turnoff. S bound only. Check signs
132 213   HEMA 47 B14   32 40 10 S   151 50 06 E

117 Olney HQ Camping Area
Olney State Forest
Watagan Forest Rd, Ravensdale
Camp Area 16 km W of Cooranbong. Via Martinsville Rd, 8 km dirt road
1300 655 687   HEMA 47 G9   33 03 47 S   151 19 55 E

NEW SOUTH WALES

118 The Pines Camping Area
Olney State Forest
M1 Watagan Forest Rd, Ravensdale
Camp Area 17 km W of Cooranbong, via Martinsville Rd. 9 km dirt road
1300 655 687   HEMA 47 G9   33 03 47 S   151 20 13 E

119 Casuarina Camping Area
Olney
Olney State Forest
M1 Watagan Forest Rd, Olney
Camp Area 18 km W of Cooranbong, via Martinsville Rd. 9 km dirt road
1300 655 687   HEMA 47 G9   33 03 33 S   151 20 01 E

120 Gap Creek Campground
Watagans National Park
B82 Bangalow Rd, Martinsville
Camp Area 20 km N from Martinsville. Head SW & L to Martinsville Rd, L to Freemans Dr, L to Mount Faulk Rd. Then L 5 km
02 4972 9000   HEMA 47 F10   33 00 49 S   151 25 50 E

121 The Basin Olney
Olney State Forest
M1 Basin Forest Rd, Laguna
Camp Area 33 km W of Cooranbong, via Martinsville Rd
1300 655 687   HEMA 47 G8   33 06 15 S   151 13 51 E

122 Morisset Showground
B53 40 Ourimbah St, Morisset
Camp Area. 4 week limit. Pre-book
0409 783 294   HEMA 47 G11   33 06 30 S   151 28 49 E

123 Freemans Campground
Munmorah State Conservation Area
A43 Birdie Beach Dr, Wybung
Camp Area 17 km S of Swansea or 23 km N of Wyong, via Elizabeth Bay Dr. Limited caravan sites. Pre-book, minimum 2 nights
1300 072 757   HEMA 47 H12   33 12 02 S   151 36 13 E

124 Gosford Showground & Greyhound Track
A1 Showground Rd, Gosford
Camp Area. Entry via Glennis St W. 6 night limit. Pre-book
02 4323 4423   HEMA 49 A13   33 24 48 S   151 20 31 E

125 Patonga Caravan & Camping Area
M1 Bay St, Patonga
Camp Area. Steep winding road. 6 week limit
02 4379 1287   HEMA 49 C12   33 33 14 S   151 16 07 E

Stanthorpe to Newcastle
New England Highway

126 Cullendore High Country

15 248 Cullendore Creek Rd, Cullendore
Camp Area 42 km NE of Stanthorpe. Via Liston Rd
0459 901 538   HEMA 57 B8   28 29 32 S   152 07 21 E

127 Aloomba Lavender Farm
15 5425 Mt Lindsay Rd, Liston
Camp Area 21 km E of Stanthorpe. Gift shop on site
07 4686 1191   HEMA 57 C9   28 37 09 S   152 05 49 E

128 Bald Rock Campground
Bald Rock National Park
A15 Bookookoorara Trail, Carrolls Creek
Camp Area 27 km S of Stanthorpe or 29 km NE of Tenterfield. Off Mt Lindsay Hwy, via Bald Rock Rd
02 6736 4298   HEMA 57 D9   28 50 44 S   152 02 45 E

129 Cypress Pine Campground
Boonoo Boonoo National Park
B60 Morgans Gully Track, Boorook
Camp Area 35 km NE of Tenterfield. Off Mt Lindsay Hwy via Boonoo Boonoo Falls Rd
02 6736 4298   HEMA 57 C9   28 50 32 S   152 09 04 E

130 Basket Swamp Campground
Boonoo State Forest
B60 Basket Swamp Rd, Boonoo Boonoo
Camp Area 24 km NE of Tenterfield. Off Mt Lindsay Hwy, via Lindrook & Woollool Woollool Rds
1300 655 687   HEMA 57 D9   28 54 33 S   152 09 11 E

131 Jennings Hotel
A15 26 Duke St, Jennings
Parking area behind hotel, check in with publican. Free for patrons. Limited space
02 4684 3237   HEMA 57 D8   28 55 29 S   151 55 56 E

132 Tenterfield Showground
A15 62 Miles St, Tenterfield
Camp Area. Turn W opposite Info Centre
02 6736 6000   HEMA 57 D9   29 03 24 S   152 00 55 E

133 Craigs Caravan Park
A15 102 Rouse St, Tenterfield
Caravan Park 800 m S of PO. Entrance off Clive St
02 6736 1585   HEMA 57 E8   29 03 40 S   152 00 59 E

134 Bluff Rock Rest Area
15 New England Hwy, Tenterfield
Rest Area 11 km S of Tenterfield or 41 km N of Deepwater
132 213   HEMA 57 E9   29 09 15 S   152 00 07 E

135 Kookaburra Camping Park
A15 98 Castlerag Rd, Deepwater
Caravan Park 35 km S of Tenterfield or 12 km N of Deepwater. Off Hwy. 28 day limit
0429 462 473   HEMA 57 F8   29 20 37 S   151 53 04 E

136 Deepwater Longhorn Inn
A15 102 Tenterfield St, Deepwater
Parking Area behind the Old Deepwater Inn. Turn E off Hwy to Cadell St, entry 100 m. Register at bar. Free for unpowered
02 6734 5111   HEMA 57 F8   29 26 12 S   151 50 53 E

137 Blatherarm Creek Camp
Torrington State Conservation Area
Blatherarm Rd, Torrington
Camp Area 11 km N of Torrington. Via Silent Grove Rd
02 6736 4298   HEMA 56 E7   29 14 25 S   151 41 59 E

138 Emmaville Caravan Park
Park Rd, Emmaville
Caravan Park 700 m SE of PO
0429 347 249   HEMA 56 F7   29 26 51 S   151 36 08 E

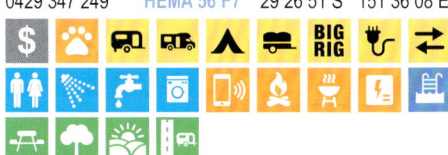

139 Beardy Creek
924 New England Hwy, Yarrowford
Rest Area at Heritage Park, 31 km S of Deepwater or 9 km N of Glen Innes
02 6730 2400   HEMA 57 G8   29 39 50 S   151 46 37 E

140 Three Waters High Country Holidays
935 Bullock Mountain Rd, Yarrowford
Camp Area 15 km NW of Glen Innes. Turn W off New England Hwy to Gwydir Hwy travel 1.4 km. Turn N off Gwydir Hwy to Emmaville Rd. 4 km to turnoff, 9 km dirt road to homestead
02 6732 4863   HEMA 57 G8   29 37 12 S   151 43 46 E

141 Bullock Mountain Homestead
1192 Bullock Mountain Rd, Yarrowford
Camp Area 17 km N of Glen Innes. Turn at Gwydir Hwy sign to Inverell. Follow 1.5 km to Emmaville, Bonshaw, Airport sign (Coronation Ave) & turn R, follow 4 km. Turn R at Bullock Mountain Rd sign, gravel road. Follow 12 km to end
0457 357 909   HEMA 57 G8   29 36 11 S   151 43 42 E

142 Glen Innes Showground
37 Torrington St, Glen Innes
Camp Area 1 km SE of PO. Caretaker collects fee. Fee for laundry
0408 809 073   HEMA 57 G8   29 44 30 S   151 44 31 E

143 Red Lion Tavern
8025 New England Hwy, Glencoe
Camp Area in paddock next to pub. Fee for hot shower. Open Fri-Sun
02 6733 3271   HEMA 57 H8   29 55 34 S   151 43 24 E

144 Ben Lomond Rec Reserve
Ben Lomond Rd, Ben Lomond
Camp Area 15 km SW of Glencoe, or 24 km N of Guyra. Donation box on the tennis shed
02 6733 2011   HEMA 56 H7   30 01 04 S   151 39 28 E

145 Mother of Ducks Lagoon
McKie Pkwy, Guyra
Rest Area S end of town, W off Hwy
02 6738 9100   HEMA 56 J7   30 13 21 S   151 40 10 E

146 Deanos Springwater
Smoked Trout Farm
Black Mountain Rd, Black Mountain
Farm Stay 10 km S of Guyra or 30 km N of Armidale. W from Hwy (A15), 5 km to entry
0427 750 182   HEMA 56 K7   30 17 52 S   151 39 52 E

147 Boorolong Creek
Bundarra Rd, Yarrowyck
Parking Area 26 km W of Armidale or 54 km SE of Bundarra. Can flood in extreme weather, avoid riverbank
132 213   HEMA 56 K7   30 28 46 S   151 25 41 E

148 Yarrowyck Gwydir River
Yarrowyck Crossing, Yarrowyck
Camp Area 25 km NW of Uralla. Via Thunderbolts Way. 5 km dirt road, causeway can be cut by floodwaters
02 6778 6300   HEMA 56 K6   30 28 03 S   151 21 34 E

149 Bundarra Lions Park
Thunderbolts Way, Bundarra
Rest Area 3 km S of Bundarra or 73 km NW of Uralla on Thunderbolts Way, riverside
02 6723 7101   HEMA 56 J5   30 11 36 S   151 04 42 E

150 Bundarra Caravan Park
Court St, Bundarra
Caravan Park. Fee for shower. Honesty box
02 6723 7101   HEMA 56 J5   30 10 14 S   151 04 35 E

151 Armidale Showgrounds
Dumaresq St, Armidale
Camp Area 1 km E of PO. 28 day limit
0400 639 630   HEMA 55 A9   30 30 54 S   151 40 47 E

152 Wooldridge Recreation & Fossicking Reserve
Devoncourt Rd, Uralla
Camp Area 6 km W of Uralla. Take Kingstown Rd for 4.5 km, turn N to Devoncourt Rd, follow to end. Cattle grid at entry
02 6778 6300   HEMA 55 B8   30 37 45 S   151 28 18 E

153 Uralla Golf Club
33 Plane Ave, Uralla
Parking Area S side of town. Limited sites. Pre-book. 7 day limit
0458 784 059   HEMA 55 B8   30 39 12 S   151 29 40 E

154 Uralla South Rest Area
New England Hwy, Kentucky
Rest Area 18 km SW of Uralla or 32 km NE of Bendemeer
132 213   HEMA 54 B7   30 45 11 S   151 23 02 E

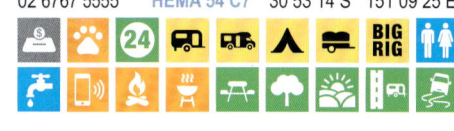

155 Bendemeer Camping Area
Selina St, Bendemeer
Camp Area behind rodeo grounds. Via 800 m dirt road, parallel to Hwy, between Hwy & service station. Honesty box. Riverside
02 6767 5555   HEMA 54 C7   30 53 14 S   151 09 25 E

156 Moonbi Park & Lookout
Moonbi Lookout Rd, Moonbi
Rest Area 6 km N of Moonbi or 11 km S of Bendemeer
02 6767 5555   HEMA 54 C6   30 58 34 S   151 05 57 E

NEW SOUTH WALES

157 Cockburn River
Kootingal-Limbri Rd, Limbri
Camp Area 11 km E of Kootingal or 2 km W of Limbri. Riverside
02 6767 5555   HEMA 54 D7   31 03 07 S   151 08 38 E

158 Hillside Farm Stay
245 Nundle Rd, Nemingha
Camp Area 6 km SE of Tamworth. SE on New England Hwy (A15), then S for 2.5 km
0402 797 196   HEMA 54 D6   31 07 54 S   151 00 42 E

159 Paceway Tamworth
24-60 Showground Rd, Tamworth
Camp Area at Showground. Entry Gate 2
02 6765 9382   HEMA 54 D6   31 05 30 S   150 54 04 E

160 Sheffield Bed & Breakfast
272 Whitehouse Ln, Kingswood
Camp Area 10 km S of Tamworth or 49 km N of Wallabadah. Pre-book
0428 485 344   HEMA 54 D6   31 10 13 S   150 56 50 E

161 LBS Musicland
348 Whitehouse Ln, Kingswood
Camp Area 12 km SE of Tamworth. Look for white gates & Australian flag
0412 605 488   HEMA 54 D6   31 10 17 S   150 57 19 E

162 Ranjen Farm Stay
658 Marsden Park Rd, Calala
Farm Stay 11 km S Nemingah. 14 night limit. Pre-book
0488 915 642   HEMA 54 D6   31 12 02 S   150 58 45 E

163 Tamworth Airport Rest Area
Oxley Hwy, Tamworth
Rest Area opposite airport. 8 km W of Tamworth or 67 km E of Gunnedah
02 6767 5555   HEMA 54 D6   31 04 40 S   150 51 01 E

164 Currabubula Rec Area
Alford St, Currabubula
Camp Area 33 km SW of Tamworth
02 6747 1226   HEMA 54 E5   31 15 40 S   150 44 22 E

165 Peel River Campground
Nundle Rd, Dungowan
Camp Area 20 km SE Tamworth or 38.5 km N Nundle. Near river, W side of road
02 6767 5555   HEMA 54 D6   31 12 08 S   151 05 13 E

166 Woolomin Reserve
Monro St, Woolomin
Camp Area beside Peel River. Fee for power payable at store
02 6767 5555   HEMA 54 E7   31 18 14 S   151 08 51 E

167 Bowling Alley Point Reserve
Nundle Rd, Tamworth Area
Camp Area at Chaffey Dam. 7 km S of Woolomin or 15 km N of Nundle. 7 day limit. Honesty box. Coins for showers
02 6767 5300   HEMA 54 E7   31 21 38 S   151 08 00 E

168 Swamp Creek
River Rd, Nundle
Camp Area 4 km N of Nundle. Beside Peel River. 2 km dirt road
02 6767 5555   HEMA 54 E7   31 26 08 S   151 08 33 E
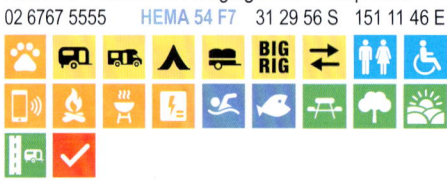

169 Sheba Dams Reserve
972 Barry Rd, Hanging Rock
Camp Area 11 km E of Nundle, via Hanging Rock Rd. 1 km SE of Hanging Rock. Steep climb
02 6767 5555   HEMA 54 F7   31 29 56 S   151 11 46 E

170 Ponderosa Park Camp
Nundle State Forest
Forest Way, Hanging Rock
Camp Area 17 km E of Nundle. Turn N off Hanging Rock Rd after 8 km to Forest Way. 8 km dirt road
1300 655 687   HEMA 54 E7   31 27 49 S   151 15 25 E

171 Teamsters Rest Campground
1532 Crawney Rd, Crawney
Camp Area 14 km S of Nundle. Beside Wombramurra Creek. 5 km dirt road
02 6767 5555   HEMA 54 F6   31 33 24 S   151 03 22 E

172 Wallabadah Camping
61 Coach St, Wallabadah
Camp Area behind First Fleet Memorial Gardens. Beside Quirindi Creek. Donation box at entrance
02 6747 1226   HEMA 54 F6   31 32 17 S   150 49 52 E

173 Willow Tree Rec Ground
84 Recreation Rd, Willow Tree
Camp Area. Visit info centre to pay for power
02 6747 1226   HEMA 54 F5   31 38 43 S   150 43 16 E

174 Nowlands Gap Rest Area
New England Hwy, Murrurundi
Rest Area 16 km SE of Willow Tree or 4 km NW of Murrurundi. Southbound only
132 213   HEMA 54 G5   31 44 26 S   150 47 52 E

175 Murrurundi SC RV Park
Teys Lane, Murrurundi
Camp Area at Wilson Memorial Oval. Donation to Visitors Centre
02 6540 1364   HEMA 54 G6   31 45 49 S   150 50 14 E

176 Burning Mountain Reserve
New England Hwy, Wingen
Rest Area 10 km S of Blandford or 23 km N of Scone. 5 km N of Wingen. 200 m in from Hwy on sloping parking area
02 6540 1100   HEMA 54 G6   31 51 21 S   150 53 58 E

177 Washpools Campground
Towarri National Park
Middlebrook Rd, Middle Brook
Camp Area 20 km NW of Scone. Last 7 km dirt road
02 6540 2300   HEMA 54 G5   31 54 11 S   150 47 12 E

178 Bunnan Rest Area
High St, Bunnan
Rest Area 56 km W of Scone or 30 km E of Merriwa. N end of town
02 6540 1300   HEMA 54 H5   32 02 04 S   150 35 08 E

179 Abercairney Terrace Camp
Abercairney Tce, Aberdeen
Parking Area 600 m NW of PO
02 6540 1300   HEMA 54 H6   32 09 40 S   150 53 16 E

180 Muswellbrook Showground
Rutherford Rd, Muswellbrook
Camp Area 3 km S of PO. Pre-book
0458 876 773   HEMA 54 J6   32 16 51 S   150 53 48 E

181 Royal Hotel Denman
10 Ogilvie St, Denman
Camp Area 27 km SW of Muswellbrook. Turn W off Golden Hwy. Check in with publican. Amenities only during opening hours
02 6547 2226   HEMA 54 J5   32 23 22 S   150 41 18 E

182 Valley View Farm
Worondi Creek Rd, Gungal
Farm Stay 31 km SE of Merriwa. Dirt road. Pre-book
0412 993 077   HEMA 54 J4   32 19 29 S   150 30 13 E

183 Gungal Rest Area
Maitland St, Gungal
Rest Area at Private Jackson VC Park. 11 km NW of Sandy Hollow or 24 km SE of Merriwa
02 6549 3891   HEMA 54 J4   32 16 24 S   150 30 06 E

184 Battery Rock Rest Area
Golden Hwy, Gungal
Rest Area 20 km NW of Sandy Hollow or 15 km SE of Merriwa
132 213   HEMA 54 J4   32 12 51 S   150 27 33 E

185 Merriwa Sports Club
King George V Ave, Merriwa
Camp Area 500 m E of PO, next to clubhouse. Entry at golf course sign. Check in at bar
02 6548 2028   HEMA 54 H4   32 08 23 S   150 21 44 E

186 Merriwa RSL RV Stop
120-126 Bettington St, Merriwa
Parking Area behind the club, entry via Bow St. Patronage appreciated. Amenities during opening hours
02 6548 2157   HEMA 54 H4   32 08 17 S   150 21 13 E
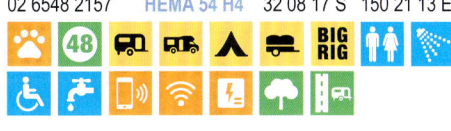

187 Merriwa RV Stop
Solly's Lane, Merriwa
Parking Area between Bow & Vennacher Sts
02 6521 7046   HEMA 54 H4   32 08 24 S   150 21 15 E

188 Jerrys Plains Rec Ground
Wambo St, Jerrys Plains
Camp Area 36 km S of Muswellbrook. S end of town. Donation box onsite
02 6578 7290   HEMA 54 K6   32 29 56 S   150 54 37 E

189 Lake Liddell Recreation Area
400 Hebden Rd, Muswellbrook
Camp Area 16 km S of Muswellbrook or 39 km NW of Singleton. Turn E off Hwy 15, 12 km S of Muswellbrook or 35 km NW of Singleton, for 4 km. Pre-book
0477 551 174   HEMA 54 J6   32 21 03 S   150 59 48 E

190 Glennies Creek Camp
Nobles Ln, Middle Falbrook
Camp Area 36 km SE of Muswellbrook or 18 km NW of Singleton. NW of Singleton on Hwy for 16 km, then N to Glennies Creek Rd for 4 km, then E for 650 m. Creekside
02 6578 7290   HEMA 54 J6   32 27 36 S   151 07 04 E

191 Singleton Showground
32 Bathurst St, Singleton
Camp Area 800 m E of PO. Access gates 2. Weekly rates available
0488 722 424   HEMA 47 A8   32 34 05 S   151 10 19 E

192 Grey Gum Cafe
8679 Putty Rd, Putty
Camp Area 86 km S of Singleton or 87 km N of Windsor. Fee for showers. Cafe open on weekend
02 6579 7015   HEMA 46 F3   33 01 49 S   150 40 25 E

193 Mountain Arm Campground
Yengo National Park
Big Yengo Loop Trail, Moruben
Camp Area 44 km W Wollombi. From Yango Creek Rd take Finchley & Yango Tracks & Wollombi Arm Trail. Gate access code. Pre-book
02 6574 5555   HEMA 46 F5   32 59 03 S   150 53 26 E

194 Blue Gums Campground
Yengo National Park
Big Yengo Loop Trail, Big Yengo
Camp Area 43 km W of Wollombi. From Yango Creek Rd take Finchley & Yango Tracks & Wollombi Arm Trail. Gate access code. Pre-book
02 6574 5555   HEMA 46 E5   32 57 22 S   150 53 14 E

195 Bulga Recreation Ground
The Inlet Rd, Bulga
Parking Area 22 km SW of Singleton
02 6578 7290   HEMA 46 B6   32 39 12 S   151 01 06 E

196 McNamara Park
1273 Milbrodale Rd, Broke
Camp Area 26 km SW of Singleton. Via Wollombi St. Riverside
02 6578 7290   HEMA 46 C7   32 44 52 S   151 06 01 E

197 Branxton Oval
John Rose Ave, Branxton
Parking Area 400 m N of PO
02 4993 6700   HEMA 45 A5   32 39 18 S   151 21 05 E

198 Drovers Camp
317 Elderslie Rd, Branxton
Camp Area 3 km N of Branxton. Pre-book 9am-3pm
02 4938 1009   HEMA 47 A9   32 37 33 S   151 21 07 E

NEW SOUTH WALES

199 Camp On Allyn
1972 Gresford Rd, East Gresford
Camp Area 1.5 km S of East Gresford. Pre-book. Signposted, GPS at entrance
0407 389 420   HEMA 55 K8   32 26 37 S   151 33 18 E

200 East Gresford Showground
44 Park St, East Gresford
Camp Area 800 m E of PO. Via Gresford-Paterson Rd
0488 139 054   HEMA 55 K8   32 25 56 S   151 33 27 E

201 Maitland Showground
50 Blomfield St, South Maitland
Camp Area 5 km SE of PO. 21 day limit. Pre-book
02 4933 5052   HEMA 47 C11   32 44 38 S   151 33 48 E

202 Kurri Kurri Sports Ground
Allworth St, Kurri Kurri
Parking Area 800 m S of PO
02 4936 1909   HEMA 47 D11   32 49 24 S   151 28 51 E

203 Abermain Bowling & Rec Club
Cnr Goulburn & Armidale St, Abermain
Parking Area beside club. 10 km W of Kurri Kurri
02 4930 4285   HEMA 45 H7   32 48 26 S   151 25 36 E

204 Cessnock Showground
111 Mount View Rd, Cessnock
Camp Area 2 km W of PO. Access gates beside indoor sports centre. 14 day limit
0412 235 447   HEMA 45 J4   32 49 51 S   151 20 26 E

205 Khartoum Hotel
19 Cessnock St, Kitchener
Parking Area 54 km W of Newcastle. Check in with publican. Limited space. Toilets opening hours only. Fee for non patrons
02 4990 1560   HEMA 47 D9   32 52 33 S   151 21 57 E

206 The Wollombi Tavern

2994 Great North Rd, Wollombi
Camp Area beside pub, check in with publican
02 4998 3261   HEMA 46 E7   32 56 19 S   151 08 25 E

Woodenbong to Grafton
Summerland Way

207 Koreelah Creek Camp
Koreelah National Park
White Swamp Rd, Woodenbong
Camp Area 35 km NW of Woodenbong. Turn N off the Mt Lindesay Rd 23 km W of Woodenbong or 22 km E of Legume at Old Koreelah to White Swamp Rd for 12 km. 3 km dirt road. Creekside
02 6632 0000   HEMA 57 A10   28 18 30 S   152 27 58 E

208 Levuka 4WD Park
Plantation Rd, Urbenville
Camp Area 16 km SW of Woodenborg. 6 km W of Woodenborg turn S to Beaury Creek Rd then W to Plantation Rd. Day fee includes overnight camp. Pre-book
02 6634 1338   HEMA 57 B10   28 25 20 S   152 30 33 E

209 Woodenbong Campground
127 Unumgar St, Woodenbong
Camp Area W end of town, next to swimming pool. Pay at service station or caretaker on site. Fee for showers
0427 612 919   HEMA 57 B11   28 23 20 S   152 36 21 E

210 Crown Hotel Urbenville
48 Urben St, Urbenville
Parking Area behind pub, opposite PO. Register at bar. Free for patrons. Amenities available in opening hours
02 6634 1213   HEMA 57 B10   28 28 20 S   152 32 53 E

211 Urbenville Showground
17638 Clarence Way, Urbenville
Camp Area near general store. Pre-book at Visitor Centre
02 6634 1254   HEMA 57 B10   28 28 15 S   152 33 09 E

212 Legume Community Hall
Mount Lindsay Rd, Legume
Camp Area behind hall. Donation to shop
07 4666 4191   HEMA 57 B10   28 24 23 S   152 18 25 E

213 Urbenville Forest Park
Urbenville Forest Reserve
Clarence Way, Urbenville
Camp Area N end of town. Fees collected
1300 655 687   HEMA 57 B10   28 28 06 S   152 32 56 E

214 Old Bonalbo Pioneers Park
Clarence Way, Old Bonalbo
Rest Area 23 km S of Urbenville or 1 km N of Old Bonalbo
02 6632 1611   HEMA 57 C11   28 38 35 S   152 35 49 E

215 Sheepstation Creek Camp
Border Ranges National Park
Sheepstation Creek Rd, Border Ranges
Camp Area 17 km NE of Wiangaree. Via Lynchs Creek Rd & Tweed Range Scenic Dr. 11 km dirt road. Pre-book
02 6632 0000   HEMA 57 B12   28 24 47 S   153 01 23 E

216 Wadeville Woolies
163 Link Rd, Wadeville
Camp Area 20 km N of Kyogle or 48 km S of Murwillumbah
02 6689 7285   HEMA 57 B13   28 33 59 S   153 07 40 E

217 Kyogle Showground
43 Summerland Way, New Park
Camp Area N end of town. Pre-book for power
02 6632 2454   HEMA 57 C12   28 36 57 S   153 00 00 E

218 Bells Bay
Toonumbar Dam
Dam Access Rd, Ghinni Ghi
Camp Area 29 km W of Kyogle, via Afterlee Rd & Dam Access Rd. Some dirt road. Closed in droughts
0459 383 498   HEMA 57 C11   28 37 00 S   152 47 39 E

219 Braemar Park

Ellangowan State Forest
Summerland Way, Ellangowan
Rest Area 28 km S of Casino or 22 km N of Whiporie
1300 655 687   HEMA 57 E12   29 05 16 S   153 00 07 E

220 Aranyani Bison Adventure
Tourist Park
670 Elliotts Rd, Myrtle Creek
Camp Area 39 km S of Casino. Pre-book
02 6661 7866   HEMA 57 E12   29 10 24 S   153 02 32 E

221 Whiporie General Store

5351 Summerland Way, Whiporie
Camp Area beside store. Ask owner's
permission. Free with spend in-store
02 6661 9100   HEMA 57 E12   29 16 56 S   152 59 22 E

222 Copmanhurst Primitive Camp

Lawrence St, Copmanhurst
Camp Area 31 km NW of Grafton. Via
Clarence Way. Pre-book
1300 886 235   HEMA 57 G11   29 35 28 S   152 47 01 E

223 Copmanhurst Rec Reserve

Lawrence St, Copmanhurst
Camp Area 31 km NW of Grafton. Via
Clarence Way
0427 449 783   HEMA 57 G11   29 35 23 S   152 46 27 E

224 Lilydale Primitive Camp

Winegrove Rd, Winegrove
Camp Area 12 km from Copmanhurst. Via
Clarence Way. SW side of Lilydale Bridge. Pre-book
1300 886 235   HEMA 57 G11   29 32 46 S   152 40 16 E

225 The Gorge

2568 Gorge Rd, Heifer Station
Farm Stay 27 km from Lilydale Bridge. Via
Copmanhurst. Dirt road. Pre-book
02 6647 2173   HEMA 57 F11   29 23 25 S   152 34 19 E

226 Wave Hill Station

543 Carnham Rd, Carnham
Farm Stay 40 km N or Copmanhurst. Via
Clarence Way. Pre-book
02 6647 2145   HEMA 57 F11   29 20 37 S   152 37 19 E

Ballina to Goondiwindi
Bruxner Highway

227 Lismore Showgrounds

Alexandra Pde, Lismore
Camp Area 2 km N of PO. Pre-book.
49 day limit
02 6621 5916   HEMA 57 C13   28 47 50 S   153 16 25 E

228 Rummery Park

Whian Whian State Conservation Area
Peates Mountain Rd, Whian Whian
Camp Area 32 km NE of Lismore. Turn N off
Dunoon Rd, 7 km NE of Dunoon to Minyon Falls
Rd (Nightcap Range Rd) & Peates Mountain Rd for
8 km. 7 km narrow, winding, dirt road. Pre-book
02 6627 0200   HEMA 57 C13   28 35 57 S   153 22 41 E

229 Nimbin Showgrounds

Cecil St, Nimbin
Camp Area 650 m E of PO. 7 day limit
0458 872 228   HEMA 57 C13   28 35 56 S   153 13 36 E

230 Ichiban Park

2486 Nimbin Rd, Nimbin
Camp Area 2 km S of Nimbin
0407 088 427   HEMA 57 C13   28 36 18 S   153 12 56 E

231 Mallanganee Oval

Pine St, Mallanganee
Camp Area 40 km W of Casino. Access
behind Bush Fire Brigade Building. See PO for
bookings. BYO water
02 6664 5266   HEMA 57 D11   28 54 29 S   152 43 17 E

232 Bonalbo Tourist Park

1 Woodenbong Rd, Bonalbo
Caravan Park 750 m SE of PO. Caretaker
onsite
0428 989 727   HEMA 57 C11   28 44 19 S   152 37 43 E

233 Peacock Creek Camp Area

Richmond Range National Park
Peacock Creek Rd, Peacock Creek
Camp Area 18 km NE of Bonalbo. Turn N off
Clarence Way 3 km E of Bonalbo. 13.5 km to
campsite. Dirt road. 4WD only when wet
02 6632 0000   HEMA 57 C11   28 39 36 S   152 42 56 E

234 West of The Range Rest Area

Bruxner Hwy, Sandilands
Rest Area 10 km E of Tabulam or 9 km W of
Mallangane. Jcn of Clarence Way
132 213   HEMA 57 D11   28 54 02 S   152 39 15 E

235 Tabulam Racecourse

Racecourse Rd, Tabulam
Camp Area 2 km S of Tabulam. Keys &
payment at the service station or co-op
02 6666 1204   HEMA 57 D11   28 54 22 S   152 33 16 E

236 Clarence River Wilderness
Lodge
Paddys Flat Rd, Tabulam
Camp Area 45 km NW of Tabulam. Turn N 3 km
S of Tabulam off the Bruxner Hwy, travel 38 km to
entrance. 7 km to camp area, 38 km of gravel road.
Pre-book
02 6665 1337   HEMA 57 C10   28 41 24 S   152 22 35 E

237 Lanikai Campground &
Wildlife Refuge
2030 Paddys Flat Rd, Tabulam
Camp Area 28 km NW of Tabulam. Turn N 3 km S of
Tabulam off Bruxner Hwy to Paddys Flat Rd. 28 km
gravel road. Book in at farmhouse for payment &
directions
0438 859 087   HEMA 57 C10   28 44 41 S   152 25 36 E

NEW SOUTH WALES

238 Crooked Creek Picnic Area
Girard State Forest
Crooked Creek Firetrail, Sandy Hill
Picnic Area 40 km E of Tenterfield or 9 km W of Drake. Steep descent for last 200 m. Inspect first
1300 655 687 HEMA 57 D10 28 55 37 S 152 18 44 E

239 Roseneath Station Farm Stay
6973 Bruxner Hwy, Dumaresq Valley
Farm Stay 70 km W of Tenterfield or 69 km SE of Texas
0427 422 639 HEMA 56 E7 29 04 58 S 151 29 32 E

240 Bonshaw Weir
Bonshaw Weir Rd, Bonshaw
Camp Area 8 km N of Bonshaw or 21 km SE of Texas
137 468 HEMA 56 D6 28 59 08 S 151 16 31 E

241 Wongalea Fishing & Camping
Bedwell Downs Rd, Yetman
Farm Stay 16 km S of Yetman. Take Bedwell Downs Rd, turn L 300 m after the Wongalea mailbox - before the grid. Follow 250 m to the creek. Phone ahead so gates are open
0427 504 198 HEMA 56 D4 29 02 28 S 150 49 25 E

242 Yetman Caravan Park
MacIntyre St, Yetman
Caravan Park 42 km W of Texas. Opposite picnic area, behind tennis courts. Pay caretaker at house next door
07 4675 3231 HEMA 56 D4 28 54 06 S 150 46 42 E

Grafton to Walgett
Gwydir Highway

243 Marr Creek Rest Area
Gwydir Hwy, Jackadgery
Rest Area (Lollback) at Jackadgery, 43 km W of South Grafton or 111 km E of Glen Innes. Beside Mann R Bridge
132 213 HEMA 57 G10 29 34 39 S 152 33 25 E

244 Mann River - Floyd Camp
Via Hermitage Rd, Coombadjha
Camp Area E off Gwydir Hwy to Cangai Bridge Rd. N to Coombadjha Rd
02 6643 0800 HEMA 57 F10 29 26 50 S 152 29 47 E

245 Cangai Bridge
Cangai Bridge Rd, Cangai
Camp Spot 20 km W of Jackadery via Gwydir Hwy. Small vehicles only, narrow bridges
02 6643 0800 HEMA 57 F10 29 29 24 S 152 28 01 E

246 Broadwater Bridge
Hanging Rock Rd, Cangai
Camp Spot 26 km W of Jackadery via Gwydir Hwy, Cangai Bridge Rd. Small vehicles only, narrow bridges
02 6643 0800 HEMA 57 F10 29 27 07 S 152 29 36 E

247 Bellbird Campground
Washpool National Park
Coombadjha Track, Gibraltar Range
Camp Area 85 km W of South Grafton or 75 km E of Glen Innes. Turn N off Gwydir Hwy 82 km W of South Grafton or 72 km E of Glen Innes, to Coachwood Rd. 3 km dirt road. Small vehicles only. Pre-book
02 6739 0700 HEMA 57 F10 29 28 27 S 152 18 58 E

248 Mulligans Hut Campground
Gibraltar Range National Park
Mulligans Dr, Gibraltar Range
Camp Area 94 km W of South Grafton or 78 km E of Glen Innes. Turn S at Info Centre 85 km W of South Grafton or 69 km E of Glen Innes, to Mulligans Dr. 9 km dirt road. Cold showers. Pre-book
02 6739 0700 HEMA 57 F10 29 30 57 S 152 21 34 E

249 Boundary Falls Campground
Gibraltar Range National Park
Boundary Creek Trail, Moogem
Camp Area 95 km W of South Grafton or 63 km E of Glen Innes. Turn N off Gwydir Hwy 93 km W of South Grafton or 61 km E of Glen Innes. 1.5 km dirt road. Pre-book
02 6739 0700 HEMA 57 F9 29 32 02 S 152 14 56 E

250 Mann River Campground
Mann River Nature Reserve
11780 Old Grafton Rd, Diehard
Camp Area 131 km W of South Grafton or 47 km E of Glen Innes. Turn S off Gwydir Hwy 119 km W of South Grafton or 35 km E of Glen Innes to Old Glen Innes-Grafton Rd. 12 km to campsites, open grassy area riverside. Narrow winding road steep in places, some dirt road. Pre-book
02 6739 0700 HEMA 57 G9 29 41 15 S 152 05 55 E

251 Jindalee River Camp
1001 Bald Nob Rd, Dundee
Camp Area 27 km NE of Glen Innes or 136 km W of South Grafton. Turn R after second bridge through gate. 14 day limit. Dirt access road. Pre-book for directions
0427 255 825 HEMA 57 G8 29 37 21 S 151 57 10 E

252 Sinclair Lookout
Gwydir Hwy, Matheson
Parking Area 15 km W of Glen Innes or 52 km E of Inverell. Steep rocky access to the lookout
132 213 HEMA 56 G7 29 43 35 S 151 35 58 E

253 Swan Brook Rest Area
Gwydir Hwy, Swan Vale
Rest Area 36 km W of Glen Innes or 35 km E of Inverell
132 213 HEMA 56 G7 29 46 18 S 151 26 09 E

254 Billabong Blue Sapphire
Fossicking Park
2479 Kings Plains Rd, Sapphire
Camp Area 26 km NE of Inverell. Look for Ned Kelly at entrance gates
02 6721 0500 HEMA 56 G6 29 41 34 S 151 19 50 E

255 Tingha Gems Caravan & Camping
91 Swimming Pool Rd, Tingha
Camp Area 28 km SE of Inverell
02 6723 3234 HEMA 56 H6 29 56 45 S 151 12 58 E

256 Green Valley Farm

161 Jones Rd, Tingha
Camp Area 37 km SE of Inverell. Via New
Valley Rd. Park access fee
02 6723 3370   HEMA 56 H6   29 59 13 S   151 18 01 E

257 Inverell Showground

10 Tingha Rd, Inverell
Camp Area 1 km E of town. Between
sporting complex & Pioneer Village. Limited sites.
Pre-book
02 6722 3435   HEMA 56 G5   29 46 57 S   151 07 14 E

258 Pindari Dam

Pindari Dam Rd, Pindaroi
Camp Area 59 km N of Inverell or 22 km SE
of Ashford. Small vehicles only. 7 day limit
02 6728 8161   HEMA 56 F6   29 23 46 S   151 15 34 E

259 Wells Crossing

Bukkulla Rd, Ashford
Camp Area 7 km E of Ashford. Via Pindari
Dam Rd
02 6728 8161   HEMA 56 F6   29 21 44 S   151 08 36 E

260 Ashford Caravan Park

Bukkulla St, Ashford
Caravan Park 57 km N of Inverell.
Honesty box
02 6728 8161   HEMA 56 F5   29 19 24 S   151 05 52 E

261 Severn River Rest Area

444 Bonshaw Rd, Ashford
Rest Area (3 Mile) 4 km N of Ashford
02 6728 8161   HEMA 56 E6   29 17 52 S   151 07 05 E

262 Lemon Tree Flat Camp

Kwiambal National Park
Lemon Tree Flat Rd, Atholwood
Camp Area 38 km NW of Ashford. Via Wallangra,
Sandy Creek, Limetone Rd. 21 km unsealed road.
Limited caravan sites
02 6736 4298   HEMA 56 E5   29 08 52 S   150 59 30 E

263 Copeton Dam (Northern Foreshore)

Auburn Vale Rd, Copeton
Camp Area 17 km SW of Inverell
02 6728 8161   HEMA 56 H5   29 53 37 S   150 59 50 E

264 Delungra Showgrounds

Reedy St, Delungra
Camp Area W end of town. Cash only to
service station
02 6728 8161   HEMA 56 G4   29 39 04 S   150 49 33 E

265 Graman Hotel

4150 Yetman Rd, Graman
Camp Area 41 km NW of Inverell. Large
grassed area behind hotel. Free for patrons. Check
in with publican
02 6725 6491   HEMA 56 F5   29 28 09 S   150 55 41 E

266 Wallangra Sports Ground

Yetman Rd, Wallangra
Rest Area 65 km NW of Inverell, or 60 km
NE of Warialda
02 6729 0046   HEMA 56 E5   29 15 31 S   150 53 52 E

267 Dumboy Creek Rest Area

Gwydir Hwy, Delungra
Rest Area 4 km NW of Delungra or 29 km
SE of Warialda
132 213   HEMA 56 G4   29 38 24 S   150 47 51 E

268 Cranky Rock Nature Reserve

Cranky Rock Rd, Warialda
Camp Area 26 km NW of Delungra or 8 km
E of Warialda. Turn N off Hwy 23 km NW of Delungra
or 5 km E of Warialda for 3 km. Pay at kiosk
02 6729 1402   HEMA 56 G4   29 33 39 S   150 38 46 E

269 The Coolatai Hall

3 Wallangra Rd, Coolatai
Camp Area 43 km NW Warialda. Donation
box for upkeep & hot showers
02 6729 0046   HEMA 56 E4   29 15 02 S   150 45 08 E

270 Saleyards Rest Area

Gwydir Hwy, Warialda
Rest Area 1 km SE of PO. E of town
02 6729 0046   HEMA 56 G4   29 32 44 S   150 34 53 E

271 Cunninghams Rest Area

Gwydir Hwy, Warialda
Rest Area 2 km W of Warialda or 78 km E
of Moree. N side of Hwy
02 6729 0046   HEMA 56 G4   29 32 46 S   150 33 14 E

272 Ezzy's Crossing

Via Gwydir Hwy, Gravesend
Camp Area 3.5 km E of Gravesend. Entry
track N side of bridge
02 6729 0046   HEMA 56 G3   29 34 37 S   150 21 31 E

273 Gravesend Rec Reserve

Warialda St, Gravesend
Camp Area 30 km W of Warialda
02 6729 0046   HEMA 56 G3   29 35 06 S   150 20 02 E

274 Gravesend Hotel

16 Railway Pde, Gravesend
Camp Area behind hotel, 30 km W of
Warialda. Check in with publican, free for patrons
02 6729 7005   HEMA 56 G3   29 34 59 S   150 20 15 E

NEW SOUTH WALES

275 Pally Pub Caravan Park
59 Bingera St, Pallamallawa
Caravan Park 33 km E of Moree
02 6754 9236　　HEMA 56 F2　29 28 28 S　150 08 07 E

276 Pallamallawa Fishing Club
55 Warialda St, Pallamallawa
Camp Area at Memorial Park, 36 km E of Moree
02 6757 3222　　HEMA 56 F2　29 28 35 S　150 08 12 E

277 Gum Flat Public Reserve
Gum Flat Rd, Biniguy
Camp Spot 58 km W of Warialda or 28 km E of Moree. Turn N 55 km W of Warialda or 25 km E of Moree to Gum Flat Rd. 3 km dirt road N of Hwy. Signposted
02 6757 3222　　HEMA 56 F2　29 27 54 S　150 04 54 E

278 Tareelaroi Weir Rec Reserve
Tareelaroi Weir Rd, Moree
Camp Area 24 km E of Moree. E on Gwydir Hwy for 18 km, N for 5 km to camp on river
02 6757 3222　　HEMA 56 F2　29 26 50 S　150 02 26 E

279 Barwon River Crossing Park
Mungindi Bridge
Carnarvon Hwy, Mungindi
Camp Area N side of bridge
07 4620 8877　　HEMA 58 C4　28 58 33 S　148 59 01 E

280 Two Mile Hotel
355 Carnarvon Hwy, Mungindi
Pub Stay behind hotel. Check in at bar, prior to setting up
02 6753 2051　　HEMA 58 C4　28 56 47 S　148 58 28 E

281 Boomi River Picnic Area
Carnarvon Hwy, Mungindi
Camp Area 10 km S of Mungindi. Turn E on tracks S side of the bridge. Large flat area 300 m from Hwy
02 6757 3222　　HEMA 58 C4　29 01 18 S　149 03 57 E

282 Mehi River Rest Area
Gwydir Hwy, Bullarah
Rest Area 91 km W of Moree or 48 km E of Collarenebri
132 213　　HEMA 58 D4　29 27 10 S　149 00 20 E

283 Collarenebri Primitive Camp
Gwydir Hwy, Collarenebri
Camp Area next to football grounds, E end of town. Gravel road
02 6828 6139　　HEMA 58 D3　29 32 56 S　148 34 55 E

Grafton / Dorrigo to Armidale

284 Coutts Tavern
13 Armidale Rd, Coutts Crossing
Pub Stay 15 km S of Grafton. Check in with publican. Parking at rear of tavern, free for patrons
02 6649 3256　　HEMA 57 H12　29 49 42 S　152 53 29 E

285 Nymboida Camping & Canoeing
3520 Armidale Rd, Nymboida
Camp Area 37 km SW of Grafton or 81 km NE of Ebor. Pre-book
02 6649 4155　　HEMA 57 H11　29 55 33 S　152 44 52 E

286 Buccarumbi Primitive Camp
3919 Old Glen Innes Rd, Buccarumbi
Camp Area 50 km SW of Grafton, via Old Grafton Rd. Adjacent to Buccarumbi Bridge
02 6643 0800　　HEMA 57 H11　29 50 07 S　152 35 16 E

287 Nymboida River Camp
Nymboida National Park
T-Ridge Rd, Jackadgery
Picnic Area 51 km W of South Grafton roundabout. Follow Gwydir Hwy through Ramornie Village to Ramornie Forest Rd. Pre-book
02 6641 1500　　HEMA 57 G10　29 42 38 S　152 33 30 E

288 Dalmorton Campground
Guy Fawkes River National Park
Chaelundi Rd, Dalmorton
Camp Area 65 km W of Grafton via Old Grafton-Glen Innes Rd. Turn to Chaelundi Rd 58 km along Grafton Rd, 1 km to campground. Pre-book
02 6739 0700　　HEMA 57 H10　29 51 56 S　152 26 52 E

289 Doon Goonge Campground
Chaelundi National Park
Chandlers Creek Trail, Buccarumbi
Camp Area 76 km SW of Grafton. Via Fitzroy, Armidale Sts, Boundary Ck Rd in Nymboida & Shannon Ck Rd. Pre-book
02 6657 5913　　HEMA 59 E12　29 54 32 S　152 30 35 E

290 Clouds Creek Campground
Armidale Rd, Clouds Creek
Camp Area at Clouds Creek. 23 km S of Nymboida
HEMA 57 H11　30 00 01 S　152 40 51 E

291 Platypus Flat Campground
Nymboi-Binderay National Park
Platypus Flat Rd, Wild Cattle Creek
Camp Area 29 km N of Dorrigo. Via Cascade, Moses Rock & Cedar Rds. Follow signs. Limited sites. Small vehicles only. Pre-book
1300 072 757　　HEMA 57 J11　30 11 09 S　152 41 29 E

292 Chaelundi Campground
Guy Fawkes River National Park
Misty Creek Rd, The Gulf
Camp Area 38 km NW of Ebor. Turn W 81 km SW of Grafton or 14 km N of Ebor to Sheepstation Creek Rd, L to Chaelundi Rd. 24 km dirt road
02 6739 0700　　HEMA 57 J10　30 04 07 S　152 19 59 E

293 Ulong Community Hall
13 Pine Ave, Ulong
Camp Area & Showground 35 km NE of Dorrigo. Pay & get key from general store during opening hours. Pre-book
02 6654 5320　　HEMA 57 J12　30 14 42 S　152 53 14 E

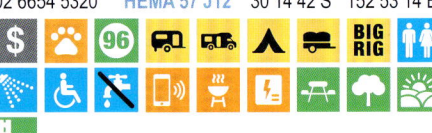

294 Dangar Falls Lodge
180 Coramba Rd, Dorrigo
B78 Camp Area 2 km N of Dorrigo. Entrance 100 m N of Dangar Falls car park. Entry through gate. Fee for shower. 7 day limit
02 6657 2131   HEMA 57 K11   30 19 18 S   152 42 51 E

295 Dorrigo Showgrounds
Waterfall Way, Dorrigo
B78 Camp Area 650 m W of PO
02 6657 1777   HEMA 55 A12   30 20 17 S   152 42 23 E

296 Ebor Sports & Rec Reserve
11822 Waterfall Way, Ebor
78 Camp Spot 600 m W of town. Next to sportsground. Opposite Ebor Falls turnoff
1300 136 833   HEMA 55 A11   30 24 28 S   152 20 46 E

297 Ebor Falls Hotel Motel
11690 Waterfall Way, Ebor
78 Camp Area behind hotel, 48 km W of Dorrigo
02 6775 9155   HEMA 55 A11   30 24 11 S   152 20 51 E

298 Native Dog Creek Camp
Cathedral Rock National Park
17 Guyra Rd, Ebor
Camp Area 12 km NW of Ebor or 67 km SE of Guyra. 200 m SW of Hwy
02 6739 0700   HEMA 55 A11   30 23 15 S   152 16 06 E

299 Barokee Campground
Cathedral Rock National Park
B78 Barokee Rd, Ebor
Camp Area 14 km SW of Ebor or 38 km E of Wollomombi. Turn W off Waterfall Way 6 km SW of Ebor or 32 km E of Wollomombi, to Round Mountain Rd. 8 km dirt road. Small vehicles only
02 6739 0700   HEMA 55 A10   30 26 38 S   152 15 02 E

300 Little Styx River Campground
971 Point Lookout Rd, Ebor
B78 Camp Area 21 km S of Ebor or 37 km E of Wollomombi. Turn E off Waterfall Way 11 km SW of Ebor or 27 km E of Wollomombi, to Point Lookout Rd. 10 km dirt road. At New England NP entry
02 6770 3888   HEMA 55 A11   30 30 28 S   152 21 59 E

301 Thungutti Camping Ground
New England National Park
B78 Point Lookout Rd, Ebor
Camp Area 23 km S of Ebor, or 35 km E of Wollomombi. Turn E off Waterfall Way. 11 km dirt road. Cold showers. Small vehicles only. Pre-book
1300 072 757   HEMA 55 A11   30 30 02 S   152 23 15 E

302 Dingo Fence Rest Area
Waterfall Way, Wollomombi
78 Rest Area 28 km SW of Ebor or 10 km E of Wollomombi
132 213   HEMA 55 A10   30 30 08 S   152 08 43 E

303 Wollomombi Rest Area
87 Wollomombi Village Rd, Wollomombi
B78 Rest Area 1 km NW off Waterfall Way. Toilets at memorial hall
02 6778 1336   HEMA 55 A10   30 30 42 S   152 02 40 E

304 Wollomombi General Store
110 Wollomombi Village Rd, Wollomombi
B78 Camp Area beside store, turn off Waterfall Way. Check in at store on arrival
02 6778 1336   HEMA 55 A10   30 30 40 S   152 02 32 E

305 Wattle Flat Camping Area
Styx River State Forest
B78 Boundary Trail, Jeogla
Camp Area 70 km E of Armidale. Access via Armidale-Kempsey Rd. Turn N to Styx River Forest Way, follow signage. Small vehicles only
1300 655 687   HEMA 55 B10   30 35 01 S   152 12 02 E

306 Georges Junction
Kempsey Rd, Carrai
B78 Camp Area 83 km SE of Armidale or 46 km W of Bellbrook. Via Armidale-Kempsey Rd, access road not suitable for caravans
1300 136 833   HEMA 55 B10   30 45 09 S   152 11 28 E

307 Cracknback Campground
8476 Armidale-Kempsey Rd, Lower Creek
B78 Camp Area 34 km NW of Bellbrook. W from Kempsey on River Rd. 14 day limit
0468 411 967   HEMA 55 B11   30 44 41 S   152 16 50 E

308 Blackbird Flat Reserve
7889 Armidale-Kempsey Rd,, Carrai
A1 Picnic Area 69 km NW of Kempsey or 68 km SE of Wollomombi near Comara. 16 km dirt road. Road not suitable for caravans. 14 day limit
02 6563 1555   HEMA 55 C11   30 45 45 S   152 21 47 E

309 Bellbrook Cabins & Camping
2 Main St, Bellbrook
A1 Camp Area opposite school. Turn off Armidale-Kempsey Rd. Book in at general store
0490 004 428   HEMA 55 C11   30 49 06 S   152 30 31 E

310 West Kunderang Wilderness Retreat
Raspberry Rd, Jeogla
Camp Area 50 km E of Armidale. Dirt road. Pre-book
0429 192 810   HEMA 55 C10   30 50 38 S   152 04 36 E

311 Budds Mare Campground
Oxley Wild Rivers NP
B56 Budds Mare Trail, Walcha
Remote campground 45 kms E of Walcha via Fitzroy/Oxley Hwy. Take Emu Ck Rd, Moona Plains Rd, Kanangra Vale Rd to Trail. Pre-book
02 6777 4700   HEMA 55 C9   30 59 01 S   151 58 14 E

312 Wollomombi Campground
Oxley Wild Rivers National Park
B78 Edgars Lookout Rd, Hillgrove
Camp Area 4 km W of Wollomombi. Turn S off Waterfall Way 2 km W of Wollomombi or 38 km E of Armidale. Near Wollomombi Gorge. Narrow entrance way. Pre-book
02 6738 9100   HEMA 55 B10   30 31 54 S   152 01 40 E

313 Gara River Rest Area
Waterfall Way, Argyle
78 Rest Area 27 km W of Wollomombi or 13 km E of Armidale
132 213   HEMA 55 B9   30 32 38 S   151 47 39 E

314 Dangars Gorge

Oxley Wild Rivers National Park

Dangars Falls Rd, Dangarsleigh
Camp Area 22 km SE of Armidale via Dangarsleigh.
10 km dirt road
02 6738 9100   HEMA 55 B9   30 40 20 S   151 43 32 E

Port Macquarie-Tamworth-Coonabarabran

Oxley Highway

315 Wauchope Showgrounds

93A High St, Wauchope
Camp Area 800 m W of PO. Limited
powered sites. Pre-book. 14 day limit
0475 111 074   HEMA 55 E12   31 27 28 S   152 43 27 E

316 Rollands Plains Rec Reserve

28 Bril Bril Rd, Rollands Plains
Camp Area 30 km N of Wauchope. Entry
via Bril Bril Rd. Caretaker on-site
0458 992 783   HEMA 55 E12   31 16 47 S   152 40 44 E

317 Brushy Mountain

Werrikimbe National Park

Brushy Trail, Forbes River
Camp Area 61 km NW of Wauchope, via
Beechwood, Bellangry & Hastings Forest Way.
38 km dirt road. Small vehicles only. Pre-book
02 6582 3355   HEMA 55 D11   31 08 52 S   152 21 42 E

318 Timbertown Heritage Park

2325 Oxley Hwy, Wauchope
Camp Area E of Wauchope and S of Hwy
0402 364 616   HEMA 55 E12   31 28 13 S   152 42 46 E

319 Long Flat Hotel

5014 Oxley Hwy, Long Flat
Pub Stay 29 km W of Wauchope. Check in
with publican
02 6587 4495   HEMA 55 E11   31 26 09 S   152 29 34 E

320 Ellenborough Reserve

Main St, Ellenborough
Camp Area 500 m N of Hwy on E side of
bridge, riverside. 14 day limit
02 6581 8111   HEMA 55 E11   31 26 25 S   152 27 40 E

321 Mooraback Campground

Werrikimbe National Park

Mooraback Rest Area Rd, Yarrowitch
Camp Area 84 km E of Walcha. Turn N off the Oxley
Hwy 111 km W of Wauchope or 54 km SE of Walcha
to Kangaroo Flat & Mooraback Rds. 30 km dirt road.
Small vehicles only
02 6777 4700   HEMA 55 D10   31 08 51 S   152 12 54 E

322 Tia Falls Campground

Oxley Wild Rivers National Park

Tia Falls Rd, Walcha
Camp Area 42 km SE of Walcha. Turn N off Oxley
Hwy 128 km NW of Wauchope or 37 km SE of
Walcha. 5 km dirt road
02 6777 4700   HEMA 55 D9   31 09 37 S   151 51 16 E

323 Tia River Rest Area

Oxley Hwy, Walcha
Rest Area 129 km NW of Wauchope or
36 km SE of Walcha
132 213   HEMA 55 D9   31 11 17 S   151 49 51 E

324 Stoney Creek Rest Area

Oxley Hwy, Walcha
Rest Area 143 km NW of Wauchope or
22 km SE of Walcha
132 213   HEMA 55 D9   31 04 35 S   151 46 39 E

325 Apsley Falls Campground

Oxley Wild Rivers National Park

Apsley Falls Rd, Walcha
Camp Area 20 km SE of Walcha. Turn N off Oxley
Hwy 146 km NW of Wauchope or 19 km SE of
Walcha for 1 km
02 6777 4700   HEMA 55 D9   31 03 16 S   151 45 45 E

326 Walcha East Rest Area

Oxley Hwy, Walcha
Rest Area 4 km E of Walcha or 161 km NW
of Wauchope
132 213   HEMA 55 D8   31 00 13 S   151 37 48 E

327 Nowendoc Memorial Hall

Brackendale Rd, Nowendoc
Picnic Area 71 km SE of Walcha. Turn off
Thunderbolts Way via The Tops Road. Near Jcn.
7 day limit
02 6777 0955   HEMA 55 F9   31 30 50 S   151 42 57 E

328 Woolbrook Rest Area

Danglemah Rd, Woolbrook
Rest Area 1 km S of Hwy, riverside. 26 km
W of Walcha or 26 km E of Bendemeer
HEMA 54 C7   30 57 55 S   151 20 50 E

329 Woolbrook Hall

Danglemah Rd, Woolbrook
Camp Area 26 km W of Walcha or 26 km E
of Bendemeer. Behind School of Arts, S side of river.
Call to obtain key. SCV rates
02 6777 5813   HEMA 54 C7   30 57 58 S   151 20 43 E

330 Eastern Foreshore Camp

Lake Keepit State Park

Keepit Dam Rd, Rushes Creek
Camp Area 56 km NW of Tamworth. Turn N off
Oxley Hwy, 46 km W of Tamworth or 29 km E of
Gunnedah. 3 km dirt road. Pre-book
02 6769 7605   HEMA 54 C4   30 53 20 S   150 31 06 E

331 Red Bank Rest Area

Oxley Hwy, Carroll
Rest Area 7 km W of Carroll or 12 km E of
Gunnedah
02 6740 2230   HEMA 54 C4   30 59 39 S   150 22 40 E

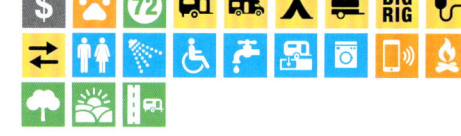

332 South St RV Park

Oxley Hwy, Gunnedah
Camp Area next to showgrounds. Caretaker
collects fees
02 6742 1589   HEMA 54 C4   30 58 44 S   150 14 42 E

333 Donnelly Field

Maitland St, Gunnedah
Camp Area 1 km NW of PO
02 6740 2230   HEMA 54 C4   30 58 20 S   150 15 10 E

334 150 Meridian Rest Area

Oxley Hwy, Mullaley
Rest Area 27 km W of Gunnedah or 10 km
E of Mullaley
132 213   HEMA 54 D3   31 03 46 S   149 59 55 E

335 Mullaley Post Office Hotel
Oxley Hwy, Mullaley
Camp Area 38 SW of Gunnedah. W end of town. Check in at bar
02 6743 7820   HEMA 54 D2   31 06 01 S   149 54 15 E

336 Oxleys Crossing Rest Area
Oxley Hwy, Rocky Glen
Rest Area 37 km W of Mullaley or 31 km E of Coonabarabran
132 213   HEMA 54 D1   31 07 56 S   149 32 38 E

Walcha to Raymond Terrace
Thunderbolts Way, Bucketts Way

337 Bretti Nature Reserve
Bretti Trail, Bretti
Camp Area 44 km S of Nowendoc or 34 km N of Gloucester. On Thunderbolts Way beside Manning River. 1 month limit
02 6538 5252   HEMA 55 G9   31 47 29 S   151 54 56 E

338 Gloryvale Reserve
Thunderbolts Way, Tibbuc
Camp Area 55 km S of Nowendoc or 23 km N of Gloucester. Beside Manning River. 1 month limit
02 6538 5252   HEMA 55 G9   31 51 25 S   151 52 42 E

339 Woko Campground
Woko National Park
Flood Detour Rd, Dewitt
Camp Area 33 km NW of Gloucester. Turn W off Thunderbolts Way 59 km S of Nowendoc or 19 km N of Gloucester to Curricarbark Rd & Flood Detour Rd for 14 km. 10 km dirt road. Riverside
1300 072 757   HEMA 55 G9   31 48 05 S   151 47 42 E

340 Jacky Barkers Campground
Nowendoc National Park
Jacky Barkers Rd, Nowendoc
Camp Area 13 km S of Nowendoc or 39 km N of Bretti. Via Thunderbolts Way and Wrights Rd. Pre-book
02 6777 4700   HEMA 55 F9   31 35 30 S   151 43 28 E

341 Barrington Reserve
Thunderbolts Way, Barrington
Camp Area 1.5 km W of Barrington. W side of bridge, beside Barrington River. Steep dip at entrance. Pay fee at Barrington Store. 14 night limit
02 7955 7777   HEMA 55 H9   31 58 17 S   151 53 59 E

342 The Steps Barrington
535 Manchester Rd, Bindera
Camp Area 23 km W of Gloucester. 5 km dirt road. 14 day limit, ebook
02 6558 2093   HEMA 55 H9   32 01 53 S   151 50 19 E

343 Poleys Place
814 Thunderbolts Way, Barrington
Farm Stay 2 km W of Barrington. 2 night minimum
02 6558 4220   HEMA 55 H9   31 58 05 S   151 53 53 E

344 Gloucester River Camp
Barrington Tops National Park
Gloucester Tops Rd, Invergordon
Camp Area 38 km W of Gloucester. Turn W off Bucketts Way 9 km S of Gloucester. 15 km dirt road
02 6538 5300   HEMA 55 H8   32 03 33 S   151 40 44 E

345 Telegherry Camping Area
Chichester State Forest
Middle Ridge Rd, Upper Karuah River
Camp Area 26 km N of Dungog. From Dungog take Chichester Dam Rd, turn N into Wangat Rd, E to Middle Ridge Rd. 8.5 km dirt road
02 9872 0111   HEMA 55 J9   32 13 21 S   151 44 40 E

346 Coachwood Camping Area
Chichester State Forest
Frying Pan Rd, Upper Karuah River
Camp Area 29 km N of Dungog. Via Chichester Dam Rd, N to Wangat Rd, E to Middle Ridge Rd. Dirt road
1300 655 687   HEMA 55 J9   32 12 58 S   151 45 39 E

347 Frying Pan Creek
Chichester State Forest
Frying Pan Rd, Upper Karuah River
Camp Area 30 km N of Dungog. Take Chichester Dam Rd N to Wangat Rd, turn E to Middle Ridge Rd, then E. Narrow track, small vehicles only
1300 655 687   HEMA 55 J9   32 13 09 S   151 45 42 E

348 Ferndale Park Camp Area
1940 Chichester Dam Rd, Bandon Grove
Camp Area 24 km N of Dungog. Signposted. 2 km gravel entrance road
02 4995 9239   HEMA 55 J9   32 14 46 S   151 41 23 E

349 Dobbie Rim Camping Area
Chichester State Forest
Paterson Forest Rd, Upper Allyn
Camp Area 40 km N of Gresford. Via Allyn River & Allyn River Forest Rds. 14 km dirt road, signposted. 28 day limit
1300 655 687   HEMA 55 H8   32 09 21 S   151 29 15 E

350 Pademelon Camping Area
Chichester State Forest
Paterson Forest Rd, Upper Allyn
Camp Area 40 km N of Gresford. Via Allyn River, Allyn River Forest & Paterson Forest Rds. 14 km dirt road. 28 day limit
1300 655 687   HEMA 55 H8   32 09 13 S   151 29 02 E

351 Old Camp
Chichester State Forest
Allyn River Forest Rd, Upper Allyn
Camp Area 40 km N of Gresford. Via Allyn River & Allyn River Forest Rds. Dirt road. Riverside opposite Dobbie Rim. 28 day limit
02 9872 0111   HEMA 55 H8   32 09 20 S   151 29 19 E

352 Dungog Showground
Chapman St, Dungog
Camp Area W side of town. Caretaker collects fee
02 4992 1810   HEMA 55 J9   32 24 19 S   151 45 03 E

NEW SOUTH WALES

353 Boothill Compound
338 Main Creek Rd, Main Creek
Camp Area 11 km NE of Dungog. Via
Stroud Hill Rd. Big Rigs pre-book.
0422 993 015   HEMA 55 J9   32 19 57 S   151 48 02 E

354 Stroud Showground
Cowper St, Stroud
Camp Area 27 km E of Dungog or 47 km S
of Gloucester
02 4994 5204   HEMA 55 J9   32 23 59 S   151 57 51 E

355 Riverwood Downs of
Barrington Tops
311 Monkerai Rd, Monkerai
Camp Area 29 km NW of Stroud via Bucketts Way.
Limited powered sites
1800 809 772   HEMA 55 J9   32 16 59 S   151 50 59 E

Kew to Scone

356 Swans Crossing
Kerewong State Forest
Via Kerewong Rd,, Swans Crossing
Camp Area 16 km NW of Kendall. Turn N 4 km W of
Kendall off Kendall-Lorne Rd to Upsalls Creek Rd
for 12 km. 10 km dirt road
02 9872 0111   HEMA 55 F12   31 36 29 S   152 34 55 E

357 Comboyne Showgrounds
Showgrounds Rd, Comboyne
Camp Area off Main St. Call into general
store or CTC centre to access. Sealed road from
Wauchope. 7 day limit. Pre-book
02 6550 4237   HEMA 55 F11   31 36 28 S   152 27 58 E

358 Little Plains Hall
Glenwarrin Rd, Elands
Camp Area 39 km N of Wingham or 24 km
W of Comboyne. Ask at shop for directions
0416 240 832   HEMA 55 F11   31 37 56 S   152 17 44 E

359 Rocks Crossing Reserve
3646 Nowendoc Rd, Number One
Camp Area 43 km NW of Wingham. Via
Killawarra & Mount George
132 213   HEMA 55 G10   31 46 07 S   152 04 30 E

360 Knorrit Flat Riverside Retreat
3109 Nowendoc Rd, Caffreys Flat
Camp Area 35 km NW of Wingham
02 6550 7541   HEMA 55 G10   31 47 49 S   152 03 36 E

361 Cundle Flat Farm
569 Cundle Flat Rd, Cundle Flat
Farm Stay 22 km NW of Bundook. Via
Gloucester or 60 km W of Taree via Wingham. Dirt
road. Pre-book. Cash only
02 6550 7565   HEMA 55 G10   31 48 45 S   151 59 02 E

362 Copeland Reserve
Scone Rd, Gloucester
Camp Area 12 km W of Gloucester.
1 month limit
02 6538 5252   HEMA 55 H9   31 58 21 S   151 51 32 E

363 Camp Cobark
2677 Scone Rd, Gloucester
Camp Area 34 km W of Gloucester.
Pre-book. Report to office on arrival. Fee for camp
kitchen
02 6558 5524   HEMA 55 G9   31 55 45 S   151 41 54 E

364 Manning River Campground
Barrington Tops State Forest
Pheasant Creek Rd, Barrington Tops
Camp Area access via Barrington Tops Forest Rd
1300 655 687   HEMA 55 G8   31 52 47 S   151 29 27 E

365 Polblue Campground
Barrington Tops National Park
Polblue Camping Area Rd, Moonan Brook
Camp Area 64 km W of Gloucester. Via Barrington,
Copeland & Barrington Tops Rd. Dirt road
02 6540 2300   HEMA 55 H8   31 57 25 S   151 25 35 E

366 Horse Swamp
Barrington Tops National Park
Tubrabucca Rd, Moonan Brook
Camp Area 80 km W of Gloucester, via Barrington,
Copeland & Barrington Tops Rd. 5 km past Polblue,
R to Tubrabucca Rd, 2 km dirt road
02 6540 2300   HEMA 54 G7   31 55 38 S   151 23 14 E

367 Belmadar Park Camp Area
Ellerston St, Moonan Flat
Camp Area on the Hunter R. Pay 3 nights,
stay 7
02 5551 6951   HEMA 54 G7   31 55 26 S   151 14 13 E

368 Stewarts Brook Rec Reserve
Stewarts Brook Rd, Stewarts Brook
Camp Area 77 km NE of Muswellbrook.
From Gundy take Hunter Rd, and turn SE, follow
to reserve, signposted. 6 week limit, pay caretaker.
10 km dirt road
02 6540 1300   HEMA 54 H7   32 00 12 S   151 18 29 E

369 Gundy Recreation Ground
Camp St, Gundy
Camp Area 23 km E of Scone or 27 km W
of Moonan Flat. Keys from store, pre-book
02 6545 8017   HEMA 54 H6   32 00 46 S   150 59 43 E

Warialda-Tamworth
Fossickers Way

370 Ti Tree Creek Rest Area
Fossickers Way, Warialda
Rest Area 11 km S of Warialda or 31 km N
of Bingara
132 213   HEMA 56 G3   29 36 50 S   150 32 36 E

371 Myall Creek Rest Area
Bingara Rd, Myall Creek
Rest Area 18 km SW of Delungra or 24 km
NE of Bingara
132 213   HEMA 56 G4   29 46 30 S   150 43 01 E

372 Bingara Riverside Camping North

Off White St, Bingara
Camp Area at Bingara. N side of River. GPS at entry. 7 night limit
02 6724 0066   HEMA 56 H4   29 51 41 S   150 34 12 E

373 Gwydir River Camps

Copeton Dam Rd, Bingara
Camps Areas within 6 km along riverbank, 5 km E of Bingara. 7 night limit
02 6724 0066   HEMA 56 H4   29 52 27 S   150 36 21 E

374 Upper Horton Caravan & Camping Area

Cobbadah St, Upper Horton
Camp Area next to tennis courts, bowling green, basketball court
02 6782 7249   HEMA 56 J3   30 08 24 S   150 26 36 E

375 Rocky Creek Glacial Area

Killarney Gap Rd, Rocky Creek
Camp Area 36 km SW of Bingara or 67 km NE of Narrabri. Some dirt road
HEMA 56 J3   30 02 04 S   150 19 01 E

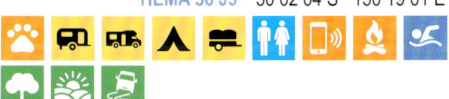

376 The Ponds Camp

Fossickers Way, Cobbadah
Rest Area 29 km S of Bingara or 32 km N of Barraba
132 213   HEMA 56 J4   30 06 39 S   150 35 51 E

377 Barraba Caravan Park

Bridge St, Barraba
Caravan Park 750 m N of PO. N end of town
02 6782 1818   HEMA 54 A5   30 22 22 S   150 36 36 E

378 Little Creek Reserve

Trevallyn Rd, Barraba
Picnic Area 21 km W of Barraba. Creekside
02 6782 1255   HEMA 54 A4   30 18 38 S   150 26 04 E

379 Barraba Lions Park

Fossickers Way, Red Hill
Rest Area 5 km S of Barraba or 40 km N of Manilla. Donation box
02 6782 1105   HEMA 54 A5   30 25 15 S   150 36 59 E

380 Glenriddle Reserve

Pera Linton Rd, Woodsreef
Camp Area 17 km S of Barraba. Turn E 9 km S of Barraba or 36 km N of Manilla to Pera Linton Rd for 8 km. 21 day limit
02 6782 1105   HEMA 54 A5   30 27 01 S   150 41 34 E

381 Split Rock Dam

Knellers Rd, Upper Manilla
Camp Area 39 km S of Barraba. Turn E 30 km S of Barraba or 15 km N of Manilla for 7 km, then N to Recreation Area Rd. Pay at council office in Barraba or Manilla
02 6782 1105   HEMA 54 B5   30 33 50 S   150 40 35 E

382 Warrabah Campground

Warrabah National Park

Warrabah Trail, Namoi River
Camp Area 35 km NE of Manilla, via Namoi Rd. 22 km dirt road. Small vehicles only
02 6792 7300   HEMA 54 B6   30 34 07 S   150 54 56 E

383 Riverside Escape

Namoi River Rd, Namoi River
Camp Area 19 km NE of Manilla. 500 m dirt track. 5 night limit
0415 388 070   HEMA 54 B5   30 38 50 S   150 50 27 E

384 Manilla Freedom Camp

Namoi St, Manilla
Camp Area town side of river. Donation to men's shed. 7 day limit
02 6785 1207   HEMA 54 B5   30 44 36 S   150 43 00 E

385 Manilla Lions Park

Fossickers Way, Klori
Rest Area 7.5 km S of Manilla or 37.5 km N of Tamworth
02 6785 1207   HEMA 54 C5   30 48 15 S   150 45 11 E

386 Attunga Creek

Manilla Rd, Attunga
Rest Area opposite pub. 24 km S of Manilla or 21 km N of Tamworth
02 6785 1207   HEMA 54 C6   30 55 45 S   150 50 48 E

Quirindi to Bourke

Kamilaroi Highway

387 Braefield Rest Area

Kamilaroi Hwy, Quirindi
Rest Area 9 km N of Willow Tree or 7 km S of Quirindi. Next to railway line
132 213   HEMA 54 F5   31 33 54 S   150 41 53 E

388 Quirindi Caravan Park

15 Rose St, Quirindi
Caravan Park 600 m E of PO. 7 day limit
0417 976 796   HEMA 54 F5   31 30 37 S   150 41 01 E

389 Imperial Hotel Quirindi

43 Henry St, Quirindi
Parking Area 500 m E of PO. Free for patrons. Pre-book. See publican on arrival. Fee for shower
02 6746 2058   HEMA 54 F5   31 30 30 S   150 41 04 E

390 Werris Creek Freedom Camp

Single St, Werris Creek
Camp Area at Hoam Park, 18 km N of Quirindi
02 6747 1226   HEMA 54 E5   31 21 14 S   150 38 47 E

391 David Taylor Oval

Park St, Werris Creek
Parking Area 18 km N of Quirindi
02 6747 1226   HEMA 54 E5   31 20 28 S   150 38 56 E

392 Square Bush Rest Area

Square Bush Rd, Breeza
Rest Area 34 km NW of Quirindi or 7 km S of Breeza. Via Kamilroi Hwy
HEMA 54 E4   31 17 55 S   150 29 43 E

NEW SOUTH WALES

393 Caroona Hall

Coonabarabran Rd, Caroona
Parking Area beside hall
02 6747 4749   HEMA 54 E4   31 24 23 S   150 25 29 E

394 Spring Ridge Showground

Darby Rd, Spring Ridge
Camp Area W side of town. Donation box
02 6747 1226   HEMA 54 E4   31 23 46 S   150 14 43 E

395 Premer Lions Park

Purlewaugh Rd, Premer
Camp Area midway between Quirindi & Coonabarabran. Donation to Lions Club. Honesty box. 7 day limit
02 6747 1226   HEMA 54 E2   31 27 09 S   149 54 03 E

396 Gunnedah South Rest Area

Kamilaroi Hwy, Gunnedah
Rest Area 11 km N of Curlewis or 7 km S of Gunnedah
132 213   HEMA 54 D4   31 01 32 S   150 16 28 E

397 Gunnedah North Rest Area
Greenwood Grange

Kamilaroi Hwy, Gunnedah
Rest Area 8 km N of Gunnedah or 31 km S of Boggabri
132 213   HEMA 54 C3   30 55 22 S   150 11 15 E

398 Boggabri Showground

Kamilaroi Hwy, Boggabri
Camp Area 1.5 km S of Boggabri. Honesty Box. Pre-book
0427 605 521   HEMA 54 B3   30 42 56 S   150 03 01 E

399 Gins Leap

Kamilaroi Hwy, Boggabri
Rest Area 6 km N of Boggabri or 51 km SE of Narrabri
132 213   HEMA 54 B3   30 39 20 S   150 02 29 E

400 Old Baan Baa School

1 Bundah St, Baan Baa
Camp Area 38 km SE of Narrabri. Pre-book
0427 289 339   HEMA 54 B3   30 35 59 S   149 57 07 E

401 Pilliga Pub

60 Dangar St, Pilliga
Camp Area 55 km SW of Wee Waa or 38 km S of Burren Jcn
02 6796 4320   HEMA 58 F4   30 21 07 S   148 53 04 E

402 Pilliga Bore Baths

Pilliga Rd, Pilliga
Camp Area 1.6 km E of Pilliga on the Wee Waa Pilliga Rd at the Hot Mineral Bore. Pay at Pilliga Cafe or Narrabri Info Centre. 21 day limit. Cold shower
02 6799 6760   HEMA 58 F4   30 21 19 S   148 54 25 E

403 Burren Junction Bore Baths

Kamilaroi Hwy, Burren Junction
Camp Area 3 km E of Burren Junction. Baths closed in summer, camping open all year
02 6828 6100   HEMA 58 F4   30 06 52 S   148 59 44 E

404 Junction City Hotel

Cnr Slackmans & Corunna Sts, Burren Junction
Pub Stay 350 m SE of PO. Check in with publican
02 6796 1440   HEMA 58 F4   30 06 19 S   148 58 12 E

405 Alex Trevallion Park

175 Fox St, Walgett
Camp Spot 2 km S of Walgett. E side of Hwy
02 6828 6139   HEMA 58 F3   30 02 04 S   148 06 55 E

406 Walgett Showground
Euroka St, Walgett
Camp Area E of town. Pay at council office or with caretaker onsite
02 6828 6139   HEMA 58 F3   30 01 14 S   148 07 57 E

407 Muddy Water Farmstay

Woodlands Rd, Walgett
Camp Area at Walgett. Head N on Castlereagh Hwy (B55) for 2 km, turn NW to unsealed Woodlands Rd for 2.5 km to camp on river
0432 250 760   HEMA 58 F3   29 59 49 S   148 06 48 E

408 Pagan Creek Bridge

Castlereagh Hwy, Walgett
Camp Spot 6 km N of Walgett. 1.5 km N of the Castlereagh Hwy & Kamilaroi Hwy Jcn
HEMA 58 F3   29 59 15 S   148 09 16 E

409 The Big Warrambool Bridge

Kamilaroi Hwy, Walgett
Parking Area 75.5 km E of Brewarrina or 56.5 km W of Walgett. N side of the road, entry W of bridge
HEMA 58 F1   30 04 39 S   147 33 36 E

410 Culgoa River Bridge
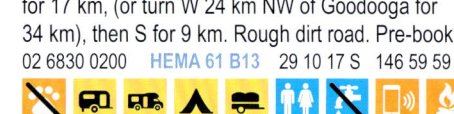
Goodooga Brenda Rd, Goodooga
Camp Area 18 km NW of Goodooga. Riverside
02 6830 5152   HEMA 61 A14   29 01 30 S   147 18 05 E

411 Culgoa River Campground
Culgoa National Park
Connellys Track, Weilmoringle
Camp Area 25 km N of Weilmoringle or 60 km W of Goodooga. Turn N 6 km W of Weilmoringle for 17 km, (or turn W 24 km NW of Goodooga for 34 km), then S for 9 km. Rough dirt road. Pre-book
02 6830 0200   HEMA 61 B13   29 10 17 S   146 59 59 E

412 Four Mile Reserve

Tarrion Yarrawin Rd, Brewarrina
Camp Area 6 km E of Brewarrina. Via Coolabah-Brewarrina Rd & Billybingbone Brae for 5 km. Follow blue signs. Cold showers
02 6830 5152   HEMA 61 D13   29 59 06 S   146 55 02 E

413 Brewarrina Caravan Park

28 Church St, Brewarrina
Caravan & Camping Park S side of town
0492 437 552   HEMA 61 D13   29 58 00 S   146 51 40 E

414 Beds on the Barwon Camp
Burban St, Brewarrina
Camp Area 2.4 km SE of PO. Just before racecourse, 600 m to entry
0428 247 824   HEMA 61 D13   29 58 28 S   146 52 31 E

415 Brewarrina Rest Area
Kamilaroi Hwy, Brewarrina
Rest Area 6 km W of Brewarrina or 92 km E of Bourke
HEMA 61 D13   29 57 29 S   146 47 53 E

416 Rossmore Station
Food & Huts by Mt Oxley
Kamilaroi Hwy, Bourke
Station Stay 28 km E of Bourke or 70 km W of Brewarrina. Check in at homestead for directions
0427 815 385   HEMA 61 D11   30 02 51 S   146 12 55 E

417 Mays Bend
Bullamunta Rd, Bourke
Camp Area 17 km NE of Bourke. Turn E off Mitchell Hwy 12 km N of Bourke to Bullamunta Rd for 3.5 km, take R fork at Y Jcn, 1.4 km to campground. Check with Bourke Info Centre for road conditions
02 6872 1321   HEMA 61 D11   30 02 20 S   146 01 23 E

Bathurst-Mudgee-Gilgandra-Nevertire

418 Capertee Rest Area
Castlereagh Hwy, Capertee
Parking Area 46 km NW of Lithgow
132 213   HEMA 52 C6   33 08 48 S   149 59 03 E

419 Royal Hotel Capertee
67 Castlereagh Hwy, Capertee
Parking Area at Capertee. Check in with publican, free for patrons. Fee for shower
0492 870 662   HEMA 52 C6   33 08 44 S   149 58 55 E

420 The Diggings Campground
Turon National Park
Turon River RD, Capertee
Camp Spot 8 km SW of Capertee. Mouth of Turon River. Pre-book
02 4787 8877   HEMA 52 C6   33 11 02 S   149 57 11 E

421 Dallis Campground
1570 Glen Davis Road, Capertee
Camp Area 15 km E of Capertee. Pre-book. 7 day limit
0419 901 993   HEMA 52 C7   33 08 22 S   150 06 18 E

422 Glen Davis Campground
Crown Cr, Glen Davis
Camp Area 35 km E of Capertee or 52 km SE of Rylestone. Signposted off Castlereagh Hwy at Capertee, 26 km dirt road. 10 km dirt road from Rylestone
02 6352 9130   HEMA 52 C7   33 07 31 S   150 16 55 E

423 Coorongooba Campground
Wollemi National Park
Glen Davis
Camp Area W side of NP. E off Hwy at Capertee. Turn to Goora St, R to Nioka St, follow signs. River crossing. Pre-book
02 6370 9000   HEMA 52 C7   33 07 21 S   150 19 20 E

424 Capertee Campground
Capertee National Park
Bogee
Camp Area 12 km SW of Bogee. Just N of Bogee turn W to Port Macquarie Rd for 11 km dirt road. At the locked gate cross river & follow signposts. Pre-book for access code
02 6370 9000   HEMA 52 C6   33 01 08 S   150 01 54 E

425 Ilford Rest Area
Ilford Hall Rd, Ilford
Rest Area 400 m E of Hwy. Beside hall
HEMA 52 B6   32 57 49 S   149 51 41 E

426 Ganguddy Dunns Swamp
Wollemi National Park
Dunns Swamp Rd, Kelgoola
Camp Area 27 km E of Rylstone. Via Narrango Rd. Beside lake. 7 km dirt road. Pre-book
02 6370 9000   HEMA 52 B7   32 50 09 S   150 12 26 E

427 Wallaby Rocks Crossing
Hill End Rd, Sofala
Camp Area 5 km W of Sofala. E side of Turon River Bridge, camp spots along river. Small vehicles only
HEMA 52 C5   33 04 31 S   149 39 01 E

428 Coles Bridge Camping Area
Turondale Rd, Turondale
Camp Area 13 km W of Sofala. Via Hill End Rd. Turn N over bridge then 200 m rough access track
HEMA 52 C5   33 03 33 S   149 37 15 E

429 Ration Point
Upper Turon Rd, Sofala
Camp Spot 3 km E of Sofala. Riverside. Small vehicles only
HEMA 52 C5   33 05 30 S   149 42 56 E

430 Greens Point
Upper Turon Rd, Sofala
Camp Area 6 km E of Sofala via Upper Turon Rd. Riverside
HEMA 52 C5   33 05 44 S   149 43 55 E

431 Wattle Flat Racecourse
Limekilns Rd, Wattle Flat
Camp Area 3 km E of Wattle Flat
1800 681 000   HEMA 52 C5   33 10 33 S   149 42 35 E

432 Wattle Flat Heritage Land (North)
Thompson St, Wattle Flat
Camp Area 800 m W of Wattle Flat. Turn W to signposted entry. GPS at gate. 14 day limit
1800 681 000   HEMA 52 C5   33 08 19 S   149 41 08 E

433 Wattle Flat Heritage Land (South)
Peel Rd, Wattle Flat
Camp Area 1 km SW of Wattle Flat via Sofala Rd
1800 681 000   HEMA 52 C5   33 08 55 S   149 41 23 E

434 Amy Anderson Reserve

The Bridle Track, Killongbutta
Camp Area 43 km N of Bathurst or 129 S of Mudgee. Contact Visitor Centre for road accessibility
1800 681 000   HEMA 52 C4   33 09 04 S   149 26 51 E

435 The Village Campground

Hill End Historic Site
9 Warrys Rd, Hill End
Camp Area 38 km W of Sofala. Via Clarke St. Coin operated hot showers. Pre-book
1300 072 757   HEMA 52 C4   33 02 03 S   149 24 48 E

436 Glendora Campground

Hill End Historic Site
31 Andersons Rd, Hill End
Camp Area 38 km W of Sofala. 1 km NW of town, via Beyers Ave & Lees Ln. Coin operated showers. Pre-book
1300 072 757   HEMA 52 C4   33 01 39 S   149 24 34 E

437 Bushlands Tourist Park

1879 Windeyer Rd, Windeyer
Caravan Park 43 km SW of Mudgee. Turn W off Hwy 86, 3 km N of Mudgee
02 6373 8252   HEMA 52 B5   32 47 44 S   149 33 25 E

438 Hargraves Pony & Tennis Club

Hill End Rd, Hargraves
Camp Area 41 km SW of Mudgee or 34 km N of Hill End. Donation at general store
02 6373 8540   HEMA 52 B4   32 47 03 S   149 27 41 E

439 Old Bara

Bara Rd, Bara
Farm Stay 28 km E of Mudgee. Via Lue Rd & Hayes Gap Rd
02 6373 6555   HEMA 52 A6   32 34 39 S   149 48 22 E

440 Mudgee Showground

Douro St, Mudgee
Camp Area 1.6 km S of PO. See caretaker
0447 111 329   HEMA 52 A5   32 36 10 S   149 34 55 E

441 Gulgong Showground

Grevillea St, Gulgong
Camp Area 1 km S of Gulgong. Off Mudgee Rd. Entrance Cnr Guntawang St
0499 246 434   HEMA 54 J1   32 22 15 S   149 31 41 E

442 Spring Gully Campground

Goulburn River National Park
Spring Gully Rd, Mogo
Camp Area at Mogo. 15 km NE of Wollar, via Mogo Rd. Small vehicles only. Pre-book
02 6370 9000   HEMA 54 J3   32 14 35 S   150 02 43 E

443 Big River Campground

Goulburn River National Park
Big River Rd, Mogo
Camp Area 22 km NE of Wollar. Via Mogo, Spring Gully & Big River Rds. Small vehicles only. Pre-book
02 6370 9000   HEMA 54 J3   32 14 15 S   150 03 20 E

444 Bylong Community Sportsground

7690 Bylong Valley Way, Bylong
Camp Area opposite general store. 80 km E of Mudgee. Coin operated shower
02 6379 8252   HEMA 54 K3   32 24 58 S   150 06 52 E

445 Cassilis Park Rest Area

Golden Hwy, Cassilis
Rest Area 9 km NE of Turill or 7 km SW of Cassilis. Shared with trucks
132 213   HEMA 54 H2   32 03 16 S   149 56 00 E

446 Cassilis Bowls Club

50 Cassilis Rd, Cassilis
Camp Area 42 km NW of Merriwa. Pay at club. Limited power
02 6376 1002   HEMA 54 H3   32 00 41 S   149 58 46 E

447 Uarbry Hall

Church St, Uarbry
Camp Area 39 km E of Dunedoo or 22 km W of Cassilis. Where the hall was before the fire. Honesty box
HEMA 54 H2   32 02 43 S   149 45 53 E

448 Nullen Rest Area

Golden Hwy, Leadville
Rest Area 43 km N of Gulgong or 9 km E of Dunedoo, 6 km S of Leadville. Jcn of Black Stump Hwy
132 213   HEMA 54 H1   32 02 08 S   149 29 33 E

449 Coolah Sporting Club

7 Goddard St, Coolah
Camp Area 48 km NE of Dunedoo. Patronage please
02 6377 1222   HEMA 54 G2   31 49 18 S   149 43 13 E

450 The Barracks Campground

Coolah Tops National Park
The Pinnacle Rd, Coolah Area
Camp Area 35 km NE of Coolah. 15 km dirt road. Pre-book
02 6825 4364   HEMA 54 G3   31 43 51 S   150 00 54 E

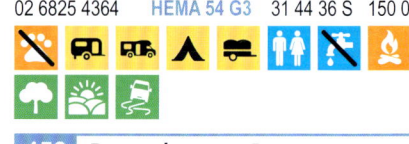

451 The Pines Campground

Coolah Tops National Park
Pine Trail, Coolah
Camp Area 37 km NE of Coolah. Via Hildegarde Rd. 16 km rough unsealed road
02 6825 4364   HEMA 54 G3   31 44 36 S   150 01 47 E

452 Pumphouse Reserve

Bullinda St, Binnaway
Camp Area Cnr Castlereagh Ave. Fees for showers & power. Limited powered sites. See notice board for access
0400 477 355   HEMA 54 F1   31 32 48 S   149 22 44 E

453 Dunedoo Caravan Park

Bolaro St, Dunedoo
Caravan Park 600 m W of PO
02 6375 1455   HEMA 54 H1   32 00 56 S   149 23 22 E

454 Mendooran Rest Area
River St, Mendooran
Rest Area 38 km NW of Dunedoo.
Riverside. Cold showers
1800 242 881   HEMA 58 K5   31 49 28 S   149 06 53 E

455 Breelong Rest Area
Castlereagh Hwy, Breelong
Rest Area 17 km E of Gilgandra or 39 km W
of Mendooran
132 213   HEMA 58 K4   31 48 40 S   148 47 43 E

456 Railway Hotel Gilgandra
6 Bundy St, Gilgandra
Parking Area 1 km W of PO. Behind hotel.
Register at bar. Free for patrons. Amenities only
during opening hours
02 6847 0575   HEMA 58 K4   31 42 46 S   148 39 17 E

457 Marthaguy West Rest Area
Oxley Hwy, Collie
Rest Area 23 km W of Gilgandra or 14 km E
of Collie. Share with trucks
132 213   HEMA 58 K3   31 39 28 S   148 26 51 E

458 Collie Hotel
Oxley Highway, Collie
Parking Area 38 km W of Gilgandra. Check
in with publican. Meals available daily
02 6847 9119   HEMA 58 K3   31 40 02 S   148 18 11 E

459 Warren North Rest Area
Oxley Hwy, Tenandra
Rest Area 44 km W of Collie or 6 km NE of
Warren
132 213   HEMA 58 K2   31 40 02 S   147 51 30 E

460 Bob Christensen Reserve
Industrial Access Rd, Warren
Parking Area 3 km NE PO. Via Burton &
Dubbo Sts
02 6847 6600   HEMA 58 K2   31 41 08 S   147 50 01 E

461 Warren Weir
Wambianna Rd, Warren
Camp Area 5 km S of Warren. N side of
weir. GPS at entrance, follow track to river
02 6847 6600   HEMA 58 K2   31 43 25 S   147 52 00 E

462 Sandy Creek
Oxley Hwy, Snakes Plain
Rest Area at Beleringar Creek, 8 km SW of
Warren or 12 km N of Nevertire
132 213   HEMA 58 K2   31 44 56 S   147 47 00 E

Greater Sydney Area

463 Bents Basin Campground
Bents Basin State Conservation Area
Bents Loop Rd, Greendale
Camp Area 25 km S of Penrith, via Northern,
Greendale & Wolstenholme Rds. Pre-book
1300 072 757   HEMA 48 H6   33 55 58 S   150 38 14 E

464 Warragamba Rec Reserve
Warradale Rd, Warragamba
Parking Area 22 km SW of Penrith. Entry
via Farnsworth Ave. Boom gate open and facilities
during daylight hours only
02 8579 0315   HEMA 48 G5   33 53 36 S   150 36 13 E

465 Wanderest Travellers Park
71 Francis St, Richmond
Camp Area 20 km N of Penrith. Fee for power
02 4578 1144   HEMA 48 D7   33 35 48 S   150 45 18 E

466 Cattai Campground
Cattai National Park
Arndells Trail, Cattai
Camp Area 800 m N of Cattai on the Wiseman Ferry
Rd. Turn W to campground road. Signposted. Small
vehicles only. Pre-book
02 4580 2750   HEMA 49 C8   33 33 33 S   150 53 24 E

467 Mill Creek
Dharug National Park
Mill Creek Rd, Gunderman
Camp 6 km E of Wisemans Ferry Crossing. N side
of the Hawkesbury River. Pre-book
02 6574 5555   HEMA 49 A10   33 24 03 S   151 02 34 E

468 St Albans Reserve
15 Wollombi Rd, St Albans
Camp Area behind the Settlers Arm Inn
  HEMA 46 K6   33 17 33 S   150 58 14 E

469 Sackville Ski Gardens
742 Tizzana Rd, Sackville
Camp Area 40 km N of Blacktown
02 4579 1036   HEMA 49 B8   33 29 47 S   150 52 59 E

470 Bielany Camp Colo River
213 Upper Colo Rd, Colo
Camp Area 32 km N of Richmond
02 4575 5311   HEMA 48 B7   33 25 26 S   150 48 34 E

471 Upper Colo Reserve
Hulbert Rd, Upper Colo
Camp Area 18 km W of Colo. Turn
off Upper Colo Rd to Colo Heights Rd, then L.
Campervans subject to approval. Pre-book
02 4560 4444   HEMA 48 A7   33 25 14 S   150 43 56 E

472 Burralow Creek Camp
Blue Mountains National Park
Burralow Rd, Kurrajong Heights
Camp Area 34 km NW of Richmond. Via Kurrajong
Rd. Lower Grose Valley section. Pre-book
02 4588 2400   HEMA 48 C5   33 33 23 S   150 36 16 E

473 Cathedral Reserve
117 Mount Irvine Rd, Mt Wilson
Camp Area at Mt Wilson
02 4723 5000   HEMA 48 B3   33 30 07 S   150 23 26 E

474 Newnes Campground
Wollemi National Park
Wolgan Rd, Newnes
Camp Area 35 km NE of Lithgow. Turn NE at
Lidsdale, 11 km N of Lithgow, 9 km dirt road. Small
vehicles only. 4WD in wet weather. Pre-book
02 4787 8877   HEMA 52 C7   33 10 19 S   150 14 17 E

475 Millionth Acre Picnic Area

Hampton State Forest

Duckmaloi Rd, Hampton
Picnic Area 4 km S of Hampton. Intersection of Jenolan Caves Rd

1300 655 687   HEMA 52 E7   33 40 37 S   150 03 00 E

476 Oberon Showgrounds

Ross St, Oberon
Camp Area 800 m S of PO. Pre-book

0417 252 685   HEMA 52 F6   33 42 37 S   149 51 24 E

477 The Reef Reserve

The Reef Rd, Lake Oberon
Camp Area 6 km SW of Oberon. W on Abercrombie Rd for 1 km, S to The Reef Rd for 2.5 km, follow to end. 7 day limit

02 6329 8210   HEMA 52 E6   33 43 01 S   149 49 38 E

478 Boyd River Campground

Kanangra-Boyd National Park

Kanangra Walls Rd, Kanangra
Camp Area 30 km S of Jenolan Cave. 27 km dirt road

02 6336 6200   HEMA 52 G7   33 58 16 S   150 03 21 E

479 Binacrombi

771 The Glen Rd, Jerrong
Camp Area 75 km S of Oberon or 40 km N of Taralga. From Taralga, turn R at Wombeyan Caves sign, after 2.5 km, turn L at Jerrong Rd, travel 21 km to Glen Rd, 8 km further. GPS at entry. Dirt roads and river crossings

1800 620 706   HEMA 50 B2   34 11 28 S   149 48 54 E

480 Black Springs Rest Area

Vulcan State Forest

Abercrombie Rd, Black Springs
Rest Area opposite general store. 24 km SW of Oberon or 26 NE of Burraga

1300 655 687   HEMA 52 F5   33 50 51 S   149 44 38 E

481 Bummaroo Ford

Abercrombie River National Park

Taralga Rd, Curraweela
Camp Area 25 km N of Taralga. Via Abercrombie Rd at Abercrombie River crossing

02 6336 6200   HEMA 50 B1   34 11 40 S   149 44 10 E

482 Wombeyan Caves

Wombeyan Karst Conservation Reserve

Victoria Arch Dr, Wombeyan Caves
Camp Area 33 km NE of Taralga. Near visitors centre. 13 km dirt road. Coins for BBQs. Pre-book

1300 072 757   HEMA 50 C3   34 18 22 S   149 58 14 E

483 Wollondilly River Station

Wombeyan Caves Rd, Wombeyan Caves
Station Stay 50 km W of Bowral on Wombeyan Caves Rd. 15 km E of Wombeyan Caves. Dirt road. Small vehicles only. Limited caravan access. Pre-book

02 4888 9207   HEMA 50 C4   34 18 28 S   150 04 00 E

484 Taralga Showgrounds

Walsh St, Taralga
Camp Area 44 km N of Goulburn. Via Bannaby Rd. Pay at Taralga General Store or Taralga Gifts & Goodies

02 4840 2558   HEMA 50 D2   34 24 16 S   149 49 26 E

485 Burraga Dam

Dam Rd, Burraga
Camp Area 3 km NE of Burraga. Turn N off Arkstone Rd 2 km E of Burraga, opposite Jeremy Station. 1 km dirt road. 4WD in wet weather

02 6337 0255   HEMA 52 F5   33 56 09 S   149 33 08 E

486 Campbells River

Dogs Rock State Forest

Swallows Nest Rd, Mount David
Camp Area 12 km N of Mount David

1300 655 687   HEMA 52 F5   33 47 07 S   149 36 17 E

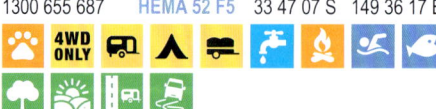

487 Trunkey Creek Showground

Arthur St, Trunkey Creek
Camp Area 63 km SW of Bathurst. Entry off opposite Lloyd St. Pay at Black Stump Hotel

02 6368 8604   HEMA 52 F4   33 49 03 S   149 19 30 E

488 Abercrombie Caves

Abercrombie Karst Conservation Reserve

272 Caves Rd, Abercrombie River
Camp Area 14 km S of Trunkey Creek. 2 km narrow, winding road. Coin operated BBQ. Pre-book

02 6368 8603   HEMA 52 F4   33 54 50 S   149 21 30 E

489 Abercrombie River Camp

The Junction

Abercrombie Rd, Tuena
Camp Area 19 km S of Trunkey Creek. S of bridge turn W. Small vehicles only

02 4832 1988   HEMA 52 G4   33 57 23 S   149 19 13 E

490 Tuena Camping Ground

Bathurst Rd, Tuena
Camp & Picnic Area at Tuena. Fee for power to general store. Coin operated showers

02 4834 5235   HEMA 52 G4   34 00 59 S   149 19 40 E

491 Binda Parking Area

Woodville Rd, Binda
Parking Area 21 km NW of Crookwell. Behind tennis courts. Toilets opposite general store

02 4835 6024   HEMA 52 H4   34 19 29 S   149 21 45 E

492 Crookwell Caravan Park

Laggan Rd, Crookwell
Caravan Park 400 m N of PO. Register at Visitor Centre or council office

02 4832 1988   HEMA 52 J5   34 27 17 S   149 28 03 E

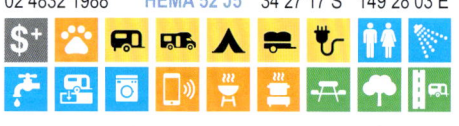

Sydney to Echuca
Great Western, Mid Western, Sturt Highways

493 Murphys Glen Campground

Blue Mountains National Park

Murphys Rd, Woodford
Camp Area 8.5 km S of Woodford or 33 km W of Penrith. Glenbrook section. Via Bedford Rd. Pre-book

02 4787 8877   HEMA 48 F4   33 46 07 S   150 29 09 E

494 Blackheath Glen Reserve

540 Megalong Rd, Megalong Valley
Camp Area 6.5 km S of Blackheath. 7 day
limit. Small vehicles only
02 4780 5000   HEMA 44 H2   33 40 30 S   150 16 08 E

495 Old Ford Reserve

1363 Megalong Rd, Megalong Valley
Camp Area 15 km S of Blackheath. Via
Shipley Rd & Megalong Valley Rd. 7 day limit
02 4780 5000   HEMA 44 K1   33 43 54 S   150 14 06 E

496 Dunphys Camping Area

Blue Mountains National Park
Bellbird Ridge Firetrail, Blackheath
Camp Area 23 km S of Blackheath. Via Megalong Rd
02 4787 8877   HEMA 48 F2   33 47 24 S   150 13 48 E

497 Lockyers Track Head Camp

Hartley Vale Rd, Lithgow
Camp Area 12 km SE of Lithgow. Small
vehicles only, limited caravan sites
02 6350 3230   HEMA 44 B1   33 32 09 S   150 13 58 E

498 Glenroy Cottages & Camp

200 Jenolan Caves Rd, Hartley
Camp Area 15 km S of Lithgow. Pre-book
02 6355 2186   HEMA 48 C1   33 32 53 S   150 08 55 E

499 Lake Lyell Campground

Magpie Hollow Rd, Rydal
Camp Area 13 km SW of Lithgow
02 6355 6347   HEMA 52 E7   33 31 30 S   150 04 38 E

500 Flat Rock

Mutton Falls Rd, Tarana
Camp Area 13 km W of Tarana or 7 km E of
O'Connell. At Rainville Creek, beside Fish River
HEMA 52 E6   33 32 54 S   149 47 31 E

501 The O'Connell Hotel

2408 O'Connell Rd, O'Connell
Parking Area 22 km S of Bathurst. Free for
patrons
02 6337 5745   HEMA 52 E5   33 32 33 S   149 43 51 E

502 Chifley Dam Primitive Camp

Chifley Dam Rd, The Lagoon
Camp Area 20 km S of Bathurst. Travel
6 km S of Bathurst along Vale Rd, turn E to Lagoon
Rd then Chifley Dam Rd for 14 km. Only 4 sites, no
bookings. Gates locked after dark
02 6632 1444   HEMA 52 E5   33 33 43 S   149 38 00 E

503 Lake Wallace

Barton Ave, Wallerawang
Camp Area 8 km W of Lithgow or 57 km E
of Bathurst. Turn N off Great Western Hwy
02 6352 9130   HEMA 52 D7   33 24 57 S   150 04 26 E

504 Kremer Park

Lime St, Portland
Camp Area at Portland Showground, 26 km
NW of Lithgow. Toilets limited opening hours
1300 760 276   HEMA 52 D6   33 21 15 S   149 58 36 E

505 Sunny Corner Rec Reserve

Vulcan State Forest
1077 Bathurst St, Sunny Corner
Camp Spot 7 km N of Meadow Flat. Turn N off Great
Western Hwy 26 km W of Lithgow or 33 km E of
Bathurst. S end of village, E side of road
1300 655 687   HEMA 52 D6   33 23 16 S   149 53 34 E

506 Bathurst Showground

Kendell Ave, Bathurst
Camp Area E side of town
02 6331 1349   HEMA 52 D5   33 25 05 S   149 35 22 E

507 Berry Park Lions Club

Lions Club Dr, Kelso
Parking Area 4 km E of town centre
02 6333-6111   HEMA 52 D5   33 25 01 S   149 35 38 E

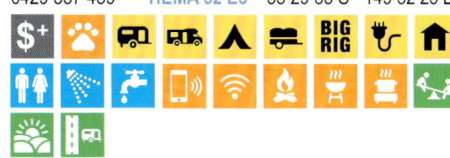

508 Barcoos Barn Farmstays

1080 Trunkey Rd, Perthville
Farm Stay 800 m over the railway line.
Pre-book
0429 337 439   HEMA 52 E5   33 29 35 S   149 32 23 E

509 Newbridge Sportsground

Three Brothers Rd, Newbridge
Camp Area 16 km SE of Blaney or 37 km SW
of Bathurst. Donation to house opposite. 7 day limit
02 6368 2104   HEMA 52 E4   33 35 11 S   149 21 52 E

510 Carcoar Dam

234 Carcoar Dam Rd, Carcoar
Camp Area 12 km SW of Blayney or 16 km
NE of Mandurama. Turn S, 9 km SW of Blayney or
6.5 km NE of Carcoar. Cold shower
02 6368 3534   HEMA 52 E4   33 36 41 S   149 10 53 E

511 Carcoar Rest Area

Fullers Ln, Carcoar
Rest Area 11 km SW of Blayney or 11 km
NE of Mandurama
132 213   HEMA 52 E3   33 35 55 S   149 09 54 E

512 Mandurama East Rest Area

Midwestern Hwy, Mandurama
Rest Area 3 km E of Mandurama or 19 km
SW of Blayney
132 213   HEMA 52 E3   33 38 24 S   149 06 06 E

513 Bakers Shaft Reserve

Junction Park Rd, Burnt Yards
Camp Area 15 km N of Mandurama. Turn
W off Mandurama-Burnt Yards Rd after 10 km to
Bakers Rd, then Junction Park Rd. 5 km dirt road.
Beside Belubula R
02 6368 2104   HEMA 52 E3   33 36 34 S   149 00 43 E

514 Lyndhurst Primitive Camp

6511 Mid Western Hwy, Lyndhurst
Camp Area in rec ground, entrance off
Harrow St. 5 day limit. Donation box
0427 201 824   HEMA 52 E3   33 40 24 S   149 02 20 E

515 Reflections Holiday Park

Wyangala Waters
2891 Reg Hailstone Way, Wyangala Dam
Camp Area 37 km SE of Cowra. Via Darbys Falls.
Pre-book
02 6345 0877   HEMA 52 G3   33 57 46 S   148 57 17 E

516 Bigga Recreation Ground
Mulgowrie St, Bigga
A41 Camp Area N of PO. Donation to general store & pub in town centre, 3 days free
02 4835 2347   HEMA 52 G3   34 04 58 S   149 09 08 E

517 Reflections Holiday Parks
Grabine Lakeside
2453 Grabine Road, Grabine
A41 Caravan Park 97 km SE of Cowra or 71 km NW of Crookwell, via Bigga & Grabine Rds. NE side of Lake Wyangala. Some dirt road
02 4835 2345   HEMA 52 G3   33 57 03 S   149 01 44 E

518 Darbys Falls River Reserve
Darbys Falls Rd, Darbys Falls
A41 Rest Area 26 km SE of Cowra or 17 km NW of Wyangala. Beside Lachlan River. 2 km S of township
02 6342 4333   HEMA 52 G2   33 56 55 S   148 51 45 E

519 Cowra Overnight Rest Area
Edgell Park
81 Lachlan Valley Way, Cowra
Rest Area 100 m S Mid Western Hwy intersection. Dump point 100 m S. Limited sites
02 6342 4333   HEMA 52 F2   33 50 08 S   148 40 55 E

520 Cowra Showground
Grenfell Rd, Cowra
B64 Camp Area 108 km SW of Bathurst. Pre-book. Weekly rates available
0411 286 858   HEMA 52 F2   33 50 04 S   148 40 29 E

521 Phillips Crossing
Phillips Crossing Rd, Cowra
B81 Camp Area 14.5 km NW of Cowra. Via North Logan Rd. Riverside
HEMA 52 F2   33 46 09 S   148 36 06 E

522 Canowindra Caravan Park
1 Tilga St, Canowindra
B81 Caravan Park 300 m SE of PO. Next to swimming pool
0428 634 410   HEMA 52 E2   33 34 08 S   148 39 50 E

523 Canowindra Showgrounds
199 Rodd St, Canowindra
B81 Parking Area N side of town
02 6344 1886   HEMA 52 E2   33 33 09 S   148 40 10 E

524 Canowindra Rest Area
Nangar Rd, Canowindra
Rest Area 2 km W of Canowindra. Riverside
HEMA 52 E2   33 33 35 S   148 39 05 E

525 Terarra Creek Camping
Nangar National Park
B81 Terarra Creek Firetrail, Eugowra
Picnic Area 18 km E of Eugowra or 76 km W of Orange. Via Escort Way. Turn S 11 km E of Eugowra to Dripping Rock Rd. 7 km to camp. 4WD in wet weather. Pre-book
02 6332 7640   HEMA 52 D1   33 25 10 S   148 29 54 E

526 Eugowra Showground
Noble St, Eugowra
B81 Camp Spot at Eugowra. 1 km E of PO
0427 639 701   HEMA 52 D1   33 26 01 S   148 23 00 E

527 Byrnes Park
Myall St, Eugowra
A39 Parking Area 37 km E of Forbes. Adjacent to bridge. Donation box near dump point
HEMA 52 D1   33 25 40 S   148 22 11 E

528 Gooloogong Primitive Camp
Cnr Main St & Warraderry Way, Gooloogong
B81 Camp Area formerly called Maisie Thompson Camping Ground
02 6340 2000   HEMA 52 E1   33 36 47 S   148 26 04 E

529 Bumbaldry Rest Area
Mid Western Hwy, Cowra
B64 Rest Area 23 km W of Cowra or 32 km E of Grenfell
HEMA 52 F1   33 54 06 S   148 28 00 E

530 John Channon Park
Mid Western Hwy, Grenfell
24 Rest Area 1 km W of Grenfell
132 213   HEMA 64 G4   33 53 25 S   148 08 43 E

531 Grenfell Old Railway Station
West St, Grenfell
B64 Rest Area 1 km from PO. W side of town. Toilets locked at night
02 6343 2059   HEMA 64 G4   33 53 43 S   148 09 21 E

532 Holy Campground
Weddin Mountains National Park
B64 Holy Camp Rd, Grenfell
Camp Area 16 km W of Grenfell, via Barmedman Rd. 4 km dirt road. Pre-book
02 6332 7640   HEMA 64 G4   33 53 52 S   148 00 12 E

533 Ben Halls Campground
Weddin Mountains National Park
B64 Northern Boundary Trail, Piney Range
Camp Area 20 km W of Grenfell. Turn W off Mid Western Hwy 5.5 km NW Grenfell to Back Piney Range Rd, follow signs for 23 km, turn L over the grid, follow to sites. Dirt road. Pre-book
02 6332 7640   HEMA 64 G3   33 54 24 S   147 57 01 E

534 Quandialla Showgrounds
Bland Rd, Quandialla
B64 Camp Area 60 km E of West Wyalong. Pre-book
02 6347 1365   HEMA 64 G3   34 00 28 S   147 47 24 E

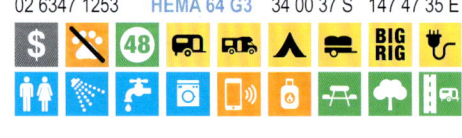

535 Bland Hotel
2 Second St, Quandialla
B64 Camp Spot next to hotel. 60 km E of West Wyalong. Check in with publican. Fee for showers & power. Pre-book
02 6347 1253   HEMA 64 G3   34 00 37 S   147 47 35 E

536 Bribbaree Showgrounds
Show Ground Rd, Bribbaree
B94 Camp Area 60 km NE of Temora. Pre-book
0427 832 224   HEMA 64 G3   34 07 16 S   147 51 44 E

537 Bogolong Creek Rest Area

Mid Western Hwy, Grenfell
Rest Area 9 km NW of Grenfell or 35 km E
of Caragabal
132 213   HEMA 64 G4   33 50 58 S   148 05 27 E

538 Ooma Creek Rest Area

Henry Lawson Hwy, Grenfell
Rest Area 14 km N of Grenfell or 50 km S
of Forbes
HEMA 64 G4   33 48 33 S   148 04 34 E

539 Ochre Arch Farm

761 Goodes Ln, Pinnacle
Farm Stay 13 km N of Piney Range. Pre-book
0425 760 596   HEMA 64 F4   33 45 12 S   148 00 54 E

540 Caragabal Rest Area

Mid Western Hwy, Caragabal
Rest Area 43 km W of Grenfell
132 213   HEMA 64 G3   33 50 38 S   147 44 23 E

541 Yalgogrin Rest Area

Paynes Rd, Yalgogrin
Rest Area at Clark Park, 36 km W of West
Wyalong or 57 km E of Rankins Springs
132 213   HEMA 63 F14   33 50 41 S   146 49 44 E

542 Weethalle Showground

Showground Rd, Weethalle
Camp Area at 58 km W of West Wyalong. If
locked call for access
0427 756 191   HEMA 63 F14   33 52 23 S   146 37 12 E

543 Selby Organic Farm Stay

431 The Springs Rd, Rankins Springs
Farm Stay 5 km N of Rankins Springs.
Discount rates for extra nights. Farm tours available.
Pre-book
02 6966 1220   HEMA 63 F13   33 48 40 S   146 13 59 E

544 John Oxley Rest Area

Mid Western Hwy, Rankins Springs
Rest Area 12 km W of Rankins Springs or
44 km E of Goolgowi. Share with trucks
132 213   HEMA 63 F13   33 52 22 S   146 11 03 E

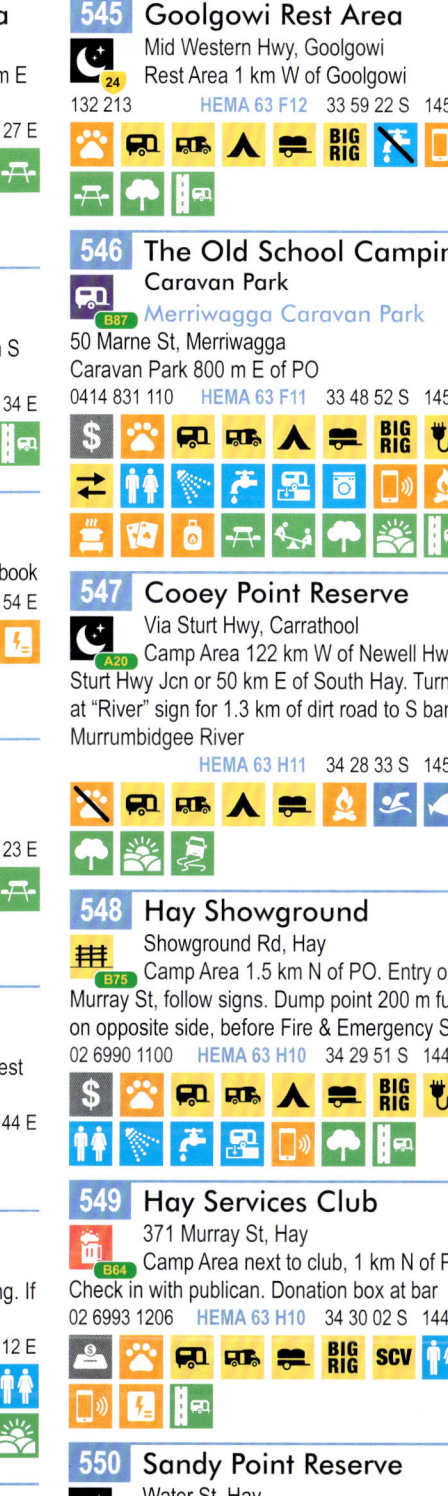

545 Goolgowi Rest Area

Mid Western Hwy, Goolgowi
Rest Area 1 km W of Goolgowi
132 213   HEMA 63 F12   33 59 22 S   145 41 42 E

546 The Old School Camping &
Caravan Park
Merriwagga Caravan Park
50 Marne St, Merriwagga
Caravan Park 800 m E of PO
0414 831 110   HEMA 63 F11   33 48 52 S   145 37 38 E

547 Cooey Point Reserve

Via Sturt Hwy, Carrathool
Camp Area 122 km W of Newell Hwy/
Sturt Hwy Jcn or 50 km E of South Hay. Turn N
at "River" sign for 1.3 km of dirt road to S bank of
Murrumbidgee River
HEMA 63 H11   34 28 33 S   145 19 18 E

548 Hay Showground

Showground Rd, Hay
Camp Area 1.5 km N of PO. Entry opposite
Murray St, follow signs. Dump point 200 m further
on opposite side, before Fire & Emergency Shed
02 6990 1100   HEMA 63 H10   34 29 51 S   144 50 08 E

549 Hay Services Club

371 Murray St, Hay
Camp Area next to club, 1 km N of PO.
Check in with publican. Donation box at bar
02 6993 1206   HEMA 63 H10   34 30 02 S   144 50 57 E

550 Sandy Point Reserve

Water St, Hay
Camp Area N side of Murrumbidgee River,
1 km SW of PO. W off Cobb Hwy, just N of bridge
onto Brunker St, S for 1 km to N riverbank. Use
entry near Hatty St for large vehicles
02 6993 4045   HEMA 63 H10   34 30 55 S   144 50 08 E

551 Soapworks Bend

Via Jackson St, Hay
Camp Spot 3 km W of Hay
02 6993 4045   HEMA 63 H10   34 30 26 S   144 49 12 E

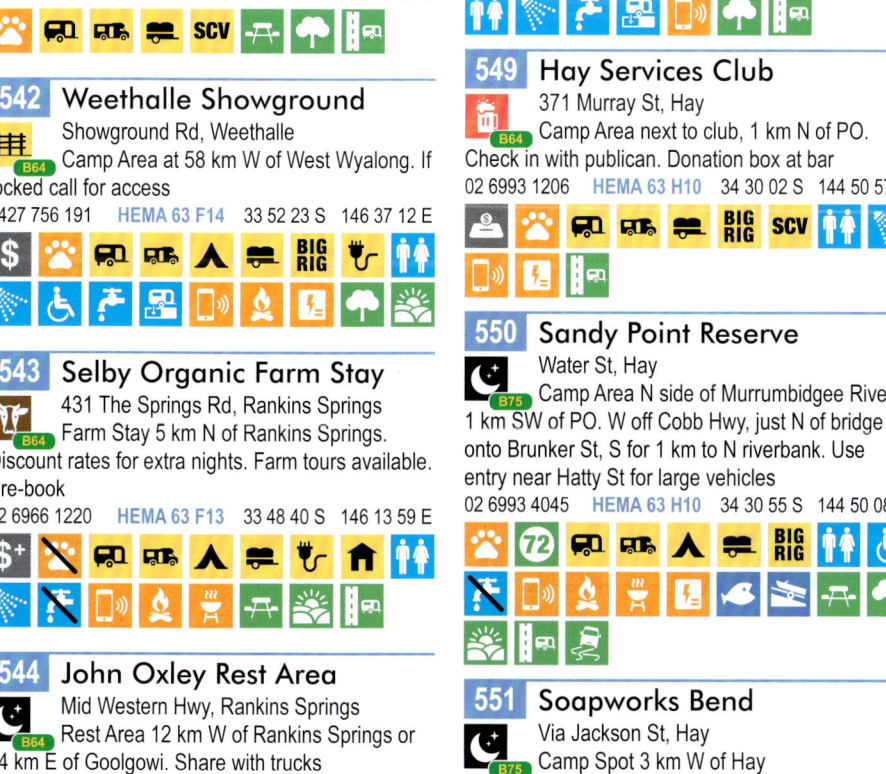

552 Hay Plains

Cobb Hwy, Booroorban
Camp Spot 40 km S of Hay or 6 km N or
Booroorban. Either side of bridge
HEMA 63 J9   34 52 43 S   144 45 34 E

553 Burraburoon Farmstay

1157 Wargam Rd, Booroorban Area
Farm Stay 12 km E of Booroorban. Turn L
at the flagpoles. GPS on entry
0419 147 455   HEMA 63 J10   34 56 01 S   144 52 59 E

554 Wanganella Weir (Reserve)

Via Cobb Hwy, Wanganella
Rest Area 43 km N of Deniliquin. Turn SW
on N side of bridge (opposite store) follow track for
1 km. Riverside
1800 650 712   HEMA 63 K10   35 13 03 S   144 48 26 E

555 Pretty Pine Hotel

Pretty Pine Rd, Deniliquin
Pub Stay 18 km N of Deniliquin. Via Cobb
Hwy towards Moulamein. Patronage welcome
03 5882 3564   HEMA 68 F6   35 24 58 S   144 52 41 E

556 Deniliquin Car O Tel &
Caravan Park
46 Crispe Street, Deniliquin
Caravan Park 700 m E of PO, opposite RSL Club
03 5881 1732   HEMA 68 G6   35 32 08 S   144 58 07 E

557 Willoughbys Beach

Murray Valley National Park
River Dr, Deniliquin
Camp Area 2 km E of PO. Take Memorial Dr
past showgrounds to regional park entrance.
200 m inside gate, various sites. Solid fuel fire ban
Oct - Mar. Pre-book
03 5483 9100   HEMA 68 G6   35 31 42 S   144 58 42 E

558 Four Post Caravan & Camping

567 Greaves Rd, Deniliquin
Camp Area 11 km S of Deniliquin. Via
Syphon, Four Post Rd
0429 647 006   HEMA 68 G6   35 35 58 S   144 59 26 E

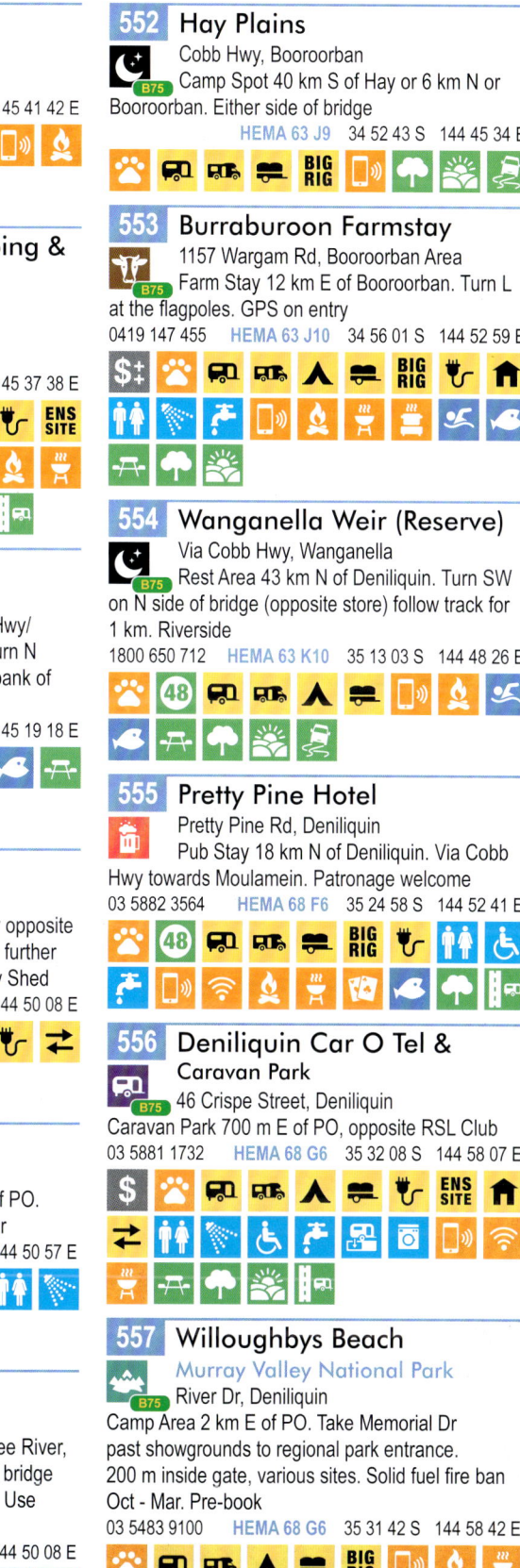
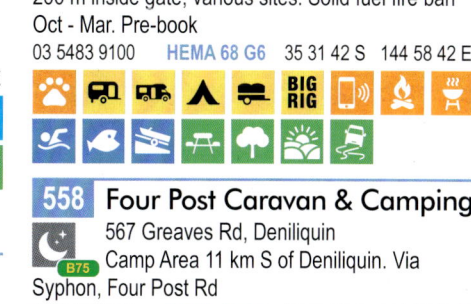

559 Gulpa Island Precinct
Murray Valley National Park
B75 Gulpa Walliston Rd, Mathoura
Dispersed Camp Areas 14 km N of Mathoura. Via Gulpa Creek, Taylor Bridge, Melvilles & Edward River Rds. GPS near entry, E of Cobb Hwy. Solid fuel fire ban Oct-Mar. Some sites require 4WD. Pre-book
03 5483 9100   HEMA 68 G6   35 42 15 S   144 54 21 E

560 Moira Precinct
Murray Valley National Park
B75 Poverty Point Rd, Mathoura
Dispersed Bush Camping S of Mathoura via Porters Creek Rd to W of Barmah, GPS near entry via Poverty Point Rd, E of Cobb Hwy. Solid fuel fire ban Oct-Mar. Pre-book
03 5483 9100   HEMA 68 H6   35 51 23 S   144 54 21 E

561 Porters Creek Road
Murray Valley National Park
B75 Porters Creek Rd, Mathoura
Dispersed Camping 13 km SE of Mathoura. Turn E 5 km S of Mathoura or 35 km N of Moama. Via Coolamon Rd. 8 km of dirt road. Solid fuel fire ban Oct-Mar. Pre-book
03 5483 9100   HEMA 68 H6   35 53 45 S   144 57 51 E

562 Mathoura Bowling Club
1 Moama St, Mathoura
B75 Camp Area 39 km N of Moama. Behind bowling club, entry from Steven St. Contact manager on arrival
03 5880 3200   HEMA 68 H6   35 48 34 S   144 53 59 E

563 Swifts Creek Campground
Murray Valley National Park
Hut Rd, Mathoura
Camp Area 15 km SE of Mathoura. E off Cobb Hwy 5 km S of Mathoura to Poverty Point Rd, 4 km to Porters Creek Rd, then R. Follow river to site. Solid fuel fire ban Oct-Mar. Pre-book
03 5483 9100   HEMA 68 H6   35 54 50 S   144 57 20 E

564 Edward River Bridge Camp
Murray Valley Regional Park
B75 Duggans Rd, Mathoura
Camp Area 8.5 km E of Mathoura. Off Mathoura-Tocumwal Rd. Bush camping riverside. Solid fuel fire ban Oct-Mar. Pre-book
03 5483 9100   HEMA 68 H6   35 48 43 S   144 57 39 E

565 Fishermans Bend
Murray Valley National Park
B75 Millewa River Rd, Mathoura
Dispersed Camping in the Millewa Precinct, 22 km E of Mathoura. Riverside at the end of Fishermans Bend Rd. Limited spaces. Solid fuel fire ban Oct-Mar. Some sites require 4WD. Pre-book
03 5483 9100   HEMA 68 H6   35 49 35 S   145 04 36 E

566 Scotts Beach
Millewa State Forest
B75 Via Millewa River Rd, Aratula
Dispersed Camp Areas 43 km E of Mathoura at Millewa Precinct. Riverside at the end of Scotts and Beach Rds. Limited spaces. Solid fuel fire ban Oct-Mar. Pre-book
03 5483 9100   HEMA 68 H7   35 51 03 S   145 15 53 E

567 Moama North Rest Area
The Keyhole
B75 Cobb Hwy, Moama
Rest Area 30 km S of Mathoura or 10 km N of Moama
132 213   HEMA 68 J5   36 02 08 S   144 46 42 E

568 Rich River Golf Club Resort
Twenty Four Ln, Moama
B75 Club Stay 5 km NW of Moama. Via Perricoota Rd. Register at reception, pay social member fee to stay. 7 day limit
03 5481 3333   HEMA 68 J5   36 04 35 S   144 43 35 E

569 Moama Five Mile
Murray Valley Regional Park
Via Perricoota Rd, Moama
Picnic Area 8 km W of Moama
03 5483 9100   HEMA 68 J5   36 04 03 S   144 41 30 E

570 Benarca Campground
Murray Valley Regional Park
B75 Benarca Forest Rd, Moama
Camp Area 18 km NW of Moama. Via Perricoota Rd (Moama-Barnham Rd) for 15 km, then S, signposted. Solid fuel fire ban Oct-Mar. Pre-book
03 5483 9100   HEMA 68 J5   36 03 15 S   144 37 25 E

571 Perricoota State Forest
Lock Rd, Womboota
B75 Camp Area 33 km NW of Moama, via Perricoota & Nineteen Mile Rds, then signposted Perricoota Forest & River Rds. Various tracks to sites
1300 655 687   HEMA 68 H4   35 56 34 S   144 28 34 E

572 Koondrook State Forest
Murray River Reserve
Barham
Camp Area 12 km SE of Barham, via East Barham & River Rds. Bush camping sites, riverside
1300 655 687   HEMA 68 G3   35 41 30 S   144 12 58 E

573 Wakool River Reserve
Werai Ln, Caldwell
Camp Area 11 km E of Wakool or 53 km W of Deniliquin. Turn E just S of Wakool River Bridge, via Wakool Rd. Follow tracks to camp spots on river
HEMA 68 F4   35 29 58 S   144 27 28 E

574 Campbells Island State Forest
Little Murray Rd, Gonn
B75 Camp Area 5 km NW of Barham. Via Cobwell St & North Barham Rd. Signposted. Bush camping sites along river
1300 655 687   HEMA 68 G3   35 35 25 S   144 06 22 E

575 Deleted

Sydney-Albury-Tocumwal
Hume and Riverina Highways

576 Coledale Camping Reserve
677 Lawrence Hargrave Dr, Coledale
Camp Area opposite beach. Pre-book and check seasonal minimum stay periods
02 4267 4302   HEMA 51 C13   34 17 13 S   150 56 54 E

577 Berrima Reserve
Oxley St, Berrima
1 Camp Area NW of town, past White Horse Inn. W to Oxley St, L at fork. No discharge of grey water, 4 sites. Permit applies
1300 657 559   HEMA 50 E7   34 29 09 S   150 19 57 E

578 Gordon VC Rest Area
Belanglo Rd, Sutton Forest
31 Rest Area 22 km SW of Mittagong or 33 km NE of Marulan. 7 km N of Illawarra Hwy Jcn near Belanglo State Forest turnoff. N bound only
132 213   HEMA 50 F6   34 32 06 S   150 16 54 E

579 Dalys Clearing

Belanglo State Forest
Dalys Rd, Belanglo
Camp Area 10 km W of Moss Vale. Turn W off Hume
Hwy 6 km N of Illawarra Hwy Jcn onto Bunnygalore
& Dalys Rds at Gordon VC Rest Area. Follow
Belanglo Rd for 4 km R for 900 m
1300 655 687   HEMA 50 F6   34 31 38 S   150 14 30 E

580 Kingsbury VC Rest Area

Penrose State Forest
Hume Hwy, Marulan
Rest Area 28 km SW of Mittagong or 25 NE of
Marulan. 6 km S of Illawarra Hwy Jcn. S bound only.
100 m off Hwy
02 9872 0111   HEMA 50 G6   34 37 10 S   150 12 48 E

581 Moss Vale Showground

16 Illawarra Hwy, Moss Vale
Camp Area 800 m E of PO. Entry via
Robertson Rd. Pre-book
0474 186 458   HEMA 50 F7   34 32 52 S   150 22 53 E

582 Gambells Rest Campground

Morton National Park
Gullies Rd, Bundanoon
Camp Area 2 km S of Bundanoon, via Church St.
Dirt road. Pre-book
1300 072 757   HEMA 50 H7   34 40 07 S   150 17 48 E

583 Wingello HQ Camp

Wingello State Forest
Forest Rd, Wingello
Camp Area 4 km SE of Wingello. Dirt road. 2 week limit
1300 655 687   HEMA 50 H5   34 42 57 S   150 11 20 E

584 Badgerys Lookout

Badgerys Lookout Rd, Tallong
Camp Spot 8 km S of Tallong. Via Caoura Rd
HEMA 50 J5   34 46 23 S   150 06 08 E

585 Bungonia Campground

Bungonia National Park
Bungonia
Camp Area 15 km NE of Bungonia, via Lookdown Rd
02 4827 4700   HEMA 50 J4   34 48 26 S   150 00 11 E

586 Derrick VC Rest Area

Hume Hwy, Boxers Creek
Rest Area 18 km W of Marulan. 100 m off
Hwy. Westbound only
132 213   HEMA 50 J2   34 44 11 S   149 49 48 E

587 Breadalbane Rest Area

Hume Hwy, Breadalbane
Rest Area 10 km W of Federal Hwy Jcn or
1 km E of Breadalbane
132 213   HEMA 52 K5   34 48 12 S   149 29 40 E

588 Barbour Park Gunning

Saxby Ln, Gunning
Parking Area N end of public pool car park.
Limited sites. Donation box at service station
02 4832 1988   HEMA 52 K4   34 46 47 S   149 16 06 E

589 Gunning Showground

80 Lerida St, Gunning
Parking Area S of town. Entry off Waratah
St. Designated camping area only. Toilet block
100 m walk
02 4830 1000   HEMA 52 K4   34 47 03 S   149 16 04 E

590 Mundoonan Rest Area

Eastbound
Hume Hwy, Gunning
Rest Area 17 km W of Gunning or 13 km E of Barton
Hwy Jcn
132 213   HEMA 52 K3   34 49 29 S   149 04 30 E

591 Mundoonan Rest Area

Westbound
Hume Hwy, Gunning
Rest Area 14 km E of Barton or 16 km W of
Gunning. W bound only
132 213   HEMA 52 K3   34 48 56 S   149 06 34 E

592 Yass Valley Way Rest Area

Yass Valley Way, Manton
Rest Area at Hume Hwy Jcn
132 213   HEMA 52 K3   34 50 16 S   149 00 50 E

593 Bowning Recreation Ground

Minehan Ln, Bowning
Parking Area 11 km NW of Yass
1300 886 014   HEMA 52 K2   34 46 13 S   148 49 17 E

594 Reflections Holiday Parks

Burrinjuck Waters
2373 Burrinjuck Rd, Burrinjuck
Camp Area 25 km S of Bookham. Turn S 27 km W
of Yass, 6 km E of Bookham. Narrow, winding road
02 6227 8114   HEMA 71 A1   34 58 46 S   148 37 11 E

595 Bookham Rest Area

Hume Hwy, Bookham
Rest Area 34 km W of Barton Hwy Jcn or
29 km E of Jugiong
132 213   HEMA 52 K2   34 48 49 S   148 38 30 E

596 Jugiong Showground

Riverside Dr, Jugiong
Camp Area S side of town. Honesty box
near toilets, 7 day limit
HEMA 52 K1   34 49 24 S   148 19 34 E

597 Coolac Cabins & Camping

100 Harvey Park Ln, Coolac
Camp Area 5 kms N of Coolac. Via Hume
Hwy & Muttama Rd
0417 446 334   HEMA 66 A5   34 53 33 S   148 10 29 E

598 Beehive Hotel

477 Coolac Rd, Coolac
Parking Area 18 km NE of Gundagai.
Check in with publican on arrival. Fee for shower
02 6945 3202   HEMA 66 A5   34 55 26 S   148 09 56 E

599 Coolac Rest Area

Hume Hwy, Coolac
Rest Area 2 km S of Coolac turnoff or
18 km N of Gundagai. Share with trucks. S bound
132 213   HEMA 66 B5   34 56 33 S   148 10 34 E

NEW SOUTH WALES

600 Gundagai North Rest Area
Hume Hwy, Gundagai
Rest Area 15 km S of Coolac or 4 km N of Gundagai. N bound only
HEMA 66 B5   35 01 27 S   148 06 36 E

601 Morleys Creek
Cnr Homer St & Oibell Dr, Gundagai
Parking Area 500 m S of PO. Off Sheridan St, just over the Yarri Bridge, L before cattle crossing
02 6944 0250   HEMA 66 B5   35 04 05 S   148 06 23 E

602 Gundagai Pumphouse
Reserve
Pope St, Gundagai
Parking Area 1.4 km E of PO. Creekside
02 6944 0250   HEMA 66 B5   35 04 00 S   148 07 06 E

603 Tumblong Rest Area
Hume Hwy, Tumblong
Rest Area 1 km N of Tumblong or 10 km SW of Gundagai turnoff
132 213   HEMA 66 B4   35 08 07 S   148 00 39 E

604 Highfield Farm & Woodland
349 Scholz Rd, Mt. Adrah
Farm Stay 3 km S of Mt Adrah. Via Snowy Mt Hwy then Oberne Ellerslie Trail. 2 night minimum. Farm tours available. Pre-book, check in at farmhouse on arrival
0429 985 222   HEMA 66 C4   35 13 33 S   147 52 39 E

605 Breaden Sports Ground
Sydney St, Tarcutta
Parking Area 1 km NE of Hume Hwy. Sports ground behind Caltex Servo. Amenities at servo
02 6928 7202   HEMA 66 C3   35 16 38 S   147 44 12 E

606 Humula Citizens Sports Club
Mate St, Humula
Camp Area 27 km S of Tarcutta or 60 NE of Holbrook. Camping always open, club opens Wed & Fri. Honesty box
0439 061 191   HEMA 66 D4   35 29 17 S   147 45 46 E

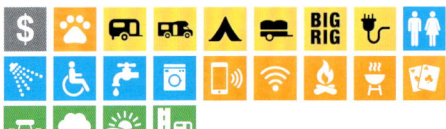

607 Woomargama Rest Area
Woomargama Way, Woomargama
Rest Area 2 km NE off Hume Hwy. Signposted
HEMA 66 E2   35 49 58 S   147 14 47 E

608 Ettamogah Pub
561 Burma Rd, Table Top
Parking Area 650 m NE off Hume Hwy. Free for patrons. Fee for shower
02 6026 2070   HEMA 66 F1   35 58 06 S   147 00 28 E

609 SS&A Club Albury
570 Olive St, Albury
Parking Area 700 m NE of PO. Entry off Wilson St. Parking Area. Check in at reception on arrival, patrons only
02 6041 2222   HEMA 66 G1   36 04 44 S   146 55 12 E

610 Albury Showgrounds
Fallon St, North Albury
Camp Area 2 km S of PO
0417 990 010   HEMA 66 G1   36 03 50 S   146 56 17 E

611 Jindera Primitive Camping
Dight St, Jindera
Camp Area 15 km N of Albury or 145 km E of Tocumwal
1300 252 879   HEMA 69 H13   35 57 27 S   146 53 19 E

612 Burrumbuttock Hall
Cnr Burrumbuttock-Walla Walla & Urana Rds, Burrumbuttock
Camp Area 30 km NW of Albury or 96 km SW of Wagga Wagga. Diagonally opposite general store, behind hall. Fee for power. Donation for unpowered
02 6029 3227   HEMA 69 H12   35 49 59 S   146 48 16 E

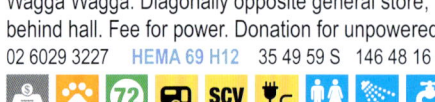

613 Collendina State Forest
Murray Valley Regional Park
Spring Drv, Corowa
Dispersed Camping 8.5 km W of Corowa or 31 km E of Mulwala. S off Mulwala-Corowa Rd. Signposted. GPS at gate. Along river. Pre-book
03 5483 9100   HEMA 69 J11   36 01 02 S   146 17 57 E

614 Kyffins Reserve
Spring Rd, Mulwala
Camp Area 32 km W of Corowa or 7 km E of Mulwala. BYO toilets & dispose appropriately offsite. Camp in marked areas only. 14 day limit in a 3 month period
02 6033 3221   HEMA 69 J10   35 58 48 S   146 03 34 E

615 Mulwala Campground
(Hinches Beach)
Mulwala Valley National Park
Via Tocumwal Rd, Mulwala
Dispersed Camping 8 km W of Mulwala. Via Mulwala-Barooga Rd. Signposted. Hinches Beach 4 km from entrance. Pre-book
03 5483 9100   HEMA 69 H9   35 58 00 S   145 56 40 E

616 Boomanoomana State Forest
Via Mulwalla-Barooga Rd, Mulwala
Dispersed Camping 18 km W of Mulwala or 21 km E of Barooga. Signposted. Sandy Beach 4.5 km, Little Pebble Beach 4 km from entrance. GPS at gate. Pre-book
03 5483 9100   HEMA 69 H9   35 55 55 S   145 53 26 E

617 One Tree Beach
Boomanoomana State Forest
Via Ruwolts Rd, Boomanoomana
Camp Area 22 km W of Mulwala. L from Mulwala through industrial estate to Tocumwal Rd. Then L, signposted. Unsealed road. Pre-book
03 5483 9100   HEMA 69 H9   35 57 33 S   145 51 29 E

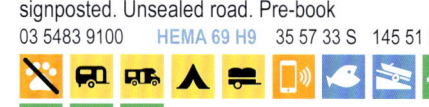

618 Quicks Beach
Murray Valley National Park
Quicks Rd, Barooga
Camp Area 4 km SE of Barooga. Turn S off Mulwala-Barooga Rd 34 km W of Mulwala or 2 km E of Barooga. Solid fuel fire ban Oct-Mar. Pre-book
03 5483 9100   HEMA 69 H8   35 55 37 S   145 42 01 E

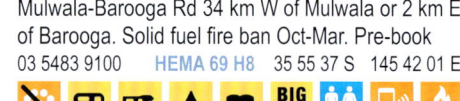

619 Paradise Beach Barooga
Murray Valley Regional Park
Via Barooga-Cobram Rd, Barooga
Camp Area 2.5 km W of Barooga. Turn S off Barooga-Cobram Rd via Ski Beach for 2 km. Signposted. Dirt road. Solid fuel fire ban Oct-Mar. Pre-book
03 5483 9100   HEMA 69 H8   35 55 46 S   145 41 07 E

620 Wattle Tree Beach

Murray Valley Regional Park
Via Barooga-Cobram Rd, Barooga
Camp Area 2 km W of Barooga. S off Barooga-Cobram Rd for 1 km then R for 0.5 km. Via Ski Beach. Signposted. Dirt road. Solid fuel fire ban Oct-Mar. Pre-book
03 5483 9100   HEMA 69 H8   35 55 27 S   145 40 27 E

621 Barooga Precinct

Murray Valley Regional Park
Barooga-Cobram Rd, Barooga
Dispersed Camping W of Barooga, riverside. GPS near entry. Solid fuel fire ban Oct-Mar. Pre-book
03 5483 9100   HEMA 69 H8   35 54 48 S   145 41 15 E

Sydney to Victorian Border via Eden

Princes Highway

622 Reflections Killalea Reserve

Killalea State Park
Killalea Dr, Shell Cove
Camp Area at Shell Cove. 6 km S of Shellharbour or 9 km N of Kiama, off Shellharbour Rd. Gates closed 7.15pm-4.30am
02 4237 8589   HEMA 51 G12   34 36 41 S   150 51 12 E

623 Nungarry Rest Area

Princes Hwy, Dunmore
Rest Area 5 km N of Kiama. S bound traffic only
132 213   HEMA 51 G12   34 37 50 S   150 50 07 E

624 Wirriwin Rest Area

Princes Hwy, Dunmore
Rest Area 5 km N of Kiama. N bound traffic only
132 213   HEMA 51 G12   34 38 05 S   150 49 56 E

625 Kevin Walsh Oval

Jamberoo Reserve
Churchill St, Jamberoo
Camp Area 11 km W of Kiama. Park in designated area. Strictly no tents. Toilets not always open
02 4232 3322   HEMA 51 G11   34 38 50 S   150 46 28 E

626 Berry Showground

35 Alexandra St, Berry
Camp Area 500 m S of PO. Pre-book, check in from 1pm, 7 day limit
02 4421 0778   HEMA 51 J10   34 46 46 S   150 41 46 E

627 Bendeela Recreation Area

Bendeela Rd, Bendeela
Camp Area 7 km W of Kangaroo Valley. Via Moss Vale Rd, N of Hampden Bridge. Short steep access into camp area. Pre-book
1300 662 077   HEMA 51 J8   34 44 21 S   150 28 15 E

628 Shoalhaven Zoo

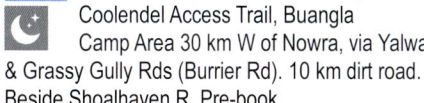

23 Rock Hill Rd, North Nowra
Camp Area. Turn W just N of Nowra Bridge via Illaroo & McMahons Rds. Riverfront
02 4421 3949   HEMA 51 K9   34 52 17 S   150 33 59 E

629 Coolendel Bush Camp

Coolendel Access Trail, Buangla
Camp Area 30 km W of Nowra, via Yalwal & Grassy Gully Rds (Burrier Rd). 10 km dirt road. Beside Shoalhaven R. Pre-book
02 4421 4586   HEMA 51 K8   34 50 38 S   150 25 18 E

630 Nowra Showground

Junction St, Nowra
Camp Area 850 m W of PO. Via West St, ebook
02 4421 0778   HEMA 51 K9   34 52 30 S   150 35 31 E

631 Green Patch Campground

Booderee National Park
Iluka Rd, Jervis Bay
Camp Area 25 km SE of Falls Creek. Via Jervis Bay Rd. Pre-book
02 4443 0977   HEMA 67 B14   35 08 17 S   150 43 17 E

632 Bewong Rest Area

Princes Hwy, Bewong
Rest Area 27 km S of Nowra or 38 km N of Ulladulla. Share with trucks
132 213   HEMA 67 B13   35 05 06 S   150 32 00 E

633 Jerrawangala Rest Area

Princes Hwy, Milton Area
Rest Area 33 km S of Nowra or 30 km N of Ulladulla
HEMA 67 B13   35 07 23 S   150 28 38 E

634 Milton Showground

107 Croobyar Rd, Milton
Camp Area W of town. Camp in designated areas only
02 4421 0778   HEMA 67 C13   35 19 09 S   150 25 48 E

635 Yadboro Flat

Yadboro State Forest
Western Distributor Rd, Yadboro
Camp Area 38 km W of Ulladulla. 8 km S of Ulladulla turn W to Wheelbarrow Rd, L to Woodburn Rd, R to Ridge Rd (Yadboro Rd). Dirt road
1300 655 687   HEMA 67 C12   35 20 24 S   150 13 01 E

636 Termeil Point Campground

Meroo National Park
Termeil Point Rd, Termeil Point
Camp Area at Termeil Point. 14 km S of Ulladulla turn E to Blackbutt Rd for 2 km, R at fork, 600 m to site. Pre-book
02 4454 9500   HEMA 67 D13   35 27 35 S   150 23 38 E

637 Pretty Beach

Murramarang National Park
Pretty Beach Rd, Pretty Beach
Camp Area 2 km S of Kioloa. Turn E off Hwy at Termeil onto Bawley Point Rd. Pre-book
02 4457 2019   HEMA 67 D13   35 34 06 S   150 22 01 E

638 Pebbly Beach Murramarang

Murramarang National Park
Pebbly Beach Access Rd, East Lynne
Camp Area 8 km E of East Lynne. Via Mount Agony Rd 5 km S of East Lynne.
1300 072 757   HEMA 67 D13   35 36 26 S   150 19 33 E

NEW SOUTH WALES

639 Depot Beach Campground
Murramarang National Park
28 Depot Beach Rd, Depot Beach
Camp Area 9 km E of East Lynne. Via Mt Agony Rd, North Durras Rd
02 4478 6582   HEMA 67 E12   35 37 45 S   150 19 20 E
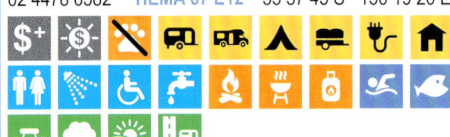

640 Shallow Crossing Camp
2350 The River Rd, Mogood
Camp Area 21 km N of Nelligan
02 4478 1183   HEMA 67 D12   35 31 55 S   150 11 55 E

641 Red Gum Campground
Clyde River National Park
Little Island Trail, Batemans Bay
Camp Area 10 km NW of Batemans Bay via Kings Hwy & Rotary Dr. Follow trail to end
02 4454 9500   HEMA 67 E12   35 40 08 S   150 09 06 E

642 Beach Campground
Clyde River National Park
Beach Camp Rd, Batemans Bay
Camp spot 10 km NW of Batemans Bay via Kings Hwy. Turn to Rotary Dr, Chinaman's Pt Trail & Beach Camp Rd
1300 072 757   HEMA 67 E12   35 41 27 S   150 07 50 E

643 Waldrons Swamp Rest Area
Princes Hwy, Moruya
Rest Area 20 km S of Batemans Bay or 7 km N of Moruya. Shared with trucks
132 213   HEMA 67 F12   35 51 54 S   150 07 09 E

644 North Head Campground
North Head Dr, Moruya
Camp Area 7 km E of Moruya. From Moruya turn E along North Head Dr just N of bridge, then to Bruce Cameron Dr beside airport. Cold showers. Fees higher in peak season
0428 633 447   HEMA 67 F12   35 54 11 S   150 08 55 E

645 Congo Campground
Eurobodalla National Park
Congo Rd, Moruya
Camp Area 10 km SE of Moruya, via South Head Dr. Beachside. Cold showers. Pre-book
02 4476 0800   HEMA 67 F12   35 57 17 S   150 09 31 E

646 Brou Lake Campground
Eurobodalla National Park
Brou Lake Rd, Bodalla
Camp Area 14 km S of Bodalla. Turn E 9 km S of Bodalla to Brou Lake Rd, L at fork. 5 km dirt road. Small vehicles only. Pre-book
02 4476 0800   HEMA 67 G12   36 08 52 S   150 07 09 E

647 Bodalla Forest Rest Area
Bodalla State Forest
Princess Hwy, Bodalla
Rest Area 9 km S of Bodalla or 9 km N of Narooma
1300 655 687   HEMA 67 G12   36 09 03 S   150 05 46 E

648 Dalmeny Campground
1 Noble Pde, Dalmeny
Camp Area on headland. Turn E off Princes Hwy to Mort Ave 38 km S of Moruya or 5 km N of Narooma
0428 635 641   HEMA 67 G12   36 09 47 S   150 07 35 E

649 Mystery Bay Campground
190 Mystery Bay Rd, Mystery Bay
Camp Area 12 km S of Narooma. Turn SE 10 km S of Narooma or 27 km NE of Cobargo. Cold showers. Fees higher in peak season
0428 622 357   HEMA 67 H12   36 17 54 S   150 08 00 E

650 Cobargo Hotel
Princes Hwy, Cobargo
Parking Area 250 m SW of PO. Check in with publican, free for patrons. Fee for showers
02 6493 6423   HEMA 67 H11   36 23 22 S   149 53 09 E

651 Bega Showgrounds
33 Upper St, Bega
Camp Area 850 m S of PO. Via East St. Caretaker on site
0424 051 901   HEMA 67 J11   36 40 40 S   149 50 50 E

652 Gillards Campground
Mimosa Rocks National Park
Gillards Rd, Nelson
Camp Area 13 km N of Tathra, via Tathra-Bermagui Rd. 4 km single lane dirt road, care needed. Pre-book
02 4476 0800   HEMA 67 J11   36 39 35 S   150 00 05 E

653 Picnic Point Campground
Mimosa Rocks National Park
Wapengo Lake Rd, Picnic Point
Camp Area 10 km SE of Wapengo. Take Tathra-Bermagui Rd then R to Wapengo Lake Rd. Not suitable for large vehicles. Private road, close gates. 1 month limit. Pre-book
1300 072 757   HEMA 67 J12   36 36 53 S   150 01 46 E

654 Hobart Beach
Bournda National Park
293 Bournda Rd, Bournda
Camp Area 13 km S of Tathra or 18 km N of Merimbula. Turn E off Sapphire Coast Dr 10 km S of Tathra or 15 km N of Merimbula. 3 km dirt road. Pre-book
02 6495 5000   HEMA 67 K11   36 47 49 S   149 56 21 E

655 Dr William Loftus Park
Williams St, Candelo
Rest Area opposite general store
02 6499 2222   HEMA 67 K10   36 46 00 S   149 41 42 E

656 East Ben Boyd Forest
Princes Hwy, Eden Area
Rest Area 18 km S of Eden or 41 km N of Genoa. Both sides of the road
HEMA 70 G6   37 12 09 S   149 50 43 E

657 Saltwater Creek Camp
Ben Boyd National Park
Via Duck Hole Rd, Green Cape
Camp Area 41 km SE of Eden. Turn E 18 km S of Eden or 7 km N of Narrabarba to Edrom, Green Cape & Saltwater Rds. 16 km winding dirt road. Limited space, small vehicles only. Pre-book. 14 day limit
02 6495 5000   HEMA 70 G6   37 10 08 S 149 59 58 E

658 Bittangabee Campground
Ben Boyd National Park
Green Cape Rd, Bittangabee Bay
Camp Area 43 km SE of Eden. Turn E 19 km S of Eden or 7 km N of Narrabarba, onto Edrom Rd. 18 km winding dirt road. Small vehicles only. Pre-book
02 6495 5000   HEMA 70 H7   37 13 04 S 150 00 58 E

659 Scrubby Creek Rest Area
East Boyd State Forest
Princes Hwy, Narrabarba
Area 20 km S of Eden or 39 km N of Genoa.
700 m W of Hwy
1300 655 687   HEMA 70 H6   37 13 20 S 149 49 49 E

660 Newtons Crossing Camp
Yambulla State Forest
Allan Brook Rd, Yambulla
Camp Area 56 km SW of Eden. Turn W to Imlay Rd 25 km S of Eden or 36 km N of Genoa. Follow for 12 km, turn S. 6 km dirt road. Last 100 m rough track. Small vehicles only
1300 655 687   HEMA 70 H5   37 16 03 S 149 40 30 E

661 Wallagaraugh River Rest Area
Princes Hwy, Timbillica
Rest Area 40 km S of Eden or 19 km N of Genoa. Small vehicles only, limited space
132 213   HEMA 70 H6   37 22 10 S 149 42 54 E

Cowra to Cann River
Lachlan Valley Way, Barton and Monaro Highways

662 Boorowa Caravan Park
Brial St, Boorowa
Caravan Park 1 km N of PO
02 6385 3658   HEMA 52 J2   34 26 04 S 148 43 10 E

663 The Ram & Stallion Hotel
72 Brial St, Boorowa
Parking Area behind pub. 60 km SE of Young. Check in with the publican. Free for patrons
02 6385 3576   HEMA 52 J2   34 26 08 S 148 43 22 E

664 Harden-Murrumburrah Showgrounds
Woolrych St, Harden
Camp Area 35 km S of Young. Call caretaker to pay fees & unlock facilities
0488 509 977   HEMA 52 J1   34 32 45 S 148 21 27 E

665 Homebush Park
23 Manning St, Binalong
Camp Area 34 km NW of Yass. Turn S off Burley Griffin Way (B94). Fee for water
0411 878 773   HEMA 52 K2   34 40 23 S 148 37 29 E

666 Yass Showgrounds
27 Grand Jct Rd, Yass
Camp Area E of town. Honesty box
02 6226 1615   HEMA 52 K3   34 50 27 S 148 55 18 E

666-1 Yass Soldiers Club
86 Meehan St, Yass
Club Stay 61 km N of Canberra or 91 km W of Goulburn. Exit Hume Hwy (M31) S to Yass Valley Hwy for 6 km, then E to Meehan St
02 6226 1911   HEMA 52 K3   34 50 31 S 148 54 47 E

667 Joe O'Connor RV Park
12 Laidlaw St, Yass
Parking Area 850 m N of PO. W side of town
1300 886 014   HEMA 52 K3   34 50 10 S 148 54 21 E

668 Bredbo Inn Hotel
Monaro Hwy, Bredbo
Parking Area 82 km SE of Canberra or 34 km N of Coma on the
02 6454 4109   HEMA 71 K5   35 57 03 S 149 08 44 E

669 Numeralla River Rest Area
Monaro Hwy, Chakola
Rest Area 14 km S of Bredbo or 20 km N of Cooma. Beside river
HEMA 67 G8   36 04 36 S 149 09 33 E

670 Badja Recreation Reserve
Numeralla Peak View Rd, Numeralla
Camp Spot 22 km E of Cooma. Beside river
02 6450 1777   HEMA 67 G9   36 10 25 S 149 21 01 E

671 Warreen Farmstay
338 Tuross Rd, Countegany
Farm Stay at Countegany. 14 km E of Numeralla via Countegany Rd
02 6453 3272   HEMA 67 G9   36 12 42 S 149 27 12 E

672 Nimmitabel Caravan Park
Boyd St, Nimmitabel
Camp Area N end of town. Call caretaker to use amenities block. Fees collected
0436 806 817   HEMA 67 J9   36 30 31 S 149 17 04 E

673 Brown Mountain
Wattle Rd, Bemboka
Parking Area 22 km SE of Nimmitabel or 17 km W of Bemboka. Behind truck parking area
HEMA 67 J9   36 36 31 S 149 25 58 E

674 Bemboka Sports Ground
Colombo Park, Bemboka
Camp Area 1 km E of Bemboka. Turn off at Colombo Creek Bridge. Fee for power & shower, phone for key & payment. 7 day limit
02 6493-0415   HEMA 67 J10   36 38 08 S 149 34 41 E

675 Nunnock Campground
South East Forests National Park
Nunnock Camp Rd, Glen Allen
Camp Area N off Mount Darragh Rd to Tantawangalo Mountain Rd. N to New Line Rd, then E into Packers Swamp Rd, on to Cattlemans Link Trail, follow to site. Small vehicles only. 15 km dirt road. Pre-book
02 6458 5900   HEMA 67 J9   36 42 12 S 149 26 49 E

676 Six Mile Creek
South East Forest National Park
Tantawangalo Mountain Rd, Tantawangalo
Camp Area 20 km NE of Cathcart or 12 km W of Candelo. Dirt road. Small vehicles only. Pre-book
1300 072 757   HEMA 67 K10   36 47 11 S 149 32 18 E

677 Bombala Caravan Park
Monaro Hwy, Bombala
Caravan Park
0488 257 928　　HEMA 67 K9　　36 54 30 S　149 14 20 E

678 Waratah Gully Campground
South East Forests National Park
Wog Way, Paddys Flat
Camp Area 19 km SE of Bombala. Via Bucky
Springs Rd & Coolangubra Forest Way. Pre-book
02 6458 5900　　HEMA 70 G4　　37 00 09 S　149 23 02 E

679 Delegate Caravan Park
Bill Jeffreys Memorial Park
Topping St, Delegate
Caravan Park
02 6458 4047　　HEMA 70 G3　　37 02 24 S　148 56 48 E

Tomerong to Braidwood
Trunk Road 92

680 Endrick River Crossing
Nerriga Rd, Coolumburra
Camp Area 55 km W of Tomerong or 5 km
NE of Nerriga on Turpentine Rd. 100 m N of bridge
on N side of the road. Dirt road
HEMA 67 B12　　35 05 22 S　150 07 15 E

681 Corang River
Nerriga Rd, Nerriga
Camp Spot 12 km S of Nerriga or 41 km NE
of Braidwood. Dirt road. E side of bridge beside river
02 4845 9190　　HEMA 67 C12　　35 12 21 S　150 03 06 E

682 Wog Wog Camping Area
Morton National Park
Charleys Forest Rd, Wog Wog
Camp Area 22 km S of Nerriga or 41 km NE of
Braidwood. Turn S off Braidwood-Nerriga Rd 17 km
S of Nerriga or 36 km NE of Braidwood. Dirt road.
Pre-book
02 4454 9500　　HEMA 67 C11　　35 16 06 S　150 02 08 E

683 Charleyong Crossing
Stuarts Crossing
6473 Stewarts Crossing Rd, Nerriga
Camp Area 31 km SW of Nerriga or 26 km NE of
Braidwood. Turn W off Braidwood-Nerriga Rd 29 km
SW of Nerriga or 24 km NE of Braidwood across
causeway, camp on R. Dirt road
1300 662 077　　HEMA 67 C11　　35 14 43 S　149 53 29 E

684 The Service Club
Cnr Coronation Ave & Victory St, Braidwood
Club Stay W side of town. Parking on
fenceline only. Patronage please
02 4842 2108　　HEMA 67 D11　　35 26 34 S　149 47 31 E

685 Braidwood Showground
Kings Hwy, Braidwood
Camp Area 2 km N of town on Kings Hwy.
Payment & keys at Colonial Motel
02 4842 2027　　HEMA 67 D11　　35 25 23 S　149 47 31 E

Batemans Bay to Canberra
Kings Highway

686 Bendethera Valley Camp
Deua National Park
Bendethera Fire Trail, Deua
Dispersed Camping 5 km along the river, 56 km W
of Moruya. Take Western Boundary Rd turnoff from
Princes Hwy, L to Little Sugarloaf Rd. Steep. Pre-book
1300 072 757　　HEMA 67 F10　　35 57 01 S　149 44 50 E

687 Dry Creek Campground
Deua National Park
Araluen Rd, Braidwood Area
Camp Area 48.5 km S of Braidwood. Dirt road,
narrow in places. steep access. No caravans
02 4476 0800　　HEMA 67 E11　　35 45 16 S　149 55 33 E

688 Deua River Campground
Deua National Park
Araluen Rd, Deua River Valley
Camp Area 48 km S of Braidwood. Dirt road, narrow
in places. Small vehicles only. Pre-book
02 4476 0800　　HEMA 67 E11　　35 44 52 S　149 55 00 E

689 Araluen Creek
Majors Creek Mountain Rd, Braidwood
Camp Area 24 km S of Braidwood or 3 km
N of Araluen Hotel
HEMA 67 E11　　35 37 27 S　149 47 37 E

690 Majors Creek Rec Reserve
Araluen St, Majors Creek
Camp Area at Majors Creek, 16 km S of
Braidwood. Donation
HEMA 67 D10　　35 34 08 S　149 44 31 E

691 Lowden Forest Park
Tallaganda State Forest
Lowden Rd, Ballalaba
Camp Area 38 km SW of Braidwood. Via the
Krawarree Rd to Ballalaba, Harolds Cross Rd
(Parlour Ck) & Coxes Ck Rd. Dirt road
1300 655 687　　HEMA 67 D10　　35 30 34 S　149 36 16 E
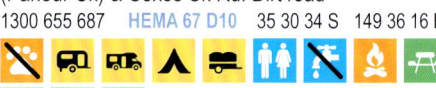

692 Wilkins Memorial Park
Foxlow St, Captains Flat
Camp Area S end of town. Small vehicles only
0423 203 041　　HEMA 71 F7　　35 35 26 S　149 26 46 E

693 Bombay Reserve
Braidwood Rd, Braidwood
Camp Spot 9 km W of Braidwood. 200 m past
bridge on R. 100 m off road by Shoalhaven River
HEMA 67 D10　　35 25 37 S　149 42 48 E

694 Warri Reserve Rest Area
Kings Hwy, Larbert
Rest Area 14 km N of Braidwood or 35 km
SE of Bungendore. By Shoalhaven River
HEMA 67 C10　　35 20 39 S　149 44 15 E

695 The Loaded Dog Hotel
1 Wallace St, Tarago
Parking Area S side of town in paddock
Check in with publican before parking
02 4849 4499　　HEMA 67 B10　　35 04 12 S　149 39 15 E

696 Bungendore Showground
Matthews Ln, Bungendore
Camp Area 4 km NW of Bungendore.
Caretaker on site. 14 day limit
0455 174 463　　HEMA 71 C7　　35 14 30 S　149 24 37 E

Goulburn to Canberra
Federal Highway

697 Edmondson VC Rest Area

Federal Hwy, Currawang
Rest Area 15 km SW of Hume/Federal Hwy Jcn or 62 km NE of Barton/Federal Hwy Jcn. Beside Rowes Lagoon, 300 m off Hwy. Signposted from S bound only. Small vehicles only
HEMA 67 A10   34 53 46 S   149 30 37 E

698 Gurney VC Rest Area

Federal Hwy, Lake George
Rest Area 33 km SW of Hume/Federal Hwy Jcn or 44 km NE of Barton/Federal Hwy Jcn
HEMA 71 A6   34 59 58 S   149 22 57 E

699 Gundaroo Sport & Recreation Ground

Cork St, Gundaroo
Camp Area W side of town, N of David St. Donation for upkeep at general store/PO. Tents in designated areas only. Short term camping preferred
0411 400 897   HEMA 71 A6   35 01 25 S   149 15 57 E

700 Anderson VC Rest Area

Hadlow Dr, Lake George
Rest Area 48 km SW of Hume/Federal Hwy Jcn or 29 km NE of Barton/Federal Hwy Jcn. 100 m off Hwy. Small vehicles only
HEMA 71 B6   35 06 01 S   149 22 36 E

701 Tin Can Ridge

Calabash Rd, Tinderry
Camp Area 67 km SE of Canberra. Via Monaro Hwy. Pets on application, toilets available on request. Pre-book
0428 460 954   HEMA 71 H6   35 45 42 S   149 17 13 E

Australian Capital Territory

702 Blue Range Hut Rec Area

Uriarra Forest
Blue Range Rd, Coree
Camp Area 42 km W of Canberra via Uriarra Rd, turn N to Blue Range Rd, 3 km to site. Pre-book
02 6237 5307   HEMA 71 D3   35 17 22 S   148 52 32 E

703 Cotter Campground

1691 Cotter Rd, Strombio
Camp Area 20 km W of Canberra. Riverside. No bookings. 14 day limit
02 6237 5307   HEMA 71 D3   35 19 33 S   148 56 52 E

704 Woods Reserve Camp

Namadgi National Park
Corin Rd, Paddys River
Camp Area 19 km NW of Tharwa, via Tidbinbilla Rd. Pre-book.14 day limit
02 6237 5307   HEMA 71 E3   35 28 52 S   148 56 26 E

705 Honeysuckle Campground

Namadgi National Park
Apollo Rd, Tennent
Camp Area 68 km SW of Canberra, via Monaro Hwy turn W to Angle Crossing Rd, S to Naas Rd, then to Apollo Rd. Travel 9.5 km to sites. Pre-book
02 6237 5307   HEMA 71 F4   35 35 00 S   148 58 35 E

706 Mount Clear Campground

Namadgi National Park
Naas Valley Firetrail, Mount Clear
Camp Area 48 km S of Tharwa via Boboyan Rd. Pre-book. Small vehicles only
02 6237 5307   HEMA 71 J4   35 51 55 S   149 00 39 E

707 Exhibition Park in Canberra

Old Well Station Rd, Lyneham
Camp Area at EPIC, 8 km N of city centre. Pre-book. Call 0466 419 099 on arrival
02 6205 5230   HEMA 72 C5   35 13 42 S   149 09 12 E

708 Hughie Edwards VC Rest Area

Federal Hwy, Canberra
Rest Area 71 km SW of Hume/Federal Hwy Jcn or 6 km NE of Barton/Federal Hwy Jcn. S bound only
132 213   HEMA 72 B6   35 12 40 S   149 11 26 E

Snowy Mountains Area
Snowy Mountains Highway

709 Fitzpatrick Trackhead Reserve

Wee Jasper Reserves
1 Nottingham Rd, Wee Jasper
Camp Area 4 km S of Wee Jasper, via Tumut-Nottingham Rd. N at T Jcn, then W. Dirt road. Pre-book
02 6227 9626   HEMA 71 B1   35 08 20 S   148 40 27 E

710 Billy Grace Reserve

Wee Jasper Reserves
5 Nottingham Rd, Wee Jasper
Camp Area 6 km S of Wee Jasper, via Tumut-Nottingham Rd. S at T Jcn, then E to reserve. 1 km dirt road. Beside Goodradigbee River. Pre-book
02 6227 9626   HEMA 71 B2   35 08 14 S   148 41 14 E

711 Swinging Bridge Reserve

Wee Jasper Reserves
524 Nottingham Rd, Wee Jasper
Camp Area 9 km S of Wee Jasper. Dirt road. By Goodradigbee River. Pre-book
02 6227 9626   HEMA 71 C2   35 09 44 S   148 41 13 E

712 Micalong Creek Reserve

Wee Jasper Reserves
524 Nottingham Rd, Wee Jasper
Camp Area 12 km S of Wee Jasper via Tumut-Nottingham Rd. S at T Jcn. Beside Micalong Creek. 7 km dirt road. Pre-book
02 6227 9626   HEMA 71 C2   35 11 19 S   148 41 10 E

713 Thomas Boyd Trackhead

Goobragandra Powerline Rd, Goobarragandra
Camp Area 23 km SE of Tumut. Via Laclamac Rd, riverside. 3 km dirt road, ebook
02 6937 2700   HEMA 66 C6   35 22 24 S   148 24 59 E

714 Rock Flat Campground

Kosciuszko National Park
Goobragandra Powerline Rd, Tumut
Camp Area 27 km SE of Tumut. Riverside. 7 km dirt road. Pre-book
02 6947 7025   HEMA 66 D6   35 24 02 S   148 25 56 E

NEW SOUTH WALES

715 Golden Gully Caravan Park
Victoria Hill Rd, Adelong
Caravan Park behind services club.
Register at reception
02 6946 2163   HEMA 66 C5   35 18 25 S   148 03 55 E

716 Adelong Showgrounds
Cromwell St, Adelong
Parking Area at Jcn of Campbell St
1300 275 782   HEMA 66 C5   35 18 55 S   148 03 49 E

717 Batlow Caravan Park
Kurrajong Ave, Batlow
Caravan Park N end of town
0437 722 697   HEMA 66 D5   35 31 02 S   148 08 47 E

718 Springfield Rest Area
Batlow Rd, Batlow
Rest Area 27 km SW of Tumut or 6 km N
of Batlow
132 213   HEMA 66 D5   35 28 17 S   148 08 51 E

719 Batlow Showground
Cnr Memorial Ave & Park St, Batlow
Camp Area E side of town
1300 275 782   HEMA 66 D5   35 31 09 S   148 09 11 E

720 Windy Point Camping Area
Blowering Reservoir
Foreshore Rd, Blowering
Camp Area 20 km NE of Batlow. W foreshore
02 6947 3911   HEMA 66 D5   35 29 43 S   148 14 30 E

721 White Gate Rest Area
Batlow Rd, Batlow
Rest Area 6 km SW of Batlow or 9 km N of
Laurel Hill. Small area
132 213   HEMA 66 D5   35 31 57 S   148 05 58 E

722 Tumbarumba RV Stop
Winton St, Tumbarumba
Parking Area opposite police station, centre
of town
1300 275 782   HEMA 66 E4   35 46 34 S   148 00 41 E

723 Mannus Creek Rest
Jingellic Rd, Tumbarumba
Camp Area 7 km W of Tumbarumba
132 213   HEMA 66 E4   35 46 46 S   147 56 44 E

724 Lake Mannus Boat Ramp
Mannus Lake Rd, Tumbarumba
Camp Area 12 km W of Tumbarumba. Turn
S at Mannus Campsite on Lake Rd, follow dirt road
for 5 km to boat ramp
1300 275 782   HEMA 66 E4   35 48 40 S   147 58 39 E

725 Jingellic Reserve
3149 River Rd, Jingellic
Camp Area beside Murray River. Fee for
showers at hotel. Dogs must be on lead. 4 week limit
02 6037 1290   HEMA 66 F3   35 55 44 S   147 42 14 E

726 Jingellic Showgrounds
3211 River Rd, Jingellic
Camp Area 66 km NW of Khancoban, or
SW of Tumbarumba. Limited spaces. Honesty box
0411 030 939   HEMA 66 F3   35 55 37 S   147 41 58 E

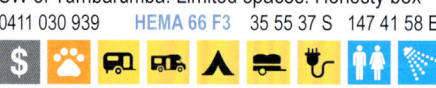

727 Paddys River Dam
Bago State Forest
Via Perkins Rd, Paddys River
Camp Area 23 km NE of Tumbarumba. Via Round
Creek & Dog Tree Rds. Dirt road
1300 655 687   HEMA 66 E5   35 42 44 S   148 10 01 E

728 Henry Angel Track Head
Tooma Rd, Tumbarumba
Camp Area 8 km SE of Tumbarumba or
26 km N of Tooma. Riverside. 4 week limit. Permit
applies after 5 days
02 6948 3444   HEMA 66 E5   35 49 41 S   148 03 38 E

729 Tooma Inn
9 Possum Point Rd, Tooma
Camp Area at park adjacent. Larger RVs
park behind hotel. Ring ahead to ensure space.
Register at bar on arrival
02 6948 4012   HEMA 66 F5   35 58 04 S   148 03 30 E

730 Paddys River Flats
Tooma Rd, Paddys River
Camp Area 18 km SE of Tumbarumba or
16 km N of Tooma. Beside river. 4 week limit. Permit
applies after 5 days
02 6948 9100   HEMA 66 F5   35 51 07 S   148 08 22 E

731 O'Hares Campground
Kosciuszko National Park
Elliott Way, Nurenmerenmong
Camp Area 22 km N of Cabramurra or 48 km SE of
Tumbarumba. Steep winding road. Pre-book
02 6947 7025   HEMA 66 E6   35 49 20 S   148 21 55 E

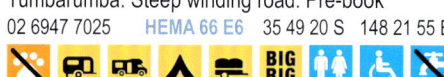

732 Three Mile Dam Camp
Kosciuszko National Park
Link Rd, Selwyn
Camp Area 6 km W of Kiandra or 12 km NE of
Cabramurra. 300 m N of road. Pre-book
02 6947 7025   HEMA 66 F6   35 53 18 S   148 26 56 E

733 Clover Flat Rest Area
Kosciuszko National Park
Tooma Rd, Jagumba
Rest Area 25 km NE of Khancoban or 35 km SW of
Cabramurra. Steep & winding road, limited space,
small vehicles only
02 6070 8400   HEMA 66 G5   36 04 21 S   148 13 02 E

734 Bradneys Gap
Kosciuszko National Park
Swampy Plains Creek Rd, Khancoban
Rest Area 10 km NE of Khancoban or 50 km SW of
Cabramurra
02 6070 8400   HEMA 66 G5   36 09 56 S   148 09 24 E

735 Towong Reserve
Towong Rd, Bringenbrong
Camp Area 25 km S of Tooma or 1 km E of
Towong. Beside Murray River bridge. 4 week limit
02 6071 5100   HEMA 66 G4   36 07 25 S   147 59 49 E

736 Geehi Flats Campground
Kosciuszko National Park
Via Alpine Way, Geehi
Camp Area 30 km S of Khancoban or 81 km W of Jindabyne. Steep & winding road. Small vehicles only. Pre-book
02 6070 8400   HEMA 66 H5   36 23 05 S   148 10 51 E

737 Tom Groggin Campground
Kosciuszko National Park
The Bicentennial National Trail, Khancoban
Camp Area 53 km S of Khancoban or 58 km W of Jindabyne. Steep & winding road. Small vehicles only. Pre-book
02 6450 5600   HEMA 66 J5   36 32 32 S   148 07 44 E

738 Ngarigo Campground
Kosciuszko National Park
Alpine Way, Thredbo
Camp Area 87 km SE of Khancoban or 24 km W of Jindabyne, beside Thredbo R. Steep & winding road. Small vehicles only. Pre-book
02 6450 5600   HEMA 66 H6   36 27 33 S   148 23 01 E

739 Thredbo Diggings Camp
Kosciuszko National Park
Alpine Way, Jindabyne
Camp Area 92 km SE of Khancoban or 19 km W of Jindabyne. Via Kosciuszko Rd. Beside Thredbo River. Steep & winding road. Pre-book
02 6450 5600   HEMA 66 H6   36 26 49 S   148 25 31 E

740 Island Bend Campground
Kosciuszko National Park
Guthega Rd, Jindabyne
Camp Area 28 km NW of Jindabyne, via Kosciuszko Rd. Small vehicles only. Pre-book
02 6450 5600   HEMA 66 H6   36 19 24 S   148 28 40 E

741 Long Plain Hut Campground
Kosciuszko National Park
Long Plain Hut Access, Long Plain
Camp Area 15 km SE of Yarrangobilly. 10.5 km S of Yarrangobilly turn E to Long Plain Rd 5 km, turn L at signpost, 1 km to sites near hut. Pre-book
02 6947 7025   HEMA 71 G1   35 41 50 S   148 32 15 E

742 Cooinbil Hut Campground
Kosciuszko National Park
Cooinbil Rd, Long Plain
Camp Area 25 km SE of Yarrangobilly. 10.5 km S of Yarrangobilly turn E to Long Plain Rd for 10.5 km, turn R at signpost, 1 km to site near hut. Pre-book. Winter closure
02 6947 7025   HEMA 71 G1   35 37 53 S   148 35 49 E

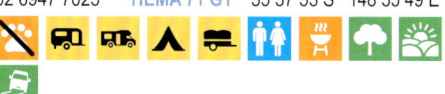

743 Cooleman Mountain Camp
Kosciuszko National Park
Blue Waterholes Trail, Bimberi
Camp Area 30 km SE of Yarrangobilly. 10.5 km S of Yarrangobilly turn E to Long Plains Rd for 17 km, turn R to Blue Waterhole Trail for 2.5 km. Pre-book. Winter closure
02 6947 7025   HEMA 71 F1   35 35 51 S   148 38 23 E

744 Magpie Flat Camping Area
Kosciuszko National Park
Blue Waterholes Trail, Cooleman
Camp Area 35 km SE of Yarrangobilly. 10.5 km S of Yarrangobilly turn E to Long Plain Rd for 16.5 km, turn R to Blue Waterholes Trail for 8 km. Pre-book. Winter closure
02 6947 7025   HEMA 71 G2   35 37 18 S   148 40 49 E

745 Blue Waterholes Camp
Kosciuszko National Park
Blue Waterholes Trail, Cooleman
Camp Area 35.5 km SE of Yarrangobilly. 10.5 km S of Yarrangobilly turn E to Long Plain Rd for 16.5 km, turn R to Blue Waterholes Trail for 8.5 km. Pre-book. Winter closure
02 6947 7025   HEMA 71 G2   35 37 23 S   148 41 00 E

746 Yarrangobilly Village Camp
Kosciuszko National Park
Snowy Mountains Hwy, Yarrangobilly
Camp Area 29 km N of Kiandra or 24 km S of Talbingo turnoff. Beside river. Pre-book
02 6947 7025   HEMA 66 E6   35 39 07 S   148 27 44 E

747 Jounama Creek Camp
Kosciuszko National Park
Jounama Creek Trail, Talbingo
Camp Area opposite Talbingo turnoff. 500 m E of Hwy. Beside creek. Pre-book
02 6947 7025   HEMA 66 D6   35 33 56 S   148 19 55 E

748 Yolde Campground
Kosciuszko National Park
Yolde Access, Blowering
Camp Area 5 km N of Talbingo turnoff or 35 km S of Tumut. Small vehicles only
02 6947 7025   HEMA 66 D5   35 32 18 S   148 17 43 E

749 Yachting Point Campground
Kosciuszko National Park
Yachting Point Access, Blowering
Camp Area 10 km N of Talbingo turnoff or 30 km S of Tumut. Pre-book
02 6947 7025   HEMA 66 D5   35 30 39 S   148 16 03 E

750 Humes Crossing Camp
Kosciuszko National Park
Via Snowy Mountains Hwy, Blowering
Camp Area 15 km N of Talbingo turnoff or 25 km S of Tumut. Pre-book
02 6947 7025   HEMA 66 D5   35 28 25 S   148 16 34 E

751 The Pines Campground
Kosciuszko National Park
The Pines Access, Blowering
Camp Area 18 km N of Talbingo turnoff or 22 km S of Tumut. Pre-book
02 6947 7025   HEMA 66 D5   35 26 51 S   148 17 06 E

752 Log Bridge Creek Camp
Kosciuszko National Park
Log Bridge Creek Access, Blowering
Camp Area 22 km N of Talbingo turnoff or 18 km S of Tumut. Turn SE off Hwy, follow road back across Hwy for 1.5 km to main camp area. Pre-book
02 6947 7025   HEMA 66 D5   35 25 11 S   148 16 16 E

753 Tumut River Jones Bridge
West Blowering Rd, Wereboldera
Rest Area 9 km S of Tumut. Turn S off Snowy Mountains Hwy to West Blowering Rd. 1.5 km to riverside sites
02 6947 7025   HEMA 66 C5   35 22 23 S   148 15 27 E

NEW SOUTH WALES

754 Tumut Valley Violets

572 Tumut Plains Rd, Tumut Plains
Camp Area 6 km SE of Township. E at 5 ways
0404 020 919   HEMA 66 C5   35 20 14 S   148 16 06 E

Cowra to Albury
Olympic Highway

755 Bendick Murrell Rest Area
Olympic Hwy, Bendick Murrell
Rest Area 44 km SW of Cowra or 26 km NE
of Young. Share with trucks
HEMA 52 H1   34 10 02 S   148 27 33 E

756 Touts Lookout
Scenic Rd, Monteagle
Parking Area 20 km N of Young. Via
Monteagle Rd
132 213   HEMA 52 H1   34 10 33 S   148 22 47 E

757 Young Showground
120 Whiteman Ave, Young
Camp Area 2 km E of PO. Free for SCV.
Fee for power. Pre-book
0427 451 133   HEMA 52 H1   34 18 58 S   148 18 50 E

758 Big Spring Creek
4129 Olympic Hwy, Young
Rest Area 8 km S of Young or 23 km NE of
Wallendbeen
132 213   HEMA 64 H4   34 22 28 S   148 15 35 E

759 Waganbah Oval
Rose St, Wombat
Camp Area 16 km S of Young. Caretaker
collects fee. Limited sites
0437 806 002   HEMA 64 H4   34 25 42 S   148 14 46 E

760 Mackay Park
Victoria St, Wallendbeen
Rest Area at the roundabout
02 6940 2190   HEMA 64 H4   34 31 45 S   148 09 46 E

761 Stockinbingal Rec Grounds
O'Brien St, Stockinbingal
Camp Area near oval, N side of town. GPS
at entry, near Dudauman St. Toilets may be open,
power limited. Cold shower
HEMA 64 H3   34 29 41 S   147 53 03 E

762 Stockinbingal
Accommodation
17 Cambria St, Stockinbingal
Camp Area W side of town
0434 604 865   HEMA 64 H3   34 29 45 S   147 52 28 E

763 Stockinbingal Rest Area
Hibernia St, Stockinbingal
Picnic Area in front of the train station, S
side of town on Burley Griffin Way. Limited space

764 Springdale Memorial Park
6250 Burley Griffin Way, Springdale
Camp Area 43.5 km W of Wallendbeen, or
19 km E of Temora
02 6977 5921   HEMA 64 H3   34 28 03 S   147 43 35 E

765 Cootamundra Showgrounds
Pinkerton Rd, Cootamundra
Camp Area 49 km S of Young or 55 km N of
Junee. Pre-book with caretaker
0428 238 516   HEMA 64 J4   34 38 24 S   148 02 27 E

766 Muttama Recreation Ground
Bridge St, Muttama
Camping Area near old tennis court
HEMA 64 J4   34 48 19 S   148 06 47 E

767 Bethungra Campground
Baylis St, Bethungra
Camp Area 23 km SW of Cootamundra or
30 km NE of Junee
02 6940 2190   HEMA 66 A4   34 45 41 S   147 51 28 E

768 Bethungra Dam
567 Bethungra Waterworks Rd, Bethungra
Camp Area 5 km E of Bethungra. 1 km
N of Bethungra Village turn E onto dirt road under
viaduct, to Bethungra Waterworks Rd, follow to dam.
5 km dirt road
02 6940 2190   HEMA 66 A4   34 45 50 S   147 54 27 E

769 Illabo Rest Area
Olympic Hwy, Illabo
Rest Area opposite hotel. Share with trucks
HEMA 66 A4   34 48 57 S   147 44 21 E

770 Junee Golf Club
Golf Ave, Junee
Parking Area W side of town. Via Gundagai
Rd. Check in at club
02 6924 3371   HEMA 66 A3   34 52 20 S   147 35 32 E

771 Old Junee Rec Ground
Goldfields Hwy, Old Junee
Camp Area at Old Junee. N side of town
HEMA 66 A3   34 50 13 S   147 31 16 E

772 Sandy Beach Reserve
Sandy Beach Ln, Wantabadgery
Camp Area 3 km SE of Wantabadgery. Via
River Rd. 14 day limit
02 6924 8100   HEMA 66 B4   35 04 06 S   147 44 23 E

773 Wallacetown Rest Area
Olympic Hwy, Yathella
Rest Area 20 km S of Junee or 21 km N of
Wagga Wagga. Opposite service station. Separate
area for caravans, follow signage
HEMA 66 B3   34 57 34 S   147 26 55 E

774 Wagga Wagga
Showgrounds
Urana St, Turvey Park
Camp Area 3 km SW of PO. Enter last gate on R
02 6925 2180   HEMA 66 B2   35 07 30 S   147 20 51 E

775 Wilks Park

Hampden Ave, Wagga Wagga
Rest Area E off Olympic Hwy at Travers St, cross bridge to Hampden Ave. N side of town, E side of Murrumbidgee River
HEMA 66 B2   35 05 59 S   147 22 17 E

776 Kohlhagens Beach

Kohlhagens Rd, Yarragundry
Camp Area 20 km W of Wagga Wagga. Via Sturt Hwy
1300 292 442   HEMA 66 B2   35 04 58 S   147 11 34 E

777 Camp Kurrajong

759 Oura Rd, Eunanoreenya
Camp Area 12 km E of Wagga Wagga. Pre-book
02 6921 7037   HEMA 66 B3   35 05 23 S   147 27 29 E

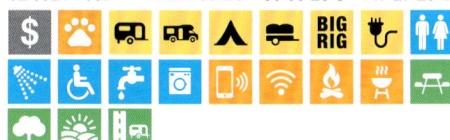

778 Oura Beach Reserve

Oura Beach Rd, Oura
Camp Area 19 km E of Wagga Wagga. At Gumly Gumly turn N off Sturt Hwy onto Eunony Bridge Rd, then E onto Wantabadgery-Oura Rd. At Oura turn S to Wagga Wagga St. Signposted. Beside Murrumbidgee River. 1 km dirt road
1300 100 122   HEMA 66 B3   35 07 25 S   147 32 32 E

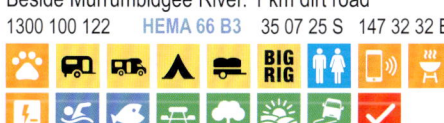

779 The Rock Recreation Ground

60 Wilson St, The Rock
Parking Area around oval via Urana & Cornwall Sts
02 6920 5674   HEMA 66 C1   35 15 55 S   147 06 37 E

780 Yerong Creek Campground

37 Yerong Creek-Mangoplah Rd, Yerong Creek
Camp Area 700 m E of town. Pay at bowling club
02 6920 3535   HEMA 66 D1   35 23 16 S   147 04 01 E

781 Henty Showground

Grubben Rd, Henty
Camp Area N end of town. Keys for amenities at Dale's Hwy Store. Entry Cnr Angaston St
02 6929 3066   HEMA 66 D1   35 30 37 S   147 01 56 E

782 Pleasant Hills Rec Ground

Crawford St, Pleasant Hills
Camp Area on NE side of town. Pay at Community Hotel in Manson St
02 6929 6429   HEMA 69 F12   35 27 43 S   146 48 04 E

783 Round Hill Hotel

38 Brownrigg St, Morven
Parking Area S of town. Register at bar on arrival
0415 862 082   HEMA 69 G13   35 39 44 S   147 07 04 E

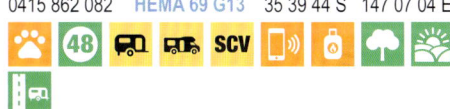

784 Walla Walla Sportsground

William St, Walla Walla
Camp Area 45km N of Albury or 95 km SW of Wagga Wagga. Off Commercial Rd. 7 day limit
0429 039 322   HEMA 69 H13   35 46 04 S   146 54 09 E

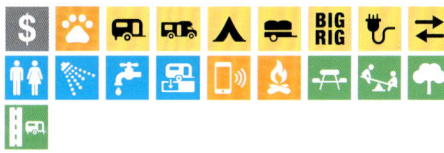

785 Billabong Creek

Urana Rd, Walbundrie
Camp Spot S side of town. Turn E over bridge
02 6036 0100   HEMA 69 G12   35 41 50 S   146 43 34 E

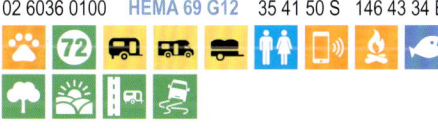

786 Walbundrie Showgrounds

Cnr Billabong & Urana St, Walbundrie
Camp Area 300 m N of PO. Entry off Billabong St. Pay at local shop
0427 299 035   HEMA 69 G12   35 41 20 S   146 43 12 E

787 Rand Camp Site

Four Corners Rd, Rand
Picnic Area beside Billabong Ck, next to the bridge
HEMA 69 G11   35 35 36 S   146 34 35 E

788 Gerogery Hotel

Olympic Hwy, Gerogery
Parking Area behind hotel. Showers available in pub hours. Register at bar on arrival
02 6026 0516   HEMA 69 H13   35 50 06 S   146 59 40 E

Tarcutta to Euston
Sturt Highway

789 Borambola Rest Area

Sturt Hwy, Alfredtown
Rest Area 7 km E of Alfredtown or 23 km W of Hume Hwy turnoff. Shared with trucks
HEMA 66 C3   35 09 42 S   147 34 54 E

790 Shanty Reserve

River Rd, Alfredtown
Dispersed Camping 7 km N of Alfred Town. N off Sturt Hwy at Alfred Town to River Rd. Signposted "Reserve", tracks along the river. 6 km dirt road. High clearance only
HEMA 66 B3   35 06 45 S   147 31 15 E

791 Coolamon Caravan Park

70 Bruce St, Coolamon
Caravan Park 41 km NW of Wagga Wagga. 600 m NE of PO
0417 610 946   HEMA 66 A2   34 48 48 S   147 12 09 E

792 Ganmain Showground

20 Showground Rd, Ganmain
Camp Area at Ganmain. 57 km NW of Wagga Wagga, or 46 km E of Narrandera. Call on arrival
02 6927 6436   HEMA 66 A1   34 47 20 S   147 02 48 E

793 Collingullie Hotel

Sturt Hwy, Collingullie
Pub Stay 24 km W of Wagga Wagga. Check in with publican. Closed Mondays
02 6920 0166   HEMA 66 B1   35 05 16 S   147 07 30 E

794 Mundowy Lane Rest Area

Mundowy Ln, Collingullie
Rest Area 5 km N of Collingullie or 32 km S of Coolamon. From Collingullie take Mundowy Lane (signposted Coolamon) to first river crossing
HEMA 66 B1   35 03 38 S   147 07 18 E

NEW SOUTH WALES

795 Berry Jerry Rest Area
Sturt Hwy, Collingullie
Rest Area 33 km W of Wagga Wagga or
62 km SE of Newell/Sturt Hwy Jcn
HEMA 66 B1   35 03 37 S   147 03 12 E

796 Pipers Reserve
Pipers Ln, Galore
Camp Area 57 km W of Wagga Wagga or
46 km SE of Newell/Sturt Hwy Jcn. 10 km N of Galore,
turn N to Weir Rd, then R at Riverside Reserve sign.
Beside Murrumbidgee River. Dirt road
HEMA 63 J14   34 55 15 S   146 51 39 E

797 Lockhart Caravan Park
162 Green St, Lockhart
Caravan Park 300 m W of PO
0458 205 303   HEMA 63 K14   35 13 13 S   146 42 46 E

798 Lockhart Showgrounds
Showground Rd, Lockhart
Parking Area via Treasure St. Groups only,
pre-book
0428 693 834   HEMA 63 K14   35 13 49 S   146 42 18 E

799 Boree Creek Hotel
Drummond St, Boree Creek
Pub Stay S side of town. Check in with
publican. Fees for shower
02 6927 1407   HEMA 63 K14   35 06 40 S   146 36 22 E

800 Sandigo Rest Area
Sturt Hwy, Sandigo
Rest Area 74 km W of Wagga Wagga or
21 km SE of Newell/Sturt Hwy Jcn
HEMA 63 J14   34 55 17 S   146 38 54 E

801 Buckingbong Reserve
Buckingbong Rd, Narrandera
Camp Area 12 km SE of Narrandera. E off
Sturt Hwy, follow 7 km to entry on L
02 6959 5545   HEMA 63 J14   34 48 15 S   146 36 58 E

802 Five Mile Reserve
Old Wagga Rd, Narrandera
Camp Area 7 km E of Narrandera. Via Bolton
St & Victoria Ave. N bank of Bundidgerry Creek
02 6959 5545   HEMA 63 J14   34 45 47 S   146 38 17 E

803 Narrandera Showground
Elizabeth St, Narrandera
Camp Area 3 km E of PO. See caretaker
0427 169 047   HEMA 63 J14   34 44 57 S   146 33 52 E

804 Narrandera Town Beach
Via Augusta St, Narrandera
Camp Area SW of town. Enter via Larmer &
Townsend Sts, under old railway line, turn S to track
to river
02 6959 5545   HEMA 63 J14   34 45 24 S   146 32 06 E

805 Brewery Flat Reserve
Old Brewery Rd, Narrandera
Parking Area 1 km S of Narrandera via
Newell Hwy. Opposite Narrandera Wetlands
02 6959 5545   HEMA 63 J14   34 45 15 S   146 33 00 E

806 Sandy Beach Camp
Murrumbidgee Valley NP
Via Grahams Grave Rd,, Cudgel
Camp Area 16 km NW of Narrandera, turn S from
Irrigation Way at MIA-Rifle Club sign, follow dirt road
& No 2 State Forest green post signs to N riverbank.
Pre-book
02 6966 8100   HEMA 63 J13   34 43 27 S   146 27 57 E

807 Markeys Beach Camp
Murrumbidgee Valley NP
Via Irrigation Way, Narrandera
Camp Area 18 km NW of Narrandera. Turn S off
Irrigation Way 12 km NW of Narrandera or 7 km SE
of Yanco for 6 km to N riverbank. Pre-book
1300 072 757   HEMA 63 J13   34 42 59 S   146 26 45 E

808 Leeton Showground
Racecourse Rd, Leeton
Camp Area 1 km S of PO. Caretaker
collects fees
02 6953 2213   HEMA 63 H13   34 33 32 S   146 24 10 E

809 Whitton Beach Camp
Murrumbidgee Valley NP
Forest Dr, Darlington Point
Camp Area 22 km W of Yanco, via River Rd. N
riverbank. Follow No 2 green sign post. Not suitable
for caravans. Pre-book
02 6966 8107   HEMA 63 H13   34 36 59 S   146 11 01 E

810 Middle Beach Yanco
Murrumbidgee Valley NP
Euroley Rd, Yanco
Camp Area 6 km SW of Yanco. Turn W 1 km S of
Yanco to Euroley Rd for 4.5 km, then W for 1.5 km
at MIA sign. N riverbank. GPS at entry. Pre-book
1300 072 757   HEMA 63 H13   34 38 08 S   146 22 31 E
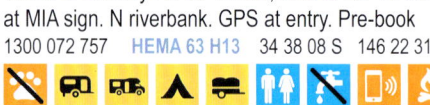

811 Gogeldrie Weir Park
1 Gogeldrie Rd, Gogeldrie
Camp Area 22 km W of Leeton. Via
Irrigation Way. Turn S to Murrami Rd 12 km W of
Leeton, W to Whitton Rd, S to Gogeldrie Rd then E
to River Rd. Signposted. Limited powered sites
02 6955 9267   HEMA 63 H13   34 36 56 S   146 15 29 E

812 East Boomerang Beach
Murrumbidgee Valley Regional Park
Beach Rd, Darlington Point
Camp Area 4 km E of Darlington Point. Turn S off
Whitton Rd 1.2 km E of PO for 3 km to N riverbank.
Follow No 1 green sign post. Not suitable for
caravans. Pre-book
1300 072 757   HEMA 63 H12   34 34 59 S   146 01 13 E

813 Horries Beach Camp
Murrumbidgee Valley Regional Park
Via Murrumbidgee River Rd, Darlington Point
Camp Area 4 km W of Darlington Point. Turn W off
Kidman Way just N of bridge, opposite caravan park
into Willbriggle State Forest, pass sawmill, follow No
1 green sign post for 4 km, then S at sign "Beach"
for 200 m to N riverbank. Not suitable for caravans.
Pre-book
1300 072 757   HEMA 63 H12   34 33 46 S   145 58 38 E

814 Alfies Beach Camp
Murrumbidgee Valley Regional Park
Via Murrumbidgee River Rd, Willbriggie
Camp Spot 7 km W of Darlington Point. Turn W off
Kidman Way just N of bridge, opposite caravan park
to Willbriggle State Forest, past sawmill, follow No1
green sign post 7 km, then S to N riverbank. Not
suitable for caravans. Pre-book
1300 072 757   HEMA 63 H12   34 33 33 S   145 57 30 E

815 Noble Beach Campground
Murrumbidgee Valley Regional Park
Via Murrumbidgee River Rd, Willbriggie
Camp Area 15 km W of Darlington Point. Turn W
3 km N of Darlington Point. N riverbank. Pre-book
1300 072 757   HEMA 63 H12   34 33 20 S 145 54 12 E

816 Common Beach
King St, Darlington Point
Rest Area W end of King St, cross grid,
immediate N to S bank of Murrumbidgee R. GPS
at entry
HEMA 63 H12   34 33 57 S 145 59 32 E

817 Bunyip Hole Reserve
Murrumbidgee Valley Regional Park
Forest Dr, Darlington Point
Camp Area at N side of town. From W end of King
St, cross grid, then 2nd track to R, then L at T Jcn,
then R to S riverbank. GPS at entry. Booking fee
1300 072 757   HEMA 63 H12   34 33 57 S 145 59 32 E

818 Birdcage Reserve Rest Area
Sturt Hwy, Darlington Point Area
Rest Area 86 km W of Newell & Sturt Hwy
Jcn or 86 km E of Hay. Both sides of the road
HEMA 63 H12   34 31 27 S 145 42 08 E

819 Tonganmain Reserve
Sturt Hwy, Darlington Point Area
Camp Area 90 km W of Newell Hwy/Sturt
Hwy Jcn or 82 km E of South Hay. Turn N at sign,
3 km of dirt road to S bank of Murrumbidgee R
1800 601 141   HEMA 63 H11   34 29 18 S 145 38 19 E

820 Carrathool Bridge Reserve
Carrathool Rd, Carrathool
Rest Area 5 km S of Carrathool or 2 km N
of Sturt Hwy Jcn. N side of bridge on river bank
02 6965 1900   HEMA 63 H11   34 26 54 S 145 25 05 E

821 Pinkers Beach
Via Murrumbidgee River Rd, Carrathool
Camp Area 5 km N of Sturt Hwy
intersection via Carrathool Rd. S off Murrumbidgee
Rd, N side of river
02 6965 1900   HEMA 63 H11   34 26 17 S 145 25 43 E

822 Rudds Point Reserve
Sturt Hwy, Carrathool
Camp Area 110 km W of Newell/Sturt
Hwy Jcn or 62 km E of South Hay. Turn N at sign,
700 m of dirt road to S bank of Murrumbidgee R
HEMA 63 H11   34 28 02 S 145 26 29 E

823 Pevensey Rest Area
Sturt Hwy, Hay South
Rest Area 27 km W of Hay or 104 km E of
Balranald. Shared with trucks
HEMA 63 H9   34 36 14 S 144 34 02 E

824 Yang Yang (Maude)
Nap Nap Rd, Maude
Rest Area W off Moulamein Rd, to Nap Nap
Rd for 300 m. S side of Murrumbidgee River
HEMA 63 H8   34 28 40 S 144 17 49 E

825 Maude Hotel
Yang Yang St, Maude
Caravan Park at Post Office Hotel, 400 m S
of PO
02 6993 6112   HEMA 63 H8   34 28 25 S 144 18 07 E

826 Tattersalls Hotel
52 Morago St, Moulamein
Camp Area behind hotel. Cnr Brougham St.
Check in with Publican, free for patrons
03 5887 5017   HEMA 63 K8   35 05 29 S 144 02 03 E

827 Willowvale Rest Area
Sturt Hwy, Keri Keri
Rest Area 91 km W of Hay or 40 km E of
Balranald. Share with trucks
HEMA 63 J8   34 43 23 S 143 55 41 E

828 The Willows Campground
Yanga National Park
Willows Visitor Access Trail, Yanga
Camp Area 3 km S of Hwy. Turn S off Sturt Hwy
100 km W of Hay or 24 km E of Balranald to Impimi
Rd. Travel 1 km to park entrance, follow track
1.5 km to camping area
03 5020 1764   HEMA 62 J7   34 45 39 S 143 45 37 E

829 Yanga Creek Rest Area
Sturt Hwy, Yanga
Rest Area 121 km W of Hay or 10 km E of
Balranald
HEMA 62 H7   34 42 05 S 143 35 31 E

830 Greenham Park RV Stop
Church St, Balranald
Parking Area next to blue towers and
swimming pool
03 5020 1599   HEMA 62 H7   34 38 07 S 143 33 43 E

831 Balranald RV Stop
83 Market St, Balranald
Parking Area behind the Discovery Centre.
Entry from River St. Gold coin donation for showers
03 5020 1599   HEMA 62 H7   34 38 21 S 143 33 52 E

832 Lake Paika Station
1725 Ivanhoe Rd, Balranald
Station Stay 18 km N of Balranald. Pre-book
0427 206 801   HEMA 62 H7   34 29 28 S 143 35 16 E

833 Homebush Hotel Camp
Ivanhoe Rd, Penarie
Camp Area at Penarie 27 km N of Balranald
or 201 km S of Ivanhoe. Pre-book
03 5020 6803   HEMA 62 H7   34 24 27 S 143 36 47 E

834 Woolpress Bend
Yanga National Park
Waugorah Rd, Waugorah
Dispersed Camping 61 km N of Balranald. Take
Sturt Hwy 10.5 km, N on Waugorah Rd for 44 km,
L to Coates Rd at intersection with old fridge
mailboxes, continue 5 km, cross Waugorah Ck
& keep R to Waugorah trail, L at info shelter to
Woolpress Bend trail, 4 km to camp. Pre-book
03 5020 1764   HEMA 62 H7   34 22 19 S 143 53 46 E

835 Mamanga Campground
Yanga National Park
Mamagna Campground Trail, Balranald
Camp Area 9 km SW Balranald. Via Sturt Hwy &
Windomal Rd. Signposted. Pre-book
03 5020 1764   HEMA 62 H7   34 40 40 S 143 31 13 E

NEW SOUTH WALES

836 Wakool River

River Rd, Kyalite
Rest Area 17 km NE of Tooleybuc or 36 km SW of Balranald, turn SE on the S side of Wakool River Bridge, dirt road to tracks by river
HEMA 62 J6   34 56 47 S   143 28 41 E

837 Kyalite Pub & Caravan Park

Kyalite Rd, Kyalite
Caravan Park E side of Kyalite Rd and Wakool R
03 5038 2221   HEMA 62 J7   34 56 58 S   143 28 59 E

838 Tooleybuc Sports Club

Lockhart Rd, Tooleybuc
Parking Area N side of town. Check in at reception. Patronage please
03 5030 5476   HEMA 62 J6   35 01 28 S   143 20 13 E

839 Tooleybuc Bridge

Tooleybuc Rd, Piangil
Camp area E off Murray Valley Hwy to Mallee Hwy, N to Tooleybuc Rd, L before the bridge
HEMA 62 J6   35 01 44 S   143 19 58 E

840 Meilman East Rest Area

Sturt Hwy, Euston
Rest Area 59 km W of Balranald or 20 km E of Euston. Share with trucks
HEMA 62 H5   34 31 45 S   142 56 17 E

841 Lake Benanee

Sturt Hwy, Euston Area
Rest Area 65 km W of Balranald or 15 km E of Euston. Lakefront. Cold shower
HEMA 62 H5   34 31 15 S   142 52 39 E

Goondiwindi to Tocumwal
Newell Highway

842 North Star Road Rest Area

Newell Hwy, Boggabilla
Rest Area 40 km S of Goondiwindi or 84 km N of Moree
HEMA 56 D2   28 50 26 S   150 13 34 E

843 North Star Caravan Park

1 Wilby St, North Star
Caravan Park 750 m SE of PO
HEMA 56 D3   28 55 55 S   150 23 39 E

844 North Star Sporting Club

North Star Rd, North Star
Parking Area E side of town
07 4676 3183   HEMA 56 D3   28 56 00 S   150 23 51 E

845 Boomi Co-Op & Caravan Park

39 Bishop St, Boomi
Caravan Park opposite police station, adjacent to artesian pools
02 6753 5150   HEMA 58 B6   28 43 30 S   149 34 43 E

846 Croppa Creek Rec Ground

Buckie Rd, Croppa Creek
Camp Area 67 km NE of Moree. Behind the hall, at the oval. Donation to Croppa Ck Store (in PO Box after hours)
02 6754 5222   HEMA 56 E3   29 07 25 S   150 18 34 E

847 Boolooroo Rest Area

Newell Hwy, Moree
Rest Area 116 km S of Goondiwindi or 8 km N of Moree. Combined truck stop
HEMA 56 F1   29 25 12 S   149 54 15 E

848 Moree Showground

25 McElhone St, Moree
Camp Area 1 km SE of PO. Entrance off River St, via Alice & Warialda Sts. Report to gate on entry for code
0428 205 098   HEMA 56 F1   29 28 07 S   149 50 53 E

849 Club Hotel Garah

17 Railway Pde, Garah
Parking Area beside hotel. Check in with publican
0432 537 717   HEMA 58 C6   29 04 27 S   149 38 07 E

850 Gurley Recreation Reserve

Millie St, Gurley
Camp Area 550 m E side of PO
0429 651 270   HEMA 56 G1   29 44 05 S   149 47 43 E

851 Royal Hotel Gurley

111 Newell Hwy, Gurley
Pub Stay 80 m N of PO. Check in with publican
0482 431 561   HEMA 56 G1   29 44 06 S   149 47 59 E

852 Tookey Creek Rest Area

Newell Hwy, Bellata
Rest Area 47 km S of Moree or 51 km N of Narrabri
HEMA 56 H1   29 52 28 S   149 47 19 E

853 Bellata Golf Club

80 Berrigal Rd, Bellata
Parking Area 800 m E off the Newell Hwy. Check in at bar
0467 937 559   HEMA 56 H1   29 55 08 S   149 47 57 E

854 Edgeroi Park

Newell Hwy, Edgeroi
Parking Area next to fuel shop
02 6793 8375   HEMA 56 J1   30 06 48 S   149 47 50 E

855 Wee Waa Showgrounds

30 Maitland St, Wee Waa
Camp Area NE side of town. Caretaker will visit to collect fee
0428 506 363   HEMA 58 F5   30 13 08 S   149 26 57 E

856 Narrabri Showground

Wukuwa St, Narrabri
Camp Area S of town. Turn off Newell Hwy to Belar St at Eathers Creek Bridge. 14 day limit
0417 006 865   HEMA 56 K1   30 20 19 S   149 45 48 E

857 Bark Hut
Mt Kaputar National Park
Bark Hut Rd, Kaputar
Camp Area 50 km E of Narrabri. Access steep & narrow in parts. Some sections of dirt road, but all steep sections are sealed. No caravans allowed
02 6792 7300   HEMA 56 K2   30 17 25 S   150 08 35 E

858 Dawsons Spring
Mt Kaputar National Park
Dawsons Spring Nature Trail, Kaputar
Camp Area 56 km E of Narrabri. Some sections of unsealed road, steep sections sealed. Access steep & narrow in parts. No caravans allowed, motorhomes up to size of coaster allowed
02 6792 7300   HEMA 56 K2   30 16 51 S   150 09 47 E

859 Namoi River
Turrawan Rd, Turrawan
Rest Area 15 km SE Narrabri via Old Gunnedah Rd. Tracks W to river. Use 2nd entry after the bridge if towing a van. Camp at the top or bank
HEMA 54 A2   30 24 18 S   149 53 39 E

860 Yarrie Lake
Yarri Lake Rd, Yarrie Lake
Camp Area 27 km W of Narrabri. W off Newell Hwy 3 km S of Narrabri to Yarrie Lake Rd, towards Australia Telescope for 19 km then S for 7 km, turn R on Lake Circuit. 1 km dirt road
0427 666 105   HEMA 54 A1   30 22 07 S   149 31 05 E

861 Bohena Creek Rest Area
Newell Hwy, Bohena Creek
Rest Area 16 km S of Narrabri or 103 km N of Coonabarabran. Share with trucks
HEMA 54 A2   30 26 12 S   149 40 42 E

862 Schwagers Bore
Pilliga State Forest
Rocky Creek Mill Rd, Pilliga
Rest Area 61 km SW of Narrabri or 50 km NE of Baradine. 27 km SW of Narrabri, via Pilliga Forest Way. Dirt road
02 6843 1607   HEMA 58 G5   30 36 13 S   149 18 57 E

863 Salt Caves Campground
Timmallallie National Park
County Line Rd, Pilliga
Camp Area next to picnic area. 68 km SW of Narrabri or 37 km NE of Baradine, turn SW to Pilliga Forest Way 27 km SW of Narrabri, then S. Dirt road. Pre-book
02 6843 4011   HEMA 58 G5   30 44 46 S   149 17 28 E

864 The Aloes
Pilliga Forest Way, Kenebri
Camp Area 88 km SW of Narrabri or 23 km N of Baradine. Dirt road. Beside Etoo Creek
02 6799 6760   HEMA 58 G5   30 44 57 S   149 06 38 E

865 Anzac Park Primitive Camp
Anzac Pde, Gwabegar
Camp Area N of Bridges St
02 6799 6760   HEMA 58 G4   30 36 30 S   148 58 15 E

866 Camp Cypress
Lachlan St, Baradine
Camp Area 1 km W of PO, at showground
02 6843 1035   HEMA 58 H4   30 56 49 S   149 03 25 E

867 Pilliga Rest Area
Newell Hwy, The Pilliga
Rest Area 52 km S of Narrabri or 68 km N of Coonabarabran
HEMA 54 B1   30 43 22 S   149 31 29 E

868 Yamminba Rest Area
Newell Hwy, The Pilliga
Rest Area 68 km S of Narrabri or 52 km N of Coonabarabran
HEMA 54 C1   30 51 14 S   149 27 26 E

869 Sculptures in the Scrub
Timmallallie National Park
Dandry Gorge Rd, Baradine
Picnic Area 33 km E of Baradine. From Baradine, N on Indian Lane for 9.5 km, E to No 1 Break Rd for 13 km, S to Top Crossing Rd for 11 km, E for 1.5 km. Signposted. 27 km dirt road. Pre-book
02 6834 4011   HEMA 58 H5   30 59 46 S   149 14 03 E

870 Barkala Farmstay
Dandry Rd, Coonabarabran Area
Camp Area at Pilliga Pottery, 34 km NW of Coonabarabran or 105 km SW of Narrabri via Newell Hwy. Turn W 23 km N of Coonabarabran to Borambitty Rd, travel about 11 km. Signposted
02 6842 2239   HEMA 58 H5   31 02 42 S   149 19 04 E

871 Gowan Rest Area
Newell Hwy, Coonabarabran
Rest Area 111 km S of Narrabri or 9 km N of Coonabarabran. 2 km N of Gowan Truck parking bay
HEMA 58 J5   31 13 05 S   149 19 34 E

872 Camp Blackman
Warrumbungle National Park
4263 John Renshaw Pkwy, Warrumbungle
Camp Area 34 km W of Coonabarabran. Pre-book
02 6825 4364   HEMA 58 J4   31 16 37 S   148 59 52 E

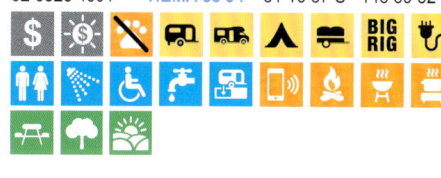

873 Camp Wambelong
Warrumbungle National Park
4001 John Renshaw Pkwy, Warrumbungle
Camp Area 35 km W of Coonabarabran. Large open area beside creek. Pre-book
02 6825 4364   HEMA 58 J4   31 16 48 S   148 58 36 E

874 Gunneemooroo Camp
Warrumbungle NP
Gunneemooroo Trail, Tonderburine
Camp Area in S section. Via John Renshaw Parkway. Access code for gate with booking
02 6825 4364   HEMA 58 J4   31 21 57 S   148 57 29 E

875 Hickeys Falls Parking Area
Coonabarabran Area
Parking Area 39 km SW of Coonabarabran or 56 km NE of Gilgandra
HEMA 58 J4   31 25 49 S   149 04 01 E

876 Tooraweenah Caravan Park
Cnr Aimee & Bridge Sts, Tooraweenah
Caravan Park central to town
02 6848 1133   HEMA 58 J4   31 26 20 S   148 54 39 E

877 Tooraweenah Rest Area
Newell/Oxley Hwy, Tooraweenah
Rest Area S of Tooraweenah, 56 km SW of
Coonabarabran or 39 km NE of Gilgandra
HEMA 58 J4   31 28 08 S   148 55 14 E

878 Biddon Rest Area
Newell Hwy, Biddon
Rest Area 72 km SW of Coonabarabran or
23 km NE of Gilgandra
HEMA 58 J4   31 33 50 S   148 47 41 E

879 Eumungerie Rec Reserve
Wheaton St, Eumungerie
Camp Area 38 km N of Dubbo or 27 km S
of Gilgandra. Turn E off Hwy, 800 m turn L just after
railway crossing. Report to caretaker. Cold showers
0412 707 920   HEMA 58 K4   31 56 58 S   148 37 25 E

880 Hows the Serenity Camping Ground
Collie Rd, Dubbo Area
Farm Stay 26 km NW of Dubbo. 20 km N of Dubbo,
L into Collie Rd for 6 km, on L. Signposted, GPS at
gate. Limited powered sites, pre-book
0478 876 255   HEMA 64 B5   32 02 25 S   148 31 21 E

881 Terramungamine Reserve
Burraway Rd, Terramungamine
Camp Area 3.5 km W of Brocklehurst.
Turn W 57 km S of Gilgandra or 10 km N of Dubbo.
Riverside
02 6801 4000   HEMA 64 B5   32 10 04 S   148 35 16 E

882 Brocklehurst Rest Area
Newell Hwy, Brocklehurst
Day Use Area 56 km S of Gilgandra or 1 km
N of Brocklehurst
132 213   HEMA 64 B5   32 10 17 S   148 37 06 E

883 Blizzardfield
Richardson Rd, Dubbo
Camp Area 4km NW of Dubbo city centre.
Off Mitchell Hwy. Pre-book. No children under 10 yrs
0407 638 990   HEMA 64 C5   32 13 32 S   148 34 21 E

884 Hair of the Dog Inn
26 Federation St, Ballimore
Parking Area behind hotel. Fee for power
02 6886 5131   HEMA 64 C5   32 11 45 S   148 53 53 E

885 Toongi Hall
220 Obley Rd, Toongi
Camp Area 26 km S of Dubbo. Turn S off
Newell Hwy 4 km SW of Dubbo PO
HEMA 64 C5   32 26 58 S   148 34 59 E

886 Red Earth Estate Vineyard
18 Camp Rd, Dubbo
Farm Stay 10 km S of Dubbo. Turn E onto
Obley Rd (Western Plains Zoo signs) for 4.5 km,
then W to Camp Rd. 1.5 km to entrance. Limited
sites. Pre-book
02 6885 6676   HEMA 64 C5   32 17 38 S   148 34 56 E

887 Wanda Wandong Camp
Goobang National Park
Tanyas Trail, Obley
Camp Area 30 km SE of Tomingley via the
Tomingley-Obley Rd, Gundong Rd. Pre-book
02 6332 7640   HEMA 52 A1   32 38 17 S   148 22 50 E

888 Tomingley North Rest Area
Newell Hwy, Tomingley
Rest Area 45 km SW of Dubbo or 25 km N
of Peak Hill. Signposted only from the S
HEMA 64 C4   32 31 19 S   148 16 43 E

889 Crossroads Hotel Tomingley
1 Newell Hwy, Tomingley
Parking Area behind pub. Check in with
publican. Fee for power
02 6869 3219   HEMA 64 C4   32 34 07 S   148 13 18 E

890 Tomingley South Rest Area
Newell Hwy, Tomingley
Rest Area 2 km S of Tomingley or 16 km N
of Peak Hill
HEMA 64 D4   32 35 42 S   148 13 10 E

891 Lyndavale Rest Area
Newell Hwy, Peak Hill
Rest Area 15 km S of Tomingley or 2 km N
of Peak Hill
HEMA 64 D4   32 41 51 S   148 11 26 E

892 Clubhouse Hotel
91 Caswell St, Peak Hill
Parking Area behind hotel. Check in with
publican (especially big rigs)
02 6869 1474   HEMA 64 D4   32 43 30 S   148 11 30 E

893 Peak Hill Showgrounds
Coradagery Rd, Peak Hill
Camp Area W of town, via Mingelo St. Stop
at caretakers cottage before entry
0429 661 382   HEMA 64 D4   32 43 42 S   148 10 33 E

894 Bogan Weir
Tullamore Rd, Peak Hill
Camp Area 7 km W of Peak Hill. Via Peak
Hill-Tullamore Rd
02 6869 1981   HEMA 64 D4   32 43 27 S   148 07 35 E

895 Greenbah Campground
Goobang National Park
Sawpit Gully Trail, Baldry
Camp Area 24 km E of Trewilga. Via Peak-Hill
Baldry Rd for 15 km, turn N to trail for 5.5 km. Dirt
road. Signposted. Pre-book
02 6332 7640   HEMA 52 A1   32 46 18 S   148 21 11 E

896 Parkes Showground
Victoria St, Parkes
Camp Area NW side of town. Access after
7pm via Mitchell St. 28 day limit per year
02 6862 2580   HEMA 64 E4   33 07 52 S   148 09 47 E

897 Railway Hotel Bogan Gate
Station St, Bogan Gate
Parking Area behind hotel
02 6864 1106   HEMA 64 E3   33 06 27 S   147 48 12 E

898 Trundle Showgrounds
Austral St, Trundle
Camp Area at SW side of town. Key and fees at hardware store
02 6892 1260   HEMA 64 D3   32 55 33 S   147 42 06 E

899 Fifield Hotel
7 Slee St, Fifield
Parking Area behind hotel. Check in with publican. Limited space. Fee for showers
02 6892 7276   HEMA 64 D2   32 48 25 S   147 27 28 E

900 Tullamore Showground
Cornet St, Tullamore
Camp Area at end of road. Keys & registration at Tullamore Hotel. 7 day limit
02 6892 5194   HEMA 61 K14   32 37 39 S   147 34 11 E

901 Tullamore Hotel
Cardigan & Haylock Sts, Tullamore
Pub Stay behind hotel. Amenities when open. Check in with publican
02 6892 5194   HEMA 64 D3   32 37 52 S   147 33 52 E

902 Wheogo Park
Junction St, Forbes
Rest Area S side of town and Lake Forbes
02 6852 4155   HEMA 64 F4   33 23 17 S   148 00 07 E

903 Forbes Showground
Show St, Forbes
Camp Area SW side of town. Caretaker collects fees. 7 day limit
02 6852 1311   HEMA 64 F4   33 23 18 S   147 59 56 E

904 Jemalong Weir
Lachlan Valley Way, Forbes Area
Camp Area 24 km W of Forbes or 76 km E of Condoblin. Entry through gates
HEMA 64 F3   33 23 59 S   147 46 32 E

905 Straneys Bridge
Hodges Rd, Jemalong
Camp Area at Jemalong. 37 km W of Forbes or 63 km E of Condobolin. Via Lachlan Valley Way, beside river
HEMA 64 F3   33 22 19 S   147 39 13 E

906 Bedgerabong Showground
Copeland Pde, Bedgerabong
Camp Area 42 km W of Forbes or 63 km E of Condoblin
02 6857 1131   HEMA 64 E3   33 21 50 S   147 41 37 E

907 Bundaburrah Rest Area
Newell Hwy, Bundaburrah
Rest Area 31 km SW of Forbes or 71 km NE of Wyalong
HEMA 64 F3   33 31 20 S   147 44 00 E

908 Marsden Rest Area
Newell Hwy, Back Creek
Rest Area 67 km SW of Forbes or 35 km NE of Wyalong. Dirt track off Hwy, near Bland Creek
HEMA 64 G3   33 45 46 S   147 31 14 E

909 Cooinda Reserve
Neeld St, Wyalong
Rest Area 500 m W of Wyalong PO or 3 km E of West Wyalong. Via Copeland St. Off Newell Hwy. Limited turning circle
HEMA 64 G2   33 55 28 S   147 14 01 E

910 West Wyalong Showground
190 Showground Rd, West Wyalong
Camp Area S of town. Caretaker collects fee
0428 518 329   HEMA 64 G2   33 56 18 S   147 12 50 E

911 Barmedman Mineral Pool
Cnr Nobbys Rd & Goldfield Way, Barmedman
Camp Area on grassed area, each side of the pool. Pool is seasonal
HEMA 64 G2   34 08 19 S   147 23 10 E

912 Barmedman Rec Ground
Star St, Barmedman
Camp Area NE side of town. Call at general store. Text for enquiries
0414 595 960   HEMA 64 G2   34 08 34 S   147 23 16 E

913 Temora Caravan Park
19 Junee Rd, Temora
Caravan Park S side of town
0418 780 251   HEMA 64 H3   34 27 22 S   147 32 06 E

914 Temora Showground
Mimosa St, Temora
Camp Area NW side of town. Honesty box at toilets
HEMA 64 H3   34 26 23 S   147 31 17 E

915 Temora Free Camp
Temora Railway Station Precinct
73 Parkes St, Temora
Parking Area next to railway station
02 6977 5921   HEMA 64 H3   34 26 43 S   147 31 42 E

916 CMCA Temora
174-182 Gardiner St, Temora
Camp Area next to sports fields. Cnr Austral St. Caretaker on site. 5 night limit
HEMA 64 H3   34 27 04 S   147 32 27 E

917 Ariah Park Camping Ground
Barnes St, Ariah Park
Camp Area 1 km N of Hwy. 33 km E of Ardlethan or 39 km W of Temora. Key from hotel during opening hours. 7 day limit
0458 184 033   HEMA 69 A14   34 21 08 S   147 13 09 E

918 Mirrool Sunshine Park
Ariah St, Mirrool
Camp Area opposite hotel. 300 m W of Hwy. Donation box at toilets. 7 day limit
02 6974 1237   HEMA 69 A13   34 18 27 S   147 05 18 E

NEW SOUTH WALES

919 Beckom RV Stop
Ariah St, Beckom
Parking Area opposite hotel, next to old bowling club
02 6930 1831   HEMA 69 A13   34 19 30 S   146 57 41 E

920 Ardlethan Recreation Park
Ariah St, Ardlethan
Rest Area on main street, next to bowling club. Coin operated power points
02 6930 1800   HEMA 69 A13   34 21 28 S   146 54 09 E

921 Ardlethan South Rest Area
Newell Hwy, Ardlethan
Rest Area 14 km S of Ardlethan or 55 km NE of Narrandera. Shared with trucks
HEMA 69 B12   34 26 50 S   146 50 20 E

922 Firetail Rest Area
Moorlands Rd, Grong Grong
Rest Area 42 km S of Ardlethan or 5 km N of Grong Grong. Share with trucks
HEMA 69 C12   34 41 36 S   146 47 12 E

923 Grong Grong Park
Junee St, Grong Grong
Rest Area with parking on roadside. Ask at store
02 6959 5545   HEMA 69 C12   34 44 19 S   146 46 59 E

924 Grong Grong Royal Hotel
Narrandera St, Grong Grong
Parking Area at rear of hotel. Check in with publican
02 6956 2117   HEMA 69 C12   34 44 24 S   146 46 58 E

925 Berembed Weir
Old Narrandera Rd, Grong Grong
Camp Area 19 km S of Grong Grong, via Old Narrandera Rd & signposted track, GPS at entry gate. Follow road across weir to campspots. Toilets at picnic area. Beside river. 12 km dirt road
02 6930 1800   HEMA 69 C12   34 50 19 S   146 50 37 E

926 Gillenbah Rest Area
Newell Hwy, Gillenbah
Rest Area 10 km SW of Narrandera or 100 km NE of Jerilderie. Share with trucks
HEMA 69 C11   34 48 54 S   146 28 42 E

927 Colombo Creek
Yamma Rd, Morundah
Camp Area 1 km S of Morundah. Limited space. Beside creek
HEMA 69 D11   34 56 11 S   146 17 40 E

928 Sandside Rest Area
Newell Hwy, Morundah
Rest Area 53 km SW of Narrandera or 57 km NE of Jerilderie. Share with trucks
132 213   HEMA 69 D10   35 03 39 S   146 09 47 E

929 Bundure Rest Area
Newell Hwy, Bundure
Rest Area 71 km SW of Narrandera or 39 km NE of Jerilderie. Share with trucks
HEMA 69 E10   35 09 01 S   146 00 36 E

930 Urana Caravan Park & Aquatic Centre
Federation Way, Urana
Caravan Park 1 km S of PO. Corowa Rd. Beside lake
02 6920 8192   HEMA 69 F10   35 20 18 S   146 16 23 E

931 Conargo Rec Grounds
Conargo Rd, Conargo
Parking Area next to tennis courts
HEMA 68 F7   35 18 18 S   145 10 53 E

932 Bills Park
Conargo Rd, Conargo
Rest Area W end of town, near school
1800 650 712   HEMA 68 F7   35 18 24 S   145 10 38 E

933 Jerilderie South Rest Area
Newell Hwy, Jerilderie
Rest Area at McPhersons Lane. 8 km S of Jerilderie or 28 km N of Finley
HEMA 69 F8   35 25 01 S   145 41 28 E

934 Oaklands RV Stop
Cnr Milthorpe & Hunter Sts, Oaklands
Camp Area 78 km NE of Tocumwal or 142 km SW of Wagga Wagga
02 6033 8999   HEMA 69 G10   35 33 28 S   146 09 52 E

935 Daysdale Recreation Reserve
Federation Way, Daysdale
Camp Area 1 km N of Daysdale Hotel
HEMA 69 G11   35 30 07 S   146 10 17 E

936 Tongaboo Rest Area
Newell Hwy, Finley
Rest Area 27 km S of Jerilderie or 9 km N of Finley. N & S bound 500 m apart
HEMA 69 G8   35 34 24 S   145 36 56 E

937 Finley Lake Caravan Park
Newell Hwy, Finley
Caravan Park 1 km N of PO
03 5883 1170   HEMA 69 G8   35 38 03 S   145 34 49 E

938 Finley RV Stop
Endeavour St, Finley
Parking Area by old railway station
HEMA 69 G8   35 38 41 S   145 34 37 E

939 Finley Showground
Tonga St, Finley
Camp Area SW side of town. Caretaker collects fee
0473 644 230   HEMA 69 G8   35 39 00 S   145 34 08 E

940 Berrigan Caravan Park
Jerilderie St, Berrigan
Caravan Park 1 km S of PO
0400 563 979   HEMA 69 G9   35 39 37 S   145 48 49 E

941 Tocumwal Town Beach

Town Beach Rd, Tocumwal
Camp Area 1 km SW of PO. S at Palm Beach Hotel. Cold showers. Caretaker on site. 6 week limit. Riverside
0408 575 479 HEMA 69 H8 35 49 06 S 145 33 36 E

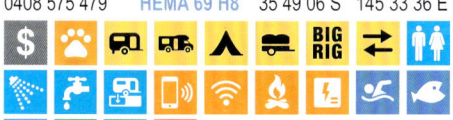

942 Sonnermans Travelling Stock Reserve

Tuppal Rd, Tocumwal
Camp Area 3 km W of Tocumwal
1300 795 299 HEMA 69 H8 35 48 16 S 145 32 10 E

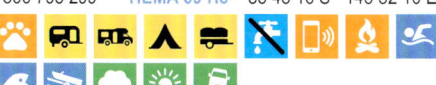

Hebel to Gilgandra
Castlereagh Highway

943 Angledool Weir

Castlereagh Hwy, Angledool
Camp Area 20 km S of Hebel. E side of Hwy and both sides of weir
HEMA 58 C2 29 06 48 S 147 54 17 E

944 Goodooga Artesian Baths

Hammond St, Goodooga
Camp Area N side of town. 74 km NW of Lightning Ridge or 40 km SW of Hebel
02 6830 5100 HEMA 58 C1 29 06 37 S 147 27 21 E

945 Carinya Station

1432 Ridge Rd, Lightning Ridge
Camp Area 32 km W of Lightning Ridge. 5 km dirt road. BYO toilet. Pre-book
0427 944 775 HEMA 58 D2 29 25 17 S 148 05 36 E

946 Lorne Station

Lorne Rd, Lightning Ridge
Farm Stay 5 km S of Lightning Ridge. Turn off 3 km S on Opal St-Lorne Rd. Pre-book
02 6829 1869 HEMA 58 D2 29 27 46 S 147 58 34 E

947 Cumborah Park Reserve

Cumborah St, Cumborah
Camp Area S end of the main road. Donation box
02 6828 6139 HEMA 58 E2 29 44 45 S 147 46 17 E

948 The Sheepyard Inn

Via Kurrajong Rd, Cumborah
Camp Area at Grawin opposite the inn. 73 km W of Lightning Ridge. Via Walgett-Cumborah. Patronage please
02 6829 3932 HEMA 58 E2 29 41 20 S 147 37 41 E

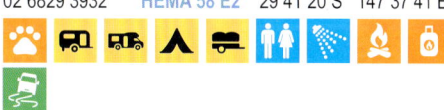

949 The Club in the Scrub

Via Wilby Wilby Rd, Grawin
Rest Area at Grawin. Lots of open area near the club, not monitored by club
02 6829 3810 HEMA 58 E2 29 35 56 S 147 40 45 E

950 Glengarry Hilton

Via Kurrajong Rd, Cumborah
Pub Stay 75 km W of Lightning Ridge. Via Walgett-Cumborah. Patronage please
02 6829 3983 HEMA 58 E2 29 40 11 S 147 36 56 E

951 Carinda Camp

Carinda Rd, Carinda
Camp Area N side of town
02 6828 6139 HEMA 58 G2 30 27 37 S 147 41 21 E

952 Carinda Hotel

Cnr Shakespear & Colin Sts, Coonamble Area
Parking area behind hotel
02 6823 2218 HEMA 58 G2 30 27 48 S 147 41 27 E

953 Wingadee Rest Area

Castlereagh Hwy, Wingadee
Rest Area 53 km S of Walgett or 62 km N of Coonamble. 4 km S of Combogolong
HEMA 58 G3 30 28 05 S 148 11 40 E

954 Nakadoo

16 Blueys Ln, Coonamble
Camp Area 4 km N of Coonamble. Via Castlereagh Hwy
0428 221 861 HEMA 58 H3 30 55 41 S 148 22 28 E

955 Coonamble Showground

Castlereagh Hwy, Coonamble
Camp Area S of town. Donation at visitors centre
02 6827 1981 HEMA 58 H3 30 57 58 S 148 23 17 E

956 Warrena Weir

Via Baradine Rd, Coonamble
Camp Area NE side of town. Call Visitor Centre first.
02 6827 1981 HEMA 58 H3 30 57 13 S 148 23 55 E

957 Quambone Primitive Camp

Mungie St, Quambone
Camp Area near swimming pool & tennis courts. Keys for pool & courts at general store. 8am-7pm
02 6827 1981 HEMA 58 H2 30 55 58 S 147 52 16 E

958 John Oxley Rest Area

Castlereagh Hwy, Gulargambone
Rest Area 32 km S of Coonamble or 13 km N of Gulargambone
HEMA 58 J3 31 13 36 S 148 27 25 E

959 Gulargambone Rest Area

Castlereagh Hwy, Gulargambone
Rest Area N of town. 42 km S of Coonamble or 3 km N of Gulargambone
HEMA 58 J3 31 18 20 S 148 28 08 E

960 Gulargambone Caravan Park

Skuthorpe St, Gulargambone
Caravan Park N side of town. Pre-book
02 6825 1666 HEMA 58 J3 31 19 51 S 148 28 12 E

961 Armatree Hotel

Merrigal St, Armatree
Camps Area beside hotel. Check in with publican on arrival
02 6848 5805 HEMA 58 J3 31 26 48 S 148 28 46 E

Bathurst to Broken Hill
Mitchell and Barrier Highways

962 The Rocks Rest Area
Mitchell Hwy, Vittoria
Rest Area 20 km W of Bathurst or 34 SE of Orange

HEMA 52 D4   33 25 56 S   149 22 48 E

963 Macquarie Woods
Vittoria State Forest
Macquarie Woods Dr, Vittoria
Camp Area 28 km W of Bathurst or 26 km SE of Orange. 2 km N of Hwy via Cashens Lane. Dirt road. Pre-book
1300 655 687   HEMA 52 D4   33 24 34 S   149 18 44 E

964 Shadforth Reserve
Millthorpe Rd, Shadforth
Rest Area 40 km NW of Bathurst or 4 km SE of Lucknow. Cnr Mitchell Hwy
HEMA 52 D4   33 22 31 S   149 11 18 E

965 Orange Showgrounds
Leeds Parade, Orange
Camp Area 2 km N of PO. Entry via Margaret St. Pre-book with Visitor Centre
1800 069 466   HEMA 52 D3   33 16 12 S   149 06 34 E

966 Cudal Caravan Park
55 Main St, Cudal
Caravan Park 400 m E of PO. Pre-book
02 6390 7100   HEMA 52 D2   33 17 03 S   148 44 39 E

967 Manildra Showground
Orange St, Manildra
Camp Area 1.2 km NW of PO. Fees collected
0458 673 164   HEMA 52 C2   33 10 38 S   148 41 16 E

968 Ophir Reserve
Lower Lewis Ponds Rd, Ophir
Camp Area 26 km NE of Orange. At Ophir goldfields. Steep sections. Best entry from the S. Pay at Orange Visitor Centre, or honesty box
02 6393 8225   HEMA 52 C4   33 10 10 S   149 14 21 E

969 Gamboola Rest Area
Mitchell Hwy, Belgravia
Rest Area 17 km NW of Orange or 17 km SE of Molong

HEMA 52 C3   33 09 44 S   149 00 36 E

970 Molong Showground
Euchareena Rd, Molong
Camp Area 2.4 km from PO. Take Euchareena Rd for 1.9 km, follow signs R. Contact caretaker
0429 722 380   HEMA 52 C2   33 05 21 S   148 53 31 E

971 Larras Lee Rest Area
Mitchell Hwy, Larras Lee
Rest Area 22 km N of Molong or 41 km S of Wellington. E side of Hwy
HEMA 52 B3   32 54 42 S   148 53 27 E

972 Two Mile Creek Rest Area
Mitchell Hwy, Cundumbul
Rest Area 31 km N of Molong or 32 km S of Wellington. W side of Hwy
HEMA 52 B3   32 50 03 S   148 54 27 E

973 Cumnock Showgrounds
McLaughlan St, Cumnock
Camp Area 21 km NW of Molong or 90 km SE of Dubbo. Key at general store
02 6367 7221   HEMA 52 B2   32 55 43 S   148 44 46 E

974 Yeoval Showground
Munro Rd, Yeoval
Camp Area 45 km NW of Molong or 40 km SW of Wellington. Caretaker will collect fees
0427 208 913   HEMA 52 A2   32 44 37 S   148 38 42 E

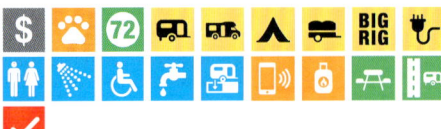

975 Royal Hotel Yeoval
13 Obley St, Yeoval
Parking Area beside hotel. Cnr Forbes St. Check in with publican, limited space
02 6846 4003   HEMA 52 A2   32 45 14 S   148 38 51 E

976 Caves Turnoff Rest Area
Mitchell Hwy, Wellington
Rest Area 56 km N of Molong or 9 km S of Wellington

HEMA 52 A3   32 37 23 S   148 56 52 E

977 Reflections Holiday Parks
Lake Burrendong
Fashions Mount Rd, Mumbil
Caravan Park 7 km NE of Mumbil or 27 km SE of Wellington, via Burrendong Dam Rd
02 6846 7435   HEMA 52 A3   32 41 24 S   149 06 34 E

978 Stuart Town Rec Ground
21 Bell St, Stuart Town
Camp Area beside Boehmes Hall. Limited power
0417 477 593   HEMA 52 B3   32 48 10 S   149 04 31 E

979 Reflections Holiday Parks
Mookerawa Waters
1000 Mookerawa Rd, Stuart Town
Caravan Park 11 km E of Stuart Town or 39 km SE of Wellington
02 6846 8426   HEMA 52 A3   32 45 58 S   149 09 27 E

980 Ponto Falls
Ponto Falls Reserve
Ponto Falls Rd, Maryvale
Camp Area 19 km NW of Wellington. Turn W off Mitchell Hwy 10 km NW of Wellington or 11 km S of Geurie. 5 km dirt road. Riverside. 14 day limit
02 6801 4000   HEMA 64 C5   32 27 57 S   148 49 12 E

981 Geurie Recreation Reserve
200 Comobella Rd, Geurie
Camp Area E side of town. Entry via Paxton St. Caretaker collects fees. Must pre-book
02 6887 1648   HEMA 64 C5   32 23 42 S   148 50 22 E

982 Geurie North Rest Area
Mitchell Hwy, Geurie
Rest Area 2 km N of Geurie or 26 km SE of Dubbo

HEMA 64 C5   32 23 17 S   148 48 57 E

983 Billyo Bush Retreat
43L Barbigal Rd, Wongarbon
Caravan Park 23 km S of Dubbo or 16 km
N of Geurie. Powered sites only. Pre-book
0418 431 334   HEMA 64 C5   32 17 58 S   148 46 46 E

984 The Rabbit Trap Hotel
1 Federation St, Albert
Parking Area 55 km SW of Trangie or
67 km N of Trundle. Donation for showers, limited
powered sites. Check in with publican
02 6892 8201   HEMA 61 K14   32 21 25 S   147 30 29 E

985 The State Centre Caravan Park
Tullamore Rd, Tottenham
Caravan Park E of town, on The Bogan Way
02 6892 4126   HEMA 61 J14   32 14 44 S   147 21 50 E

986 Nyngan Leisure & Van Park
12 Old Warren Rd, Nyngan
Caravan Park S end of town, via Hospital Rd
02 6832 2366   HEMA 61 H13   31 34 00 S   147 12 29 E

987 Flood Memorial Park
Nymagee St, Nyngan
Parking Area next to Mid-State Shearing
Shed. Toilets locked at night
02 6832 1052   HEMA 61 H13   31 33 44 S   147 11 49 E

988 Nyngan Weir
Ski Ln, Nyngan
Camp Area 5 km S of Nyngan. Turn off
Barrier Hwy to Temples Ln for 2 km, then E
HEMA 61 H13   31 34 50 S   147 10 23 E

989 Hermidale Hotel
Quanda St, Hermidale
Parking Area behind hotel. Check in with
publican
02 6833 0725   HEMA 61 H12   31 32 49 S   146 43 34 E

990 Hermidale West Rest Area
Barrier Hwy, Hermidale
Rest Area 1.5 km W of Hermidale
HEMA 61 H12   31 32 53 S   146 42 28 E

991 Florida Rest Area
Barrier Hwy, Canbelego
Rest Area 82 km W of Nyngan or 50 km E
of Cobar
HEMA 61 G12   31 31 57 S   146 21 03 E

992 Glenhope Camp
Barrier Hwy, Cobar
Camp Area 5.5 km E Cobar. GPS at Hwy
turn off. Ring on arrival for details of camp area
0428 463 413   HEMA 61 G11   31 30 17 S   145 54 09 E

993 Old Reservoir Cobar
Old Reservoir Rd, Cobar
Camp Spot 3 km N of Cobar. Via Old
Bourke Rd. Turn NE before Pistol Club. Bush
camping, 1 km dirt road.
HEMA 61 G11   31 28 51 S   145 51 32 E

994 Cornish (Cobar) Rest Area
Cnr Barrier Hwy and Kidman Way, Cobar
Rest Area 500 m S of Info Centre. Shared
truck stop, park on grass area behind toilet to avoid
truck area
HEMA 61 G11   31 29 57 S   145 50 41 E

995 Cobar Memorial Services Club
Cnr Barrier Hwy & Lewis St, Cobar
Parking Area beside club
02 6836 2102   HEMA 61 G11   31 29 54 S   145 50 24 E

996 Louth Camp Spot
Weelong Rd, Louth
Camp Area beside Darling River. W over
bridge, on L. Showers at park, opposite hotel for
donation
HEMA 61 E9   30 32 07 S   145 06 45 E

997 Shindys Inn
Bloxham St, Louth
Caravan Park next to pub. Pre-book
02 6874 7422   HEMA 61 E9   30 32 07 S   145 06 56 E

998 Trilby Station
Louth Tilpa Rd, Louth Area
Farm Stay 160 km NW of Cobar via Louth
or 125 km SW of Bourke via Louth. Western side of
the Louth to Tilba Rd. GPS at gate. Unpowered sites
riverside. Pre-book
02 6874 7420   HEMA 61 E9   30 37 16 S   144 55 37 E

999 Dunlop Station
10045 Toorale Rd, Louth
Station Stay 16 km SW Louth. On the
Darling River
0458 472 698   HEMA 61 E9   30 38 02 S   145 00 57 E

1000 Kallara Station
Tilpa-Louth Rd, Tilpa
Farm Stay 208 km NW of Cobar via Louth
or 175 km SW of Bourke via Louth. Signed turn off
80 km SW of Louth or 10 km NE of Tilpa on the
Western side of Tilpa-Louth Rd. 2 km from turn off to
homestead office
02 6837 3964   HEMA 61 F8   30 53 27 S   144 30 55 E

1001 Tilpa Flats
Tilpa-Tonga Rd, Tilpa
Camp Area opposite pub, donation to hotel
02 6837 3928   HEMA 61 F8   30 56 07 S   144 24 57 E

1002 Meadow Glen Rest Area
Barrier Hwy, Cubba
Rest Area 63 km W of Cobar or 196 km E
of Wilcannia. Tracks off site, not sign-posted
HEMA 61 H9   31 33 33 S   145 11 16 E

1003 Lilydale Rest Area
Barrier Hwy, Noona
Rest Area 94 W of Cobar or 167 E of Wilcannia. Shared truck stop

HEMA 61 H9   31 35 12 S   144 52 26 E

1004 Bulla Park Rest Area
Barrier Hwy, Noona
Rest Area 119 km W of Cobar or 140 km E of Wilcannia

HEMA 61 H8   31 33 30 S   144 37 35 E

1005 Emmdale Roadhouse
15981 Barrier Hwy, Wilcannia
Parking Area 159 km W of Cobar or 100 km E of Wilcannia. Limited power

02 6837 3979   HEMA 60 H7   31 39 11 S   144 16 06 E

1006 Baden Park Rest Area
Barrier Hwy, Wilcannia
Rest Area 172 km W of Cobar or 89 km E of Wilcannia

HEMA 60 H7   31 42 50 S   144 08 34 E

1007 MacCullochs Rest Area
Barrier Hwy, Wilcannia
Rest Area 204 km W of Cobar or 55 km E of Wilcannia

HEMA 60 H6   31 41 42 S   143 48 53 E

1008 Coach & Horses Camp
Paroo - Darling National Park
E Tipla Rd, Wilcannia
Camp Area 52 km NE of Wilcannia or 282 km SW of Bourke on the Bourke-Wilcannia Rd. E side of Darling River. Pre-book

08 8084 2880   HEMA 60 G6   31 27 23 S   143 49 37 E

1009 Warrawong on the Darling
Barrier Hwy, Wilcannia
Camp Area 3 km S of Wilcannia

0437 010 105   HEMA 60 H6   31 34 03 S   143 23 39 E

1010 Victory Park Caravan Park
Barrier Hwy, Wilcannia
Caravan Park at Wilcannia. Fees payable to caretaker

08 8083 8900   HEMA 60 H6   31 33 36 S   143 22 52 E

1011 Tilpa Weir
Via Curranyalpa Rd, Tilpa
Camp Area 6 km NE of Tilpa on E side of Darling River. 139 km NE of Wilcannia or 186 km SW of Bourke

02 6837 3928   HEMA 61 F8   30 55 10 S   144 27 29 E

1012 Wanaaring Store
O'Grady St, Wanaaring
Caravan Park 192 km W of Bourke or 234 km E of Tibooburra. Pre-book

02 6874 7720   HEMA 60 C7   29 42 09 S   144 08 57 E

1013 Hungerford-Wanaaring
Rest Area
Mooleyarra Rd, Wanaaring
Rest Area 53 km S of Hungerford or 46 km N of Wanaaring. W side of Hwy

HEMA 61 B8   29 27 01 S   144 25 08 E

1014 Wanaaring Town Common
Bourke-Milparinka Rd, Wanaaring
Rest Area 1.3 km E of town, S of Paroo River Bridge

HEMA 60 C7   29 41 51 S   144 09 31 E

1015 Wanaaring Riverside Camp
Bourke-Milparinka Rd, Wanaaring
Camp Area opposite Outback Inn Hotel

02 6874 7758   HEMA 60 C7   29 42 13 S   144 09 00 E

1016 White Cliffs Opal Pioneer
Reserve
Johnston St, White Cliffs
Caravan Park 200 m N of PO. Pre-book

08 8091 6688   HEMA 60 F5   30 51 02 S   143 05 22 E

1017 Glen Hope Stationstay
1305 Reola Rd, White Cliffs
Station Stay 15 km N of White Cliffs, 200 m on the R, facilities at shearer's quarters on the L of the driveway

0414 935 803   HEMA 60 F5   30 44 21 S   143 04 06 E

1018 Goodwood Station Stay
1025 Glendara Rd, Wilcannia
Camp Area 46 km NE of White Cliffs. Via Keraro Rd, turn N onto Wilcannia-Wanaaring Rd for 4 km, then NW to Glendara Rd. 9.5 km to mailbox. Pre-book

0448 220 336   HEMA 60 E6   30 42 43 S   143 22 09 E

1019 Netallie Rest Area
Barrier Hwy, Wilcannia
Rest Area 18 km W of Wilcannia or 176 km E of Broken Hill

HEMA 60 H5   31 34 07 S   143 13 00 E

1020 Spring Hill Rest Area
Barrier Hwy, Little Topar
Rest Area 74 km W of Wilcannia or 122 km E of Broken Hill

HEMA 60 H4   31 43 23 S   142 41 09 E

1021 Little Topar Roadhouse
11908 Barrier Hwy, Little Topar
Rest Area 128 km W of Wilcannia or 76 km E of Broken Hill

08 8091 9428   HEMA 60 H3   31 46 47 S   142 13 39 E

1022 Round Hill Rest Area
Barrier Hwy, Broken Hill
Rest Area 190 km W of Wilcannia or 6 km E of Broken Hill. Combined truck stop

HEMA 60 J2   31 56 15 S   141 31 06 E

1023 Broken Hill Racecourse
Racecourse Rd, Broken Hill
Camp Area & Regional Events Centre 5 km NE of Broken Hill, off Tibooburra Rd. Pre-book, limited space

0437 250 286   HEMA 60 H2   31 54 48 S   141 28 51 E

1024 Starview Primitive Campsite

Living Desert State Park

Nine Mile Rd, Broken Hill
Camp Area 12 km N of Broken Hill. Entry 7.5 km N of town, via Nine Mile Rd. Pre-book
08 8080 3560   HEMA 60 H2   31 54 27 S   141 26 34 E

1025 Eldee Station

2886 Wilangee Rd, Silverton
Farm Stay 52 km NW of Broken Hill
08 8091 2578   HEMA 60 H1   31 40 10 S   141 15 33 E

1026 Penrose Park

Penrose Park Rd, Silverton
Camp Area NE of town centre, 24 km NW of Broken Hill
08 8088 5307   HEMA 60 H1   31 52 57 S   141 13 48 E

1027 Thackaringa Rest Area

Barrier Hwy, Broken Hill
Rest Area 36 km W of Broken Hill or 14 km E of Cockburn
HEMA 60 K1   32 02 44 S   141 07 39 E

1028 Border Gate Roadhouse

Barrier Hwy, Cockburn
Rest Area on NSW/SA Border. Share with trucks. Fee for shower
0422 705 571   HEMA 60 J1   32 04 42 S   141 00 06 E

Barringun to Jerilderie
Kidman Way

1029 Bush Tucker Inn Roadhouse

Mitchell Hwy, Barringun
Camp Area beside service station. Check in at office
02 6874 7584   HEMA 61 A10   29 00 36 S   145 42 44 E

1030 Comeroo Cattle Station

Via Yantabulla Enngonia Rd, Yantabulla
Station Stay 97 km SE of Hungerford. Take Hungerford Rd SE from Hungerford for 80 km, E on Yantabulla-Enngonia Rd 13 km, then N for 2.5 km
02 6874 7735   HEMA 61 B9   29 14 36 S   145 08 25 E

1031 Enngonia South Rest Area

Mitchell Hwy, Enngonia
Rest Area 31 km S of Enngonia or 66 km N of Bourke
HEMA 61 C11   29 35 10 S   145 50 32 E

1032 Warrego Hotel

16 Aubrey St, Fords Bridge
Parking Area next to pub. 70 km NW of Burke or 145 km SE of Hungerford on Bourke-Hungerford Rd
02 6874 7877   HEMA 61 C10   29 45 09 S   145 25 30 E

1033 Kinchela Rest Area

Kidman Way, Bourke
Rest Area 41 km S of Bourke or 120 km N of Cobar
HEMA 61 E11   30 27 27 S   145 56 07 E

1034 Dry Tank Campground

Gundabooka National Park

Dry Tank Trail, Gundabooka
Camp Area 49 km S of Bourke or 111 km N of Cobar. Turn W onto Ben Lomond Rd for 18 km to sites. Dirt road. Pre-book
02 6830 0200   HEMA 61 E10   30 31 04 S   145 42 53 E

1035 Yanda Campground

Gundabooka National Park

Yanda Campground Trail, Gundabooka
Camp Area 46 km S of Bourke or 114 km N of Cobar. Turn W off Louth Rd opposite Telstra tower, follow signs. GPS at turn off
02 6830 0200   HEMA 61 E10   30 19 28 S   145 36 21 E

1036 Rose Isle Station

Bourke-Louth Road, Louth
Farm Stay 30 km E of Louth or 70 km W of Bourke on the Darling River Run. Pre-book
02 6874 7371   HEMA 61 E10   30 26 16 S   145 22 42 E

1037 Curraweena Rest Area

Kidman Hwy, Gunderbooka
Rest Area 61 km S of Bourke or 100 km N of Cobar
HEMA 61 E11   30 38 14 S   145 52 22 E

1038 Four Corners Farm Stay

Burthong Rd, Nymagee
Camp Area 8 km S of Nymagee township. Limited powered sites, pre-book
0438 683 626   HEMA 63 A13   32 09 02 S   146 18 07 E

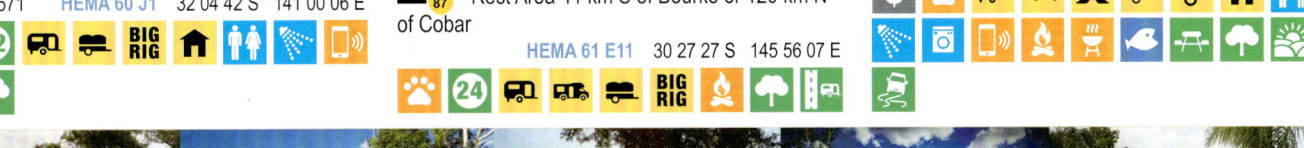

1039 Gilgunnia Rest Area

Kidman Way, Gilgunnia
Rest Area 109 km S of Cobar or 51 km N of Mount Hope

HEMA 63 B12   32 25 04 S   146 02 05 E

1040 Royal Hotel Mt Hope
Kidman Way, Mount Hope
Parking Area next to pub. 161 km S of Cobar or 94 km N of Hillston
02 6897 7988   HEMA 63 C12   32 50 24 S   145 52 47 E

1041 Mount Hope Community Hall
Via Kidman Way, Mount Hope
Parking Area 161 km S of Cobar or 94 km N of Hilston. Honesty box
HEMA 63 C12   32 50 19 S   145 52 44 E

1042 Lachlan River Rest Area
Mount Grace Rd, Wallanthery
Rest Area 218 km S of Cobar or 37 km N of Hillston. Beside old bridge
HEMA 63 E12   33 20 29 S   145 50 10 E

1043 Billabourie Riverside Tourist Park
5801 Mt Grace Rd, Hillston
Caravan Park 48 km NE of Hillston. Turn E 38 km N of Hillston at Wallanthery Bridge to Mt Grace Rd. Entry 10 km along road. Signposted
0427 674 131   HEMA 63 E12   33 22 32 S   145 55 38 E

1044 Hillston Rest Area
Kidman Way, Hillston
Rest Area 1.5 km S of Hillston. Shared with trucks
HEMA 63 E11   33 30 15 S   145 31 56 E

1045 Duke of Edinburgh Hotel
8 Lachlan St, Booligal
Parking Area beside pub (Booligal Hotel). Check in with publican. Fee for shower
02 6993 8123   HEMA 63 F10   33 52 08 S   144 53 06 E

1046 Lachlan River
Mossgiel Rd, Hillston
Parking Area 3 km NE of the town off Mossgiel Rd, turn N just E of the bridge
HEMA 63 E11   33 28 19 S   145 31 55 E

1047 Group Campground
Willandra National Park
Willandra Creek Trail, Hillston
Camp Area 62 km NW of Hillston, via Hillston-Mossgeil Rd. Dirt road
02 6966 8100   HEMA 63 D10   33 11 36 S   145 07 05 E

1048 Lake View Caravan Park
10 City St, Lake Cargelligo
Caravan Park 1 km SE of PO
02 6898 1077   HEMA 63 D13   33 18 08 S   146 22 39 E

1049 Frogs Hollow
Via Lake Cargelligo Rd, Lake Cargelligo
Camp Area 1.5 km SE of PO, via Canada & Narrandera Sts. Turn E at foreshore, beside lake
02 6898 1501   HEMA 63 D13   33 18 18 S   146 22 57 E

1050 Dead Mans Point
McInnes St, Lake Cargelligo
Camp Area 3.5 km NE of Lake Cargelligo, via Canada & Uabba Sts. Beside lake
02 6898 1501   HEMA 63 D13   33 16 46 S   146 23 44 E

1051 Euabalong Campground
Lachlan St, Euabalong
Camp Area 28 km N of Lake Cargelligo. Signposted "Caravan Park". Fee payable in honesty box
0428 951 875   HEMA 63 D13   33 06 42 S   146 28 20 E

1052 Royal Hotel Euabalong
19 Lachlan St, Euabalong
Parking Area behind hotel. Check in with publican
02 6896 6605   HEMA 63 D13   33 06 34 S   146 28 22 E

1053 Booberoi Weir
Booberoi Rd, Euabalong
Dispersed Camping 20 km NE of Euabalong or 56 km W of Condobolin. Access from Euabalong via Euabalong West Rd & Booberoi Rd (15 km dirt) or from Condobolin via Kiacatoo & Euabalong West Rds. Turn S just E of radio tower for 1 km to river
02 6836 5888   HEMA 63 D14   33 02 13 S   146 38 36 E

1054 Gum Bend Lake
Gum Bend Rd, Condobolin
Camp Area 4 km W of Condobolin, via Bathurst St. Pets not permitted on bank
02 6895 1900   HEMA 64 E2   33 04 45 S   147 06 03 E

1055 River View Caravan Park
Diggers Ave, Condobolin
Caravan Park S end of town
02 6895 2611   HEMA 64 E2   33 05 40 S   147 08 50 E

1056 Wallaroi Creek Rest Area
The Gipps Way, Condobolin
Rest Area 15 km S of Condobolin or 90 km N of West Wyalong. Creekside
HEMA 64 E2   33 12 34 S   147 06 10 E

1057 Burcher Camping Ground
Kurrajong St, Burcher
Camp Area in town. Donation to pub, PO or box
02 6972 5244   HEMA 64 F2   33 31 00 S   147 15 07 E

1058 Ungarie Showground
Crown Camp Rd, Ungarie
Camp Area N side of town. Entrance beyond school, signposted
02 6979 0272   HEMA 64 F2   33 38 07 S   146 58 43 E

1059 Tullibigeal Sportsground
Burgooney Rd, Tullibigeal
Camp Area N of town. 44 km SE of Lake Cargelligo or 82 km NW of West Wyalong
02 6972 9176   HEMA 63 E14   33 25 00 S   146 43 28 E

1060 Tullibigeal Pioneer Park

Cargelligo St, Tullibigeal
Rest Area central to town. 44 km SE of
Lake Cargelligo or 82 km NW of West Wyalong
02 6972 9176   HEMA 63 E14   33 25 16 S   146 43 40 E

1061 Woolshed Flat

Cocoparra National Park
Woolshed Flat Trail, Binya
Camp Area 25 km NE of Griffith. Access via
Beelbangera Rd to Yenda, N along Myall Park Rd
(Whitton Stock Route) then E onto Mt Bingar Rd.
Signposted. Some dirt road. Pre-book
02 6966 8100   HEMA 63 G13   34 04 53 S   146 13 16 E

1062 Lake Wyangan

Lakes Rd, Lake Wyangan
Camp Area 11 km NW of Griffith
02 6962 8400   HEMA 63 G12   34 12 46 S   146 01 02 E

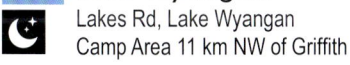

1063 Griffith Boat Club

Lakes Rd, Lake Wyangan
Campground 8 km N of Griffth. Pre-book
02 6963 4847   HEMA 63 G12   34 13 02 S   146 00 57 E

1064 Griffith Showground

Cnr Merrigal St & Walla Ave, Griffith
Caravan Park at Griffith. Call on arrival for
gate codes
0403 655 123   HEMA 63 G12   34 17 25 S   146 01 46 E

1065 Willow Park

Kookora St, Griffith
Rest Area at Griffith. 1.5 km W of PO, near
TAFE college
02 6962 4145   HEMA 63 G12   34 17 16 S   146 01 55 E

1066 Garoolgan Rest Area

Burley Griffin Way, Garoolgan
Rest Area 40 km E of Griffith or 45 km W of
Ardlethan
HEMA 63 G13   34 15 10 S   146 26 56 E

1067 Barellan Showground

Barellan Showground Rd, Barellan
Camp Area N of town. Call on arrival. Pay
fee at general store or PO
0429 639 378   HEMA 63 G14   34 16 48 S   146 34 37 E

1068 Nugan Bend

Kidman Way, Hanwood
Rest Area 10 km S of Griffith or 24 km N of
Darlington Point
HEMA 63 H12   34 22 08 S   146 02 03 E

1069 The Coly Club

Coleambally Community Club
3 Falcon St, Coleambally
Parking Area W side of town. Check in at club.
Showers at footy oval
02 6954 4170   HEMA 63 J12   34 48 26 S   145 53 01 E

1070 Brolga Hotel Motel

Brolga Pl, Coleambally
Parking Area in town. Check in with
publican. Toilets open during pub hours
02 6954 4009   HEMA 63 J12   34 48 20 S   145 52 49 E

Tibooburra to Mildura
Silver City Highway

1071 Cameron Corner Store

Camerons Corner Rd, Cameron Corner
Camp Area behind store. Pre-book
08 8091 3872   HEMA 60 A1   28 59 48 S   140 59 59 E

1072 Fort Grey Campground

Sturt National Park
Fort Grey Camping Area Trail, Tibooburra
Camp Area 109 km NW of Tibooburra, via
Tibooburra-Cameron Corner Rd. Dirt road. Pre-book
08 8091 3308   HEMA 60 A1   29 05 17 S   141 12 45 E

1073 The Granites Motel

Cnr of King & Brown Sts, Tibooburra
Caravan Park SE side of town
0427 913 477   HEMA 60 B3   29 26 02 S   142 00 33 E

1074 Tibooburra Beds and Camping

Cnr Briscoe & Brown Sts, Tibooburra
Camp Area S side of town. Pay at Corner Country
Store. Pre-book
08 8091 3333   HEMA 60 B3   29 26 03 S   142 00 36 E

1075 Tibooburra Aboriginal Reserve Campground

Burgess St, Tibooburra
Camp Area at Tibooburra. S from Tibooburra Rd for
1 km. Pay at land council office or other businesses
08 8091 3435   HEMA 60 B3   29 26 29 S   142 01 03 E

1076 Dead Horse Gully Camp

Sturt National Park
Dead Horse Campground Trail, Tibooburra
Camp Area 2.5 km N of Tibooburra. Turn W off
Silver City Hwy 1 km N of Tibooburra. Signposted.
Pre-book
08 8091 3308   HEMA 60 B3   29 25 02 S   142 00 03 E

1077 Olive Downs Campground

Sturt National Park
Jump-Up Loop Rd, Tibooburra
Camp Area 55 km N of Tibooburra. Signposted off
Silver City Hwy. Access road can be rough. Pre-book
08 8091 3308   HEMA 60 A2   29 03 32 S   141 51 48 E

1078 Mount Wood Campground

Sturt National Park
Mt Wood Camping Area Trail, Tibooburra
Camp Area 26 km E of Tibooburra. Via Tibooburra &
Gorge Loop Rds. Dirt road. Pre-book
08 8091 3308   HEMA 60 B3   29 28 49 S   142 14 14 E

1079 Milparinka Camping & Caravan Site

Tompson St, Milparinka
Camp Area behind heritage centre. Pay at info centre
0499 164 919   HEMA 60 C3   29 44 18 S   141 53 06 E

1080 Cobham Lake North

Silver City Hwy, Packsaddle
Camp Area 235 km N Broken Hill. GPS at
track entrance. SW side of Hwy
HEMA 60 D3   30 08 05 S   142 05 36 E

NEW SOUTH WALES

1081 Cobham Lake South
Silver City Hwy, Packsaddle
Dispersed Camping 229 km N Broken Hill.
GPS at track entrance
HEMA 60 D3   30 10 04 S   142 06 08 E

1082 Pincally Station
6611 Mount Shannon Rd, Milparinka
Camp Area 70 km S of Milparinka. Faciltes
for a fee. Pre-book
08 8091 3571   HEMA 60 D2   30 11 25 S   141 33 13 E

1083 Pimpara Lake Station
4244 Pimpara Lake Rd, Packsaddle
Station Stay 130 km S of Milparinka or
200 km N of Broken Hill. Via Mount Arrowsmith Rd.
Bush camping, call for directions
0499 164 919   HEMA 60 E2   30 25 19 S   141 44 02 E

1084 Packsaddle Rest Area
Silver City Hwy, Packsaddle
Rest Area N of roadhouse
HEMA 60 E3   30 36 07 S   141 57 52 E

1085 Packsaddle Roadhouse
17242 Silver City Hwy, Packsaddle
Camp Area 175 km N of Broken Hill
08 8091 2539   HEMA 60 E3   30 36 37 S   141 58 00 E

1086 Pine View Station
Border Downs Rd, Broughams Gate
Station Stay 180 km NW of Broken Hill. Via
Silverton to Hawker Gate Rd. Dirt road. Pre-book
08 8091 2513   HEMA 60 E1   30 41 46 S   141 04 22 E

1087 Fowlers Gap
Silver City Hwy, Fowlers Gap
Rest Area 66 km S of Packsaddle or
110 km N of Broken Hill
HEMA 60 F2   31 06 07 S   141 42 07 E

1088 Homestead Creek Camp
Mutawintji National Park
Mutawintji-Waterbag Rd, Mutawintji
Camp Area 130 km NE of Broken Hill. Turn E 56 km
S of Fowlers Gap or 54 km N of Broken Hill for
59 km. Dirt road. Pre-book
08 8084 2880   HEMA 60 G3   31 16 56 S   142 17 37 E

1089 Yanco Glen
Silver City Hwy, Fowlers Gap
Rest Area 31 km N Broken Hill
HEMA 60 H2   31 43 07 S   141 34 26 E

1090 Lake Pamamaroo Campsites
Main Weir Rd, Menindee
Dispersed Camping along lake. 16 km NE
of Menindee. 8 km N of Menindee on Menindee Rd,
turn E on Main Weir Rd
08 8091 4274   HEMA 62 B4   32 18 59 S   142 27 58 E

1091 Burke and Wills Campground
Main Weir Rd, Menindee
Camp Area 18 km NE of Menindee. 8 km N of
Menindee on Menindee Rd, turn E. Beside Darling R
08 8091 4274   HEMA 62 B4   32 18 18 S   142 29 55 E

1092 Main Weir Campground
Main Weir Rd, Menindee
Camp Area 19 km NE of Menindee. 8 km
N of Menindee on Menindee Rd, turn E. Beside
Darling R
08 8091 4274   HEMA 62 B4   32 18 49 S   142 30 26 E

1093 Nelia Gaari Station
W Wilcannia Rd, Menindee
Farm Stay 80 km E of Menindee or 90 km W
of Wilcannia. W side of River Rd. 4WD in wet weather
08 8091 6496   HEMA 62 A5   32 06 08 S   142 51 04 E

1094 Menindee Bridge Caravan Park
Cnr Menindee St and Pooncarie Rd, Menindee
Caravan Park at Menindee
08 8091 4282   HEMA 62 B4   32 23 59 S   142 24 48 E

1095 Darling River Campgrounds
Kinchega National Park
River Dr, Menindee
Camp Area 4.5 km SW of Menindee. 34 sites beside
Darling River, first site starts at park entry point.
Gold coin showers & bore water available at the
Shearer's Quarters. Pre-book
08 8084 2880   HEMA 62 B4   32 23 52 S   142 22 30 E

1096 Emu Lake Campground
Kinchega National Park
Woolshed Dr, Menindee
Camp Area 24 km S of Menindee. Turn off
Menindee-Pooncarie Rd onto Emu Lake Dr,
signposted. Gold coin showers & bore water
available at the Shearer's Quarters. Pre-book
08 8084 2880   HEMA 62 B4   32 28 13 S   142 20 47 E

1097 Bindara Station
Old Pooncarie Rd, Menindee Area
Station Stay 92 km N of Pooncarie. Cross the
Darling River at Pooncarie, 3 km turn R at Polia Rd.
Continue about 20 km. At T intersection turn R onto
Polia/RooRoo Rd. Follow about 68 km to Bindara
08 8091 7412   HEMA 62 C4   32 45 30 S   142 22 22 E

1098 Tolarno Station
Pooncarie Rd, Menindee
Station Stay 45 km S of Menindee or 77 km
N of Pooncarie via Pooncarie-Menindee Rd. Pre-
book. Bush camping by river
0427 073 971   HEMA 62 C4   32 46 59 S   142 23 52 E

1099 Ivanhoe Caravan Park
30 Columbus St, Ivanhoe
Caravan Park at Ivanhoe Servo
02 6995 1187   HEMA 63 C8   32 54 03 S   144 18 05 E

1100 Popiltah Lake Rest Area
Silver City Hwy, Scotia
Rest Area 137 km S of Broken Hill or
129 km N of Wentworth
HEMA 62 D2   33 04 02 S   141 38 37 E

1101 Seven Trees Rest Area
Silver City Hwy, Anabranch South
Rest Area 185 km S of Broken Hill or 82 km
N of Wentworth. W side of Hwy
HEMA 62 E2   33 27 49 S   141 42 37 E

1102 Bunnerungee Rest Area

Silver City Hwy, Anabranch South
Rest Area 200 km S of Broken Hill or 67 km N of Wentworth. Both sides of bridge

HEMA 62 E3   33 34 50 S   141 45 21 E

1103 Milpara Rest Area

Silver City Hwy, Anabranch South
Rest Area 240 km S of Broken Hill or 26 km N of Wentworth. Small vehicles only

HEMA 62 F3   33 55 34 S   141 47 45 E

1104 Pooncarie Multi Purpose Park

(Wakefied Oval)
Cemetery Rd, Pooncarie
Dispersed Camping at Pooncarie. 140 km NE of Mildura, 52 km W of Mungo NP. Pay at hotel, coin showers. Key deposit for power

03 5029 5205   HEMA 62 E4   33 22 49 S   142 33 53 E

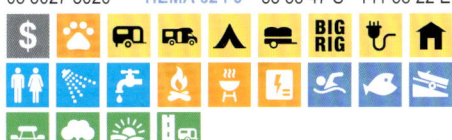

1105 Avoca on Darling

1122A Low Darling Rd, Wentworth
Camp Area 26 km N of Wentworth, via Pomona & Low Darling Rds. Pre-book

03 5027 3020   HEMA 62 F3   33 55 47 S   141 58 22 E

1106 Yankabilly Island

45 Yankabilly Rd, Wentworth
Camp Area 14 km N of Wentworth. Via Silver City Hwy (B79) for 6 km, NE to Pomona Rd for 7 km, E for 750 m

0407 328 004   HEMA 62 F3   34 00 03 S   141 54 06 E

1107 Fort Courage Caravan Park

1703 Old Renmark Rd, Wentworth
Caravan Park 20 km W of Wentworth. Beside Murray River

03 5027 3097   HEMA 62 G3   34 05 22 S   141 44 01 E

1108 Wentworth RV Park

Beverley St, Wentworth
Parking Area at the sporting complex

HEMA 62 G3   34 06 17 S   141 54 51 E

1109 Thegoa Lagoon & Reserve

Cadell St, Wentworth
Camp Area 2.5 km W of Wentworth. Turn at boat ramp sign

03 5027 5080   HEMA 62 G3   34 06 34 S   141 53 49 E

1110 Curlwaa Caravan Park

3 Williamsville Rd, Curlwaa
Caravan Park 5 km E of Wentworth

03 5027 6210   HEMA 62 G3   34 06 45 S   141 59 21 E

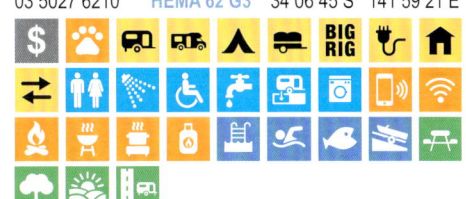

Nyngan to Bourke
Mitchell Highway

1111 CWA Memorial Park

Arcturus St, Girilambone
Rest Area E of Hwy. See signage for access.
Check in with publican opposite

0492 983 824   HEMA 61 G13   31 14 52 S   146 54 24 E

1112 Willie Retreat Macquarie

Marshes
Carinda Rd & Gibson Way, Warren
Camp Area 110 km N of Warren or 76 km S of Carinda on the Carinda-Nyngan Rd, turn E into Gibson Way, entrance 1.5 km on the S side of road. Bush camping available. GPS at gate

02 6824 4361   HEMA 61 F14   30 53 49 S   147 29 08 E

1113 Glenariff (Byrock) Rest Area

Mitchell Hwy, Byrock
Rest Area 26 km NW of Coolabah or 25 km SE of Byrock

HEMA 61 F12   30 49 51 S   146 32 46 E

1114 Mulga Creek Hotel

Mitchell Hwy, Byrock
Caravan Park behind hotel. Pre-book

02 6874 7311   HEMA 61 E12   30 39 47 S   146 24 10 E

1115 Maroona Rest Area

Mitchell Hwy, Bourke
Rest Area 56 km NW of Byrock or 22 km SE of Bourke

HEMA 61 D11   30 14 44 S   146 03 31 E

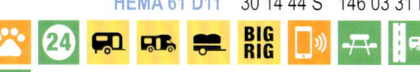

Euston to Mildura

1116 Mail Route Rest Area

Sturt Hwy, Mallee
Rest Area 23 km NW of Euston or 47 km SE of Gol Gol. Combined truck stop

HEMA 62 H4   34 27 53 S   142 32 26 E

1117 Malleefowl Rest Area

Sturt Hwy, Mallee
Rest Area 38 km NW of Euston or 33 km SE of Gol Gol. Observe local signage

HEMA 62 H4   34 23 26 S   142 25 36 E

1118 Bottle Bend Nature Reserve

Bottle Bend Rd, Mildura Area
Camp Area 57 km NW of Euston or 18 km SE of Gol Gol. Turn S 56 km NW of Euston or 15 km SE of Gol Gol at signpost. 2 km dirt road. Beside river

HEMA 62 G4   34 18 12 S   142 17 55 E

1119 Mungo Lodge

Arumpo Rd, Arumpo
Camp Area 150 km NW of Balranald or 110 km NE of Mildura. Dirt road. Pre-book

03 5029 7297   HEMA 62 F5   33 44 29 S   143 00 08 E

1120 Main Campground

Mungo National Park
Arumpo Rd, Arumpo
Camp Area 150 km NW of Balranald or 110 km NE of Mildura. Signposted. Dirt road. Pre-book

1300 072 757   HEMA 62 F5   33 44 07 S   143 00 55 E

1121 Belah Campground

Mungo National Park
Arumpo Rd, Arumpo
Camp Area 136 km NW of Balranald or 142 km NE of Mildura. From visitor centre follow signposted directions. Small offroad caravans. Pre-book

1300 072 757   HEMA 62 F6   33 42 46 S   143 10 36 E

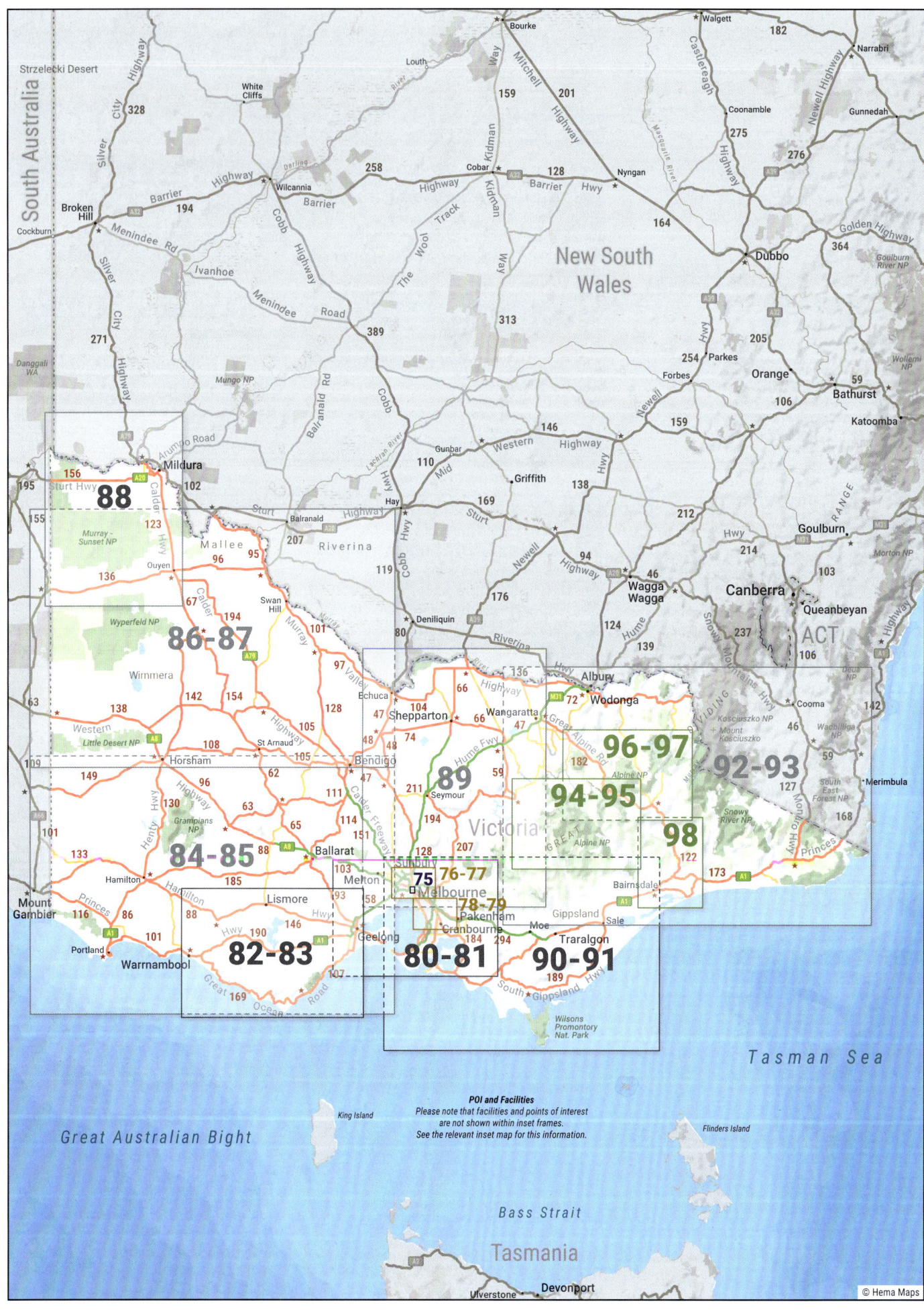

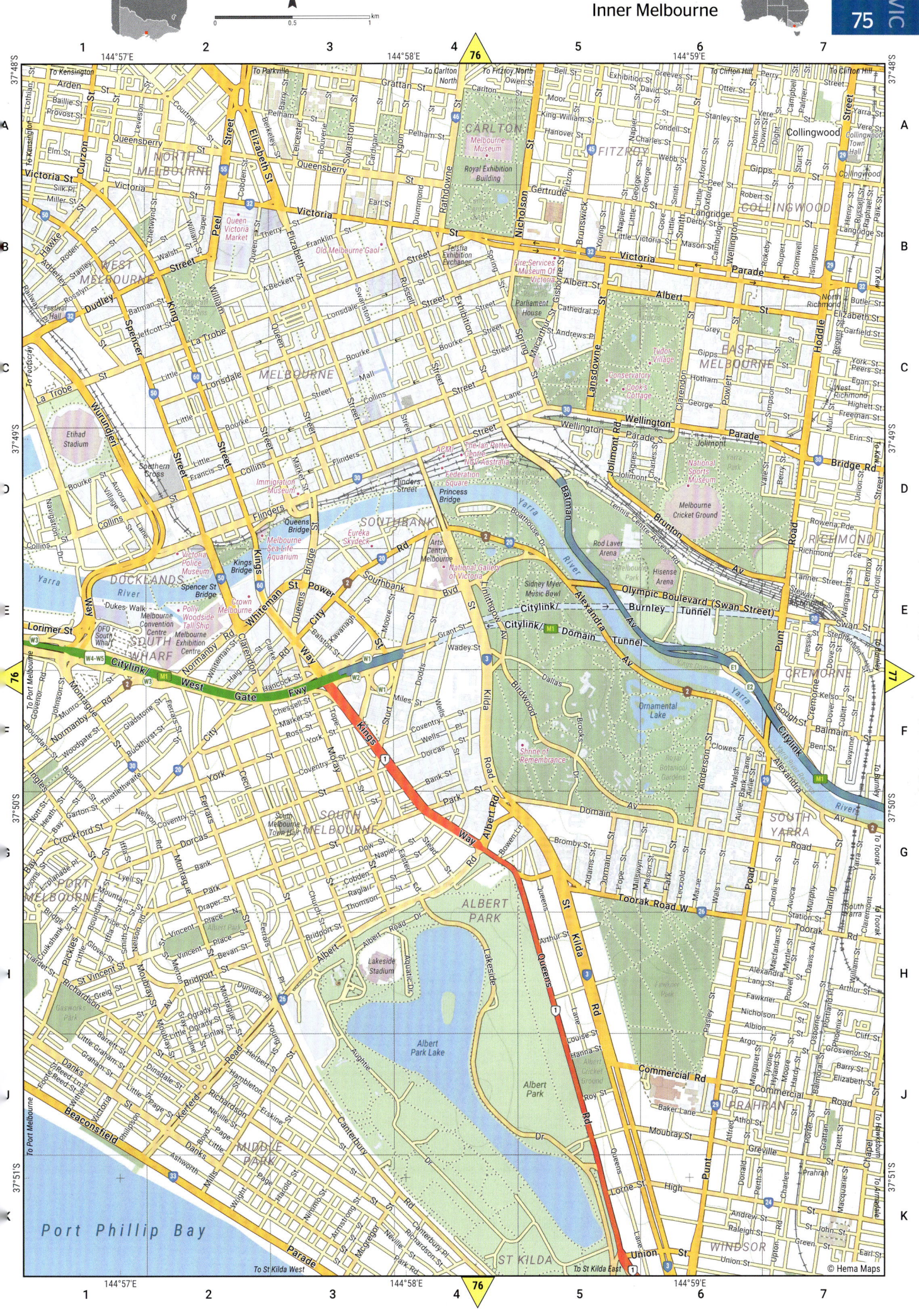

Inner Melbourne Suburbs

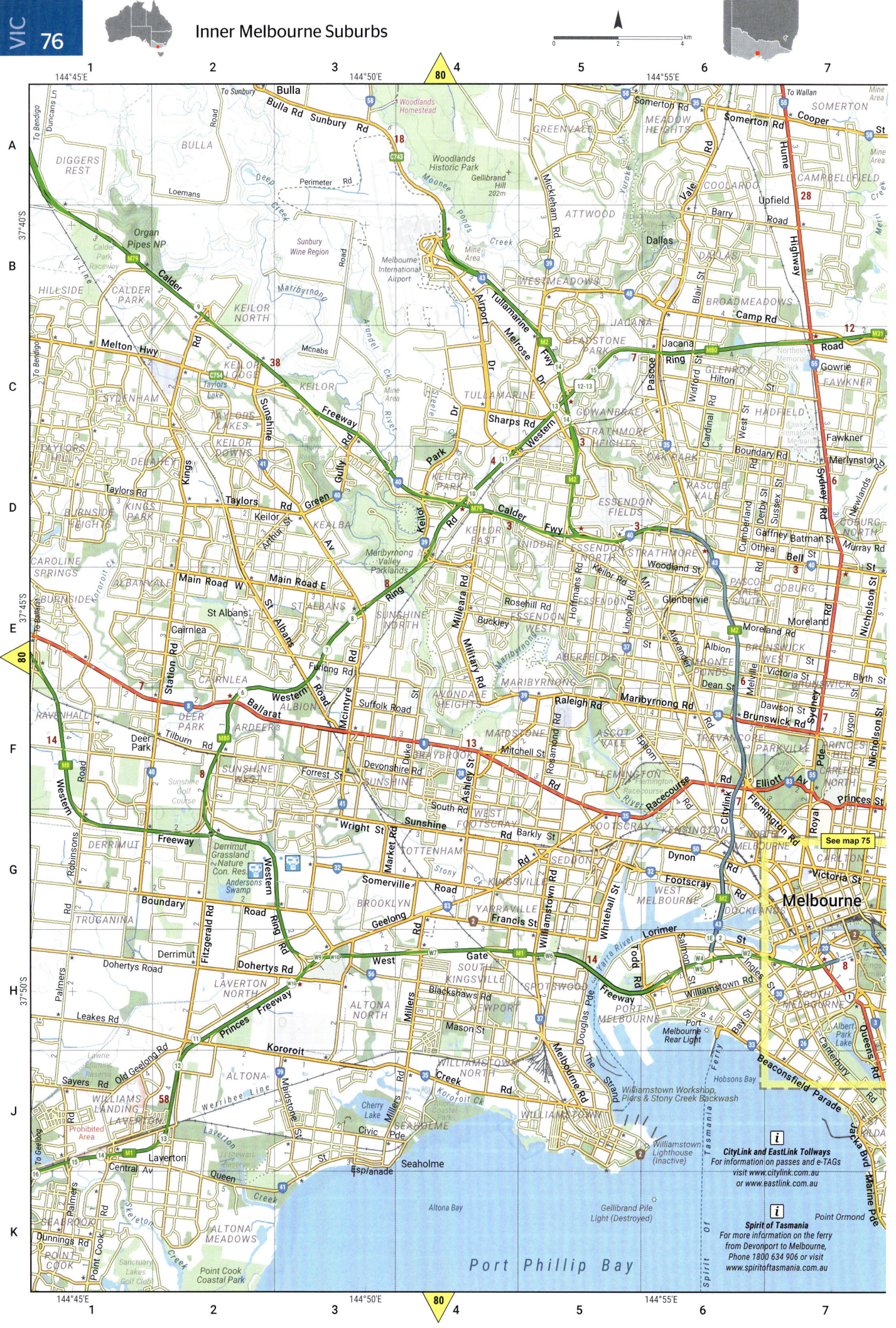

Bayside and Southern Melbourne Suburbs

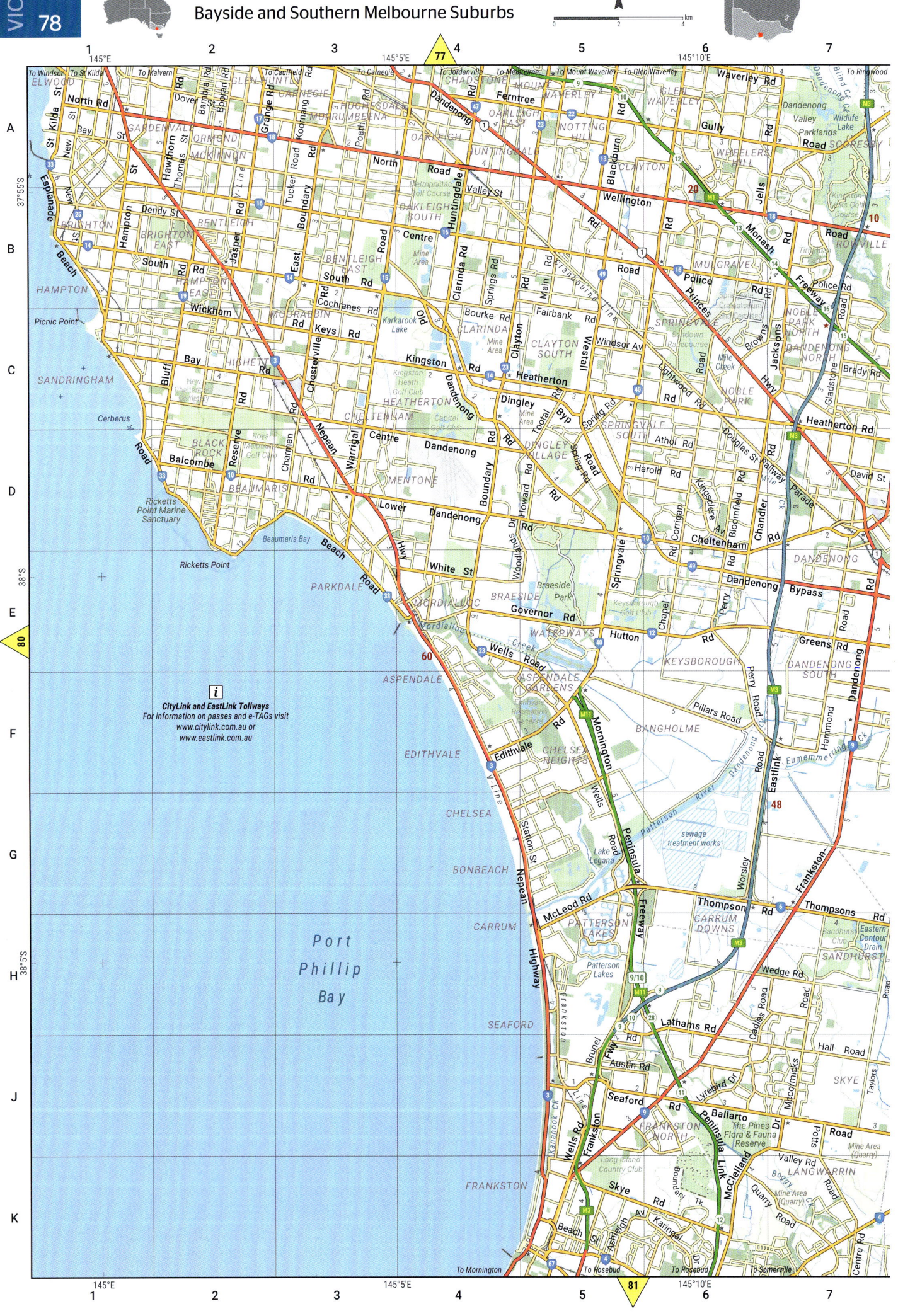

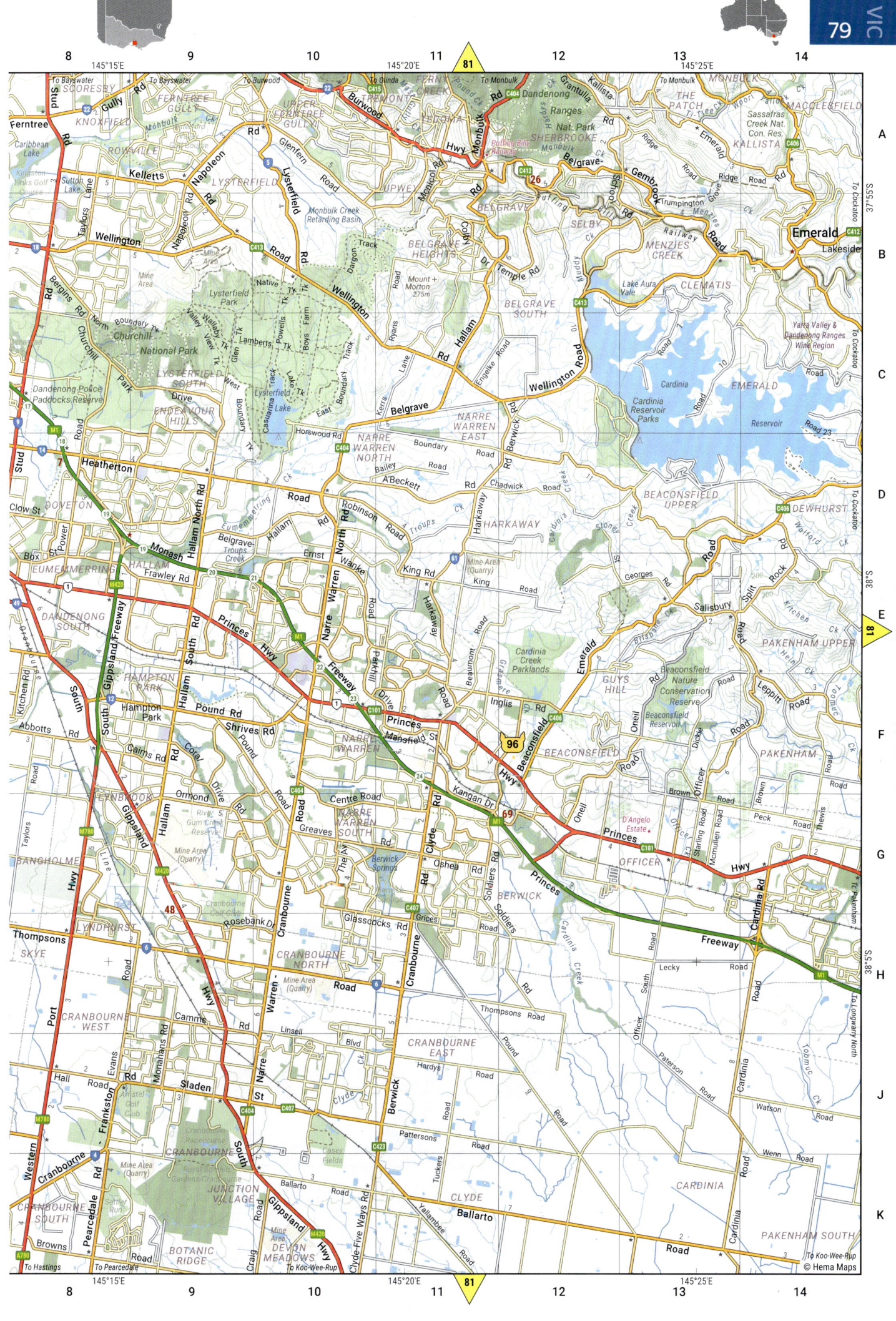

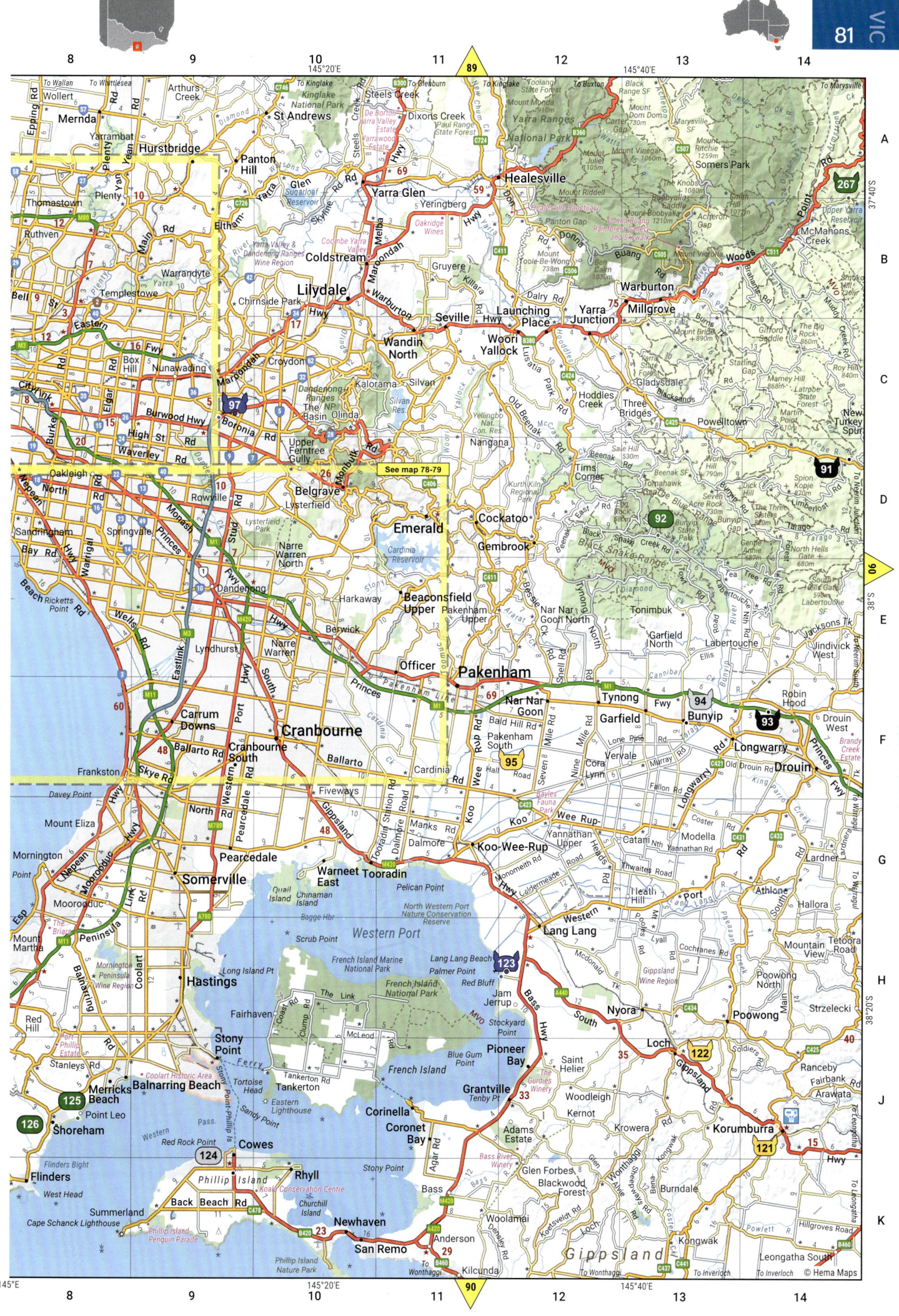

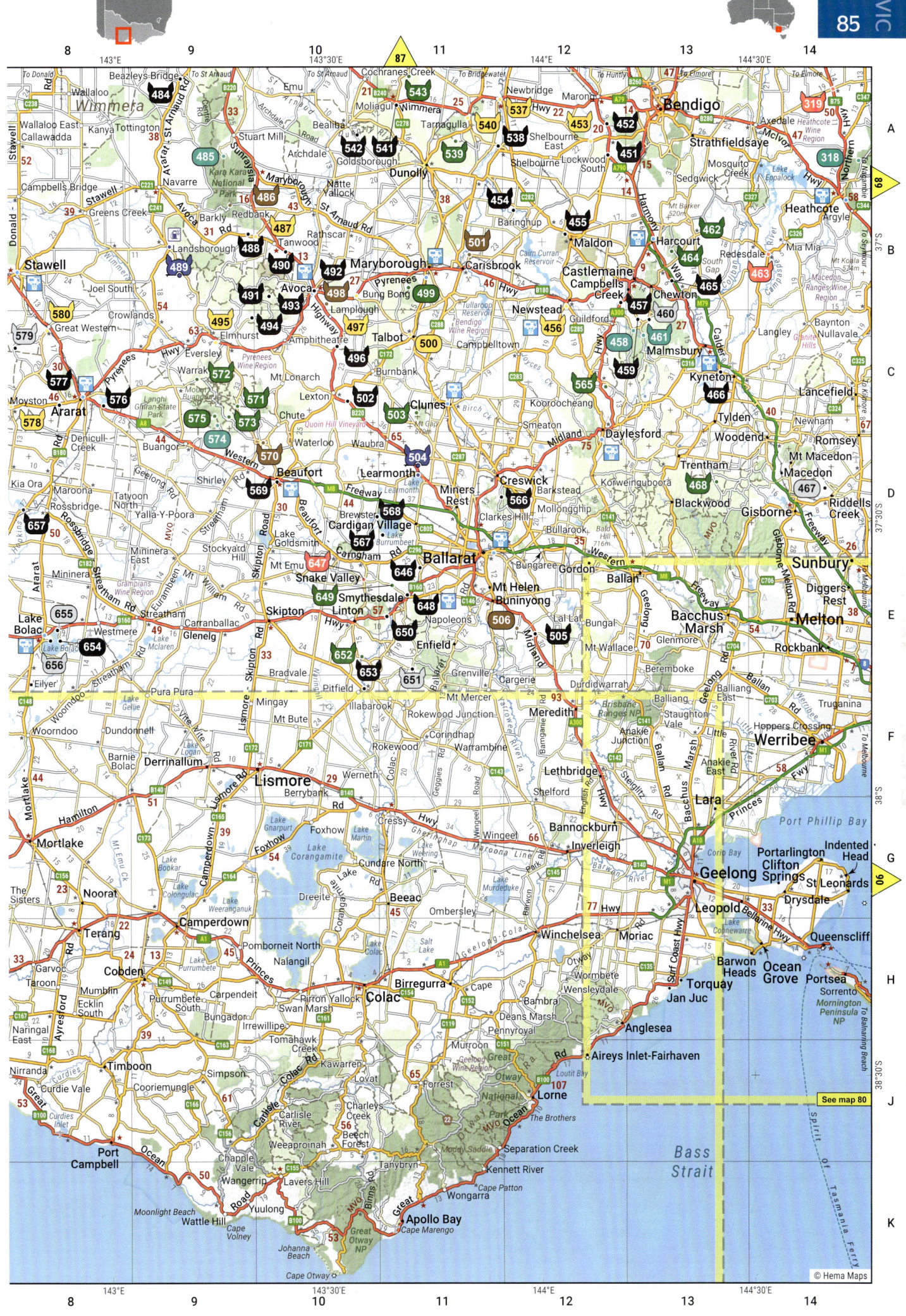

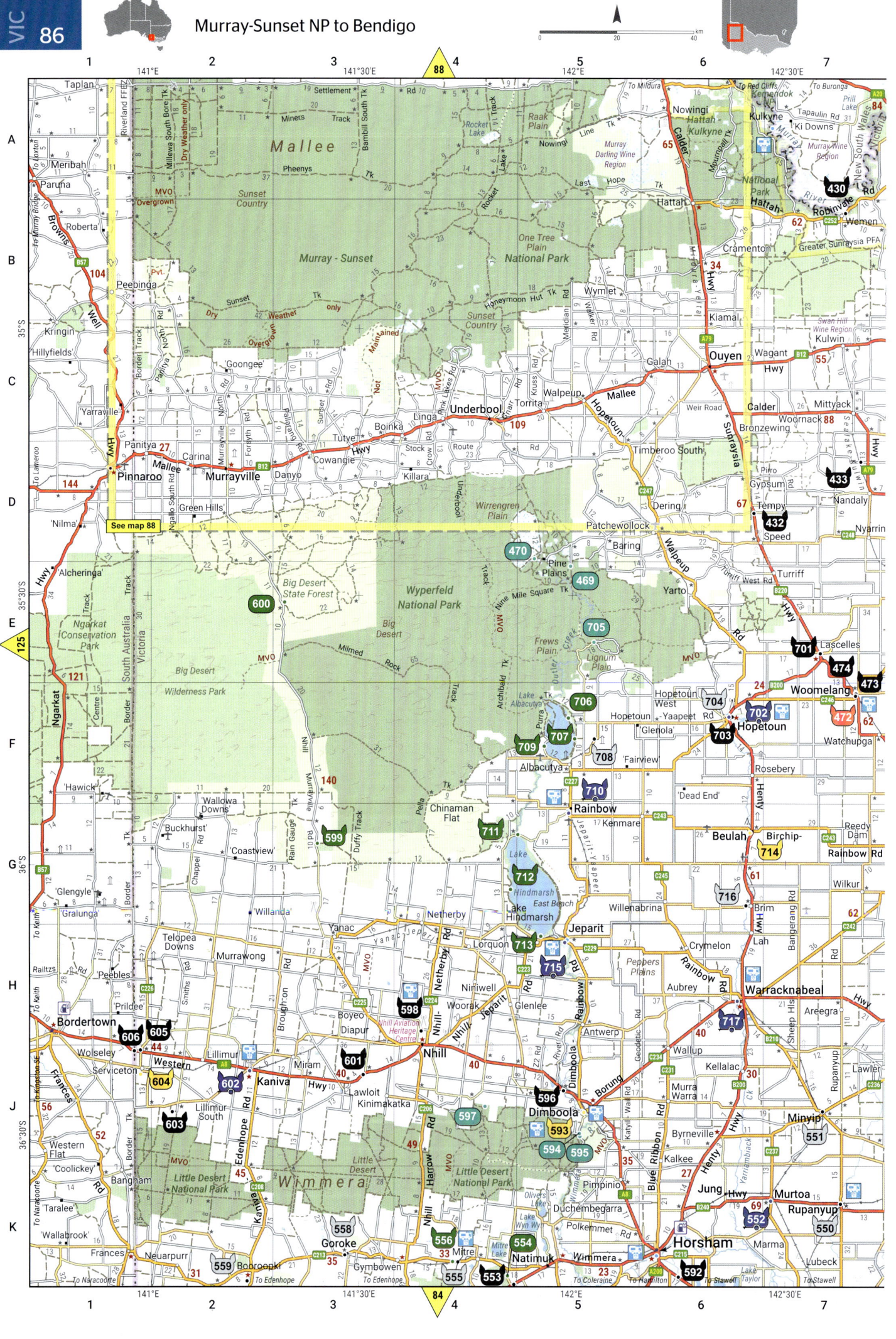

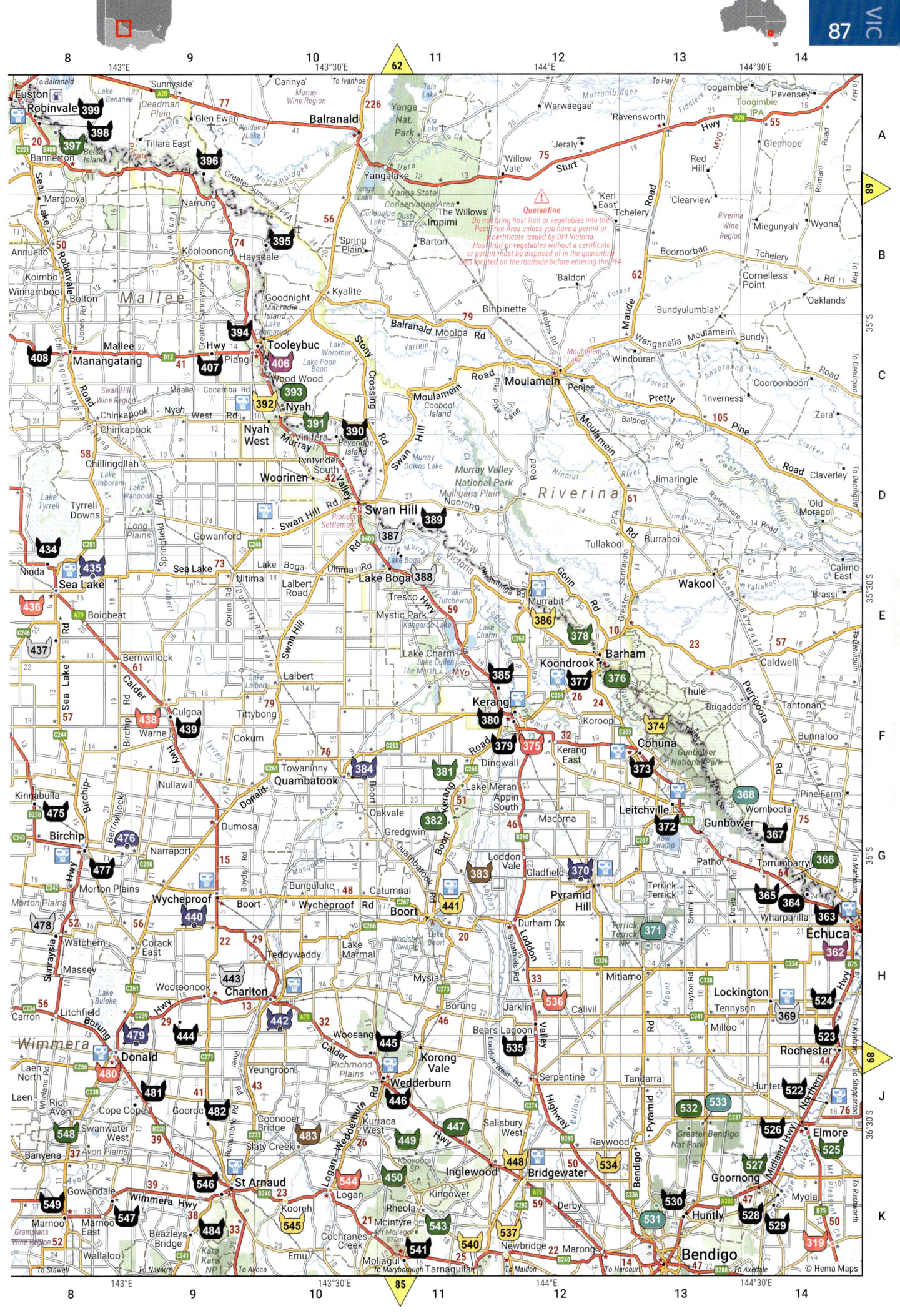

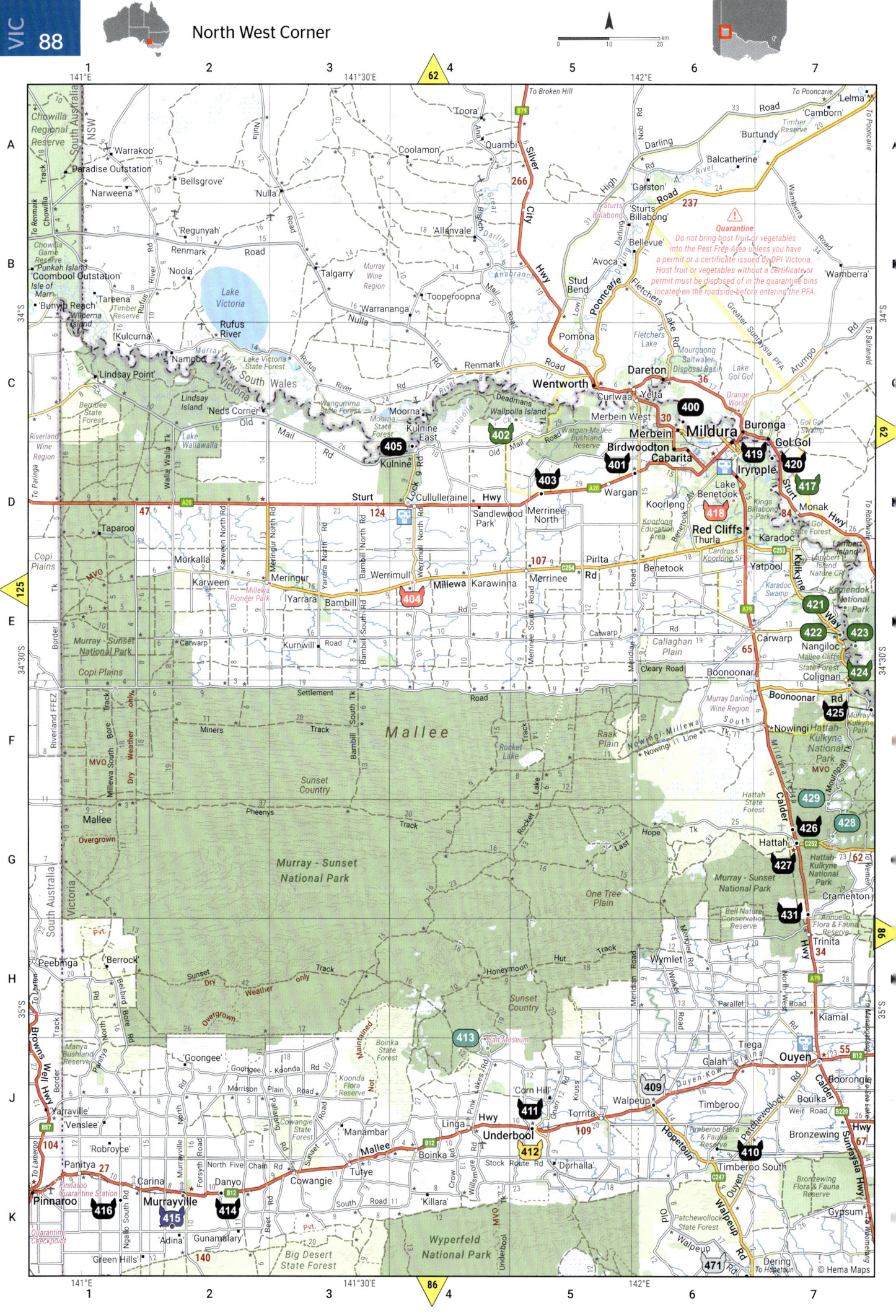

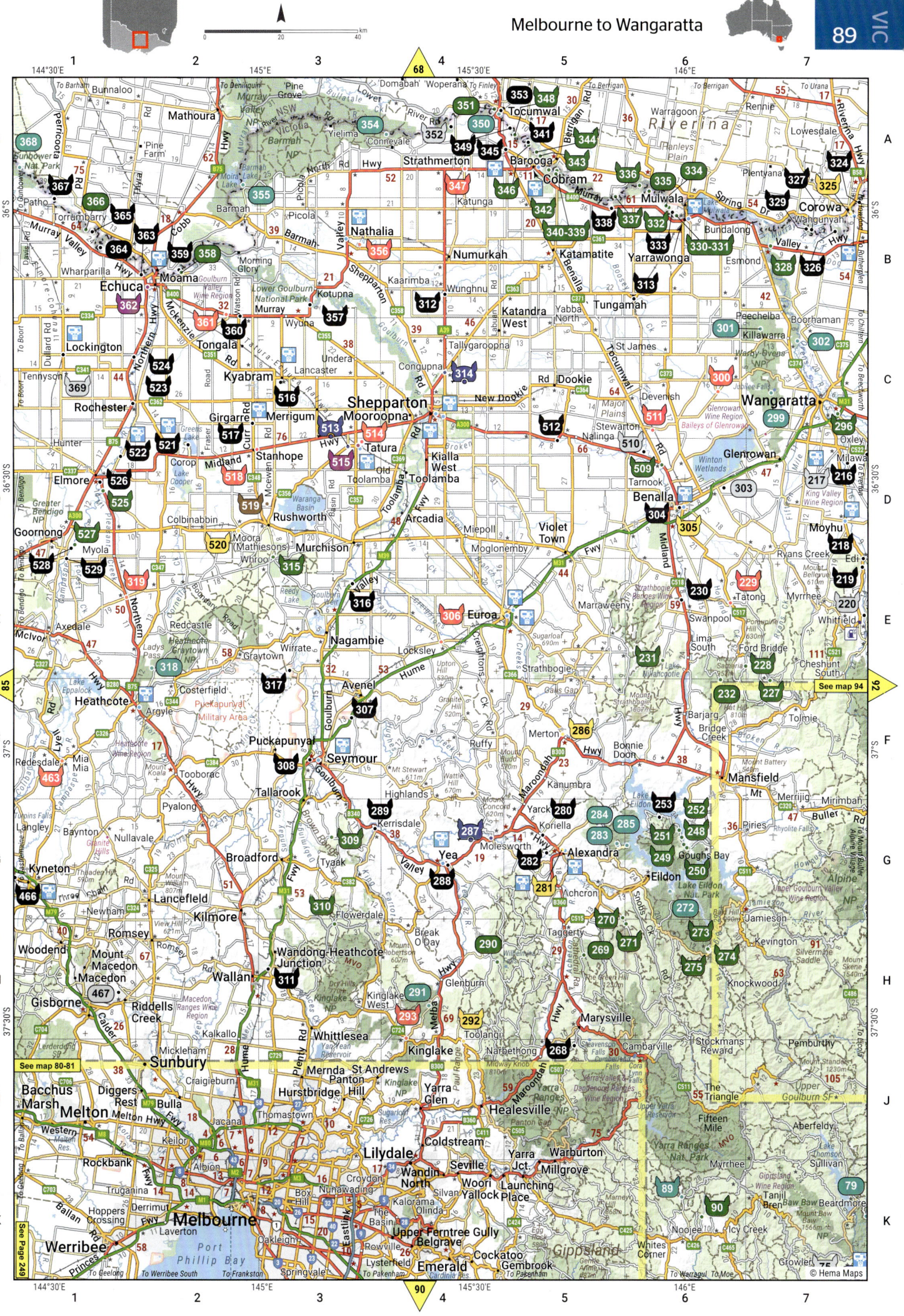

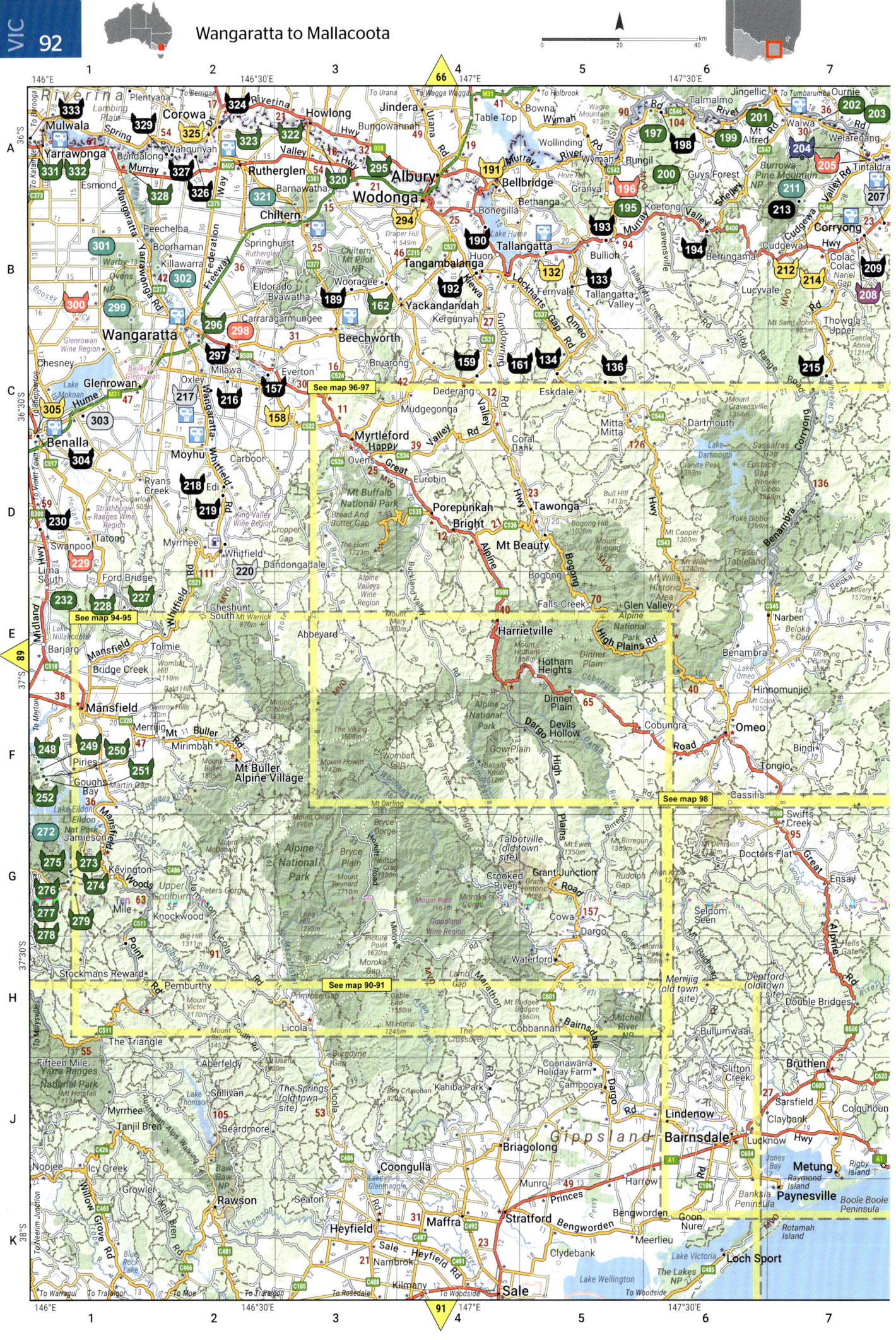

Mansfield to Dargo

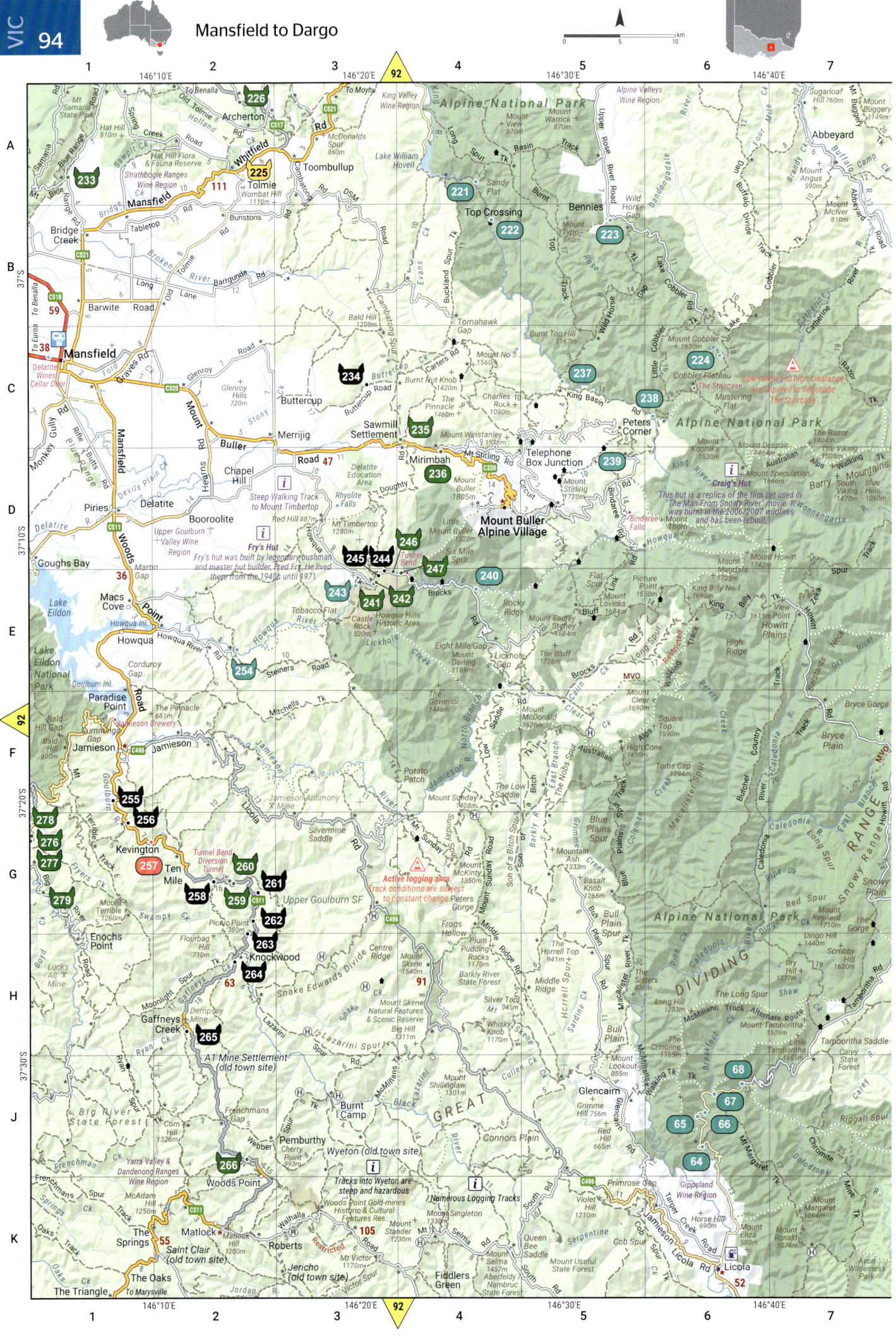

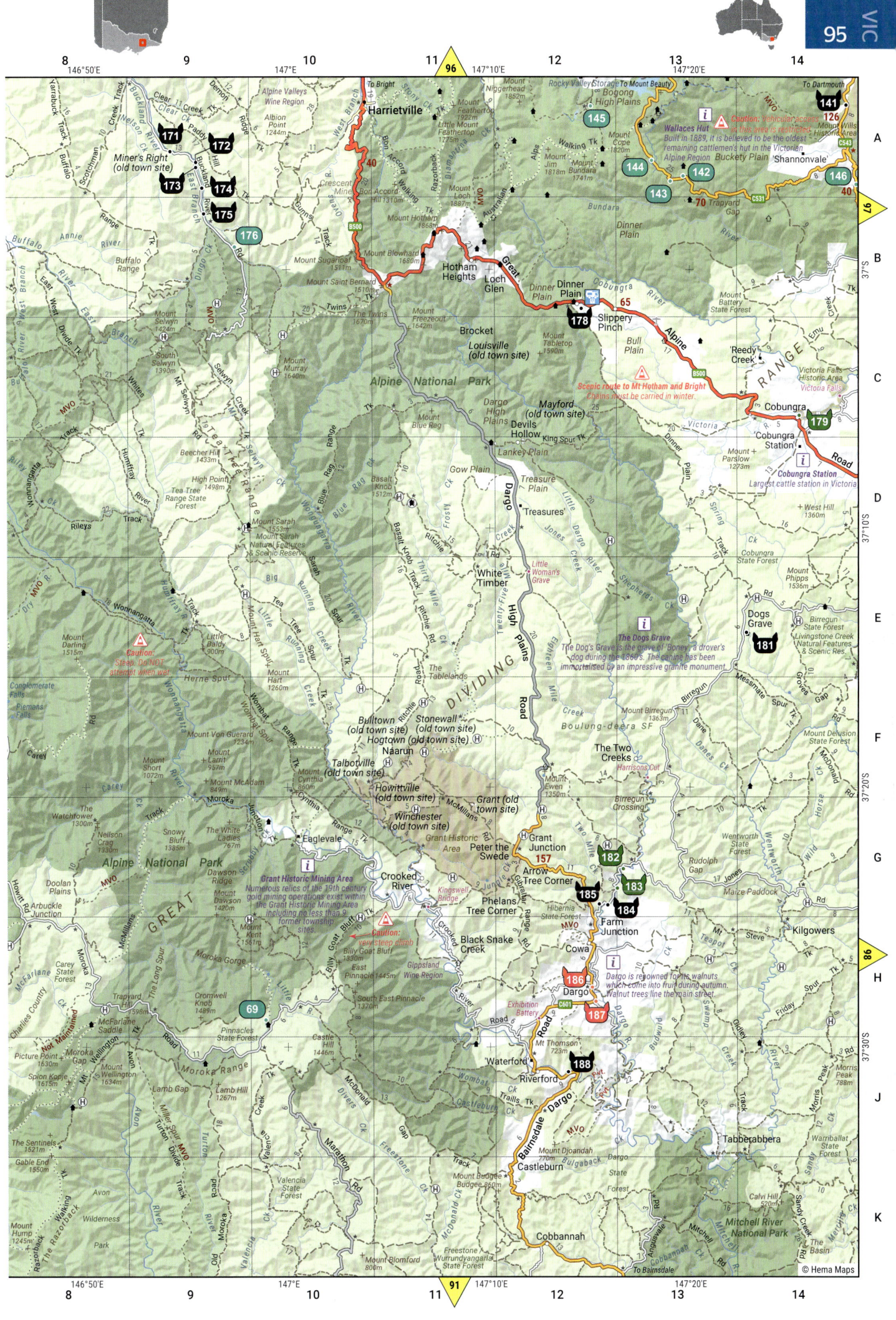

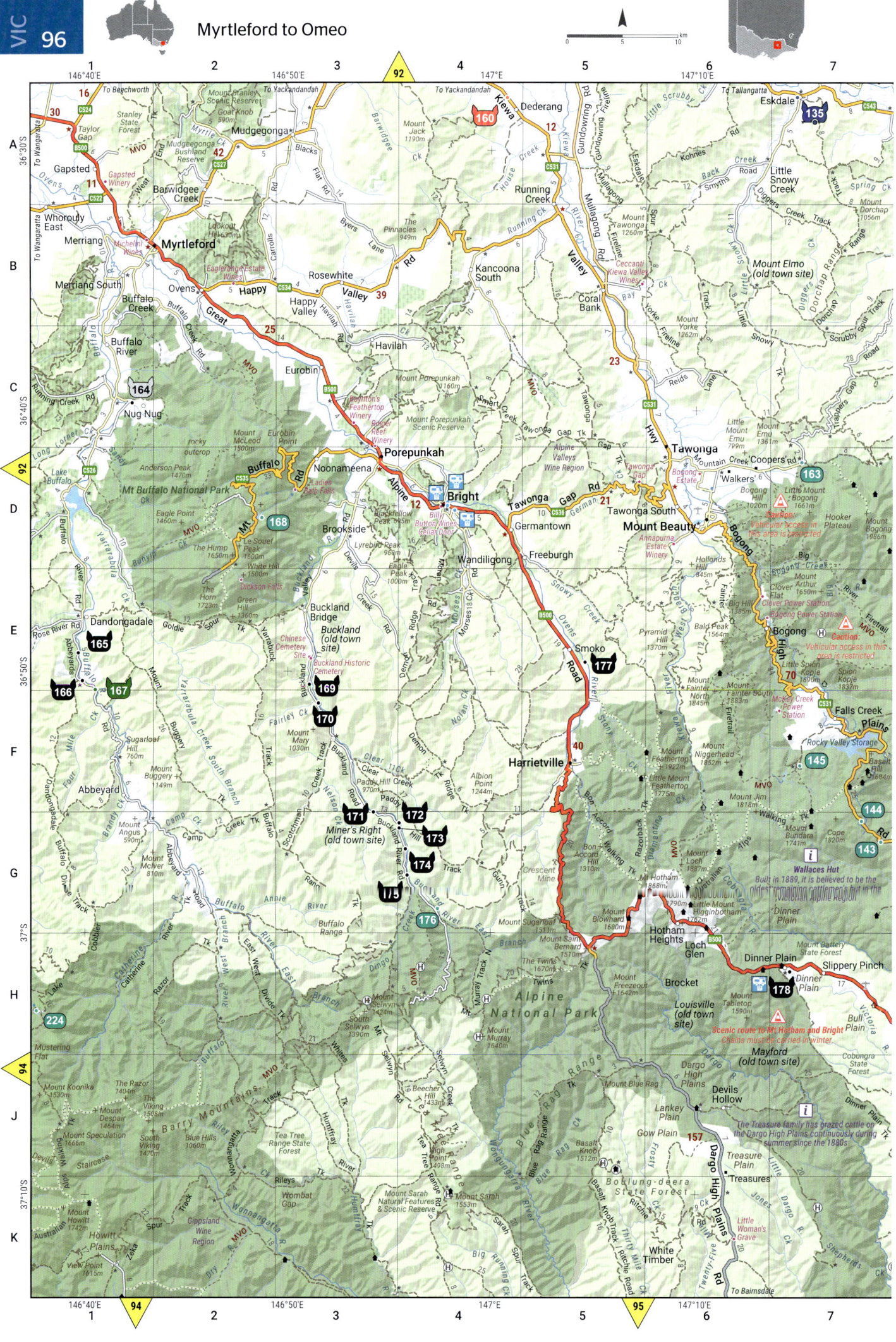

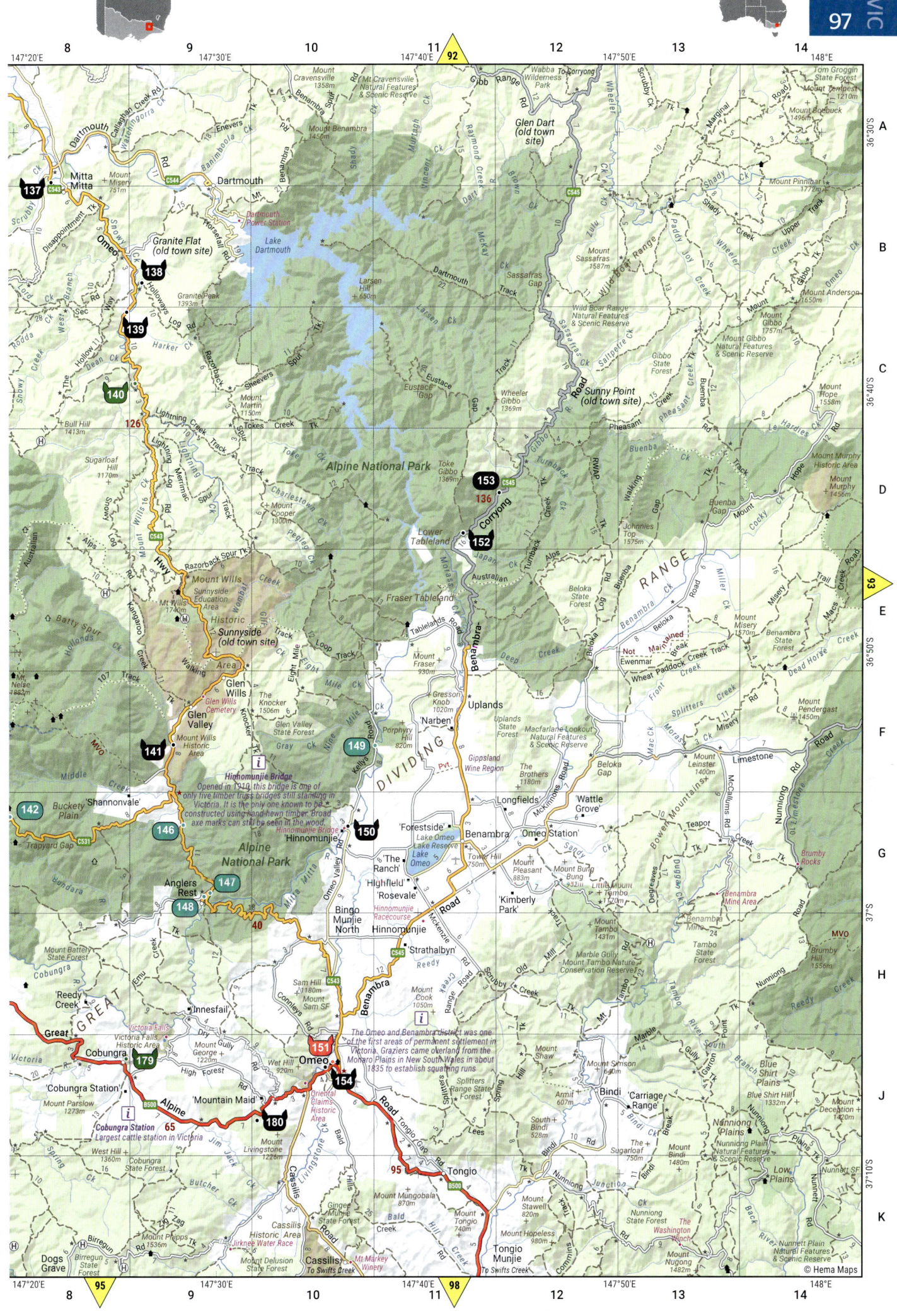

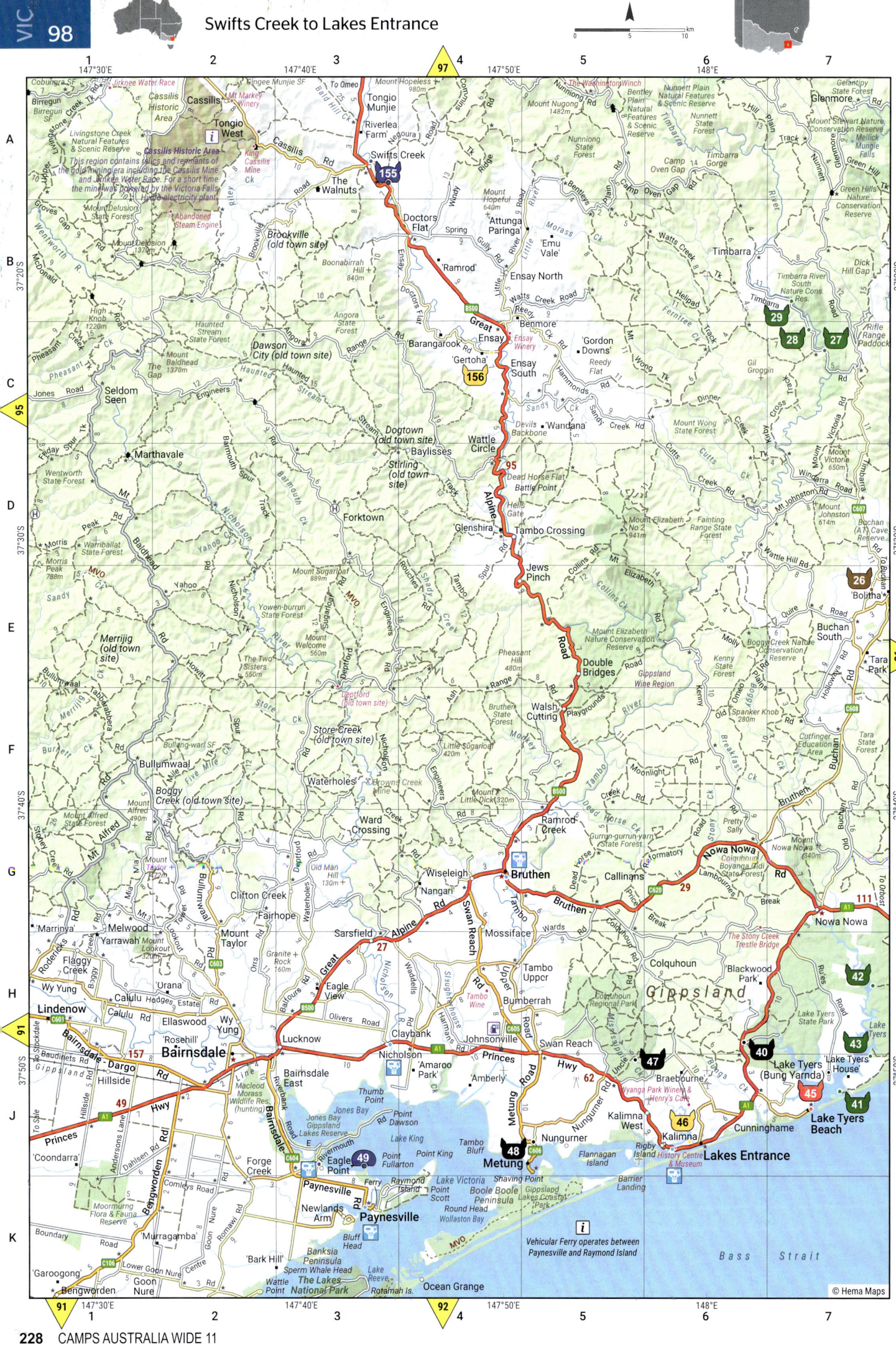

Murray River, Victoria by Annette Hobbs

Victoria

VICTORIA

1 Wallagaraugh River Retreat
73 Peisleys Rd, Genoa
Camp Area 17 km S of Timbillica. Turn E just N of bridge, 9 km S of Timbillica or 9 km N of Genoa. 8 km dirt road. Generator power
03 5158 8211   HEMA 93 G13   37 27 09 S   149 41 29 E

2 Genoa Camping Reserve
4 Park Rd, Genoa
Camp Area 1 km N of Genoa before bridge. Park inside fence
03 5153 9500   HEMA 93 H13   37 28 19 S   149 35 29 E

3 Shipwreck Creek
Croajingolong National Park
Betka Rd, Mallacoota
Camp Area 13 km S of Mallacoota on Betka Rd. Changeable road conditions. 21 day limit
131 963   HEMA 93 H13   37 38 45 S   149 42 02 E

4 Drummer Rainforest
Via Princes Highway, Cann River
Picnic Area on Thurra River. 36 km W of Genoa or 11 km E of Cann River. 200 m off Hwy
136186   HEMA 93 H12   37 34 08 S   149 16 20 E

5 Cann River Rainforest
Tourist Park
7536 Princes Hwy, Cann River
Caravan Park on W entry to town, before river. Council run
03 5153 9500   HEMA 93 H12   37 33 59 S   149 08 46 E

6 Thurra River Campground
Croajingolong National Park
Bald Hill Track, Tamboon
Camp Area 42 km S of Cann River. At the Thurra River mouth, near Point Hicks. Dirt road. Not suitable for caravans. 21 day limit
131 963   HEMA 93 J12   37 46 38 S   149 19 25 E

7 Peachtree Creek
Croajingolong National Park
Fishermans Tr, Tamboon Inlet
Area 27 km S of Cann River. Turn S to Tamboon Rd for 21 km, veer R to Fishermans Tr. 6 km to sites. Dirt road. Small vehicles only. 21 day limit
131 963   HEMA 93 J12   37 44 33 S   149 08 12 E

8 Ada River Campground
Errinundra Valley Rd, Club Terrace
Camp Area 22 km N of Club Terrace. Turn NW off the Club Terrace-Combienbar Rd 11 km N of Club Terrace to Errinundra Valley Rd. 12 km dirt road. Riverside
136186   HEMA 93 G11   37 24 15 S   148 53 33 E

9 Goongerah Campground
Yalmy State Forest
Ellery Ck Rd, Goongerah
Camp Area 25 km S of Bonang or 68 km N of Orbost. Signposted off Bonang Hwy
HEMA 93 G10   37 20 34 S   148 42 02 E

10 Delegate River Camp
Errinundra National Park
1017-1032 Bendoc-Orbost Rd, Bendoc
Camp Area 9 km SW of Bendoc. 21 day limit
131 963   HEMA 93 F10   37 11 48 S   148 49 41 E

11 McKillops Bridge
Snowy River National Park
McKillops Rd, Wulgulmerang
Camp Area 30 km E of Wulgulmerang or 53 km W of Bonang. Tight winding road not suitable for caravans. 21 day limit
131 963   HEMA 93 F9   37 05 25 S   148 24 42 E

12 Bemm River Caravan Park
2-18 Sydenham Inlet Rd, Bemm River
Caravan Park E of PO
03 5158 4216   HEMA 93 J11   37 45 31 S   148 57 56 E

13 Bellbird Hotel
3872 Princes Hwy, Bellbird Creek
Rest Area 38 km W of Cann River or 38 km E of Orbost. Toilets at hotel with permission. Fee for shower. See the publican on arrival
03 5158 1239   HEMA 93 H10   37 39 08 S   148 49 04 E

14 Banksia Bluff Campground
Cape Conran Coastal Park
Yeerung River Rd, Cape Conran
Camp Area 19 km E of Marlo, via Marlo Rd. 1.5 km dirt road. Cold showers. Cabins closed due to bushfire damage
03 5154 8438   HEMA 93 J10   37 47 33 S   148 44 53 E

15 Murrungowar Rest Area
Via Princes Hwy, Orbost
Rest Area 18 km W of Bellbird or 20 km E of Orbost
133 778   HEMA 93 J10   37 41 22 S   148 37 06 E

16 Orbost Caravan Park
2-6 Lochiel St, Orbost
Caravan Park 450 m S of PO
03 5154 1097   HEMA 93 J9   37 42 38 S   148 27 14 E

17 Orbost Club Hotel
63 Nicholson St, Orbost
Parking Area behind pub. Register at bar on arrival. Fee for showers. Entry via McLeod St or Clarke St. Patrons only
03 5154 1003   HEMA 93 J9   37 42 26 S   148 27 16 E

18 Woods Point Camping Area
Via Wood Point Track, Orbost
Camp Area 23 km NW of Orbost. Take McLeod St / "B" road, along river to Garnets Track, follow signs, 4 km to campsite. Small off road caravans only. Riverside
136 186   HEMA 93 H9   37 38 30 S   148 19 13 E

19 Snowy River Rest Area 6
Via Marlo Rd, Orbost
Rest Area 7 km S of Orbost or 8 km N of Marlo. Riverside
HEMA 93 J9   37 44 11 S   148 30 16 E

20 Snowy River Rest Area 1
Marlo Rd, Orbost
Rest Areas 7 km S of Orbost or 8 km N of Marlo. 6 riverside camps, each GPS & details in the Camps Australia Wide App
HEMA 93 J9   37 44 24 S   148 30 26 E

21 Corringle Slips Campground

Corringle Foreshore Reserve
1017 Corringle Rd, Marlo
Camp Area 18 km S of Newmerella. Dirt road
131963   HEMA 93 J9   37 48 00 S   148 31 21 E

22 Snowy Riverside

764 Lochend Rd, Newmerella
Camp Area 10.5 km SE of Orbost, S side of river

HEMA 93 J9   37 45 08 S   148 31 08 E

23 Mantos Landing

722-764 Lochend Rd, Newmerella
Camp Area 10 km SE of Orbost, S of river
HEMA 93 J9   37 44 57 S   148 30 58 E

24 Hospital Creek Rest Area

3026 Princes Hwy, Tostaree
Rest Area E of Tostaree
HEMA 93 J8   37 45 07 S   148 11 21 E

25 Tostaree Cottages

Lot 34D3 Jonsons Rd, Tostaree
Farm Stay N of Hwy. Check in with office before parking
0408 031 668   HEMA 93 J8   37 44 51 S   148 11 03 E

26 Stonehenge Farmstay

163 Buchan South Gillingal Rd, Buchan
Camp Area W of Buchan. 9 km N of Nowa
Nowa turn N onto Buchan Caves Rd, 15 km to
Buchan South Rd, then onto Buchan South Gillingall
Rd. Signposted
0417 727 389   HEMA 98 E7   37 31 51 S   148 08 08 E

27 Timbarra Bridge

Timbarra Rd, Buchan
Camp Area 28 km NW of Buchan. Turn
onto Timbarra Rd 4 km S of Buchan for 24 km.
Riverside just S of bridge. 4 km dirt road. Off road
caravans only
HEMA 98 C7   37 22 49 S   148 05 48 E

28 Timbarra Central

Via Timbarra Rd, Buchan
Camp Area 30 km NW of Buchan. Turn to
Timbarra Rd 4 km S of Buchan for 26 km. Riverside.
7 km dirt road. GPS at entrance, follow track to site
HEMA 98 C7   37 22 02 S   148 05 01 E

29 Timbarra North

Via Timbarra Rd, Buchan
Camp Area 32 km NW of Buchan. Turn to
Timbarra Rd 4 km S of Buchan for 28 km. Riverside.
9 km dirt road. Suitable for off road caravans,
access track narrow in parts
HEMA 98 B7   37 20 57 S   148 04 10 E

30 Buchan Caves Camping

Snowy River National Park
Buchan Caves Rd, Buchan
Camp Area & Reserve W of Buchan. 21 day limit
131 963   HEMA 93 H8   37 29 43 S   148 09 50 E

31 Jacksons Crossing Camp

Snowy River National Park
Gelantipy Rd & Running Ck Tr, Buchan
Camp Area 45 km NE of Buchan
03 5162 1904   HEMA 93 G9   37 23 38 S   148 20 07 E

32 Balley Hooley

Snowy River National Park
Balley Hooley Rd, Buchan
Camp Area 18 km E of Buchan. Via Buchan-Orbost
Rd. Steep & windy in places, not suitable for
caravans. 21 day limit
131 963   HEMA 93 H8   37 31 03 S   148 15 48 E

33 Raymond Creek Falls

Snowy River National Park
Via Moorsford Rd., Yalmy
Camp Area 40 km N of Orbost via B Rd & Garnets
Track in Yalmy. 21 day limit
131 963   HEMA 93 H9   37 29 05 S   148 18 28 E

34 Hicks Campground

Snowy River National Park
Via Varney's Track, Yalmy
Camp Area 42 km N of Orbost via Yalmy Rd. Veer L
to Varney's Track. 21 day limit
131 963   HEMA 93 G9   37 24 37 S   148 21 39 E

35 Little River Falls

Snowy River National Park
McKillops Rd, Wulgulmerang
Camp Area 65 km N of Buchan via Gelantipy Rd.
Veer R at Wulgulmery East, site on L. 21 day limit
131 963   HEMA 93 F9   37 03 40 S   148 18 35 E

36 Wulgulmerang Rec Reserve

Snowy River Rd, Wulgulmerang
C608   Camp Area 133 km NE of Bairnsdale or
112 km SW of Jindabyne
03 5155 0253   HEMA 93 F8   37 04 06 S   148 15 37 E

37 Suggan Buggan Camp

Via Snowy River Rd, Wulgulmerang
Camp Area 80 km N of Buchan or 87 km
S of Jindabyne. Tight winding road in places, not
suitable for caravans. 21 day limit
HEMA 93 E9   36 57 09 S   148 19 27 E

38 Willis Campground

Via Snowy River Rd, Wulgulmerang
Camp Area 99 km N of Buchan or 68 km
S of Jindabyne. Tight winding road in places, not
suitable for caravans
HEMA 93 E9   36 53 41 S   148 25 22 E

39 Running Waters Creek

Kosciuszko National Park
Barry Way, Wulgulmerang
Camp Area 102 km N of Buchan or 65 km S of
Jindabyne. Tight winding road in places, not suitable
for caravans
HEMA 93 E9   36 48 47 S   148 24 16 E

40 Burnt Bridge Reserve

Via Princes Hwy, Nowa Nowa
A1   Rest Area 12 km E of Lakes Entrance or
10 km W of Nowa Nowa
HEMA 98 H6   37 48 56 S   148 01 50 E

41 The Glasshouse Camp Area

Lake Tyers State Park
11 Lake Tyers House Rd, Lake Tyers
Camp Area 22 km SE of Nowa Nowa. Turn S 6 km E
of Nowa Nowa or 32 km W of Orbost, follow to end.
16 km dirt road. 21 day limit
131 963   HEMA 98 J7   37 50 47 S   148 06 33 E

42 Camerons Arm No 1

Lake Tyers State Park
Camerons Arm No 1 Tr, Lake Tyers
Camp Area 16 km SE of Nowa Nowa. Turn S 6 km
E of Nowa Nowa or 32 km W of Orbost via Tyers
House Rd
131 963   HEMA 98 H7   37 46 48 S   148 08 12 E

43 Trident Arm Campground

Lake Tyers State Park
Trident Arm Track, Lake Tyers
Camp Area 18 km SE of Nowa Nowa. Turn S 6 km E
of Nowa Nowa or 32 km W of Orbost to Tyers House &
Lake Tyers Beach Rds. 14 km dirt road. Limited space
131 963   HEMA 98 J7   37 49 27 S   148 08 05 E

44 Pettmans Beach

Lake Tyers State Park
Pettmans Rd, Pettmans Beach
Camp Area W of Orbost. Turn S 6 km E of Nowa
Nowa or 32 km W of Orbost. Via Tyers House Rd,
site at end of 12 km dirt road
131 963   HEMA 93 J8   37 49 44 S   148 11 08 E

45 Waterwheel Beach Tavern

577 Lake Tyers Beach Rd, Lake Tyers Beach
Parking Area on L at end of road. Check
in at bar for parking instructions. First 2 nights free.
Limited caravan sites, narrow
03 5156 5855   HEMA 98 J7   37 51 26 S   148 05 08 E

46 Lakes Entrance Rec Reserve

1 Rowe S, Lakes Entrance
Camp Area on the waterfront
03 5155 1647   HEMA 98 J6   37 52 40 S   147 59 09 E

47 Log Crossing

Log Crossing Rd, Kalimna West
Camp Area N of Kalimna, turn N off Hwy to
Uncle Rd, then E
   HEMA 92 J5   37 49 36 S   147 56 29 E

---

48 Chinamans Creek

402-404 Rosherville Rd, Metung
Parking Area N of town. Small area
   HEMA 98 J5   37 52 41 S   147 51 28 E

49 Eagle Point Caravan Park

40 School Rd, Eagle Point
Caravan Park opposite school
03 5156 1183   HEMA 98 J3   37 53 32 S   147 40 53 E

50 Providence Ponds

3502 Princes Hwy, Stratford
Rest Area at Flora & Fauna Reserve. 34 km
W of Bairnsdale or 18 km E of Stratford
   HEMA 91 C13   37 55 14 S   147 16 16 E

51 Avon River Streamside

Reserve
Avon Turton, Perry Bridge
Camp Spot 4 km S of Perry Bridge. Via Springberg
Ln. 3 km dirt road
131 963   HEMA 91 C13   38 01 49 S   147 14 54 E

52 Marlay Point

696 Marlay Point Rd, Marlay Point
Camp Area on Foreshore Reserve. Turn E
off Hwy to Clydebank Rd 8 km S of Stratford or 9 km
N of Sale. Signposted
   HEMA 91 D13   38 03 40 S   147 14 58 E

53 Sale Showground

2 Sale-Maffra Rd, Sale
Caravan Park N end of town
03 5144 6432   HEMA 91 D12   38 05 31 S   147 03 58 E

54 Maffra Golf Club

13 Fulton Rd, Maffra
Camp Area behind clubrooms. Via Stratford Rd
03 5147 1884   HEMA 91 C11   37 57 04 S   147 00 01 E

---

55 Maffra RV Park

187 Johnson St, Maffra
Parking Area Cnr of Johnson St
   HEMA 91 C11   37 58 11 S   146 58 50 E

56 Newry RV Rest Area

838 Three Chain Rd, Newry
Parking Area at Rec Reserve, next to golf
course. 2 km N of Newry via Newry-Boisdale Rd
   HEMA 91 C11   37 54 20 S   146 54 28 E

57 Farmers Arms Tavern

61 Main St, Newry
Parking Area behind hotel. Register at bar.
Patrons only
03 5145 1312   HEMA 91 C11   37 55 20 S   146 53 27 E

58 Willow Park Farm Stay

Heyfield-Upper Maffra Rd, Tinamba
Farm Stay 16 km W of Maffra. Via
Traralgon-Maffra Rd travel W 13 km turn R & follow
Tinamba-Newry & Tinamba-Glenmaggie Rd, turn R,
on R. Pre-book
0428 506 731   HEMA 91 C11   37 55 48 S   146 51 04 E

59 Briagolong Quarry Reserve

365 Freestone Creek Rd, Briagolong
Camp Area 4 km N of Briagolong. Pay at
Briagolong cafe or hotel. Riverside
0439158982   HEMA 91 B12   37 48 50 S   147 05 19 E

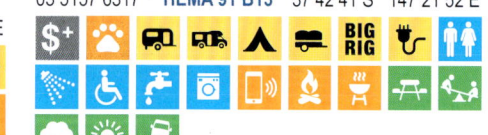

60 Echo Bend Bark Hut

1555 Dunbars Rd, Glenaladale
Camp Area 12 km NE of Glenaladale. Via
Bairnsdale-Dargo Rd, Wallers Rd
03 5157 6317   HEMA 91 B13   37 42 41 S   147 21 52 E

61 Heyfield RV Park

Cnr MacFarlane & Clark Sts, Heyfield
Rest Area 700 m SE of Heyfield PO, S area
of reserve
0418 108 691   HEMA 91 C10   37 59 06 S   146 47 15 E

62 Paradise Valley Camp Park

51 Gells Rd, Glenmaggie
Camping Area 16 km N of Glenmaggie.
Pre-book
03 5148 0291   HEMA 91 B10   37 50 24 S   146 42 31 E

63 Cheynes Bridge

Via Licola Rd, Glenmaggie
Camp Area 20 km S of Licola or 32 km N of
Heyfield, beside Macalister R
HEMA 91 B10   37 45 50 S   146 40 07 E

64 Currawong Camp

Alpine National Park
Via Tamboritha Rd, Licola
Camp Area 11 km N of Licola. Beside Wellington R.
21 day limit
131 963   HEMA 94 J6   37 33 07 S   146 36 44 E

65 Manna Gum Licola

Alpine National Park
Tamboritha Rd, Licola
Camp Area 16 km N of Licola. Beside Wellington R.
21 day limit
131 963   HEMA 94 J6   37 31 58 S   146 36 30 E

66 Muttonwood Camp

Alpine National Park
Via Tamboritha Rd, Licola
Camp Area 16.5 km N of Licola. Beside Wellington
R. 21 day limit
131 963   HEMA 94 J6   37 31 49 S   146 36 52 E

67 Red Box Camp

Alpine National Park
Via Tamboritha Rd, Licola
Camp Area 20 km N of Licola. Beside Wellington R.
21 day limit
131 963   HEMA 94 J6   37 31 07 S   146 37 19 E

68 Platypus Camp

Alpine National Park
Via Tamboritha Rd, Licola
Camp Area 22 km N of Licola. Beside Wellington R.
21 day limit
131 963   HEMA 94 J6   37 30 43 S   146 38 40 E

69 Horseyard Flat

Alpine National Park
Cromwell Knob Tr, Licola
Dispersed Camping 70 km E of Licola. Via
Tamboritha Rd, Moroka Rd to 300 m rough gravel
road. Small vehicles only. 21 day limit
131 963   HEMA 95 H10   37 28 59 S   146 58 53 E

70 Nambrok Hall

173 Nambrok Hall Rd, Nambrok
Camp Area 13 km NE of Rosedale. N off
Hwy to Nambrok Rd
0429 422 207   HEMA 91 D11   38 04 13 S   146 51 12 E

71 Willow RV Park

Princes Hwy, Rosedale
Camp Spot 1 km N of Rosedale. Beside La
Trobe River
HEMA 91 D10   38 08 31 S   146 47 28 E

72 Harriers Swamp

Holey Plains State Park
Rosedale
Camp Area 10 km SE of Rosedale. Turn E 3.5 km S
of Rosedale off Willung Rd to Rosedale-Stradbroke
Rd 7 km, then S, 2 km of dirt road. 21 day limit
131 963   HEMA 91 E11   38 12 31 S   146 50 45 E

73 Holey Hill Campground

Holey Plains State Park
Holey Hill Track, Longford
Camp Area 19 km SE from Rosedale on Rosedale-
Stradbroke Rd, then E
HEMA 91 E11   38 13 54 S   146 56 19 E

74 Seninis Campground

Moondarra State Park
Via Seninis Track, Moondarra
Camp Area 26 km NE of Moe. Turn W off C466
25 km NE of Moe or 6 km S of Erica. Over 1 km
dirt road, steep in parts. Small vehicles only, limited
caravan sites
131 963   HEMA 91 C8   38 01 24 S   146 20 24 E

75 Caringal Scout Camp

Via Telbit Rd, Erica
Camp Area 9 km W of Erica. Turn W off
C466 29 km NE of Moe or 2 km S of Erica to Telbit
Rd. 7 km dirt road. Beside Tyers River. Limited
power. Pre-book
03 5165 3210   HEMA 91 C8   37 57 36 S   146 20 02 E

76 Mountain Rivers Tourist Park

11 Depot Rd, Rawson
Caravan Park N side of town. Vans no
larger than 6 metres
03 5165 3231   HEMA 91 C9   37 57 10 S   146 23 55 E

77 Walhalla North Gardens

Via Black Diamond Track, Walhalla
Camp Area 1 km N of PO. Other campsites
& Big Rigs at S entrance to town
131 963   HEMA 91 C9   37 55 57 S   146 26 55 E

78 Chinese Gardens Camping

288 Main Rd, Walhalla
Camp Area 1 km N of Walhalla, via
Walhalla Rd. Permit required, pay & key at store
03 5165 6250   HEMA 91 C9   37 55 50 S   146 26 58 E

79 Aberfeldy River

Baw Baw National Park
Via Walhalla-Aberfeldy Rd, Walhalla
Camp Area 17 km N of Walhalla. Signposted off
Walhalla-Aberfeldy Rd. Not suitable for caravans,
narrow windy road. 21 day limit
131 963   HEMA 91 B9   37 51 13 S   146 25 52 E

80 Coopers Creek

Via Coopers Ck Rd, Rawson
Camp Area 9 km SE of Rawson or 9 km
SW of Walhalla. Turn S off C461, 5 km from Tyers-
Walhalla Rd Jcn or 7 km S of Walhalla. Signposted.
2 camp areas
136 186   HEMA 91 C9   37 58 52 S   146 25 29 E

81 Boolarra Community Hotel
2760 Monash Way, Boolarra
Camp Area beside pub and parklands.
Check in with publican. Booking fee returned as
credit in bar & bistro
03 5169 6420   HEMA 91 F8   38 22 48 S   146 16 36 E

82 Jack Richards Park
2684 Monash Way, Boolarra
Rest Area S off Hwy
HEMA 91 F8   38 23 03 S   146 16 55 E

83 Boolarra Apex Park
Via Morwell River Rd, Boolarra
Camp Area 8.5 km SE of Boolarra, via
Morwell River Rd. Turn W at Boolarra South sign,
after 30 m S into Morwell River Rd follow for 7.5 km.
Grassed area on R side of road
HEMA 91 F8   38 25 45 S   146 18 32 E

84 Primrose Park
240 Morwell River Rd, Boolarra
Camp Spot 2 km SE of Boolarra. Turn W at
Boolarra S sign, 1 km to entry
HEMA 91 F8   38 23 50 S   146 16 55 E

85 Cafe Escargot
10 Old Nichols Rd, Mirboo North
Parking Area SE of town via Grand Ridge
East Rd, free overnight parking with a purchase
03 5668 1589   HEMA 91 F8   38 25 05 S   146 10 17 E

86 The Darnum Hotel
1 Princes Hwy, Darnum
Parking Area near pub. Amenities available
in open hours. Pre-book. Check in with publican on
arrival
03 5627 8133   HEMA 90 D7   38 11 16 S   146 00 18 E

87 Gippsland Food & Wine
123 Princes Hwy, Yarragon
Parking Area behind Visitor Centre. Open
after 5pm. Pre-book
03 5634 2451   HEMA 90 E7   38 12 12 S   146 03 43 E

88 Neerim South Caravan Park
410 Neerim East Rd, Neerim South
Caravan Park 4 km E of Neerim South
03 5628 1248   HEMA 90 C7   38 00 46 S   145 59 25 E

89 Poplars Reserve
Great Forest National Park
670 Loch Valley Rd, Lock Valley
Camp Area 9 km N of Noojee via narrow road.
Riverside. Steep access
03 5624 8100   HEMA 90 B7   37 49 08 S   145 59 38 E

90 Noojee Toorongo Falls
Toorongo Falls Reserve
640 Toorongo Valley Rd, Noojee
Camp Area 9 km NE of Noojee. N off Mt Baw Baw
Rd 4 km E of Noojee. 5 km bitumen road. After third
bridge, site 1 is on R. Unlevel & riverside
131 963   HEMA 90 B7   37 51 19 S   146 02 28 E

91 Latrobe River Camping Area
Via Yarra Junction-Noojee Rd, Noojee
Camp Area 15 km W of Noojee. Turn N
off C425, 11 km W of C425/C426 Jcn or 14 km
E of Powelltown to Ada River Rd. Entry track is
350 m from Hwy on the L. Small vehicles only,
limited turning space
136 186   HEMA 90 C6   37 53 02 S   145 53 30 E

92 Nash Creek Campground
Bunyip State Park
Black Snake Ck Rd, Gembrook
Camp Area in 65 km E of Melbourne. From
Gembrook via Beenak East Rd. 1.4 km E of Dyers
Picnic Area. Small vehicles only
131 963   HEMA 90 C5   37 56 48 S   145 41 15 E

93 Longwarry North Rest Area
Via Princes Hwy, Robin Hood
Rest Area on Princes Hwy 2 km W of Robin
Hood turn off. W bound traffic only
HEMA 90 D6   38 05 26 S   145 48 25 E

94 Bunyip Reserve
80 Nar Nar Goon Rd-Longwarry Rd,
Bunyip
Camp Area in Bunyip, 3 km W of Longwarry. Call
ahead to book or pay at Top Pub. Sites at grassy
area, before the oval
0408 558 307   HEMA 90 D5   38 05 59 S   145 43 08 E

95 South Pakenham
Community Hall
Cnr Hall Rd & McDonald Drain Rd W,
South Pakenham
Parking Area N side of town. Pre-book. Fees collected
0429 326 272   HEMA 90 D4   38 07 52 S   145 30 29 E

96 Akoonah Park Showground
via Cardinia St, Berwick
Camp Area 2.5 km SE of Berwick on Hwy,
entry via Cardinia St, Gate 5. Pre-book. 21 day limit
0427 057 768   HEMA 79 F12   38 02 20 S   145 21 51 E
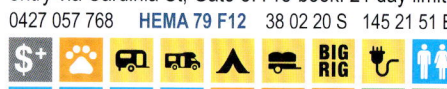
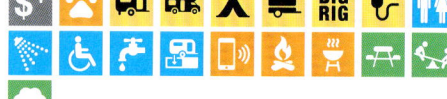

97 Wantirna Park Caravan Park
203 Mountain Hwy, Wantirna
Caravan Park on main street, W of town
03 9887 1157   HEMA 77 J14   37 51 04 S   145 13 18 E

Sale - Leongatha - Dandenong
South Gippsland Highway

98 Golden Beach RV Rest Stop
1/19 Surf Edge Dr, Golden Beach
Camp Area opposite beach. Crn Shoreline Dr
HEMA 91 E13   38 12 40 S   147 23 56 E

99 Paradise Beach Camp
via Shoreline Dr, Golden Beach
Camp Area 2.5 km N of Golden Beach, via
Shoreline Dr. Pre-book
131 963   HEMA 91 D13   38 11 39 S   147 25 20 E

100 Spoon Bay Campground
Gippsland Lakes Coastal Park
Lakeside Track, Loch Sport
Camp Area W of Loch Sport. Turn N off Longford-Loch Sport Rd 12 km W of Lock Sport to Spoon Bay Tr. Follow to T Jcn, turn L, 300 m. Signposted
131 963   HEMA 91 D13   38 04 36 S   147 27 42 E

101 Red Bluff Campground
Gippsland Lakes Coastal Park
Via Loch Sport Rd, Loch Sport
Camp Area W of Loch Sport. Turn off Longford-Loch Sport Rd 7 km W onto Beacon Swamp Track, veer R at end to camp area. Signposted
131 963   HEMA 91 D14   38 03 20 S   147 31 28 E

102 Emu Bight Campground
The Lakes National Park
Via Lake Victoria Track, Loch Sport
Camp Area 6 km E of Loch Sport, via Lake Victoria Track. Dirt road. Pre-book. 21 day limit
131 963   HEMA 91 C14   37 59 44 S   147 39 10 E
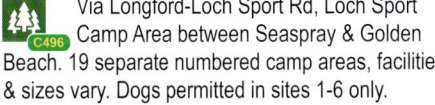

103 Gippsland Lakes Coastal Park
Via Longford-Loch Sport Rd, Loch Sport
Camp Area between Seaspray & Golden Beach. 19 separate numbered camp areas, facilities & sizes vary. Dogs permitted in sites 1-6 only. Showers at Golden Beach
131 963   HEMA 91 E12   38 20 07 S   147 14 36 E

104 McGaurans Beach
Seaspray Coastal Reserve
26 McGaurans Rd, Giffard
Camp Area E off South Gippsland Hwy to Giffard Rd, E to McGaurans Beach Rd
HEMA 91 F12   38 26 51 S   147 06 04 E

105 Reeves Beach
Seaspray Coastal Reserve
Reeves Beach Rd, Woodside
Camp Area 10 km S of Woodside. Via Woodside Beach, Balloong & Reeves Beach Rds
131 963   HEMA 91 G11   38 34 24 S   146 57 08 E

106 White Womans Waterhole
Won Wron State Forest
Napier Rd, Won Wron
Picnic Area 5 km E of Won Wron. 5 km dirt road
03 5183 9100   HEMA 91 F10   38 28 55 S   146 46 19 E

107 Won Wron North Rest Area
Hyland Hwy, Won Wron
Rest Area 2 km N of Won Wron or 25 km S of Gormandale
HEMA 91 F10   38 27 32 S   146 43 47 E
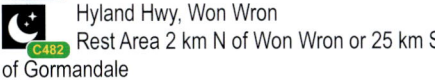

108 Gormandale Rec Reserve
Via Morleys Ln, Gormandale
Camp Spot 20 km SE of Traralgon, off Hyland Hwy
03 5197 7200   HEMA 91 E10   38 17 32 S   146 42 03 E

109 Yarram Tarra River Rest Area
Via South Gippsland Hwy, Yarram
Rest Area 1 km NE of Yarram, N of road
HEMA 91 G10   38 33 02 S   146 40 59 E

110 Port Albert Parking Area
37 Wharf St, Port Albert
Parking Area on foreshore. 6 parks available
HEMA 91 G10   38 40 22 S   146 41 38 E

111 Agnes River Rest Area
Via South Gippsland Hwy, Welshpool
Rest Area 5 km W of Welshpool or 6 km E of Toora
HEMA 91 G9   38 40 18 S   146 23 11 E

112 Dingo Creek
Via Dingo Cr Rd, Wonyip
Camp Area 20 km N of Port Welshpool. Head N off Hwy, via Woorarra Rd
HEMA 91 G8   38 34 34 S   146 22 24 E

113 Minnehaha Falls
1223 Albert River R, Yarram
Camp Area 25 km W of Yarram
HEMA 91 F9   38 31 15 S   146 27 58 E

114 Meeniyan Rec Reserve
15 Hanily St, Meeniyan
Parking Area N of town
HEMA 90 G7   38 34 32 S   146 00 44 E

115 Shallow Inlet Campground
Via Lester Rd, Yanakie
Camp Area 8 km W of Yanakie. Turn W off C444 19 km S of Foster or 4 km N of Yanakie to Lester Rd. Past caravan park. 4 km dirt road. Bush camping adjacent to beach. Open Nov - Apr, pre-book peak periods
03 5687 1365   HEMA 91 H8   38 49 16 S   146 10 18 E

116 Tidal River
Wilsons Promontory National Park
Ring Rd, Tidal River
Camp Area 63 km S of Foster. Via Wilsons Promontory Rd. 21 day limit
131 963   HEMA 91 K8   39 01 48 S   146 19 16 E

117 Fish Creek Hotel
7 Old Waratah Rd, Fish Creek
Parking Area 17 SE of Meeniyan or 13 km SW of Foster. From Meeniyan exit Hwy (A440) S to Meeniyan-Promontory Rd (C444) for 17 km, then S. Toilets available in opening hours. Free for patrons
03 5683 2404   HEMA 90 H7   38 41 41 S   146 04 58 E
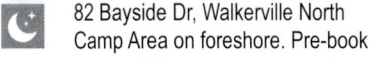

118 Bear Gully Campground
Cape Liptrap Coastal Park
Via Bear Gully Rd, Walkerville
Camp Area 35 km SW of Fish Creek, via Walkerville-Fish Creek Rd. Turn SE at Cape Liptrap turnoff to Walkerville South Rd for 3 km, then S for 5 km to beach. Dirt road. Pre-book. 21 day limit
131 963   HEMA 90 J7   38 53 18 S   145 59 14 E

119 Walkerville Camping Reserve
82 Bayside Dr, Walkerville North
Camp Area on foreshore. Pre-book
03 5663 2224   HEMA 90 H7   38 50 26 S   146 00 02 E

VICTORIA

120 Riverview Hotel

15 River Dr, Tarwin Lower
Camp Area 7 km SW of Tarwin. S off S
Gippsland Hwy on Tarwin Lower Rd. Free for patrons
03 5663 5211   HEMA 90 H6   38 41 50 S   145 51 55 E

121 Korumburra Showgrounds
Victoria St, Korumburra
Camp Area at Korumburra. Pre-book. Call
and deposit for dump point key
0408 353 785   HEMA 90 F6   38 25 40 S   145 49 02 E

122 Loch Memorial Reserve
35 Loch-Poowong Rd, Loch
Camp Area on E side of Hwy
0492911213   HEMA 90 F5   38 22 03 S   145 42 44 E

123 Lang Lang Foreshore
Caravan Park
174 Jetty Rd, Jam Jerrup
Caravan Park S of Lang Lang
03 5997 5220   HEMA 90 E5   38 18 25 S   145 31 16 E

124 Woodbyne Resort
2185 Phillip Island Rd, Cowes
Camp Area S of Cowes on Phillip Island.
Pre-book
03 5952 3086   HEMA 90 F3   38 28 02 S   145 14 17 E

125 Point Leo Foreshore
Camping Reserve
1 Point Leo Ring Rd, Point Leo
Camp Area opposite foreshore. Pre-book peak
periods
03 5989 8333   HEMA 90 F2   38 25 23 S   145 04 23 E

126 Shoreham Foreshore Reserve
57 Prout Webb Rd, Shoreham
Camp Area 850 m E of PO. Pre-book
peak periods
03 5989 8325   HEMA 90 F2   38 25 44 S   145 03 03 E

127 Rosebud Foreshore Reserve
1380 Point Nepean Rd, Rosebud
Camp Area opposite shops. Pre-book peak
periods. Open Nov - Apr
03 5950 1011   HEMA 90 E2   38 21 41 S   144 53 01 E

128 Capel Sound Foreshore
Reserve
1681 Point Nepean Rd, Capel Sound
Camp Area at Rosebud West & Tootgarook. Pre-
book peak periods. Closed for winter
03 5986 4382   HEMA 90 E2   38 21 46 S   144 52 49 E

129 Rye Foreshore Reserve
2376 Point Nepean Rd, Rye
Camp Area along shore. Pre-book peak
periods. Open Nov - Apr
03 5950 1011   HEMA 90 F1   38 22 13 S   144 49 29 E

130 White Cliffs Foreshore
2120 Point Nepean Rd, Rye
Camp Area 1 km W of town. Pre-book
03 5985 3288   HEMA 80 H6   38 21 22 S   144 45 58 E

131 Sorrento Foreshore Reserve
Point Nepean Rd, Sorrento
Camp Area at Sorrento Front Beach. Pre-
book. Open Nov - Apr
03 5950 1011   HEMA 90 E1   38 20 39 S   144 45 08 E

Tallangatta to Bairnsdale
Omeo Highway

132 Tallangatta Showgrounds
10 Coorilla St, Tallangatta
Camp Area. Caretaker on site
02 6071 2621   HEMA 92 B5   36 13 10 S   147 10 05 E

133 Pigs Point Streamside Reserve
Lot 2 Omeo Hwy, Tallangatta South
Camp Area 9 km S of Tallangatta or 30 km
N of Eskdale. Beside Mitta Mitta River
HEMA 92 B5   36 16 49 S   147 14 15 E

134 Tallandoon Rest Area
Via Omeo Hwy, Eskdale
Rest Area 33 km S of B400/C543 Jcn or 6 km
N of Eskdale. Beside Mitta Mitta River & Peters Bridge
HEMA 92 C5   36 26 25 S   147 12 11 E

135 Eskdale Caravan Park
3762 Omeo Hwy, Eskdale
Caravan Park beside Little Snowy Ck
0438 645 846   HEMA 96 A7   36 27 57 S   147 14 53 E

136 Katie Peters Reserve
Via Mitta N Rd, Eskdale Area
Camp Area 8 km E of Eskdale. 6.5 km from
turn off. Riverside
HEMA 92 C5   36 27 22 S   147 18 54 E

137 The Mill
Via Omeo Hwy, Mitta Mitta
Camp Area 1.5 km N of Mitta Mitta. 18 km
SE of Eskdale. E side of the road, track to bush
camping spots
HEMA 97 A8   36 31 53 S   147 21 49 E

138 Snowy Creek
Via Holloway Log Rd, Dartmouth
Camp Area 11 km S of Mitta Mitta or 94 km
N of Omeo. Turn N to Holloway Log Rd, 600 m to
campsite. Small vehicles only, both sides of the road
02 6072 3410   HEMA 97 B9   36 35 46 S   147 26 19 E

139 The Walnuts
6961 Omeo Hwy, Mitta Mitta
Camp Area 14 km S of Mitta Mitta or 91 km
N of Omeo. Beside Snowy Ck
02 6072 3410   HEMA 97 C8   36 36 54 S   147 25 33 E

140 Lightning Creek Camping
Via Omeo Hwy, Mitta Mitta
Picnic Area 22 km S of Mitta Mitta or 83 km
N of Omeo. Creekside

HEMA 97 C9   36 39 39 S   147 25 58 E

141 Big River Camping Area
Mount Wills Historic Area
Via Omeo Hwy, Glen Valley
Camp Area 58 km S of Mitta Mitta or 47 km N of
Omeo. Riverside

136 186   HEMA 97 F9   36 53 34 S   147 27 51 E

142 Buckety Plain Campground
Alpine National Park
Via Bogong High Plains Rd, Bundara
Camp Area 19 km S of Falls Creek or 18 km W
of Omeo Hwy. Signposted. Steep & winding road.
21 day limit

131 963   HEMA 95 G8   36 56 20 S   147 19 43 E

143 Raspberry Hill Campground
Alpine National Park
Via Bogong High Plains Rd, Bundarra
Camp Area 18 km S of Falls Creek or 19 km W
of Omeo Hwy. Signposted. Steep & winding road.
21 day limit

131 963   HEMA 95 A13   36 56 32 S   147 19 05 E

144 Langford West Camp Area
Alpine National Park
Via Langford West Aqueduct Rd, Nelse
Camp Area 15 km S of Falls Creek or 22 km W of
Omeo Hwy. Signposted. Steep & winding road. Not
suitable for caravans. 21 day limit

131 963   HEMA 95 A13   36 55 44 S   147 18 08 E

145 Pretty Valley
Alpine National Park
Pretty Valley Rd, Falls Creek
Dispersed Camping 7 km SW Falls Creek. No camping
within 200 m of Bogong High Plains or Pretty Valley Rd,
historic hut & horse yards. Overlooks pondage

HEMA 95 A12   36 53 37 S   147 15 05 E

146 Jokers Flat Campground
Alpine National Park
Via Omeo Hwy, Glen Valley
Camp Area 67 km S of Mitta Mitta or 38 km N of Omeo.
Beside Mitta Mitta R. Steep access. 21 day limit

131 963   HEMA 97 G9   36 56 39 S   147 28 21 E

147 CRB Campground
Alpine National Park
2855 Omeo Hwy, Anglers Rest
Camp Area 77 km S of Mitta Mitta or 28 km N of
Omeo. Beside Cobungra R. 21 day limit

131 963   HEMA 97 G9   36 59 16 S   147 29 41 E

148 Anglers Rest
Alpine National Park
2855 Omeo Hwy, Anglers Rest
Camp Area 76 km S of Mitta Mitta or 29 km N of
Omeo. Beside Cobungra R. 21 day limit

131 963   HEMA 97 G9   36 59 24 S   147 29 23 E

149 Ferny Flat Campground
Alpine National Park
Kellys Rd, Benambra
Camp Area 26 km N of Omeo via Omeo Valley Rd.
Beside Mitta Mitta R. 5.5 km dirt road. 21 day limit

131 963   HEMA 97 F11   36 53 36 S   147 37 53 E

150 Hinnomunjie Bridge Camp
Via Omeo Valley Rd, Omeo
Camp Area 18 km N of Omeo, 840 Omeo
Valley Rd, over Mitta Mitta R

HEMA 97 G10   36 56 42 S   147 36 32 E

151 Omeo Hilltop Hotel
107 Day Ave, Omeo
Parking Area behind hotel. Register at bar

03 5159 1303   HEMA 97 J10   37 05 44 S   147 35 45 E

152 Gibbo River Bush Camping
Via Corryong Rd, Benambra
Camp Spot 26 km N of Benambra or 97 km
S of Corryong. From Benambra 15 km winding
dirt road. Not suitable for caravan access from
Corryong. Steep creek crossing at entry. Large open
area beside river

131 963   HEMA 97 D11   36 45 25 S   147 42 15 E

153 Ah Syes Camping Area
Via Corryong Rd, Benambra
Camp Area 31 km N of Benambra or 93 km
S of Corryong. From Benambra 20 km winding dirt
road. Not suitable for caravan access from Corryong

131 963   HEMA 97 D12   36 43 52 S   147 44 02 E

154 Omeo RV Stop
Creek St, Omeo
Parking Area behind RV signage at
Livingstone Park

HEMA 97 J10   37 05 57 S   147 35 24 E

155 Swifts Creek Tourist Park
11 McLarty Rd, Swifts Creek
Caravan Park 500 m E of PO. Adjacent to
the Tambo River. Pre-book Swifts Ck General Store

03 5159 4205   HEMA 98 A3   37 15 40 S   147 43 28 E

156 Ensay Recreation Ground
Via Doctors Flat Rd, Ensay
Camp Area S of river. Phone for key &
payment

03 5157 3227   HEMA 98 C4   37 22 54 S   147 49 25 E

Wangaratta to Omeo
Great Alpine Road

157 Pioneer Bridges
3678/285 Markwood-Everton Rd, Markwood
Rest Area beside Ovens River. 2 km SW of
Everton or 3 km NE of Markwood. Turn S 700 m W
of Everton

HEMA 92 C2   36 26 32 S   146 31 30 E

158 Whorouly Rec Reserve
Via Church St, Whorouly
Camp Area S side of town. Honesty box

HEMA 92 C3   36 30 27 S   146 35 10 E

159 Dederang North Rest Area
Via Dederang Rd, Dederang
Rest Area 5 km N of Dederang or 13 km S
of Kergunyah

HEMA 92 B4   36 26 40 S   147 01 01 E

VICTORIA

160 Dederang Hotel

4326 Kiewa Valley Hwy, Dederang
Parking Area behind hotel. Check in with publican. Toilets at hotel when open
02 6028 9325   **HEMA 96 A4**   36 27 58 S   147 00 46 E

161 Boyds Bridge
Boyd Rd, Gundowring
Camp Spot 42 km SE Wodonga. Beside Kiewa R
  HEMA 92 B5   36 25 33 S   147 02 50 E

162 Yackandandah Creek
Yackandandah State Forest

Yack Gate Rd, Yackandandah
Camp Areas 4.5 km SW of Yackandandah. Follow Bell's Flat Rd 2.5 km to Service Basin Rd
136 186   **HEMA 92 B3**   36 20 18 S   146 48 24 E

163 Mountain Creek
Alpine National Park
978 Mountain Ck Rd, Tawonga
Camp Area 11 km E of Tawonga. 21 day limit
131 963   **HEMA 96 D7**   36 41 59 S   147 15 09 E

164 Nug Nug Reserve
Nug Nug Reserve Rd, Buffalo River
Camp Area 15 km S of Myrtleford. Turn E off Buffalo River Rd (C526), 13 km S of Myrtleford before McGuffies Bridge. Turn L after 1 km, then next R. Cold showers
0428 336 272   **HEMA 96 C1**   36 39 42 S   146 42 20 E

165 Blades Camping Area
Via Abbeyards Rd, Buffalo River
Camp Area 36 km S of Myrtleford. Via Buffalo River & Abbeyards Rds
1800 111 885   **HEMA 96 E1**   36 49 17 S   146 39 41 E

166 Tea Tree Camping Area
Via Abbeyards Rd, Buffalo River
Camp Area 38 km S of Myrtleford. Via Buffalo River Rd. Riverside
1800 111 885   **HEMA 96 E1**   36 50 21 S   146 39 53 E

167 Manna Gum Myrtleford
Via Abbeyards Rd, Buffalo River
Camp Area 40 km S of Myrtleford. Via Buffalo River Rd. Riverside
1800 111 885   **HEMA 96 E1**   36 50 42 S   146 40 31 E

168 Lake Catani Campground
Mount Buffalo National Park
Via Mt Buffalo Rd, Porepunkah
Camp Area 28 km W of Porepunkah. Closed May - Oct. Pre-book. Limited sites for small caravans & campervans. 21 day limit
131 963   **HEMA 96 D2**   36 44 07 S   146 48 43 E

169 Ah Youngs Camping Area
Via Buckland Valley Rd, Buckland
Camp Area 18 km S of Porepunkah. From Porepunkah roundabout turn S to riverside sites. 4 km dirt road
1800 111 885   **HEMA 96 E3**   36 50 30 S   146 51 04 E

170 Camp Flat
Buckland Valley Rd, Porepunkah
Camp Area 23 km S of Porepunkah. From Porepunkah roundabout turn S riverside sites. 7 km dirt road
136 186   **HEMA 96 F3**   36 51 13 S   146 51 32 E

171 Shippens Flat
Buckland River Rd, Buckland
Camp Area 30 km S of Porepunkah. Riverside. 15 km dirt road
1800 111 885   **HEMA 95 A9**   36 55 23 S   146 54 15 E

172 Leinster Flat
Buckland Valley Rd, Porepunkah
Camp Area 31 km S of Porepunkah, beside river. 17 km dirt road
1800 111 885   **HEMA 95 A9**   36 55 48 S   146 55 32 E

173 Good Hope Flat
Via Buckland Valley Rd, Porepunkah
Camp Area 32 km S of Porepunkah, beside river. 18 km dirt road
1800 111 885   **HEMA 95 A9**   36 56 00 S   146 55 32 E

174 Headrace Flat
Via Buckland Valley Rd, Porepunkah
Camp Area 33 km S of Porepunkah, beside river. 20 km dirt road
1800 111 885   **HEMA 95 A9**   36 56 48 S   146 55 50 E

175 The Bend
Via Buckland River Rd, Buckland
Camp Area 36 km S of Porepunkah. Riverside. 21 km dirt road
1800 111 885   **HEMA 95 B9**   36 57 48 S   146 55 55 E

176 Beveridges Station
Alpine National Park
Via Selwyn Ck Rd, Porepunkah
Camp Area 39 km S of Porepunkah. Via Buckland Valley Rd, follow for 37 km, then veer L onto Selwyn Creek Rd. 2.5 km narrow windy road to camp, riverside. 25 km dirt road. 21 day limit
131 963   **HEMA 95 B9**   36 59 05 S   146 57 25 E

177 Smoko Camping Area
Via Miley Lane, Bright
Camp Area 16 km S of Bright or 11.5 km N of Harrietville. Turn E off Great Alpine Rd (opposite house) follow track for 700 m veering R to campsite. Beside river
1800 111 885   **HEMA 96 E5**   36 49 39 S   147 04 36 E

178 Scrubbers End
Scrubbers End Ln, Dinner Plain
Parking Area at Dinner Plain Alpine Village. Enter via Big Muster Dr, E side of village. Permit required Jun - Sept. Best in summer. Dogs need a permit
1800 444 066   **HEMA 95 B12**   37 01 29 S   147 14 36 E

179 Victoria Falls Camping Area
Victoria Falls Historic Area
43 Victoria Falls Rd, Cobungra
Camp Area near Cobungra Station. 25 km W of Omeo or 90 km SE of Bright. Off Great Alpine Rd
131 963   **HEMA 95 C14**   37 05 37 S   147 25 30 E

180 Mt Kosciuszko Lookout
703 Great Alpine Rd, Omeo
Parking Area 9 km W of Omeo or 100 km SE of Bright
  HEMA 97 J10   37 07 59 S   147 32 01 E

Omeo-Dargo-Bairnsdale

181 Dogs Grave Campground

Birregun Rd, Omeo
Camp Area 22 km SW of Omeo or 44 km NE of Dargo. Turn S off B500, 3 km W of Omeo to Swifts Creek-Omeo Rd for 7 km, SW to Upper Livingstone Rd for 6 km, then W 6 km. Winding dirt road

HEMA 95 E14   37 14 01 S   147 22 51 E

182 Ollies Jump Up Camp

Dargo State Forest
Dargo
Camp Area 61 km SW of Omeo or 12 km N of Dargo. 5.5 km N of Dargo turn NE onto Upper Dargo Rd. Winding dirt road. Signposted

HEMA 95 G13   37 23 09 S   147 16 39 E

183 Jimmy Iversons Camp

Upper Dargo Rd, Dargo
Camp Area 63 km SW of Omeo or 10 km N of Dargo. 5.5 km N of Dargo turn NE. The camp is located at the 3.9 km mark. Winding dirt road. Riverside. Signposted

HEMA 95 G13   37 23 54 S   147 16 21 E

184 Italian Flat Campground

Upper Dargo Rd, Dargo
Camp Area 65 km SW of Omeo or 8 km N of Dargo. 5.5 km N of Dargo turn NE. Winding dirt road. Riverside. Signposted

HEMA 95 G12   37 24 33 S   147 15 53 E

185 Two Mile Creek

Upper Dargo Rd, Cowa
Camp Area 66 km SW of Omeo or 7 km N of Dargo. 5.5 km N of Dargo turn NE. Winding dirt road. Beside Two Mile Creek. Signposted

HEMA 95 G12   37 24 31 S   147 15 28 E

186 Dargo Hotel

Via Lind Ave & Omeo Rd, Dargo
Camp Area in paddock behind pub. Register at bar

03 5140 1231   HEMA 95 H12   37 27 43 S   147 15 06 E

187 Dargo River Inn

13 Lower Dargo Rd, Dargo
Camp Area behind Inn. 20 powered sites avaliable

03 5140 1330   HEMA 95 H12   37 28 16 S   147 15 17 E

188 Meyers Flat Campsite

Via Dargo Bairnsdale Rd, Dargo
Camp Area 12.5 km S of Dargo. Signposted access, riverside

HEMA 95 J12   37 30 59 S   147 13 53 E

Far North East Victoria

189 Yackandandah North

Via Wodonga-Yackandandah Rd, Yackandandah
Rest Area 22 km SW of Wodonga or 5 km NW of Yackandandah. Jcn of C532 & C315

HEMA 92 B3   36 16 33 S   146 48 15 E

190 Ludlows Reserve

Murray Valley Hwy, Ebden
Rest Area 5 km SE of Bonegilla or 22 km NW of Tallangatta. Beside Lake Hume

HEMA 92 B4   36 10 16 S   147 02 09 E

191 Bethanga Rec Reserve

2 Hollow St, Bethanga
Camp Area N side of town. Payment box at front gate

0468 350 930   HEMA 92 A4   36 07 11 S   147 05 56 E

192 Kiewa Memorial Park

Via Kiewa Valley Hwy & Kiewa East Rd, Kiewa
Camp Area 20 km SE of Wodonga, opposite general store

HEMA 92 B4   36 15 20 S   147 00 56 E

193 Tallangatta Creek Rest Area

8078 Murray Valley Hwy, Tallangatta
Rest Area 13 km E of Tallangatta or 2 km W of B400/C546 Jcn

HEMA 92 B5   36 11 43 S   147 19 01 E

194 Tom Mitchell Reserve

40 Avondale Rd, Shelley
Rest Area 6.5 km E of Koetong or 24 km W of Cudgewa-Tintaldra Rd intersection. Cnr of Murray Valley Hwy

HEMA 92 B6   36 10 43 S   147 32 59 E

195 Cotton Tree Creek

Mount Granya State Park
Webbs Lane, Granya
Camp Area 2 km W of Granya. Dirt road

131 963   HEMA 92 A5   36 06 53 S   147 18 18 E

196 Hotel Granya

3100 Murray River Rd, Granya
Camp Area and Farm Stay. Register at bar. Fee for shower

02 6072 9548   HEMA 92 A5   36 04 45 S   147 19 02 E

197 The Kurrajongs Camping

Mount Lawson State Park
Via Kurrajong Track, Thologolong
Camp Area 40 km W of Walwa or 16 km NE of Bungil Junction. Via Murray River Rd. Small vehicles only

131 963   HEMA 92 A6   35 57 22 S   147 25 11 E

198 Kennedys Reserve

4951-5901 Murry River Rd, Thologolong
Rest Area 37 km W of Walwa or 23 km NE of C542/C546 Jcn. Riverside

HEMA 92 A6   35 57 33 S   147 26 37 E

199 Burrowye Bend

Murray River Reserve
Via Murray River Rd, Burrowye
Camp Area 25 km W of Walwa or 35 km NE of C542/C546 Jcn. Riverside

131963   HEMA 92 A6   35 59 15 S   147 31 39 E

200 Koetong Creek Camping

Mount Lawson State Park
Via Koetong Ck Track, Koetong
Camp Area 7 km NW of Koetong. Off Mount Lawson Rd. Small vehicles only

131 963   HEMA 92 A6   36 05 54 S   147 26 49 E

VICTORIA

201 Gadds Bend Reserve
Murray River Reserve
8243 Murray River Rd, Walwa
Camp Spot 8.5 km E of Walwa
131963   HEMA 92 A6   35 56 45 S   147 40 24 E

202 Neils Bend
Murray River Reserve
C546
Via Murray River Rd, Walwa
Camp Spot 7 km E of Walwa or 17 km NW of
Tintaldra. 300 m dirt road off Hwy. Riverside
131 963   HEMA 92 A7   35 58 22 S   147 48 46 E

203 Clarke Lagoon Wildlife
Reserve
C546
10918-11038 Murray River Rd, Tintaldra
Camp Area 19 km SE of Walwa or 5 km NW of
Tintaldra. 300 m dirt road off Hwy. Riverside. 7 day
limit
02 6076 2277   HEMA 92 A7   36 01 27 S   147 54 38 E

204 Clear Water Upper Murray
17 Tintaldra Back Rd, Tintaldra
Caravan Park W of main street
0400 232 872   HEMA 92 A7   36 02 47 S   147 55 44 E

205 Tintaldra Hotel
2 Main St, Tintaldra
Pub Stay near bridge. Pre-book, 7 day limit
02 6077 9261   HEMA 92 A7   36 02 47 S   147 55 51 E

206 Lighthouse Crossing Reserve
12158 Murray River Rd, Towong
Camp Spot 6 km N of Towong
HEMA 93 A8   36 05 40 S   147 59 18 E

207 The Resting Place - Poets
Paradise
568 Murray Valley Hwy, Towong
Camp Area 6 km S of Towong
0429 100 279   HEMA 92 B7   36 09 48 S   147 57 53 E

208 Corryong RV Parking
Strezlecki Way, Cooryong
Parking Area N side of town. Showgrounds
Rd via Jardine St. Park in gravel area between trees
& old tennis courts, not in Rec Reserve
02 6076 2277   HEMA 92 B7   36 11 36 S   147 54 02 E

209 Corryong East Rest Area
Via Murray Valley Hwy, Corryong
Camp Area E of Corryong
HEMA 92 B7   36 11 10 S   147 55 03 E

210 Indi Bridge
Murray River Reserve
818 Upper Murray Rd, Towong Upper
Camp Area 4 km S of Towong Upper or 16 km S of
Towong
02 6076 2277   HEMA 93 B8   36 14 05 S   148 02 00 E

211 Bluff Creek Camp
Burrowa - Pine Mountain NP
385 Bluff Falls Rd, Cudgewa North
Camp Area 21 km SW of Tintaldra. Take the
Cudgewa-Tintaldra Rd, turn N to Cudgewa N Rd,
then S. Dirt road. Small caravans only. 21 day limit
131 963   HEMA 92 A7   36 07 19 S   147 46 40 E

212 Cudgewa Football &
Netball Club
245 Main St, Cudgewa
Camp Area around oval & paddocks. Via Mary
Valley Hwy to Cudgewa-Tintaldra Rd. Pre-book
0429 665014   HEMA 92 B7   36 10 38 S   147 46 42 E

213 Blue Gum Campground
Via Bluff Falls Rd, Cudgewa
Camp Area 27 km SW of Tintaldra. Take the
Cudgewa-Tintaldra Rd, turn N into Cudgewa N Rd,
then S. Dirt road. Small caravans only
HEMA 92 A7   36 07 23 S   147 45 54 E

214 Nariel Creek Rec Reserve
C545
Via Corryong-Benambra Rd, Corryong
Camp Area 12 km S of Corryong or 21 km
N of Nariel Creek. Honesty box
02 6076 2277   HEMA 92 B7   36 14 34 S   147 50 04 E
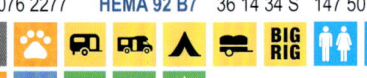

215 Staceys Bridge Reserve
C545
Via Benambra-Corryong Rd, Nariel
Camp Area 44 km S of Corryong
02 6076 2277   HEMA 92 C7   36 26 37 S   147 49 45 E

Wangaratta-Mansfield-
Healesville
North East Victoria

216 Brown Brothers Vineyard
239 Milawa Bobinawarrah Rd, Milawa
Parking Area beside winery. Follow signs
03 5720 5520   HEMA 89 D7   36 27 16 S   146 25 50 E

217 Oxley Rec Reserve
300 Oxley-Meadowcreek Rd, Oxley
Camp Area 3 km S of Oxley. Honesty box
HEMA 89 D7   36 28 14 S   146 23 06 E
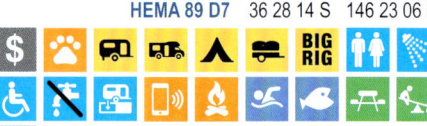

218 Edi Turnoff Rest Area
14 Porters Ln, Moyhu
C521
Rest Area 9 km S of Moyhu or 15 km N
of Whitfield. Beside King River. Camp in permitted
areas only
HEMA 89 D7   36 38 51 S   146 25 19 E

219 Edi Cutting Reserve
3741 Wangaratta-Whitefield Rd, Edi
C521
Camp Area 10 km S of Moyhu or 14 km
N of Whitfield. 1 km S of Edi turnoff. Dirt track to
camps along King River. Small vehicles
HEMA 89 E7   36 39 48 S   146 25 11 E

220 Gentle Annie Caravan &
Camping
98 Gentle Annie Lane, Whitfield
Camp Area 24 km S of Moyhu or 2 km N of
Whitfield. Turn E 23 km S of Moyhu or 1 km N of
Whitfield 1 km. Beside King River
03 5729 8205   HEMA 89 E7   36 45 08 S   146 25 27 E

221 Sandy Flat Camp
Alpine National Park
Via Sandy Flat Track, Wabonga
Camp Area 77 km S of Wangaratta or 91 km NE of Mansfield. From Whitfield, S on King Valley Rd 5 km, S to Upper King River Rd 22 km to Top Crossing Tr, after 500 m turn E
HEMA 94 A4 36 56 20 S 146 25 44 E
4WD ONLY SCV

222 Top Crossing Hut
Alpine National Park
Via Top Crossing Track, Wabonga
Camp Area 81 km S of Wangaratta or 97 km NE of Mansfield. From Whitfield, S on King Valley Rd 5 km, S to Upper King River Rd 22 km to Top Crossing Tr, 5 km to camp. 21 day limit
131 963 HEMA 94 B4 36 57 48 S 146 26 29 E
4WD ONLY SCV

223 Bennies Camping Area
Alpine National Park
Lake Cobbler Rd, Wabonga
Camp Area 31 km S of Whitfield. Via King Valley, Rose River & Upper Rose River Rds. Riverside. Dirt road, rough in places. 21 day limit
131 963 HEMA 94 B5 36 57 49 S 146 32 17 E

224 Lake Cobbler Camping Area
Alpine National Park
Via Lake Cobbler Rd, Wobonga
Camp Area 48 km S of Whitfield. Via King Valley, Rose River & Upper Rose River Rds. Dirt road rough in places. 21 day limit.
131 963 HEMA 94 C6 37 02 59 S 146 37 35 E
4WD ONLY

225 Tolmie Recreation Reserve
C521
1528 Old Tolmie Rd, Tolmie
Camp Area 20 km NE Mansfield or 20 km SW of Whitfield. Pay via registration envelopes on site. 7 day limit
03 5776 2113 HEMA 94 A2 36 56 05 S 146 14 14 E
$ BIG RIG

226 Toombullup School Site
Toombullup State Forest
C517
Tolmie-Mahaikah Rd, Toombullup
Camp Area 6 km NW of Tolmie or 33 km SE of Tatong. Windy narrow dirt road. Small area 100 m off road
136 186 HEMA 94 A2 36 53 16 S 146 14 06 E

227 Stringybark Creek
Toombullup State Forest
C517
Via Tolmie-Tatong Rd, Tolmie
Camp Area 11 km NW of Tolmie or 28 km SE of Tatong. Windy narrow dirt road. Large area 400 m off road
136 186 HEMA 89 F7 36 52 22 S 146 12 06 E

228 Jones Camping Reserve
Toombullup State Forest
Via Jones Rd, Tolmie
Camp Area 23 km NW of Tolmie or 16 km SE of Tatong, via Tolmie-Tatong Rd. Signposted. 5 km dirt road from Tatong. Seasonal
136 186 HEMA 89 E6 36 50 48 S 146 08 38 E

229 Tatong Tavern
2581 Benalla-Tatong Rd, Tatong
Camp Area beside pub. Patronage please
03 5767 2210 HEMA 89 E6 36 43 48 S 146 06 27 E
$ SCV

230 Lima East Creek Rest Area
B300
Via Midland Hwy, Swanpool
Rest Area 18 km S of B300/M31 Jcn or 2 km N of Swanpool
HEMA 89 E6 36 43 28 S 145 59 31 E
BIG RIG

231 James Camping Reserve
Strathbogie Ranges State Forest
1121 Lima East Rd, Lima East
Camp Area 13 km SW of Swanpool. From Swanpool turn W onto Swanpool-Lima Rd, then turn S for 11 km. 5.5 km dirt road. Beside Black Charlies Creek
136 186 HEMA 89 E6 36 50 11 S 145 56 49 E

232 Spring Creek Sawmill
Mount Samaria State Park
Via Mount Samaria Rd, Bridge Creek
Camp Area 30 km N of Mansfield, via Mansfield-Whitfield & Mount Samaria Rds. Windy dirt road
131 963 HEMA 89 F6 36 52 18 S 146 05 04 E
4WD ONLY

233 Blue Range Creek Camping
Blue Range Rd, Bridge Creek
Camp & Picnic Area 14 km N of Mansfield. Turn N 18 km W of Tolmie or 10 km N of Mansfield. 4 km dirt road
136186 HEMA 94 A1 36 56 07 S 146 05 42 E

234 Buttercup Creek
Buttercup Rd, Mirimbah
Camp Area 10 km E of Merrijig or 3 km NW of Mirimbah. Via Carters Rd, turn W for 7 km of dirt road to the first site. 4 more sites over the next 4 km. 4WD only beyond Buttercup 4
131 963 HEMA 94 C3 37 04 05 S 146 20 21 E

235 Carters Mill Camping
C320
Via Carters Rd, Merrijig
Camp & Picnic Area 10 km E of Merrijig or 3 km W of Mirimbah. Turn N along Carters Rd for 400 m. Unlevel area, small vehicles only
03 5775 7000 HEMA 94 C4 37 06 11 S 146 22 02 E

236 Klingsporn Bridal Track
Via Mt Buller Rd, Mirimbah
Camp Area at Mirimbah, S of Mt Buller Rd on S side opposite Mt Sterling Rd. 16 km NW of Mt Buller. Often closed in winter
HEMA 94 D4 37 06 39 S 146 24 00 E

237 Pineapple Flat
Alpine National Park
Via Burnt Top Track, Mount Buller
Camp Area 55 km W of Mansfield. W on Mount Buller Rd 30 km, N 23 km via Mount Stirling & Circuit Rds & Black Landing Tr
HEMA 94 C6 37 03 58 S 146 29 57 E
4WD ONLY

238 King Hut
Alpine National Park
Via King Basin Rd, Wabonga
Camp Area 15 km E of Mt Stirling
03 5775 7000 HEMA 94 C6 37 05 18 S 146 34 20 E
4WD ONLY

239 Craigs Hut
Alpine National Park
Via Circuit Rd, Mount Buller
Camp Area 19 km E of Telephone Box Jcn, Mt Buller. High clearance only, steep sections. open Dec - May
03 5775 7000 HEMA 94 D6 37 06 22 S 146 32 07 E
4WD ONLY

240 8 Mile Flat Camping Area
Alpine National Park
Via Brocks Rd, Merrijig
Camp Area 29 km SE of Merrijig. Turn S off C320 2 km E of Merrijig to Howqua Track. 27 km dirt road, steep in places. Small vehicles only. 21 day limit
131 963 HEMA 94 E4 37 11 54 S 146 25 44 E
4WD ONLY

241 Blackbird Flat
Via Howqua Track, Merrijig
Camp Area 19 km SE of Merrijig. Turn S off C320 2 km E of Merrijig onto the Howqua Track for 16.5 km. 200 m W of Sheepyard Flat, before the bridge. 17 km windy dirt road. Riverside. 21 day limit
131 963   HEMA 94 E4   37 11 41 S   146 20 42 E

242 Sheepyard Flat
Howqua Hills HA
Via Brocks Rd, Howqua Hills
Camp Area 19 km SE of Merrijig. Turn S off C320 2 km E of Merrijig to the Howqua Track for 16.5 km then to Brocks Rd. 17 km windy dirt road. Riverside
131 963   HEMA 94 E3   37 11 38 S   146 20 49 E

243 Frys Flat
Howqua Hills Historia Area
Via Howqua Track, Merrijig
Camp Area 20 km SE of Merrijig. Turn S off C320 2 km E of Merrijig to the Howqua Track for 16.5 km. Access track is at the rear of Sheepyards Flat. 19 km windy dirt road. Riverside
131 963   HEMA 94 E3   37 11 46 S   146 19 48 E

244 Davons Flat
Via Brocks Rd, Merrijig
Camp Area 23 km SE of Merrijig. Turn S off C320 2 km E of Merrijig to the Howqua Track for 16.5 km. Brocks Rd, 500 m beyond Sheepyard Flat. 17 km windy dirt road. Riverside
131 963   HEMA 94 E3   37 11 23 S   146 20 56 E

245 Pickerings Flat
Via Brocks Rd, Merrijig
Camp Area 24 km SE of Merrijig. Turn S off C320 2 km E of Merrijig onto the Howqua Track for 16 km. 1 km beyond Sheepyard Flat. 17 km windy dirt road. Riverside
131 963   HEMA 94 E3   37 11 12 S   146 21 14 E

246 Noonans Flat
Howqua Hills Historic Area
Via Brocks Rd, Merrijig
Camp Area 24 km SE of Merrijig. Turn S off C320 2 km E of Merrijig to the Howqua Track for 16.5 km. 1.4 km beyond Sheepyard Flat. 17 km windy dirt road. Riverside
131 963   HEMA 94 E3   37 11 14 S   146 21 40 E

247 Tunnel Bend Flat
Howqua Hills Heritage Area
Via Noonams Flat Track, Howqua Hills
Camp Area 25 km SE of Merrijig. Turn S off C320 2 km E of Merrijig to the Howqua Track for 16.5 km. Brocks Rd, 2.3 km beyond Sheepyard Flat. 17 km windy dirt road. Riverside
131 963   HEMA 94 E4   37 11 17 S   146 22 03 E

248 The Orchard
Delatite Arm Reserve
Via Walshs Rd, Lake Eildon
Camp Area at Lake Eildon. 8 km N of Goughs Bay. Via Howes Creek Rd, turn 500 m before Goughs Bay. Mostly dirt road
131 963   HEMA 89 G6   37 10 52 S   146 00 34 E

249 Newtons Campground
Delatite Arm Reserve
Via Howes Creek Rd, Goughs Bay
Camp Area 8 km N of Goughs Bay. Turn 500 m before Goughs Bay, via Walshs Rd. Mostly dirt road
131 963   HEMA 89 G6   37 10 51 S   146 00 20 E

250 Blue Gum Flat
Delatite Arm Reserve
Via Howes Creek Rd, Goughs Bay
Camp Area 9 km N of Goughs Bay. Turn 500 m before Goughs Bay, via Walshs Rd. Mostly dirt road
131 963   HEMA 89 G6   37 10 29 S   145 59 54 E

251 Picnic Point
Delatite Arm Reserve
Via Howes Creek Rd, Goughs Bay
Camp Area 10 km N of Goughs Bay. Turn 500 m before Goughs Bay, via Walshs Rd. Mostly dirt road
131 963   HEMA 89 G6   37 09 43 S   145 59 36 E

252 Long Gully
Delatite Arm Reserve
Via Howes Creek Rd, Goughs Bay
Camp Areas W of Goughs Bay, turn 500 m before Goughs Bay, via Walshs Rd. Designated camping sites along shoreline. Dirt road. GPS is at Long Gully
131 963   HEMA 89 G6   37 08 55 S   145 59 13 E

253 Harrops Flat
Via Walshs Rd, Lake Eildon
Camp Area N from Lake Eildon on Delatite Plantation Rd
   HEMA 89 G6   37 07 29 S   145 56 20 E

254 Running Creek Camping Reserve
Yarra Ranges National Park
Via Steiners Rd, Howqua
Camp Area 7 km E of Howqua. From Howqua turn E to Howqua River Rd. Cross bridge turn down signposted track to the L. Dirt road, steep in places, numerous sites. Water is from the river
136 186   HEMA 94 E2   37 14 11 S   146 13 54 E

255 Doctors Creek Reserve
Via Mansfield Wood Points Rd, Jamieson
C511
Camp Area 5 km S of Jamieson or 51 km N of Woods Point. Riverside
136 186   HEMA 94 F1   37 19 55 S   146 07 50 E

256 Skipworth Reserve
Mansfield-Woods Point Rd, Jamieson
C511
Camp Area 7.5 km S of Jamieson or 48.5 km N of Woods Point. Riverside
136 186   HEMA 94 G1   37 20 46 S   146 08 34 E

257 Kevington Hotel
1 Mansfield-Woods Point Road, Kevington
C511
Camp Spot next to pub. Pay at hotel. Fee for showers
03 5777 0543   HEMA 94 G1   37 21 30 S   146 09 41 E

258 Flour Bag Creek Reserve
Via Mansfield Woods Pt Road, Kevington
C511
Camp Area 20.5 km S of Jamieson or 35.5 km N of Woods Point
131 963   HEMA 94 G2   37 23 01 S   146 12 44 E

259 Tunnel Bend Reserve
Via Mansfield-Woods Point Rd, Kevington
C511
Camp Area 22 km S of Jamieson or 34 km N of Woods Point
131 963   HEMA 94 G2   37 22 59 S   146 13 31 E

260 Twelve Mile Reserve
5419 Mansfield-Woods Point Rd, Kevington
Camp Area 23 km S of Jamieson or 33 km N of Woods Point
131 963   **HEMA 94 G2**   37 23 05 S   146 13 43 E

261 Blue Hole Reserve
6419 Mansfield-Woods Point Rd, Kevington
Camp Area 26 km S of Jamieson or 29.5 km N of Woods Point
131 963   **HEMA 94 G2**   37 23 26 S   146 14 56 E

262 Picnic Point Reserve
Via Mansfield-Woods Point Rd, Kevington
Camp Area 29 km S of Jamieson or 26.5 km N of Woods Point
131 963   **HEMA 94 G2**   37 24 31 S   146 14 41 E

263 Snakes Reserve
Via Mansfield-Woods Point Rd, Kevington
Camp Area 30 km S of Jamieson or 26 km N of Woods Point. Dirt road
131 963   **HEMA 94 H2**   37 25 00 S   146 14 24 E

264 Knockwood Reserve
Via Mansfield-Woods Point Rd, Kevington
Camp Area 33 km S of Jamieson or 23 km N of Woods Point. Dirt road
131 963   **HEMA 94 H2**   37 26 04 S   146 13 46 E

265 Gaffneys Creek Reserve
7537 Mansfield-Woods Point Rd, Gaffneys Creek
Camp Area 39 km S of Jamieson or 17 km N of Woods Point
131 963   **HEMA 94 H2**   37 28 42 S   146 11 23 E

266 Scotts Reserve
Via Mansfield-Woods Point Rd, Woods Point
Camp Area 3 km NW of Woods Point or 53 km S of Jamieson. Dirt road
131 963   **HEMA 94 J2**   37 33 34 S   146 14 21 E

267 Upper Yarra Reservoir Park
Via Office Access Rd, Reefton
Camp Area 24 km NE of Warburton. Turn E 21 km NE of Warburton onto Woods Point Rd. Pre-book. Gates close at 5pm
131 963   **HEMA 81 A14**   37 40 10 S   145 53 25 E

268 Andersons Mill
Marysville State Forest
Via Anderson Mill Rd, Marysville
Camp Area 6 km SW of Marysville. Turn off Marysville Rd
   HEMA 89 J5   37 32 35 S   145 44 11 E
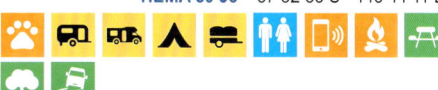

269 Cooks Mill Campground
Cathedral Range State Park
Via Little River Tr, Taggerty
Camp Area 10 km SE of Taggerty. Turn E off B360 9 km N of Buxton or 2 km S of Taggerty to Cathedral Ln. 6 km dirt road. 21 day limit
131 963   **HEMA 89 H5**   37 22 40 S   145 45 34 E

270 Kendalls Camping Area
Rubicon Rd, Rubicon
Camp Area 9 km S of Thornton. Via Thornton-Taggerty Rd then turn E for 6 km. Closed mid Jun - late Oct
136 186   **HEMA 89 G5**   37 18 35 S   145 51 07 E

271 The Boys Camping Area
Rubicon Valley Historic Area
Rubicon Rd, Rubicon
Camp Area 10 km S of Thornton. Via Thornton-Taggerty Rd then turn E for 7 km
136 186   **HEMA 89 H6**   37 19 15 S   145 51 36 E

272 Jerusalem Creek Camping
Lake Eildon National Park
Via Jerusalem Ck Rd, Eildon
Camp Areas 1-8 at Jerusalem Inlet. 10 km SE of Eildon. Pre-book sites. GPS is at Area 1. 21 day limit
131 963   **HEMA 89 G6**   37 15 41 S   145 57 55 E

273 Taponga
Big River State Forest
Via Bull Range Rd, Eildon
Camp Area 33 km S of Eildon or 28 km SE of Jamieson, via Eildon-Jamieson Rd. Signposted, entry just S of bridge. Small caravans only. Riverside
136 186   **HEMA 89 H6**   37 22 11 S   146 03 27 E

274 Jim Bullock
Big River State Forest
Via Eildon-Jamieson Rd, Eildon
Camp Area 33 km S of Eildon or 28 km SE of Jamieson. Signposted, on E side of road. Small vehicles only, low trees tight turns. Riverside
136 186   **HEMA 89 H6**   37 22 05 S   146 03 26 E

275 Horseshoe Bend (Big Bend)
Big River State Forest
Via Eildon-Jamieson Rd, Eildon
Camp Area 34 km S of Eildon or 27 km SE of Jamieson, via Eildon-Jamieson Rd. Signposted, on W side of road. Small vehicles only, low trees tight turns. Riverside
136 186   **HEMA 89 H6**   37 21 59 S   146 03 19 E

276 The Pines
Big River State Forest
Via Eildon-Jamieson Rd, Kevington
Camp Area 35 km S of Eildon or 26 km SE of Jamieson. Signposted, on W side of road. Small vehicles only, not suitable for caravans, low trees. Riverside
136 186   **HEMA 94 G1**   37 21 27 S   146 03 45 E

277 Bulldog Flat
Big River State Forest
Via Eildon-Jamieson Rd, Kevington
Camp Area 35 km S of Eildon or 26 km SE of Jamieson. Signposted, on W side of road. Small vehicles only, not suitable for caravans, low trees. Riverside
136 186   **HEMA 94 G1**   37 21 15 S   146 03 49 E

278 Burnt Bridge
Big River State Forest
Via Eildon-Jamieson Rd, Eildon
Camp Area 35 km S of Eildon or 26 km SE of Jamieson. Signposted, on W side of road. Riverside. Small caravans only
136 186   **HEMA 94 G1**   37 20 52 S   146 03 42 E

VICTORIA

279 Chaffe Creek Camping Area
Big River State Forest
Via Big River Rd, Enochs Point
Camp Area 38 km S of Eildon or 35 km SE of Jamieson, via Eildon-Jamieson & Big River Rds. 4.5 km dirt road, steep & windy in parts
136 186   HEMA 94 G1   37 23 24 S   146 04 23 E

280 Koriella Rest Area
Via Moorandah Hwy, Koriella
Rest Area 6 km NW of Alexandra or 11 km E of Molesworth
          HEMA 89 G5   37 09 28 S   145 39 42 E

281 Alexandra Showground
17 William St, Alexandra
Camp Area N side of town. Caretaker onsite
0417 179 313   HEMA 89 G5   37 11 06 S   145 42 27 E

282 Brookes River Reserve
3714/19 Brooks Cutting Rd, Alexandra
Camp Area 5 km W of Alexandra. Turn W off Maroonda Hwy 1.5 km N of Alexandra onto Swann Rd. 3 km to sites. Signposted. Riverside
136 186   HEMA 89 G5   37 11 25 S   145 40 16 E

283 Lakeside - Fraser Block
Lake Eildon National Park
Via Lakeside Rd, Devils River
Camp Area 19 km NE of Alexandra (via U.T. Creek Rd) or 18 km NW of Eildon (via Alexandra or Skyline Rd). Pre-book. 21 day limit
131 963   HEMA 89 G6   37 10 37 S   145 51 44 E

284 Candlebark Campground
Lake Eildon National Park
Via Fraser Park Rd, Devils River
Camp Area 17 km NE of Alexandra (U.T. Creek Rd) or 16 km NW of Eildon (via Alexandra or Skyline Rd). Pre-book. 21 day limit
131 963   HEMA 89 G5   37 10 36 S   145 50 26 E

285 Devil Cove Campground
Lake Eildon National Park
Via Fraser Park Rd, Devils River
Camp Area 18 km NE of Alexandra (via U.T. Creek Rd) or 17 km NW of Eildon (via Alexandra or Skyline Rd). Open peak periods only. Pre-book. 21 day limit
131 963   HEMA 89 G5   37 10 25 S   145 50 21 E

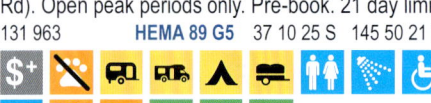

286 Merton Racecourse Reserve
3138 Merton-Euroa Rd, Merton
Camp Area N of town. Gold coin donation
          HEMA 89 F5   36 58 21 S   145 42 32 E

287 Molesworth Rec Reserve
Recreation Reserve Rd, Molesworth
Caravan Park opposite hall, 300 m off Hwy. Limited powered sites
03 5797 6278   HEMA 89 G4   37 09 49 S   145 32 23 E

288 Yea East Rest Area
Via Valley Hwy, Yea
Rest Area 1 km E of town, S of Goulburn Valley Hwy (B340)
          HEMA 89 G4   37 12 46 S   145 26 18 E

289 King Parrot Creek Rest Area
7441-7522 Goulbourn, Kerrisdale
Rest Area 18 km NW of Yea or 20 km SE of Seymour
          HEMA 89 G3   37 08 46 S   145 16 01 E

290 Murrindindi Scenic Reserve
Murrindindi Natural Features & Scenic Reserve
Via Murrindindi Rd, Murrindindi
Camp Areas 34 km NE of Toolangi. Turn E off B300 at Devlins Bridge. Via Wilhelmina Falls Rd. 6 areas. Alternative access from Toolangi via Myers Creek Rd. Dirt road
136 186   HEMA 89 H4   37 23 26 S   145 33 14 E

291 The Gums Campground
Kinglake National Park
Kinglake-Glenburn Rd, Kinglake West
Camp Area 10 km N of Kinglake. Via Eucalyptus Rd (Glenburn Rd). Limited caravan sites for vans up to 20 ft, tight turns. Pre-book. 21 day limit
131 963   HEMA 89 H4   37 28 15 S   145 23 37 E

292 Toolangi Rec Area
68 Cherrys Ln, Toolangi
Camp Area near Toolangi Streamside Reserve. Exit Healesville-Kinglake Rd (C724) N at primary school. Creekside
0447 330 863   HEMA 89 J4   37 32 07 S   145 28 28 E

293 Kinglake Pub
28 Whittlesea-Kinglake Rd, Kinglake
Parking Area on Cnr Kinglake-Glenburn Rd. Register at bar on arrival
03 5786 1230   HEMA 89 H4   37 31 49 S   145 20 24 E

Wodonga to Melbourne
Hume Highway

294 Wodonga Showground
Lot 2 Wilson St, Wodonga
Camp Area E of Hume Link Hwy. Limited sites, call on arrival
02 6024 1872   HEMA 92 A4   36 07 56 S   146 53 31 E

295 Richardsons Bend
Murray River Reserve
Richardsons Rd, Barnawartha
Camp Area 14 km NE of Barnawartha. N from Hume Hwy to Old Barnawartha Rd for 9.5 km. R into Kings Rd, to Geering & Moss Rds, follow to river. Signposted
          HEMA 92 A3   36 02 54 S   146 44 39 E

296 Ovens Billabong
Ovens Billabong Bushland Reserve
Via Oxley Flats Rd, Wangaratta
Camp Spot 5 km SE Wangaratta. GPS at turnoff to dirt road
          HEMA 92 C2   36 22 46 S   146 21 44 E

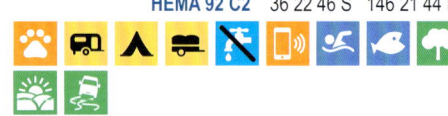

297 River Road Reserve
Via River Rd, Tarrawingee
Camp Area 16km SE of Wangaratta via Great Alpine Rd. Turn R 1 km past Tarrawingee turn off
1800 801 065   HEMA 92 C2   36 24 42 S   146 27 15 E

298 Plough Inn
2322 Wangaratta Beechworth Rd, Tarrawingee
Parking Area behind hotel. Pre-book. Check in on arrival
03 5725 1609   HEMA 92 C2   36 23 23 S   146 27 04 E

299 Wenhams Camp
Warby-Ovens National Park
Via Wenhams Track, Taminick
Camp Area 15 km W of Wangaratta, via Wangandry, Gerrett & Booth Rds. Small vehicles only, limited space. 4.4 km dirt road
131 963   HEMA 92 B1   36 20 27 S   146 12 15 E

300 Thoona Pub
59 Sargeant St, Thoona
Parking Area behind pub. See hotel before parking
03 5765 2224   HEMA 92 B1   36 20 20 S   146 04 41 E

301 The Forest Camp
Warby-Ovens National Park
Via Camp Rd, Killawarra
Camp Area 21 km NW of Wangaratta or 17 km SW of Peechelba. Turn W 13 km N of Wangaratta or 9 km S of Peechelba along Boweya Rd, then N after 6 km. Pre-book. 21 day limit
131 963   HEMA 92 B1   36 13 19 S   146 10 43 E

302 Frosts Reserve
Warby-Ovens National Park
Via Francis Rd, Peechelba
Dispersed Camping 14 km NW of Wangaratta. Turn E 14 km NW of Wangaratta or 8 km S of Peechelba along Francis Rd. Follow to various sites on Ovens River. Higher clearance may be needed, water crossings
    HEMA 92 B2   36 14 40 S   146 16 01 E

303 Winton Motor Raceway Camp
Via Wattle Creek Rd, Winton
Camp Area 12 km NE of Benalla or 17 km SW of Glenrowan. Exit Hume Hwy (M31) to Winton-Glenrowan Rd, S to entry
03 5760 7100   HEMA 89 D6   36 31 02 S   146 05 31 E

304 Jaycee Island Car Park
Via Fawckner Dr, Benalla
Parking Area in Benalla. From Fawckner Dr through library carpark to dirt track past skate park. No parking on the grass. Limited space
03 5762 1749   HEMA 89 D6   36 33 14 S   145 59 13 E

305 Benalla Showgrounds
Via Cecil St, Benalla
Camp Area S of Lake Benalla bridge. Honesty box
03 5762 2323   HEMA 89 D6   36 33 18 S   145 58 46 E

306 White Hart Hotel
63 Hill St, Longwood
Parking Area 16 km SW of Euroa or 39 NE of Seymour. Exit Hume Hwy at Depot Rd for 2.5 km. Patronage please
03 5798 5203   HEMA 89 E4   36 48 10 S   145 25 21 E

307 Coach Road Rest Area
Via Hume Hwy, Avenel
Rest Area 33 km SW of Euroa or 6 km NE of A39/M31 Jcn. S bound only
131 171   HEMA 89 F3   36 56 32 S   145 12 43 E

308 Northwood Reserve
230 Northwood Rd, Seymour
Parking Area 5 km from Seymour via Emily St & Manse Hill Rd
    HEMA 89 F3   37 01 11 S   145 06 53 E

309 Freemans Camp
Tallarook State Forest
Via Main Rd, Tallarock
Camp Area 30 km S of Seymour or 21 km NE of Broadford. Turn off Hume Hwy to Ennis Rd. Dirt road, steep in places. Not suitable for caravans
136 186   HEMA 89 G3   37 09 44 S   145 09 56 E

310 Number 1 Camp Horseyards
Mt Disappointment State Forest
Via Flowerdale Rd, Mount Disapointment
Camp Area 25 km SE of Broadford or 32 km NE of Whallan. Exit Hume Fwy (M31) E at Waterford Park to Spur Rd 7 km, continue E on Main Mountain Rd 5 km, then NE to Flowerdale Rd 2 km, S 200 m to camp
136 186   HEMA 89 H3   37 19 17 S   145 10 20 E

311 Great Divide Rest Area
Via Hume Hwy, Wallan
Rest Area 44 km S of C384/M31 Jcn or 6 km N of B75/M31 Jcn. Both sides of road
    HEMA 89 H3   37 24 12 S   145 00 56 E

Tocumwal to Seymour
Goulburn Valley Highway

312 Wunghnu Rec Reserve
Goulburn Valley Hwy, Wunghnu
Parking Area S side of town
    HEMA 89 B4   36 09 30 S   145 25 56 E

313 Tungamah Lions Park
Via Boyd St, Tungamah
Parking Area at Tennis Reserve. Via Bailey St, creekside. Donation at the pub
    HEMA 89 B6   36 10 00 S   145 52 42 E

314 Four Corners Motel
Via Goulburn Valley Hwy, Congupna
Caravan Park 350 m S of PO
03 5829 9404   HEMA 89 C4   36 18 13 S   145 25 55 E

315 Greens Campground
Whroo Historic Reserve
Via Greens Rd, Whroo
Camp Area 8 km S of Rushworth, via Rushworth-Nagambie Rd & Reedy Creek Rd. 1 km dirt road. Beyond Balaclava Hill Info Centre
13 19 63   HEMA 89 D3   36 38 45 S   145 01 41 E

316 Nagambie North Rest Area
Via Goulburn Valley Hwy, Nagambie
Rest Area 41 km S of Shepparton or 12 km N of Nagambie. S bound only. Share with trucks
    HEMA 89 E3   36 41 43 S   145 12 51 E

317 Major Creek Reserve
Via Mitchellstown Rd, Nagambie
Camp Spot 14 km SW of Nagambie. 6 km S of Nagambie, turn W off Hwy for 8 km
131 963   HEMA 89 E3   36 51 19 S   145 04 01 E

318 Dargile Camping Area
Heathcote-Graytown NP
Plantation Rd, Heathcote
Camp & Picnic Area 15 km NE of Heathcote. Via Heathcote-Costerfield Rd. Check fire restrictions
136 186   HEMA 89 E2   36 51 04 S   144 44 34 E

319 Toolleen Hotel
Northern Hwy, Toolleen
Pub Stay Cnr Toolleen-Cornella Rd. Patrons only
03 5433 6220   HEMA 89 E1   36 43 14 S   144 40 58 E

Wodonga to Mildura
Murray Valley Highway

320 Doolans Bend
Murray River Reserve
Via Fleggs Rd, Rutherglen
Camp Area 16 km E of Rutherglen. Turn N off
Barnawartha Rd, follow track for 800 m into reserve.
Bush camping riverside

HEMA 92 A3　36 01 20 S　146 39 12 E

321 Tuan Campground
Chiltern Box-Ironbark National Park
Depot Rd, Cornishtown
Camp Area N off Humc Fwy to C377 Main St then
W to Chiltern-Rutherglen Rd, then NE. 7 day limit
131 963　HEMA 92 A3　36 07 42 S　146 35 23 E

322 Police Paddocks
Gooramadda State Forest
Via Robbs Lne, Rutherglen
Camp Area 12 km NE of Rutherglen, via
Gooramadda/Up River Rd (1.7 km E of
Rutherglen) & Police Paddocks Rd. Beside
Murray River. 1 km dirt road
131 963　HEMA 92 A2　35 58 45 S　146 30 34 E

323 Shaws Flat
Via Shaws Flat Rd, Carlyle
Camp Area N of Rutherglen. Via Corowa-
Wahgunyah and Up River Rds. 800 m to the
entrance. Various bush camps riverside
HEMA 92 A2　35 59 10 S　146 29 12 E

324 Granthams Bend
Via Federation Way, Wahgunyah
Camp Area 6 km N of Wahgunyah or 1 km
S of Riverina Hwy. Turn E just S of John Foord
Bridge, follow track. Signposted
131 963　HEMA 92 A2　35 59 08 S　146 24 45 E

325 Willows Camping
Via Short St, Wahgunyah
Camp Area at Rec Reserve. Donation per
day for park projects
HEMA 92 A2　36 00 28 S　146 23 26 E

326 Stantons Bend
Via Moodemere Rd, Wahgunyah
Camp Area 11 km W of Rutherglen. Turn N
off Hwy, 4 km to entry. Bush camping riverside
131 963　HEMA 92 A2　36 02 26 S　146 21 21 E

327 Lumbys Bend
Via Raitts Rd, Brimin
Camp Area 18 km W of Rutherglen. Turn N
off Hwy 14 km W of Rutherglen or 4 km E of Brimin
Rd. Follow for 3.5 km, becomes Kellys Rd. Enter
forest & follow track. Bush camping riverside
131 963　HEMA 92 A2　36 02 14 S　146 18 02 E

328 Parolas Bend
Lower Ovens Wildlife Reserve
Via Old Murray Valley Hwy, Bundalong
Camp Area 24 km W of Rutherglen or 7 km SE of
Bundalong. Turn N off B400 just E of Ovens River,
opposite Riverside Caravan Park, along Parolas Tr.
Big rigs just inside entry. Beside Ovens River. GPS
at entrance
131 963　HEMA 92 A1　36 04 03 S　146 12 10 E

329 Taylors Bend
Clarke Ln, Brimin
Camp Area 12 km NW of Brimin. N off
Murray Valley Hwy to Brimin Rd
HEMA 92 A2　36 02 09 S　146 17 15 E

330 Forges Beach No 1
Yarrawonga Regional Park
Via Forges Bend Track, Yarrawonga
Camp Area 10 km NW of Yarrawonga via Hwy,
Forges Pump Ln & Forges Bend Tr
HEMA 89 B6　35 59 46 S　145 57 46 E

331 Green Bank
Murray River Reserve
Via Cullens Rd, Yarrawonga
Camp Area 5 km W of Yarrawonga. Turn N off B400,
3 km W of Yarrawonga or 34 km SE of Cobram. L
fork at info board
131 963　HEMA 89 A6　36 00 35 S　145 58 38 E

332 Yarrawonga River Camp
Yarrawonga Regional Park
Via Cullen Rd, Yarrawonga
Camp Area 5 km W of Yarrawonga. Turn N off Hwy,
on loop near river
HEMA 89 B6　36 00 43 S　145 58 51 E

333 Chinamans Bend
Murray River Reserve
Via Chinamans Track, Yarrawonga
Camp Area 7 km W of Yarrawonga. Turn N off B400,
4 km W of Yarrawonga or 33 km SE of Cobram to
Brears Rd. L at gate
131 963　HEMA 89 A6　36 00 20 S　145 58 15 E

334 Forges Beach No 2

 Yarrawonga Regional Park
Via Forges Bend Track, Yarrawonga
Camp Area 10.6 km NW of Yarrawonga. Turn N off
B400, 8 km W of Yarrawonga or 29 km SE of Cobram
onto Forges Pump Rd. Signposted. Riverside
131 963   HEMA 89 A6   35 59 35 S   145 57 21 E

335 Bruces Beach No 2

 Murray River Reserve
Via Bruces Rd, Burramine
Camp Area 13 km NW of Yarrawonga. Turn N
off B400, 9 km W of Yarrawonga or 28 km SE of
Cobram to Bruces Rd. L at fork to Bruces Track
131 963   HEMA 89 A6   35 57 58 S   145 54 52 E

336 Nevins Beach East

 Murray River Reserve
Via Collins Lane, Burramine
Camp Area 20 km NW of Yarrawonga. Turn N off B400,
14 km W of Yarrawonga or 23 km SE of Cobram to Thoms
Rd. R at info board along Collins Ln & Nevins Track
131 963   HEMA 89 A6   35 57 20 S   145 53 31 E

337 Bourkes Beach 1 - 3

 **Murray River Reserve**
Via Bourkes Bend Tr, Burramine
Camp Areas N off B400 19 km W of Yarrawonga 18 km
SE of Cobram to Bourkes Bend Tr, GPS for Area 1, other
sections detailed in the Camps Australia Wide App
HEMA 89 A6   35 58 35 S   145 50 07 E

338 Bourkes Bridge Rest Area

 Via Bourkes Bend Track, Burramine
Rest Area 10 km W of Burramine. Off
Murray Valley Hwy
HEMA 89 B5   35 59 53 S   145 49 34 E

339 Big Toms Beach

 Cobram Regional Park
Wondah St, Cobram
Camp Area 3 km N of Cobram. Turn N from C370
(Cobram Barooga Rd). At end of street take track
over the levee. After grid, follow middle dirt track for
2 km. Riverside. Toilet block 1 km away
131 963   HEMA 89 A5   35 53 37 S   145 38 52 E

340 Little Toms Beach

 Cobram Regional Park
Wondah St, Cobram
Camp Area 2.4 km N of Cobram. Turn N from C370
(Cobram Barooga Rd). Cross over levy at end of
road, take middle track for 0.6 km. Signposted
HEMA 89 A5   35 54 03 S   145 39 24 E

341 Davies Beach

 Via Cobram-Koonoomoo Rd, Cobram
Camp Area 12 km N of Cobram
HEMA 89 A5   35 52 31 S   145 37 40 E

342 Horseshoe Bend Cobram

 Cobram Regional Park
Via River Rd, Cobram
Camp Area 6.8 km E of Cobram. Turn S off Barooga
Rd for 4.8 km, then N to Horseshoe Track. Riverside
131 963   HEMA 89 A5   35 55 41 S   145 41 45 E

343 Horse Shoe Lagoon

 Cobram Regional Park
Via River Rd, Cobram
Camp Area 7 km E of Cobram. Turn S off Barooga
Rd onto River Rd for 5 km, then N onto Horseshoe
Track. Riverside
HEMA 89 A5   35 56 03 S   145 41 37 E

344 Scotts Beach

 Cobram Regional Park
Via River Rd, Cobram
Camp Area 3.5 km E of Cobram. Turn S off Barooga
Rd for 3 km. Riverside. 14 day limit
131 963   HEMA 89 A5   35 55 36 S   145 40 36 E

345 The Big Strawberry

 7034 Goulburn Valley Hwy, Koonoomoo
Parking Area next to cafe. Check in with the
cafe. Limited power available for a fee
03 5871 1300   HEMA 89 A5   35 53 19 S   145 34 28 E

346 Dead River Beach

 Murray River Reserve
Via Dead River Track, Cobram
Camp Area 5.5 km NW of Cobram. Turn N off
Cobram-Koonoomo Rd 1.7 km W of Cobram onto
Racecourse Rd. Travel to end of road through gate/
grid. After 200 m take middle track for 500 m, then
R. Riverside
131 963   HEMA 89 A5   35 52 49 S   145 37 45 E

347 Railway Hotel Strathmerton

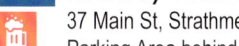 37 Main St, Strathmerton
Parking Area behind hotel, off Murray Valley
Rd. Check in at bar on arrival. Fee for amenities and
laundry
03 5874 5203   HEMA 89 A4   35 55 29 S   145 28 46 E

348 Weiss Beach

 Cobram Regional Park
Via Levings Rd, Koonoomoo
Camp Area 13.5 km N of Cobram or 17.5 km S
of Tocumwal. Turn E off Cobram Koonoomoo Rd
(C357) to Fresian Rd, L to Levings Rd, cross levy at
end of road to Cobram Tr 3.5 km. Signposted
HEMA 89 A5   35 51 41 S   145 35 45 E

349 Green Beach

 Via Cobram Track, Koonoomoo
Camp Area 38 km NE of Koonoomoo. Turn
E off A39 to Cobram Track. Check access road may
need 4WD
HEMA 89 A5   35 50 56 S   145 35 04 E

350 Finley Beach on Murray

 **Tocumwal Regional Park**
Via Bushlands Rd, Tocumwal
Camp Area 2.5 km S of Tocumwal. Turn E off A39,
2 km S of Tocumwal along Finley Track. Riverside
131 963   HEMA 89 A5   35 49 20 S   145 33 32 E

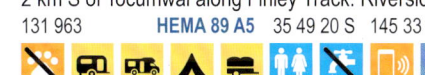

351 Apex Beach on Murray

 **Tocumwal Regional Park**
Via Pump Bend Track, Tocumwal
Camp Area 2.5 km SW of Tocumwal. Turn W off
A39, 200 m S of bridge, signposted "Time-Out
Resort", L over railway line for 1 km. Riverside
131 963   HEMA 89 A5   35 48 47 S   145 32 54 E

352 Red Gum Retreat

 311 Ulupna Bridge Rd, Ulupna
Camp Area 29 km NW of Cobram. Pre-book
03 5874 5531   HEMA 89 A4   35 50 47 S   145 26 50 E

353 Pebble Beach Campground

 Via Newell Hwy, Koonoomoo
Camp Area S of Murray R, off Goulburn
Valley Hwy
HEMA 89 A4   35 48 56 S   145 33 47 E

354 Barmah National Park

Via Barmah Rd, Barmah
Dispersed Camping 20 km W of Tocumwal.
Various sites along 112 km frontage of Murray R.
Only Barmah Lake has a toilet
131 963   HEMA 89 A4   35 51 39 S   145 17 44 E

355 Barmah Lakes Campground
Barmah National Park
Via Moira Lakes Rd, Barmah
Camp Area 7 km N of Barmah. Turn N at hotel to
Moira Lake Rd, follow to entry. 21 day limit
131 963   HEMA 89 A2   35 57 17 S   144 57 32 E

356 Nathalia Golf Club
444 Paynes Rd, Nathalia
Parking Area 4 km E of Nathalia. Play &
stay. Limited space, pre-book
03 5866 2289   HEMA 89 B3   36 03 58 S   145 13 56 E

357 McCoys Bridge
Via Murray Valley Hwy, Katupna
Rest Area 18 km S of Nathalia or 8 km E of
Wyuna, beside Goulburn River
          HEMA 89 B3   36 10 41 S   145 06 58 E

358 Christies Beach
Echuca Regional Park
Simmies Rd, Echuca
Camp Area 8.5 km E of Echuca. Turn N off Echuca-
Bangerang Rd 6 km E of Echuca to Simmie Rd,
2 km to various camping areas. 2.5 km dirt road.
Riverside. GPS at entry
131 963   HEMA 89 B2   36 07 04 S   144 48 48 E

359 Rivers Edge Campground
Via Simmie Rd, Echuca
Camp Area E of village. Via Goulburn Rd
then N
131 963   HEMA 89 B2   36 06 47 S   144 48 28 E

360 Tongala Turnoff
Via Murray Valley Hwy, Tongala
Rest Area 10 km W of Wyuna or 21 km E
of Echuca
          HEMA 89 B2   36 11 57 S   144 57 05 E

361 Falcon Hotel
7784 Murray Valley Hwy, Kanyapella
Camp Area 18 km E of Echuca. Register at
bar. Hotel patrons only
03 5859 2304   HEMA 89 B2   36 11 46 S   144 55 08 E

362 Echuca Rotary Park RV Stop
Via Rose St, Echuca
Parking Area W side of town. Entry Cnr
Crossen St. Donation box on site
          HEMA 87 H14   36 08 43 S   144 44 02 E

363 Wharparilla Flora Reserve
120 Murray Valley Hwy, Echuca
Rest Area 4 km NW of Echuca or 38 km SE
of Gunbower
          HEMA 87 G14   36 07 20 S   144 43 09 E

364 Point Bend
Via O'Sullivan Rd, Wharparilla
Camp Area 5 km NW of Wharparilla.
N from Hwy
          HEMA 87 G14   36 04 19 S   144 37 20 E

365 Betha Bend
Via Glyn Rd, Wharparilla
Camp Area 6 km NW of Wharparilla. Turn N
off Hwy to Farley Rd for 3.6 km, then E
          HEMA 87 G14   36 02 33 S   144 36 11 E

366 Arnold Bend
River Murray Reserve
Via Fraser Rd, Torrumbarry
Dispersed Camping 26 km SE of Gunbower, or
21 km NW of Echuca. Turn N off Hwy. Riverside
          HEMA 87 G14   36 02 18 S   144 35 19 E

367 Turner Bend
565 Headworks Rd, Torrumbarry
Camp Area 3 km E of Torrumbarry. N off Hwy
          HEMA 87 G14   35 58 50 S   144 30 57 E

368 Masters Landing
Gunbower National Park
Via River Track, Gunbower
Camp Area 8.6 km NE of Gunbower. Take
Gunbower Island Rd NE 4.4 km, E to Brereton Rd
3.8 km, then S to unsealed track 700 m. Riverside.
21 day limit
131 963   HEMA 87 G14   35 55 21 S   144 25 59 E

369 Lockington Travellers Rest
Via Pannoo Rd, Lockington
Camp Area behind Lions Park. Call to
access facilities. 14 night limit, permit for 4 nights
or more
0447 787 581   HEMA 87 J14   36 16 15 S   144 32 08 E

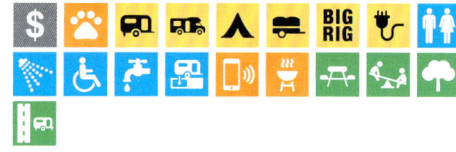

370 Pyramid Hill Caravan Park
Via Victoria St, Pyramid Hill
Caravan Park 1 km E of PO. Ring caretaker
on arrival
0456 478 558   HEMA 87 G12   36 03 19 S   144 07 30 E

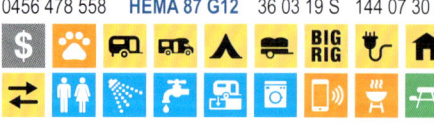

371 Terrick Terrick Campground
Terrick Terrick National Park
Via Picnic Track, Mitiamo
Camp Area 6 km N of Mitiamo. Take Mitiamo Forest
Rd N for 4.2 km, E to Cemetery Track. 1.6 km to
picnic access track. Signposted. Small vehicles only.
21 day limit
131 963   HEMA 87 H13   36 10 05 S   144 14 35 E

372 Travellers Rest Leitchville
2 King George St, Leitchville
Rest Area N side of town. Off Leitchville Rd
          HEMA 87 G13   35 54 14 S   144 18 06 E

373 Cohuna RV Rest Area
Cnr Cohuna Island & Tennis Rd, Cohuna
Parking Area on Cohuna Island
          HEMA 87 F13   35 48 31 S   144 13 24 E

374 Cohuna Golf Club
Golf Rd, Cohuna
Camp Area 6 km N of Cohuna via
Weymouths Rd
03 5456 2820   HEMA 87 F13   35 46 14 S   144 13 25 E

375 Kerang Golf & Bowls Club
193 Kerang-Koondrook Rd, Kerang
Parking Area E of town. Play & stay
03 5452 1506   HEMA 87 F12   35 44 27 S   143 56 19 E

376 Gunbower State Forest

Murray River Reserve
Via Kerang-Koondrook Rd, Gunbower
Dispersed Camping 2.5 km SE of Koondrook, via
weir along Canoe Trail. Riverside
131 963   **HEMA 87 E12**   35 39 47 S   144 07 47 E

377 Koondrook Wetland Reserve

Via View St, Koondrook
Parking Area W of Koondrook-Murrabit Rd
HEMA 87 E12   35 38 00 S   144 07 29 E

378 Guttrum State Forest

Brays Ln, Koondrook
Camp Area 4 km NW of Koondrook, via
Murray Pde & Cassidy Ln. Bush camping, riverside
131 963   **HEMA 87 E12**   35 36 45 S   144 06 55 E

379 Kerang Turf Club

Via Park Rd, Kerang
Parking Area opposite Keats Rd
HEMA 87 F11   35 43 52 S   143 55 31 E

380 Bills Astro Garden

14 Collins Rd, Kerang
Parking Area 1 km S of town. Look for
yellow gate & mural. Pre-book
0428 419 744   **HEMA 87 F12**   35 44 56 S   143 55 23 E

381 Lake Meran

Leaghur State Park
Via Boort Kerang Rd, Lake Meran
Camp Area 21 km S of Kerang
HEMA 87 F11   35 52 07 S   143 48 11 E

382 Leaghur Campground

Leaghur State Park
Via Boort Kerang Rd, Leaghur
Camp Areas 29 km S of Kerang. At entrance & S
end of Lake Meran Track. GPS at entrance
03 5452 1266   **HEMA 87 G11**   35 55 43 S   143 47 02 E

383 Simply Tomatoes

479 Parkers Rd, Boort
Camp Area 19 km N of Boort via Boort
Kerang Rd. Honesty box. Mon-Thurs only. Pre-book
03 5455 4237   **HEMA 87 G11**   36 01 41 S   143 47 57 E

384 Quambatook Caravan Park

Via Quambatook-Boort Rd, Quambatook
Caravan Park next to golf course
0428 857 122   **HEMA 87 F10**   35 51 10 S   143 31 31 E

385 Reedy Lake RV Rest Area

Via Apex Park Rd, Kerang
Parking Area 8.5 km N of Kerang or 12 km
S of Lake Charm. 1 km E of Hwy. Beside lake
03 5456 2047   **HEMA 87 E11**   35 41 10 S   143 53 11 E

386 Murrabit Rec Reserve

Via Browning Ave, Murrabit
Camp Area W of town. Caretaker collects fees
HEMA 87 E12   35 31 49 S   143 57 09 E

387 Lake Boga Area 4 Camping

Via Lakeside Dr, Lake Boga
Camp Area NW side of lake. Register & pay
at caravan park
03 5037 2386   **HEMA 87 E11**   35 26 02 S   143 39 09 E

388 Lake Boga Area 5 Camping

Via Lakeside Dr, Lake Boga
Camp Area NW side of lake. Register & pay
at caravan park
03 5037 2386   **HEMA 87 E11**   35 26 19 S   143 39 33 E

389 Loddon Floodway

Via Caelli Lane, Swan Hill
Camp Spot 19 km SE of Swan Hill. Turn E
2 km S of Swan Hill to Pental Island Rd for 14 km,
then N. 3 km dirt road. Small vehicles only
HEMA 87 D11   35 22 40 S   143 41 22 E

390 Speewa Ferry Crossing

Via Speewa Punt Rd, Speewa
Camp Area 16 km N of Swan Hill. Turn W
off Hwy
HEMA 87 D10   35 12 50 S   143 30 31 E

391 Nyah-Vinifera Park South

River Murray Reserve
Via Forest Rd, Vinifera
Camp Areas 10.5 km NW of Beverford or 4.5 km SE
of Vinifera. Turn N 7.5 km NW of Beverford or 1 km
S of Vinifera. 3 km dirt road. Riverside
131 963   **HEMA 87 C10**   35 11 42 S   143 25 02 E

392 Nyah Rec Reserve

37 River St, Nyah
Camp Spot on riverbank behind Harness
Club. 7 day limit. Honesty box
HEMA 87 C10   35 10 18 S   143 22 53 E

393 Nyah-Vinifera Park North

River Murray Reserve
Via Byrnes Ln, Nyah
Camp Area between Nyah & Wood Wood. W bank
of river
131 963   **HEMA 87 C10**   35 09 19 S   143 22 56 E

394 Piangil North Rest Area

Via Murray Valley Hwy, Piangil
Rest Area 2 km N of B12/B400 Jcn or
45 km S of Boundary Bend. Riverside
HEMA 87 C9   35 02 34 S   143 19 29 E

395 Wakool Junction

Via Kenley Rd, Kenley
Camp Area 7 km E of Piambie. Turn E off
B400 27 km N of B400/B12 Jcn or 20 km SE of
Boundary Bend to Coghill Rd. Dirt road. Riverside.
Small vehicles only
HEMA 87 B9   34 51 08 S   143 20 43 E

396 Passage Camp

Via Mills Lane, Boundary Bend
Camp Area 5 km SE of Boundary Bend.
Turn E to Mills Ln. Veer N at end of lane to Passage
Camp Track. Signposted. 2 km to river. Small 4WD
vehicles only
HEMA 87 A9   34 43 01 S   143 11 58 E

397 Beggs Bend State Forest
Via Tol Tol Rd, Tol Tol
Camp Spot 15 km SE of Robinvale. From Hwy, turn NE 5 km E of Robinvale 5 km to signposted entry. Follow tracks to river. GPS at entry
131 963 HEMA 87 A8 34 38 19 S 142 51 03 E

398 Walshs Bend Camp
Via Tol Tol Rd, Tol Tol
Camp Spot 5 km E of Robinvale. Turn N for 600 m. Turn N to track, signposted. Follow dirt track for 2 km to sites. Low branches. GPS at entrance
HEMA 87 A8 34 37 16 S 142 48 45 E

399 Pump Road Camp
Pump Rd, Robinvale
Camp Area 2 km E of Robinvale. E of Cemetery, turn N for 500 m. Bridge has a 2 t weight limit. Turn E over water pipes, follow dirt tracks to riverside
HEMA 87 A8 34 36 25 S 142 48 10 E

Mildura to Yamba
Sturt Highway

400 Merbein Common
Via Wentworth Rd, Merbein
Camp Areas 11 km NW of Mildura via McEdward St & Red Gum Tr
131 963 HEMA 88 C6 34 09 22 S 142 04 30 E

401 Merbein South Weighbridge
Via Sturt Hwy, Merbein
Rest Area 14 km W of Mildura
HEMA 88 C6 34 13 51 S 141 59 23 E

402 Wallpolla Island
Wallpolla Island State Forest
Old Mail Rd, Wargan
Camp Spot 26 km W of Merbein. Via Channel Rd. Dirt road. Riverside
HEMA 88 C5 34 09 13 S 141 46 45 E

403 Merrinee North Rest Area
A20
Via Sturt Hwy, Cullulleraine
Rest Area 35 km W of Mildura or 22 km E of Cullulleraine
HEMA 88 D5 34 15 37 S 141 49 27 E

404 Werrimull Hotel
5543 Millewa Rd, Werrimull
Parking Area behind pub (limited space) & opposite. Fees for power and shower. Open Wed-Sun. Check in with publican
03 5028 1200 HEMA 88 E4 34 23 17 S 141 35 41 E

405 Lock 9
Via Crozier Rock Tr, Cullulleraine
Camp Spot 10 km N of Cullulleraine. Turn N 1 km W of Cullulleraine. 9 km dirt road. Turn W at boat ramp sign, follow track. Camp near boat ramp, not at Lock carpark
HEMA 88 D4 34 11 30 S 141 35 39 E

Tooleybuc to Pinnaroo
Mallee Highway

406 Piangil RV Rest Area
Via Hall St, Piangil
Picnic Area at Memorial Park, S of Mallee Hwy
HEMA 87 C10 35 03 19 S 143 18 43 E

407 Piangil West Rest Area
B12
Via Mallee Hwy, Piangil
Rest Area 9 km W of Piangil or 31 km E of Manangatang
HEMA 87 C9 35 03 25 S 143 13 01 E

408 Manangatang Travellers Rest
B12
Via Wattle St, Manangatang
Rest Area opposite hotel, donation for upkeep
HEMA 87 C8 35 03 10 S 142 53 00 E

409 Walpeup Wayside Stop
B12
Via Murphys Rd, Walpeup
Camp Area centre of town. Fees in box at toilet block
03 5018 8100 HEMA 88 J6 35 08 10 S 142 01 30 E

410 Lake Walpeup Reserve
Via Mclivena Rd, Walpeup
Camp Spot 14 km SE of Walpeup. Take Walpeup-Patchewollock Rd, turn N to Walpeup Lake Rd then E. 6 km dirt road
HEMA 88 J6 35 11 53 S 142 08 18 E

411 Underbool Campground
B12
Cotter St, Underbool
Rest Area next to Mallee Hwy. Honesty box for power & shower
HEMA 88 J5 35 10 10 S 141 48 35 E

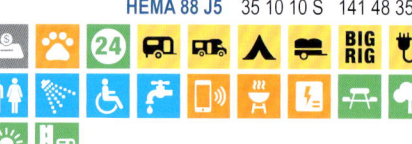

412 Underbool Rec Reserve
B12
Via Gnarr Rd, Underbool
Camp Area N of railway line. Power box & water on W side of grounds, access around oval. Honesty box at toilet block
HEMA 88 J5 35 10 08 S 141 48 47 E

413 Lake Crosbie Campground
Murray Sunset National Park
Via Pink Lakes Rd, Murray-Sunset
Camp Area 13.5 km N of Linga. Turn N 60 km W of Ouyen or 76 km E of Pinnaroo. 13 km dirt road. Signposted. 21 day limit
131 963 HEMA 88 J4 35 03 19 S 141 43 49 E

414 Murrayville East Rest Area
B12
Via Mallee Hwy, Murrayville
Rest Area 12 km W of Cowangie or 7 km E of Murrayville
HEMA 88 K2 35 15 43 S 141 15 03 E

415 Murrayville Caravan Park
Reed St, Murrayville
Caravan Park 200 m S of PO. Honesty box
0457 241 186 HEMA 88 K2 35 15 57 S 141 10 54 E

416 Ngallo Park
Ngall S Rd, Panitya
Camp Area 21 km SW of Murrayville. Turn S off Mallee Hwy. E side of road. 3 km dirt road
HEMA 88 K1 35 16 20 S 141 04 10 E

Mildura to Melbourne
Calder Highway

417 Psyche Bend Camp 1
Kings Billabong Park
Psyche Bend Rd, Mildura
Camp Area 12 km SE of Mildura, via Eleventh St.
R into Cureton Ave, then L at sign. 4 km dirt road.
Riverside. 7 day limit
131 963   HEMA 88 D7   34 15 16 S   142 13 55 E

418 Red Cliffs Golf Club
274 Twenty Second St, Red Cliffs
Camp Area W off Calder Hwy
03 5024 1531   HEMA 88 D6   34 16 11 S   142 09 56 E
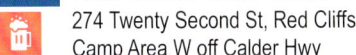

419 Marina Campground
Billabong Rd, Mildura
Camp Area 15 km E of Mildura, off
Billabong Rd at Nichols Point
HEMA 88 C7   34 12 30 S   142 14 01 E

420 McDougall Wines
Cnr Eleventh St and Ginquam Ave, Mildura
Camp Area 3 km from Calder Hwy (A79).
Free for patrons. 7 day limit
0417 104 065   HEMA 88 D7   34 13 50 S   142 12 24 E

421 Johnsons Bend
River Murray Reserve
Blake Rd, Red Cliffs
Camp Area 8.5 km N of Nangiloc. N on Kulkyne Way
4 km, turn W to Rudds Rd 2 km, N on Barko Rd 400
m, then W 1.8 km, riverside. Last 1 km gravel track.
131 963   HEMA 88 E7   34 25 25 S   142 21 53 E

422 Spences Bend
Milduras Murray River Parklands
Via Kulkyne Way, Nangiloc
Camp Area 2 km N of Nangiloc. N on Kulkyne Way
1.6 km, turn W to dirt track for 230 m, riverside
131 963   HEMA 88 E7   34 27 46 S   142 21 20 E

423 Police Bend
Murray River Reserve
Via Kulkyne Way, Nangiloc
Camp Area 2.7 km W of Nangiloc. Entry S of Rec
Reserve, dirt track to riverside
131 963   HEMA 88 E7   34 28 43 S   142 23 00 E

424 Watts Bend
Milduras Murray River Parklands
9 Kulkyne Way, Coligan
Camp Spot 7.6 km S of Nagiloc. Turn W 850 m after
Lewis Rd. Riverside
131 963   HEMA 88 F7   34 32 07 S   142 22 20 E

425 Emmerts Bend
Murray Kulkyne Park
Kulkyne Way, Coligan
Camp Spot 7 km S of Colignan. Dirt track for last
2.8 km. Turn W at Info board. Riverside
131 963   HEMA 88 F7   34 34 12 S   142 24 41 E

426 Hattah North Rest Area
Via Calder Hwy, Hattah
Rest Area 51 km S of Red Cliffs or 3 km N
of Hattah
HEMA 88 G7   34 44 31 S   142 16 18 E

427 Hattah Roadhouse
3478 Calder Hwy, Hattah
Camp Area N of Hattah-Robinvale Rd,
separate area for campers
03 5029 3250   HEMA 88 G7   34 45 41 S   142 16 45 E

428 Lake Hattah Campground
Hattah-Kulkyne National Park
Via Bugle Ridge Walking Track, Hattah
Camp Area 6 km E of Hattah. Turn N 5 km E of
Hattah 1 km. Dirt road. Narrow for last 100 m. Pre-
book. 21 day limit
131 963   HEMA 88 G7   34 45 06 S   142 20 36 E

429 Lake Mournpall
Hattah-Kulkyne National Park
Via Mournpall Track, Hattah
Camp Area 15 km NE of Hattah. Turn N 5 km E
of Hattah for 10 km. 9 km sandy road. Pre-book.
21 day limit
131 963   HEMA 88 G7   34 42 18 S   142 20 08 E

430 Wemen Rest Area
Via Hattah-Robinvale Rd, Wemen
Rest Area beside river. Small vehicles only
HEMA 86 B7   34 46 56 S   142 38 13 E

431 Hattah South Rest Area
Via Calder Hwy, Hattah
Rest Area 12 km S of Hattah or 22 km N of
Ouyen
HEMA 88 G7   34 51 49 S   142 17 58 E

432 Tempy Memorial Park
Via Sunraysia Hwy, Tempy
Camp Area W of Sunraysia Hwy
HEMA 86 D6   35 20 44 S   142 25 28 E

433 Old Pier-Millan Post Office
Pier Millan-Chinkapook Rd, Pier Millan
Camp Spot with entry at old PO building.
Turn W off Calder Hwy, travel 700 m
0447 850 308   HEMA 86 D7   35 14 57 S   142 40 29 E

434 Lake Tyrrell Rest Area
Via Lake Tyrell Rd, Sea Lake
Rest Area 20 km S of Daytrap Corner or
7 km N of Sea Lake
HEMA 87 E8   35 27 12 S   142 49 44 E

435 Sea Lake Rec Reserve
71-91 Calder Hwy, Sea Lake
Caravan Park at 71-91 Calder Hwy.
Honesty box. SCV rates available
0427 701 261   HEMA 87 E8   35 30 11 S   142 50 57 E

436 Royal Hotel Sea Lake
74 Best St, Sea Lake
Parking Area behind pub. Check in at bar
on arrival, Free for patrons
03 5070 1050   HEMA 87 E8   35 30 15 S   142 51 01 E

437 Green Lake Camping
Birchip-Sea Lake Rd, Boigbeat
Camp Area & Caravan Park 10 km S of
Sea Lake
03 5070 1448   HEMA 87 E8   35 35 48 S   142 50 54 E

438 Kaneira Hotel

24 Main St, Culgoa
Camp Area beside hotel, register with publican. Toilets during open hours
0431 188 117   HEMA 87 F9   35 43 00 S   143 06 25 E

439 Culgoa Rest Area

Calder Hwy, Culgoa
A79 Rest Area 3 km S of Culgoa or 39 km N of Wycheproof
HEMA 87 F9   35 44 22 S   143 06 59 E

440 Wycheproof Caravan Park

462 Broadway, Wycheproof
A79 Caravan Park on Hwy, 500 m N of PO
03 5493 7278   HEMA 87 G9   36 04 10 S   143 13 33 E

441 Boort Park Showground

Via Malone St, Boort
Camp Area N of town. Donation please
0419 445 060   HEMA 87 H11   36 06 37 S   143 43 46 E

442 Travellers Rest Caravan Park

43-45 High St, Charlton
Caravan Park central to town. Via John Curtin Dr. SCV rates
0448 276 631   HEMA 87 H10   36 16 02 S   143 21 05 E

443 Wooroonook Lakes

Via Borung Hwy, Charlton
B239 Camp Area 14 km W of Charlton or 27 km E of Donald. 300 m W of C239/C271 (N bound) Jcn
HEMA 87 H9   36 15 38 S   143 11 46 E

444 Mount Jeffcott Campground

Via Camerons Mail Rd, Jeffcott
Camp Area 4 km S of Jeffcott. Turn S off Borung Hwy at Jeffcott
HEMA 87 H9   36 18 30 S   143 08 18 E

445 Skinners Flat Reservoir

153 Mount Kerang Rd, Wedderburn
Camp Area 27 km SE of Charlton or 6 km NW of Wedderburn. Turn E 26 km SE of Charlton or 5 km NW of Wedderburn. 1 km dirt road
131 963   HEMA 87 J10   36 21 58 S   143 35 09 E

446 Hard Hill Tourist Reserve

Via Wilson St, Wedderburn
Camp Area 600 m N of Info Centre
03 5494 3489   HEMA 87 J11   36 24 47 S   143 36 59 E

447 Glenalbyn Forest Camp

Kooyoora State Park
Sunday Morning Hills Rd, Brenanah
Camp Area 16 km W of Inglewood via Brenanah-Glenalbyn & Forbes Ck Rds
HEMA 87 J11   36 32 01 S   143 44 34 E

448 Bridgewater Rec Reserve

Via Bridgewater-Maldon Rd, Bridgewater
Camp Area SE side of town. Dump point key at bakery in Main St
03 5494 1257   HEMA 87 K12   36 36 23 S   143 56 41 E

449 Camp Kooyoora

Kooyoora State Park
792 Brenanah-Whehla Road, Inglewood
Camp Area 10 km W of Kurting. Turn W at Kurting, travel past the dip sign to T Jcn. Signposted. Pre-book
03 5438 3428   HEMA 87 J11   36 33 14 S   143 41 33 E

450 Melville Caves Campground

Kooyoora State Park
Via Melville Caves Rd, Brenanah
Camp Area 21 km W of Inglewood, via Kingower. Turn N 19 km W of Inglewood
131 963   HEMA 87 K11   36 36 03 S   143 41 55 E

451 Happy Jacks Rec Reserve

48 Glen Rd, Lockwood South
A790 Camp Area W side of Hwy
HEMA 85 A12   36 50 30 S   144 09 19 E

452 Bullock Picnic Camp

Via Bullock Rd, Marong
Camp Area at Green Gully Reservoir. 7 km S of Marong, E from Calder Alternative Hwy. Limited sites
13 19 63   HEMA 85 A12   36 47 06 S   144 09 11 E

453 East Shelbourne Rec Reserve

Via Bendigo-Maryborough Rd, East Shelbourne
Rest Area 18.5 km SW of Bendigo
HEMA 85 A12   36 49 00 S   144 06 52 E

454 Hamiltons Crossing

Via Baringhup-Eastville Rd, Baringhup
Camp Spot 12 km S of Eddington or 2 km N of Baringhup. S side of bridge to sites
HEMA 85 B12   36 56 33 S   143 56 01 E

455 Butts Reserve

Maldon Historic Area
Via Mt Tarrengower Rd, Tarrengower
Dispersed Camping 2 km W of Maldon. N from town, then W to Franklin St
13 19 63   HEMA 85 B12   36 59 10 S   144 03 14 E

456 Newstead Racecourse

Via Racecourse Rd, Newstead
Camp Area at Rec Reserve. Key for shower at Rural Transaction Centre. Donation box
03 5476 2360   HEMA 85 B12   37 07 01 S   144 03 23 E

457 Jessie Kennedy Reserve

Via Midland Hwy, Campbells Creek
A300 Rest Area 6 km S of Castlemaine or 5 km N of Guildford
HEMA 85 B12   37 06 37 S   144 11 04 E

458 Vaughan Springs Reserve

Castlemaine Diggings National Heritage Park
29 Greville St, Vaughan
Camp Area 15 km S of Castlemaine or 8 km E of Guildford. Turn E 9 km S of Castlemaine or 2 km NE of Guildford, via Yapeen along Vaughan Springs Rd. Campground on top level
131 963   HEMA 85 C13   37 09 41 S   144 12 51 E

459 Chokem Flat
Via Campbell's Creek-Fryers Rd, Irishtown
Camp Area 38 km N of Daylesford. SE off
Midland Hwy to camp N of Irishtown
131 963   HEMA 85 C13   37 08 27 S   144 13 29 E

460 Fryerstown School Camp
5 Camp St, Fryerstown
Camp Area SE of Midland Hwy. Via
Vaughan Springs Rd. Pre-book. 14 day limit
0422 301 008   HEMA 85 C13   37 08 28 S   144 15 05 E

461 Warburton Bridge Reserve
Castlemaine Diggings National Heritage Park
Via Drummond-Vaughan Rd, Glenluce
Camp Area 18 km S of Castlemaine or 11 km E of
Guildford. Turn E 9 km S of Castlemaine or 2 km NE
of Guildford, via Yapeen along Vaughan Springs Rd.
At Loddon R bridge
131 963   HEMA 85 C13   37 10 11 S   144 14 16 E

462 The Oaks
Mount Alexander Regional Park
93 Picnic Gully Rd, Harcourt
Parking Area 3 km E of Harcourt. E end of Market St
from BP servo. Follow sign to Picnic Gully along dirt
road. L at Xmas Tree sign, then R at Oak Plantation
sign. Small vehicles only. Low trees
HEMA 85 B13   36 59 54 S   144 17 26 E

463 The Redesdale Hotel
2640 Kyneton-Heathcote Rd, Redesdale
Pub Stay opposite reserve. Pre-book.
Patrons only
03 4405 0601   HEMA 85 B14   37 01 20 S   144 31 55 E

464 Leanganook Picnic Area
Mount Alexander Regional Park
Faraday Sutton Grange Rd, Harcourt
Dispersed Camping 13 km SE of Harcourt. Via
Harmony Way
131 963   HEMA 85 B13   37 01 02 S   144 18 22 E

465 Elphinstone North Rest Area
Via Harmony Way, Elphinstone
Rest Area 10 km S of Harcourt or 8 km N
of Taradale
HEMA 85 B13   37 04 14 S   144 18 23 E

466 South Kyneton Mineral Springs
219 Burton Ave, Kyneton
Parking Area 3.5 km W of Kyneton
HEMA 85 C13   37 14 09 S   144 25 10 E

467 Treetops Scout Camp
140 Royal Parade, Riddells Creek
Camp Area NW side of town. Via Gap Rd, off
Melvins Rd. Do not enter via Bolithos Rd. Pre-book
03 5428 6756   HEMA 85 D14   37 26 47 S   144 39 49 E
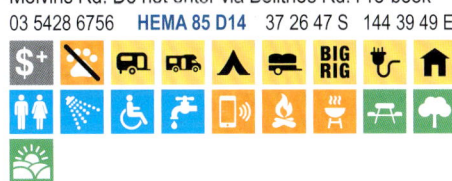

468 Firth Park Campground
Wombat State Park
Via Firth Rd, Trentham East
Camp Area 24 km W of Gisborne. Take Woodend
exit off Calder Hwy. Turn W to Ashbourne Rd,
11 km turn S to Chanters Ln, W to Pearson Rd, S to
Beatties Rd. 5 km dirt road
HEMA 85 D13   37 26 07 S   144 24 35 E

Ouyen-Ballarat-Geelong
Sunraysia and Midland Highways

469 Casuarina Campground
Wyperfeld National Park
Via Meridian Rd, Patchewollock
Camp Area 23 km W of Patchewollock, via Pine
Plains & Meridian Rds from Baring. 15 km dirt road.
Signposted
03 5395 1345   HEMA 86 E5   35 26 43 S   141 59 46 E

470 Snowdrift Campground
Wyperfeld National Park
Pine Plains Rd, Big Desert
Camp Area 30 km W of Patchewollock. W on Baring
Rd, L to Pine Plains Rd toward Lodge, follow signs
to camp. S from Underbool via Gunners Track is
4WD only, no towing permitted
131963   HEMA 86 E5   35 25 52 S   141 54 41 E

471 Patche Sunset Retreat
Via Algerian St, Patchewollock
Camp Area on Cnr Barley & Kernot Sts.
Book at hotel
0499 110 807   HEMA 88 K6   35 22 44 S   142 11 26 E

472 Woomelang Hotel
57 Brook St, Woomelang
Parking Area 30 km E of Hopetoun or
60 km S of Ouyen. Turn N off Hwy to Brook St.
Register at bar. Dump point opposite
03 5081 2148   HEMA 86 F7   35 40 49 S   142 39 50 E

473 Woomelang Free Caravan Park
16 Proctor St
Cnr Gloucester Ave & Proctor St, Woomelang
Camp Area in Lions Park, E of Hwy. Donation at PO
Store
HEMA 86 F7   35 40 55 S   142 39 51 E

474 Cronomby Tanks
Cronomby Tanks Rd, Woomelang
Parking Area at Bushland Reserve. Via the
Hopetoun-Sea Lake Rd
HEMA 86 F7   35 41 10 S   142 39 48 E

475 Kinnabulla Rest Area
Via Sunraysia Hwy, Kinnabulla
Rest Area 24 km NW of Birchip
HEMA 87 G8   35 54 06 S   142 47 49 E

476 Tchum Lake Caravan Park
Via Birchip-Wycheproof, Birchip
Camp Area 8 km E of Birchip
0447 557 837   HEMA 87 G8   35 59 44 S   143 00 14 E

477 Taylor Park
Via Sunraysia Hwy, Birchip
Rest Area S of town
HEMA 87 G8   35 59 22 S   142 54 54 E

478 Watchem Lake
Watchem-Warracknabeal Rd, Watchem
Camp Area 1 km W of Watchem. Fees to
community store, or onsite at the boat ramp
0411 890 172   HEMA 87 H8   36 08 54 S   142 50 51 E

479 Donald Caravan Park
2 Corack Rd, Donald
Caravan Park 1 km N of PO
C261
0497 770 064   **HEMA 87 J8**   36 21 52 S   142 59 16 E

480 Donald Hotel
126 Woods St, Donald
Camp Area on the main road. Patrons only
03 5497 1410   **HEMA 87 J8**   36 22 22 S   142 59 03 E

481 Browns Lake Campground
Camerera Rd, Cope Cope
Camp Area W of Sunraysia Hwy & Lake
Cope Cope
      HEMA 87 J9   36 27 44 S   143 01 56 E

482 Gooroc Roadside Camp
1505 St Arnaud-Wycheproof Rd, Gooroc
Camp Area 14 km N of St Arnaud
131 963   **HEMA 87 J9**   36 29 49 S   143 12 15 E

483 The Farm
54 Gowar Berrimal Rd, Gowar East
Farm Stay 17 km to St Arnaud or 28 km to
Wedderburn. Via old St Arnaud Rd
03 5496 5263   **HEMA 87 J10**   36 32 25 S   143 24 58 E

484 Beazleys Bridge Reserve
Via Ararat-St Arnaud Rd, Beazleys Bridge
C241
Rest Area 24 km N of Navarre or 14 km SW
of St Arnaud
      HEMA 85 A9   36 42 07 S   143 09 45 E

485 Teddington Reservoir
Kara Kara National Park
385 Teddington Rd, Stuart Mill
Camp Area 6 km SW of Stuart Mill. Turn W at Stuart
Mill. 21 day limit
131 963   **HEMA 85 A9**   36 50 36 S   143 15 46 E

486 Wishbone Therapy Farm
436 Redbank-Barkly Rd, Barkly
Camp Area 5.5 km W of Redbank. Free
camping for volunteers. Pre-book
0410 483 763   **HEMA 85 B9**   36 55 58 S   143 16 37 E

---

487 Moonambel Rec Reserve
Via Stawell-Avoca Rd, Moonambel
Camp Area S of road. Call for payment & key
0408 148 261   **HEMA 85 B10**   36 59 24 S   143 20 12 E

488 Mountain Creek Picnic Area
Via Greens Lane, Moonambel
Picnic Area 400 m N of Moonambel
      HEMA 85 B10   36 59 07 S   143 19 09 E

489 Landsborough Caravan Park
Via Burke St, Landsborough
Caravan Park opposite the hotel. Call into
general store to pick up key & pay fees
03 5356 1000   **HEMA 85 B9**   37 00 30 S   143 08 11 E

490 Tanwood South Rest Area
Sunraysia Hwy, Avoca Area
B220
Rest Area 29 km S of Stuart Mill or 10 km
N of Avoca
      HEMA 85 B10   37 01 03 S   143 24 22 E

491 Pyrenees Waterfalls
Via Vinoca Rd, Avoca
Camp Area 12.5 km W of Avoca. Turn W
200 m N of PO to Duke St, then R at T Jcn to Vinoca
Rd & Waterfall Track
03 5465 1000   **HEMA 85 B10**   37 05 55 S   143 22 01 E

492 Avoca Lions Park
Via Creek St, Avoca
Parking Area S of Hwy. Riverside
      HEMA 85 B10   37 05 26 S   143 28 21 E

493 Avoca Riverside
Via Dundas St, Avoca
Parking Area N side of bridge
      HEMA 85 B10   37 05 19 S   143 28 19 E

494 Glenpatrick Reserve
Via Elmhurst Glenpatrick Rd, Glenpatrick
Camp Area 9 km NE of Elmhurst. Pre-book
03 5354 8290   **HEMA 85 B9**   37 08 15 S   143 19 38 E

---

495 Elmhurst Recreation Reserve
Via Green St, Elmhurst
Camp Area SW of Hwy. Pay at hotel
0438 272 861   **HEMA 85 C9**   37 10 56 S   143 14 34 E

496 Bet Bet Creek Rest Area
4236 Sunraysia Hwy, Lexton
Rest Area 11 km N of Lexton or 13 km S of
Avoca. Sunraysia Hwy N of Greenhill Creek Rd
      HEMA 85 C10   37 11 22 S   143 31 26 E

497 Bung Bong Hall Rest Area
Pyrenees Hwy, Bung Bong
B180
Rest Area 8 km E of Avoca or 18 km W of
Maryborough. Next to historical church
      HEMA 85 B10   37 05 53 S   143 34 09 E

498 Avoca Farm Stay
104 Mitchell Rd, Avoca
Farm Stay off Sunraysia Hwy, S of Avoca.
Pre-book. 7 day limit
0438 614 175   **HEMA 85 B10**   37 06 45 S   143 30 00 E

499 Karri Track Camping Area
Paddys Ranges State Park
Via Karri Track, Maryborough
Camp Area 8 km SW of Maryborough or 25 km E of
Avoca, via Old Avoca Rd to dirt road
131 963   **HEMA 85 B11**   37 04 58 S   143 41 27 E

500 Talbot Recreation Reserve
Via Barnes & McCleary Sts, Talbot
Camp Area NW side of town. Caretaker
collects fee. Power metered
      HEMA 85 C11   37 10 07 S   143 41 38 E

501 Lochinver Farm Homestead
245 Baringhup Rd, Carisbrook
Farm Stay 63 km SW of Bendigo. Pre-book
0427 444 436   **HEMA 85 B11**   37 01 23 S   143 49 54 E

502 Lexton South Rest Area

Sunraysia Hwy, Lexton
Rest Area 4 km SE of Lexton or 21 km NW of Learmonth

HEMA 85 C10   37 17 20 S   143 32 53 E

503 The Cork Oaks Picnic Area

Mount Beckworth Scenic Reserve
Cork Oaks Track, Mount Beckworth
Camp Area 8 km W of Clunes. Via Kierces Rd, Mountain Creek Rd. Dirt road, rough in places. Limited caravan sites

131 963   HEMA 85 C11   37 18 36 S   143 42 29 E

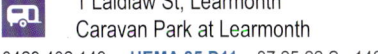

504 Lake Learmonth Caravan Park

1 Laidlaw St, Learmonth
Caravan Park at Learmonth

0429 402 149   HEMA 85 D11   37 25 22 S   143 42 39 E

505 Clarendon Rest Area

Midland Hwy, Clarendon
Rest Area 2 km S of Clarendon or 8 km N of Elaine

HEMA 85 E12   37 42 33 S   143 58 56 E

506 Galwiji Homestead

309 Pryors Rd, Clarendon
Farmstay near Scotsburn, 8 km NW of Clarendon. Sun-Thurs only. Pre-book

0424 750 555   HEMA 85 E12   37 41 57 S   143 56 21 E

507 Hunts Bridge

Via Egerton Rd, Bungal
Camp Area 13 km NE of Elaine. From N side of town take Settlement Rd for 5.5 km, R at T Jcn onto Doran-Egerton Rd for 5 km, L at T Jcn for 400 m, L at Jcn for 2 km. Beside river. 6 km dirt road

131 963   HEMA 80 B1   37 42 37 S   144 05 41 E

508 Meredith Hotel

53/51 Staughton St, Meredith
Camp Area behind pub. Register at bar, fee for power

03 5286 1311   HEMA 83 A12   37 50 43 S   144 04 22 E

Benalla to Naracoorte
Midland and Wimmera Highways

509 Casey Weir Rest Area

5017 Midland Hwy, Benalla
Rest Area 10 km NW of Benalla or 52 km E of Shepparton

HEMA 89 D6   36 28 29 S   145 56 41 E

510 Broken Creek Bush Camp

100 Quinn Rd, Broken Creek
Camp Area 14 km N of Benalla or 48 km E of Shepparton

0428 574 799   HEMA 89 D6   36 27 01 S   145 54 05 E

511 Railway Hotel Goorambat

59 Halls Rd, Goorambat
Parking Area behind pub. Register at bar

03 5764 1206   HEMA 89 C6   36 24 38 S   145 55 21 E

512 Nalinga West Rest Area

Midland Hwy, Nalinga
Rest Area 33 km NW of Benalla or 29 km E of Shepparton

HEMA 89 D5   36 25 47 S   145 41 47 E

513 Country Gardens Caravan Park

270 Winter Rd, Tatura
Caravan Park 2 km W of Tatura

03 5824 2652   HEMA 89 D3   36 26 29 S   145 12 16 E

514 Hilltop Golf & Country Club

71 Gowrie St, Tatura
Camp Area N of town. Pre-book, limited sites

03 5824 1689   HEMA 89 D3   36 25 57 S   145 14 13 E

515 Tatura RV Rest Stop

Douglas St, Tatura
Parking Area 21 km SW of Shepparton in Douglas St carpark. Limited space - 3 vehicles

03 5832 9330   HEMA 89 D3   36 26 22 S   145 13 41 E

516 John Pilley Reserve

20 Fauna Park Dr
75 Lake Rd, Kyabram
Parking Area Cnr Fauna Park Dr. Permit for longer stays

03 5481 2200   HEMA 89 C3   36 19 19 S   145 02 48 E

---

517 Girgarre Town Park

Morgan Cr, Girgarre
Camp Area on outer grounds of Town Park, cnr Winter & Station Sts, either side of hall. Not available 2nd Sunday of the month due to markets. Donation box

0474 114 397   HEMA 89 C2   36 23 53 S   144 58 48 E

518 The Stanhope Pub

67 Midland Hwy, Stanhope
Parking Area N of Hwy. Check in with publican before parking

03 5857 2293   HEMA 89 D2   36 26 47 S   144 59 25 E

519 Sunny Acres Farm

1353 Middle Rd, Rushworth
Camp Area 5 km N of Rushworth. Turn NW off Bendigo-Murchison Rd (C345), at Rushworth, after 2 km turn NE, 2 km to camp

0419 518 729   HEMA 89 D3   36 32 51 S   145 00 51 E

520 Moora Racecourse

47 Heathcote-Moora Rd, Moora
Parking Area 7 km W of Rushworth or 13 km E of Colbinabbin. Donation box is on the shed

HEMA 89 D2   36 35 49 S   144 56 46 E

521 Greens Lake Rec Reserve

Via Greens Lake Rd, Corop
Camp Area 16 km W of Stanhope or 24 km E of Elmore. Turn N off Midland Hwy 14 km W of Stanhope or 22 km E of Elmore. 1 km dirt road. Donation for upkeep

HEMA 89 D2   36 26 16 S   144 49 42 E

522 Aysons Reserve (Campaspe River)

Via Burnewang Rd, Rochester
Camp Area 8 km NE of Elmore. From Midland Hwy 32 km W of Stanhope or 5 km NE of Elmore, turn N 3 km. Permit required for stays over 3 days

03 5481 2200   HEMA 87 J14   36 27 34 S   144 40 08 E

VICTORIA

523 Rochester Silo Stop
9 Ramsay St, Rochester
Rest Area W of Main St

HEMA 89 C1   36 21 42 S   144 41 55 E

524 Rochester North Rest Area
Northern Hwy, Ballendella
B75 Rest Area 11 km N of Rochester or 18 km S of Echuca. Beside Campaspe River

HEMA 89 C1   36 16 31 S   144 42 05 E

525 Runnymede Highway Park
Northern Hwy, Runnymede
B75 Rest Area at Elmore Hwy Park, W of Hwy.
47 km N of Heathcote or 5 km SE of Elmore. Riverside

HEMA 87 J14   36 31 25 S   144 37 38 E

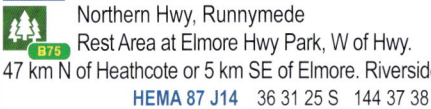

526 Potters Lane
Potters Lane, Elmore
A300 Camp Area S of town. Head S on Elmore-Barnadown Rd, then W. Riverside

HEMA 87 J14   36 30 27 S   144 37 12 E

527 Englishs Bridge Streamside
Reserve
Englishs Rd, Goornong
Camp Spot 3 km E of Goornong. Turn E off A300
3 km NE of Goornong to Axedale Rd, E to Englishs
Rd for 2.5 km. Beside Campaspe River

136 186   HEMA 87 K14   36 37 23 S   144 33 42 E

528 Rocky Crossing
Via Rocky Crossing Rd, Goornong
A300 Camp Area 30 km NE of Bendigo or 5 km
SE of Goornong. Exit Midland Hwy (A300) S to
Chute St, to Goornong-Barnadown Rd for 4 km,
N to Elmore-Barnadown Rd for 400 m, then E for
900 m to riverside

HEMA 87 K14   36 37 47 S   144 33 11 E

529 Muskerry Campground
2140 Epsom-Barnadown Rd, Muskerry
A300 Camp Area 27 km NE of Bendigo or 6 km
SE of Goornong. Exit Midland Hwy (A300) S to
Chute St, then to Goornong-Barnadown Rd for 4km
to Elmore-Barnadown Rd for 2 km to riverside

HEMA 87 J14   36 38 56 S   144 32 32 E

530 Huntly Lions Park
Midland Hwy, Huntly
A300 Rest Area S end of town. Small area

HEMA 87 K13   36 40 11 S   144 19 36 E

531 Notley Picnic Area
Greater Bendigo National Park
Via Notley Rd, Whipstick
Camp Area 21 km N of Eaglehawk. Turn E off
Bendigo-Pyramid Rd (C336) 12 km N of Eaglehawk
to Evans Rd for 4 km, S at T Jcn along Neilborough-
Eaglehawk Rd for 5 km. 21 day limit

131 963   HEMA 87 K13   36 39 01 S   144 15 46 E

532 Rush Dam
Kamarooka State Park
Camp Rd, Kamarooka
Camp Area 27 km W of Elmore or 20 km E of
Raywood. Via Millwood

131 963   HEMA 87 J13   36 30 27 S   144 20 24 E

533 Mulga Dam
Greater Bendigo National Park
Via Bendigo-Tennyson Rd, Kamarooka
Camp Area 23 km W of Elmore or 23 km W of
Raywood. 21 day limit

131 963   HEMA 87 J13   36 29 56 S   144 22 23 E

534 Sebastian Rec Ground
Recreation Rd, Sebastian
Camp Area around oval (not trotting track).
Via Main St & Vogele Rd. 7 night limit

HEMA 87 K13   36 35 32 S   144 11 14 E

535 Bears Lagoon Fruit Fly
Loddon Valley Hwy, Bears Lagoon
B260 Rest Area 2 km N of Bears Lagoon or
21 km S of Durham Ox

HEMA 87 H12   36 18 47 S   143 58 28 E

536 Four Post Hotel
6696 Loddon Valley Hwy, Jarklin
Parking Area E of Hwy. Check in at bar.
Toilets only during trading hours

03 5437 9241   HEMA 87 H12   36 16 08 S   143 58 01 E

537 Newbridge Rec Reserve
Via Lyons St, Newbridge
B240 Camp Area E side of Loddon R on
Wimmera Hwy. Pay at hotel or general store

0417 471 558   HEMA 85 A11   36 44 25 S   143 54 10 E

538 Laanecoorie River Reserve
River St, Laanecoorie
C277 Camp Area on Main Rd, N end on town by
Loddon River

03 5435 7200   HEMA 85 A11   36 49 32 S   143 53 55 E

539 Waanyarra Camp Ground
Waanyarra Nature Conservation
Reserve
Waanyarra Cemetery Rd, Waanyarra
Camp Area 10 km NE of Dunolly or 33 km S of
Bridgewater. Turn E to Waanyarra Cemetery Rd.
2 km dirt road

136 186   HEMA 85 A11   36 49 00 S   143 48 02 E

540 Tarnagulla Recreation Park
25 Wayman St, Tarnagulla
Camp Area off Commercial Rd. Caretaker
on site

0400 976 970   HEMA 85 A11   36 46 28 S   143 49 42 E

541 Moliagul Rest Area
Via Dunolly-Moliagul Road, Moliagul
C240 Rest Area 14 km N of Dunolly or 21 km S
of Logan

HEMA 85 A11   36 45 02 S   143 39 50 E

542 Bealiba Reservoir Rec Area
Bealiba Cycle Track, Bealiba
Camp Area 4 km S of Bealiba. W at
Inkerman to St Arnaud-Donolly Rd, S to Mount Rd at
Bealiba, then to Scent Farm Rd

HEMA 85 A10   36 48 18 S   143 34 21 E

543 Longbush State Forest
Long Bush Rd, Bealiba
Camp Area 4 km SE of McIntyre, N off
Wimmera Hwy to Wedderburn-Dunolly Rd, S to
Long Bush & Cains Rds

HEMA 85 A11   36 41 53 S   143 41 34 E

544 Logan Pub

6742 Wimmera Hwy, Logan
Parking Area behind pub. 23 km E of St
Arnaud or 35 km NW of Dunolly. Check in with publican
03 5496 2220   HEMA 87 K10   36 37 17 S   143 29 28 E

545 Kooreh Hall

Wimmera Hwy, Kooreh
Parking Area 36 km SW of Wedderburn or
12 km E of St Arnaud
HEMA 87 K10   36 38 28 S   143 23 05 E

546 St Arnaud Rest Area West

Wimmera Hwy, St Arnaud Area
Camp Area 2.5 km SW of St Arnaud
HEMA 87 K9   36 37 40 S   143 14 09 E

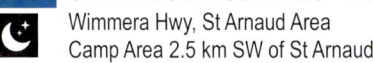

547 Avon River

Via McPherson Rd, Gre Gre South
Rest Area 27 km W of St Arnaud or 50 km
E of Murtoa
HEMA 87 K8   36 38 25 S   142 58 42 E

548 Walkers Lake

Avon Plains Wilderness Reserve
Via Walker Rd, Avon Plains
Camp Area 23 km S of Donald. Via Donald-Avon
Plains Rd
HEMA 87 J8   36 32 20 S   142 55 19 E

549 Marnoo Memorial Park

Via Park Rd, Marnoo
Camp Area 40 km W of St Arnaud. Turn S
off Wimmera Hwy to Donald-Stawell Rd, then W
HEMA 87 K8   36 40 16 S   142 51 59 E

550 Rupanyup Memorial Park

Jack Emmet Billabong
89 Wimmera Hwy, Rupanyup
Camp Area 63 km W of St Arnaud or 14 km E of
Murtoa. Cnr of Minyip-Rupanyup Rd. 7 day limit
0448 782 834   HEMA 86 K7   36 37 35 S   142 37 46 E

551 Minyip Caravan Rest Stop

89 Wimmera Way, Minyip
Camp Area at Minyip Wetlands. Cnr Petering
St & Stawell-Warracknabeal Rd. Limited power. See
notice board for payment details, honesty box
0429 942 471   HEMA 86 J7   36 27 23 S   142 35 12 E

552 Murtoa Caravan Park

47 Lake St, Murtoa
Caravan Park beside Lake Marma
0448 511 879   HEMA 86 K7   36 37 18 S   142 27 58 E

553 Philip of Sherewoods

Wimmera Hwy, Natimuk
Rest Area 9 km W of Natimuk or 61 km NE
of Edenhope
HEMA 84 A4   36 46 29 S   141 51 56 E

554 Centenary Park Camp

Mount Arapiles-Tooan State Park
Via Centenary Park Rd, Natimuk
Camp Area 12 km W of Natimuk or 60 km NE of
Edenhope. 2 km N of Wimmera Hwy
131 963   HEMA 84 A4   36 45 33 S   141 51 03 E

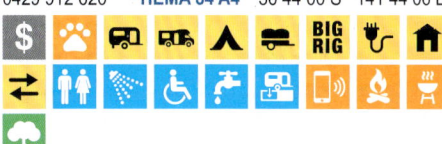

555 Duffholme Cottages

1859 Natimuk-Frances Rd, Mitre
Camp Area 1.5 km E of Mitre. Turn NW
from Hwy B240 to Mitre on Mitre-Nurcoung Rd then
W. Pre-book
0429 912 620   HEMA 84 A4   36 44 00 S   141 44 06 E

556 Jane Duff Highway Park

Natimuk-Frances Road, Duffholme
Camp Area 21 km W of Natimuk or 24 km
E of Goroke
HEMA 84 A4   36 43 59 S   141 43 21 E

557 Lake Ratzcastle Camp Area

Via Edenhope-Goroke Rd, Karnak
Camp Area 10 km S of Goroke, 2 km
off Edenhope-Goroke & Exells Rds. Donation at
general store
HEMA 84 A3   36 48 38 S   141 27 59 E

558 Goroke Apex Accommodation Park

69-85 Main St, Goroke
Camp Area next to swimming pool. See noticeboard
for fees
0429 672 791   HEMA 84 A3   36 43 13 S   141 28 01 E

559 Lake Charlegrark Camp

Via Charlegrark Rd, Goroke
Camp Area 33 km N of Edenhope or 23 km
W of Goroke. 2 km S off C213
03 5386 6281   HEMA 84 A2   36 46 06 S   141 14 04 E

560 Lake Bringalbert

Old Bringalbert Rd, Bringalbert
Camp Area 5 km N of Bringalbert
HEMA 84 A2   36 49 58 S   141 09 40 E

561 Apsley Border Inn

65 Wallace St, Apsley
Parking Area behind pub, on Splatt St.
Check in at the bar
03 5586 1205   HEMA 84 B2   36 58 06 S   141 04 57 E

562 Parsons (Collins) Lake

Parson Lake Reserve
Via Sullivan Rd, Edenhope
Picnic Area 63 km SW of Natimuk or 7 km NE of
Edenhope
13 19 63   HEMA 84 B3   37 00 05 S   141 21 05 E

563 Johnny Mullagh Reserve

Blair St, Harrow
Camp Area S side of Harrow, beside
Glenelg R. Pay at Harrows Cafe
0455 881 210   HEMA 84 C3   37 10 12 S   141 35 21 E

Melbourne to Bordertown
Western Highway

564 Boar Gully Campground

Brisbane Ranges National Park
Little River Tr, Mount Wallace
Camp Area 6 km E of Mount Wallace. Turn E off
C141, 18 km S of Ballan to Brisbane Ranges Rd.
Pre-book. Limited vehicle sites. 21 day limit
131 963   HEMA 80 B2   37 46 00 S   144 15 47 E

VICTORIA

565 Lalgambook Mount Franklin Reserve
Hepburn Regional Park
Mount Franklin Rd, Daylesford
Camp Area 11 km N of Daylesford. Turn E 9 km N of Daylesford
131 963   **HEMA 85 C12**   37 15 47 S   144 08 57 E

566 Slaty Creek Campground
Creswick Regional Park
Slaty Creek Rd, Creswick
Camp Area 5 km SE of Creswick. Turn W off C291, 2 km SE of Creswick. 3 km dirt road. 2 other camp areas within 400 m with no facilities
131 963   **HEMA 85 D11**   37 27 46 S   143 54 15 E

567 Lake Burrumbeet South
Canico Dr, Burrumbeet
Camp Spot at Carngham, near boat club
03 5320 5500   **HEMA 85 D11**   37 31 51 S   143 37 45 E

568 Lake Burrumbeet
Dobsons Ln, Burrumbeet
Camp Area W side of lake, 16 km W of Cardigan Village
03 5320 5500   **HEMA 85 D11**   37 29 53 S   143 36 59 E

569 Beaufort RV Park
1 Park Rd, Beaufort
Parking Area behind church. Follow Lawrence St S, L at Jcn of South St to Audus Ln
1300 797 363   **HEMA 85 D10**   37 26 07 S   143 23 03 E

570 Valdara Rustic Farmstay
8 Dundas St, Raglan
Farm Stay 10 km N of Beaufort or 55 km NW of Ballarat. N from Western Hwy to Main Lead Rd for 7 km, Raglan-Elmhurst Rd for 1 km, N 500 m. Pre-book
0414 082 754   **HEMA 85 D10**   37 21 50 S   143 21 09 E

571 Smiths Bridge Camp Area
Mount Cole State Forest
Fiery Creek Rd, Raglan
Camp Area 8 km N of town. Via Raglan-Elmhurst Rd
136 186   **HEMA 85 C9**   37 17 52 S   143 17 35 E

572 Chinamans Campground
Mount Cole State Forest
Chinaman Rd, Raglan
Camp Area 25 km NW of Ararat or 39 km NE of Beaufort. Exit Western Hwy N to Buangor-Ben Nevis Rd at Buangor for 13 km, then W to Mount Cole Rd for 4.5 km, 650 m to campground
136 186   **HEMA 85 C9**   37 14 56 S   143 11 57 E

573 Ditchfield Campsite
Mount Buangor State Park
Camp Rd, Raglan
Camp Area 9 km NW of Raglan or 19 km NW of Beaufort. W from Raglan to Raglan-Mount Cole Rd 3 km, Mount Cole Rd 4.5 km, then N 800 m to camp
136 186   **HEMA 85 C9**   37 19 01 S   143 16 23 E

574 Middle Creek Campground
Mount Buangor State Park
Middle Ck Walk, Beaufort
Camp Area 20 km NW of Beaufort or 16 km NE of Buangor. Turn N off Western Hwy 12 km NW of Beaufort or 8 km SE of Buangor to Ferntree Gully Rd. 8 km dirt road. Pre-book
136 186   **HEMA 85 C9**   37 19 57 S   143 14 47 E

575 Bailes Camping Area
Mount Buangor State Park
Middle Ck Walk, Beaufort
Camp Area 22 km NW of Beaufort or 18 km NE of Buangor. Turn N off Western Hwy 12 km NW of Beaufort or 8 km SE of Buangor to Ferntree Gully Rd. 8 km dirt road. Pre-book
136 186   **HEMA 85 C9**   37 18 56 S   143 14 24 E

576 Green Hill Lake Reserve
Green Hill Lake Rd, Ararat
Camp Area 19 km W of Buangor or 3 km E of Ararat. 500 m N of Hwy. Turn at offical sign to the lake & cross railway line to track. Free 28 day permit required for longer stays
1800 657 158   **HEMA 85 C8**   37 17 47 S   142 58 53 E

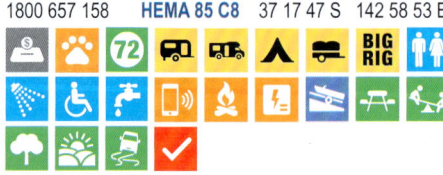

577 Cathcart Rest Area
Ararat-Halls Gap Rd, Ararat
Rest Area 6 km W of Ararat
132 213   **HEMA 85 C8**   37 17 43 S   142 52 42 E

578 Moyston Sports Ground
Moyston-Great Western Rd, Moyston
Camp Area N side of town. Honesty box
1800 657 158   **HEMA 85 C8**   37 17 54 S   142 45 55 E

579 Suma Lodge
751 Sugarloaf Rd, Rhymney
Camp Area 20 km NW of Ararat. Turn SW off Western Hwy at Great Western to Moyston Great Western Rd then W. Pre-book
0417 666 729   **HEMA 85 C8**   37 11 30 S   142 46 33 E

580 Great Western Rec Reserve
Great Western-Moyston Rd, Great Western
Camp Area E side of road, S of town centre. Fee for power/facilities. 14 day limit. SCV are free for 3 days then site fee applies
0438 532 557   **HEMA 85 C8**   37 09 38 S   142 51 00 E

581 Grampians Old Man Emu Stay
3971 Ararat Hlls Gap Rd, Halls Gap
Camp Area 8 km E of Halls Gap. Via Grampian Rd
0427 519 691   **HEMA 84 C7**   37 09 00 S   142 34 17 E

582 Dadswells Bridge South
Western Hwy, Dadswells Bridge
Rest Area 22 km NW of Stawell turnoff or 7 km SE of Dadswells Bridge
133 778   **HEMA 84 B7**   36 57 15 S   142 34 45 E

583 Dadswells Bridge Motel
5385 Western Hwy, Dadswells Bridge
Parking Area behind hotel. Register at bar
03 5359 5251   **HEMA 84 B7**   36 55 03 S   142 30 48 E

584 Plantation Campground
Grampians National Park
Mount Zero Rd, Halls Gap
Camp Area 10 km N of Halls Gap Info Centre. Turn N off C216 before bridge, for 8.8 km (mostly dirt road). 21 day limit
131 963   **HEMA 84 B7**   37 03 34 S   142 30 53 E

585 Stapylton Campground

Grampians National Park
Olive Plantation Rd, Halls Gap
Camp Area 33 km SE of Horsham. Turn S off Western Hwy 17 km SE of Horsham to Northern Grampians Rd 14 km, E for 2 km (dirt road). Permit applies. Small vehicles only. 21 day limit
131 963   HEMA 84 B6   36 55 28 S   142 23 00 E

586 Troopers Creek Camp

Grampians National Park
Roses Gap Rd, Halls Gap
Camp Area 41 km N of Halls Gap. E off C222, 32 km NW of Halls Gap. Permit applies. Pre-book. 21 day limit
131 963   HEMA 84 B6   37 00 59 S   142 25 34 E

587 Borough Huts Campground

Grampians National Park
C216 Grampians Rd, Halls Gap
Camp Area 11 km S of Halls Gap. Access near Fyans Creek. Pre-book. 21 day limit
131 963   HEMA 84 C7   37 13 27 S   142 32 25 E

588 Jimmy Creek Campground

Grampians National Park
C216 Grampians Rd, Halls Gap
Camp Area 29 km S of Halls Gap. Pre-book. 21 day limit
131 963   HEMA 84 D7   37 22 19 S   142 30 11 E

589 Wannon Crossing Camp

Grampians National Park
Grampians Rd, Mafeking
Camp Area 35 km S of Halls Gap, at Knight Bridge on Wannon River. Small vehicles only
03 5361 4000   HEMA 84 D7   37 26 00 S   142 28 33 E

590 Boreang Campground

Grampians National Park
Glenelg River Rd, Halls Gap
Camp Area 18 km SW of Halls Gap. Access via Mount Victory Rd. Dirt road. Not suitable for caravans. Pre-book
03 5361 4000   HEMA 84 C6   37 10 27 S   142 25 07 E

591 Smiths Mill Campground

Grampians National Park
Old Mill Rd, Halls Gap
Camp Area 17 km NW of Halls Gap. Turn N off C222 to Wartook Rd (C228), then R for 1 km, L to Smiths Rd (dirt road). Pre-book
03 5361 4000   HEMA 84 B6   37 06 28 S   142 25 24 E

592 Burnt Creek

Western Hwy, Horsham
Rest Area 32 km NW of Dadswells Bridge or 5 km SE of Horsham
133 778   HEMA 84 A6   36 45 39 S   142 15 01 E

593 Dimboola Rec Reserve

Lloyd St, Dimboola
Parking Area S of town, near PO. Riverside
HEMA 86 J5   36 27 30 S   142 01 44 E

594 Ackle Bend

Little Desert National Park
River Tr, Dimboola
Camp Area 6 km S of Dimboola. Access via Riverside & Horseshoe Bend Rds. 3 km dirt road. Pre-book. 21 day limit
131 963   HEMA 86 J5   36 30 10 S   142 01 11 E

595 Horseshoe Bend Dimboola

Little Desert National Park
Horseshoe Bend Rd, Dimboola
Camp Area 7 km S of Dimboola. Via Riverside Rd. 4 km dirt road. Pre-book. 21 day limit
131 963   HEMA 86 J5   36 29 51 S   142 01 05 E

596 Lochiel Rest Area

Western Hwy, Dimboola
Rest Area 6 km W of Dimboola or 32 km E of Nhill
133 778   HEMA 86 J5   36 25 06 S   141 58 52 E

597 Kiata Campground

Little Desert National Park
Campground Tr, Winiam East
Camp Area 12 km S of Kiata, via Kiata South Rd. Signposted. 4 km dirt road. 21 day limit
131 963   HEMA 86 J4   36 26 51 S   141 47 53 E

598 Nhill Aerodrome RV Stop

Aerodrome Rd, Nhill
Camp Spot 3 km N of Nhill. Via Propodollah Rd
0437 351 753   HEMA 86 H4   36 18 29 S   141 38 51 E

599 Broken Bucket Camp Area

Broken Bucket Tank Bushland Reserve
Broken Bucket Tr, Nhill
Camp Area 55 km N of Nhill. Access via Murrayville-Nhill Tr, then R
HEMA 86 G3   35 57 39 S   141 24 04 E

600 Big Billy Bore Camp

Big Desert State Forest
Nhill-Murrayville Rd, Murrayville
Camp Area 34 km S of Murrayville or 108 km N of Nhill. Well signposted, check road conditions as sometimes impassable

601 Lawloit Rest Area

Western Hwy, Lawloit
Rest Area 14 km W of Nhill or 27 km E of Kaniva
133 778   HEMA 86 J3   36 23 18 S   141 30 36 E

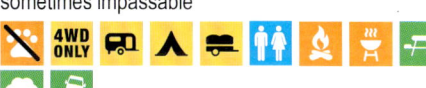

602 Kaniva Poolside Caravan Park

Baker St, Kaniva
Caravan Park 400m S of PO
0458 687 054   HEMA 86 J2   36 22 54 S   141 14 25 E

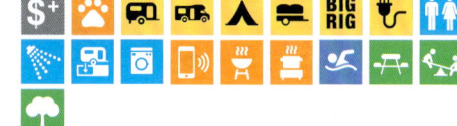

603 Mooree Reserve

Leeor Rd, Kaniva
Camp Area 26 km SW of Kaniva. Turn SW at the roundabout via South Lillmur Rd & L. Track is rough
HEMA 86 J2   36 27 25 S   141 03 26 E

604 Serviceton Rec Reserve

52 Baldocks-Grossers Rd, Serviceton
Camp Area S of township. Call for access to facilities & payment
0419 032 418   HEMA 86 J1   36 23 16 S   140 58 56 E

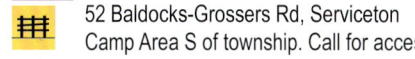

605 Serviceton Reservoir
Via Western Hwy, Serviceton
Camp Area 3.5 km NE of Serviceton via
Serviceton North-Telopea Downs Rd. Turn R to
Kings & Madderns Rds. On L

HEMA 86 J2   36 20 35 S   140 58 54 E

606 Tolmer Reserve
Western Hwy, Serviceton
A8   Rest Area 25 km W of Kaniva or 18 km E of
Bordertown at VIC/SA border

HEMA 86 J1   36 20 40 S   140 58 02 E

Melbourne to Mt Gambier
Princes Highway

607 Geelong Showground
77 Breakwater Rd, Breakwater
C112   Camp Area at East Geelong. Contact
Caretaker

03 5221 1707   HEMA 80 G3   38 10 17 S   144 22 20 E

608 Winchelsea RV Parking
Barwon River Reserve
A1   Cnr Barwon Tce & Mercer St, Winchelsea
Parking Area at Winchelsea

03 5261 0600   HEMA 83 D11   38 14 19 S   143 59 20 E

609 Barwon Hotel
1 Main St, Winchelsea
A1   Parking Area E side of Main St. Check in
with publican on arrival

03 5267 2046   HEMA 83 D11   38 14 34 S   143 59 27 E

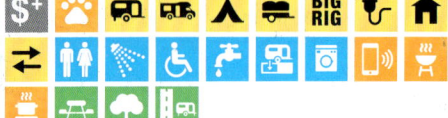

610 Meredith Park
Lake Colac
C146   175 Meredith Park Rd, Ondit
Camp Area 12 km N of Colac or 11 km S of Beeac.
W off C146, 10 km N of Colac or 9 km S of Beeac

03 5232 9400   HEMA 83 E9   38 16 07 S   143 36 38 E

611 Central Caravan Park
Bruce St, Colac
A1   Caravan Park at showground

03 5231 3586   HEMA 83 E9   38 20 09 S   143 36 12 E

612 Simpson Recreation Reserve
Lavers Hill Codben Rd, Simpson
C166   Parking Area N end of town. Seasonal.
Pre-book to access

0428 363 604   HEMA 82 G6   38 29 41 S   143 12 40 E

613 Cobden Freedom Camp
1236 Camperdown Rd, Cobden
C164   Camp Area behind BP Roadhouse

03 5595 1535   HEMA 82 E5   38 19 13 S   143 04 46 E

614 Lake Elingamite
Oates Rd, Elingamite North
C167   Camp Area 7 km SW of Cobden. Turn W
off Cobden-Warrnambool Rd 5 km SW of Cobden.
2 km dirt road

131 963   HEMA 82 E5   38 20 56 S   143 00 56 E

615 Timboon Rec Reserve
45 Curdies Rd, Timboon
C163   Parking Area 17 km N of Port Campbell.
Dump point key at Timboon Fuel

0407 504 374   HEMA 82 G4   38 28 41 S   142 57 56 E

616 Brucknell Park Scout Camp
Timboon-Nullawarre Rd, Nirranda East
Camp Area 30 km E of Allansford or 12 km
W of Timboon. Pre-book

03 5566 5205   HEMA 82 G4   38 28 14 S   142 51 27 E

617 Terang Community Caravan Park
A1   Princes Hwy, Terang
Caravan Park 1 km W of PO

0409 518 795   HEMA 82 D4   38 14 31 S   142 54 34 E

618 Panmure Rest Area
1 Harris St, Panmure
A1   Rest Area on Princes Hwy

131 171   HEMA 82 E3   38 20 11 S   142 43 39 E

619 Hawkesdale Apex Park
2621 Penshurst-Warrnambool Rd, Hawkesdale
C178   Camp Spot 200 m N of PO

0469 694 404   HEMA 84 G6   38 06 15 S   142 19 19 E

620 Hawkesdale Racecourse
Racecourse St, Hawkesdale
C178   Camp Area & Rec Reserve 28 km N of
Killarney. N off Princes Hwy between Rosebrook and
Killarney to Penshurst-Warrnambool Rd. Cnr Irving St

HEMA 84 G6   38 06 36 S   142 20 02 E

621 Warrnambool Showgrounds
331 Koroit St, Warrnambool
Camp Area beside greyhound race track.
Turn R at gate, go all the way past another gate,
camp near row of trees

0409 009 473   HEMA 82 F1   38 22 37 S   142 28 08 E

622 Macarthur Rec Reserve
Hamilton-Port Fairy Rd, Macarthur
C184   Camp Area 700 m S of town. Entry just S of
river crossing. Contact caretaker on arrival

HEMA 84 G5   38 02 15 S   142 00 27 E

623 Budj Bim Campground
Budj Bim National Park
Mount Eccles Rd, Macarthur
Camp Area 10 km SW of Macarthur. Pre-book.
21 day limit

131 963   HEMA 84 G5   38 03 28 S   141 55 26 E

624 Byaduk Rec Reserve
Byaduk-Penshurst Rd, Byaduk
C184   Camp Area 57 km N of Port Fairy off
Hamilton-Port Fairy Rd, then E

HEMA 84 F5   37 57 06 S   141 57 26 E

625 Yambuk Inn
Princes Hwy, Yambuk
Camp Area 18 km NW of Port Fairy. Pre-book.
Check in with publican

03 5568 4310   HEMA 84 H5   38 18 55 S   142 04 06 E

626 Fitzroy River Reserve

Thompsons Rd, Tyrendarra
Camp Area 26 km NW of Yambuk or 11 km
SE of Tyrendarra. S off A1, 22 km NW of Yambuk
or 7 km SE of Tyrendarra, signposted River Outlet.
At river mouth
03 5523 2671   HEMA 84 H4   38 15 29 S   141 50 51 E

627 Sawpit Picnic Area

Mount Clay State Forest
242 Boyers Rd, Narrawong
Picnic Area 4 km NW of Narrawong. Turn N 1 km W
of Narrawong to Boyers Rd for 3 km
1800 035 567   HEMA 84 H4   38 14 07 S   141 41 17 E

628 Henty Park

2 Bentinck St, Portland
Parking Area near Vintage Cable Tram
depot
03 5523 2671   HEMA 84 H4   38 21 16 S   141 36 22 E

629 Surrey Ridge Camp Area

Cobboboonee National Park
Cut Out Dam Rd, Heywood
Camp Area 18 km W of Heywood. Turn W off
A1, 6 km S of Heywood or 21 km N of Portland
to Coffeys Lane. L at Jackys Swamp Rd, then R.
9 km dirt road
13 61 86   HEMA 84 G3   38 11 02 S   141 30 15 E

630 Jackass Fern Gully Camp

Cobboboonee National Park
T&W Rd, Lyons
Camp Area 24 km NW of Heywood. Turn W off A1,
7 km NW of Heywood to Sinclair Settlement & Mt
Deception Rds. Alternative route via T&W Rd off A1,
5 km SE of Greenwald. 9 km dirt road
13 61 86   HEMA 84 G3   38 04 29 S   141 25 32 E

631 Heywood RV Stop

Hunter St East, Heywood
Parking Area NE side of town
HEMA 84 G4   38 07 51 S   141 37 57 E

632 Annya Campground

Annya State Forest
Annya Rd, Heywood
Camp Area 15 km NW of Heywood or 25 km S of
Digby. E off C195, 7.5 km NW of A1/C195 Jcn or
24.5 km S of Digby. 500 m off Hwy. Dirt road
03 5581 2070   HEMA 84 G3   38 01 07 S   141 34 58 E

633 Hotspur Bridge (Crawford River)

C195
Portland-Casterton Rd, Hotspur
Camp Area 20 km NW of A1/C195 Jcn or 13 km S of
Digby. Riverside
03 5523 2671   HEMA 84 F3   37 55 33 S   141 33 40 E

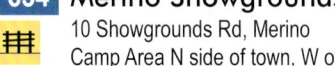

634 Merino Showgrounds

10 Showgrounds Rd, Merino
Camp Area N side of town, W of C195
HEMA 84 E3   37 42 34 S   141 32 46 E

VICTORIA

635 Hiscocks Crossing
Crawford River Regional Park
Big Hill Rd, Greenwald
Dispersed Camping 16 km W of Hotspur. W off C195, 600 m N of Hotspur Bridge to Mill Rd & The Boulevard. Dirt road. Alternative route from Greenwald. 9 km dirt road. Riverside
13 19 63   HEMA 84 F3   37 56 19 S   141 26 47 E

636 Fort O'Hare Campground
Gambier Rd, Dartmoor
Camp Area 500 m E of PO, via Greenham St. Riverside
03 5523 2671   HEMA 84 F2   37 55 33 S   141 17 06 E

Portland to Mt Gambier
via Nelson

637 Cape Bridgewater Coastal Camp
1721 Blowholes Rd, Cape Bridgewater
Camp Area via Bridgewater Rd, SW of town
03 5526 7247   HEMA 84 H3   38 22 15 S   141 24 05 E

638 Swan Lake Campground
Discovery Bay Coastal Park
Great South West Walk, Kentbruck
Camp Area 36 km W of Portland or 45 km E of Nelson. Turn S onto Swan Lake Rd 30 km W of Portland or 38 km E of Nelson. 6 km to site. Dirt road, steep in places. Pre-book. Not suitable for caravans
131 963   HEMA 84 G2   38 12 54 S   141 18 41 E

639 Lake Mombeong Camp
Discovery Bay Coastal Park
Lake Mombeong Rd, Nelson
Camp Area 72 km W of Portland or 23 km E of Nelson. Turn S onto Lake Mombeong Rd 65 km W of Portland or 16 km E of Nelson. 7 km to campsite. Pre-book. Not suitable for caravans
131 963   HEMA 84 G2   38 08 02 S   141 11 08 E

640 Dartmoor Turnoff Rest Area
Portland-Nelson Rd, Nelson Area
Rest Area 54 km NW of Portland or 15 km E of Nelson
133 778   HEMA 84 G2   38 04 31 S   141 09 54 E

641 Pritchards Campground - Southern Shore
Lower Glenelg National Park
Post & Rail Tr, Nelson
Camp Area 18 km NW of Kentbruck, 21 km E of Nelson or 21 km S of Winnap. Turn N off C192, 12 km W of Kentbruck or 15 km E of Nelson. Access via Winnap-Nelson Rd. 1.5 km dirt road. Pre-book. 21 day limit
131 963   HEMA 84 G2   38 03 23 S   141 13 05 E

642 Forest Camp
Lower Glenelg National Park
Glenelg Dr, Nelson
Camp Area 26 km E of Nelson off Winnap-Nelson Rd. 8 km dirt road. Permit applies. 21 day limit
131 963   HEMA 84 G2   38 01 52 S   141 08 18 E

643 Wilson Hall Camping Area
Lower Glenelg National Park
Wilson Hall Tr, Nelson
Camp Area on north shore. Signposted access off Wanwin Rd turn S. Dirt road. Small to medium vehicles. Some low trees. Pre-book. 21 day limit
131 963   HEMA 84 G2   38 01 09 S   141 06 25 E

644 Red Gum Landing
Lower Glenelg National Park
River Fire Line Tr, Wanwin
Camp Area 20 km SW of Dartmoor. 12 km on Wanwin Rd, veer L 2 km on Wanwin Rd, continue S 3 km on The Fence Track, then R 2 km, L down a sandy track, 200 m to river, ebook
131 963   HEMA 84 G2   38 02 35 S   141 09 41 E

645 Princess Margaret Rose Caves - Northern Shore
Lower Glenelg National Park
Princess Margaret Rose Caves Rd, Nelson
Camp Area 16 km N of Nelson or 28 km SE of Mt Gambier. Turn N 4 km W of Nelson or S 10 km E of Mt Gambier off the A1. Permit applies
08 8738 4171   HEMA 84 F1   37 59 12 S   140 59 31 E

Ballarat to Mt Gambier
Glenelg Highway

646 Haddon Woady Lions Park
Via Racecourse Rd, Haddon
Parking Area opposite general store, near Smythes Ck. 5 day limit. Donation envelopes at amenities
HEMA 85 E11   37 35 26 S   143 42 54 E

647 Snake Valley Royal Hotel
886 Carngham-Linton Rd, Snake Valley
Parking Area next to pub. Check in with publican. Fee for showers.
03 5344 9224   HEMA 85 E10   37 36 41 S   143 35 05 E

648 Smythesdale Gardens
35 Garden St, Smythesdale
Rest Area 500 m N of Hwy
03 5342 8752   HEMA 85 E11   37 38 21 S   143 41 09 E

649 Chill Crest Campground
396 Smythesdale-Snake Valley Rd, Hillcrest
Camp Area E of Hillcrest. N from Glenelg Hwy. Pre-book
0418 503 938   HEMA 85 E10   37 37 19 S   143 39 04 E

650 Woady Yaloak Creek
Old Glenelg Hwy, Scarsdale
Rest Area 2 km W of Scarsdale or 7 km E of Linton
HEMA 85 E11   37 40 41 S   143 38 19 E

651 Berringa Recreation Reserve
9 Recreational Rd, Berringa
Camp Area S of Derwent Jacks Rd. Caretaker collects fee
0439 534 223   HEMA 85 E11   37 46 22 S   143 41 49 E

652 Happy Valley Crossing
Happy Valley Streamside Reserve
264 Happy Valley Crossing Rd, Linton Area
Camp Area 8 km SE of Linton. Exit Glenelg Hwy (B160) S to Linton-Naringhil Rd for 5 km, then E 3 km to creek
HEMA 85 E10   37 45 02 S   143 34 49 E

653 Pitfield Streamside Reserve
Rokewood-Skipron Rd, Pitfield
Rest Area near Jcn of C143 & C171
HEMA 85 F10   37 48 28 S   143 35 08 E

654 East Beach Reserve
Via East Beach Rd, Lake Bolac
Camp Area 4 km SE of Lake Bolac. Turn S off B160. Ranger collects fees
03 5350 2204   HEMA 85 E8   37 43 17 S   142 52 43 E

655 Lake Bolac Campground

Frontage Rd, Lake Bolac
Camp Area S off Glenelg Hwy. Via East
Beach Rd

HEMA 85 E8   37 42 07 S   142 52 21 E

656 Lake Bolac Foreshore

Via Frontage Rd, Lake Bolac
Camp Area 2 km S of Lake Bolac, via Sago
Rd. Various sites on W side of lake. Ranger collects fee
03 5350 2204   HEMA 85 E8   37 43 16 S   142 51 22 E

657 Lake Buninjon

Maroona-Glenthompson Rd, Willaura
Rest Area 7 km SW of Maroona or 8 km NE
of Willaura
B180

HEMA 85 D8   37 29 05 S   142 47 38 E

658 Willaura Rec Grounds

1 Delacome Way, Willaura
Camp Area E of Main St. Limited powered
sites. Call caretaker on arrival
0429 953 150   HEMA 84 D7   37 32 41 S   142 44 36 E

659 Yuppeckiar Park

Glenelg Hwy, Glenthompson
Rest Area at Nine Mile Creek. 6 km W of
Glenthompson or 12 km E of Dunkeld
B160

HEMA 84 E7   37 38 08 S   142 28 58 E

660 Dunkeld Caravan Park

Victoria Valley Rd, Dunkeld
Caravan Park Cnr Glenelg Hwy
03 5577 2578   HEMA 84 E6   37 38 59 S   142 20 44 E

661 Freshwater Lake Reserve

753 Victoria Valley Rd, Dunkeld
Camp Area 8 km N of Dunkeld

13 19 63   HEMA 84 E6   37 35 07 S   142 19 07 E

662 Wannon Falls Campground

Wannon Falls State Reserve

Camerons Rd, Wannon
B160
Camp Area 15 km NW of Hamilton or 17 km SE of
Coleraine. Entry via Camerons Rd or Wannon Falls
Rd, 1 km S of Wannon
1800 807 056   HEMA 84 E4   37 40 31 S   141 50 49 E

663 Coleraine Caravan Park

4 Winter St, Coleraine
Caravan Park behind PO. Cnr of Turnbull St.
Pay at PO
03 5575 2268   HEMA 84 E4   37 35 50 S   141 41 29 E

664 Wando Vale Memorial Hall

Casterton-Edenhope Rr, Wando Vale
Camp Area 7 km N of Glenelg Hwy. Pre-book
03 5582 0272   HEMA 84 D3   37 30 43 S   141 26 40 E

665 Island Park Caravan Park

Malcolm Carmichael Dr, Casterton
Caravan Park off Murray St, adjacent to
swimming pool. Phone for payment & key access
0457 414 187   HEMA 84 E3   37 34 58 S   141 24 19 E

666 Ess Lagoon

Ess Lagoon Rd, Casterton
Camp Spot N side of town. 1 month limit

HEMA 84 E3   37 34 51 S   141 23 56 E

667 Casterton Angling Camp

27 Warrock Rd, Warrock
Camp Area 27 km N of Casterton. E off
Casterton Apsley Rd. Pre-book
0488 063352   HEMA 84 D2   37 26 30 S   141 16 22 E

668 Wattle Glen (Carmichaels)

Carmichaels Track, Corndale
Picnic Area 11 km W of Casterton.
Signposted off Penola Rd, S for 1 km
136 186   HEMA 84 E2   37 35 28 S   141 17 22 E

669 Long Lead

Via Casterton-Penola Rd, Casterton
Camp Area 18 km W of Casterton. From
Casterton-Penola Rd, turn N to Long Lead Track, L
to Blue Line, veer R. GPS at entry. Popular with trail
bike riders
HEMA 84 E2   37 35 07 S   141 12 33 E

670 Mill Swamp Camp Area

Wilkin Flora & Fauna Reserve

Grubbed Rd, Strathdownie
Camp Area 12 km E of Strathdownie. Access via
Hwy. Signposted. Small vehicles only
03 5554 2440   HEMA 84 E2   37 42 08 S   141 13 29 E

671 Baileys Rocks Campground

Dergholm State Park

Via Baileys Rocks Rd, Dergholm
Camp Area 45 km NW of Casterton or 27 km SE of
Langkoop. Turn E 9 km N of Dergholm or 25 km SE
of Langkoop. 3 km dirt road
131 963   HEMA 84 C2   37 17 17 S   141 10 38 E

Geelong to Hamilton
Hamilton Highway

672 Inverleigh Rest Area

Hamilton Hwy, Inverleigh
B140
Rest Area 28 km W of Geelong or 1 km E of
Inverleigh. E of river/bridge only
HEMA 83 C12   38 05 58 S   144 03 47 E

673 Cressy Rec Reserve

Brown St, Cressy
B140
Camp Area 63 km W of Geelong. Exit
Hamilton Hwy (B140) at Cressy to Colac-Ballarat Rd
for 1.4 km to Dennis St, 250 m to sites
HEMA 83 C9   38 02 07 S   143 37 59 E

674 Corindhap Rec Reserve

Hall St, Corindhap
Camp Area 44 km NW of Inverleigh, or
39 km S of Ballarat. Donation box in building next to
bathrooms
HEMA 83 A10   37 52 25 S   143 44 26 E

VICTORIA

675 Browns Water Hole

High St, Lismore
Caravan Park E side of town. Contact caretaker for key
0417 071 523   HEMA 82 B7   37 57 16 S   143 20 48 E

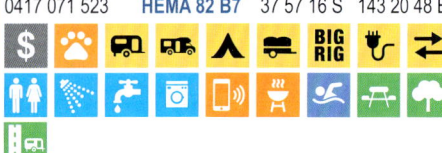

676 Lake Tooliorook

Lake Tooliorook Rd, Derrinallum
Camp Area 6 km S of Lismore. Turn W off C165, 5 km S of Lismore. 1 km dirt road. Check availability with caretaker, tokens for showers
0487 337 946   HEMA 82 B7   37 58 38 S   143 17 05 E

677 Derrinallum Rec Reserve

Hamilton Hwy, Derrinallum
B140
Camp Area E end of town
HEMA 82 B6   37 56 56 S   143 13 39 E

678 Deep Lake Rec Reserve

Via Chatsworth Rd, Derrinallum
Camp Area 5 km NW of Derrinallum. Pay fees at cafe, tokens for showers
0407 201 735   HEMA 82 B6   37 55 53 S   143 10 37 E

679 Nuggets Flat

2810 Hamilton Hwy, Darlington
B140
Camp Area 27 km SW of Lismore or 23 km NE of Mortlake. Opposite Elephant Bridge Hotel. Creekside
0418 324 007   HEMA 82 B5   37 59 59 S   143 02 39 E

680 Mortlake Caravan Park

31 Montgomery Way, Mortlake
Caravan Park 1 km E of PO. Off Jamieson Ave
0409 428 870   HEMA 82 C3   38 05 04 S   142 48 32 E

681 Caramut Hotel

16 Brown St, Caramut
Camp Area just off B140, behind hotel. Patrons only. Check in at bar on arrival
03 55998381   HEMA 82 B1   37 57 31 S   142 31 09 E

682 Penshurst Caravan Park

78-96 Cox St, Penshurst
Caravan Park 100 m from PO. Pay at PO
03 5576 5220   HEMA 84 F6   37 52 26 S   142 17 26 E

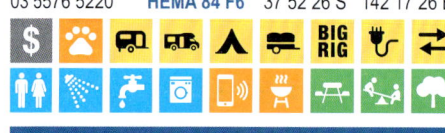

Geelong to Warrnambool
Great Ocean Road

683 Hammonds Campground

Great Otway National Park
Hammond Rd, Aireys Inlet
Camp Area 12 km NW of Aireys Inlet. Via Bambra Rd. Dirt road. 21 day limit
131 963   HEMA 83 F12   38 23 55 S   144 01 23 E

684 Tanners Road Bend

Otway Forest Park
Tanners Rd, Gherang
Camp Area S from Princes Hwy at Winchelsea to Barwon Tce/Atkins Rd, then S to Gherang Rd
HEMA 83 E12   38 19 49 S   144 04 38 E

685 Big Hill Track Camping

Great Otway National Park
Big Hill Tr & Lorne-Deans March Rd Jcn, Lorne
Camp Area 12 km NW of Lorne or 13 km SE of Deans Marsh. Signposted. Open Nov - Apr. 21 day limit
131 963   HEMA 83 G11   38 28 29 S   143 55 57 E

686 Sharps Campground

Great Otway National Park
Sharps Rd, Lorne
Camp Area 3 km W of Lorne via Allenvale Rd. 21 day limit
131 963   HEMA 83 G11   38 33 05 S   143 55 55 E

687 Wye River Foreshore Reserve

37-41 Great Ocean Rd, Wye River
Camp Area 15 km S of Lorne, 30 km N of Apollo Bay. Pre-book peak periods. Open Oct - Apr, call to confirm
03 5289 0412   HEMA 83 H11   38 38 02 S   143 53 32 E

688 Stevenson Falls Scenic Reserve

Great Otway State Park
Colac Water Pipeline Track, Forrest
Camp Area 5 km W of Barramunga. Turn W off C119, 26 km N of Apollo Bay or 8 km S of C119/C154 Jcn to Upper Gellibrand Rd. Narrow winding dirt road
136 186   HEMA 83 G9   38 33 49 S   143 39 23 E

689 Dandos Campground

Otway Forest Park
Lardners Tr, Barramunga
Camp Area 13 km SE of Gellibrand. Turn E off C155, 1 km S of Gellibrand to Gellibrand East Rd, Lardners & Sayers Tracks. Dirt road. Riverside
HEMA 83 G9   38 33 16 S   143 37 05 E

690 Beauchamp Falls Reserve

Great Otway National Park
Beauchamp Falls Rd, Beech Forest
Camp Area 4 km SE of Beech Forest. Turn S off C159, 1 km E of Beech Forest to Aire Valley Rd. Dirt road. 21 day limit
131 963   HEMA 83 H9   38 39 05 S   143 36 24 E

691 Apollo Bay Rec Reserve

70 Great Ocean Rd., Apollo Bay
Camp Area 1 km S of PO
03 5237 6577   HEMA 83 J9   38 45 50 S   143 40 06 E

692 The Dairy Farmstay

200 Barham River Rd, Apollo Bay
Farm Stay SW on Barham River Rd, 2 km to camp. GPS at entrance. Pre-book. 7 day limit
0429 140 170   HEMA 83 J9   38 46 08 S   143 38 56 E

693 Barham Park Farm Stay

Barham River Rd, Apollo Bay
Farm Stay SW on Barham River Rd, 3 km to camp. GPS at entrance. Pre-book
0434 196 061   HEMA 83 J9   38 45 58 S   143 38 16 E

694 Blanket Bay Campground

Great Otway National Park
Blanket Bay Rd, Point Lewis
Camp Area 36 km W of Apollo Bay. Turn S to Cape Otway Lighthouse Rd. Pre-book. BYO firewood. 21 day limit
131 963   HEMA 83 K9   38 49 41 S   143 34 58 E

695 Parker Hill Campground

Great Otway National Park
Parker Hill Tr, Cape Otway
Camp Area S off Great Ocean Rd (E of Hordern Vale) to Otway Lighthouse Rd to Blanket Bay Rd, then SE to track. 21 day limit, ebook
131 963   HEMA 83 K8   38 50 48 S   143 33 30 E

696 Aire River East Campground
Great Otway National Park
Via Hordern Vale Rd, Glenaire
Camp Area 29 km W of Apollo Bay or 29 km SE of Lavers Hill. Turn S off B100, 24 km W of Apollo Bay or 24 km SE of Lavers Hill to Hordern Vale Rd. 4.5 km to campsites. 2 km dirt road. First camp on R, larger area over bridge. Pre-book. 21 day limit
131 963   HEMA 83 K8   38 48 02 S   143 28 55 E

697 Aire River West

Great Otway National Park
Sand Rd, Glenaire
Camp Area 38 km W of Apollo Bay or 20 km S of Lavers Hill. Turn S off B100, 33 km W of Apollo Bay or 15 km S of Lavers Hill. 5 km narrow dirt track. Riverside. Pre-book. 21 day limit
131 963   HEMA 83 K8   38 48 06 S   143 28 40 E

698 Johanna Beach

Great Otway National Park
Red Johanna Rd, Johanna
Camp Area 15 km S of Lavers Hill. Turn W off B100, 38 km W of Apollo Bay or 10 km S of Lavers Hill. Pre-book. 21 day limit
131 963   HEMA 82 J7   38 45 32 S   143 22 33 E

699 Princetown Rec Reserve

93 Old Coach Rd, Princetown
Camp Area 1 km S of Princetown, beside Gellibrand River
0429 985 176   HEMA 82 J6   38 41 56 S   143 09 31 E

700 Port Campbell Rec Reserve

Hennessy St, Port Campbell
Camp Area close to town
0431 128 790   HEMA 82 H5   38 36 58 S   143 00 06 E

---

701 Lascelles Camping Ground

Via Mallee St, Lascelles
Camp Area E of Hwy. Pay at Minapre Hotel
03 5081 6242   HEMA 86 E7   35 36 26 S   142 34 47 E

702 Hopetoun Caravan Park
Austin St, Hopetoun
Caravan Park E side of town, near lake
0417 237 587   HEMA 86 F6   35 43 33 S   142 22 02 E

703 Lake Lascelles
Via Rifle Butts Rd, Hopetoun
Rest Area E foreshore of lake. Turn N at the end of Austin St, follow track around lake. 1.5 km dirt road. Donation box
0439 529 973   HEMA 86 F6   35 43 31 S   142 22 29 E

704 Mallee Bush Retreat
Via Strachan St, Hopetoun
Camp Area on the W foreshore of lake. E end of Austin St
0439 529 973   HEMA 86 F6   35 43 39 S   142 22 15 E

705 Wonga Campground

Wyperfeld National Park
Via James Barrett Nature Dr, Yaapeet
Camp Area 28 km N of Yaapeet. Turn W 3 km N of Yaapeet, then N after 3 km onto Wyperfeld Entrance. Pre-book. 21 day limit
131 963   HEMA 86 E5   35 35 12 S   142 03 02 E

706 OTIT Campground
Lake Albacutya Regional Park
Via Jordan Valley Track, Yaapeet
Camp Area 8 km NW of Yaapeet. W end of Rifle Butts Rd. 2 km dirt road past OTIT Well sign. Lake can be dry
131 963   HEMA 86 F5   35 43 40 S   141 59 30 E

---

707 Yaapeet Beach Campground

Lake Albacutya Regional Park
Via Yaapeet West Rd, Yaapeet
Camp Area 4 km W of Yaapeet. Dirt road. Lake can be dry
131 963   HEMA 86 F5   35 46 01 S   142 00 23 E

708 Yaapeet Campground
Yaapeet-Kenmare Rd, Yaapeet
Camp Area at rear of hall, honesty box or pay at school
03 5395 7243   HEMA 86 F5   35 46 01 S   142 03 07 E

709 Western Beach Campground
Lake Albacutya Regional Park
Via Western Beach Rd, Yaapeet
Camp Area 17 km NW of Rainbow. Via Albacutya Rd. Lake can be dry
131 963   HEMA 86 F5   35 46 50 S   141 56 08 E

710 Rainbow Caravan Park
2 Railway St, Rainbow
Caravan Park 1 km SW of PO
03 5395 1062   HEMA 86 G5   35 54 17 S   141 59 35 E

711 The Wattles
Lake Hindmarsh Lake Reserve
Via Rainbow-Nhill Rd, Rainbow
Camp Area 16 km SW of Rainbow
131 963   HEMA 86 G5   35 56 41 S   141 52 27 E

712 Schulzes Beach
Lake Hindmarsh Lake Reserve
Via Schulzes Beach Rd, Jeparit
Camp Area 22 km SW of Rainbow. Via Rainbow-Nhill Rd. Lakeside, sandy track
131 963   HEMA 86 G4   36 02 46 S   141 51 25 E

713 Four Mile Beach Camping
Lake Hindmarsh Lake Reserve
Via Nhil-Jeparit Rd, Jeparit
Camp Area 7 km W of Jeparit on Nhil-Jeparit Rd
131 963   HEMA 86 H5   36 07 59 S   141 55 41 E

VICTORIA

714 Beulah Caravan Park
Via Higgbotham St, Beulah
Caravan Park in sportsground. Payment & keys from cafe, 67 Phillip St
03 5390 2200   **HEMA 86 G6**   35 56 28 S   142 25 01 E

715 Jeparit Caravan Park
Via Peterson Ave, Jeparit
Caravan Park 500 m SW of PO. See noticeboard for caretaker details
0408 107 851   **HEMA 86 H5**   36 08 41 S   141 59 03 E

716 Brim Reddas (Highway) Park
Via Swann St, Brim
Camp Area 1 km W of Brim. Fee for power, pay at Dixon Garage
03 5390 4212   **HEMA 86 G6**   36 04 32 S   142 24 26 E

717 Warracknabeal Caravan Park
2 Lyle St / Dimboola Rd, Warracknabeal
Caravan Park 1 km SW of PO
0400 915 125   **HEMA 86 H6**   36 15 11 S   142 23 15 E

718 Balmoral Mural Square
11 Bell St, Balmoral
Parking Area central to town. Via Glendinning St
HEMA 84 C4   37 14 53 S   141 50 24 E

719 Glendinning Campground
Rocklands Reservoir
1237 Yarramyljup Rd, Balmoral
Camp Area 20 km SE of Balmoral, via Yarramyljup or Glendinning Rds
1800 807 056   **HEMA 84 C5**   37 17 51 S   141 59 57 E

720 Mountain Dam Camp
Rocklands Reservoir
Via Rocklands-Cherrypool Rd, Balmoral
Camp Area 23 km SW of Cherrypool. Turn W off A200, 49 km S of Horsham or 55 km N of Cavendish, then L at HGH Cnr after 7 km. Dirt road
1800 807 056   **HEMA 84 C5**   37 13 39 S   142 05 16 E

721 Cherrypool Highway Park
Via Henty Hwy, Cherrypool
Rest Area 49 km S of Horsham or 55 km N of Cavendish. Along Glenelg River near bridge
03 5382 1832   **HEMA 84 B6**   37 06 29 S   142 11 14 E

722 Hynes Camping Reserve
Rocklands Reservoir
Via Hynes Rd, Glenisla
Camp Area 9 km W of Glenisla. Turn W off A200, 63 km S of Horsham or 41 km N of Cavendish
0438 561 772   **HEMA 84 C5**   37 13 29 S   142 06 18 E

723 Buandik Campground
Grampians National Park
Via Goat Track, Glenisla
Camp Area 10 km E of Glenisla. Turn E off A200, 66 km S of Horsham or 38 km N of Cavendish to Billiwing Rd & Harrop Tr. 9 km dirt road. 21 day limit
131 963   **HEMA 84 C6**   37 15 09 S   142 16 43 E

724 Fergusons Campground
Rocklands State Forest
530 Shilcocks Rd, Woohlpooer
Camp Area 27 km N of Cavendish. Turn W off A200, 78 km S of Horsham or 26 km N of Cavendish to Gartons Rd. After 3.7 km turn N, after 5 km turn W. Dirt road
1800 807 056   **HEMA 84 C5**   37 17 44 S   142 03 36 E

725 Wongaburra Camping
Via Snells Rd, Mooralla
Camp Area 19 km NE of Cavendish. E off Hwy. Pre-book
HEMA 84 D6   37 25 24 S   142 10 56 E

726 Cavendish Rec Reserve
Via Cadden St, Cavendish
Camp Area 1 km N of Cavendish. 300 m E of Hwy, next to picnic area. Pay at hotel or see notice board
0499 048 184   **HEMA 84 D5**   37 31 20 S   142 02 38 E

727 Greenhills Hotel
5191 Henry Hwy, Condah
Camp Area 4 km N of Myamyn. Patrons only. Register at bar
03 5578 2220   **HEMA 84 F4**   37 57 08 S   141 44 51 E

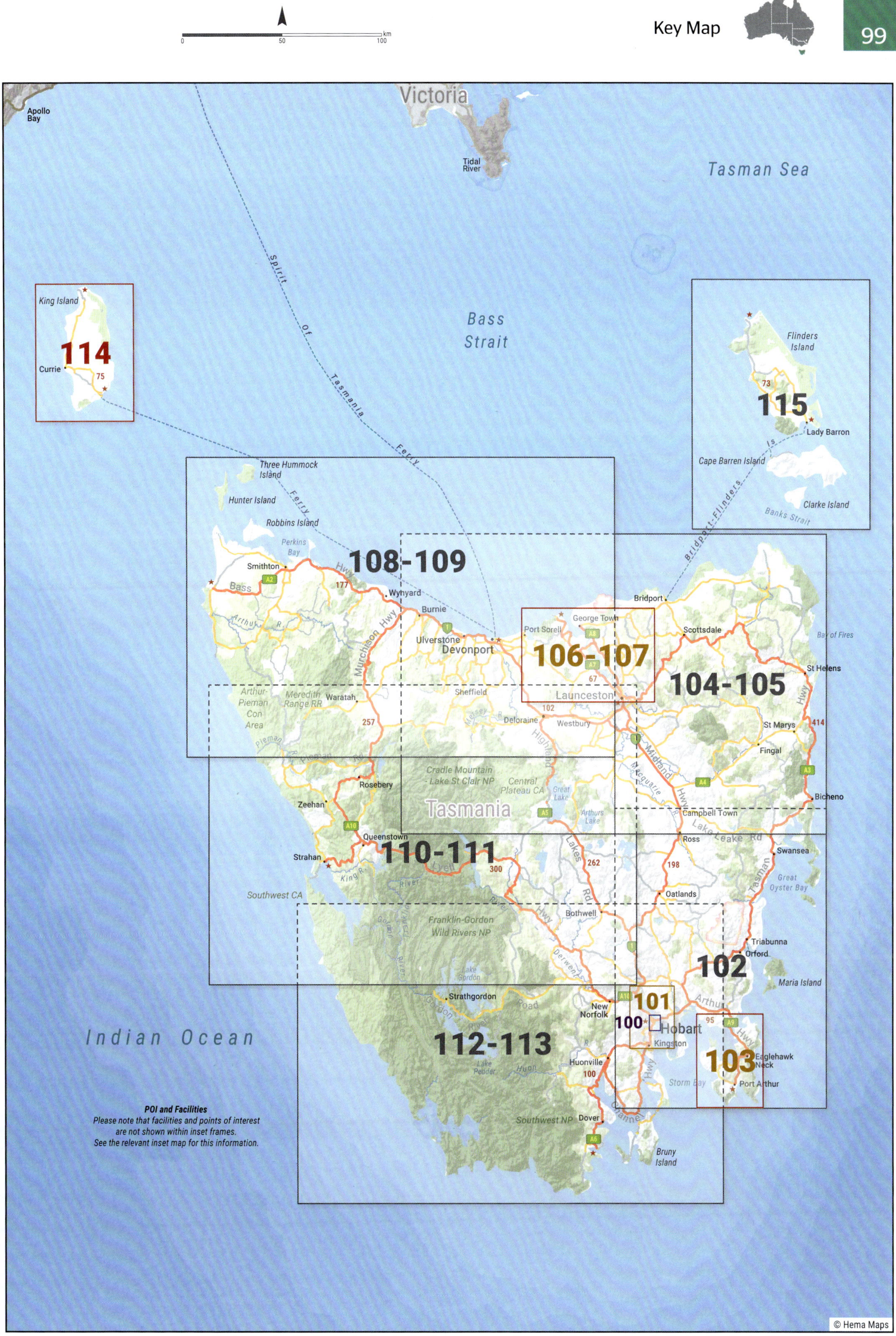

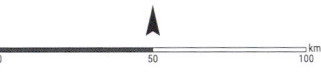

0 50 100 km

Victoria

Tasman Sea

Apollo
Bay

Tidal
River

Bass
Strait

Spirit of Tasmania Ferry

King Island
Currie
114
75

Flinders
Island
73
Lady Barron
115
Cape Barren Island
Clarke Island
Banks Strait
Bridport-Flinders Is

Three Hummock
Island
Hunter Island
Robbins Island
Perkins
Bay
Smithton
Bass
Arthur R.
108-109
177
Wynyard
Burnie
Ulverstone
Devonport
Port Sorell
George Town
Bridport
Scottsdale
Bay of Fires
St Helens
106-107
Launceston
67
104-105
102
Westbury
St Marys
Fingal
414
Bicheno

Arthur-
Pieman Con
Area
Meredith
Range RR
Waratah
257
Sheffield
Deloraine

Murchison Hwy
Pieman R.

Cradle Mountain
Lake St Clair NP
Central
Plateau CA
Great
Lake
Tasmania
Arthurs
Lake
Campbell Town
Ross
Lake Leake Rd
Swansea
Great
Oyster Bay

Rosebery
Zeehan
Queenstown
Strahan
110-111
300
262
198
Oatlands

Midland Hwy
Macquarie R.
A4
A3
A5

Southwest CA

Franklin-Gordon
Wild Rivers NP
Lake
Gordon
Strathgordon
Bothwell

Lakes Rd
Derwent R.

Triabunna
Orford
Maria Island
102

112-113
Lake
Pedder
Huon R.
Huonville
100
Dover
Southwest NP
A6

New
Norfolk
100
101
Hobart
Kingston
Storm Bay
95 A9
103
Eaglehawk
Neck
Port Arthur
Arthur Hwy

Channel Hwy

Bruny
Island

Indian Ocean

POI and Facilities
Please note that facilities and points of interest
are not shown within inset frames.
See the relevant inset map for this information.

© Hema Maps

Hobart Suburbs - Kingston to Richmond

See map 100

Port Arthur
The Tasman Peninsula offers phenomenal coastal scenery with towering dolerite cliffs and pinnacles. No visit to Tasmania is complete without a trip to the former convict settlement at Port Arthur – Australia's most famous convict settlement.

© Hema Maps

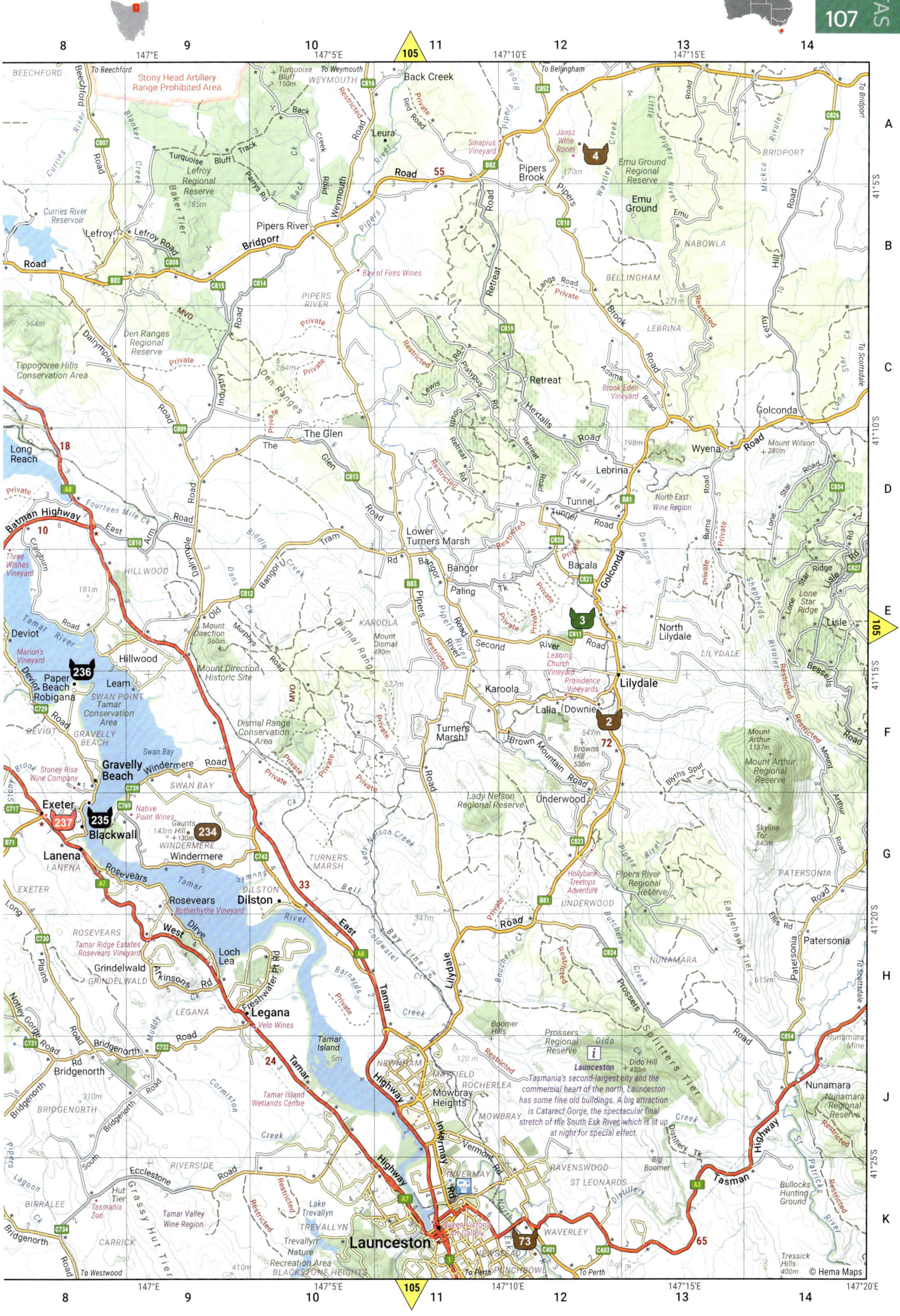

Three Hummock Island
Cape Rochon
Highland Bluff Lighthouse (new)
North West Cape
Cape Keraudren
Coulomb Bay
Burgess Point
Three Hummock Island State Reserve
Cape Adamson
Cuvier Bay
Cuvier Point
West Point Lighthouse
Wallaby Point
Hunter Is
Hunter Island Conservation Area
Perigo Point
Middle Bank
Cape Buache
Walker Island
Trefoil Island
Hunter Pass.
Weber Point
Woolnorth Point
Boullanger Bay
Kangaroo Island
Remarkable Banks
Ransonnet Bay
Robbins Island
Guyton Point
Cape Grim
Woolnorth
Woolnorth Bluff Point Wind Farm
Welcome Heath
Cape Elie
Robbins Pass.
Stony Point
Swan Bay Plain
Harcus Plain
Dluff Point
West Montagu
Montagu
Montagu Plains
Big Bay
Shipwreck Point
Perkins Island
Perkins Bay
North Point
Highland Bluff Lighthouse (new)
Highfield Historic Site
The Nut Chairlift
Stanley
Circular Head
Sawyer Bay
Stanley
Stanley sits at the base of a distinctive, 150m-high volcanic plug called Circular Head but better known as the Nut. For a panoramic view, visitors can climb the Nut or take the chairlift.
Bass Strait
Ferry
Dodgers Point
Calm Bay State Reserve
Jims Plain
Scopus
Duck Bay
Tatlows Folly
Leesville
Mella
Smithton
Scotchtown
Smokers Bank
North Forest
Forest
Wiltshire
Black River
Cowrie Point
Port Latta
Crayfish Creek
Edgcumbe Beach
Hellyer
Rocky Cape Beach
Rocky Cape
Sisters Beach
Boat Harbour Beach
Boat Harbour
Preminghana IPA
Ann Bay
Green Point
Marrawah
Broadmeadows
Pulbeena
Mengha
South Forest
Seventeen Mile Plain
Redpa
Christmas Hills
Brittons Swamp
Togari
Irishtown
Jones Plain
Alcomie
Eurebia
Mawbanna
Montumana
Sisters Creek
Flowerdale
Wynyard
West Point
West Point State Reserve
Mawson Bay
Bluff Hill Point
Richardsons Flats
Tarkine Forest Adventures - Dismal Swamp
Duffs Flat
Waratah Plain
Edith Creek
Lileah
Nabageena
Gibson Plains
Junction Plain
Roger River
Trowutta
Roger River West
Montagu Swamp Regional Reserve
Detention Falls Con. Area
Detention Peak
Rulla
Myalla
Moorleah
Lapoinya
Seabrook
Doctors Rocks
Milabena
Upper Calder
Calder
Oldina
Upper Mount Hicks
Mount Hicks
Lower Mount Hicks
Elliott
South Elliott
Yolla
East Yolla
Arthur River
Edge Of The World Viewing Platform
Sundown Point
Couta Rocks
Dip Range Regional Reserve
Preolenna
Meunna
Kellatier
Pruana Regional Reserve
West Ridgley
Henrietta
Takone
West Takone
Tewkesbury
Balfour Track Regional Reserve
Rebecca Creek Conservation Area
Kaywood
Temma
Sumac Regional Reserve
Balfour
Mount Bertha 703m
Mt Leslie 530m
Oonah
Hampshire
Parrawe
Hellyer Gorge State Reserve
Companion Hill 816m
Ridgley
Arthur-Pieman Conservation Area
Ordnance Point
Savage River Pipeline Regional Reserve
Savage River National Park
Mount Hazelton 650m
Mount Lily 560m
West Bluff 577m
Mount Holloway 585m
Kenneth Bay
Donaldson River Nature Recreation Area
Savage River Regional Reserve
Deep Gully Regional Reserve
Guildford
Fingerpost
Talbots Lagoon
Sandy Cape Lighthouse
Mount Mabel 665m
Mount Edith 740m
Mount Hadman 720m
Mount Norfolk 740m
Mount Vero 660m
Burgess Hill 520m
Mt Cleveland 855m
Magnet
Waratah
Knole Plain
Mount Pearse 1001m
Wombat Flat
Hatfield
Moory Mount 710m
Surrey Hills
Badger Plains
Long Plains
Savage River
Mount Youngbuck 631m
Mount Sunday 699m
Meredith Range Regional Reserve
West Plain
Mount Meredith 792m
Yellowband Plain
Mount Ramsay 855m
Hatfield River Regional Reserve
Mount Cripps 948m
Mt Charter 850m
Lake Mackintosh
Reynolds Falls Nature Recreation Area
Mt Block 790m
Pieman River State Reserve
Ford
Corinna
Brown Plains
Parsons Hood 915m
Mount Livingstone 781m
John Lynch Regional Reserve
Bulgobac Sawmill Creek Regional Reserve
Boco
To Rosebery
Granite Tor Cons. Area
Rupert Point
Pieman Head
Tikkawoppa Plateau Regional Reserve
To Zeehan
Ferry
Bass Hwy
Murchison Hwy
Western Explorer Road
Norfolk Rd
Heemskirk Rd
Norfolk Range
Meredith Range
Restricted
144°40'E
145°E
145°20'E
145°40'E
40°40'S
41°S
41°20'S
41°40'S

Strahan to Launceston

Strahan
While visiting Strahan, the tourist centre of the west coast, a cruise up the Gordon River is a must. Other options in the area include harbour cruises, a jet boat up the King River, kayaking, yachting, and plane or helicopter flights.

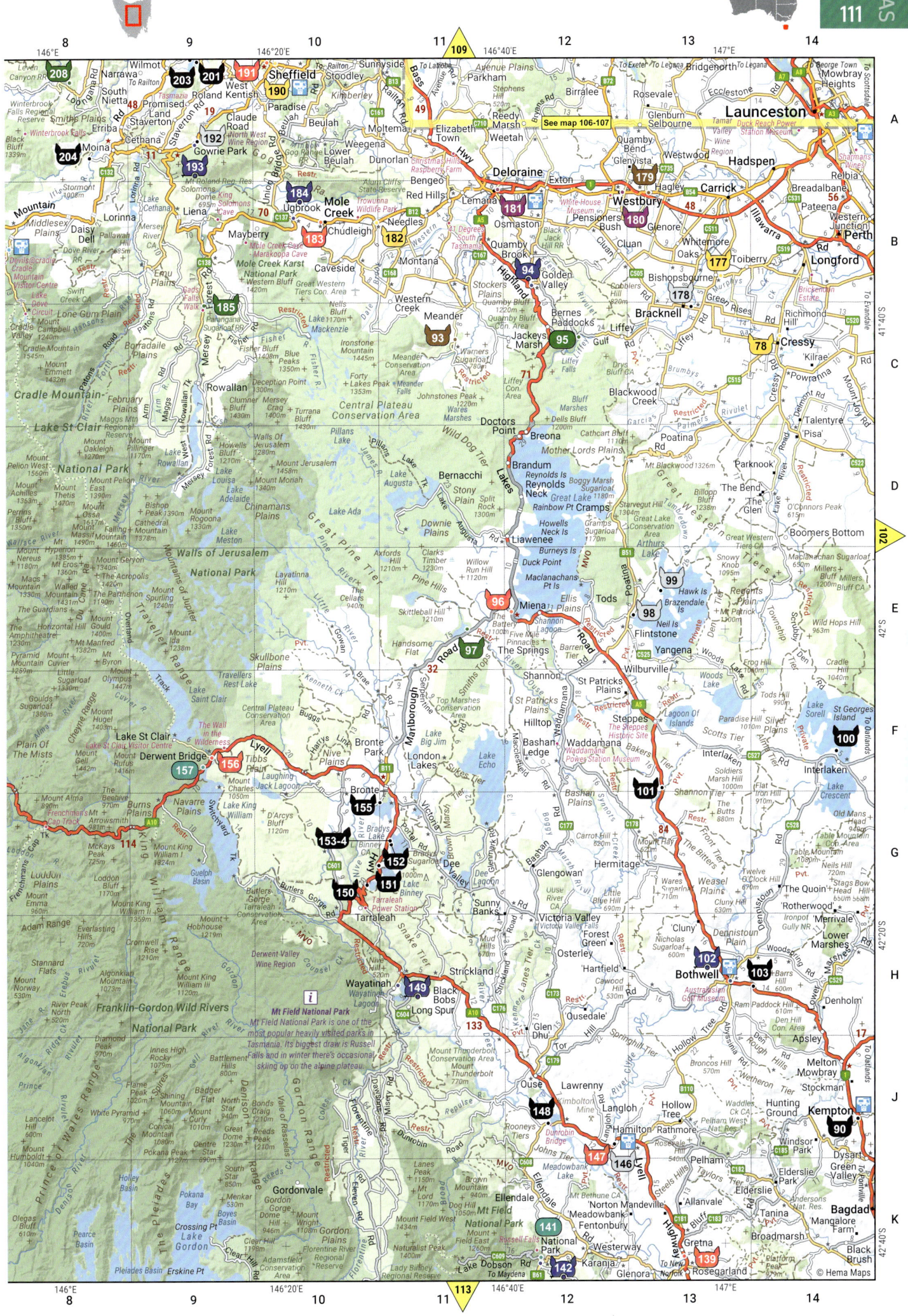

© Hema Maps

King Island

Make Travelling Easy

with Australia's favourite & most complete Caravan Park Guide

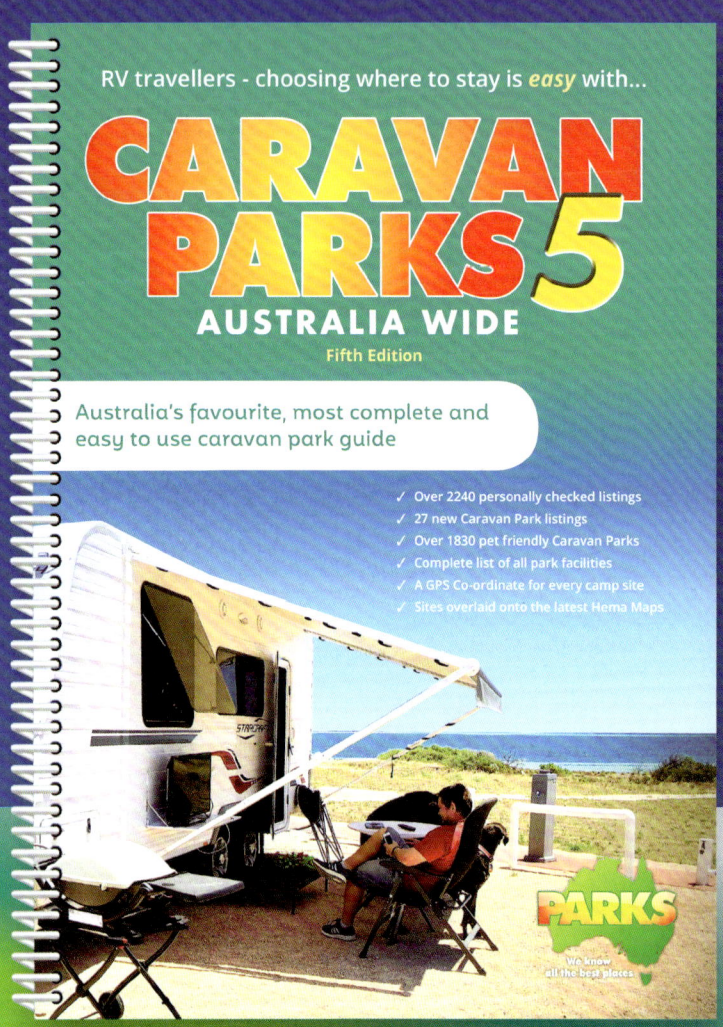

✔ 100% researched & updated

✔ New fold out map of Australia to plot your journey

✔ Location Map for each state

✔ Sites overlaid on Hema's most detailed road atlas ever

✔ Colourful symbols show facilities at a glance

✔ Every state is colour coded

✔ Search caravan parks by town - one index for the whole country

✔ Full GPS coordinates for every site

✔ Complete list of public dump points

"Excellent guide to caravan parks in Australia, much better than the motoring associations guides as this one covers all tourist parks, plus the bonus of maps for each state."

Eddie Young

"Being new to the camping scene I have found the book extremely valuable in being able to pre-plan a trip and review our park sites. Well done."

Neville C

AVAILABLE at most leading Book Stores, Outdoor & 4WD Centres, Caravan Dealers or Online

www.campsaustraliawide.com
(07) 5474 2542
info@campsaustraliawide.com

Mayfield Bay, Tasmania

Tasmania

Launceston - St Helens - Hobart
Tasman Highway

1 Myrtle Park Rec Ground

38250 Tasman Hwy, Targa
Camp Area 32 km NE of Launceston or 31 km SW of Scottsdale, riverside, 7 day limit
0439 216 695   HEMA 105 E9   41 18 31 S   147 21 55 E

2 Cherry Top Farm Stay
81 Lalla Road, Lilydale
Farm Stay 28 km E of Launceston via East Tamar Hwy & Lilydale Rd exit. Pre-book
03 6395 1167   HEMA 107 F12   41 15 37 S   147 12 31 E

3 Lilydale Falls Reserve
231 Golconda Road, Lilydale
Camp Area 30 km E of Launceston, via East Tamar Hwy, towards Georgetown, Lilydale Rd exit, 2 km N of town
HEMA 107 E12   41 13 47 S   147 12 34 E

4 Pipers Brook Vineyard
1216 Pipers Brook Rd, Pipers Brook
Parking Area 56 km E of Launceston, R off East Tamar Hwy towards Georgetown, Lilydale Rd exit. Register at cellar door by 5pm
03 6382 7555   HEMA 107 A12   41 04 09 S   147 11 56 E

5 Northeast Park
41 Ringarooma Rd, Scottsdale
Camp Area 1 km E of PO on Tasman Hwy. 14 day limit
03 6352 6500   HEMA 105 D10   41 09 56 S   147 31 23 E

6 Blackmans Lagoon
Waterhouse Conservation Area
Blackmans Lagoon Rd, Waterhouse
Camp Area 27 km NE of Bridport. N off B82, 24 km NE of Bridport. 2 km dirt road. Beside pine forest. Small vehicles only. 4 week limit
03 6778 8520   HEMA 105 B10   40 54 46 S   147 35 44 E

7 Big Waterhouse Lake
Waterhouse Conservation Area
Via Homestead Rd, Waterhouse
Camp Area 34 km NE of Bridport. Turn N off B82, 27 km NE of Bridport to Homestead Rd, L after 4 km for 2 km. 7 km dirt road. 4 week limit
03 6778 8520   HEMA 105 B10   40 53 32 S   147 36 57 E

8 South Croppies Point
Waterhouse Conservation Area
Via Homestead Rd, Waterhouse
Camp Area 37 km NE of Bridport. N off B82, 27 km NE of Bridport to Homestead Rd, L after 6 km for 4 km. 10 km dirt road. Sites beside road after fork. 4 week limit
03 6778 8520   HEMA 105 B10   40 51 56 S   147 35 37 E

9 Waterhouse Point
Waterhouse Conservation Area
Via Homestead Rd, Waterhouse
Camp Area 40 km NE of Bridport. N off B82, 27 km NE of Bridport to Homestead Rd, L after 12 km for 800 m. 13 km dirt road. Small vehicles only. Beachfront. 4 week limit
03 6778 8520   HEMA 105 A11   40 49 49 S   147 40 19 E

10 Village Green
Waterhouse Conservation Area
Via Homestead Rd, Waterhouse
Camp Area 41 km NE of Bridport. N off B82, 27 km NE of Bridport to Homestead Rd, L after 12 km for 1 km. 14 km rough dirt road. 4 week limit
03 6778 8520   HEMA 105 A11   40 49 36 S   147 39 40 E

11 Mathers Camping Area
Waterhouse Conservation Area
Via Homestead Rd, Waterhouse
Camp Area 40 km NE of Bridport. N off B82, 27 km NE of Bridport to Homestead Rd, follow signs. 13 km dirt road. Beachfront. 4 week limit
03 6778 8520   HEMA 105 A11   40 49 40 S   147 40 09 E

12 Ransons Beach
Waterhouse Conservation Area
Via Homestead Rd, Waterhouse
Camp Area 41 km NE of Bridport. N off B82, 27 km NE of Bridport to Homestead Rd for 14 km of corrugated dirt road. Beachfront. 4 week limit
03 6778 8520   HEMA 105 A11   40 50 24 S   147 41 14 E

13 Branxholm Park
3 Scott St, Branxholm
Camp Area opposite IGA. Shower fee
03 6352 6500   HEMA 105 D11   41 10 06 S   147 44 15 E

14 Legerwood Memorial Park
RV Stop
Ringarooma Rd, Legerwood
Parking Area 86 kms N of Launceston & 24 km E of Scottsdale on Tasman Hwy, turn R into Carlsbrook Lane 2 km to park
03 6352 6500   HEMA 105 D11   41 12 58 S   147 41 42 E

15 Ringarooma RV Park
37 East Maurice Rd, Ringarooma
Parking Area at oval. S off Tasman Hwy to Legerwood Rd. E to Ringarooma Rd, then R
03 6352 6500   HEMA 105 E11   41 14 45 S   147 44 13 E

16 Derby Park
Main St, Derby
Camp Area beside river. 4 week limit. Shower fee
HEMA 105 D11   41 08 31 S   147 47 50 E

17 Derby Works Depot Big Rig
Camp
Tasman Hwy, Derby
Parking Area at E end of town, beside council depot
HEMA 105 D11   41 09 00 S   147 48 16 E

18 Dorset Hotel
29 Main St, Derby
Parking Area behind hotel, register at bar, shower fee
03 6354 2360   HEMA 105 D11   41 08 38 S   147 47 56 E

19 Winnaleah Hotel
12 Main St, Winnaleah
Parking Area at rear, free for patrons. Register at bar, shower fee
03 6354 2331   HEMA 105 C12   41 05 52 S   147 49 29 E

20 Winnaleah RV Park
Winnaleah Rd, Winnaleah
Parking Area in Rec Grounds, L off Tasman Hwy to S side of town. 14 day limit
HEMA 105 C11   41 06 06 S   147 49 24 E

21 Gladstone Hall

1 Carr St, Gladstone
Parking Area 18 km N of Pioneer on the Gladstone Rd. In town at rear of hall
HEMA 105 B13   40 57 36 S   148 00 32 E

22 Petal Point Campground

Cape Portland Conservation Area
Via Cape Portland Rd, Rushy Lagoon
Camp Area 21 km N of Gladstone, dirt road. Camp only in existing sites
HEMA 105 A12   40 46 38 S   147 57 02 E

23 Musselroe Bay

Musselroe Bay Conservation Area
Musselroe Rd, Musselroe Bay
Camp Area 24 km NE of Gladstone, via C843, C845 & Forester Kangaroo Dr. 800 m N of fire station. Dirt road. Oceanfront. 4 week limit
03 6387 5510   HEMA 105 A13   40 50 07 S   148 10 39 E

24 Top Camp

Mt William National Park
Via Main Rd, Musselroe Bay
Camp Area 27 km NE of Gladstone, via C843, C845 & Forester Kangaroo Dr. Turn E 300 m N of Musselroe Bay township for 2 km. Narrow access track, mostly dirt, small vehicles only. Oceanfront. Parks Pass applies
03 6387 5510   HEMA 105 B14   40 50 34 S   148 12 12 E

25 Stumpys Bay

Mt William National Park
Forester Kangaroo Dr, St Helens
Dispersed Camping Area 26 km NE of Gladstone, via C843 & C845.Mostly dirt road. Turn E 6 km N of park entrance. Small vehicles only. 4 camps. Parks Pass applies
03 6387 5510   HEMA 105 B14   40 52 16 S   148 13 19 E

26 Deep Creek Eddystone Pt

Mt William National Park
North Ansons Rd, Ansons Bay
Camp Area 37 km E of Gladstone. Turn N off C846, 34 km E of Gladstone at Eddystone Point Rd Jcn for 3 km. Mostly dirt road. Small vehicles only. Parks pass applies
03 6387 5510   HEMA 105 C14   40 58 11 S   148 18 44 E

27 Policemans Point

Bay of Fires Conservation Area
South Ansons Rd, St Helens Area
Camp Area 40 km E of Gladstone. Turn S off C843, 35 km E of Gladstone at South Ansons Bay Rd for 5 km. Mostly dirt road. 4 week limit
03 6387 5510   HEMA 105 C14   41 03 44 S   148 17 27 E

28 Weldborough Hotel

Tasman Hwy, Weldborough
Camp Area 21 km E of Derby or 44 km NW of St Helens. Behind hotel. Register at bar. Shower fee
03 6354 2223   HEMA 105 D12   41 11 38 S   147 54 16 E

29 Pub in the Paddock

250 St Columba Falls Rd, Pyengana
Pub Stay 750 m W of the Pyengana Dairy Company
03 6373 6121   HEMA 105 E12   41 17 28 S   147 59 44 E

30 Pyengana Rec Ground

St Columba Falls Rd, Pyengana
Camp Area at Pyengana, 400 m W of the Dairy Company. Donations at gate, shower fee
HEMA 105 E12   41 17 31 S   148 00 03 E

31 Lottah Recreation Ground

Lottah Rd, Lottah
Parking Area 27 km NW of St. Helens N off Tasman Hwy at Anchor Rd, N to Lottah Rd
HEMA 105 D13   41 13 38 S   148 01 40 E

32 RC Ranch

27464 Tasman Hwy, Goulds Country
Camp Area 19 km W of St Helens. Riverside, pre-book
0406 306 981   HEMA 105 E13   41 15 28 S   148 02 18 E

33 Moulting Bay

Humbug Point Nature Rec Area
Moulting Bay Beach Rd, St Helens
Camp Area 8 km NE of St Helens. Follow Binalong Bay Rd (C850) 7 km. Turn E for 1 km dirt road. Bayside. 4 week limit
03 6387 5510   HEMA 105 E14   41 16 46 S   148 16 57 E

34 Dora Point Camping Area

Humbug Point Nature Rec Area
286 Dora Point Rd, Binalong Bay
Dispersed Camping 13 km NE of St Helens, 10 km N on Binalong Bay Rd (C850). Turn R, sites behind sand dunes. Cold showers. 4 week limit
03 6387 5510   HEMA 105 E14   41 16 37 S   148 19 36 E

35 Grants Lagoon

Bay of Fires Conservation Area
Via Gardens Rd, Binalong Bay
Camp Area 10 km NE of St Helens, via Binalong Bay Rd (C850) & The Gardens Rd (C848). Turn E off C848, 9 km NE of St Helens, then R after 300 m. Near lagoon. 4 week limit
03 6387 5510   HEMA 105 E14   41 15 17 S   148 17 25 E

36 Jeanneret Beach

Bay of Fires Conservation Area
Jeanneret Beach Rd, Binalong Bay
Camp Area 12 km NE of St Helens, via Binalong Bay Rd (C850) & The Gardens Rd (C848). Turn E off C848. Small vehicles only. Beachfront. 4 week limit
03 6387 5510   HEMA 105 E14   41 14 16 S   148 17 23 E

37 Swimcart Beach

Bay of Fires Conservation Area
Swimcart Beach Rd, Binalong Bay
Camp Area 13 km NE of St Helens, via Binalong Bay Rd (C850) & The Gardens Rd (C848). Turn E off C848, 1 km dirt road. Beachfront. 4 week limit
03 6387 5510   HEMA 105 D14   41 13 44 S   148 17 03 E

38 Cosy Corner South

Bay of Fires Conservation Area
Gardens Rd, Binalong Bay
Camp Area 14 km NE of St Helens, via Binalong Bay Rd (C850) & The Gardens Rd (C848). Turn E off C848, 300 m dirt road. Beachfront. 4 week limit
03 6387 5510   HEMA 105 D14   41 13 23 S   148 16 59 E

39 Cosy Corner North

Bay of Fires Conservation Area
Gardens Rd, Binalong Bay
Camp Area 15 km NE of St Helens, via Binalong Bay Rd (C850) & The Gardens Rd (C848). Turn E off C848, 500 m dirt road. Beachfront. 4 week limit
03 6387 5510   HEMA 105 D14   41 13 16 S   148 16 55 E

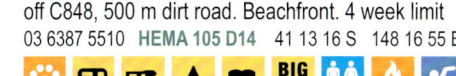

40 Seatons Cove
Bay of Fires Conservation Area
Seatons Rd, Binalong Bay
Camp Area 17 km N of St. Helens, take Gardens Rd, then R, camp on N side of road. 4 week limit
03 6387 5510   HEMA 105 D14   41 12 43 S   148 16 51 E

41 Sloop Reef
Bay of Fires Conservation Area
Seaton Tramway Tr, Binalong Bay
Camp Area 17 km N of St. Helens, take Gardens Rd, R to Seaton Rd. L to camp. 4 week limit
03 6387 5510   HEMA 105 D14   41 12 33 S   148 16 42 E

42 The Big Lagoon
Bay of Fires Conservation Area
Gardens Rd, The Gardens
Parking Area 19 km N of St Helens via Binalong Bay Rd & Gardens Rd to camp near Fire Rd. Environmentally sensitive area. 4 week limit
HEMA 105 D14   41 10 49 S   148 16 10 E

43 St Helens Rec Ground
Cnr Young & Tully Sts, St Helens
Camp Area 2 km from St Helens PO
03 6376 7900   HEMA 105 E14   41 19 00 S   148 14 08 E

44 Bay of Fires RV Park
17 Colchis Creek Dr, St Helens
Camp Area 1 km from PO. Turn L off Cecilia St. to Quail St. L to Cameron, R to Park
0476 214 950   HEMA 105 E14   41 19 10 S   148 15 17 E

45 Dianas Basin
St Helens Point Conservation Area
Tasman Hwy, St Helens
Camp Area 9 km S of St Helens or 4 km N of Beaumaris. Turn E 8 km S of St Helens or 3 km N of Beaumaris for 900 m. Turn L after 500 m. Waterfront. 4 week limit
03 6387 5510   HEMA 105 F14   41 22 33 S   148 17 16 E

46 Paddys Island Campground
Scamander Conservation Area
St Helens Area
Camp Area 10.5 km S of St Helens or 2.5 km NW of Beaumaris. Small area, limited sites. Beachfront
03 6387 5510   HEMA 105 F14   41 23 43 S   148 17 21 E

47 Shelly Point
Scamander Conservation Area
Tasman Hwy, Scamander
Camp Area 2 km S of Beaumaris or 3 km N of Scamander Bridge. 400 m off Hwy. No camping on oceanfront, small vehicles only
03 6387 5510   HEMA 105 F14   41 26 05 S   148 16 36 E

48 Scamander Forest Reserve
Trout Rd, Scamander
Camp Area at Trout Creek. 11 km W of Beaumaris, via Upper Scamander & Eastern Creek Rds. Dirt road
03 6387 5510   HEMA 105 F14   41 26 05 S   148 13 30 E

49 St Marys Sportsground
22 Harefield Rd, St Marys
Camp Area near the Golf Course. Shower fee
03 6372 2177   HEMA 105 G13   41 35 05 S   148 11 02 E

50 Serenity Camp
326 Davies Gully Rd, Four Mile Creek
Camp Area 48 km N of Bicheno. Pre-book
0419 612 292   HEMA 105 G14   41 34 59 S   148 16 25 E

51 Iron House Brewery White
Sands Estate
21554 Tasman Hwy, Four Mile Creek
Parking Area 9 km S of Falmouth Jcn, follow signs. Pool & laundry fees
03 6372 2228   HEMA 105 G14   41 34 46 S   148 18 23 E

52 Little Beach Campground
Little Beach Conservation Area
Tasman Hwy, Chain of Lagoons
Camp Area 17 km S of A3/A4 Jcn or 5 km N of Chain of Lagoons. 200 m off Hwy. Beachfront. 4 week limit
03 6387 5512   HEMA 105 G14   41 37 35 S   148 18 44 E

53 Lagoons Beach
Lagoons Beach Conservation Area
Tasman Hwy, Chain of Lagoons
Camp Area 20 km S of A3/A4 Jcn or 2 km N of Chain of Lagoons. 300 m off Hwy. Beachfront. 4 week limit
03 6387 5512   HEMA 105 H14   41 38 48 S   148 17 52 E

54 Douglas River Cabins
19029 Tasman Hwy, Douglas River
Camp Area 31 km S of St Marys or 13 km N of Bicheno. Pre-book. BYO chemical toilet
03 6375 1164   HEMA 105 J14   41 46 57 S   148 15 22 E

55 Friendly Beaches Camp
Freycinet National Park
Friendly Beaches Rd, Friendly Beaches
Camp Area at Isaacs Pt. 13 km S of A3/C302 Jcn. Turn E off C302, 9 km S of Jcn. 3 km dirt road. Beachfront. Parks pass applies. 2 week limit
03 6256 7000   HEMA 102 A7   41 59 27 S   148 17 15 E

56 Campground at Freycinet
Paintball
961 Coles Bay Rd, Coles Bay
Camp area 9 km past Friendly Beaches turn off
0407 251 095   HEMA 102 A7   42 00 28 S   148 14 22 E

57 River & Rocks Campground
Moulting Lagoon Game Reserve
River & Rocks Rd, Coles Bay
Camp Area 19 km S of A3/C302 Jcn or 8 km N of Coles Bay, 1 km dirt road W of Hwy
03 6256 7000   HEMA 102 B7   42 05 12 S   148 14 03 E

58 Bagot Point
Bagot Point Coastal Reserve
Dolphin Sands Rd., Dolphin Sands
Parking Area 21 km E of Swansea to Swan River Rd, turn R follow to end. Subject to tides
03 6233 6413   HEMA 102 B7   42 05 44 S   148 14 01 E

59 Freycinet Golf Club
1 Swanwick Rd, Coles Bay
Parking Area 6 km W of Coles Bay. Pay at clubhouse. 5 day limit. Toilet access when club open
03 6257 0053   HEMA 102 B7   42 05 45 S   148 14 40 E

60 Richardsons Beach Camp
Freycinet National Park
Freycinet Dr, Coles Bay
Camp Areas 17 km S of Bicheno. W off Tasman Hwy to Coles Bay Rd, camp near Visitor Centre or coastal strip. Pre-book. Parks Pass applies
03 6256 7004   HEMA 102 B7   42 07 27 S   148 17 47 E

61 The Pondering Frog
Tearoom
16494 Tasman Hwy, Bicheno
Parking Area 11 km S of Bicheno. Entry 400 m S of Coles Bay turn off
0412 631 299   HEMA 102 A7   41 56 35 S   148 12 51 E

62 Lake Leake Campground
via Lake Leake Rd, Lake Leake
Camp Area 39 km NW of Swansea via Lake Leake Rd. 4 km dirt road. Limited space
03 6381 1319   HEMA 102 A4   42 00 44 S   147 48 02 E

63 Lake Leake Inn
320 Lake Leake Rd, Lake Leake
Pub Stay 35 km E of Campbell Town via Lake Leake Hwy. Register at bar
03 6381 2092   HEMA 102 A4   42 00 22 S   147 47 37 E

64 Swan River Boat Ramp
Swan River Rd, Dolphin Sands
Parking Area 10 km NE of Swansea off Tasman Hwy follow to end
1300 135 513   HEMA 102 B6   42 04 59 S   148 05 53 E

65 Swansea RV Park
13110 Tasman Hwy, Swansea
Camp Area 2.5 km S of Swansea town. Check-in booth at entrance
0400 019 613   HEMA 102 B6   42 08 40 S   148 04 07 E

66 Mayfield Bay Campground
Mayfield Bay Conservation Area
Tasman Hwy, Rocky Hills
Camp Area 16 km S of Swansea or 34 km N of Triabunna. Beachfront
03 6256 7000   HEMA 102 C5   42 14 21 S   148 00 45 E

67 Tandara Hotel
17 Tasman Hwy, Triabunna
Parking Area 1 km from PO. Register at bar. Free for patrons
03 6257 3333   HEMA 102 E5   42 30 06 S   147 54 40 E

68 Triabunna Spring Bay Hotel
Charles St, Triabunna
Camp Area in paddock behind hotel. Register at bar. SCV 4 night limit
03 6257 3115   HEMA 102 E5   42 30 33 S   147 54 51 E

69 Triabunna RV Stop
Cnr Charles St & Esplanade, Triabunna
Parking Area opposite Info Centre. Pay at takeaway
03 6257 3344   HEMA 102 E5   42 30 32 S   147 54 54 E

70 Ye Olde Buckland Inn
Kent St, Buckland
Parking Area behind hotel. Register at bar
03 6257 5114   HEMA 102 F4   42 36 24 S   147 43 12 E

71 Sorell RV Stop
6 Montagu St, Sorell
Camp Area at Sorell. Permit available from council office or honesty box. 10 day limit
03 6269 0000   HEMA 102 G3   42 47 02 S   147 33 24 E

72 South Arm RSL
2972 South Arm Rd, South Arm
Camp Spot 2 km SE of PO. Register at bar. Use large car park & grass area. Shower fee
03 6239 9171   HEMA 102 J2   43 01 46 S   147 25 41 E

Launceston to Hobart
Midland Highway

73 Old Macs Caravan & Motorhome Farm Stay
55 Sandown Rd, Norwood
Farm Stay 5 km N of Launceston. Open Oct - May
0408 443 696   HEMA 107 K12   41 26 52 S   147 10 46 E

74 Ben Lomond Camping Roses Cottage
287 Burns Creek Rd, Burns Creek
Camp Area 41 km E of Launceston
03 6390 6274   HEMA 105 F10   41 27 45 S   147 29 39 E

75 Ben Lomond Camp
Ben Lomond National Park
Ben Lomond Rd, Blessington
Camp Area 1 km inside NP. Take C401 through White Hills, R at Blessington to Ben Lomond Rd (C432). Follow signs. Parks Pass applies
03 6349 1020   HEMA 105 F10   41 30 08 S   147 36 50 E

76 Honeysuckle Banks
Leighlands Rd, Evandale
Rest Area 1km E of PO. Epermit applies. Open Nov - Apr
03 6397 7303   HEMA 105 G8   41 34 21 S   147 14 15 E

77 Falls Park Reserve
14 Logan Rd, Evandale
Camp Area 700 m E of PO at market site. Mon - Fri only. Epermit
03 6397 7303   HEMA 105 G8   41 34 16 S   147 15 14 E

78 Cressy Recreation Ground
Macquarie St, Cressy
Camp Area 1 km E of PO past Bowling Club. Epermit
03 6397 7303   HEMA 104 H7   41 40 55 S   147 04 59 E

79 Rossarden Rest Area
Schell St, Rossarden
Rest Area in town, camp on L. Donation for RFDS
03 6397 7303   HEMA 105 H11   41 40 00 S   147 44 49 E

80 Fingal Park
Talbot St, Fingal
Parking Area behind toilet block at the info board. Shower fee
03 6376 7900   HEMA 105 H12   41 38 17 S   147 58 06 E

81 Mathinna Rec Ground
High St, Mathinna
Picnic Area past Chapman St
0409 239 415   HEMA 105 F12   41 28 31 S   147 53 19 E

82 South Esk River Picnic Area
Griffin Rd, Mathinna
Camp Area 3 km N of Mathinna, W to Griffin Rd after bridge. Camp at Jcn
03 6376 7900   HEMA 105 F12   41 27 49 S   147 53 21 E

TASMANIA

83 Griffin Camping Area

Griffin Rd, Mathinna
Camp Area 25 km N of Fingal to Mathinna turnoff. R after bridge, then L, past picnic area 5 km. Follow signs to riverside camps
03 6376 7900   HEMA 105 F12   41 28 10 S   147 50 39 E

84 Blackburn Park Rest Area

Franklin St, Campbell Town
Rest Area SE side of Red Bridge, enter via Franklin St. E-permit
03 6397 7303   HEMA 102 A3   41 55 58 S   147 29 38 E

85 Tooms Lake Camp Ground

Tooms Lake Rd, Tooms Lake
Camp Area 42 km SE of Ross via C305. 20 km dirt road
03 6397 7303   HEMA 102 C4   42 12 48 S   147 46 56 E

86 Oatlands Overflow Paddock

The Esplanade, Oatlands
Camp Area via High St
03 6254 5000   HEMA 102 C2   42 17 59 S   147 22 32 E

87 Lake Dulverton Rest Area

The Esplanade, Oatlands
Rest Area 700 m from PO. Enter from N end of Oatlands to foreshore
03 6254 5000   HEMA 102 C2   42 18 03 S   147 22 34 E

88 Blue Haven Retreat

Tunnack Oval
27 Scotts Rd, Tunnack
Camp Area at SW Oval. Exit Midland Hwy SW at Oatlands to Tunnack Rd for 21 km. Honesty box
0409 145 407   HEMA 102 D2   42 27 21 S   147 27 33 E

89 Colebrook Tavern

2120 Mud Walls Rd, Colebrook
Camp Spot 1 km N of PO. Register at bar
03 6259 7164   HEMA 102 E2   42 31 34 S   147 21 32 E

90 Kempton Roadside Stopover

90 Main St, Kempton
Camp Area 48 km N of Hobart. Key from PO or council offices. Amenities fee
03 6254 5014   HEMA 102 E1   42 31 55 S   147 12 07 E

91 Brighton Pontville RV Stop

3 Glen Lea Rd, Pontville
Parking Area W off Midland Hwy. Permit from IGA
03 6268 1254   HEMA 102 F1   42 41 12 S   147 15 37 E

92 Hobart Showgrounds

2 Howard Rd, Glenorchy
Camp Area. Register at admin building. If closed, ebook
03 6272 6812   HEMA 101 E3   42 50 02 S   147 17 06 E

Deloraine to Hobart
Lake Highway

93 Hill Top Farm Meander

296 Huntsman Rd, Meander
Farm Stay 4 km S of Meander, 20 km S of Deloraine, or 76 km N of Miena. 2WD and 4WD sites available. 7 day limit
0414 952 729   HEMA 104 H5   41 41 04 S   146 35 51 E

94 Quamby Corner

15 Golden Valley Rd, Golden Valley
Camp Area 16 km S of Deloraine. Highland Lakes Rd toward Miena, continue on A5, turn E, 150 m to entrance
03 6369 5156   HEMA 104 G5   41 37 35 S   146 42 39 E

95 Lower Liffey Reserve

Liffey Falls State Reserve
Bogan Rd, Liffey
Camp Area 7 km W of Liffey. Best access via Gulf Rd (C513)
03 6701 2104   HEMA 104 H6   41 40 58 S   146 46 54 E

96 Great Lake Hotel

3096 Marlborough Hwy, Miena
Parking Area 3 km from Miena via Highland Lakes Rd
03 6259 8163   HEMA 104 K5   41 58 50 S   146 40 39 E

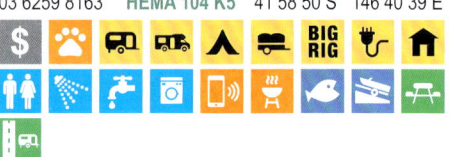

97 Little Pine Lagoon

Conservation Area
34 Little Pine Lagoon Rd, Miena
Camp Area 10 km SW of Miena or 24 km NE of Bronte Park, via B11. Dirt road
03 6701 2104   HEMA 104 K5   41 59 57 S   146 36 44 E

98 Pump House Bay Camp

Arthurs Lake Recreation Area
Poatina Rd, Flintstone
Camp Area 7 km NE of A5/B51 Jcn or 35 km S of Poatina. Turn E off B51, 6 km N of Jcn or 34 km S of Poatina. 1 km dirt road. Lakeside. Closed May - July
0439 202 436   HEMA 104 K6   41 59 05 S   146 51 41 E

99 Jonah Bay Campground

Arthurs Lake Recreation Area
Gunns Marsh Rd, Arthurs Lake
Camp Area 15 km NE of A5/B51 Jcn or 40 km S of Poatina. Turn E off B51, 10 km N of Jcn or 30 km S of Poatina, then R at Y Jcn. 5 km dirt road. Lakeside. Closed May - July
0439 202 436   HEMA 104 K6   41 57 31 S   146 54 10 E

100 Dago Point Campground

Lake Sorrell
2716 Interlaken Rd, Interlaken
Camp Area 26 km E of Steppes or 1.4 km W of Interlaken. Turn N 600 m W of Interlaken. Dirt road. Lakeside. Big rigs at boat ramp. Closed May - Aug
HEMA 111 F14   42 07 57 S   147 10 07 E

101 Blackburn Creek

Highland Lakes Rd, Steppes
Parking Area 9 km S of Steppes or 25 km N of Bothwell. Creekside
HEMA 111 F13   42 10 21 S   146 54 17 E

102 Bothwell Caravan Park

6-8 Market Place, Bothwell
Caravan Park behind Info Centre
03 6259 5503   HEMA 111 H13   42 22 58 S   147 00 29 E

103 Pub With No Beer

1755 Highland Lakes Rd, Bothwell
Camp Area 3 km E of Bothwell or 17 km
NW of Melton Mowbray. Via Midland Hwy to
Bothwell turn off

03 6286 3202   HEMA 111 H14   42 23 18 S   147 02 36 E

Sorell to Port Arthur
Arthur Highway

104 Eldee Camp Spot

179 Josephs Rd, Carlton
Camp Area 2 km E of Carlton. Shower fee,
10 night limit

0418 135 647   HEMA 103 A1   42 51 19 S   147 39 20 E

105 Primrose Sands RSL Club

415 Primrose Sands Rd, Primrose Sands
Parking Area 22 km SE of Sorell. Toilet
access when open

03 6265 5655   HEMA 103 B2   42 53 09 S   147 40 09 E

106 Derford Farm

285 Bream Ck Rd, Bream Creek
Farm Stay 6 km NE of Copping. Via Marion
Bay Rd. Honesty box

03 6253 5294   HEMA 102 G4   42 48 08 S   147 50 08 E

107 Dunalley Golf Club

28 Florence St, Dunalley
Camp Area 700 m from PO. Free for patrons

0417 900 331   HEMA 103 B4   42 53 12 S   147 48 17 E

108 Dunalley Hotel

210 Arthur Hwy, Dunalley
Camp Area 1 km from PO. Register at bar

03 6253 5101   HEMA 103 B4   42 53 36 S   147 48 18 E

109 Sunset Beach Holiday Spot

3532 Arthur Hwy, Murdunna
Camp Area 4 km S of Dunalley. Pre-book

03 6253 5257   HEMA 103 B4   42 55 02 S   147 49 27 E

110 Rosedale Homestead & Self Contained Campers

19 Nubeena Rd, Taranna
Camp Area near Cnr of Arthur Hwy

0418 126 151   HEMA 103 F5   43 03 45 S   147 51 43 E

111 Fortescue Bay Banksia Camp
Tasman National Park

Fortescue Rd, Fortescue Bay
Camp Area 24 km NE of Port Arthur. Turn E off the
A9, 6 km S of Taranna or 5 km N of Port Arthur.
12 km dirt road. Pre-book. Shower tokens, Parks
Pass applies

03 6250 2433   HEMA 103 H7   43 008 32 S   147 58 002 E

112 Mill Creek Campground
Tasman National Park

Fortescue Rd, Fortescue Bay
Camp Area 24 km NE of Port Arthur. Turn E off the
A9, 6 km S of Taranna or 5 km N of Port Arthur.
12 km dirt road. Pre-book. Shower tokens & Parks
Pass applies

03 6250 2433   HEMA 103 H7   43 08 35 S   147 58 07 E

113 Raoul Bay Retreat

925 Stormlea Rd, Stormlea
Camp Area 13 km S of Nubeena. 2 km S
of Nubeena or 8 km W of Port Arthur to the turn off,
10 km to camp

03 6250 2739   HEMA 103 J3   43 11 42 S   147 46 43 E

114 Tasman RSL Club Nubeena

Cnr Main & Alfred St, Nubeena
Parking Area next to RSL. Shower fee

03 6250 2135   HEMA 103 G3   43 06 29 S   147 44 46 E

115 Lime Bay Campground
Lime Bay State Reserve

Coal Mines Road, Nubeena
Camp Area 16 km N of Premaydena. 6 km dirt road.
Waterfront

03 6250 3980   HEMA 103 C2   42 57 23 S   147 42 16 E

Hobart-Cockle Creek-Bruny Island
Huon and Channel Highways

116 The Lea Scout Centre
Lea Conservation Area

Gilwell Dr, Kingston
Camp Area 10 km S of Hobart via Southern Outlet &
Gilwell Dr. Open Dec - Mar

0427 249 576   HEMA 101 J4   42 56 58 S   147 19 37 E

117 Longley International Hotel

Huon Rd, Longley
Parking Area opposite hotel. Free for
patrons. Register at bar

03 6239 6378   HEMA 101 K1   42 58 20 S   147 11 42 E

118 Huon Bush Retreats

300 Browns Rd, Ranelagh
Camp Area at Ranelagh. 10 km NW of
Huonville. Via North Huon Rd (C619). Pre-book.
Small vehicles only

03 6264 2233   HEMA 113 E10   42 58 56 S   146 59 57 E

119 Rivers Edge Wilderness Camping

1322 Lonnavale Rd, Lonnavale
Camp Area 28 km W of Huonville. R off Huon Hwy
at Grove before Huonville, follow yellow-on-blue
tourism signs for 25 km. Closed Jun - Aug

03 6266 0007   HEMA 113 E9   42 56 50 S   146 48 01 E

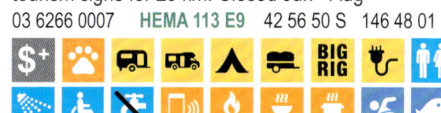

120 Franklin Camping Ground
Franklin Foreshore Reserve

3445 Huon Hwy, Franklin
Camp Area opposite hotel, behind fire station,
beside river. Fees collected

03 6264 0326   HEMA 113 F10   43 05 34 S   147 00 33 E

121 Shipwrights Point Regatta Ground

Huon Hwy, Port Huon
Camp Area 17 S of Huonville N of wharf area beside
river. No dogs in playground. Fee collected

03 6264 0300   HEMA 113 G10   43 09 31 S   146 58 47 E

122 Geeveston Ex Servicemen & Womens Club
11 Memorial Dr, Geeveston
Parking Area 1 km S of town
03 6297 1105   HEMA 113 G10   43 10 08 S   146 55 37 E

123 Heritage Park
Arve Rd, Geeveston
Parking Area opposite roadhouse. Fees collected
03 6264 0300   HEMA 113 G10   43 09 44 S   146 55 28 E

124 Arve River Picnic Area
Arve River Nature Walk, Geeveston
Picnic Area 13 km W of Geeveston. Small vehicles only
03 6297 1120   HEMA 113 G9   43 09 31 S   146 48 22 E

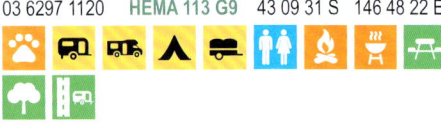

125 Tahune Airwalk Forest Reserve
Arve Road, Geeveston
Camp Area 29 km W of Geeveston at Air Walk Info Centre. In overflow car park
03 6251 3903   HEMA 113 F9   43 05 43 S   146 43 49 E

126 Gilhams Beach
Recherche Bay Nature Rec Area
Cockle Creek Rd, Recherche
Camp Area 21 km S of A6/C635 Jcn. Dirt road. 30 day limit
03 6121 7026   HEMA 113 K10   43 32 36 S   146 53 25 E

127 Finns Beach Campground
Recherche Bay Nature Rec Area
Cockle Creek Rd, Recherche
Camp Area 22 km S of A6/C635 Jcn. Dirt road. 30 day limit
03 6121 7026   HEMA 113 K10   43 32 56 S   146 53 14 E

128 Catamaran River
Recherche Bay Nature Rec Area
Cockle Creek Rd, Recherche
Camp Area 23 km S of A6/C635 Jcn. Signposted. Dirt road. 30 day limit
03 6121 7026   HEMA 113 K10   43 33 16 S   146 53 14 E

129 Cockle Creek Campground
Recherche Bay Nature Rec Area
Cockle Creek Rd, Recherche
Camp Area 26 km S of A6/C635 Jcn. Dirt road. 30 day limit
03 6121 7026   HEMA 113 K10   43 34 42 S   146 53 12 E

130 Boltons Green Campground
Southwest National Park
Cockle Creek Rd, Recherche
Camp Area 27 km S of A6/C635 Jcn. Dirt road. 5 tonne load limit on bridge. 30 day limit. Parks Pass applies
03 6121 7026   HEMA 113 K10   43 34 58 S   146 53 42 E

131 Gordon Foreshore Reserve
4775 Channel Hwy, Gordon
Camp Area at Gordon. Honesty box at amenities
03 6211 8200   HEMA 113 G12   43 15 39 S   147 14 33 E

132 Bruny Island Landscape Supplies
1751 Bruny Island Main Rd, Great Bay
Parking Area 15 km S of Ferry on B66. Pre-book
0429 011 840   HEMA 113 G12   43 11 55 S   147 23 11 E

133 The Neck Campground
Lutregala Rd, Bruny Island
Camp Area 26 km S of ferry terminal. 2 km S of Penguin Rookery
03 6121 7026   HEMA 113 H12   43 17 27 S   147 19 44 E

134 Hotel Bruny
3959 Bruny Island Main Rd, Alonnah
Parking Area at hotel. Register at bar
03 6293 1148   HEMA 113 H12   43 19 18 S   147 14 32 E

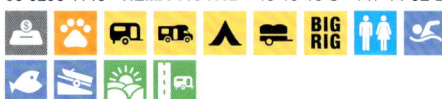

135 Jetty Beach Camp Area
South Bruny National Park
Old Jetty Rd, Bruny Island
Camp Area 57 km S of Ferry Terminal. 17 km SW of Lunawanna off Lighthouse Rd. Parks Pass applies
03 6121 7026   HEMA 113 J11   43 27 33 S   147 09 10 E

136 The Pines Camp Area
South Bruny National Park
Cloudy Bay Rd, Bruny Island
Camp Area 49 km S of Ferry Terminal. 8 km S of Lunawanna. Parks Pass applies
03 6121 7026   HEMA 113 J12   43 26 15 S   147 14 48 E

137 Cloudy Bay Corner
South Bruny National Park
980 Cloudy Bay Rd, Bruny Island
Camp Area 49 km S of Ferry Terminal. Beach access only for 3 km. Check tides. Parks pass applies
03 6121 7026   HEMA 113 J12   43 27 55 S   147 15 09 E

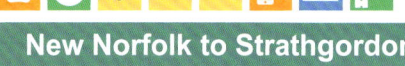

138 Oyster Cove Inn
1 Ferry Rd, Kettering
Pub Stay 32 km S of Hobart. Turn E off Channel Hwy (B68) into Ferry Rd, hotel on L
03 6267 4446   HEMA 113 F12   43 07 39 S   147 14 53 E

New Norfolk to Strathgordon
Gordon River Road

139 Gretna Green Hotel
3423 Lyell Hwy, Gretna
Pub Stay beside hotel. N end of town. Register at bar
03 6286 1332   HEMA 111 K13   42 40 54 S   146 56 16 E

140 Bushy Park Camping Ground
451 Gordon River Rd, Bushy Park
Camp Area 18 km NW of New Norfolk. Private property. Shower fee
0407 523 839   HEMA 113 C10   42 42 33 S   146 53 55 E

141 Mount Field Campground
Mount Field National Park
66 Lake Dobson Rd, National Park
Camp Area adjacent to Visitor Centre. Limited sites. Parks Pass applies
03 6288 1149   HEMA 111 K12   42 40 56 S   146 43 06 E

142 Left of Field Camping Gardens
2440 Gordon River Rd, Mount Field
Camp Area 9 km W of Westerway
0418 136 434   HEMA 111 K12   42 41 19 S   146 43 02 E

143 Edgar Dam Campground
Scotts Peak Dam Rd, Edgar Dam
C607 Camp Area S end of Lake Pedder.
30 km gravel road. Signposted off B61, 42 km E of
Strathgordon or 51 km W of Westerway
03 6288 1149 **HEMA 112 F7** 43 01 52 S 146 20 35 E

144 Huon Campground
Southwest National Park
C607 Port Davey Tr, Strathgordon
Camp Area 7 km W of Edgar Campground. L off
Scotts Peak Rd opposite dam. 1 km to camping
area. Small vehicles only. Parks Pass applies
03 6288 1149 **HEMA 112 F7** 43 02 18 S 146 17 57 E

145 Teds Beach Campground
Lake Pedder
B61 **Southwest National Park**
Gordon River Rd, Strathgordon
Camp Area 4 km E of town
03 6288 1149 **HEMA 112 D5** 42 47 13 S 146 03 39 E

Hobart-Queenstown-Burnie
Lyell, Zeehan and Murchison Highways

146 Hamilton Camping Ground
River St, Hamilton
A10 Camp Area W end of town, riverside.
Honesty box. Shower fee. 7 day limit
03 6286 3202 **HEMA 111 J12** 42 33 33 S 146 49 50 E

147 Hamilton Inn
10 Tarleton St, Hamilton
Pub Stay opposite hotel. Register at bar.
Pre-book
03 6286 3204 **HEMA 111 J12** 42 33 39 S 146 49 44 E

148 Bethune Park
Ellendale Rd, Ouse
C608 Camp Area 10 km W of Hamilton. W side of
Lake Meadowbank. 7 day limit
03 6286 3202 **HEMA 111 J12** 42 32 11 S 146 43 49 E

---

149 Wayatinah Lakeside Caravan Park
131 Wayatinah Rd, Wayatinah
A10 Caravan Park 24 km NW of Ouse or 16 km S of
Tarraleah. 1 km sealed road from Lyell Hwy
03 6289 3317 **HEMA 111 H11** 42 23 09 S 146 30 19 E

150 Tungatinah Lagoon
Lyell Hwy, Tarraleah
Camp Spot 10 km N of town off the A10
near boat ramp. 7 day limit
1300 360 441 **HEMA 111 G10** 42 16 34 S 146 27 36 E

151 Lake Binney Boat Ramp
Lyell Hwy, Tarraleah
Camp Area 13 km NE of town. W side of
Lake Binney near boat ramp
1300 360 441 **HEMA 111 G10** 42 15 20 S 146 28 41 E

152 Lake Binney Camp Corner
Lyell Hwy, Tarraleah
Camp Area 13 km NE of town. W side of
Lake Binney
1300 360 441 **HEMA 111 G10** 42 15 18 S 146 28 41 E

153 Bradys Lake Whitewater Point Campground
Bradys Lake Rd, Bradys Lake
A10 Camp Area 17 km N of Tarraleah or 8 km S of A10/
B11 Jcn. 800 m dirt road E of Hwy. 14 day limit
1300 360 441 **HEMA 111 G11** 42 13 57 S 146 29 49 E

154 Bradys Lake Woodwards Canal Campground
Bradys Lake Rd, Bronte
A10 Camp Area 17 km N of Tarraleah or 8 km S of A10/
B11 Jcn. 800 m dirt road E of Hwy. 7 day limit
1300 360 441 **HEMA 111 G11** 42 13 42 S 146 29 43 E

155 Bronte Lagoon
Bronte Lagoon Rd, Bronte Park
A10 Camp Area 26 km N of Tarraleah. Turn
S 250 m S of A10/B11 Jcn. 2 km to campsites.
Signposted. Limited space, small vehicles only.
7 day limit
1300 360 441 **HEMA 111 G11** 42 11 12 S 146 28 49 E

---

156 Derwent Bridge Wilderness Hotel
A10 Lyell Hwy, Derwent Bridge
Pub Stay in hotel car park. Register at bar
03 6289 1144 **HEMA 111 F9** 42 08 11 S 146 13 48 E

157 Lake King William
Franklin-Gordon Wild Rivers NP
A10 Lyell Hwy, Derwent Bridge
Parking Area 2 km W of Derwent Bridge or 85 km E
of Queenstown. L at fork after narrow access track.
100 m off Hwy, lakeside. Parks pass applies
03 6289 1172 **HEMA 111 F9** 42 08 47 S 146 13 01 E

158 Lake Burbury Campground
Lyell Hwy, Gormanston
A10 Camp Area 23 km E of Queenstown.
Turn N 86 km W of Derwent Bridge or 22 km E of
Queenstown. 800 m off Hwy. Caretaker on site
03 6471 2762 **HEMA 110 F6** 42 05 47 S 145 40 27 E

159 Thureau Hills Camping Area
Lyell Hwy, Gormanston
A10 Camp Area 76 km W of Derwent Bridge
or 20 km E of Queenstown. Turn S 72 km W of
Derwent Bridge or 16 km E of Queenstown. 3.5 km
to lakeside camping
1300 360 441 **HEMA 110 F6** 42 08 37 S 145 39 03 E

160 Lake Burbury Foreshore
Lyell Hwy, Gormanston
A10 Parking Area 12 km E of Queenstown.
Turn N 77 km W of Derwent Bridge or 11 km E of
Queenstown. W side of lake, 800 m N of Hwy along
old bitumen road. Limited space
03 6471 4700 **HEMA 110 F6** 42 004 25 S 145 38 19 E

161 Railway Hotel Queenstown
27-35 Driffield St, Queenstown
Parking Area behind hotel. Register at bar
03 6471 1511 **HEMA 110 F6** 42 04 49 S 145 33 11 E

162 Lake Burbury Darwin Dam Campground
A10 Mt Jukes Rd, Gormanston
Rest Area 23 km SW of Queenstown
03 6471 4700 **HEMA 110 G6** 42 12 24 S 145 37 08 E

163 Queenstown Oval
Wilsdon St, Queenstown
B24 Camp Area off Batchelor St
0438 454 962 **HEMA 110 F6** 42 04 30 S 145 33 32 E

164 Strahan Golf Club
Via Meredith St, Strahan
Parking Area 400 m W of clubhouse via gravel road. Register in clubhouse
03 6471 7242   HEMA 110 F4   42 08 46 S   145 18 59 E

165 Macquarie Heads Pine Forest
Macquarie Heads Rd, Strahan
Camp Area 5 km SW of town
03 6433 2636   HEMA 110 G4   42 13 06 S   145 15 14 E

166 Macquarie Heads Camp
Via Ocean Beach Rd, Strahan
Camp Area 15 km S of town. 12 km dirt road
03 6471 7382   HEMA 110 G4   42 13 16 S   145 13 44 E

167 Zeehan Golf Club
Fowler St, Zeehan
Parking Area beside golf club
0437 293 439   HEMA 110 D4   41 53 19 S   145 19 24 E

168 Trial Harbour
Trial Harbour Rd, Trial Harbour
Camp Area 24 km W of Zeehan. Winding road, not suitable caravans or motorhomes
HEMA 110 E3   41 55 39 S   145 10 21 E

169 Rosebery Golf Club
12399 Murchison Hwy, Rosebery
Parking Area 5 km SW of town. Honesty box at clubhouse
03 6473 1112   HEMA 110 D5   41 47 11 S   145 30 06 E

170 Lake Rosebery Foreshore
Murchison Hwy, Tullah
Parking Area 12 km E of Rosebery or 3 km S of Tullah. Turn W 50 m N of Murchison Bridge or 200 m S of Murchison Dam Rd intersection. Sharp turn from S. 200 m off Hwy. Limited space, small vehicles only
1800 352 200   HEMA 110 C6   41 45 39 S   145 37 08 E

171 Lake Mackintosh Camping
Mackintosh Dam Rd, Tullah
Camp Area 2 km N of Dam. Signposted from Tullah. Access over Mackintosh Dam wall. No access when dam spilling. 7 day limit
1800 352 200   HEMA 110 C6   41 41 07 S   145 39 23 E

172 Reece Dam
Pieman Rd, West Coast
Parking Area 44 km NW of Zeehan or 58 km W of Tullah. At boat ramp off Pieman Rd
1800 352 200   HEMA 110 C3   41 43 51 S   145 08 05 E

173 Corinna Campground
Corinna Rd, Corinna
Camp Area 49 km NW of Zeehan or 26 km SW of Savage River (dirt road). Limited small campsites, pre-book. Access from S by barge (9 m from mid front hub to mid rear hub maximum)
03 6446 1170   HEMA 110 C3   41 39 03 S   145 04 39 E

174 Granville Harbour
Top Farm Tr, Granville Harbour
Camp Area 2 km W of town, turn R & follow track along coastline to various bush campsites. 8 km gravel road
HEMA 110 D3   41 48 19 S   145 01 43 E

175 Waratah Camping Ground
William St, Waratah
Camp Area behind council. Key required
03 6439 7100   HEMA 108 J6   41 26 44 S   145 31 58 E

176 Yolla Tavern
1610 Murchison Hwy, Yolla
Pub Stay 22 km SW of Burnie or 19 km SE of Wynyard. Free for patrons. Register at bar
03 6438 1144   HEMA 108 F7   41 07 37 S   145 42 52 E

Launceston to Stanley
Bass Highway

177 Bishopsbourne RV Stop
1111 Bishopsbourne Rd, Bishopsbourne
Camp Area W side of reserve. E-permit
03 6397 7303   HEMA 104 G7   41 36 59 S   146 59 41 E

178 Bracknell River Reserve
Bracknell Ln, Bracknell
Parking Area 700 m E of general store, via Louisa St & Esplanade. Check in with roadhouse, permit applies
HEMA 104 H7   41 39 00 S   146 57 01 E

179 Hagley RV Farmstay
62 Meander Valley Rd, Hagley
Farm Stay 30 km W of Launceston
03 6392 2273   HEMA 104 G7   41 31 34 S   146 53 12 E

180 Westbury Private RV Camp
4 Peyton St, Westbury
Camp Area off Meander Valley Rd
03 6393 1480   HEMA 104 G6   41 31 32 S   146 50 51 E

181 Deloraine RV Rest Stop
6 Racecourse Dr, Deloraine
Camp Area 700 m E of PO. Turn N off A5 at police station. 4 day limit. Permit fee
03 6393 5300   HEMA 104 G5   41 31 19 S   146 39 43 E

182 Chudleigh Showground
Burnett & Sorrel Sts, Chudleigh
Camp Area in town. Pay at general store
03 6363 6138   HEMA 104 G4   41 33 25 S   146 28 58 E

183 Mole Creek Hotel
90 Pioneer Dr, Mole Creek
Pub Stay W end of town. Free for patrons, register at bar, fee for power
03 6363 1102   HEMA 104 G4   41 33 21 S   146 24 02 E

184 Mole Creek Caravan Park
2 Union Bridge Rd, Mole Creek
Caravan Park 4 km W of town. Creekside
03 6363 1150   HEMA 104 G4   41 33 04 S   146 21 37 E

185 Lake Parangana Rec Area
Parangana Sugarloaf Forest Reserve
Mersey Forest Rd, Mole Creek
Camp Area 29 km SW of Mole Creek. 1 km S of dam wall, via picnic area. Beside lake
HEMA 104 H3   41 38 43 S   146 13 35 E

186 Gewilebon Railton
Railton Kimberley Rd, Railton
Camp Area near Railton. Limited sites. Pre-book
0429 077 102   HEMA 104 E4   41 20 55 S   146 25 52 E

187 Railton Hotel
5 Foster St, Railton
Parking Area behind hotel. Register at bar. Shower fee, first 3 days free
03 6496 1232   HEMA 104 E4   41 20 44 S   146 25 27 E

188 Railton Motorhome Stop
Esplanade & Foster Sts, Railton
Parking Area on N side of Foster St opposite hotel. Park on gravel
03 6491 0200   HEMA 104 E4   41 20 39 S   146 25 23 E

189 CMCA Railton RV Park
15 Esplanade, Railton
Camp Area in town
02 4978 8788   HEMA 104 H11   41 20 34 S   146 25 21 E

190 Sheffield Recreation Ground
30 Spring St, Sheffield
Camp Area behind sportsground. Display permit
03 6491 1179   HEMA 104 F3   41 22 58 S   146 20 09 E

191 Sheffield Hotel
38 Main St, Sheffield
Pub Stay in town. Register at bar. Free for patrons. Closed in wet season
03 6491 1130   HEMA 104 H10   41 22 55 S   146 19 24 E

192 O'Neills Creek Picnic Reserve
Claude Rd, Gowrie Park
Picnic Area E end of town. Park on concrete pad. Honesty box
03 6491 1179   HEMA 104 F3   41 28 00 S   146 13 11 E

193 Gowrie Park Wilderness Village
1447 Claude Rd, Gowrie Park
Camp Area 15 km S of Sheffield, towards Cradle Mt
03 6491 1385   HEMA 104 F3   41 28 14 S   146 12 56 E

194 Farm on Franklin
Lades Rd, Harford
Farm Stay 31 km SE of Devonport via Frankford. Riverside. Pre-book
0438 951 067   HEMA 106 E2   41 14 36 S   146 35 44 E

195 Horse Yards Campground
Narawntapu National Park
Bakers Beach Rd, Port Sorell
Camp Area 12 km N of B71/C740 jcn. 1 km dirt road. Parks Pass applies
03 6428 6277   HEMA 106 C2   41 09 15 S   146 36 31 E

196 Springlawn Campground
Narawntapu National Park
Bakers Beach Rd, Bakers Beach
Camp Area 13 km N of B71/C740 Jcn. 2 km dirt road, shower token from Visitor Centre. Parks Pass applies
03 6428 6277   HEMA 106 C2   41 08 52 S   146 36 09 E

197 Bakers Point Campground
Narawntapu National Park
Bakers Point Rd, Bakers Beach
Camp Area 18 km N of B71/C740 Jcn. From Frankford Rd via N to Bakers Beach Rd. 6 km dirt road. Parks Pass applies
03 6428 6277   HEMA 106 C1   41 09 44 S   146 34 05 E

198 Latrobe Overnight Stop
via Cotton St, Latrobe
Camp Area at Latrobe. Access from Cotton St, behind IGA. Fees collected
03 6426 4444   HEMA 104 D4   41 14 14 S   146 24 37 E

199 Girdlestone Park
John St, East Devonport
Camp Area in town. Permit from Visitor Centre at 145 Rooke St. Toilets locked at night
03 6424 4466   HEMA 104 D4   41 11 10 S   146 22 45 E

200 Horsehead Creek Riverside Park
Devonport Rd, Quoiba
Camp Area N side of Mersey R Bridge. Permit from Visitor Centre, 92 Formby Rd
03 6424 4466   HEMA 104 D4   41 12 04 S   146 21 30 E

201 Kentish Park
1093 West Kentish Rd, West Kentish
Camp Area 6 km W of town on E shore of Lake Barrington, gravel road, 21 day limit
03 6491 0200   HEMA 104 F3   41 22 49 S   146 13 12 E

202 Forth Recreation Ground
Mell St, Forth
Camp Area at Football Ground. Designated area only
03 6429 8900   HEMA 104 D3   41 11 19 S   146 15 00 E

203 Lake Barrington
Lake Barrington Rd, Wilmot
Camp Area 4 km E of town on W shore of Lake Barrington. Take track on R, 100 m before boat ramp. 2.5 km dirt road
03 6491 0200   HEMA 104 F3   41 22 40 S   146 12 37 E

204 Lake Gairdner Campground
Moina Rd, Moina
Camp Area 5 km W of town. W off C132, 1 km S of Moina. Lakeside. 4 km narrow dirt road
1300 360 441   HEMA 104 F2   41 29 01 S   146 03 33 E

205 O.C. Ling Memorial Caravan Park
45 Esplanade, Turners Beach
Caravan Park at Turners Beach
0499 949 584   HEMA 104 D3   41 09 29 S   146 14 35 E

206 The Berry Patch
4 Blackburn Dr, Turners Beach
Camp Area at 5 km E of Ulverstone. Exit Hwy interchange to Turners Beach Rd. Free for patrons
03 6428 3967   HEMA 104 D3   41 09 44 S   146 14 18 F

207 Nicholson Point
Off Riverside Ave, Ulverstone
Parking Area via Lovett & Ihlata Sts. L to open area past railway line
HEMA 104 D2   41 09 32 S   146 09 46 E

208 Leven Canyon Reserve
Leven Canyon Rd, Nietta
Picnic Area 9 km SW of town via Loongana Rd
03 6425 2839   HEMA 104 F2   41 24 03 S   146 01 53 E

TASMANIA

209 Ulverston Golf Club

Golf Club Rd, West Ulverstone
Parking Area at Ulverstone West. Turn
SW off Bass Hwy to South Rd for 2 km, then SW to
Lobster Creek Rd, then S for 400 m. Register at bar
03 6425 2322   HEMA 104 D2   41 09 18 S   146 06 43 E

210 Wings Wildlife Park

137 Winduss Rd, Gunns Plains
Camp Area 2 km NW of Gunns Plains or
12 km S of Ulverston
03 6429 1151   HEMA 104 E2   41 15 49 S   146 02 43 E

211 The Blue Wren RV Park

225 Penguin Rd, Ulverston
Camp Area E off Bass Hwy to South Rd, N
via Queen St
0428 990 223   HEMA 104 D2   41 08 14 S   146 08 05 E

212 Riana Pioneer Park

1399 Pine Rd, Riana
Camp Area 1.5 km S of town. Caretaker
collects fees. Limited sites. 4 week limit. Shower fee
03 6437 6137   HEMA 104 D2   41 12 59 S   145 59 59 E

213 Preservation Bay

68/62 Preservation Dr, Penguin
Rest Area on E side of surf club. Honesty
box on wall near playground
03 6437 2639   HEMA 104 C2   41 06 07 S   146 03 09 E

214 Midway Point

196 Preservation Dr, Sulphur Creek
Camp Area 1 km E of Sulphur Ck or 3.5 km
W of Penguin
03 6429 8900   HEMA 104 C2   41 05 48 S   146 02 25 E

215 Hall Point

Preservation Dr, Sulphur Creek
Camp Area 8 km W of Penguin. 700 m E of
shop. Oceanfront
03 6429 8900   HEMA 104 C2   41 05 38 S   146 01 42 E

216 Upper Natone Forest Reserve

1 Bythe Rd, Hampshire
Camp Area 30 km SE of Ridgley, E off
Ridgley Hwy to Upper Natone Rd, R to Blythe Rd
03 6430 5700   HEMA 104 E1   41 15 08 S   145 51 45 E

217 Lake Kara Campsite

Lake Kara Rd, Upper Natone
Camp Area 32 km S of Burnie. S to the
Ridgley Hwy (B18) 23km past Ridgley turn L to Upper
Natone Rd (C102) for 6 km. R to Osbourns Rd then L
03 6433 2666   HEMA 104 E1   41 15 45 S   145 50 41 E

218 Ridgley Campground

Parker Ct, Ridgley
Camp Area S off Bass Hwy, at Burnie to
Ridgley Hwy (B18)
0408 126 166   HEMA 104 D1   41 08 46 S   145 49 59 E

219 Cooee Point Reserve

Cooee Point Rd, Burnie
Parking Area 3 km W of town. Oceanfront.
Permits online (2 permits per year)
03 6430 5831   HEMA 104 C1   41 02 19 S   145 52 37 E

220 Wynyard Showgrounds

59 Jackson St, Wynyard
Parking Area N side of town
03 6443 8333   HEMA 108 E7   40 59 13 S   145 43 37 E

221 Rocky Cape Tavern

19375 Bass Hwy, Rocky Cape
Caravan Park 31 km NW of Wynyard
beside tavern. Register at bottleshop. Shower fee
03 6443 4110   HEMA 108 D6   40 53 07 S   145 27 56 E

222 Peggs Beach Campground

Peggs Beach Conservation Area
Bass Hwy, Cowrie Point
Camp Area 14km W of Rocky Cape turnoff or 11 km
E of Stanley turnoff. Closed May - Oct
03 6458 1480   HEMA 108 D5   40 51 03 S   145 21 10 E

223 Black River Campground

Peggs Beach Conservation Area
Bass Hwy, Black River
Camp Area 5 km W of Port Latta or 9 km E of A2/
B21 Jcn. 1 km of dirt road N of Hwy. 30 day limit
03 6458 1480   HEMA 108 D5   40 50 36 S   145 19 00 E

224 Stanley Recreation Ground

23 Marine Esplanade, Stanley
Parking Area beachside adjacent to golf
club. Fees collected. 7 day limit
03 6458 1266   HEMA 108 D5   40 45 51 S   145 17 22 E

225 Irishtown Recreation Ground

602 Irishtown Rd, Irishtown
Camp Area 11 km past Stanley turnoff
towards Smithton, L to Irishtown Rd (B22) to
Irishtown/Edith Creek/Tarkine Dr
0448 654 384   HEMA 108 E4   40 54 45 S   145 08 43 E

226 Tall Timbers Free RV Parking

5-15 Scotchtown Rd, Smithton
Pub Stay beside hotel, Jcn Bass Hwy &
Scotchtown Rd. Open Oct - May
1800 628 476   HEMA 108 D4   40 51 24 S   145 07 10 E

227 Montagu Recreation Reserve

Camping Area
380 Old Port Rd, Montagu
Camp Area 20 km NW of Smithton. Turn N off C215,
16 km NW of Smithton, 4 km dirt road. Caretaker
collects fees, closed October
03 6452 1181   HEMA 108 C3   40 44 40 S   144 58 44 E

228 Marrawah Green Point

Beach Camping Area
Green Point Rd, Marrawah
Camp Area 3 km W of Marrawah, via Beach Rd.
Outside cold shower. Oceanfront
03 6452 4800   HEMA 108 E1   40 54 35 S   144 40 45 E

229 Manuka Campground

Arthur-Pieman Conservation Area
Arthur River Rd, Arthur River
Camp Area 15 km S of Marrawah or 1 km N of
Arthur River
03 6457 1225   HEMA 108 F1   41 02 41 S   144 40 04 E

230 Peppermint Campground

Arthur-Pieman Conservation Area

C214 1413 Arthur River Rd, Arthur River

Camp Area next to ranger station. Cold showers

03 6457 1225   HEMA 108 F1   41 02 53 S   144 40 03 E

231 Prickly Wattle Campground

Arthur-Pieman Conservation Area

C214 Temma Rd, Arthur River

Camp Area 1 km S of Arthur River. 4 entry points, 2 & 3 easiest access for caravans

03 6457 1225   HEMA 108 F1   41 03 36 S   144 40 45 E

232 Nelson Bay

Arthur-Pieman Conservation Area

Nelson Bay Rd, Nelson Bay

Camp Area 15 km S of Arthur River. Turn R at beach, past boats. Camp beachside of road

03 6457 1225   HEMA 108 F1   41 07 39 S   144 40 19 E

233 Julius River Motorhome Campground

The Tarkine

C218 Sumac Rd, Kanunnah Bridge

Camp Area 10 km E of Kanunnah Bridge. 7 km gravel road. Toilets are 600 m W at picnic area

03 6458 1480   HEMA 108 G3   41 09 08 S   145 02 02 E

George Town to Beaconsfield

East/West Tamar Highways

234 Fortrose Naturist Farmstay

320 Windemere Rd, Windemere

Farm Stay 20 km N of Launceston. Book ahead. Clothing optional, open Oct - Apr

0418 222 970   HEMA 107 G9   41 18 15 S   147 01 07 E

235 Rose Bay Park

C728 243 Gravelly Beach Rd, Gravelly Beach

Rest Area S end of town, riverside. 6 sites available between 5pm - 9am

03 6394 4454   HEMA 107 G8   41 17 38 S   146 58 20 E

236 Paper Beach Reserve

Paper Beach Rd, Swan Point

Rest Area 2 km S of Exeter

1800 651 827   HEMA 107 F8   41 15 12 S   146 57 55 E

237 Exeter Hotel

A7 Main Rd, Exeter

Camp Area 24 km N of Launceston or 23 km S of Beauty Pt. In paddock behind hotel. Register at bar

03 6394 4216   HEMA 107 G8   41 17 53 S   146 57 08 E

238 Fork n Farm Homestead

91 Blackberrys Rd, Glengarry

Farm Stay 4 km S of Frankford Rd & Loop Rd Jcn. Turn S off Loop Rd to Blackberrys Rd. Pre-book

0456 649 088   HEMA 106 H7   41 21 02 S   146 54 09 E

239 Beaconsfield Rec Ground

A7 Grubb St, Beaconsfield

Parking Area at E end of Grubb St

03 6394 4454   HEMA 106 D6   41 11 57 S   146 49 19 E

240 Watermill Cottage

C741 30 Bowens Rd, York Town

Camp Area 6 km N of Beaconsfield at York Town. Closed during winter

0417 151 153   HEMA 106 C5   41 09 01 S   146 45 47 E

241 Garden Island Clarence Point

A7 Bevic Rd, Clarence Point

Parking Area 11 km N of Beaconsfield. Follow Greens Beach Rd, R to Bevic. Keep dogs leashed, seals in the area

HEMA 106 B5   41 06 40 S   146 48 16 E

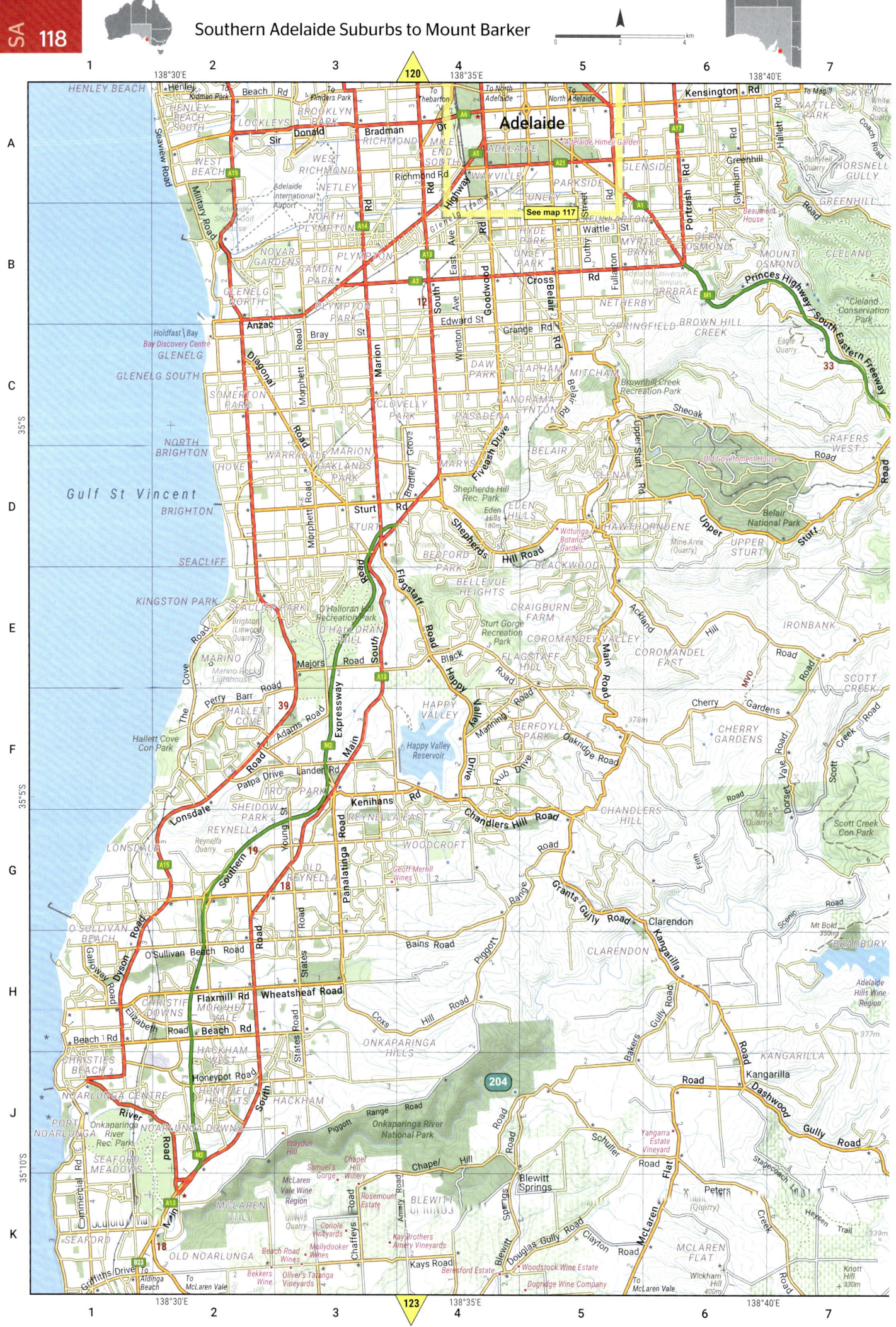

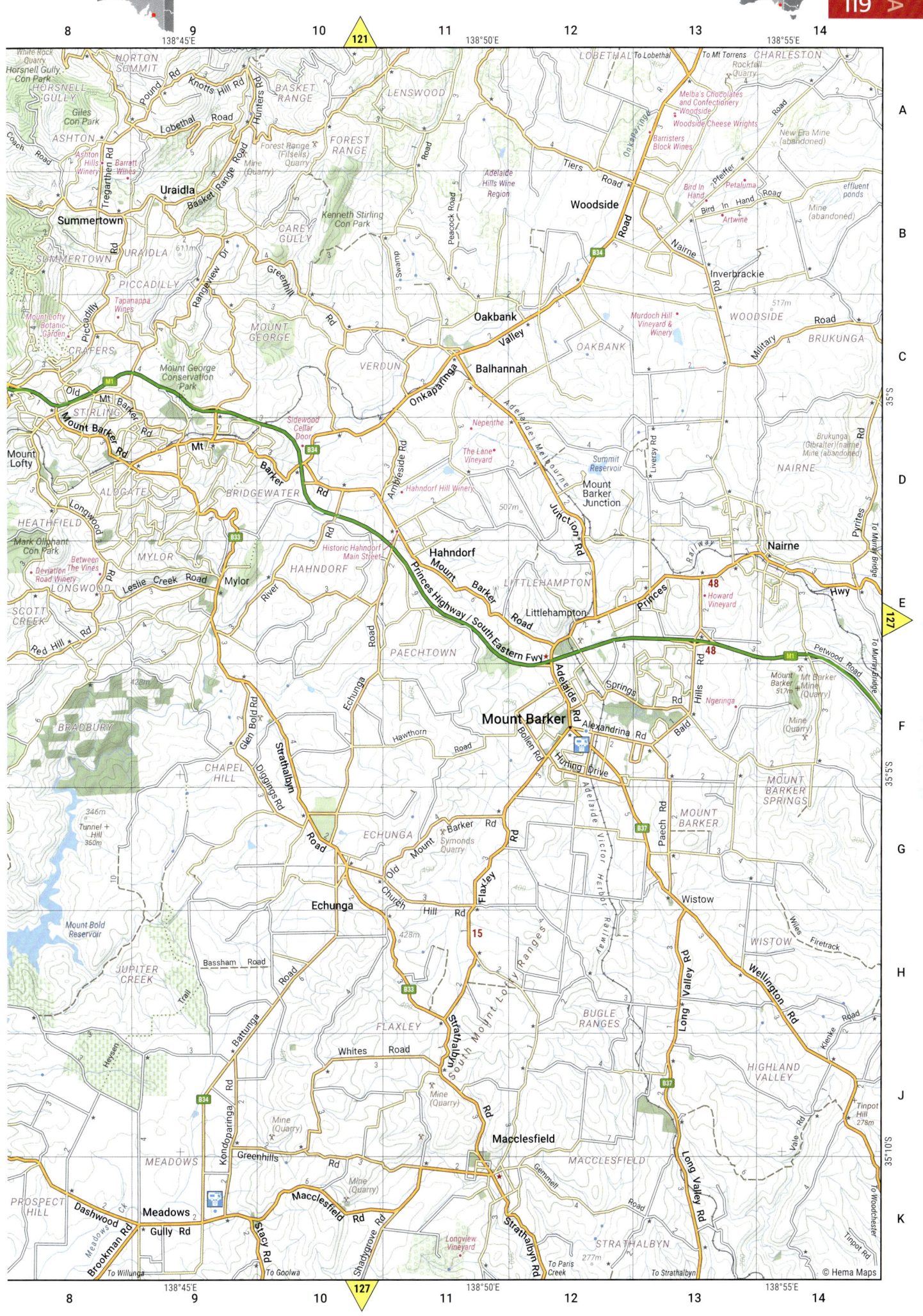

© Hema Maps

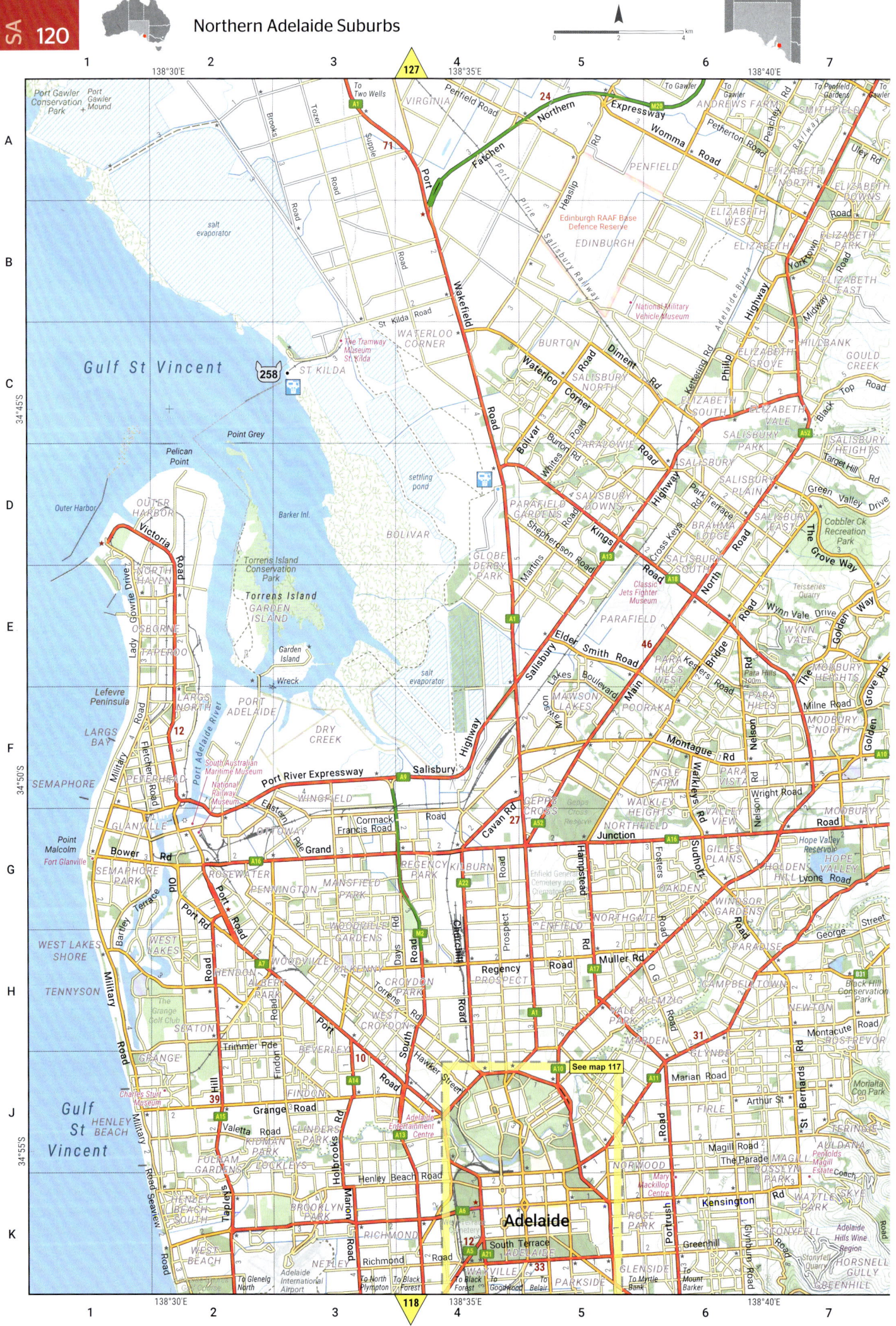

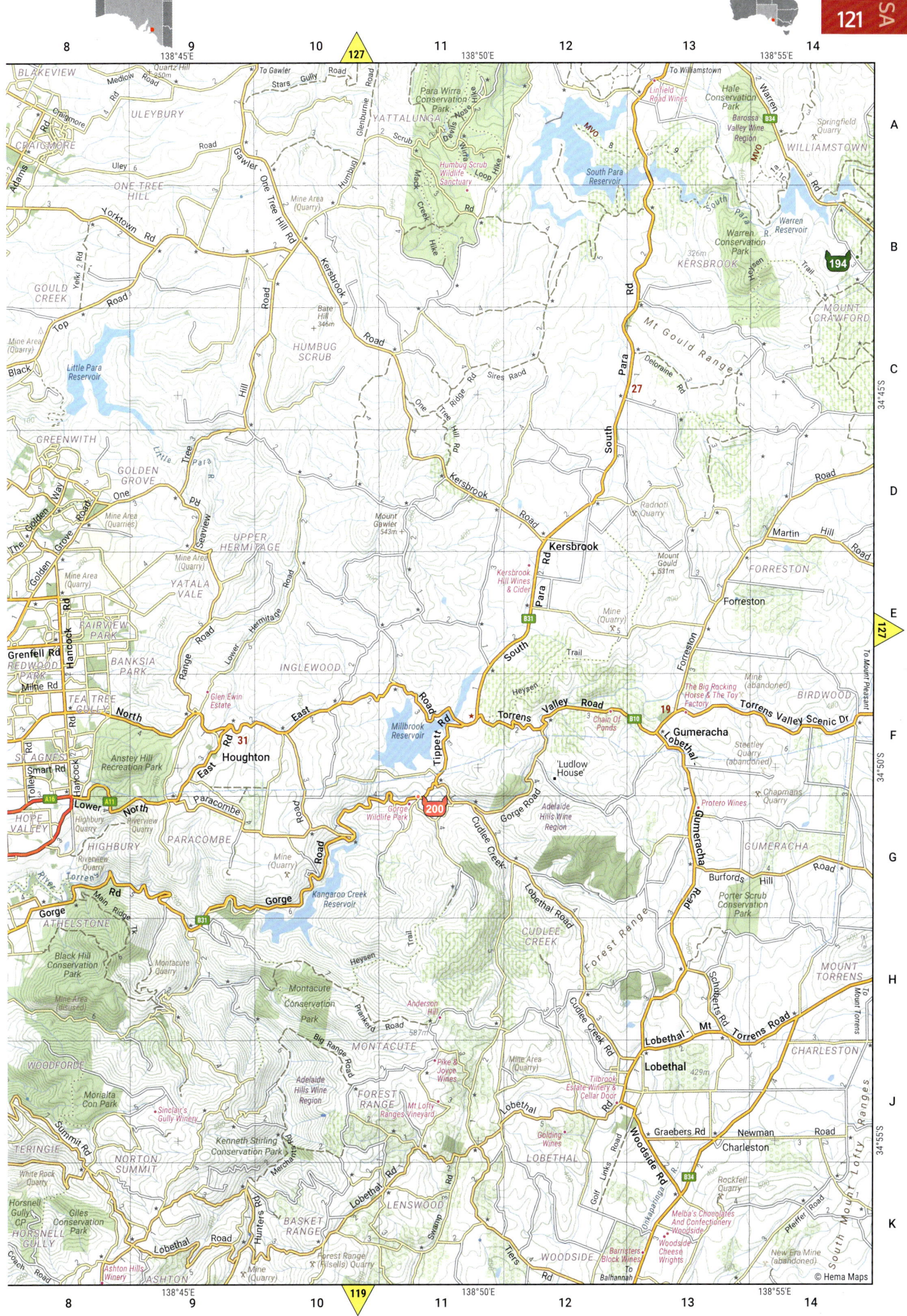

© Hema Maps

Barossa Valley

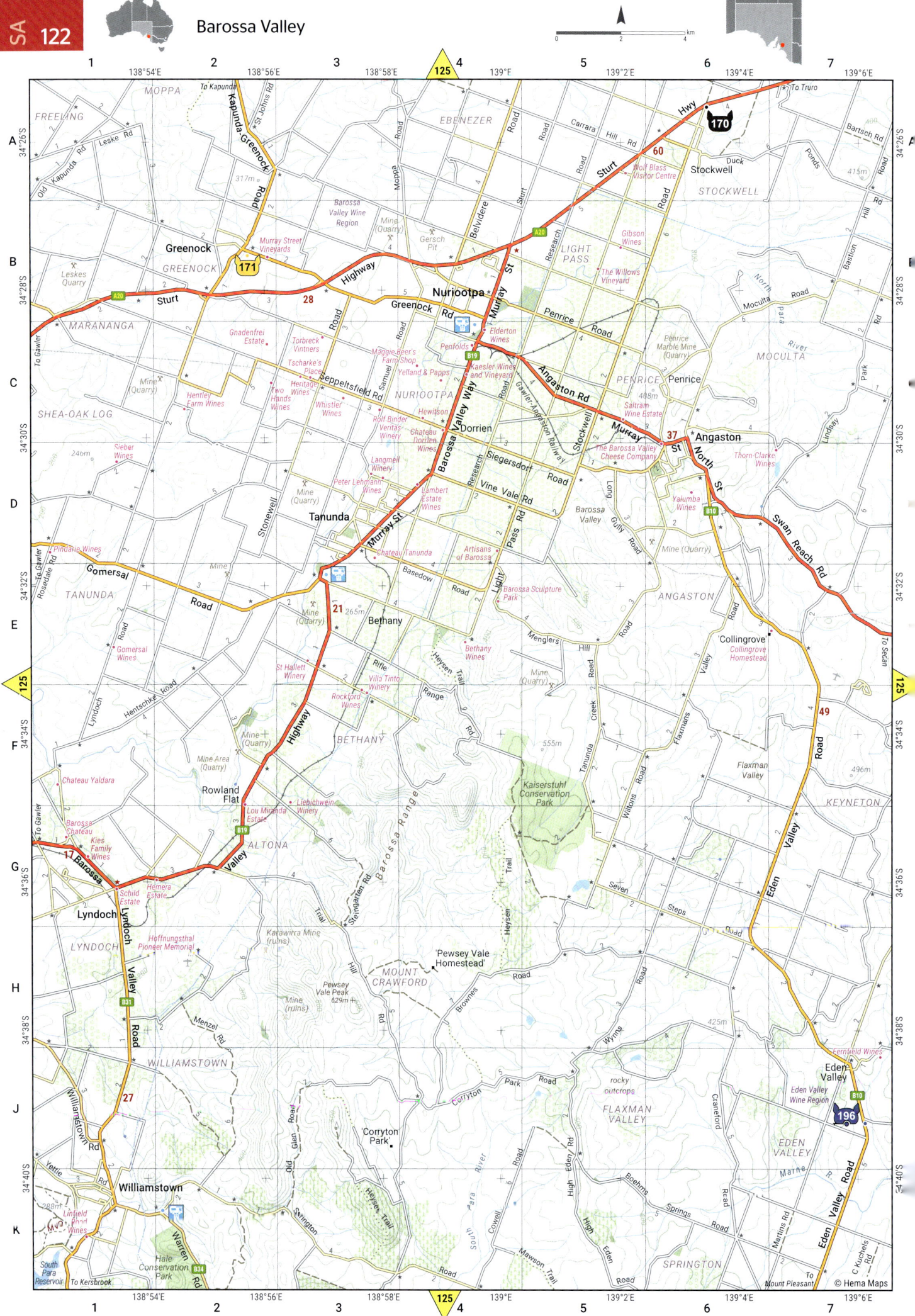

© Hema Maps

139°10'E · 140°E · 140°50'E

8 | 9 | 10 | 11 | 12 | 13 | 14

131 (top marker) · **125** (bottom marker)

Strzelecki Desert

Lake Frome
Lake Frome Regional Reserve

North Flinders Ranges · Jubilee Range · Grindstone Range

'Mulga View' · Wearing (ruins) · To Arkaroola Village · 'Broughams Gate House' · 'Quinyambie'

Mount Gill 914m · 'Pinda Springs' · Mount Chambers Gorge · Mt Chambers Ck · Lake Kuturu · Lake Karpi · Lake Moko · Lake Carnanto

'Narrina' · Ann Hill 798m · 'Point Well' · First Hill · Mount Lyall 595m · Wirrealpa · Lake Millyera · Lake Tarkarooloo

Blinman North · See map 142 · Balcanoona Creek · Yunta · Eurilla Creek

Blinman · Wirrealpa Ck · Balcatacana Creek · 'Wyambana Outstation' · 'Frome Downs' · Billeroo Creek · Lake Namba

Gum Creek · Second Plain · Watkins Well · Kemp Bore · 'Billeroo West' · 'Benagerie'

Ikara-Flinders Ranges NP · Fifteen Mile Well

'Oraparinna' · 'Erudina' · 'Mulyungarie'

'Willow Springs' · 'Martins Well' · 'Curnamona' · 'Yarramba'

'Warcowie' · 'Willipa' · Wilyerpa Hill 870m · 'Killawarra Outstation' · 'Strathearn' · Road · Kalkaroo

Shaggy Ridge · Bibliando · Windowarta Hut (Ruin) · Old Woolshed Bore · Kalbity · 'Kalbity' · Mundi Mundi Plain · 'Mundi Mundi'

'Holowiliena' · Black Range · 'Glenorchy' · Bimbowrie Con Park · 'Boolcoomata' · To Broken Hill

'Worumba' · 'Holowilena South' · Baratta · 'Nillinghoo' · 'Plumbago' · 'Bimbowrie' · Bimbowrie · Wiperaminga Gap · Road

'Three Creeks' · Milang · Koonamore · 'Mount Victor' · 'Old Boolcoomata' · **212** · Cockburn

Weira Hill 620m · 'Witchitie' · 'Four Brothers' · Weekeroo Hill 540m · 'Outalpa' · Cutana · **213** · Mingary · 'Pine Creek'

Mares Cave · Belton · Marchant Hill 780m · Waukaringa Historic Site · 'Morialpa' · 'Weekeroo' · Olary · **214** · Highway · 'Aroona' · 'Corella'

Bendleby Settlers Monument · Gum Dale · Waukaringa · 'Melton' · Karkala Peak 510m · 'Bonnie Brae' · **215** · 'Wiawera' · 'Ballara' · 'Coutra Hut'

Bendleby Warna Plain · 'The Springs' · **249** · Barrier · Outalpa · **216** · 'Eringa Park' · 'Devonborough Downs' · Mutooroo

Minburra Plain · 'Wabricoola' · 'Old Wabricoola' · Manna Hill · Wawirra · Duffields

Meadow Downs · 'Winnininnie' · **217** · Oulnina · Benda Range

Bob Gap · Hope Bank Range · Waroonee Range · **267** · 'Wadnaminga' · 'Taltabooka'

Steve Gap · 'Yalpara' · 'Mccoys Well' · Yunta · **218** · 'Oulnina Park' · Ocalia Creek

Peaked Hill 550m · 'Whyngoon' · **219** · 'Panaramatee' · 'Netley Gap' · Netley Gap

'Kylmorn' · 'Oakdowns' · Buttanuck Hill 520m · 'Old Whydown' · Paratoo · 'Tiverton' · Manunda

Black Rock · Dawson · White Well · **220** · Barrier · 'Spring Dam' · Woolshed Range

244 · **221** · **222** · Nackara · 'Oak Park' · Manunda

Yatina · **242** · **240** · Oodla Wirra · 'Hill Grange' · Pualco Range · Lilydale

Yongala · **241** · Peterborough · Nantabibbie · 'Pitcairn' · Pualco Range Con Park · **Quarantine** – Do not take fruit, vegetables, plants or flowers across State and quarantine borders. Penalties apply. Phone 1800 084 881

Enwby · Wandre Plain · **243** · Sunnybrae · 'Blue Hills' · Zevir Range · Ironback Gorge · 'Quondong Vale' · **Danggali Conservation Park** · Australia's first Biosphere Reserve. Birdwatching, historical significance, mallee scrubland

Canowie Belt · **223** · Terowie · Franklyn · 'The Oaks' · 'Loch Winnoch' · 'Faraway Hill Outstation' · 'Oakbank Outstation' · 'Oakvale'

Belalie East · Whyte-Yarcowie · 'Pine Creek' · 'Bendigo' · 'Braemar' · Block Seven Gorge · 'Aldermans Outstation' · 'Sturt Vale' · Tom Allison Waterhole · Tipperary · Birthday Hut

Old Canowie · Moorowie Plain · Mallett · 'Pulpara' · 'Woolamba' · 'Alexandrina Outstation' · 'Pine Valley' · **Danggali Wilderness Protection Area**

'Yellowie' · Hallett · Uloolloo · 'Ketchowla' · 'Willara' · 'Kia-Ora' · Danggali Con Park

Tommy Gap · Mount Bryan East · Collinsville · 'Hog Back' · 'Lords Well Outstation' · Danggali Con FFEZ

Tiverville · **224** · Caroona Ck Con Park · New Caroona · 'Glenora' · 'Murkaby' · 'Dustholes Station' · 'Canopus' · 'Hypurna'

Booborowie · **225** · Mount Bryan · Caroona · Chowilla Regional Reserve

Leighton · Tracy · 'Chalk Cliffs' · 'Koomooloo' · 'Old Koomooloo' · 'Parcoola'

'Arlie' · To Burra

South Australia / New South Wales

© Hema Maps

Blinman — The township of Blinman was named after Robert 'peg leg' Blinman, a miner with a wooden leg who discovered copper nearby in 1859. At its peak Blinman had a population of 1,500, currently it is 22.

Roxby Downs to Cameron Corner

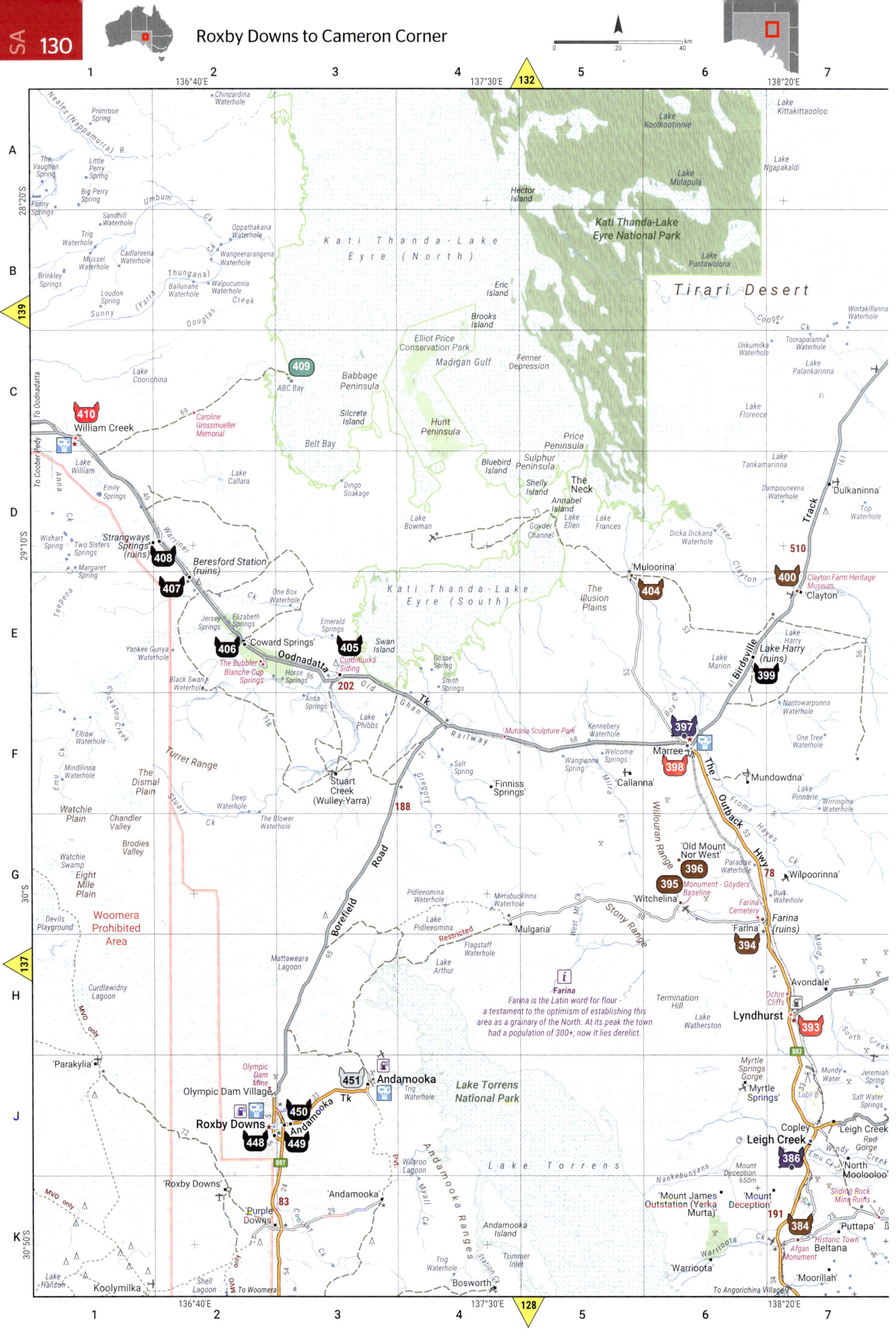

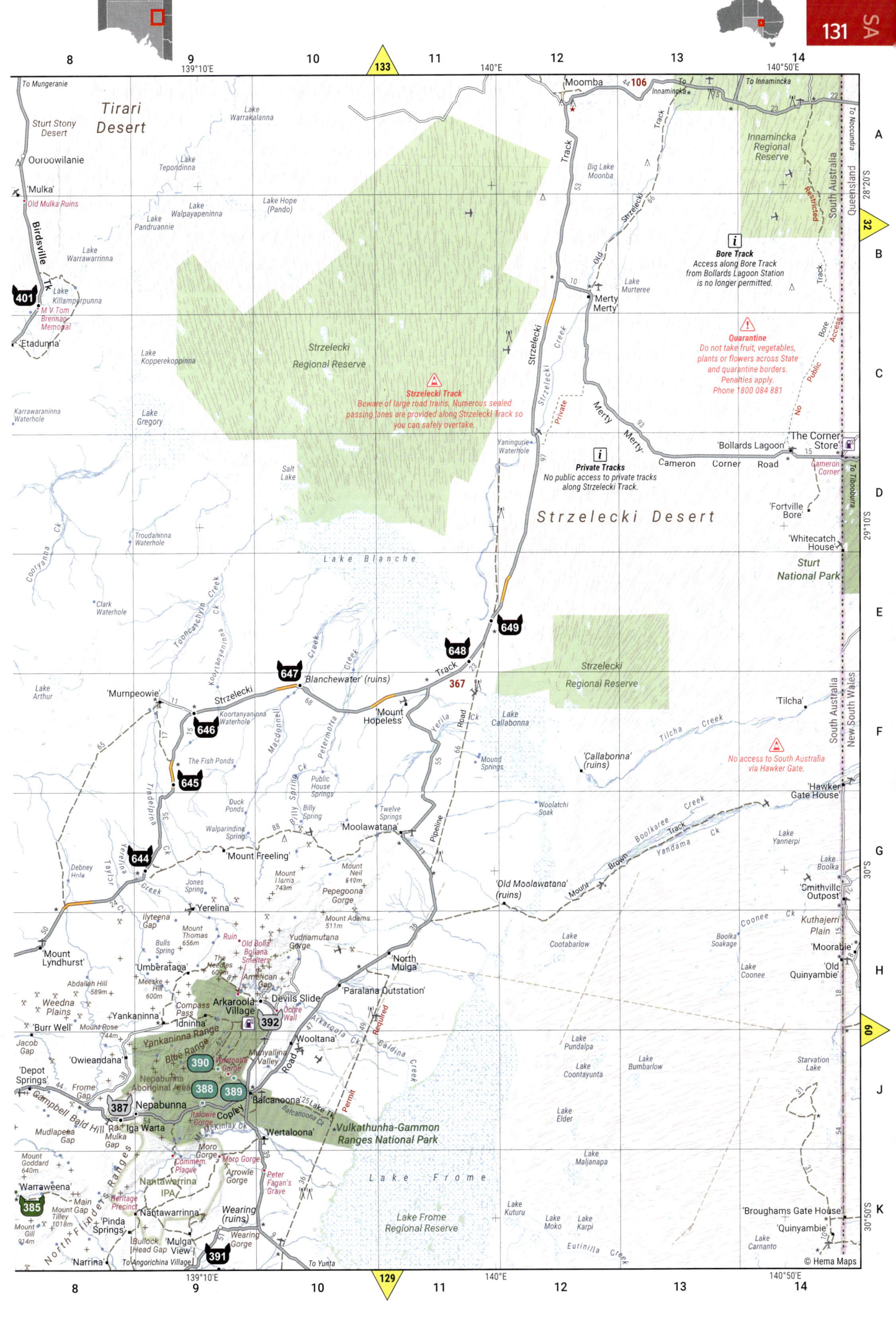

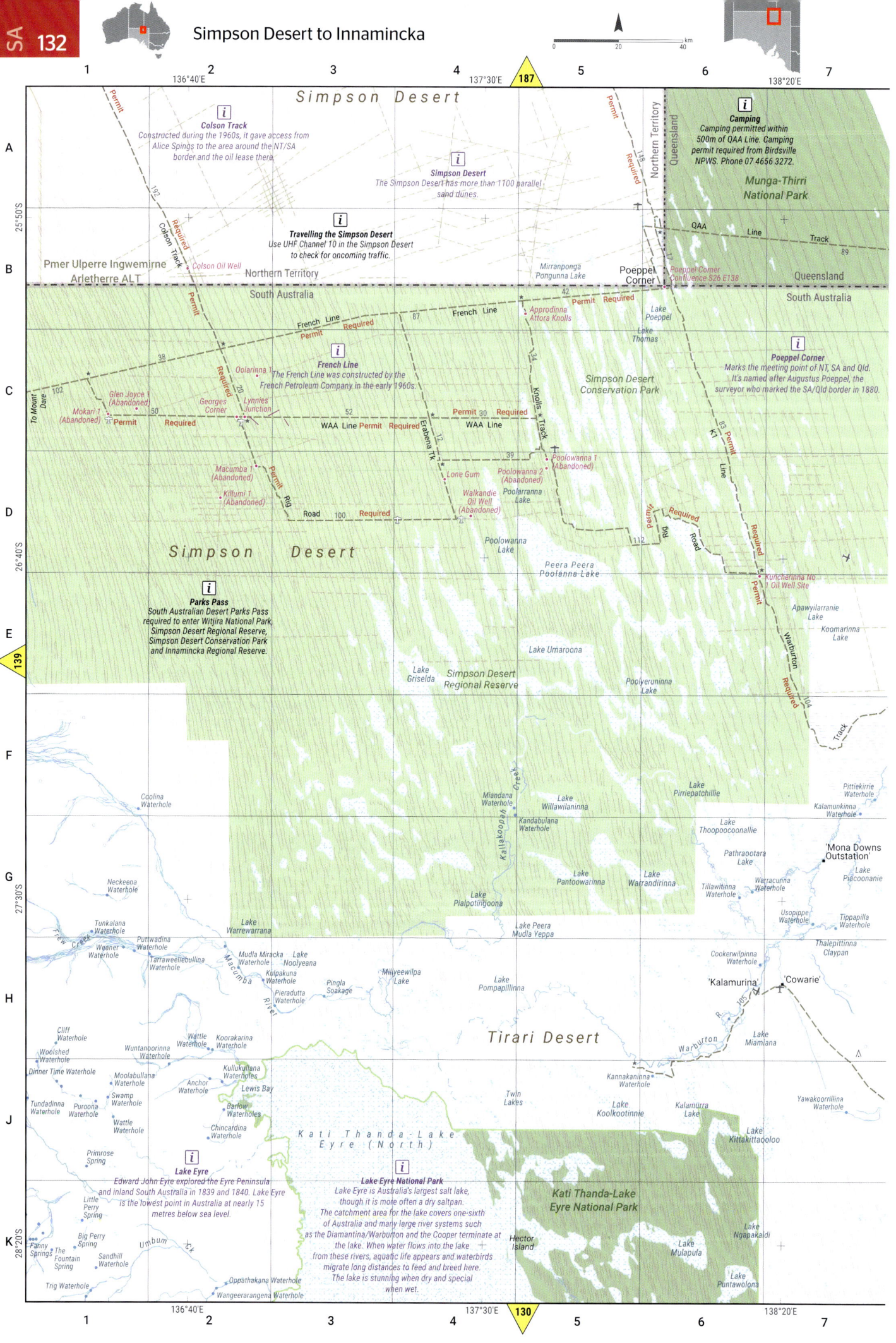

Colson Track
Constructed during the 1960s, it gave access from Alice Springs to the area around the NT/SA border and the oil lease there.

Simpson Desert
The Simpson Desert has more than 1100 parallel sand dunes.

Camping
Camping permitted within 500m of QAA Line. Camping permit required from Birdsville NPWS. Phone 07 4656 3272.

Travelling the Simpson Desert
Use UHF Channel 10 in the Simpson Desert to check for oncoming traffic.

French Line
The French Line was constructed by the French Petroleum Company in the early 1960s.

Poeppel Corner
Marks the meeting point of NT, SA and Qld. It's named after Augustus Poeppel, the surveyor who marked the SA/Qld border in 1880.

Parks Pass
South Australian Desert Parks Pass required to enter Witjira National Park, Simpson Desert Regional Reserve, Simpson Desert Conservation Park and Innamincka Regional Reserve.

Lake Eyre
Edward John Eyre explored the Eyre Peninsula and inland South Australia in 1839 and 1840. Lake Eyre is the lowest point in Australia at nearly 15 metres below sea level.

Lake Eyre National Park
Lake Eyre is Australia's largest salt lake, though it is more often a dry saltpan. The catchment area for the lake covers one-sixth of Australia and many large river systems such as the Diamantina/Warburton and the Cooper terminate at the lake. When water flows into the lake from these rivers, aquatic life appears and waterbirds migrate long distances to feed and breed here. The lake is stunning when dry and special when wet.

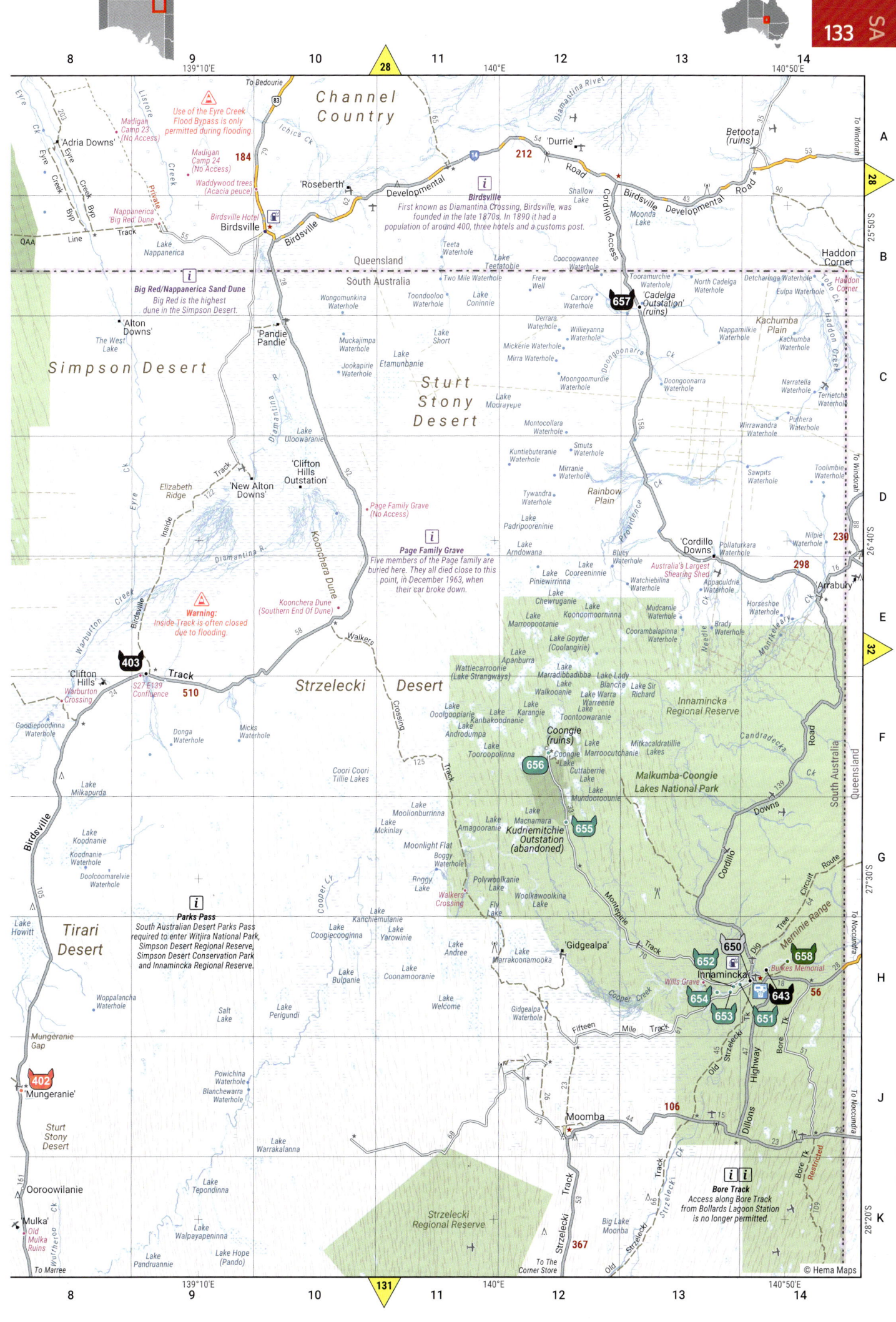

Use of the Eyre Creek Flood Bypass is only permitted during flooding

Madigan Camp 23 (No Access)

Madigan Camp 24 (No Access)   184

Waddywood trees (Acacia peuce)

Nappanerica 'Big Red' Dune   Private

QAA   Line   Track

'Adria Downs'

Channel Country

To Bedourie

Ichica Ck

'Durrie'   212

'Roseberth'

Developmental

Birdsville Hotel
Birdsville

Lake Nappanerica

Birdsville
First known as Diamantina Crossing, Birdsville was founded in the late 1870s. In 1890 it had a population of around 400, three hotels and a customs post.

Shallow Lake

Moonda Lake

Betoota (ruins)

To Windorah

28

Haddon Corner

Queensland
South Australia

Big Red/Nappanerica Sand Dune
Big Red is the highest dune in the Simpson Desert.

'Alton Downs'

The West Lake

Simpson Desert

'Pandie Pandie'

Muckajimpa Waterhole

Jookapirie Waterhole

Lake Short

Lake Etamunbanie

Teeta Waterhole

Lake Teetatobie

Two Mile Waterhole

Lake Coninnie

Frew Well

Coocoowannee Waterhole

Tooramurchie Waterhole

Carcory Waterhole

North Cadelga Waterhole

657   'Cadelga Outstation' (ruins)

Detcharinga Waterhole

Eulpa Waterhole

Kachumba Plain

Nappamilkie Waterhole

Kachumba Waterhole

Haddon Ck

Haddon Creek

Sturt Stony Desert

Derrara Waterhole

Willieyanna Waterhole

Mickerie Waterhole

Mirra Waterhole

Lake Mourayepe

Moongoomurdie Waterhole

Doongoonarra Waterhole

Doongoonarra Ck

158

Narratella Waterhole

Wirrawandra Waterhole

Puthera Waterhole

Ternetcha Waterhole

Toolimbie Waterhole

To Windorah

Lake Uloowaranie

'Clifton Hills Outstation'

Montocollara Waterhole

Kuntiebuteranie Waterhole

Smuts Waterhole

Mirranie Waterhole

Rainbow Plain

Sawpits Waterhole

Elizabeth Ridge

'New Alton Downs'

Page Family Grave (No Access)

Tywandra Waterhole

Lake Padripooreninie

Diamantina R.

Page Family Grave
Five members of the Page family are buried here. They all died close to this point, in December 1963, when their car broke down.

Lake Arndowana

'Cordillo Downs'

Pollaturkara Waterhole

Nilpie Waterhole   230

Australia's Largest Shearing Shed

Appaculdrie Waterhole

298

Arrabury

Koonchera Dune

Warning:
Inside Track is often closed due to flooding.

Koonchera Dune (Southern End Of Dune)

Lake Cooreeninnie

Lake Piniewirrinna

Watchiebillina Waterhole

Mudcarnie Waterhole

Horseshoe Waterhole

Brady Waterhole

Needle Ck

Monitelery

32

Warburton Creek

Birdsville

403

'Clifton Hills'

Warburton Crossing

S27 E139 Confluence   510

Track

Strzelecki   Desert

Crossing

Walkers

Lake Chewrugan

Lake Marroopootanie

Lake Koohoomoorninna

Cooram-balapinna Waterhole

Lake Goyder (Coolangirie)

Innamincka Regional Reserve

Candradecka Ck

Road

Queensland
South Australia

Goodiepoodinna Waterhole

Lake Milkapurda

Donga Waterhole

Micks Waterhole

Coori Coori Tillie Lakes

125

Wattiecarroonie (Lake Strangways)

Lake Apanburra

Lake Marradibbadibba

Lake Walkooanie

Lake Lady Blanche

Lake Warra Warreenie

Lake Sir Richard

Malkumba-Coongie Lakes National Park

Tree

Circuit

Merninie Range

To Noccundra

Lake Koodnanie

Koodnanie Waterhole

Doolcoomarelvie Waterhole

Lake Ooolgoopiarie

Lake Androdumpa

Lake Karangie

Lake Tooroopolina

Coongie (ruins)

656

Coongie Lake

Cuttaberrie Lake

Marroocutchanie

Mitkacaldratillie Lakes

Toontoowaranie

Cordillo

Downs

139

Tirari Desert

Lake Howitt

Parks Pass
South Australian Desert Parks Pass required to enter Witjira National Park, Simpson Desert Regional Reserve, Simpson Desert Conservation Park and Innamincka Regional Reserve.

Lake Moolionburrinna

Lake Mckinlay

Lake Amagooranie

Moonlight Flat

Boggy Waterhole

Lake Macnamara

Lake Mundoorounie

Kudriemitchie Outstation (abandoned)

655

Birdsville

105

Woppalancha Waterhole

Boggy Lake

Polywolbolkanie Lake

Woolkawoolkina Lake

Fly Lake

Walkers Crossing

Kanchiemiulanie

Lake Coogiecooginna

Lake Yarowinie

Lake Andree

Lake Marrakoonamooka

'Gidgealpa'

Montepie

650

652

Innamincka

658

Burkes Memorial

56

Salt Lake

Lake Perigundi

Lake Bulpanie

Lake Coonamooranie

Lake Welcome

Gidgealpa Waterhole

Cooper   Creek

Wills Grave

654   653   651   643

Old Strzelecki Tk

Strzelecki   Tk

Bore   Tk

Mungeranie Gap

402   'Mungeranie'

Powichina Waterhole

Blanchewarra Waterhole

Fifteen   Mile   Track

45

47

Dillons

Highway

Sturt Stony Desert

23

26

106

Moomba

44   15

Bore Tk

Restricted

Warburtho

161

Ooroowilanie

Lake Warrakalanna

Strzelecki Regional Reserve

658

Old

Strzelecki

Track

Bore Track
Access along Bore Track from Bollards Lagoon Station is no longer permitted.

To Noccundra

'Mulka'
Old Mulka Ruins

Lake Tepondinna

Lake Walpayapeninna

Lake Hope (Pando)

Strzelecki Regional Reserve

53

Strzelecki Ck

Big Lake Moomba

Strzelecki

367

To Marree

To The Corner Store

© Hema Maps

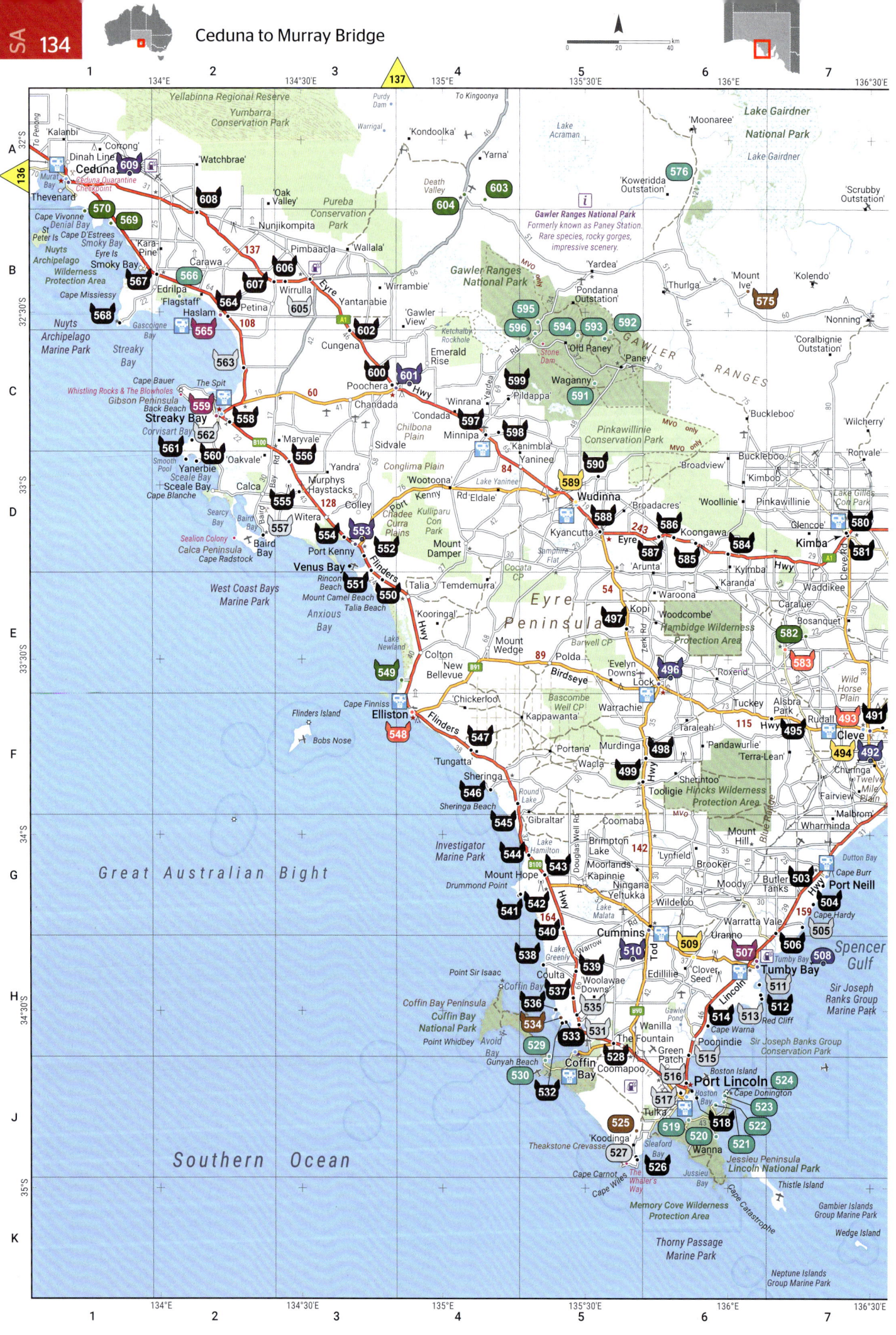

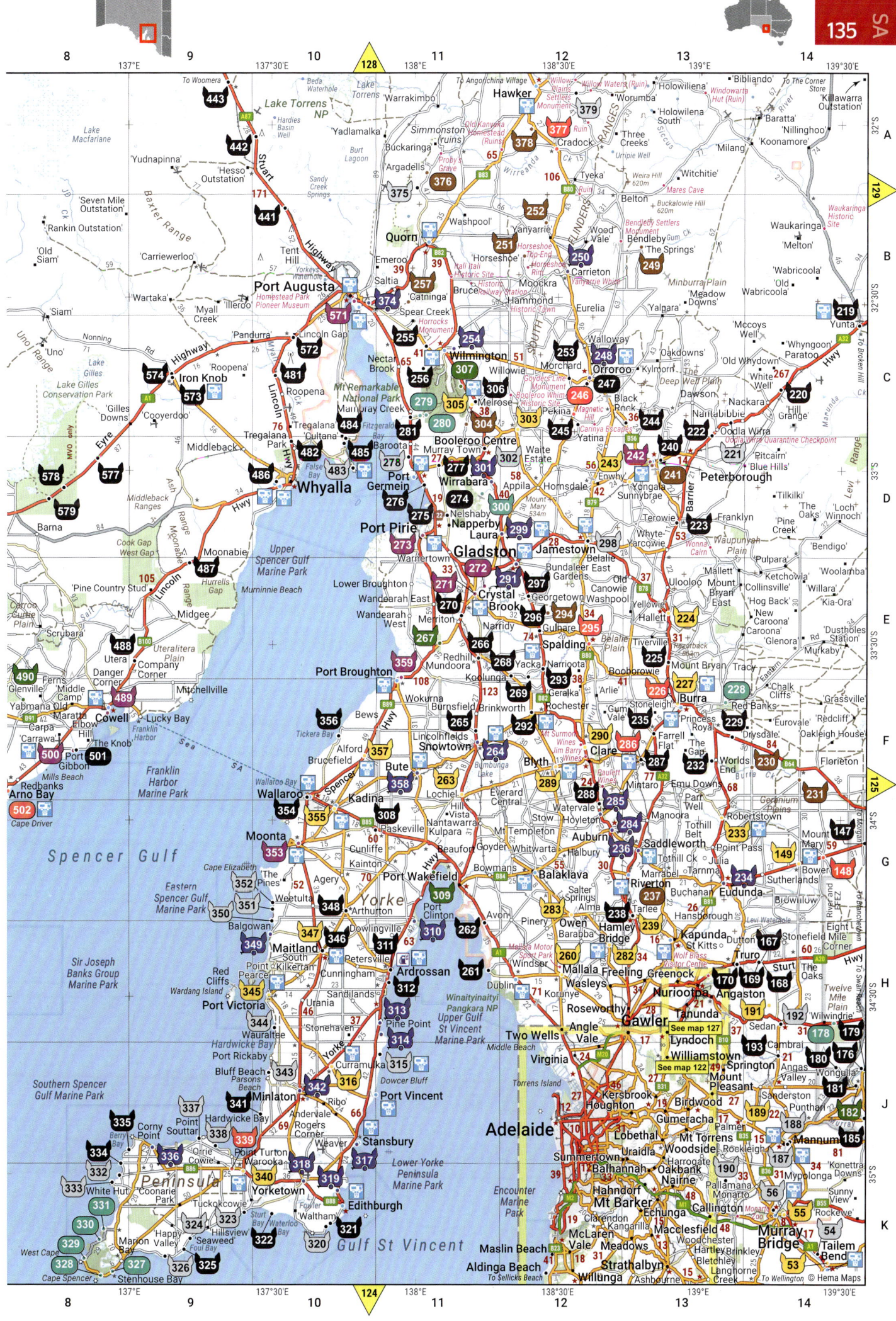

Nundroo to Woomera

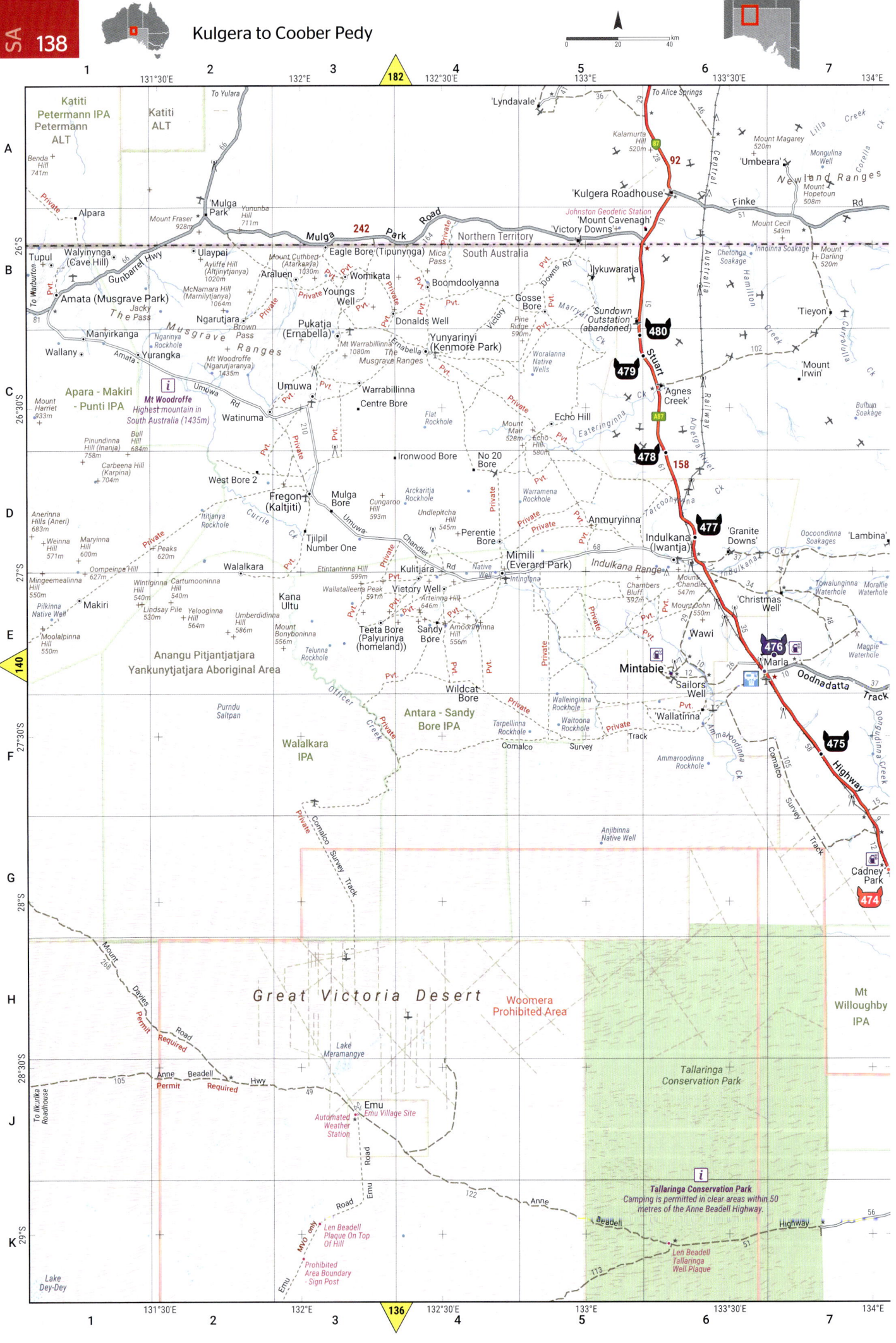

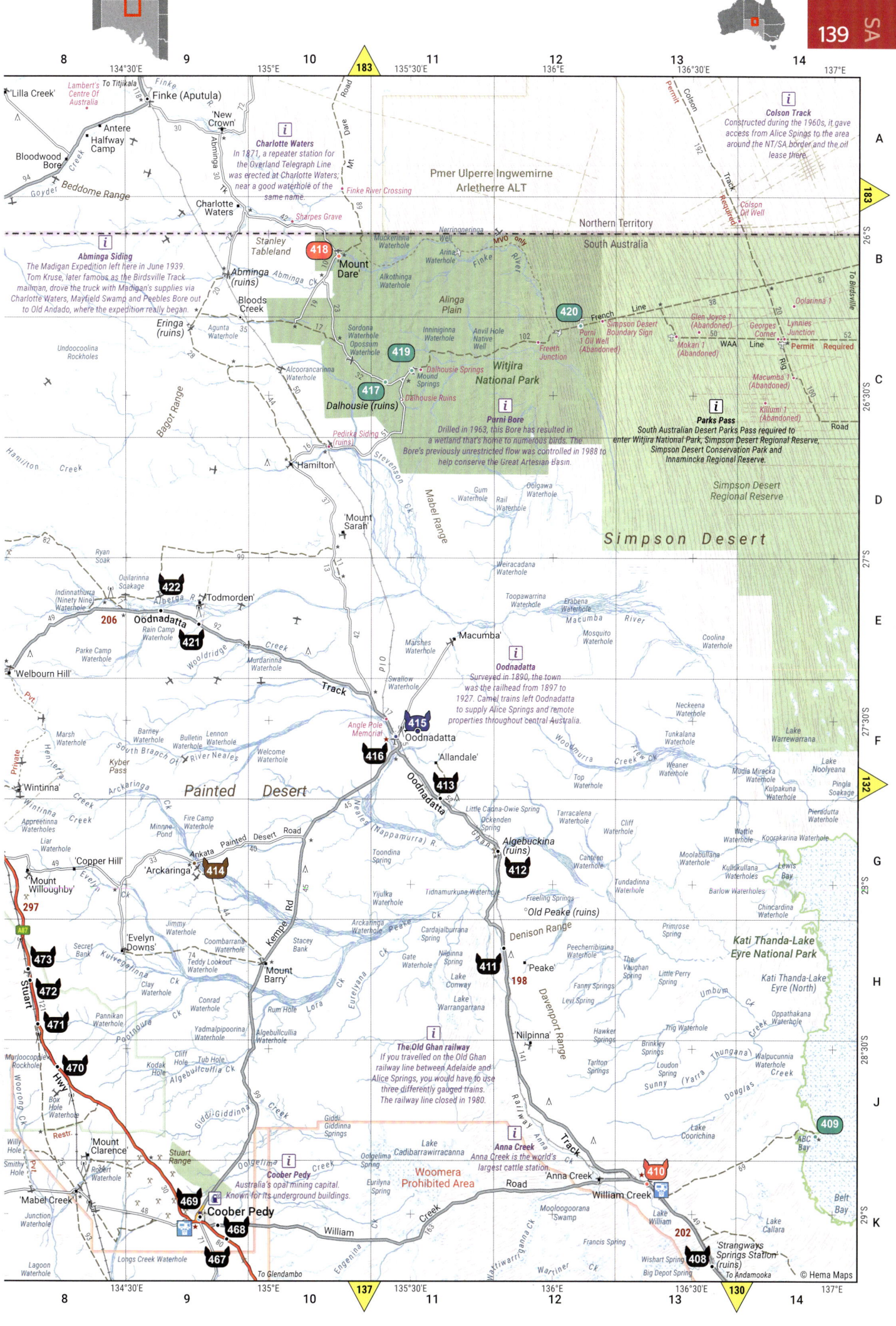

Great Victoria Desert

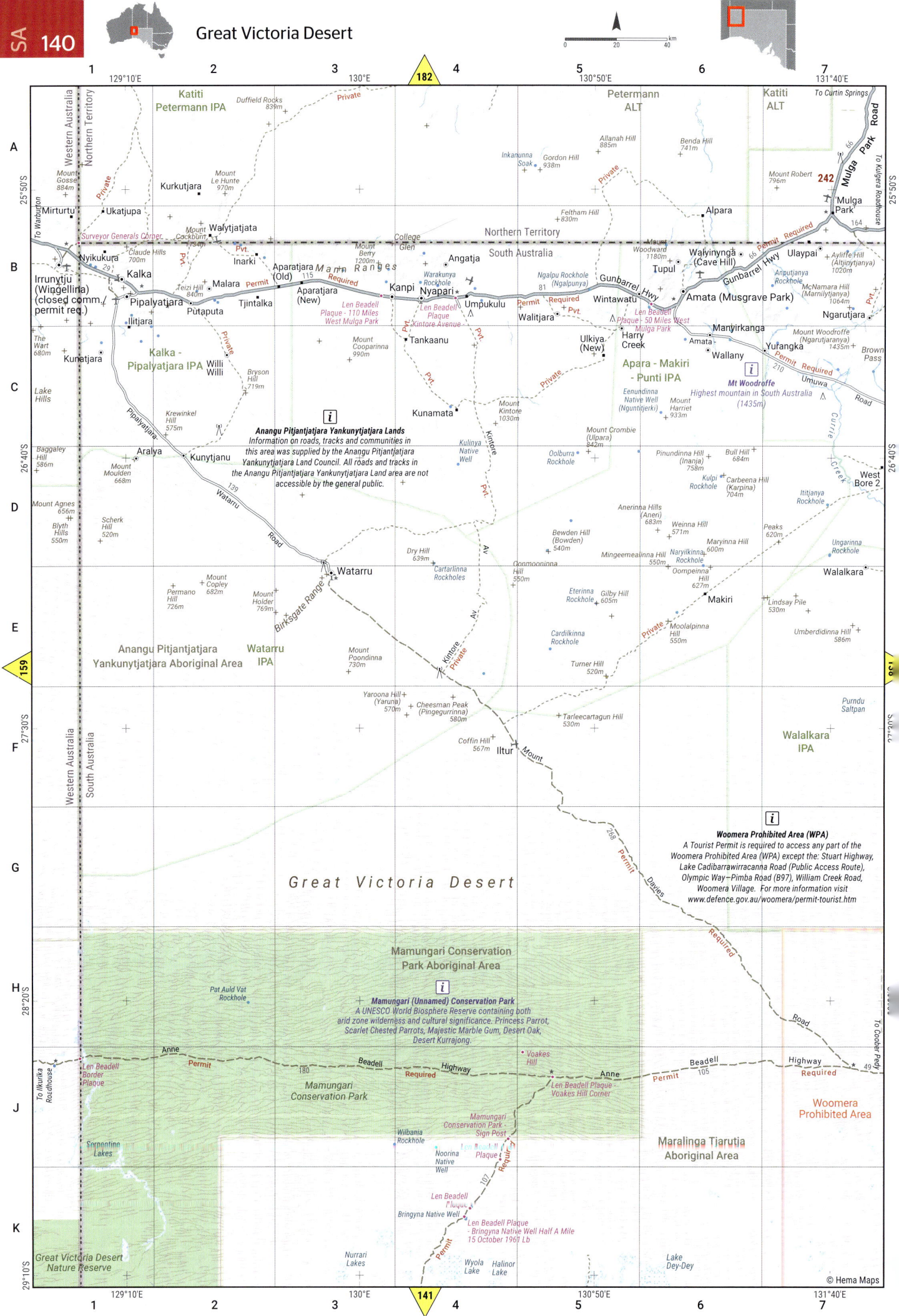

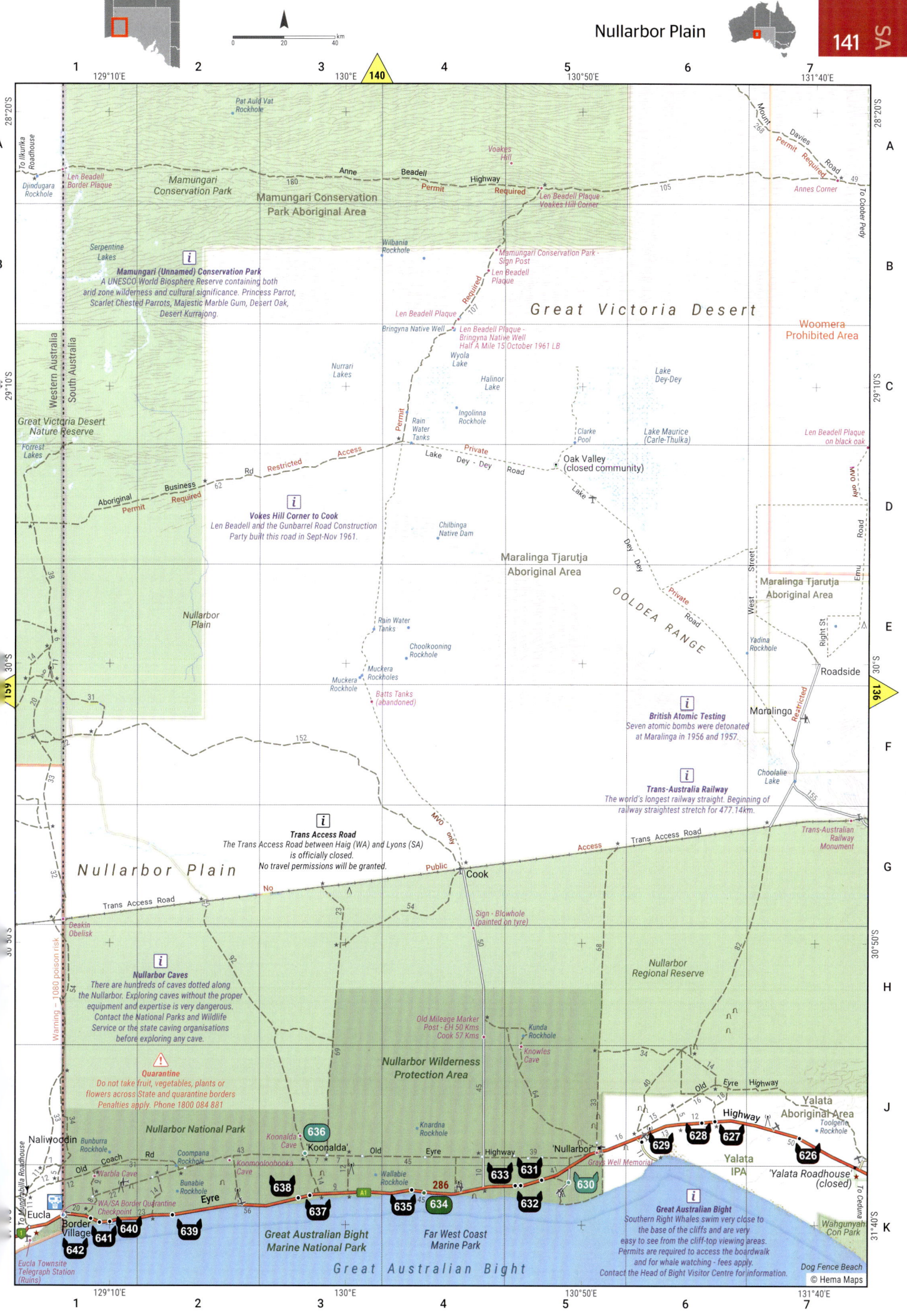

Ikara - Flinders Ranges National Park

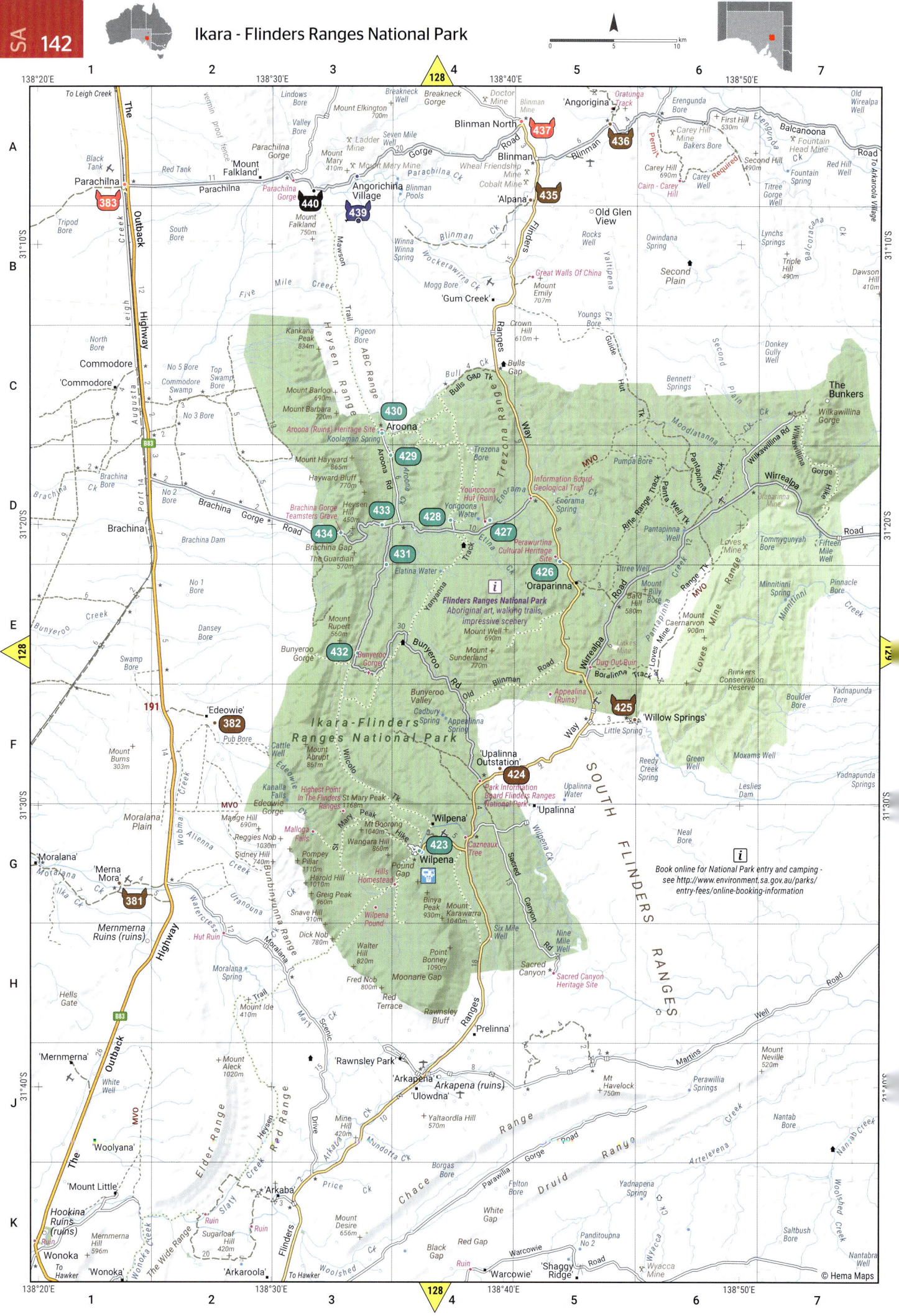

Murray River, South Australia

South Australia

Mt Gambier to Tailem Bend
Princes Highway

1 Kromelite Rd Rest Area
Cnr Princes Hwy & Kromelite Rd, Glenburnie
Rest Area 23 km W of Mumbannar or 16 km E of Mt Gambier. 1 km W of border
HEMA 126 J6   37 50 47 S   140 55 15 E

2 Glenburnie Rest Area
Glenelg Hwy, Glenburnie
Rest Area 11 km E of Glenburnie & 4 km W of border
1300 872 677   HEMA 126 H6   37 46 38 S   140 56 27 E

3 Mount Gambier Showground
34 Pick Ave, Mount Gambier
Camp Area 400 m from PO. Caretaker on site. 28 day limit. Pre-book
0408 492 182   HEMA 126 J5   37 50 16 S   140 47 51 E

4 Brown Bay Car Park
Eight Mile Creek Rd, Port MacDonnell
Parking Area 13 km E of Port MacDonnell. Cold shower
08 8721 0444   HEMA 126 J5   38 02 24 S   140 50 07 E

5 Bellum Hotel
22339 Riddoch Hwy, Mount Schank
Camp Area 13 km S of Mount Gambier or 14 km N of Port Macdonnell. Near Bellum Ln. Free for patrons. Register at bar
08 8738 5269   HEMA 126 J5   37 55 43 S   140 43 10 E

6 Cape Northumberland 1
Cape Northumberland Rd, Port MacDonnell
Parking Area 4 km W of Port MacDonnell
08 8721 0444   HEMA 126 K5   38 03 32 S   140 39 44 E

7 Cape Northumberland 2
54 Finger Pt Rd, Port MacDonnell
Parking Area 4 km W of Port MacDonnell
08 8721 0444   HEMA 126 K5   38 03 20 S   140 39 35 E

8 Cape Banks Lighthouse
Canunda National Park
via Cape Banks Rd, Carpenter Rocks
Camp Area 4 km N of Carpenter Rocks, ebook
08 8735 1177   HEMA 126 J4   37 53 51 S   140 22 37 E

9 Carpenter Rocks Rec Reserve
24 Carpenter Rocks Rd, Carpenter Rocks
Camp Area 35 km SW of Mount Gambier behind hall. No camping in carpark. Donation to store
08 8721 0444   HEMA 126 J4   37 54 49 S   140 23 55 E

10 Blackfellows Caves Camp
Coastal Rd, Blackfellows Caves
Parking Area S off Hwy to Burrungule Rd to Dixon Rd, W to Blackfellows Rd, then E
HEMA 126 J4   37 56 57 S   140 28 07 E

11 Tantanoola East
31921 Princes Hwy, Tantanoola
Rest Area 31 km NW of Mt Gambier or 19 km SE of Millicent. Opposite Tantanoola Roadhouse, do not block trucks
08 8734 4177   HEMA 126 H4   37 42 21 S   140 29 54 E

12 Tantanoola Parklands
22 Railway Tce East, Tantanoola
Parking Area opposite hotel
08 8733 0900   HEMA 126 H4   37 41 46 S   140 27 20 E

13 Millicent South
Princes Hwy, Millicent
Parking Area 45 km NW of Mt Gambier or 5 km S of Millicent
08 8733 0900   HEMA 126 H4   37 38 01 S   140 23 29 E

14 Oil Rig Square Campground
Canunda National Park
Oil Rig Square Rd, Canunda
Camp Area 14 km W of Millicent, via Canunda Causeway Rd. Small caravans only. 5 day limit, ebook
08 8735 1177   HEMA 126 H3   37 39 16 S   40 13 50 E

15 Geltwood Beach
Canunda National Park
Oil Rig Square Rd, Southend
Camp Area 14 km W of Millicent, via Canunda Causeway Rd. Sandy track. Small caravans only. 5 day limit, ebook
08 8735 1177   HEMA 126 H3   37 39 34 S   140 14 11 E

16 Millicent North
Princes Hwy, Millicent
Rest Area 4 km N of Millicent or 103 km S of Kingston SE
08 8733 0900   HEMA 126 G4   37 33 50 S   140 21 16 E

17 Thornlea Rest Area
Princes Hwy, Furner
Parking Area 23 km N of Millicent or 84 km S of Kingston SE
08 8733 0904   HEMA 126 G3   37 23 37 S   140 14 17 E

18 Reedy Creek South
Princes Hwy, Reedy Creek
Parking Area 77 km N of Millicent or 30 km S of Kingston SE
08 8767 2033   HEMA 126 E3   37 00 49 S   140 00 34 E
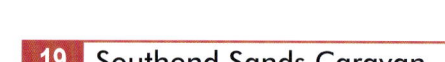

19 Southend Sands Caravan Park
4-8 Leake St, Southend
Caravan Park at Southend
08 8735 6200   HEMA 126 G3   37 34 08 S   140 07 38 E

20 Kotgee Camping Area
Canunda National Park
Bevilaqua Ford Rd, Southend
Camp Area 2 km S of Southend, turn E off Bevilaqua Ford Rd 2 km sandy dirt road. Small caravans only. 5 day limit, ebook
08 8735 1177   HEMA 126 G3   37 34 50 S   140 08 14 E

21 Nalawort Campground
Canunda National Park
Bevilaqua Ford Rd, Canunda
Camp Area 2 km S of Southend, 2 km sandy dirt road, pass Kotgee Camp. Small caravans only. 5 day limit, ebook
08 8735 1177   HEMA 126 G3   37 34 53 S   140 08 20 E

22 Southend Foreshore Camp

Leake St, Southend
Camp Area 26 km NW of Millicent W off
Princes Hwy to Leake St. Bush camping. Cold
showers. Register at Southend-on-Sea Tourist Park
08 8735 6035   HEMA 126 G3   37 34 01 S   140 07 40 E

23 Wakelin Park Rest Area

Southern Ports Hwy, Beachport
Rest Area 25 kms NW of Millicent. W off
Princes Hwy
HEMA 126 G3   37 30 40 S   140 06 55 E

24 Three Mile Bend Camp

Beachport Conservation Park
Lake George Rd, Beachport
Camp Area 3 km NW of Beachport. Small vehicles
only. 2 km dirt road, ebook
08 8735 1177   HEMA 126 G3   37 27 07 S   139 59 40 E

25 Nora Creina Rest Area

Southern Ports Hwy, Nora Creina
Rest Area 54 km NW of Millicent or 106 km
W of Penola
08 8768 2003   HEMA 126 F2   37 19 14 S   139 57 14 E

26 Long Gully Campground

Little Dip Conservation Park
Nora Creina Rd, Robe
Camp Area 12 km N of Nora Creina or 14 km S of
Robe, 6 km dirt road. 5 day limit, ebook. Tent and
camper trailer only campgrounds in the Camps
Australia Wide App
08 8735 1177   HEMA 126 F2   37 15 17 S   139 48 03 E

27 Robe Rest Stop

3819 Southern Ports Hwy, Robe
Parking Area 5.5 km N of Robe
08 8768 2003   HEMA 126 E2   37 09 12 S   139 48 27 E

28 Wrights Bay Caravan Park

Wrights Bay Rd, Mount Benson
Camp Area 19 km N of Robe or 25 km S of
Kingston. See caretaker
0427 007 006   HEMA 126 E2   37 02 31 S   139 44 33 E

29 Kingston South

Southern Ports Hwy, Kingston SE
Parking Area 32 km N of Robe or 12 km S
of Kingston SE
08 8767 2033   HEMA 126 D2   36 55 30 S   139 49 16 E

30 Maria Creek RV Park

Marine Pde, Kingston SE
Parking Area. Cold shower. TPay via ticket
system
08 8767 2033   HEMA 126 D2   36 49 40 S   139 51 01 E

31 Mount Scott Conservation Park

Mount Scott Rd, Blackford
Camp Area 22 km NE of Kingston SE, just N of
Conservation Park. Turn SE off Desert Camp-
Kingston Rd (Rowney Rd) 19 km NE of Kingston
SE. 5 km dirt road
08 8767 2033   HEMA 126 D3   36 46 49 S   140 03 19 E

32 The Granites

Granites Rd, Coorong
Parking Area 21 km N of Kingston SE. Turn
W off Princes Hwy 18 km N of Kingston SE to Old
Coorong Rd for 2.5 km
08 87672036   HEMA 126 C2   36 39 28 S   139 51 17 E

33 Coorong Rest Area

Princes Hwy, Coorong
Rest Area 25 km N of Kingston SE or 59 km
S of Salt Creek
08 8767 2033   HEMA 126 C2   36 37 15 S   139 52 36 E

34 42 Mile Crossing

Coorong National Park
42 Mile Crossing Rd, Salt Creek
Camp Area 69 km N of Kingston SE or 21 km S
of Salt Creek. Turn W 66 km N of Kingston SE
or 18 km S of Salt Creek. 3 km dirt road. 5 day
limit. Book online, more tent & camper trailer only
campground in Camps Australia Wide App
08 8735 1200   HEMA 126 B2   36 17 15 S   139 42 42 E

35 Pelican Campground

Coorong National Park
Parnka Pt, Magrath Flat
Camp Area 42 km N of Salt Creek or 28 km S of
Meningie. Turn W 38 km N of Salt Creek or 24 km S
of Meningie. 3 km dirt road. 5 day limit, ebook
08 8575 1200   HEMA 125 K9   35 53 49 S   139 24 05 E

36 Long Point

Coorong National Park
Long Point Rd, Meningie
Camp Area 23 km W of Meningie. Take Narung Rd
for 19 km then L to Long Point Rd. 5 day limit, ebook
08 8735 1200   HEMA 125 J8   35 41 40 S   139 09 49 E

37 Mark Point

Coorong National Park
Kartoo Rd, Meningie
Camp Area 34 km W of Meningie. 11 km unsealed
road, tracks to camp sites on sandy track. 5 day
limit, ebook
08 8735 1200   HEMA 125 J8   35 37 30 S   139 04 37 E

38 Narrung Jetty Reserve

Alexandrina Dr, Meningie
Rest Area at Narrung, beside ferry terminal.
W side
1300 785 277   HEMA 125 H9   35 30 49 S   139 11 04 E

39 Tailem Bend South Rest Area

Mowantji Willauwar Conservation Park
Princes Hwy, Tailem Bend
Rest Area 45 km N of Meningie or 7 km S of Tailem
Bend
1300 785 277   HEMA 125 G9   35 18 16 S   139 25 51 E

Bordertown to Adelaide

Dukes Highway

40 Poocher Swamp Rest Area

Cannawigara Rd, Bordertown
Rest Area 8 km W of Bordertown
08 8204 1910   HEMA 126 B5   36 17 55 S   140 40 56 E

41 Brimbago Rest Area

Dukes Hwy, Brimbago
Rest Area 29 km NW of Bordertown or
16 km SE of Keith
08 8752 1044   HEMA 126 A4   36 10 19 S   140 28 52 E

42 Keith Showgrounds

Showground Pde, Keith
Camp Area NE side of town
0428 124 093   HEMA 125 K12   36 05 44 S   140 21 30 E

SOUTH AUSTRALIA

43   Tintinara South Rest Area
Dukes Hwy, Tintinara
Rest Area 29 km NW of Keith or 9 km S of Tintinara
1300 785 277   HEMA 125 K11   35 56 17 S   140 07 26 E

44   Lake Indawarra
Kings Rd, Tintinara
Camp Area 34 km NW of Keith. SW off Dukes Hwy at Tintinara to Woods Well Rd then SE to Kings Rd. Honesty box on toilet wall
1300 785 277   HEMA 125 K11   35 53 16 S   140 03 29 E

45   Tolmer Rocks
Tolmer Rocks (Homestead) Rd, Colebatch
Camp Area 22 km SW of Tintinara
1300 785 277   HEMA 125 K11   35 54 36 S   139 51 22 E

46   Boothby Rocks
Boothby Rd, Colebatch
Camp Area 20 km SW of Tintinara on Boothby Rocks Rd. Look for blue sign post at entry on R side. Small vehicles only
1300 785 277   HEMA 125 K10   35 53 31 S   139 45 58 E

47   Culburra Hall RV Park
1396 Prosser Rd, Culburra
Camp Area 41 km NW of Keith on Dukes Hwy then E. Hall near intersection
1300 785 277   HEMA 125 J11   35 48 51 S   139 57 58 E

48   Culburra North Rest Area
Dukes Hwy, Culburra
Rest Area 3 km NW of Culburra, 14 km NW of Tintinara or 13 km SE of Coonalpyn
1300 785 277   HEMA 125 J11   35 47 48 S   139 56 39 E

49   Coonalpyn Soldiers Memorial Caravan Park
Malcolm Tce, Coonalpyn
Caravan Park next to swimming pool. Honesty box by toilets
0427 399 089   HEMA 125 J10   35 41 33 S   139 51 27 E

50   Coonalpyn Hotel
45 Poyntz Tce, Coonalpyn
Parking Area. Register at bar
08 8571 1006   HEMA 125 J10   35 41 47 S   139 51 25 E

51   Ki Ki South Rest Area
Dukes Hwy, Ki Ki
Rest Area 10 km NW of Coonalpyn or 6 km SE of Ki Ki
HEMA 125 H10   35 36 52 S   139 48 43 E

52   Coomandook Rest Area
3189 Dukes Hwy, Coomandook
Rest Area. Toilet across the road
1300 785 277   HEMA 125 H10   35 28 16 S   139 41 49 E

53   Tailem Bend Football Oval
Cnr Granite Rd & Second Ave, Tailem Bend
Parking Area 750 m N of PO. Access to amenities on request
0419 187 446   HEMA 125 G9   35 14 56 S   139 27 20 E

54   Old Tailem Town Village
Princes Hwy, Tailem Bend
Parking Area in front car park. 5 km N of Tailem Bend. Check in by 4pm. Gates locked 4pm - 9am
08 8572 3838   HEMA 125 G9   35 13 26 S   139 25 21 E

55   Murray Bridge Showgrounds
113 Old Princes Hwy, Murray Bridge
Camp Area 3 km from PO. Entry via gate 2. 7 day limit. Fee collected or use silver honesty box at office
0400 880 578   HEMA 125 G9   35 06 49 S   139 18 13 E

56   A La Folly B&B & Camp
41 Doyle Rd, Northern Heights
Camp Area. Turn N off South Eastern Fwy at Murray Bridge to Swanport & Mannum Rds, then E
0414 949 348   HEMA 125 G9   35 06 02 S   139 16 68 E

57   IAKFM Farm
Eclair Mine Rd, St Ives
Camp Area at St. Ives. Pre-book
0409 278 123   HEMA 125 G8   35 06 50 S   138 59 16 E

Mt Gambier to Keith
Riddoch Highway

58   Tarpeena Sports Ground
Edward St, Tarpeena
Parking Area 24 km N of Mount Gambier. 7 day limit
08 8721 0444   HEMA 126 H5   37 37 39 S   140 47 52 E

59   Lake Leake
949 Glencoe West Rd, Koorine
Camp Area 14 km W of Kalangadoo, via Kangaroo Flat Rd & Lake Leake Rd. Outdoor cold shower, honesty box
08 8733 0904   HEMA 126 H5   37 36 42 S   140 35 34 E

60   Kalangadoo Railway Reserve
Railway Tce, Kalangadoo
Parking Area
08 8733 0900   HEMA 126 G5   37 33 44 S   140 41 58 E

61   Forestry Information Bay
Bookers Ln, Nangwarry
Rest Area 4 km N of Nangwarry or 15 km S of Penola. Opposite Yeates Rd on the E side of Hwy
08 8733 0900   HEMA 126 G5   37 30 39 S   140 49 06 E

62   Penola South Rest Area
Riddoch Hwy, Penola
Rest Area 10 km S of Penola or 8 km N of Nangwarry
08 8733 0900   HEMA 126 G5   37 28 25 S   140 49 47 E

63   Greenrise Lake
Riddoch Hwy, Penola
Picnic Area 18 km N of Nangwarry or 3 km S of Penola. 800 m off Hwy. Toilets in adjacent day use area
08 8733 0900   HEMA 126 G5   37 23 48 S   140 50 11 E

64   CMCA Penola RV Park
John St, Penola
Camp Area at MacCorquindale Sports Grounds
02 49788788   HEMA 126 F5   37 22 20 S   140 50 23 E

65 Coonawarra North

Riddoch Hwy, Coonawarra
Rest Area 12 km N of Penola on W side of
Riddoch Hwy
08 8733 0900   **HEMA 126 E5**   37 16 10 S   140 50 15 E

66 Bellwether Wines & Camp

14183 Riddoch Hwy, Coonawarra
Farm Stay 7 km N of Coonawarra. Limited
sites, pre-book
0447 334 545   **HEMA 126 F5**   37 13 52 S   140 51 11 E

67 Bool Lagoon Turnoff

Riddoch Hwy, Naracoorte
Rest Area 33 km N of Penola or 17 km S of
Naracoorte
08 8760 1100   **HEMA 126 E5**   37 06 09 S   140 47 35 E

68 Bool Lagoon Game Reserve

Bool Lagoon & Hacks Lagoon
Conservation Park
Bool Lagoon Access Rd, Naracoorte
Camp Area 43 km N of Penola or 27 km S of
Naracoorte. Turn W 33 km N of Penola or 17 km S
of Naracoorte. 5 day limit. Permit applies
08 8762 3412   **HEMA 126 E5**   37 06 18 S   140 43 11 E

69 Naracoorte Caves Camp

Naracoorte Caves National Park
Caves District Rd, Joanna
Camp Area 45 km N of Penola or 13 km SE of
Naracoorte. Turn E onto Caves Rd 41 km N of
Penola or 9 km S of Naracoorte. Permit applies.
5 day limit
08 8760 1210   **HEMA 126 E5**   37 02 09 S   140 47 49 E

70 Naracoorte Showgrounds

Cnr Smith St & Cadgee Rd, Naracoorte
Camp Area. Enter beside bowls club. 7 day
limit
0414 453 360   **HEMA 126 E5**   36 57 16 S   140 44 48 E

71 Lucindale Caravan Park

Oak Ave, Lucindale
Caravan Park in showgrounds, next to
Yakka Park
08 8766 2038   **HEMA 126 E4**   36 58 08 S   140 21 59 E

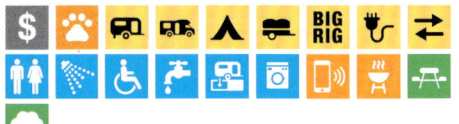

72 Black Cockatoo Bush Camp

596 Chapples Rd, Naracoorte Area
Camp Area 14 km NE of Naracoorte. Via
Cadgee Rd for 11 km, then E for 3 km
0428 621 613   **HEMA 126 D5**   36 52 00 S   140 49 33 E

73 Frances Recreation Ground

Lot 69 East Tce, Frances
Camp Area off Second St
08 8760 1100   **HEMA 126 C6**   36 42 45 S   140 57 30 E

74 Mullinger Swamp

Kybybolite Rec Reserve
Mullinger Rd, Kybybolite
Camp Area N side of park. E off Riddoch Hwy to
Wimmera Hwy, N to Frances Rd, E to Mullinger /
Butterworth Rd. S to camp
08 8762 1399   **HEMA 126 D6**   36 50 57 S   140 58 11 E

75 Cockatoo Lake Rec Reserve

Grubbed Rd, Lochaber
Camp Area 105 km S of Keith or 30 km N of
Naracoorte. Turn W 93 km S of Keith or 18 km N of
Naracoorte. 12 km unsealed road
08 8762 3139   **HEMA 126 D5**   36 44 58 S   140 34 46 E

76 Morambro Creek

Naracoorte Rd Jcn, Cadgee
Rest Area 26 km N of Naracoorte or 21 km
S of Padthaway
HEMA 126 D5   36 44 46 S   140 37 37 E

77 Western Flat Sports Oval

2606 Naracoorte Rd, Western Flat
Camp Area. S off Dukes Hwy or N off
Riddoch Hwy
HEMA 126 C5   36 31 22 S   140 45 03 E

78 Padthaway Caravan Park

75 Beeamma-Parsons Rd, Padthaway
Caravan Park 1 km E of PO at Padthaway.
600 m off Riddoch Hwy
08 8765 5212   **HEMA 126 C4**   36 35 59 S   140 30 14 E

79 Padthaway North Rest Area

Keith-Mt Gambier Road, Marcollat
Rest Area 14 km N of Padthaway or 48 km
S of Keith
HEMA 126 C4   36 30 24 S   140 23 38 E

80 Desert Camp Conservation

Reserve
Rowney Rd, Marcollat
Parking Area 20 km N of Padthaway or 42 km S of
Keith
08 8124 4707   **HEMA 126 B4**   36 28 00 S   140 21 54 E

81 Willalooka Tavern

3449 Riddoch Hwy, Willalooka
Parking Area 34 km S of Keith. Register at
bar. Patrons only
08 8757 8242   **HEMA 126 B4**   36 23 35 S   140 21 01 E

82 Willalooka Rest Area

Petherick Rd & Riddoch Hwy, Willalooka
Parking Area on old tennis courts behind
the oval, amenities at Hwy rest area
HEMA 126 B4   36 23 27 S   140 21 02 E

83 Mount Monster

Conservation Park
Riddoch Hwy, Keith
Camp Area, 14 km S of Keith, W side of Riddoch
Hwy
08 8755 1620   **HEMA 126 A4**   36 11 52 S   140 19 41 E

84 Keith South Rest Area

Riddoch Hwy, Keith
Rest Area 50 km N of Padthaway or 12 km
S of Keith
HEMA 126 A4   36 11 39 S   140 20 29 E

Pinnaroo to Tailem Bend
Mallee Highway

85 Border Rest Area

Mallee Hwy, Pinnaroo
Rest Area 6 km E of Pinnaroo or 21 km W
of Murrayville
HEMA 125 G14   35 14 22 S   140 57 39 E

86 Pinnaroo Caravan Park

Lot 532 Mallee Hwy, Pinnaroo
Caravan Park between Day St & South Tce
0430 465 304   **HEMA 125 G14**   35 15 46 S   140 54 35 E

SOUTH AUSTRALIA

87 Pinnaroo RV Stop
Cnr South Tce & Mann St, Pinnaroo
Parking Area behind old croquet club
HEMA 125 G13   35 15 48 S   140 54 25 E

88 Parilla Rest Area
Mallee Hwy, Pinnaroo
Rest Area 20 km W of Pinnaroo or 6 km E of Parilla. Both sides of road, share with trucks
HEMA 125 G13   35 17 47 S   140 43 54 E

89 Parilla Campsite
Mallee Hwy, Parilla
Rest Area opposite hotel
08 8577 8002   HEMA 125 G13   35 17 47 S   140 40 00 E

90 Karte Campground
Karte Conservation Park
Colwill Rd, Karte
Camp Area 31 km NW of Pinnaroo, via Parilla Well Rd. Pre-book. 5 day limit. Permit applies
08 8580 1800   HEMA 125 G13   35 05 25 S   140 44 12 E

91 Lameroo Lakeside Caravan Park
Cnr Mallee Hwy & Varden Tce, Lameroo
Caravan Park beside Lake Robert. Book, pay & keys at hotel. Free RV Park for SCV at N end
08 8576 3006   HEMA 125 G12   35 19 41 S   140 31 17 E

92 Baan Hill Soak
Bews South Rd, Lameroo Area
Picnic Area 25 km SW of Lameroo. Turn S 8 km W of Lameroo 19 km dirt road
08 8577 8002   HEMA 125 H12   35 30 01 S   140 26 19 E

93 Parrakie East Rest Area
Malley Hwy, Parrakie
Rest Area 20 km W of Lameroo or 6 km E of Parrakie
08 8577 8002   HEMA 125 H12   35 21 42 S   140 18 37 E

94 Geranium Rest Area
Mallee Hwy, Geranium
Rest Area opposite Geranium turnoff
08 8577 8002   HEMA 125 H11   35 22 40 S   140 09 42 E

95 Geranium Oval
Geranium Tce, Geranium
Camp Area S of Hwy, cnr Small Rd
08 8577 8002   HEMA 125 H11   35 23 01 S   140 09 35 E

96 Peake Rest Area
Mallee Hwy, Peake
Rest Area S of Hwy. Toilets opposite at hall
1300 785 277   HEMA 125 H11   35 21 58 S   139 57 05 E

97 Sherlock Rest Area
3 Mallee Hwy, Sherlock
Rest Area opposite hall
1300 785 277   HEMA 125 G10   35 19 07 S   139 48 04 E
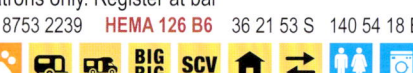

Bordertown to Pinnaroo

98 Wolseley Community Club
Grice St, Wolseley
Camp Area. Access via Railway Tce. N near playground. Limited power. Call prior to arrival
0410 121 796   HEMA 126 B6   36 21 53 S   140 54 34 E

99 Wolseley Hotel
Railway Tce, Wolseley
Camp Area 15 km S of Bordertown off Dukes Hwy into Ridgway Rd, W to Railway Tce. Patrons only. Register at bar
08 8753 2239   HEMA 126 B6   36 21 53 S   140 54 18 E

100 Creecoona Waterhole
Dukes Hwy, Bordertown
Rest Area 5 km E of Bordertown
HEMA 126 B5   36 18 49 S   140 48 02 E

101 Safe Haven Wildlife Sanctuary
104 Western Dr, Bordertown
Camp Area 3 km S of Bordertown. Limited sites. Pre-book. No children under 10
0400 262 713   HEMA 126 B5   36 19 30 S   140 46 43 E

102 Mundulla Showground
North Tce, Mundulla
Camp Area at Mundulla. Cnr North Tce & Mile Ln. Honesty box
0475 920 837   HEMA 126 B5   36 21 30 S   140 41 25 E

103 Bordertown Recreation Lake
Golf Course Rd, Bordertown
Rest Area N of Hwy, turn R to lake
08 8752 1044   HEMA 126 B5   36 18 21 S   140 46 31 E

104 Bordertown Golf Club
624 Golf Course Rd, Bordertown
Camp Area NW off Dukes Hwy. Register at clubhouse
0427 853 720   HEMA 126 B5   36 15 18 S   140 45 49 E

105 Hawick Rest Area
Ngarkat Hwy, Shaugh
Rest Area 20 km S of Ngarkat
HEMA 125 J13   35 49 49 S   140 47 26 E

106 Comet Bore Campground
Ngarkat Conservation Park
Ngarkat Hwy, Pinnaroo Area
Camp Area 61 km S of Pinnaroo or 72 km N of Bordertown. Permit applies. 5 day limit
08 8204 1910   HEMA 125 J13   35 44 37 S   140 48 03 E

107 Pertendi Hut Campground
Ngarkat Conservation Park
Pertendi Tr off Ngarkat Hwy, Pinnaroo Area
Camp Area 48 km S of Pinnaroo or 84 km N of Bordertown. Permit applies. Pre-book. 5 day limit
08 8580 1800   HEMA 125 J13   35 38 24 S   140 46 43 E

108 Pine Soak Hut
Ngarkat Conservation Park
Pine Hut Soak Tr, Pinnaroo Area
Camp Area 24 km S of Pinnaroo via Rosy Pine Rd & Centre Tr. Follow signs, 5 day limit
08 8580 1800   HEMA 125 H13   35 25 26 S   140 52 44 E

Renmark to Adelaide
Sturt Highway

109 Yamba East Rest Area
Sturt Hwy, Yamba
Rest Area 119 km W of Mildura or 23 km E of Renmark. 5 km W of VIC/SA border. S area quieter
08 8580 3000   HEMA 125 D13   34 16 10 S   140 54 22 E

110 Murtho Forest Landing

Heading Rd, Renmark
Camp Area 17 km NE of Paringa, via Paringa - Murtho Rd. 7 day limit. 4 km steep dirt road. Riverside
1300 661 704 HEMA 125 C13 34 03 56 S 140 46 50 E

111 Border Cliffs Campground
Chowilla Game Reserve
Murtho Rd, Renmark Area
Camp Area 30 km NE of Paringa. Take road E of river. 5 day limit. Permit from general store. Pre-book & check for declared duck hunting open season
08 8580 1800 HEMA 125 B14 33 58 20 S 140 57 28 E

112 Little Gums Campground
Chowilla Game Reserve
Old Wentworth Rd, Renmark Area
Camp Area 32 km NE of Renmark. Turn S to signposted road to park entrance (6.5 km). Dirt road. 2WD in dry conditions only. Permit applies
08 8580 1800 HEMA 125 C13 34 00 32 S 140 51 25 E

113 Chowilla Creekside Camps
Chowilla Game Reserve
Via Old Wentworth Rd, Renmark
Dispersed Camping 48 km N of Renmark. 35 sites. Pre-book & check website for declared duck hunting open season. 5 day limit. Loose gravel, potholes, GPS at turnoff
1300 661 704 HEMA 125 C13 33 57 06 S 140 51 00 E

114 Plushs Bend
Plushs Bend Rd, Renmark Area
Camp Area 6 km S of Renmark. Turn S 2 km SW of Renmark for 3 km on Twentythird St, 1 km to river sites. Tents in designated areas only, ebook
1300 661 704 HEMA 125 C13 34 12 56 S 140 45 15 E

115 T M Price Rotary RV Park
Cnr Sturt Hwy & 28th St, Renmark Area
Camp Area 6 km W of Renmark or 12 km E of Berri. Numbered sites in carpark area, ebook
1300 661 704 HEMA 125 C13 34 12 23 S 140 42 10 E

116 Lyrup Flats Colligans
Murray River National Park
Lyrup Rd, Berri Area
Camp Area 17 km W of Renmark. Turn S 12 km W of Renmark (just past country club). Bush camping riverside. 5 km dirt road. Permit applies. 5 day limit
08 8580 1800 HEMA 125 D13 34 15 14 S 140 41 49 E

117 Lyrup Flats Black Box Camp
Murray River National Park
Old Calperum
Camp Area 2.5 km NE of Lyrup. Turn S 8 km SW of Renmark or 8 km E of Berri. 3 km dirt road. Bush camping, riverside. Low trees. Permit applies. 5 day limit
08 8580 1800 HEMA 125 C13 34 14 39 S 140 39 44 E

118 Lyrup Flats Tea Tree Camp
Murray River National Park
Berri Area
Camp Area 1.5 km N of Lyrup. Turn S 9 km SW of Renmark or 6 km E of Berri. Enter next to ferry crossing. 500 m dirt road. Bush camping riverside. Permit applies. 5 day limit
08 8580 1800 HEMA 125 C13 34 14 57 S 140 39 07 E

119 SS Ellen RV Park

Thayne Tce, Lyrup
Rest Area at Lyrup S side of river. W of ferry crossing. Numbered sites in carpark area, ebook
1300 661 704   HEMA 125 D13   34 15 14 S   140 38 52 E

120 Martins Bend Reserve

Martins Bend Dr, Berri
Camp Area 3 km E of Berri, via Riverview Rd. Riverside. 21 night limit. See caretaker on arrival
08 8582 5511   HEMA 125 D13   34 17 21 S   140 37 52 E

121 Rilli Reserve

189 Briers Rd, Loxton
Camp Area 7km N of Loxton. Turn W 6.5 km N of Loxton, 2 km to riverside bush camping
08 8584 8071   HEMA 125 D13   34 23 36 S   140 34 59 E

122 Loxton Golf Club

196 Edwards Rd, Loxton North
Camp Area at Loxton North. Honesty box
08 8584 1490   HEMA 125 D13   34 25 26 S   140 38 45 E

123 Thieles Sandbar

Tower Dr, Loxton
Camp Area 3.5 km NE of Loxton via Bookpurnong Rd. Turn W at water tower, turn R at crossroads, 1.5 km dirt track to river. GPS at entry. 21 day limit
08 8584 8071   HEMA 125 D13   34 26 29 S   140 35 02 E

124 Paruna Camping Park

Cnr Railway Tce & First St, Paruna
Camp Area 34 km S of Loxton or 70 km N of Pinaroo on Browns Well Hwy. Honesty box & sign for key
08 8587 3003   HEMA 125 E13   34 43 11 S   140 43 44 E

125 Pata Rest Area

Karoonda Hwy, Pata
Camp Area 21 km S of Pata, E of Hwy
HEMA 125 E12   34 37 05 S   140 30 49 E

126 Mindarie

Karoonda Hwy, Mindarie
Parking Area 500 m SW of town
08 8578 1004   HEMA 125 F11   34 48 59 S   140 12 50 E

127 Halidon Parking Area

Harris Tce, Halidon
Parking Area 1 km W of Halidon on Karoonda Hwy
08 8578 1004   HEMA 125 F11   34 53 02 S   140 09 50 E

128 Karoonda East

Karoonda Hwy, Karoonda
Parking Area 1 km E of Karoonda
08 8578 1004   HEMA 125 G11   35 05 14 S   139 54 34 E

129 Perponda Oval

Cnr. Schiller Rd, Perponda
Parking Area 16 km N of Karoonda
0429 411 658   HEMA 125 F10   34 59 06 S   139 48 55 E

130 Karoonda Cabin & Caravan Park

11 Railway Tce, Karoonda
Caravan Park next to oval. Free RV Park for SCV next to oval toilet block, via Caravan Park
08 8578 1004   HEMA 125 G11   35 05 47 S   139 53 23 E

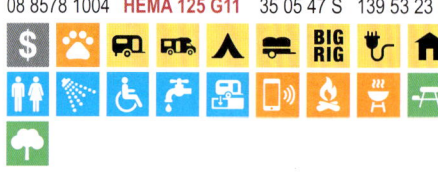

131 Wynarka Rec Grounds

Karoonda Hwy, Karoonda
Parking Area at Wynarka. 16 km W of Karoonda or 32 km E of Tailem Bend
0417 348 106   HEMA 125 G10   35 07 49 S   139 43 49 E

132 Lock 4 Section Katarapko

Murray River National Park
Draper Rd, Berri Area
Camp Area 5 km SW Berri. Via Draper Rd, under Murray River Bridge, 4.5 km dirt road to park entrance. Designated sites. Small vehicles only. Pre-book. Permit applies. 5 day limit
08 8580 1800   HEMA 125 D13   34 19 06 S   140 34 16 E

133 Eckerts Creek Katarapko

Murray River National Park
Migga Rd, Berri Area
Camp Area 13 km SW of Berri. From Old Sturt Hwy turn S to Lower Winkie Rd (3.5 km) & E to Migga Rd, R fork to park entry (1 km). Bush camping riverside. Permit applies. 5 day limit. Pre-book
08 8580 1800   HEMA 125 D12   34 20 09 S   140 32 47 E

134 Katarapko Creek Section

Murray River National Park
Katarapko Cres, Berri Area
Camp Area 18 km SW of Berri, via Winkie, Bulpitt & Plush Rds. Turn S 5 km W of Berri or 2 km E of Glossop for 3 km dirt road. Bush camping beside river. 5 day limit, small vehicles
08 8580 1800   HEMA 125 D12   34 21 37 S   140 32 28 E

135 Lake Bonney Reserve

Queen Elizabeth Dr, Barmera
Camp Area 11 km NW of Barmera, via Morgan Rd & Nappers Bridge. 200 m E of Nappers Bridge, lakeside. Sandy area, walk in first to check
08 8588 2289   HEMA 125 C12   34 11 43 S   140 25 37 E

136 Loch Luna Farm Stay

Morgan Rd, Barmera
Camp Area 20 km NW of Barmera. Pre-book
0418 894 289   HEMA 125 C12   34 11 23 S   140 22 34 E

137 Overland Corner Hotel

Old Coach Rd, Overland Corner
Camp Area S of Hwy, via Morgan Rd. Patrons only. Register at bar. Fee for showers
08 8588 7021   HEMA 125 C12   34 09 07 S   140 20 26 E

138 Herons Bend Reserve

Overland Corner Conservation Reserve
34 Herons Bend Rd, Overland Corner
Camp Area 1.2 km W of hotel. GPS at entry from road, follow track to the river
08 8588 2289   HEMA 125 C12   34 08 59 S   140 19 50 E

139 Devlins Pound Rest Area

Goyder Hwy, Markaranka
Rest Area 12 km W of Overland Corner or 57 km E of Morgan
08 8584 8000   HEMA 125 C11   34 09 01 S   140 13 00 E

140 Pooginook Conservation Park

Goyder Hwy, Waikerie Area
Camp Area 45 km E of Morgan or 43 km W of B64/Sturt Hwy Jcn. Signposted, 1.9 km N to site. GPS at entrance
08 8580 1800   HEMA 125 C11   34 08 21 S   140 07 17 E

141 Morgan East Rest Area
Goyder Hwy, Markaranka
Rest Area 44 km W of Overland Corner or 25 km E of Morgan. Both sides of Hwy
08 8584 8000 **HEMA 125 C11** 34 03 29 S 139 53 52 E

142 Graeme Claxton Reserve
Kings Riverside Drive, Cadell
Camp Area R side of boat ramp. Via Cadell Valley Rd. Ticket machine near toilet
08 8569 0100 **HEMA 125 C10** 34 01 36 S 139 45 35 E

143 Cadell Recreation Ground
81 Dalzell Rd, Cadell
Camp Area. Via Heinrich Rd. 14 day limit. Caretaker on site
0497 799 284 **HEMA 125 C10** 34 02 12 S 139 45 27 E

144 Morgan Camp North
Morgan Conservation Park
Morgan-Cadell Rd, Morgan
Camp Area 1 km E of Morgan, signposted 750 m E of ferry crossing. Various tracks. Permit applies. 5 day limit. Pre-book. GPS at entrance
08 8580 1800 **HEMA 125 C10** 34 02 19 S 139 40 57 E

145 Morgan Camp South
Morgan Conservation Park
via Tennanabie St, Morgan
Camp Area 1.6 km E of Morgan. 1.2 km S of ferry crossing E side of river. Dirt road. Small area only. Permit applies. 5 day limit. Pre-book
08 8580 1800 **HEMA 125 C10** 34 02 43 S 139 41 04 E

146 Cordola Camping & Rec
42 Hausler Road, Morgan
Camp Area 11 km SW of Morgan. Turn S off B81 to Murraylands Rd for 8.5 km, E to Pelican Point Rd for 2 km. S into property gate (500 m). Follow River Rd to riverside sites. Honesty box
0427 716 560 **HEMA 125 C10** 34 07 47 S 139 39 54 E

147 Morgan West
Theile Hwy, Morgan
Parking Area 7 km W of Morgan or 26 km E of Bower
HEMA 125 C10 34 03 52 S 139 35 09 E

148 Mount Mary Hotel
4 North Tce, Mount Mary
Camp Area 22 km W of Morgan or 11 km E of Bower via Mount Mary Rd. Limited powered sites. Register at bar
08 8581 0581 **HEMA 125 C9** 34 06 17 S 139 26 22 E

149 Bower Reserve
Thiele Hwy, Bower
Camp Area next to tennis court. Fee for power & use of dump point. Fee box near BBQ
08 8892 0100 **HEMA 125 C9** 34 07 23 S 139 21 11 E

150 Barmera RV Park
Sims St, Barmera
Camp Area at Bruce Oval. 4 night limit. Pay at Visitor Centre
08 8588 2289 **HEMA 125 D12** 34 15 13 S 140 28 03 E

151 Cobdogla Pump Station
Schell Rd, Loveday
Camp Area 2 km S of Cobdogla. From Shueard Rd turn S to Park Tce, Schell Rd for 2 km. Turn W across causeway. Camping N & S of pump station
08 8588 2289 **HEMA 125 D12** 34 15 45 S 140 24 02 E

152 Kaiser Strip Campground
Loch Luna & Moorook Game Reserve
Via Shueard Dr, Overland Corner
Camp Area 2 km W of Cobdogla, 14 riverside sites either side of Hwy. Pre-book. Permit applies. 5 day limit. Check hunting season
08 8580 1800 **HEMA 125 C12** 34 14 00 S 140 23 16 E

153 Loch Luna Campground
Loch Luna & Moorook Game Reserve
Via Morgan Rd, Barmera
Camp Area 18 km NW of Barmera. 7 km W of Nappers Bridge. Dirt road. 11 sites along Chambers Ck. Pre-book. Permit applies. Check for hunting season
08 8580 1800 **HEMA 125 C12** 34 13 20 S 140 23 39 E

154 Moorook Campground
Loch Luna & Moorook Game Reserve
Via Kingston Rd, Moorook
Camp Area 4 km N of Moorook. 1 km dirt road. 23 bush riverside sites. Pre-book, permit applies. 5 day limit
08 8580 1800 **HEMA 125 D12** 34 15 59 S 140 22 10 E

155 Moorook Riverfront Camp

Kingston-Loxton Rd, Moorook
Picnic Area beside Murray River. Honesty box. 7 night limit
08 8584 8000   HEMA 125 D12   34 17 17 S   140 22 06 E

156 Wunkar Rest Area

Main St, Wunkar
Rest Area opposite Golden Grain Tavern
08 8587 6233   HEMA 125 D12   34 29 23 S   140 18 00 E

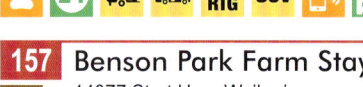

157 Benson Park Farm Stay

14077 Sturt Hwy, Waikerie
Camp Area 14 km E of Waikerie
0431 207 828   HEMA 125 C11   34 11 17 S   140 07 47 E

158 Lowbank Landing

Lowbank Rd, Waikerie
 Camp Area 10 km E of Waikerie. Turn N off Sturt Hwy 1 km dirt road. 21 day limit. Riverside
08 8541 0720   HEMA 125 C11   34 11 01 S   140 04 08 E

159 Holder Bend Reserve & Boat Ramp

Holder Bottom Rd, Waikerie
Camp Area 5 km E of Waikerie. Turn N 3 km E of Waikerie to Holder Top Rd 300 m, NW 1 km, W to reserve via dirt road. Riverside. 7 day limit
08 8541 0720   HEMA 125 C11   34 11 04 S   140 00 48 E

160 Maize Island Lagoon

Maize Island Lagoon Conservation Park

Hawkes Hill Rd, Waikerie
Camp Area 7 km E of Waikerie. Turn N 3 km E of Waikerie to Holder Top Rd for 4 km. R at intersection, take R fork dirt road. Bush camping riverside
08 8541 0720   HEMA 125 C11   34 09 47 S   140 01 22 E

161 Hart Lagoon

via Edgar Bartlett Dr, Waikerie
Camp Area N of town, W bank of river. Tracks to bush camping. Limited space for caravans & RVs, more suitable for tents. 7 day limit
08 8541 0708   HEMA 125 C11   34 09 47 S   139 58 11 E

162 Ramco Point

Ramco Point Rd, Ramco
Camp Area 7.5 km W of Waikerie via Peake Tce & Ramco Rd. Turn R past primary school, signposted, follow 3 km. No camping on grassed area. 7 day limit
08 8541 0720   HEMA 125 C11   34 09 53 S   139 55 50 E

163 Hogwash Bend
Conservation Park

Hogwash Rd, Cadell
Camp Area 25 km NW of Waikerie or 22 km E of Morgan, via Morgan-Waikerie Rd. Turn N 23 km NW of Waikerie or 20 km E of Morgan to Hogwash Rd (signposted Caudo Vineyard) continue 2.5 km. Bush camping by river
08 8541 0720   HEMA 125 C10   34 03 57 S   139 51 12 E

164 Caudo Vineyard

92 Riverboat Rd, Cadell
Camp Area 23 km W of Waikerie via Cadell Valley & Hogwash Rd. Pre-book & check in at cellar door for directions. Open Tue - Sun
0418 715 661   HEMA 125 C10   34 03 57 S   139 50 15 E

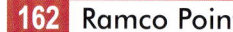

WAIKERIE HOLIDAY PARK

Fun, family and pet friendly Holiday Park!

08 8541 2651 | waikerieholidaypark.com.au

165 Stockyard Plain Rest Area
Stuart Hwy, Stockyard Plain
Rest Area 20 km SW of Waikerie or 22 km
NE of Blanchetown
08 8584 8000   HEMA 125 D10   34 15 53 S   139 48 28 E

166 Roonka Water Activities Centre
309B Boy Scout Rd, McBean Pound
Camp Area 11 km N of Blanchetown. 2 night
minimum on weekends. Pre-book, fee for power
08 8339 3333   HEMA 125 D10   34 17 42 S   139 37 55 E

167 Bear Fence Lookout
Sturt Hwy, Truro
Rest Area 8 km E of Truro or 38 km W of
Blanchetown
08 8569 0100   HEMA 125 D9   34 24 07 S   139 13 03 E

168 Accommodation Hill
Sturt Hwy, Truro
Rest Area 8 km E of Truro or 38 km W of
Blanchetown
08 8569 0100   HEMA 125 D9   34 24 09 S   139 12 47 E

169 Truro Centenary
Sturt Hwy, Truro
Rest Area 1 km E of Truro
08 8569 0100   HEMA 125 D8   34 24 30 S   139 08 09 E

170 Stockwell Rest Area
Sturt Hwy, Stockwell
Rest Area 6 km E of Nuriootpa or 9 km W
of Truro
HEMA 122 A6   34 25 31 S   139 03 27 E

171 Greenock Centenary Park
Martin Street, Greenock
Camp Area at oval, via Murray St. 7 day
limit. Register & pay at entrance
0409 177 657   HEMA 122 B2   34 27 32 S   138 55 43 E

172 Sandy Creek Hotel
Barossa Valley Hwy, Sandy Creek
Parking Area. Register at bar. Patrons only
08 8524 5162   HEMA 127 A5   34 36 10 S   138 49 32 E

Blanchetown to Murray Bridge

173 Tenbury Hunter Reserve
Sedan Swan Reach Rd, Swan Reach
Camp Area at Swan Reach, take ferry N
across to W side of river. Bush camping on river
bank. 500 m E of ferry crossing. 5 night limit
08 8569 0100   HEMA 125 E10   34 33 43 S   139 36 01 E

174 Big Bend River Camp
Riverside Drive, Swan Reach
Camp Area 6 km S of Swan Reach or
17 km N of Nildottie, turn W to Old Loxton Rd, 4 km
dirt road, bush camping riverside
08 8569 0100   HEMA 125 E10   34 38 12 S   139 36 50 E

175 Big Bend Lookout
Hunter Rd, Swan Reach
Rest Area 10 km S of Swan Reach or 5 km
N of Nildottie via Walker Flat Rd. E side of river
08 8569 0100   HEMA 125 E10   34 37 56 S   139 39 56 E

176 Kroehns Landing Lookout
Hunter Rd, Nildottie
Parking Area 8 km S of Nildottie or 6 km
N of Walker Flat turnoff. E side of river
08 8569 0100   HEMA 125 E10   34 42 13 S   139 35 16 E

177 Sunnydale Boat Ramp
Christians Rd, Sunnydale
Camp Area 44 km S of Blanchetown at end
of road. 5 day limit
08 8569 0100   HEMA 125 E10   34 41 08 S   139 36 50 E

178 Swan Reach Conservation Park
Old Punyelroo Rd, Swan Reach
Camp Area 14 km W of Swan Reach or 16 km E of
Sedan via Angaston-Swan Reach Rd. 2 km of dirt
road S of Hwy, self-sufficient bush camping
08 8532 9100   HEMA 125 E9   34 34 29 S   139 28 44 E

179 Wongulla Campground
Cliff View Dr, Wongulla
Camp Area 53 km S of Blanchetown
08 8569 0100   HEMA 125 E10   34 42 05 S   139 34 32 E

180 John Christian Reserve
Black Hill Rd, Black Hill
Camp Area 19 km NW of Walker Flat, via
Walker Flat-Mt Pleasant Rd (10 km), Mannum-Swan
Reach Rd (5 km N) & Black Hill Rd (4 km W). 9 km
dirt road
08 8569 0100   HEMA 125 E9   34 41 56 S   139 29 11 E

181 Hettner Landing
Via Cliff View Dr, Walker Flat
Camp Area 50 m N of general store. Access
track opposite Walker Flat Rd. Bush camping
08 8569 0100   HEMA 125 E10   34 45 03 S   139 33 23 E

182 Walker Flat Boat Ramp
Lakeside Dr, Walker Flat
Camp Area at Walker Flat (Swamp Hen
Reserve) 1 km NW of ferry landing on W side of river
08 8569 0100   HEMA 125 E10   34 45 08 S   139 33 43 E

183 Purnong Reserve
Evans Tce, Caurnamont
Parking Area E side of river, downstream
side of ferry crossing
08 8569 0100   HEMA 125 F10   34 51 15 S   139 37 02 E

184 Caurnamont Reserve
Purnong Rd, Caurnamont
Camp Area 100 m N of Purnong ferry
crossing on W side of river
08 8564 6020   HEMA 125 F10   34 51 17 S   139 36 55 E

185 Caurnamont North
Thompsons Rd, Caurnamont
Parking Area 3.5 km N of Purnong Ferry on
W side of river
08 8569 0100   HEMA 125 F10   34 50 32 S   139 35 11 E

186 Lakeside Camping Ground
248 Craignook Rd, Caurnamont
Camp Area 5.5 km SE of Caurnamont
Ferry. From ferry follow road through Caurnamont
for 3.5 km. Turn SE. 2 km dirt road
08 8570 4309   HEMA 125 F10   34 51 25 S   139 36 28 E

SOUTH AUSTRALIA

187 Haythorpe Reserve

Hunter Rd, Mannum
Camp Area 1 km NE of Mannum, on Bowhill
Rd. E side of river. N of ferry crossing. 5 night limit.
Permit applies, pay machine at amenities
08 8569 0100   HEMA 125 F9   34 54 33 S   139 19 24 E

188 Bolto Reserve

Via Khartoum-Centre Rd, Mannum
Camp Area 1 km SE of Mannum. E side of
river. S of ferry crossing. 5 night limit. Permit applies,
pay machine
08 8564 6020   HEMA 125 F9   34 54 56 S   139 18 58 E

189 Palmer Oval

Cnr Olive Grove & Randell Rd, Palmer River
Parking Area on gravel ring road. 7 day limit
08 8569 0100   HEMA 125 F8   34 51 11 S   139 09 44 E

190 Rockleigh Bush Camp

380 Critchley Rd, Rockleigh
Camp Area 25 km NE of Murray Bridge
on South Eastern Fwy, N to Ferries McDonald &
Schenscher Rds, W to Thile Rd, N to Peach Rd,
then N. Call ahead, gates locked
0417 833 640   HEMA 125 F8   35 01 06 S   139 05 48 E

191 Towitta Hall

Towitta Rd, Towitta
Camp Area 10 km NW of Sedan via
Angaston-Swan Reach Rd. Turn R into Towitta Rd
for 3 km, on L
08 8569 0100   HEMA 125 D9   34 31 28 S   139 14 56 E

192 Sedan Recreation Park

Ridley Rd, Sedan
Camping Area. Volunteer caretaker onsite
HEMA 125 E9   34 34 38 S   139 17 28 E

193 Rhine Villa Reserve

Ridley Road, Cambrai
Picnic Area 1.7 km S of Cambrai or 34 km
N of Mannum. 5 day limit
08 8569 0810   HEMA 125 E9   34 39 59 S   139 16 56 E

Adelaide Greater Area

194 Rocky Paddock Campground

Mount Crawford Forest
Warren Rd, Williamstown
Camp Area 8 km SE of Williamstown. 1 km S of
Forest Info Centre, via Tower Rd. Permit applies.
Apr – Nov, pre-book
08 8391 8800   HEMA 121 B14   34 43 09 S   138 56 22 E

195 Chalks Campground

Mount Crawford Forest
Chalks Rd, Williamstown
Camp Area 3.5 km from Forest Info Centre. Dirt
road. Permit applies. Apr – Nov
08 8391 8800   HEMA 127 B6   34 44 26 S   138 57 33 E

196 Eden Valley Caravan Park

1845 Eden Valley Road, Eden Valley
Caravan Park 1 km S of PO at Murray Rec
Park. Pre-book
08 8568 1934   HEMA 122 J7   34 39 15 S   139 06 07 E

197 Totness Inn Hotel

148 Melrose St, Mount Pleasant
Parking Area in town. Register at bar,
patrons only
08 8568 2637   HEMA 127 C7   34 46 18 S   139 03 07 E

198 Talunga Park Caravan Park

Melrose St, Mount Pleasant
Caravan Park at showgrounds
08 8568 1934   HEMA 127 C7   34 46 34 S   139 02 34 E

199 Mount Torrens Hotel

1 Townsend St, Mount Torrens
Parking Area. Register at bar, patrons only.
Toilet access during pub hours
08 8389 4252   HEMA 127 D6   34 52 32 S   138 57 31 E

200 Cudlee Creek Tavern

2121 Gorge Rd, Cudlee Creek
Caravan Park 30 km E of Adelaide, riverside
08 8389 2319   HEMA 121 G11   34 50 23 S   138 49 00 E

201 Frank Potts Reserve

Wellington Rd, Langhorne Creek
Camp Area 1 km E of Langhorne Creek,
riverside
08 8555 7000   HEMA 125 G8   35 17 56 S   139 02 33 E

202 Tolderol Game Reserve

via Dog Lake Rd, Langhorne Creek
Camp Area 14 km SE of Langhorne Creek.
Turn S 5 km E of Langhorne Creek. Dirt road. 5 day
limit. Permit applies, ebook
08 8580 1800   HEMA 125 H8   35 22 12 S   139 08 59 E

203 Mundoo Island Station Stay

Denver Rd, Goolwa
Camp Area via Hindmarsh Is. Pre-book. No
public access - meet at the barrages for guidance to
site. Minimum camping fee applies. BYO toilet
08 8555 2242   HEMA 125 H8   35 31 55 S   138 54 05 E

204 Pink Gum Campground

Onkaparinga River NP
360 Chapel Hill Rd, Blewitt Springs
Camp Area 12 km N of McLaren Vale. W off
McLaren Flat Rd. into Bakers Gully Rd then W.
5 day limit
08 8550 3400   HEMA 118 J4   35 08 58 S   138 35 50 E

205 Chookarloo Campground

Kuitpo Forest Reserve
Brookman Rd, Kuitpo
Camp Area 5 km SW of Meadows. Permit from
Kuitpo Forest Info Centre. 1 April – 30 November
08 8391 8800   HEMA 127 H4   35 12 10 S   138 42 51 E

206 Eagle Dell

453 Frome Rd, Currency Creek
Camp Area 13 km N of Goolwa. Pre-book.
Gates locked. GPS at turnoff
0439 832 804   HEMA 124 H7   35 25 24 S   138 43 58 E

207 Port Elliot Showground

Cameron St, Port Elliot
Camp Area. Enter via Kurramin Ct. Call
ahead, locked gates
0417 218 029   HEMA 124 H7   35 31 31 S   138 40 40 E

208 Breakaway Farmstay

790 Waitpinga Road, Waitpinga
Farm Stay 2.4 km E of Waitpinga. SW from
Victor Harbour on Bay Rd, then S. Pre-book
08 8552 9317   HEMA 124 H7   35 35 53 S   138 31 12 E

209 Stringybark Campground

Deep Creek Conservation Park
Via Tapanappa Rd, Delamere Area
Camp Area 9 km SE of Delamere. Dirt road.
5 day limit, ebook. Tapanappa, Trig & Cobbler Hill
Campgrounds (no showers) also in park, listed in
Camps Australia Wide App
08 8598 0263   HEMA 124 H6   35 36 24 S   138 14 20 E

210 Rapid Bay Camping Area

Essington Lewis Dr, Rapid Bay
Camp Area. Outside cold shower
0418 833 653   HEMA 124 H6   35 31 29 S   138 11 30 E

211 Cape Jervis Station

9351 Main South Rd, Cape Jervis
Caravan Park 105 km S of Adelaide
08 8598 0288   HEMA 124 H5   35 36 19 S   138 07 41 E

Broken Hill to Adelaide
Barrier Highway

212 Cockburn Village

14 Elder Tce, Cockburn
Camp Area 50 km W of Broken Hill.
Register at hotel opposite water tower
08 8091 1634   HEMA 129 E14   32 04 37 S   140 59 46 E

213 Mingary Siding

Barrier Hwy, Mingary
Parking Area 25 km SW of Cockburn or
42 km NE of Olary
08 8648 5970   HEMA 129 E14   32 07 43 S   140 44 27 E

214 Cutana Rest Area

Barrier Hwy, Cutana
Rest Area 32 km SW of Cockburn or 35 km
NE of Olary. Both sides of the road
08 8648 5970   HEMA 129 E13   32 11 10 S   140 34 56 E

215 Olary Creek

Barrier Hwy, Olary
Rest Area 2 km E of Olary. 65 km SW of
Cockburn or 39 km NE of Mannahill
08 8648 5970   HEMA 129 F12   32 16 08 S   140 20 46 E

216 Olary Rest Area

Cnr Barrier Hwy & High St, Olary
Rest Area
08 8648 5970   HEMA 129 F12   32 16 53 S   140 19 39 E

217 Manna Hill Rest Area

Barrier Hwy, Manna Hill
Rest Area 38 km SW of Olary or 44 km NE
of Yunta
08 8648 5970   HEMA 129 F11   32 25 51 S   139 59 12 E

Relax, explore and rediscover!

08 8261 1091 | windsorgardenscaravanpark.com.au

SOUTH AUSTRALIA

218 Winnininnie Creek
Barrier Hwy, Winnininnie
Rest Area 36 km SW of Mannahill or 9 km NE of Yunta
08 8648 5970   HEMA 129 G10   32 32 38 S   139 39 21 E

219 Yunta Centennial Park
Barrier Hwy, Yunta
Rest Area next to Telecentre on Hwy. Donation box
0439 845 940   HEMA 129 G10   32 34 54 S   139 33 46 E

220 Nackara East
Barrier Hwy, Nackara
Parking Area 35 km SW of Yunta or 25 km NE of Oodla Wirra. W side of road
08 8651 3566   HEMA 129 G9   32 46 03 S   139 17 13 E

221 Peechara Hills Bush Camp
Barrier Hwy, Oodla Wirra
Camp Area 6 km NE of Oodla Wirra. Exit S from Barrier Hwy (A32). GPS at gate. 4WD adventure track onsite
0477 817 430   HEMA 129 H9   32 51 44 S   139 06 38 E

222 Oodla Wirra Rest Area
Barrier Hwy, Oodla Wirra
Rest Area 4 km SW of Oodla Wirra or 7 km NE of Hwy 56 Jcn
HEMA 129 H9   32 53 58 S   139 02 40 E

223 Terowie Railway Yard
Railway Tce, Terowie
Camp spot at the old railway siding. Toilets in Main St. Donations at Info Centre or PO box slot. 7 day limit
0413 003 586   HEMA 129 J8   33 09 01 S   138 55 17 E

224 Hallett Recreation Ground
West Tce, Hallett
Parking Area past bowling club into oval, far side of grandstand. Fee & key from Mini Mart, or hotel if after hours
0438 072 904   HEMA 129 K8   33 24 34 S   138 53 28 E

225 Mount Bryan Rest Area
Railway Pde, Mount Bryan
Rest Area 16 km N of Burra or 16 km S of Hallett. Opposite Mount Bryan Hotel
HEMA 125 A8   33 33 01 S   138 53 32 E

226 Bon Accord Hotel
Cnr. West St & Copperhouse Rd, Burra
Parking Area. Register at bar
08 8892 2122   HEMA 125 A8   33 40 17 S   138 55 17 E

227 Burra Showgrounds
Lot 4 Hall Tce, Burra North
Camp Area. Via Young St. Fees collected
0417 938 152   HEMA 125 A8   33 40 05 S   138 55 28 E

228 Red Banks Conservation Park
Eastern Rd, Red Banks
Camp Area 17 km E of Burra. Access via Burra-Morgan Hwy & Eastern Rd. 11 km dirt road
08 8841 3400   HEMA 125 A8   33 39 53 S   139 05 37 E

229 21 Peg Rest Area
Goyder Hwy, Worlds End
Rest Area 20 km SE of Burra or 64 km NW of Morgan. Small area
HEMA 125 B8   33 45 48 S   139 07 02 E

230 Burra Creek Camping
Junction Rd, Bundey
Station Stay 22 km NE of Robertstown, or 42 km SE via Goyder Hwy. Creek crossings. Multiple campgrounds, pre-book
0477 087 709   HEMA 125 B9   33 50 56 S   139 11 11 E

231 Bundey Bore Station
Bundey Church Rd, Bundey
Station Stay 42 km NW of Morgan. Boundary Rd via Goyder Hwy. Pre-book
0477 087 709   HEMA 125 B9   33 53 04 S   139 21 16 E

232 Burra Creek Gorge Reserve (Worlds End)
Worlds End Gorge Rd, Worlds End
Camp Area 26 km SE of Burra. Turn S off Burra-Morgan Rd 16 km to Robertstown Rd for 10 km, then W for 2 km
08 8892 2154   HEMA 125 B8   33 49 52 S   139 02 44 E

233 Robertstown Oval
10 Main Rd, Robertstown
Parking Area. Entry from Main Rd/Church St
08 8581 7100   HEMA 125 C8   33 59 35 S   139 04 49 E

234 Eudunda Caravan Park
Thiele Hwy, Eudunda
Caravan Park at Oval Cr, adjacent to the pool. 4 sites, fees collected. Free camping at rear
0498 858 186   HEMA 125 C8   34 10 44 S   139 05 19 E

235 Hanson Parking Area
Barrier Hwy, Hanson
Parking Area 13 km S of Burra
1300 872 677   HEMA 125 B8   33 45 14 S   138 50 21 E

236 Saddleworth Caravan Park

Belvidere/Marrabel Rd, Saddleworth
Caravan Park at oval, N of road
0417 847 971   HEMA 124 C7   34 05 10 S   138 47 05 E

237 Edgehill Farm Stay

Ryelands Rd, Riverton
Farm Stay at Ryelands Rd N on Horrocks
Hwy, E via Tralee Rd. Various sites
0477 087 709   HEMA 124 C7   34 11 06 S   138 48 42 E

238 Tarlee Rest Area

Horrocks Hwy, Tarlee
Rest Area 1 km N of Tarlee. 54 km S of
Clare or 39 km N of Gawler
1300 872 677   HEMA 124 D7   34 16 15 S   138 45 52 E

239 Tarlee Recreation Ground

Main North Rd, Tarlee
Parking Area on Horrocks Hwy. Honesty
box or pay at store
0418 843 136   HEMA 124 D7   34 16 21 S   138 46 08 E

Peterborough to Port Augusta

240 Peterborough East

Petersburg Rd, Peterborough
Rest Area 2 km E of Peterborough
1300 872 677   HEMA 129 H8   32 58 11 S   138 51 45 E

241 Willangi Bush Escapes

119 Hurlstone St, Peterborough
Station Stay. Pre-book. Collect key, map
& directions in Peterborough office, Hurlstone St
extension, past the hospital. Bond payable
0427 014 215   HEMA 129 H8   32 59 04 S   138 49 53 E

242 Peterborough West RV Stop

Telford Ave, Peterborough
Parking Area W of Steamtown Heritage Rail
Centre. Via Tripney Ave
08 8651 3566   HEMA 129 H8   32 58 27 S   138 49 28 E

243 Yongala Recreation Park

Belalie Rd, Yongala
Camp Area S end of town. Donation to
Globe Hotel
08 8651 3566   HEMA 129 H8   33 01 56 S   138 44 58 E

244 Black Rock South

Petersburg Rd, Peterborough
Parking Area 15 km NW of Peterborough or
22 km SE of Orroroo
1300 872 677   HEMA 129 H8   32 51 45 S   138 44 14 E

245 Carinya Escapes

74 Hogshead Rd, Pekina
Station Stay 15 km S of Orroroo.
Environmental road fee
08 8658 6038   HEMA 128 H7   32 52 02 S   138 34 05 E

246 Pekina Hotel

1334 Price-Maurice Rd, Pekina
Camp Area. Register on arrival. Patrons only
08 8658 6184   HEMA 128 H7   32 50 12 S   138 33 12 E

247 Bush Camp Orroroo

Price Maurice Rd, Orroroo
Camp Area 2 km S from Orroroo. Signed
access gate on E side of road, opposite road to
Pekina Ck Reservoir. Private property
HEMA 128 G7   32 45 00 S   138 36 01 E

248 Orroroo Caravan Park

21 West Tce, Orroroo
Caravan Park 200 m W of PO
08 8658 1444   HEMA 128 G7   32 43 57 S   138 36 36 E

249 Bendleby Ranges Bush Camp

741 Crotta Road, Belton
Station Stay 50 km N of Orroroo. Take
Johnburgh Rd for 42 km, turn E 8 km. Pre-book
08 8658 9064   HEMA 129 F8   32 21 15 S   138 47 33 E

250 Carrieton Caravan Park

Fourth St, Carrieton
Caravan Park off RM Williams Way. Follow
Second St to park sign
08 8658 9090   HEMA 128 F7   32 25 29 S   138 31 55 E

251 Horseshoe Top-End

1133 Horseshoe Rd, Moockra
Station Stay 25 km W of Carrieton or 11 km
N of Moockra. Pre-book
0448 048 836   HEMA 128 F7   32 22 49 S   138 22 49 E

252 Almerta Station Stay

235 Almerta Rd, Yanyarrie
Station Stay 18 km N of Carrieton or 65 km
S of Hawker on the RM Williams Way. 12 km N of
Carrieton, turn W on Carrieton Quorn Rd, 6 km dirt
road. Signposted
08 8658 9076   HEMA 128 F7   32 17 02 S   138 27 24 E

253 Orroroo Rest Area

Willowie Rd, Morchard
Rest Area 8 km W of Orroroo or 5 km E of
Morchard
1300 872 677   HEMA 128 G7   32 44 02 S   138 32 13 E

254 Stony Creek Bush Camp

23 Burnett Rd, Wilmington
Caravan Park 4 km E of Wilmington via
Second St & Stony Ck Rd. 1 km dirt road
0400 150 050   HEMA 128 G0   32 30 54 3   138 08 00 E

255 Horrocks Pass Parking

Horrocks Pass Rd, Wilmington
Parking Area 6 km NW of Wilmington or
36 km SE of Port Augusta
HEMA 128 G6   32 38 29 S   138 02 15 E

256 Hancocks Lookout

Hancocks Lookout Rd, Nectar Brook
Camp Spot 13 km W of Wilmington. Turn
S off Horrocks Pass Rd 3 km W of Wilmington or
40 km SE of Port Augusta. 7 km dirt road
1300 726 252   HEMA 128 G6   32 42 21 S   138 01 37 E

SOUTH AUSTRALIA

257 Catninga Station

655 Catninga Rd, Saltia
Station Stay 24 km E of Port Augusta via Spear Creek Rd
08 8643 6327   HEMA 135 B11   32 30 49 S   137 58 33 E

Adelaide to Port Augusta

258 St Kilda Adventure Park

Cockle St, St Kilda
Parking Area. Permit from Tackle & Tucker Store
08 8280 9355   HEMA 120 C3   34 44 31 S   138 32 00 E

259 Middle Beach Campground

555 The Esplanade, Middle Beach
Camp Area 51 km N of Adelaide on Port Wakefield Hwy, W to Middle Beach Rd, N to Two Wells, N to Esplanade
08 8520 2374   HEMA 127 A1   34 36 04 S   138 24 30 E

260 Mallala Sports Ground

1 Wasleys Rd, Mallala
Camp Area 200 m E of PO. 30 km NW of Gawler, or 51 km SE of Port Wakefield Renovations
08 8527 0200   HEMA 124 D7   34 26 18 S   138 30 49 E

261 Parham Camping Ground

The Esplanade, Port Parham
Camp Area. Limit 5 tonne. Self-register onsite. 14 day limit
08 8527 0200   HEMA 124 D6   34 25 34 S   138 15 20 E

262 Dublin North Rest Area

Port Wakefield Rd, Dublin
Rest Area 21 km N of Dublin or 14 km S of Port Wakefield. N bound only
1300 872 677   HEMA 124 D6   34 17 29 S   138 14 30 E

263 Lochiel Memorial Hall

Robert St / Princes Hwy, Lochiel
Parking Area next to hotel, N end of town
HEMA 124 B6   33 55 37 S   138 09 40 E

264 Snowtown Centenary Park

North Tce, Snowtown
Caravan Park N side of town. See notice board for payment details & keys
08 8865 2252   HEMA 124 B6   33 46 42 S   138 12 59 E

265 Snowtown (North) Rest Area

Augusta Hwy, Snowtown
Rest Area 3 km N of Snowtown or 13 km S of Lake View
HEMA 124 B6   33 44 45 S   138 12 36 E

266 Redhill RV Area

Ellis St Reserve, Redhill
Parking Area between railway line & Mundoora Tce. Gold coin donation to Redhill Corner Store. Toilets 100 m from site
08 8633 9777   HEMA 124 A6   33 32 16 S   138 13 10 E

267 Clements Gap Old School

Clements Gap Conservation Park
Clements Rd, Clements Gap
Camp Area 20 km NE of Port Broughton or 10 km SW of Merriton. In old school grounds, second entrance for high vehicles
08 8633 8700   HEMA 124 A5   33 29 45 S   138 05 04 E

268 Bunyip Park

Seventh St, Koolunga
Camp Area 45 km NE of Clare or 11 km SW of Red Hill. Park at S end of town, turn into First St. Limited power sites. Key from garage or hotel
HEMA 124 A6   33 35 20 S   138 20 01 E

269 White Cliffs Reserve

Yacka Rd, Koolunga
Camp Spot 5 km E of Koolunga, via Koolunga. Dirt road
08 8633 9777   HEMA 124 A6   33 35 29 S   138 23 38 E

270 Merriton Rest Area

Augusta Hwy, Merriton
Rest Area 2 km N of Merriton or 8 km SW of Crystal Brook
HEMA 128 K6   33 24 59 S   138 09 36 E

271 Jubilee Park Crystal Brook

Railway Tce, Crystal Brook
Rest Area near PO
08 8633 8700   HEMA 128 J6   33 21 13 S   138 12 23 E

272 Bowman RV Park

140 Bowman Park Rd, Crystal Brook
Parking Area 5 km NE of Crystal Brook, via Huddlestone Rd
0404 138 544   HEMA 128 J6   33 19 54 S   138 14 24 E

273 Port Pirie Overnight Parking

Service Rd, Port Pirie
Parking Area E of Globe Oval, in service lane. Via Warnertown Rd. Limited space
08 8633 9777   HEMA 128 J6   33 11 09 S   138 01 27 E

274 Lawrie Park

Flinders View Dr, Nelshaby
Camp Spot 10 km NE of Port Pirie. Turn E off Port Augusta Hwy to Nelshaby Rd for 5 km then E. Signposted
08 8633 9777   HEMA 128 J6   33 07 43 S   138 06 37 E

275 Port Germein South 2

Augusta Hwy, Port Germein
Rest Area 21 km N of Port Pirie turnoff or 4 km S of Port Germein turnoff. Northbound only
HEMA 128 H6   33 02 46 S   138 01 51 E

276 Port Germein South 1

Augusta Hwy, Port Germein
Rest Area 22 km N of Port Pirie turnoff or 3 km S of Port Germein turnoff. Southbound only
HEMA 128 H6   33 02 31 S   138 01 48 E

277 Germein Gorge

Telowie Gorge Rd, Port Germein
Parking Area 9 km E of Port Germein turnoff, 20 km W of Murray Town or 17 km W of B82 Hwy Jcn. Follow 200 m S
HEMA 128 H6   32 59 07 S   138 04 52 E

278 Baroota Camping Park

57 Buggy Rd, Baroota
Camp Area 6 km N of Port Germein turnoff or 14 km S of Mambray Creek Roadhouse. 1 km W of Hwy. Dirt road. Call if gate is locked
0439 558 374   HEMA 128 H6   32 57 39 S   137 58 33 E

279 Baroota Ruins Campground
Mount Remarkable National Park
Park Rd, Mambray Creek
Camp Area 23 km N of Port Germein. N on Port
Augusta Hwy, E to Park Rd before Mambray Ck
08 8841 3400   HEMA 128 H6   32 50 31 S   138 00 59 E

280 Mambray Creek Camp
Mount Remarkable National Park
Via Park Rd, Mambray Creek
Camp Area 26 km NE of Port Germein. Turn E
46 km S of Port Augusta or 21 km N Port Germein.
Signposted. 5 day limit, ebook
08 8841 3400   HEMA 128 H6   32 50 26 S   138 02 14 E

281 Mambray Creek Rest Area
Augusta Hwy, Mambray Creek
Rest Area 46 km S of Port Augusta or
21 km N of Port Germein. E side of road
1300 872 677   HEMA 128 H6   32 50 47 S   137 58 55 E

Gawler to Wilmington
Main North Road

282 Hamley Bridge Community
& Sports Centre
17 Stockport Rd, Hamley Bridge
Parking Area. Entry off Stockport Rd
08 8862 0800   HEMA 124 D7   34 21 14 S   138 40 53 E

283 Owen Oval
Off Railway Tce, Owen
Parking Area. Enter behind grain silos
08 8862 0800   HEMA 124 D7   34 16 07 S   138 32 49 E

284 Auburn Community
Caravan Park
Saddleworth Rd, Auburn
Caravan Park. Via Ford St. Signposted
0417 550 781   HEMA 124 C7   34 01 42 S   138 41 30 E

285 Leasingham Village Cabins
11 Wakefield Rd, Leasingham
Caravan Park 6 km N of Auburn or 14 km
S of Clare
08 8843 0136   HEMA 124 C7   33 58 56 S   138 39 01 E

286 Farrell Flat Hotel
12 Patterson Tce, Farrell Flat
Parking Area at rear of hotel. Register at
bar. Pay fee or spend in the bar
08 8843 8187   HEMA 124 B7   33 49 48 S   138 47 40 E

287 Farrell Flat Oval
Cnr Cameron & South Terrace, Farrell Flat
Parking Area. Entry off Cameron Tce
08 8892 0100   HEMA 124 B7   33 49 40 S   138 47 36 E

288 Watervale Rest Area
Main North Rd, Watervale
Rest Area 125 km N of Adelaide City. On
Horrocks Hwy
  HEMA 124 B7   33 57 10 S   138 38 47 E

289 Blyth Sportsground
15-17 South Tce, Blyth
Parking Area S side of town, close to PO
0428 445 218   HEMA 124 B7   33 50 53 S   138 29 24 E

290 Clare Valley Racecourse
100 Horrocks Hwy, Clare
Camp Area 4 km N of Clare Horrocks Hwy.
Pre-book. GPS near entry, exit via Stradbrooke Rd
0447 271 840   HEMA 124 B7   33 47 32 S   138 35 38 E

291 Gladstone Caravan Park
West Tce, Gladstone
Caravan Park 1 km W of PO. S side of town
08 8662 2522   HEMA 128 J7   33 16 08 S   138 21 05 E

292 Brinkworth Travellers
Overnight Stay
Cnr East Tce & Edgar St, Brinkworth
Camp Area E off Main St, enter via East Tce
0427 462 023   HEMA 124 A6   33 41 33 S   138 24 18 E

293 Yackamoorundie Park
Cnr Main North Rd & North Tce, Yacka
Camp Area N side of town on Broughton R.
Refundable key deposit, see sign on gate
08 8846 4038   HEMA 124 A6   33 34 06 S   138 26 43 E

294 Ossies Homestead Farmstay
1029 Pipeline Rd, Gulnare
Farm Stay 55 km N of Clare, 7 km NE of
Gulnare. Pre-book
0417 813 095   HEMA 128 K7   33 26 59 S   138 28 52 E

295 Spalding Hotel
19 Main St, Spalding
Parking Area behind hotel. Free for patrons.
Register at bar. Pre-order meals. Amenities fee
08 8845 2006   HEMA 128 K7   33 29 49 S   138 36 29 E

296 Gulnare Rest Area
Main North Rd, Gulnare
Rest Area 5 km N of turnoff to Gulnare.
1.5 km S of Crystal Drook turnoff
1300 872 677   HEMA 128 K7   33 27 34 S   138 25 58 E

297 Georgetown RV Park Area
Cnr James & Fisher St, Georgetown
Parking Area at Georgetown Memorial
Playground. Coin shower, donation at general store
08 8662 4011   HEMA 128 J7   33 21 38 S   138 23 37 E

298 Robinson Park
Vohr St (RM Williams Way), Jamestown
Parking Area. Permit from Foodland in Ayr St
08 8664 0070   HEMA 128 J7   33 12 06 S   138 36 12 E

SOUTH AUSTRALIA

299 Laura Community Caravan Park

Cnr Main North Rd & North Tce, Laura
Caravan Park 500m N of PO. SCV rates available
08 8663 2296   HEMA 128 J7   33 10 54 S   138 18 02 E

300 Ippinitchie Campground

Wirrabara Range Conservation Park

Wirrabara-Forest Rd, Wirrabara
Camp Area 8 km SW of Wirrabara. Dirt road. Permit applies. Open April - Nov
08 8841 3400   HEMA 128 H6   33 04 01 S   138 13 58 E

301 Wirrabara Camping Ground

Via Crew Rd, Wirrabara
Caravan Park next to football oval, N end of town. 400 m dirt road. Key at Wirrabara Craft House
08 8668 4250   HEMA 128 H6   33 01 56 S   138 15 54 E

302 Murray Town Park

Main North Rd, Murray Town
Camp Area. Honesty box
08 8666 4253   HEMA 128 H6   32 56 10 S   138 14 26 E

303 Arthur Street Town Oval

42 Arthur St, Booleroo
Camp Area 66 km NE of Port Pirie. Off B82 at Murray Town to Booleroo Centre Oval
0438 823 896   HEMA 128 H7   32 52 54 S   138 21 23 E

304 Bartagunyah Estate

1277 Survey Rd, Melrose
Camp Area 5 km S of Melrose. Keep driving until cellar door. Pre-book
08 8666 2136   HEMA 128 H6   32 51 59 S   138 10 37 E

305 Melrose Showground

Horrocks Hwy, Melrose
Camp Area 1 km N of Melrose
0401 002 658   HEMA 128 G6   32 48 36 S   138 11 46 E

306 Goyder Line Rest Area

Horrocks Hwy, Melrose
Parking Area 3 km N of Melrose or 22 km S of Wilmington
1300 872 677   HEMA 128 G6   32 48 06 S   138 12 31 E

307 Kookaburra Creek Retreat

96 Shanks Rd, Melrose
Camp Area NW of Melrose. N on Horrocks Hwy. April - Nov only. Pre-book
0439 618 378   HEMA 128 G6   32 45 27 S   138 09 31 E

Yorke Peninsula

308 The Acreage

Cnr New Holland & Paskeville Rd, Paskeville
Camp Spot 4 km W of Paskeville. Entry off New Holland Rd. Signposted. 7 day limit
0428 272 083   HEMA 124 C5   34 01 42 S   137 51 41 E

309 Port Arthur Rest Area

Clinton Conservation Reserve

Yorke Hwy, Port Arthur
Rest Area 4 km S of Port Arthur on Yorke Hwy
1800 202 445   HEMA 124 C5   34 08 53 S   138 03 50 E

310 Price Caravan Park

14 Fowler Tce, Price
Caravan Park E side of town, near shops
08 8837 6311   HEMA 124 D5   34 17 14 S   137 59 48 E

311 Ardrossan RV Stop

Cnr Second St & West Terrace, Ardrossan
Parking Area. Enter from West Tce at rear of bowling club & tennis court. Park in designated bays only. Donations at info centre
1800 202 445   HEMA 124 D5   34 25 28 S   137 54 52 E

312 Parara

Parara Rd, Ardrossan
Camp Area 4 km S of Ardrossan. Via Yorke Hwy. Camp sites are located S of the Whale Memorial. Permit applies
1800 202 445   HEMA 124 D5   34 27 37 S   137 54 32 E

313 Pine Point Caravan Park

46-48 Main Coast Rd, Pine Point
Caravan Park S of township, E of road
08 8838 2239   HEMA 124 E5   34 34 28 S   137 52 40 E

314 Black Point Camp Ground

Black Point Rd, Pine Point
Camp Area 4 km S of Pine Point (known as Harvey Camp Ground), next to boat ramp. Caretaker collects fees
08 8838 2239   HEMA 124 E5   34 36 26 S   137 52 55 E

315 Port Julia Oval

Cnr Port Julia Rd & Osprey St, Port Julia
Camp Spot at Reichenbach Memorial Park. Caretaker collects fees in the afternoon
0417 877 316   HEMA 124 E5   34 39 46 S   137 52 38 E

316 Curramulka Overnight Stay

Mount Rat Rd, Curramulka
Parking Area next to bowling club & tennis courts
08 8854 2234   HEMA 124 E4   34 41 52 S   137 42 24 E

317 Oyster Point Drive Caravan Park

Oyster Point Dr, Stansbury
Caravan Park 2 km S of PO
08 8852 4171   HEMA 124 F4   34 55 00 S   137 47 46 E

318 Yorketown Community Caravan Park

10 Memorial Dr, Yorketown
Caravan Park E side of town
0499 213 605   HEMA 124 F4   35 01 13 S   137 36 37 E

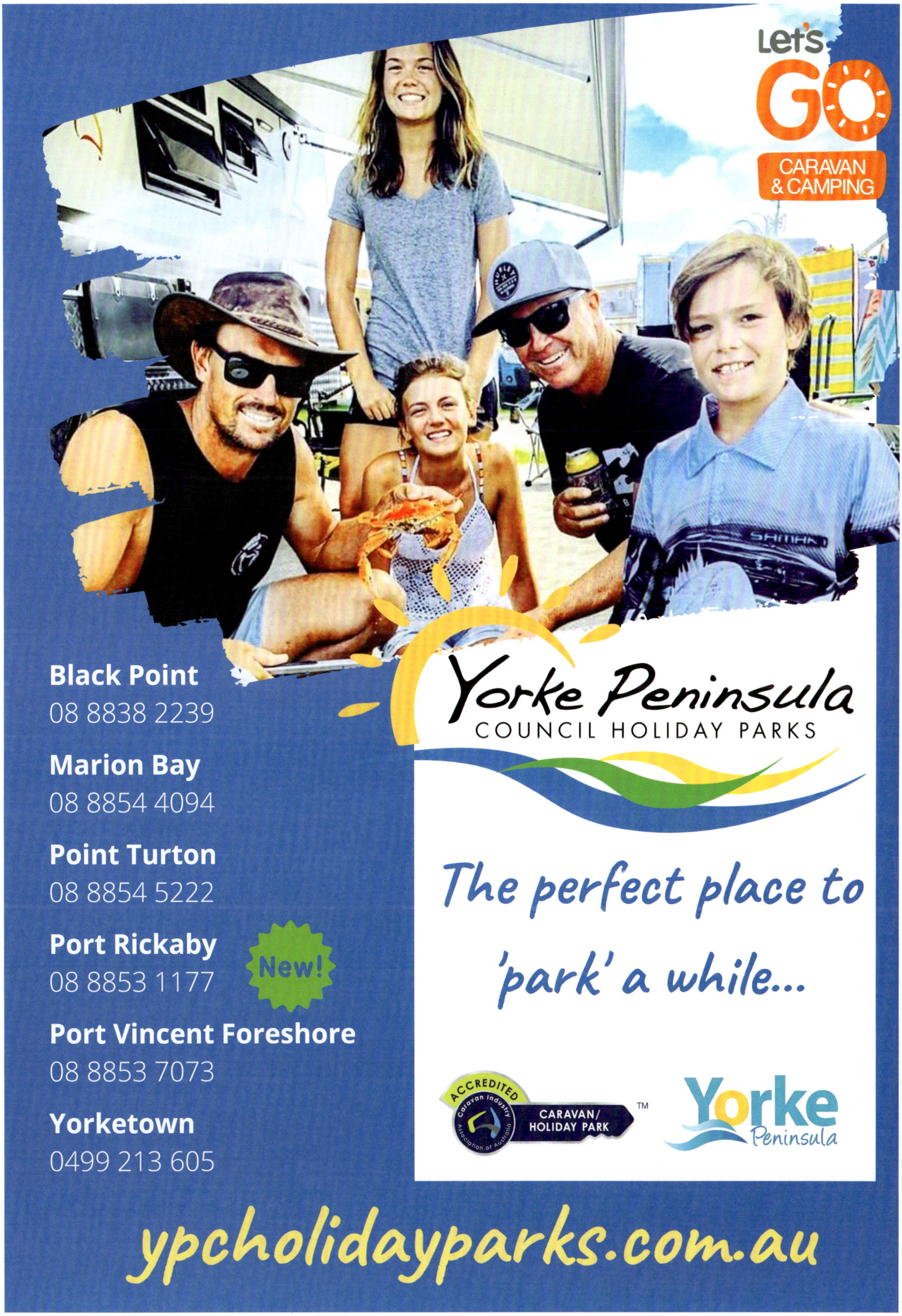
Let's GO
CARAVAN & CAMPING
Black Point
08 8838 2239
Marion Bay
08 8854 4094
Point Turton
08 8854 5222
Port Rickaby
08 8853 1177
New!
Port Vincent Foreshore
08 8853 7073
Yorketown
0499 213 605
Yorke Peninsula
COUNCIL HOLIDAY PARKS
The perfect place to 'park' a while...
ACCREDITED
Caravan Industry Association of Australia
CARAVAN/ HOLIDAY PARK
TM
Yorke Peninsula
ypcholidayparks.com.au

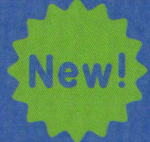

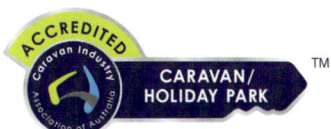

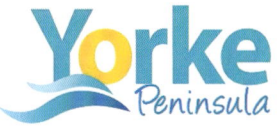

SOUTH AUSTRALIA

319 Coobowie Caravan Park
23 Beach Rd, Coobowie
Caravan Park 5 km N of Edithburgh or 8 km S of Wool Bay. 400 m S of PO
08 8852 8132   HEMA 124 F4   35 02 47 S   137 43 39 E

320 Wattle Point
Heel Rd, Edithburgh
Camp Area 8 km SW of Edithburgh. Access via Wattle Point Rd. Dirt road. Permit applies
1800 202 445   HEMA 124 G4   35 08 19 S   137 42 08 E

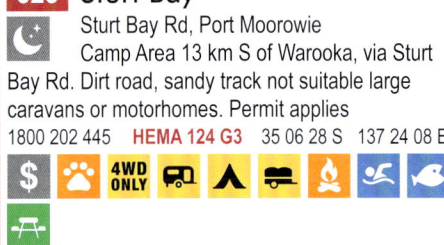

321 Goldsmith Beach
Troubridge Point Dr, Edithburgh
Camp Areas 8 km SW of Edithburgh. Near Cnr of Heel Rd. Camp in various spots along coastal reserve. Dirt road. Permit applies
1800 202 445   HEMA 124 G4   35 08 51 S   137 41 13 E

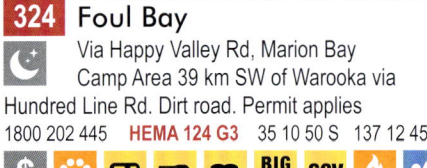

322 Mozzie Flat
South Coast Rd, Edithburgh
Camp Area 17 km SW of Yorketown or 23 km SE of Warooka. Off road vehicles only, small area. Dirt road. Permit applies
1800 202 445   HEMA 124 G4   35 06 42 S   137 29 56 E

323 Sturt Bay
Sturt Bay Rd, Port Moorowie
Camp Area 13 km S of Warooka, via Sturt Bay Rd. Dirt road, sandy track not suitable large caravans or motorhomes. Permit applies
1800 202 445   HEMA 124 G3   35 06 28 S   137 24 08 E

324 Foul Bay
Via Happy Valley Rd, Marion Bay
Camp Area 39 km SW of Warooka via Hundred Line Rd. Dirt road. Permit applies
1800 202 445   HEMA 124 G3   35 10 50 S   137 12 45 E

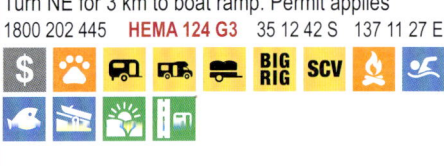

325 Foul Bay Boat Ramp
South Coast Rd, Marion Bay Area
Camp Area 41 km SW of Warooka & 1 km S of Foul Bay, via Yorke Hwy to Hundred Line Rd. Turn NE for 3 km to boat ramp. Permit applies
1800 202 445   HEMA 124 G3   35 12 42 S   137 11 27 E

326 Hillocks Drive, Butlers Beach
South Coast Rd, Marion Bay
Camp Area 16 km E of Marion Bay. Permit, toilet, water & shower at homestead. Dirt road. Fires permitted May - Oct, BYO equipment
08 8854 4002   HEMA 124 G3   35 13 52 S   137 07 29 E

327 Stenhouse Bay Campground
Innes National Park
Pondalowie Inneston Rd, Stenhouse Bay
Camp Area 6 km SW of Marion Bay. Pre-book. 5 day limit
08 8854 3200   HEMA 124 G2   35 16 26 S   136 56 29 E

328 Cable Bay Campground
Innes National Park
Pondalowie Bay Rd, Stenhouse Bay
Camp Area 10 km SW of Marion Bay. Pre-book. 5 day limit
08 8854 3200   HEMA 124 G2   35 17 07 S   136 53 59 E

329 Pondalowie Campground
Innes National Park
Stenhouse Bay
Camp Area 20 km SW of Marion Bay. Pre-book. 5 day limit
08 8854 3200   HEMA 124 G2   35 14 15 S   136 50 24 E

330 Browns Beach Campground
Innes National Park
Browns Beach Rd, Stenhouse Bay
Camp Area 12 km NW of Marion Bay. Off Marion Bay Rd. Pre-book. Small vehicles only. 5 day limit
08 8854 3200   HEMA 124 G2   35 11 03 S   136 53 40 E

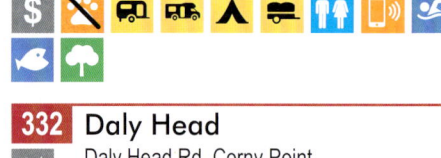

331 Gym Beach
Innes National Park
Gym Beach Rd, Inneston
Camp Area 14 km NW of Marion Bay, W off Marion Bay Rd
08 8854 3200   HEMA 124 G2   35 09 16 S   136 54 36 E

332 Daly Head
Daly Head Rd, Corny Point
Camp Area 25 km S of Corny Point, via Daly Head Rd. Dirt road. Permit applies
1800 202 445   HEMA 124 F2   35 01 26 S   136 56 23 E

333 Gleesons Landing
Gleesons Rd, Corny Point
Camp Area 19 km SW of Corny Point. Via Marion Bay Rd. Dirt road. Permit applies
1800 202 445   HEMA 124 F2   35 00 14 S   136 57 57 E

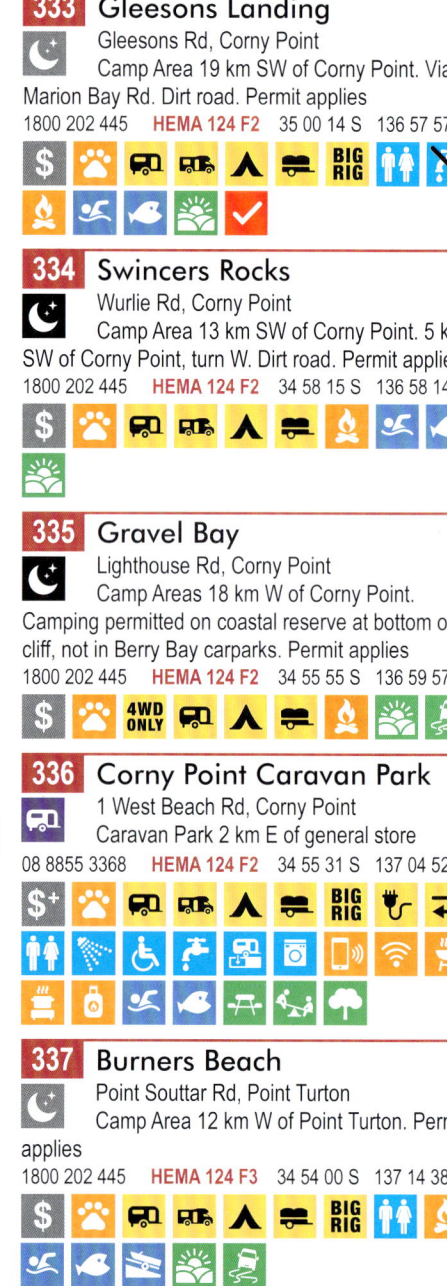

334 Swincers Rocks
Wurlie Rd, Corny Point
Camp Area 13 km SW of Corny Point. 5 km SW of Corny Point, turn W. Dirt road. Permit applies
1800 202 445   HEMA 124 F2   34 58 15 S   136 58 14 E

335 Gravel Bay
Lighthouse Rd, Corny Point
Camp Areas 18 km W of Corny Point. Camping permitted on coastal reserve at bottom of cliff, not in Berry Bay carparks. Permit applies
1800 202 445   HEMA 124 F2   34 55 55 S   136 59 57 E

336 Corny Point Caravan Park
1 West Beach Rd, Corny Point
Caravan Park 2 km E of general store
08 8855 3368   HEMA 124 F2   34 55 31 S   137 04 52 E

337 Burners Beach
Point Souttar Rd, Point Turton
Camp Area 12 km W of Point Turton. Permit applies
1800 202 445   HEMA 124 F3   34 54 00 S   137 14 38 E

338 Len Barker Reserve
North Coast Rd, Point Turton
Camp Area 7 km NW of Point Turton. Near Jcn with West Cowie Rd. Permit applies
1800 202 445   HEMA 124 F3   34 55 14 S   137 18 05 E

339 Inland Sea Restaurant
12918 Yorke Hwy, Warooka
Camp Spot 4 km W of Warooka. Cold showers. Patrons only
08 8854 5499   HEMA 124 F3   34 59 06 S   137 21 33 E

340 Warooka Camp Ground
Oval Ave & Fifth St, Warooka
Camp Area at Warooka Oval. Donation envelopes in cylinder on site
08 8854 5004   HEMA 124 F3   34 59 32 S   137 23 53 E

341 Port Minlacowie

Beegoodye Wells Rd, Minlaton
Camp Area 17 km SW of Minlaton.
Via Minlacowie Rd. 650 m N of Minlacowie Rd
intersection. Permit applies
1800 202 445　HEMA 124 F4　34 49 54 S　137 27 32 E

342 Minlaton Caravan Park

Cnr Bluff & Maitland Rds, Minlaton
Caravan Park NW side of town
08 8853 2435　HEMA 124 E4　34 45 58 S　137 35 47 E

343 Barkers Rocks

Via Barkers Rocks Rd, Minlaton
Camp Area 12 km NW of Minlaton. Turn
W 10 km NW of Minlaton. 3 km dirt road. Small
vehicles only. Permit applies
1800 202 445　HEMA 124 E4　34 42 52 S　137 29 14 E

344 Wauraltee Beach

Wauraltee Beach Rd, Wauraltee
Camp Area 4 km W of Wauraltee. Turn W at
Wauraltee, 17 km S of Port Victoria. 4 km dirt road.
Permit required
1800 202 445　HEMA 124 E4　34 35 16 S　137 30 28 E

345 Port Victoria Oval

1 Kuhn Tce, Port Victoria
Parking Area NE side of town
0429 702 234　HEMA 124 D4　34 29 46 S　137 29 16 E

346 Maitland Rest Area

Robert St, Maitland
Rest Area N end of town, opposite hospital.
Small vehicles only
08 8832 2174　HEMA 124 D4　34 22 14 S　137 40 29 E

347 Maitland Showground SA

Rogers Tce, Maitland
Camp Area NE side of town. Caretaker
collects fees
08 8832 2171　HEMA 124 D4　34 22 18 S　137 40 39 E

348 Arthurton Rest Area

Third St, Arthurton
Rest Area 15 km NE of Maitland or 35 km
SW of Kulpara. Behind St Agatha's Church
HEMA 124 D4　34 15 27 S　137 45 25 E

349 Balgowan Camping Area

4 Main St, Balgowan
Caravan Park on headland
0498 744 415　HEMA 124 D4　34 19 26 S　137 29 38 E

350 Tiparra Rocks

Coastal Track, Balgowan
Camp Area 8 km N of Balgowan. Take
Tiparra West Rd, then L fork after 1 km. Dirt road,
access track sandy. Not suitable for larger caravans
or motorhomes. Permit applies
1800 202 445　HEMA 124 D4　34 17 10 S　137 29 56 E

351 The Bamboos

Via Tiparra West Rd, Balgowan
Camp Area 12 km N of Balgowan. Take
Tiparra West Rd, then L fork after 1 km. Dirt road,
access track sandy. Permit applies
1800 202 445　HEMA 124 C4　34 15 10 S　137 30 05 E

352 The Gap

Gap Rd, Balgowan
Camp Area 15 km N of Balgowan. Take
Tiparra West Rd, then L fork after 1 km. Alternate route
from Moonta, head S 24 km to Weetulta turn W on Gap
Rd, campsite is 15 km on dirt road. Permit applies
1800 202 445　HEMA 124 C4　34 14 03 S　137 30 06 E

353 Moonta RV Overnight Stop

Cnr Blyth Tce & Old Wallaroo Rd, Moonta
Parking Area. Overflow opposite
08 8825 1891　HEMA 124 C4　34 03 55 S　137 35 32 E

354 Wallaroo Overnight Area

Cnr Cornish Tce & Wildman St, Wallaroo
Parking Area W end of town
08 8821 2333　HEMA 124 B4　33 56 04 S　137 37 18 E

355 Kadina Showgrounds

Moonta Rd, Kadina
Camp Area. Entry off Agery St. Fee, key &
water access from Copper Coast Info Centre, Mines
Rd. 7 night limit
08 8821 2333　HEMA 124 B4　33 58 03 S　137 42 57 E

356 Tickera North

Coast Rd, Tickera
Parking Area 4.5 km N of Tickera. Turn W
to beach
08 8635 2107　HEMA 124 B4　33 45 37 S　137 43 49 E

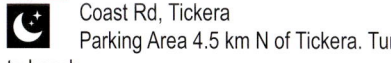

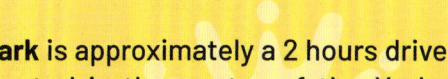

357 Alford Recreation Park

South Tce, Alford
Camp Area opposite tennis courts, via Port Broughton-Kadina Rd
0400 005 859   HEMA 124 B5   33 49 01 S   137 49 18 E

358 Bute Caravan Park

21 Railway Tce, Bute
Caravan Park 250 m W of PO
08 8826 2011   HEMA 124 B5   33 51 57 S   138 00 22 E

359 Broughton Bay RV

17 Hornby Rd, Port Broughton
Camp Area 2 km W of Port Broughton. Exit Spencer Hwy N to Hornby Rd. Payment box onsite. Separate area for dogs off leash
08 8635 2608   HEMA 124 A5   33 35 34 S   137 57 02 E

Kangaroo Island

360 Antechamber Bay North

Lashmar Conservation Park
Willoughby Rd, Antechamber Bay
Camp Area on the N side of the Chapman River, 11 sites. 5 day limit, ebook
08 8553 4444   HEMA 124 J5   35 47 03 S   138 03 59 E

361 Antechamber Bay South

Lashmar Conservation Park
Creek Bay Rd, Antechamber Bay
Camp Area 20 km SE of Penneshaw on the SE side of Chapman River. 12 sites. 5 day limit, ebook
08 8553 2381   HEMA 124 J5   35 47 11 S   138 03 59 E

362 Brown Beach Campground

Hog Bay Rd, Dudley West
Camp Area at Browns Bay. Permit applies. Self registration
08 8553 4500   HEMA 124 J5   35 47 38 S   137 51 27 E

363 D'Estrees Bay Campground

Cape Gantheaume Conservation Park
D'Estrees Bay Rd, D'Estrees Bay
Camp Area. Permit applies. Pre-book. Dirt road. 5 day limit
08 8553 4444   HEMA 124 K4   35 57 58 S   137 36 19 E

364 Vivonne Bay Campground

Samedi Dr, Vivonne Bay
Camp Area. Permit applies. Self registration. Limited power sites
08 8553 4500   HEMA 124 K3   35 59 04 S   137 10 37 E

365 Western River Caravan Park
& Wildlife Reserve

South Coast Rd, Karatta
Caravan Park 3 km E of Flinders Chase
08 8559 7201   HEMA 124 K2   35 57 39 S   136 48 28 E

366 Rocky River Camping Area

Flinders Chase National Park
Cape Du Couedic Rd, Flinders Chase
Camp Area 300 m S of Visitor Centre, ebook
08 8553 4470   HEMA 124 K1   35 57 11 S   136 44 07 E

367 Western River Cove

Western River Rd, Western River
Camp Area 29 km W of Parndana. Dirt road. Steep in places. Small vehicles only. Permit applies. Self registration
08 8553 4500   HEMA 124 J2   35 40 40 S   136 58 18 E

368 Stokes Bay

North Coast Rd, Stokes Bay
Camp Area 38 km W of Kingscote. Via Stokes Bay Rd, 4 km W of Parndana. Behind café, check-in & pay at café
8553 4500   HEMA 124 J3   35 37 30 S   137 12 23 E

369 Parndana Hotel

Cnr Wedgwood Rd & Cook St, Parndana
Camp Area at rear of hotel
08 8559 6071   HEMA 124 J3   35 47 27 S   137 15 51 E

370 Discovery Lagoon Camping

948 North Coast Rd, Wisanger
Camp Area 3 km S of Emu Bay or 12 W of Kingscote
0412 422 618   HEMA 124 J4   35 37 25 S   137 31 23 E

371 Emu Bay Campground

Bates Rd, Emu Bay
Camp Area NE on Playford Hwy. W on North Coast Rd, N to Emu Bay Rd, N on Gap Rd, then W
08 8553 4500   HEMA 124 H4   35 35 41 S   137 30 20 E

372 American River Camp

Tangara Dr, American River
Camp Area. Self registration. Small vehicles only. Fee for showers
08 8553 4500 **HEMA 124 J4** 35 47 15 S 137 46 14 E

Port Augusta to Birdsville

373 Augusta Caravan Park

9 Brook St, Stirling North
Caravan Park 6 km SE of PO

08 8643 6357 **HEMA 128 F5** 32 30 58 S 137 50 14 E

374 Quorn Town Oval

Park Tce, Quorn
Camp Area N of town centre, via Oval Rd. Pay at the Visitor Info Centre on Railway Tce. SCV rates. May be limited turning circle for big rigs

375 Warren Gorge

Via Arden Vale Rd, Quorn
Camp Area 21 km N of Quorn. Dirt road last 8 km, after grid, veer L & stay on main road. Camp spots after steep hill
08 8620 0500 **HEMA 128 E6** 32 10 57 S 138 00 26 E

376 Argadells Homestead

Via Arden Vale Rd, Quorn
Farm Stay 26 km N of Quorn. 5 km of dirt. Bush camping or powered sites. Pre-book
08 8648 6246 **HEMA 128 E6** 32 08 20 S 138 02 25 E

377 Cradock Hotel

RM Williams Way, Cradock
Pub Stay 27 km SE of Hawker or 43 km N of Carrieton. Free for patrons. Tues - Sun. Fee for showers
08 8648 4107 **HEMA 128 E7** 32 04 10 S 138 29 36 E

378 Three Creeks Station

21425 RM Williams Way, Kanyaka
Station Stay 103 km NE of Port Augusta between Cradock & intersection with B83 to Wilpena
0429 019 230 **HEMA 128E7** 32 00 45 S 138 24 17 E

379 Flinders Bush Retreats
- Willow Waters Gorge

651 Willow Waters Rd, Hawker
Camp Area 20 km E of Hawker. Take Cradock Rd for 7.4 km then signposted road to Willow Waters. Follow road for 6 km, turn L at first house on L. Bush camping. Pre-book
08 8648 4441 **HEMA 128 D7** 31 54 27 S 138 33 41 E

380 Nooltana Creek Parking

The Outback Hwy, Hawker
B83
Parking Area 13 km N of Hawker or 76 km S of Parachilna

HEMA 128 D7 31 48 33 S 138 22 01 E

381 Merna Mora Station

Merna Mora Rd, Hookina
B83
Station Stay 47 km N of Hawker. 3 km W off the Hwy opposite the Moralana Scenic Dr
08 8648 4717 **HEMA 142 G1** 31 32 46 S 138 23 28 E

382 Edeowie Station Stay

309 Edeowie Rd, Flinders Ranges
Camp Area S of Parachilna. N from Hawker on B83 for 45 km, E to Edeowie Rd. Pre-book. Shower fee
08 8648 4714 **HEMA 142 F2** 31 27 04 S 138 27 34 E

383 Parachilna Campground

West Tce, Parachilna
Camp Area E of Hwy. Payment & keys at Prairie Hotel if no caretaker onsite. Open Mar - mid Dec
08 8648 4895 **HEMA 142 A1** 31 07 52 S 138 23 42 E

384 Beltana Station

Beltana Station Rd, Beltana
Station Stay 10 km E of Beltana Roadhouse on Beltana Rd. Turn S on Beltana Station Rd. Pre-book re pets. Honesty box. Bush camping or powered sites at the Woolshed for Restoration
0432 236 131 **HEMA 130 K7** 30 49 18 S 138 22 17 E

385 Warraweena Conservation
Park

Warraweena Rd, Warraweena
Camp Area 25 km E of Beltana. Pre-book. Call at homestead prior. Dirt road. Bush camping rates available. Signposted
08 8675 2770 **HEMA 131 K8** 30 46 04 S 138 38 12 E

386 Leigh Creek Caravan Park

Acacia Dr, Leigh Creek
Caravan Park N of town, W of Hwy
0429 012 445 **HEMA 130 J7** 30 35 17 S 138 24 29 E

387 Iga Warta Community Camp

Via Gammon Ranges Rd, Iga Warta
Camp Area 62 km E of Copley. Pre-book. Dirt road
08 8648 3737 **HEMA 131 J8** 30 35 45 S 138 56 05 E

388 Italowie Gap Campground

Vulkathunha-Gammon Ranges NP
Copley-Arkaroola Rd, Arkaroola Village
Camp Area 22 km E of Nepabunna or 17 km W of the Park HQ. Self registration required. 5 day limit
08 8648 5300 **HEMA 131 J9** 30 33 22 S 139 10 11 E

389 Weetootla Gorge Camp

Vulkathunha-Gammon Ranges NP
Arkaroola Rd, Arkaroola Village
Camp Area 110 km W of Copley. Turn N at Balcanoona into Arkaroola Rd, turn W 2.3 km N of Balcanoona. 4.5 km to campsites. Small vehicles only. Self registration required. 5 day limit
08 8648 5300 **HEMA 131 J9** 30 29 49 S 139 15 33 E

390 Grindells Hut Campground

Vulkathunha-Gammon Ranges NP
Arkaroola Village
Camp Area 118 km W of Copley. Turn N 9 km N of Balcanoona into Arkaroola Rd, continue 17 km. 4WD & camper trailers only
08 8648 5300 **HEMA 131 J9** 30 28 30 S 139 12 51 E

391 Chambers Gorge

Chambers Gorge Rd, Arkaroola Village
Camp Area 27 km NE of Wirrealpa
HEMA 129 A9 30 57 12 S 139 12 53 E

SOUTH AUSTRALIA

392 Arkaroola Wilderness
Sanctuary
Northern Flinders Ranges, Arkaroola Village
Camp Area 130 km E of Leigh Creek. Bush camping
also available
08 8648 4848   HEMA 131 H10   30 18 42 S   139 20 10 E

393 Lyndhurst Hotel Motel
3 Short St, Lyndhurst
Caravan Park on the Strzelecki Track
08 8675 7781   HEMA 130 H7   30 17 16 S   138 21 08 E

394 Farina Station Campground
North Tce, Lyndhurst
Station Stay 26 km N of Lyndhurst. Turn
W 25 km N of Lyndhurst or 56 km S of Marree.
Signposted
08 8675 7790   HEMA 130 G6   30 03 41 S   138 16 22 E

395 Witchelina Homestead
Witchelina Nature Reserve
Witchelina Tr, Lyndhurst
Station Stay 30 km NW of Lyndhurst, along Station
Ck, fee for showers & nature drives, may be
restricted access - pre-book. 7 day limit
08 8340 2880   HEMA 130 G6   30 01 19 S   138 02 37 E

396 Old Mt NorWest Witchelina
Witchelina Nature Reserve
The Outback Hwy, Lyndhurst
Station Stay about 30 km NW of Lyndhurst to the
gate, fee for nature drives, may be restricted access.
Pre-book. 7 day limit. 19 km from homestead. Well
signed
08 8340 2880   HEMA 130 G6   29 55 11 S   138 02 20 E

397 Marree Oasis Caravan Park
Railway Tce South, Marree
Caravan Park S of Oodnadatta Track
08 8675 8352   HEMA 130 F6   29 38 49 S   138 03 46 E

398 Marree Hotel
Railway Tce South, Marree
Camps Spot S of Oodnadatta Track.
Patrons only. Register at bar. Donation for amenities
08 8675 8344   HEMA 130 F6   29 38 54 S   138 03 52 E

Birdsville to Marree
Birdsville Track
*This road is seasonal and more
suitable to 4WD vehicles, camper
trailers and off road caravans. Road
conditions phone 1300 361 033*

399 Lake Harry Ruins
Birdsville Tr, Birdsville Track
Camp Spot 38 km NE of Marree or 168 km
SW of Mungerannie Roadhouse
HEMA 130 E6   29 26 03 S   138 14 46 E

400 Clayton Wetlands
Birdsville Track, Clayton Station
Camp Area 54 km NE of Marree or 152 km S
of Mungerannie Roadhouse. Honesty box by toilets
08 8675 8311   HEMA 130 E7   29 16 32 S   138 22 17 E

401 Cooper Creek
Birdsville Track, Cooper Creek
Camp Area 146 km NE of Marree or 60 km
S of Mungerannie Roadhouse
08 8675 9591   HEMA 131 B8   28 37 25 S   138 42 36 E

402 Mungerannie Hotel
Birdsville Track, Mungerannie
Camp Area 206 km NE of Marree or
308 km SW of Birdsville. Register before setting up.
Beside Derwent River, do not camp in signed area.
BYO firewood
08 8675 8317   HEMA 133 J8   28 01 07 S   138 39 47 E

403 Tippipila Creek Bush Camp
Birdsville Inside Track, Tippipila Creek
Camp Spot N of road, 134 km N of
Mungerannie or 181 km S of Birdsville
HEMA 133 E9   26 59 42 S   139 01 01 E

Marree to Marla
Oodnadatta Track
*This road is seasonal and more
suitable to 4WD vehicles, camper
trailers and off road caravans. Road
conditions phone 1300 361 033*

404 Muloorina Station
Muloorina Rd, Maree
Station Stay 54 km NW of Marree. Turn N
off Oodnadatta Track 2 km W of Maree. Honesty box
08 8675 8386   HEMA 130 E5   29 14 20 S   137 54 23 E

405 Curdimurka Railway Siding
Oodnadatta Tr, Curdimurka
Parking Area 104 km W of Marree or
100 km SE of William Ck. Parking around the ruins
HEMA 130 E3   29 28 36 S   137 05 04 E

406 Coward Springs Camp
Oodnadatta Tr, Stuarts Creek
Camp Area 131 km W of Marree or 73 km
SE of William Creek
08 8675 8336   HEMA 130 E2   29 24 14 S   136 48 44 E

407 Beresford Siding
Oodnadatta Tr, Anna Creek
Parking Area 154 km W of Marree or 50 km
SE of William Creek
HEMA 130 E2   29 14 34 S   136 39 23 E

408 Strangways Siding
Oodnadatta Tr, William Creek
Parking Area 167 km W of Marree or 37 km
SE of William Creek
HEMA 139 K13   29 09 23 S   136 34 21 E

409 Halligan Bay Campground
Kati Thanda - Lake Eyre NP
Halligan Bay Access Tr, Halligan Bay
Camp Area beside Lake Eyre. Turn N 7 km SE of
William Creek to track (57 km). High clearance.
Check conditions, desert pass required
08 8648 5300   HEMA 139 J14   28 45 49 S   136 56 23 E

410 William Creek Camp Ground
Oodnadatta Tr, William Creek
Camp Area at hotel
08 8670 7880   HEMA 139 K13   28 54 28 S   136 20 18 E

411 Warrina Siding
Oodnadatta Tr, Oodnadatta Area
Parking Area 108 km NW of William Creek
or 95 km S of Oodnadatta
HEMA 139 H12   28 11 38 S   135 49 42 E

412 Algebuckina Bridge, Neals
Creek
Oodnadatta Tr, Oodnadatta Area
Rest Area 55 km SE of Oodnadatta
HEMA 139 G12   27 53 57 S   135 48 27 E

413 North Creek
Oodnadatta Tr, Oodnadatta Area
Camp Spot 175 km NW of William Creek
or 28 km S of Oodnadatta, N side of road by old
railway bridge
HEMA 139 F11   27 44 15 S   135 36 15 E

414 Arckaringa Station
Painted Desert Rd, Oodnadatta Area
Station Stay 140 km N of Coober Pedy or
86 km SW of Oodnadatta
08 8670 7992   HEMA 139 G9   27 56 12 S   134 44 18 E

415 The Pink Roadhouse
Ikaturka Tce, Oodnadatta
Caravan Park behind the roadhouse
1800 802 074   HEMA 139 F11   27 32 56 S   135 26 53 E

416 Oodnadatta Town Camp
Oodnadatta Tr, Oodnadatta
Camp Spot opposite health service
08 8670 7865   HEMA 139 F11   27 32 42 S   135 26 48 E

417 3 O'Clock Creek Camp
Witjira National Park
Mount Dare Dalhousie Springs Rd, Witjira
Camp Area 183 km NE of Oodnadatta or 58 km S
of Mt Dare Hotel. Turn N 18 km from Oodnadatta,
91 km to Hamilton HS then turn NE 71 km to
Dalhousie. Turn W 3 km. Dirt road. 21 day limit
08 8648 5328   HEMA 139 C11   26 27 34 S   135 24 41 E

418 Mount Dare Hotel
Mount Dare Rd, Mount Dare
Camp Area 75 km SE of Finke or 70 km
NW of Dalhousie Springs. BYO firewood
08 8670 7835   HEMA 139 B10   26 04 10 S   135 14 52 E
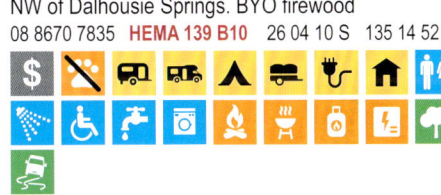

419 Dalhousie Springs Camp
Witjira National Park
Dalhousie
Camp Area 183 km NE of Oodnadatta or 68 km S
of Mt Dare Hotel. Turn N 18 km from Oodnadatta,
91 km to Hamilton HS then turn NE 71 km to
Dalhousie. Turn E 3 km. Dirt road. 21 day limit
08 8648 5328   HEMA 139 C11   26 25 23 S   135 30 13 E

420 Purni Bore
Witjira National Park
Spring Creek Tr, Dalhousie
Camp Area 248 km NE of Oodnadatta or 65 km E
of Dalhousie Springs. Dirt road. Desert Parks Pass
applies
08 8648 5328   HEMA 139 C12   26 17 03 S   136 05 54 E

421 Kathleen Creek
Oodnadatta Tr, Oodnadatta Area
Camp Spot 89 km NW of Oodnadatta or
129 km E of Marla. Tracks along creek
HEMA 139 E9   27 12 17 S   134 45 13 E

422 Olarinna Creek
Oodnadatta Tr, Oodnadatta Area
Camp Spot 104 km NW of Oodnadatta or
114 km E of Marla. Turn N on W side of creek, follow
track
HEMA 139 E9   27 09 48 S   134 37 09 E

Flinders Ranges National Park

423 Wilpena Pound Resort
Ikara Flinders Ranges NP
Wilpena Pound, Parachilna
Caravan Park 60 km N of Hawker. Book at Visitor
Centre or resort
08 8648 0048   HEMA 142 G4   31 31 37 S   138 36 23 E

424 Upalinna Station
Flinders Ranges Way, Wilpena
Station Stay 56 km NE of Hawker. N from
Hawker to Wilpena Pound, 6 km from Pound turnoff,
ebook
08 8648 0184   HEMA 142 F4   31 28 41 S   138 39 49 E

425 Willow Springs Station
Willow Springs Rd, Wilpena
Station Stay 21 km NE of Wilpena. Some
dirt road
08 8648 0016   HEMA 142 F5   31 26 56 S   138 45 32 E

426 Dingley Dell Campground
Ikara-Flinders Ranges NP
Flinders Ranges Way, Wilpena
Camp Area 28 km N of Wilpena. Signposted. 5 day
limit
08 8648 0049   HEMA 142 D5   31 21 19 S   138 42 20 E

427 Youngoona Campground
Ikara-Flinders Ranges NP
Brachina Gorge Rd, Wilpena
Camp Area 36 km N of Wilpena. Turn W 33 km N of
Wilpena turnoff or 29 km S of Blinman to Brachina
Gorge Geological Trail for 3 km. Dirt road. 4 sites
only. 5 day limit
08 8648 5300   HEMA 142 D4   31 19 51 S   138 39 21 E

428 Trezona Campground
Ikara-Flinders Ranges NP
Brachina Gorge Rd, Wilpena
Camp Area 45 km N of Wilpena. Turn W 33 km N
of Wilpena to Brachina Gorge Geological Trail for
6 km, then turn N. Dirt road. 5 day limit, ebook
08 8648 5300   HEMA 142 D4   31 19 51 S   138 37 42 E

429 Koolamon Campground
Ikara-Flinders Ranges NP
Aroona Valley Rd, Wilpena
Camp Area 53 km N of Wilpena. Turn W 33 km N of
Wilpena turnoff or 29 km S of Blinman to Brachina
Geological Trail for 10 km. Then turn N to Aroona
Valley Rd 4.6 km. Dirt road. 5 day limit
08 8648 5300   HEMA 142 D3   31 17 32 S   138 35 08 E

430 Aroona Ruins Campground

Ikara-Flinders Ranges NP
Aroona Valley Rd, Blinman
Camp Area 54 km N of Wilpena. Turn W 33 km N of Wilpena turnoff or 29 km S of Blinman to Brachina Geological Trail for 10 km. Then turn N to Aroona Valley Rd for 6 km. Dirt road. 5 day limit
08 8648 5300 HEMA 142 C3 31 16 45 S 138 34 45 E

431 Cambrian Campground

Ikara-Flinders Ranges NP
Bunyeroo Rd, Wilpena
Camp Area 33 km NW of Wilpena. Turn W 5 km N of Wilpena turnoff to Bunyeroo Valley Scenic Dr. Dirt road. 5 day limit
08 8648 5300 HEMA 142 E3 31 21 26 S 138 34 57 E

4WD ONLY

432 Acraman Campground

Ikara-Flinders Ranges NP
Bunyeroo Valley Scenic Dr, Wilpena
Camp Area 28 km NW of Wilpena. Turn W 5 km N of Wilpena turnoff to Bunyeroo Valley Scenic Dr. Dirt road. 4 sites only. Not suitable for caravans. 5 day limit
08 8648 5300 HEMA 142 E3 31 24 35 S 138 33 42 E

433 Brachina East Campground

Ikara-Flinders Ranges NP
Brachina Gorge Rd, Wilpena
Camp Area 38 km NW of Wilpena. Turn W 5 km N of Wilpena turnoff to Bunyeroo Valley Scenic Dr. Then turn W at T-intersection of Brachina Gorge Rd for 1 km. Dirt road. 5 day limit
08 8648 5300 HEMA 142 D3 31 20 01 S 138 34 46 E

434 Teamsters Campground

Ikara-Flinders Ranges NP
Brachina Gorge Rd, Wilpena
Camp Area 42 km NW of Wilpena. Turn W 5 km N of Wilpena turnoff to Bunyeroo Valley Scenic Dr. Then turn W at T-intersection of Brachina Gorge Rd for 4.5 km. Dirt road. 5 day limit
08 8648 5300 HEMA 142 D3 31 20 18 S 138 32 59 E

435 Alpana Station

Wilpena Rd, Blinman
Station Stay 55 km N of Wilpena Pound or 5 km S of Blinman. Sealed road from Wilpena Pound. Fee for ensuite
08 8648 4626 HEMA 142 A5 31 08 25 S 138 41 04 E

ENS SITE

436 Angorichina Station

Narinna Rd, Blinman
Station Stay 9 km E of Blinman turn E approx 2.2 km S of Blinman into N Flinders Rd. Pre-book
08 8648 4863 HEMA 142 A5 31 05 42 S 138 44 25 E

437 North Blinman Hotel

1 Mine Rd, Blinman
Pub Stay 59 km N of Wilpena or 32 km E of Parachilna. Dirt road from Parachilna
08 8648 4867 HEMA 142 A5 31 05 37 S 138 40 40 E

438 Moolooloo Station

636 Moolooloo Rd, Blinman
Station Stay 21 km NW or 30 km NE of Parachilna along Glass Gorge Rd. Variety of sites, SCV rates. Pre-book
08 8648 4861 HEMA 128 A7 30 59 24 S 138 34 42 E

4WD ONLY

439 Angorichina Tourist Village

Parachilna Gorge Rd, Angorichina Village
Caravan Park 17 km E of Parachilna or 16 km W of Blinman
08 8648 4842 HEMA 142 A3 31 07 35 S 138 33 39 E

BIG RIG

440 Parachilna Gorge

Parachilna Gorge Rd, Parachilna
Camp Area 10 km E of Parachilna. Various sites on riverbank
HEMA 142 A3 31 08 06 S 138 31 48 E

Port Augusta to Kulgera

Stuart Highway

441 North Tent Hill Rest Area

A87
Stuart Hwy, Tent Hill
Rest Area 35 km NW of Port Augusta or 136 km SE of Pimba
1300 872 677 HEMA 128 E4 32 14 30 S 137 32 45 E

BIG RIG

442 Ranges View Rest Area

A87
Stuart Hwy, Kootaberra
Rest Area 62 km NW of Port Augusta or 108 km SE of Pimba
1300 872 677 HEMA 128 E4 32 02 04 S 137 26 41 E

BIG RIG

443 Bookaloo Rest Area

A87
Stuart Hwy, Bookaloo
Rest Area 79 km NW of Port Augusta or 91 km SE of Pimba
1300 872 677 HEMA 128 D4 31 52 31 S 137 20 52 E

BIG RIG

444 Maslin Rest Area

A87
Stuart Hwy, Bookaloo
Rest Area 94 km NW of Port Augusta or 76 km SE of Pimba
1300 872 677 HEMA 128 D4 31 46 25 S 137 17 23 E

BIG RIG

445 Monalena Lagoon Rest Area

A87
Stuart Hwy, Oakden Hills
Rest Area 102 km NW of Port Augusta or 68 km SE of Pimba
1300 872 677 HEMA 128 D3 31 43 06 S 137 13 47 E

BIG RIG

446 Island Lagoon Lookout East

A87
Stuart Hwy, Pimba
Rest Area 153 km NW of Port Augusta or 17 km SE of Pimba
HEMA 128 B3 31 22 45 S 136 55 24 E

BIG RIG

447 Pimba Community Camp

A87
Olympic Dam Hwy, Pimba
Rest Area 480 km N of Adelaide next to Spuds Roadhouse. Coins for hot showers
08 8673 7473 HEMA 128 B2 31 15 23 S 136 48 16 E

BIG RIG

448 Roxby Downs South

Olympic Way, Roxby Downs
Parking Area 2 km S of Roxby Downs
HEMA 130 J2 30 34 30 S 136 53 38 E

48 BIG RIG

449 Champagne Corner

Andamooka Rd, Andamooka
Camp Area 64 km N of Woomera on B97 to Roxby Downs, E to Andamooka Rd
HEMA 130 J3 30 33 02 S 136 55 21 E

BIG RIG

450 Roxby Downs

B97
Roxby Downs-Andamooka Rd, Roxby Downs
Camp Spot 5 km E of Roxby Downs & 1.8 km E of Roxby Downs/Andamooka turnoff. Large open bush area with many tracks
HEMA 130 J3 30 32 50 S 136 56 24 E

BIG RIG

451 Andamooka Caravan & Camping Ground
Cnr Water Rd & Opan Ck Rd, Andamooka Camp Area. Honesty box
0477 184 485 HEMA 130 J3 30 27 11 S 137 09 39 E

452 Island Lagoon Lookout West
Stuart Hwy, Pimba
Rest Area 19 km W of Pimba. Northbound
1300 872 677 HEMA 137 G13 31 15 52 S 136 35 58 E

453 Arcoona Bush Camp
Vulkathunha-Gammon Ranges NP
Arcoona
Rest Area 24 km W of Pimba. 5 day limit
08 8648 5300 HEMA 131 J8 31 14 49 S 136 32 44 E

454 Lake Hart Lookout
Stuart Hwy, Wirraminna
Rest Area 42 km W of Pimba or 71 km SE of Glendambo, camp in designated area only
HEMA 137 G13 31 14 01 S 136 24 17 E

455 Glendambo South Rest Area
Stuart Hwy, Glendambo
Rest Area 89 km W of Pimba or 24 km SE of Glendambo
HEMA 137 F12 31 07 11 S 135 55 39 E

456 Glendambo Outback Resort
Stuart Hwy, Glendambo
Caravan Park E of Hwy, behind pub and roadhouse
08 8672 1030 HEMA 137 F11 30 58 10 S 135 45 01 E

457 Glendambo North
Stuart Hwy, Glendambo
Parking Area 8 km N of Glendambo on Stuart Hwy
HEMA 137 F11 30 54 57 S 135 42 00 E

458 Lake Site 1
Stuart Hwy, Glendambo
Parking Area 15 km N of Glendambo
HEMA 137 F11 30 52 45 S 135 38 30 E

459 Kingoonya Camp
Via Tarcoola Rd, Kingoonya
Camp Area 43 km W of Glendambo. 300 m from hotel on the W side
HEMA 137 F10 30 54 42 S 135 18 51 E

460 Kingoonya Caravan Park
27 Harvey St, Kingoonya
Caravan Park behind the hotel. Call on arrival
0409 401 715 HEMA 137 F10 30 54 52 S 135 19 01 E

461 Mulga Well Rest Area
Stuart Hwy, Glendambo
Rest Area 27 km N of Glendambo or 225 km S of Coober Pedy
HEMA 137 F11 30 48 36 S 135 32 38 E

462 Mulga Well North Rest Area
Stuart Hwy, Glendambo Area
Rest Area 63 km N of Glendambo or 189 km S of Coober Pedy
HEMA 137 E10 30 32 04 S 135 21 33 E

463 Bon Bon Rest Area
Stuart Hwy, Kingooya
Rest Area 84 km N of Glendambo or 168 km S of Coober Pedy. Emergency phone
1300 872 677 HEMA 137 D10 30 21 20 S 135 19 44 E

464 The Twins Rest Area
Stuart Hwy, Glendambo Area
Rest Area 124 km N of Glendambo or 128 km S of Coober Pedy
HEMA 137 C10 30 01 41 S 135 11 43 E

465 Ingomar Rest Area
Stuart Hwy, Ingomar
Rest Area 161 km N of Glendambo or 91 km S of Coober Pedy. Emergency phone
1300 872 677 HEMA 137 C10 29 42 44 S 135 07 39 E

466 Ingomar North Rest Area
Stuart Hwy, Ingomar
Rest Area 207 km N of Glendambo or 47 km S of Coober Pedy
HEMA 137 B10 29 21 00 S 134 59 12 E

467 Hutchison Memorial
Stuart Hwy, Coober Pedy
Parking Area 240 km N of Glendambo or 12 km S of Coober Pedy
HEMA 137 A9 29 04 30 S 134 51 12 E

468 William Creek Road
William Ck Rd, Coober Pedy
Parking Area 10 km E of Coober Pedy. Dirt road
HEMA 137 A9 29 02 03 S 134 49 20 E

469 Old Timers Mine
Crowders Gully Rd, Coober Pedy
Camp Area 2 km N of Stuart Hwy via Hutchison St
08 8672 5555 HEMA 139 K9 29 00 32 S 134 45 34 E

470 Pootnoura Rest Area
Stuart Hwy, Pootnoura
Rest Area 75 km N of Coober Pedy or 75 km S of Cadney Roadhouse. Emergency phone
HEMA 139 J8 28 33 17 S 134 15 19 E

471 Evelyn Downs Rest Area
Stuart Hwy, Pootnoura
Rest Area 90 km N of Coober Pedy or 60 km S of Cadney Roadhouse
HEMA 139 H8 28 25 32 S 134 11 07 E

472 Pootnoura Bush Site
Stuart Hwy, Pootnoura
Parking Area 107 km N Coober Pedy or 43 km S of Cadney Roadhouse
HEMA 139 H8 28 17 33 S 134 09 28 E

473 Matheson Bore
Stuart Hwy, Pootnoura
Parking Area 110 km N of Coober Pedy or 40 km S of Cadney Roadhouse
HEMA 139 H8 28 15 29 S 134 09 04 E

474 Cadney Park Homestead
Lot 69 Stuart Hwy, Wintinna
Pub Stay & Caravan Park at Cadney Roadhouse. 150 km N of Coober Pedy
08 8670 7994 HEMA 138 G7 27 54 18 S 134 03 24 E

SOUTH AUSTRALIA

475 Marla South Rest Area
Stuart Hwy, Marla Area
Rest Area 46 km NW of Cadney
Roadhouse or 35 km SE of Marla
A87
HEMA 138 F7   27 33 21 S   133 49 13 E

476 Marla Travellers Rest
Stuart Hwy, Marla
Caravan Park at roadhouse, hotel & motel
A87
08 8670 7001   HEMA 138 E6   27 18 15 S   133 37 20 E

477 Tarcoonyinna Rest Area
Stuart Hwy, Indulkana
Rest Area 53 km N of Marla or 125 km S of
Kulgera
A87
HEMA 138 D6   26 53 47 S   133 22 51 E

478 Agnes Creek Rest Area
Stuart Hwy, Marla Area
Rest Area 85 km N of Marla or 93 km S of
Kulgera
A87
HEMA 138 D6   26 38 14 S   133 16 45 E

479 The Marryat Rest Area
Stuart Hwy, Indulkana
Rest Area 120 km N of Marla, 39 km S of
NT Border or 58 km S of Kulgera. Emergency phone
A87
HEMA 138 C6   26 20 29 S   133 12 04 E

480 Marryat Creek North
Stuart Hwy, Marla Area
Rest Area 128 km N of Marla or 31 km S of
NT Border. 52 km S of Kulgera
A87
HEMA 138 C5   26 16 42 S   133 11 20 E

Eyre Peninsula
Lincoln and Flinders Highways

481 Half Way Rest Area
Lincoln Hwy, Whyalla
Rest Area 40 km S of Port Augusta or
34 km N of Whyalla. Both sides of Hwy
B100
1300 872 677   HEMA 128 G4   32 43 33 S   137 30 38 E

482 Lincoln Highway Rest Area
Lincoln Hwy, Cultana
Rest Area 72 km S of Pt Augusta, on
Lincoln Hwy 2.5 km N of Cultana. Share wth trucks
HEMA 128 H4   32 54 56 S   137 33 59 E

---

483 Point Lowly
Lighthouse Dr, Point Lowly
Camp Area 35 km NE of Whyalla. E off
B100, 65 km SW of Port Augusta or 8 km N of
Whyalla to Point Lowly Rd. Adjacent to toilet block,
near boat ramp. Dump point 500 m N campsite.
14 day limit. Display ticket
08 8645 7900   HEMA 128 H5   32 59 34 S   137 46 51 E

484 Shingles Beach Ridges
Fitzgerald Bay Rd, Whyalla
Camp Area at Fitzgerald Bay. E off B100 to
Port Bonython Rd, 65 km SW of Port Augusta or 8 km
N of Whyalla, N after 16 km to the end of bitumen.
Turn L, then 2 km dirt road. Site on R. Signposted
08 8645 7900   HEMA 128 H5   32 55 17 S   137 44 57 E

485 Fitzgerald Bay Bush Camp
Fitzgerald Bay Rd, Whyalla
Camp Area at Fitzgerald Bay. E off B100
to Port Bonython Rd, 65 km SW of Port Augusta
or 8 km N of Whyalla, N after 16 km to the end of
bitumen. Turn L, then 3.7 km dirt road. Track on R.
Signposted. Limited space, small vehicles only
08 8645 7900   HEMA 128 H5   32 54 25 S   137 45 18 E

486 Stuart Park
215 Cartledge Ave, Whyalla
Camp Area at Weeroona Bay Football Club.
8 km W of PO. Via McDouall Stuart Ave. Caretaker
collects fee. 7 day limit
0458 600 036   HEMA 128 H4   33 01 54 S   137 30 50 E

487 Hancocks Shaft Rest Area
Lincoln Hwy, Middleback Range
Rest Area 49 km S of Whyalla or 57 km N
of Cowell
B100
1300 872 677   HEMA 128 J3   33 15 55 S   137 12 34 E

488 Minbrie Rest Area
Lincoln Hwy, Mitchellville
Rest Area 87 km S of Whyalla or 14 km N
of Cowell
HEMA 128 K3   33 32 46 S   137 01 03 E

489 Cowell RV Park
Beach Rd, Cowell
Camp Area at S end of town. Via Wellington
Rd. 14 day limit. Display permit
08 8629 2019   HEMA 124 A2   33 41 40 S   136 55 20 E

---

490 Cleve Hills Lookout
Yeldulknie Conservation Park
426 Scenic Rd, Cleve
Camp Area 35 km W of Cowell. N off Birdseye Hwy
to Wangaraleednie Rd, then NW
08 8628 2004   HEMA 124 A1   33 39 25 S   136 37 34 E

491 Yeldulknie Weir
Lot 1 Yeldulknie Weir Road, Cleve
Picnic Area 37 km W of Cowell or 5 km E of
Cleve. Via Cowell Rd then N to Yeldulknie Rd
08 8628 2004   HEMA 124 A1   33 41 35 S   136 32 39 E

492 Birdseye Roadhouse
1 Cowell Rd, Cleve
Caravan Park E of town, S of Hwy
08 8628 2019   HEMA 124 B1   33 42 08 S   136 29 59 E

493 Cleve Hotel
32 Fourth St, Cleve
Parking Area. Free for patrons. Register at
bar on arrival
08 8628 2011   HEMA 124 B1   33 42 12 S   136 29 37 E

494 Cleve Showgrounds
Cnr Rudall Rd & West Tce, Cleve
Camp Area W side of town, N of Hwy.
Honesty box
0438 137 774   HEMA 124 A1   33 42 03 S   136 29 26 E

495 Rudall West Rest Area
Birdseye Hwy, Rudall
Rest Area 12 km W of Rudall or 40 km E of
Lock. S side of Hwy
HEMA 134 F7   33 40 04 S   136 09 09 E

496 Lock Caravan Park
South Tce, Lock
Caravan Park near town centre. Pay at PO
weekdays, caretaker on weekends
B90
0417 896 991   HEMA 134 E6   33 34 10 S   135 45 24 E

497 Lock North Rest Area
Tod Hwy, Lock Area
Rest Area 22 km NW of Lock or 21 km SE
of Warramboo
HEMA 134 E5   33 24 41 S   135 38 44 E

498 Peachna Rest Area

Murdinga
Rest Area 26 km S of Lock or 55 km N of Cummins

HEMA 134 F6   33 46 54 S   135 42 47 E

499 Tooligie Rest Area

Tod Hwy, Tooligie
Rest Area 1 km N of Tooligie Station or 34 km S of Lock

HEMA 134 F6   33 50 55 S   135 42 11 E

500 Port Gibbon Foreshore

Beach Rd, Port Gibbon
Rest Area. Access from B100 at Port Gibbon sign via Igloo Rd. 6 km dirt road. Caretaker issues permit on site. 14 day limit
08 8629 2019   HEMA 124 B2   33 48 07 S   136 48 06 E

501 Cliff Top Camp

Beach Rd, Port Gibbon
Camp Area 23 km S of Cowell, E of Port Gibbon

HEMA 124 B2   33 48 02 S   136 48 41 E

502 The Arno Bay Hotel

Cnr Creek Rd & Tel El Kebir Tce, Arno Bay
Camp Area at Foreshore end of Arno Bay, behind hotel. Register at bar
08 8628 0001   HEMA 124 B1   33 54 59 S   136 34 22 E

503 Carrow Wells

North Coast Rd, Port Neill
Camp Spot 4 km S of Port Neill, via Coast Rd. Alternatively turn E 25 km NE of Tumby Bay for 5 km, then NE for 10 km. Dirt road

HEMA 134 G7   34 08 39 S   136 20 01 E

504 Cowleys Beach

Kiandra Rd, Port Neill
Camp Area 11 km S of Port Neill via Coastal Rd. Turn E into Kiandra Rd or turn E 22 km NE of Tumby Bay along Kiandra Rd for 6 km. 7 day limit

HEMA 134 G7   34 11 50 S   136 17 56 E

505 Lipson Cove

Lipson Cove Rd, Port Neill
Camp Area 13 km NE of Lipson. At 52 km SW of Arno Bay or 18 km NE of Tumby Bay, turn E. 8 km dirt road. Honesty box. 14 day limit
08 8688 2101   HEMA 134 G7   34 15 43 S   136 15 38 E

506 Lipson Rest Area

Butler Centre Rd, Lipson
Rest Area 100 km SW of Cowell on Lincoln Hwy NE of Lipson

HEMA 134 G7   34 16 46 S   136 10 04 E

507 Tumby Bay Self Contained RV Park

Lipson Rd, Tumby Bay
Parking Area 1 km N of Tumby Bay. Opposite airport turnoff & golf course. 10 day limit. Honesty box
08 8688 2087   HEMA 134 H6   34 21 31 S   136 06 03 E

508 Tumby Bay CWA & Caravan Park

3 The Esplanade, Tumby Bay
Caravan Park N side of town. Limited sites
0438 031 476   HEMA 134 H6   34 22 29 S   136 06 13 E

509 Yallunda Flat Showgrounds

Yallunda Flat Rd, Yallunda Flat
Camp Area between Tumby Bay & Cummins on Bratten Way. Honesty box
08 8688 5004   HEMA 134 H6   34 20 51 S   135 52 49 E

510 Cummins Community Caravan Park

Roe St, Cummins
Caravan Park 2 km S of PO. Check in at Cummins Takeaway in Bruce Tce
08 8676 2011   HEMA 134 G6   34 16 15 S   135 43 23 E

511 Second Creek Beach

Trinity Haven Rd, Tumby Bay
Camp Area 9 km S from Tumby Bay on Thuruna Rd then SE. Honesty box
08 8688 2101   HEMA 134 H6   34 25 31 S   136 06 36 E

512 Red Cliff Beach

Trinity Haven Rd, Tumby Bay
Camp Area 13 km S of Tumby Bay. E off Lincoln Hwy to end of White River Rd, then S

HEMA 134 H6   34 27 16 S   136 06 53 E

513 Redcliff Church of Christ Campsite

789 Trinity Haven Rd, Tumby Bay
Camp Area 15 km S of Tumby Bay. E off Lincoln Hwy to White River Rd, to end S to camp, ebook
0429 788 008   HEMA 134 H6   34 27 56 S   136 07 05 E

514 Louth Bay Campground

Louth Tce, Louth Bay
Camp Area 27 km SW of Tumby Bay. Turn E 25 km SW of Tumby Bay or 21 km N of Port Lincoln for 2 km. First L past golf club. 5 sites, 14 day limit. Honesty box
08 8676 0400   HEMA 134 H6   34 32 30 S   135 55 47 E

515 Port Lincoln Lions Hostel

1055 Lincoln Hwy, North Shields
Camp Area S of airport. Pre-book
0499 039 458   HEMA 134 H6   34 37 29 S   135 51 45 E

516 Axel Stenross Boat Ramp

97 Lincoln Hwy, Port Lincoln
Parking Area N end of town. Upper car park only, limited turning space. Permit applies
1300 788 378   HEMA 134 J6   34 42 14 S   135 51 14 E

517 John Martin Caravan Repairs

165 New West Rd, Port Lincoln
Parking Area W side of town
0418 837 849   HEMA 134 J6   34 43 55 S   135 50 04 E

518 Billy Lights Point Boat Ramp

St Andrews Dr, Port Lincoln
Parking Area S side of town. Via Ravendale Rd & Marina Dr. Car park area adjacent to bush and bay. Permit applies
1300 788 378   HEMA 134 J6   34 44 43 S   135 53 28 E

SOUTH AUSTRALIA

519 Horse Rock Campground
Lincoln National Park
Lincoln Tr, Port Lincoln Area
Camp Area 9 km NE of park entrance on access road. Dirt road. Small sites. 5 day limit, ebook
08 8688 3111   HEMA 134 J6   34 48 28 S   135 51 44 E

520 Taylors Landing Camp
Lincoln National Park
Taylors Landing Rd, Port Lincoln Area
Camp Area 24 km SE of park entrance on access road. Dirt road. 5 day limit, ebook
08 8688 3111   HEMA 134 J6   34 51 16 S   135 57 32 E

521 Surfleet Cove Campground
Lincoln National Park
Surfleet Cove Rd, Port Lincoln Area
Camp Area 22 km NE of park entrance on wide bitumen access road. 5 day limit, ebook
08 8688 3111   HEMA 134 J6   34 45 57 S   135 57 25 E

522 Fishermans Point Camp
Lincoln National Park
Fishermans Point Tr, Port Lincoln Area
Camp Area 24 km NE of park entrance on access road. Dirt road. 5 day limit, ebook
08 8688 3111   HEMA 134 J6   34 45 25 S   135 59 09 E

523 September Beach Camp
Lincoln National Park
via Donington Rd, Port Lincoln Area
Camp Area 28 km NE of park entrance on access road. Dirt road. Pay at park entry. 5 day limit
08 8688 3111   HEMA 134 J6   34 44 02 S   135 59 47 E

524 Engine Point Campground
Lincoln National Park
Engine Point Tr, Port Lincoln Area
Camp Area 25 km NE of park entrance on access road. Pay at park entry. 5 day limit
08 8688 3111   HEMA 134 J6   34 44 21 S   135 59 20 E

525 Mikkira Station
261 Mikkira Lane, Port Lincoln Area
Station Stay 25 km SW of Port Lincoln via Fishery Bay Rd. Dirt road. Key, book & permit from Visit Port Lincoln Accommodation. May - Sept
0419 302 300   HEMA 134 J5   34 50 18 S   135 40 51 E

526 Fishery Bay
Fishery Bay Rd, Port Lincoln Area
Parking Area 31 km SW of Port Lincoln. Via Proper Bay Rd. 12 km dirt road. Stay in car park area
0419 302 300   HEMA 134 J5   34 54 40 S   135 40 44 E

527 Whalers Way
Fishery Bay Rd, Sleaford
Camp Area 32 km S of Port Lincoln W to Fishery Bay Rd. Day permit applies and includes first night stay
1300 788 378   HEMA 134 J5   34 55 10 S   135 40 59 E

528 Memorial Rest Area
Flinders Hwy, Fountain
Rest Area 32 km NW of Port Lincoln, near Coffin Bay Rd
HEMA 134 H5   34 35 29 S   135 36 01 E

529 Yangie Bay Campground
Coffin Bay National Park
Yangie Trail, Coffin Bay
Camp Area 19 km W of Coffin Bay. Some dirt road. 5 day limit, ebook
08 8688 3111   HEMA 134 J5   34 38 24 S   135 21 38 E

530 Big Yangie Campground
Coffin Bay National Park
Big Yangie Track, Coffin Bay
Camp Area 19 km W of Coffin Bay. 5 day limit, ebook
08 8688 3111   HEMA 134 J5   34 37 43 S   135 22 28 E

531 Mount Dutton Bay Woolshed
Woolshed Dr, Wangary
Camp Area 5 km W of Wangary. Fee for showers
08 8685 4031   HEMA 134 H5   34 31 53 S   135 25 58 E

532 Ricky Bates Reserve
Dolphin Dr, Mount Dutton Bay
Parking Area 2 km W of Mount Dutton Bay. Limited space, small vehicles only
HEMA 134 H5   34 32 04 S   135 25 12 E

533 Marble Range Community & Sports Centre
Flinders Hwy, Wangary
Camp Area near intersection of Morgan Ln
08 8685 4050   HEMA 134 H5   34 32 21 S   135 28 42 E

534 Shelly Beach Lodge
148 Shelly Beach Rd, Mount Dutton Bay
Camp Area 6 km NW of Wangary via Farm Beach Rd, then W
0459 254 192   HEMA 134 H5   34 31 09 S   135 24 56 E

535 Farm Beach Campground
Hull Rd, Farm Beach
Camp Area 10 km NW of Wangary, via Farm Beach Rd. Payment box on site. Cold showers
08 8676 0400   HEMA 134 H5   34 29 48 S   135 23 52 E

536 Nyroca Camp
223 Flinders Hwy, Wangary
Camp Area & Function Centre 9 km N of Wangary
0417 837 760   HEMA 134 H5   34 27 48 S   135 27 30 E

537 Wangary Rest Area
Flinders Hwy, Wangary
Camp Area 8 kms N of Wangary
HEMA 134 H5   34 30 41 S   135 28 14 E

538 Coles Point
Coles Point Rd, Coulta
Camp Spot at 26 km N of Wangary. Turn W 15 km N of Wangary. 10 km to coastal bush sites
HEMA 134 H5   34 22 10 S   135 21 14 E

539 Coulta Rest Area
South Tce, Coulta
Rest Area behind Fire Brigade shed. Payment in red PO box across the road
HEMA 134 H5   34 23 14 S   135 28 03 E

540 Warrow North Rest Area
Flinders Hwy, Mount Drummond
Rest Area 9 km NW of Warrow or 18 km of Mount Hope
HEMA 134 G5   34 15 57 S   135 25 21 E

541 Point Drummond Camp 1
Point Drummond Rd, Mount Hope
Camp Area 42 km NW of Coulta or 88 km SE of Elliston. Exit Flinders Hwy (B100) W for 18 km. Follow track S at lookout, camp at end
08 8676 0400   HEMA 134 G4   34 10 20 S   135 16 03 E

542 Point Drummond Camp 2
Point Drummond Rd, Mount Hope
Camp Area 42 km NW of Coulta or 88 km
SE of Elliston. Exit Flinders Hwy (B100) W for
18 km. Follow track S at lookout, camp at end
08 8676 0400   HEMA 134 G4   34 10 09 S   135 16 23 E

543 Mount Hope Rest Area
Flinders Hwy, Mount Hope
Rest Area between Kiana & Coast Rds
HEMA 134 G5   34 06 51 S   135 21 34 E

544 Kiana Park
10002 Flinders Hwy, Kiana Area
Camp Area S of Lake Hamilton. GPS at
entrance, 2.4 km to campsite. Limited powered sites
0427 876 049   HEMA 134 G5   34 03 30 S   135 18 10 E

545 Sheringa South Rest Area
Flinders Hwy, Sheringa
Rest Area 25 km N of Mount Hope or 8 km
S of Sheringa
HEMA 134 F4   33 54 40 S   135 15 50 E

546 Sheringa Beach
Sheringa Beach Rd, Sheringa
Camp Area 8 km W of Sheringa. Turn W
off B100, 40 km SE of Elliston or 33 km N of Mount
Hope. Dirt road. Permits from store. Cold shower
08 8687 9200   HEMA 134 F4   33 52 19 S   135 10 10 E

547 Dry Stone Walling Rest Area
Flinders Hwy, Sheringa
Rest Area 16 km NW of Sheringa or 24 km
SE of Elliston
HEMA 134 F4   33 45 33 S   135 06 05 E

548 Elliston Golf Club
Beach Tce, Elliston
Camp Area S of town. Permit & pay at Info
Centre on Memorial Dr
08 8687 9200   HEMA 134 F4   33 39 04 S   134 53 36 E

549 Walkers Rocks Campground
Lake Newland Conservation Park
Walkers Rocks Rd, Elliston
Camp Area 10 km N of Elliston or 117 km SE of
Streaky Bay. Turn W off B100. Honesty box on site.
Cold showers
08 8687 9200   HEMA 134 E4   33 33 34 S   134 51 21 E

550 Coodlie Park
Flinders Hwy, Venus Bay
Camp Area in Coodlie Park 49 km N of
Elliston or 16 km S of Port Kenny. Signposted turn
off to W. Call at office for site directions
08 8687 0411   HEMA 134 E3   33 16 20 S   134 47 17 E

551 Charlies Camp
Flinders Hwy, Venus Bay
Camp Area 291 km N of Port Lincoln, or
72 km S of Streaky Bay, S of Venus Bay Rd
HEMA 134 E3   33 14 43 S   134 44 53 E

552 Port Kenny Rest Area
Flinders Hwy, Venus Bay
Rest Area 9 km N of Venus Bay
HEMA 134 D3   33 12 11 S   134 43 23 E

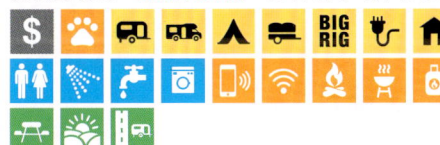

553 Port Kenny Caravan Park
Flinders Hwy, Port Kenny
Caravan Park on main road
08 8625 5076   HEMA 134 D3   33 10 12 S   134 41 32 E

554 Old Highway Rest Area
Flinders Hwy, Port Kenny
Rest Area 58 km SE of Streaky Bay on
Flinders Hwy, NW of Port Kenny
HEMA 134 D3   33 08 58 S   134 39 10 E

555 Murphys Haystacks
Benbarber Rd, Mortana
Parking Area 22 km NW of Port Kenny. Turn
W off B100 or 39 km SE of Streaky Bay for 2 km
HEMA 134 D3   33 01 09 S   134 29 28 E

556 Streaky Bay South Rest Area
Flinders Hwy, Maryvale
Camp Area 28 km SE of Streaky Bay &
34 km N of Port Kenny on Flinders Hwy
HEMA 134 D3   32 55 57 S   134 27 19 E

557 Baird Bay
23 Baird Bay Rd, Baird Bay
Camp Area 48 km NW of Port Kenny
or 50 km S of Streaky Bay, via Calca Rd. Small
vehicles only, limited space. Dirt road. Payment box.
7 day limit
08 8626 7033   HEMA 134 D2   33 08 38 S   134 21 47 E

558 Eyres Waterhole
Flinders Hwy, Streaky Bay
Rest Area 59 km NW of Port Kenny or 5 km
SE of Streaky Bay
HEMA 134 C2   32 49 05 S   134 14 46 E

559 Streaky Bay RV Stop
Alec Baldock Dr, Streaky Bay
Parking Area next to town oval. Honesty
box. Display permit
08 8626 7033   HEMA 134 C2   32 48 02 S   134 11 58 E

560 Speeds Point Campground
Yanerbie Rd, Streaky Bay
Camp Area 16 km S of Streaky Bay. Small
vehicles only. Dirt road. Honesty box. Display permit
08 8626 7033   HEMA 134 D2   32 55 51 S   134 07 45 E

561 Rubys Beach
Westall Way Loop, Westall
Camp Area 22 km S from Streaky Bay on
Sceale Bay Rd, then W
HEMA 134 D2   32 55 31 S   134 05 30 E

562 Tractor Beach
Westall Way Loop, Streaky Bay
Camp Area 17 km SW of Streaky Bay. Dirt
road. Honesty box. Display permit
08 8626 7033   HEMA 134 C2   32 52 13 S   134 06 47 E

563 Perlubie Beach
Via Wharf Dr, Streaky Bay
Camp Area 21 km N of Streaky Bay or
49 km SE of Smoky Bay via Flinders Hwy & The
Grub Rd. Camp only on beach. Beware tide & soft
sand. Honesty box
08 8626 7033   HEMA 134 C2   32 39 40 S   134 17 41 E

SOUTH AUSTRALIA

564 Haslam Rest Area
Flinders Hwy, Haslam
Rest Area 3 km S of Haslam Hwy exit,
39 km N of Streaky Bay or 31 km SE of Smoky Bay
HEMA 134 B2   32 30 45 S   134 14 25 E

565 Haslam RV Camping
Cnr Main St & South Tce, Haslam
Camp Area on the foreshore. Honesty box
08 8626 7033   HEMA 134 B2   32 30 32 S   134 12 50 E

566 Acraman Creek
Acraman Creek Conservation Park
Acramans Ck Rd, Haslam
Camp Area 23 km SE of Smoky Bay. Turn W 12 km
NW of Haslam turnoff or 17 km SE of Smoky Bay
for 6 km of dirt road. Small vehicles only. Permit
applies. 5 day limit
08 8625 3144   HEMA 134 B2   32 27 15 S   134 04 12 E

567 Smoky Road Rest Area
Flinders Hwy, Smoky Bay
Rest Area 2.5 km SE of the Smoky Bay turn off
HEMA 134 B2   32 23 25 S   133 59 26 E

568 Point Brown Campground
Point Brown Rd, Smoky Bay
Camp Spot 30 km S Smoky Bay via
Flinders Hwy, 23 km dirt road. No swimming
HEMA 134 B1   32 31 53 S   133 51 35 E

569 Laura Bay Campground
Laura Bay Conservation Park
Flinders Hwy, Laura Bay
Camp Spot 19 km NW of Smoky Bay or 21 km SE of
Ceduna. 3 km dirt road. Limited space. 5 day limit
08 8625 3144   HEMA 134 B1   32 14 32 S   133 49 47 E

570 Wittelbee Campground
Wittelbee Conservation Park
Decres Bay Rd, Laura Bay
Camp Area 10 km SE of Ceduna. Signposted. 5 day
limit
08 8625 3144   HEMA 134 B1   32 12 22 S   133 44 17 E

Port Augusta to Eucla
Eyre Highway

571 Port Augusta Motorhome Park
58 Old Power Station Rd, Port Augusta
Camp Spot behind the Port Augusta Sports
& Recreation facility, 4 km E of town. 7 day limit
08 8642 5282   HEMA 128 F5   32 30 40 S   137 47 09 E

572 Lincoln/Eyre Highway Junction
Eyre Hwy, Port Augusta
Rest Area 25 km SW of Port Augusta or
42 km E of Iron Knob
HEMA 128 G4   32 36 58 S   137 34 26 E

573 Iron Knob Rest Area
Iron Knob Rd, Iron Knob
Rest Area 1 km W of Iron Knob, at Hwy A1 Jcn
HEMA 128 G3   32 43 15 S   137 08 54 E

574 Knobbies Camping &
Caravan Area
Moroney St, Iron Knob
Camp Area at Iron Knob. Donation box near dump
point. 5 day limit
HEMA 128 G3   32 43 56 S   137 09 02 E

575 Mount Ive Station
373 Mount Ive Rd, Mount Ive
Station Stay 128 km W of Iron Knob via
Kingoonya - Iron Knob Rd
08 8648 1817   HEMA 134 B6   32 26 18 S   136 04 05 E

576 Waltumba Camping Area
Lake Gairdner National Park
Moonaree Station Rd, Mount Ive
Camp Area 30 km NW of N Mt Ive Station. Private
access road, book & gate key via Mt Ive Station
08 8648 1817   HEMA 134 A6   32 07 20 S   135 53 46 E

577 Iron Knob West Park Area
Eyre Hwy, Iron Knob Area
Parking Area 37 km SW of Iron Knob or
50 km NE of Kimba
1300 872 677   HEMA 128 H2   32 57 50 S   136 53 16 E

---

578 Kimba East Parking Area
Eyre Hwy, Kimba
Parking Area 52 km SW of Iron Knob or
35 km E of Kimba
HEMA 128 H2   33 02 56 S   136 46 09 E

579 Carradoo Tanks
Eyre Hwy, Barna
Camp Area 128 km S of Port Augusta on
Eyre Hwy, E of Sectus Tanks Rd
HEMA 128 H2   33 04 51 S   136 42 59 E

580 The Gums
Eyre Hwy & South Tce, Kimba
Rest Area at Kimba opposite IGA
08 8627 2026   HEMA 128 J1   33 08 31 S   136 25 11 E

581 Kimba Recreation Reserve
North Tce, Kimba
Camp Area at Buckleboo Rd, extension of
North Tce. Entry through Kimba Pioneer Memorial
archway. Coin shower. 5 night limit
08 8627 2026   HEMA 128 J1   33 08 04 S   136 24 54 E

582 Carappee Hill Campground
Carappee Hill Conservation Park
Carapee Hill Rd, Darke Peak
Camp Area 8 km NE of Darke Peak or 42 km SW
of Kimba
08 8688 3111   HEMA 128 K1   33 25 56 S   136 16 20 E

583 Darke Peak Hotel
Cnr Howard Tce & Balumbah Kinnard Rd,
Darke Peak
Camp Spot. Patrons only. Register at bar on arrival
08 8620 7009   HEMA 134 E7   33 28 13 S   136 11 57 E

584 Koongawa East
Eyre Hwy, Koongawa
Parking Area 44 km W of Kimba or 45 km E
of Kyancutta
HEMA 134 D6   33 11 40 S   135 50 57 E

585 Darkes Memorial Rest Area
Eyre Hwy, Koongawa
Rest Area 55 km W of Kimba or 34 km E of
Kyancutta
HEMA 134 D6   33 09 56 S   135 53 12 E

586 Kooma View Old Farmhouse

Eyre Hwy, Koongawa
Camp Area 65 km W of Kimba or 24 km E of Kyacutta

HEMA 134 D6   33 08 58 S   135 48 37 E

587 Goyders Line Memorial

Eyre Hwy, Koongawa
Parking Area 11 km W of Koongawa or 20 km E of Kyacutta

HEMA 134 D6   33 08 50 S   135 45 24 E

588 Polkdinney Park

Eyre Hwy, Kyacutta
Parking Area next to Kyacutta general store

HEMA 134 D5   33 07 59 S   135 33 09 E

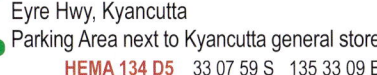

589 Wudinna Showgrounds

Naylor Tce, Wudinna
Camp Area. Pay & self register onsite

0427 802 177   HEMA 134 D5   33 02 50 S   135 27 59 E

590 Wattle Grove Rock

1661 Edmonds Rd, Wuddina
Camp Area 14 km NE of Wuddina. Via Standley Rd & Mt Wuddina Access. Mar - Oct

0473 907 094   HEMA 134 D5   32 58 26 S   135 32 47 E

591 Waganny Campground

Gawler Ranges National Park
Old Paney Scenic Route, Gawler Ranges
Camp Area 63 km NW of Widunna. Access via Old Paney Scenic Route. Signposted. 3 km S to campsite. 5 day limit. BYO firewood

08 8688 3111   HEMA 134 C5   32 42 20 S   135 32 00 E

592 Chillunie Campground

Gawler Ranges National Park
Chillunie Campground Tr, Gawler Ranges
Camp Area 70 km N of Wudinna. Via Barns Rd, Loop Track. Signposted turn off 10 km N of Paney Homestead, 3.6 km track to campsites. 5 day limit. BYO firewood

08 8688 3111   HEMA 134 C5   32 34 33 S   135 34 06 E

593 Kolay Hut Campground

Gawler Ranges National Park
Wudinna
Camp Area 69 km N of Wudinna. Via Barns Rd, Loop track. 13 km N of Paney Homestead, signposted. 5 day limit. BYO firewood

08 8688 3111   HEMA 134 C5   32 33 25 S   135 35 18 E

594 Mattera Campground

Gawler Ranges National Park
Mattera Campground Tr, Gawler Ranges
Camp Area 80 km NW of Wudinna. Via Old Paney Scenic Route, Loop & Mattera Trs. Signposted. 3 km very narrow track. 5 day limit. BYO firewood

08 8688 3111   HEMA 134 C5   32 34 00 S   135 28 22 E

595 Scrubby Peak Campground

Gawler Ranges National Park
Scrubby Campground Tr, Gawler Ranges
Camp Area 41 km N of Minnipa via Yardea Rd. Signposted turn off 8 km N of Old Paney Scenic Route intersection. 5 day limit. BYO firewood

08 8688 3111   HEMA 134 B5   32 31 42 S   135 20 00 E

596 Yandinga Campground

Gawler Ranges National Park
Yandinga Campground Tr, Gawler Ranges
Camp Area 36 km N of Minnipa via Yardea Rd. Signposted turn off 3 km N of Old Paney Scenic Route intersection. 500 m to campground. BYO firewood

08 8688 3111   HEMA 134 C5   32 33 41 S   135 19 28 E

597 Minnipa Apex Park

Cnr. Crabb Rd & Eyre Hwy, Minnipa
Rest Area opposite silos. Donation box

08 8680 2002   HEMA 134 C4   32 51 16 S   135 09 03 E

598 Tcharkuldu Rock

via Bockelberg Rd, Minnipa
Camp Area 6 km E of Minnipa. Dirt road. 7 day limit. Donation box

08 8680 2969   HEMA 134 C4   32 50 50 S   135 11 45 E

599 Pildappa Rock

via Pildappa Rd, Minnipa
Camp Area 15 km NE of Minnipa. Donation box

08 8680 2969   HEMA 134 C4   32 45 03 S   135 13 47 E

600 Poochera Parking Area

Eyre Hwy, Poochera
Parking Area 2 km W of Poochera or 45 km SE of Wirrulla

HEMA 134 C3   32 42 39 S   134 49 22 E

601 Poochera Hotel

6-8 Barnes St, Poochera
Caravan Park. Entry on Railway Tce

08 8626 3257   HEMA 134 C3   32 43 10 S   134 50 12 E

602 Yantanabie South Rest Area

Eyre Hwy, Yantanabie
Rest Area 25 km NW of Poochera or 22 km SE of Wirrulla

HEMA 134 C3   32 33 12 S   134 40 21 E

603 Pretty Point Camp - Hiltaba

Hiltaba Nature Reserve
Wirrulla-Kingoonya Rd, Poochera
Camp Area 70 km N of Poochera, fee for nature drives, may be restricted access. Pre-book. 7 day limit

08 8340 2880   HEMA 134 A4   32 10 22 S   135 08 53 E

604 Old Shearers Quarters

Hiltaba Nature Reserve
Wirrulla-Kingoonya Rd, Poochera
Camp Area 70 km north of Poochera, fee for shower and nature drives, may be restricted access. Pre-book. 7 day limit. GPS at station entry

08 8340 2880   HEMA 134 A4   32 09 29 S   135 04 36 E

605 Wirrulla Camp Rec Ground

25 Hay St, Wirrulla
Camp Area at Walker Tce, opposite town centre reserve. Pay & shower key at general store or hotel

08 8626 7033   HEMA 134 B3   32 24 16 S   134 31 57 E

606 Wirrulla West Rest Area

Eyre Hwy, Wirrulla
Rest Area 9 km W of Wirrulla or 84 km E of Ceduna

HEMA 134 B3   32 24 41 S   134 26 32 E

SOUTH AUSTRALIA

607 Old Perlubie School Site
Eyre Hwy, Wirrulla
Rest Area 13 km W of Wirrulla or 80 km E of Ceduna
HEMA 134 B2   32 24 44 S   134 24 10 E

608 Puntabie East Rest Area
Eyre Hwy, Puntabie
Rest Area 48 km W of Wirrulla or 45 km E of Ceduna
HEMA 134 B2   32 12 38 S   134 07 56 E

609 A1 Cabins & Caravan Park
41 McKenzie St, Ceduna
Caravan Park S of A1. Pre-book
08 8625 2578   HEMA 134 A1   32 07 25 S   133 40 49 E

610 Koonibba Parking Area
Eyre Hwy, Ceduna Area
Parking Area 33 km W of Ceduna or 40 km E of Penong
HEMA 136 J6   31 57 05 S   133 25 09 E

611 Watraba Parking Area
Eyre Hwy, Ceduna Area
Parking Area 51 km W of Ceduna or 25 km E of Penong
HEMA 136 J6   31 56 26 S   133 16 31 E

612 Penong Caravan Park
4 Stiggants Rd, Penong
Caravan Park 500 m N of PO
08 8625 1111   HEMA 136 J5   31 55 31 S   133 00 32 E

613 Cactus Beach Point Sinclair
Point Sinclair Rd, Penong Area
Camp Area 21 km S of Penong. Dirt road
08 8625 1036   HEMA 136 J5   32 05 19 S   132 59 00 E

614 Cohen Old School Site
Eyre Hwy, Penong Area
Parking Area 14 km W of Penong or 66 km E of Nundroo. N side of the road, 2 km E of Cohen Rest Area
HEMA 136 J5   31 52 16 S   132 53 02 E

615 Cohen Rest Area
Eyre Hwy, Penong Area
Rest Area 16 km W of Penong or 63 km E of Nundroo
HEMA 136 J5   31 51 40 S   132 51 50 E

616 Scotts Point
Fowlers Bay Conservation Park
Scotts Bay Rd, Fowlers Bay
Camp Spot 13 km W of Fowlers Bay. Via Fowlers Bay or Corrabie Rd, then S for 6.6 km. W end behind dunes, sand tracks. 5 day limit
08 8625 3144   HEMA 136 J4   32 00 15 S   132 23 05 E

617 Mexican Hat Campground
Fowlers Bay Conservation Park
Via Coorabie Rd, Fowlers Bay
Camp Spot on Mexican Hat Rd, W of Fowlers Bay. 5 day limit, ebook
08 8625 3144   HEMA 136 J3   32 00 57 S   132 20 23 E

618 Coorabie Farm
Coorabie Rd, Coorabie
Farm Stay 15 km SE of Nundroo, turn S 5 km E of Nundroo into Fowlers Bay Rd. 10 km gravel, turn R into farm just before Coorabie
0428 256 126   HEMA 136 J3   31 53 28 S   132 17 19 E

619 Rushys Balcony 2
Eyre Hwy, Coorabie
Camp Area 24 km W of Bookabie on Eyre Hwy at Coorabie
HEMA 136 H4   31 49 27 S   132 25 10 E

620 Nundroo East Rest Area
Eyre Hwy, Nundroo
Rest Area 69 km W of Penong or 10 km E of Nundroo
HEMA 136 H3   31 49 34 S   132 18 51 E

621 Nundroo Hotel Motel
Eyre Hwy, Nundroo
Caravan Park at Nundroo Roadhouse
08 8625 6120   HEMA 136 H3   31 47 33 S   132 13 29 E

622 Nallanippi Parking Area
Eyre Hwy, Nundroo
Parking Area 6 km W of Nundroo or 56 km E of Yalata. Cnr of Nallanippi Rd
HEMA 136 H3   31 45 11 S   132 11 02 E

623 Kidnippy Rest Area
Eyre Hwy, Nundroo
Camp Area 172 km W of Ceduna on Eyre Hwy at Nundroo, E of Yalata
HEMA 136 H3   31 39 38 S   132 05 40 E

624 Colona Rest Area
Eyre Hwy, Yalata
Rest Area 27 km W of Nundroo or 25 km E of Yalata
HEMA 136 H3   31 36 21 S   132 02 09 E

625 Yalata East Parking Area
Eyre Hwy, Yalata
Parking Area 44 km W of Nundroo or 8 km E of Yalata. Share with trucks, caravan parking at rear of sealed area
HEMA 136 H2   31 31 44 S   131 53 36 E

626 Yalata West Rest Area
Eyre Hwy, Yalata
Rest Area 21 km W of Yalata or 70 km E of Nullarbor Roadhouse
HEMA 136 G2   31 24 34 S   131 36 51 E

627 Red Gate Tank Parking Area
Eyre Hwy, Yalata
Parking Area 41 km W of Yalata or 42 km E of Nullarbor Roadhouse. Share with trucks
HEMA 136 G1   31 21 38 S   131 18 45 E

628 222k Peg Rest Area
Eyre Hwy, Yalata
Rest Area 54 km W of Yalata or 37 km E of Nullarbor Roadhouse
HEMA 136 G1   31 21 55 S   131 15 58 E

629 Whitewell Tank
Eyre Hwy, Yalata
Parking Area on Head of Bight Rd, 2 km SW of Eyre Hwy
HEMA 136 G1   31 25 17 S   131 03 00 E

630 Gilgerabbie Hut
Nullabor National Park & Regional Reserve
Eyre Hwy, Border Village
Camp Area at Gilgerabbie, 313 km W of Ceduna or 190 km E of Eucla
HEMA 141 K5   31 32 29 S   130 47 17 E

631 164k Peg Rest Area
Eyre Hwy, Border Village
Rest Area 20 km W of Nullarbor Roadhouse or 164 km E of Border Village
HEMA 141 K5   31 32 05 S   130 41 32 E

632 157k Peg Rest Area
Eyre Hwy, Nullabor
Rest Area 27 km W of Nullarbor Roadhouse or 157 km E of Border Village
HEMA 141 K5   31 33 02 S   130 37 03 E

633 Mallabie Parking Area 155
K Peg
Eyre Hwy, Nullabor
Parking Area 29 km W of Nullarbor Roadhouse or 155 km E of Border Village. Large gravel area, caravans at the back
HEMA 141 K5   31 33 04 S   130 35 55 E

634 Bunda Cliffs
Nullabor Wilderness Protection Area
Eyre Hwy, Bunda Cliffs
Parking Area 60 km W of Nullarbor Roadhouse or 124 km E of Border Village
HEMA 141 K4   31 34 21 S   130 16 39 E

635 Knardna South
Eyre Hwy, Nullarbor Area
Rest Area, 66 km W of Nullarbor Roadhouse or 130 km E of Eucla
HEMA 141 K4   31 33 51 S   130 14 02 E

636 Koonalda Homestead
Nullarbor National Park
Old Eyre Hwy, Border Village
Camp Area. Turn N 94 km W Nullarbor Roadhouse or 88 km E of Border Village. 14 km to old Homestead. 5 day limit.
08 8625 3144   HEMA 141 J3   31 27 22 S   129 51 28 E

637 85k Peg Rest Area
Eyre Highway, Nullarbor Area
Rest Area 100 km W of Nullarbor Roadhouse or 84 km E of Border Village
HEMA 141 K3   31 34 49 S   129 52 27 E

638 81k Peg Rest Area
Eyre Highway, Nullarbor Area
Rest Area 103 km W of Nullarbor Roadhouse or 81 km E of Border Village
HEMA 141 K3   31 35 16 S   129 50 03 E

639 38k Peg Parking Bay
Eyre Hwy, Border Village
Parking Area 146 km W of Nullarbor Roadhouse or 38 km E of Border Village
HEMA 141 K2   31 38 17 S   129 23 19 E

640 17k Peg Parking Bay
Eyre Hwy, Border Village
Parking Area 167 km W of Nullarbor Roadhouse or 17 km E of Border Village
HEMA 141 K1   31 39 27 S   129 10 04 E

641 13k Peg Parking Bay
Eyre Hwy, Border Village
Parking Area 171 km W of Nullarbor Roadhouse or 13 km E of Border Village
HEMA 141 K1   31 39 35 S   129 07 52 E

642 10k Peg Parking Area
Eyre Highway, Border Village
Parking Area 174 km W of Nullarbor Roadhouse or 10 km E of Border Village
HEMA 141 K1   31 38 54 S   129 05 59 E

Lyndhurst to Innamincka
Strzelecki Track
This road is seasonal and more suitable to 4WD vehicles, camper trailers and off road caravans. Road conditions phone 1300 361 033

643 Burkes Grave Camp Area
Adventure Way, Innamincka
Camp Area 11 km NE of Innamincka. Take Innamincka - Nappa Merrie Rd E from Innaminka. Turn N 7 km. 21 day limit
08 8675 9909   HEMA 133 H14   27 43 22 S   140 46 43 E

644 Freeling Rest Area
Strzelecki Track, Lyndhurst
Rest Area 76 km NE of Lyndhurst or 387 km SW of Innamincka
HEMA 131 G9   29 59 48 S   139 00 28 E

645 Dog Fence Rest Area
Strzelecki Track, Lyndhurst
Rest Area 104 km NE of Lyndhurst or 338 km SW of Innamincka
HEMA 131 F9   29 47 21 S   139 05 22 E

646 Murnpeowie Rest Area
Strzelecki Track, Lyndhurst
Rest Area 126 km NE of Lyndhurst or 338 km SW of Innamincka. Opposite Murnpeowie Station turnoff
HEMA 131 F9   29 37 01 S   139 08 57 E

647 Blanchewater Ruins
Strzelecki Tr, Lyndhurst
Camp Spot 158 km NE of Lyndhurst or 307 km SW of Innamincka. W side of creek on the N side of road
HEMA 131 F10   29 33 01 S   139 27 01 E

648 Art Baker Rest Area
Strzelecki Tr, Lyndhurst Area
Rest Area 209 km NE of Lyndhurst or 255 km SW of Innamincka
HEMA 131 E11   29 29 37 S   139 55 47 E

649 Montecollina Bore Rest Area
Strzelecki Tr, Lyndhurst Area
Rest Area 222 km NE of Lyndhurst or 223 km SW of Innamincka
08 8648 5307   HEMA 131 E11   29 23 43 S   139 59 35 E

650 Innamincka Town Common
Old Strzelecki Track, Innamincka
Camp Area 1 km S of township on banks of Cooper Creek. Signposted, honesty box at entrance
08 8675 9901   HEMA 133 H14   27 44 59 S   140 43 56 E

651 Policemans Waterhole
Innamincka Regional Reserve
Fifteen Mile Tr, Innamincka
Camp Area SW of Innamincka. At 3.5 km turn R to Policeman's Water Hole. 5 day limit, ebook
08 8648 5328   HEMA 133 H13   27 45 31 S   140 42 12 E

652 Ski Beach
Innamincka Regional Reserve
Fifteen Mile Tr, Innamincka Area
Camp Area SW of Innamincka. Drive 5.6 km, turn R to Ski Beach. 5 day limit, ebook
08 8648 5328   HEMA 133 H13   27 45 52 S   140 41 06 E

SOUTH AUSTRALIA

653 Kings Site

Innamincka Regional Reserve
Fifteen Mile Tr, Innamincka Area
Camp Area SW of Innamincka. 7 km turn R to campground. 5 day limit, ebook
08 8648 5328 **HEMA 133 H13** 27 46 42 S 140 40 33 E

654 Minkie Waterhole

Innamincka Regional Reserve
Fifteen Mile Tr, Innamincka Area
Camp Area SW of Innamincka. 10.8 km turn R to Minkie Waterhole. 5 day limit, ebook
08 8648 5328 **HEMA 133 H13** 27 46 45 S 140 38 19 E

655 Kudriemitchie Campground

Malkumba-Coongie Lakes NP
Coongie Rd, Innamincka Area
Camp Spot on the Coongie Lake track NW of Innamincka. 83 km turn L into camp site. 5 day limit, ebook
08 8648 5328 **HEMA 133 G12** 27 21 41 S 140 12 15 E

656 Coongie Lakes Campground

Malkumba-Coongie Lakes NP
Coongie Rd, Innamincka Area
Camp Spot NW of Innamincka. 104 km turn L into camp site. Subject to flooding, check ahead to make sure road is open
1800 816 078 **HEMA 133 F12** 27 11 27 S 140 09 12 E

657 Cadelga Ruins

Cordillo Rd, Innamincka Area
Camp Area 155 km SE of Birdsville
HEMA 133 B13 26 05 13 S 140 24 39 E

658 Cullyamurra Waterhole

Innamincka Regional Reserve
Innamincka - Nappa Merrie Rd, Innamincka
Camp Area 14 km N from road, ebook
08 8648 5328 **HEMA 133 H13** 27 42 07 S 140 50 20 E

Timor Sea

Indian Ocean

POI and Facilities
Please note that facilities and points of interest
are not shown within inset frames.
See the relevant inset map for this information.

164-165

162-163

166-167

160-161

168-169

170-171

158-159

146-147
144-145
148-149

150-151

152-153

156-157

154-155

Great Australian Bight

Southern Ocean

© Hema Maps

Western Australia

Northern Territory

South Australia

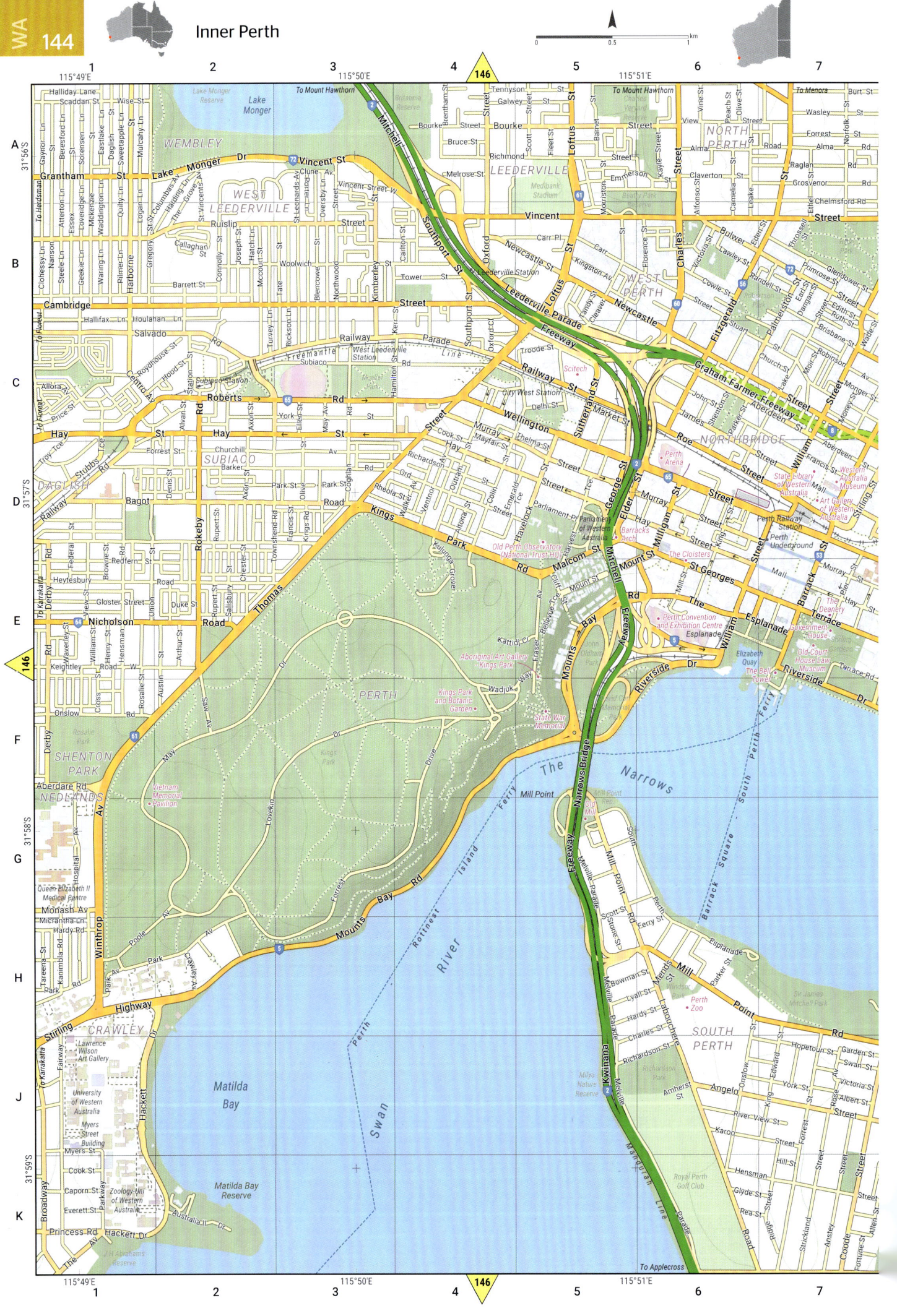

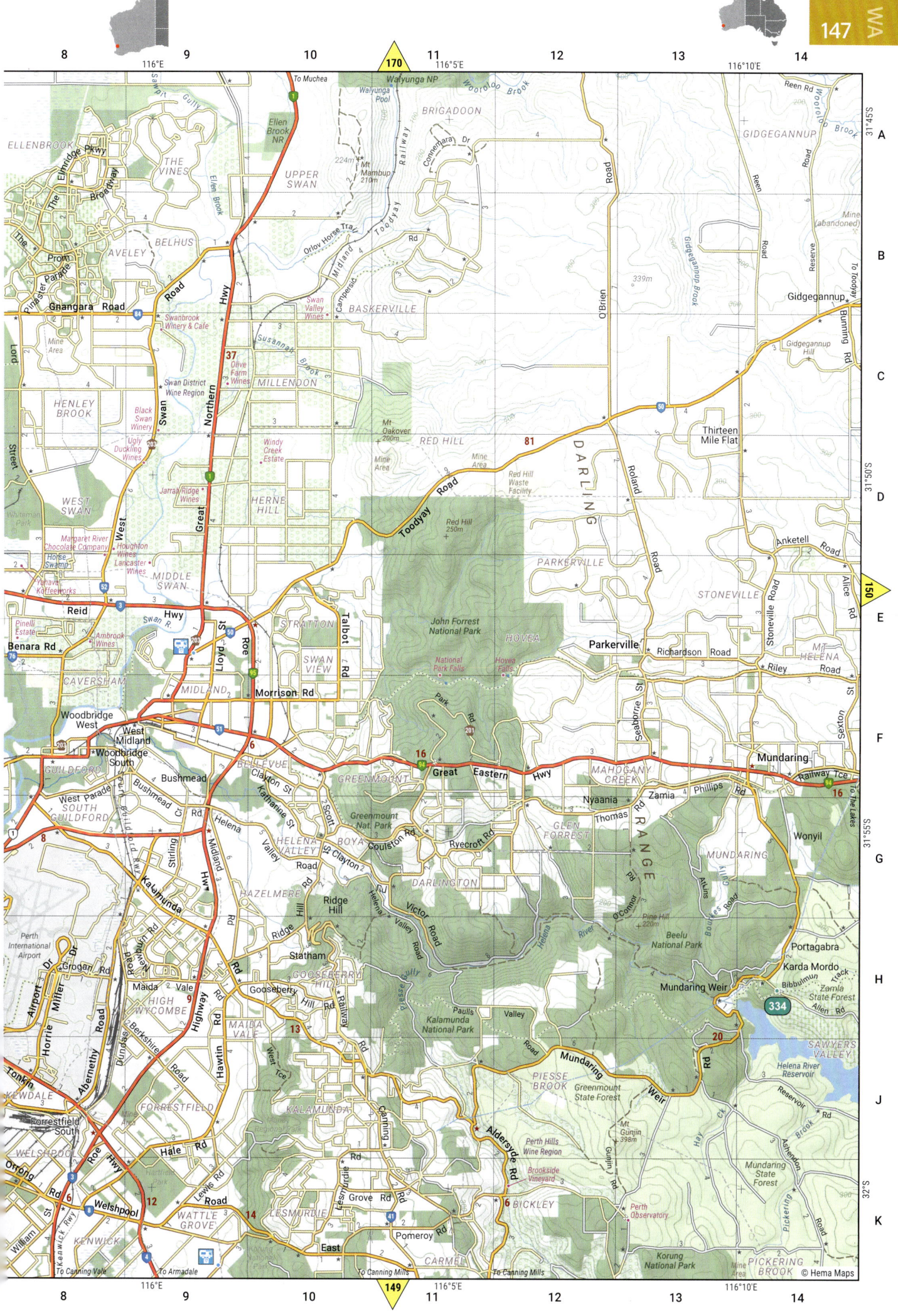

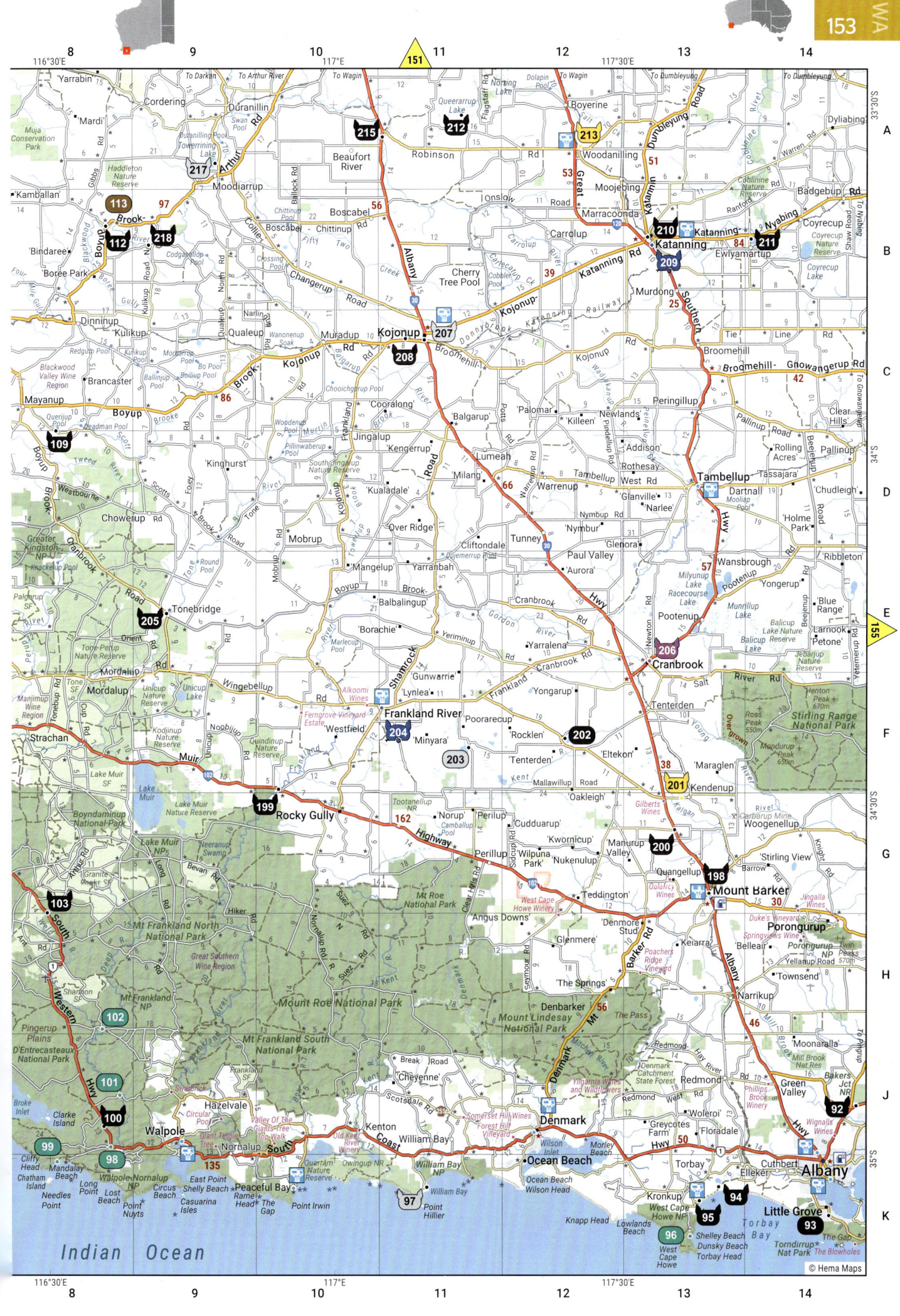

Perth to Ravensthorpe

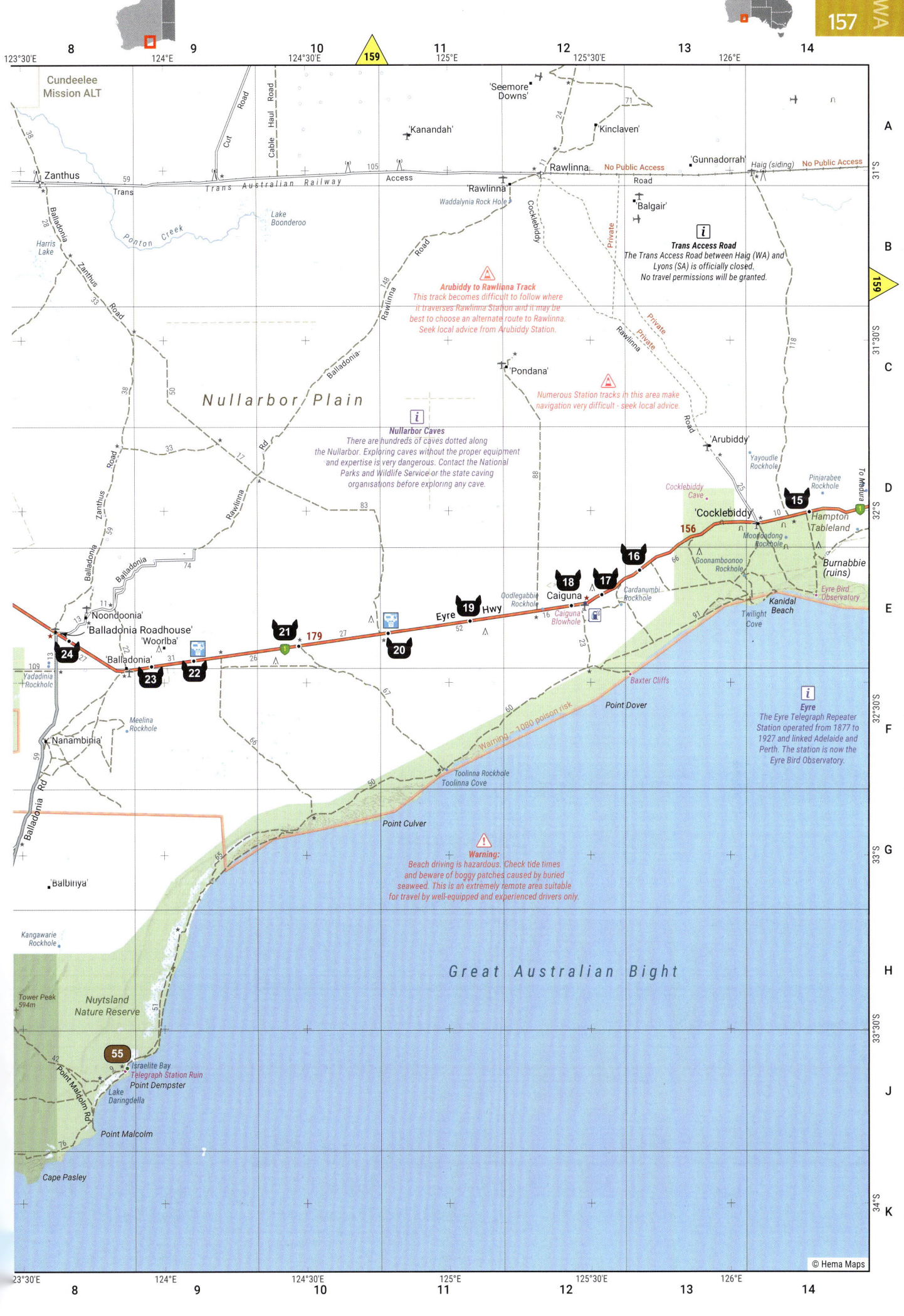

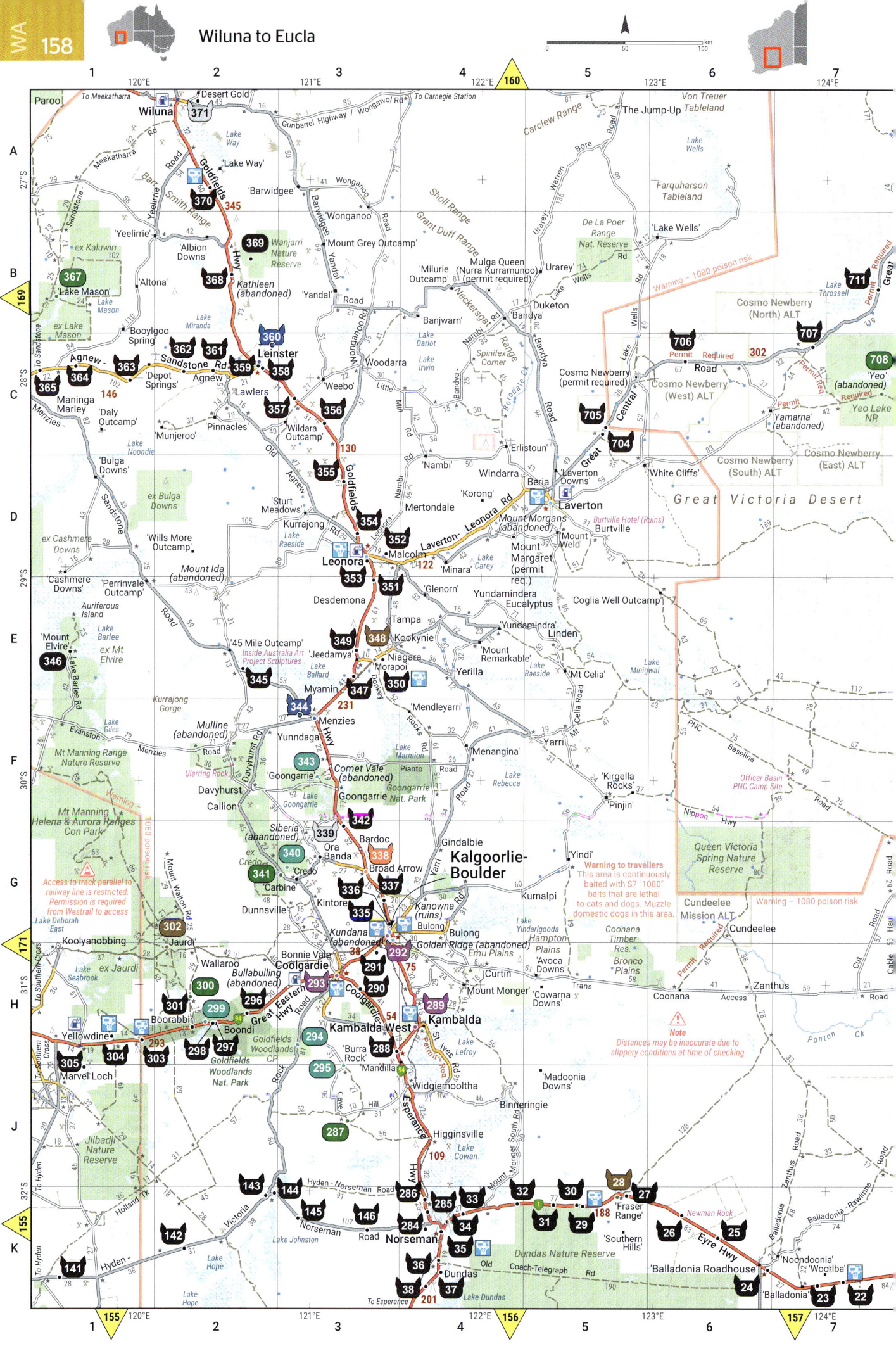

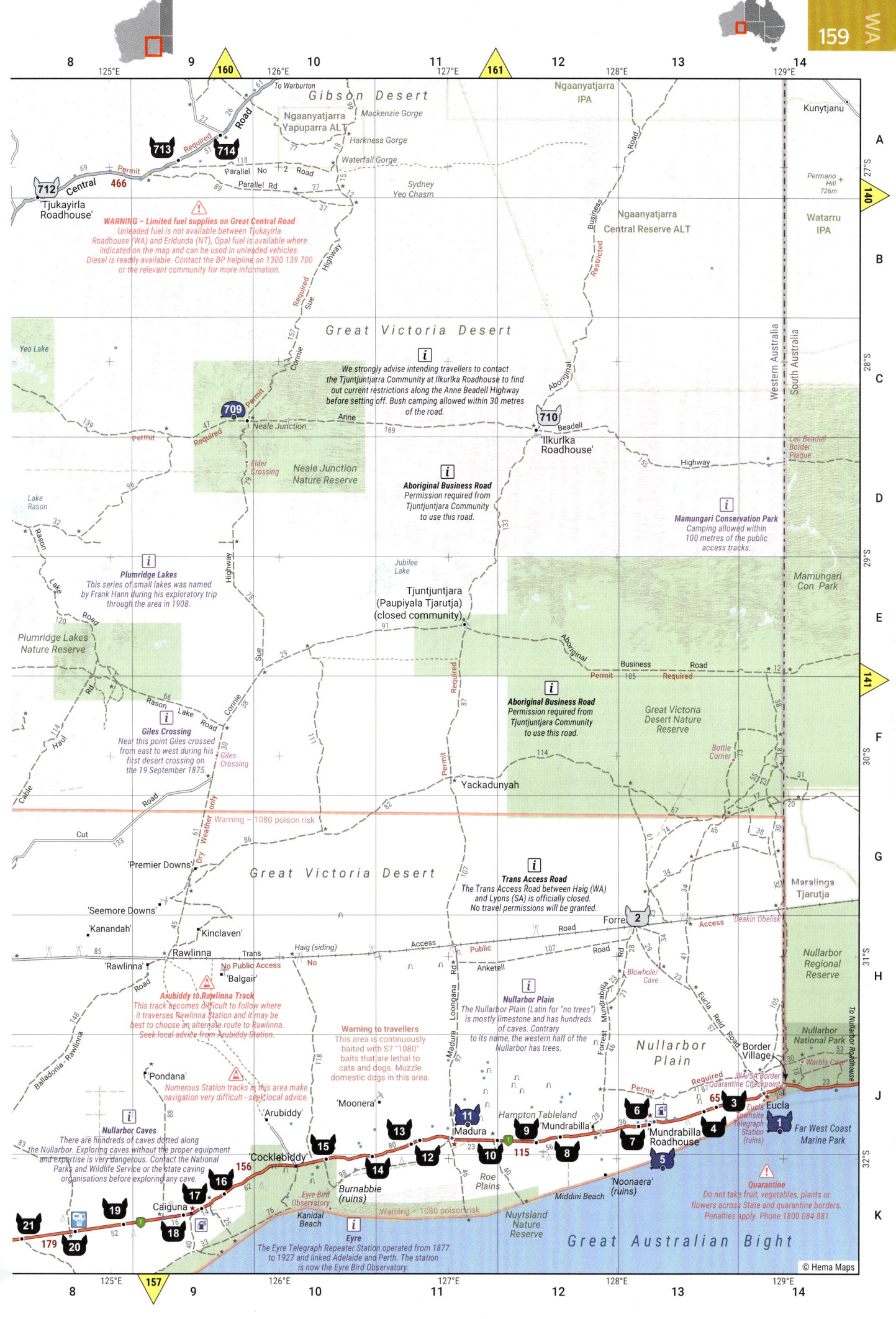

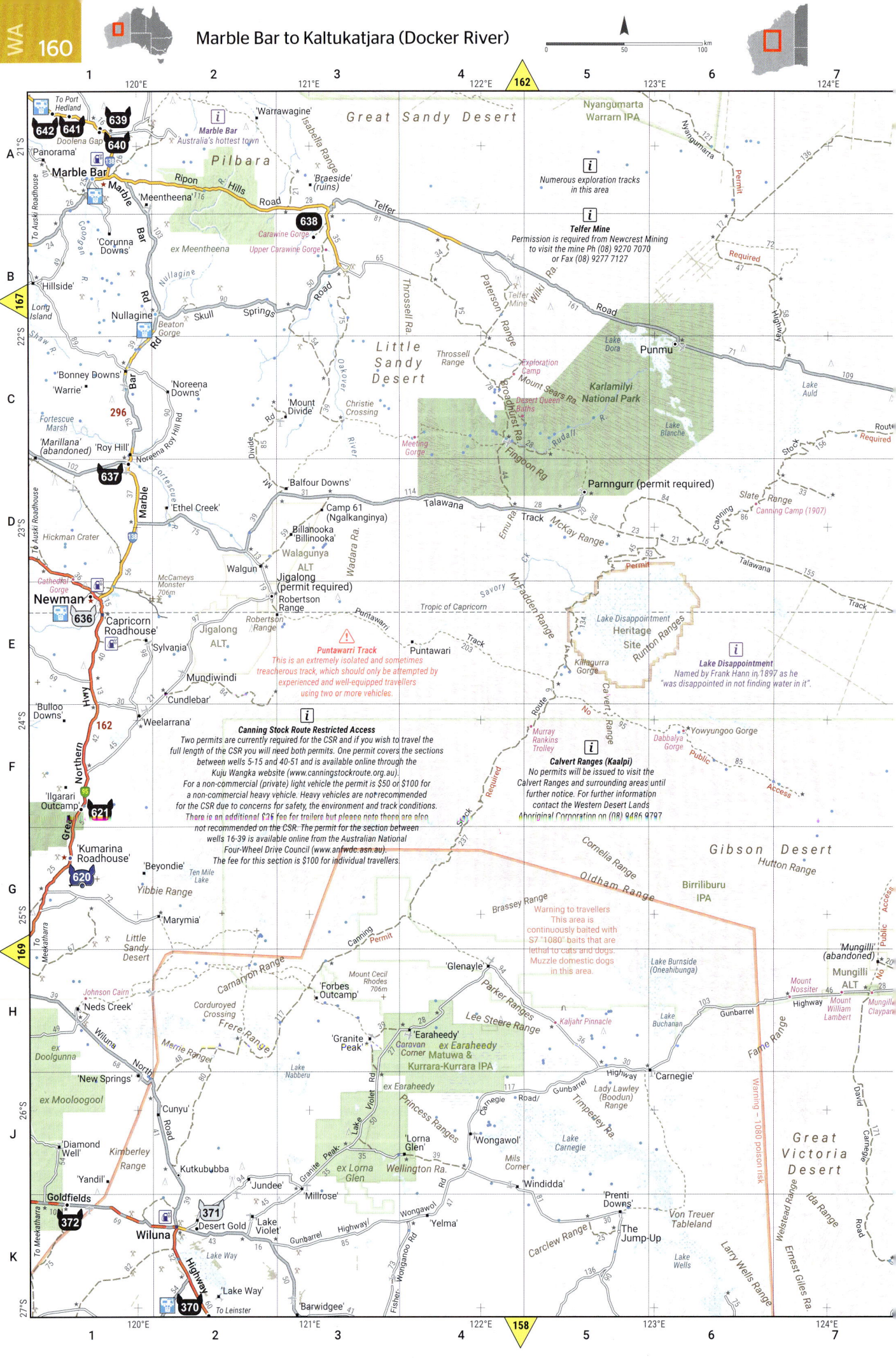

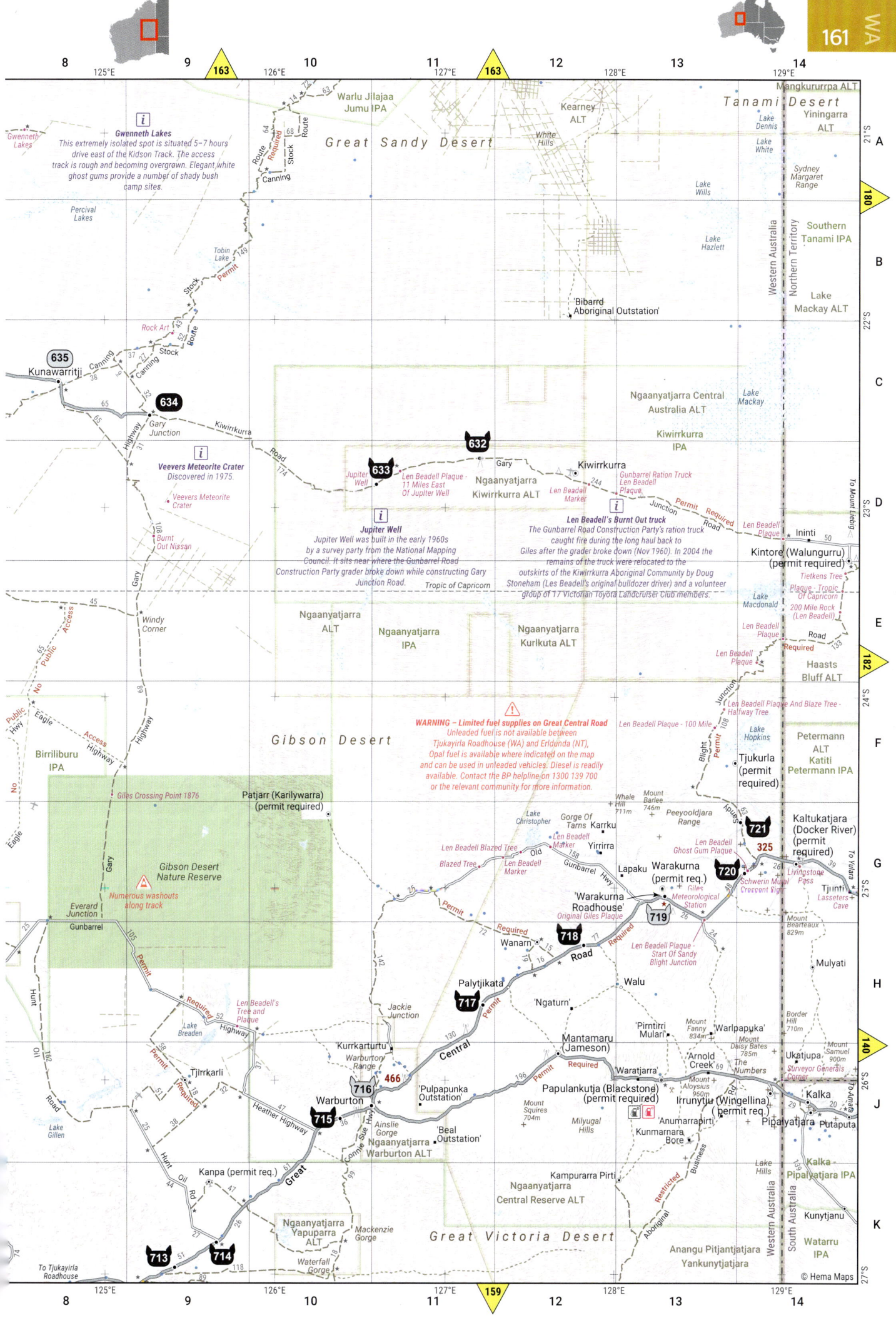

The following text is embedded within the map image:

Gwenneth Lakes
This extremely isolated spot is situated 5-7 hours drive east of the Kidson Track. The access track is rough and becoming overgrown. Elegant white ghost gums provide a number of shady bush camp sites.

Great Sandy Desert

Tanami Desert

Warlu Jilajaa Jumu IPA

Kearney ALT

White Hills

Mangkururrpa ALT

Yiningurra ALT

Lake Dennis

Lake White

Sydney Margaret Range

Percival Lakes

Lake Wills

Lake Hazlett

Southern Tanami IPA

Tobin Lake

'Bibarrd' Aboriginal Outstation'

Lake Mackay ALT

635 Kunawarritji

634

Gary Junction

Rock Art

Canning Stock Route

Veevers Meteorite Crater
Discovered in 1975.

Veevers Meteorite Crater

Burnt Out Nissan

Ngaanyatjarra Central Australia ALT

Lake Mackay

Kiwirrkurra IPA

632

633 Jupiter Well

Len Beadell Plaque - 11 Miles East Of Jupiter Well

Ngaanyatjarra Kiwirrkurra ALT

Len Beadell Marker

Gary

Kiwirrkurra

Gunbarrel Ration Truck Len Beadell Plaque

Kintore (Walungurru) (permit required)

Ininti

To Mount Liebig

Jupiter Well
Jupiter Well was built in the early 1960s by a survey party from the National Mapping Council. It sits near where the Gunbarrel Road Construction Party grader broke down while constructing Gary Junction Road.

Len Beadell's Burnt Out truck
The Gunbarrel Road Construction Party's ration truck caught fire during the long haul back to Giles after the grader broke down (Nov 1960). In 2004 the remains of the truck were relocated to the outskirts of the Kiwirrkurra Aboriginal Community by Doug Stoneham (Les Beadell's original bulldozer driver) and a volunteer group of 17 Victorian Toyota Landcruiser Club members.

Tropic of Capricorn

Tietkens Tree Plaque - Tropic Of Capricorn

200 Mile Rock (Len Beadell)

Windy Corner

Ngaanyatjarra ALT

Ngaanyatjarra IPA

Ngaanyatjarra Kurlkuta ALT

Lake Macdonald

Len Beadell Plaque

Len Beadell Plaque

Haasts Bluff ALT

Gibson Desert

WARNING – Limited fuel supplies on Great Central Road
Unleaded fuel is not available between Tjukayirla Roadhouse (WA) and Erldunda (NT). Opal fuel is available where indicated on the map and can be used in unleaded vehicles. Diesel is readily available. Contact the BP helpline on 1300 139 700 or the relevant community for more information.

Len Beadell Plaque - 100 Mile

Len Beadell Plaque And Blaze Tree - Halfway Tree

Petermann ALT Katiti Petermann IPA

Tjukurla (permit required)

Lake Hopkins

Birriliburu IPA

Giles Crossing Point 1876

Patjarr (Karilywarra) (permit required)

Lake Christopher

Gorge Of Tarns

Karrku

Whale Hill

Mount Barlee 746m

Peeyooldjara Range

Mount Beadeaux 829m

Kaltukatjara (Docker River) (permit required)

721

325

To Yulara

Gibson Desert Nature Reserve

Numerous washouts along track

Len Beadell Blazed Tree

Blazed Tree

Old Gunbarrel Hwy

Len Beadell Marker

Yirrira

Lapaku

Warakurna (permit req.)

Len Beadell Ghost Gum Plaque

720

Schwerin Mural Crescent Sign

Livingstone Pass

Tjunti

Lasseters Cave

Everard Junction

Gunbarrel

'Warakurna Roadhouse' Original Giles Plaque

Giles Meteorological Station

719

Len Beadell Plaque - Start Of Sandy Blight Junction

Len Beadell's Tree and Plaque

Wanarn

718

Road

Walu

Mulyati

Lake Breaden

Palytjikata

717

'Ngaturn'

'Pirntirri Mulari'

Mount Fanny 834m

'Warlpapuka'

Border Hill 710m

Jackie Junction

'Kurrkarturtu'

Warburton Range

466

Central

Required

Mantamaru (Jameson)

Mount Daisy Bates 785m

The Numbers

'Arnold Creek'

Mount Aloysius 1107m

Ukatjupa

Mount Samuel 900m

Surveyor Generals Corner

Tjirrkarli

716

'Pulpapunka Outstation'

Waratjarra

Papulankutja (Blackstone) (permit required)

Irrunytju (Wingellina) (permit req.)

Kalka

715 Warburton

Ainslie Gorge

'Beal Outstation'

Mount Squires 704m

Milyugal Hills

'Anumarrapiti'

Kunmarnara Bore

Pipalyatjara

Putaputa

Oil

Lake Gillen

Ngaanyatjarra Warburton ALT

Kanpa (permit req.)

Great

Ngaanyatjarra Central Reserve ALT

Kampurarra Pirti

Kampurarra Pirti

Lake Hills

Kalka Pipalyatjara IPA

Kunytjanu

Ngaanyatjarra Yapuparra ALT

Mackenzie Gorge

Great Victoria Desert

Anangu Pitjantjatjara Yankunytjatjara

Watarru IPA

To Tjukayirla Roadhouse

713

714

Waterfall Gorge

© Hema Maps

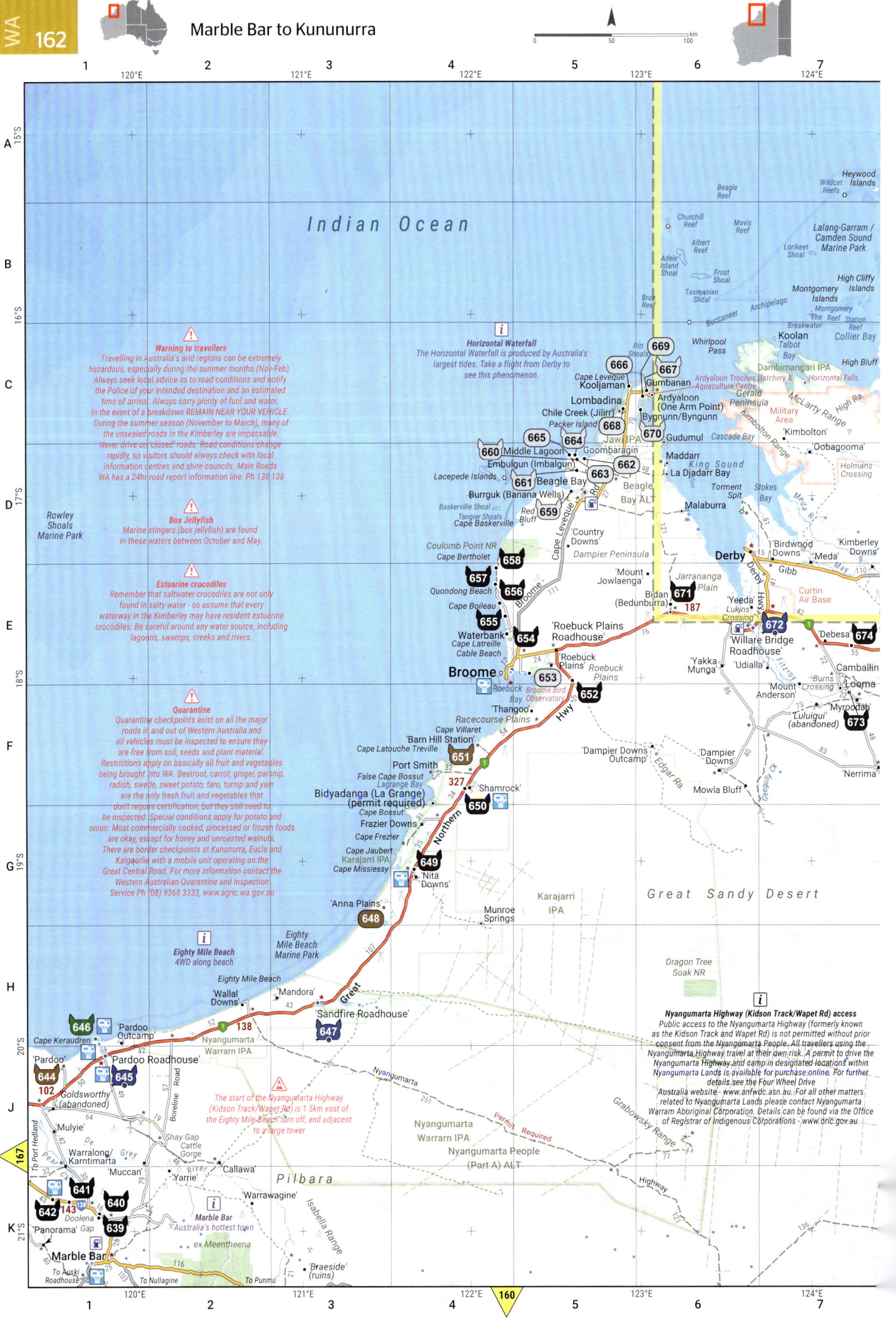

Warning to travellers
Travelling in Australia's arid regions can be extremely hazardous, especially during the summer months (Nov-Feb). Always seek local advice as to road conditions and notify the Police of your intended destination and an estimated time of arrival. Always carry plenty of fuel and water. In the event of a breakdown REMAIN NEAR YOUR VEHICLE. During the summer season (November to March), many of the unsealed roads in the Kimberley are impassable. Never drive on closed roads. Road conditions change rapidly, so visitors should always check with local information centres and shire councils. Main Roads WA has a 24hr road report information line: Ph 138 138

Box Jellyfish
Marine stingers (box jellyfish) are found in these waters between October and May.

Estuarine crocodiles
Remember that saltwater crocodiles are not only found in salty water - so assume that every waterway in the Kimberley may have resident estuarine crocodiles. Be careful around any water source, including lagoons, swamps, creeks and rivers.

Quarantine
Quarantine checkpoints exist on all the major roads in and out of Western Australia and all vehicles must be inspected to ensure they are free from soil, seeds and plant material. Restrictions apply on basically all fruit and vegetables being brought into WA. Beetroot, carrot, ginger, parsnip, radish, swede, sweet potato, taro, turnip and yam are the only fresh fruit and vegetables that don't require certification, but they still need to be inspected. Special conditions apply for potato and onion. Most commercially cooked, processed or frozen foods are okay, except for honey and unroasted walnuts. There are border checkpoints at Kununurra, Eucla and Kalgoorlie with a mobile unit operating on the Great Central Road. For more information contact the Western Australian Quarantine and Inspection Service Ph (08) 9368 3333, www.agric.wa.gov.au

Horizontal Waterfall
The Horizontal Waterfall is produced by Australia's largest tides. Take a flight from Derby to see this phenomenon.

Eighty Mile Beach
4WD along beach

Nyangumarta Highway (Kidson Track/Wapet Rd) access
Public access to the Nyangumarta Highway (formerly known as the Kidson Track and Wapet Rd) is not permitted without prior consent from the Nyangumarta People. All travellers using the Nyangumarta Highway travel at their own risk. A permit to drive the Nyangumarta Highway and camp in designated locations within Nyangumarta Lands is available for purchase online. For further details see the Four Wheel Drive Australia website - www.anfwdc.asn.au. For all other matters related to Nyangumarta Lands please contact Nyangumarta Warram Aboriginal Corporation. Details can be found via the Office of Registrar of Indigenous Corporations - www.oric.gov.au

The start of the Nyangumarta Highway (Kidson Track/Wapet Rd) is 1.5km east of the Eighty Mile Beach turn off, and adjacent to a large tower.

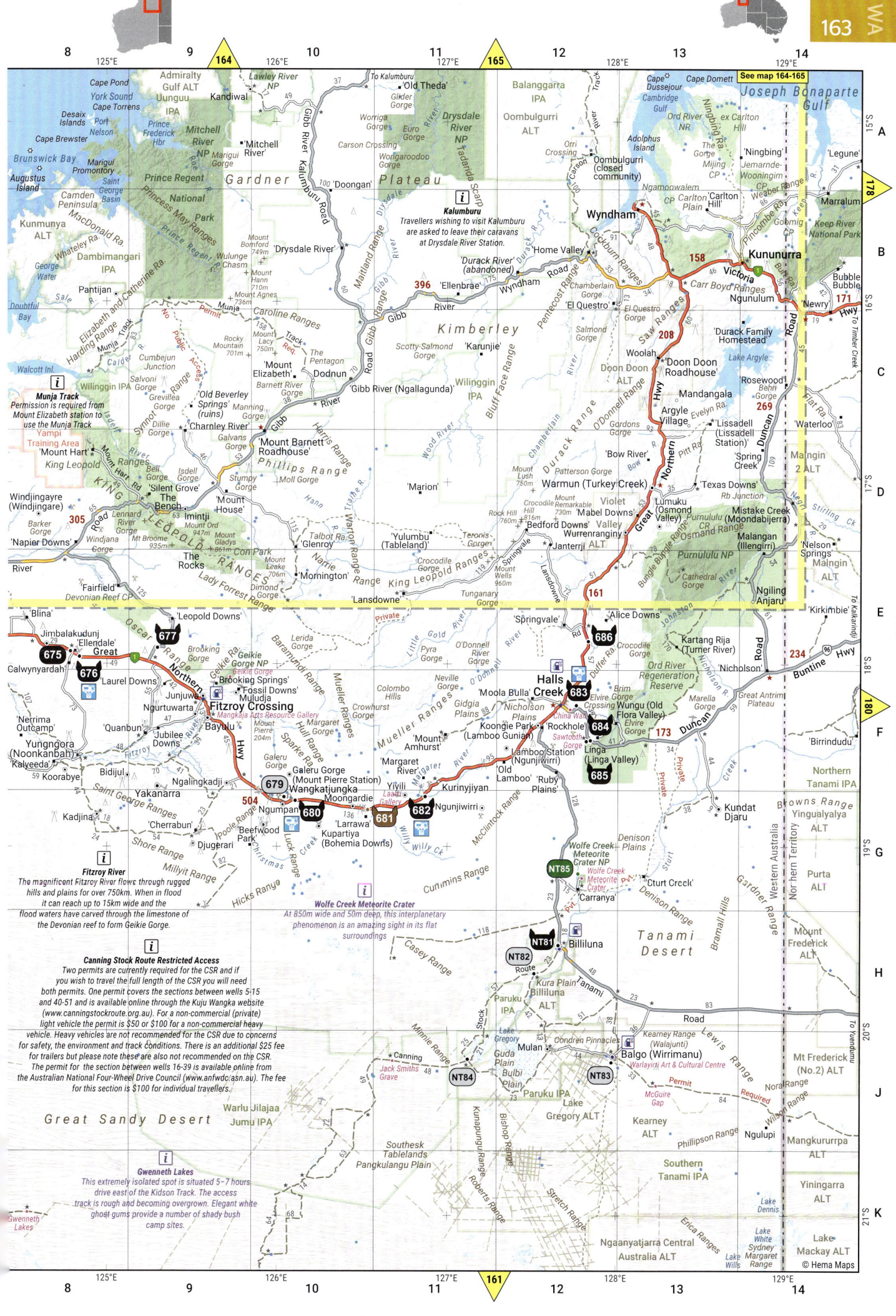

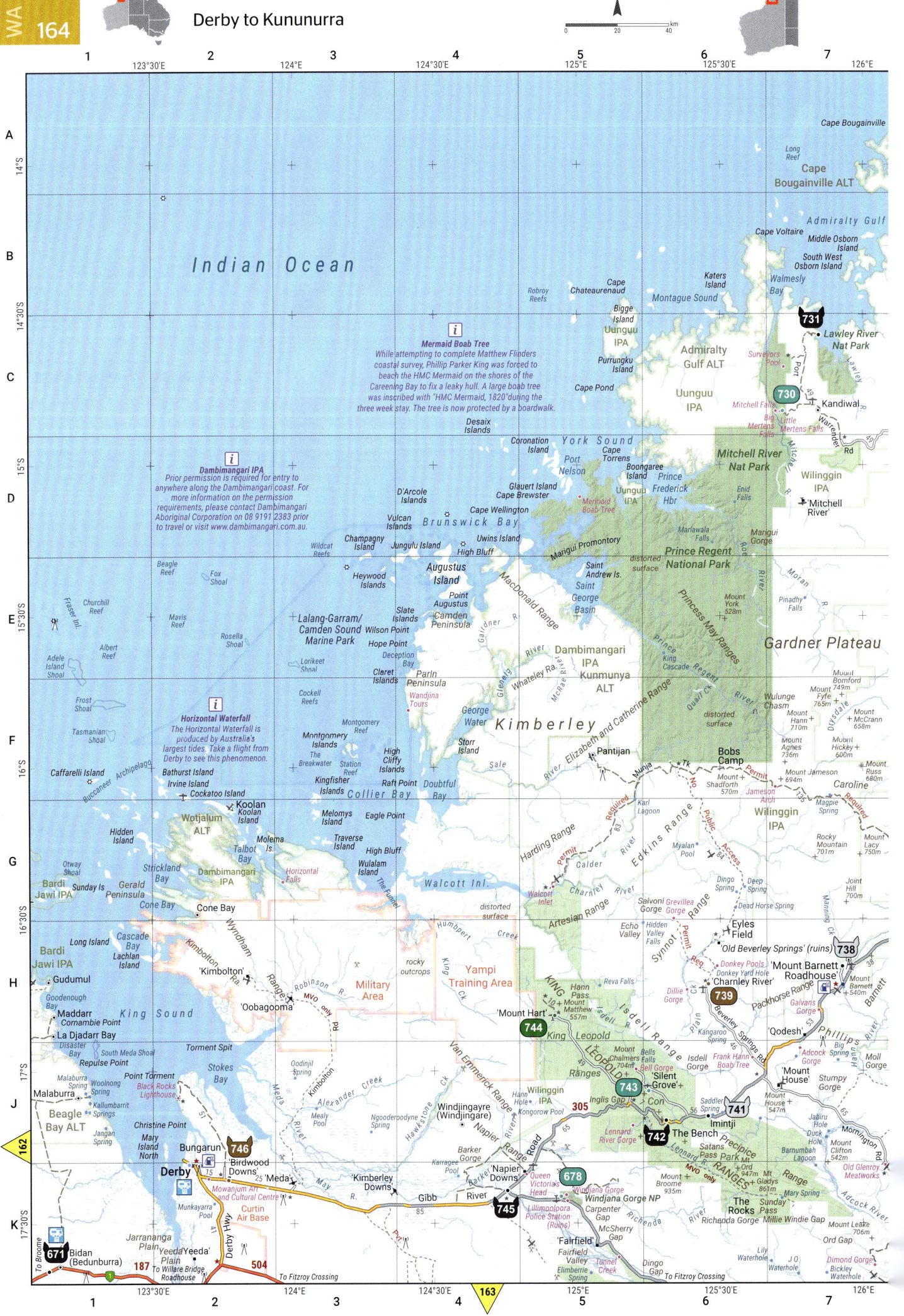

© Hema Maps

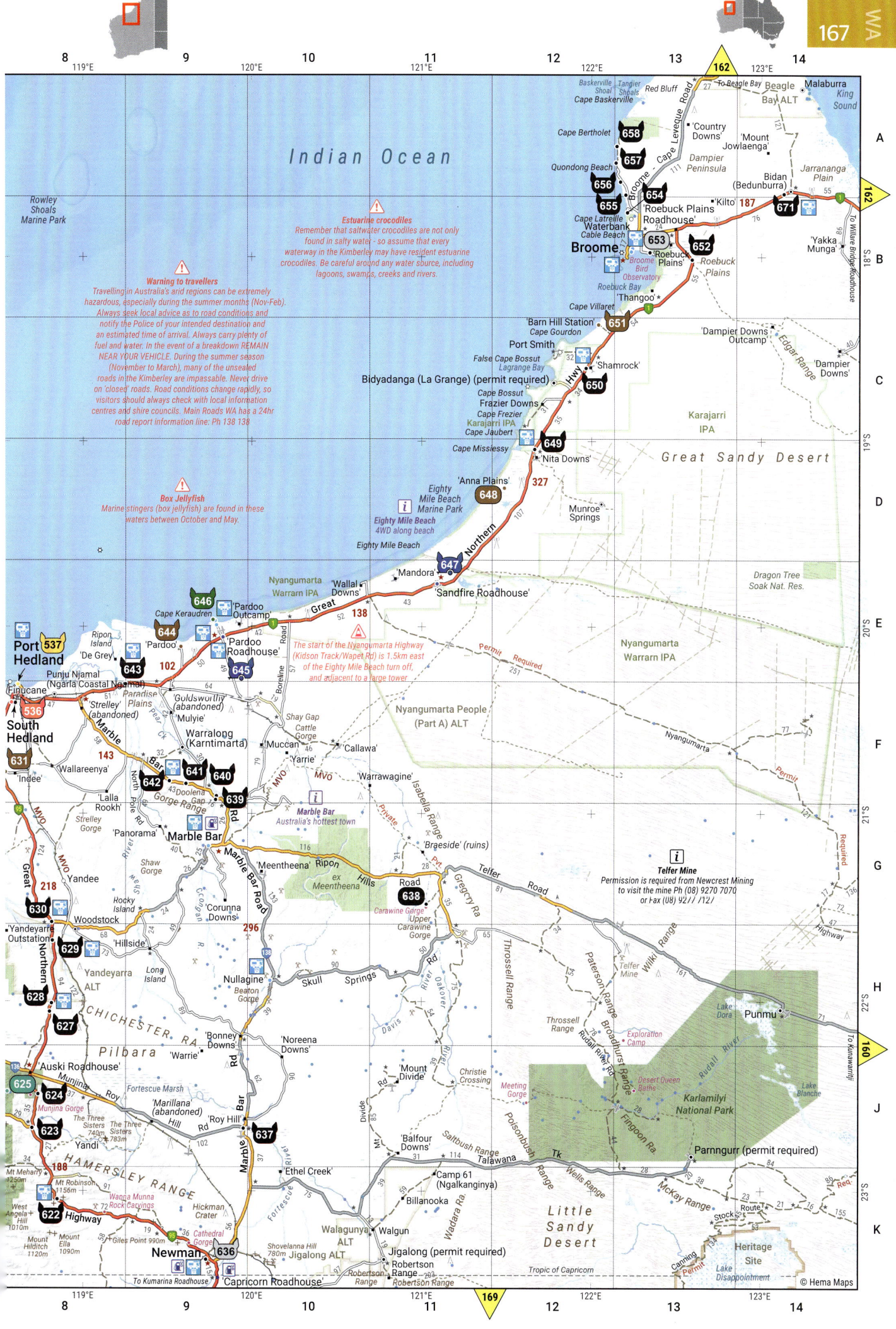

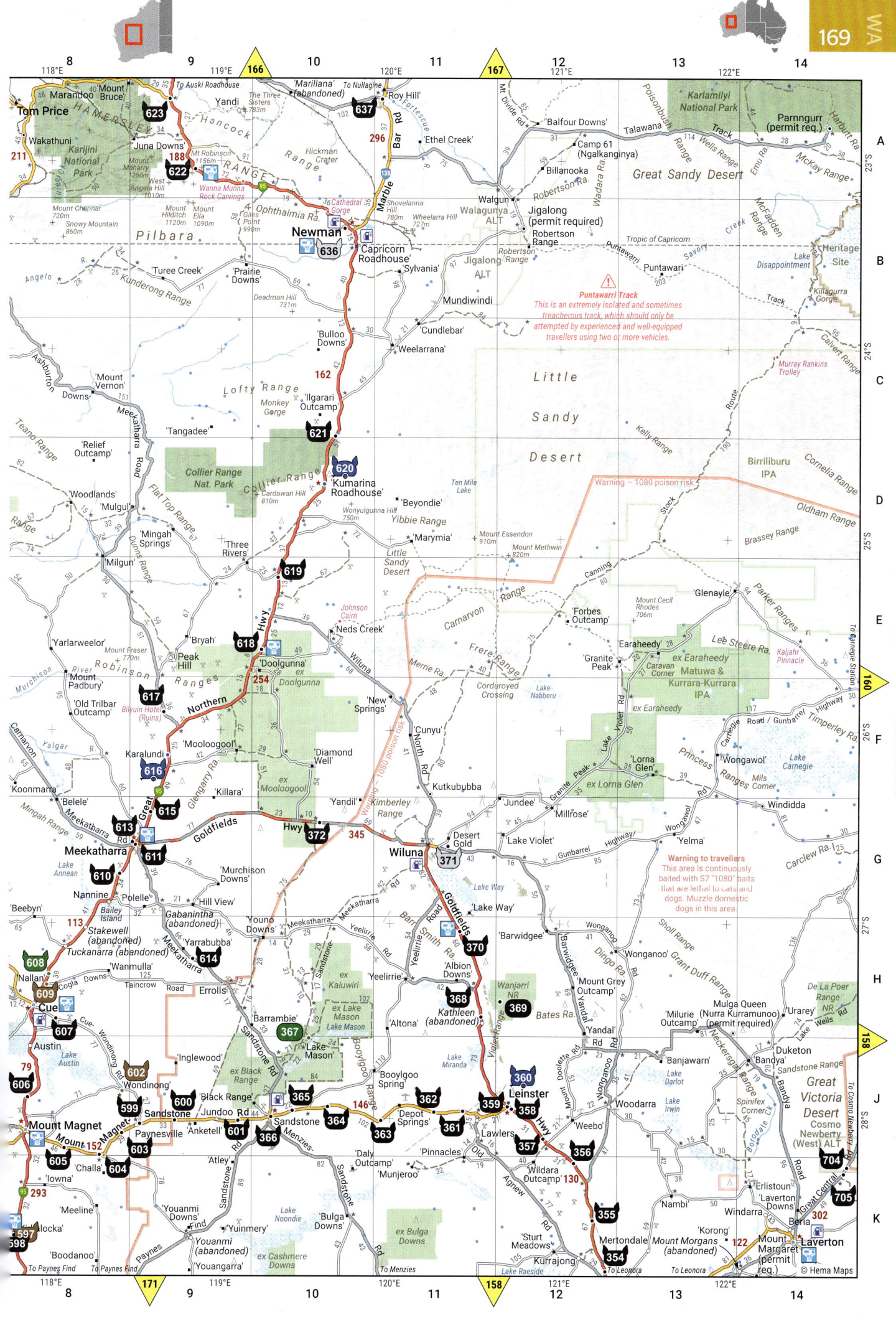

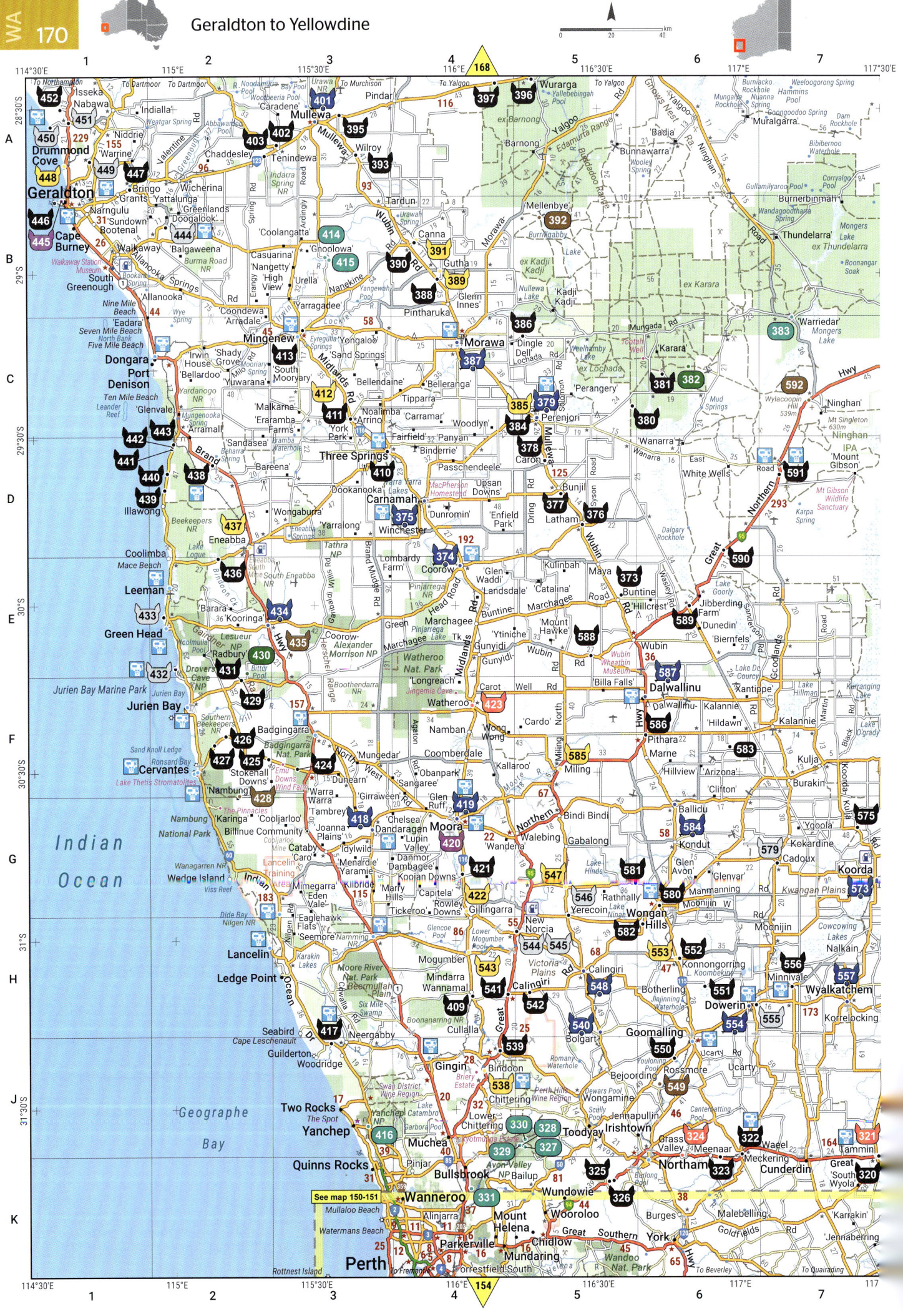

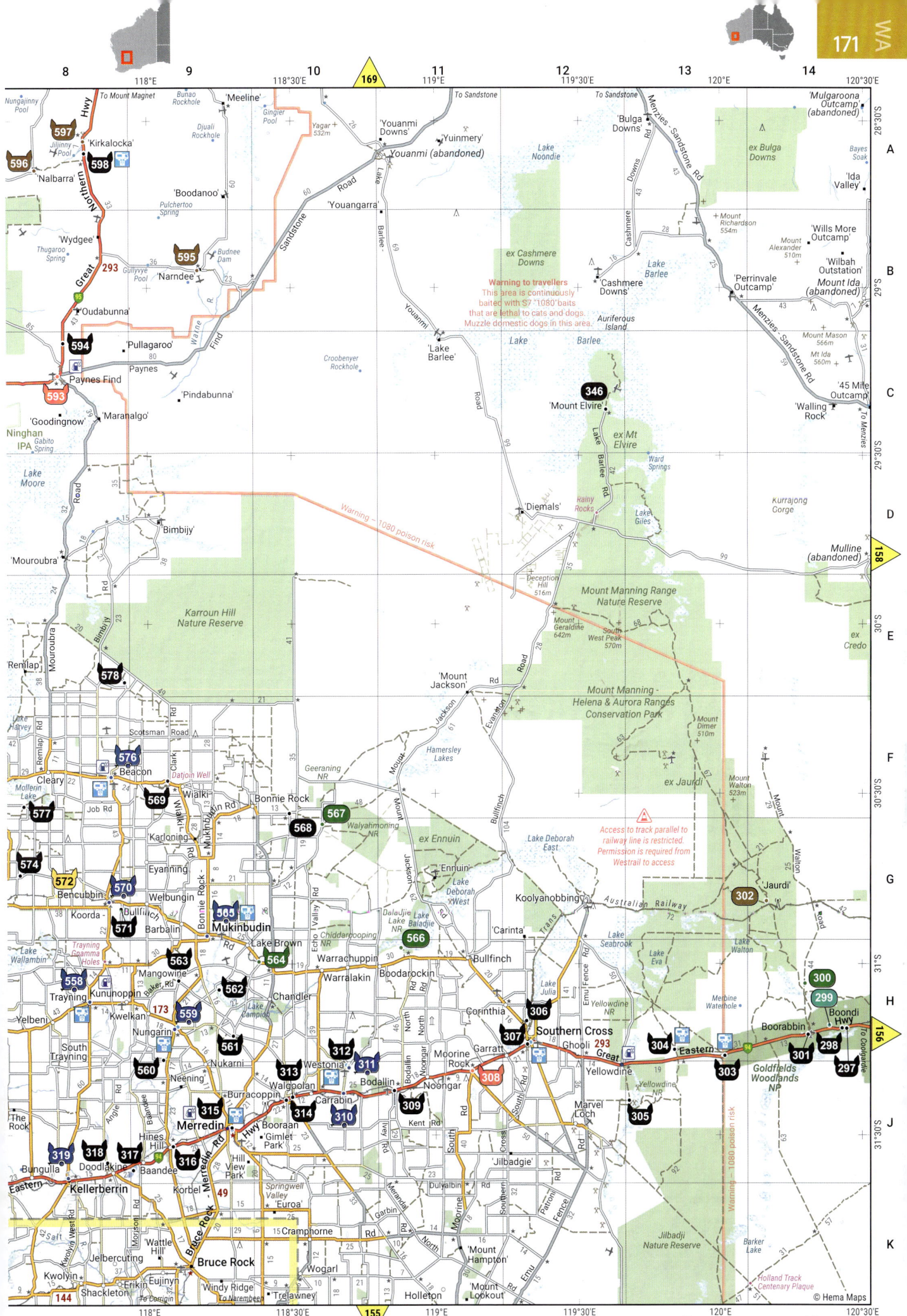

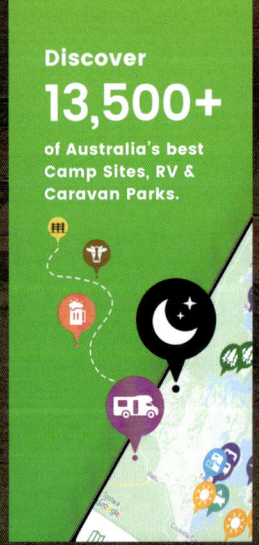

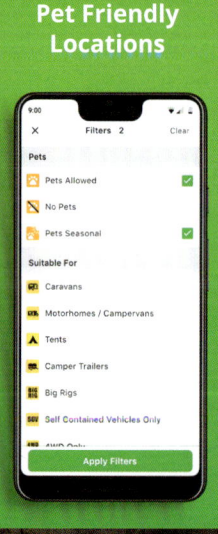

Coronation Beach, Western Australia by Stephanie Lopaten

Western Australia

WESTERN AUSTRALIA

Eyre and Coolgardie-Esperance Highways

1 Eucla Roadhouse

Eyre Hwy, Eucla
Caravan Park 12 km W of the WA/SA Border. Eucla-Reid Rd. No water except showers & toilet
08 9039 3468   HEMA 159 J14   31 40 37 S   128 53 04 E

2 Forrest Airport

Trans Access Rd, Forrest
Camp Area 122 km NW of Eucla. Off road vehicles only. Fee for shower
08 9022 6403   HEMA 159 G13   30 50 53 S   128 06 30 E

3 Najada Rockhole

Eyre Hwy, Eucla Area
Rest Area 30 km W of Eucla or 35 km E of Mundrabilla
138 138   HEMA 159 J13   31 44 46 S   128 36 01 E

4 Hearder Hill

Eyre Hwy, Eucla Area
Parking Area 36 km W of Eucla or 29 km E of Mundrabilla
138 138   HEMA 159 J13   31 46 02 S   128 31 42 E

5 Mundrabilla Roadhouse

Eyre Hwy, Mundrabilla
Caravan Park 65 km W of Eucla
08 9039 3465   HEMA 159 J13   31 49 06 S   128 13 31 E

6 Kuthala Tank

Eyre Hwy, Mundrabilla Area
Parking Area 3 km W of Mundrabilla or 113 km E of Madura. 500 m S of Hwy
HEMA 159 J13   31 49 53 S   128 11 43 E

7 Jallah Rockhole

Eyre Hwy, Mundrabilla Area
Rest Area 10 km W of Mundrabilla or 106 km E of Madura
HEMA 159 J13   31 50 26 S   128 07 49 E

8 Boolaboola Parking Area

Eyre Hwy, Mundrabilla Area
Parking Area 54 km W of Mundrabilla or 62 km E of Madura
HEMA 159 J12   31 53 33 S   127 39 42 E

9 Carlabeencabba Rockhole

Eyre Hwy, Madura Area
Parking Area 69 km W of Mundrabilla or 47 km E of Madura. Emergency phone
138 138   HEMA 159 J12   31 55 14 S   127 31 09 E

10 Moodini Bluff

Eyre Hwy, Madura Area
Rest Area 90 km W of Mundrabilla or 26 km E of Madura
138 138   HEMA 159 J11   31 54 35 S   127 17 15 E

11 Madura Pass Roadhouse

Eyre Hwy, Madura
Caravan Park. No water except showers & toilets
08 9039 3464   HEMA 159 J11   31 53 58 S   127 01 10 E

12 The Old Quarry

Eyre Hwy, Madura Area
Camp Area 19 km W of Madura or 81 km E of Cocklebiddy. GPS at turn off. 1 km from Hwy
HEMA 159 J11   31 54 33 S   126 49 46 E

13 Olwolgin Bluff

Eyre Hwy, Madura Area
Parking Area 24 km W of Madura or 66 km E of Cocklebiddy
138 138   HEMA 159 J11   31 55 40 S   126 46 43 E

14 Moonera Tank

Eyre Hwy, Cocklebiddy Area
Parking Area 47 km W of Madura or 43 km E of Cocklebiddy. Emergency phone
138 138   HEMA 159 K10   31 59 23 S   126 32 50 E

15 Observatory Turnoff

Eyre Hwy, Cocklebiddy Area
Parking Area 73 km W of Madura or 17 km E of Cocklebiddy. 1 km E of Eyre Bird Observatory turnoff
138 138   HEMA 159 K10   32 00 10 S   126 16 38 E

16 Jillbunya Rockhole

Eyre Hwy, Caiguna
Parking Area 44 km W of Cocklebiddy or 21 km E of Caiguna
138 138   HEMA 159 K9   32 10 25 S   125 40 25 E

17 Caiguna East

Eyre Hwy, Caiguna
Camp Spot 6 km E of Caiguna, 59 km W of Cocklebiddy, GPS on entry, 500 m S of Hwy
HEMA 159 K9   32 14 42 S   125 32 24 E

18 Caiguna Blowhole

Eyre Hwy, Caiguna
Camp Spot 5 km W of Caiguna, 177 km E of Balladonia, GPS on entry
HEMA 159 K9   32 16 36 S   125 25 52 E

19 Domblegabby Rest Area

Eyre Hwy, Caiguna
Rest Area 39 km W of Caiguna or 143 km E of Balladonia
138 138   HEMA 157 E11   32 19 17 S   125 04 30 E

20 Baxter Rest Area

Eyre Hwy, Caiguna
Rest Area 67 km W of Caiguna or 115 km E of Balladonia
HEMA 157 E11   32 21 26 S   124 47 14 E

21 Woorlba East Parking Area

Eyre Hwy, Balladonia
Parking Area 97 km W of Caiguna or 85 km E of Balladonia
HEMA 157 E10   32 23 39 S   124 28 21 E

22 Woorlba Homestead

Eyre Hwy, Balladonia
Rest Area 132 km W of Caiguna or 50 km E of Balladonia Roadhouse. Emergency phone
138 138   HEMA 157 E9   32 26 12 S   124 06 17 E

23 90 Mile Sign

Eyre Hwy, Balladonia Area
Parking Area 147 km W of Caiguna or 35 km E of Balladonia
HEMA 157 E9   32 27 12 S   123 57 17 E

24 Afghan Rock

Eyre Hwy, Balladonia Area
Parking Area 177 km W of Caiguna or 5 km E of Balladonia

HEMA 157 E8   32 22 42 S   123 39 54 E

25 Harms Lake

Eyre Hwy, Balladonia Area
Rest Area 25 km W of Balladonia or 167 km E of Norseman

HEMA 156 E7   32 13 28 S   123 22 34 E

26 Newman Rock

Via Eyre Hwy, Fraser Range Area
Camp Spot 50 km W of Balladonia or 142 km E of Norseman. N at sign follow track 1 km

HEMA 156 E7   32 06 58 S   123 10 04 E

27 Mt Pleasant

Eyre Hwy, Fraser Range Area
Parking Area 82 km W of Balladonia or 110 km E of Norseman. Emergency phone

HEMA 156 D6   32 01 20 S   122 50 50 E

28 Fraser Range Station

Dempster Dr, Norseman
Station Stay 90 km W of Balladonia 103 km E of Norseman turn S off the Hwy. Signposted

08 9039 3210   HEMA 156 D6   32 01 45 S   122 47 40 E

29 Southern Hill 24 Hr Rest Area

Eyre Hwy, Norseman Area
Rest Area 108 km W of Balladonia or 84 km E of Norseman

138 138   HEMA 156 D5   32 04 24 S   122 35 36 E

30 Ten Mile Rocks

Eyre Hwy, Norseman Area
Rest Area 113 km W of Balladonia or 79 km E of Norseman

HEMA 156 D5   32 04 04 S   122 33 34 E

31 Dundas Reserve Park Area

Eyre Hwy, Norseman Area
Parking Area 125 km W of Balladonia or 67 km E of Norseman. Emergency phone

HEMA 156 D5   32 04 01 S   122 25 32 E

32 Kevin Lanceley Parking Area

Eyre Hwy, Norseman Area
Parking Area 145 km W of Balladonia or 47 km E of Norseman. Emergency phone

HEMA 156 D5   32 03 41 S   122 12 52 E

33 Norseman East Park Area

Eyre Hwy, Norseman
Parking Area 176 km W of Balladonia or 16 km E of Norseman

HEMA 156 E4   32 06 36 S   121 54 06 E

34 Jimberlana Hill Rest Area

Eyre Hwy, Norseman Area
Rest Area 7 km NE of Norseman. Follow Eyre Hwy for 5 km towards Eucla. On R

HEMA 156 E4   32 08 50 S   121 48 37 E

35 Norseman RV Park

Cnr Richardson & Mildura St, Norseman
Parking Area beside Rec Reserve, access via Mildura St

08 9039 1205   HEMA 156 E4   32 11 42 S   121 46 28 E

36 Dundas North

Coolgardie-Esperance Hwy, Dundas
Rest Area 15 km S of Norseman or 6.5 km N of Dundas

HEMA 156 E4   32 19 54 S   121 45 34 E

37 Dundas Rocks

Old Coach Rd, Dundas
Camp Spot 25 km S of Norseman or 46 km N of Kumarl. 2 km E of Hwy. 2 km dirt road, signposted. Access track narrows towards site, small vehicles only. Larger vehicles side tracks to stop in before rocks

HEMA 156 E4   32 23 25 S   121 46 23 E

38 Bromus Dam

Coolgardie-Esperance Hwy, Dundas
Camp Spot 32 km S of Norseman or 39 km N of Kumarl. Signposted

08 9039 1205   HEMA 156 E3   32 27 31 S   121 41 03 E

39 Kumarl Rest Area

Coolgardie-Esperance Hwy, Salmon Gums
Rest Area 73 km S of Norseman or 24 km N of Salmon Gums

138 138   HEMA 156 F3   32 47 16 S   121 33 16 E

40 Peak Charles Campground

Peak Charles National Park
Peak Charles Rd, North Cascade
Camp Area 106 km SW of Norseman or 46 km W of Kumarl. Turn W off Coolgardie Esperance Hwy 56 km S of Norseman to Lake King-Norseman Rd for 29 km, then S for 21 km. 50 km dirt road

08 9083 2100   HEMA 156 G2   32 52 45 S   121 10 25 E

41 Salmon Gums Community

Caravan Park
Nulsen St, Salmon Gums
Caravan Park E side of town. Caretaker collects fees

0467 880 443   HEMA 156 G3   32 58 55 S   121 38 53 E

42 Grass Patch Park & Stay

Shepherd St, Grass Patch
Caravan Park in town. Limited sites. Phone on arrival. Cash only. No EFTPOS in town

0488 510 701   HEMA 156 H3   33 13 44 S   121 42 52 E

43 Cape Le Grand

Cape Le Grand NP
Cape Le Grand Rd, Esperance Area
Camp Area 55 km SE of Esperance, via Merivale Rd

08 9083 2102   HEMA 156 K4   33 58 42 S   122 07 11 E

44 Lucky Bay Campground

Cape Le Grand NP
Lucky Bay Rd, Esperance
Camp Area 59 km SE of Esperance, via Merivale & Cape Le Grand Rds

08 9083 2102   HEMA 156 K5   33 59 30 S   122 13 12 E

WESTERN AUSTRALIA

45 Dunn Rocks
Cape Le Grand NP
Dunn Rock Rd, Esperance Area
Camp Spot 58 km E of Esperance. Via Merivale Rd
for 33 km turn R to for 12 km turn R for 4 km
08 9083 2102 　HEMA 156 K5　 33 55 34 S　 122 20 23 E

46 Condingup Community Hall
Sutcliffe St, Condingup
Parking Area via Parish St or Howick Rd
　HEMA 156 J5　 33 45 03 S　 122 31 48 E

47 Membinup Beach
Daniels Rd, Howick
Camp Area 90 km E of Esperance. Via
Merivale Rd. 12 km dirt road, suitable for offroad
caravans, limited sites. Honesty box
08 9083 1555　 HEMA 156 K6　 33 53 26 S　 122 38 58 E

48 Alexander Bay
Alexander Rd, Howick
Camp Area 105 km E of Esperance via
Merivale Rd. 10 km dirt road. Honesty box & ranger
08 9083 1555　 HEMA 156 K6　 33 53 06 S　 122 44 53 E

49 Thomas River Yokinup Mia
Mia Campground
Cape Arid National Park
Thomas River Rd, Cape Arid
Camp Area 118 km E of Esperance, via Fisheries
Rd & Tagon Rd. Dirt road
08 9083 2102　 HEMA 156 K6　 33 51 08 S　 123 00 48 E

50 Belinup Thomas River Shire
Campground
Cape Arid National Park
Thomas River Rd, Condingup
Camp Area 118 km E of Esperance, via Fisheries
Rd & Tagon Rd. Dirt road
08 9083 2100　 HEMA 156 K6　 33 51 15 S　 123 01 04 E

51 Thomas Fishery
Cape Arid National Park
Fisheries Rd, Cape Arid
Camp Area 164 km E of Esperance. Small vehicles only
08 9083 2102　 HEMA 156 K7　 33 59 32 S　 123 13 19 E

52 Jorndee Creek
Cape Arid National Park
Via Poison Ck Rd, Boyatup Area
Camp Area 163 km E of Esperance via Fisheries
Road & Baring Rds. Small vehicles only. No
campfires or solid fuel appliances
08 9083 2102　 HEMA 156 K7　 33 55 56 S　 123 19 23 E

53 Seal Creek
Cape Arid National Park
Poison Ck Rd, Boyatup Area
Camp Area 163 km E of Esperance via Fisheries
Road & Baring Rds. Small vehicles only
08 9083 2102　 HEMA 156 K7　 33 55 03 S　 123 19 44 E

54 Mount Ragged
Cape Arid National Park
Fisheries & Balladonia Rds, Boyatup Area
Camp Area 170 km E of Esperance or 134 km S of
Balladonia. Small vehicles only
08 9083 2102　 HEMA 156 H7　 33 27 58 S　 123 27 39 E

55 Israelite Bay
Nuytsland Nature Reserve
Fisheries Tr, Israelite Bay
Camp Area 198 km E of Esperance via Telegraph
Track, or 182 km S of Balladonia via Balladonia &
Gora Tracks. Honesty box & ranger
08 9219 9000　 HEMA 157 J8　 33 36 48 S　 123 52 03 E

Esperance to Albany
South Coast Highway

56 Quagi Beach
Via Farrells Rd, Munglinup
Camp Area 71 km W of Esperance or
51 km E of Munglinup. Turn S off South Coast Hwy
63 km W of Esperance or 43 km E of Munglinup to
8 km of dirt road. Honesty box & ranger
08 9083 1533　 HEMA 156 J2　 33 49 45 S　 121 17 31 E

57 Fanny Cove Camp Area
Stokes National Park
Fanny Cove Rd, Esperance Area
Camp Areas 89 km W of Esperance. W for 61 km on
Hwy, L to Farrells Rd 7 km, R 11 km, slight L 4 km, R
900 m, R 1 km, sites on L
08 9083 2100　 HEMA 156 J2　 33 51 21 S　 121 11 32 E

58 Benwenerup Campground
Stokes National Park
Stokes Inlet Rd, Munglinup
Camp Area 83 km W of Esperance. Turn S off Hwy
78 km W of Esperance or 28 km E of Munglinup for
7 km of dirt
08 9083 2100　 HEMA 156 J2　 33 49 03 S　 121 08 58 E

59 Coomalbidgup Rest Area
South Coast Hwy, Munglinup Area
Rest Area 88 km W of Esperance or 19 km
E of Munglinup
138 138　 HEMA 156 J2　 33 45 49 S　 121 02 56 E

60 Skippy Rock Campground
Stokes National Park
Torradup Rd, Esperance Area
Camp Area 103 km W of Esperance. W 87 km on
Hwy, L to Springdale Rd 6 km & L 7 km
08 9083 2100　 HEMA 156 K2　 33 51 33 S　 121 02 20 E

61 Munglinup Rest Area
Tubada St, Ravensthorpe
Rest Area opposite roadhouse. Fee for
shower
0890 751 041　 HEMA 156 J1　 33 42 17 S　 120 51 39 E

62 Munglinup Beach
Munglinup Beach Rd, Munglinup
Camp Area 31 km S of Munglinup. Turn
S off Hwy 4 km E of Munglinup to Fuss Rd 10 km,
Springdale Rd 10 km, then Munglinup Beach Rd
7 km. 9 km dirt road
08 9075 1155　 HEMA 155 K1　 33 53 13 S　 120 48 18 E

63 Starvation Bay Camping
Starvation Boat Harbour Rd, Munglinup
Camp Area 50 km E of Hopetoun, via
Springdale Rd. 40 km dirt road
0427 264 377　 HEMA 155 G14　 33 55 10 S　 120 33 19 E

64 Mason Bay
Speciosa Rd, Jerdacuttup
Camp Area 40 km E of Hopetoun, via
Springdale & Mason Bay Rds. 30 km dirt road
0427 264 377　 HEMA 155 G14　 33 57 16 S　 120 28 45 E

65 Hopetoun 48 RV Site

Esplanade, Hopetoun
Parking Area along Southern Ocean Rd.
Park between the signs
0400 499 267   HEMA 155 G13   33 56 48 S   120 07 53 E

66 Four Mile Campground

Fitzgerald River National Park
Hamersley Dr, Hopetoun
Camp Area 10 km W of Hopetoun. Via Southern
Ocean West Rd. Limited caravan sites
0488 451 119   HEMA 155 G13   33 55 22 S   120 02 14 E

67 Wonjarup (Hamersley Inlet)

Fitzgerald River National Park
Hamersley Inlet Dr, Hopetoun Area
Camp Area 26 km SW of Hopetoun. Via Southern
Ocean West Rd, Hamersley Inlet Dr & Moir Rd. No
booking, first in self-service stations & cash only
0427 264 377   HEMA 155 G12   33 57 22 S   119 55 02 E

68 Kundip Rest Area

Hopetoun-Ravensthorpe Rd, Ravensthorpe
Rest Area 19 km S of Ravensthorpe or
30 km N of Hopetoun
0400 499 267   HEMA 155 F13   33 41 25 S   120 11 10 E

69 Ravensthorpe Parking Area

Cnr Morgan & Queen Sts, Ravensthorpe
Parking Area opposite BP Roadhouse
0400 499 267   HEMA 155 F13   33 34 55 S   120 02 41 E

70 Meridian Rest Area

South Coast Hwy, Ravensthorpe
Rest Area 4 km W of Ravensthorpe or
109 km E of Jerramungup
08 9839 0000   HEMA 155 F13   33 34 26 S   120 00 08 E

71 Fitzgerald Old School Site

Fitzgerald Rd, Fitzgerald
Parking Area 60 km W of Ravensthorpe. Turn
N off Hwy to Fitzgerald Rd then second road on L
0400 499 267   HEMA 155 F11   33 44 53 S   119 27 25 E

72 Fitzgerald River (Jacup)

South Coast Hwy, Fitzgerald
Rest Area 80 km W of Ravensthorpe or
33 km E of Jerramungup midway between Lake
Magenta Rd & Jacup Rd North
08 9892 0555   HEMA 155 F11   33 49 53 S   119 15 13 E

73 Needilup Rest Area

Gnowangerup-Jerramungup Rd,
Jerramungup
Rest Area only 14 km W of Jerramungup or 25 km E
of Ongerup near Jcn Needilup Rd North, behind hall
138 138   HEMA 155 G10   33 57 09 S   118 46 19 E

74 Ongerup Caravan Park

Cnr Walker & Lamont Sts, Ongerup
Caravan Park S side of town
0476 379 291   HEMA 155 G9   33 58 04 S   118 29 12 E

75 Gnowangerup Caravan Park

5 Richardson St, Gnowangerup
Caravan Park 150 km NE of Albany. Pay at
IGA. Key bond applies
08 9827 1109   HEMA 155 G8   33 56 32 S   118 00 32 E

76 Borden Rest Area

Moir St, Borden
Rest Area opposite general store
08 9827 1007   HEMA 155 G9   34 04 16 S   118 15 46 E

77 Borden Recreation Ground

Stone St, Borden
Parking Area W side of town
08 9827 1007   HEMA 155 G9   34 04 22 S   118 15 31 E

78 Moingup Springs Camp

Stirling Range National Park
Chester Pass Rd, Borden
Camp Area 76 km N of Albany, 65 km N of Bakers
Junction or 45 km S of Borden
08 9842 4500   HEMA 155 H8   34 24 03 S   118 06 08 E

79 St Mary Inlet

Fitzgerald River National Park
Point Ann Rd, Point Ann
Camp Area 97 km SE of Jerramungup, access from
Bremer Bay side of NP
0488 451 119   HEMA 155 G12   34 09 51 S   119 34 35 E

80 Quaalup Homestead

Wilderness Retreat
Gairdner Rd, Bremer Bay
Camp Area 77 km SW of Jerramungup or 48 km
N of Bremer Bay. From Jerramungup turn E after
28 km to Devils Ck Rd 34 km, E to Collets Rd 4km,
SE to Gairdner Rd 9km. Gravel road for last 9 km.
From Bremer Bay via Swamp Rd route. Fires with
restrictions, BYO timber
08 9837 4124   HEMA 155 H11   34 15 37 S   119 24 35 E

81 Tozers Bush Camp

54 Oucomup Rd, Bremer Bay
Camp Area 85 km S of Jerramungup or
88 km E of Wellstead
0428 371 015   HEMA 155 H11   34 20 37 S   119 12 07 E

82 Millers Point Reserve

Millers Point Rd, Boxwood
Camp Area 20 km E of Boxwood Hill or
53 km W of Bremer Bay. Turn S off Borden Bremer
Bay Rd 14 km E of Boxwood Hill to Millers Point Rd.
6 km dirt road. Small vehicles only
08 9835 1022   HEMA 155 H10   34 27 14 S   118 52 42 E

83 Pallinup River

South Coast Hwy, Boxwood Area
Rest Area 67 km S of Jerramungup or
15 km NE of Wellstead. 5 km S Bremer Bay turnoff
08 9892 0555   HEMA 155 H10   34 24 24 S   118 43 35 E

84 Boat Harbour Camp

171 Boat Harbour Rd, Parryville
Camp Area 26 km W of Denmark & 2 km
SE of Hwy turnoff
0419 775 957   HEMA 153 K11   34 31 01 S   118 48 12 E

85 Cape Riche Campground

Sandlewood Rd, Cape Riche
Camp Area 18 km SE of Wellstead. Limited
space for big rigs, cold shower. Dirt road, 7 day limit
08 9847 3088   HEMA 155 J10   34 35 52 S   118 44 56 E

WESTERN AUSTRALIA

86 Wellstead Bush Park
37743 South Coast Hwy, Wellstead
Camp Area N side of town
0427 473 035   HEMA 155 H9   34 29 25 S   118 36 23 E

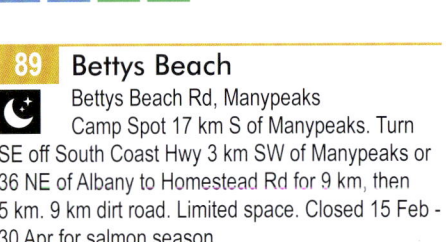

87 Green Range Rest Area
South Coast Hwy, Green Range
Rest Area 25 km SW of Wellstead or 73 km NE of Albany
08 9892 0555   HEMA 155 J9   34 37 41 S   118 22 51 E

88 Normans Beach
Normans Beach Rd, Manypeaks
Camp Spot 14 km S of Manypeaks. SE off Hwy 3 km SW of Manypeaks or 36 km NE of Albany to Homestead Rd 9 km, then to Normans Beach Rd 2 km. 6 km dirt road. 7 day limit
08 6820 3000   HEMA 155 K8   34 55 17 S   118 12 51 E

89 Bettys Beach
Bettys Beach Rd, Manypeaks
Camp Spot 17 km S of Manypeaks. Turn SE off South Coast Hwy 3 km SW of Manypeaks or 36 NE of Albany to Homestead Rd for 9 km, then 5 km. 9 km dirt road. Limited space. Closed 15 Feb - 30 Apr for salmon season
08 6820 3000   HEMA 155 K8   34 56 12 S   118 12 30 E

90 East Bay Campground
East Bay Rd, Manypeaks
Camp Area 15 km E of Hwy at Manypeaks. Turn L to Homestead Rd for 9 km & continue to Betty's Beach Rd for 3 km and turn R. 7 day limit
08 6820 3000   HEMA 155 K8   34 56 17 S   118 10 48 E

91 Napier Creek
Chester Pass Rd, Napier
Parking Area 25 km N of Albany or 23 km S of Porongurup. S of Napier Bridge on L
138 138   HEMA 155 J8   34 49 51 S   117 57 36 E

92 Bakers Junction Rest
South Coast Hwy, King River
Rest Area 16 km NE of Albany. At Hwy roundabout travel 10 km, turn R to stay on Hwy for 1 km, on L
138 138   HEMA 153 J14   34 55 30 S   117 55 28 E

93 Grove Park Golf Links
780 Frenchman Bay Rd, Little Grove
Camp Area 11 km S of Albany at Golf Links, turn to Torndirrup Rd
08 9844 4277   HEMA 153 K14   35 04 47 S   117 52 34 E

Albany-Bunbury-Perth
South Western Highway

94 Torbay Inlet
Torbay Inlet Rd, Torbay
Camp Area 28 km W of Albany or 38 km E of Denmark. Turn S off Lower Denmark Rd 24 km W of Albany or 34 E of Denmark to Perkins Beach & Torbay Inlet Rds. Dirt road for 4 km. Small area. 7 day limit
08 6820 3000   HEMA 153 K13   35 02 22 S   117 40 47 E

95 Cosy Corner East
Cosy Corner East Rd, Kronkup
Camp Area 35 km W of Albany or 38 km E of Denmark. Turn S off Lower Denmark Rd 25 km W of Albany or 33 km E of Denmark. 7 day limit
08 6820 3000   HEMA 153 K13   35 03 33 S   117 38 44 E

96 Shelley Beach Camp Area
West Cape Howe National Park
Shelley Beach Rd, Torbay
Camp Area 38 km W of Albany. Via Cosy Corner & Coombes Rds. 5.5 km dirt road, very steep descent. No caravans, small vehicles only, small area.
08 9844 4090   HEMA 153 K13   35 06 32 S   117 37 45 E

97 Parry Beach
Parry Rd, Parryville
Camp Area 28 km W of Denmark or 43 km E of Walpole. Turn S 22 km W of Denmark or 43 km E of Walpole for 6 km. Height limit 2.7m. Small vehicles only. No bookings, arrive before 5pm. Large vehicle overflow adjacent - no facilities. 3 week limit
08 9848 0300   HEMA 153 K11   35 02 25 S   117 09 42 E

98 Crystal Springs Camp
D'Entrecasteaux National Park
Mandalay Beach Rd, Crystal Springs
Camp Area 13 km W of Walpole
08 9840 0400   HEMA 153 J8   34 59 00 S   116 36 21 E

99 Banksia Camp
D'Entrecasteaux National Park
Banksia Tr, Broke
Camp Area 19 km W of Broke. Travel W along South Western Hwy 6 km turn L and follow Mandalay Beach Rd, signposted
08 9840 0400   HEMA 153 K8   35 00 16 S   116 30 43 E

100 Walpole West Rest Area
South Western Hwy, Walpole
Rest Area 16 km NW of Walpole or 104 km SE of Manjimup
138 138   HEMA 153 J8   34 57 16 S   116 35 39 E

101 Centre Road Crossing
Mount Frankland South NP
Centre Rd, Walpole
Camp Area 32 km NW of Walpole. Travel 27 km on the Hwy turn R for 5 km
08 9840 0400   HEMA 153 J8   34 54 37 S   116 37 20 E

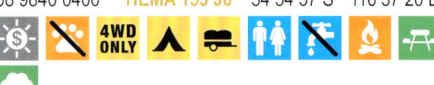

102 Fernhook Falls Campground
Mount Frankland South NP
Beardmore Rd, Walpole
Camp Area 39 km NW of Walpole or 88 km SE of Manjimup. Turn E 35 km NW of Walpole or 83 km SE of Manjimup, travel 5 km. Small sites, no caravans
08 9840 0400   HEMA 153 H8   34 49 01 S   116 35 28 E

103 Mount Burnside Rest Area
South Western Hwy, Walpole
Rest Area 56 km NW of Walpole or 64 km SE of Manjimup
138 138   HEMA 153 G8   34 39 10 S   116 29 42 E

104 Shannon Campground
Shannon National Park
Lower Shannon Rd, Shannon
Camp Area 53 km SE of Manjimup. Parks pass applies
08 9776 1207   HEMA 152 G7   34 35 40 S   116 24 43 E

105 Quinninup Eco Tourist Park
11 Wheatley Coast Rd, Quinninup
Caravan Park W side of road
08 9773 1329   HEMA 152 F7   34 26 11 S   116 14 44 E

106 Rooneys Bridge Camp

South Western Hwy, Quinninup
Camp Spot 25 km S of Manjimup or 2 km N
of Quinninup beside Rooneys Bridge
HEMA 152 F6   34 25 02 S   116 12 59 E

107 Greens Island

One Tree Bridge Conservation Park
Greens Island Rd, Manjimup
Camp Spot 26 km W of Manjimup via Graphite
Rd. N to Donnelly Dr 1.7 km past bridge to Greens
Island Rd. 2 km dirt road. Small vehicles only
08 9771 7988   HEMA 152 E5   34 12 00 S   115 56 46 E

108 Jayes Bridge

Jayes Rd, Mayanup
Picnic Area 15 km S of Boyup Brook. Turn
W off Boyup Brook-Kojonup Rd 6 km S of Boyup
Brook to Aegers Bridge Rd. Dirt road. Beside
Blackwood River
HEMA 152 C7   33 54 48 S   116 24 25 E

109 Querijup Pool

Scotts Brook Rd, Mayanup
Camp Spot 6 km SE of Mayanup. E on
Boyup Brook-Kojonup Rd 1 km, S to Scotts Brook
Rd 5.5 km. Track to camp spots, small vehicles only
08 9765 1200   HEMA 153 D8   33 58 01 S   116 30 38 E

110 Flax Mill Caravan Park

Jackson St, Boyup Brook
Caravan Park E end of town, run by council
08 9765 1200   HEMA 152 C7   33 50 06 S   116 23 59 E

111 Harvey Dicksons Country

Music Centre Campground
Boyup Brook Arthur Rd, Boyup Brook
Camp Area 5 km NE of Boyup Brook
08 9765 1125   HEMA 152 C7   33 48 25 S   116 25 18 E

112 Trigwells Bridge

Trigwell Bridge Rd, Dinninup
Parking Area 24 km SW of Moodiarrup or
36 km NE of Boyup Brook via Boyup Brook-Arthur
Rd. At the bridge over the Blackwood River
08 9765 1200   HEMA 153 B8   33 40 27 S   116 35 55 E

113 Wedge Tailed Eagle Retreat

3772 Boyup Brook-Arthur Rd, Trigwell
Farm Stay 39 km NE of Boyup Brook
0460 509 610   HEMA 153 B8   33 40 10 S   116 37 07 E

114 Maranup Ford Caravan Park

600 Maranup Ford Rd, Maranup
Caravan Park 20 km W of Bridgetown. Turn
N to Maranup Ford Rd or 10 km S of Greenbushes,
turn S. Entrance opposite 5 Gates Rd
0448 600 190   HEMA 152 C6   33 56 08 S   116 01 34 E

115 Karri Gully Picnic Site

Brockman Hwy, Nannup
Picnic Area 19 km E of Nannup or 27 km W
of Bridgetown. Small area
HEMA 152 D5   34 00 28 S   115 56 28 E

116 Nannup Lavender

4365 Graphite Rd, Nannup
Farm Stay 14 km S of Nannup
0428 302 370   HEMA 152 D5   34 05 47 S   115 46 53 E

117 Workmans Pool

St Johns Brook Conservation Park
Brook Rd, Nannup
Camp Area 8 km NW of Nannup. Turn W 2 km N of
Nannup to Mowen Rd. Signposted
08 9752 5555   HEMA 152 C4   33 57 14 S   115 41 16 E

118 Greenbushes Pool

Norm Lindsay Reserve
Spring Gully Rd, Greenbushes
Camp Area W of town. Donation at roadhouse.
Camp only in designated areas, see sign
08 9761 1740   HEMA 152 C6   33 51 01 S   116 02 43 E

119 Greenbushes Sportsground

Cnr South Western Hwy & Blackwood Rd,
Greenbushes
Camp Area 2 km N of Greenbushes or 8 km S of
Balingup, near N exit to Greenbushes. 7 day limit
08 9761 1740   HEMA 152 C6   33 50 13 S   116 02 49 E

120 Balingup Transit Park

Walter St, Balingup
Camp Area 1 km NE of PO. Turn R to
Jayes Rd, then L. Beside Balingup Brook
08 9764 1818   HEMA 152 B5   33 46 55 S   115 59 10 E

121 Wrights Bridge

Powlalup Nature Reserve
Ridge Rd, Southampton
Camp Area 29 km NE of Nannup or 11 km SW
of Balingup take Balingup-Nannup Rd. Beside
Blackwood River
08 9731 6232   HEMA 152 C5   33 50 45 S   115 55 07 E

122 Kirup Tavern Caravan Park

47 South Western Hwy, Kirup
Caravan Park behind pub
08 9731 6311   HEMA 152 B5   33 42 28 S   115 53 34 E

123 Donnybrook Transit Park

18 Reserve St, Donnybrook
Caravan Park at Egan Park entry at W end
of the oval. Book in at BP & collect key
08 9731 1897   HEMA 152 A5   33 34 16 S   115 49 12 E

124 Thomson Brook Wines

131 Thomson Rd, Donnybrook
Parking Area 5.5 km E of Donnybrook via
Donnybrook-Boyup Rd. Register at cellar door on
arrival. Patrons only
08 9731 0590   HEMA 152 A5   33 34 12 S   115 52 36 E

125 Wyalup Rocky Point

Ocean Dr, Bunbury
Parking Area at Cnr Upper Esplanade &
Ocean Dr. Permit from Visitor Centre
08 9792 7205   HEMA 150 K1   33 19 20 S   115 37 54 E

126 Ocean Drive

Cnr Ocean Dr & Scott St, Bunbury
Parking area S of intersection. Permit from
Bunbury Visitor Centre
08 9792 7205   HEMA 150 K1   33 19 47 S   115 37 45 E

WESTERN AUSTRALIA

127 Belvidere Campground
Leschenault Peninsula Conservation Park
Buffalo Rd, Australind
Camp Area 25 km N of Bunbury or 14 km NW of Australind. Follow Buffalo Rd, along Preston Lake continue along dirt road to campsites for 4.4 km
08 9219 9000   HEMA 150 J1   33 14 07 S   115 41 48 E

128 Buffalo Road Rest Area
Forrest Hwy, Australind
Rest Area 25 km N of Bunbury or 81 km S of Mandurah
138 138   HEMA 150 J2   33 11 58 S   115 43 02 E

129 Old Whittakers Mill
Bagieau Rd, Myalup
Rest Area 16 km N of Myalup on Forrest Hwy/Old Coast Rd. Turn R to Bagieau Rd site on L
138 138   HEMA 150 G2   32 57 39 S   115 43 36 E

130 Preston Beach
87 Mitchell Rd, Preston Beach
Parking Area 66 km N of Bunbury or 60 km S of Mandurah. From Mandurah, S on Forrest Hwy 50 km, W to Preston Beach Rd 8 km, continue on Mitchell Rd 1.5 km to sites. Open May - Oct
08 9733 7800   HEMA 150 G1   32 52 57 S   115 39 00 E

131 Martins Tank Lake
Yalgorup National Park
Preston Beach Rd, Preston Beach
Camp Area 74 km N of Bunbury or 58 km S of Mandurah. Turn W off Bunbury Hwy 61 km N of Bunbury or 45 km S of Mandurah for 12 km. 5 km dirt road. Small vehicles only. Pre-book
08 9405 0750   HEMA 150 G1   32 50 44 S   115 40 02 E

132 Lake Clifton Tavern Motel
3236 Old Coast Rd, Lake Clifton
Parking Area W of road. Pre-book
08 9739 1010   HEMA 150 F1   32 47 20 S   115 40 19 E

133 John Tognela Rest Area
Forrest Hwy & Lake Clifton Rd, Preston Beach
Rest Area 32 km S of Ravenswood. 2 areas, N & S bound traffic
138 138   HEMA 150 G2   32 48 52 S   115 44 28 E

WESTERN AUSTRALIA

Ravensthorpe-Hyden-Perth
Brookton Highway

134 Overshot Hill Nature Reserve
Newdegate-Ravensthorpe Rd, Ravensthorpe
Rest Area 9 km N of Ravensthorpe or 61 km S of Lake King
138 138   HEMA 155 F13   33 31 39 S   119 59 36 E

135 Lake King Caravan Park
Critchley Ave, Lake King
Caravan Park 500 m N of PO. Honesty box. Pay at tavern
08 9874 4048   HEMA 155 D12   33 05 02 S   119 41 18 E

136 Lake Camm Tennis Club
Lake Newton Rd, Lake Camm
Camp Area 90 km N of Ravensthorpe. Follow Newdegate-Ravensthorpe Rd 87 km. On R off Lake Newton Rd. Take the track behind the tennis courts to lake
08 9890 2500   HEMA 155 D12   32 57 29 S   119 36 22 E

137 Varley Chicken Ranch
Seward St, Varley
Parking Area 40 km S of Hyden. Donation box
08 9865 2140   HEMA 155 D11   32 47 41 S   119 30 35 E

138 Orange Gravel Resort
Hyden-Lake King Rd, Lake Grace
Camp Spot 67 km N of Lake King. Follow Hyden-Lake King Rd 66 km
HEMA 155 C11   32 37 35 S   119 21 27 E

139 Holt Rock North Road RV Stop
Holt Rock Rd North, Holt Rock
Camp Spot 250 m N of Lake King Rd/Brookton Hwy Jcn, 17 km N of Varley & 65 km S of Hyden
08 9880 1204   HEMA 155 C11   32 40 28 S   119 24 56 E

140 Anderson Rock
Anderson Rock Rd, Woolocutty
Camp Spot 40 km N of Hyden. Follow Hyden-Mt Walker Rd for 36 km turn R for 2.5 km & R again 2 km. Entry on L
08 9064 7308   HEMA 155 B10   32 10 08 S   118 51 04 E

141 The Forrestania Plots
Hyden Norseman Rd, Forrestania
Camp Spot 64.5 km E of Hyden. Dirt road. Signposted
08 9889 1006   HEMA 155 B11   32 24 55 S   119 32 01 E

142 The Breakaways
Hyden-Norseman Rd, Hyden Area
Camp Area 137 km E of Hyden. Signposted follow track for 500 m to sites. Dirt road
08 9039 1205   HEMA 155 B13   32 16 34 S   120 15 46 E

143 McDermid Rock
Hyden-Norseman Rd, Norseman Area
Camp Area 192 km E of Hyden, or 141 km W of Norseman. Turn N, travel 1.5 km to rock
08 9039 1205   HEMA 155 A14   32 01 18 S   120 44 20 E

144 Lake Johnston
Hyden-Norseman Rd, Norseman
Camp Area 200 km E of Hyden or 102 km W of Norseman. Access track S side of road
08 9039 1205   HEMA 155 A14   32 00 37 S   120 47 22 E

145 Disappointment Rock
Off Hyden-Norseman Rd, Norseman Area
Camp Area 87 km W of Norseman or 246 km E of Hyden. Dirt road. Narrow access track S side of road, limited space
08 9039 1205   HEMA 156 E2   32 07 48 S   120 55 44 E

146 Woodlands Picnic Area
Hyden-Norseman Rd, Norseman Area
Picnic Area 48 km W of Norseman or 285 km E of Hyden. Dirt road
08 9039 1205   HEMA 156 E3   32 11 15 S   121 20 16 E

147 Tressies Museum & Caravan Park
4313 Konbinin-Hyden Rd, Karlgarin
Caravan Park 17 km W of Hyden. N of road
0475 895 043   HEMA 155 C10   32 29 44 S   118 42 43 E

148 Kulin Caravan Park

82 Johnston St, Kulin
Caravan Park N side of town. Donation - conditions apply
0439 469 850 HEMA 151 F13 32 40 02 S 118 09 31 E

149 Kulin Overnight Stop
Johnston St South Side, Kulin
Camp Spot E of road. Entry between toilets & skate park
08 9880 1204 HEMA 151 F13 32 40 13 S 118 09 20 E

150 Harrismith Caravan Park
Cnr Railway Ave & Baylon St, Harrismith
Caravan Park. Check in at the pub
08 9883 1010 HEMA 151 G11 32 56 10 S 117 51 44 E

151 Kondinin Caravan Park
32 Gordon St, Kondinin
Caravan Park. Key & payment at shire office or roadhouse
08 9889 1006 HEMA 151 E13 32 29 43 S 118 15 49 E

152 Kondinin Town Hall Parking
25 Jones St, Kondinin
Parking Area opposite town hall, vehicles to 11 m only
08 9041 1666 HEMA 151 E13 32 29 45 S 118 16 04 E

153 Roe Dam
Yeomans Rd, Mount Walker
Camp Area 54 km N of Hyden. Follow Hyden-Mt Walker Rd for 46 km, Mt Walker & Roe Dam Rds
08 9064 7308 HEMA 155 A10 31 59 50 S 118 48 55 E

154 Narembeen Caravan Park
11 Currall St, Narembeen
Caravan Park. Free RV Park for SCV
08 9064 7308 HEMA 151 B14 32 03 49 S 118 23 46 E

155 Bruce Rock Caravan Park
Dunstal St, Bruce Rock
Caravan Park by the swimming pool
08 9061 1377 HEMA 151 A13 31 52 26 S 118 09 05 E

156 Bruce Rock RV Stop
59 Dunstal St, Bruce Rock
Parking Area near old tennis courts. Veer R after entry, signposted. Permit applies
08 9041 1666 HEMA 151 A13 31 52 23 S 118 09 04 E

157 Kwolyin Camp
Bruce Rock-Quairading Rd, Kwolyin
Camp Area on the Old Kwolyin town site
08 9061 1377 HEMA 151 B11 31 55 56 S 117 45 46 E

158 Quairading Caravan Park

McLennan St, Quairading
Caravan Park keys available from shire office at Quairading
08 9645 2400 HEMA 151 B9 32 00 44 S 117 24 09 E

159 Quairading RV Club Permit Area
McLennan St, Quirading
Camp Area at Travellers Rest Area Greater Sports Ground. Permit from shire office,10 Jennaberring Rd
08 9041 1666 HEMA 151 B9 32 00 42 S 117 24 10 E

160 Toapin Weir
Toapin Rd, Quairading
Rest Area 8 km N of Quairading. Signposted, turn W from Cunderdin-Quairading Rd 5.5 km N of Quairading. 3 km gravel road to weir
HEMA 151 B9 31 58 44 S 117 21 36 E

161 Wamenusking Sports Club
2789 Corrigin-Quairading Rd, Wamenusking
Parking Area 36 km N of Corrigin. Phone for key to amenities
0427 042 036 HEMA 151 C10 32 08 50 S 117 37 04 E

Lake King to Bunbury

162 Jam Patch
Lake Grace Land Conservation District
Lake Grace-Karlgarin Rd, Lake Grace Area
Camp Spot 20 km N of Lake Grace, via Kulin-Lake Grace Rd for 16 km, GPS at turn off on R
08 9890 2500 HEMA 151 G14 32 57 14 S 118 29 46 E

163 Lake Grace Caravan Park
Mather St, Lake Grace
Caravan Park NW side of town. SCV rates
08 9865 1263 HEMA 151 H14 33 05 59 S 118 27 33 E

164 Kukerin Caravan Park
31 Bath St, Kukerin
Caravan Park. Pay at store or hotel
08 9863 4012 HEMA 151 J12 33 11 09 S 118 04 59 E

165 Dumbleyung Caravan Park
35 Harvey St, Dumbleyung
Caravan Park central to town. Check in at shire office opposite
08 9863 4012 HEMA 151 J11 33 18 49 S 117 44 25 E

166 Stubbs Park
Bahrs Rd, Dumbleyung
Parking Area at Sporting Ground, S of town
08 9863 4012 HEMA 151 J11 33 19 04 S 117 44 36 E

167 Darkan Caravan Park
274 Coalfields Rd, Darkan
Caravan Park 1 km W of PO
08 9736 2222 HEMA 150 K6 33 20 04 S 116 43 30 E

168 Collie River - Buckingham
Coalfields Hwy, Collie River
Camp Spot 19 km E of Collie off Hwy 18 km turn R, 500 m on L
08 9734 9000 HEMA 150 K4 33 23 36 S 116 19 08 E

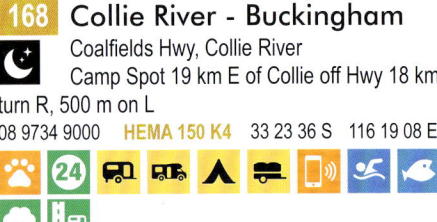

169 Stockton Lake
Stockton Lake Rec Area
Piavanini Rd, Collie
Camp Area 8 km E of Collie. Turn S off Hwy 107, 53 km W of Darkan or 6 km E of Collie
08 9735 1988 HEMA 150 K4 33 23 05 S 116 13 43 E

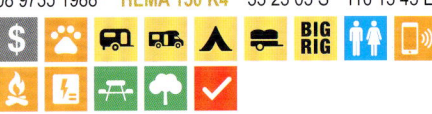

170 Yourdamung Road Retreat
708 Yourdamung Rd, Collie
Camp Area 20 km NE of Collie, 8.5 km off Collie-Williams Rd. Pre-book
0408 224 562 HEMA 150 J4 33 15 09 S 116 16 41 E

171 Glen Mervyn Dam
Collie-Preston Rd, Mumballup
Camp Spot 18 km S of Collie. Camping on the W side only. Small vehicles only via a narrow unsealed track. Road is potholed
08 9734 2051 HEMA 152 A6 33 29 49 S 116 05 53 E

172 The Mumby Tavern
2751 Donnybrook-Boyup Brook Rd, Mumballup
Parking Area opposite Mumby Pub
08 9732 2550 HEMA 152 A6 33 31 41 S 116 06 45 E

173 Potters Gorge
Wellington National Park
Tom Jones Dr, Burekup Area
Camp Area 29 km W of Collie, via Coalfields & Wellington Dam Rds. Concession applies
08 9735 1988 HEMA 150 K3 33 23 25 S 115 58 55 E

174 Coalfields Road Rest Area
Coalfields Rd, Collie
Rest Area 23 km W of Collie or 13 km E of South West Hwy/Coalfields Rd Jcn
138 138 HEMA 150 J3 33 17 30 S 115 56 56 E

Cranbrook to Northam
Great Southern Highway

175 Nyabing Caravan Parking Facility
Martin St, Nyabing
Caravan Park at Sports Rec Grounds. Key at shire office
08 9829 1051 HEMA 155 F8 33 32 40 S 118 08 49 E

176 Pingrup Caravan Park
18 Sanderson St, Pingrup
Caravan Park. Pay at CRC 2 Burston St
08 9820 1101 HEMA 155 F9 33 32 05 S 118 30 40 E

177 Wagin Caravan Park
39 Scadden St, Wagin
Caravan Park 1 km W of PO, off Arthur Rd. Cash only or pay at shire office
0419 611 057 HEMA 151 J9 33 18 39 S 117 20 05 E

178 Wagin Showgrounds RV Area
Ballagin St, Wagin
Camp Area NW of PO
08 9861 1177 HEMA 151 J9 33 18 20 S 117 20 10 E

179 Highbury Rest Area
Great Southern Hwy, Highbury
Rest Area E side of Hwy, opposite Highbury Store, in town centre between Burley & Campbell Sts
08 9881 2064 HEMA 151 H9 33 03 23 S 117 14 26 E

180 Downderry Winery
Lot 2 Graham Rd, Dumberning
Farm Stay 12 km SW of Narrogin via William & Williams-Kondinin Rd for 6.5 km, L to Tarwonga Rd for 5.5 km, turn R
0429 814 903 HEMA 151 H8 33 00 46 S 117 06 25 E

181 Narrogin RV Stop
Fairway St, Narrogin
Camp Area in the old Goods Shed Yard. Dump point opposite
08 9881 2064 HEMA 151 G8 32 56 12 S 117 10 47 E

182 Wickepin Caravan Park
Wogolin Rd, Wickepin
Caravan Park behind police station. Reduced fee for RV
0487 257 036 HEMA 151 F10 32 46 52 S 117 30 12

183 Wickepin RV Stop
Wogolin Rd, Wickepin
Parking Area behind 24 hour fuel depot
08 9888 1005 HEMA 151 F10 32 46 53 S 117 29 59

184 Lake Yealering Caravan Park
Sewell Rd, Yealering
Caravan Park beside lake
0428 787 426 **HEMA 151 E10** 32 35 37 S 117 37 32 E

185 Laze-Away Holiday Farm
Great Southern Hwy, Popanyinning
Caravan Park 4 km S of PO
08 9887 5027 **HEMA 151 F8** 32 41 34 S 117 08 40 E

186 Pingelly Caravan Park
26 Sharrow St, Pingelly
Caravan Park E of Hwy. Pay & amenities
code at craft centre
08 9887 1351 **HEMA 151 E8** 32 32 09 S 117 05 07 E

187 Kulyaling Picnic Area
Kulyaling Rd, East Pingelly
Picnic Area 10 km N of Pingelly or 10 km S
of Brookton
HEMA 151 E8 32 27 37 S 117 02 55 E

188 Brookton Caravan Park
Brookton Hwy, Brookton
Caravan Park behind rec ground. Pre-book
with council & honesty box onsite
08 9642 1106 **HEMA 150 D7** 32 22 07 S 117 00 08 E

189 Brookton Lions Park
Brookton-Corrigan Rd, Brookton
Parking Area on Hwy. Near Reynolds St
08 9642 1106 **HEMA 151 D8** 32 21 53 S 117 00 46 E

190 Jelcobine Rest Area
Coles Rd, Jelcobine
Rest Area 30 km W of Brookton. Follow
Hwy for 27 km, L to Woods Loop, sharp R
HEMA 150 D6 32 23 59 S 116 44 14 E

191 Beverley Caravan Park
Council Rd, Beverley
Caravan Park N end of town. Via Hunt Rd
0457 344 434 **HEMA 150 C7** 32 06 28 S 116 55 25 E

192 Beverley RV Stop
Lukin St, Beverley
Rest Area opposite Avon R. Donation box
08 9646 1200 **HEMA 150 C7** 32 06 27 S 116 55 52 E

193 Gwambygine Avon Ascent Park
Great Southern Hwy, Gwambygine
Picnic Area 23 km N of Beverley or 11 km S of York
08 9641 2233 **HEMA 150 B7** 31 58 20 S 116 48 35 E

194 Janet Millet Lane RV Stop
Janet Millet Lane, York
Parking Area adjacent to croquet club
08 9641 1301 **HEMA 150 A6** 31 53 15 S 116 46 19 E

195 Whitegum Farm
680 Cameron Rd, York Area
Camp Area 20 km SE of York via Northam-
York & Goldfields Rd
0408 906 520 **HEMA 150 A7** 31 52 10 S 116 57 32 E

196 Greenhills Inn
444 Greenhills Rd, Greenhills
Parking Area. Check in with publican
08 9641 4095 **HEMA 150 B7** 31 55 17 S 116 57 47 E

197 Woottating Roadside Rest
1093 Great Southern Hwy, Woottating
Rest Area 27 km E of Madaring or 34 km
W of York. E from Mundaring on Great Eastern Hwy
(94) 16 km, E to Great Southern Hwy 11 km
138 138 **HEMA 150 A5** 31 52 50 S 116 26 15 E

Albany to Perth
Albany Highway

198 Mount Barker RV Stop
Muir St, Mount Barker
Parking Area W of the Hall, on bitumen
08 9892 1111 **HEMA 153 G13** 34 37 29 S 117 39 45 E

199 Muirs Bridge Rest Area
Muir Hwy, Rocky Gully
Rest Area 11 km NW of Rocky Gully or
87 km SE of Manjimup, beside Frankland River
HEMA 153 F10 34 28 38 S 116 54 07 E

200 Sturdee Road Rest Area
Albany Hwy, Kendenup
Rest Area 12 km N of Mt Barker or 94 km S
of Kojonup
138 138 **HEMA 153 G13** 34 32 05 S 117 36 05 E

201 Kendenup Agricultural Grounds
Beverley Rd, Kendenup
Camp Area W of PO. 7 day limit
0418 855 669 **HEMA 153 G13** 34 29 23 S 117 36 50 E

202 Lake Nunijup
Stockyard Rd, Cranbrook
Picnic Area 39 km NW of Mount Barker. W
off Albany Hwy at Kendenup to Martagallup Rd. NW
for 20 km, E to dirt road 700 m
08 9826 1008 **HEMA 153 F12** 34 24 19 S 117 24 20 E

203 Lake Poorrarecup
Poorrarecup Rd, Frankland River
Camp Area 42 km SW of Cranbrook. Turn S
off Cranbrook-Frankland Rd 33 km W of Cranbrook
or 13 km E of Frankland. 9 km dirt road
08 9826 1008 **HEMA 153 F11** 34 25 06 S 117 14 08 E

204 Frankland River Caravan Park
Marlock St, Frankland
Caravan Park behind town hall. Access via
Wingebellup Rd. Caretaker collects fees
0428 302 489 **HEMA 153 F11** 34 21 42 S 117 04 57 E

205 Tonebridge Rest Area
Cranbrook-Boyup Brook Rd, Tonebridge
Rest Area 1.5 km NW of Tonebridge. S side
of bridge by river
08 9765 1200 **HEMA 153 E9** 34 13 39 S 116 42 16 E

206 Cranbrook RV Stop
29 Gathorne St, Cranbrook
Parking Area opposite hotel, behind
museum. Pay at shire office
08 9826 1008 **HEMA 153 E13** 34 17 42 S 117 33 19 E

207 Kojonup RV Rest Area

Cnr Albany Hwy & Gordon St, Kojonup
Rest Area S end of town next to Giant Wool
Wagon. Permit from Info Centre at 143 Albany Hwy
08 9831 2400   HEMA 153 C11   33 50 13 S   117 09 32 E

208 Froggle Forest

26 Denny Rd, Kojonup
Camp Spot 4 km W of Kojonup. From
Blackwood Pensioner Rd Jcn travel 3 km W, turn R
for 230 m turn R. Pre-book
0400 648 937   HEMA 153 C11   33 50 07 S   117 07 32 E

209 Katanning BP Roadhouse

68 Cornwall St, Katanning
Caravan Park with 25 powered sites
08 9821 1155   HEMA 153 B13   33 42 04 S   117 33 36 E

210 Katanning RV Rest Area

15 Aberdeen St, Katanning
Rest Area behind the library. Donation at
Visitors Info Centre
08 9821 9999   HEMA 153 B13   33 41 23 S   117 33 09 E

211 Lake Ewlyamartup

Langaweira Rd, Katanning
Camp Area 19 km E of Katanning. Via
Katanning-Nyabing Rd 15 km, R 1 km, L 120 m, on L
08 9821 9999   HEMA 153 B14   33 41 31 S   117 44 12 E

212 Queererrup Lake

Queererrup Rd, Woodanilling
Camp Area 28 km NW of Woodanilling.
Turn N off Robinson Rd 15 km W of Woodanilling to
Reshke Rd, follow 3 km, L to Douglas Rd, R & turn
R at T Jcn
08 9823 1506   HEMA 153 A11   33 30 55 S   117 13 27 E

213 Woodanilling Rec Reserve

Yairabin St, Woodanilling
Parking Area. Limited sites. Honesty box
onsite
08 9823 1506   HEMA 153 A12   33 33 36 S   117 25 59 E

214 Norring Lake

Norring Rd, Woodanilling
Camp Area 20 km SW of Wagin. From Hwy
take Beaufort St via Umbra St 7 km, L for 7 km, slight
R for 3 km & turn L stay on Norring Rd for 1 km
08 9861 1177   HEMA 151 K9   33 26 50 S   117 17 04 E

215 Martup Pool

Albany Hwy, Beaufort River
Camp Spot 32 km N of Kojonup or 24 km S
of Arthur River. Some low trees, track to river
HEMA 153 A11   33 32 47 S   117 05 07 E

216 Old Minding School

Arthur Rd, Arthur River
Camp Area 22 km W of Wagin
138 138   HEMA 151 K8   33 20 07 S   117 07 18 E

217 Lakeside Camping (Lake Towerrinning)

64 Towerrinning Rd, Moodiarrup
Camp Area 40 km SW of Arthur River or 64 km NE of
Boyup Brook. 2 km N of Moodiarrup, via Darkan Rd S
0419 765 196   HEMA 153 A9   33 35 02 S   116 47 32 E

218 Eulin Crossing

Eulin Crossing Rd, Eulin Crossing
Camp Spot 20 km SW of Moodiarrup or
49 km NE of Boyup Brook. Turn SE 16 km from
Moodiarrup or 45 km from Boyup Brook to Kulikup N
Rd for 4 km. Turn W for 1 km, track down to sites
08 9765 1200   HEMA 153 B9   33 42 04 S   116 40 27 E

219 Congelin Campground

Dryandra Woodland
York-Williams Rd, Congelin
Camp Area 27 km N of Williams. Turn N off Hwy 30,
3 km NW of Williams. Signposted
08 9881 9200   HEMA 150 G7   32 49 15 S   116 53 20 E

220 Gnaala Mia Campground

Dryandra Woodland
Godfrey Rd, Congelin
Camp Area 27 km N of Williams via Albany Hwy. Turn
N off Hwy 3 km NW of Williams to York-Williams Rd
08 9881 9200   HEMA 150 G7   32 48 34 S   116 52 25 E

221 Lions Dryandra

Lol Gray State Forest
Kawana Rd, Dryandra
Camp Area S of Dryandra. Take Stevens Rd
4 km turn R to Wandering-Narrogin Rd, 6 km R to
Kawana Rd, 3 km turn L 850 m
08 9881 9200   HEMA 150 F7   32 46 46 S   116 58 12 E

222 Pumphreys Bridge Lions Park

Pumphreys Rd, Pumphreys Bridge
Camp Area 43 km N Narrogin via Wandering-
Narrogin Rd. NW side of the CWA building
HEMA 150 F7   32 39 45 S   116 54 17 E

223 Codjatotine Rest Area

1878 Wandering Pingelly Rd, Codjatotine
Rest Area 30 km W of Pingelly via N
Bannister-Pingelly Rd
08 9884 1056   HEMA 150 F7   32 39 36 S   116 49 37 E

224 Williams River Farm Stay

10845 Pinjarra-Williams Rd, Williams
Farm Stay 19 km W of Williams Woolshed.
Unpowered sites exclude facilities. Pre-book
08 9885 1181   HEMA 150 H6   33 06 02 S   116 42 59 E

225 Quindanning Hotel

9197 Pinjarra-Williams Rd, Quindanning
Parking Area E of road. Check in at bar on
arrival. Patrons only
08 9885 7053   HEMA 150 H5   33 02 38 S   116 34 05 E

226 Williams Roadside RV Stop

Albany Hwy, Williams
Rest Area 6 km N of Williams, or 29 km S
of Crossman
138 138   HEMA 150 H7   32 59 22 S   116 50 26 E

227 Armoin Nature Based Camp

9721 Albany Hwy, Crossman
Camp Area 6 km S of Crossman or 34 km
N of Williams. Pre-book. Hire toilet available
0437 906 510   HEMA 150 G6   32 49 26 S   116 36 53 E

228 Crossman Rest Area

Albany Hwy, Crossman
Rest Area 93 km S of Armadale, or 39 km N of Williams. Between Crossman-Dwarda Rd and Crossman Rd

138 138   HEMA 150 F6   32 46 40 S   116 35 42 E

229 Boddington RV Stop

Bannister Rd, Boddington
Parking Area at Boddington opposite intersection of Bannister & Crossmans Rds

08 9883 4999   HEMA 150 G5   32 47 52 S   116 28 39 E

230 Wandering Caravan Park

Lot 27 Cheetanning S, Wandering
Caravan Park S side of town. Register & pay at shire office, or at tavern after hours

08 9884 1056   HEMA 150 F6   32 41 03 S   116 40 29 E

231 Bannister Parking Area

Albany Hwy, Bannister
Parking Area 11 km N of Crossman or 4 km S of Bannister

138 138   HEMA 150 F5   32 42 47 S   116 32 47 E

232 North Bannister Threeways Roadhouse

6519 Albany Hwy, North Bannister
Rest Area opposite Threeways Tavern

138 138   HEMA 150 E5   32 34 49 S   116 26 38 E

233 Jarrahdale 24 Hr Rest Area

Albany Hwy, Jarrahdale
Rest Area 29 km S of Albany, or 69 km N of Crossman. 2 km S of Jarrahdale Rd

138 138   HEMA 150 D4   32 18 55 S   116 12 25 E

234 Gleneagle Rest Area

Albany Hwy, Gleneagle
Rest Area 25 km S of Armadale & 68 km N of the Boddington turnoff. 2 km N of Jarrahdale Rd & Serpentine Dam turnoff on E side of Hwy. Some low trees at entrance

138 138   HEMA 150 D4   32 17 21 S   116 11 29 E

235 Jarrahdale Old Mill

Millars Rd, Jarradale
Parking Area off Jarrahdale Road, near Cnr of Kingsbury Dr

08 9526 1111   HEMA 150 D3   32 20 03 S   116 04 07 E

Perth to Bunbury
South Western Highway

236 Serpentine South Rest Area

South Western Hwy, Serpentine Area
Rest Area 11 km S of Serpentine, or 24 km N of Pinjarra

138 138   HEMA 150 D3   32 27 12 S   115 58 57 E

237 Pinjarra RV Parking Area

21 Pinjarra-Williams Rd, Pinjarra
Parking Area 200 m from Hwy Cnr

08 9531 7777   HEMA 150 F2   32 37 46 S   115 52 45 E

238 Blythwood Rest Area

South Western Hwy, Blythwood
Rest Area 7.5 km S of Pinjara

138 138   HEMA 150 F2   32 40 49 S   115 51 46 E

239 Blythwood South

South Western Hwy, Blythwood
Rest Area 10 km S of Pinjara via S Western Hwy

138 138   HEMA 150 F2   32 41 57 S   115 52 35 E

240 Herron Point Reserve

Herron Point Rd, Birchmont
Camp Area 30 km S of Pinjarra near Lake Clifton. Turn N off Old Bunbury Rd 16 km SW of Pinjarra or 14 km E of Old Coast Rd/Old Bunbury Rd Jcn. Ranger collect fees

08 9531 7777   HEMA 150 F2   32 44 28 S   115 42 38 E

241 Marrinup Townsite Camp

Marrinup State Forest
Grey Rd, Dwellingup
Camp Area 5 km NW of Dwellingup. Turn N 2.2 km W of Dwellingup or 25 km E of Pinjarra to Grey Rd. Travel 2.7 km, cross railway line, follow signposted track up hill

08 9538 1078   HEMA 150 F3   32 42 07 S   116 01 40 E

242 Nanga Mill

Lane Poole Reserve
Via Nanga Rd, Dwellingup
Camp Area 18 km S of Dwellingup. Dirt road. 500 m from Nanga gate

08 9538 1078   HEMA 150 G3   32 48 10 S   116 06 14 E

243 Chuditch Campground

Lane Poole Reserve
Nanga Rd, Dwellingup
Camp Area 16 km S of Dwellingup. 8.5 km from entry station, via Murray Valley Rd. Small vehicles only, limited caravan sites, ebook

08 9538 1078   HEMA 150 F3   32 47 18 S   116 06 43 E

244 Baden Powell Campground

Lane Poole Reserve
Via Nanga Rd, Dwellingup
Camp Area 9 km S of Dwellingup & 1.5 km from entry station, ebook

08 9538 1078   HEMA 150 F3   32 46 18 S   116 05 12 E

245 Charlies Flat Campground

Lane Poole Reserve
via Nanga Rd, Dwellingup Area
Camp Area 14.5 km S of Dwellingup & 7 km from entry station on River Rd. Dirt road. Small vehicles only, limited caravan sites, ebook

08 9538 1078   HEMA 150 G3   32 46 53 S   116 06 22 E

246 Waroona North Rest Area

South Western Hwy, Waroona Area
Rest Area 21 km S of Pinjarra or 18 km N or Yarloop

138 138   HEMA 150 F2   32 48 25 S   115 54 12 E

247 Waroona Showgrounds

South Western Hwy, Waroona
Camp Area entry from Millar St. May - Oct

08 9733 7800   HEMA 150 G2   32 50 46 S   115 55 16 E

248 Wagerup Parking Area

South Western Hwy, Wagerup
Parking Area 6 km N of Yarloop or 6 km S of Waroona

138 138   HEMA 150 G2   32 53 36 S   115 54 30 E

WESTERN AUSTRALIA

249 Drakesbrook Weir

Weir Rd, Waroona
Camp Area 10 km E of Waroona to Lake Moyanup via SW Hwy, McLarty St & Weir Rd. May - Oct
08 9733 7800   HEMA 150 G2   32 51 34 S   115 57 01 E

250 Logue Brook North Camp

Dwellingup State Forest
Logue Brook Dam Rd, Yarloop
Dispersed Camping at Lake Brockman, NW side. 20 km NE of Harvey. Turn E off SW Hwy 6 km S of Yarloop. Continue over dam wall, 3 km to end. Ranger collects fees
08 9735 1988   HEMA 150 H3   32 59 17 S   115 58 49 E

251 Logue Brook South Camp

Dwellingup State Forest
Logue Brook Dam Rd, Yarloop
Camp Area at Lake Brockman. Turn E off South Western Hwy 6 km S of Yarloop, to Scarp Rd. Pay fees at tourist park kiosk. Pre-book
08 9733 5402   HEMA 150 H3   33 00 19 S   115 58 26 E

252 Hoffman Mill

Dwellingup State Forest
Clarke Rd, Yarloop
Camp Area 22 km E of Yarloop. Turn E 5 km S of Yarloop or 9 km N of Harvey, to Logue Brook Dam Rd. 11 km dirt road. Open Nov - Easter
08 9735 1988   HEMA 150 H3   33 00 15 S   116 04 59 E

253 Waterloo Rest Area

South Western Hwy, Waterloo
Rest Area 13 km E of Bunbury, or 12 km SW of Brunswick. Old State School site
138 138   HEMA 150 K2   33 19 46 S   115 45 33 E

Bunbury-Margaret River-Northcliffe

Bussell, Brockman and Vasse Highways

254 Capel RV Stop

Berkshire St, Capel
Parking Area S of PO
08 9727 0222   HEMA 152 A3   33 33 33 S   115 33 36 E

255 Christian Brethren Campsite

172 Caves Rd, Siesta Park
Campground 11 km W of Busselton
08 9755 4561   HEMA 152 B2   33 39 29 S   115 14 27 E

256 Busselton Farm Stay

394 Kaloorup Rd, Busselton
Farm Stay at Vasse Lawn Farm, 16 km SW of Busselton, or 37 km NE of Margaret River. Pre-book. Limited sites, 7 day limit
0408 931 168   HEMA 152 B2   33 42 45 S   115 14 41 E

257 Olive Hill Farm RV Camp

232 Bramley River Rd, Osmington Area
Camp Area 13 km E of Margaret River. No campervans
0448 095 428   HEMA 152 C2   33 55 18 S   115 10 10 E

258 Canebrake Pool

Rapids Conservation Park
Crossing Rd, Margaret River Area
Camp Area 25 km E of Margaret River via Mowen & Great North Rd. 5 km dirt road
08 9752 5555   HEMA 152 C2   33 52 55 S   115 16 52 E

259 RAC Margaret River Nature Park

Wooditjup National Park
Carters Rd, Margaret River Area
Camp Area 280 km S of Perth or 2 km N of Margaret River
08 9758 8227   HEMA 152 C1   33 56 04 S   115 04 07 E

260 Big Valley Campsite

46 Boronia Rd, Rosa Glen
Camp Area 12 km SE of Margaret River. Via Bussell Hwy 2 km, turn E to Rosa Brook Rd for 5 km & S to Wallis Rd for 2 km over cattle grid
08 9757 5020   HEMA 152 D2   33 59 04 S   115 09 18 E

261 Glenbrook Country Retreat

38 Darch Rd, Margaret River
Camp Area 5 km S of Margaret River, or 25 km N of Karridale. Pre-book
0448 681 868   HEMA 152 D1   33 59 13 S   115 05 32 E

262 Warner Glen (Chapman Pool)

Blackwood River National Park
Warner Glen Rd, Forest Grove Area
Camp Area 15 km SE of Witchcliffe or 21 km NE of Karridale. Turn E 6 km S of Witchcliffe or turn N 11 km E of Karridale
08 9752 5555   HEMA 152 D2   34 05 33 S   115 12 23 E

Logue Brook Campground is set in the state forest overlooking the clear blue waters of **Logue Brook Dam** and caters for all sizes and types of camping set ups, including:

- a specialised tent area
- a fire ring *(in winter months)* and a park bench for each site.
- drop toilets and undercover areas with gas BBQs.
- 2 BMX pump tracks.
- We are pet friendly
- Bushwalking and birdwatching - we are close to the Munda Biddi bike trail and the Bibbulman walking track.

Logue Brook Dam is a water lovers paradise where you can waterski, canoe, kayak and swim in the fresh water.

Fish for trout all year round *(must have a freshwater fishing license)*

Book online: www.lakebrockman.com.au | Ph: (08) 9733 5402 | Email: lakebrockman@gmail.com

263 Conto Chuditch Camp

Leeuwin-Naturaliste National Park
Conto Rd, Forest Grove Area
Camp Area 19 km SW of Margaret River or 20 km NW of Karridale. Turn W off Caves Rd 16 km SW of Margaret River or 18 km NW of Karridale, ebook
08 9757 7025   HEMA 152 D1   34 04 50 S   115 00 43 E

264 Conto Quenda Camp
Leeuwin-Naturaliste National Park
Conto Rd, Forest Grove Area
Camp Area 19 km SW of Margaret River. Turn W off Caves Rd
08 9757 7025   HEMA 152 D1   34 04 57 S   115 00 47 E

265 Conto Whistlers Camp

Leeuwin-Naturaliste National Park
Conto Rd, Forest Grove Area
Camp Area 20 km SW of Margaret River. Turn W off Caves Rd
08 9757 7025   HEMA 152 D1   34 04 58 S   115 00 56 E

266 Jarrahdene Campground

Leeuwin-Naturaliste National Park
Jarrahdene Rd, Forest Grove Area
Camp Area 21 km SW of Margaret River. Turn W off Caves Rd, ebook
08 9757 7025   HEMA 152 D1   34 06 40 S   115 04 37 E

267 Boranup Campground

Leeuwin-Naturaliste National Park
Boranup Rd, Karridale
Camp Area 35 km SW of Margaret River or 8 km NW of Karridale, via Caves Rd. Small vehicles only
08 9757 7025   HEMA 152 E1   34 10 41 S   115 04 04 E

268 Deepdene Farm Stay
10517 Caves Rd, Deepdene
Farm Stay 5.1 km NW of Augusta. Turn L to Bussell Hwy 450 m, turn L 4.3 km. Pre-book
0438 905 627   HEMA 152 E1   34 16 32 S   115 06 21 E

269 Boogaloo Campground
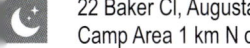
22 Baker Cl, Augusta
Camp Area 1 km N of Augusta, coast side of Hwy
0478 899 398   HEMA 152 E2   34 17 47 S   115 08 39 E

270 Alexandra Bridge Camp
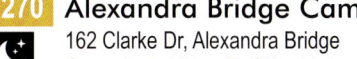
162 Clarke Dr, Alexandra Bridge
Camp Area 10 km E of Karridale or 65 km SW of Nannup. Veer L, beside Blackwood River. Cold showers
08 9780 5676   HEMA 152 E2   34 09 51 S   115 11 10 E

271 Sues Bridge Campground
Blackwood River National Park
Sues Rd, Alexandra Bridge Area
Camp Area 40 km NE of Karridale. Turn N 30 km E of Karridale or 46 km SW of Nannup for 9 km
08 9752 5555   HEMA 152 D3   34 04 37 S   115 23 24 E

272 Canebreak Rest Area

Brockman Hwy, Darradup
Rest Area 42 km E of Karridale or 34 km SW of Nannup
138 138   HEMA 152 E3   34 09 20 S   115 31 09 E

273 Lake Jasper
D'Entrecasteaux National Park
Scott Rd, Lake Jasper
Camp Area 20 km E of Beedelup. Turn R to Vasse Hwy 6 km.Continue on Scott Rd via Woodarburrup Rd 14 km. Park fees apply
HEMA 152 F4   34 25 15 S   115 41 28 E

274 Black Point
D'Entrecasteaux National Park
Black Point Rd, Lake Jasper Area
Campground 50 km W of Beedelup. Turn R to Vasse Hwy 20 km, L to Stewart Rd 7 km. Continue to Black Point Rd in Lake Jasper 23 km. Park fees apply
08 9776 1207   HEMA 152 F3   34 25 03 S   115 32 36 E

275 Grass Tree Hollow Camp
Greater Hawke National Park
Boat Landing Rd, Pemberton Area
Camp Area 84 km E of Karridale or 25 km NW of Pemberton. Turn S. Limited tent only sites, small vehicles only. 2 km dirt road
08 9776 1207   HEMA 152 F5   34 25 33 S   115 48 20 E

276 Snottygobble Loop
Greater Hawke National Park
Boat Landing Rd, Yeagarup
Camp Area 55 km S of Nannup. S via Brockman Hwy, Vasse Hwy & Warren Rd 52 km, R for 3 km, on R
08 9776 1207   HEMA 152 F5   34 26 04 S   115 47 55 E

277 Yeagarup Hut

D'Entrecasteaux National Park
Yeagarup Rd, Yeagarup
Camp Area 21 km S of Beedelup. From Beedelup turn L to Vasse Hwy, 9 km slight R to Old Vasse Rd, 500 m turn R to Ritter Rd, 11 km turn R. Draftys and Leaning Marri campsites listed in Camps Australia Wide App (tent & camper trailer only)
08 9776 0484   HEMA 152 F4   34 34 16 S   115 51 10 E

278 Big Brook Arboretum
Big Brook State Forest
Rainbow Tr, Pemberton
Camp Area 10 km N of Pemberton, via Club Rd, Pump Hill Rd & Tramway Trail. Small vehicles only
08 9776 1207   HEMA 152 F6   34 24 14 S   116 00 14 E

279 River Road Bridge

River Rd, Pemberton
Camp Areas on both E & W side of River Rd Bridge, 17 km SE of Pemberton. Via Burma & Spring Gully Rds 16 km
08 9219 9000   HEMA 152 G6   34 30 35 S   116 06 09 E

280 Moons Crossing
Warrens State Forest
Moon Crossing Rd, Pemberton
Camp Spot 17 km SE of Pemberton via Spring Gully & Moons Crossing Rds. Parks pass applies
08 9776 1133   HEMA 152 G6   34 30 23 S   116 08 45 E

281 Sids Campground

157 Riverway Rd, Northcliffe
Camp Area via Boorara Brook. 4 km E of Northcliffe. 28 day limit
0427 767 127   HEMA 152 H6   34 39 55 S   116 08 18 E

282 Moores Hut

D'Entrecasteaux National Park
Moores Rd, Broke
Camp Area 35 km S of Northcliffe. Follow Windy Harbour Rd for 6 km, Chesapeake Rd for 11.5 km, R to Gardner Rd for 4.5 km, R to Lake Rd, 2 km turn R, 3 km slight L, 5 km turn R 1 km
08 9776 1207   HEMA 152 J7   34 51 24 S   116 13 54 E

283 Windy Harbour Campground
D'Entrecasteaux National Park
Windy Harbour Rd, Windy Harbour
Camp Area 28 km SW of Northcliffe. 3 month limit
08 9776 8398   HEMA 152 J6   34 50 19 S   116 01 27 E

Norseman to Perth
Coolgardie-Esperance and Great Eastern Highways

284 Gem Fields Picnic Area
Mort Harslett Dr, Norseman Area
Camp Area 10 km W of Norseman. On RHS
08 9039 1205   HEMA 158 K4   32 11 00 S   121 40 53 E

285 Mount Thirsty
Coolgardie-Esperance Hwy, Norseman
Parking Area 15 km N of Norseman or
151 km S of Coolgardie
138 138   ·   HEMA 158 K4   32 06 03 S   121 41 40 E

286 Lake Cowan
Coolgardie-Esperance Hwy, Norseman
Rest Area 23 km N of Norseman on R
138 138   HEMA 158 K4   32 02 28 S   121 40 43 E

287 Cave Hill Nature Reserve
Higginsville Pump Station Rd, Higginsville
Camp Spot 50 km SW of Widgiemooltha or
87 km S of Coolgardie. Turn W. Small off road caravans
08 9080 5555   HEMA 158 H3   31 39 41 S   121 13 25 E

288 Kambalda Turn Off
Cnr Goldfields & Coolgardie-Esperance
Hwys, Kambalda West
Rest Area 56 km SW of Coolgardie. Site on L 250 m
after Hwy Jcn
138 138   HEMA 158 H3   31 19 24 S   121 30 48 E

289 Kambalda West RV Stop
Barnes Dr, Kambalda
Parking Area behind Rec Centre Pool &
Skate Park. Facilities at centre during opening hours
08 9080 2111   HEMA 158 H4   31 12 23 S   121 37 17 E

290 Londonderry
Coolgardie-Esperance Hwy, Coolgardie
Rest Area 15 km SE of Coolgardie, E side
of Hwy
138 138   HEMA 158 H3   31 01 14 S   121 17 43 E

291 Lake Douglas Rec Reserve
Lake Douglas Rd, Kalgoorlie
Camp Spot 12 km SW of Kalgoorlie or
26 km NE Coolgardie. Turn S & follow signs for
3.5 km. 2 km dirt road
08 9021 1966   HEMA 158 G3   30 50 38 S   121 23 35 E

292 Centennial Park
Cnr Hannan St & Patroni Rd, Kalgoorlie
Rest Area. Must display sticker
08 9021 1966   HEMA 158 G3   30 45 45 S   121 27 27 E

293 Coolgardie RV Stop
75 Woodward St, Coolgardie
Parking Area beside railway buidling
08 9080 2111   HEMA 156 A2   30 57 22 S   121 09 43 E

294 Victoria Rock
Goldfields Woodlands NP
Victoria Rock Rd, Coolgardie Area
Camp Spot 45 km SW of Coolgardie. Via Jobson St.
Dirt road
08 9080 5555   HEMA 158 H3   31 17 35 S   120 55 32 E

295 Burra Rock
Goldfields Woodlands NP
Burra Rock Rd, Coolgardie Area
Camp Area 59 km S of Coolgardie via Hunt St.
33 km dirt road
08 9080 5555   HEMA 158 H3   31 23 35 S   121 12 02 E

296 Yerdani Well
Great Eastern Hwy, Boorabbin Area
Rest Area 56 km W of Coolgardie or
129 km E of Southern Cross
138 138   HEMA 158 H2   31 08 22 S   120 37 41 E

297 Boondi Lookout
Great Eastern Hwy, Boorabbin Area
Parking Area 75 km W of Coolgardie or 109 km
E of Southern Cross. S side of road, follow old road
138 138   HEMA 158 H2   31 11 21 S   120 26 43 E

298 Boondi Rest Area
Great Eastern Hwy, Boorabbin Area
Rest Area 76 km W of Coolgardie or
108 km E of Southern Cross
138 138   HEMA 158 H2   31 11 18 S   120 25 45 E

299 Boondi Rock
Goldfields Woodlands NP
Great Eastern Hwy, Boorabbin Area
Camp Area 83 km W of Coolgardie or 107 km E
of Southern Cross. Turn N 81 km W of Coolgardie
or 105 km E of Southern Cross, 3 km of dirt road.
7.5 km E of Boorabbin-Jaurdi Rd. Signposted
08 9080 5555   HEMA 158 H2   31 10 52 S   120 23 04 E

300 Wallaroo Rock
Wallaroo Rock Conservation Park
Boorabbin Area
Camp Area 103 W of Coolgardie. Turn N off Hwy 64 km
W of Coolgardie or 123 km E of Southern Cross at the
Old Woolgangie Township sign. 39 km 4WD track to rock
08 9080 5555   HEMA 158 H2   31 03 29 S   120 17 53 E

301 Boorabbin Memorial
Great Eastern Hwy, Boorabbin
Rest Area 90 km W of Coolgardie or 96 km
E of Southern Cross
138 138   HEMA 158 H2   31 12 26 S   120 18 33 E

302 Jaurdi Station Homestead
Ryans Find Rd, Boorrabin
Station Stay 189 km E of Kalgoorlie. W
on Great Eastern Hwy 127 km, R at Boorabin for
45 km, L for 16 km, R for 1 km, on L
08 9219 9000   HEMA 158 H2   30 48 59 S   120 09 46 E

303 Boorabbin Rest Area
Great Eastern Hwy, Southern Cross Area
Rest Area 114 km W of Coolgardie or
68 km E of Southern Cross
138 138   HEMA 158 H1   31 16 08 S   120 01 00 E

304 Karalee Rock & Dam
Great Eastern Hwy, Southern Cross
Camp Area 137 km W of Coolgardie or
52 km E of Southern Cross. Turn N 133 km W of
Coolgardie or 48 km E of Southern Cross for 5 km of
dirt road. Signposted
08 9049 1001   HEMA 158 H1   31 15 03 S   119 50 24 E

305 Mount Palmer
Palmer St, Mount Palmer
Camp Spot 45 km SE of Southern Cross.
Take Great Eastern Hwy E for 33 km, turn R to
Marvel Loch-Yellowdine Rd for 12 km, R for 200 m
08 9049 1001   HEMA 158 J1   31 23 58 S   119 40 40 E

306 Lake Koorkoordine
Turkey Hill Rd, Southern Cross
Camp Area 8 km N of Southern Cross.
From Great Eastern Hwy, turn N via Antares St to
Bullfinch St for 6 km. Turn R travel 140 m then R
again. 1.3 km to site. End of road can be rough
08 9049 1001   HEMA 171 H12   31 10 00 S   119 18 59 E

307 Southern Cross Parking
Cnr Great Eastern Hwy & Three Boys Rd,
Southern Cross
Parking Area W of town
08 9049 1001   HEMA 171 H12   31 14 06 S   119 19 09 E

308 Moorine Rock Hotel
Great Eastern Hwy, Moorine Rock
Parking Area behind hotel, 22 km SW of
Southern Cross. From Hwy, turn S to Driver St. Free
for patrons
08 9049 1235   HEMA 171 J11   31 18 48 S   119 07 38 E

309 Bodallin Pioneers Park
Great Eastern Hwy, Boballin
Rest Area at Bodallin E of town
08 9049 1001   HEMA 171 J11   31 22 12 S   118 51 23 E

310 Carrabin Roadhouse Motel
Cnr Carrabin South Rd & Great Eastern
Hwy, Carrabin
Caravan Park behind roadhouse
08 9047163   HEMA 171 J10   31 22 44 S   118 40 41 E

311 Westonia Caravan Park
Wolfram St, Westonia
Caravan Park S side of town
08 9046 7063   HEMA 171 J10   31 18 16 S   118 41 50 E

312 St Lukes Church Park Area
Wolfram St, Westonia
Parking Area N off Hwy at Carrabin 7.5 km,
R on Carrabin-Westonia Rd 1.2 km. 650 m on L
08 9046 7063   HEMA 171 J10   31 17 59 S   118 41 50 E

313 Rabbit Proof Fence Parking
Bay
Great Eastern Hwy, Burracoppin
Parking Area 6 km W of Walgoolan or 2 km E of
Burracoppin
138 138   HEMA 171 J10   31 23 23 S   118 30 05 E

314 Burracoppin Centenary Park
Great Eastern Hwy, Burracoppin
Rest Area in town
HEMA 171 J10   31 23 54 S   118 28 46 E

315 Merredin Peak Reserve
Benson Rd, Merredin
Parking Area at Merredin Peak Heritage
Trail. Entry at Cnr Watson Rd
08 9041 1666   HEMA 171 J9   31 28 42 S   118 17 25 E

316 Hines Hill
Great Eastern Hwy, Hines Hill
Camp Area off Hwy, E side of Hines Hill.
Look for area on L after MacKenzie St
138 138   HEMA 171 J9   31 31 58 S   118 05 07 E

317 Baandee Lake
Ski Lake Rd, Doodalkine
Camp Area 23 km E of Kellerberrin or 38 km
W of Meredin. 20 km E of Kellerberrin, S for 2 km
08 9045 4006   HEMA 171 J9   31 36 06 S   117 56 43 E

318 Old Doodlakine / Well Site
Yilgarn Rd, Doodalkine
Camp Area 4 km NW of Doodalkine on
Doodlakine-Kununoppin Rd, then W
HEMA 171 J8   31 34 47 S   117 51 16 E

319 Kellerberrin Caravan Park
Cnr George & Moore Sts, Kellerberrin
Caravan Park N side of town
0428 138 474   HEMA 171 J8   31 37 30 S   117 43 01 E

320 Puma Tammin Roadhouse
Great Eastern Hwy, Tammin
Parking Area adjacent to roadhouse
08 9637 1321   HEMA 170 J7   31 38 25 S   117 29 30 E

321 Tammin Hotel
23 Donnan Street, Tammin
Parking Area behind pub. Free for patrons,
gold coin for shower
08 9637 1777   HEMA 170 J7   31 38 29 S   117 29 14 E

322 Meckering Memorial Park
Kelly St, Meckering
Rest Area opposite PO
08 9635 2700   HEMA 170 J6   31 37 58 S   117 00 26 E

323 Meenaar Rest Area
Great Eastern Hwy, Northam
Rest Area 3 km W of Meenaar, 26 km E of
Northam or 9 km W of Meckering
138 138   HEMA 170 K6   31 38 30 S   116 55 47 E

324 Grass Valley Tavern
8 Carter Rd, Grass Valley
Parking Area 16 km E of Northam. Pre-book
0407 205 068   HEMA 170 J6   31 38 06 S   116 47 46 E

325 Eadine Springs Picnic Area
Great Eastern Hwy, Northam
Picnic Area 14 km SW of Northam or
32 km NE of The Lakes. 1 km dirt road off Hwy.
Unlevel area
08 9622 6100   HEMA 170 K5   31 42 45 S   116 32 23 E

326 Clackline Rest Area
Great Eastern Hwy, Mokine
Rest Area 3 km E of Clackline
138 138   HEMA 170 K5   31 42 37 S   116 33 23 E

327 Homestead Campground
Avon Valley National Park
Governors Dr, Moondyne
Camp Area 40 km W of Toodyay or 35 km N of Gidgegannup. Turn W off Toodyay Rd 24 km S of Toodyay or 19 km N of Gidgegannup to Morangup Rd for 5 km, via Quarry Rd for 9 km then 2 km
08 9290 6100   HEMA 170 J5   31 36 36 S   116 14 29 E

328 Drummonds Campground
Avon Valley National Park
Governors Dr, Moondyne
Camp Area 43 km W of Toodyay or 38 km N of Gidgegannup. Turn W off Toodyay Rd 24 km S of Toodyay or 19 km N of Gidgegannup to Morangup Rd for 5 km, then to Quarry Rd for 9 km, 5 km to camp. Small vehicles only
08 9290 6100   HEMA 170 J5   31 36 21 S   116 13 45 E

329 Bald Hill Campground
Avon Valley National Park
Governors Dr, Moondyne
Camp Area 44 km W of Toodyay or 39 km N of Gidgegannup. W off Toodyay Rd 24 km S of Toodyay or 19 km N of Gidgegannup to Morangup Rd for 5 km, Quarry Rd for 9 km, 6 km to camp. Small vehicles only, off road caravans only
08 9290 6100   HEMA 170 J5   31 36 20 S   116 13 22 E

330 Valley Campground
Avon Valley National Park
41 Mile Rd, Moondyne
Camp Area 41 km W of Toodyay or 36 km N of Gidgegannup. Turn W off Toodyay Rd 24 km S of Toodyay or 19 km N of Gidgegannup to Morangup Rd 5 km, Quarry Rd 9 km. 3 km to camp. Small vehicles only
08 9290 6100   HEMA 170 J5   31 35 15 S   116 14 31 E

331 Walyunga Campground
Walyunga National Park
Walyunga Rd, Bullsbrook
Camp Area 10 km S of Bullsbrook. From Great Northern Hwy turn L. Signposted. Entry fee applies. Pre-book for gate code
08 9290 6100   HEMA 170 K4   31 43 59 S   116 03 09 E

332 Lake Leschenaultia
Rosedale Rd, Chidlow
Camp Area 12 km NE of Mundaring. Pre-book. Small vehicles only, vehicle size limit applies, ring for details
08 9290 6645   HEMA 150 A4   31 51 01 S   116 15 08 E

333 Gidgedales Retreat
20 Leyburn Retreat, Gidgegannup
Camp Area 4 km SE of Gidgegannup. S on Bunnings Rd 3 km L to Askrigg St. 900 m straight into Walden Cl 450 m. Pre-book
08 9574 6394   HEMA 150 A4   31 48 33 S   116 13 22 E

334 Perth Hills Discovery Centre
Beelu National Park
380 Allen Rd, Mundaring
Camp Area 40 km E of Perth. 7.5 km S of Mundaring
08 9295 2244   HEMA 147 H14   31 57 13 S   116 10 36 E

Coolgardie-Leonora-Meekatharra

335 Kalgoorlie North
Goldfields Hwy, Kalgoorlie
Rest Area 5 km N Kalgoorlie-Boulder either side of Hwy
138 138   HEMA 158 G3   30 42 48 S   121 28 19 E

336 Kalgoorlie RV Stop
Goldfields Hwy, Kalgoorlie
Rest Area 6 km N of Kalgoorlie
138 138   HEMA 158 G3   30 42 16 S   121 28 13 E

337 Kanowna South
Goldfields Hwy, Kanowna
Rest Area 20 km N of Kalgoorlie
HEMA 158 G3   30 35 15 S   121 26 11 E

338 Broad Arrow Tavern
492 Railway St, Kanowna
Parking Area 42 km N of Boulder opposite tavern. Register at bar
08 9024 2058   HEMA 158 G3   30 26 55 S   121 19 47 E

339 Ora Banda Historical Inn
Davyhurst-Ora Banda Rd, Ora Banda
Camp Area 70 km NW of Kalgoorlie. 40 km N of Kalgoorlie, W to Broad Arrow-Ora Banda Rd
HEMA 158 G3   30 22 34 S   121 03 41 E

340 Rowles Lagoon
Rowles Lagoon Conservation Park
Coolgardie North Rd, Ora Banda
Camp Area 70 km N of Coolgardie via Kunanalling & Kintore. Dirt road
08 9080 5555   HEMA 158 G3   30 25 38 S   120 51 50 E

341 Credo Homestead
Coolgardie North Rd, Ora Banda
Camp Area 75 km NW of Coolgardie via Kununalling & Kintore. Pre-book at DEC Kalgoorlie
08 9024 2063   HEMA 158 G3   30 27 55 S   120 49 38 E

342 Baden Powell Mine
Goldfields Hwy, Kanowna
Rest Area 67 km N of Kalgoorlie or 64 km S of Menzies
138 138   HEMA 158 G3   30 13 28 S   121 12 02 E

343 Goongarrie Homestead
Goongarrie National Park
Goldfields Hwy, Goongarrie
Camp Area 104 km NW of Kalgoorlie. Signposted turnoff 90 km N of Kalgoorlie or 43 km S of Menzies. Book at DEC Kalgoorlie
08 9080 5555   HEMA 158 F3   29 58 56 S   121 02 43 E

344 Menzies Caravan Park
Shenton St, Menzies
Caravan Park in town, access via Brown St
08 9024 2702   HEMA 158 F3   29 41 40 S   121 01 44 E

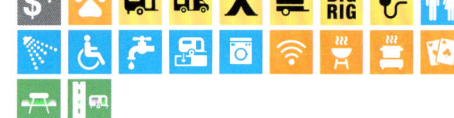

345 Lake Ballard
Menzies-Sandstone Rd, Menzies
Camp Area 55 km NW of Menzies. Road closes with rain, check at Menzies before travelling
08 9024 2702   HEMA 158 E2   29 26 56 S   120 36 11 E

346 Mount Elvire Reserve
Lake Barlee Rd, Ularring
Camp Area 179 km NW of Menzies. Travel W on Menzies-Evanston Rd for 137 km turn N near Bullfinch Rd for 42 km. Signposted. Pre-book
08 9080 5555   HEMA 158 E1   29 21 47 S   119 35 51 E

347 Kookynie Well Rest Area
Goldfields Hwy, Kookynie
Rest Area 32 km N of Menzies or 72 km S of Leonora
138 138   HEMA 158 E3   29 29 14 S   121 15 25 E

348 Morapoi Station
Kookynie Rd, Kookynie
Station Stay 53 km NE of Menzies or 74 km S of Leonora. E to Kookynie Mount Remarkable Rd 42 km N of Menzies. 10 km dirt road
0417 911 485　HEMA 158 E3　29 24 18 S　121 22 49 E

349 Kookynie Rest Area
Goldfields Hwy, Menzies
Rest Area 47 km N of Menzies or 57 km S of Leonora
138 138　HEMA 158 E3　29 21 29 S　121 16 15 E

350 Niagara Dam
Niagara Dam Rd, Kookynie
Camp Area 60 km NE of Menzies via Kookynie Rd
08 9024 2041　HEMA 158 E3　29 24 15 S　121 25 40 E

351 Leonora South
Goldfields Hwy, Leonora
Rest Area 16 km S of Leonora
138 138　HEMA 158 E3　29 00 37 S　121 22 21 E

352 Malcolm Dam
Malcolm Dam Rd, Leonora
Camp Spot 13 km E of Leonora. Turn N 10 km along Laverton-Leonora Rd. 3 km dirt road, veer R at fork for spots along edge of dam
08 9037 6044　HEMA 158 D3　28 52 44 S　121 26 49 E

353 Gwalia Museum
Leonora Area
Parking Area 3.7 km S side of Leonora. Signposted Museum & Hoover House, follow road to the end, turn L up the hill. Register at museum
08 9037 7122　HEMA 158 D3　28 54 52 S　121 19 59 E

354 Station Creek Camp
Goldfields Hwy, Leonora
Camp Spot 13 km N of Leonora. Take Hwy N for 13 km & turn R
138 138　HEMA 158 D3　28 46 40 S　121 16 36 E

355 King of the Hills Gold Mine North
Goldfields Hwy, Leonora
Rest Area 44 km N of Leonora or 90 km S of Leinster
138 138　HEMA 158 D3　28 31 07 S　121 11 55 E

356 Ford Run Rest Area
Goldfields Hwy, Leinster
Rest Area 52 km S of Leinster or 79 km N of Leonora
138 138　HEMA 158 C3　28 13 40 S　121 05 08 E

357 Thunderbox Gold Mine North
Goldfields Hwy, Leinster Area
Rest Area 32 km SE of Leinster or 102 km NW of Leonora
138 138　HEMA 158 C3　28 06 11 S　120 54 15 E

358 Leinster South
Goldfields Hwy, Leinster
Rest Area 3 km S of Leinster or 128 km NW of Leonora
138 138　HEMA 158 C2　27 57 03 S　120 43 01 E

359 Leinster West
Agnew-Leinster Rd, Leinster
Rest Area 4 km W of Leinster or 131 km NW of Leonora
138 138　HEMA 158 C2　27 56 22 S　120 41 31 E

360 Leinster Caravan Park
Mansbridge St, Leinster
Caravan Park. Pay at supermarket
0436 661 725　HEMA 158 C2　27 55 07 S　120 41 53 E

361 Agnew Gold Mine North
Agnew-Sandstone Rd, Leinster
Rest Area 33 km W of Leinster or 118 km E of Sandstone
138 138　HEMA 158 C2　27 57 45 S　120 25 44 E

362 Munjeroo East
Agnew-Sandstone Rd, Leinster
Rest Area 50 km W of Leinster or 101 km E of Sandstone
138 138　HEMA 158 C2　27 58 02 S　120 15 32 E

363 Depot Springs West
Agnew-Sandstone Rd, Sandstone
Rest Area 67 km E of Sandstone or 84 km W of Leinster
138 138　HEMA 158 C1　28 00 38 S　119 56 50 E

364 Peter Denny Lookout
Agnew-Sandstone Rd, Sandstone
Rest Area 114 km W of Leinster or 39 km E of Sandstone
138 138　HEMA 158 C1　27 56 21 S　119 37 55 E

365 Sandstone East
Agnew-Sandstone Rd, Sandstone
Rest Area 13 km E of Sandstone or 138 km W of Leinster
138 138　HEMA 169 J10　27 57 35 S　119 25 22 E

366 Sandstone South
Mount Magnet-Sandstone Rd, Sandstone
Rest Area N of main road
138 138　HEMA 169 J9　27 59 29 S　119 17 53 E

367 Lake Mason Homestead
Lake Mason Conservation Park
Unnamed Rd, Sandstone
Camp Area 56 km N of Sandstone & 5 km off the Gidgee Mine Rd. Pre-book at DEC Kalgoorlie
08 9080 5555　HEMA 158 B1　27 35 16 S　119 31 13 E

368 Jones Creek Parking Area
Goldfields Hwy, Leinster
Rest Area 58 km N of Leinster or 114 km S of Wiluna. Small area, parking for larger vehicles 100 m N on W side road
138 138　HEMA 158 B2　27 28 45 S　120 32 12 E

369 Wanjarri Natural Reserve
off Goldfields Hwy, Leinster
Camp Area 125 km S of Wiluna or 84 km N of Leinster. From Wiluna take Goldfields Hwy 109 km turn L & continue straight for 7 km. Site on R
HEMA 158 B2　27 24 05 S　120 38 53 E

370 Lake Way Rest Area
Goldfields Hwy, Wiluna
Rest Area 117 km N of Leinster or 58 km S of Wiluna. Just off the road GPS at turnoff
138 138　HEMA 158 A2　27 02 25 S　120 24 39 E

371 Gunbarrel Laager
Travellers Rest
Lot 25 Wongawol Rd, Wiluna
Camp Area 12 km E of Wiluna. Signposted off Gunbarrel Hwy
08 9981 7161　HEMA 158 A2　26 36 01 S　120 20 26 E

372 Black Well Truck Stop
Goldfields Hwy, Meekatharra
Rest Area 114 km E of Meekatharra or 67 km W of Wiluna
138 138　HEMA 169 G10　26 28 43 S　119 34 59 E

WESTERN AUSTRALIA

Wubin - Mullewa - Geraldton

373 Buntine Rocks
Buntine East Rd, Buntine
Camp Spot 18 km NW of Wubin or 25 km
SE of Latham. 3 km dirt road
08 9661 0500   HEMA 170 E5   29 58 13 S   116 35 07 E

374 Coorow Caravan Park
Station St, Coorow
Caravan Park W of Midlands Rd
08 9952 0100   HEMA 170 E4   29 52 51 S   116 01 02 E

375 Carnamah Caravan Park
King St, Carnamah
Caravan Park 1 km NE of PO, beside
Niven Park
08 9951 1785   HEMA 170 D4   29 41 10 S   115 53 28 E

376 Latham Community Centre
Mullewa-Wubin Rd, Latham
Camp Area in town
08 9973 0100   HEMA 170 D5   29 45 31 S   116 26 50 E

377 Bunjil Rocks
Iona Rd, Latham
Camp Area 57 km N of Wubin or 29 km S
of Perenjori. At the Bunjil Rocks signpost turn W for
1 km. Signposted to track on R. Dirt road
08 9973 0100   HEMA 170 D5   29 39 56 S   116 22 18 E

378 Caron Dam Reserve
Mullewa-Wubin Rd, Perenjori
Camp Spot 13 km S of Perenjori or 65 km
N of Wubin. W at Caron Dam Signposted 1 km
08 9973 0100   HEMA 170 D5   29 33 56 S   116 18 57 E

379 Perenjori Caravan Park
137 Crossing Rd, Perenjori
Caravan Park in town
08 9973 1193   HEMA 170 C5   29 26 09 S   116 17 17 E

380 Camel Soak
Rabbit Proof Fence Rd, Perenjori
Camp Area 47 km NE of Perenjori. Drive
14 km SE on Wanarra Rd, L for 13 km, site on R
08 9973 0100   HEMA 170 C5   29 24 07 S   116 37 31 E

381 John Forrest Lookout
Forrest Rd, Perenjori
Picnic Area via Perenjori Rothsay & Morton
Rds to base of lookout
08 9973 0100   HEMA 170 C6   29 18 20 S   116 43 50 E

382 Damperwah Camp Area
Karara Rangeland Park
Perenjori-Rothsay Rd, Paynes Find
Camp Areas 80 km NE of Perenjori. Permit applies
08 9219 9000   HEMA 170 C6   29 16 57 S   116 49 20 E

383 Warriedar
Karara Rangeland Park
Yalgoo-Ninghan Rd, Paynes Find
Camp Areas 110 km NE of Perenjori. GPS at
entrance. Permit applies
08 9964 0901   HEMA 170 C7   29 08 02 S   117 11 10 E

384 Perenjori Rest Area
Mullewa-Wubin Rd, Perenjori
Rest Area between Anzac Memorial &
Village Green
138 138   HEMA 170 C5   29 26 30 S   116 17 11 E

385 Perenjori Sports Ground
Fowler St, Perenjori
Parking Area at the oval
08 9973 0100   HEMA 170 C5   29 26 13 S   116 16 57 E

386 Koolanooka Springs
Kalanooka Springs Rd, Morawa Area
Camp Spot 30 km E of Morawa, via
Morawa-Yalgoo, Munckton, Fallon & Mungada Rds.
16 km dirt road
HEMA 170 C5   29 11 25 S   116 14 19 E

387 Morawa Caravan Park
White Ave, Morawa
Caravan Park in town
08 9971 1204   HEMA 170 C4   29 12 31 S   116 00 27 E

388 Ross Road Parking Bay
Ross Rd, Gutha
Parking Area 23 km NW of Morawa or
75 km SE of Mullewa off the Wubin-Mullewa Rd
138 138   HEMA 170 B4   29 01 02 S   115 56 20 E

389 Gutha Hall
216 Evaside Rd, Gutha
Camp Area 74 km SE of Mullewa. Take
Mullewa-Wubin Rd for 69 km, L to Gutha West Rd
for 3.5 km, on R
08 9971 1204   HEMA 170 B4   28 59 32 S   115 56 53 E

390 Old Canna Camp Site
Offszanka Rd, Canna
Camp Area 62 km SE of Mullewa. Take
Mullewa-Wubin Rd for 58 km then L for 2 km
08 9971 1204   HEMA 170 B4   28 54 25 S   115 51 27 E

391 Canna Hall
Canna North East Rd, Canna
Camp Area via Wubin-Mullewa & Offszanka
Rds, travel 3 km to hall. Box at hall for power fee
08 9971 1204   HEMA 170 B4   28 53 51 S   115 51 50 E

392 Mellenbye Station
Morawa-Yalgoo Rd, Morawa
Station Stay 120 km SE of Mullewa. Follow
Mullewa-Wubin Rd 46 km, L to Gutha Rd 20 km, L to
Morawa-Yalgoo Rd 23.5 km, turn R 7 km. Jul - Oct
08 9972 3072   HEMA 170 B5   28 49 51 S   116 17 53 E

393 Wilroy Nature Reserve
Wubin-Mullewa Rd, Mullewa
Rest Area 79 km NW of Morawa or 19 km
SE of Mullewa
08 9961 1500   HEMA 170 A3   28 38 25 S   115 38 56 E

394 Tallering Station
Beringarra-Pindar Rd, Pindar
Station Stay 13 km NE of Pindar on L
08 9962 3007   HEMA 168 K5   28 22 39 S   115 51 08 E

395 Mullewa East
Geraldton-Mount Magnet Rd, Mullewa
Rest Area 8 km E of Mullewa or 20 km W
of Pindar
138 138   HEMA 168 K5   28 31 10 S   115 35 28 E

396 Wurarga Dam
Wurarga Rd, Yalgoo
Camp Spot 48 km W of Yalgoo via
Geraldton-Mt Magnet Rd. Take a sharp L about
km, travel 3 km
8 9962 8042   HEMA 168 K5   28 24 39 S   116 16 12 E

397 Pindar East
Geraldton-Mount Magnet Rd, Pindar
Rest Area 35 km E of Pindar or 54 km W
f Yalgoo
38 138   HEMA 168 K5   28 25 20 S   116 08 29 E

398 Yalgoo Caravan Park
Gibbons St, Yalgoo
Caravan Park in main street
8 9962 8472   HEMA 168 K6   28 20 40 S   116 40 54 E

399 Gabyon Station
Gabyon-Tardie Rd, Yalgoo
Station Stay 54 km W of Yalgoo or 99 km E
f Mullewa. From the Geraldton-Mount Magnet Rd,
rn N. 17 km gravel road. Signposted
8 9963 7993   HEMA 168 K6   28 15 01 S   116 20 29 E

400 Melangata Station Stay
Melangata Rd, Yalgoo
Station Stay 285 km NE of Geraldton on NW
oastal Hwy. Follow Geraldton-Mt Magnet Rd turn at
algoo for 68 km via Yalgoo N & Dalgaranga Rd
8 9963 7777   HEMA 168 J6   27 48 14 S   116 53 06 E

401 Mullewa Caravan Park
Lovers Ln, Mullewa
Caravan Park at W outskirts of town. Pay at
ervice Station
439 898 762   HEMA 170 A3   28 32 19 S   115 30 14 E

402 Tenindewa Pioneer Well
(Woolya)
Yuna-Tenindewa Rd, Tenindewa
icnic Area 22 km W of Mullewa or 84 km E of
eraldton. Turn N off Hwy 123 to Yuna Rd, 18 km W
f Mullewa or 80 km E of Geraldton for 50 m, turn R
o Well Site Rd for 1 km
HEMA 170 A3   28 36 38 S   115 21 52 E

403 Indarra
Geraldton-Mount Magnet Rd, Tenindewa
Parking Area 22 km W of Mullewa or 76 km
E of Geraldton
058 9961 1500   HEMA 170 A2   28 38 37 S   115 19 19 E

404 Greenough River
Carnarvon-Mullewa Rd, Mullewa
Parking Area 47 km N of Mullewa or
161 km S of Murchison Roadhouse
HEMA 168 J5   28 11 03 S   115 41 14 E

405 Ballinyoo Bridge
Carnarvon-Mullewa Rd, Murchison
Parking Area 132 km N of Mullewa or
76 km S of Murchison Roadhouse. Various tracks
along river, N side better. Dirt road
HEMA 168 H5   27 31 35 S   115 46 29 E

406 Stock Well 9
Carnarvon-Mullewa Rd, Murchison
Camp Spot 53 km S of Muchison
Settlement or 148 km N of Mullewa. Turn E, follow
track to well
HEMA 168 H5   27 20 40 S   115 53 41 E

407 Wooleen Station
Twin Peaks-Wooleen Rd, Murchison
Station Stay 50 km SE of Muchison
Settlement. Signposted on Carnarvon-Mullewa Rd.
Open Apr - Oct. Pre-book
08 9963 7973   HEMA 168 H5   27 05 15 S   116 09 43 E

408 Murchison Oasis Roadhouse
Carnarvon Mullewa Rd, Murchison
Caravan Park at Murchison Settlement
08 9961 3875   HEMA 168 G5   26 53 46 S   115 57 26 E

Bindoon to Dongara
Midlands Road

409 Wannamal (Robert Hindmarsh) Rest Area
Bindoon-Moora Rd, Wannamal
Rest Area 26 km N of Bindoon or 59 km S of Moora,
opposite hall
08 9576 4600   HEMA 170 H4   31 09 54 S   116 03 29 E

410 Three Springs Short Stay
Parking
Hunt St, Three Springs
Parking Area next to sports oval, key from shire
office 8am - 4pm
08 9954 1001   HEMA 170 D3   29 32 15 S   115 45 39 E

411 Arrino Siding
Midlands Rd, Arrino
Rest Area 18 km N of Three Springs or
35 km S of Mingenew opposite Arrino wheatbin
HEMA 170 C3   29 26 22 S   115 37 41 E

412 Yandanooka Town Hall
Yandanooka North East Rd, Yandanooka
Camp Area 20 km S of Mingenew. 500 m
from Hwy
08 9928 1102   HEMA 170 C3   29 18 43 S   115 34 01 E

413 Enanty Barn
Mingenew-Mullewa Rd, Mingenew
Parking Area 3.5 km NE of Mingenew
08 9928 1128   HEMA 170 C3   29 10 19 S   115 27 27 E

414 Breakaway Campground
Coalseam Conservation Park
Coalseam Rd, Mingenew
Camp Area 34 km N of Mingenew (dirt road) or 50 km
S of Mullewa (steep in places). 3 night limit. Aug - Oct
08 9921 5955   HEMA 170 B3   28 57 01 S   115 32 23 E

415 Miners Camp
Coalseam Conservation Park
Via Lookout Rd, Mingenew Area
Camp Area 35 km N of Mingenew (dirt road) or 52 km
S of Mullewa (steep in places). 3 night limit. Aug - Oct
08 9964 0901   HEMA 170 B3   28 57 29 S   115 33 15 E

Perth to Port Hedland
Brand and North West Coastal Highways

416 Henry White Oval
Yanchep National Park
Indian Ocean Dr, Yanchep
Camp Area 55 km N of Perth CBD. Turn R to NP.
Must register. 7 day limit
08 9303 7759   HEMA 170 J3   31 32 55 S   115 41 07 E

417 Moore River Bridge
Indian Ocean Dr, Moore River
Rest Area 33 km N of Yanchep NP turnoff
or 2 km SE of Guilderton turnoff. Site access parallel
to Glenrowan Rd
138 138   HEMA 170 J3   31 18 14 S   115 33 18 E

418 Dandaragan Transit Park
3550 Dandaragan Rd, Dandaragan
Caravan Park at Pioneer Park
08 9652 0800   HEMA 170 G3   30 40 13 S   115 42 12 E

419 Moora Shire Caravan Park
Dandaragan St, Moora
Caravan Park opposite Moora IGA,
adjacent swimming pool & Apex Park
08 9651 0000   HEMA 170 G4   30 38 17 S   116 00 16 E

420 Moora RV Short Stay
Padbury St, Moora
Parking Area behind Performing Arts Centre
08 9651 0000   HEMA 170 G4   30 38 33 S   116 00 28 E

421 Koojan Salmon Gum Reserve
Bindoon-Moora Rd, Koojan
Rest Area 18 km S of Moora, or 28 km N of
Mogumber. Set back off the road
08 9651 0000   HEMA 170 G4   30 48 10 S   116 01 24 E

422 Gillingarra Sport & Rec Club
Bindoon-Moora Rd, Gillingarra
Camp Area 30 km S of Moora, or 15 km N
of Mogumber. Payment via drop box
0427 364 167   HEMA 170 G4   30 54 43 S   116 02 14 E

423 Watheroo Station Tavern
George St, Watheroo
Rest Area next to pub, 37 km N of Moora
via Midlands Rd
08 9651 7007   HEMA 170 F4   30 17 55 S   116 03 31 E

424 Drummonds Reserve
Bibby Rd, Cervantes
Camp Spot 4 km W of Brand Hwy or 45 km
E of Indian Ocean Dr
08 9652 0800   HEMA 170 F3   30 29 20 S   115 26 04 E

425 Hakea Reserve
Bibby Rd, Cervantes
Rest Area 15 km W of Brand Hwy or 35 km
E of Indian Ocean Dr
08 9652 0800   HEMA 170 F2   30 27 37 S   115 19 55 E

426 Banksia Reserve
Cervantes Rd, Cervantes
Rest Area 35 km W of Brand Hwy or 14 km
E of Indian Ocean Dr. Small area
08 9652 0800   HEMA 170 F2   30 23 32 S   115 10 50 E

427 Tuarts Reserve
Cervantes Rd, Jurien Bay
Camp Spot 40 km W of Brand Hwy or 9 km
E of Indian Ocean Dr. Small area
08 9652 0800   HEMA 170 F2   30 25 07 S   115 08 24 E

428 Nambung Station Stay and B&B
Wongonderrah Rd, Cervantes
Station Stay 44 km E of Cervantes via Cervantes &
Munbinea Rds. GPS at gate
08 9652 4048   HEMA 170 F2   30 34 10 S   115 13 44 E

429 Smokebush Reserve
Jurien East Rd, Jurien Bay
Rest Area 10.5 km W of Brand Hwy or
37.5 km E of Indian Ocean Dr
08 9652 0800   HEMA 170 F2   30 13 27 S   115 14 16 E

430 Karda Campground
Karda Reserve
Benovich Rd, Hill River
Camp Area 20 km E of Jurien Bay. Via Jurien Rd,
some unsealed roads. Pre-book
08 9688 6000   HEMA 170 E2   30 12 09 S   115 15 22 E

431 Wandoo Reserve
Jurien East Rd, Jurien Bay
Camp Spot 16.5 km W of Brand Hwy or
32 km E of Indian Ocean Dr
08 9652 0800   HEMA 170 F2   30 13 25 S   115 14 09 E

432 Sandy Cape Rec Park
Sandy Cape Rd, Jurien Bay
Camp Area 12 km N of Jurien Bay or 18 km
S of Green Head. Caretaker on site
08 9652 0800   HEMA 170 E2   30 11 23 S   115 00 07 E

433 Milligan Island Camping Node
Green Head Rd, Milligan Island
Camp Area 2.5 km N of Green Head. Turn W off
Indian Ocean Dr to Green Head Rd and follow
signs. 7 day limit
0428 521 106   HEMA 170 E2   30 02 04 S   114 57 40 E

434 Halfway Mill Roadhouse
Brand Hwy, Eneabba
Caravan Park 30 km S of Eneabba, enter
Cnr of Coorow Rd
08 9952 9054   HEMA 170 E2   30 03 27 S   115 19 50 E

435 Hi Vallee Farm
Tootbardi Rd, Badgingarra
Farm Stay 250 km N of Perth. GPS at gate,
3 km to sites, W of the house. Pre-book. No cats
08 9652 3035   HEMA 170 E3   30 08 52 S   115 24 41 E

436 Lake Indoon
Coolimba-Eneabba Rd, Eneabba
Camp Area 12 km SW of Eneabba or 16 km
E of Coolimba, donation box. Obey fire restrictions
08 9951 7000   HEMA 170 E2   29 51 37 S   115 09 17 E

437 Eneabba Overnight Stay
Eneabba Dr, Eneabba
Parking Area behind Rec Centre.
Signposted entry. Fees collected
08 9951 7000   HEMA 170 D2   29 49 31 S   115 15 59 E

438 Arrowsmith Rest Area
Brand Hwy, Eneabba
Rest Area 30 km N of Eneabba or 50 km S of Dongara
138 138   HEMA 170 D2   29 34 43 S   115 08 09 E

439 Knobby Head
Indian Ocean Dr, Illawong
Camp Spot 35 km N of Leeman or 22 km S of Brand Hwy Jcn
08 9927 1404   HEMA 170 D2   29 39 14 S   114 57 56 E

440 Freshwater Point
Indian Ocean Dr, Arrowsmith
Camp Spot 42 km N of Leeman or 16 km S of Brand Hwy Jcn
08 9927 1404   HEMA 170 D2   29 36 15 S   114 58 31 E

441 Cliff Head South
Indian Ocean Dr, Illawong
Camp Spot 49 km N of Leeman or 8 km S of Brand Hwy Jcn
08 9927 1404   HEMA 170 D2   29 31 40 S   114 59 30 E

442 Cliff Head Central
Indian Ocean Dr, Illawong
Camp Spot 50 km N of Leeman or 7 km S of Brand Hwy Jcn
08 9927 1404   HEMA 170 D2   29 31 17 S   114 59 41 E

443 Cliff Head North
Indian Ocean Dr, Illawong
Camp Spot 51 km N of Leeman or 6 km S of Brand Hwy Jcn
08 9927 1404   HEMA 170 D2   29 30 54 S   114 59 51 E

444 Ellendale Pool
Ellendale Pool Rd, Greenough
Camp Area 45 km SE of Geraldton or 22 km NE of Walkaway via Walkaway-Nangetty & Ellendale Rd
08 9956 6670   HEMA 170 B2   28 51 33 S   114 58 22 E

445 Geraldton RV Park
Cnr Francis St & Marine Tce, Geraldton
Parking Area at Cnr of Marine Tce. Park in marked bays. Toilets locked at night
08 9956 6670   HEMA 168 K3   28 46 33 S   114 36 11 E

446 Bob Davies Park (Point Moore)
45 Marine Tce, West End
Parking Area opposite Point Moore Lighthouse. Small non SCV only. Cold showers
08 9956 6600   HEMA 168 K3   28 46 56 S   114 34 45 E

447 Bringo Lookout
2087 Geraldton-Mount Magnet Rd, Geraldton
Camp Spot 26 km E of Geraldton. S side of road
138 138   HEMA 168 K3   28 44 35 S   114 50 46 E
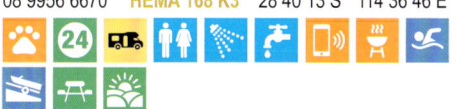

448 John Batten Community Hall
Whitehill Rd, Drummond Cove
Parking Area 13 km N of Geraldton or 38 km S of Northampton. Non SC campervans only. Cold showers
08 9956 6670   HEMA 168 K3   28 40 13 S   114 36 46 E

449 Fig Tree Camping Ground
Chapman Valley Rd, Geraldton
Camp & Picnic Area 21 km NE of Geraldton
08 9920 5011   HEMA 168 K3   28 39 32 S   114 42 15 E

450 Coronation Beach
Coronation Beach Rd, Coronation Beach
Camp Area 36 km N of Geraldton or 32 km S of Northampton. Turn W 28 km N of Geraldton or 24 km S of Northampton. 1 month limit
08 9920 5011   HEMA 168 K3   28 33 12 S   114 33 52 E

451 Goodies Eco Camp
2975 North West Coastal Hwy, Chapman Valley
Camp Area 23 km S of Northampton or 30 km N of Geraldton
0400 800 661   HEMA 168 K3   28 32 24 S   114 37 46 E

452 Oakabella Homestead
423 Starling Rd, Bowes
Camp Area 35 km N of Geraldton or 17 km S of Northampton. Follow signs
08 9925 1033   HEMA 168 K3   28 30 00 S   114 35 58 E

453 Northampton Golf Club
Stephen St, Northampton
Parking Area near the club
08 9934 1488   HEMA 168 K3   28 21 23 S   114 38 41 E

454 Yuna Hall
6967 Chapman Valley Rd, Yuna
Camp Spot NE of Yuna Hall, E of tavern. Turn at school sign. Signposted
08 9920 5011   HEMA 168 K4   28 19 40 S   115 00 10 E

455 Elbenjo Sanctuary
485 Swamps Rd, Yallabatharra
Camp Area 24 km NE of Northhampton. Take Hwy N to Rob Rd in Alma turn L and follow signs 15 km
0409 685 877   HEMA 168 K3   28 15 55 S   114 29 06 E

456 Northbrook Farm Stay
5800 North West Coastal Hwy, Northhampton
Farm Stay 6 km N of Northampton
08 9934 1222   HEMA 168 K3   28 17 54 S   114 37 49 E

457 Baddera Rest Area
North West Coastal Hwy, Alma
Rest Area 8 km N of Northampton or 3 km W of Alma
138 138   HEMA 168 K3   28 16 49 S   114 37 18 E

458 Little Bay
Little Bay Rd, Horrocks Beach
Camp Area 3.5 km NW of Horrocks. Site on your R. 5 day limit. Ranger collects fees
08 9934 1202   HEMA 168 K3   28 20 56 S   114 24 30 E

459 Linga Longa Lynton Station

3530 Port Gregory Rd, Gregory Downs
Station Stay 40 km W of Northampton or
62 km S of Kalbarri
0438 916 202   HEMA 168 K3   28 12 40 S   114 18 18 E

460 Ogilvie Rest Area
North West Coastal Hwy, Ogilvie
Rest Area 19 km N of Northampton, or
42 km S of Ajana
138 138   HEMA 168 J3   28 11 29 S   114 38 10 E

461 Lucky Bay Camping Kalbarri
Via Balline Road, Kalbarri
Camp Area 60 km N of Northampton or
46 km S of Kalbarri. W off George Grey Dr to Balline
Rd, 2 km sandy road. Camp only in designated
areas if not SCV. 28 day limit
08 9937 1140   HEMA 168 J3   28 03 01 S   114 09 52 E
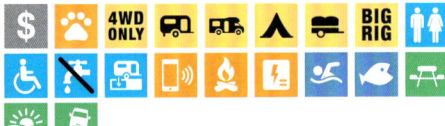

462 Wagoe Chalets & Camping
4043 George Grey Dr, Kalbarri
Camp Area 84 km NW of Northampton or
20 km S of Kalbarri. Turn W off Kalbarri Coast Rd.
3 km dirt road
08 9936 6060   HEMA 168 J2   27 53 10 S   114 08 09 E

463 Big River Ranch
1149 Ajana-Kalbarri Rd, Kalbarri
Farm Stay 4 km NE of Kalbarri
08 9937 1214   HEMA 168 J3   27 41 21 S   114 11 17 E

464 Murchison House Station
Ajana-Kalbarri Rd, Kalbarri
Station Stay 10 km E of Kalbarri. 4 km dirt
road. Pre-book. Closed Nov - Mar. Bush camping
4WD only rates available on N side
08 9937 1998   HEMA 168 J3   27 38 49 S   114 14 08 E

465 Galena Bridge (Murchison River)
North West Coastal Hwy, Northampton
Rest Area 13 km N of Kalbarri turnoff or 115 km S of
Billabong Roadhouse
138 138   HEMA 168 J3   27 49 39 S   114 41 24 E
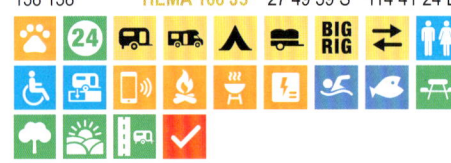

466 Nerren Nerren Rest Area
North West Coastal Hwy, Nerren Nerren
Rest Area 82 km N of Kalbarri turnoff or
46 km S of Billabong Roadhouse
138 138   HEMA 168 H3   27 12 43 S   114 36 44 E

467 Billabong Roadhouse
Lot 2 North West Coastal Hwy, Meadow
Parking Area 51 km S of Hamelin Pool
08 9942 5919   HEMA 168 G3   26 48 58 S   114 36 51 E

468 Overlander Roadhouse
North West Coastal Hwy, Overlander
Camp Area 700 km N of Perth at the Shark
Bay Monkey Mia turnoff
08 9942 5916   HEMA 168 G3   26 24 42 S   114 27 51 E

469 Hamelin Outback Station
Shark Bay Rd, Denham Area
Station Stay 30 km W of Overlander
Roadhouse or 100 km SE of Denham
08 9948 5145   HEMA 168 G3   26 26 03 S   114 12 00 E

470 Steep Point Camp Sites
Edel Land NP (Proposed)
Denham
Camp Areas at Steep Point on the mainland at base
of Dirk Hartog Is. Access via Useless Loop Rd. Pre-
book. GPS at Steep Pt Rangers Station
08 9948 3993   HEMA 168 F1   26 10 37 S   113 12 53 E

471 Dirk Hartog Island NP
Dirk Hartog Island
Denham
Camp Areas on E & W coast of Dirk Hartog Island.
Access via barge landing at Cape Ransonnet.
Pre-book. Barge transfer max vehicle length 10.6 m,
GPS position at entry to island, up to 9 official sites
08 9948 1211   HEMA 168 F1   26 09 35 S   113 12 53 E

472 The Homestead Camp
Dirk Hartog Island
Denham
Camp Areas on E coast of Dirk Hartog Island, 20 km
N of the barge landing at Cape Ransonnet. Pre-
book. Barge transfer max vehicle length 10.6 m
08 9948 1211   HEMA 168 F1   26 00 07 S   113 11 48 E

473 Goulet Bluff
Shark Bay Rd, Denham
Camp Area 95 km W of Overlander
Roadhouse or 36 km SE of Denham. Turn W off
Shark Bay Rd 36 km SE of Denham, 2 km dirt
road. 1 night permits only, on the day required from
Discovery Centre, no pre-bookings. Signposted
08 9948 1590   HEMA 168 F2   26 12 52 S   113 41 36 E

474 Whalebone Bay
Denham-Hamelin Rd, Denham
Camp Area 102 km W of Overlander
Roadhouse or 27 km SE of Denham. Turn W off
Shark Bay Rd 26 km SE of Denham, 1 km dirt rd.
Permits booked on the day required from Discovery
Centre, no advance bookings. Signposted
08 9948 1590   HEMA 168 F2   26 07 47 S   113 38 25 E

475 Fowlers Camp
Fowlers Camp Rd, Denham
Camp Area 109 km W of Overlander
Roadhouse or 22 km SE of Denham. Turn W off
Shark Bay Rd 22 km SE of Denham, 2 km dirt road.
Permits booked on the day required from Discovery
Centre, no advance bookings
08 9948 1590   HEMA 168 F2   26 06 22 S   113 37 12 E

476 Eagle Bluff
Francois Peron NP
Eagle Bluff Lagoon Rd, Denham
Camp Area 114 km W of Overlander Roadhouse
or 22 km SE of Denham. Turn W off Shark Bay
Rd 19 km SE of Denham, 3 km dirt road. Permits
booked on the day required from Discovery Centre,
Denham, no advance bookings
08 9948 1590   HEMA 168 F2   26 04 28 S   113 34 56 E

477 Big Lagoon Campground
Francois Peron NP
Big Lagoon Tr, Denham
Camp Area 23 km N of Denham. L from Dampier Rd to Monkey Mia Rd 3 km turn L to Peron Rd for 6 km, L again, 10 km to camp. Park fees apply.
08 9948 2226   HEMA 168 F2   25 46 29 S   113 28 34 E

478 South Gregories
Francois Peron NP
Peron Rd, Denham
Camp Area 44 km N of Denham. Turn L from Dampier Rd to Monkey Mia Rd 3 km, turn L to Peron Rd for 39 km camp site on L. Parks Pass applies. Herald Bight, Bottle Bay & Gregories Camp Areas are tent and camper trailer only, listed in Camps Australia Wide App
08 9948 2226   HEMA 168 E2   25 34 43 S   113 27 55 E

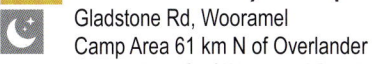

479 Gladstone Bay Camp
Gladstone Rd, Wooramel
Camp Area 61 km N of Overlander Roadhouse or 27 km S of Wooramel Roadhouse. Turn W opposite Yaringa Homestead, 55 km N of Overlander Roadhouse or 21 km S of Wooramel Roadhouse. 6 km dirt road
08 9942 5952   HEMA 168 F3   25 57 08 S   114 14 55 E

480 Wooramel Roadhouse
North West Coastal Hwy, Wooramel
Caravan Park at Wooramel Roadhouse. 70 km N of Overlander Roadhouse or 124 km S of Carnarvon
08 9942 5910   HEMA 168 F3   25 46 13 S   114 17 40 E

481 Wooramel River Retreat
Wooramel Rd, Carnarvon
Station Stay turn off 120 km S of Carnarvon or 2.6 km N of Wooramel Roadhouse. Signposted. Closed Dec - Feb
0499 425 888   HEMA 168 F3   25 44 27 S   114 17 02 E

482 Edaggee Rest Area
North West Coastal Hwy, Wooramel
Rest Area 43 km N of Wooramel Roadhouse or 81 km S of Carnarvon
138 138   HEMA 168 E2   25 27 34 S   114 03 31 E

483 New Beach
New Beach Rd, New Beach
Camp Area 99 km N of Wooramel Roadhouse or 41 km S of Carnarvon. Turn W 91 km N of Wooramel Roadhouse or 33 km S of Carnarvon. 8 km dirt road. Low lying, check tide charts. Chemical toilet required
08 9941 0019   HEMA 168 E2   25 09 22 S   113 47 53 E

484 Bush Bay
Bush Bay Rd, New Beach
Camp Area 101 km N of Wooramel Roadhouse or 43 km S of Carnarvon. Turn W 91 km N of Wooramel Roadhouse or 33 km S of Carnarvon. 6 km N of New Beach. 10 km dirt road. Low lying, check tide charts. Chemical toilet required
08 9941 0019   HEMA 168 E2   25 07 50 S   113 45 14 E

485 Junction Pub & Tourist Park
4 Viveash Way, Gascoyne Junction
Caravan Park central in town
08 9943 0868   HEMA 168 D4   25 03 13 S   115 12 25 E

486 Bilung Pool
Off Carnarvon-Mullewea Rd, Murchison
Camp Spot 152 km N of Murchison Roadhouse or 147 km SE of Gascoyne Junction. Turn W at sign just S of Bilung Creek, follow track about 200 m to pool
08 9963 7999   HEMA 168 E5   25 42 22 S   115 59 09 E

487 Temple Gorge Campground
Kennedy Range NP
Lyons River Rd, Gascoyne Junction
Camp Area 59 km N of Gascoyne Junction. Turn W 47 km N of Gascoyne Junction to Ullawarra Rd for 12 km. Mostly dirt road
08 9948 2226   HEMA 168 D4   24 39 38 S   115 10 57 E

488 Mount Augustus Tourist Park
Cobra-Mt Augustus Rd, Mount Augustus
Caravan Park 280 km NE of Gascoyne Junction via Dairy Creek or 360 km NW of Meekatharra
08 9943 0527   HEMA 168 C6   24 18 29 S   116 54 32 E

489 Blowholes (Point Quobba)
Beach Rd, Carnarvon
Camp Area 72 km N of Carnarvon. Turn W off North West Coastal Hwy 24 km N of Carnarvon or 115 km S of Minilya Roadhouse. BYO chemical toilet. 30 day limit
08 9941 0019   HEMA 168 D1   24 29 16 S   113 24 44 E

490 Quobba Station
Gnaraloo Rd, Quobba
Station Stay 82 km N of Carnarvon. Turn W off North West Coastal Hwy 24 km N of Carnarvon or 115 km S of Minilya Roadhouse. 10 km dirt road N of Blowholes
08 9948 5098   HEMA 168 C1   24 23 43 S   113 24 19 E

491 Red Bluff
Gnaraloo Rd, Quobba Station
Camp Area 54 km N of Quobba Homestead. Signposted turnoff 44 km N of station, 10 km rough dirt road to campsite. Suitable for off road caravans
08 9948 5001   HEMA 168 C2   24 01 56 S   113 26 56 E

492 Gnaraloo Station 3 Mile
Gnaraloo Rd, Quobba
Station Stay at Gnaraloo Station. 150 km N of Cararvon via Blowholes Rd turnoff. At King Waves sign turn R travel N for 75 km through Gnaraloo Stone Arch. Camp is 11.5 km past arch
08 9315 4809   HEMA 168 C2   23 52 39 S   113 29 48 E

493 Lake MacLeod Rest Area
North West Coastal Hwy, Yalabia
Rest Area 49 km S of Minilya Roadhouse or 90 km N of Carnarvon
138 138   HEMA 168 C2   24 14 57 S   114 02 11 E

494 Minilya River
North West Coast Hwy, Minilya
Rest Area 500 m S of Minilya Roadhouse. S side of Minilya R Bridge or 141 km N of Carnarvon
138 138   HEMA 168 B2   23 49 01 S   114 00 38 E

495 Lyndon Station
Lyndon-Towera Rd, Lyndon
Camp Area 110 km E Lyndon or 159 km E
Minilya Roadhouse. Pre-book
08 9943 0540   HEMA 168 B4   23 38 13 S   115 14 45 E

496 Minilya Bridge Roadhouse
North West Coastal Hwy, Minilya
Caravan Park N side of river at roadhouse
0456 998 547   HEMA 168 B2   23 48 53 S   114 00 33 E

497 Lyndon River
North West Coastal Hwy, Minilya
Rest Area 48 km NE of Minilya Roadhouse
or 179 km SW of Nanutarra Roadhouse
138 138   HEMA 168 B3   23 28 58 S   114 16 32 E

498 Lyndon River (West)
Minilya-Exmouth Rd, Minilya
Rest Area 32 km N of Minilya Roadhouse or
190 km S of Exmouth on Minilya-Exmouth Rd
138 138   HEMA 168 B2   23 32 32 S   113 57 47 E

499 Bruboodjoo (9 Mile Camp)
Minilya-Exmouth Rd, Coral Bay
Camp Area 19 km north of Coral Bay. Turn
off 15 km N of Coral Bay off Minilya-Exmouth Rd.
Sandy dirt road. Report to caretaker before setting
up. Beach camping. BYO chemical toilet.
08 9941 3814   HEMA 168 A2   22 58 32 S   113 49 32 E

500 Ningaloo Coast
Ningaloo Rd, Ningaloo
Camp Areas along the coast via Minilya-
Exmouth Rd. Turn W 40 km N of Coral Bay turn off
to Ningaloo Rd. BYO chemical toilet. Rough road
08 9947 8013   HEMA 166 J1   22 41 46 S   113 40 32 E

501 Neds Campground
Cape Range NP
Yardie Ck Rd, Exmouth
Camp Area 48 km S of Exmouth via Murat Rd.
Limited sites. No generators. Public phone & DP at
Milyering Visitor Centre
08 9949 2808   HEMA 166 H1   22 00 01 S   113 55 58 E

502 Mesa Campground
Cape Range National Park
Yardie Ck Rd, Exmouth
Camp Area 77 km S of Exmouth via Murat &
Learmonth-Minilya Rd. Limited sites. Public phone &
DP at Milyering Visitor Centre. Pre-book
08 9949 2808   HEMA 166 H1   22 00 24 S   113 55 38 E

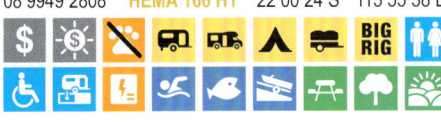

503 Tulki Beach Campground
Cape Range National Park
Yardie Ck Rd, Exmouth
Camp Area 60 km S of Exmouth via Murat Rd.
Limited sites. Public phone & DP at Milyering
Visitor Centre
08 9949 2808   HEMA 166 H1   22 04 31 S   113 53 56 E

504 Kurrajong Campground
Cape Range National Park
Yardie Ck Rd, Exmouth
Camp Area 70 km S of Exmouth via Murat Rd.
Limited sites. Public phone & DP at Milyering Visitor
Centre
08 9949 2808   HEMA 166 H1   22 10 44 S   113 51 34 E

505 North Kurrajong
Cape Range NP
Yardie Ck Rd, Exmouth
Camp Area 70 km S of Exmouth via Murat Rd.
Limited sites. Public phone & DP at Milyering Visitor
Centre
08 9949 2808   HEMA 166 H1   22 10 24 S   113 51 39 E

506 Osprey Bay Campground
Cape Range National Park
Yardie Creek Rd, Exmouth
Camp Area 77 km SW of Exmouth. Limited sites.
Public phone & DP at Milyering Visitor Centre
08 9949 2808   HEMA 166 J1   22 14 19 S   113 50 21 E

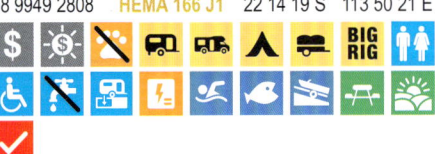

507 Yardie Creek Campground
Cape Range National Park
Yardie Ck Rd, Exmouth
Camp Area 90 km S of Exmouth via Murat Rd.
Limited sites. Public phone & DP at Milyering Visitor
Centre
08 9949 2808   HEMA 166 J1   22 19 13 S   113 48 53 E

508 Bullara Station
Burkett Rd, Exmouth Gulf
Station Stay 86 km S of Exmouth or 60 km
N of Coral Bay. 8 km E of NW Coastal Hwy Jcn.
Signposted
08 9942 5938   HEMA 166 J1   22 40 39 S   114 03 15 E

509 Giralia Station
2 Burkett Rd, Exmouth Gulf
Station Stay 125 km S of Exmouth or
110 km N of Coral Bay. 45 km E of NW Coastal Hwy
Jcn. 4 km dirt road
08 9942 5937   HEMA 166 J2   22 42 31 S   114 20 20 E

510 Burkett Road Rest Area
North West Coastal Hwy, Learmonth
Rest Area 116 km NE of Minilya Roadhouse
or 111 km SW of Nanutarra Roadhouse. 1 km N of
Exmouth turnoff
138 138   HEMA 166 K2   22 59 01 S   114 36 47 E

511 Yannarie Rest Area
North West Coastal Hwy, Yannarie River
Rest Area 156 km NE of Minilya Roadhouse
or 70 km SW of Nanutarra Roadhouse
138 138   HEMA 166 J3   22 51 49 S   114 57 05 E

512 Emu Creek Station
1 Nyang Rd, Yannarie
Station Stay 156 km N of Minilya
Roadhouse or 49 km S of Nanutarra Roadhouse.
Turn E on Nyang. 22 km to station. Dirt road
08 9943 0534   HEMA 166 K3   23 01 54 S   115 02 31 E

513 Nanutarra Roadhouse
North West Coastal Hwy, Nanutarra
Caravan Park 280 km S of Karratha
08 9943 0521   HEMA 166 J3   22 32 32 S   115 30 01 E

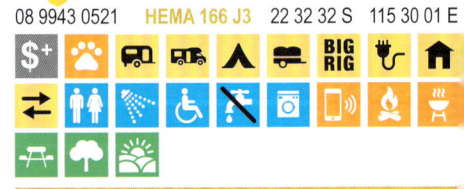

514 House Creek Bridge
Nanutarra Munjina Rd, Nanutarra
Rest Area 62 km E of Nanutarra Roadhouse
or 162 km W of Paraburdoo/Wittenoom Rd Jcn
138 138   HEMA 166 J4   22 27 51 S   116 02 12 E

515 Beasley River Rest Area
Nanutarra Munjina Rd, Beasley River Rest Area 171 km E of Nanutarra Roadhouse or 53 km W of Paraburdoo/Wittenoom Rd Jcn

138 138   HEMA 166 K5   22 56 56 S   116 58 40 E

516 Cheela Plains Station Stay
Nanutarra Munjina Rd, Paraburdoo Station Stay 181 km E of Nanutarra Roadhouse or 43 km W of Paraburdoo/Wittenoom Rd Jcn. Turnoff N side of road, after crossing Beasley R bridge. Follow gravel 2 km over hill to camp. Open Apr - Oct

08 9189 8251   HEMA 166 K5   22 57 26 S   116 59 02 E

517 Onslow Turnoff
North West Coastal Hwy, Onslow Parking Area 44 km N of Nanutarra Roadhouse or 119 km S of Fortesque River Roadhouse. 1 km S of turnoff

138 138   HEMA 166 H3   22 09 03 S   115 32 28 E

518 Three Mile Pool
Old Onslow Rd, Onslow Dispersed Camping 36 km S of Onslow or 5 km S of Old Onslow Township. Turn W 64 km NW of Hwy 1 Jcn or 17 km S of Onslow to Twitchen Rd & Old Onslow Rd. 19 km dirt road to sites on Ashburton R

08 9184 6644   HEMA 166 H3   21 45 44 S   114 57 05 E

519 Peedamulla Campground
Onslow-Peedamulla Rd, Peedamulla Campground 80 km N of Nanutarra Roadhouse or 73 km E of Onslow. 7 km off Hwy. Open Apr - Oct. Pre-book

0467 308 479   HEMA 166 H3   21 50 38 S   115 37 37 E

520 Robe River
North West Coastal Hwy, Robe River Rest Area 117 km N of Nanutarra Roadhouse or 43 km S of Fortescue River Roadhouse

138 138   HEMA 166 H4   21 36 55 S   115 55 21 E

521 Pannawonica Transit Park
Sports Way, Pannawonica Caravan Park next to Tony Lyons Park. Book & pay at the library

08 9134 9501   HEMA 166 H4   21 38 12 S   116 19 29 E

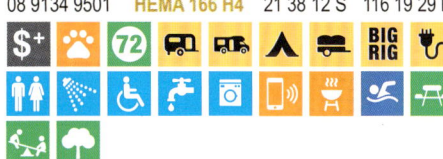

522 Fortescue River Roadhouse
North West Coastal Hwy, Mardie Caravan Park 108 km S of Karratha at Roadhouse

08 9184 5126   HEMA 166 G4   21 17 42 S   116 08 17 E

523 Gnoorea Point (40 Mile)
Forty Mile Beach Rd, Gnoorea Point Camp Area 66 km N of Fortescue River Roadhouse or 92 km W of Roebourne. Turn N off NW Coastal Hwy. 11 km dirt road. Fees apply May - Sep. 28 day limit. Chemical toilet required

08 9186 8055   HEMA 166 F4   20 50 26 S   116 20 51 E

524 Miaree Pool
North West Coastal Hwy, Karratha Rest Area 76 km NE of Fortescue River Roadhouse or 60 km W of Roebourne. S of NW Hwy. Signposted. 1 km dirt road

138 138   HEMA 166 F5   20 51 14 S   116 36 46 E

525 Karratha Council Seasonal Camp
Bayview Rd, Karratha Camp Area beside Discovery Balmoral Caravan Park, pay at their office. Open May - Sept

08 9144 4600   HEMA 166 F5   20 43 54 S   116 48 35 E

526 Coles Express Karratha Travel & Truck
Cnr NW Coastal Hwy & Madigan Rd, Karratha Rest Area 12 km SW of Karratha, or 96 km NE of Fortescue Roadhouse. Park in designated area

08 9185 3684   HEMA 166 F5   20 47 43 S   116 46 39 E

527 Cleaverville Beach
Cleaverville Rd, Cleaverville Beach Camp Area 26 km NW of Roebourne, or 33 km NE of Karratha. Turn N off NW Coastal Hwy. 13 km dirt road. Fees apply Apr - Sep, 28 day limit. No fees Oct - Mar, 3 day limit. BYO chemical toilet

08 9186 8055   HEMA 166 F5   20 39 40 S   116 59 53 E

528 Settlers Beach Campground
Settlers Beach Rd, Cossack Camp Area 16 km NE of Roebourne. Follow Pt Samson-Roebourne Rd 9 km, turn R to Cossack Rd Wickham for 9 km to Settlers Beach Rd for 7 km. See caretaker

08 6373 1440   HEMA 166 F6   20 40 09 S   117 11 42 E

529 Miliyanha Campground
Millstream Chichester NP
Via Dawson Ck Rd, Roebourne Camp Area 144 km S of Roebourne. Turn S 27 km E of Roebourne or 55 km W of Whim Creek, then SE after 79 km, then SW for 18 km. Alternative access via Pannawonica, 92 km dirt road

08 9182 2000   HEMA 166 G5   21 35 18 S   117 04 22 E

530 Stargazers Campground
Millstream Chichester NP
Off Kanjenjie-Millstream Rd, Roebourne Camp Area 144 km S of Roebourne. Turn S 27 km E of Roebourne or 55 km W of Whim Creek, then SE after 79 km, then SW for 18 km. Alternative access via Pannawonica, 92 km dirt road

08 9182 2000   HEMA 166 H5   21 35 40 S   117 05 17 E

531 Kialrah Pool Camp
Roebourne-Wittenoom Rd, Sherlock Camp Spot 38 km SE of Roebourne or 44 km W of Whim Creek. Turn off North West Coastal Hwy for 10 km to camp. Call on arrival

0472 515 239   HEMA 166 G6   20 58 37 S   117 23 20 E

532 Sherlock River
North West Coastal Hwy, Whim Creek Camp Spot 56 km E of Roebourne or 27 km W of Whim Creek. Turn N 100 m W of bridge. Small area

HEMA 166 G6   20 56 41 S   117 36 41 E

533 Koy Hill
North West Coastal Hwy, Whim Creek Camp Area 29 km E of Whim Creek. Turn off is on the S side

HEMA 166 F7   20 51 30 S   118 03 33 E

534 Peawah River
North West Coastal Hwy, Whim Creek area
Rest Area 26 km NE of Whim Creek or
92 km SW of Port Hedland
138 138   HEMA 166 F7   20 50 51 S   118 04 06 E

535 Herbert Parker (Yule River)
North West Coastal Hwy, Port Hedland
Rest Area 56 km NE of Whim Creek or
62 km SW of Port Hedland. Limited space. Do not
enter station
138 138   HEMA 166 F7   20 42 00 S   118 18 00 E

536 Port Hedland Golf Club
Great Northern Hwy, Port Hedland
Camp Area 17 km S of Port Hedland
08 9172 2046   HEMA 167 F8   20 24 13 S   118 34 29 E

537 Port Hedland Racecourse
2 McGregor St, Port Hedland
Parking Area opposite Koombana Lookout.
Peak season May - Sept. Managed by shire
08 9158 9300   HEMA 167 F8   20 18 32 S   118 36 45 E

Perth to Port Hedland
Great Northern Highway

538 Bindoon Transit Park
Great Northern Hwy, Bindoon
Camp Area at Rec Oval, S end of town,
entry near PO
08 9576 4600   HEMA 170 J4   31 23 08 S   116 05 52 E

539 Bindoon Hill
Great Northern Hwy, Bindoon
Rest Area 9 km N of Bindoon or 38 km S of
New Norcia. Share with trucks
138 138   HEMA 170 J4   31 19 35 S   116 09 15 E

540 Bolgart Caravan Park
George St, Bolgart
Caravan Park with honesty box. Key pad
entry
08 9628 7004   HEMA 170 H5   31 16 17 S   116 30 31 E

541 Wannamal East Rest Area
Great Northern Hwy, Wannamal
Rest Area 28 km N of Bindoon or 22 km S
of New Norcia
138 138   HEMA 170 H4   31 09 35 S   116 10 58 E

542 Yarrawinda South Rest Area
Caingiri Rd, Yarrawinda
Rest Area at Yarrawinda. 36 km NE of
Bindoon or 22 km SW of Calingiri
138 138   HEMA 170 H5   31 09 15 S   116 15 33 E

543 Mogumber Hall
Bindoon-Moora Rd, Mogumber
Camp Spot N of town at the sports ground.
Honesty box in shed for Progress Association
08 9628 7004   HEMA 170 H4   31 02 04 S   116 02 38 E

544 New Norcia Roadhouse
New Norcia Rd, New Norcia
Camp Area at New Norcia off bypass. Great
Northern Hwy near oval S of Monastery. Pay at
Visitor Centre. Signposted. Facilities in roadhouse.
Limited space
08 9654 8020   HEMA 170 H5   30 58 25 S   116 12 45 E

545 New Norcia
New Norcia Rd, New Norcia
Parking Area at New Norcia. Great
Northern Hwy beside oval S of Monastery. Pay at
Visitor Centre
08 9654 8056   HEMA 170 H5   30 58 24 S   116 12 48 E

546 Yerecoin Wayside Rest Area
Yerecoin South East Rd, Yerecoin
Parking Area. Payment at Yerecoin Traders.
7 day limit
0428 546 062   HEMA 170 G5   30 55 33 S   116 23 44 E

547 Piawaning Hall
Waddington-Wongan Hills Rd, Piawaning
Camp Spot 29 km S of Bindi-Bindi or 36 km
W of Wongan Hills. Cnr Denton St
08 9654 5015   HEMA 170 G5   30 50 28 S   116 23 09 E

548 Calingiri Caravan Park
21 Cavell St, Calingiri
Caravan Park E of main road
08 9628 7004   HEMA 170 H5   31 05 25 S   116 26 54 E

549 Trapwell Farm
Bebakine Rd, Rossmore
Farm Stay 20 km SW of Goomalling. Pre-book
0438 537 171   HEMA 170 J6   31 25 32 S   116 43 02 E

550 Mortlock River Rest
Goomalling-Toodyay Rd, Goomalling
Camp Spot 9 km SW of Goomalling. Site on R
138 138   HEMA 170 J6   31 20 59 S   116 46 10 E

551 Oak Park & Gnamma Holes
Oak Park Rd, Goomalling
Picnic Area 17 km NE of Goomalling
08 9629 1101   HEMA 170 H6   31 08 15 S   116 52 37 E

552 Gabby Quoi Quoi Lookout
Dowerin-Konnongorring Rd, Konnongorring
Camp Area 4 km W of Konnongorring.
Site on R
HEMA 170 H6   31 03 15 S   116 47 18 E

553 Konnongorring Hall
7122 Northam-Pithara Rd, Konnongorring
Parking Area just N of Dowerin-
Konnongorring Rd Jcn
08 9629 1101   HEMA 170 H6   31 03 14 S   116 46 36 E

554 Dowerin Roadhouse & Caratel Park
12 Goldfields Rd, Dowerin
Caravan Park. Pay at the roadhouse. Limited sites
08 9631 1135   HEMA 170 H6   31 11 43 S   117 01 55 E

555 Dowerin Short Stay Accommodation
Cnr Fraser & East Sts, Dowerin
Camp Area. SCV rates, ebook
08 9631 1202   HEMA 170 H6   31 11 25 S   117 01 59 E

556 Minnivale Camp Site
Hughes St, Minnivale
Rest Area next to disused tennis courts.
Turn N off the Goomalling-Wyalkatchem Rd 15 km
E of Dowerin or 20 km W of Wyalkatchem, along
Cunderdin-Minnivale Rd for 5 km. Honesty box
08 9631 1202   HEMA 170 H7   31 08 20 S   117 11 04 E

557 Wyalkatchem Travellers Park
Hands Dr, Wyalkatchem
Caravan Park S side of town
08 9681 1166   HEMA 170 H7   31 10 59 S   117 22 46 E

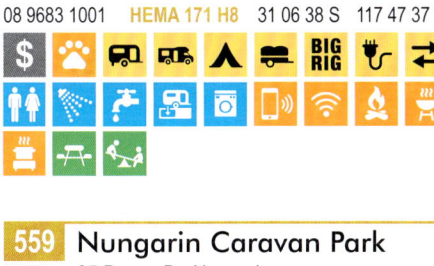

558 Trayning Caravan Park
Bencubbin/Kellerberrin Rd, Trayning
Caravan Park N side of town
08 9683 1001   HEMA 171 H8   31 06 38 S   117 47 37 E

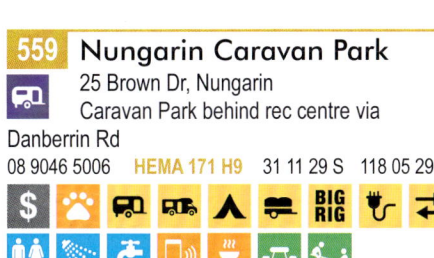

559 Nungarin Caravan Park
25 Brown Dr, Nungarin
Caravan Park behind rec centre via
Danberrin Rd
08 9046 5006   HEMA 171 H9   31 11 29 S   118 05 29 E

560 Danberrin Rock
Baird Rd, Burran Rock
Camp Spot 15.5 km S of Nungarin via
Danberrin Rd. Signposted
HEMA 171 H9   31 16 51 S   118 03 08 E

561 Talgomine Reserve
Off Talgomine Reserve Rd, Nungarin
Camp Spot 24 km E of Nungarin via
Nungarin-Chandler Rd. Signposted
HEMA 171 H9   31 12 39 S   118 17 45 E

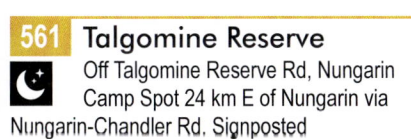

562 Eaglestone Rock
Lake Brown Rd, Nungarin
Camp Spot 21 km NE of Nungarin towards
Lake Brown. Via Danberrin Rd, Knungajin Rd &
Lake Brown South Rd. 4.5 km dirt road
08 9046 5006   HEMA 171 H9   31 04 31 S   118 14 48 E

563 Mangowine Homestead
Karomin Rd, Nungarin
Camp Area 14.5 km N of Nungarin or 24 km
S of Mukinbudin in homestead grounds
08 9046 5149   HEMA 171 H9   31 02 55 S   118 06 21 E

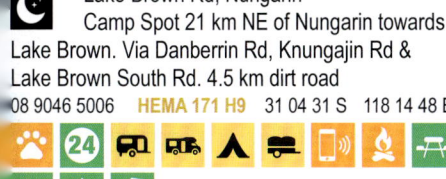

564 Weira Reserve
Via Koorda-Bullfinch Rd, Mukinbudin
Camp Spot 13 km E of Mukinbudin.
Signposted
08 9047 2100   HEMA 171 H10   30 59 40 S   118 23 13 E

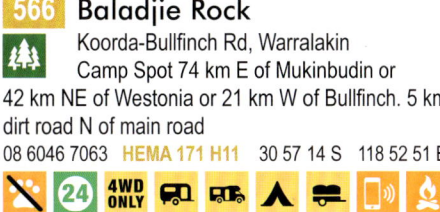

565 Mukinbudin Caravan Park
Cruickshank St, Mukinbudin
Caravan Park 700 m SW of PO
0429 471 103   HEMA 171 G9   30 55 09 S   118 12 21 E

566 Baladjie Rock
Koorda-Bullfinch Rd, Warralakin
Camp Spot 74 km E of Mukinbudin or
42 km NE of Westonia or 21 km W of Bullfinch. 5 km
dirt road N of main road
08 6046 7063   HEMA 171 H11   30 57 14 S   118 52 51 E

567 Elachbutting Rock
Elachbutting Nature Reserve
Echo Valley Rd, Mukinbudin
Camp Spot 100 km N of Westonia via Stoneman
Rd past Boodalin Soak, N to Warralakin Rd. L to
Koorda-Bullfinch Rd, R. GPS at entrance, follow
signposted track around rock to camping area
08 9046 7063   HEMA 171 G10   30 35 27 S   118 36 25 E

568 Beringbooding Rock
1487 Cunderin Rd, Mukinbudin
Camp Spot via Beringbooding Rd
08 9047 2100   HEMA 171 F10   30 33 30 S   118 29 32 E

569 Datjoin Well & Rock Reserve
Burakin-Wialki Rd, Wialki
Camp Spot 5 km W of Wialki. Signposted
to narrow track entrance to well & camping. Rock a
further 2 km E on Clark Rd on L at top of rise
HEMA 171 F9   30 27 44 S   118 04 07 E

570 Bencubbin Caravan Park
Kellerberrin Rd, Bencubbin
Caravan Park S outskirts of town
08 9685 1202   HEMA 171 G8   30 49 07 S   117 51 44 E

571 Marshall Rock Camping
Marshall Rock South Rd, Bencubbin
Camp Area 10 km S of Bencubbin via
Mukinbudin Rd. 1.7 km dirt road
08 9685 1202   HEMA 171 G8   30 50 19 S   117 54 15 E

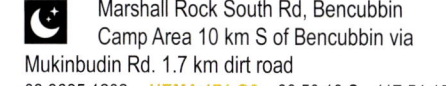

572 Gabbin Community Hall
Cnr Scarlett & Brindle Sts, Gabbin
Camp Spot next to community heritage hall
HEMA 171 G8   30 48 01 S   117 40 48 E

573 Koorda Caravan Park
Scott St, Koorda
Caravan Park 1 km N of PO
08 9684 1219   HEMA 170 G7   30 49 20 S   117 29 12 E

574 Koorda Native Flora Reserve
Mulji Rd, Koorda
Camp Area 16 km N of Koorda via Koorda-
Mollerin Rd. Signposted
08 9684 1219   HEMA 171 G8   30 44 25 S   117 33 10 E

575 Newcarlbeon Rock
Newcarleon Rd, Koorda
Camp Area 20 km N of Koorda via Koorda-
Kulja Rd. Signposted
08 9041 1666   HEMA 170 G7   30 39 59 S   117 25 05 E

576 Beacon Caravan Park
Lucas St, Deacon
Caravan Park in town
0488 025 853   HEMA 171 F8   30 27 07 S   117 52 13 E

577 Mollerin Rock
Kulja-Mollerin Rock Rd, Beacon
Camp Area 45 km N of Koorda. Via Koorda-
Mollerin Rd. Signposted
HEMA 171 F8   30 32 19 S   117 33 57 E

578 Billiburning Rock
White Rd, Beacon
Camp Area 34 km N of Beacon, via Ingleton
Rd. 18 km dirt road
HEMA 171 E8   30 10 20 S   117 55 04 E

WESTERN AUSTRALIA

579 Cadoux Rest Area

Dowerin-Kalannie Rd, Cadoux
Rest Area. Access key & pay at Cadoux
Trader
08 9673 1040   HEMA 170 G7   30 46 18 S   117 08 00 E

580 Wongan Hills Rest Area

Sadler Rd, Wongan Hills
Rest Area next to swimming pool & PCYC.
S on Wongan Rd take a R to Ninan St then L. Site
on R. Donation at Visitor Centre
08 9671 1973   HEMA 170 G6   30 53 51 S   116 43 03 E

581 The Gap

Waddington-Wongan Hills Rd, Wongan Hills
Camp Spot 12 km W of Wongan Hills or
36 km E of Waddington. Signposted on the L from
Wongan Hills
08 9671 1973   HEMA 170 G5   30 49 49 S   116 38 02 E

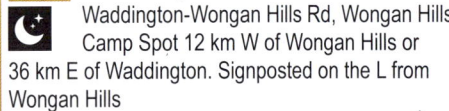

582 Lake Ninan Rest Area

Calingiri-Wongan Hill Rd, Wongan Hills
Rest Area 10 km SW of Wongan Hills
08 9671 2500   HEMA 170 H6   30 57 07 S   116 39 31 E

583 Petrudor Rock

Petrudor Rd, Kalannie
Camp Spot 31 km E of Pithara, S off
Pithara East Rd. 8 km dirt road
08 9661 0500   HEMA 170 F6   30 25 30 S   116 58 00 E

584 Ballidu Caravan Park

Wallis St, Ballidu
Caravan Park. Payment & caretaker info
at site
0427 088 885   HEMA 170 G6   30 35 44 S   116 46 22 E

585 Miling Sports Reserve

11 Miling E Rd, Miling
Camp Area. Pay & access code at Miling
General Store or phone
08 9654 1013   HEMA 170 F5   30 29 22 S   116 22 03 E

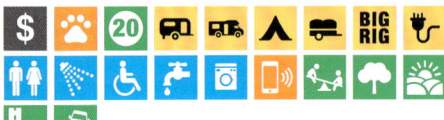

586 Pithara Tavern

Pearn Rd, Pithara
Parking Area behind disused tavern. Via
Pithara E Rd
08 9662 1032   HEMA 170 F6   30 23 22 S   116 40 12 E

587 Dalwallinu Caravan Park

10 Dowie St, Dalwallinu
Caravan Park NE side of town
08 9661 1253   HEMA 170 F6   30 16 27 S   116 40 08 E

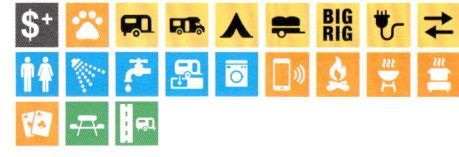

588 Mia Moon

Gunyidi-Wubin Rd, Miamoon
Camp Spot 17 km W of Wubin via Mullewa-
Wubin Rd
08 9661 0500   HEMA 170 E5   30 09 07 S   116 28 37 E

589 Jibberding Nature Reserve

Great Northern Hwy, Wubin
Rest Area 22 km NE of Wubin or 131 km
SW of Paynes Find. 200 m N of Rabbit Proof Fence
Rd. Follow track to open area
138 138   HEMA 170 E6   30 00 09 S   116 49 29 E

590 White Wells

Great Northern Hwy, Jibberding
Parking Area 47 km NE of Wubin or 107 km
SW of Paynes Find
HEMA 170 D6   29 50 10 S   116 56 45 E

591 Mount Gibson Rest Area

Great Northern Hwy, Paynes Find
Rest Area 83 km NE of Wubin. W side of road
138 138   HEMA 170 D7   29 36 34 S   117 08 31 E

592 Ninghan Station

Ninghan Road, Paynes Find
Station Stay 191 km W of Mount Magnet.
48 km S of Paynes Find. GPS at Hwy turnoff. Pre-
book, check in at homestead
08 9963 6517   HEMA 170 C7   29 23 06 S   117 14 48 E

593 Paynes Find Roadhouse

Great Northern Hwy, Paynes Find
Camp Area & Tavern 145 km S of Mt Magnet
08 9963 6111   HEMA 171 C8   29 15 48 S   117 41 09 E

594 Paynes Find Camp

Great Northern Hwy, Paynes Find
Camp Spot 12 km N of Paynes Find or
132 km S of Mt Magnet. From Paynes Find turn W
1.2 km before parking area, several access tracks.
From Mt Magnet turn W 1.2 km S of parking area,
veer L to access track, various campsites
08 9962 8042   HEMA 171 C8   29 09 55 S   117 42 22 E

595 Narndee Station

Narndee West Rd, Paynes Find
Station Stay 70 km NE of Paynes Find.
Signposted
08 9963 5414   HEMA 171 B9   28 56 54 S   118 10 34 E

596 Nalbarra Station

Burnerbinmah-Nalbarra Rd, Mount Magnet
Station Stay 80 km SW of Mt Magnet. Turn
W off Hwy 63 km S of Mt Magnet or 70 km N of
Paynes Find, 17 km to station. Signposted, dirt road
08 9963 5829   HEMA 171 A8   28 38 55 S   117 36 29 E

597 Kirkalocka Station

Great Northern Hwy, Mount Magnet
Station Stay 60 km S of Mt Magnet or
84 km N of Paynes Find. Turn E at signpost 500 m.
Limited power available. Closed in Summer
08 9963 5827   HEMA 171 A8   28 33 42 S   117 46 40 E

598 Kirkalocka Rest Area

Great Northern Hwy, Mount Magnet
Rest Area 64 km S of Mt Magnet or 80 km
N of Paynes Find. Park behind toilets
138 138   HEMA 171 A8   28 35 50 S   117 46 51 E

599 Windsor Rest Area

Mt Magnet-Sandstone Rd, Mount Magnet
Rest Area 77 km W of Sandstone or 76 km
E of Mt Magnet
138 138   HEMA 169 J9   28 01 41 S   118 31 25 E

600 Jundoo Dam West

Mount Magnet-Sandstone Rd, Sandstone
Area
Rest Area 57 km W of Sandstone or 97 km E of
Mt Magnet
138 138   HEMA 169 J9   28 00 36 S   118 43 47 E

601 Jundoo Dam East

Mount Magnet-Sandstone Rd, Sandstone
Rest Area 19 km W of Sandstone or
134 km E of Mt Magnet
138 138   HEMA 169 J9   28 00 40 S   119 06 17 E

602 Wondinong Station Stay

Cue-Wondinong Rd, Paynesville
Station Stay 103 km NE of Mt Magnet.
Travel 75 km on Mt Magnet-Sandstone Rd, to Mt
Magnet-Windsor Rd for 27 km. On R. Access from
Cue or Sandstone via Cue/Paynesville Rd
08 9963 5823   HEMA 169 J8   27 51 36 S   118 25 04 E

603 Paynesville West

Mt Magnet-Sandstone Rd, Mt Magnet Area
Rest Area 65 km E of Mt Magnet or 89 km
W of Sandstone
138 138   HEMA 169 J8   28 04 29 S   118 24 59 E

604 Challa Station West

Mt Magnet-Sandstone Rd, Mt Magnet Area
Rest Area 46 km E of Mt Magnet or 108 km
W of Sandstone
138 138   HEMA 169 J8   28 11 12 S   118 16 59 E

605 Mt Magnet East

Mt Magnet-Sandstone Rd, Mt Magnet Area
Rest Area 25 km E of Mt Magnet or 129 km
W of Sandstone
138 138   HEMA 169 J8   28 09 09 S   118 04 33 E

606 Old Wynyangoo Park Area

Great Northern Hwy, Mount Magnet
Parking Area 20 km N of Mt Magnet or
60 km S of Cue. Tracks away from road
HEMA 169 J8   27 53 38 S   117 51 40 E

607 Garden Rock

Cue-Wondinong Rd, Cue
Camp Spot 16 km SE from Cue.
Signposted from Cue. Dirt road. 4WD when wet
HEMA 169 H8   27 29 21 S   118 01 36 E
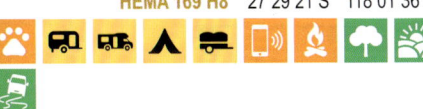

608 Lake Nallan

Lake Nallan Nature Reserve
Cue
Camp Spot 20 km N of Cue or 96 km SW of
Meekatharra. Camp in the 2 designated areas
08 9963 8600   HEMA 169 H8   27 15 41 S   117 59 07 E

609 Nallan Station Stay

Cogla Downs-Taincrow Rd, Cue
Station Stay 14 km NE of Cue. Pre-book
08 9963 1054   HEMA 169 H8   27 18 58 S   117 58 20 E
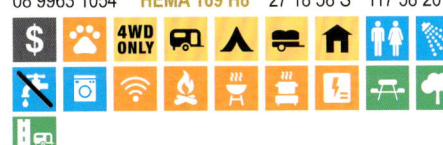

610 Bluebird Parking Area

Great Northern Hwy, Meekatharra
Parking Area 19 km S of Meekatharra or
106 km N of Cue
HEMA 169 G8   26 44 36 S   118 24 14 E

611 Lions Park Meekatharra

Cnr Hill & Savage Sts, Meekatharra
Parking Area at Meekatharra
08 9980 0600   HEMA 169 G9   26 35 35 S   118 29 49 E

612 Mount Gould

Landor-Meekatharra Rd, Meekatharra
Camp Spot 157 km NW of Meekatharra,
behind old police station
HEMA 168 F7   25 48 12 S   117 18 47 E

613 Peace Gorge

Peace Gorge Rd, Meekatharra
Picnic Area 3.4 km W of Meekatharra.
Turn N 1.5 km W of Meekatharra on the Landor
Meekatharra Rd
08 9980 1811   HEMA 169 G9   26 34 46 S   118 28 45 E

614 Barlangi Rock

Meekatharra-Sandstone Rd, Meekatharra
Parking Area 79 km SE of Meekatharra or
114 km NW of Sandstone
08 9980 0600   HEMA 169 H9   27 10 52 S   118 50 09 E

615 Meekatharra Boulders

Great Northern Hwy, Meekatharra
Camp Spot 20 km N of Meekatharra,
both sides of road, follow 100 m dirt track behind
distinctive boulder outcrops
08 9980 0600   HEMA 169 G9   26 25 28 S   118 35 14 E

616 Karalundi Caravan & Camping Park

1 Karalundi Dr, Karalundi
Caravan Park 58 km N of Meekatharra
08 9981 2000   HEMA 169 F9   26 07 42 S   118 41 09 E

617 Bilyuin Pool

Ashburton Downs-Meekatharra Rd,
Karalundi
Camp Spot 88 km N of Meekatharra. Turn W 74 km N
of Meekatharra or 182 km S of Kumarina Roadhouse
to Ashburton Downs Rd. On L after Murchison River,
tracks 1 km to riverside. 14 km dirt road
08 9980 0600   HEMA 169 F9   25 54 15 S   118 39 47 E

618 Gascoyne River (South Branch)

Great Northern Hwy, Meekatharra
Rest Area 148 km NW of Meekatharra, 276 km S of
Newman or 108 km S of Kumarina Roadhouse
138 138   HEMA 169 E10   25 34 44 S   119 14 19 E

619 Gascoyne River (Middle Branch)

Great Northern Hwy, Meekatharra
Rest Area 192 km NW of Meekatharra, 230 km S of
Newman or 64 km S of Kumarina Roadhouse. Sites
along river
HEMA 169 E10   25 12 05 S   119 20 06 E

620 Kumarina Roadhouse

Goldfields Hwy, Kumarina
Roadhouse Caravan Park behind roadhouse, W of road
08 9981 2930   HEMA 169 D10   24 42 38 S   119 36 27 E

621 Collier Range Rest Area

Great Northern Hwy, Kumarina
Rest Area 287 km NW of Meekatharra,
135 km S of Newman or 30 km N of Kumarina
Roadhouse
138 138   HEMA 169 C10   24 27 30 S   119 40 18 E

622 Mt Robinson Rest Area

Great Northern Hwy, Newman
Rest Area 109 km NW of Newman or 86 km
SE of Auski Roadhouse. 800 m E of Hwy
138 138   HEMA 169 A9   23 02 34 S   118 50 57 E

623 Tom Price Turn Off Rest Area

Karijini Dr, Karijini
Rest Area 155 km NW of Newman or 48 km
S of Auski Roadhouse. Turn to Karijini Dr on the L
138 138   HEMA 169 A9   22 40 04 S   118 42 00 E
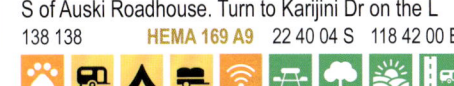

WESTERN AUSTRALIA

624 Albert Tognolini Rest Area
Great Northern Hwy, Auski
Rest Area 179 km NW of Newman or 17 km S of Auski Roadhouse. 2 km E of Hwy. Follow tracks to the R along ridge
138 138   HEMA 167 J8   22 29 23 S   118 44 09 E

625 Dales Gorge Campground
Karijini National Park
Auski
Camp Area 8 km E of Karijini Visitors Centre. Showers at Info Centre for fee
08 9189 8121   HEMA 167 J8   22 28 30 S   118 33 05 E

626 Karijini Eco Resort
Karijini National Park
Off Weano Gorge Rd, Auski
Camp Area 35 km W of Karijini Visitors Centre or 79 km NE of Tom Price via Karijini & Banjima Dr & Weano Gorge Rd. Rough dirt road
08 9286 1731   HEMA 166 J7   22 23 10 S   118 15 46 E

627 Mulga Parking Area
Great Northern Highway, Munjina (Auski)
Parking Area 39 km N of Auski Roadhouse or 180 km S of Hwy 1 Jcn
HEMA 167 H8   22 03 10 S   118 48 10 E

628 Bea Bea
Great Northern Highway, Auski
Rest Area 42 km N of Auski Roadhouse or 177 km S of Hwy 1 Jcn
318 138   HEMA 167 H8   22 00 32 S   118 48 55 E

629 Two Camel Creek
Great Northern Highway, Yule River
Rest Area 83 km N of Auski Roadhouse or 137km S of Hwy 1 Jcn, GPS at entry - 1 km to area, share with trucks
138 138   HEMA 167 H8   21 40 32 S   118 49 10 E

630 Marble Bar Turn Off
Great Northern Highway, Yule River
Parking Area 95 km N of Auski Roadhouse or 124 km S of Hwy 1 Jcn. Share with trucks
138 138   HEMA 167 G8   21 34 40 S   118 48 57 E

631 Indee Station
Indee Rd, Port Hedland
Station Stay 185 km N of Auski Roadhouse or 25 km S of Hwy 1 Jcn. E for 9 km dirt road. GPS at gate, signs to homestead
0408 890 797   HEMA 167 F8   20 46 41 S   118 32 23 E

Kiwirrkurra - Newman - Port Hedland

Gary Junction Road

This road is seasonal and more suitable to 4WD vehicles, camper trailers and off road caravans. Road conditions phone 1800 013 314. Permits are required to travel on this road

632 Top Up Rise
Kiwirrikurra Rd, Kiwirrikurra
Camp Area 313 km W of Kunawarritji & 227 km E of Kintore. Permits apply
HEMA 161 D11   22 44 16 S   127 12 11 E

633 Jupiter Well
Kiwirrikurra Rd, Kiwirrikurra
Camp Area 223 km E of Kunawarritji & 317 km W of Kintore. Permits apply
HEMA 161 D11   22 52 36 S   126 35 47 E

634 Gary Junction
Cnr of Gary Hwy & Kiwirrikurra Rd, Kunawarritji
Camp Area 65 km E of Kunawarritji. Permit applies
HEMA 161 C9   22 30 33 S   125 15 55 F

635 Kunawarritji Community
Canning Stock Route, Kunawarritji
Camp Area on the Kidson Track 4 km W of the Stock Route. Permits apply
08 9176 9040   HEMA 161 C8   22 19 51 S   124 43 35 E

Kiwirrkurra - Newman - Port Hedland

Marble Bar Road

636 Newman Visitors Centre
2 Fortescue Ave, Newman
Parking Area. Pay & obtain key at centre, open 8am - 5pm daily
08 9175 2888   HEMA 160 E1   23 21 33 S   119 43 40 E

637 Roy Hill Rest Area
Jcn Roy Hill & Marble Bar Rds, Roy Hill
Rest Area 93 km N of Newman or 96 km S of Nullagine
HEMA 160 D1   22 40 10 S   119 57 01 E

638 Carawine Gorge
Warrawagine Station
Woodie Woodie Rd, Marble Bar
Camp Area 174 km E of Marble Bar, via Rippon Hills & Woodie Woodie Mine Rd. Signposted to Gorge. 14 km, veer R to sites. Dirt road. No firearms. Watch for cattle at all times
08 9176 5900   HEMA 160 B3   21 28 55 S   121 01 43 E

639 Coongan Pool
Marble Bar-Port Hedland Rd, Marble Bar
Camp Spot 110 km SE of the Great Northern Hwy or 33 km N of the Marble Bar turn off. Turn NE opposite parking area on Marble Bar side of river, follow tracks to Y Jcn, veer L. Small vehicles only, dirt track
HEMA 160 A1   20 54 18 S   119 47 25 E

640 Doolena Gorge
Marble Bar-Port Hedland Rd, Marble Bar
Camp Spot 109 km SE of the Great Northern Hwy or 34 km N of Marble Bar turn off. Turn S dirt track on Port Hedland side of river. Follow track for 1.5 km. Watch for overhanging trees
HEMA 160 A1   20 55 32 S   119 47 08 E

641 Pear Creek
Marble Bar Rd, Marble Bar Area
Camp Spot 89 km SE of the Great Northern Hwy or 55 km NW of the Marble Bar turn off. Turn NE on Marble Bar side of creek & follow track. Small vehicles only, limited space
HEMA 160 A1   20 50 24 S   119 36 38 E

642 Des Streckfuss Rest Area
Marble Bar Rd, Port Hedland Area
Rest Area 74 km NW of Marble Bar or 79 km SE of Hwy 1 Jcn. 129 km SE of Port Hedland
HEMA 160 A1   20 49 33 S   119 30 44 E

Port Hedland to Kununurra

Great Northern Highway

643 De Grey River
Great Northern Hwy, De Grey River
Rest Area 82 km NE of Port Hedland or 71 km SW of Pardoo Roadhouse
08 9173 1711   HEMA 167 F8   20 18 28 S   119 15 11 E

644 Pardoo Station

Pardoo Station Rd, Pardoo
Station Stay 133 km N of Port Hedland
or 44 km S of Pardoo Roadhouse. 32 km S of
Roadhouse or 120 km N of Port Hedland, turn N.
13 km dirt road
08 9176 4930   HEMA 162 J1   20 06 23 S   119 34 46 E

645 Pardoo Roadhouse

Great Northern Highway, Pardoo
Caravan Park & Tavern 153 km N of Port
Hedland
08 9176 4916   HEMA 162 J1   20 03 14 S   119 49 39 E

646 Cape Keraudren

Cape Keraudren Coastal Reserve
Cape Keraudren Access Rd, Pardoo
Camp Area 12 km NW of Pardoo Roadhouse. Turn
N off Hwy 1 at Pardoo Roadhouse. 2 km good
gravel track. 28 day limit, entry fee
0419 968 123   HEMA 162 H1   19 57 38 S   119 46 08 E

647 Sandfire Roadhouse

Great Northern Hwy, Eighty Mile Beach
Caravan Park 291 km N of Port Headland.
No bookings
08 9176 5944   HEMA 162 H3   19 46 07 S   121 05 26 E

648 Anna Plains Station

Great Northern Hwy, Eighty Mile Beach
Camp Area 250 km S of Broome on Great
Northern Hwy, W to Anna Plains Rd 17 km dirt.
Short stay with limited sites. Pre-book via phone
0419 845 490   HEMA 162 G3   19 15 09 S   121 29 13 E

649 Stanley Rest Area

Great Northern Hwy, Eighty Mile Beach Area
Rest Area 108 km NE of Sandfire
Roadhouse or 181 km SW of Roebuck Plains
Roadhouse. 4 km N of Nita Downs turnoff
HEMA 162 G4   19 02 36 S   121 39 56 E

650 Goldwire Rest Area

Great Northern Hwy, Port Smith Area
Rest Area 168 km NE of Sandfire
Roadhouse or 121 km SW of Roebuck Plains
Roadhouse
HEMA 162 F4   18 36 14 S   121 57 59 E

651 Barn Hill Station

Great Northern Hwy, Roebuck
Station Stay 205 km N of Sandfire
Roadhouse or 95 km SW of Roebuck Plains
Roadhouse. Turn W off Hwy 1, 195 km N of
Sandfire Roadhouse or 95 km S of Roebuck Plains
Roadhouse for 10 km of sand & dirt road. Crocodile
area. Closed Nov - Apr
08 9192 4975   HEMA 162 F4   18 22 05 S   122 02 27 E

652 Roebuck Plains Rest Area

Great Northern Highway, Roebuck Plains
Parking Area 267 km N of Sandfire
Roadhouse or 22 km SW of Roebuck Plains
Roadhouse
HEMA 162 E5   18 00 51 S   122 35 42 E

653 Broome Bird Observatory

Crab Creek Rd, Broome
Camp Area 20 km E of Broome. Turn R
off Broome Rd. At T Jcn turn L. Signposted, small
vehicles only
08 9193 5600   HEMA 162 E5   17 58 32 S   122 20 39 E

654 Willie Creek

Willie Creek Rd, Broome Area
Camp Spot 35 km N of Broome. Turn
N 9 km E of Broome, along Cape Leveque Rd
& Manari Rd. Follow red markers around lake.
Camping area just past picnic shelter, veer R. Small
vehicles only. Dirt road
08 9191 3456   HEMA 162 E4   17 45 33 S   122 12 40 E

655 Barred Creek

Barred Ck Rd, Broome Area
Camp Spot 39 km N of Broome. Turn
N 9 km E of Broome, along Cape Leveque Rd &
Manari Rd then turn W 9 km N of Willie Creek Rd,
1.5 km to various sites. Stay alert for crocs
08 9191 3456   HEMA 162 E4   17 39 42 S   122 12 07 E

656 Quondong

Manari Rd, Broome Area
Camp Spot 45 km N of Broome. Turn N 9 km
E of Broome, along Cape Leveque Rd. Dirt road
08 9191 3456   HEMA 162 E4   17 35 28 S   122 10 11 E

657 James Price Point

Manari Rd, Cape Leveque
Camp Spot 58 km N of Broome. Turn N 9 km
E of Broome, along Cape Leveque Rd. Dirt road
08 9191 3456   HEMA 162 E4   17 29 15 S   122 08 39 E

658 Flat Rock Free Camp

Manari Rd, Broome Area
Dispersed Camping 69 km N of Broome
& 11 km N of James Price Pt, along Broome-Cape
Leveque Rd. Dirt road & soft sand
08 9191 3456   HEMA 162 E4   17 23 53 S   122 08 58 E

659 Banana Well Getaway

Via Cape Leveque Rd, Beagle Bay Area
Camp Area 135 km N of Broome.
109 km on Cape Leveque Rd, turn W at sign called
Loongabid (Steve Arrow Rd), 7 km to signpost, then
6 km to site. Stay alert for crocs
08 9192 4040   HEMA 162 D5   16 58 35 S   122 35 18 E

660 Gnylmarung Retreat

Middle Lagoon Rd, Beagle Bay Area
Camp Area 150 km N of Broome. Travel Cape
Leveque Rd for 134 km, turn W & follow signs for 28 km
08 9192 4097   HEMA 162 D5   16 51 40 S   122 37 15 E

661 Natures Hideaway at Middle Lagoon

Cape Leveque Rd, Beagle Bay Area
Camp Area 180 km N of Broome. Travel 134 km
along Cape Leveque Rd, W to Middle Lagoon Rd,
follow signs. 40 km to site. Open Apr - Oct
08 9192 4002   HEMA 162 D5   16 46 26 S   122 34 37 E

WESTERN AUSTRALIA

662 Pender Bay Escape
Two Moons Rd, Beagle Bay Area
Camp Area 175 km N of Broome. Follow the Cape Leveque Rd for 134 km, turn W to Middle Lagoon Rd, follow Pender Bay signs for 30 km. Pre-book
0429 845 707   HEMA 162 D5   16 46 31 S   122 36 37 E

663 Whalesong Cafe & Camp
Pender Bay, Beagle Bay Area
Camp Area 175 km N of Broome. Follow the Cape Leveque Rd for 134 km, turn W to Middle Lagoon Rd, follow Whalesong signs for 30 km. Pre-book, limited sites, open in dry season
08 9192 4000   HEMA 162 D5   16 47 59 S   122 37 22 E

664 Smithy's Seaside Adventures
Embalgun Outstation, Beagle Bay Area
Camp Area 175 km N of Broome. Follow the Cape Leveque Rd for 134 km, turn W onto Middle Lagoon Rd, then follow the Embalgun Community signs about 30 km. Pre-book
0429 086 388   HEMA 162 D5   16 48 01 S   122 37 39 E

665 Goombaragin Eco Retreat
Pender Bay, Beagle Bay Area
Camp Area 175 km N of Broome. Follow the Cape Leveque Rd for 134 km, turn W to Middle Lagoon Rd, turn R after 16 km, follow signs. Pre-book, limited sites
0429 505 347   HEMA 162 D5   16 47 43 S   122 39 58 E

666 Kooljaman at Cape Leveque
1 Cape Leveque Rd, Cape Leveque
Camp Area 220 km N of Broome. Small campervans only, no caravans. 2 night minimum
08 9192 4970   HEMA 162 C5   16 23 47 S   122 55 38 E

667 Gumbanan Wilderness Retreat
One Arm Point Rd, Bardi
Camp Area 4.5 km NW of One Arm Point. Signposted, 1.5 km track 344
0499 330 169   HEMA 162 C6   16 25 14 S   123 01 54 E

668 Lombadina
Lombadina Rd, Lombadina Community
Camp Area 196 km N of Broome. Turn to Diaradgin Rd, follow signs
08 9192 4936   HEMA 162 C5   16 31 13 S   122 53 37 E

669 Cygnet Bay Pearl Farm
Dampier Peninsula
Cygnet Bay Rd, Cape Leveque
Camp Area 10 km E of One Arm Point, 220 km N of Broome, via Cape Leveque Rd to One Arm Point Rd. Turn R, travel 3 km
08 9192 4283   HEMA 162 C6   16 27 05 S   123 00 31 E

670 Bullys Camp Djoodoon
Cape Leveque Rd, Cape Leveque
Camp Area 10 km E of Djarindjin Roadhouse. Turn R 800 m after the roadhouse on Cape Leveque Rd and 8 km to camp
08 9192 4359   HEMA 162 C6   16 31 32 S   122 59 44 E

671 Nillibubbica Rest Area
Great Northern Hwy, Roebuck Plains Area
Rest Area 71 km E of Roebuck Plains Roadhouse or 60 km W of Willare Bridge Roadhouse
HEMA 162 E6   17 39 21 S   123 07 57 E

672 Willare Bridge Roadhouse
Lot 64, Great Northern Hwy, Willare
Caravan Park 14 km SW of Derby turn off or 165 km E of Broome
08 9191 4775   HEMA 162 E6   17 43 35 S   123 39 15 E

673 Myroodah Crossing
Myroodah-Luluigui Rd, Geegully Creek
Camp Spot 38 km S of Camballin Rd & Great Northern Hwy Jcn. At 3 way intersection continue straight ahead to river crossing. Various sites both sides of river. Dirt road
HEMA 162 F7   18 04 44 S   124 13 18 E

674 The Boab Rest Area
Great Northern Hwy, Camballin
Rest Area 55 km SE of Derby turnoff or 158 km W of Fitzroy Crossing
HEMA 162 E7   17 49 26 S   124 14 04 E

675 The Lake Ellendale
Mt Hardman
Camp Area 118 km SE of Derby turnoff or 95 km W of Fitzroy Crossing. Entry is 6 km W of Ellendale Rest Area
HEMA 163 E8   17 55 52 S   124 47 00 E

676 Ellendale Rest Area
Great Northern Hwy, Mt Hardman
Rest Area 125 km SE of Derby turnoff or 88 km W of Fitzroy Crossing
HEMA 163 E8   17 57 38 S   124 50 10 E

677 RAAF Boab Quarry
Leopold Downs Rd, Fitzroy Crossing Area
Camp Spot 54 km NW of Fitzroy Crossing. Turn N 43 km W of Fitzroy Crossing. 11 km to Y Jcn, take R fork 700 m down track to various campspots. 58 km S of Tunnel Creek turnoff. Dirt road
HEMA 163 E9   17 54 44 S   125 17 48 E

678 Windjana Gorge
Windjana Gorge National Park
Leopold Downs Rd, Fitzroy Crossing Area
Camp Area 144 km E of Derby or 146 km NW of Fitzroy Crossing. Turn S off Gibb River Rd 125 km E of Derby for 18 km or turn N 43 km W of Fitzroy Crossing for 105 km. Dirt road. Open dry season
08 9195 5500   HEMA 164 K5   17 24 42 S   124 56 33 E

679 Jarlarloo Riwi Mimbi Camp
Mt Pierre Station Rd, Fitzroy Crossing Area
Camp Area 90 km E of Fitzroy Crossing or 202 km W of Halls Creek. 3 km from Hwy, follow signs. Pay & book at Mimbi Caves Tours
08 9191 5355   HEMA 163 G10   18 43 43 S   126 02 36 E

680 Ngumban Cliff Lookout
Great Northern Hwy, Fitzroy Crossing Area
Rest Area 96 km SE of Fitzroy Crossing or 192 km W of Halls Creek
HEMA 163 G10   18 44 53 S   126 06 31 E

681 Larrawa Nature Stay

Great Northern Hwy, Halls Creek Area
Camp Area 143 km E of Fitzroy Crossing
or 147 km W of Halls Creek. 4 km on dirt road to
station. Open Apr - Sept. GPS at gate
08 9191 7025   HEMA 163 G10   18 47 57 S   126 32 04 E

682 Mary Pool (Mary River)

Great Northern Hwy, Mary River
Rest Area 180 km E of Fitzroy Crossing or
108 km W of Halls Creek
HEMA 163 G11   18 43 37 S   126 52 19 E

683 Caroline Pool

Sophie Downs Access, Halls Creek Area
Camp Spot 15 km SE of Halls Creek, via
Duncan Rd. Turn E 13 km SE of Halls Creek. Sandy
road, small area limited turning space
08 9168 6262   HEMA 163 F12   18 13 36 S   127 45 35 E

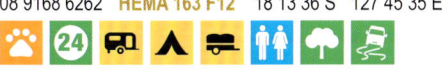

684 Palm Springs

Via Duncan Rd, Halls Creek Area
Picnic Spot 40 km SE of Halls Creek. Small
area close to road
08 9168 6262   HEMA 163 F12   18 25 12 S   127 50 42 E

685 Sawpit Gorge

Via Duncan Rd, Halls Creek Area
Camp Spot 46 km SE of Halls Creek. Last
3 km winding & corrugated. Small vehicles only.
Small area
08 9168 6262   HEMA 163 F12   18 25 30 S   127 49 14 E

686 Little Panton River

Great Northern Hwy, Halls Creek Area
Parking Area 46 km N of Halls Creek or
117 km S of Turkey Creek
HEMA 163 E12   17 52 32 S   127 49 54 E

687 Leycesters Rest Ord River

Via Great Northern Hwy, Ord River
Rest Area 100 km N of Halls Creek or
63 km S of Turkey Creek
HEMA 165 K12   17 28 45 S   127 57 04 E

688 Spring Creek

Warmun (Turkey Creek) Area
Rest Area 107 km NE of Halls Creek or
56 km SW of Turkey Creek. Big rigs at top car park
HEMA 165 K12   17 25 59 S   127 59 21 E

689 Muluks Rest Area

Great Northern Hwy, Warmun
Rest Area 121 km N of Halls Creek or
39 km S of Turkey Creek
HEMA 165 K12   17 20 19 S   128 03 08 E

690 Kurrajong Campground

Purnululu NP (Bungle Bungles)
Warmun (Turkey Creek) Area
Camp Area 7 km N of Visitor Centre. 56 km rough
dirt road. Accessed by high clearance, single axle,
towable units, caravan & camper trailers
08 9168 4200   HEMA 165 K13   17 23 20 S   128 19 50 E

691 Walardi Campground

Purnululu NP (Bungle Bungles)
Warmun (Turkey Creek) Area
Camp Area 12 km S of visitor centre. 56 km rough
dirt road. Accessed by high clearance, single axle,
towable units, caravan & camper trailers
08 9168 4200   HEMA 165 K13   17 31 16 S   128 18 02 E

692 Doon Doon Roadhouse

Great Northern Hwy, Doon Doon
Camp Area & Caravan Park 93 km N of
Turkey Creek or 60 km S of Victoria Hwy Jcn
08 9167 8004   HEMA 165 G12   16 18 30 S   128 14 53 E

693 Dunham River

Great Northern Hwy, Kununurra Area
Rest Area 118 km N of Turkey Creek or
35 km S of Victoria Hwy Jcn
HEMA 165 G13   16 07 54 S   128 22 52 E

694 Wuggubun Aboriginal
Community Campground

Great Northern Hwy, Kununurra Area
Camp Area 157 km N of Turkey Creek or 40 km SW
of Kununurra. Turn W off Hwy. Signposted. Open
Apr - Oct
HEMA 165 F13   15 57 13 S   128 22 45 E

695 Cockburn Rest Area

Great Northern Hwy, Kununurra Area
Rest Area at Victoria Hwy Jcn or 152 km N
of Turkey Creek, 56 km S of Wyndham or 45 km W
of Kununurra
HEMA 165 F13   15 52 07 S   128 22 17 E

696 Maggie Creek

Great Northern Hwy, Wyndham Area
Rest Area 28 km N of Victoria Hwy Jcn or
28 km S of Wyndham. Unlevel area
HEMA 165 F12   15 40 42 S   128 14 50 E

697 Diggers Rest Station

King River Rd, Wyndham Area
Camp Area 38 km N of Victoria Hwy Jcn
or 34 km SW Wyndham. Signposted on Great
Northern Hwy
08 9161 1029   HEMA 165 E12   15 38 19 S   128 04 48 E

698 Kununurra Showground

Coolibah Dr, Kununurra
Camp Area. Open in dry season
08 9168 2885   HEMA 165 F14   15 46 19 S   128 43 54 E

699 Maxwell Camp

Crossing Falls Rd, Kununurra
Camp Area 16 km S of Kununurra. Turn R
off Victoria Hwy. Pre-book
1300663369   HEMA 165 F14   15 51 34 S   128 45 19 E

700 Lake Argyle Spillway

Lake Argyle Rd, Lake Argyle
Rest Area S of Kununurra. Drive 36 km on
Victoria Hwy turn R, travel about 23 km
HEMA 165 14 F   16 01 48 S   128 46 56 E

701 Mambi Island

Parry Creek Rd, Kununurra Area
Camp Area 54 km NW Kununurra. Turn
N to Valentine Springs Rd, travel 14.5 km to Parry
Creek Rd, turn L travel 31.5 km. Signposted access
to camp. Dirt road. Steep entry
HEMA 165 E13   15 34 58 S   128 28 24 E

702 Halls Creek Camp
Via Valentine Spring Rd, Kununurra
Camp Spot on the Ord River 32 km NW of Kununurra. Turn N off Victoria Hwy 13 km W of Kununarra, or 32 km NE of Jcn Victoria & Great Northern Hwys,14 km from Hwy. Turn NE at T Jcn for 4.5 km. Crocodile area
HEMA 165 E14   15 37 20 S   128 41 28 E

703 Cape Domett
Cambridge Gulf, Kununurra Area
Camp Spot N of Kununurra on E side of Cambridge Gulf. Remote area. Crocodile area
HEMA 165 C13   14 48 29 S   128 24 04 E

Leonora to Yulara (NT)

Great Central Road

This road is seasonal and more suitable to 4WD vehicles, camper trailers and off road caravans. Road conditions phone 1800 013 314. Permits are required to travel on this road

704 Giles Breakaway
Great Central Rd, Laverton Area
Camp Spot 50 km N of Laverton or 262 km SW of Tjukayirla Roadhouse. At Outback Way sign turn S to track to Breakaway
HEMA 158 C5   28 16 49 S   122 42 03 E

705 Giles Breakaway Park Area
Great Central Rd, Laverton Area
Parking Area 56 km N of Laverton or 256 km SW of Tjukayirla Roadhouse
HEMA 158 C5   28 14 49 S   122 43 10 E

706 Limestone Well Parking Area
(The Pines)
Great Central Rd, Laverton Area
Parking Area 120 km NE of Laverton or 191 km SW of Tjukayirla Roadhouse
HEMA 158 C6   27 54 55 S   123 10 41 E

707 Minnie Creek Rd Park Area
Great Central Rd, Tjukayirla Area
Parking Area 197 km NE of Laverton or 115 km SW of Tjukayirla Roadhouse
HEMA 158 C7   27 50 32 S   123 55 03 E

708 Yeo Lake Homestead
Yeo Lake Nature Reserve
Great Central Rd, Yeo Station
Camp Area 93 km E of Cosmo Newbery via Neale Jct Rd. Buy permits from DEC & Ngaanyatjarra (08) 8950 1711
08 9080 5555   HEMA 158 C7   28 04 36 S   124 19 05 E

709 Neale Junction
Neale Jct Rd, Neale Junction
Camp Area 257 km E of Cosmo Newbery. Permits from DEC & Ngaanyatjarra (08) 8950 1711
08 9080 5555   HEMA 159 C9   28 18 11 S   125 48 52 E

710 Ilkurlka Roadhouse
Serpentine Lakes Rd, Ilkurlka
Camp Area. Facilities at roadhouse
08 9037 1147   HEMA 159 C12   28 21 01 S   127 31 05 E

711 Lake Throssell Parking Area
Great Central Rd, Tjukayirla Area
Parking Area 57 km SW of Tjukayirla Roadhouse or 250 km NE of Laverton. Long area with 2 entries, N side turn to old road
HEMA 158 B7   27 33 09 S   124 17 51 E

712 Tjukayirla Roadhouse
Great Central Rd, Tjukayirla
Camp Area next to roadhouse. Fee for WiFi
08 9037 1108   HEMA 159 A8   27 09 19 S   124 34 29 E

713 Camp Paradise
Great Central Rd, Tjukayirla Area
Camp Spot 92 km NE of Tjukayirla Roadhouse or 163 km SW of Warburton. Turn N off road
HEMA 159 A9   26 57 55 S   125 24 43 E

714 Mananytja Rockhole
Great Central Rd, Great Central Road
Camp Spot 122 km NE of Tjukayirla Roadhouse or 133 km SE of Warburton. Turn N 100m W of rockhole follow track to breakaway
HEMA 159 A9   26 50 10 S   125 39 29 E

715 Rock Holes Camp
Great Central Rd, Warburton Area
Camp Area 235 km NE of Tjukayirla Roadhouse or 20 km SE of Warburton
HEMA 161 J10   26 11 52 S   126 23 03 E

716 Warburton Roadhouse
Great Central Rd, Warburton
Camp Area 245 km E of Tjukayirla and 230 km W of Warakurna
08 8956 7656   HEMA 161 J10   26 07 56 S   126 34 09 E

717 Yarla Kutjarra
Great Central Rd, Warburton Area
Camp Spot 95 km NE of Warburton or 136 km SE of Warakurna
08 8956 7966   HEMA 161 H11   25 36 37 S   127 13 24 E

718 Gnamma Holes
Great Central Rd, Warakurna
Camp Spot 61 km W of Warakurna Roadhouse, camp on N side of Hwy, waterholes S of Hwy
HEMA 161 H12   25 17 58 S   127 49 02 E

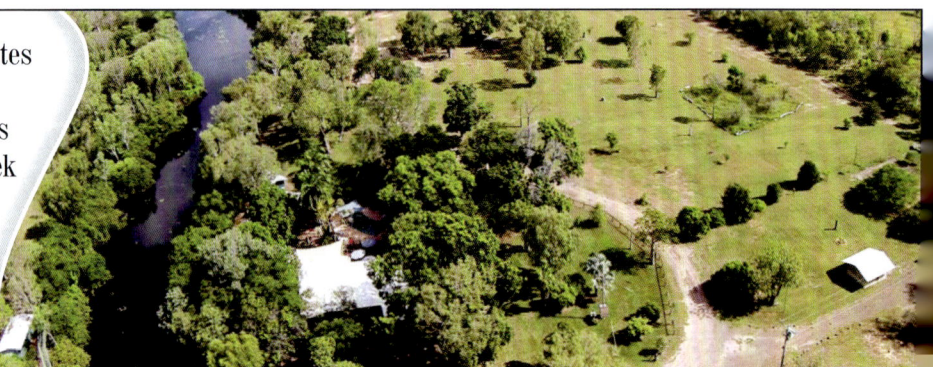

719 Warakurna Roadhouse

Via Nineteenth St, Warakurna
Camp Area in the Great Victoria Desert,
781 km W of Alice Springs and 331 km from Yulara
08 8956 7344   HEMA 161 G13   25 02 34 S   128 18 12 E

720 Gill Pinnacle

Great Central Rd, Ngaanyatjarra Lands
Camp Spot 65 km E of Warakurna
Roadhouse, GPS at Hwy, 500 m further. Small
vehicles only
HEMA 161 G14   24 55 22 S   128 46 35 E

721 Bungabiddy Rock Hole

Sandy Blight Junction Rd, Warakurna Area
Camp Spot 102 km NE of Warakurna
Roadhouse, 26 km from Great Central Rd
HEMA 161 G14   24 39 26 S   128 45 05 E

Gibb River Road

*This road is seasonal and more
suitable to 4WD vehicles, camper
trailers and off road caravans. Road
conditions phone 1800 013 314*

722 El Questro Station

Gibb River Rd, Kununurra
Station Stay 87 km W of Kununurra on
the Gibb River-Wyndham Rd. GPS at turn off to El
Questro Rd. Water crossings
1800 837 168   HEMA 165 F12   15 55 10 S   128 02 04 E

723 Pentecost River Camp

Gibb River Rd, Kununurra
Camp Area 110 km W of Kununurra on the
Gibb River-Wyndham Rd
HEMA 165 F12   15 47 50 S   127 52 57 E

724 Home Valley Station

Gibb River Rd, Kununurra
Station Stay 66 km W of Wyndham -
Kununurra turnoff. 1.7 km from Gibb River Rd
08 9161 4322   HEMA 165 F12   15 43 15 S   127 49 24 E

725 Durack River Crossing

Gibb River Rd, Durack
Camp Area 150 km W of Wyndham
- Kununurra turnoff & 198 km E of Mt Barnett
Roadhouse. Crocodile area
HEMA 165 F10   15 56 17 S   127 13 17 E

726 Ellenbrae Station

Gibb River Rd, Durack
Station Stay 171 km W of Wyndham-
Kununurra turnoff & 180 km E of Mt Barnett
Roadhouse. 5 km N of Gibb River Rd. Pay fees at
homestead. Open Apr - Oct
08 9161 4325   HEMA 165 F10   15 57 27 S   127 03 47 E

727 Russ Creek

Gibb River Rd, Durack
Camp Spot 46 km W of Ellenbrae Station
turnoff or 43 km E of Kalumburu Rd. On N side of
road, E of creek
HEMA 165 G9   16 02 53 S   126 42 04 E

728 Drysdale River Station
- Homestead Campground

Kalumburu Rd, Drysdale River
Station Stay 59 km N of Gibb River Rd & Kalumburu
Rd intersection. Limited powered sites. Register &
pay at the shop or bar prior to setting up
08 9161 4326   HEMA 165 F8   15 42 13 S   126 22 45 E

729 Munurra/King Edward River

Mitchell River National Park
Port Warrender Rd, Mitchell Plateau
Camp Spot 8 km W of Kalumburu Rd via the
Mitchell Plateau Rd
08 9168 4200   HEMA 165 D8   14 53 03 S   126 12 05 E

730 Mitchell Falls Campground

Mitchell River National Park
Twelfth St, Mitchell Plateau
Camp Area 16 km W of the Mitchell Plateau & Port
Warrender Rd
08 9168 4200   HEMA 164 C7   14 49 12 S   125 43 06 E

731 Walsh Point Campground

Port Warrender Rd, Mitchell Plateau
Camp Area 38 km N of Mitchell Falls turnoff
08 9161 4205   HEMA 164 C7   14 34 05 S   125 50 47 E

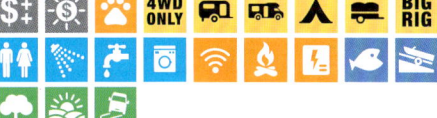

732 Kalumburu Mission

Gibb River Rd
Kalumburu Boulevard, Kalumburu
Camp Area & Caravan Park. Pre-book. Crocodile area
08 9161 4333   HEMA 165 B9   14 17 44 S   126 38 29 E

733 McGowan Island Beach

2000 Kalumburu Airport Rd, Kalumburu
Camp Area 16 km N of Kalumburu. Open
Apr - Nov
08 9161 4748   HEMA 165 B9   14 08 44 S   126 38 56 E

734 Honeymoon Bay

Lot 42 Honeymoon Beach, Kalumburu
Camp Area 30 km N of Kalumburu.
Crocodile area
08 9161 4378   HEMA 165 B9   14 06 16 S   126 40 50 E

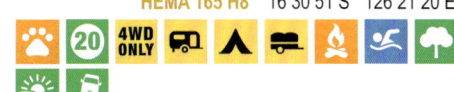

735 Ngallagunda - Gibb River
Station

Gibb River Rd, Durack
Camp Area next to homestead and store. 370 km E
of Derby at Ngallagunda
08 9191 4600   HEMA 165 G8   16 25 37 S   126 26 03 E

736 Hann River

Gibb River Rd, Gibb
Rest Area 54 km W of Kalumburu Rd Jcn or
54 km E of Mt Barnett Roadhouse
HEMA 165 H8   16 30 51 S   126 21 20 E

737 Mt Elizabeth Station

Mt Elizabeth Rd, Gibb
Station Stay 38 km NE of Mt Barnett
Roadhouse or 70 km S of the Kalumburu Rd Jcn,
then 30 km N to campsite
08 9191 4644   HEMA 165 G8   16 25 10 S   126 06 17 E

WESTERN AUSTRALIA

738 Manning Gorge Camp Area
Gibb River Rd, King Leopold Ranges
Camp Area 7 km N of Mt Barnett
Roadhouse. Permit required, fees payable at
roadhouse
08 9191 7007   HEMA 164 H7   16 39 25 S   125 55 39 E

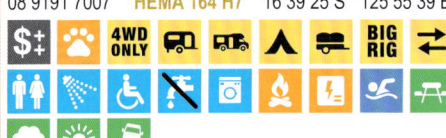

739 Charnley River Station
Gibb River Rd, Imintji
Station Stay with turn off 27 km NE of
Imintji Store or 47 km SW of Mt Barnett Roadhouse.
Travel N for 42 km to station. Open in dry season
08 9191 4646   HEMA 164 H6   16 42 53 S   125 27 29 E

740 Mornington Wilderness Camp
Gibb River Rd, Imintji
Camp Area 90 km S of Gibb River Rd.
Turn S 25 km E of Imintji Store or 53 km W of Mt
Barnett Roadhouse. Report in at radio booth before
entering. No fires
08 9191 7406   HEMA 165 K8   17 30 29 S   126 06 45 E

741 Imintji Campground
Derby - Gibb River Rd, Imintji
Camp Area E of store & art centre. No need
to book, check in at store. Open May - Oct
08 9191 7227   HEMA 164 J6   17 08 58 S   125 27 24 E

742 March Fly Glen Rest Area
Derby-Gibb River Rd, King Leopold Ranges
Rest Area 9.7 km W of Silent Grove Rd or
220 km E of Derby. Small vehicles only
HEMA 164 J6   17 09 47 S   125 18 37 E

743 Silent Grove Camp Area
Wunaamin Miliwundi Ranges Conservation Park
Silent Grove Rd, King Leopold Ranges
Camp Area 20 km N of Gibb River Rd on Silent
Grove Rd. Turn N 8 km W of Imintji Roadhouse or
95 E of Gibb River Rd & Leopold Downs Rd Jcn
08 9192 5500   HEMA 164 J6   17 03 59 S   125 14 57 E

744 Mt Hart Wilderness Lodge
King Leopold Ranges Conservation Park
Gibb River Rd, Mount Hart
Camp Area at Mt Hart Station. Turn N 65 km E of
Leopold Downs Rd Jcn or 38 km W of Imintji Store.
49 km to station. Fee for WiFi. Open dry season
08 9191 4645   HEMA 164 H5   16 49 06 S   124 55 14 E

745 Lennard River Rest Area
Gibb River Rd, King Leopold Ranges
Rest Area 72 km W of Silent Grove Rd or
128 km E of Derby
HEMA 164 K4   17 23 34 S   124 45 22 E

746 Birdwood Downs Station
Gibb River Rd, Derby Area
Station Stay 18 km E of Derby. Bush
camping. Gravel road 750 m to gate
08 9191 1275   HEMA 164 K2   17 21 28 S   123 46 06 E

  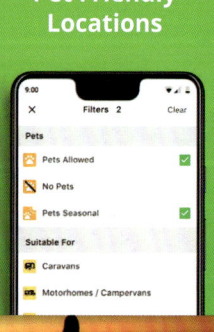 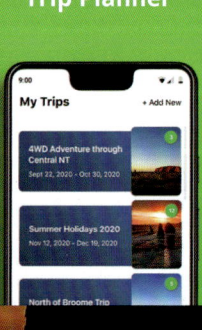

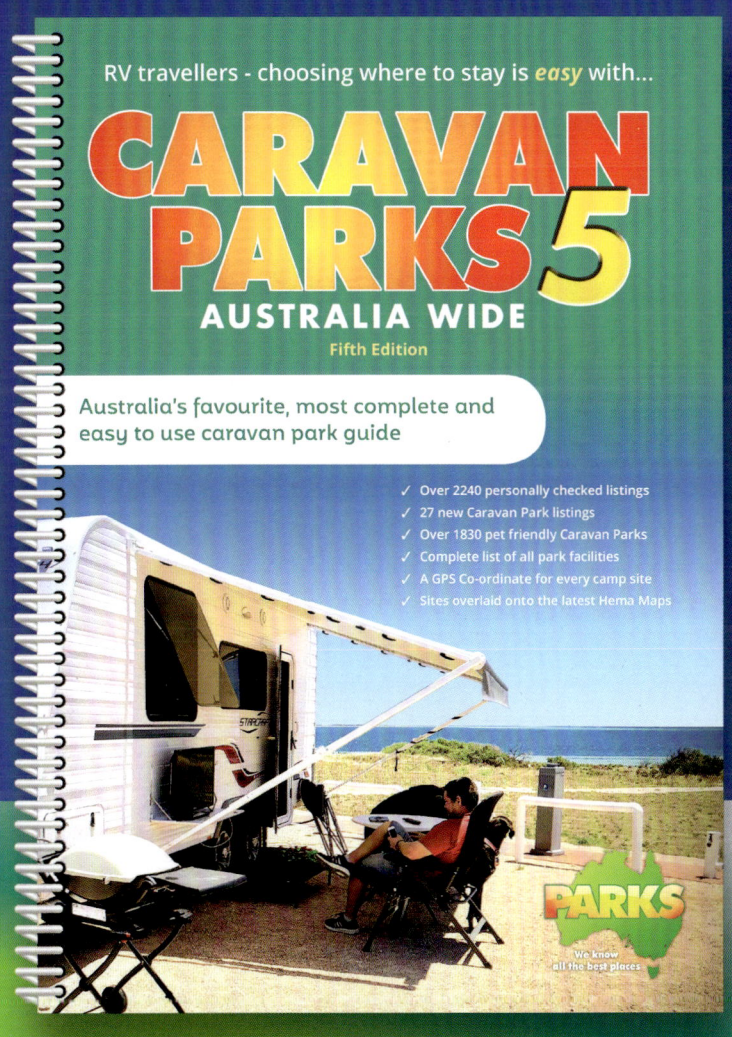

Key Map

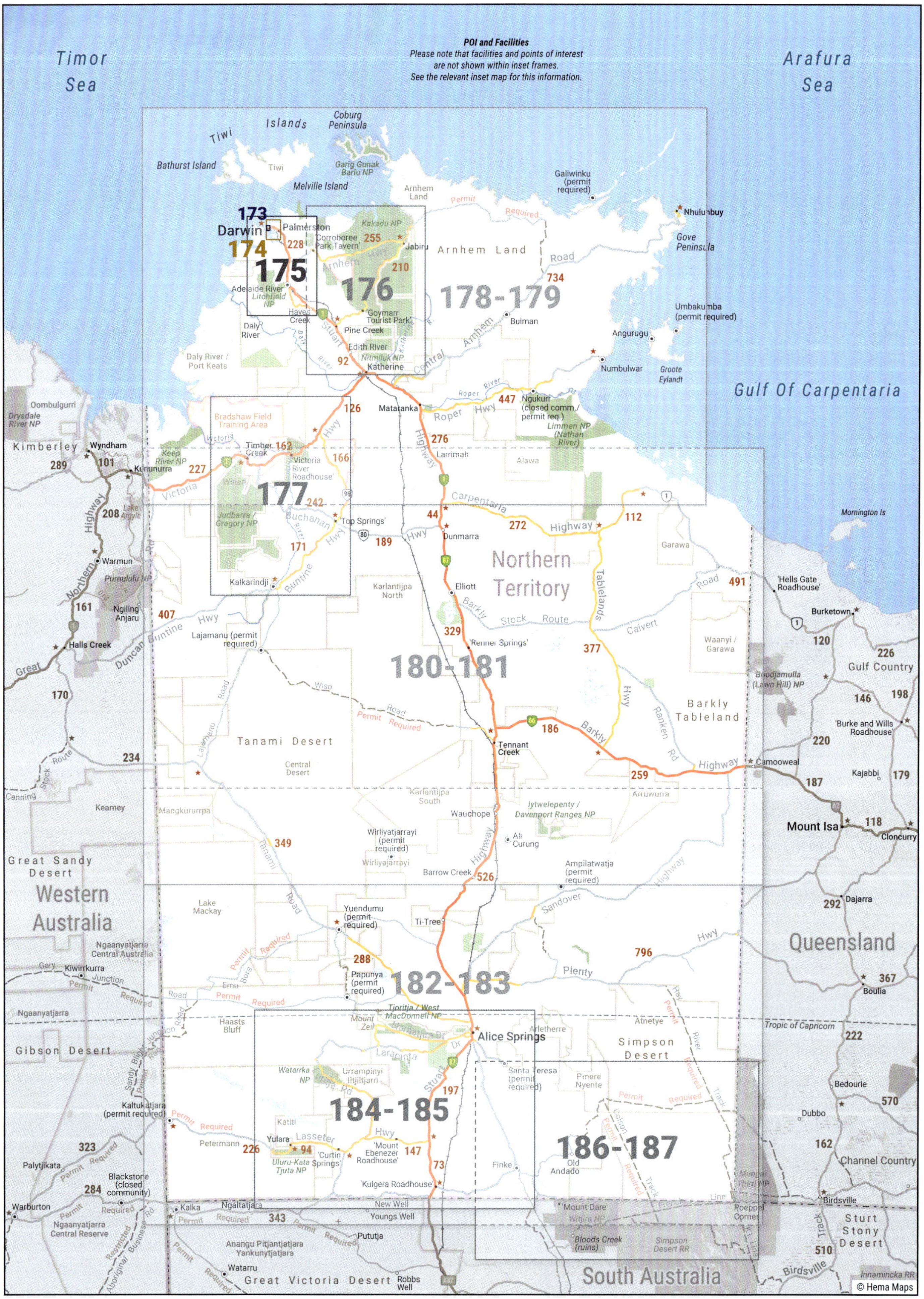

km
0   100   200

Timor Sea

Arafura Sea

POI and Facilities
Please note that facilities and points of interest
are not shown within inset frames.
See the relevant inset map for this information.

Islands

Coburg Peninsula

Tiwi Islands

Bathurst Island

Melville Island

Tiwi

Garig Gunak Barlu NP

Galiwinku (permit required)

Arnhem Land

Nhulunbuy

Gove Peninsula

173
Darwin   Palmerston
174   228
175   Corroboree Park Tavern' 255   Kakadu NP   Jabiru
176   210
178-179   734

Adelaide River
Litchfield NP

'Goymarr Tourist Park'

Pine Creek

Bulman

Umbakumba (permit required)

Hayes Creek

Daly River

Edith River

Angurugu

Daly River / Port Keats

92   Nitmiluk NP   Katherine

Roper River

Ngukurr (closed comm./ permit req)   447

Numbulwar   Groote Eylandt

Gulf Of Carpentaria

Kimberley   Wyndham

126   Mataranka   Roper Hwy

Limmen NP (Nathan River)

289   101   Kununurra

Bradshaw Field Training Area

Keep River NP   Timber Creek 162   276   Larrimah   Alawa

227   Victoria Hwy   166   'Victoria River Roadhouse'

Mornington Is

208   Lake Argyle

177   242   90   Top Springs   44   Dunmarra   272   Highway   112   Garawa

Judbarra / Gregory NP   171   189   329   'Renner Springs'   377   Waanyi / Garawa

Warmun   Purnululu NP   Buntine Hwy   Kalkarindji   Karlantijpa North

'Hells Gate Roadhouse'   Burketown   120

161   Ngiling Anjaru   407   Lajamanu (permit required)

180-181   Northern Territory   Barkly Tableland   491

Halls Creek   170   Duncan   234   Wiso   Barkly Stock Route   186   259   Camooweal

Boodjamulla (Lawn Hill) NP   226   146   198

'Burke and Wills Roadhouse'   220

Canning   Kearney   Karlantijpa South   Tennant Creek   Ranken Rd   187   Mount Isa   118   Cloncurry   179

Tanami Desert   Central Desert   Kajabbi

Great Sandy Desert

Western Australia   Mangkururrpa   349   Wirliyatjarrayi (permit required)   Wauchope   Iytwelepenty / Davenport Ranges NP   Ali Curung   Sandover Hwy   292   Dajarra

Lake Mackay   Wirliyatjarrayi   Barrow Creek 526   Ampilatwatja (permit required)   796   Plenty   *Queensland*

Gary Junction   Kiwirrkurra   Yuendumu (permit required)   Ti-Tree   367   Boulia

Ngaanyatjarra Central Australia   288   Papunya (permit required)   **182-183**   Atnetye   222

Ngaanyatjarra   Haasts Bluff   Tjoritja / West MacDonnell NP   Alice Springs   Simpson Desert   Tropic of Capricorn

Gibson Desert   Mount Zeil   Larapinta Dr   Aretherre   Bedourie

Watarrka NP   Urrampinyi Iltjiltjarri   Santa Teresa (permit required)   Pmere Nyente

Kaltukatjara (permit required)   226   94   Yulara   197   **184-185**   570   Dubbo   162

323   Palytjikata   Petermann   Uluru-Kata Tjuta NP   'Curtin Springs'   'Mount Ebenezer Roadhouse'   147   73   **186-187**   Channel Country

284   Blackstore (closed community)   'Kulgera Roadhouse'   Finke   Old Andado   510   Birdsville

Warburton   Kalka   New Well   'Mount Dare'   Witjira NP   Roeppel Corner

343   Youngs Well   Bloods Creek (ruins)   Simpson Desert RR   *Sturt Stony Desert*

Ngaanyatjarra Central Reserve   Pututja   *South Australia*   Birdsville

Anangu Pitjantjatjara Yankunytjatjara   Robbs Well   Innamincka RR

Watarru   *Great Victoria Desert*   © Hema Maps

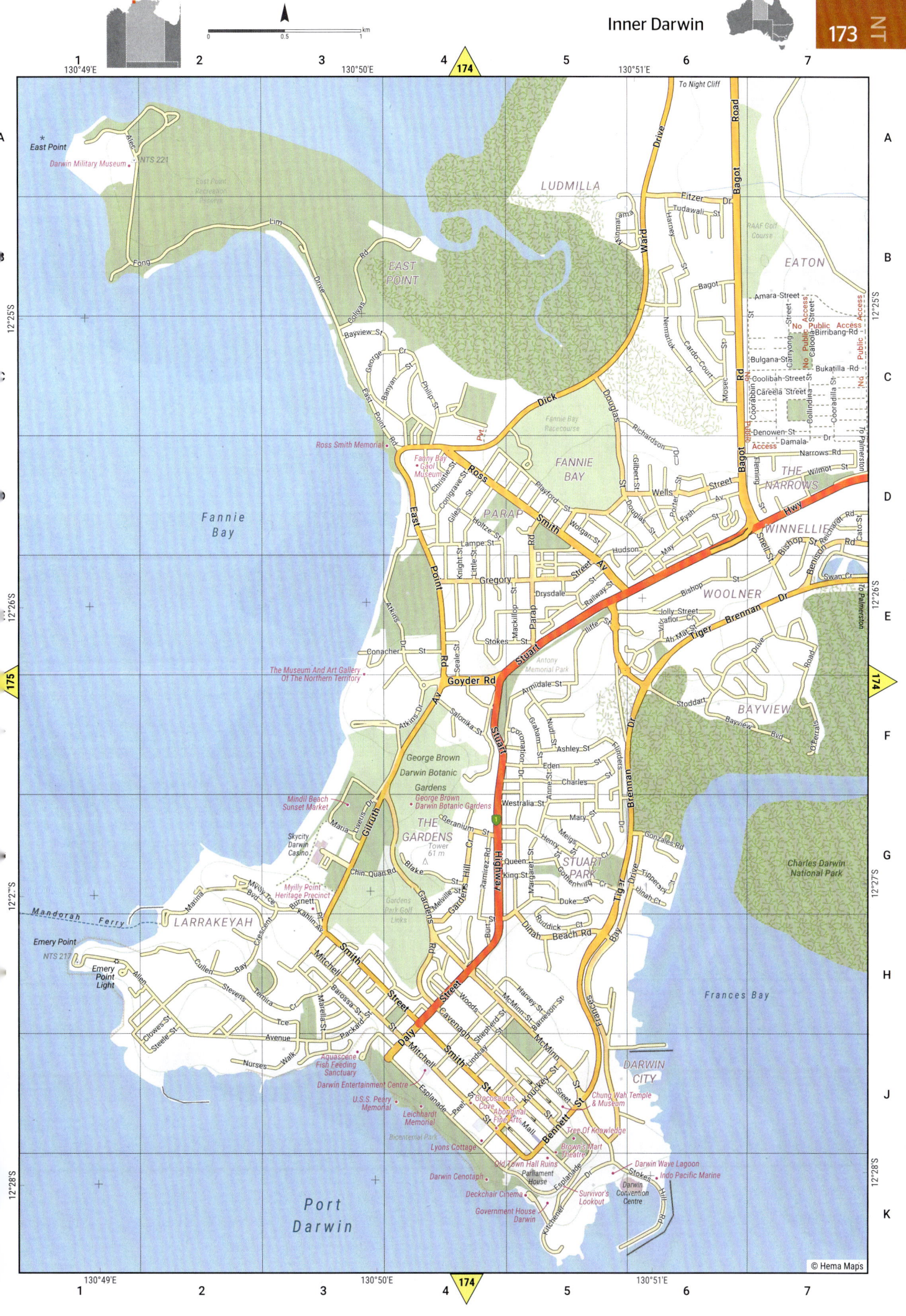

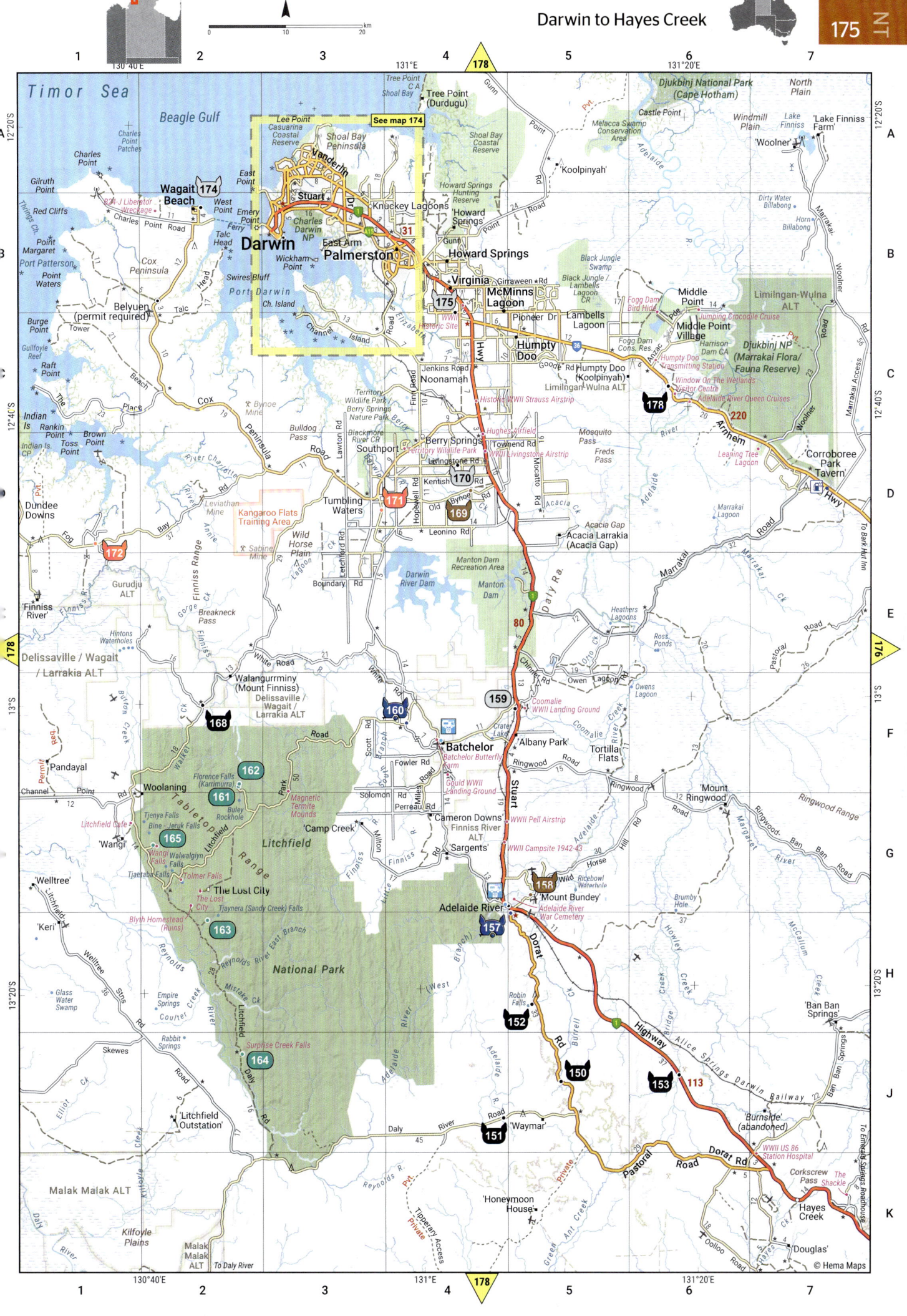

Kakadu National Park

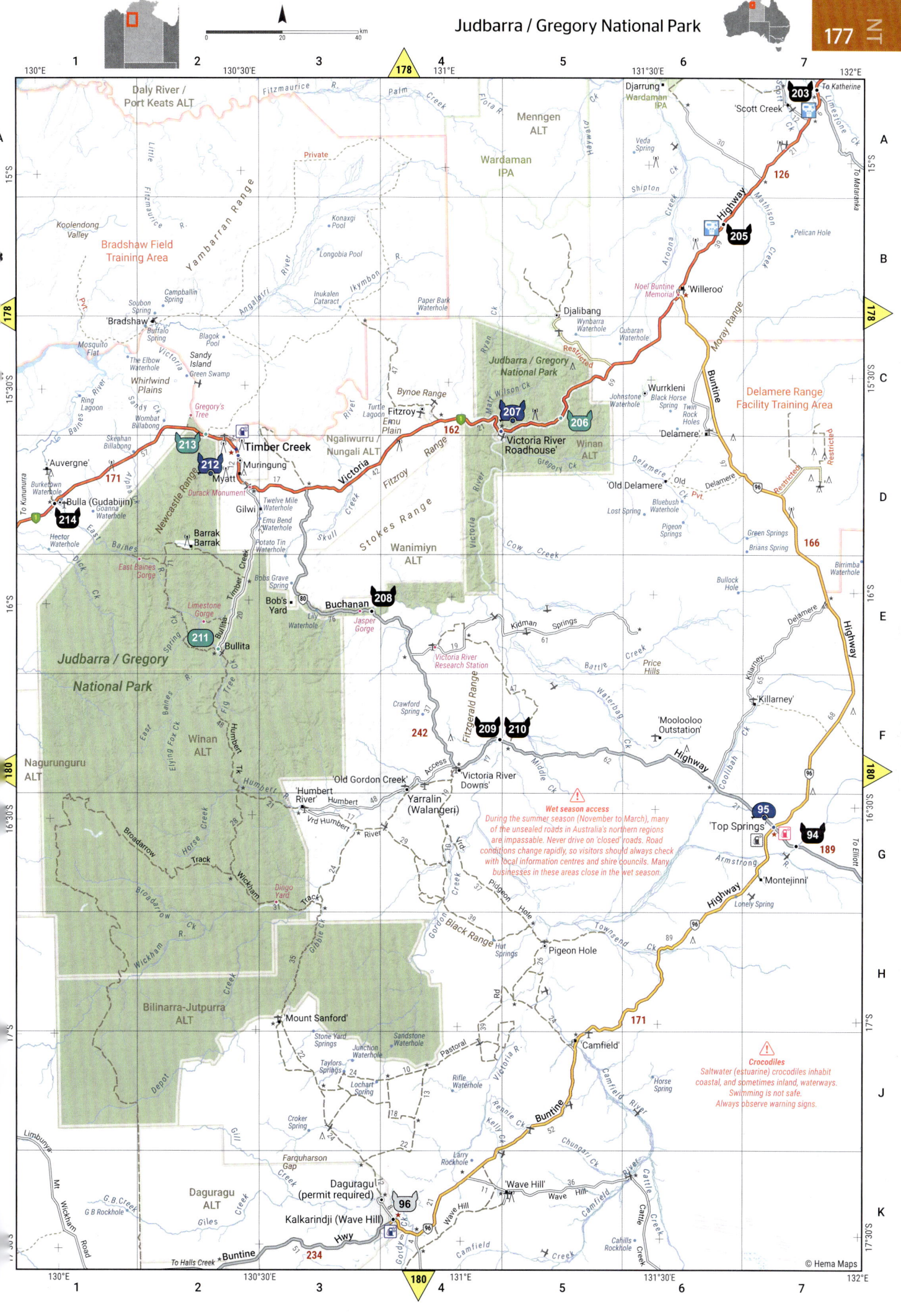

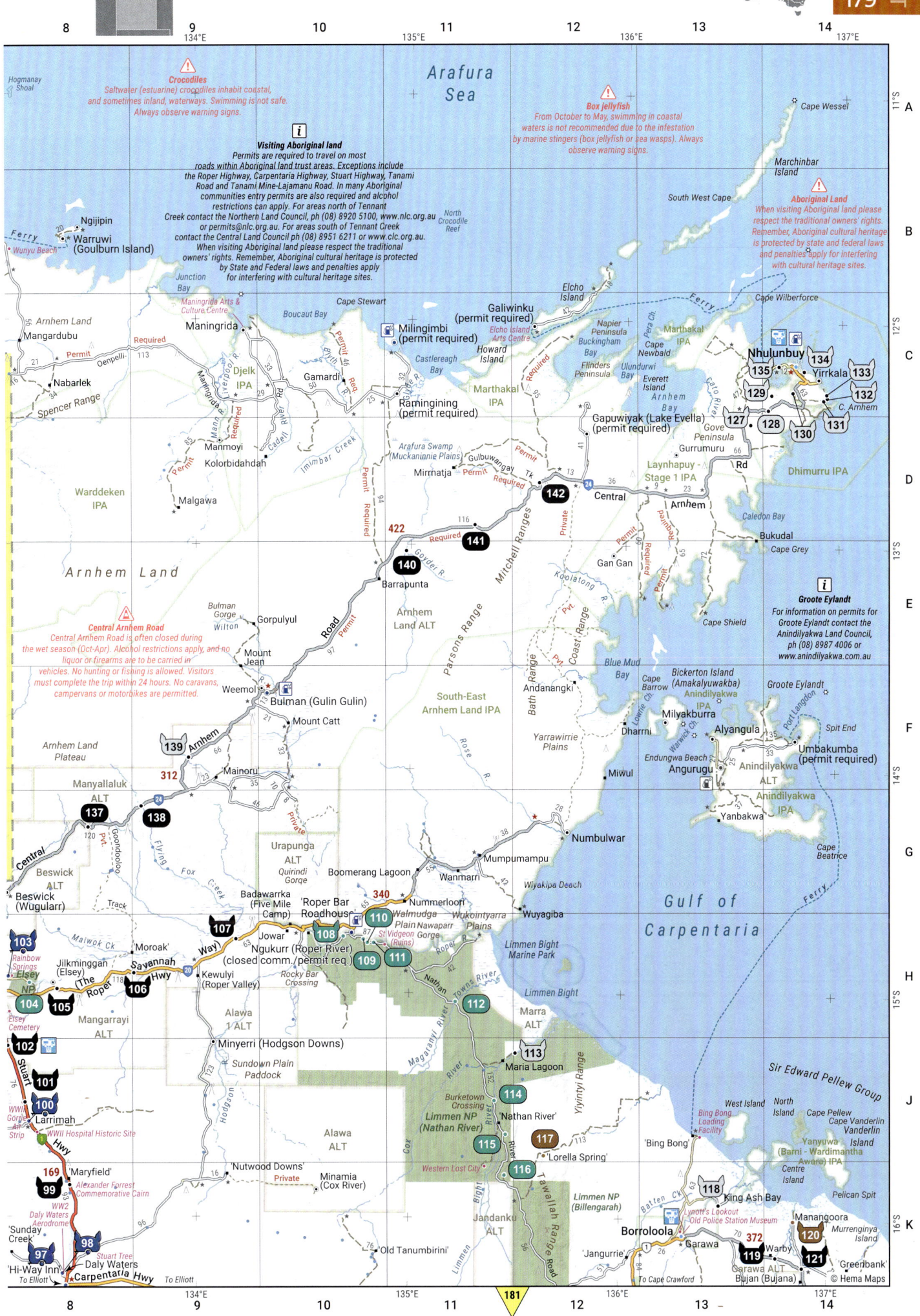

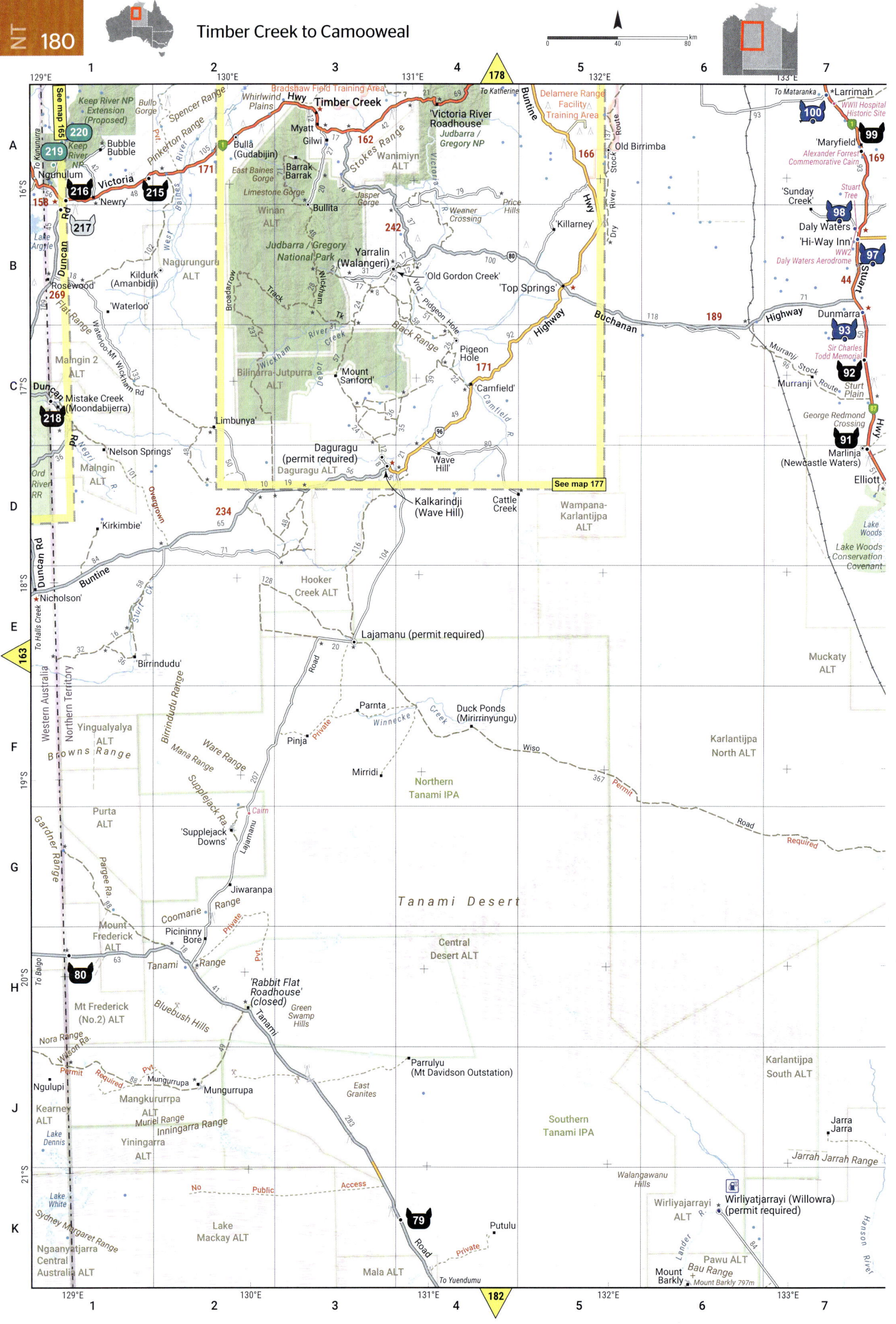

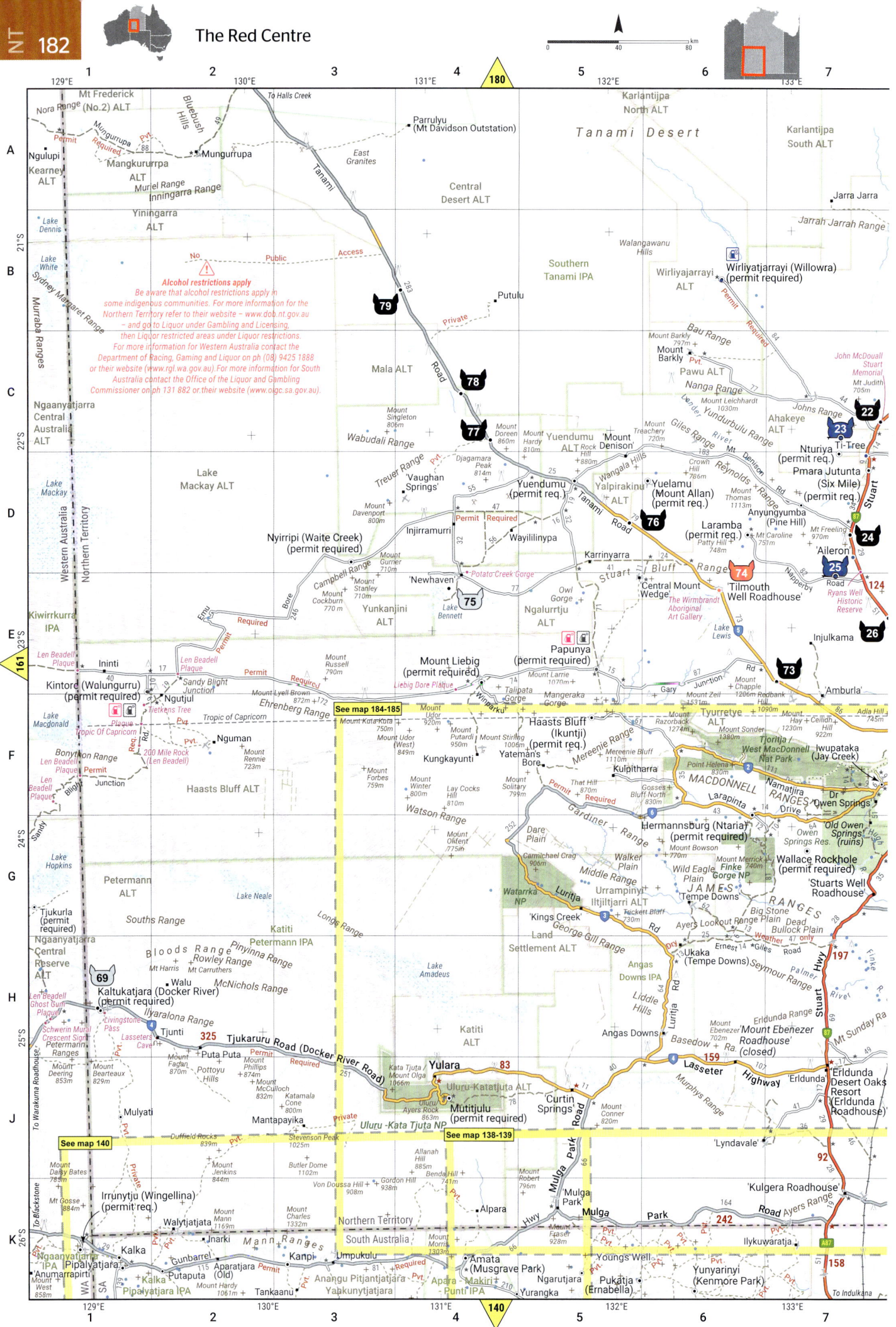

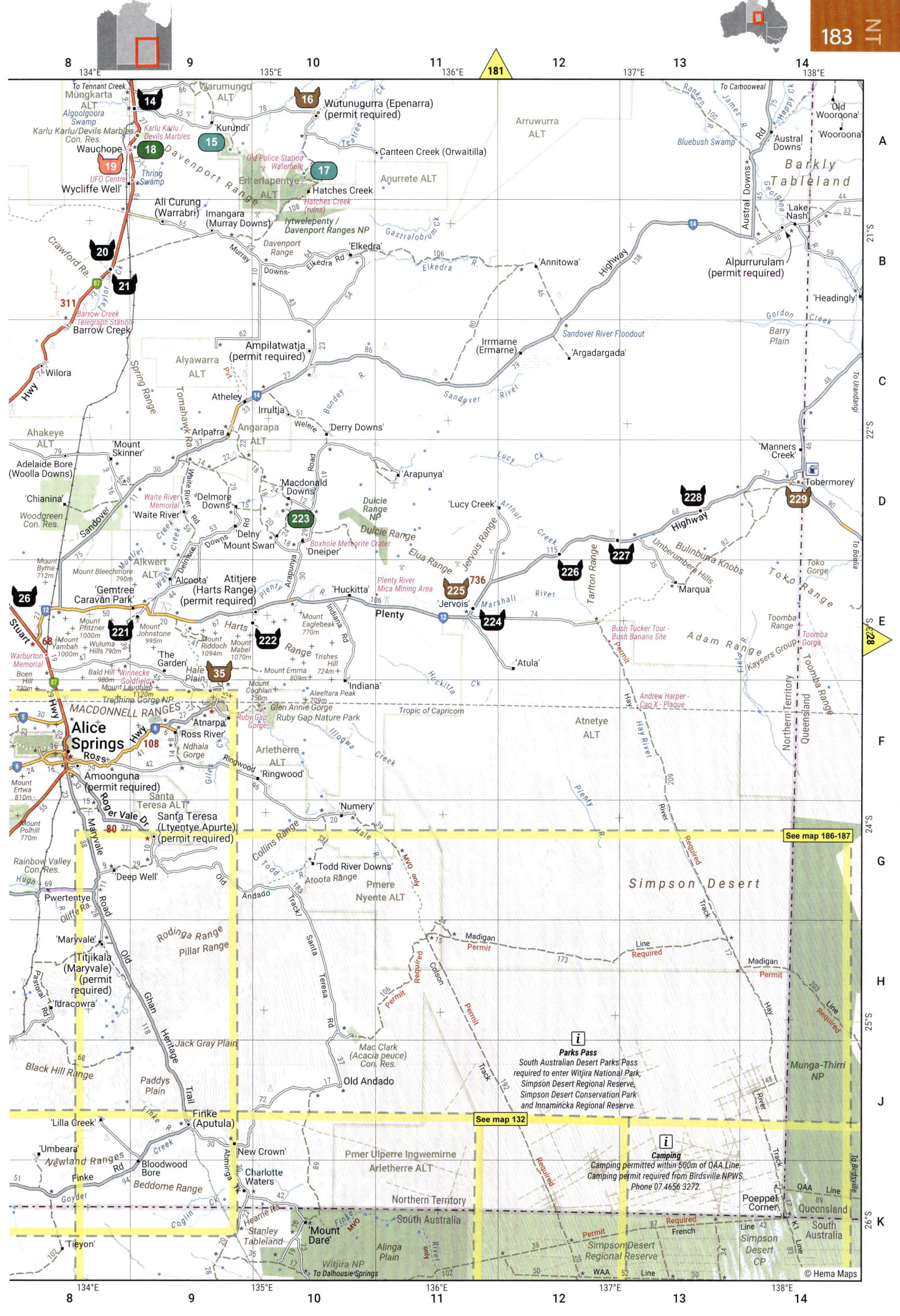

Uluru / Ayers Rock to Alice Springs

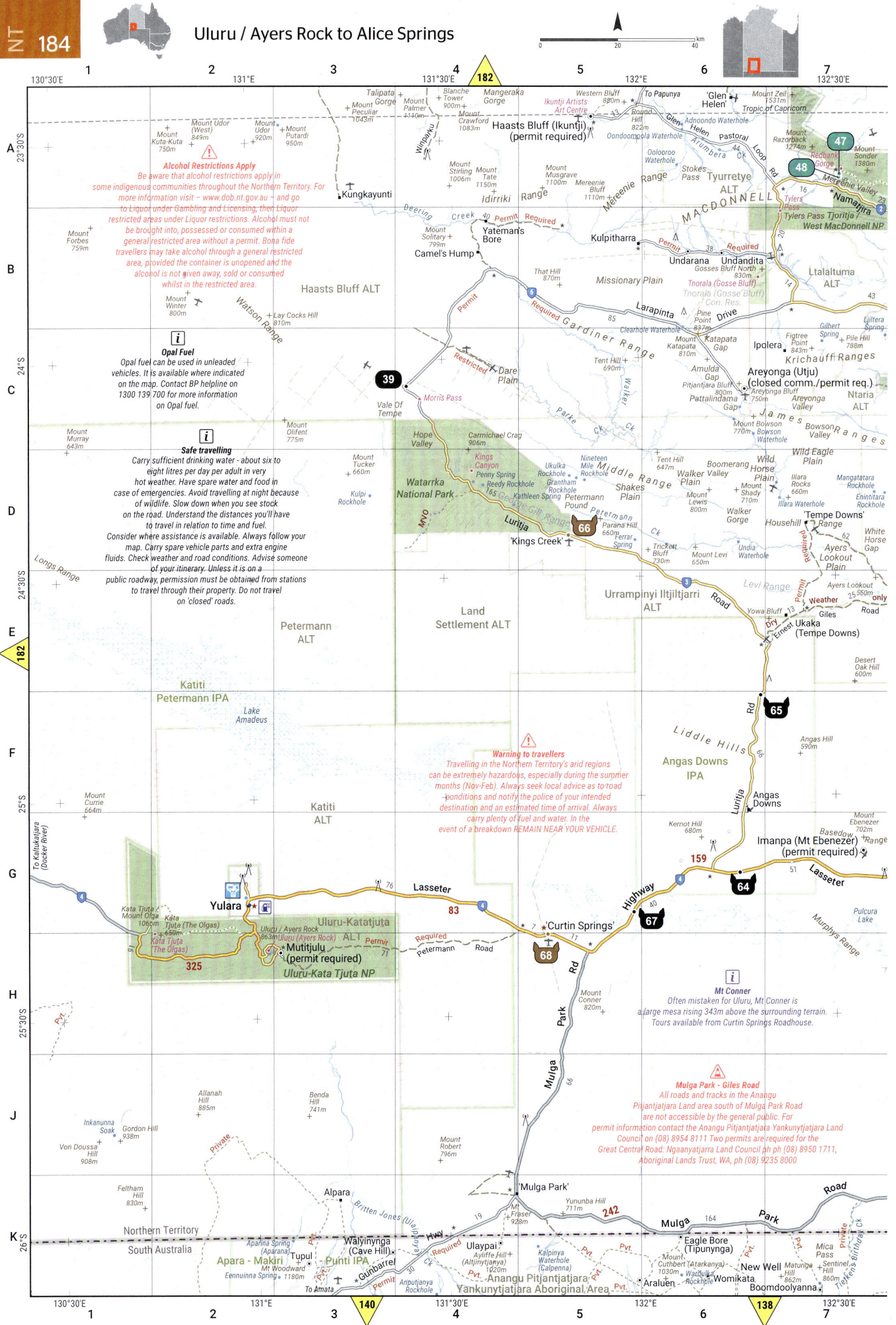

Alcohol Restrictions Apply
Be aware that alcohol restrictions apply in some indigenous communities throughout the Northern Territory. For more information visit – www.dob.nt.gov.au – and go to Liquor under Gambling and Licensing, then Liquor restricted areas under Liquor restrictions. Alcohol must not be brought into, possessed or consumed within a general restricted area without a permit. Bona fide travellers may take alcohol through a general restricted area, provided the container is unopened and the alcohol is not given away, sold or consumed whilst in the restricted area.

Opal Fuel
Opal fuel can be used in unleaded vehicles. It is available where indicated on the map. Contact BP helpline on 1300 139 700 for more information on Opal fuel.

Safe travelling
Carry sufficient drinking water - about six to eight litres per day per adult in very hot weather. Have spare water and food in case of emergencies. Avoid travelling at night because of wildlife. Slow down when you see stock on the road. Understand the distances you'll have to travel in relation to time and fuel. Consider where assistance is available. Always follow your map. Carry spare vehicle parts and extra engine fluids. Check weather and road conditions. Advise someone of your itinerary. Unless it is on a public roadway, permission must be obtained from stations to travel through their property. Do not travel on 'closed' roads.

Warning to travellers
Travelling in the Northern Territory's arid regions can be extremely hazardous, especially during the summer months (Nov-Feb). Always seek local advice as to road conditions and notify the police of your intended destination and an estimated time of arrival. Always carry plenty of fuel and water. In the event of a breakdown REMAIN NEAR YOUR VEHICLE.

Mt Conner
Often mistaken for Uluru, Mt Conner is a large mesa rising 343m above the surrounding terrain. Tours available from Curtin Springs Roadhouse.

Mulga Park - Giles Road
All roads and tracks in the Anangu Pitjantjatjara Land area south of Mulga Park Road are not accessible by the general public. For permit information contact the Anangu Pitjantjatjara Yankunytjatjara Land Council on (08) 8954 8111 Two permits are required for the Great Central Road: Ngaanyatjarra Land Council ph ph (08) 8950 1711, Aboriginal Lands Trust, WA, ph (08) 9235 8000

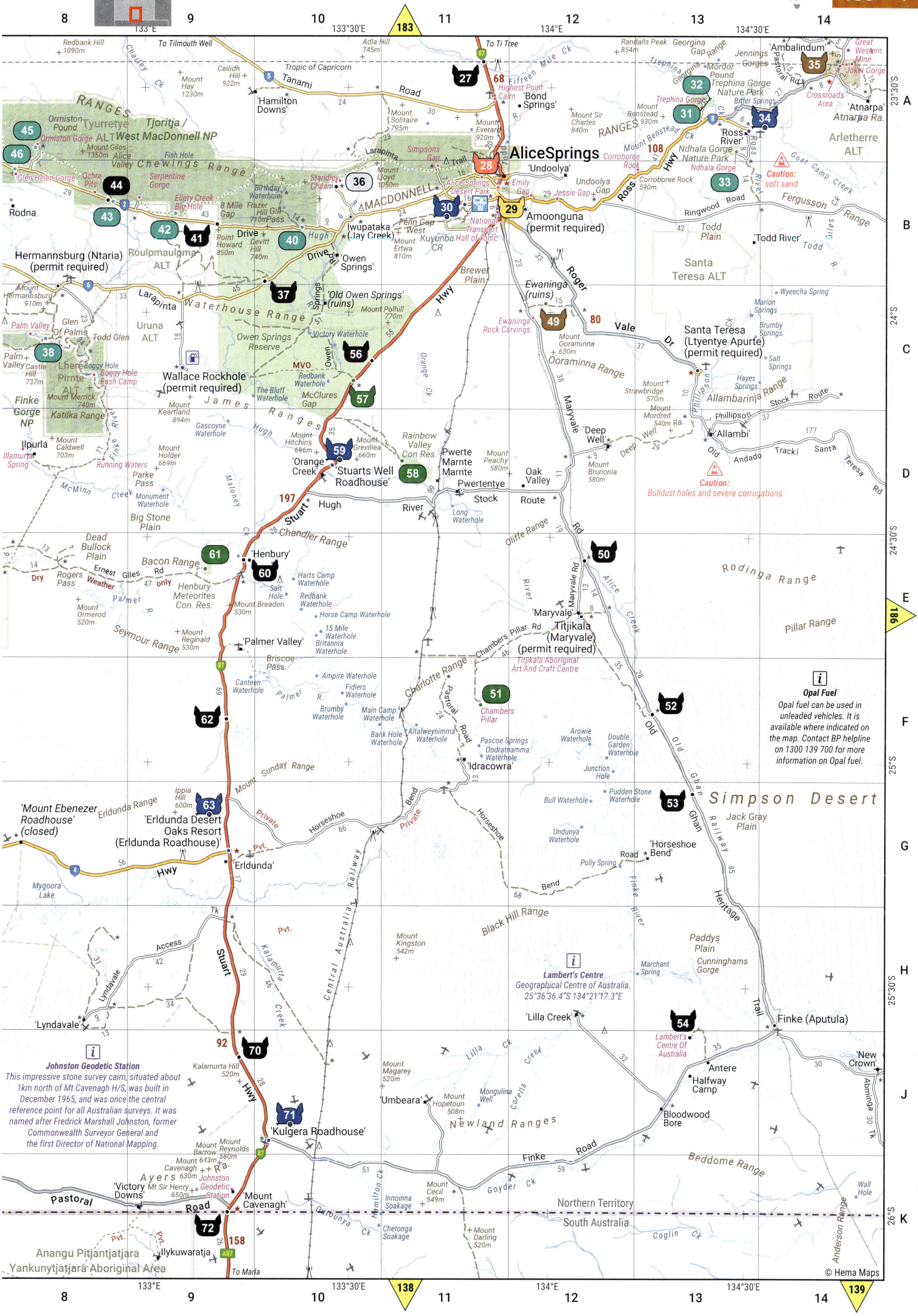

AliceSprings

West MacDonnell NP
Tjoritja / Tjuurretye
RANGES
Ormiston Pound
Ormiston Gorge
Glen Helen Gorge
Ochre Pits
Serpentine Gorge
Ellery Creek Big Hole
Hermannsburg (Ntaria) (permit required)
Roulpmaulpma ALT
Uruna ALT
Wallace Rockhole (permit required)
Finke Gorge NP
Katilka Range
Lhere Pirnte ALT
Palm Valley
Ilpurla
Illamurta Spring

Chewings Range
Waterhouse Range
James Ranges
Owen Springs Reserve
'Old Owen Springs' (ruins)
Victory Waterhole
Redbank Waterhole
McClures Gap
Stuart Hwy
'Orange Creek'
Stuarts Well Roadhouse
Rainbow Valley Con. Res.
Pwerte Marnte Marnte
Pwertentye
Oak Valley Route

MACDONNELL RANGES
Simpsons Gap
Standley Chasm
Iwupataka (Jay Creek)
'Owen Springs'
Brewer Plain
National Transport Hall of Fame
Amoonguna (permit required)
Ewaninga (ruins)
Ewaninga Rock Carvings
Ooraminna Range
Santa Teresa (Ltyentye Apurte) (permit required)
Allambarinja Range
'Allambi'

Ross River
'Ross River'
Trephina Gorge Nature Park
Ndhala Gorge Nature Park
'Undoolya'
Emily Gap
Jessie Gap
Corroboree Rock
'Ambalindum'
Great Western Mine
'Atnarpa' Atnarpa Ra.
Arletherre ALT
Santa Teresa ALT

Tropic of Capricorn
To Tilmouth Well
To Ti Tree
'Hamilton Downs'
'Bond Springs'
Tanami Road

'Henbury'
Henbury Meteorites Con. Res.
'Palmer Valley'
Chandler Range
Ernest Giles Rd
Seymour Range
Bacon Range
'Maryvale'
Titjikala (Maryvale) (permit required)
Titjikala Aboriginal Art And Craft Centre
Chambers Pillar
'Idracowra'
Simpson Desert
Rodinga Range
Pillar Range

Opal Fuel
Opal fuel can be used in unleaded vehicles. It is available where indicated on the map. Contact BP helpline on 1300 139 700 for more information on Opal fuel.

'Mount Ebenezer Roadhouse' (closed)
Erldunda Range
Erldunda Desert Oaks Resort (Erldunda Roadhouse)
'Erldunda'
Ippia Hill
'Lyndavale'
Mount Sunday Range
Central Australia Railway
Old Ghan Railway
'Horseshoe Bend'
Jack Gray Plain
Paddys Plain
Cunninghams Gorge

Lambert's Centre
Geographical Centre of Australia.
25°36'36.4"S 134°21'17.3"E
'Lilla Creek'
Lambert's Centre Of Australia
Finke (Aputula)
'New Crown'

Johnston Geodetic Station
This impressive stone survey cairn, situated about 1km north of Mt Cavenagh H/S, was built in December 1965, and was once the central reference point for all Australian surveys. It was named after Fredrick Marshall Johnston, former Commonwealth Surveyor General and the first Director of National Mapping.

Kalamurta Hill
Mount Barrow
Mount Reynolds
'Kulgera Roadhouse'
Ayers Rra.
Mount Cavenagh
'Victory Downs'
Mt Sir Henry
Johnston Geodetic Station
'Mount Cavenagh'

Northern Territory
South Australia

Anangu Pitjantjatjara Yankunytjatjara Aboriginal Area
'Illykuwaratja'
To Marla

© Hema Maps

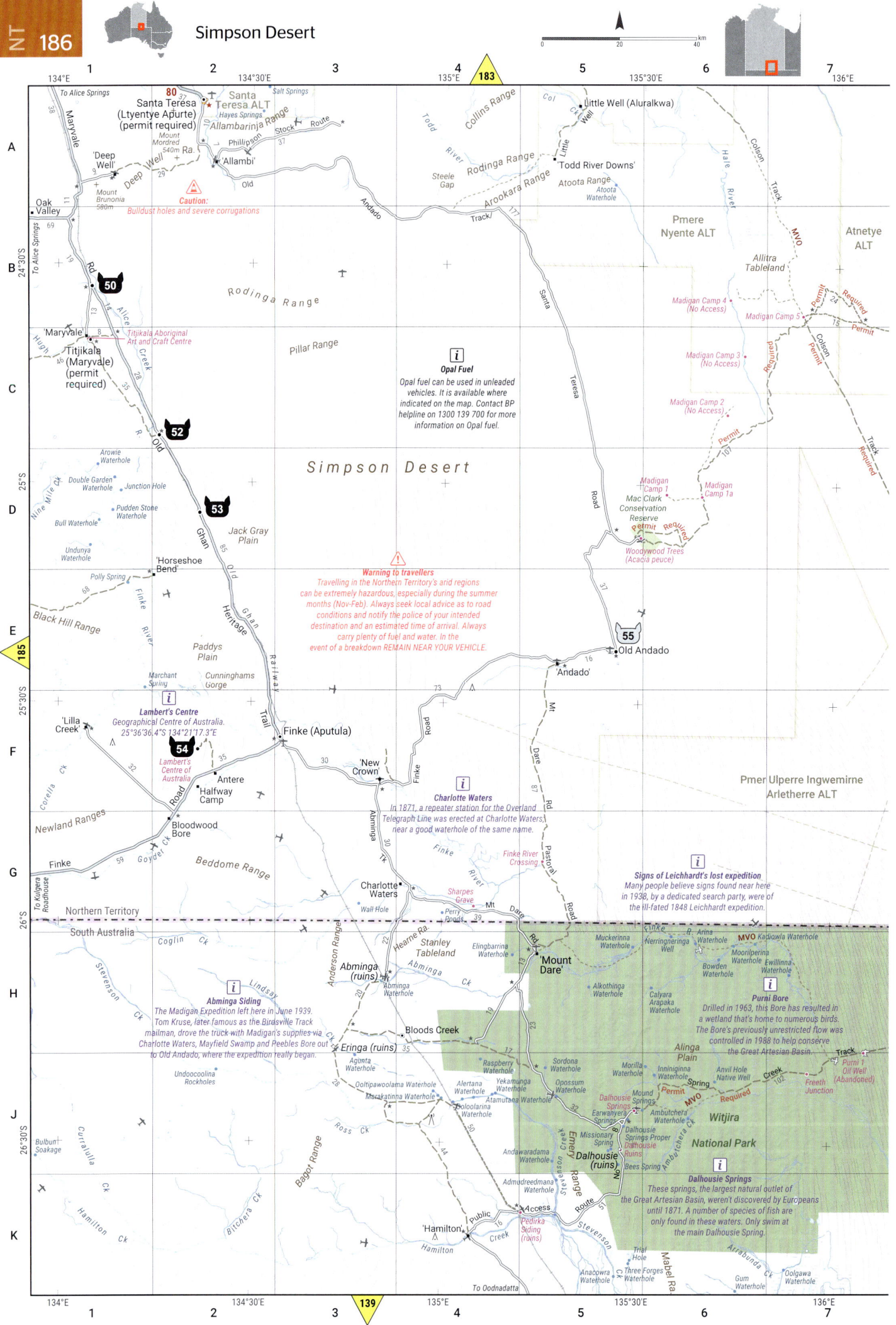

Simpson Desert

Opal Fuel
Opal fuel can be used in unleaded vehicles. It is available where indicated on the map. Contact BP helpline on 1300 139 700 for more information on Opal fuel.

Warning to travellers
Travelling in the Northern Territory's arid regions can be extremely hazardous, especially during the summer months (Nov-Feb). Always seek local advice as to road conditions and notify the police of your intended destination and an estimated time of arrival. Always carry plenty of fuel and water. In the event of a breakdown REMAIN NEAR YOUR VEHICLE.

Lambert's Centre
Geographical Centre of Australia.
25°36'36.4"S 134°21'17.3"E

Charlotte Waters
In 1871, a repeater station for the Overland Telegraph Line was erected at Charlotte Waters, near a good waterhole of the same name.

Signs of Leichhardt's lost expedition
Many people believe signs found near here in 1938, by a dedicated search party, were of the ill-fated 1848 Leichhardt expedition.

Abminga Siding
The Madigan Expedition left here in June 1939. Tom Kruse, later famous as the Birdsville Track mailman, drove the truck with Madigan's supplies via Charlotte Waters, Mayfield Swamp and Peebles Bore out to Old Andado, where the expedition really began.

Purni Bore
Drilled in 1963, this Bore has resulted in a wetland that's home to numerous birds. The Bore's previously unrestricted flow was controlled in 1988 to help conserve the Great Artesian Basin.

Dalhousie Springs
These springs, the largest natural outlet of the Great Artesian Basin, weren't discovered by Europeans until 1871. A number of species of fish are only found in these waters. Only swim at the main Dalhousie Spring.

Caution:
Bulldust holes and severe corrugations

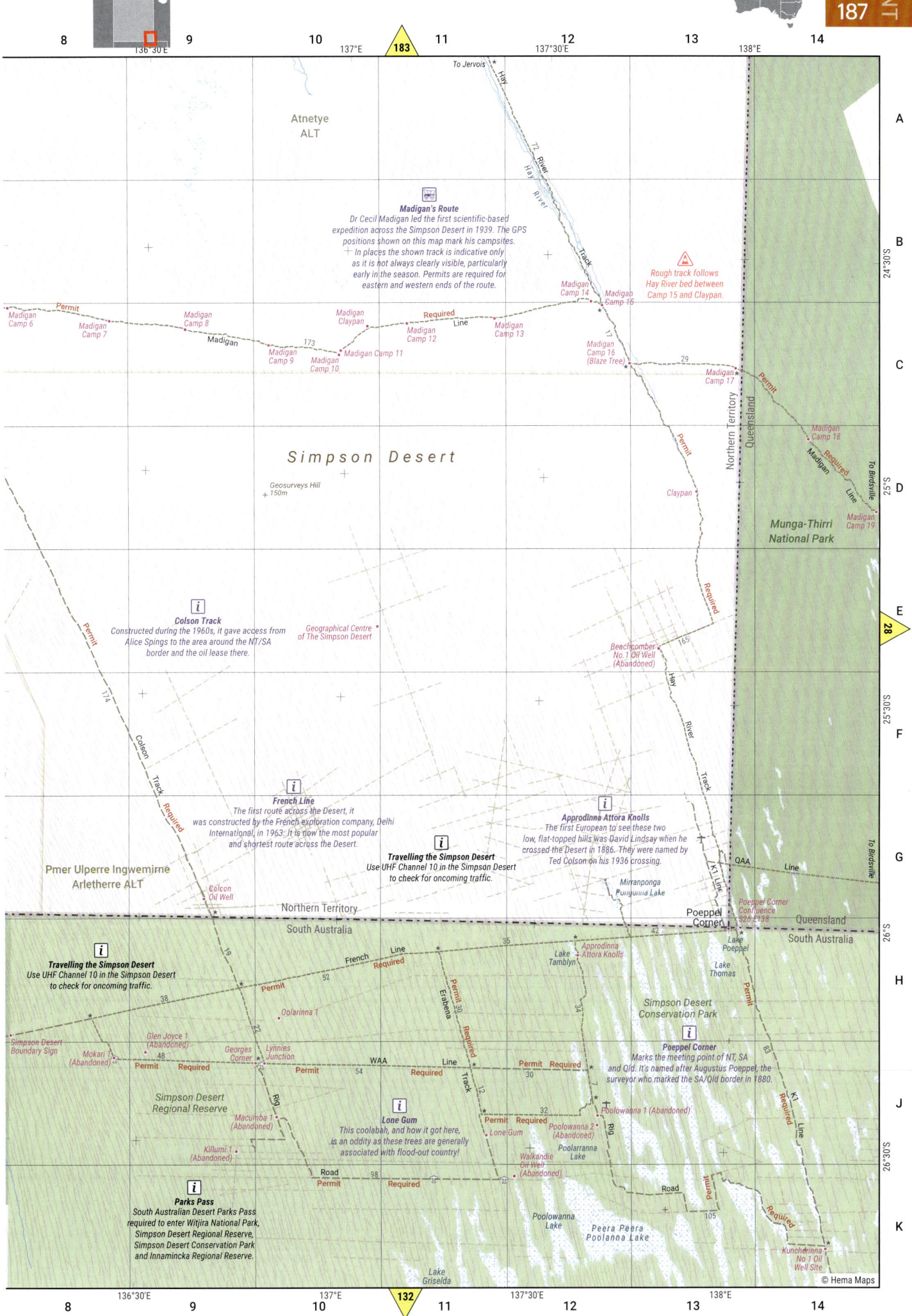

Atnetye ALT

Madigan's Route
Dr Cecil Madigan led the first scientific-based expedition across the Simpson Desert in 1939. The GPS positions shown on this map mark his campsites. In places the shown track is indicative only as it is not always clearly visible, particularly early in the season. Permits are required for eastern and western ends of the route.

⚠ Rough track follows Hay River bed between Camp 15 and Claypan.

Madigan Camp 6
Permit
Madigan Camp 7
Madigan Camp 8
Madigan
Madigan Claypan
Required Line
Madigan Camp 12
Madigan Camp 13
Madigan Camp 14
Madigan Camp 15
173
Madigan Camp 9
Madigan Camp 10
Madigan Camp 11
Madigan Camp 16 (Blaze Tree)
29
Madigan Camp 17
Permit
Madigan Camp 18
Required
Madigan Line
Madigan Camp 19

Simpson Desert

Geosurveys Hill
150m

Claypan

Munga-Thirri National Park

Colson Track
Constructed during the 1960s, it gave access from Alice Springs to the area around the NT/SA border and the oil lease there.

Geographical Centre of The Simpson Desert

Beachcomber No.1 Oil Well (Abandoned)
165

Permit
Required

Hay River Track

French Line
The first route across the Desert, it was constructed by the French exploration company, Delhi International, in 1963. It is now the most popular and shortest route across the Desert.

Approdinna Attora Knolls
The first European to see these two low, flat-topped hills was David Lindsay when he crossed the Desert in 1886. They were named by Ted Colson on his 1936 crossing.

Travelling the Simpson Desert
Use UHF Channel 10 in the Simpson Desert to check for oncoming traffic.

Mirranponga Punguinna Lake

Pmer Ulperre Ingwemirne Arletherre ALT

Colson Track
Required

Colson Oil Well

Northern Territory
South Australia

QAA Line
K1 Line

Poeppel Corner

Poeppel Corner Confluence S26 E138
Queensland
South Australia

Travelling the Simpson Desert
Use UHF Channel 10 in the Simpson Desert to check for oncoming traffic.

French Line
Required
35
Lake Poeppel
Lake Thomas

Approdinna Attora Knolls
Lake Tamblyn
42

Permit
52
38
Erabena
Required

Simpson Desert Conservation Park

Simpson Desert Boundary Sign

Oolarinna 1

Glen Joyce 1 (Abandoned)

Mokari (Abandoned)
48
Permit Required

Georges Corner

Lynnies Junction

WAA Line
54

Permit Required
30

Poeppel Corner
Marks the meeting point of NT, SA and Qld. It's named after Augustus Poeppel, the surveyor who marked the SA/Qld border in 1880.

Simpson Desert Regional Reserve

Macumba 1 (Abandoned)

Rig

Lone Gum
This coolabah, and how it got here, is an oddity as these trees are generally associated with flood-out country!

Lone Gum
Permit Required
32

Poolowanna 1 (Abandoned)

Poolowanna 2 (Abandoned)

Poolarranna Lake

Killumi 1 (Abandoned)

Walkandie Oil Well (Abandoned)

Road
Permit
98
Required

Rig
Road
105

Permit
Required
K1 Line

Parks Pass
South Australian Desert Parks Pass required to enter Witjira National Park, Simpson Desert Regional Reserve, Simpson Desert Conservation Park and Innamincka Regional Reserve.

Poolowanna Lake

Peera Peera Poolanna Lake

Kuncherinna No.1 Oil Well Site

Lake Griselda

© Hema Maps

   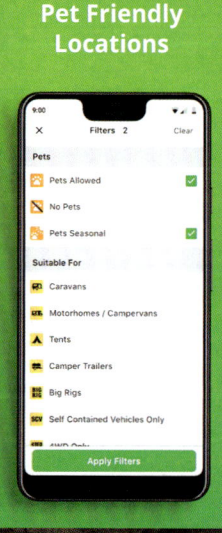 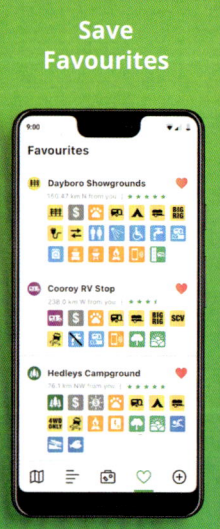

Cape Arnhem, Wanuwuy Northern Territory by 20000ksinacampertrailer

NORTHERN TERRITORY

Camooweal to Three Ways
Barkly Highway

1 Avon Downs Rest Area
Barkly Hwy, Ranken
Rest Area 69 km W of Camooweal or 66 km E of Soudan. Opposite police station
HEMA 181 H13   20 01 30 S   137 29 23 E

2 Soudan Bore Rest Area
Barkly Hwy, Ranken
Rest Area 66 km W of Avon Downs or 85 km E of Wonarah Bore
HEMA 181 H12   20 04 25 S   136 52 42 E

3 Wonarah Bore
Barkly Hwy, Tablelands
Rest Area 85 km W of Soudan Bore or 40 km E of Barkly Homestead
HEMA 181 H11   19 50 33 S   136 09 23 E

4 Barkly Homestead
Crn Barkly & Tablelands Hwys, Tablelands
Caravan Park 260 km E of Camooweal or 187 km E of Three Ways
08 8964 4549   HEMA 181 G11   19 42 38 S   135 49 39 E

5 Frewena Rest Area
Barkly Hwy, Tablelands
Rest Area 55 km W of Barkly Homestead or 132 km E of Three Ways
HEMA 181 G10   19 25 59 S   135 24 04 E

6 41 Mile Bore
Barkly Hwy, Warumungu
Rest Area 116 km W of Barkly Homestead or 70 km E of Three Ways
HEMA 181 G9   19 19 13 S   134 51 03 E

Barkly Homestead - Borroloola - Daly Waters
Tablelands and Carpentaria Highways

7 Brunette Downs Rest Area
Tablelands Hwy, Tablelands
Rest Area 145 km N of Barkly Homestead or 232 km S of Cape Crawford. At old windmill
HEMA 181 E11   18 28 27 S   135 58 46 E

8 Kiana Turnoff Rest Area
Tablelands Hwy, Tablelands
Rest Area 271 km N of Barkly Homestead or 107 km S of Cape Crawford
HEMA 181 D11   17 31 41 S   135 41 02 E

9 Heartbreak Hotel
Cnr Carpentaria & Tablelands Hwys, Cape Crawford
Caravan Park behind motel & bar. Fuel available
08 8975 9928   HEMA 181 B11   16 40 59 S   135 43 36 E

10 Little River
Carpentaria Hwy, Cape Crawford
Camp Area 10 km W of Cape Crawford or 259 km E of Daly Waters. E of bridge, riverside
HEMA 181 B11   16 42 00 S   135 38 22 E

11 Goanna Creek Rest Area
Carpentaria Hwy, Cape Crawford Area
Rest Area 39 km W of Cape Crawford or 230 km E of Daly Waters. Limited space, 100 m N of Hwy
HEMA 181 B10   16 42 16 S   135 22 03 E

12 October Creek Rest Area
Carpentaria Hwy, Cape Crawford Area
Rest Area 99 km W of Cape Crawford or 170 km E of Daly Waters
HEMA 181 B9   16 37 54 S   134 51 31 E

13 Bullwaddy Rest Area
Carpentaria Hwy, Daly Waters
Rest Area 179 km W of Cape Crawford or 90 km E of Daly Waters
HEMA 181 B8   16 27 03 S   134 11 40 E

Three Ways to Kulgera
Stuart Highway

14 Bonney Well Rest Area
Stuart Hwy, Warumungu
Rest Area 89 km S of Tennant Creek or 15 km N of Devils Marbles
HEMA 181 J9   20 25 48 S   134 14 46 E

15 Whistleduck Creek
Iytwelepenty Davenport Ranges NP
Whistleduck Creek Rd, Davenport
Camp Area 87 km S of Tennant Creek. E to Kurundi Rd for 69 km, then S for 25 km. Dirt road
08 8962 4599   HEMA 181 J9   20 38 11 S   134 46 46 E

16 Epenarra Station
Epenarra/Murray Downs, Davenport
Station Stay 208 km SE of Tennant Creek or 290 km NE of Wilora. Turn E off Stuart Hwy to Kurundi Rd for 120 km. Support station store
08 8964 1511   HEMA 181 J10   20 26 38 S   135 15 45 E

17 Old Police Station Waterhole
Iytwelepenty Davenport Ranges NP
Old Police Station Waterhole, Davenport
Camp Area 87 km S of Tennant Creek. E to Kurundi Rd for 119 km, turn S for 43 km. Dirt road
08 8962 4499   HEMA 181 J10   20 45 15 S   135 11 12 E

18 Karlu Karlu / Devils Marbles
Karlu Karlu Conservation Reserve
Devils Marbles, Davenport
Camp Area 103 km S of Tennant Creek or 81 km N of Taylor Creek. 1 km E of Hwy
08 8962 4499   HEMA 181 J9   20 34 05 S   134 15 51 E

19 Devils Marbles Hotel
Stuart Hwy, Wauchope
Caravan Park at Wauchope. Behind hotel
08 8964 1963   HEMA 181 J9   20 38 26 S   134 13 20 E

20 Taylor Creek
Stuart Hwy, Barrow Creek
Rest Area 81 km S of Devils Marbles or 129 km N of Ti Tree. Limited space
HEMA 181 K8   21 14 52 S   134 06 53 E

21 Barrow Creek WWII Area
Stuart Hwy, Barrow Creek
Camp Area 28 km N of Barrow Creek or 60 km S of Wycliffe Well. 1 km S from Hwy at the sign. GPS at entry
HEMA 181 K8   21 18 07 S   134 03 07 E

22 McDouall Stuart Memorial
Stuart Hwy, Ti Tree
Rest Area 68 km S of Barrow Creek or 21 km N of Ti Tree at Central Mount Stuart Historical Reserve
HEMA 182 C7   21 57 38 S   133 29 48 E

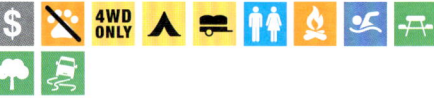

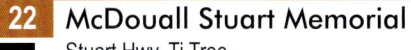

23 Ti Tree Roadhouse
Stuart Hwy, Ti Tree
Caravan Park with a bar, motel & service station
08 8956 9741 HEMA 182 D7 22 07 53 S 133 25 00 E

24 Prowse Gap
Stuart Hwy, Aileron
Rest Area 45 km S of Ti Tree or 14 km N of Aileron
HEMA 182 D7 22 31 52 S 133 19 44 E

25 Aileron Hotel & Roadhouse
Stuart Hwy, Aileron
Caravan Park 135 km N of Alice Springs or 60 km S of Ti Tree
08 8956 9703 HEMA 182 D7 22 38 38 S 133 20 43 E

26 Connors Well
Stuart Hwy, Aileron
Rest Area 38 km S of Aileron or 95 km N of Alice Springs
HEMA 183 E8 22 57 02 S 133 32 35 E

27 Tropic of Capricorn
Stuart Hwy, Alice Springs
Rest Area 103 km S of Aileron or 30 km N of Alice Springs
HEMA 185 A11 23 26 31 S 133 49 58 E

28 Gap View Hotel
123 Gap Rd, Alice Springs
Camp Area beside hotel. 7 day limit
08 8952 6578 HEMA 185 B11 23 43 19 S 133 52 10 E

29 Blatherskite Park
Len Kettle Dr, Alice Springs
Camp Area 5 km S of PO. Pre-book
0439 998 381 HEMA 185 B11 23 44 07 S 133 51 45 E

30 Temple Bar Caravan Park
875 Ilparpa Rd, Arumbera
Caravan Park 14 km SW of PO. Metered power. Cash only
0455 922 533 HEMA 185 B11 23 45 37 S 133 47 13 E

31 Panorama Campground
Trephina Gorge Nature Park
Via Ross Hwy, Trephina Gorge
Camp Area 85 km E of Alice Springs. Follow Ross Hwy for 76 km, turn N for 9 km. Last 5 km dirt road
08 8956 9765 HEMA 185 A13 23 31 20 S 134 23 49 E

32 Trephina Gorge Camp
Trephina Gorge Nature Park
Off Ross Hwy, Trephina Gorge
Camp Area 85 km E of Alice Springs. Via Ross Hwy for 76 km, turn N for 9 km. Last 5 km dirt road. 4WD & tent sites in the Camps Australia Wide App
08 8956 9765 HEMA 185 A13 23 31 18 S 134 23 48 E
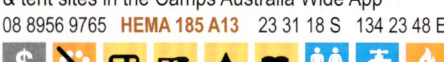

33 N'Dhala Gorge
N'Dhala Gorge Nature Park
Off Ross Hwy, Ross River
Camp Area 90 km E of Alice Springs. Signposted S off Ross Hwy. 11 km of 4WD track, 3 water crossings, first one deepest
08 8956 9765 HEMA 185 A13 23 38 19 S 134 27 47 E

34 Ross River Resort
Ross Hwy, Ross River
Caravan Park 83 km E of Alice Springs
08 8956 9711 HEMA 185 A13 23 35 34 S 134 29 35 E

35 Hale River Homestead at Old Ambalindum
Altunga Rd, Ross River
Camp Area 124 km NE of Alice Springs. E on Ross Hwy for 70 km, then N for 47 km, dirt road. Call ahead for road advice
08 8956 9993 HEMA 185 A14 23 23 05 S 134 41 00 E

36 Angkerle Atwatye / Standley Chasm
Off Larapinta Dr, Hugh
Camp Area 50 km W of Alice Springs. Rate includes chasm entry, reduction for additional nights. Gates close 5 pm. Pre-book
08 8956 7440 HEMA 185 B10 23 43 17 S 133 28 10 E

37 Mueller Creek
Larapinta Dr, West MacDonnell NP
Rest Area 70 km SW of Alice Springs or 56 km E of Hermannsburg. 23 km SW of Namatjira Dr Jcn
HEMA 185 B10 23 55 54 S 133 17 34 E

38 Palm Valley Campground
Finke Gorge National Park
Off Larapinta Dr, Hermannsburg
Camp Area 138 km W of Alice Springs via Larapinta Dr. Turn S 1.5 km W of Hermannsburg. 16 km dirt road. Cash only
08 8956 7401 HEMA 185 C8 24 03 29 S 132 44 49 E

39 Gintys Lookout
Larapinta Dr, Mereenie Loop Road
Camp Area 302 km NW of Erldunda or 295 km W of Alice Springs. Dirt road extends 5 km S, and 120 kms N. Permit applies
HEMA 184 C4 24 03 38 S 131 24 30 E

40 Hugh River Bush Camping
Tjoritja / West MacDonnell NP
Namatjira Dr, Alice Springs Area
Dispersed Camping along Hugh River. From Larapinta Dr Jcn, turn W to Namatjira Dr for 9.5 km, then N to access track. 200 m to info board, 1 km to camps along river. GPS at entrance
HEMA 185 B10 23 48 40 S 133 23 07 E

41 Point Howard Lookout
Namatjira Dr, West MacDonnell NP
Rest Area 78 km W of Alice Springs or 53 km E of Glen Helen. Steep access
HEMA 185 B9 23 48 15 S 133 10 34 E

NORTHERN TERRITORY

42 Ellery Creek Big Hole

Tjoritja / West MacDonnell NP
Namatjira Dr, Rodna
Camp Area 80 km W of Alice Springs or 43 km E of Glen Helen. 2 km access road N of Hwy, dirt road. Small vehicles only. Emergency phone onsite. Cash only
08 8956 7799   HEMA 185 B9   23 46 48 S   133 04 22 E

43 Serpentine Chalet Bush
Camping

Tjoritja / West MacDonnell NP
Namatjira Dr, Rodna
Camp Area 108 km W of Alice Springs or 23 km E of Glen Helen. 600 m to 2WD camping. 4WD only beyond. No caravans
08 8956 7799   HEMA 185 B8   23 45 13 S   132 55 03 E

44 Neil Hargrave Lookout

Namatjira Dr, Rodna
Rest Area 107 km W of Alice Springs or 24 km E of Glen Helen. 800 m S off Hwy
HEMA 185 B8   23 45 02 S   132 54 19 E

45 Ormiston Gorge

Tjoritja / West MacDonnell NP
Namatjira Rd, Rodna
Camp Area 135 km W of Alice Springs or 12 km NE of Glen Helen. 7 km N of road
08 8956 7799   HEMA 185 A8   23 37 57 S   132 43 29 E

46 Two Mile

Tjoritja / West MacDonnell NP
Namatjira Dr, Rodna
Dispersed Camping 147 km W of Alice Springs. 700m N of Glen Helen, to dirt track. Sites on Finke R
HEMA 185 B8   23 40 50 S   132 40 24 E

47 Woodland Camping Area

Tjoritja / West MacDonnell NP
Redbank Gorge Rd, Redbank Gorge
Camp Area 155 km W of Alice Springs. Turn N for 5 km off Namatjira Dr, 20 km W of Glen Helen. High clearance recommended. Cash only. Limited space
08 8956 7799   HEMA 184 A7   23 35 25 S   132 30 46 E

48 Ridgetop Camping Area

Tjoritja / West MacDonnell NP
Redbank Gorge Rd, Redbank Gorge
Camp Area 156 km W of Alice Springs. Turn N for 6 km off Namatjira Dr 20 km W of Glen Helen. High clearance recommended. Cash only. Limited space
08 8956 7799   HEMA 184 A7   23 34 58 S   132 30 52 E

49 Ooraminna Station

Maryvale Rd, Hale
Station Stay 23 km SE of Alice Springs. Turn off Hwy 11 km S Alice Springs to Roger Vale Rd, immediate S to Maryvale Rd for 23 km to signed gate. 4 km E to Homestead. 15 km dirt road
08 8953 0477   HEMA 185 C12   23 58 48 S   133 59 15 E

50 Rodinga Ruins

Maryvale Rd, Hugh
Parking Area 106 km SE Alice Springs. 11 km S Alice Springs off Hwy to Roger Vale Rd, immediate S to Maryvale Rd 94 km. Turn E 500 m
HEMA 185 E12   24 33 07 S   134 05 10 E

51 Chambers Pillar

Maryvale (Old South) Rd, Titjikala
Camp Area & Historical Reserve 160 km S of Alice Springs. W at Maryvale store to Chambers Pillars track 45 km to site. Steep sections. Cash only
08 8952 1013   HEMA 185 F11   24 52 22 S   133 49 41 E

52 Bundooma Siding

Ghan Heritage Rd, Titjikala
Parking Area 151 km S of Alice Springs or 94 km N of Finke on the Old Ghan Railway track
HEMA 186 C2   24 53 34 S   134 15 34 E

53 Engoordina Ruins

Ghan Heritage Rd, Ghan
Parking Area 173 km S of Alice Springs or 72 km N of Finke on the Old Ghan Railway track
HEMA 186 D2   25 04 10 S   134 21 51 E

54 Lambert Centre

Finke Rd, Finke
Camp Area 127 km NE of Kulgera. Turn E at Kulgera for 114 km, N to track for 7.5 km, SW for 5 km. Road restrictions may apply
HEMA 186 F2   25 36 32 S   134 21 42 E

55 Old Andado Homestead

Finke Rd / Santa Teresa, Ghan
Camp Area at Old Andado Station, 268 km E of Kulgera. Road restrictions may apply
0411 667 110   HEMA 186 E5   25 22 49 S   135 26 30 E

56 Mount Polhill Rest Area

Stuart Hwy, Hugh
Rest Area 61 km S of Alice Springs or 140 km N of Erldunda. 32 km N of Stuarts Well. Limited space
HEMA 185 C10   24 06 30 S   133 33 28 E

57 Redbank Waterhole

Owen Springs Reserve
Stuart Hwy, Hugh
Dispersed Camping 66 km S of Alice Springs or 25 km N of Stuarts Well. 6 km to waterhole from Hwy. Signposted. GPS at entry
08 8956 7300   HEMA 185 C10   24 09 09 S   133 30 40 E

58 Rainbow Valley

Conservation Reserve
Stuart Hwy / Access Rd, Hugh
Camp Area in Reserve. Turn off 75 km S of Alice Springs or 14 km N of Stuarts Well. 22 km dirt road, sandy patches
08 8952 1013   HEMA 185 D11   24 19 51 S   133 37 57 E

59 Stuarts Well Roadhouse

Stuart Hwy, Stuarts Well
Caravan Park 90 km S of Alice Springs or 104 km N of Erldunda
08 8956 0808   HEMA 185 D10   24 20 26 S   133 27 31 E

60 Finke River Rest Area

Stuart Hwy, Ghan
Rest Area 126 km S of Alice Springs or 75 km N of Erldunda. Riverside
HEMA 185 E9   24 33 05 S   133 14 20 E

61 Henbury Meteorites

Conservation Reserve
Ernest Giles Rd, Ghan
Camp Area 145 km SW of Alice Springs or 85 km N or Erldunda. W of Hwy to Ernest Giles Rd 11 km, N 5 km. Dirt road
08 8952 1013   HEMA 185 E9   24 34 16 S   133 08 35 E

62 Desert Oaks Rest Area
Stuart Hwy, Ghan
Rest Area 167 km S of Alice Springs or 32 km N of Erldunda
HEMA 185 F9   24 54 18 S   133 11 46 E

63 Erldunda Roadhouse
Cnr Stuart Hwy & Lasseter Hwy, Erldunda
Caravan Park 200 km S of Alice Springs, or 95 km N of SA/NT border
08 8956 0984   HEMA 185 G9   25 11 50 S   133 12 03 E

64 Kernot Range Rest Area
Lasseter Hwy, Curtin Springs
Rest Area 101 km W of Erldunda or 59 km E of Curtin Springs. 7 km E of Luritja Rd Jcn
HEMA 184 G6   25 10 37 S   132 15 06 E

65 Salt Creek Rest Area
Luritja Rd, Erldunda
Rest Area 48 km N of Lasseter Hwy or 20 km S of Ernest Giles Rd Jcn
HEMA 184 F6   24 46 21 S   132 18 24 E

66 Kings Creek Station
Luritja Rd, Petermann
Station Stay 35 km SE Kings Canyon. Pre-book for power
08 8956 7474   HEMA 184 D5   24 24 15 S   131 49 06 E

67 Curtin Springs East
Lasseter Hwy, Curtin Springs
Rest Area 136 km W of Erldunda or 27 km E of Curtin Springs. 25 km W of Luritja Rd Jcn
HEMA 184 G5   25 15 57 S   131 58 43 E

68 Curtin Springs Wayside Inn
Lasseter Hwy, Curtin Springs
Camp Area 163 km W of Erldunda or 84 km E of Yulara. Limited powered sites, pre-book. Fee for facilities. Unpowered camping free, no bookings
08 8956 2906   HEMA 184 H5   25 18 52 S   131 45 27 E
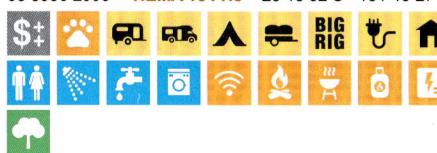

69 Kaltukatjara Campground (Docker River)
Tjukaruru Rd, Kaltukatjara (Docker River)
Camp Area 1 km W of town turnoff. Pay and collect keys at store. Permit required
08 8956 7373   HEMA 161 G14   24 51 50 S   129 03 42 E

70 Alex Warne Stop
Stuart Hwy, Ghan
Rest Area behind truck stop. 23 km N of Kulgera or 52 km S of Lassiter Hwy Jcn. Enter S end of truck area
HEMA 185 J9   25 39 19 S   133 13 35 E

71 Kulgera Roadhouse
Cnr Kulgera Cr & South Stuart Hwy, Kulgera
Caravan Park with hotel & pub
08 8956 0973   HEMA 185 J10   25 50 22 S   133 18 01 E

72 NT-SA Border
Stuart Hwy, Kulgera
Rest Area 159 km N of Marla or 19 km S of Kulgera
HEMA 185 K9   25 59 54 S   133 11 47 E

Alice Springs to Halls Creek - Tanami Track
Tanami Road
This road is seasonal and more suitable to 4WD vehicles, camper trailers and off road caravans. Road conditions phone 1800 246 199 (NT) or 138 138 (WA)

73 Charley Creek Rest Area
Tanami Rd, Burt Plain
Rest Area 123 km NW of Alice Springs or 62 km SE of Tilmouth Well Roadhouse
HEMA 182 E7   23 16 15 S   132 55 06 E

74 Tilmouth Well Roadhouse
Tanami Rd, Tilmouth Well
Camp Area 187 km NW of Alice Springs or 106 km SE of Yuendumu. Limited powered sites
08 8956 8777   HEMA 182 E6   22 48 35 S   132 35 54 E

75 Newhaven Wildlife Sanctuary
Tanami Rd / Access Tr, Newhaven
Camp Area 363 km NW of Alice Springs off the Tanami Track. Pre-book. Limited sites. Cash only. Open May - Sept
08 8964 6000   HEMA 182 E4   22 47 15 S   131 05 03 E

76 Yuelamu Roadside Stop
Tanami Rd, Anmatjere
Camp Area 253 km NW of Alice Springs or 472 km SE of NT/WA border. W on Tanami Rd for 232 km from Hwy. From NT/WA border, turn off Tanami Rd 37 km past Yuendum Jcn. Tracks to SW. GPS at turn off. Opposite turnoff to Yuelamu Community
HEMA 182 D5   22 28 00 S   132 06 09 E

77 Mount Doreen Ruins
Tanami Rd, Southern Tanami
Camp Area 101 km SE of Renahans Bore or 162 km N of Tilmouth Well Roadhouse
HEMA 182 C4   22 02 29 S   131 20 03 E

78 Floodout Creek
Tanami Rd, Southern Tanami
Rest Area 69 km SE of Renehans Bore or 194 km NW of Tilmouth Well Roadhouse
HEMA 182 C4   21 48 22 S   131 10 38 E

79 Renahans Bore Rest Area
Tanami Rd, Central Desert
Rest Area 152 km SE of Rabbit Flat or 263 km NW of Tilmouth Well Roadhouse. Tracks to bore off road
HEMA 182 B4   21 16 39 S   130 50 57 E

80 Border Rest Area
Tanami Rd, Mt Frederick
Rest Area on NT side of border, N of road
HEMA 180 H1   19 53 50 S   129 01 22 E

81 Sturt Creek
Tanami Rd, Halls Creek
Camp Area 46 km S of Wolfe Creek Crater turnoff or 176 km S of Halls Creek. 3 km E of Billiluna Community, creekside
HEMA 163 H12   19 33 36 S   127 41 37 E

82 Lake Stretch (Nyarna)
Paruku IPA
Canning Stock Route, Sturt Creek
Camp Area 18 km S of Bililuna. Permit applies from Bililuna
HEMA 163 H12   19 40 46 S   127 35 18 E

83 Lake Gregory (Paruku)

Lake Gregory Rd, Sturt Creek
Camp Area 344 km S of Halls Creek along Tanami Rd via Balgo or 212 km via the Canning Stock Route. Permits at Bililuna, Balgo & Mulan stores
08 9425 2099 HEMA 163 J12 20 10 56 S 127 59 11 E

84 Yunpu

Canning Stock Route, Sturt Creek
Camp Area 113 km S of Bililuna on the W side of Lake Gregory. Permits from Bililuna Store
08 9168 8259 HEMA 163 J11 20 13 08 S 127 16 31 E

85 Wolfe Creek Camp

Wolfe Creek Crater NP
Tanami Rd / Carranya Rd, Halls Creek
Camp Area. Turnoff 130 km SE of Halls Creek or 196 km W of NT/WA Border. Turn E off Tanami Rd, 20 km to campsite
08 9168 4200 HEMA 163 G12 19 10 35 S 127 47 10 E

Three Ways to Mataranka
Stuart Highway

86 Warrego Gold

Warrego Rd / Access track, Warumungu
Camp Area 62 km NW of Tennant Creek. Via Stuart Hwy 1.5 km N to the Warrego Rd turnoff, then W for 45.5 km. Take Kalumpurlpa dirt track N for 15 km to old mine
HEMA 181G8 19 19 32 S 133 51 55 E

87 Stuart Monument

Attack Creek Historical Reserve
Stuart Hwy, Tablelands
Rest Area 72 km N of Tennant Creek or 87 km S of Renner Springs
08 8962 4499 HEMA 181 F8 19 01 24 S 134 08 29 E

88 Old Stuart Highway -
Churchills Head
Old Stuart Hwy, Tablelands
Parking Area 80 km N of Tennant Creek or 80 km S of Renner Springs. Signposted Churchills Head at both N & S entry. S entry is 800 m N of Stuart Monument
HEMA 180 D7 18 56 21 S 134 06 58 E

89 Banka Banka Station

Stuart Hwy, Tablelands
Station Stay 74 km N of Three Ways or 60 km S of Renner Springs. Pre-book
08 8964 4511 HEMA 181 F8 18 47 32 S 134 01 50 E

90 Renner Springs Desert Inn

Stuart Hwy, Renner Springs
Caravan Park at Renner Springs. 92 km S of Elliott or 161 km N of Tennant Creek
08 8964 4505 HEMA 181 E8 18 19 08 S 133 47 43 E

91 Newcastle Waters Rest Area

Stuart Hwy, Newcastle Waters
Rest Area 25 km N of Elliott or 77 km S of Dunmarra. Just S of Newcastle Waters turnoff. Limited space
HEMA 180 D7 17 22 31 S 133 26 22 E

92 Sir Charles Todd Memorial

Stuart Hwy, Birdum
Rest Area 74 km N of Elliott or 25 km S of Dunmarra
HEMA 180 C7 16 55 15 S 133 25 21 E

93 Dunmarra Wayside Inn

Stuart Hwy, Dunmarra
Caravan Park at roadhouse, motel & bar
08 8975 9922 HEMA 180 B7 16 40 47 S 133 24 45 E

94 Illawarra Creek

Buchanan Hwy, Top Springs
Camp Area 181 km W of Dunmarra or 250 km SE of Timber Creek. 173 km W from Stuart Hwy or 7 km E Top Springs. Both sides of road & E side of creek
HEMA 177 G7 16 35 19 S 131 51 10 E

95 Top Springs Hotel

Cnr Buchanan & Buntine Hwys, Top Springs
Caravan Park 225 km W of Daly Waters or 293 km S of Katherine. Limited powered sites
08 8975 0767 HEMA 177 G7 16 32 36 S 131 47 49 E

96 Kalkarindji (Wave Hill)

Buntine Hwy, Kalkarindji
Camp Area 350 km W of Stuart Hwy or 480 km SW of Katherine. Next to general store
08 8975 0788 HEMA 177 K4 17 26 49 S 130 50 03 E

97 Daly Waters Hi-Way Inn

Cnr Stuart & Carpentaria Hwys, Daly Waters
Caravan Park at motel, bar & roadhouse
08 8975 9925 HEMA 179 K8 16 18 28 S 133 23 06 E

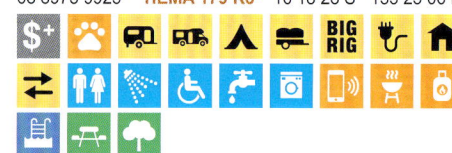

98 The Daly Waters Pub

Stuart St., Daly Waters
Caravan Park 3 km W off Stuart Hwy
08 8975 9927 HEMA 179 K8 16 15 14 S 133 22 11 E

99 Alexander Forrest Memorial

Stuart Hwy, Birdum
Rest Area 65 km N of Dunmarra or 37 km S of Larrimah
HEMA 179 K8 15 51 37 S 133 24 17 E

100 Larrimah Pink Panther Hotel

5 Mahoney St, Larrimah
Caravan Park next to pub & motel
08 8975 9931 HEMA 179 J8 15 34 27 S 133 12 52 E

101 WWII Gorrie Airfield

Stuart Hwy, Larrimah
Camp Area. Turn off Hwy 66 km S of Mataranka or 10 km N of Larrimah to signed track. Follow 1 km, R at Y intersection & immediately R again, follow to runway. GPS at entry
HEMA 179 J8 15 29 25 S 133 11 43 E

102 Warloch Rest Area

Stuart Hwy, Larrimah
Rest Area 41 km N of Larrimah or 37 km S of Mataranka
HEMA 179 J8 15 14 12 S 133 06 53 E

Mataranka to Borroloola
Roper Highway

103 Little Roper Stock Camp

547 Homestead Rd, Mataranka
Camp Area 7.5 km E of Mataranka, via Homestead Rd
0427 880 819 HEMA 179 H8 14 55 31 S 133 07 10 E

104 Jalmurark Campground
Elsey National Park
John Hauser Dr, Mataranka
Camp Area 18 km E of Mataranka, via Homestead Rd
08 8975 4560 　HEMA 179 H8 　14 57 18 S 　133 13 09 E

105 Elsey Rest Area
Roper Hwy, Mataranka
Rest Area 31 km E of Stuart Hwy or 140 km W of Roper Bar. 1 km E of Elsey Station turnoff
HEMA 179 H8 　14 59 06 S 　133 20 53 E

106 Mount Price Rest Area
Roper Hwy, Roper Bar Area
Rest Area 75 km E of Stuart Hwy or 96 km W of Roper Bar
HEMA 179 H9 　14 54 48 S 　133 42 35 E

107 Roper Valley East Rest Area
Roper Hwy, Mataranka
Rest Area 136 km E of Stuart Hwy or 35 km W of Roper Bar
HEMA 179 H9 　14 45 41 S 　134 11 22 E

108 Munbililla Campground
(Tomato Island)
Limmen National Park
Nathan River Rd, Mataranka
Camp Area 45 km SE of Roper Bar or 303 km N of Cape Crawford
08 8975 9940 　HEMA 179 H10 　14 44 49 S 　134 41 31 E

109 Yurrlmundji (Bullshark) Camp
Limmen National Park
Nathan River Rd, Mataranka
Camp Area 57 km E of Roper Bar or 281 km N of Cape Crawford
08 8975 9940 　HEMA 179 H10 　14 45 36 S 　134 47 13 E

110 Mountain Creek
Limmen National Park
Nathan River Rd, Mataranka
Camp Area 60 km E of Roper Bar or 278 km N of Cape Crawford
08 8975 9940 　HEMA 179 H10 　14 46 28 S 　134 48 23 E

111 Didi Baba (Jacana) Camp
Limmen National Park
Nathan River Rd, Mataranka
Camp Area 63 km E of Roper Bar or 275 km N of Cape Crawford
08 8975 9940 　HEMA 179 H10 　14 46 28 S 　134 50 11 E

112 Towns River
Limmen National Park
Nathan River Rd, Mataranka
Camp Area 117 km SE of Roper Bar or 221 km N of Cape Crawford. Sandy access to sites on S side of river for 1.5 km. Small vehicles only
08 8975 9940 　HEMA 179 H11 　15 02 10 S 　135 13 10 E

113 Limmen Bight Fishing Camp
Nathan River Rd, Limmen
Camp Area 176 km SE of Roper Bar or 162 km N of Cape Crawford. Pre-book
08 8975 9844 　HEMA 179 J12 　15 15 52 S 　135 30 05 E

114 Limmen Bight River Camp
Limmen National Park
Nathan River Rd, Borroloola
Camp Area 180 km S of Roper Bar or 163 N of Cape Crawford
08 8975 9940 　HEMA 179 J11 　15 28 36 S 　135 24 22 E

115 Butterfly Falls
Limmen National Park
Nathan River Rd, Borroloola
Camp Area 199 km S of Roper Bar or 146 km N of Cape Crawford. Turn E. Signposted Butterfly Springs, 2 km dirt track to site. Small vehicles only
08 8975 9940 　HEMA 179 J11 　15 37 36 S 　135 27 36 E

116 Southern Lost City
Limmen National Park
Nathan River Road, Borroloola
Camp Area 224 km S of Roper Bar or 114 km N of Cape Crawford. Turn N at sign, follow track 4 km
08 8975 9940 　HEMA 179 K11 　15 48 31 S 　135 27 21 E

117 Lorella Springs Wilderness Park
Lorella Access Rd, Borroloola
Station Stay 275 km SE of Roper Bar or 180 km NW of Borroloola. Turn E off Nathan River Rd at 237 km SE of Roper Bar or 102 km N of Cape Crawford, 30 km to site
08 8975 9917 　HEMA 179 J12 　15 43 15 S 　135 38 26 E

118 King Ash Bay Fishing Club
Batten Rd, King Ash Bay
Camp Area 42 km NE of Borroloola. Take Bing Bong Rd for 21 km, turn SE to Batten Point, 22 km dirt road. Beside McArthur River
08 8975 9800 　HEMA 179 K13 　15 56 08 S 　136 28 44 E

119 Wearyan River
Carpentaria Hwy / Wollogorang Rd, Borroloola
Camp Area 55 km SE of Borroloola or 209 km NW of NT/QLD border. Tracks along both sides of river
HEMA 179 K14 　16 10 01 S 　136 45 22 E

120 Manangoora Station
Manangoora Rd, Borroloola
Camp Area 96 km E of Borroloola or 210 km NW of Wollogorang. Turn N off Carpentaria Hwy at Foelsche River Crossing for 25 km. Signposted. Check in at the shed
08 8975 9549 　HEMA 181 A13 　16 00 12 S 　136 50 18 E

121 Foelsche River Crossing
Carpentaria Hwy / Wollogorang Rd, Borroloola
Camp Area 70 km E of Borroloola or 452 km W of Burketown. Both sides Hwy on E side of river
HEMA 181 A13 　16 12 39 S 　136 53 01 E

122 Seven Emu Station
Seven Emu Rd, Borroloola
Dispersed Camping 85 km SE of Borroloola or 212 km NW of Wollogorang. On Carpentaria Hwy at Foelsche River Crossing, turn N on Manangoora Rd for 1 km, then E. Check in at homestead
08 8975 9904 　HEMA 181 B13 　16 17 49 S 　137 05 00 E

NORTHERN TERRITORY

123 Robinson River Crossing
Carpentaria Hwy / Wollogorang Rd, Borroloola
Camp Area 107 km SE of Borroloola or 149 km NW of Wollogorang. Tracks 2 km on the NW side of Robinson River crossing
HEMA 181 B13   16 28 10 S   137 02 52 E

124 Calvert Creek
Carpentaria Hwy / Wollogorang Rd, Borroloola
Camp Area 177 km E of Borroloola or 80 km W of Wollogorang. Tracks on both sides of the river
HEMA 181 C13   16 56 01 S   137 21 29 E

125 Calvert River
Calvert Rd, Calvert Hills
Camp Area 219 km SE of Borroloola or 340 km NW Burketown. Turn SW off Carpentaria Hwy to Calvert Rd for 18 km. N side of river
HEMA 181 C13   17 12 24 S   137 25 29 E

126 Calvert Rest Stop
Carpentaria Hwy / Wollogorang Rd, Calvert Hills
Rest Area 224 km SE of Borroloola or 229 km NW of Burketown
HEMA 181 C14   17 09 10 S   137 41 22 E

Mataranka to Nhulunbuy
Mainoru and Central Arnhem Roads
This road is seasonal and more suitable to 4WD vehicles, camper trailers and off road caravans. Road conditions phone 1800 013 314. Permits are required to travel on this road

127 Gapuru (Memorial Park)
Central Arnhem Rd, Nhulunbuy
Camp Area 65 km SW of Nhulunbuy. Access track 10 km S from road. Pre-book. Exclusive site. Permits apply
08 8939 2700   HEMA 179 D13   12 27 12 S   136 34 42 E

128 Guwatjurumurru (Giddy River)
Central Arnhem Rd, Nhulunbuy
Dispersed Camping 51 km SW of Nhulunbuy. GPS at entrance of access track S of road. Permit applies
08 8939 2700   HEMA 179 C14   12 23 19 S   136 39 37 E

129 Manangaymi (Scout Camp)
Central Arnhem Rd, Nhulunbuy
Camp Area 48 km SW of Nhulunbuy. Turn N off Central Arnhem Rd 45.5 km S of Nhulunbuy to dirt track. Shallow creek crossing. Permits apply, 5 vehicle limit
08 8939 2700   HEMA 179 C14   12 19 16 S   136 40 32 E

130 Wathawuy (Latram River / Goanna Lagoon)
Dhupuma Rd Access Track, Nhulunbuy
Camp Area 25 km S of Nhulunbuy. Turn SW 21 km from Nhulunbuy from Dhupuma Rd, to dirt track. Permits apply
08 8939 2700   HEMA 179 C14   12 18 32 S   136 46 29 E

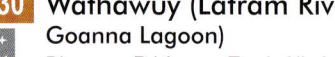

131 Binydjarrna (Daliwuy Bay)
Old Dhupuma Rd, Nhulunbuy
Camp Area 35 km SE of Nhulunbuy. Turn E off Central Arnhem Hwy 25 km S Nhulunbuy, to Old Dhupuma Rd for 10 km, turn SE on access track to site. Permit applies
08 8939 2700   HEMA 179 C14   12 20 29 S   136 55 05 E

132 Garanhan (Macassan Beach)
Macassan Beach Rd, Nhulunbuy
Camp Area 37 km SE of Nhulunbuy. E off Hwy, 25 km S Nhulunbuy to Old Dhupuma Rd for 12 km, then E. Permits apply
08 8939 2700   HEMA 179 C14   12 19 51 S   136 56 03 E

133 Ngumuy (Turtle Beach)
Turtle Beach Rd, Nhulunbuy
Camp Area 40 km SE of Nhulunbuy. Turn E off Hwy 25.5 km S Nhulunbuy to Old Dhupuma Rd for 16.5 km, then E for 500 m. Limited spots. Permit applies
08 8939 2700   HEMA 179 C14   12 18 53 S   136 55 53 E

134 Banambarrnga (Rainbow Cliffs)
Rainbow Cliff Rd, Nhulunbuy
Camp Area 10 km SE of Nhulumbuy. Turn E off Melville Bay Rd 5 km SE from Nhulunbuy to Rainbow Cliff Rd for 2 km, NE on unnamed track for 2.5 km. Permit applies
08 8939 2700   HEMA 179 C14   12 12 48 S   136 49 32 E

135 Manyimi Campground (Gove Boat Club)
1 Drimmie Head Rd, Nhulunbuy
Camp Area 9.5 km W of Nhulunbuy via Melville Bay Rd. Check in at clubhouse. Permit applies
08 8927 3077   HEMA 179 C14   12 11 35 S   136 42 28 E

Mataranka to Darwin
Stuart Highway

136 King Rest Area
Stuart Hwy, Katherine
Rest Area 59 km N of Mataranka or 46 km S of Katherine. 4.5 km S of King River bridge
HEMA 178 G7   14 38 40 S   132 37 58 E

137 Lookout Camp
Central Arnhem Rd, Beswick Creek
Camp Area 160 km E Katherine. From Stuart Hwy 50 km S of Katherine, turn E, 110 km dirt. Permit applies
HEMA 179 G8   14 15 49 S   133 29 44 E

138 Flying Fox Creek
Central Arnhem Rd, Flying Fox
Camp Area 206 km E of Katherine. From Hwy, 152 km E. Permit applies
HEMA 179 G9   14 10 13 S   133 44 41 E

139 Mainoru Outstation Store
Central Arnhem Rd, Flying Fox
Camp Area 250 km NE of Katherine, or 57 km SW of Bulman Weemol. From Hwy turn E for 178 km. Permit applies
08 8977 4200   HEMA 179 F9   13 57 08 S   133 57 53 E

140 Goyder River (East Bank)
Central Arnhem Rd, Flying Fox
Rest Area 390 km E Katherine or 391 km NE Mataranka. From Hwy, turn E for 371 km. On 'old' road, two river crossings. Permit applies
HEMA 179 E11   13 01 43 S   134 58 40 E

141 Rocky Bottom Creek
Central Arnhem Rd, Nhulunbuy
Dispersed Camping 422 km E Katherine or 423 km NE Mataranka. N side of track bend. Permit applies
HEMA 179 D11   12 54 37 S   135 17 38 E

142 Flat Rock Rest Area
Central Arnhem Rd, Nhulunbuy
Rest Area 572 km NE of Katherine or 573 km NE of Mataranka. From Hwy, turn E for 457 km. Permit applies
HEMA 179 D12   12 43 18 S   135 35 30 E

143 Leliyn (Edith Falls) Camp
Nitmiluk National Park
Edith Falls, Roper Gulf
Camp Area 61 km N of Katherine. Turn E off Stuart Hwy, 42 km N of Katherine or 49 km S of Pine Creek
08 8972 2884   HEMA 176 J4   14 10 45 S   132 11 17 E

144 Umbrawarra Gorge
Umbrawarra Rd, Pine Creek
Camp Area & Nature Park 24 km SW of Pine Creek. Turn W off Stuart Hwy 3 km S of Pine Creek. 22 km dirt road. Limited space
08 8976 0282   HEMA 176 H2   13 57 56 S   131 41 52 E

145 Pine Creek Service Station
44 Moule St, Pine Creek
Caravan Park next to pub and service station
08 8976 1217   HEMA 176 H2   13 49 29 S   131 50 06 E

146 Emerald Springs Roadhouse
721 Stuart Hwy, Douglas-Daly
Caravan Park 32 km N of Pine Creek or 76 km S of Adelaide River
08 8975 4109   HEMA 176 G1   13 37 53 S   131 37 47 E

147 Tjuwaliyn (Douglas) Hot Springs Park
Hot Spring Rd, Hayes Creek
Camp Area 100 km NW of Pine Creek or 87 km SE of Adelaide River. Turn W off Hwy 61 km NW of Pine Creek or 62 km SE of Adelaide River to Dorat Rd for 5 km, SW to Oolloo Rd for 25 km, SE for 7 km of dirt road. Pre-book
08 8999 3947   HEMA 176 G1   13 45 53 S   131 26 22 E

148 Douglas River Esplanade Conservation Area
Oolloo Rd, Douglas-Daly
Dispersed Camping 2 km S of Douglas Daly Tourist Park along Daly R. Check in at tourist park, fee includes use of their facilites. Small vehicles only
08 8978 2479   HEMA 178 F5   13 47 14 S   131 21 09 E

149 Oolloo Crossing
Oolloo Rd, Douglas-Daly
Camp Area on Daly R bank, 37 km S of Douglas Daly Tourist Park. Small vehicles only. 28 km dirt road
HEMA 178 F4   14 04 09 S   131 15 02 E

150 Burrell Creek Camp
Dorat Rd, Robin Falls
Rest Area 27 km S of Adelaide River or 101 km NW Pine Creek. Turn W off Stuart Hwy
HEMA 175 J5   13 26 32 S   131 10 04 E

151 Adelaide River Crossing
Daly River Rd, Robin Falls
Camp Area 31 km SE of Adelaide River or 105 km NW of Pine Creek. Turn W off Stuart Hwy on Dorat Rd, then W into Daly River Rd for 10 km
HEMA 175 J4   13 28 59 S   131 05 52 E

152 Robin Falls
Dorat Rd, Robin Falls
Rest Area 14 km S of Adelaide River or 113 km NW of Pine Creek. 500 m W of road. Dirt road. Small vehicles only, limited space & turnaround
HEMA 175 H5   13 21 10 S   131 08 01 E

153 Bridge Creek
Stuart Hwy, Douglas-Daly
Rest Area 79 km NW of Pine Creek or 33 km S of Adelaide River
HEMA 175 J6   13 26 11 S   131 18 48 E

154 Sinclairs Fishing Retreat
Wooliana Rd, Daly River
Camp Area 13 km N of Daly River township, via Daly-River Rd
08 8978 2267   HEMA 178 F3   13 42 11 S   130 40 14 E

155 Lee & Jennys Bush Camp
Wooliana Rd, Daly River
Camp Area 18 km N of Daly River township via Daly-River Rd
0427 030 556   HEMA 178 F3   13 39 53 S   130 39 25 E

156 Mount Nancar Wilderness Retreat
Nanaar Rd, Daly River
Camp Area 6 km SE of Daly River off Daly-River Rd. Open Apr - Sept. Pre-book
0427 014 714   HEMA 178 F3   13 47 57 S   130 43 32 E

157 Adelaide River Show Society
51 Dorat Rd, Adelaide River
Caravan Park 2 km SW of Adelaide River
08 8976 7032   HEMA 175 H5   13 14 49 S   131 06 36 E

158 Mount Bundy Station
Haynes Rd, Adelaide River
Station Stay 5.5 km NW of Adelaide River. Turn off 1 km S of Adelaide River. Weekends only. Pre-book
08 8976 7009   HEMA 175 G5   13 13 39 S   131 08 02 E

NORTHERN TERRITORY

159 Community Church Camp

Batchelor Rd, Coomalie Creek
Camp Area 29 km N of Adelaide River or 86 km S of Darwin. W off Stuart Hwy to Batchelor Rd 700 m, 300 m bush track. Pre-book
08 8976 0280   HEMA 175 F5   13 00 43 S   131 07 05 E

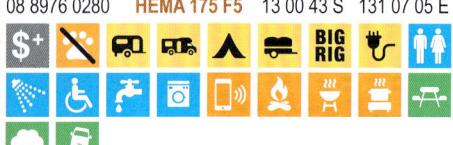

160 Pandanus on Litchfield

275 Litchfield Park Rd, Batchelor
Caravan Park 9 km W of Batchelor via Rum Jungle Rd
08 8976 0242   HEMA 175 F4   13 01 35 S   130 59 17 E

161 Florence Falls 2WD Camp

Litchfield National Park
Litchfield Park Rd, Batchelor
Camp Area 43 km W of Batchelor, or 120 km SW of Darwin
08 8999 3947   HEMA 175 F2   13 05 47 S   130 47 05 E

162 Florence Falls 4WD Camp

Litchfield National Park
Litchfield Park Rd, Batchelor
Camp Area 43 km W of Batchelor. Small vehicles only, no caravans
08 8999 3947   HEMA 175 F2   13 05 36 S   130 47 09 E

163 Tjaynera Falls (Sandy Creek)

Litchfield National Park
Litchfield Park Rd, Batchelor
Camp Area 57 km W of Batchelor or 7 km S of Wangi Falls. 9 km dirt road. Dry season only
08 8999 3947   HEMA 175 H2   13 15 00 S   130 44 41 E

164 Surprise Creek Falls

Litchfield National Park
Litchfield Park Rd, Batchelor
Camp Area 88 km SW of Batchelor. Pre-book. Dry season only
08 8999 3947   HEMA 175 J2   13 24 17 S   130 47 03 E

165 Wangi Falls Campground

Litchfield National Park
Litchfield Park Rd, Litchfield Park
Camp Area 66 km SW of Batchelor
08 8999 3947   HEMA 175 G2   13 09 44 S   130 40 50 E

166 Channel Point Coastal

Reserve
Marindja Rd, Rakula
Camp Area 67 km W of Wangi Falls. Dirt road. Open May - Oct. Pre-book. Permit & refundable key deposit required, limited sites
08 8999 4795   HEMA 178 E2   13 10 23 S   130 08 22 E

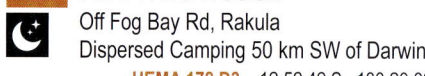

167 Five Mile Beach

Off Fog Bay Rd, Rakula
Dispersed Camping 50 km SW of Darwin
HEMA 178 D3   12 52 42 S   130 20 09 E

168 Litchfield Park Road Rest Area

Litchfield Park Rd, Rakula
Rest Area 58 km SW Berry Springs (9 km dirt road), or 92 km NW Batchelor (2.5 km dirt road)
HEMA 175 F2   13 00 09 S   130 44 34 E

169 Ozzy As

335 Old Bynoe Rd, Livingstone
Station Stay 59 km SE of Darwin, 3 km W of Hwy. Limited sites. Pre-book
0476 513 400   HEMA 175 D4   12 45 36 S   131 04 08 E

170 Rosies Rural

Off Stuart Hwy, Livingstone
Camp Area 55 km S of Darwin. 4 km W of Hwy, secured property. Pre-book
0421 908 088   HEMA 175 D4   12 43 51 S   131 03 12 E

171 Darwin River Tavern

195 Darwin River Rd, Darwin River
Camp Area 12 km SW of Berry Springs. Via Cox Peninsula Rd 10 km past Berry Springs into Darwin River Rd for 2 km. Check in with publican
08 8988 6044   HEMA 175 D3   12 46 51 S   130 57 42 E

172 Sandpalms Roadhouse

Tropical Motel
29 Bynoe Haven Rd, Bynoe
Camp Area 64 km W of Livingstone
08 8978 2822   HEMA 175 D1   12 48 50 S   130 37 00 E

173 Dundee Forest Retreat

4294 Fog Bay Rd, Dundee Forest
Camp Area 500 m W of Barramundi Dr. Signposted. Pre-book, limited sites
0447 082 200   HEMA 178 D3   12 47 52 S   130 29 21 E

174 Beachfront Beauty

29 De Lissa Dr, Wagait Beach
Camp Area 74 km NW of Berry Springs via Cox Peninsula Rd. Turn E into Charles Point Rd for 700 m, N into Wagait Tower Rd for 2 km, turn E. Private camp, pre-book
0499 995 851   HEMA 175 B2   12 25 46 S   130 45 04 E

175 Bees Creek Heights

185 Lowther Rd, Bees Creek
Camp Area 32 km SE Darwin. BYO toilet. Pre-book
0419 039 080   HEMA 175 B4   12 33 18 S   131 03 12 E

176 Leaders Creek Fishing Base

Gunn Point Rd, Koolpinyah
Camp Area 49 km N of Hwy & Howard Springs Rd Jcn. Signed. 39 km dirt road. Pre-book
08 8983 5009   HEMA 178 C4   12 13 26 S   131 05 33 E

177 Robbie Robbins Reserve

Wongabilla St, Berrimah
Camp Area. Pre-book
0407 413 314   HEMA 174 E5   12 26 36 S   130 56 33 E

Darwin-Jabiru-Arnhem Land-Pine Creek

Arnhem and Kakadu Highways

178 Beatrice Hill Parking Area

Arnhem Hwy, Humpty Doo
Parking Area 30 km E of Stuart Hwy Jcn or 53 km W of Bark Hut Inn. 1 km W of visitor centre
HEMA 175 C6   12 38 35 S   131 18 35 E

179 Couzens Lookout & Camp
Mary River National Park
Rockhole Rd, Mount Bundey
Camp Area 130 km SE Humpty Doo, 153 km W Jabiru. Turn N off Arnhem Hwy to Point Stuart Rd for 17 km, W on Rockhole Rd for 16 km, then SW 2 km. 19 km dirt road
08 8978 8986   HEMA 176 C2   12 44 03 S   131 40 07 E

180 Point Stuart Wilderness Lodge
Mary River National Park
Point Stuart Rd, Point Stuart
Camp Area 132 km E of Humpty Doo or 154 km NW of Jabiru. N off Arnhem Hwy 97 km E Humpty Doo or 119 km W Jabiru to Point Stuart Rd for 33 km, then W for 400 m. Open Feb - Nov
08 8978 8914   HEMA 176 B2   12 35 09 S   131 45 38 E

181 Shady Camp
Mary River National Park
Shady Camp Rd, Point Stuart
Camp Area 149 km NE of Humpty Doo or 172 km W of Jabiru. N off Arnhem Hwy to Point Stuart Rd, N Harold Knowles Rd, then W. 30 km dirt road. GPS at entry
08 8978 8986   HEMA 176 B2   12 29 04 S   131 43 33 E

182 Two Mile Hole Camp
Kakadu National Park
Arnhem Hwy, Jabiru Area
Dispersed Camping 12 km N of Hwy. Turn off 1.5 km NE of Kakadu entry station. Dirt track
08 8938 1120   HEMA 176 C4   12 41 32 S   132 09 05 E

183 Four Mile Hole
Kakadu National Park
Via Arnhem Hwy, Jabiru Area
Dispersed Camping 30 km NE of Hwy. Turn off 2 km NE from Kakadu entry station. Dirt road
08 8938 1120   HEMA 176 B4   12 34 15 S   132 13 08 E

184 Alligator Billabong
Kakadu National Park
Via Arnhem Hwy, Jabiru Area
Dispersed Camping 24 km S of Aurora Kakadu Resort. 2 km W of Resort, turn off to Bucket Billabong. 23 km dirt track. Entry fees. Not recommended for rooftop tinnies
08 8938 1120   HEMA 176 D5   12 51 57 S   132 26 41 E

185 Red Lily Billabong
Kakadu National Park
Via Arnhem Hwy, Jabiru Area
Dispersed Camping 62 km SW of Jabiru or 166 km E of Humpty Doo. S off Arnhem Hwy 2 km W of Aurora Kakadu Resort to bush track for 18 km
08 8938 1120   HEMA 176 C   12 51 06 S   132 29 40 E

186 Bucket Billabong Camp
Kakadu National Park
Via Arnhem Hwy, Jabiru Area
Dispersed Camping 22 km S of Aurora Kakadu Resort. 2 km W of resort, follow sign. 20 km dirt track. Entry fees
08 8938 1120   HEMA 176 C5   12 51 16 S   132 27 16 E

187 Merl Campground
Kakadu National Park
Arnhem Hwy / Ooenpelli Rd, Jabiru Area
Camp Area near Ubirr Rock, 36 km N of Jabiru turnoff
08 8938 1120   HEMA 176 B7   12 25 30 S   132 57 26 E

188 Malabanjbanjdju Camp
Kakadu National Park
Kakadu Hwy, Jabiru
Camp Area 16 km S of Jabiru turnoff or 32 km N of Cooinda
08 8938 1120   HEMA 176 C6   12 45 56 S   132 45 17 E

189 Djarradjin Billabong
(Muirella Park) Campground
Kakadu National Park
Kakadu Hwy, Jabiru
Camp Area 34 km S of Jabiru. Turn E 28 km S of Jabiru turnoff or 20 km NE of Cooinda for 6 km. Signposted
08 8938 1120   HEMA 176 C6   12 51 15 S   132 45 18 E

190 Sandy Billabong Camp
Kakadu National Park
Kakadu Hwy, Jabiru
Camp Area 6 km S of Muirella Park. Dirt road
08 8938 1120   HEMA 176 D6   12 54 02 S   132 46 25 E

191 Garnamarr Campground
Kakadu National Park
Jim Jim Falls Rd, Jabiru Area
Camp Area 95 km S of Bowali Centre. E off Kakadu Hwy 43 km S of Bowali Centre, 52 km dirt road
08 8938 1120   HEMA 176 E6   13 13 04 S   132 48 58 E

192 Jim Jim Billabong Camp
Kakadu National Park
Kakadu Hwy, Cooinda
Camp Area 6 km SE of Cooinda. Just N of Cooinda turnoff, turn S for 3 km, then SW for 2 km of dirt road. Heavy rainfall may affect site, contact Parks
08 8938 1120   HEMA 176 D5   12 56 38 S   132 33 11 E

193 Mardugal Camp One
(Mardukal)
Kakadu National Park
Kakadu Hwy, Cooinda
Camp Area 2 km S of Cooinda or 96 km NE of Mary River Roadhouse. Turn W from Hwy for 500 m
08 8938 1120   HEMA 176 D5   12 55 47 S   132 32 17 E

194 Maguk Campground
Kakadu National Park
Kakadu Hwy, Cooinda
Camp Area 58 km S of Cooinda turnoff or 65 km NE of Mary River Roadhouse. Turn E off Hwy 46 km S of Cooinda turnoff or 53 km NE of Mary River Roadhouse. 12 km dirt road
08 8938 1120   HEMA 176 E5   13 18 12 S   132 26 00 E

195 Gungurul Campground
Kakadu National Park
Kakadu Hwy, Cooinda
Camp Area 58 km S of Cooinda turnoff or 50 km NE of Mary River Roadhouse
08 8938 1120   HEMA 176 E4   13 17 25 S   132 20 08 E

196 Kambolgie Campground
Kakadu National Park
Gunlom Rd, Jabiru Area
Dispersed Camping 100 km S of Cooinda turnoff or 24 km NE of Mary River Roadhouse. Turn E off Kakadu Hwy 87 km S of Cooinda turnoff or 11 km NE of Mary River Roadhouse. 10 km dirt road
08 8938 1120   HEMA 176 F5   13 30 13 S   132 23 37 E

NORTHERN TERRITORY

197 Gunlom Campground
Kakadu National Park
Kakadu Hwy, Jabiru Area
Camp Area 124 km S of Cooinda turnoff or 48 km NE of Mary River Roadhouse. Turn E off Hwy 87 km S of Cooinda turnoff or 11 km NE of Mary River Roadhouse. 36 km dirt road
08 8938 1120   HEMA 176 F5   13 26 05 S   132 24 53 E

198 Jarrangbarnmi Campground
(Koolpin Gorge)
Kakadu National Park
Via Gimbat Access Rd, Kakadu National Park
Camp Area 56 km E of Mary River Roadhouse. Turn E off Kakadu Hwy onto dirt road 2 km NE after Park Entrance Station for 26 km. Turn SE 10 km, then E on dirt track for 7 km. Pre-book. Permit applies
08 8938 1120   HEMA 176 F5   13 29 58 S   132 34 41 E
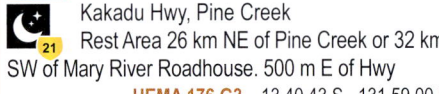

199 Harriet Creek
Kakadu Hwy, Pine Creek
Rest Area 26 km NE of Pine Creek or 32 km SW of Mary River Roadhouse. 500 m E of Hwy
HEMA 176 G3   13 40 43 S   131 59 00 E

200 Pussy Cat Flats
Kakadu Hwy, Pine Creek
Camp Area 56 km SW of Mary River Roadhouse or 2 km E of Pine Creek
0483 389 347   HEMA 176 H2   13 48 29 S   131 50 18 E

Katherine to NT/WA Border
Victoria Highway

201 Manbulloo Homestead
275 Murnburlu Rd, Cossack
Caravan Park 11 SW of Katherine. Turn N off Victoria Hwy 9 km W of Katherine, follow signs
08 8972 1559   HEMA 178 G6   14 31 09 S   132 11 57 E

202 King West Rest Area
Victoria Hwy, Manbulloo
Rest Area 34 km SW of Katherine or 163 km NE of Victoria River
HEMA 178 H6   14 40 38 S   132 05 11 E

203 Vince Connolly Crossing
(Limestone Creek)
Victoria Hwy, Manbulloo
Rest Area 58 km SW of Katherine or 138 km NE of Victoria River
HEMA 177 A7   14 49 42 S   131 55 00 E

204 Lorrngurl Campground
Giwining / Flora River Nature Park
Via Victoria Hwy, Giwining
Camp Area 132 km SW of Katherine. Turn NW 86 km SW of Katherine or 110 km NE of Victoria River. 46 km dirt road. Closed Nov - May
08 8973 8888   HEMA 178 H5   14 45 30 S   131 35 46 E

205 Mathison Rest Area
Victoria Hwy, Delamere
Rest Area 104 km SW of Katherine or 92 km NE of Victoria River
HEMA 177 B6   15 08 23 S   131 41 01 E

206 Sullivan Creek Campground
Judbarra / Gregory National Park
Victoria Hwy, Gregory
Camp Area 178 km SW of Katherine or 18 km E of Victoria River. Pets allowed in campground only
08 8975 0888   HEMA 177 C5   15 35 13 S   131 16 29 E

207 Victoria River Roadhouse
Victoria Hwy, Gregory
Caravan Park 90 km E of Timber Creek
08 8975 0744   HEMA 177 C4   15 36 57 S   131 07 38 E

208 Charlies Crossing
Buchanan Hwy, Timber Creek
Camp Area 55 km S of the Victoria Hwy & Buchanan Hwy Jcn or 157 km N of Top Springs. Dirt road
HEMA 177 E3   16 01 51 S   130 48 10 E

209 Dashwood Crossing West
Victoria River Ford
Buchanan Hwy, Victoria River
Camp Area 127 km S of Victoria Hwy, 86 km NW of Top Springs. Level sites prior to descent to river
HEMA 177 F4   16 20 02 S   131 06 45 E

210 Dashwood Crossing East
Victoria River Ford
Buchanan Hwy, Victoria River
Camp Area 127 km S of Victoria Hwy or 86 km NW of Top Springs. Tracks on E side of river to N. Small vehicles only
HEMA 177 F5   16 20 01 S   131 06 52 E
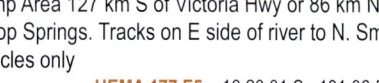

211 Bullita Homestead Camp
Judbarra / Gregory National Park
Bullita / Timber Creek, Baines
Camp Area 60 km SE of Timber Creek on the Binns Track. Turn S 12 km SE of Timber Creek. 48 km dirt road. Open May - Nov
08 8975 0888   HEMA 177 E2   16 06 46 S   130 25 25 E

212 Wirib Tourism Park & Store
Victoria Hwy, Timber Creek
Caravan Park at Supermarket, Takeaway & Bakery. Creekside
08 8975 0602   HEMA 177 D2   15 39 46 S   130 28 52 E

213 Big Horse Creek Camp
Judbarra / Gregory National Park
Victoria Hwy, Gregory
Camp Area 10 km W of Timber Creek, 216 km E of Kununurra or 177 km E of NT/WA border. Pets allowed in campground only. No large caravans
08 8975 0888   HEMA 177 C2   15 36 44 S   130 24 09 E

214 East Baines River
Victoria Hwy, Baines
Rest Area 57 km W of Timber Creek, 169 km E of Kununurra or 130 km E of border
HEMA 177 D1   15 46 02 S   130 01 35 E

215 Saddle Creek
Victoria Hwy, Baines
Rest Area 117 km W of Timber Creek, 109 km E of Kununurra or 70 km E of NT/WA border
HEMA 178 K2   15 57 26 S   129 33 42 E

216 Alan Kellet Rest Area
Victoria Hwy, Baines
Rest Area 167 km W of Timber Creek, 79 km E of Kununurra or 16 km E of NT/WA Border
HEMA 177 D1   16 03 28 S   129 06 48 E

217 Zebra Rock Mine

Duncan Rd, Baines

Camp Area at Zebra Rock Mine. Turn S to Duncan Rd off Hwy 10 km E of WA border or 170 km W of Timber Creek. Travel 5 km, R to access road. 10 km dirt road. Open Apr - Sept. Signposted. GPS at entry road. Pre-book

0400 767 650   HEMA 180 B1   16 06 13 S   129 05 06 E

218 Negri River

Duncan Rd, Buchanan

Dispersed Camping near NT/WA border 302 km SW Timber Creek or 373 km NW Kalkarindji (Wave Hill) via Buntine Hwy. S into Duncan Rd from Victoria Hwy for 133 km, or N 9 km W border from Buntine Hwy for 136 km

HEMA 180 C1   17 04 35 S   129 00 10 E

219 Goorrandalng Campground

Keep River National Park

Via Victoria Hwy, Zebra Rock Area

Camp Area 202 km W of Timber Creek. Turn N 184 km W of Timber Creek or 3 km E of NT/WA border. 18 km rough, dirt road. Open May - October

08 9167 8827   HEMA 180 A1   15 52 31 S   129 03 05 E

220 Jarnem Campground

Keep River National Park

Keep River Access Tr, Baines

Camp Area 215 km W of Timber Creek. Off Victoria Hwy turn N 184 km W of Timber Creek or 3 km E of NT/WA border. 32 km rough, dirt road

08 9167 8827   HEMA 180 A1   15 45 44 S   129 05 57 E

Plenty Highway

This road is seasonal and more suitable to 4WD vehicles, camper trailers and off road caravans. Road conditions phone 1800 246 199 (NT)

221 Mud Tank Zircon Field

Fossicking Area

Alatyeye Rd, Anmatjere

Dispersed Camping 17 km SE of Gemtree. Turn S off Plenty Hwy 7.5 E of Gemtree. 9 km to access gate. Sites 500 m after gate

HEMA 183 E9   23 00 45 S   134 16 13 E

222 Spotted Tiger Campground

Racecourse Rd, Hart

Dispersed Camping 8 km S of Harts Range Police Station. Turn S 500m W of station. Follow 8 km to sites

HEMA 183 E9   23 02 21 S   134 55 04 E

223 Mac & Rose Chalmers

Conservation Reserve (Tower Rock)

Off Plenty Hwy, Sandover

Dispersed Camping 75 km N of Plenty Hwy. Turn N 20 km E of Harts Range Police Station or 335 km W of QLD border. 75 km to site

08 8956 9745   HEMA 183 D10   22 28 08 S   135 05 01 E

224 Marshall River Rest Area

Plenty Hwy, Anatye

Rest Area 202 km E of Stuart Hwy or 222 km W of NT/QLD border. Dirt road. Riverside

HEMA 183 E11   22 57 12 S   136 09 06 E

225 Jervois Station

Plenty Hwy, Plenty

Station Stay 202 km E of Stuart Hwy or 222 km W of NT/QLD border. Dirt road

08 8956 6307   HEMA 183 E11   22 57 04 S   136 08 39 E

226 Arthur River

Plenty Hwy, Anatye

Rest Area 62 km NE of Jervois Station or 159 km W of NT/QLD Border. Tracks beside creek. Dirt road

HEMA 183 D12   22 40 11 S   136 37 51 E

227 Mount Guide

Plenty Hwy, Anatye

Rest Area 101 km NE of Jervois Station or 123 km W of NT/QLD border. Tracks N side of road

HEMA 183 D12   22 35 36 S   136 57 30 E

228 Mount Pozieres

Plenty Hwy, Anatye

Rest Area 153 km NE of Jervois Station or 69 km W of NT/QLD border. S side of road, tracks to gravel area

HEMA 183 D13   22 26 01 S   137 25 38 E

229 Tobermorey Station

Plenty Hwy, Mount Isa

Station Stay 218 km E of Jervois Station or 4 km W of NT/QLD border

07 4748 3280   HEMA 183 D14   22 16 27 S   137 58 26 E

Public Dump Points

With environmental issues becoming more of a concern to travellers, the disposal of grey and black water is of major importance. A comprehensive public dump point list has been compiled to assist you in locating the facilities for responsible disposal of your waste water.

The list is alphabetical by town within each State or Territory, with location details and contact phone numbers where available. Note that public dump points are also indicated on the maps. See "Symbols used on the maps" below for an explanation of the meaning of these map symbols.

Be aware that some situations may change and the accuracy of accessibility and type of facility cannot be guaranteed.

The use of chemicals in 'black water' is of concern, so it is advisable to use those which are biodegradable and eco-friendly rather than those containing chemicals such as formaldehyde.

Most of the dump points accessible by big rigs would require the use of a waste hose, preferably 3 metres or more in length.

Please leave the facility clean and tidy, otherwise the use may be withdrawn if abused.

Where the information is available, listings show whether the dump point is suitable for cassettes or holding tanks and whether big rigs can access it.

Please respect the courtesy extended to you if you avail yourself of this service.

Explanation of a sample Public Dump Point listing

Town/city — Karatta
Site name — Western River Caravan Park & Wildlife Reserve **CT HT $ BIG RIG** — Facilities available at the park
Location and access details — South Coast Rd. Dump point 3 km E of Flinders Chase. Fee for non guests, must call into reception
Contact phone number — 08 8559 7201   HEMA 124 K2   35 57 39 S   136 48 28 E — GPS coordinates
— Map reference

Symbols used in listing

CT *Cassette Toilet Use*

BIG RIG *Access Suitable for Big Rigs*

HT *Holding Tank Use*

$ *Fees Applicable*

Water Available

Symbols used on the maps

  Public Dump Point

Devils Marbles, Northern Territory by Annette Hobbs

QUEENSLAND

Adels Grove
Adels Grove Dump Point `CT` `HT` `tap`
Adels Grove Airfield. Outside the Airport fence. GPS is approximate. Donation
07 4748 5502   **HEMA 25 F3**   18 41 29 S   138 31 53 E

Allora
Allora Apex Park `CT` `HT` `BIG RIG`
New England Hwy. S end of town near Anglican Church, opposite Dalrymple Rd
1300 697 372   **HEMA 12 H1**   28 02 09 S   151 59 18 E

Alpha
Alpha Dump Point `CT` `HT` `BIG RIG`
Clermont-Alpha Rd. Opposite showgrounds
07 4985 1166   **HEMA 29 F14**   23 38 47 S   146 38 11 E

Aramac
Aramac Caravan Park `CT` `HT` `BIG RIG` `tap`
Booker St. Public access
07 4652 9999   **HEMA 29 E12**   22 58 02 S   145 14 20 E

Atherton
Atherton Sewerage Works `CT` `HT` `BIG RIG` `tap`
69 Grove St. Off Tolga Rd, over railway. N end of town. 730am-3.30pm weekdays only
07 4091 7937   **HEMA 22 J2**   17 15 18 S   145 28 49 E

Augathella
Augathella Dump Point `CT` `HT` `BIG RIG` `tap`
Old Charleville Augathella Rd. Brassington Park, Bendee St
07 4656 8355   **HEMA 34 A3**   25 48 08 S   146 35 18 E

Ellangowan Hotel `CT` `HT` `BIG RIG` `tap`
90 Main St. At Caravan Park, behind pub
0411 545 194   **HEMA 34 A3**   25 47 46 S   146 34 58 E

Ayr
Shell Burdekin Travel Centre `CT` `HT` `BIG RIG` `tap`
249 Queen St. Cnr Bruce Hwy
07 4783 9800   **HEMA 18 B1**   19 34 59 S   147 23 56 E

Babinda
Babinda Rotary Park `CT` `HT` `BIG RIG` `tap`
Howard Kennedy Dr. Rest Area at Babinda. Just east of town over railway. S end of Howard Kennedy Dr
07 4067 1008   **HEMA 21 H6**   17 20 54 S   145 55 35 E

Balgal Beach
Balgal Beach `CT` `HT` `BIG RIG` `tap`
3 Tooth St. At Rest Area 6 km E of Rollingstone. Turn E off Bruce Hwy 1 km S of Rollingstone. 5 km E of Hwy. N end of town near boat ramp
134 810   **HEMA 19 F3**   19 00 37 S   146 24 18 E

Baralaba
Baralaba Dump Point `CT` `HT` `BIG RIG` `tap`
12 Wooroonah St. Near caravan park, behind the showgrounds
07 4992 9500   **HEMA 31 G9**   24 11 09 S   149 49 06 E

Barcaldine
Barcaldine Showground `CT` `HT` `BIG RIG` `tap`
Cnr Pine & Wilga Sts. Capricorn Hwy, E end of town
07 4651 5600   **HEMA 29 F12**   23 33 02 S   145 17 37 E

Lloyd Jones Weir `CT` `HT` `BIG RIG`
Lloyd Jones Weir Rd. 15 km SW of Barcaldine. Turn W off Landsborough Hwy 5 km S of Barcaldine for 9 km. 1 km dirt road
07 4651 5600   **HEMA 29 F12**   23 39 00 S   145 12 57 E

Basalt
Fletcher Creek `CT` `HT` `BIG RIG` `tap`
Gregory Hwy. Rest Area 42 km N of Charters Towers or 157 km SE of Greenvale
07 4761 5533   **HEMA 19 J2**   19 48 58 S   146 03 14 E

Beaudesert
Beaudesert Caravan & Tourist Park `CT` `HT` `$` `BIG RIG` `tap`
57 Albert St. Fee applies. Must call at office first
07 5541 1368   **HEMA 6 G7**   27 59 31 S   153 00 16 E

Bedourie
Bedourie Dump Point `CT` `HT` `BIG RIG` `tap`
Diamantina Dev Rd. 500 m N of roadhouse
07 4746 1630   **HEMA 28 G3**   24 21 07 S   139 28 05 E

Monkira Rest Area `CT` `HT` `BIG RIG` `tap`
Diamantina Dev Rd. Rest Area 121 km E of Eyre Dev Rd Jcn or 138 km W of Birdsville Dev Rd Jcn
132 380   **HEMA 28 H5**   24 49 11 S   140 32 28 E

No 3 Bore Rest Area `CT` `HT` `BIG RIG`
Diamantina Dev Rd. Rest Area on Diamantina Dev Rd. 28 km E of Eyre Dev Rd Jcn
132 380   **HEMA 28 G4**   24 28 31 S   139 48 33 E

Bedourie
Cuttaburra Crossing `CT` `HT` `BIG RIG`
Eyre Developmental Rd. Rest Area 121 km N of Birdsville or 68 km S of Bedourie
07 4564 2000   **HEMA 28 H3**   24 54 49 S   139 38 58 E

Beenleigh
Hugh Muntz Park `CT` `HT` `BIG RIG` `tap`
Reisers Rd. Exit Pacific Hwy to George St
07 3412 3412   **HEMA 4 H6**   27 43 01 S   153 12 33 E

Beerwah
Beerwah Caravan Park `CT` `HT` `BIG RIG` `tap`
205 Burys Rd. SE of town
07 5494 0365   **HEMA 11 H12**   26 52 30 S   152 58 43 E

Beerwah Sportsground `CT` `HT` `$` `tap`
32 Sportsground Dr. Entry via Simpson St, off roundabout. Donation
07 5494 0513   **HEMA 11 H12**   26 51 50 S   152 57 21 E

Benaraby
Boyne River Rest Area `CT` `HT` `BIG RIG` `tap`
48739 Bruce Hwy. At Rest Area 49 km SE of Mount Larcom or 49 km N of Miriam Vale. 1 km S of Benaraby
132 380   **HEMA 16 D4**   24 00 39 S   151 20 26 E

Biggenden
Biggenden Dump Point `CT` `HT` `BIG RIG` `tap`
Isis Hwy. 50 m W of caravan park
07 4160 3555   **HEMA 13 C2**   25 30 52 S   152 02 20 E

Biloela
Lake Callide Retreat `CT` `HT` `BIG RIG` `tap`
119 Lake Callide Drive. E of town
07 4993 9010   **HEMA 16 F2**   24 22 19 S   150 36 41 E

Queensland Heritage Park `CT` `HT` `BIG RIG` `tap`
11 Exhibition Ave. Only available 0900-1600, near carpark
07 4992 2400   **HEMA 16 F1**   24 24 17 S   150 29 59 E

Visitor Information Centre `CT` `HT` `BIG RIG` `tap`
Callide St. In the carpark
07 4992 2405   **HEMA 16 F1**   24 24 18 S   150 30 51 E

Birdsville
Birdsville Dump Point `CT` `HT` `BIG RIG` `tap`
Simpson Desert NP Rd. South side of road past the Airstrip
07 4746 1600   **HEMA 28 K3**   25 54 14 S   139 20 41 E

Birdsville East Dump Point `CT` `HT` `BIG RIG` `tap`
Eyre Dev Rd. E of Birdsville. 500 m E of windmill
07 4746 1600   **HEMA 28 K3**   25 54 28 S   139 22 39 E

Blackall
Blackall Dump Point `CT` `HT` `BIG RIG` `tap`
Garden St. Cnr Blackall - Isisford Rd. Opposite Barcoo River Camp
07 4621 6600   **HEMA 29 G13**   24 25 31 S   145 27 45 E

Blackall Showgrounds `CT` `HT` `BIG RIG`
Blackall-Jericho Rd. E side of town, N of road
07 4621 6600   **HEMA 29 G13**   24 25 33 S   145 28 29 E

Blackbutt North
Blackbutt Showgrounds `CT` `HT` `BIG RIG` `tap`
23 Bowman Rd. By water tanks
0437 665 199   **HEMA 10 H1**   26 52 52 S   152 06 08 E

Blackwater
Blackwater Dump Point `CT` `HT` `BIG RIG` `tap`
3 Turpentine St. Near the showgrounds
1300 242 686   **HEMA 30 F7**   23 35 35 S   148 52 31 E

Bluewater
Bluewater Park `CT` `HT` `BIG RIG`
Bruce Hwy. Rest Area at Bluewater, 80 km S of Ingham or 29 km N of Townsville
134 810   **HEMA 19 G4**   19 10 34 S   146 33 06 E

Bollon
Bollon Dump Point `CT` `HT` `BIG RIG`
William St. Behind fire station
07 4620 8888   **HEMA 34 G5**   28 01 51 S   147 28 40 E

Boonah
Boonah Showgrounds `CT` `HT` `BIG RIG` `tap`
8 Melbourne St. Just E of main street
07 5463 4080   **HEMA 6 G3**   27 59 51 S   152 41 06 E

Boulia
Boulia Dump Point `CT` `HT` `BIG RIG` `tap`
Diamantina Hwy. W side of Hwy, 1 km N of Boulia
07 4746 3188   **HEMA 28 E4**   22 54 28 S   139 54 15 E

Bowen
Bowen Showground `CT` `HT` `BIG RIG` `tap`
25 Mount Nutt Rd. N side of town
0414 339 081   **HEMA 18 D4**   19 59 42 S   148 13 42 E

Boynedale
Boynedale Bush Camp `CT` `HT` `BIG RIG`
Bush Camp Rd. At the camp lookout. 26 km W of Calliope on the Gladstone-Monto Rd
07 4972 9000   **HEMA 16 E4**   24 13 23 S   151 15 15 E

Bribie Island
Ocean Beach Zone 2 `CT`
Beach Access Rd. N side of island. Near toilets on Access Track P. 4WD access
137 468   **HEMA 11 H14**   26 53 14 S   153 07 59 E

Poverty Creek `CT` `HT` `tap`
Poverty Creek Rd. W side of island. Campertrailers and tents, 4WD only
137 468   **HEMA 11 K13**   26 59 29 S   153 05 42 E

QUEENSLAND

Bundaberg
Hinkler Lions Park | CT HT BIG RIG 🚰
6 University Dr. Opposite airport. If locked, key at Waste Transfer Station
1300 722 099 **HEMA 16 G7** 24 53 49 S 152 18 51 E

Burketown
Burketown Dump Point | CT HT BIG RIG 🚰
Wills Developmental Rd. Just W of township, washdown station and water refill available
07 4745 5100 **HEMA 25 D4** 17 44 26 S 139 31 59 E

Cairns
Cairns Wastewater Depot | CT HT BIG RIG 🚰
Macnamara St. Available 7am-4pm daily, excluding public holidays. In Manunda
1300 692 247 **HEMA 22 C7** 16 54 46 S 145 45 00 E

Calliope
Calliope Dump Point | CT HT BIG RIG 🚰
Cnr Taragoola Rd & Dawson Hwy. Key for lock from Calliope Store
07 4970 0700 **HEMA 16 D3** 24 00 27 S 151 12 02 E

Caloundra
Caloundra Dump Point | CT HT 🚰
7 Caloundra Rd. Behind the Information Centre. Showers and toilets available
07 5475 7272 **HEMA 11 G14** 26 47 53 S 153 06 51 E

Camooweal
Camooweal Dump Point | CT HT BIG RIG 🚰
Barkly Hwy. E end of town, opposite the water tower
07 4748 2110 **HEMA 25 H2** 19 55 18 S 138 07 27 E

Capalaba
John Fredericks Park | CT HT BIG RIG 🚰
2 -14 Old Cleveland Rd. Cross Tingalpa Creek bridge, take an immediate sharp turn left (before the tavern). Inside the park, close to the entry.
07 3829 8999 **HEMA 4 F6** 27 31 09 S 153 11 19 E

Capella
Bridgeman Park Showground | CT HT BIG RIG 🚰
32-42 Hibernia Rd. SW corner of grounds near horse stables
07 4988 7200 **HEMA 30 E6** 23 05 21 S 148 00 58 E

Carmila Beach
Carmila Beach | CT HT BIG RIG
35 Esplanade. 6 km E of Carmila. 1 km dirt road. Last 300 m narrow, sandy track
1300 472 227 **HEMA 17 D3** 21 54 50 S 149 27 47 E

Carnarvon Gorge
Takarakka Bush Resort | CT $
O'Briens Rd. Via Carnarvon Gorge Rd. Fee for all users
07 4984 4535 **HEMA 30 H6** 25 04 13 S 148 16 17 E

Cecil Plains
Cecil Plains Rural Retreat | CT HT BIG RIG 🚰
Warfield Ave. In Caravan Park
0457 275 310 **HEMA 35 E14** 27 31 59 S 151 11 45 E

Charleville
Charleville Dump Point | CT HT BIG RIG 🚰
Qantas Drv. Airport Access Rd
07 4656 8359 **HEMA 34 B2** 26 24 59 S 146 15 07 E

Charters Towers
Columbia Mine Poppet Head | CT HT BIG RIG 🚰
New Queen Rd. At Picnic Area on Flinders Hwy Bypass, near toilets
07 4761 5300 **HEMA 19 K3** 20 04 21 S 146 16 35 E

Childers
Childers RV | CT HT BIG RIG 🚰
3 Crescent St. Behind PO
1300 722 099 **HEMA 13 A3** 25 14 06 S 152 16 44 E

Chillagoe
Chillagoe Rodeo Grounds | CT HT BIG RIG 🚰
Frew St. From Queen St turn W onto Frew St, enter 700 m on R
07 4094 7090 **HEMA 27 D8** 17 09 29 S 144 30 58 E

Chinchilla
Chinchilla Dump Point | CT HT BIG RIG 🚰
28 Park St. N of town, on the Wondai Rd
07 4679 4000 **HEMA 35 C12** 26 44 07 S 150 37 50 E

Clermont
Clermont Dump Point | CT HT BIG RIG
Lime St. Next to bowls club
1300 472 227 **HEMA 30 D5** 22 49 08 S 147 38 40 E

Cleveland
William St Marine Facility | CT HT BIG RIG 🚰
1-9 William St. Off Shore St North
07 3829 8999 **HEMA 4 F7** 27 30 54 S 153 17 15 E

Clifton
Clifton Rec Grounds | CT HT BIG RIG 🚰
12 Morton St. N side of town, via Clark & Devonport Sts
131 872 **HEMA 12 H1** 27 55 34 S 151 54 45 E

Cloncurry
Cloncurry Dump Point | CT HT BIG RIG 🚰
34 Flinders Hwy, Cloncurry QLD. Mary Kathleen Memorial Park, adjacent to Info Centre
07 4742 1361 **HEMA 25 J6** 20 42 26 S 140 31 06 E

Coen
Coen Dump Point | CT HT BIG RIG 🚰
Peninsula Developmental Rd. E side of Rd. S side of library
07 4082 0500 **HEMA 23 G4** 13 56 43 S 143 12 06 E

Collinsville
Collinsville Showgrounds | CT HT BIG RIG 🚰
11 Conway St. Entry from Railway Rd next to showgrounds
0418 556 560 **HEMA 18 F3** 20 33 24 S 147 50 57 E

Cooktown
Cooktown Dump Point | CT HT 🚰
Adelaide St. Access from Charlotte St, opposite Sovereign Hotel
07 4082 0500 **HEMA 20 A3** 15 27 58 S 145 14 57 E

Cooroy
Cooroy RV Stop | CT HT BIG RIG 🚰
17 Mary River Rd. Enter at driveway between Car Club & Horse & Pony Club
0458 650 285 **HEMA 11 A11** 26 24 49 S 152 54 25 E

Craiglie
Willie Pye Teamsters Memorial Park | CT HT
Captain Cook Hwy. S end of town
07 4099 9444 **HEMA 21 B3** 16 32 22 S 145 28 11 E

Croydon
Croydon Dump Point | CT HT BIG RIG 🚰
Alldridge St. Outside the Caravan Park
07 4748 7152 **HEMA 26 F5** 18 12 05 S 142 14 43 E

Cunnamulla
Cunnamulla Council Dump Point | CT HT BIG RIG 🚰
Williams St. Adjacent to showground fence
07 4655 8470 **HEMA 33 G14** 28 04 05 S 145 41 49 E

Dalby
Dalby Dump Point | CT HT BIG RIG 🚰
5 Black St. S side of Hwy
07 4679 4000 **HEMA 35 D14** 27 10 34 S 151 14 41 E

Dalveen
Jim Mitchell Park | CT HT BIG RIG 🚰
Mountain Park Rd. Rest Area at Dalveen
1300 697 372 **HEMA 12 K1** 28 29 21 S 151 58 14 E

Dayboro
Dayboro Showgrounds | CT HT BIG RIG 🚰
3512 Mount Mee Rd. N side of town, W of main road
0403 952 198 **HEMA 4 B3** 27 11 25 S 152 49 24 E

Dirranbandi
Dirranbandi Dump Point | CT HT BIG RIG 🚰
Castlereagh Hwy. S end of town, opposite service station
07 4620 8888 **HEMA 34 H7** 28 35 16 S 148 13 25 E

Duaringa
Duaringa Rest Area | CT HT BIG RIG 🚰
30 Theresa St. Rest Area at Duaringa. E end of town
1300 242 686 **HEMA 31 F8** 23 43 18 S 149 40 20 E

Dululu
Dululu Rest Area | CT HT BIG RIG 🚰
Bryant St. Next to toilet block
07 4992 9500 **HEMA 16 D1** 23 50 54 S 150 15 40 E

Eidsvold
Eidsvold Dump Point | CT HT BIG RIG 🚰
Cnr Burnett Hwy & Esplanade St.
07 4160 3555 **HEMA 16 J3** 25 22 18 S 151 07 24 E

Einasleigh
Einasleigh Dump Point | CT HT BIG RIG 🚰
Baroota St.
07 4079 9090 **HEMA 26 F7** 18 30 44 S 144 05 36 E

Emerald
Emerald Showgrounds | CT HT BIG RIG 🚰
Capricorn Hwy.
0448 824 333 **HEMA 30 F6** 23 31 23 S 148 09 07 E

Eromanga
Eromanga Hall | CT HT
Deacon St.
07 4656 0540 **HEMA 33 C9** 26 40 12 S 143 16 00 E

Eulo
Eulo Dump Point | CT HT BIG RIG 🚰
Bulloo Development Rd. Outside airport, adjacent to toilets
07 4655 8470 **HEMA 33 G13** 28 09 46 S 145 02 43 E

Eumundi
Eumundi RV Stop Over | CT HT BIG RIG 🚰
Cnr Napier Rd & Albert St. At Parking Area
0412 566 671 **HEMA 11 B12** 26 28 34 S 152 57 13 E

QUEENSLAND

Fernvale
Fernvale Dump Point `CT` `HT` `BIG RIG`
Clive St.
07 5424 4000   **HEMA 4 E1**   27 27 14 S   152 39 01 E

Forsayth
Forsayth Rest Area `CT` `HT` `⛲`
Einasleigh-Forsayth Rd. Next to
the public toilet block
07 4079 9090   **HEMA 26 F6**   18 35 10 S   143 36 10 E

Fraser Island K'gari
Cornwells `CT` `HT`
75 Mile Beach Rd. 6 km N Eurong, at
beach entrance of Cornwells Break Rd. 4WD only
137 468   **HEMA 15 E6**   25 27 30 S   153 08 58 E

Dundubara `CT`
Fraser Island Beach Rd. Camp Area 8 km W
of Eurong, 75 km N of Hook Pt or 19 km S of Indian
Head. High clearance, off road 4WD only, sandy &
beach tracks
137 468   **HEMA 14 D7**   25 10 06 S   153 17 01 E

Hook Point `CT` `⛲`
75 Mile Beach Rd. 12 km N of Hook
Point Barge landing. Hook Point inland road and
11km beach access track intersection. 4WD only
137 468   **HEMA 14 J5**   25 42 23 S   153 04 32 E

Orchid Beach `CT` `HT`
Ngkala Rd. 400 m S of service station.
4WD only
137 468   **HEMA 14 C7**   24 57 37 S   153 18 54 E

Wanggoolba Creek Barge Landing `CT`
Wanggoolba Rd. Adjacent to toilet facilities.
4WD only
137 468   **HEMA 15 D1**   25 26 50 S   152 59 22 E

Woralie Road `CT`
75 Mile Beach Rd. At beach entrance Woralie
Rd, near K'gari private camp area. 4WD only
137 468   **HEMA 14 D6**   25 14 54 S   153 14 47 E

Gatton
Gatton Dump Point `CT` `HT` `⛲`
23 East St. William Kemp Park
1300 005 872   **HEMA 12 F2**   27 33 19 S   152 16 29 E

Gatton Showgrounds `CT` `HT` `BIG RIG`
Yates St. Behind toilet block, near
grassed area at rear of grounds
07 5462 2577   **HEMA 12 F2**   27 33 39 S   152 16 51 E

Gayndah
Zonhoven Park `CT` `HT` `⛲`
Burnett Hwy. E end of town
1300 696 272   **HEMA 16 K5**   25 37 44 S   151 37 33 E

Georgetown
Georgetown Dump Point `CT` `HT` `BIG RIG`
Normanton St. Opposite toilets in Heritage Park
07 4079 9090   **HEMA 26 F6**   18 17 30 S   143 32 53 E

Gin Gin
Gin Gin Dump Point `CT` `HT` `BIG RIG` `⛲`
Bruce Hwy. N end of town. L
side of gravel parking area opposite service stations
07 4130 4130   **HEMA 16 H6**   24 59 02 S   151 57 01 E

Glenden
Glenden Dump Point `CT` `HT` `BIG RIG`
Gilbert Ave. At Golf Club
1300 472 227   **HEMA 18 H3**   21 21 01 S   148 07 23 E

Goomeri
Goomeri Showgrounds `CT` `HT` `$` `BIG RIG` `⛲`
Burnett Hwy. Cnr Laird St. S end of town
0419 720 407   **HEMA 13 E2**   26 11 11 S   152 04 09 E

Goondiwindi
Caltex Truck Stop `CT` `HT` `BIG RIG` `⛲`
Boundary Rd. E end of town
07 4671 0999   **HEMA 35 H11**   28 31 42 S   150 18 37 E

Redmond Park `CT` `HT` `BIG RIG`
4 Andersen St. Near the
driver reviver area. Opposite Jolly Swagman Motor
Inn
07 4671 7400   **HEMA 35 H12**   28 33 01 S   150 19 12 E

Gordonvale
Greenpatch Reserve `CT` `HT` `BIG RIG`
Bruce Hwy. Exit N from Hwy
to service road, 500 m to camp entrance. Subject to
closures during flood events
1300 692 247   **HEMA 22 F7**   17 06 01 S   145 47 15 E

Gregory Downs
Council Dump Point `CT` `HT` `BIG RIG`
Wills Development Rd. Next
to the toilets
07 4745 5100   **HEMA 25 E4**   18 38 59 S   139 15 14 E

Gunpowder
World War 2 Historical Site `CT` `HT` `BIG RIG`
Barkly Hwy. Rest Area 50 km
NW of Mt Isa or 139 km E of Camooweal. Near
monument on Barkly Hwy
07 4747 3200   **HEMA 25 J4**   20 22 23 S   139 15 53 E

Gympie
Archery Park `CT` `HT` `BIG RIG`
Cross St. 4 km N of town
centre
1300 307 800   **HEMA 12 A4**   26 11 19 S   152 39 13 E

Six Mile Creek Rest Area `CT` `HT` `BIG RIG`
Bruce Hwy. 6 km S of Gympie
1300 307 800   **HEMA 13 E4**   26 13 54 S   152 41 49 E

Hervey Bay
Hervey Bay RV Stop `CT` `HT` `BIG RIG` `⛲`
227 Maryborough Hervey
Bay Rd. Hervey Bay Information Centre. Cnr
Urraween Rd, Urraween
1800 811 728   **HEMA 14 E4**   25 17 59 S   152 48 34 E

Home Hill
Home Hill Dump Point `CT` `HT` `BIG RIG`
Sixth St. W of railway
crossing
07 4783 9800   **HEMA 18 C1**   19 39 59 S   147 24 52 E

Hughenden
Allen Terry Caravan Park `CT` `HT` `BIG RIG`
2 Resolution St.
07 4741 1190   **HEMA 26 K7**   20 50 57 S   144 11 46 E

Hughenden Dump Point `CT` `HT` `BIG RIG`
Cnr McLaren & Swanston Sts. Near white tower
07 4741 2900   **HEMA 26 K7**   20 51 03 S   144 11 32 E

Ilfracombe
Ilfracombe Dump Point `CT` `HT` `BIG RIG`
Murray St. Opposite Caravan Park
07 4658 4111   **HEMA 29 F11**   23 29 27 S   144 30 37 E

Imbil
Imbil Showgrounds `CT` `HT` `BIG RIG`
Imbil Brooloo Rd.
0488 566 131   **HEMA 11 B8**   26 27 50 S   152 40 42 E

Ingham
Frances Creek `CT` `HT` `BIG RIG` `⛲`
Bruce Hwy. In Helens Hill, S
of Ingham. W of Hwy
132 380   **HEMA 19 E2**   18 44 52 S   146 08 14 E

Tyto Wetlands RV Stop
`CT` `HT` `BIG RIG` `⛲`
48 Cooper St. Cnr Bruce
Hwy. S of town on W side of Hwy
07 4776 4792   **HEMA 19 E2**   18 39 18 S   146 09 11 E

Inglewood
Inglewood Rest Area `CT` `HT` `BIG RIG`
Brook St. Off Hwy at E end
of town. Good access for Big Rigs
07 4671 7400   **HEMA 35 H13**   28 24 51 S   151 05 02 E

Injune
Injune Truck Stop `CT` `HT` `BIG RIG`
Hutton St. Near roadhouse
1300 007 662   **HEMA 34 A7**   25 50 24 S   148 34 03 E

Innisfail
Innisfail Dump Point `CT` `HT` `BIG RIG`
Bruce Hwy. Haddrell Park,
Opposite Barrier Reef Motel. S side of town
07 4030 2222   **HEMA 21 J6**   17 32 01 S   146 01 47 E

Ipswich
Ipswich Showgrounds `CT` `HT` `BIG RIG` `⛲`
Cnr Warwick & Salisbury Rds.
07 3281 1577   **HEMA 4 G2**   27 37 38 S   152 45 33 E

Isisford
Barcoo River Weir `CT` `HT` `BIG RIG` `⛲`
St Frances St. At toilet
block, SE end of town
07 4658 8900   **HEMA 29 G11**   24 15 28 S   144 26 36 E

Jandowae
Jandowae Dump Point `CT` `HT` `BIG RIG` `⛲`
Dalby St. Between High &
Hickey Sts. Adjacent to Lions Park, N side of town
07 4679 4000   **HEMA 35 C13**   26 46 45 S   151 06 33 E

Jandowae Showgrounds `CT` `HT` `BIG RIG` `⛲`
80 Warra St. Older style system with manual cover
0458 595 796   **HEMA 35 C13**   26 47 13 S   151 06 38 E

Jericho
Jericho Showground `CT` `HT` `BIG RIG` `⛲`
Showgrounds Rd. 1 km NE
of Jericho, at E end of town, turn N just E of railway
crossing
07 4651 4129   **HEMA 29 F14**   23 35 45 S   146 07 53 E

Jondaryan
Jondaryan Woolshed `CT` `HT` `BIG RIG`
264 Jondaryan Evanslea Rd. 3 km
S of Jondaryan
07 4692 2229   **HEMA 35 E14**   27 23 32 S   151 34 30 E

Julia Creek
Julia Creek Dump Point `CT` `HT` `BIG RIG` `⛲`
Hickman St. Near Jcn of Allison St
07 4746 7166   **HEMA 26 K4**   20 39 10 S   141 44 30 E

Julia Creek Racecourse `CT` `HT` `BIG RIG` `⛲`
Kynuna Road. Via main entrance, go straight then
verge left to other gate. Near the blue toilet block.
GPS at entry
0428 464 001   **HEMA 28 A7**   20 39 50 S   141 44 32 E

Jundah
Jundah Dump Point `CT` `HT` `BIG RIG` `⛲`
Thomson Developmental
Rd. 800 m N of Jundah, near turn off to outpatient
entrance
07 4658 6900   **HEMA 29 H9**   24 49 11 S   143 03 52 E

Kalbar
Kalbar Showground `CT` `HT` `BIG RIG` `⛲`
107 George St. N end of
town
0499 970 119   **HEMA 6 G3**   27 56 15 S   152 37 32 E

Public Dump Points

Karumba
Truck Stop CT HT BIG RIG 💧
Cnr of Yappar and Walker St.
07 4745 2200   HEMA 25 C7   17 29 29 S   140 50 07 E

Kenilworth
Kenilworth Showground CT HT BIG RIG
3742 Maleny Kenilworth Rd. Elizabeth St. S side of town
0438 849 947   HEMA 11 D9   26 35 57 S   152 43 35 E

Kerry
Darlington Park CT HT $ BIG RIG
2505 Kerry Rd.
07 5544 8120   HEMA 7 K8   28 11 04 S   153 02 26 E

Kia Ora
Standown Park CT HT $ BIG RIG 💧
91 Radtke Rd. Turn N of Tin Can Bay Rd
07 5486 5144   HEMA 13 E5   26 02 08 S   152 47 32 E

Kilcoy
Kilcoy Showgrounds HT BIG RIG
26 Showground Rd.
07 5422 0440   HEMA 10 J6   26 56 37 S   152 32 45 E

Kilkivan
Weir Oval CT HT BIG RIG 💧
Wide Bay Hwy. Beside the toilet block
1300 307 800   HEMA 13 E3   26 05 01 S   152 14 33 E

Killarney
Killarney Sundown Motel HT $ BIG RIG 💧
2 Pine St. Free for guests
07 4664 1318   HEMA 12 J3   28 20 29 S   152 17 46 E

Kingaroy
Kingaroy Dump Point CT HT BIG RIG
Via Alford St. In carpark behind main street shops
07 4189 9100   HEMA 12 B1   26 32 25 S   151 50 25 E

Lions Park CT HT 💧
Baron St. Off Kingaroy St
07 4189 9100   HEMA 12 B1   26 32 47 S   151 50 16 E

Laidley
Laidley Dump Point CT HT BIG RIG 💧
John St. Near swimming pool
1300 005 872   HEMA 12 F3   27 37 55 S   152 23 34 E

Lawnton
Pine Rivers Showground CT HT BIG RIG
757 Gympie Rd. Sun-Fri from 8am-5pm. Water for washdown only, no filling tanks, water limited
0459 023 346   HEMA 4 C4   27 17 07 S   152 59 13 E

Longreach
Longreach Dump Point CT HT BIG RIG 💧
Cnr Landsborough Hwy & Kite St.
07 4658 4111   HEMA 29 F11   23 26 24 S   144 14 57 E

Lowood
Lowood Showgrounds CT HT BIG RIG 💧
14 Station St. Turn L at entry, between buildings
0455 187 201   HEMA 8 H2   27 27 45 S   152 35 01 E

Mackay
Mackay Visitor Centre CT HT BIG RIG 💧
320 Nebo Rd. In West Mackay. Access from N bound only. Turn in between BP & Info Centre. On L
07 4961 9444   HEMA 17 A1   21 09 56 S   149 09 14 E

Maleny
Maleny Showgrounds CT HT $ BIG RIG 💧
13 Maleny Stanley River Rd. Donation for water
07 5494 2008   HEMA 11 F10   26 45 47 S   152 50 44 E

Manly
Manly Boat Harbour CT 💧
Davenport Dr.
133 263   HEMA 4 E6   27 27 37 S   153 11 21 E

Mareeba
Eales Park Dump Point CT HT BIG RIG 💧
Doyle St. Opposite Davies Park. W side of town
07 4086 4500   HEMA 22 D1   16 59 42 S   145 24 50 E

Maroochydore
Maroochydore Dump Point CT HT BIG RIG 💧
Commercial Rd. Business hours only. For key contact treatment plant admin office
07 5431 8333   HEMA 11 E13   26 39 09 S   153 03 34 E

Maryborough
Maryborough Airport CT HT BIG RIG 💧
Airport Dr. Via Saltwater Creek Rd. Follow signs around to right. 2 km from town on way to Hervey Bay
1300 794 929   HEMA 14 G3   25 31 06 S   152 42 33 E

Maryborough
Maryborough Showground & Equestrian Park CT HT BIG RIG 💧
23349 Bruce Hwy. N end of town. Veer R past entry gates
07 4122 3584   HEMA 14 G3   25 30 22 S   152 39 46 E

McKinlay
McKinlay Dump Point CT HT BIG RIG 💧
Middleton St. At the truck stop
07 4746 7166   HEMA 26 K3   21 16 14 S   141 17 23 E

Meandarra
Leo Gordon Apex Park CT HT BIG RIG 💧
Payne St.
07 4679 4000   HEMA 35 E10   27 19 24 S   149 52 50 E

Miles
Miles Council Dump Point CT HT BIG RIG 💧
Industry Lane. Via Leichhardt Hwy
07 4679 4000   HEMA 35 C11   26 39 59 S   150 11 07 E

Millmerran
Millmerran Showgrounds CT HT BIG RIG 💧
Millmerran Cecil Plains Rd.
07 4695 4151   HEMA 35 F14   27 51 37 S   151 16 40 E

Walpole Park CT HT BIG RIG 💧
6 Walpole St. Charles St, between Walpole & Charlotte Sts. Dump Point opposite park
131 872   HEMA 35 F14   27 52 17 S   151 16 28 E

Mirani
Mirani Dump Point CT HT BIG RIG 💧
Victoria St. Opposite council customer service centre
07 4961 9444   HEMA 18 G6   21 09 34 S   148 51 52 E

Miriam Vale
Miriam Vale Dump Point CT HT BIG RIG 💧
Blomfield St. Cnr Dougall St. Opposite train station, open 24 hrs
07 4970 0700   HEMA 16 E5   24 19 42 S   151 33 41 E

Mission Beach
Mission Beach Dump Point CT HT BIG RIG 💧
53 Porter Promenade. Outside caravan park
07 4030 2222   HEMA 19 B2   17 51 53 S   146 06 29 E

Mitchell
Mitchell Showgrounds CT HT BIG RIG 💧
Alice St. Near entrance
07 4622 2325   HEMA 34 B6   26 29 47 S   147 58 45 E

Moffatdale
Yallakool Caravan Park CT HT BIG RIG 💧
Haager Dr. Bjelke Petersen Dam. In parking area opposite tennis courts
07 4168 4746   HEMA 12 A1   26 18 17 S   151 59 41 E

Monto
Monto Community Rest Stop CT HT BIG RIG 💧
Lister St. At railway yard and RV park, turn L
07 4166 9999   HEMA 16 G3   24 51 46 S   151 07 15 E

Monto Showground CT HT BIG RIG 💧
Oxley St. W side of town
07 4160 3555   HEMA 16 G3   24 51 57 S   151 06 53 E

Morven
Morven Rec Ground CT HT BIG RIG 💧
Nebine Rd. S side of town via Victoria St
07 4656 8355   HEMA 34 B4   26 25 06 S   147 06 58 E

Mossman
Mossman Dump Point CT HT BIG RIG 💧
Cnr Foxton Ave & Park St. Outside aquatic centre
07 4099 9444   HEMA 21 A2   16 27 18 S   145 22 18 E

Mount Isa
Mount Isa Dump Point CT HT BIG RIG 💧
Arline St. Rear of complex, next to Royal Flying Doctor Service
07 4747 3200   HEMA 25 J4   20 43 16 S   139 30 10 E

Mount Molloy
Rifle Creek Rest Area CT HT BIG RIG 💧
Mulligan Hwy. Rest Area 1 km N of Mt Molloy, 33 km S of Mossman or 41 km N of Mareeba
07 4086 4500   HEMA 21 C2   16 39 58 S   145 19 42 E

Mount Morgan
Mount Morgan Motel CT HT $ BIG RIG
Cnr Burnett Hwy & Showgrounds Rd.
07 4938 1952   HEMA 16 C1   23 39 41 S   150 23 15 E

Mount Perry
Mount Perry Dump Point CT HT BIG RIG 💧
54 Heusman St. In front of Caravan Park
07 4160 3555   HEMA 13 A1   25 10 29 S   151 38 24 E

Mount Surprise
Mount Surprise Dump Point CT HT BIG RIG 💧
Gulf Developmental Rd. Outside toilet block
07 4079 9090   HEMA 26 F7   18 08 50 S   144 19 03 E

Moura
Moura Dump Point CT HT BIG RIG 💧
Moura Bindaree Rd. E end of town
07 4992 9500   HEMA 31 H9   24 33 54 S   149 58 27 E

Mundubbera
Mundubbera Dump Point CT HT BIG RIG 💧
Bauer St, near Lyons St & tennis courts
07 4160 3555   HEMA 16 K4   25 35 33 S   151 18 03 E

QUEENSLAND

Mungallala
Mungallala RV Stop
CT HT BIG RIG 💧
4379 Warrego Hwy. Camp
Spot at Mungallala
1300 007 662　　HEMA 34 B5　26 26 44 S　147 32 29 E

Murgon
Murgon RV Stop
CT HT BIG RIG
3 Krebs St.
07 4189 9387　　HEMA 12 A1　26 14 32 S　151 56 17 E

Muttaburra
Muttaburra Caravan
Park
CT HT BIG RIG 💧
17 Bridge St. Caravan Park at Muttaburra. Cnr Mary St
07 4658 7191　　HEMA 29 D11　22 35 36 S　144 33 07 E

Nambour
Nambour Dump Point
CT HT BIG RIG 💧
Bli Bli Rd. Located in the
side road on the S side of roundabout when taking
the W exit off Hwy. Signposted. Open 24/7
07 5431 8333　　HEMA 11 D12　26 36 59 S　152 58 44 E

Nanango
Tipperary Flat Park
CT HT BIG RIG 💧
D'Aguilar Hwy. Apex Park
1.5 km S of PO. Next to BP service station
07 4189 9446　　HEMA 13 G2　26 40 48 S　151 59 47 E

Nebo
Nebo Rest Area
CT HT BIG RIG
Peak Downs Hwy.
1300 472 227　　HEMA 18 J5　21 40 58 S　148 41 34 E

Nindigully
Nindigully Pub
CT HT BIG RIG
Sternes St. At the rear of
new toilet block, near hotel
07 4625 9637　　HEMA 35 G8　28 21 17 S　148 49 15 E

Normanton
Normanton Works
Depot
CT HT BIG RIG 💧
Old Hospital Rd. Business hours only. Own hose
required for HT
07 4745 2200　　HEMA 25 D7　17 40 51 S　141 04 36 E

Oakey
Oakey Dump Point
CT HT BIG RIG 💧
York St. Next to Works
Depot. Cnr Lorrimer St
07 4688 6611　　HEMA 12 F1　27 26 27 S　151 43 27 E

Petrie
Wyllie Park Rest Area
CT HT BIG RIG
980 Gympie Rd. Old Bruce Hwy,
beside North Pine River. Gates open 8am-6pm
132 380　　HEMA 4 C4　27 16 22 S　152 58 49 E

Pittsworth
Pittsworth Dump Point
CT HT BIG RIG 💧
Railways St. Outside
showgrounds next to SES building
131 872　　HEMA 36 F2　27 42 41 S　151 38 31 E

Pomona
Pomona Showgrounds
CT HT BIG RIG
15 Pavilion St. Entry via
Exhibition St
0490 195 374　　HEMA 12 A4　26 21 36 S　152 51 28 E

Proserpine
Proserpine Dump Point
CT HT BIG RIG
79 Anzac Rd. On road outside
Caravan Park
1300 972 753　　HEMA 18 E5　20 24 14 S　148 34 17 E

Quilpie
Quilpie Dump Point
CT HT BIG RIG 💧
Quarrion St. John Waugh
Park
07 4656 0540　　HEMA 33 C11　26 36 57 S　144 15 46 E

Rainbow Beach
Rainbow Beach
Sewerage Works
CT HT BIG RIG 💧
Clarkson Dr. By sewerage pumping station
1300 307 800　　HEMA 14 K6　25 54 03 S　153 05 18 E

Ravenshoe
Ravenshoe Dump Point
CT HT BIG RIG 💧
Ascham St. Outside
sewerage works
1300 362 242　　HEMA 21 K3　17 36 55 S　145 28 49 E

Ravenswood
Burdekin Falls Dam
Caravan Park
HT BIG RIG 💧
11950 Burdekin Falls Dam Rd.
07 4770 3177　　HEMA 18 F1　20 38 29 S　147 08 47 E

Redcliffe
Redcliffe Showgrounds
CT HT BIG RIG 💧
Scarborough Rd. Near
hospital. Daylight hours only. Unavailable during
events & Jun-Aug
07 3284 5387　　HEMA 4 C5　27 13 30 S　153 06 22 E

Richmond
Richmond RV Park
CT HT BIG RIG 💧
1 Hillier St. 300 m E of main
road, via Harris St
07 4719 3390　　HEMA 26 K6　20 43 44 S　143 08 36 E

Rockhampton
Music Bowl Park
CT HT BIG RIG 💧
Nuttall Rd. Off Hwy, N of
city at Parkhurst. Across from sports fields
07 4932 9000　　HEMA 16 B2　23 19 08 S　150 30 51 E

Rolleston
Beazley Park
CT HT BIG RIG 💧
Meteor St. In Beazley Park,
opposite side of Dawson Hwy
132 380　　HEMA 30 G7　24 27 48 S　148 37 28 E

Rollingstone
Bushy Parker Park
CT HT BIG RIG 💧
Rollingstone St. Turn E off
Hwy, just N of Rollingstone, across railway line to
Rest Area
134 810　　HEMA 19 F3　19 02 46 S　146 23 37 E

Roma
Roma Dump Point
CT HT BIG RIG 💧
Station St. Between Lewis
& Major Sts
1300 007 662　　HEMA 35 C8　26 34 34 S　148 47 46 E

Roma Showgrounds
CT HT BIG RIG 💧
Carnarvon Hwy. Northern
Rd. N end of town
1300 007 662　　HEMA 35 C8　26 33 13 S　148 47 06 E

Rosewood
Rosewood Showground
CT HT BIG RIG 💧
Railway St.
0481 382 049　　HEMA 8 K2　27 38 25 S　152 35 58 E

Sandstone Point
Sandstone Point
CT HT BIG RIG 💧
1813 – 1819 Bribie Island Rd.
07 3205 0555　　HEMA 4 A6　27 04 25 S　153 08 29 E

Sapphire
Sapphire Reserve
CT HT BIG RIG
Rifle Range Rd. Opposite
general store
1300 242 686　　HEMA 30 F5　23 27 57 S　147 43 12 E

Sarina
Sarina Dump Point
CT HT BIG RIG 💧
1 Railway Square. Tourist
Centre, off the Bruce Hwy
07 4961 9444　　HEMA 17 B2　21 25 33 S　149 13 02 E

Scarborough
Scarborough Boat Ramp
CT HT
Thurecht Pde. Next to public
toilets, raised off the ground, open 24/7
07 3205 0555　　HEMA 4 B5　27 11 39 S　153 06 15 E

Seisia
Seisia Holiday Park
CT HT 💧
6 Koraba Rd.
07 4203 0992　　HEMA 24 B4　10 50 51 S　142 22 05 E

Seventeen Seventy
Council Depot 1770
CT HT BIG RIG 💧
Captain Cook Dr. 4.2 km N
of Round Hill Rd intersection. Turn L at SES HQ sign
07 4970 0700　　HEMA 16 E5　24 10 49 S　151 52 59 E

Shorncliffe
Shorncliffe Boat Ramp
CT 💧
Sinbad St. In boat ramp car park. Next
to toilet block. Cassettes only, raised off ground
133 263　　HEMA 4 D5　27 20 02 S　153 04 50 E

Springsure
Springsure Dump Point
CT HT 💧
William St. At toilet block near
museum, on Hwy
1300 242 686　　HEMA 30 G6　24 07 05 S　148 05 22 E

St George
St George Showground
CT HT BIG RIG
McGahan St. Behind E end
of showground
07 4620 8888　　HEMA 35 G8　28 01 39 S　148 35 27 E

St Lawrence
St Lawrence Rec
Reserve
CT HT BIG RIG
624 St Lawrence Connection Rd. 1 km W of St
Lawrence
1300 472 227　　HEMA 17 F3　22 21 04 S　149 31 11 E

Stanthorpe
Apex Park
CT HT BIG RIG 💧
Folkestone St. Off Maryland
St at toilet block
1300 697 372　　HEMA 36 H3　28 39 29 S　151 55 55 E

Stokes
Bang Bang Rest Area
CT HT BIG RIG 💧
Burke Developmental Rd.
Rest Area 112 km S of Normanton or 90 km N of
Burke & Wills Roadhouse
132 380　　HEMA 25 E6　18 31 36 S　140 39 11 E

Stonehenge
Isisford Road Rest Area
CT HT BIG RIG
Jundah Longreach Rd. Rest Area
121 km S of Longreach or 96 km N of Jundah
132 380　　HEMA 29 G10　24 14 01 S　143 33 27 E

Surat
Surat Fishing &
Restocking Club Park
CT HT BIG RIG 💧
Carnarvon Hwy. 1 km N of Surat at Noorindoo
07 4626 5136　　HEMA 35 D9　27 08 57 S　149 04 23 E

Talwood
Talwood Rec Ground
CT HT BIG RIG 💧
Recreation St.
07 4671 7400　　HEMA 35 H10　28 29 12 S　149 28 08 E

QUEENSLAND

Tambo
Tambo Lake `CT` `HT` `BIG RIG` `tap`
Landsborough Hwy. S end of town
132 380   **HEMA 29 H14**   24 52 55 S   146 15 35 E

Tara
Tara Lagoon Parklands `CT` `HT` `BIG RIG` `tap`
Showground Rd. In Camp Area at Tara Lagoon
07 4679 4000   **HEMA 35 E12**   27 16 21 S   150 27 36 E

Taroom
Taroom Dump Point `CT` `HT` `BIG RIG` `tap`
Wolsey St. 700 m N of PO. Outside council depot
07 4992 9500   **HEMA 31 J9**   25 38 03 S   149 47 56 E

Texas
Texas Dump Point `CT` `HT` `BIG RIG` `tap`
Flemming St. Outside council depot
07 4671 7400   **HEMA 35 J13**   28 51 12 S   151 10 25 E

Thallon
Thallon Rec Ground `CT` `HT` `BIG RIG` `tap`
William Rd.
07 4620 8888   **HEMA 35 H8**   28 37 58 S   148 51 59 E

Thargomindah
Thargomindah Dump Point `CT` `HT` `BIG RIG` `tap`
Watts St. Off Adventure Way. N of town, opposite council building near cooling ponds
07 4621 8095   **HEMA 33 F10**   27 59 23 S   143 49 11 E

Theodore
Theodore Dump Point `CT` `HT` `BIG RIG` `tap`
Eastern Lane. Off 7th Avenue. Next to tennis courts
07 4992 9500   **HEMA 31 H9**   24 56 43 S   150 04 36 E

Three Rivers
Terry Smith Lookout `CT` `HT` `BIG RIG`
Burke Developmental Rd. Rest Area 103 km S of Burke & Wills Roadhouse or 78 km N of Cloncurry
132 380   **HEMA 25 H6**   20 04 49 S   140 13 39 E

Tin Can Bay
Tin Can Bay Dump Point `CT` `HT` `BIG RIG` `tap`
Snapper Creek Rd. Turning point 100 m further, near the Tin Can Bay Tip
1300 307 800   **HEMA 14 K5**   25 55 24 S   152 59 27 E

Tinnanbar
Hedleys Campground `CT` `HT`
Reserved Esplanade. Follow Cooloola Coast Rd 38 km SE of Maryborough, E to Tinnanbar Rd for 10.5 km to turn off, located midway along campground access road. 4WD only
137 468   **HEMA 14 J5**   25 47 55 S   152 56 50 E

Toogoolawah
Toogoolawah Showgrounds `CT` `HT` `$` `BIG RIG`
30 Ivory Creek Rd. Drive straight ahead through gate, on your R
0417 738 590   **HEMA 12 D3**   27 04 41 S   152 22 31 E

Toowoomba
Toowoomba Showground `CT` `HT` `$` `BIG RIG` `tap`
Glenvale Rd. 8am-5pm Mon to Fri
07 4634 7400   **HEMA 12 F1**   27 33 36 S   151 53 04 E

Townsville
Puma Bohle Little Acre `CT` `HT` `BIG RIG` `tap`
900 Ingham Rd. At rear of service station. Daylight hours only. Key deposit
07 4766 9581   **HEMA 19 G4**   19 15 43 S   146 42 53 E

Ross River Dam `CT` `HT` `BIG RIG` `tap`
Riverway Drv. At Kelso, S of Townsville. Near entrance to Ross River Dam Park
134 810   **HEMA 19 H4**   19 24 27 S   146 44 00 E

Willows Shopping Centre `CT` `HT` `BIG RIG` `tap`
Kern Brothers Dr. In shopping centre car park, Thuringowa Central. S side on far right
07 4799 9100   **HEMA 19 G4**   19 19 02 S   146 43 31 E

Tully
Tully Showground `CT` `HT` `BIG RIG` `tap`
Butler St. Outside showgrounds
07 4030 2222   **HEMA 19 B2**   17 56 02 S   145 55 47 E

Wallumbilla
Wallumbilla Showgrounds `CT` `HT` `BIG RIG` `tap`
Warrego Hwy. On main road, W end of town
1300 007 662   **HEMA 35 C9**   26 35 14 S   149 11 01 E

Wandoan
Wandoan Dump Point `CT` `HT` `BIG RIG` `tap`
28-30 Jerrard St. Near water tower
07 4679 4000   **HEMA 35 A11**   26 07 21 S   149 57 35 E

Warwick
Matilda Roadhouse `CT` `HT` `BIG RIG` `tap`
Cnr Cunningham Hwy & Ogilvie Rd. N end of town
1300 697 372   **HEMA 12 J2**   28 11 41 S   152 02 39 E

Weipa
Weipa Dump Point `CT` `HT` `BIG RIG` `tap`
Kerr Point Rd. Outside Weipa Camping Ground
07 4030 9400   **HEMA 23 D1**   12 38 23 S   141 51 42 E

Windorah
Morney Rest Area `CT` `HT` `BIG RIG` `tap`
Diamantina Dev Rd. Rest Area 108 km W of Windorah or 95 km E of Betoota on the Diamantina Dev Rd
132 380   **HEMA 28 J7**   25 22 50 S   141 37 24 E

Windorah Dump Point `CT` `HT` `BIG RIG` `tap`
Diamantina Dev Rd. Near water tower. E side of town
07 4658 6900   **HEMA 29 J8**   25 25 04 S   142 39 35 E

Winton
Winton Dump Point `CT` `HT` `BIG RIG` `tap`
Landsborough Hwy. Cnr of Riley & Jundah Rds
07 4658 6900   **HEMA 29 D9**   22 23 30 S   143 02 23 E

Winton Rec Ground `CT` `HT` `BIG RIG` `tap`
Vindex St. Next to skate park
07 4658 6900   **HEMA 29 D9**   22 23 14 S   143 01 56 E

Wondai
Wondai RV Stop `CT` `HT` `BIG RIG`
Haly St. Adjacent to old rail station
07 4189 9251   **HEMA 12 A1**   26 19 02 S   151 52 26 E

Woodford
Woodford Showgrounds `CT` `HT` `BIG RIG`
38 Neurum Rd.
0437 390 862   **HEMA 11 J9**   26 56 51 S   152 46 12 E

Wyandra
Wyandra Dump Point `CT` `HT` `BIG RIG` `tap`
Mack St. Near Cooper St
07 4655 8470   **HEMA 34 D1**   27 14 44 S   145 58 43 E

Yeppoon
Merv Anderson Park `CT` `HT` `BIG RIG` `tap`
Yeppoon Emu Park Rd. 200 m E of Visitor Info Centre
07 4913 5000   **HEMA 16 B2**   23 08 16 S   150 45 00 E

Yowah
Yowah Rest Area `CT` `HT` `BIG RIG` `tap`
Gemwood St. First turn L after school
07 4655 8470   **HEMA 33 F12**   27 58 01 S   144 37 59 E

Yungaburra
Yungaburra Dump Point `CT` `HT` `BIG RIG` `tap`
Lot 550 Mulgrave Rd. On road outside sewerage works
1300 362 242   **HEMA 22 J4**   17 15 45 S   145 34 44 E

NEW SOUTH WALES

Aberdeen
Taylor Park `CT` `HT` `BIG RIG` `tap`
New England Hwy. N end of town. At fence on N side of park
02 6549 3891   **HEMA 54 H6**   32 09 39 S   150 53 18 E

Abermain
Abermain Bowling & Rec Club `CT` `HT` `BIG RIG` `tap`
Cnr Goulburn & Armidale Sts. Key at reception
02 4930 4285   **HEMA 45 H7**   32 48 26 S   151 25 36 E

Adelong
Adelong Dump Point `CT` `HT` `BIG RIG` `tap`
Travers St. Off Snowy Mountain Hwy
02 6947 7025   **HEMA 66 C5**   35 18 24 S   148 03 42 E

Albury
Albury City Dump Point `CT` `HT` `BIG RIG` `tap`
Railway Pl. Enter at Cnr Smollett & Young Sts to railway station, turn S to dump location
1300 252 879   **HEMA 66 G1**   36 05 07 S   146 55 26 E

Appin
Appin Park Rest Area `CT` `HT` `BIG RIG`
Appin Rd. Entry at N of Park
HEMA 51 B11   34 11 53 S   150 47 19 E

Arakoon
Trial Bay Gaol Dump Point `CT` `HT` `tap`
Trial Bay Gaol Access Rd. Next to amenities block in day use area. Deposit & key collection from office at campground
1300 072 757   **HEMA 55 C13**   30 52 37 S   153 04 19 E

Ariah Park
Ariah Park Dump Point `CT` `HT` `tap`
Cnr Barnes St & Mary Gilmore Way. Entry via Barnes St. For vehicles less than 11 m. Potable water
HEMA 69 A14   34 21 11 S   147 13 16 E

Armidale
Armidale Dump Point `CT` `HT` `BIG RIG` `tap`
Galloway St. 1 km S of city, off Waterfall Way. Follow signs for Arboretum
02 6770 3888   **HEMA 55 A8**   30 31 15 S   151 38 47 E

Arrawarra
Arrawarra Rest Area `CT` `HT` `BIG RIG` `tap`
Arrawarra Beach Rd. Turn off Hwy via overpass to E side of Hwy & turn N onto Eggins Rd. 4 hour limit
132 213   **HEMA 57 J13**   30 03 34 S   153 11 10 E

NEW SOUTH WALES

Ashford
Ashford Caravan Park [CT] [HT] [BIG RIG] [tap]
Bukkulla St. 57 km N of Inverell
02 6728 8161 HEMA 56 F5 29 19 24 S 151 05 52 E

Balranald
Greenham Park RV Stop [CT] [HT] [BIG RIG]
Church St. In car park next to water tower
03 5020 1599 HEMA 62 H7 34 38 07 S 143 33 43 E

Baradine
Baradine Dump Point [CT] [HT] [BIG RIG] [tap]
Cnr Wellington & Darling Sts. At Lions Park
02 6843 4011 HEMA 58 H4 30 56 59 S 149 04 00 E

Barellan
Barellan Dump Point [CT] [HT] [BIG RIG] [tap]
Myall St. Beside hall
02 6959 5545 HEMA 63 G14 34 17 06 S 146 34 16 E

Barmedman
Barmedman Dump Point [CT] [HT] [BIG RIG] [tap]
67 De Boos St. At Rec Ground & Camp Area near Cnr Star St. Potable water separate to wash down tap
0414 595 960 HEMA 64 G2 34 08 33 S 147 23 18 E

Barooga
Barooga Dump Point [CT] [HT] [BIG RIG]
Nangunia St. Adjacent to the Lions bus shelter
03 5888 5100 HEMA 69 H8 35 54 25 S 145 41 44 E

Barraba
Council Works Depot [CT] [HT] [BIG RIG] [tap]
77 Cherry St. Outside depot
02 6782 1255 HEMA 54 A5 30 22 49 S 150 36 46 E

Batehaven
City Park [CT]
Beach Rd. Car park opposite shops. Access may be blocked by cars
1800 802 528 HEMA 67 E12 35 43 53 S 150 12 00 E

Bathurst
Bathurst Council Depot [CT] [HT] [BIG RIG] [tap]
Morrisset St. Access 24/7, both sides of road
02 6336 6011 HEMA 52 D5 33 24 10 S 149 34 26 E

Bathurst Showground [CT] [HT] [BIG RIG] [tap]
Kendell Ave. Fee for water
02 6331 1349 HEMA 52 D5 33 25 05 S 149 35 22 E

Batlow
Batlow Dump Point [CT] [HT] [BIG RIG] [tap]
Memorial Ave. Opposite Wakehurst Ave
02 6947 7025 HEMA 66 D5 35 31 12 S 148 09 00 E

Bega
Bega Showgrounds [CT] [HT] [BIG RIG] [tap]
33 Upper St. Beside toilets
0424 051 901 HEMA 67 J11 36 40 40 S 149 50 50 E

Bellingen
Bellingen Dump Point [CT] [HT] [tap]
Black St. Opposite Bellingen Showground
02 6655 2310 HEMA 55 A13 30 26 55 S 152 53 54 E

Bendeela
Bendeela Recreation Area [CT] [tap]
Bendeela Rd. In Camp Area 7 km W of Kangaroo Valley. Near toilet block in campgrounds 1 & 2
1300 662 077 HEMA 51 J8 34 44 21 S 150 28 15 E

Berridale
Berridale Dump Point [CT] [HT] [tap]
1 Middlingbank Rd. At rear of the Southern Cross Motor Inn
02 6456 3289 HEMA 66 H7 36 21 30 S 148 49 52 E

Berrigan
Berrigan Dump Point [CT] [HT]
Jerilderie St. Hayes Park
03 5888 5100 HEMA 69 G9 35 39 38 S 145 48 50 E

Berry
Berry Showground [CT] [HT] [BIG RIG]
35 Alexandra St. 500 m S of PO
02 4421 0778 HEMA 51 J10 34 46 46 S 150 41 46 E

Bigga
Bigga Recreation Ground [CT] [HT] [BIG RIG]
Mulgowrie St. 250 m N of PO
02 4835 2347 HEMA 52 G3 34 04 58 S 149 09 08 E

Bingara
Bingara Saleyards Dump Point [CT] [HT] [BIG RIG]
Riddell St. Inside 2nd entrance gate
02 6724 0066 HEMA 56 H4 29 52 49 S 150 34 19 E

Cunningham Park [CT] [HT] [BIG RIG]
Copeton Dam Rd. Fee for water
02 6724 0066 HEMA 56 H4 29 51 51 S 150 34 35 E

Binnaway
Pumphouse Reserve [CT] [HT] [BIG RIG]
Bullinda St. At Camp Area Cnr Castlereagh Ave
0400 477 355 HEMA 54 F1 31 32 48 S 149 22 44 E

Blayney
Henry St Toilet Block [CT] [HT] [tap]
Henry St. S end, behind PO
02 6368 2104 HEMA 52 E4 33 31 58 S 149 15 23 E

Boggabri
Jubilee Park [CT] [HT] [BIG RIG]
Hull St. In sportsground, next to the entrance
02 6799 6760 HEMA 54 B3 30 42 20 S 150 02 56 E

Bombala
Bombala Caravan Park [CT] [HT]
Monaro Hwy. Pay fee to office
0488 257 928 HEMA 67 K9 36 54 30 S 149 14 20 E

Bonalbo
Bonalbo Tourist Park [CT] [HT] [$] [BIG RIG]
1 Woodenbong Rd. Free for guests
0428 989 727 HEMA 57 C11 28 44 19 S 152 37 43 E

Boomi
Boomi Dump Point [CT] [HT] [BIG RIG]
36 Boomi St. Behind a shed and tree
HEMA 58 B6 28 43 30 S 149 34 42 E

Boorowa
Boorowa Dump Point [CT] [HT] [BIG RIG]
Park St. Next to Caravan Park
1800 628 233 HEMA 52 J2 34 26 01 S 148 43 12 E

Bourke
Back O Bourke Information Centre [CT] [HT] [BIG RIG]
Mitchell Hwy.
08 6872 1321 HEMA 61 D11 30 04 51 S 145 57 00 E

Braidwood
Braidwood Dump Point [CT] [HT] [BIG RIG]
McKellar St. N side of town
02 4842 9231 HEMA 67 D11 35 26 24 S 149 48 07 E

Branxton
Branxton Oval [CT] [HT] [BIG RIG] [tap]
John Rose Ave.
02 4993 6700 HEMA 45 A5 32 39 18 S 151 21 05 E

Brewarrina
Brewarrina Dump Point [CT] [HT] [BIG RIG]
50 Bathurst St. Behind Info Centre, only accessible when open. 0900-1700 weekdays
02 6830 5152 HEMA 61 D13 29 57 35 S 146 51 28 E

Broken Hill
Broken Hill Info Centre [CT] [HT] [BIG RIG] [tap]
Cnr Bromide & Blende Sts. Key at Kintore Headframe Reserve, near Info Centre
08 8080 3560 HEMA 62 A2 31 57 34 S 141 27 39 E

Broken Hill Racecourse [CT] [HT] [$] [BIG RIG]
Racecourse Rd. 5 km NE of Broken Hill, off Tibooburra Rd. Fee if not staying at racecourse
0437 250 286 HEMA 60 H2 31 54 48 S 141 28 51 E

Bulahdelah
Bulahdelah Showgrounds [CT] [HT] [BIG RIG]
17 Prince St. Near helipad
02 4997 4981 HEMA 55 J10 32 24 18 S 152 12 16 E

Bungendore
Bungendore Showground [CT] [HT] [BIG RIG] [tap]
Matthews Ln. On the Bungendore-Sutton Rd. See caretaker
0455 174 463 HEMA 71 C7 35 14 30 S 149 24 37 E

Burren Junction
Burren Junction Bore Baths [CT] [HT] [BIG RIG]
Kamilaroi Hwy.
02 6828 6100 HEMA 58 F4 30 06 52 S 148 59 44 E

Bylong
Bylong Community Sportsground [CT] [HT] [BIG RIG] [tap]
7690 Bylong Valley Way. Oopposite store
02 6379 8252 HEMA 54 K3 32 24 58 S 150 06 52 E

Canowindra
Canowindra Caravan Park [CT] [HT] [BIG RIG] [tap]
1 Tilga St. Next to swimming pool. 300 m S of PO
0428 634 410 HEMA 52 E2 33 34 08 S 148 39 50 E

Canowindra Showgrounds [CT] [HT] [BIG RIG] [tap]
199 Rodd St.
02 6344 1886 HEMA 52 E2 33 33 09 S 148 40 10 E

Casino
Casino Showground [CT] [HT] [BIG RIG] [tap]
Grafton Rd. S end of town
02 6660 0300 HEMA 57 D12 28 53 02 S 153 02 48 E

Cessnock
Cessnock Showground [CT] [HT] [BIG RIG]
111 Mount View Rd. Access gates beside indoor sports centre. Close Feb-early Mar for show
0412 235 447 HEMA 45 J4 32 49 51 S 151 20 26 E

Clarence Town
Bridge Reserve [CT] [HT] [BIG RIG]
Durham St.
02 4996 4231 HEMA 47 A14 32 34 58 S 151 46 56 E

Public Dump Points

Cobar
Cobar Dump Point `CT` `HT` `🚰`
Cnr Lewis St & Barrier Hwy.
Opposite Info Centre (Great Cobar Heritage Centre)
in the large vehicle parking area. Potable water
HEMA 61 G11   31 29 52 S   145 50 31 E

Cobar Visitors Centre `CT` `HT` `BIG RIG` `🚰`
Marshall St. Barrier Hwy,
opposite Memorial Services Club also Great Cobar
Heritage Centre. Non-potable water with hose for
clean ups
02 6836 2448   HEMA 61 G11   31 29 53 S   145 50 33 E

Cobargo
Cobargo Hotel `CT` `HT` `BIG RIG` `🚰`
Princes Hwy.
02 6493 6423   HEMA 67 H11   36 23 22 S   149 53 09 E

Coffs Harbour
Coffs Harbour Dump Point `CT` `HT` `BIG RIG` `🚰`
Phil Hawthorne Dr. Off Stadium Dr roundabout. S of
town off Pacific Hwy
02 6648 4000   HEMA 55 A13   30 19 26 S   153 05 47 E

Coleambilly
Lion's Park `CT`
Kingfisher Ave. Adjacent to Caravan Park
1300 676 243   HEMA 63 J12   34 47 52 S   145 52 47 E

Collarenebri
Collarenebri Primitive Camp `CT` `HT` `BIG RIG`
Gwydir Hwy. E end of town. Next to football grounds.
Beside toilet block
02 6828 6139   HEMA 58 D3   29 32 56 S   148 34 55 E

Conargo
Bills Park `CT` `HT` `BIG RIG` `🚰`
Conargo Rd. W end of town,
near school
1800 650 712   HEMA 68 F7   35 18 24 S   145 10 38 E

Condobolin
Condobolin Dump Point `CT` `HT`
216 Bathurst Rd. Near Moulder St
HEMA 64 E2   33 05 09 S   147 08 04 E

River View Caravan Park `CT` `HT` `BIG RIG` `🚰`
Diggers Ave. S end of town
02 6895 2611   HEMA 64 E2   33 05 40 S   147 08 50 E

Coolongolook
Coolongolook Dump Point `CT`
King St. Off Pacific Hwy
HEMA 55 J11   32 13 08 S   152 19 21 E

Cooma
Cooma Dump Point `CT` `HT` `BIG RIG`
Cnr of Geebung St & Polo
Flat Rd.
HEMA 67 G8   36 13 30 S   149 08 52 E

Coonabarabran
Neilson Park `CT` `HT` `BIG RIG`
6 Essex St. E end of Rest Area
HEMA 58 J5   31 16 16 S   149 16 46 E

Coonamble
Coonamble Riverside Caravan Park `CT` `HT` `BIG RIG`
138 Castlereagh St. Inside caravan park, public
access. Big Rigs call ahead
02 6822 1926   HEMA 58 H3   30 57 48 S   148 23 21 E

Cootamundra
Cootamundra Dump Point `CT` `HT` `BIG RIG`
Hurley St. Apex Park, off Olympic
Hwy. Near toilet block
HEMA 64 J4   34 38 40 S   148 01 30 E

Corowa
Corowa Dump Point `CT` `HT` `BIG RIG`
Bridge Rd. Rowers Park. Near the
toilets
02 6033 8999   HEMA 69 J11   36 00 15 S   146 23 38 E

Cowra
Cowra Overnight Rest Area `CT` `HT` `BIG RIG` `🚰`
Lachlan Valley Way.
02 6342 4333   HEMA 52 F2   33 50 08 S   148 40 55 E

Crookwell
Crookwell Caravan Park `CT` `HT` `BIG RIG` `🚰`
Laggan Rd.
02 4832 1988   HEMA 52 J5   34 27 17 S   149 28 03 E

Culcairn
Culcairn Dump Point `CT` `HT` `BIG RIG` `🚰`
Cnr Balfour & Federal Sts. At
Rest Area near railway, well signed. Potable water
HEMA 66 E1   35 39 59 S   147 02 20 E

Cullendore
Cullendore High Country `CT` `HT` `BIG RIG` `🚰`
248 Cullendore Creek Rd.
0459 901 538   HEMA 57 B8   28 29 32 S   152 07 21 E

Cumnock
Cumnock Showgrounds `CT` `HT` `BIG RIG`
McLaughlan St. Off Baldry Rd
02 6367 7221   HEMA 52 B2   32 55 43 S   148 44 46 E

Dareton
Dareton Dump Point `CT` `🚰`
Tiltao St. Next to service station
HEMA 62 G3   34 05 44 S   142 02 29 E

Darlington Point
Darlington Point Lions Park `CT` `BIG RIG`
Darlington St. N side of town, 200 m E
of caravan park
02 6968 4166   HEMA 63 H12   34 34 00 S   146 00 29 E

Delungra
Delungra Showgrounds `CT` `HT` `BIG RIG` `🚰`
Reedy St. W end of town
02 6728 8161   HEMA 56 G4   29 39 04 S   150 49 33 E

Deniliquin
Deniliquin Rest Area `CT` `HT` `BIG RIG` `🚰`
135 Davidson St. Cobb Hwy,
N side of town, next to public toilet
132 213   HEMA 68 G6   35 31 31 S   144 58 41 E

Denman
Denman Dump Point `CT` `HT` `BIG RIG` `🚰`
Via Turner St. At Rec Sports
Field. Potable water
02 6547 2799   HEMA 54 J5   32 23 16 S   150 40 54 E

Dorrigo
Dorrigo Dump Point `CT` `HT` `BIG RIG`
Waterfall Way. S of
showground
0412 948 700   HEMA 55 A12   30 20 29 S   152 42 02 E

Dubbo
Western Plains Zoo `CT` `HT` `BIG RIG` `🚰`
Obley Rd. Turn R after
entering through main gate. In caravan parking area
HEMA 64 C5   32 16 18 S   148 35 09 E

Dunedoo
Dunedoo Dump Point `CT` `HT` `BIG RIG` `🚰`
156 Bolaro St. Next to town
hall
02 6378 5000   HEMA 54 H1   32 00 58 S   149 23 24 E

Dungog
Dungog Showground `CT` `HT` `BIG RIG` `🚰`
Chapman St.
02 4992 1810   HEMA 55 J9   32 24 19 S   151 45 03 E

Eugowra
Byrnes Park `CT` `HT` `BIG RIG` `🚰`
Myall St. Adjacent to bridge
HEMA 52 D1   33 25 40 S   148 22 11 E

Euston
Euston Dump Point `CT` `HT` `BIG RIG` `🚰`
Nixon St. Entrance between
Euston Club & motel. If locked key at club
03 5026 4244   HEMA 62 H5   34 34 47 S   142 44 41 E

Evans Head
Evans Head Industrial Estate `CT` `HT` `BIG RIG`
Memorial Airport Dr. Near council depot, between
Winjeel Dr & Sir Valston Hancock Dr
02 6682 4392   HEMA 57 E13   29 06 15 S   153 25 20 E

Finley
Finley RV Stop `CT` `HT` `BIG RIG`
Endeavour St. Beside old railway
station
HEMA 69 G8   35 38 41 S   145 34 37 E

Forbes
Wheogo Park `CT` `HT` `BIG RIG` `🚰`
Junction St. At Rest Area
S side of town and Lake Forbes, on the Taylor
Underpass. Beside toilets. Non potable water
02 6852 4155   HEMA 64 F4   33 23 17 S   148 00 07 E

Glen Innes
Glen Innes Lions Park `CT` `HT` `BIG RIG` `🚰`
Cnr East Ave & Ferguson St.
02 6730 2400   HEMA 57 G8   29 44 03 S   151 44 04 E

New England Highlands RV Park `CT` `HT` `$` `BIG RIG` `🚰`
209 Grafton St.
0428 483 099   HEMA 57 G8   29 43 36 S   151 44 20 E

Glenreagh
Glenreagh Rec Grounds `CT` `HT` `BIG RIG`
14 Bridge St. Potable water onsite
0428 582 314   HEMA 57 J12   30 03 08 S   152 58 26 E

Gloucester
Gloucester Holiday Park `CT` `$` `🚰`
1 Denison St. 700 m W of PO.
Call at reception for payment & directions
02 6558 1720   HEMA 55 H9   32 00 23 S   151 57 12 E

Goodooga
Goodooga Artesian Baths `CT` `HT` `BIG RIG`
Hammond St. At Camp Area N side of town. 74 km
NW of Lightning Ridge or 40 km SW of Hebel
02 6830 5100   HEMA 58 C1   29 06 37 S   147 27 21 E

Goolgowi
Goolgowi Caravan Park `CT` `HT` `BIG RIG` `🚰`
Combo St. 1 km NE of PO
02 6965 1900   HEMA 63 F12   33 58 47 S   145 42 22 E

Goolgowi Dump Point `CT` `HT`
Napier St. In the lane beside the fire station
HEMA 63 F12   33 58 47 S   145 42 28 E

Goulburn
Goulburn Recreation Area `CT` `BIG RIG`
Braidwood Rd.
HEMA 50 J1   34 46 12 S   149 42 52 E

Marsden Weir Park `CT`
Fitzroy St. Off Crookwell Rd. Limited access
HEMA 50 J1   34 44 08 S   149 42 25 E

NEW SOUTH WALES

Grafton
Grafton Greyhound Racing Club Campground CT HT BIG RIG 🚰
70 Cranworth St.
02 6642 3713 HEMA 57 G12 29 40 27 S 152 55 32 E

Grafton Showground CT HT BIG RIG 🚰
208 Prince St.
02 6642 2240 HEMA 57 G12 29 41 03 S 152 56 24 E

The Grafton Vintage Motor Vehicle Club CT HT BIG RIG 🚰
Minden St. In South Grafton, Cnr Vere St. Potable water. Follow signs
0482 561 246 HEMA 57 G12 29 42 09 S 152 55 24 E

Grenfell
Grenfell Old Railway Station CT HT BIG RIG
West St. Near old railway station. Take 2nd driveway from Cnr of Camp St
02 6343 2059 HEMA 64 G4 33 53 43 S 148 09 21 E

Griffith
Willow Park CT BIG RIG 🚰
Kookora St. Beside toilet block
02 6962 4145 HEMA 63 G12 34 17 16 S 146 01 55 E

Gulgong
Gulgong Dump Point CT HT BIG RIG
Saleyards Lane. Off Station St, front of shire depot
02 6374 1202 HEMA 54 J1 32 21 30 S 149 32 46 E

Gundagai
Gundagai Dump Point CT HT BIG RIG 🚰
Railway Parade.
02 6944 0250 HEMA 66 B5 35 03 55 S 148 06 45 E

Gunnedah
Gunnedah Lions RV Park CT HT BIG RIG
Oxley Highway. Water filling station for a fee
HEMA 54 C3 30 58 43 S 150 14 24 E

Gunnedah Showground CT HT BIG RIG
South St. Located just inside entrance
02 6740 2125 HEMA 54 C4 30 58 48 S 150 14 53 E

Gunning
Gunning Dump Point CT HT BIG RIG 🚰
Cnr of Yass & Gundaroo Sts.
02 4832 1988 HEMA 52 K4 34 46 49 S 149 16 13 E

Guyra
Mother of Ducks Lagoon CT HT BIG RIG 🚰
McKie Pkwy. S end of town, W off Hwy
02 6738 9100 HEMA 56 J7 30 13 21 S 151 40 10 E

Harden
Harden-Murrumburrah Showgrounds CT HT BIG RIG 🚰
Woolrych St.
0488 509 977 HEMA 52 J1 34 32 45 S 148 21 27 E

Hay
Hay Showground CT HT BIG RIG 🚰
Showground Rd. Dunera Way, N end of town. Outside emergency service building. 200 m W of showground
02 6990 1100 HEMA 63 H10 34 29 51 S 144 50 08 E

Henty
Henty Dump Point CT HT BIG RIG 🚰
Henty Pleasant Hills Rd. Behind the library
02 6036 2422 HEMA 66 D1 35 30 57 S 147 01 58 E

Hillston
Hillston Lions Park CT HT BIG RIG 🚰
Kidman Way-Lachlan River Rd. 100 m N of Caravan Park, adjacent to swimming pool
02 6967 1594 HEMA 63 E11 33 28 47 S 145 32 04 E

Holbrook
Gallipoli Victoria Cross Rest Area CT HT BIG RIG 🚰
146 Albury St. Off Prospect St. Potable water
02 6036 2422 HEMA 66 E2 35 43 03 S 147 19 03 E

Howlong
Lowe Square Recreation Reserve CT HT BIG RIG 🚰
Riverina Hwy. Between High & Larmer Sts. Near toilet block
02 6026 5055 HEMA 69 J12 35 58 50 S 146 38 02 E

Illabo
Illabo Dump Point CT HT BIG RIG 🚰
Cnr Wood St & Olympic Hwy. At hall & tennis courts. Potable water
HEMA 66 A4 34 48 50 S 147 44 33 E

Inverell
Inverell Showground CT HT BIG RIG 🚰
10 Tingha Rd. 1 km E of town, in between Sporting Complex & Pioneer Village
02 6722 3435 HEMA 56 G5 29 46 57 S 151 07 14 E

Jamberoo
Jamberoo Dump Point CT HT 🚰
Churchill St. Kevin Walsh Oval
02 4232 3322 HEMA 51 G11 34 38 49 S 150 46 28 E

Jerilderie
Lakeside Parking Area CT HT BIG RIG 🚰
Newell Hwy. At carpark, 100 m W of Civic Centre, beside church
03 5886 1200 HEMA 63 K12 35 21 19 S 145 43 23 E

Jerrys Plains
Jerrys Plains Rec Ground CT HT BIG RIG 🚰
Wambo St. S end of town
02 6578 7290 HEMA 54 K6 32 29 56 S 150 54 37 E

Jugiong
Jugiong Showground CT HT BIG RIG 🚰
Riverside Dr. Donation requested
HEMA 52 K1 34 49 24 S 148 19 34 E

Junee
Laurie Daley Oval CT HT BIG RIG 🚰
Park Ln. 70 m from entry
02 6924 8100 HEMA 66 A3 34 51 34 S 147 34 24 E

Kempsey
Kempsey Showground CT HT BIG RIG 🚰
19 Sea St.
0438 625 235 HEMA 55 D12 31 04 24 S 152 49 45 E

Kew
Kew Information & Community Centre CT HT BIG RIG 🚰
133 Nancy Bird Walton Dr.
02 6559 4400 HEMA 55 F12 31 38 06 S 152 43 19 E

Khancoban
Khancoban Dump Point CT HT BIG RIG 🚰
Scott St. Near Cnr Mitchell Ave
02 6948 9100 HEMA 66 G5 36 13 03 S 148 07 24 E

Kurri Kurri
Kurri Kurri Sports Ground CT HT BIG RIG 🚰
Allworth St.
02 4936 1909 HEMA 47 D11 32 49 24 S 151 28 51 E

Kyogle
Kyogle Showground CT HT $ BIG RIG
43 Summerland Way. N end of town, at New Park
02 6632 2454 HEMA 57 C12 28 36 57 S 153 00 00 E

Lake Cargelligo
Lake Cargelligo Shire Dump Point CT HT BIG RIG
Narrandera St.
02 6895 1900 HEMA 63 D13 33 18 17 S 146 22 23 E

Leeton
Leeton Showground CT HT BIG RIG 🚰
Racecourse Rd.
02 6953 2213 HEMA 63 H13 34 33 32 S 146 24 10 E

Lightning Ridge
Lightning Ridge Dump Point CT HT BIG RIG
Onyx St. W end of town
02 6829 1670 HEMA 58 D2 29 25 32 S 147 58 21 E

Lismore
Lismore Showgrounds CT HT $ BIG RIG
Alexandra Pde.
02 6621 5916 HEMA 57 C13 28 47 50 S 153 16 25 E

Lithgow
Lithgow Showground CT HT BIG RIG 🚰
George Coates St. Daylight hours
02 6353 1775 HEMA 48 B1 33 28 51 S 150 08 42 E

Lockhart
Lockhart Caravan Park CT HT 🚰
162 Green St. 300 m W of PO
0458 205 303 HEMA 63 K14 35 13 13 S 146 42 46 E

Lyndhurst
Lyndhurst Primitive Camp CT HT BIG RIG 🚰
6511 Mid Western Hwy. In Rec Ground, entrance off Harrow St
0427 201 824 HEMA 52 E3 33 40 24 S 149 02 20 E

Macksville
Gumma Crossing Reserve CT HT BIG RIG 🚰
Boultons Crossing Rd. 7.5 km E of Macksville at Camp Area
02 6568 2555 HEMA 55 B13 30 42 24 S 152 59 00 E

Macksville Aquatic Centre CT HT BIG RIG 🚰
23 Cooper St. Potable water
02 6568 2555 HEMA 55 B13 30 42 32 S 152 55 14 E

Maclean
Maclean Showground CT HT BIG RIG
12 Cameron St.
0487 101 151 HEMA 57 F13 29 27 50 S 153 11 58 E

Maitland
Maitland Dump Point CT HT BIG RIG 🚰
High St. In Visitor Info car park. Limited turrning circle
02 4931 2800 HEMA 47 C11 32 44 32 S 151 34 01 E

Manildra
Manildra Showground CT HT BIG RIG 🚰
Orange St.
0458 673 164 HEMA 52 C2 33 10 38 S 148 41 16 E

NEW SOUTH WALES

Manilla
Manilla Park CT HT BIG RIG 🚰
Charles St. Coronation Park
02 6785 1304   HEMA 54 B5   30 44 21 S   150 42 57 E

Mathoura
Mathoura Dump Point CT HT BIG RIG 🚰
1 Moama St. Laneway behind Bowling Club. Enter off Mitchell St. Drive through
03 5880 3200   HEMA 68 H6   35 48 30 S   144 53 56 E

Menindee
Menindee Dump Point CT HT 🚰
Perry St. At Burke & Wills Oval, near shed. Potable water
HEMA 62 B4   32 23 31 S   142 25 06 E

Merriwa
Merriwa Dump Point CT HT BIG RIG 🚰
Blaxland St. Next to caravan park, opposite showgrounds
02 6548 2607   HEMA 54 H4   32 08 17 S   150 21 03 E

Milton
Milton Showground CT HT BIG RIG 🚰
107 Croobyar Rd.
02 4421 0778   HEMA 67 C13   35 19 09 S   150 25 48 E

Moama
Rich River Golf Club Resort CT HT BIG RIG 🚰
Twenty Four Ln. Via Perricoota Rd. ID required, report to reception for key
03 5481 3333   HEMA 68 J5   36 04 35 S   144 43 35 E

Moree
Moree Dump Point CT HT BIG RIG 🚰
Webb Ave. Off Newell Hwy. Webb Oval
02 6757 3350   HEMA 58 D6   29 27 26 S   149 50 40 E

Moruya
Moruya Dump Point CT HT BIG RIG 🚰
Shore St. Near sewer pump station, opposite tennis courts. Via Church St off Princes Hwy
0427 744 999   HEMA 67 F12   35 54 27 S   150 04 35 E

Moruya Showground CT HT BIG RIG 🚰
Albert St. GPS at entry to showgrounds. Potable water
HEMA 67 F12   35 55 06 S   150 04 50 E

Moulamein
Moulamein Dump Point CT HT BIG RIG 🚰
Moulamein Rd. Between Tallow & Sainsberry Sts
03 5480 7555   HEMA 63 K8   35 05 16 S   144 01 53 E

Mudgee
Mudgee Showground CT HT BIG RIG 🚰
Douro St. 200 m from Cnr Nicolson St. Phone first to check if dump open
0447 111 329   HEMA 52 A5   32 36 10 S   149 34 55 E

Mulwala
Owen Bridges Park CT HT BIG RIG 🚰
Corowa Rd. Opposite Caravan Park, on foreshore in front of toilet block
02 6033 8999   HEMA 69 J10   35 58 32 S   146 01 31 E

Purtle Park CT HT BIG RIG 🚰
Melbourne St. Key at Newsagent
02 6033 8999   HEMA 69 J10   35 59 08 S   146 00 34 E

Mungindi
WH Smith Park CT HT BIG RIG 🚰
Cnr Wirrah & Loftus Sts.
02 6757 3350   HEMA 58 C4   28 58 53 S   148 59 30 E

Murrurundi
Wilson Memorial Park CT HT BIG RIG 🚰
Teys Lane. Via New England Hwy. S end of town. Best entrance via Mount St through back gate
02 6540 1364   HEMA 54 G6   31 45 51 S   150 50 11 E

Nabiac
Nabiac Dump Point CT HT BIG RIG 🚰
Nabiac St. By the tennis courts and public toilets
02 6554 8799   HEMA 55 H11   32 05 56 S   152 22 52 E

Nambucca Heads
Nambucca Service Centre CT HT BIG RIG 🚰
5 Boggy Creek Rd. Within the Service Centre, off Pacific Hwy
02 6568 9536   HEMA 55 B13   30 37 38 S   152 58 18 E

Narrabri
Cameron Park Narrabri CT HT BIG RIG 🚰
Cameron St. 700 m S of Information Centre
02 6799 6760   HEMA 54 A2   30 19 37 S   149 46 43 E

Narrabri Showground CT HT BIG RIG 🚰
Wukuwa St.
0417 006 865   HEMA 56 K1   30 20 19 S   149 45 48 E

Narrandera
Narrandera Showground CT HT BIG RIG 🚰
Elizabeth St. E side of town. Behind hall in grounds
0427 169 047   HEMA 63 J14   34 44 57 S   146 33 52 E

Narromine
Narromine Dump Point CT HT BIG RIG 🚰
Manildra St. S off Mitchell Hwy. Next to stockyards, W side of long vehicle parking area at railway station
02 6889 9999   HEMA 64 C4   32 14 15 S   148 14 49 E

Nimbin
Nimbin Showgrounds CT HT $ BIG RIG 🚰
Cecil St.
0458 872 228   HEMA 57 C13   28 35 56 S   153 13 36 E

Norah Head
Norah Head Holiday Park CT HT $ 🚰
Victoria St.
02 4396 3935   HEMA 47 J11   33 17 00 S   151 33 58 E

Nowra
Nowra Showground CT HT BIG RIG 🚰
Junction St.
02 4421 0778   HEMA 51 K9   34 52 30 S   150 35 31 E

Nyngan
Flood Memorial Park CT HT BIG RIG 🚰
Nymagee St. Mitchell Hwy
02 6832 1052   HEMA 61 H13   31 33 44 S   147 11 49 E

Oaklands
Oaklands Rec Ground & Oval CT HT 🚰
Patey St. Potable water
HEMA 69 G10   35 33 20 S   146 10 15 E

Oberon
Jenolan Caravan Park CT HT $ 🚰
Cunynghame St.
02 6336 0344   HEMA 52 E6   33 42 06 S   149 51 28 E

Oberon Dump Point CT HT BIG RIG 🚰
Cnr North & Albion Sts. At old recycling centre space. Potable water & tourist boards
02 6329 8210   HEMA 52 E6   33 41 56 S   149 51 17 E

Orange
Total Park CT HT BIG RIG 🚰
Bathurst Rd. Behind service station. E end of town
1800 069 466   HEMA 52 D3   33 17 27 S   149 06 34 E

Parkes
Kelly Reserve CT HT BIG RIG 🚰
Peak Hill Rd. N end of town
02 6862 6000   HEMA 64 E4   33 07 29 S   148 10 25 E

Parkes Showground CT HT BIG RIG 🚰
Victoria St. Not available during show in Aug or Elvis Festival 1-14 Jan
02 6862 2580   HEMA 64 E4   33 07 52 S   148 09 47 E

Peak Hill
Peak Hill Dump Point CT HT BIG RIG 🚰
Warrah St. Between Mingelo & Bogan Sts. W side of Hwy. Lindner Oval
02 6869 1981   HEMA 64 D4   32 43 38 S   148 11 10 E

Picton
Picton Dump Point CT HT 🚰
Walton Ln. Next to the car park. Off Menangle St W
02 4677 1100   HEMA 51 A10   34 10 04 S   150 36 40 E

Pooncarie
Pooncarie Multi Purpose Park (Wakefied Oval) CT HT BIG RIG 🚰
Off Cemetery Rd. Near banks of Darling River, on R. Potable water
03 5029 5205   HEMA 62 E4   33 22 49 S   142 33 53 E

Port Macquarie
Port Macquarie Dump Point CT HT BIG RIG 🚰
Chestnut Rd. Off Lake Rd. Adjacent to sewer pumping station
1300 303 155   HEMA 55 E13   31 27 06 S   152 53 23 E

Portland
Kremer Park CT HT BIG RIG 🚰
Lime St.
1300 760 276   HEMA 52 D6   33 21 15 S   149 58 36 E

Quirindi
Rose Lee Park CT HT BIG RIG 🚰
Kamilaroi Hwy.
02 6747 1226   HEMA 54 F5   31 31 04 S   150 40 34 E

Raymond Terrace
Raymond Terrace Dump Point CT HT BIG RIG 🚰
Adelaide St. S bound traffic only, between Sketchley & Wahroonga Sts
HEMA 47 C13   32 46 08 S   151 44 29 E

Rylstone
Rylstone Caravan Park CT HT $ BIG RIG 🚰
7 Carwell St.
0448 251 440   HEMA 52 B6   32 48 02 S   149 58 04 E

Scone
Scone Sports Club CT HT BIG RIG 🚰
Aberdeen St. Cnr Kingdon St
02 6540 1300   HEMA 54 H6   32 03 10 S   150 51 37 E

Seal Rocks
Seal Rocks Dump Point CT HT BIG RIG 🚰
Seal Rocks Rd. Opposite entry to Caravan Park. Near public toilets
1800 642 480   HEMA 55 K11   32 25 57 S   152 31 28 E

Talbingo
Talbingo Dump Point CT HT BIG RIG 🚰
Miles Franklin Dr. Between Lampe & Bridle Sts. At entrance to water depot station
02 6941 2555   HEMA 66 D5   35 34 43 S   148 17 59 E

NEW SOUTH WALES

Tamworth

South Tamworth Rest Area `CT` `HT` `BIG RIG` 🚰
470 Goonoo Goonoo Rd. Lions Park, New England Hwy, opposite power sub-station
02 6767 5300 HEMA 54 D6 31 07 57 S 150 55 22 E

Tamworth Airport Rest Area `CT` `HT` `BIG RIG` 🚰
Oxley Hwy. On Hwy, opposite airport
02 6767 5555 HEMA 54 D6 31 04 40 S 150 51 01 E

Tamworth Rest Area `CT` `HT` 🚰
New England Hwy. 3 km NE of Tamworth. Limited turning circle
02 6767 5555 HEMA 54 D6 31 06 30 S 150 57 16 E

Tarcutta

Tarcutta Dump Point `CT` `HT` `BIG RIG` 🚰
Sydney St. In truck changeover bay. Beside toilets
1300 100 122 HEMA 66 C4 35 16 33 S 147 44 17 E

Taree

Taree Rotary Park `CT` `HT` `BIG RIG` 🚰
Manning River Dr. Via Victoria St. Just W of Info Centre
1800 182 733 HEMA 55 G11 31 53 57 S 152 29 27 E

Tea Gardens

Tea Gardens Rest Area `CT` `HT` 🚰
Myall Way. 1 km W of Tea Gardens. Cnr Viney Creek Rd
02 4997 0111 HEMA 53 A14 32 38 23 S 152 08 39 E

Temora

Temora Dump Point `CT` `HT` `BIG RIG` 🚰
Airport St. N end of street. 200 m from Hwy
02 6980 1100 HEMA 64 H3 34 25 40 S 147 31 09 E

Temora Showground `CT` `HT` `BIG RIG` 🚰
Mimosa St.
02 6977 5921 HEMA 64 H3 34 26 23 S 147 31 17 E

Tenterfield

Tenterfield Showground `CT` `HT` `$` `BIG RIG` 🚰
62 Miles St. Entry at back gate
02 6736 6000 HEMA 57 D9 29 03 24 S 152 00 55 E

The Rock

The Rock Rec Ground `CT` `HT` `BIG RIG` 🚰
60 Wilson St. Via Urana & Cornwall Sts
02 6920 5674 HEMA 66 C1 35 15 55 S 147 06 37 E

Tilligerry

Lemon Tree Passage Boat Ramp `CT` `HT` `BIG RIG` 🚰
Cook Pde. Near wharf
132 213 HEMA 53 A13 32 43 47 S 152 02 23 E

Tiona

Camp Elim `CT` `HT` `$` `BIG RIG` 🚰
4859 The Lakes Way.
02 6554 0277 HEMA 55 J11 32 16 08 S 152 31 42 E

Tocumwal

Tocumwal Town Beach `CT` `HT` `BIG RIG` 🚰
Town Beach Rd. From Tocumwal-Corawa Rd turn W to Hennessy St, then S on Town Beach Rd. 700 m dirt road
0408 575 479 HEMA 69 H8 35 49 06 S 145 33 36 E

Tooleybuc

Tooleybuc Rec Reserve `CT` `HT` `BIG RIG` 🚰
Lockhart Rd.
02 6977 5921 HEMA 62 J6 35 01 22 S 143 20 17 E

Trundle

Trundle Showgrounds `CT` `HT` `BIG RIG` 🚰
Austral St.
02 6892 1260 HEMA 64 D3 32 55 33 S 147 42 06 E

Tullamore

Tullamore Showground `CT` `HT` `BIG RIG` 🚰
Cornet St.
02 6892 5194 HEMA 61 K14 32 37 39 S 147 34 11 E

Tumbarumba

Tumbarumba Dump Point `CT` `HT` `BIG RIG` 🚰
Cnr Cape & Bridge Sts. 100 m from Visitors Centre
02 6948 3333 HEMA 66 E4 35 46 37 S 148 00 33 E

Tumut

Tumut Dump Point `CT` `HT` `BIG RIG` 🚰
Elm Drive.
02 6941 2555 HEMA 66 C5 35 18 11 S 148 13 42 E

Tuncurry

Tuncurry Sporties RV Park `CT` `HT` `BIG RIG`
65 Beach St.
02 6554 9270 HEMA 55 H11 32 09 59 S 152 30 04 E

Tyalgum

Tyalgum Diggers Camp `CT` `HT` `$` 🚰
Carraboi Tce.
0490 780 181 HEMA 57 B13 28 21 11 S 153 12 20 E

Ungarie

Ungarie Showground `CT` `HT` `BIG RIG` 🚰
Crown Camp Rd. Entrance beyond school. Behind toilets, signposted
02 6979 0272 HEMA 64 F2 33 38 07 S 146 58 43 E

Uralla

Uralla Dump Point `CT` `HT` `BIG RIG` 🚰
John St. At Pioneer Cemetery
02 6778 6420 HEMA 55 B8 30 38 31 S 151 29 35 E

Uranquinty

Uranquinty Rest Area `CT` `HT` `BIG RIG` 🚰
Morgan St. In the main street
1300 100 122 HEMA 66 C2 35 11 34 S 147 14 46 E

Urunga

Urunga Rec Reserve `CT` `HT` `BIG RIG` 🚰
Morgo St. S of town centre heading to Hungry Head. 250 m S of intersection with South St E
02 6655 5711 HEMA 55 A13 30 30 06 S 153 01 16 E

Wagga Wagga

Wagga Wagga Showgrounds `CT` `HT` `$` `BIG RIG` 🚰
Urana & Bourke Sts. 8am-5pm
02 6925 2180 HEMA 66 B2 35 07 35 S 147 21 15 E

Wilks Park `CT` `HT` `BIG RIG` 🚰
Hampden Ave. E off Olympic Hwy at Travers St, across bridge to Hampden Ave. N side of town, E side of Murrumbidgee River
1300 100 122 HEMA 66 B2 35 05 59 S 147 22 17 E

Walcha

Walcha Dump Point `CT` `HT` `BIG RIG` 🚰
North St. In front of council depot
02 6774 2460 HEMA 55 C8 30 58 40 S 151 35 18 E

Walgett

Alex Trevallion Park `CT` `HT` `BIG RIG` 🚰
175 Fox St. Castlereagh Hwy. S end of town
02 6828 6139 HEMA 58 F3 30 02 04 S 148 06 55 E

Walla Walla

Walla Walla Sportsground `CT` `HT` `BIG RIG` 🚰
William St. Off Commercial Road, 20 m on the R, inside main entry gate
0429 039 322 HEMA 69 H13 35 46 04 S 146 54 09 E

Wallerawang

Lake Wallace `CT` `HT` `BIG RIG` 🚰
Barton Ave.
02 6352 9130 HEMA 52 D7 33 24 57 S 150 04 26 E

Warialda

Saleyards Rest Area `CT` `HT` `BIG RIG` 🚰
Gwydir Hwy. E side of town
02 6729 0046 HEMA 56 G4 29 32 44 S 150 34 53 E

Warragamba

Warragamba Picnic Area `CT` `HT` 🚰
Warradale Rd.
02 4774 4437 HEMA 48 G5 33 53 37 S 150 36 06 E

Warren

Warren Dump Point `CT` `HT` `BIG RIG` 🚰
4 Coonamble Rd. Oxley Park. Near the water tower
02 6847 6665 HEMA 58 K2 31 41 48 S 147 50 23 E

Wauchope

Timbertown Heritage Park `CT` `HT` `BIG RIG` 🚰
2325 Oxley Hwy.
0402 364 616 HEMA 55 E12 31 28 13 S 152 42 46 E

Wauchope Showgrounds `CT` `HT` `BIG RIG` 🚰
93A High St. Camp Area, enter via High St. Fee for water. Call caretaker before use
0475 111 074 HEMA 55 E12 31 27 28 S 152 43 27 E

Wee Waa

Dangar Park `CT` `HT` `BIG RIG`
Cnr Cowper & George Sts. Next to toilet block
02 6799 6760 HEMA 58 F5 30 13 25 S 149 26 39 E

Weethalle

Weethalle Dump Point `CT` `HT` 🚰
Teamster Dr. Next to toilets
HEMA 63 F14 33 52 09 S 146 37 24 E

Wellington

Wellington Showground `CT` `HT` `BIG RIG` 🚰
Bushranger Creek Rd.
1800 621 614 HEMA 52 A3 32 33 15 S 148 56 03 E

Wentworth

Fort Courage Caravan Park `CT` `HT` `BIG RIG`
1703 Old Renmark Rd. 20 km W of Wentworth on Old Renmark Rd. Beside Murray River
03 5027 3097 HEMA 62 G3 34 05 22 S 141 44 01 E

Willow Bend Caravan Park `CT` `HT` `$` 🚰
14-16 Darling St. Donation
03 5027 3213 HEMA 62 G3 34 06 36 S 141 55 12 E

West Wyalong

Ace Caravan Park `CT` `HT` `$` 🚰
Cnr Newell & Mid Western Hwys.
02 6972 3061 HEMA 64 G2 33 55 23 S 147 11 55 E

West Wyalong Showground `CT` `HT` `BIG RIG` 🚰
190 Showground Rd. Entry by Duffs Rd only. Off the West Wyalong bypass road
0428 518 329 HEMA 64 G2 33 56 18 S 147 12 50 E

Public Dump Points

NEW SOUTH WALES

White Cliffs
White Cliffs Opal Pioneer Reserve `CT` `HT` `BIG RIG` `💧`
Johnston St.
08 8091 6688   HEMA 60 F5   30 51 02 S   143 05 22 E

Wilcannia
Wilcannia Dump Point `CT` `HT` `BIG RIG`
Myers St
HEMA 60 H6   31 33 23 S   143 22 29 E

Wingham
Wingham Showground `CT` `HT` `BIG RIG` `💧`
1274 Gloucester Rd.
0434 144 722   HEMA 55 G11   31 52 25 S   152 21 43 E

Woodburn
Woodburn Dump Point `CT`
Pacific Hwy. Pacific Hwy. Beside public toilets next to Coraki turnoff
02 6660 0267   HEMA 57 E13   29 04 25 S   153 20 20 E

Woodenbong
Woodenbong Campground `CT` `HT` `BIG RIG` `💧`
127 Unumgar St. W end of town, next to swimming pool. Deposit for key at Ampol
0427 612 919   HEMA 57 B11   28 23 20 S   152 36 21 E

Wyalong
Cooinda Reserve `CT` `HT` `BIG RIG`
Neeld St. Copeland St, off Newell Hwy
HEMA 64 G2   33 55 28 S   147 14 01 E

Wyangala Dam
Reflections Holiday Park Wyangala Waters `CT` `$` `BIG RIG`
2891 Reg Hailstone Way. Day fee to enter park. See reception
02 6345 0877   HEMA 52 G3   33 57 46 S   148 57 17 E

Wyong
Caltex Service Station `CT`
Both sides of F3 Freeway. Both sides of F3 Freeway. Go through truck parking to find the site
02 4352 2944   HEMA 47 J10   33 15 10 S   151 24 12 E

Yass
Yass Dump Point `CT` `HT` `BIG RIG`
1428 Yass Valley Way, outside council depot
HEMA 52 K3   34 49 18 S   148 54 21 E

Yerong Creek
Yerong Creek Campground `CT` `HT` `BIG RIG` `💧`
37 Yerong Creek-Mangoplah Rd. In Rec Grounds, past tennis club. Potable water
02 6920 3535   HEMA 66 D1   35 23 16 S   147 04 01 E

Yetman
Apex Park Yetman `CT` `HT` `BIG RIG` `💧`
River St (Bruxner Hwy) next to picnic area
HEMA 59 C8   28 54 10 S   150 46 48 E

Young
Young Showground `CT` `HT` `BIG RIG` `💧`
120 Whiteman Ave.
0427 451 133   HEMA 52 H1   34 18 58 S   148 18 50 E

AUSTRALIAN CAPITAL TERRITORY

Canberra
Epic Exhibition Park `CT` `HT` `BIG RIG`
Cnr Flemington Rd & Northbourne Ave. In Mitchell. Adjacent to camping area. Call ahead as site often closed during Dec-Jan/Easter
02 6205 5230   HEMA 72 B5   35 13 36 S   149 08 55 E

VICTORIA

Alexandra
Alexandra Showground `CT` `HT` `💧`
17 William St. Dump Point on L side as you come in the gate. Caretaker on site.
0417 179 313   HEMA 89 G5   37 11 06 S   145 42 27 E

Leckie Park Dump Point `CT` `HT` `BIG RIG` `💧`
23 Station St. Right beside helicopter pad opposite Lamont St. Non-potable water
HEMA 89 G5   37 11 11 S   145 42 54 E

Ararat
Ararat Dump Point `CT` `HT` `BIG RIG`
Green Hill Lake Rd. Dump Point at Green Hill Lake Reserve, 4 km E of town
03 5355 0200   HEMA 85 C8   37 16 50 S   142 55 59 E

Avoca
Avoca Caravan Park `CT` `HT` `BIG RIG`
2 Liebig St. Dump Point outside the Caravan Park, 1.2 km W of PO
03 5465 3073   HEMA 85 B10   37 05 36 S   143 28 07 E

Ballarat
Eureka Stockade Caravan Park `CT` `HT` `$` `BIG RIG`
104 Stawell St South. Dump Point 3 km E of PO. Visit reception
03 5331 2281   HEMA 85 D11   37 33 49 S   143 53 09 E

Beaufort
Beaufort Dump Point `CT` `HT` `BIG RIG` `💧`
27 Lawrence St. On a 50 m one way street, long hoses required if tank is on your driver's side. Potable water & toilets also opposite at Wotherspoon Park
HEMA 85 D10   37 25 53 S   143 23 01 E

Beechworth
Lake Sambell Caravan Park `CT` `HT` `$` `BIG RIG`
Peach Dr. 1.5 km E of PO. Call at reception first
03 5728 1421   HEMA 92 C3   36 21 28 S   146 42 00 E

Benalla
Benalla Dump Point `CT` `HT` `BIG RIG`
Airport Dr. Dump Point at old airport terminus building off Samaria Rd. Signposted
HEMA 89 D6   36 33 11 S   145 59 50 E

Birchip
Birchip Dump Point `CT` `HT` `BIG RIG`
Cnr Morrison & Johnson Sts. At Community Leisure Centre. Veer L to toilets
HEMA 87 G8   35 58 46 S   142 54 41 E

Boort
Boort Park Showground `CT` `HT` `BIG RIG` `💧`
Via Malone St. Dump Point on left behind main building near water tank
0419 445 060   HEMA 87 H11   36 06 37 S   143 43 46 E

Bright
BIG4 Bright `CT` `HT` `$` `BIG RIG` `💧`
1 Mountbatten Ave. Dump Point 500 m E of PO
03 5755 1064   HEMA 96 D4   36 43 31 S   146 57 54 E

Bright Caravan Park `CT` `HT` `$` `BIG RIG` `💧`
7 Churchill Ave. At Caravan Park. 1 km E of PO
03 5755 1010   HEMA 96 D4   36 43 50 S   146 58 15 E

NRMA Bright Holiday Park `CT` `HT` `$` `BIG RIG` `💧`
Cherry Ln. 900 m E of PO
1800 706 685   HEMA 96 D4   36 43 39 S   146 57 53 E

Bruthen
Bruthen Caravan Park `CT` `HT` `$` `BIG RIG`
Tambo Upper Rd. Off Bruthen-Nowa Nowa Rd. 600 m E of PO. Pay DP fee at reception
03 5157 5753   HEMA 98 G4   37 42 43 S   147 50 08 E

Cann River
Cann River Rainforest Tourist Park `CT`
7536 Princes Hwy. Just W of bridge
03 5153 9500   HEMA 93 H12   37 33 59 S   149 08 46 E

Casterton
Island Park Caravan Park `CT` `BIG RIG`
Malcolm Carmichael Dr. DP off Murray St, next to swimming pool & amenities block
0457 414 187   HEMA 84 E3   37 34 58 S   141 24 19 E

Charlton
Travellers Rest Caravan Park `CT`
43-45 High St.
0448 276 631   HEMA 87 H10   36 16 02 S   143 21 05 E

Chiltern
Chiltern Dump Point `CT` `HT` `BIG RIG`
Lake Anderson Dr. Dump Point adjacent to caravan park
HEMA 92 B3   36 09 08 S   146 36 44 E

Clunes
Clunes Dump Point `CT`
70 Bailey St. Dump Point at Info Centre
03 5345 3359   HEMA 85 C11   37 17 37 S   143 46 50 E

Cobden
Cobden Freedom Camp `CT` `HT` `💧`
1236 Camperdown Rd. Dump Point behind roadhouse at W end. Potable water
03 5595 1535   HEMA 82 E5   38 19 13 S   143 04 46 E

Cobram
Cobram Dump Point `CT` `HT` `BIG RIG`
Ivy St. Dump Point at Cobram Showgrounds. Enter from Banks St. Follow past tennis court to S corner
HEMA 89 A5   35 55 18 S   145 39 09 E

Cohuna
Cohuna Dump Point `CT` `HT` `BIG RIG`
58 Cohuna Island Rd. Dump Point opposite caravan park
HEMA 87 F13   35 48 17 S   144 13 33 E

Colac
Central Caravan Park `CT` `HT` `$` `BIG RIG` `💧`
Bruce St. Dump Point at Caravan Park in showground
03 5231 3586   HEMA 83 E9   38 20 09 S   143 36 12 E

Coleraine
Coleraine Tourist & Exhibition Centre `CT` `HT` `💧`
27 Pilleau St. Dump Point located outside Tourist Centre. Potable water, playground, BBQ & toilets
03 5575 2733   HEMA 84 E4   37 36 05 S   141 41 51 E

Corop
Greens Lake Rec Reserve `CT` `HT` `BIG RIG`
Via Greens Lake Rd. Dump Point next to the toilet block
HEMA 89 D2   36 26 16 S   144 49 42 E

Corryong
Corryong Dump Point `CT` `BIG RIG` `💧`
Donaldson St. Dump Point next to toilet block at saleyards
HEMA 92 B7   36 11 17 S   147 53 56 E

VICTORIA

Cullulleraine
Bushmans Rest Caravan Park `CT` `HT` `BIG RIG`
68 Sturt Hwy. Dump Point at the back of the park
03 5028 2252   HEMA 88 D4   34 16 23 S   141 35 13 E

Daylesford
Daylesford Holiday Park `CT` `HT` `$` `BIG RIG`
Cnr Ballan Rd & Burrall St.
1.7 km S of PO. 1.7 km S of PO. Key at reception. Deposit applies
03 5348 3821   HEMA 85 D12   37 21 31 S   144 08 23 E

Dimboola
Dimboola Dump Point `CT` `🔧`
8 Wimmera St. Dump Point near caravan park entrance
03 5391 4444   HEMA 86 J5   36 27 24 S   142 01 30 E

Dimboola Rec Reserve `CT` `HT` `🔧`
Lloyd St. At the rec reserve
HEMA 86 J5   36 27 30 S   142 01 44 E

Dinner Plain
Scrubbers End `CT` `HT`
Scrubbers End Ln. Dump Point at Dinner Plain Alpine Village. Enter via Big Muster Dr, E side of village, in carpark
1800 444 066   HEMA 95 B12   37 01 29 S   147 14 36 E

Donald
Donald Apex Park `CT` `HT` `BIG RIG`
2 Aitken Ave. N end of town
HEMA 87 J8   36 22 03 S   142 58 39 E

Dunkeld
Dunkeld Caravan Park `CT` `HT` `🔧`
Victoria Valley Rd. Inside gate, potable water. See caretaker
03 5577 2578   HEMA 84 E6   37 38 59 S   142 20 44 E

Eagle Point
Eagle Point Caravan Park `CT` `HT` `BIG RIG`
40 School Rd. Opposite reception
03 5156 1183   HEMA 98 J3   37 53 32 S   147 40 53 E

Echuca
Echuca Rotary Park RV Stop `CT` `HT` `BIG RIG` `🔧`
Via Rose St. Dump Point entry Cnr Crossen St
HEMA 87 H14   36 08 43 S   144 44 02 E

Euroa
Kirkland Ave Rest Area `CT`
Kirkland Ave. Near Caravan Park
HEMA 89 E5   36 45 15 S   145 34 34 E

Foster
Foster Dump Point `CT` `HT` `BIG RIG`
Cnr Nelson & Main Sts. Dump Point at service station
HEMA 91 G8   38 39 08 S   146 12 13 E

Girgare
Girgarre Town Park `CT` `HT` `BIG RIG`
Morgan Cr. At rear of hall. Cnr Winter & Station Sts
0474 114 397   HEMA 89 C2   36 23 53 S   144 58 48 E

Glenmaggie
Paradise Valley Camp Park `CT` `HT` `BIG RIG` `🔧`
51 Gells Rd. At private Camping Area 16 km N of Glenmaggie
03 5148 0291   HEMA 91 B10   37 50 24 S   146 42 31 E

Hamilton
Hamilton Dump Point `CT` `HT` `🔧`
8 Ballarat Rd (Glenelg Hwy). At the front of Lake Hamilton Caravan Park, before entry, close to Hwy. Potable water (another DP is located in the Caravan Park for guests)
HEMA 84 E5   37 44 33 S   142 02 03 E

Harcourt
Harcourt Dump Point `CT` `HT` `BIG RIG` `🔧`
Cnr Bridge & High Sts.
Dump Point near the swimming pool
HEMA 85 B13   36 59 40 S   144 15 43 E

Heathcote
Heathcote Dump Point `CT` `HT` `BIG RIG`
Barrack St. Dump Point outside entry of Queen Meadow Caravan Park
03 5433 3121   HEMA 85 B14   36 55 24 S   144 42 47 E

Heyfield
Heyfield RV Park `HT`
Cnr MacFarlane & Clark Sts. Dump Point 700 m SE of PO
0418 108 691   HEMA 91 C10   37 59 06 S   146 47 15 E

Heywood
Heywood RV Stop `CT` `HT` `BIG RIG` `🔧`
Hunter St East. Dump Point alongside the asphalt open area
HEMA 84 G4   38 07 51 S   141 37 57 E

Hollands Landing
Hollands Landing Dump Point `CT` `BIG RIG`
Hollands Landing Rd. Near jetty toilets
1300 366 244   HEMA 91 D13   38 03 13 S   147 27 36 E

Hopetoun
Hopetoun Rest Area `CT` `BIG RIG` `🔧`
Cnr Henty Hwy & Evelyn St.
Dump Point at Rest Area 1 km NE of Hopetoun
HEMA 86 F6   35 43 21 S   142 21 53 E

Horsham
Horsham Dump Point `CT` `HT` `BIG RIG`
Firebrace St. Dump Point outside caravan park
03 5382 9777   HEMA 84 A6   36 43 21 S   142 11 58 E

Jeparit
Jeparit Dump Point `CT` `HT` `BIG RIG`
Lower Roy St. Dump Point near the bowling green
03 5391 4450   HEMA 86 H5   36 08 24 S   141 59 23 E

Kaniva
Kaniva Poolside Caravan Park `CT` `BIG RIG`
Baker St. DP at Caravan Park
0458 687 054   HEMA 86 J2   36 22 54 S   141 14 25 E

Kerang
Kerang Dump Point `CT` `HT` `BIG RIG`
2 Markets Rd.
HEMA 87 F12   35 44 14 S   143 55 39 E

Koondrook
Koondrook Wetland Reserve `CT` `HT` `BIG RIG` `🔧`
Via View St. Next to RV Camp Area at 62 Penglase St. Potable water
HEMA 87 E12   35 38 00 S   144 07 29 E

Korumburra
Korumburra Showgrounds `CT` `HT` `BIG RIG` `🔧`
Victoria St. Dump Point at rear entrance gate, next to toilets. If locked, key at Korumburra Tourist Park or BP Service Station. Deposit applies
0408 353 785   HEMA 90 F6   38 25 40 S   145 49 02 E

Kyabram
Kyabram Dump Point `CT`
24 Fauna Park Rd. Dump Point at the front of park. Next to toilet block. If locked, obtain key from Fauna Park office
03 5852 2883   HEMA 89 C3   36 19 16 S   145 02 52 E

Kyneton
South Kyneton Mineral Springs `CT` `🔧`
219 Burton Ave. Parking Area 3.5 km W of Kyneton
HEMA 85 C13   37 14 09 S   144 25 10 E

Lake Bolac
Lake Bolac Dump Point `CT` `HT` `BIG RIG`
Glenelg Hwy. Dump Point on service road
HEMA 85 E8   37 42 40 S   142 50 32 E

Lakes Entrance
Lakes Entrance-Gippsland Lakes Fishing Club `CT` `HT` `BIG RIG`
23 Bullock Island Rd. DP opposite Info Centre
HEMA 98 J6   37 52 58 S   147 58 18 E

Leitchville
Leitchville Dump Point `CT` `HT` `BIG RIG`
Leitchville-Kerang Rd. Dump Point at the Rec Reserve
HEMA 87 G13   35 54 13 S   144 17 55 E

Leongatha
Leongatha Caravan Park `CT` `$`
14 Turner St. Dump Point 800 m N of PO. Fee for non guests
03 5662 2753   HEMA 90 F6   38 28 18 S   145 56 52 E

Lockington
Lockington Travellers Rest `CT` `HT` `🔧`
Via Pannoo Rd. Dump Point In Camp Area
0447 787 581   HEMA 87 J14   36 16 15 S   144 32 08 E

Lorne
Lorne Dump Point `CT`
Otway St. DP behind Info Centre. Follow road towards the spit. On the R side at 2nd toilet block, in Council Caravan Park
1300 614 219   HEMA 83 G11   38 32 06 S   143 58 37 E

Macarthur
Macarthur Rec Reserve `CT` `HT` `BIG RIG`
Hamilton-Port Fairy Rd. Dump Point entry to reserve just S of river crossing. Signposted
HEMA 84 G5   38 02 15 S   142 00 27 E

Maffra
Gippsland Vehicle Collection `CT` `HT` `$` `BIG RIG`
1A Sale Rd. Call ahead
03 5147 3223   HEMA 91 C11   37 58 24 S   146 59 05 E

Maffra RV Park `CT` `HT` `🔧`
187 Johnson St. Dump Point at Cnr Moroney St
HEMA 91 C11   37 58 11 S   146 58 50 E

Mallacoota
Mallacoota Dump Point `CT`
Buckland Dr. Dump Point next to toilet block near Wharf
03 5153 9500   HEMA 93 H14   37 33 20 S   149 45 21 E

Mallacoota Foreshore Holiday Park `CT` `HT` `BIG RIG`
7 Allan Dr. Dump Point at the Caravan Park
03 5158 0300   HEMA 93 H14   37 33 26 S   149 45 32 E

VICTORIA

Mansfield
Mansfield Dump Point CT HT BIG RIG 🚰
Stock Route off High St. At
N side of rail trail. 200 m W of Info Centre
1800 039 049   HEMA 94 C1   37 03 00 S   146 04 43 E

Maryborough
Maryborough Dump Point CT HT BIG RIG 🚰
Reservoir Rd. Off Ballarat-Maryborough Rd
HEMA 85 B11   37 03 52 S   143 43 55 E

Meeniyan
Meeniyan Rec Reserve CT HT BIG RIG
15 Hanily St.
HEMA 90 G7   38 34 32 S   146 00 44 E

Mildura
Mildura Dump Point CT HT BIG RIG
Benetook Ave. Dump Point
between 11th & 14th Sts. Front of council depot,
opposite TAFE
03 5018 8450   HEMA 88 D6   34 12 17 S   142 10 06 E

Mirboo North
BP Service Station CT HT $ BIG RIG
106 Ridgway St. Dump
Point key from attendant, fee if no fuel purchased
HEMA 90 F7   38 24 04 S   146 09 39 E

Mitre
Duffholme Cottages CT HT BIG RIG
1859 Natimuk-Frances Rd.
0429 912 620   HEMA 84 A4   36 44 00 S   141 44 06 E

Moyhu
Moyhu Lions Park CT HT BIG RIG 🚰
Moyhu Meadow Creek Rd.
Potable water
137 468   HEMA 89 D7   36 34 42 S   146 22 46 E

Murrabit
Murrabit Rec Reserve CT HT BIG RIG 🚰
Via Browning Ave.
HEMA 87 E12   35 31 49 S   143 57 09 E

Murtoa
Murtoa Dump Point CT HT BIG RIG
47 Lake St. Dump Point near the
showground & Caravan Park
HEMA 86 A7   34 37 20 S   142 27 59 E

Nathalia
Nathalia Dump Point CT HT BIG RIG 🚰
23 Weir St. Dump Point next
to the toilets
HEMA 89 B3   36 03 20 S   145 12 03 E

Neerim South
Neeerim South Recreation Reserve CT HT BIG RIG
17 Neerim East Rd.
03 5624 2411   HEMA 90 C7   38 00 59 S   145 57 24 E

Newstead
Newstead Racecourse CT HT BIG RIG 🚰
Via Racecourse Rd.
03 5476 2360   HEMA 85 B12   37 07 01 S   144 03 23 E

Nhill
Nhill Aerodrome RV Stop CT HT BIG RIG
Aerodrome Rd. 3 km N of Nhill.
Via Propodollah Rd
0437 351 753   HEMA 86 H4   36 18 29 S   141 38 51 E

Nicholson
Nicholson River Reserve CT
Princes Hwy. Dump Point beside toilet block
at boat ramp car park
03 5153 9500   HEMA 98 H3   37 49 02 S   147 44 24 E

Nyah
Nyah Rec Reserve CT BIG RIG
37 River St. Dump Point adjacent to
Harness Club
HEMA 87 C10   35 10 18 S   143 22 53 E

Orbost
Murrungowar Rest Area CT HT BIG RIG
Via Princes Hwy. Dump Point
18 km W of Bellbird or 20 km E of Orbost
133 778   HEMA 93 J10   37 41 22 S   148 37 06 E

Orbost Dump Point CT HT 🚰
20 Forest Rd. Dump Point behind
the truck wash
HEMA 93 J9   37 42 28 S   148 27 05 E

Ouyen
Ouyen Caravan Park CT HT BIG RIG 🚰
Calder Hwy. Dump Point
300 m S of railway station
03 5092 1426   HEMA 88 J7   35 04 26 S   142 19 08 E

Oxley
Oxley Rec Reserve CT HT BIG RIG
300 Oxley-Meadowcreek Rd.
Dump Point 3 km S of Oxley. Run by locals.
Donation requested. Honesty box
HEMA 89 D7   36 28 14 S   146 23 06 E

Paynesville
Paynesville Progress Jetty CT
Esplanade. Dump Point at toilet block
03 5153 9500   HEMA 98 K3   37 55 09 S   147 43 10 E

Port Albert
Port Albert Parking Area CT HT BIG RIG
37 Wharf St. Dump Point in
Parking Area near boat ramp. Collect key from Port
Albert General Store
HEMA 91 G10   38 40 22 S   146 41 38 E

Port Fairy
Gardens Caravan Park HT 🚰
111 Griffith St. Dump Point 700 m NE
of PO
03 5568 1060   HEMA 84 H6   38 22 44 S   142 14 30 E

Southcombe Caravan Park HT 🚰
James St.
03 5568 2677   HEMA 84 H6   38 23 20 S   142 14 03 E

Portland
Henty Park CT HT BIG RIG 🚰
2 Bentinck St. Dump Point
adjacent to amenities block, near the Cable Tram depot
03 5523 2671   HEMA 84 H4   38 21 16 S   141 36 22 E

Pyramid Hill
Pyramid Hill Caravan Park CT HT BIG RIG
Via Victoria St. Dump Point in
Caravan Park. 1 km E of PO. Behind amenities
0456 478 558   HEMA 87 G12   36 03 19 S   144 07 30 E

Rainbow
Rainbow Dump Point CT HT BIG RIG
Park St. Dump Point off the
Rainbow-Nhill Rd. Next to the bowling club
HEMA 86 G5   35 54 05 S   141 59 30 E

Rawson
Rawson Dump Point CT HT BIG RIG 🚰
4 Pinnacle Dr. Dump Point
key available at Rawson General Store
HEMA 91 C9   37 57 22 S   146 23 49 E

Robinvale
Robinvale Dump Point CT HT BIG RIG
6 Robin St. Dump Point at
Riverside Park by toilet block
HEMA 87 A1   34 34 52 S   142 46 24 E

Rochester
Aysons Reserve (Campaspe River) CT HT BIG RIG 🚰
Via Burnewang Rd. Dump Point at Camp Area 8 km
NE of Elmore
03 5481 2200   HEMA 87 J14   36 27 34 S   144 40 08 E

Rosedale
Rosedale Bowling Club CT 🚰
1 Dawson St. Dump Point near Wood St
HEMA 91 D10   38 09 21 S   146 46 49 E

Rupanyup
Rupanyup Memorial Park CT HT 🚰
89 Wimmera Hwy. Dump Point
Cnr Minyip-Rupanyup Rd
0448 782 834   HEMA 86 K7   36 37 35 S   142 37 46 E

Sale
Port of Sale CT
Cnr Grand Canal Rd & Punt Ln. Dump Point
near toilet block
1300 366 244   HEMA 91 D12   38 06 50 S   147 03 56 E

Sale Showground CT HT BIG RIG 🚰
2 Sale-Maffra Rd. Dump
Point at Showground
03 5144 6432   HEMA 91 D12   38 05 31 S   147 03 58 E

Sea Lake
Sea Lake Rec Reserve CT HT BIG RIG
71-91 Calder Hwy. Dump Point in
the middle of town
0427 701 261   HEMA 87 E8   35 30 11 S   142 50 57 E

Seymour
Seymour Dump Point CT HT
40 High St. Dump Point Cnr Wallis St
HEMA 89 F3   37 01 14 S   145 08 05 E

Shepparton
Ken Muston Automotive Dump Point CT HT $ BIG RIG
Enterprise Dr. At the rear of business. Enter via
Florence St or Doyles Rd to laneway, through gates,
signposted. Business hours only, donation
03 5821 6688   HEMA 89 C4   36 23 08 S   145 25 41 E

Shepparton Dump Point CT HT 🚰
Fryers St. Dump Point rear of
Showgrounds. Access from Archer St at E end
1800 808 839   HEMA 89 C4   36 22 50 S   145 24 39 E

Simpson
Simpson Recreation Reserve CT HT
Lavers Hill Codben Rd. At Parking Area
N end of town
0428 363 604   HEMA 82 G6   38 29 41 S   143 12 40 E

Smythesdale
Smythesdale Gardens CT HT 🚰
35 Garden St. Potable water
03 5342 8752   HEMA 85 E11   37 38 21 S   143 41 09 E

St Arnaud
St Arnaud Sports Club CT HT BIG RIG 🚰
Dunstan St. Off Charlton St
& Arnaud Rd, behind sports club
03 5495 1268   HEMA 87 K9   36 36 32 S   143 15 34 E

Stawell
Stawell Dump Point CT 🚰
35 Scallan St. Dump Point near public
toilets. Please obey No Standing signs
HEMA 85 B8   37 03 15 S   142 46 52 E

Stratford
Stratford On the River Tourist Park CT HT $ BIG RIG 🚰
16 McMillan St. Dump Point at park, 400 m S of PO
03 5145 6588   HEMA 91 C12   37 58 11 S   147 04 40 E

VICTORIA

Strathmerton
Strathmerton Dump Point `CT` `HT` `BIG RIG` 🚰
Murray Valley Hwy. Dump Point in lane behind toilet block. Opposite pub
HEMA 89 A4   35 55 33 S   145 28 46 E

Sunshine
Sunshine 7 Eleven Service Station Northbound `CT` `BIG RIG`
Western Ring Rd Northbound. Dump Point. Take truck lane, past diesel pumps. Marked as Bus Effluent point
03 9310 2694   **HEMA 76 G2**   37 48 16 S   144 48 16 E

Sunshine 7 Eleven Service Station Southbound `CT` `BIG RIG`
Western Ring Rd Southbound. Dump Point. Take truck lane, past diesel pumps. Marked as Bus Effluent point
03 9310 2615   **HEMA 76 G3**   37 48 16 S   144 48 33 E

Swan Hill
Swan Hill Showgrounds `CT` `HT` `BIG RIG`
Stradbroke Ave. Dump Point entry via Stradbroke Ave, left of the grandstand
HEMA 87 D10   35 20 20 S   143 22 04 E

Tallangatta
Tallangatta Showgrounds `CT` `HT` `BIG RIG` 🚰
10 Coorilla St. At showground entry near Weeramu St. Gold coin donation for water
02 6071 2621   **HEMA 92 B5**   36 13 10 S   147 10 05 E

Tatura
Tatura Park `CT` `BIG RIG`
Hastie St. At entry opposite Davy St
HEMA 89 D3   36 26 44 S   145 13 58 E

Terang
Terang Community Caravan Park `CT` `HT` `BIG RIG` 🚰
Princes Hwy. Dump Point access easiest from E entrance Camperdown side
0409 518 795   **HEMA 82 D4**   38 14 31 S   142 54 34 E

Tidal River
Tidal River `CT` `HT` 🚰
Ring Rd. Dump Point at Camp Area
131 963   **HEMA 91 K8**   39 01 48 S   146 19 16 E

Timboon
Timboon Rec Reserve `CT` `HT` `BIG RIG` 🚰
45 Curdies Rd. Dump Point Key at Timboon Fuel
0407 504 374   **HEMA 82 G4**   38 28 41 S   142 57 56 E

Wahgunyah
Wahgunyah `CT` `HT` `BIG RIG`
Cnr Victoria & Distillery Rd. Dump Point opposite Main St
HEMA 92 A2   36 00 44 S   146 24 04 E

Walwa
Walwa Dump Point `CT` `HT` `BIG RIG`
O'Halloran St. Dump Point off River Rd. At the football oval
HEMA 92 A7   35 57 44 S   147 44 11 E

Wangaratta
Wangaratta Dump Point `CT` `HT` `BIG RIG` 🚰
2 Swan St. Next to toilets, open during business hours
HEMA 92 B2   36 21 32 S   146 18 34 E

Warracknabeal
Warracknabeal Caravan Park `CT` `HT`
2 Lyle St / Dimboola Rd. Dump Point at local Council Park
0400 915 125   **HEMA 86 H6**   36 15 11 S   142 23 15 E

Warrnambool
Surfside Holiday Park `CT` `HT` `$`
120 Pertobe Rd. Dump Point within the park. Fee for non guests
03 5559 4700   **HEMA 82 F1**   38 23 31 S   142 29 02 E

Warrnambool Holiday Village `CT` `HT` `$`
81 Henna St.
03 5562 3376   **HEMA 82 F1**   38 22 41 S   142 28 43 E

Warrnambool Showgrounds `CT` `HT` `$` 🚰
331 Koroit St. Dump Point located at the back of the park near toilets. Honesty box for donation
0409 009 473   **HEMA 82 F1**   38 22 37 S   142 28 08 E

Wedderburn
Wedderburn Pioneer Caravan Park `CT` `HT` `BIG RIG`
63 Hospital St. 1 km E of PO. Report to office
03 5494 3301   **HEMA 87 J11**   36 24 47 S   143 36 59 E

Willaura
Willaura Rec Grounds `CT` `HT` `BIG RIG` 🚰
1 Delacome Way. Dump Point beside public toilet
0429 953 150   **HEMA 84 D7**   37 32 41 S   142 44 36 E

Winchelsea
Barwon Hotel `CT` `HT` `BIG RIG` 🚰
1 Main St. Dump Point adjacent hotel. If locked, see hotel or information on sign
03 5267 2046   **HEMA 83 D11**   38 14 34 S   143 59 27 E

Woomelang
Woomelang Dump Point `CT` `HT` `BIG RIG`
67 Brook St. Dump Point behind undercover seating area
HEMA 86 F7   35 40 50 S   142 39 49 E

Wulgulmerang
Wulgulmerang Rec Reserve `CT` `HT` `BIG RIG`
Snowy River Rd. Dump Point beside amenities building
03 5155 0253   **HEMA 93 F8**   37 04 06 S   148 15 37 E

Wycheproof
Wycheproof Caravan Park `CT` `HT` `BIG RIG` 🚰
462 Broadway. Dump Point at Caravan Park on Calder Hwy 500 m N of PO
03 5493 7278   **HEMA 87 G9**   36 04 10 S   143 13 33 E

Yarram
Yarram Rec Reserve `CT` `HT` `BIG RIG` 🚰
Cnr Railway Ave & Buckley St. Dump Point at Showground
HEMA 91 G10   38 33 25 S   146 40 25 E

Yarrawonga
Yarrawonga Showgrounds `CT` `HT` `BIG RIG`
46 Dunlop St. Dump Point next to cream brick amenities block
03 5744 1989   **HEMA 89 B6**   36 01 03 S   146 00 32 E

Yea
Yea Water Discovery Centre `CT` `HT` `BIG RIG`
2 Hood St. Dump Point near Info Centre
03 5797 2663   **HEMA 89 G4**   37 12 36 S   145 25 37 E

TASMANIA

Arthur River
Arthur River Dump Point `CT` `BIG RIG`
Airey St. S side of river, turn R to Gardiner Point. End of the road at the "Edge of the World Lookout"
03 6452 4800   **HEMA 108 F1**   41 03 27 S   144 39 37 E

TASMANIA

Bakers Beach
Bakers Point Campground `CT`
Bakers Point Rd. Camp Area 18 km N of B71/C740 Jcn. 6 km dirt road
03 6428 6277   **HEMA 106 C1**   41 09 44 S   146 34 05 E

Springlawn Campground `CT`
Bakers Beach Rd. Camp Area 13.5 km N of B71/C740 Jcn. 2 km dirt road
03 6428 6277   **HEMA 106 C2**   41 08 52 S   146 36 09 E

Beaconsfield
Beaconsfield Rec Ground `CT` `HT` `BIG RIG`
Grubb St. E side of town, via York St
03 6394 4454   **HEMA 106 D6**   41 11 57 S   146 49 19 E

Bicheno
Bicheno Dump Point `CT` `HT` `BIG RIG`
The Esplanade. Cnr of Fraser St
03 6256 4777   **HEMA 105 J14**   41 52 19 S   148 18 25 E

Bothwell
Bothwell Dump Point `CT`
Market place. Rear of Council CP, behind golf museum
03 6259 5503   **HEMA 111 H13**   42 22 59 S   147 00 31 E

Bruny Island
Alonnah Dump Point `CT` `BIG RIG` 🚰
3915 Bruny Island Main Rd. Flushing Dump Point. Tap water & toilets nearby, park roadside and walk cartridge in
HEMA 113 H12   43 18 58 S   147 14 36 E

Burnie
Cooee Point Reserve `CT` `HT` `BIG RIG`
Cooee Point Rd. 3 km W of Burnie, via Turrung St
03 6430 5831   **HEMA 104 C1**   41 02 19 S   145 52 37 E

South Burnie Dump Point `CT` `HT`
Esplanade. Reeve St public toilets, near yacht club
HEMA 104 C1   41 03 44 S   145 54 54 E

Cambridge
Cambridge Memorial Oval `CT` `HT` `BIG RIG`
Bungana Way. Cambridge Rd
03 6245 8600   **HEMA 101 E7**   42 50 10 S   147 26 41 E

Campbell Town
King Street Oval `CT` `HT` `BIG RIG`
24 King St. W end of oval
03 6397 7303   **HEMA 102 A3**   41 55 47 S   147 29 17 E

Cradle Mountain
Cradle Mountain Dump Point `CT` `HT` `BIG RIG`
Cradle Mountain Rd. N end of main carpark, near 24 hour pump
03 6492 7799   **HEMA 104 G1**   41 34 52 S   145 56 16 E

Cygnet
Cygnet Dump Point `CT` `HT` `BIG RIG`
Esplanade. S end of town, Channel Hwy Jcn
03 6264 0300   **HEMA 113 G11**   43 09 48 S   147 05 00 E

Deloraine
Deloraine RV Rest Stop `CT` `HT` `BIG RIG`
6 Racecourse Dr. Near tennis courts
03 6393 5300   **HEMA 104 G5**   41 31 19 S   146 39 43 E

Devonport
Devonport South Dump Point `CT` `HT` `BIG RIG`
Miandetta-Devonport Rd. Sewerage facility, next to bridge near Horsehead Creek
03 6424 0511   **HEMA 104 D3**   41 11 59 S   146 21 19 E

TASMANIA

East Devonport
Girdlestone Park `CT` `HT` `BIG RIG` `[tap]`
John St. Car park at football ground
03 6424 4466   HEMA 104 D4   41 11 10 S   146 22 45 E

Evandale
Morven Park `CT` `HT` `BIG RIG`
Barclay St. W end of town. Behind clubhouse
03 6397 7303   HEMA 105 G8   41 34 04 S   147 14 38 E

Fingal
Fingal Park `CT` `BIG RIG`
Talbot St. Beside public toilets
03 6376 7900   HEMA 105 H12   41 38 17 S   147 58 06 E

Franklin
Franklin Camping Ground `CT` `HT` `BIG RIG`
3445 Huon Hwy. Next to toilet block
03 6264 0326   HEMA 113 F10   43 05 34 S   147 00 33 E

Geeveston
Heritage Park `CT` `HT` `BIG RIG`
Arve Rd. Parking Area, entry opposite roadhouse
03 6264 0300   HEMA 113 G10   43 09 44 S   146 55 28 E

George Town
George Town Rest Area `CT` `HT` `BIG RIG`
Main Rd. S end of town, behind information centre
6382 1700   HEMA 106 B6   41 06 33 S   146 50 18 E

Glenorchy
Hobart Showgrounds `CT` `HT`
2 Howard Rd. Inside grounds
03 6272 6812   HEMA 101 E3   42 50 02 S   147 17 06 E

Gordon
Gordon Foreshore Reserve `CT` `HT` `BIG RIG`
4775 Channel Hwy. Near Camp Area
03 6211 8200   HEMA 113 G12   43 15 39 S   147 14 33 E

Hamilton
Hamilton Camping Ground `CT` `HT` `$` `BIG RIG`
River St. W end of town. Riverside
03 6286 3202   HEMA 111 J12   42 33 33 S   146 49 50 E

Hobart
Montrose Bay Reserve `CT` `HT` `BIG RIG`
Foreshore Rd. Off Brooker Hwy
03 6216 6800   HEMA 101 D3   42 49 17 S   147 16 08 E

Huonville
Huonville Foreshore `CT` `HT` `BIG RIG`
The Esplanade. Channel Hwy. Next to toilets
03 6264 0300   HEMA 113 F11   43 02 06 S   147 03 02 E

Kempton
Victoria Memorial Hall `CT`
Old Hunting Ground Rd. Off Main St, next to toilets. Difficult for large motorhomes to back into
03 6259 3011   HEMA 102 E1   42 31 54 S   147 12 01 E

Kingston
Kingston Wetlands Site `CT` `HT` `BIG RIG`
Channel Hwy. At entrance to Wetlands Reserve
03 6211 8200   HEMA 101 K4   42 58 27 S   147 18 50 E

Latrobe
Latrobe Overnight Stop `CT` `HT` `BIG RIG`
via Cotton St. Rear of Wells Supermarket
03 6426 4444   HEMA 104 D4   41 14 14 S   146 24 37 E

Launceston
Inveresk Showgrounds (York Park Precinct) `CT` `HT` `BIG RIG`
Forster St. All day parking area near the Round House. Via Invermay Rd, entry near South St
03 6323 3383   HEMA 107 K11   41 25 22 S   147 08 24 E

New Norfolk
New Norfolk Dump Point `CT` `HT` `BIG RIG`
4 Page Ave. Next to caravan park
03 6261 8500   HEMA 113 D11   42 46 34 S   147 03 57 E

Nubeena
Nubeena Dump Point `CT` `HT` `BIG RIG`
27 Nubeena Rd. N end of town, opposite Police Station
03 6250 9200   HEMA 103 G3   43 05 44 S   147 44 36 E

Oatlands
Oatlands Dump Point `CT` `HT` `BIG RIG` `[tap]`
Cnr William & Wellington Sts. L off main road, drive to end
HEMA 102 C2   42 17 52 S   147 21 58 E

Penguin
Penguin Dump Point `CT` `HT` `BIG RIG`
Johnsons Beach Rd. Close to Main Rd, beach side. If locked, key at Info Centre
03 6429 8979   HEMA 104 D2   41 06 36 S   146 04 10 E

Pontville
Brighton Pontville RV Stop `CT` `HT` `BIG RIG`
3 Glen Lea Rd. Off Midland Hwy
03 6268 1254   HEMA 102 F1   42 41 12 S   147 15 37 E

Port Huon
Shipwrights Point Regatta Ground `CT` `HT` `BIG RIG`
Huon Hwy. Camp Area N of wharf, beside river. Signposted
03 6264 0300   HEMA 113 G10   43 09 31 S   146 58 47 E

Port Sorell
Port Sorell Jetty `CT` `HT` `BIG RIG`
Darling St. N end, next to caravan park
03 6426 4444   HEMA 106 C1   41 09 51 S   146 33 23 E

Queenstown
Queenstown Dump Point `CT` `BIG RIG`
Batchelor St (Lyell Hwy). Near Mary St, beside works building
03 6471 4700   HEMA 110 F6   42 04 38 S   145 33 34 E

Railton
Railton Motorhome Stop `CT` `HT` `BIG RIG`
Esplanade & Foster Sts. At Camp Spot opposite hotel, N side of street
03 6491 0200   HEMA 104 E4   41 20 39 S   146 25 23 E

Rosebery
Rosebery Dump Point `CT` `HT` `BIG RIG`
Park Rd. Opposite caravan park
HEMA 110 D5   41 46 38 S   145 32 06 E

Scottsdale
Northeast Park `CT` `HT` `BIG RIG`
41 Ringarooma Rd. 1 km E of Post Office
03 6352 6500   HEMA 105 D10   41 09 56 S   147 31 23 E

Sheffield
Sheffield Rec Ground `CT` `HT` `BIG RIG` `[tap]`
30 Spring St. On route to Rec Ground
03 6491 1179   HEMA 104 F3   41 22 58 S   146 20 09 E

Sisters Beach
Sisters Beach Dump Point `CT`
cnr Honeysuckle Ave & Cumming St. Behind Fire Station
03 6443 8333   HEMA 108 E6   40 55 05 S   145 33 54 E

Smithton
Smithton Esplanade `CT` `HT` `BIG RIG`
West Esplanade. W side of Duck River Bridge. RH side
HEMA 108 D4   40 50 20 S   145 07 12 E

Sorell
Sorell RV Stop `CT` `BIG RIG`
6 Montagu St.
03 6269 0000   HEMA 102 G3   42 47 02 S   147 33 24 E

St Helens
St Helens Rec Ground `CT` `HT` `BIG RIG` `[tap]`
Cnr Young & Tully Sts. Near Camp Area 2 km from PO
03 6376 7900   HEMA 105 E14   41 19 00 S   148 14 08 E

St Leonards
St Leonards Park Dump Point `CT` `HT` `BIG RIG`
Station Rd. Off Johnston Rd
03 6323 3000   HEMA 105 F8   41 27 45 S   147 11 35 E

St Marys
St Marys Sportsground `CT` `HT` `BIG RIG`
22 Harefield Rd. Near golf course
03 6372 2177   HEMA 105 G13   41 35 05 S   148 11 02 E

Stanley
Stanley Public Dump Point `CT` `HT` `[tap]`
23 Marine Esp. At RV Rec Ground
HEMA 108 D5   40 45 50 S   145 17 45 E

Strahan
Council Depot `CT` `HT` `BIG RIG`
96 Harvey St (Ocean Beach Rd). Outside depot
HEMA 110 F4   42 08 59 S   145 18 48 E

Swansea
Boat Ramp Car Park `CT` `HT` `BIG RIG`
The Esplanade. Near toilets & playground
03 6257 8155   HEMA 102 B6   42 07 51 S   148 04 28 E

Triabunna
Triabunna Dump Point `CT` `HT` `BIG RIG`
Cnr of Esplanade & Charles St. Veer L over bridge, W of Info Centre
03 6257 4772   HEMA 102 E5   42 30 33 S   147 55 10 E

Ulverstone
Ulverstone Dump Point `CT`
Cnr of Victoria St & Beach Rd. In car park, access can be limited if busy. Key at Information Centre
03 6425 2839   HEMA 104 D3   41 09 06 S   146 10 27 E

Waratah
Waratah Dump Point `CT` `HT` `BIG RIG`
Annie St. Opposite Council Works Depot
03 6443 8342   HEMA 108 J6   41 26 36 S   145 31 51 E

Wynyard
Wynyard Solid Waste Transfer Station `CT` `HT` `BIG RIG`
Goldie St. W end of street, outside Transfer Station
03 6443 8342   HEMA 108 E7   40 59 31 S   145 43 01 E

Zeehan
Zeehan Dump Point `CT` `HT` `BIG RIG`
Cnr. Mulcahy & Packer St. Off B27, 300 m from intersection on R
03 6471 4700   HEMA 110 D4   41 53 25 S   145 20 45 E

SOUTH AUSTRALIA

Alford
Alford Recreation Park CT HT BIG RIG
South Tce. Camp Area at Alford opposite tennis courts in South Tce
0400 005 859   **HEMA 124 B5**   33 49 01 S   137 49 18 E

Andamooka
Andamooka Caravan & Camping Ground CT HT BIG RIG [water]
Cnr Water & Opan Ck Rds. Camp Area 1 km W of Andamooka
0477 184 485   **HEMA 130 J3**   30 27 11 S   137 09 39 E

Ardrossan
Ardrossan RV Stop CT HT BIG RIG
Cnr Second St & West Tce. Dump Point at rear of bowling club & tennis courts, enter from West Tce
1800 202 445   **HEMA 124 D5**   34 25 28 S   137 54 52 E

Arno Bay
The Arno Bay Hotel CT HT BIG RIG [water]
Cnr Creek Rd & Tel El Kebir Tce. Camp Area at Arno Bay foreshore end
08 8628 0001   **HEMA 124 B1**   33 54 59 S   136 34 22 E

Balaklava
Balaklava Caravan Park CT HT BIG RIG
Short Tce. Next to swimming pool
0400 264 075   **HEMA 124 C6**   34 08 57 S   138 25 08 E

Barmera
Barmera RV Park CT HT BIG RIG [water]
Sims St. Dump Point in town
08 8588 2289   **HEMA 125 D12**   34 15 13 S   140 28 03 E

Beachport
Beachport Surf Beach CT HT BIG RIG [water]
Millicent Rd. Located at the front of the Visitor Info Centre. Potable water
08 8733 0900   **HEMA 126 G3**   37 28 26 S   140 01 52 E

Berri
Martins Bend Reserve CT
Martins Bend Dr. At Camp Area 3 km E of Berri via Riverview Rd. Follow signs. See caretaker before using
08 8582 5511   **HEMA 125 D13**   34 17 21 S   140 37 52 E

Blanchetown
Blanchetown Oval CT HT BIG RIG
South Tce. S of town, at Lower Blanchetown Oval
08 8540 0901   **HEMA 125 D10**   34 21 19 S   139 37 00 E

Blyth
Blyth Sportsground CT HT BIG RIG
15-17 South Tce. Parking Area at Blyth. Entry off South Tce
0428 445 218   **HEMA 124 B7**   33 50 53 S   138 29 24 E

Bolivar
Bolivar Service Station Dump Point CT HT BIG RIG
885 Port Wakefield Rd. Behind OTR service station. Cnr Hodgson Rd
08 8250 0700   **HEMA 120 D4**   34 46 05 S   138 35 33 E

Booleroo
Arthur Street Town Oval CT HT BIG RIG [water]
42 Arthur St. Dump Point near athletic club. Potable water
0438 823 896   **HEMA 128 H7**   32 52 54 S   138 21 23 E

Border Village
Border Village Caravan Park CT HT BIG RIG
Eyre Hwy. Outside entrance
08 9039 3474   **HEMA 141 K1**   31 38 18 S   129 00 12 E

Bordertown
Bordertown Recreation Lake CT HT BIG RIG
Golf Course Rd. At Rest Area N of Hwy, turn R to lake
08 8752 1044   **HEMA 126 B5**   36 18 21 S   140 46 31 E

Bower
Bower Reserve CT HT $ BIG RIG
Thiele Hwy. At Camp Area next to tennis court.
08 8892 0100   **HEMA 125 C9**   34 07 23 S   139 21 11 E

Brinkworth
Brinkworth Travellers Overnight Stay CT HT BIG RIG [water]
Cnr East Tce & Edgar St. Turn E off Main St. Entry off East Tce. Outside Camp Area, potable water
0427 462 023   **HEMA 124 A6**   33 41 33 S   138 24 18 E

Brownlow
Brownlow CT HT BIG RIG
Third St. Dump Point adjacent to Nepean Bay Tourist Park
HEMA 124 J4   35 40 15 S   137 36 42 E

Burra
Burra Caravan & Camping Park CT HT $ BIG RIG
12 Bridge Tce. Dump Point in Burra
0488 513 101   **HEMA 125 A8**   33 40 44 S   138 56 15 E

Burra North
Burra Showgrounds CT HT $ BIG RIG
Lot 4 Hall Tce. Dump Point at showgrounds
0447 938 152   **HEMA 125 A8**   33 40 05 S   138 55 28 E

Bute
Bute Dump Point CT BIG RIG
Railway Tce. Dump Point at Lions Park
HEMA 124 B5   33 51 54 S   138 00 32 E

Cadell
Cadell Recreation Ground CT HT BIG RIG
81 Dalzell Rd. Near Camp Area. Via Heinrich Rd
0497 799 284   **HEMA 125 C10**   34 02 12 S   139 45 27 E

Callington
Callington Recreation Grounds CT HT BIG RIG [water]
Callington Rd. Toilets available
08 8539 1100   **HEMA 127 G7**   35 06 47 S   139 02 22 E

Carpenter Rocks
Carpenter Rocks Rec Reserve CT
24 Carpenter Rocks Rd. Near Camp Area behind hall
08 8721 0444   **HEMA 126 J4**   37 54 49 S   140 23 55 E

Ceduna
BP Service Station CT HT BIG RIG
Eyre Hwy. Dump Point W end of town at Fruit Fly Checkpoint
08 8625 3407   **HEMA 134 A1**   32 06 48 S   133 40 21 E

Clayton Bay
Clayton Bay Dump Point CT HT BIG RIG
Island View Dr. Dump Point next to boat club entrance
08 8555 7000   **HEMA 125 H8**   35 29 33 S   138 55 21 E

Cleve
Cleve Dump Point CT HT BIG RIG
Rudall Road. Dump Point 1.8 km W of PO
08 8628 2004   **HEMA 124 A1**   33 41 52 S   136 28 33 E

Coffin Bay
Coffin Bay Boat Ramp CT HT BIG RIG
Esplanade. Dump Point near toilets
08 8676 0400   **HEMA 134 H5**   34 36 58 S   135 27 51 E

Coober Pedy
Coober Pedy Dump Point CT HT BIG RIG [water]
Hutchinson St. 900m N of PO, next to Info Centre
HEMA 137 A9   29 00 55 S   134 45 22 E

Coonalpyn
Coonalpyn Soldiers Memorial Caravan Park CT HT BIG RIG
Malcolm Tce. Dump Point at Coonalpyn after Caravan Park sign
0427 399 089   **HEMA 125 J10**   35 41 33 S   139 51 27 E

Cowell
Cowell CT HT BIG RIG
16073 Lincoln Hwy. Dump Point opposite BP Roadhouse
HEMA 124 A2   33 40 48 S   136 55 32 E

Crystal Brook
Jubilee Park Crystal Brook CT HT BIG RIG
Railway Tce. Dump Point between Cunningham & Bowman Sts
08 8633 8700   **HEMA 128 J6**   33 21 13 S   138 12 23 E

Cummins
Cummins Community Caravan Park CT HT BIG RIG
Roe St. Dump Point 2 km S of PO
08 8676 2011   **HEMA 134 G6**   34 16 15 S   135 43 23 E

Curramulka
Curramulka Overnight Stay CT HT BIG RIG
Mount Rat Rd. At Parking Area next to bowls club & tennis court
08 8854 2234   **HEMA 124 E4**   34 41 52 S   137 42 24 E

Dublin
Dublin Lions Park CT HT BIG RIG
Sixth St. Dump Point in Rest Area behind toilet block
08 8527 0200   **HEMA 124 D6**   34 27 07 S   138 21 05 E

Edithburgh
Edithburgh Dump Point CT HT BIG RIG
65 Blanche St. Dump Point opposite caravan park
1800 202 445   **HEMA 124 G4**   35 05 24 S   137 44 44 E

Elliston
Elliston Dump Point CT HT BIG RIG [water]
Memorial Dr. Dump Point near the hall
08 8687 9200   **HEMA 134 F4**   33 38 51 S   134 53 28 E

Farrell Flat
Farrell Flat Oval CT HT BIG RIG [water]
Cnr Cameron & South Tces. Dump Point in Duncan Park, next to toilets
08 8892 0100   **HEMA 124 B7**   33 49 40 S   138 47 36 E

Gawler
Gawler Caravan Park CT HT $
7 Main North Rd. Dump Point 500 m N of PO
08 8522 3805   **HEMA 127 A4**   34 35 33 S   138 44 48 E

Gladstone
Gladstone Dump Point CT HT BIG RIG
Main North Rd. Dump Point behind caravan park
08 8664 1139   **HEMA 128 J7**   33 16 06 S   138 20 59 E

SOUTH AUSTRALIA

Goolwa South
Bristow-Smith Park `CT` 💧
92-94 Barrage Rd. Bristow Smith
Reserve next to toilet block at S end of Aquatic
Centre carpark
08 8555 7000   **HEMA 124 H7**   35 30 51 S   138 47 04 E

Hamley Bridge
Hamley Bridge `CT` `HT` `BIG RIG` 💧
Community & Sports
Centre
17 Stockport Rd. Dump Point at the oval
08 8862 0800   **HEMA 124 D7**   34 21 14 S   138 40 53 E

Haslam
Haslam RV Camping `CT` `HT` 💧
Cnr Main St & South Tce. Dump
Point & potable water at Doc Woods Rec Area
08 8626 7033   **HEMA 134 B2**   32 30 32 S   134 12 50 E

Hawker
Hawker Town Park `CT` `HT` `BIG RIG`
Elder Tce. Rest Area at Hawker off
the Outback Hwy
HEMA 128 D7   31 53 15 S   138 25 16 E

Innamincka
Innamincka Town Common `CT` `HT` `BIG RIG`
Old Strzelecki Track. Dump Point
1 km S of Innamincka Township
08 8675 9901   **HEMA 133 H14**   27 44 59 S   140 43 56 E

Iron Knob
Knobbies Camping & `CT` `HT` `$` `BIG RIG`
Caravan Area
Moroney St. Dump Point at the Caravan Park
HEMA 128 G3   32 43 56 S   137 09 02 E

Jamestown
Jamestown Dump Point `CT` `HT` `BIG RIG`
103 Ayr St. Dump Point outside
caravan park
08 8664 0077   **HEMA 128 J7**   33 12 19 S   138 36 03 E

Kadina
Kadina Dump Point `CT` `HT` `BIG RIG`
Doswell Tce. Dump Point to the
end on L near dog park
08 8828 1200   **HEMA 124 B4**   33 57 32 S   137 43 16 E

Kangaroo Island
American River Dump Point `CT` `HT` `BIG RIG`
Tangara Dr. In front of toilet block
08 8553 4500   **HEMA 124 J4**   35 47 15 S   137 46 15 E

Christmas Cove - Penneshaw `CT`
Howard Dr. In the carpark next to the old
Tourism KI Gateway building. Access is limited
HEMA 124 J5   35 43 09 S   137 56 02 E

Kapunda
Kapunda Harness `CT` `HT` `BIG RIG` 💧
Racing Club
Hancock Rd. Gold coin donation
0428 956 462   **HEMA 125 D8**   34 20 26 S   138 54 08 E

Karatta
Western River Caravan `CT` `HT` `$` `BIG RIG`
Park & Wildlife Reserve
South Coast Rd. Dump Point 3 km E of Flinders
Chase. Fee for non guests, must call into reception
08 8559 7201   **HEMA 124 K2**   35 57 39 S   136 48 28 E

Karoonda
Karoonda Cabin & `CT` `HT` `BIG RIG`
Caravan Park
11 Railway Tce. Entry off Karoonda Rd, follow track
to back of oval toilet block. Signposted
08 8578 1004   **HEMA 125 G11**   35 05 47 S   139 53 23 E

Keith
Keith Caravan Park `CT` `HT`
Naracoorte Rd. Dump Point at Caravan
Park. Small fee for public access
0427 876 993   **HEMA 125 K12**   36 06 04 S   140 21 04 E

Kimba
Kimba Rec Reserve `CT` `HT` `BIG RIG` 💧
North Tce. Dump Point on
Buckleboo Rd extension. Entry through archway
08 8627 2026   **HEMA 128 J1**   33 08 04 S   136 24 54 E

Kingston SE
Kingston SE Dump Point `CT` `HT` `BIG RIG`
Railway Tce. Dump Point off Cape
Jaffa/Robe Hwy, at sale yards
08 8767 2033   **HEMA 126 D2**   36 50 03 S   139 51 45 E

Maria Creek RV Park `CT` `HT`
Marine Pde. At beachfront Parking Area
08 8767 2033   **HEMA 126 D2**   36 49 40 S   139 51 01 E

Langhorne Creek
Langhorne Creek Dump Point `CT` `HT`
Meechi Rd. Behind town hall
08 8555 7000   **HEMA 127 J7**   35 17 44 S   139 02 11 E

Laura
Laura Dump Point `CT` `HT` `BIG RIG`
North Tce. Dump Point on road
outside Laura Caravan Park
08 8663 2296   **HEMA 128 J7**   33 10 54 S   138 18 03 E

Lock
Lock Caravan Park `CT` `HT` `BIG RIG` 💧
South Tce. Dump Point at
Caravan Park near town centre
0417 896 991   **HEMA 134 E6**   33 34 10 S   135 45 24 E

Loxton
Loxton Dump Point `CT` `HT` `BIG RIG`
AW Traeger Dr. Dump Point at the
end of Pine Ave behind swimming pool
08 8584 8000   **HEMA 125 D13**   34 27 06 S   140 34 42 E

Loxton Lions Park Reserve `CT` `HT` `BIG RIG`
Grant Schubert Dr. Dump Point
beside park and toilets
08 8584 8071   **HEMA 125 D12**   34 26 53 S   140 33 01 E

Lucindale
Lucindale Dump Point `CT` `HT` `BIG RIG`
Centenary Ave. In Sports Oval near
the toilets, via W entry before agriculture field grounds
08 8762 1399   **HEMA 126 E4**   36 58 18 S   140 21 51 E

Maitland
Maitland Showground SA `CT` `HT` `BIG RIG`
Rogers Tce. Dump Point near
shed on right. Signposted
08 8832 2171   **HEMA 124 D4**   34 22 18 S   137 40 39 E

Mallala
Mallala Sports Ground `CT` `HT` `BIG RIG`
1 Wasleys Rd. At Camp Area
200 m E of PO, near Cnr Marshman St
08 8527 0200   **HEMA 124 D7**   34 26 18 S   138 30 49 E

Mannum
Haythorpe Reserve `CT` 💧
Hunter Rd. In parking area 1 km NE of
Mannum on Bowhill Rd. E side of river. N of ferry
crossing. Non potable water
08 8569 0100   **HEMA 125 F9**   34 54 33 S   139 19 24 E

Marla
Marla Dump Point `CT` `HT` `BIG RIG`
Cockatoo Cr. Near toilets and
roadhouse
08 8670 7001   **HEMA 138 E6**   27 18 08 S   133 37 22 E

Meadows
Meadows Rec Ground `CT` `HT` `BIG RIG`
Mawson Rd. Dump Point not
available during sports or events
08 8391 7200   **HEMA 119 K9**   35 10 47 S   138 45 35 E

Melrose
Melrose Showground `CT` `HT` `BIG RIG`
Horrocks Hwy. Dump Point on
Main North Rd. N end of town
0401 002 658   **HEMA 128 G6**   32 48 36 S   138 11 46 E

Meningie
Meningie Dump Point `CT` `HT` `BIG RIG`
Princes Hwy. Dump Point in
parking bay at S entrance to town
1300 785 277   **HEMA 125 J9**   35 41 40 S   139 20 12 E

Millicent
Millicent Info Centre `CT` `HT` `BIG RIG`
1 Mt Gambier St. Dump Point
behind Info Centre in Towers Rd, but access through
Mt Gambier St
08 8733 0904   **HEMA 126 G4**   37 35 50 S   140 21 27 E

Minlaton
Minlaton Dump Point `CT` `HT` 💧
Cnr West & North Tce. At football
ground, near toilets and potable water
HEMA 124 E4   34 46 07 S   137 35 30 E

Moonta
Moonta Dump Point `CT` `HT` `BIG RIG` 💧
Cnr Blyth & Frances Tces.
Drive through Dump Point at Moonta
08 8828 1200   **HEMA 124 C4**   34 03 43 S   137 35 15 E

Moorook
Moorook Riverfront Camp `CT` `HT`
Kingston-Loxton Rd. Dump Point at
Moorook Rec Area
08 8584 8000   **HEMA 125 D12**   34 17 17 S   140 22 06 E

Morgan
Morgan Dump Point `CT` `HT` `BIG RIG`
4 North East Tce. Dump Point
near the Morgan Sporting Complex
HEMA 125 C10   34 01 46 S   139 40 08 E

Mount Barker
Mount Barker Dump Point `CT`
Alexandrina Rd. Dump Point at the oval
HEMA 119 F12   35 04 26 S   138 51 43 E

Mount Gambier
Frew Park Public Dump Point `CT` `BIG RIG`
48 Penola Rd. Dump Point at RV Day
parking only
HEMA 126 J5   37 49 29 S   140 46 58 E

Mount Gambier `CT` `HT` `$` `BIG RIG`
Showground
34 Pick Ave. Dump Point at showgrounds. Fee if not
staying overnight
0408 492 182   **HEMA 126 J5**   37 50 16 S   140 47 51 E

Mount Pleasant
Talunga Park Caravan Park `CT` `HT` `BIG RIG`
Melrose St. Dump Point at oval
08 8568 1934   **HEMA 127 C7**   34 46 34 S   139 02 34 E

Mundulla
Mundulla Showground `CT` `HT` `BIG RIG`
Cnr North Tce & Mile Ln. Dump
Point at showground toilets
0475 920 837   **HEMA 126 B5**   36 21 30 S   140 41 25 E

Murray Bridge
Murray Bridge Dump Point `CT` `HT` `BIG RIG`
Railway Terrace. Dump Point
200 m NE of PO
HEMA 125 G9   35 06 57 S   139 16 25 E

SOUTH AUSTRALIA

Naracoorte
Naracoorte Showgrounds `CT` `HT` `BIG RIG`
Cnr Smith St & Cadgee Rd. Dump Point at showground
0414 453 360   HEMA 126 E5   36 57 16 S   140 44 48 E

Nuriootpa
Barossa Co-op Shopping Centre `CT` `HT` `BIG RIG` `tap`
3 Murray St. Dump Point from Tanunda, turn L after bridge, drive straight through car park, over speed bumps & pedestrian crossing, past underground carpark side entrance, opposite the wall, in the garden on the L side
08 8568 6000   HEMA 122 B4   34 28 28 S   138 59 34 E

Orroroo
Orroroo Caravan Park `CT` `$` `BIG RIG`
21 West Tce. Dump Point 200 m W of PO, at back of park. Pay fee at reception
08 8658 1444   HEMA 128 G7   32 43 57 S   138 36 36 E

Parndana
Parndana Dump Point `CT` `BIG RIG`
Jubilee Ave. Dump Point in carpark near the health centre and playground
08 8553 4500   HEMA 124 J3   35 47 17 S   137 15 38 E

Penola
McCorquindale Park `CT` `HT` `BIG RIG`
19 Cameron St. Dump Point entrance between Portland & Gordon Sts
HEMA 126 F5   37 22 29 S   140 50 27 E

Peterborough
Peterborough Dump Point `CT` `HT` `BIG RIG`
Don Ferguson Drive. Dump Point entry beside Info Centre opposite Railway Hotel
08 8651 3566   HEMA 129 H8   32 58 25 S   138 50 02 E

Pinnaroo
Pinnaroo `CT` `HT` `BIG RIG`
Cnr Mallee Hwy & Homburg Tce. Dump Point beside toilets and wetlands
08 8577 8002   HEMA 125 G14   35 15 37 S   140 54 46 E

Point Lowly
Point Lowly `CT` `HT` `BIG RIG`
Lighthouse Dr. Dump Point on Port Bonython Rd. 500 m N of Camp Spot, S side past gas plant
08 8645 7900   HEMA 128 H5   32 59 34 S   137 46 51 E

Port Augusta
OTR Port Augusta `CT` `HT`
Cnr Augusta Hwy & Northern Power Station Rd. Dump Point at BP carpark
HEMA 128 F5   32 31 45 S   137 48 11 E

Port Augusta Motorhome Park `CT` `HT` `BIG RIG`
58 Old Power Station Rd. Dump Point on site
08 8642 5282   HEMA 128 F5   32 30 40 S   137 47 09 E

Port Broughton
Port Broughton Dump Point `CT` `HT` `BIG RIG`
Cnr Mundoora & Bute Rds. Dump Point next to council depot
08 8635 2107   HEMA 124 A5   33 36 10 S   137 56 09 E

Port Clinton
Port Clinton Dump Point `CT` `HT` `BIG RIG` `tap`
Cnr Emeu St & Cumberland Rd. Near toilets, potable water
HEMA 124 C5   34 13 28 S   138 01 09 E

Port Germein
Port Germein Rec Grounds `CT` `HT` `BIG RIG`
Esplanade. Dump Point near Cnr Mozart & Kobenhavn Jcn
08 8666 2014   HEMA 128 H6   33 01 09 S   137 59 39 E

Port Gibbon
Port Gibbon Foreshore `CT` `HT` `BIG RIG`
Beach Rd. Access from B100 at Port Gibbon sign, through Igloo Rd
08 8629 2019   HEMA 124 B2   33 48 07 S   136 48 06 E

Port Julia
Port Julia Oval `CT` `$`
Cnr Port Julia Rd & Osprey St. Behind toilets. Fee if not staying
0417 877 316   HEMA 124 E5   34 39 46 S   137 52 38 E

Port Lincoln
Port Lincoln Dump Point `CT` `HT` `BIG RIG` `tap`
Windsor Ave. Dump Point off Proper Bay Rd next to Ravendale sportsgrounds. Locked at sunset
08 8621 2300   HEMA 134 J6   34 44 35 S   135 51 18 E

Port MacDonnell
Port MacDonnell Rec Reserve `CT` `HT` `BIG RIG`
Elizabeth St. Dump Point at Rec grounds
08 8721 0444   HEMA 126 K5   38 03 04 S   140 42 01 E

Port Neill
Port Neill Dump Point `CT` `HT` `BIG RIG` `tap`
Wallis St. Dump Point near tennis court, potable water and public toilets
08 8688 9027   HEMA 134 G7   34 07 03 S   136 20 49 E

Port Parham
Parham Camping Ground `CT` `tap`
The Esplanade. At N end of Camp Area. Potable water
08 8527 0200   HEMA 124 D6   34 25 34 S   138 15 20 E

Port Pirie
Port Pirie Dump Point `CT` `HT` `BIG RIG`
Geddes Rd. At Globe Oval
08 8633 8700   HEMA 128 J6   33 11 09 S   138 01 25 E

Port Victoria
Port Victoria Oval `CT` `HT` `BIG RIG` `tap`
1 Kuhn Tce. Dump Point at the oval
0429 702 234   HEMA 124 D4   34 29 46 S   137 29 16 E

Port Vincent
Port Vincent Foreshore Caravan Park `CT` `HT`
12 Marine Pde. Dump Point next to Caravan Park
08 8853 7073   HEMA 124 E5   34 46 41 S   137 51 48 E

Quorn
Quorn Dump Point `CT` `HT` `BIG RIG` `tap`
Silo Rd. Dump Point with bore water
08 8620 0500   HEMA 128 F6   32 20 26 S   138 02 52 E

Renmark
Renmark Swimming Pool Car Park `CT` `HT` `BIG RIG`
Cnr Cowra & Fifteenth Sts. Dump Point in swimming pool car park
08 8580 3000   HEMA 125 C13   34 10 08 S   140 44 41 E

Riverton
Riverton Caravan Park `CT` `HT` `$`
Cnr Oxford Tce & Torrens Rd. Dump Point at town oval. Fee if not a guest
08 8847 2419   HEMA 124 C7   34 09 20 S   138 44 59 E

Robe
Robe Dump Point `CT` `HT` `BIG RIG` `tap`
Cnr White & Robe Sts. Near Parking Area
08 8768 2003   HEMA 126 F2   37 10 30 S   139 45 40 E

Robertstown
Robertstown Oval `CT` `HT` `BIG RIG`
10 Main Rd. Dump Point. Entry from Church St
08 8581 7100   HEMA 125 C8   33 59 35 S   139 04 49 E

Roxby Downs
Roxby Downs Dump Point `CT` `HT` `BIG RIG` `tap`
Olympic Way. Dump Point near BP Service Station. Key deposit
08 8671 0010   HEMA 130 J2   30 33 15 S   136 53 36 E

Saddleworth
Saddleworth Caravan Park `CT` `HT` `BIG RIG` `tap`
Belvidere/Marrabel Rds. At oval off main road
0417 847 971   HEMA 124 C7   34 05 10 S   138 47 05 E

Snowtown
Snowtown Centenary Park `CT` `HT` `BIG RIG`
North Tce. In Caravan Park at Snowtown. Use E entry for higher vehicles
08 8865 2252   HEMA 124 B6   33 46 42 S   138 12 59 E

Southend
Southend Dump Point `CT` `BIG RIG`
22 Bridges Dr. Dump Point behind the public toilet at beach car park, new bitumen
08 8733 0900   HEMA 126 G3   37 34 14 S   140 07 05 E

St Kilda
St Kilda Adventure Park `CT`
Cockle St. Parking Area at St Kilda, via Mangrove St. At W end of boat ramp car park. Key at kiosk
08 8280 9355   HEMA 120 C3   34 44 31 S   138 32 00 E

Stansbury
Stansbury Dump Point `CT` `HT` `BIG RIG`
Anzac Pde. Dump Point just past caravan park rear entrance
08 8852 4577   HEMA 124 F5   34 54 48 S   137 48 12 E

Streaky Bay
Streaky Bay Lions Park `CT` `HT` `BIG RIG` `tap`
East Tce. Dump Point beside toilets. Small fee for water
08 8626 1001   HEMA 134 C2   32 47 42 S   134 13 05 E

Swan Reach
Tenbury Hunter Reserve `CT` `HT` `BIG RIG`
Sedan Swan Reach Rd. Take ferry N across to W side of river. 500 m E of ferry crossing. Next to toilets
08 8569 0100   HEMA 125 E10   34 33 43 S   139 36 01 E

Tailem Bend
Tailem Bend Dump Point `CT` `HT` `BIG RIG`
Princes Hwy. Dump Point in parking bay at S end of town
1300 785 277   HEMA 125 G9   35 16 07 S   139 27 30 E

Tantanoola
Tantanoola Parklands `CT` `HT` `BIG RIG`
22 Railway Tce East. Dump Point opposite hotel in rest area
08 8733 0900   HEMA 126 H4   37 41 46 S   140 27 20 E

Tanunda
Discovery Holiday Parks Barossa Valley `CT` `HT` `$`
Barossa Valley Way. Dump Point 1.5 km S of PO
08 8563 2784   HEMA 122 E3   34 31 51 S   138 57 03 E

Tintinara
Tintinara Lions Park `CT` `HT` `BIG RIG` `tap`
Dukes Hwy. Dump Point beside railway station and info centre
08 8757 2220   HEMA 125 J11   35 53 06 S   140 03 26 E

Public Dump Points

SOUTH AUSTRALIA

Tumby Bay
Tumby Bay Self Contained RV Park `CT` `HT` `BIG RIG`
Lipson Rd. Northern Access Rd. N end of town
08 8688 2087   HEMA 134 H6   34 21 31 S   136 06 03 E

Waikerie
Waikerie Dump Point `CT` `HT` `BIG RIG` `🚰`
Cnr. Civic Ave & Dowling St. Dump Point access off Civic Ave
08 8541 0708   HEMA 125 C11   34 10 56 S   139 59 14 E

Wallaroo
Wallaroo Dump Point `CT` `HT` `BIG RIG`
Owen Tce. Dump Point next to service station
08 8823 2023   HEMA 124 B4   33 56 04 S   137 37 53 E

Warooka
Warooka Camp Ground `CT` `HT`
Oval Ave & Fifth St. Gold coin donation
08 8854 5004   HEMA 124 F3   34 59 32 S   137 23 53 E

Whyalla
Foreshore Rest Area `CT` `HT` `BIG RIG`
Lincoln Hwy. Dump Point 350 m S of McDouall Stuart Ave
08 8645 7900   HEMA 128 H4   33 02 46 S   137 31 35 E

Jubilee Park Dump Point (Whyalla Showgrounds) `CT` `HT` `BIG RIG`
Jenkins Ave. Dump Point signposted at entry. Daytime only, gates locked at night
08 8645 7900   HEMA 128 H4   33 02 20 S   137 30 31 E

William Creek
William Creek Camp Ground `CT`
Oodnadatta Tr. At public toilets just outside campground
08 8670 7880   HEMA 139 K13   28 54 28 S   136 20 18 E

Williamstown
Williamstown Queen Victoria Jubilee Park `CT` `HT`
Cnr Springton & Mt Crawford Rds. At Caravan Park 3 km E of PO
08 8524 6363   HEMA 122 K2   34 40 26 S   138 54 15 E

Wilmington
Wilmington Centenary Park `CT` `HT` `BIG RIG` `🚰`
Cudmore Tce. Dump Point outside park
08 8666 2014   HEMA 128 G6   32 39 13 S   138 06 06 E

Wilpena Pound
Wilpena Pound Dump Point `CT` `BIG RIG`
Wilpena Rd. Dump Point at the back of the long term car park near Visitor Centre. GPS approximate
08 8620 0500   HEMA 142 G4   31 31 40 S   138 36 29 E

Wudinna
Gawler Ranges Motel & Caravan Park `CT` `HT` `BIG RIG`
Eyre Hwy. Dump Point 1 km E from PO behind the caravan park ablution block
08 8680 2090   HEMA 134 D5   33 03 20 S   135 28 01 E

Yacka
Yackamoorundie Park `CT` `BIG RIG`
Cnr Main North Rd & North Tce. Dump Point at park
08 8846 4038   HEMA 124 A6   33 34 06 S   138 26 43 E

Yankalilla
Yankalilla Dump Point `CT` `HT` `BIG RIG`
Cnr Main & Arthur Sts. Dump Point in town
08 8558 0200   HEMA 124 H6   35 27 31 S   138 21 06 E

Yunta
Yunta Centennial Park `CT` `HT` `BIG RIG`
Barrier Hwy. Dump Point next to Telecentre on Hwy
0439 845 940   HEMA 129 G10   32 34 54 S   139 33 46 E

WESTERN AUSTRALIA

Albany
Brig Amity Park `CT` `HT` `BIG RIG` `🚰`
Off Princess Royal Dr.
08 9841 9290   HEMA 153 K14   35 01 44 S   117 52 45 E

Augusta
Turners `CT` `HT` `$` `🚰`
Off Blackwood Ave. Dump Point at Turner Caravan Park between Hardy St & Albany Tce. Free for guests
08 9780 5633   HEMA 152 F2   34 19 22 S   115 09 45 E

Badgingarra
Badgingarra Community Rec Centre `CT` `HT` `BIG RIG` `🚰`
Meagher Dr.
08 9652 0800   HEMA 170 F3   30 23 14 S   115 30 01 E

Balladonia
Woorlba Homestead `CT` `HT` `BIG RIG`
Eyre Hwy. 132 km W of Caiguna or 50 km E of Balladonia Roadhouse
138 138   HEMA 157 E9   32 26 12 S   124 06 17 E

Beacon
Beacon Dump Point `CT` `HT`
Lucas St. Dump Point adjacent to Information Bay, opposite the Beacon Co-op
08 9685 1202   HEMA 171 F8   30 27 04 S   117 51 49 E

Beasley River
Beasley River Rest Area `CT` `HT` `BIG RIG`
Nanutarra Munjina Rd. Dump Point 171 km E of Nanutarra Roadhouse or 53 km W of Paraburdoo/Wittenoom Rd Jcn
138 138   HEMA 166 K5   22 56 56 S   116 58 40 E

Beverley
Beverley Dump Point `CT` `HT` `BIG RIG`
Council Rd. Dump Point just past & opposite the caravan park entrance
HEMA 150 C7   32 06 27 S   116 55 26 E

Bindoon
Bindoon Transit Park `CT` `HT` `🚰`
Great Northern Hwy. Dump Point next to toilets at the oval
08 9576 4600   HEMA 170 J4   31 23 08 S   116 05 52 E

Boddington
Boddington Dump Point `CT` `HT` `🚰`
Cnr Johnstone St & Farmers Ave. Dump Point at old council depot
08 9883 4999   HEMA 150 G5   32 48 20 S   116 28 15 E

Bridgetown
Bridgetown Dump Point `CT` `HT`
Peninsula Rd. Enter showgrounds & NE side of main building, signed
HEMA 152 C6   33 56 59 S   116 07 45 E

Brookton
Brookton Caravan Park `CT` `HT` `BIG RIG`
Brookton Hwy.
08 9642 1106   HEMA 150 D7   32 22 07 S   117 00 08 E

Broome
Broome Dump Point `CT` `HT` `BIG RIG` `🚰`
Hamersley St. Dump Point at Info Centre. Ask for key to access water
08 9195 2200   HEMA 162 E4   17 57 12 S   122 14 28 E

WESTERN AUSTRALIA

Brunswick Junction
Brunswick Junction Showgrounds `CT` `HT` `BIG RIG`
Ridley St. Turn R inside grounds. Key at Eziway Supermarket, business hours
08 9726 1244   HEMA 150 J2   33 15 11 S   115 50 14 E

Busselton
Busselton Dump Point `CT` `HT` `BIG RIG`
Adelaide St. Dump Point behind Churchill Park Hall. Call to receive access code to unlock
08 9781 0444   HEMA 152 B3   33 38 47 S   115 21 03 E

Caiguna
Baxter Rest Area `CT` `HT` `BIG RIG`
Eyre Hwy. Dump Point at Rest Area 67 km W of Caiguna or 115 km E of Balladonia
HEMA 157 E11   32 21 26 S   124 47 14 E

Capel
Capel Park `CT` `HT` `BIG RIG`
Buchanan Rd. Refundable deposit for key payable at Colroys Cafe
HEMA 152 A3   33 33 10 S   115 33 44 E

Carnamah
Carnamah Caravan Park `HT` `BIG RIG` `🚰`
King St. Dump Point 1 km NE of PO. Next to Niven Park
08 9951 1785   HEMA 170 D4   29 41 10 S   115 53 28 E

Carnarvon
Blowholes (Point Quobba) `CT`
Beach Rd. Dump Point is before Camp Area entry. 72 km N of Carnarvon. Turn W off North West Coastal Hwy 24 km N of Carnarvon or 115 km S of Minilya Roadhouse
08 9941 0019   HEMA 168 D1   24 29 16 S   113 24 44 E

Carnarvon Dump Point `CT` `HT` `BIG RIG`
Hill St. Dump Point off Robinson St. Piyarli Yardi Aboriginal Cultural Centre toilet block
08 9941 1146   HEMA 168 D2   24 52 55 S   113 39 34 E

Cervantes
Cervantes 24 Hour Dump Point `CT` `HT` `BIG RIG` `🚰`
Cadiz St. Dump Point near Visitor Centre
08 9652 0800   HEMA 170 F2   30 30 07 S   115 04 03 E

Waste Transfer Station `CT` `HT` `BIG RIG`
Estella Pl. Dump Point front of local dump. Limited opening hours
08 9652 0800   HEMA 170 F2   30 29 52 S   115 04 48 E

Cleaverville Beach
Cleaverville Beach `CT`
Cleaverville Rd. Dump Point at Camp Area. Turn N 28 km E of Karrratha Roadhouse or 14 km W of Roebourne. 13 km dirt road. Open May - Sep
08 9186 8055   HEMA 166 F5   20 39 40 S   116 59 53 E

Collie
Collie River Valley Tourist Park `CT`
Porter St. Dump Point 2 km W of PO. Visit reception first, donation jar for local firies if public use
08 9734 5088   HEMA 150 K4   33 21 44 S   116 08 44 E

Collie Visitor Centre `CT` `HT` `BIG RIG` `🚰`
156 Throssell St. Donation for water, fee for hot showers, caravan parking
08 9734 2051   HEMA 150 K4   33 21 31 S   116 08 57 E

Eddie Woods Memorial Park `CT` `HT` `BIG RIG`
Throssell St. Dump Point opposite Federal Hotel
HEMA 150 K4   33 21 40 S   116 09 33 E

WESTERN AUSTRALIA

Coolgardie
Coolgardie RV Stop CT HT BIG RIG
75 Woodward St. Dump Point Cnr
of Lefroy St at old railway station
08 9080 2111 HEMA 156 A2 30 57 22 S 121 09 43 E

Coorow
Coorow Caravan Park CT HT BIG RIG
Thomas St.
08 9952 0100 HEMA 170 E4 29 52 51 S 116 01 02 E

Coronation Beach
Coronation Beach CT
Coronation Beach Rd. Dump Point at Camp
Area. Turn W 28 km N of Geraldton or 24 km S of
Northampton
08 9920 5011 HEMA 168 K3 28 33 12 S 114 33 52 E

Corrigin
Corrigin Dump Point CT
Walton St. Dump Point behind toilet block
08 9063 2203 HEMA 151 D12 32 19 51 S 117 52 23 E

Cuballing
Cuballing RV Parking Area CT HT 🚰
Great Southern Hwy. Dump Point
& Parking Area, W side of road between Hwy &
Railway line
08 9883 6031 HEMA 151 G8 32 49 15 S 117 10 48 E

Cue
Cue Dump Point CT HT BIG RIG
Dowley St. Next to shire hall
HEMA 169 H8 27 25 21 S 117 53 46 E

Dalwallinu
Dalwallinu Caravan Park CT $
10 Dowie St.
08 9661 1253 HEMA 170 F6 30 16 27 S 116 40 08 E

Dandaragan
Dandaragan Transit Park CT HT BIG RIG 🚰
3550 Dandaragan Rd. Dump Point at Pioneer Park
08 9652 0800 HEMA 170 G3 30 40 13 S 115 42 12 E

De Grey River
De Grey River CT
Great Northern Hwy. Dump Point at Rest Area
82 km NE of Port Hedland or 71 km SW of Pardoo
Roadhouse
08 9173 1711 HEMA 167 F8 20 18 28 S 119 15 11 E

Denham
Denham Dump Point CT HT BIG RIG
Denham-Hamelin Rd. Dump Point
in info bay on approach to town
HEMA 168 F2 25 55 37 S 113 32 36 E

Denmark
Denmark Dump Point CT HT BIG RIG 🚰
17 Ocean Beach Rd. Dump
Point at the Info Centre
08 9848 2055 HEMA 153 J12 34 57 46 S 117 21 01 E

Derby
Kimberley Entrance Caravan Park CT HT BIG RIG
Rowan St. See reception, donation to RFDS
08 9193 1055 HEMA 164 K2 17 18 25 S 123 37 45 E

Dongara
Dongara Dump Point CT HT BIG RIG
Waldeck St. Beside Oval
HEMA 170 C2 29 14 51 S 114 55 58 E

Donnybrook
Donnybrook Transit Park CT HT BIG RIG
18 Reserve St. Dump Point W end
of oval
08 9731 1897 HEMA 152 A5 33 34 16 S 115 49 12 E

Dowerin
Dowerin Dump Point CT HT
Stewart St. Opposite the hotel
HEMA 170 H6 31 11 43 S 117 01 50 E

Dumbleyung
Stubbs Park CT HT BIG RIG 🚰
Bahrs Rd. Dump Point at oval
08 9863 4012 HEMA 151 J11 33 19 04 S 117 44 36 E

Eighty Mile Beach Area
Stanley Rest Area CT HT BIG RIG
Great Northern Hwy. Dump Point
at Rest Area 108 km NE of Sandfire Roadhouse or
181 km SW of Roebuck Plains Roadhouse. 5 km N
of Nita Downs turnoff
HEMA 162 G4 19 02 36 S 121 39 56 E

Eneabba
Arrowsmith Rest Area CT HT BIG RIG
Brand Hwy. Dump Point at Rest
Area 30 km N of Eneabba or 50 km S of Dongara
138 138 HEMA 170 D2 29 34 43 S 115 08 09 E

Esperance
Esperance Dump Point CT HT BIG RIG
Shelden Rd. Off Norseman Rd
HEMA 156 J4 33 50 35 S 121 53 54 E

Exmouth
Sports & Rec Ground CT HT BIG RIG
Willersdorf Rd. Dump Point N of
Info Centre off Murat Rd. Directions Info Centre
08 9949 3070 HEMA 166 H1 21 55 56 S 114 07 47 E

Fitzroy Crossing Area
Ngumban Cliff Lookout CT HT BIG RIG
Great Northern Hwy. Dump
Point at Rest Area 96 km SE of Fitzroy Crossing or
192 km W of Halls Creek
HEMA 163 G10 18 44 53 S 126 06 31 E

Forest Grove Area
Jarrahdene Campground CT HT 🚰
Jarrahdene Rd. Dump Point
350 m from the intersection of Caves & Jarrahdede Rds
08 9757 7025 HEMA 152 D1 34 06 40 S 115 04 37 E

Frankland
Frankland River Caravan Park CT HT BIG RIG 🚰
Marlock St. Dump point at L side on entry. Near
amenity block & hall. Potable water available
0428 302 489 HEMA 153 F11 34 21 42 S 117 04 57 E

Geraldton
Fig Tree Camping Ground CT
Chapman Valley Rd. Dump Point 21 km NE of
Geraldton. North West Coast Hwy, Chapman Valley
Scenic Drive for 12 km
08 9920 5011 HEMA 168 K3 28 39 32 S 114 42 15 E

Geraldton RV Park CT HT BIG RIG 🚰
Cnr Francis St & Marine
Tce. Dump Point & Parking Area at Geraldton
08 9956 6670 HEMA 168 K3 28 46 33 S 114 36 11 E

Gingin
Gingin CT HT
Brockman & Weld Sts. Dump Point
heading NW on the L after intersection. Opposite
shire office
HEMA 170 J4 31 20 49 S 115 54 12 E

Gnoorea Point
Gnoorea Point (40 Mile) CT HT BIG RIG
Forty Mile Beach Rd. Near Camp
Area. Turn W 54 km N of Fortescue River Roadhouse
or 40 km S of Karratha Roadhouse.12 km dirt road.
Open May-Sep
08 9186 8055 HEMA 166 F4 20 50 26 S 116 20 51 E

Gnowangerup
Gnowangerup Caravan Park CT
5 Richardson St.
08 9827 1109 HEMA 155 G8 33 56 32 S 118 00 32 E

Goomalling
Goomalling Caravan Park CT HT BIG RIG
Throssell St. Dump Point 1 km
SE of PO
08 9629 1183 HEMA 170 J6 31 17 59 S 116 49 57 E

Green Head
Green Head Dump Point CT HT BIG RIG 🚰
Green Head Rd. Dump Point in rec centre carpark
08 9952 0100 HEMA 170 E2 30 04 01 S 114 58 07 E

Greenough
Ellendale Pool CT
Ellendale Pool Rd. Dump Point at Camp Area
22 km NE of Walkaway, via Walkaway-Nangetty &
Ellendale Rds
08 9956 6670 HEMA 170 B2 28 51 33 S 114 58 22 E

Halls Creek
Halls Creek Dump Point CT HT BIG RIG 🚰
Lot 7 Egan St. Between
the Shell Service Station and Hall. Open 8am-5pm
weekdays, 8am-4pm weekends. Potable water
HEMA 163 F12 18 13 24 S 127 40 04 E

Harrismith
Harrismith Caravan Park CT HT BIG RIG
Cnr Railway Ave & Baylon St.
Dump Point at Caravan Park
08 9883 1010 HEMA 151 G11 32 56 10 S 117 51 44 E

Hoffman Area
Lake Brockman CT HT
Scarp Rd. From Logue Brook Dam Rd
turn L 300 m. Dump Point on L
HEMA 150 H3 33 00 16 S 115 58 26 E

Hopetoun
Hopetoun Dump Point CT HT BIG RIG 🚰
Cnr Hopetoun-Ravensthorpe
Rd & Senna Rd. Dump Point 3 km N of Hopetoun
08 9839 0000 HEMA 155 G13 33 55 08 S 120 08 13 E

Jarradale
Jarrahdale Old Mill CT HT BIG RIG 🚰
Millars Rd. Dump Point off
Jarradale Rd
08 9526 1111 HEMA 150 D3 32 20 03 S 116 04 07 E

Jurien Bay
Jurien Bay Dump Point CT HT BIG RIG 🚰
Bashford St. Dump Point
adjacent to Caltex Service Station
08 9652 0800 HEMA 170 F2 30 18 10 S 115 02 35 E

Sandy Cape Rec Park CT HT BIG RIG 🚰
Sandy Cape Rd. Dump
Point at the info bay. 10 km N of Jurien Bay or
18 km S of Green Head. 6 km dirt road
08 9652 0800 HEMA 170 E2 30 11 23 S 115 00 07 E

Kalbarri
Kalbarri Dump Point CT HT BIG RIG 🚰
141 Porter St. Dump Point
in front of shire workshops
HEMA 168 J3 27 42 47 S 114 10 47 E

Kalgoorlie
Boulder Dump Point CT HT BIG RIG
Hamilton St. Dump Point between
Piesse & Richardson Sts
08 9021 9600 HEMA 156 A3 30 47 00 S 121 29 29 E

WESTERN AUSTRALIA

Kalgoorlie Dump Point
CT HT BIG RIG
Forrest St. Dump Point N of railway station
08 9021 9600   HEMA 156 A3   30 44 38 S   121 28 12 E

Kambalda
Kambalda West RV Stop
CT HT BIG RIG
Barnes Dr. Dump Point behind rec centre
08 9080 2111   HEMA 158 H4   31 12 23 S   121 37 17 E

Karlgarin
Tressies Museum & Caravan Park
HT $ BIG RIG 🚰
4313 Konbinin-Hyden Rd.
0475 895 043   HEMA 155 C10   32 29 44 S   118 42 43 E

Karratha
BP Karratha West
CT HT BIG RIG
9 Exploration Dr. Dump Point on Cnr Dampier Hwy, Gap Ridge
08 9143 0116   HEMA 166 F5   20 44 13 S   116 45 58 E

Karratha Dump Point
CT HT BIG RIG
North Coast Hwy. Dump Point near intersection of De Witt Rd
HEMA 166 F5   20 47 36 S   116 51 47 E

Katanning
Katanning RV Rest Area
CT BIG RIG 🚰
15 Aberdeen St. Dump Point behind the library
08 9821 9999   HEMA 153 B13   33 41 23 S   117 33 09 E

Kojonup
Kojonup RV Rest Area
CT HT BIG RIG
Cnr Albany Hwy & Gordon St. Dump Point at S end of town
08 9831 2400   HEMA 153 C11   33 50 13 S   117 09 32 E

Kondinin
Kondinin Caravan Park
CT HT BIG RIG
32 Gordon St.
08 9889 1006   HEMA 151 E13   32 29 43 S   118 15 49 E

Kookynie
Niagara Dam
CT HT
Niagara Dam Rd. Dump Point downstream from dam wall
08 9024 2041   HEMA 158 E3   29 24 15 S   121 25 40 E

Kronkup
Cosy Corner East
CT
Cosy Corner East Rd. Dump Point at Camp Area 30 km W of Albany or 38 km E of Denmark
08 6820 3000   HEMA 153 K13   35 03 33 S   117 38 44 E

Kukerin
Kukerin Dump Point
CT HT BIG RIG 🚰
Bath St. At Nenke Park. Potable water
HEMA 151 J12   33 11 05 S   118 04 51 E

Kulin
Kulin Overnight Stop
CT BIG RIG
Johnston St South Side. Dump Point at S end of town, at public toilets
08 9880 1204   HEMA 151 F13   32 40 13 S   118 09 20 E

Kununurra
Kununurra Dump Point
CT HT $
5 Messmate Way, BP Ord River Roadhouse. At BP Ord River Roadhouse, ask for key at counter
08 9169 1188   HEMA 165 F14   15 46 42 S   128 44 25 E

Kununurra Area
Cockburn Rest Area
CT HT BIG RIG
Great Northern Hwy. Dump Point Victoria Hwy Jcn or 152 km N of Turkey Creek, 56 km S of Wyndham or 45 km W of Kununurra
HEMA 165 F13   15 52 07 S   128 22 17 E

Dunham River
CT HT BIG RIG
Great Northern Hwy. Dump Point 118 km N of Turkey Creek or 35 km S of Victoria Hwy Jcn
HEMA 165 G13   16 07 54 S   128 22 52 E

Lake Grace
Lake Grace Dump Point
CT HT BIG RIG
Stubbs St. Dump Point next to Sportsmans Club
08 9890 2500   HEMA 151 H14   33 06 03 S   118 27 22 E

Lancelin
Lancelin Dump Point
CT BIG RIG
Rock Way. Dump Point off Gingin Rd
HEMA 170 H2   31 01 14 S   115 19 58 E

Laverton
Laverton Dump Point
CT HT BIG RIG 🚰
10 Weld Dr.
08 9031 1202   HEMA 158 D5   28 37 29 S   122 24 08 E

Learmonth
Burkett Road Rest Area
CT HT BIG RIG
North West Coastal Hwy. 16 km NE of Minilya Roadhouse or 111 km SW of Nanutarra Roadhouse. 1 km N of Exmouth turnoff
138 138   HEMA 166 K2   22 59 01 S   114 36 47 E

Leeman
Leeman Dump Point
CT HT BIG RIG 🚰
Rudduck St. At Wann Park Oval
HEMA 170 E2   29 56 42 S   114 58 52 E

Leonora
Leonora Dump Point
CT HT BIG RIG
Goldfields Hwy. Dump Point at info bay, S of town
HEMA 158 D3   28 53 37 S   121 19 47 E

Mandurah
Mandurah Dump Point
CT HT BIG RIG
Cnr Sholl & Hackett Sts. Dump Point in car park
HEMA 150 E2   32 31 42 S   115 43 21 E

Manjimup
Manjimup
CT HT BIG RIG 🚰
53 Mottram St. Dump Point opposite Manjimup Central Caravan Park
HEMA 152 E6   34 14 27 S   116 08 53 E

Marble Bar
Marble Bar Dump Point
CT HT BIG RIG
General St. Dump Point at Rest Area near general store & service station
HEMA 160 A1   21 10 17 S   119 44 37 E

Margaret River
Margaret River Dump Point
CT HT BIG RIG
51 Walcliffe Rd. At W end entrance of Gloucester Park, next to the Rec Centre
08 9780 5911   HEMA 152 C1   33 57 14 S   115 04 12 E

Mary River
Mary Pool (Mary River)
CT
Great Northern Hwy. Rest Area 180 km E of Fitzroy Crossing or 108 km W of Halls Creek
HEMA 163 G11   18 43 37 S   126 52 19 E

Meckering
Meckering Memorial Park
CT HT BIG RIG 🚰
Kelly St.
08 9635 2700   HEMA 170 J6   31 37 58 S   117 00 26 E

Meekatharra
Gascoyne River (South Branch)
CT HT BIG RIG
Great Northern Hwy. Rest Area 148 km NW of Meekatharra, 276 km S of Newman or 108 km S of Kumarina Roadhouse
138 138   HEMA 169 E10   25 34 44 S   119 14 19 E

Meekatharra Dump Point
CT HT
In lane way between Savage & Porter Sts, behind shire office. Follow signs on main road
08 9981 1002   HEMA 169 G9   26 35 37 S   118 29 45 E

Merredin
Merredin Tourist Park
CT HT
2 Oats St. Cnr Great Eastern Hwy, 1.5 km E of PO
08 9041 1535   HEMA 171 J9   31 29 05 S   118 17 29 E

Midland
Midland Tourist Park
CT HT $ BIG RIG 🚰
2 Toodyay Rd. At Middle Swan
08 9274 3002   HEMA 147 E9   31 52 30 S   116 00 42 E

Mingenew
Mingenew Dump Point
CT HT BIG RIG 🚰
Midlands Rd. In parking bay 100 m W of Palm Roadhouse
HEMA 170 C3   29 11 25 S   115 26 19 E

Minilya
Lyndon River
CT HT BIG RIG
North West Coastal Hwy. Rest Area 48 km NE of Minilya Roadhouse or 179 km SW of Nanutarra Roadhouse
138 138   HEMA 168 B3   23 28 58 S   114 16 32 E

Lyndon River (West)
CT HT BIG RIG
Minilya-Exmouth Rd. Rest Area 32 km N of Minilya Roadhouse or 190 km S of Exmouth
138 138   HEMA 168 B2   23 32 32 S   113 57 47 E

Minilya River
CT HT BIG RIG
North West Coast Hwy. Rest Area 1 km S of Minilya Roadhouse or 141 km N of Carnarvon
138 138   HEMA 168 B2   23 49 01 S   114 00 38 E

Minnivale
Minnivale Camp Site
CT HT BIG RIG
Hughes St. Cnr of Amery Benjaberring & Berry Rd. Next to disused tennis courts
08 9631 1202   HEMA 170 H7   31 08 20 S   117 11 04 E

Moora
Moora RV Short Stay
BIG RIG 🚰
Padbury St. Cnr Clinch St, behind shire chambers
08 9651 0000   HEMA 170 G4   30 38 33 S   116 00 28 E

Moora Shire Caravan Park
CT HT BIG RIG
Dandaragan St. Roberts St. Opposite service station
08 9651 0000   HEMA 170 G4   30 38 17 S   116 00 16 E

Moore River
Moore River Bridge
CT HT BIG RIG
Indian Ocean Dr. Rest Area 33 km N of Yanchep NP turnoff or 2 km SE of Guilderton turnoff
138 138   HEMA 170 J3   31 18 14 S   115 33 18 E

Morawa
Morawa Dump Point
CT HT BIG RIG 🚰
Winfield St. S side on L after McGlew St
HEMA 170 C4   29 12 59 S   116 00 33 E

WESTERN AUSTRALIA

Mount Barker
Mount Barker Visitors Centre CT HT BIG RIG
Albany Hwy.
08 9851 1163   HEMA 153 G13   34 37 38 S   117 39 49 E

Mount Magnet
Kirkalocka Rest Area CT HT BIG RIG
Great Northern Hwy. Rest Area
64 km S of Mt Magnet or 80 km N of Paynes Find
138 138   HEMA 171 A8   28 35 50 S   117 46 51 E

Mount Magnet Caravan Park CT $
100 Hepburn St. Gold coin donation for public use
08 9963 4198   HEMA 169 J8   28 03 42 S   117 50 58 E

Mt Hardman
Ellendale Rest Area CT BIG RIG
Great Northern Hwy. Rest Area 125 km SE of Derby turnoff or 88 km W of Fitzroy Crossing
HEMA 163 E8   17 57 38 S   124 50 10 E

Mukinbudin
Mukinbudin Caravan Park CT HT
Cruickshank St.
0429 471 103   HEMA 171 G9   30 55 09 S   118 12 21 E

Munjina (Auski)
Mulga Parking Area CT HT BIG RIG
Great Northern Hwy. Parking Area
39 km N of Auski Roadhouse or 180 km S of Hwy 1 Jcn
HEMA 167 H8   22 03 10 S   118 48 10 E

Murchison
Murchison Oasis Roadhouse CT HT BIG RIG
Carnarvon Mullewa Rd. Roadside of toilet block
08 9961 3875   HEMA 168 G5   26 53 46 S   115 57 26 E

Nannup
Nannup Dump Point CT HT BIG RIG
Brockman St. Next to the caravan park, drinking water & taps on wood fence
HEMA 152 D4   33 58 34 S   115 45 47 E

Nanutarra
House Creek Bridge CT HT BIG RIG
Nanutarra Munjina Rd. Rest Area
62 km E of Nanutarra Roadhouse or 162 km W of Paraburdoo/Wittenoom Rd Jcn
138 138   HEMA 166 J4   22 27 51 S   116 02 12 E

Narembeen
Narembeen Caravan Park CT HT BIG RIG
11 Currall St.
08 9064 7308   HEMA 151 B14   32 03 49 S   118 23 46 E

Narrogin
Narrogin Dump Point CT HT
Fairway St. Located at the RV site in the Old Goods Shed Yard
08 9881 2064   HEMA 151 G8   32 56 10 S   117 10 45 E

Nerren Nerren
Nerren Nerren Rest Area CT
North West Coastal Hwy. 82 km N of Kalbarri turnoff or 46 km S of Billabong Roadhouse
138 138   HEMA 168 H3   27 12 43 S   114 36 44 E

Newdegate
Newdegate Rest Area CT
Maley St. Behind public toilets next to roadhouse
HEMA 155 D10   33 05 34 S   119 01 27 E

Newman
Mt Robinson Rest Area CT HT BIG RIG
Great Northern Hwy. Rest Area
109 km NW of Newman or 86 km SE of Auski Roadhouse. 800 m E of Hwy
138 138   HEMA 169 A9   23 02 34 S   118 50 57 E

Newman Visitors Centre CT HT BIG RIG
2 Fortescue Ave. Key required from Information centre open 8am-5pm daily
08 9175 2888   HEMA 160 E1   23 21 33 S   119 43 40 E

Nilgen
Nilgen Nature Reserve CT HT BIG RIG
Indian Ocean Dr. From Nilgen turn off, go N about 5.5 km. Site on L
138 138   HEMA 170 G3   30 55 14 S   115 22 03 E

Norseman
Norseman Rest Area CT HT $ ⚒
68 Roberts St. Key required from Info Centre. Open business hours
08 9039 1071   HEMA 156 E4   32 11 46 S   121 46 51 E

Norseman Area
Southern Hill 24 Hr Rest Area CT HT BIG RIG
Eyre Hwy. 109 km W of Balladonia or 83 km E of Norseman
138 138   HEMA 156 D5   32 04 24 S   122 35 36 E

Northam
Northam Dump Point CT HT BIG RIG ⚒
Peel St. Opposite fast food restaurant
08 9622 2100   HEMA 170 K6   31 38 59 S   116 40 38 E

Northampton
Galena Bridge (Murchison River) CT HT BIG RIG
North West Coastal Hwy. Rest Area 13 km N of Kalbarri turnoff or 115 km S of Billabong Roadhouse
138 138   HEMA 168 J3   27 49 39 S   114 41 24 E

Hampton Gardens CT HT ⚒
Bateman St, access off Essex St. In the long vehicle car park, opposite IGA (Hampton Road)
08 9934 1202   HEMA 168 K3   28 20 54 S   114 37 49 E

Northcliffe
Northcliffe Tourist Centre CT HT BIG RIG
Muirillup Rd. At the Northcliffe Visitor Centre, E of Wheatley Coast Rd Jcn
HEMA 152 G6   34 37 58 S   116 07 31 E

Nullagine
Nullagine CT HT BIG RIG ⚒
Cnr Cooke & Walter Sts. In the rest stop
08 9175 8000   HEMA 160 B2   21 53 10 S   120 06 28 E

Nungarin
Nungarin Dump Point CT HT BIG RIG
Main St. Opposite Heritage Machinery & Army Museum
HEMA 171 H9   31 11 05 S   118 06 10 E

Nyabing
Nyabing Caravan Parking Facility CT HT BIG RIG ⚒
Martin St. Dump Point beside toilets, at sports rec grounds. Potable water
08 9829 1051   HEMA 155 F8   33 32 40 S   118 08 49 E

Onslow
Onslow Dump Point CT HT BIG RIG
Cameron Avenue. Adjacent to basketball court. S of PO
08 9184 6644   HEMA 166 H3   21 38 28 S   115 06 47 E

Onslow Area
Old Onslow Dump Point CT HT BIG RIG
Onslow Rd. 17.5 km on North West Coastal Hwy, turn R & follow signs to Old Onslow Historical Site. Signposted
HEMA 166 H3   21 42 42 S   114 56 55 E

Orana
Albany Dump Point CT HT BIG RIG ⚒
Albany Hwy. At Info Bay N of town opposite Le Grande Ave
08 6820 3000   HEMA 153 J14   34 59 28 S   117 51 21 E

Orange Grove
Crystal Brook Caravan Park WA CT $
388 Kelvin Rd.
08 9453 6226   HEMA 147 K9   32 01 05 S   116 01 08 E

Ord River
Leycesters Rest Ord River CT HT BIG RIG
Via Great Northern Hwy. Rest Area
100 km N of Halls Creek or 63 km S of Turkey Creek
HEMA 165 K12   17 28 45 S   127 57 04 E

Pardoo
Cape Keraudren CT HT BIG RIG
Cape Keraudren Access Rd. Dump Point 11 km NW of Pardoo Roadhouse. Turn N off Hwy 1 at Pardoo Roadhouse. Dirt road, entry fee
0419 968 123   HEMA 162 H1   19 57 38 S   119 46 08 E

Cape Keraudren - Rangers Station Dump Point CT HT BIG RIG ⚒
Dump Point 8.5 km NW of Pardoo Roadhouse. Turn N off Hwy 1 at Pardoo Roadhouse. Dirt road, entry fee
0419 968 123   HEMA 162 J1   19 59 23 S   119 47 24 E

Sandy Beach Dump Point CT HT BIG RIG
Via Cape Keraudren Rd. Dump Point 12 km NW of Pardoo Roadhouse. Turn N off Hwy 1 at Pardoo Roadhouse. Dirt road, entry fee
0419 968 123   HEMA 162 H1   19 57 57 S   119 46 55 E

Paynes Find
Mount Gibson Rest Area CT HT BIG RIG
Great Northern Hwy. At the Rest Area 83 km NE of Wubin on the Great Northern Hwy
138 138   HEMA 170 D7   29 36 34 S   117 08 31 E

Peaceful Bay
Peaceful Bay Dump Point CT HT BIG RIG
Peaceful Bay Rd. Near toilets
HEMA 153 K10   35 02 30 S   116 55 40 E

Perenjori
Perenjori Caravan Park CT HT BIG RIG ⚒
137 Crossing Rd. Caravan Park Cnr North Rd
0408 731 100   HEMA 170 C5   29 26 09 S   116 17 17 E

Pingelly
Pingelly Dump Point CT HT BIG RIG
Hall St. Behind caravan park
08 9887 1066   HEMA 151 E8   32 32 05 S   117 05 06 E

Pingelly Recreation Ground CT HT BIG RIG
Somerset St. Behind swimming pool
08 9887 1066   HEMA 151 E8   32 31 53 S   117 05 25 E

Pingrup
Pingrup Caravan Park CT HT ⚒
18 Sanderson St. Potable water available
08 9820 1101   HEMA 155 F9   33 32 05 S   118 30 40 E

Pinjarra
Pinjarra RV Parking Area CT HT BIG RIG
21 Pinjarra-Williams Rd. 100 m E of Premier Hotel, just before RV stop
08 9531 7777   HEMA 150 F2   32 37 46 S   115 52 45 E

Port Hedland
Port Hedland Racecourse CT HT BIG RIG ⚒
2 McGregor St. Enter via McGregor St opposite Civic Centre
08 9158 9300   HEMA 167 F8   20 18 32 S   118 36 45 E

WESTERN AUSTRALIA

Port Hedland Area
Des Streckfuss Rest Area `CT` `HT` `BIG RIG`
Marble Bar Rd. Rest Area 74 km
NW of Marble Bar or 79 km SE of Hwy 1 Jcn
HEMA 160 A1   20 49 33 S   119 30 44 E

Mundabullangana `CT` `HT` `BIG RIG`
Cnr Great Northern & North West
Coastal Hwys. At Rest Area 40 km S of Port Hedland
HEMA 166 F7   20 34 27 S   118 26 18 E

Port Smith Area
Goldwire Rest Area `CT` `HT` `BIG RIG`
Great Northern Hwy. Rest Area
168 km NE of Sandfire Roadhouse or 121 km SW of
Roebuck Plains Roadhouse
HEMA 162 F4   18 36 14 S   121 57 59 E

Quairading
Quairading Dump Point `CT` `HT` `BIG RIG`
Quairading-York Rd. Nearby info
bay & amenities block, opposite stockyards on W
side of town
08 9645 1001   HEMA 151 B9   32 00 43 S   117 23 42 E

Ravensthorpe
Ravensthorpe Dump Point `CT` `HT` `BIG RIG`
32 Dunn St. Next to CRC
HEMA 155 F13   33 34 50 S   120 02 46 E

Regans Ford
Regans Ford Rest Area `CT` `HT` `BIG RIG`
Brand Hwy. Rest Area 43 km N of
Gingin or 32 km S of Cataby. Dirt. No camping
HEMA 170 H3   30 59 13 S   115 42 19 E

Robe River
Robe River `CT` `HT` `BIG RIG`
North West Coastal Hwy. Rest
Area 117 km N of Nanutarra Roadhouse or 43 km S
of Fortescue River Roadhouse
138 138   HEMA 166 H4   21 36 55 S   115 55 21 E

Roebuck Plains Area
Nillibubbica Rest Area `CT` `HT` `BIG RIG`
Great Northern Hwy. At rest area
71 km E of Roebuck Plains Roadhouse or 60 km W
of Willare Bridge Roadhouse
HEMA 162 E6   17 39 21 S   123 07 57 E

Southern Cross
Karalee Rock & Dam `CT` `HT` `BIG RIG`
Great Eastern Hwy. At Camp Area
137 km W of Coolgardie or 52 km E of Southern
Cross. Turn N 133 km W of Coolgardie or 48 km E
of Southern Cross. 5 km dirt road
08 9049 1001   HEMA 158 H1   31 15 03 S   119 50 24 E

Southern Cross `CT` `HT` `BIG RIG` `water`
Dump Point
Cnr Achernar & Sirius Sts. E end near old shire yards
HEMA 171 H12   31 13 50 S   119 19 51 E

Southern Cross Area
Boorabbin Rest Area `CT` `HT` `BIG RIG`
Great Eastern Hwy. Rest Area
114 km W of Coolgardie or 68 km E of Southern Cross
138 138   HEMA 158 H1   31 16 08 S   120 01 00 E

Tambellup
Tambellup Dump Point `CT` `HT` `BIG RIG` `water`
22 Norrish Street.
HEMA 153 D3   34 02 45 S   117 38 31 E

Tammin
Tammin Dump Point `CT` `HT` `BIG RIG` `water`
Station Rd. S side of
Tammin Sporting Oval
08 9637 0300   HEMA 170 J7   31 38 18 S   117 29 01 E

Three Springs
Three Springs Dump `CT` `HT` `BIG RIG` `water`
Point
Hall St. Adjacent to council building
HEMA 170 D3   29 32 10 S   115 45 52 E

Trayning
Trayning Caravan Park `CT` `HT` `BIG RIG` `water`
Bencubbin/Kellerberrin Rd.
At Caravan Park. Behind the swimming pool
08 9683 1001   HEMA 171 H8   31 06 38 S   117 47 37 E

Wagin
Wagin Showgrounds RV `CT` `HT` `BIG RIG`
Area
Ballagin St. Great Southern Hwy
08 9861 1177   HEMA 151 J9   33 18 20 S   117 20 10 E

Walpole
Walpole Visitor Info Centre `CT` `HT` `water`
South Coast Hwy. N side of town
08 9840 1111   HEMA 153 J9   34 58 31 S   116 43 51 E

Warmun (Turkey Creek) Area
Spring Creek `CT` `HT` `BIG RIG`
Great Northern Hwy. Rest Area
107 km NE of Halls Creek or 56 km SW of Turkey Creek
HEMA 165 K12   17 25 59 S   127 59 21 E

Waroona
Waroona Town Oval `CT` `HT` `BIG RIG`
Millar St. Off South Western Hwy.
Next to Walmsley Pavilion
08 9733 7800   HEMA 150 G2   32 50 42 S   115 55 25 E

Wellstead
Wellstead Dump Point `CT` `HT` `BIG RIG` `water`
South Coast Hwy. On
service road, in truck stop
HEMA 155 H9   34 29 36 S   118 36 15 E

Westonia
Westonia Dump Point `CT` `HT` `BIG RIG`
Cnr Westonia-Carrabin &
Boodarockin Rds.
HEMA 171 J10   31 17 48 S   118 41 21 E

Whim Creek area
Peawah River `CT`
North West Coastal Hwy. 26 km NE of Whim
Creek or 92 km SW of Port Hedland
138 138   HEMA 166 F7   20 50 51 S   118 04 06 E

Wickepin
Wickepin Caravan Park `CT` `HT`
Wogolin Rd. At Caravan Park, behind
Police Station
0487 257 036   HEMA 151 F10   32 46 52 S   117 30 12 E

Wiluna
Lake Way Rest Area `CT` `HT` `BIG RIG`
Goldfields Hwy. Rest Area 117 km
N of Leinster or 58 km S of Wiluna. Just off the road
GPS at turnoff
138 138   HEMA 158 A2   27 02 25 S   120 24 39 E

Wongan Hills
Wongan Hills Dump Point `CT` `BIG RIG`
Wongan Hills Rd. Opposite supermarket,
near Info Centre
08 9671 1973   HEMA 170 G6   30 53 35 S   116 42 59 E

Woodanilling
Woodanilling Rec Reserve `CT` `HT` `BIG RIG`
Yairabin St. At Parking Area
08 9823 1506   HEMA 153 A12   33 33 36 S   117 25 59 E

Wooramel
Edaggee Rest Area `CT` `HT` `BIG RIG`
North West Coastal Hwy. Rest
Area 43 km N of Wooramel Roadhouse or 81 km S
of Carnarvon
138 138   HEMA 168 E2   25 27 34 S   114 03 31 E

Yalabia
Lake MacLeod Rest Area `CT` `HT` `BIG RIG`
North West Coastal Hwy. Rest Area
49 km S of Minilya Roadhouse or 90 km N of Carnarvon
138 138   HEMA 168 C2   24 14 57 S   114 02 11 E

Yannarie River
Yannarie Rest Area `CT` `HT` `BIG RIG`
North West Coastal Hwy. Rest
Area 156 km NE of Minilya Roadhouse or 70 km SW
of Nanutarra Roadhouse
138 138   HEMA 166 J3   22 51 49 S   114 57 05 E

Yealering
Lake Yealering Caravan Park `CT` `HT` `BIG RIG`
Sewell Rd. Near PO
0428 787 426   HEMA 151 E10   32 35 37 S   117 37 32 E

York
Janet Millet Lane RV `CT` `HT` `BIG RIG` `water`
Stop
Janet Millet Lane. Parking Area adjacent to
croquet club
08 9641 1301   HEMA 150 A6   31 53 15 S   116 46 19 E

Yule River
Marble Bar Turn Off `CT` `HT` `BIG RIG`
Great Northern Highway. Parking
Area 95 km N of Auski Roadhouse or 124 km S of
Hwy 1 Jcn
138 138   HEMA 167 G8   21 34 40 S   118 48 57 E

Two Camel Creek `CT` `HT` `BIG RIG`
Great Northern Highway. Rest
Area 83 km North of Auski Roadhouse or 137 km
South of Hwy 1 Jcn, GPS at entry - 1 km to area
138 138   HEMA 167 H8   21 40 32 S   118 49 10 E

NORTHERN TERRITORY

Adelaide River
Adelaide River Dump Point `CT` `HT` `water`
Stuart Hwy Service Rd. Off Stuart
Hwy, adjacent to fire station
08 8976 0058   HEMA 175 G4   13 14 13 S   131 06 13 E

Alice Springs
Alice Springs Dump Point `CT` `HT` `BIG RIG`
Commonage Rd. S of The Gap. L
of road, next to Blatherskite Park
1800 645 199   HEMA 185 B11   23 43 57 S   133 51 37 E

Batchelor
Batchelor Dump Point `CT` `HT` `BIG RIG`
Numdina St. Adjacent to public toilets
08 8976 0058   HEMA 175 F4   13 02 49 S   131 01 43 E

Borroloola
Tamarind Park `CT` `HT` `water`
Broad St. Near airport gate
1800 245 091   HEMA 179 K13   16 04 19 S   136 18 22 E

Delamere
Mathison Rest Area `CT` `HT` `BIG RIG`
Victoria Hwy. Rest Area 104 km
SW of Katherine or 92 km NE of Victoria River
HEMA 177 B6   15 08 23 S   131 41 01 E

Jabiru
Jabiru Dump Point `CT` `HT` `BIG RIG`
Jabiru Drive. 300 m past tourist
info board, opposite turnoff to cemetery
08 8979 2230   HEMA 176 C6   12 39 52 S   132 50 19 E

NORTHERN TERRITORY

Katherine
Katherine Dump Point
Lindsay St. 200 m from Info
Centre. 300 m along Lindsay St, just beyond Second St
HEMA 176 K4   14 27 53 S   132 16 02 E

King Rest Area
Stuart Hwy. Rest Area 59 km N of
Mataranka or 46 km S of Katherine
HEMA 178 G7   14 38 40 S   132 37 58 E

Larrimah
Warloch Rest Area
Stuart Hwy. Rest Area 41 km N of
Larrimah or 37 km S of Mataranka
HEMA 179 J8   15 14 12 S   133 06 53 E

Manbulloo
**Vince Connolly Crossing
(Limestone Creek)**
Victoria Hwy. Rest Area 58 km SW of Katherine or
138 km NE of Victoria River
HEMA 177 A7   14 49 42 S   131 55 00 E

Mataranka
Mataranka Dump Point
Cnr Stuart Hwy & Martin Rd.
Near white tower
HEMA 178 H7   14 55 17 S   133 03 56 E

Nhulunbuy
Nhulunbuy Dump Point
Bottlebrush Ave. Turn NE off
Melville Bay Rd to Matthew Flinders Way 2 km, S to
Bottlebrush Ave 330 m (between Hindle Oval 1 & 2).
Signposted
08 8939 2200   **HEMA 179 C14**   12 11 20 S   136 47 19 E

Pine Creek
Pine Creek Dump Point
27 Ward St. Outside council
depot
08 8972 0777   **HEMA 176 H2**   13 49 28 S   131 49 55 E

Tennant Creek
Tennant Creek Dump Point
82 Ambrose St. Via Stuart St, near
showgrounds
08 8962 3388   **HEMA 181 G8**   19 38 36 S   134 11 34 E

Winnellie
**Winnellie Greyhound
Club**
15 Hook Rd. Winnellie
08 8984 3167   **HEMA 174 D3**   12 25 41 S   130 53 40 E

Yulara
Yulara Dump Point
Cnr Berry Rd & Tuit Crescent. Off
Giles St. Behind AAT Kings depot, on the ground
under metal plate
08 8956 2171   **HEMA 184 G2**   25 13 24 S   130 58 31 E

Make Travelling Easy

with Australia's favourite & most complete Caravan Park Guide

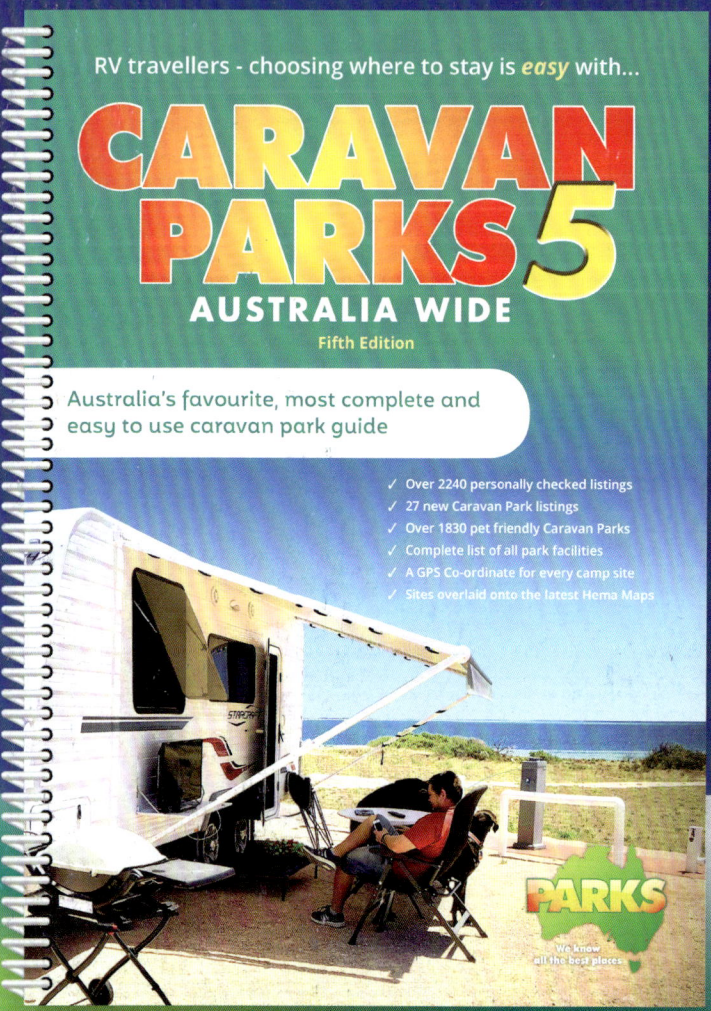

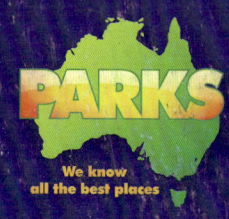

Lovicks Hut, High Country Victoria by John Nieddu Photography

AUSTRALIA WIDE

H

AUSTRALIA WIDE

AUSTRALIA WIDE

U

Important Contacts

National Parks and Wildlife Service

Western Australia
Department of Parks and Wildlife (DPAW)
Ph: 08 9219 9000 | www.dpaw.wa.gov.au

Queensland
Dept of National Parks, Sport & Racing
Ph: 13 74 68 | www.nprsr.qld.gov.au

New South Wales
NSW National Parks and Wildlife Service Ph: 1300 072 757
www.nationalparks.nsw.gov.au

South Australia
Dept of Environment, Water and Natural Resources
Ph: 08 8204 1910 | www.environment.sa.gov.au/parks

Tasmania
Parks and Wildlife Service Ph: 1300 827 727
www.parks.tas.gov.au

Northern Territory
Parks and Wildlife Commission Northern Territory
Ph: 08 8999 4555 | www.parksandwildlife.nt.gov.au

Victoria
Parks Victoria Ph: 13 19 63 | www.parkweb.vic.gov.au

Australian Capital Territory
Environment and Planning Development
Ph: 13 22 81 | www.environment.act.gov.au

Aboriginal Land Permits

Western Australia
Department of Indigenous Affairs Ph: 1300 651 077
On-line Permits:
www.daa.wa.gov.au/land/entry-permits

Northern Territory, Central Land Council Alice Springs
Main Office Ph: 08 8951 6211 | www.clc.org.au

South Australia
Maralinga -Tjarutja Admin Office
Ph: 08 8625 2946 | www.maralingatjarutja.com

Road Conditions

Live Traffic NSW www.livetraffic.com | Ph: 132 701
New South Wales (Outback) Ph: 08 8082 6660 –
24-hour recorded message
Queensland Ph: 13 19 40
South Australia Ph: 1300 361 033
Western Australia Ph: 13 81 38
Northern Territory Ph: 1800 246 199
Victoria Ph: 13 11 70

Vehicle Assistance

AANT, NRMA, RAA, RAC, RACQ, RACT, RACV
Ph: 131 111

Royal Flying Doctor Service

Queensland Medical & Emergency Calls
Ph: 1300 697 337

New South Wales
Medical & Emergency Calls
Ph: 08 8088 1188

South Australia & Northern Territory
Medical & Emergency Calls
Ph: 1800 733 772 (SA) 1800 733 768 (NT)
1800 167 222 (Central Australia)
HF Radio: 4010kHz, 6890kHz or 8165kHz
Satphones: 08 8648 9555

Western Australia
Medical & Emergency Calls
Ph: 1800 625 800
Satphones: 08 9417 6389

Weather Information

Bureau of Meterology www.bom.gov.au

Other Useful Contacts

DFES Western Australia Ph: 133 337
New South Wales Rural Fire Service Ph: 1800 679 737
Queensland Fire & Emergency Services Ph: 13 74 68
Victoria Country Fire Authority – Fire Restrictions
Ph: 1800 226 226
South Australia Country Fire Service Ph: 1800 362 361
Bushfires Council Northern Territory Ph: 08 8922 0844
Tasmanian Fire Service Ph: 1800 000 699
Australian National 4WD Radio Network
Ph: 08 7325 2600 | www.vks737.radio
Birdsville Hotel, Queensland Ph: 07 4656 3244
Innaminka Hotel Ph: 08 8675 9901
Spirit of Tasmania - Information and Reservations
Ph: 1800 634 906 | www.spiritoftasmania.com.au
Pink Roadhouse, Oodnadatta, SA Ph: 08 8670 7822
www.pinkroadhouse.com.au
Aussie Travel Code www.aussietravelcode.com.au

Fruit and Quarantine Zones

www.interstatequarantine.org.au
Western Australian Quarantine & Inspection Service
Kununurra border checkpoint Ph: 08 9168 7354
Eucla/Eyre Hwy (WA/SA Border) Ph: 08 9039 3227
South Australia Fruit Fly & Quarantine Ph: 1300 666 010
Queensland DPI & F Coen Quarantine & Inspection Point
Ph: 07 4060 1135 | www.qld.gov.au